D1065893

500
MASTER GAMES
OF CHESS

This work comprises
BOOK I   OPEN GAMES

&

BOOKS II and III   SEMI-OPEN and
CLOSED GAMES

500

MASTER GAMES

OF CHESS

BY

Dr. S. TARTAKOWER

AND

J. du MONT

DOVER PUBLICATIONS, INC.
NEW YORK

TO SIR GEORGE THOMAS, BART.

A GREAT FIGURE IN BRITISH CHESS

This Dover edition, first published in 1975, is an
unabridged, unaltered republication of the work first
published in 1952. This edition is published by
special arrangement with G. Bell & Sons, Ltd., York
House, Portugal Street, London W.C. 2, publisher
of the original edition.

International Standard Book Number: 0-486-23208-5
Library of Congress Catalog Card Number: 75-11306

Manufactured in the United States of America
Dover Publications, Inc.
180 Varick Street
New York, N.Y. 10014

PREFACE

THE games in this collection have been selected for their intrinsic merit, and although there are many examples of extreme brilliance among them, the guiding idea has been to reproduce masterpieces representative of the style of the respective periods in the history of Chess.

It is hoped that, by grouping the games according to openings and within their particular sections, chronologically, the pedagogical value of the work will have been increased, without any loss in other directions.

It should be remembered that the character of an opening is often kept up throughout the middle-game and because of the peculiarities of its pawn formation can, and frequently does, have an influence even on the end-game. A collection such as this can be looked upon as complementary to the standard works on the theory of the openings.

The authors wish to express their gratitude to Messrs. D. Castello and R. N. Coles, who have undertaken the gigantic task of reading the whole of the proofs, and others who have assisted in this work.

Also, and in particular, to Miss Joan Kealey, now Mrs. Ronald Smith, who, out of over 8,000 games, copied and in part translated well over 2,000 for final selection, an undertaking which she carried out with exemplary thoroughness and accuracy.

S. TARTAKOWER.
J. DU MONT.

CONTENTS

OF THE COMPLETE WORK

BOOK I OPEN GAMES

3. TWO KNIGHTS DEFENCE

4. HUNGARIAN DEFENCE

5. RUY LOPEZ

10. PETROFF'S DEFENCE

11. GRECO'S COUNTER-GAMBIT

xiv

CONTENTS

BOOK II SEMI-OPEN GAMES

16. FRENCH DEFENCE

17. CARO-KANN DEFENCE

19. THE CENTRE COUNTER

20. ALEKHINE'S DEFENCE

26. QUEEN'S PAWN GAME

APPENDIX

GAMES AT ODDS, BLINDFOLD, ETC.

BOOK I

OPEN GAMES

1. GIUOCO PIANO

1

White	Black
BLEDOW	VON DER LASA

(Berlin, 1839)

Morphy's great principles—the formation of a pawn centre, the most rapid development of the pieces (even at the cost of material), the opening up of lines of attack, the deadly effect of an advanced pawn—all are already in evidence in the following old-time game.

1 P—K4	P—K4
2 Kt—KB3	Kt—QB3
3 B—B4	B—B4
4 P—B3	

With the idea—known and appreciated ever since chess was played—of establishing a pawn centre by P—Q4.

4	Q—K2

One of the earliest defences.

5 P—Q4	B—Kt3

A complement of his last move. Black evidently wishes to maintain a hold on his K4. If he abandons the centre by 5 .... P×P; White plays 6 Castles, and his pressure, at the expense of a pawn (6 .... P×P; 7 Kt×P, etc.), would become irksome.

6 Castles	P—Q3
7 P—QR4	

This flank attack already threatens to win a piece by 8 P—R5, B×RP (or 8 .... Kt×RP; 9 R×Kt, B×R; 10 Q—R4 ch, winning the Bishop); 9 R×B, Kt×R; 10 Q—R4 ch, Kt—B3; 11 P—Q5, P—QR3; 12 P×Kt, P—QKt4; 13 B×P, and White has the last word.

7	P—QR4

7 .... P—QR3; 8 P—QKt4.

8 B—K3	Kt—B3

Here the gain of a pawn by 8 .... P×P; 9 P×P, Q×P; would be refuted by 10 R—K1, with a winning frontal attack.

B

9 P×P
It is also feasible to maintain the tension in the centre by 9 QKt—Q2.

9	QKt×P
10 Kt×Kt	P×Kt
11 B×B	P×B
12 Kt—Q2	Castles
13 Q—K2	B—Q2

Instead of seeking simplification by 13 .... B—K3; Black pursues more ambitious plans.

14 QR—Q1
Disregarding the loss of a pawn, White speeds up his development.

14	B×P
15 P—QKt3	B—B3
16 P—B4	

The opening of the KB file is important.

16	QR—Q1
17 P×P	Q×P
18 R—B5	Q—Q3

Or 18 .... Q—K2; 19 P—K5, P—QKt4; 20 Kt—K4, and White's pressure is more effective still.

19 P—K5	Q—B4 ch
20 K—R1	Kt—K5

Black's hope of obtaining relief by exchanges is doomed to disappointment. But if 20 .... Kt—Q4; 21 P—K6, and if 20 .... Kt—Q2; or 20 .... QR—K1; 21 QR—KB1, and in either case White has the advantage.

21 Kt×Kt	R×R ch
22 Q×R	B×Kt

Hoping to drive away the bellicose Rook (e.g.: 23 R—Kt5, P—R3; 24 R—R5, B—Kt3; followed by .... Q×P; or 23 R—R5, B—Kt3; 24 R—Kt5, Q—K6); the more interesting is the ensuing drama which unfolds round the sensitive point KB7. (*Diagram. See p. 2.*)

23 R×P	R×R
24 Q—Q8 ch	Q—B1
25 B×R ch	K×B
26 P—K6 ch	K—Kt1
27 P—K7	Resigns.

The mobility of this pawn has played the decisive *rôle* in the attack.

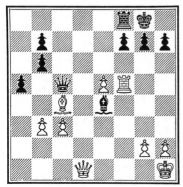

Position after 22 .... B × Kt

2

White	Black
TARRASCH	ALEKHINE

(Baden-Baden, 1925)

In this game Black's strategy abounds in manœuvres which are deeply conceived, but very hard to fathom; such are the subtle waiting moves 11 .... Q—Q1; and 13 .... B—R2; and such also is the challenging sortie 21 .... B—B4; which heralds the winning coup 22 .... B×P.

1 P—K4	P—K4
2 Kt—KB3	Kt—QB3
3 B—B4	B—B4
4 P—B3	B—Kt3

On the same lines as the ancient continuation 4 .... Q—K2; 5 P—Q4, B—Kt3; etc. But there is a subtle improvement, for if now White were to reply 5 P—Q3 (instead of 5 P—Q4), Black has no need to mobilise his Queen for the "overprotection" of his KP.

5 P—Q4	Q—K2
6 Castles	Kt—B3

Another refinement of the opening and more energetic than 6 .... P—Q3. Now White has to take measures to protect his KP, and this lessens his prospects of attack.

7 R—K1

The most lively continuation here is 7 B—KKt5. 7 P×P simplifies the game too much, whilst 7 P—Q5, Kt—QKt1 results in a congested position.

7	P—Q3
8 P—QR4	P—QR3
9 P—R3	

After the energetic 8 P—QR4, this move shows over-anxiety and could prove a weakness in the King's field. An ambitious continuation is 9 Kt—R3.

9	Castles
10 B—KKt5	P—R3
11 B—K3	

A trap (11 .... KKt×P; 12 P—Q5, winning a piece).

11 ......   Q—Q1

Having fulfilled the task of guarding the KP, the Queen returns home, leaving the square available for the Knight (12 P—Q5, Kt—K2).

12 B—Q3

Here White had an opportunity of simplifying the game by: 12 P×P, QKt×P; 13 Kt×Kt, P×Kt; 14 B×B, P×B; 15 Q—K2, etc. with equal chances.

12	R—K1
13 QKt—Q2	B—R2

A fresh preventive manœuvre. Black's KB not only anticipates an eventual 14 Kt—B4, but also 14 P—Q5, followed by 15 B × B, by which the structure of the black pawn formation would have deteriorated.

14 Q—B2   P×P
15 Kt×P

If 15 P×P, Kt—QKt5.

15 ......   Kt—K4
16 B—B1

Better than this full retreat is 16 B—K2.

16 ......   P—Q4

By this thrust in the centre Black assumes the initiative.

17 QR—Q1

If 17 P—KB4, Kt—Kt3; 18 P—K5, Kt—R4; with advantage to Black.

17	P—B4
18 Kt (Q4)—Kt3	Q—B2
19 B—KB4	

Hoping to ease the tension by exchanges.

19 ......   Kt—B6 ch

Well thought out, for Black not only succeeds in massing his shock troops on the K side, but his sacrifice of a pawn is well grounded.

20 Kt×Kt   Q×B
21 P×P
He accepts the proffered pawn as he does not fear the reply 21 .... B×P; 22 P×B, Q×Kt; 23 B—Kt2, after which White would then have a strong position.

21 ......   B—B4
The idea underlying this challenging manœuvre is to turn aside the adverse KB from his post of observation and then to pounce upon the denuded King's field.

22 B—Q3
Plausible, but in the light of the preceding remark, it would have been wiser to play 22 Q—B1 or 22 Q—Q2, although in either case Black would have regained his pawn with advantage.

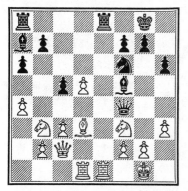

22 ......   B×P
Breaking down the hostile bastions (see note to White's 9th move) and threatening .... B×P.

23 P×B
Here 23 Q—Q2, offered more resistance.

23 ......   Q×Kt
24 R×R ch
By playing 24 B—B1, at once with the continuation 24 .... R×R ch; 25 R×R, Q×QP, etc., White would have lost a pawn, but he would have avoided the subsequent catastrophe.

24 ......   R×R
25 B—B1   R—K4
This frontal assault is decisive.

26 P—B4   R—Kt4 ch
27 K—R2   Kt—Kt5 ch
Super-brilliance.

28 P×Kt
After 28 K—Kt1, there is a mate in two by 28 .... Kt×P dis. ch; etc.

28 ......   R×KtP
29 B—R3   R—R5
Resigns.

3

White	Black
ELISKASES	GRÜNFELD

(Mährisch-Ostrau, 1933)

This game is typical of the modern style, and recalls a modern war of attrition. We observe what may be termed liquidating *sacrifices.*

Thus the beautiful move 27 Kt—B5, loses a piece temporarily only, but White secures a breach in the open KKt file. Later on, 40 P—R5, abandons the QKtP only to regain it forthwith, obtaining thereby a base for action on the QKt file. In the sequel, 45 Q—B7 ch gives up a valuable pawn in order to obtain the still more valuable asset of an irruption by a Rook into the hostile camp.

Even the final move 53 R—R8 represents, theoretically speaking, the sacrifice of the well-advanced QP with the sole object of liquidating the last remaining pieces.

1 P—K4   P—K4
2 Kt—KB3   Kt—QB3
3 B—B4   B—B4
4 P—B3   B—Kt3
5 P—Q4   Q—K2
6 Castles   Kt—B3
7 P—Q5   Kt—QKt1
Hoping to return later to the fray via Q2, whereas, after 7 .... Kt—Q1; this piece would remain restricted for a long time. After 7 .... Kt—QR4; 8 B—Q3, followed by P—QKt4, Black's QKt would have suffered an inglorious death.

8 B—Q3
Although the central zone is closed, White counts on exerting an enduring pressure. An energetic line of play, not however devoid of risk, consists in the sacrifice of a pawn by 8 P—Q6, Q×P; 9 Q×Q, P×Q; 10 B—Q5, and White dominates the field in spite of the absence of Queens.

8 ......   P—Q3
9 QKt—Q2   P—QR3
In view of the menace of 10 Kt—B4,
Black wishes to preserve his active KB.

10 Kt—B4   B—R2
11 P—QR4   Castles
12 P—QKt4   Kt—K1
Intending the aggressive advance 13 ....
P—KB4; which, however, is prevented by
White's next move.

13 Q—B2   P—KKt3
Still hankering after .... P—KB4; and
trying at the same time to mobilise the
inactive KKt. But Black's position remains
cramped.

14 B—R6   Kt—Kt2
15 Kt—K3   P—KB3
Black sees himself compelled to abandon
the projected advance .... P—KB4.

16 QR—K1   R—B2
17 K—R1   Kt—Q2
Or, for example, 17 .... K—R1;
18 R—KKt1, and White will still initiate
a lively attack by P—Kt4.

18 P—Kt4   Kt—B1
19 R—KKt1   B×Kt
20 P×B   B—Q2
21 R—Kt3   P—B3
If Black wanted to prepare for this
counter-action by 21 .... R—B1; White
could prevent it altogether by 22 B—QB4.

22 B—QB4   P×P
23 B×QP   B—K3
24 QR—KKt1   R—B1
25 Kt—R4   B×B
26 P×B   R—B2
Against 26 .... K—R1; White would
reply with the same move as in the text,
namely 27 Kt—B5, for after 27 .... P×Kt;
28 P×P, Black's KKt is tied to its
post because of the threat 29 R—Kt8
mate.

27 Kt—B5
Having in masterly fashion concentrated
his forces on the critical sector, White at
last forces the enemy defences.

27 ......   P×Kt
If 27 .... Kt×Kt; 28 P×Kt, P—KKt4;
in the hope of keeping the KKt file closed,
then 29 P—R4, or more speedily still,
29 B×P, P×B; 30 R×P ch would break
down all resistance.

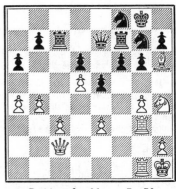

Position after 26 .... R—B2

28 P×P   Q—K1
29 Q—KKt2   Q—Q2
30 R×Kt ch   R×R
31 B×R   Q×B
32 Q—QB2   Kt—Kt3
33 P×Kt   P—R3
If 33 .... P—KR4; White's reply in the
text would be still more effective. But, on
the whole, Black has succeeded in holding
back the hostile attack and, in the next
phase, White has to look for a fresh
opening.

34 Q—B5   Q—B1
If 34 .... R×P; 35 Q—K6 ch, K—R1
(35 .... K—B1; 36 Q×QP ch, etc.);
36 Q—K8 ch, Q—Kt1; 37 P—Kt7 ch,
K—R2; 38 Q—Kt6 mate.

35 P—B4   K—Kt2
If instead, 35 .... R×P; 36 Q—K6 ch,
K—Kt2 (36 .... K—R1; 37 P—Kt7 ch);
37 Q—Q7 ch, K any; 38 Q—R7 mate.

36 R—QB1   P—Kt3
37 P—K4   Q—K2
38 Q—B2   R—Kt2
39 P—R4   P—QR4
A better defence would result from 39 ....
Q—Q2. Suicidal in any case would be
39 .... K×P; because of 40 R—Kt1 ch,
and the attack on the KKt file revives in
full vigour.

40 P—R5   P×P
41 R—QKt1   P—Kt6
42 R×P   Q—Q2
43 Q—B5
With a decisive gain of territory, for
Black can neither afford to exchange Queens
(43 .... Q×Q; 44 P×Q, threatening
45 P—R5), nor try to escape the worst by
43 .... Q×P (because of 44 R—KB3).

43 ...... Q—K2
44 Q—K6 Q—QB2
45 Q—B7 ch Q × Q
46 P × Q R—R2

Trying to obviate the threat 47 P—R5, but the entry of the white Rook into the hostile camp will decide the issue.

47 R × P R × RP
48 R × P R × P
49 R × P K—B1
50 P—Q6 R × P
51 P—Q7 R—Q5
52 R × P K × P
53 R—R8 Resigns

Compulsory but also compelling, for after 53 .... R × P; 54 R—R7 ch, K—K3; 55 R × R, K × R; 56 P—R6, the black King is "outside the square" and can no longer stop the pawn's victorious progress.

4

White   *Black*

DE LA
BOURDONNAIS McDONNELL

(Match, 1834)

The following game is a good example of how Rooks should be handled. It shows that their work can be far more flexible than is generally supposed.

1 P—K4 P—K4
2 Kt—KB3 Kt—QB3
3 B—B4 B—B4
4 P—B3 P—Q3

Combining development with a threat by 4 .... Kt—B3 is a more active procedure.

5 P—Q4 P × P
6 P × P B—Kt3

After 6 .... B—Kt5 ch, White would have the choice between 7 Kt—B3, or even 7 K—B1 (threatening 8 P—Q5, followed by Q—R4 ch). Now, however, Black's KB continues to control the hostile centre.

7 P—Q5

Closing the centre and particularly the diagonal occupied by his KB. But he hopes, in return, to obtain free play for his remaining pieces. The most intensive continuation is 7 Kt—B3.

7 ...... Kt—K4

A mistake would be 7 .... Kt—R4, because of 8 B—Q3, with the threat 9 P—QKt4. And if 7 .... QKt—K2; 8 P—K5 favours White's chances.

8 Kt × Kt P × Kt
9 Kt—B3 Kt—B3

Instead of this routine move, 9 .... Q—R5 was a promising *sortie* because of the absence of a defending white Knight.

10 B—Kt5 Castles

If, in order to relieve the pin as quickly as possible, Black plays 10 .... P—KR3, White plays neither 11 B—R4, P—Kt4; 12 B—KKt3, Q—K2, etc., nor 11 B × Kt, Q × B, etc., with an even game, but— as an effective intermediary manœuvre— 11 B—Kt5 ch, B—Q2; 12 B × B ch, Q × B; 13 B × Kt, P × B; 14 Q—B3, Q—Q3; 15 Castles KR, and White dominates the field.

11 Q—B3 Q—Q3

This unpins the Knight or, alternatively, achieves simplification; more effective— with the same kind of idea—was 11 .... P—KR3; 12 B × Kt, Q × B; 13 Q × Q, P × Q; and if 14 P—KKt4, K—R2; preparing without delay for eventualities.

12 B × Kt Q × B
13 Q × Q P × Q

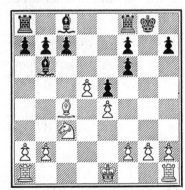

14 P—KKt4

A fine conception, which combines defence (prevention of the liberating move 14 .... P—KB4) with attack (breakthrough on the KKt file). It is clear that Black cannot reply with 14 .... B × P; because of 15 R—KKt1, P—KR4; 16 P—KR3, winning the Bishop.

14 ...... K—Kt2
An impetuous player, McDonnell prepares an aggressive counter-action (18 .... P—KR4), but 14 .... K—R1 would have been more level-headed. Other lines of defence would be 14 .... P—KR3 or 14 .... B—R4, in order to eliminate a dangerous unit; but Black does not seem to fear his adversary's machinations.

15 Kt—K2   R—R1
16 R—KKt1   K—B1
17 R—Kt2
With the double mission of rendering the King mobile (by guarding the KBP) and of doubling Rooks on the critical file.

17 ......   K—K2
18 Castles   P—KR4
See note to Black's 14th move. A sounder continuation would be 18 .... B—Q2, to be followed by .... QR—KKt1.

19 P—Kt5   P—KB4
A critical juncture. Again Black seems to underestimate his opponent's resources and to assess his own chances too highly. There was a complicated continuation as follows: 19 .... P×P; 20 R×P, B×P (threatening 21 .... B—K6 ch), e.g.:

A. 21 R×P ch, K—Q3; and Black wins.

B. 21 K—Q2 (to parry 21 .... B—K6 ch), B—R5; overcoming the attack.

C. 21 P—Q6 ch, P×P; 22 R—Kt7, B—K3; 23 B×B, K×B; 24 R—B1, B—K6 ch; 25 K—Q1, QR—KB1; and Black has consolidated his position.

D. 21 R—Kt7 (threatening 22 P—Q6 ch); 21 .... K—B1; 22 R—Kt2, B—K6 ch; 23 K—B2, R—KKt1; putting his house in order.

E. 21 R—Kt2 (the best continuation of the attack); 21 .... B—K6 ch; 22 K—B2, etc., with even chances.

20 Kt—B3   B—B4
Providing against the threat which has suddenly arisen: 21 P—Q6 ch, P×P; 22 Kt—Q5 ch.

21 P—Kt6   B—Q3
22 KtP×P   K×P
23 P—B4
If 23 QR—Kt1, at once, Black plays 23 .... P—B5; barring the way.

23 ......   KP×P
24 QR—Kt1   K—B1
Or 24 .... B—Q2; 25 R—Kt7 ch, K—K1; 26 P—K5, B—KB1 (26 .... B×P; 27 R—K1); 27 R (Kt7)—Kt6; and White has his own way.

25 R—Kt6
Preparing the final onslaught which White conducts with great ability.

25 ......   P—B6
26 P×P   B—K4
27 P—Q6
Reopening the diagonal, closed for the last 20 moves (7 P—Q5), with overwhelming effect.

27 ......   P×P
28 R—Kt8 ch R×R
29 R×R ch   K—K2
30 Kt—Q5 ch K—Q2
31 B—Kt5 mate

5

White	Black
SPIELMANN	JANOWSKI

(Carlsbad, 1907)

The feature of the following beautiful game is the thorough manner in which White takes advantage of the K file, which he opens at the cost of the temporary sacrifice of a pawn (8 Castles), and finally controls at the cost of another pawn (19 P—Q6).

His forces penetrate into the hostile position (18 R—K7, 25 KKt—K7 ch, and 29 Kt—K7), with the most damaging results.

1 P—K4   P—K4
2 Kt—KB3 Kt—QB3
3 B—B4   B—B4
4 P—B3   P—Q3
5 P—Q4   P×P
6 P×P   B—Kt3
7 P—KR3
As in reply to 7 B—K3, or 7 Kt—B3, Black's 7 .... B—KKt5 might prove irksome, White decides to sacrifice a *tempo* in his development in order to eliminate this threat once and for all.

7 ......   Kt—B3
8 Castles
If 8 Kt—B3, there follows the well-known simplification: 8 .... KKt×P; 9 Kt×Kt (or 9 B×P ch, K×B; 10 Kt×Kt, R—K1, with artificial castling, advantageous in this case; or 9 Q—K2, Castles); 9 .... P—Q4.

For this reason White gives up the threatened pawn for the sake of an attack.

8	Kt×KP
9 R—K1	Castles
10 R×Kt	P—Q4
11 B—KKt5	

White gains an important *tempo* by this intermediary manœuvre, as Black could not very well reply 11.... P—B3, on account of 12 B—Kt3, P×B; 13 Kt—B3, with advantage to White.

11	Q—Q3
12 B×P	Q×B
13 Kt—B3	Q—Q2
14 P—Q5	

Although isolated, this centre pawn assumes the *rôle* of a blockader.

14	P—B3
15 B—K3	Kt—Q1

In order to control the square at his K3, for if 15 .... Kt—K2, there follows 16 B×B, RP×B; 17 Q—Kt3, K—R1; 18 Kt—Q4, with many threats.

16 B×B	RP×B
17 Q—K2	

Increasing the pressure on the K file.

17	Kt—B2
18 R—K7	Q—Q1

With the counter-threat 19 .... Kt—K4.

19 P—Q6

A *vacating sacrifice*.

19	Kt×P

A crucial moment. It is obvious that after 19 .... Q×P; 20 Kt—QKt5 (as also 20 R—Q1) is to White's advantage. Similarly, if 19 .... P—B3, the following beautiful continuation secures White an advantage in material: 20 P—Q7, B×P; 21 R—Q1, Kt—K4; 22 QR×B, Kt×R; 23 Q—K6 ch, K—R1; 24 R×Kt. Less clear is the ultimate result of 19 .... P×P; e.g. 20 Kt—QKt5 (the most logical move is 20 R—K3, anticipating future weaknesses on Black's Q side); 20 .... R—R4; 21 R—Q1, Kt—K4; threatening 22 .... R×Kt.

20 Kt—Q5	R—B2
21 R—K1	B—Q2
22 Kt—R4	

This Knight wishes even to surpass its companion in usefulness.

22	R—R4

Instead of thus relinquishing the greatest possible control of his first rank, Black would have done better to play 22 .... P—B3.

23 R×R	Kt×R
24 Kt—B5	

A tactical finesse which is to bring yet another piece into the firing line (24 .... B×Kt; 25 Q—K8 ch, Q×Q; 26 R×Q mate).

24	Kt—K4

Ordre, contre-ordre, désordre. The black King should have looked after his own defence by 24 .... K—B1.

25 KKt—K7 ch	K—R1
26 P—QKt4	R—R1
27 P—B4	Kt—Kt3
28 Kt×Kt ch	P×Kt
29 Kt—K7	Q—K1

Black's precarious situation is well illustrated also in the following variation: 29 .... B—K1; 30 R—Q1, and the black Queen has only one pitiful retreat, namely 30 .... Q—Kt1; after which follows: 31 Q—Kt4, threatening 32 Q—R4 mate.

30 Q—KB2	P—KKt4
31 P×P	P×P

In order to save the mate, Black must already leave corpses by the way.

32 Q—Q2	P—Kt4
33 Q×P	R—R3
34 R—K4	R—R3

Black has no valid defence, e.g. 34 .... Q—B2; 35 R—R4 ch, R—R3; 36 R×R ch, P×R; 37 Q×P ch, Q—R2; 38 Kt—Kt6 ch (or 38 Q—B8 ch, with mate to follow), 38 .... K—Kt1; 39 Q—B8 mate.

35 Kt—B5	Q—Kt3

Saving the exchange, but losing a piece. As, however, neither 35 .... Q×R nor 35 .... R—K3 is feasible (because of 36 Q×P mate), Black disdains the continuation 35 .... Q—KB1; 36 Kt×R, P×Kt; with a slightly prolonged agony.

36 Q—Q8 ch

If 36 Kt×R, Black plays, not 36 .... Q×Q (because of 37 Kt—B7 ch and Kt×Q), but 36 .... Q×R; and Black is safe!

36	K—R2
37 Q×B	R—R4
38 R—Kt4	R—Kt4
39 R—R4 ch	Resigns

6

White	Black
BECKER	MATTISON

(Carlsbad, 1929)

The strategic basis of many brilliant games consists in the attack against the sensitive point KB7. The following game offers some novel aspects of this ancient theme in the evolutions of the white Knights, which alternately mask and unmask the critical KB file.

1 P—K4	P—K4
2 Kt—KB3	Kt—QB3
3 B—B4	B—B4
4 P—B3	P—Q3
5 P—Q4	P×P
6 P×P	B—Kt3
7 Kt—B3	

With the firm intention of maintaining a compact and, at the same time, a flexible centre.

7	Kt—B3
8 Castles	B—Kt5

Trying to demonstrate that White's centre can be challenged.

9 B—K3	Castles

After .... B×Kt; 10 P×B, the strengthening of White's centre would counterbalance the doubled pawns, whilst the open KKt file would also (after K—R1 and R—KKt1) further White's interests.

10 B—Kt3
Parrying a possible threat of 10 .... KKt×P; 11 Kt×Kt, P—Q4, which would have eased Black's position in the centre.

10	R—K1
11 Q—Q3	B—KR4

Here also 11 .... B×Kt; 12 P×B would serve White's cause, whereas now Black hopes to initiate a lasting pressure against the hostile KP by .... B—Kt3.

12 Kt—Q2	Kt—KKt5

A premature counter-plan. More in the spirit of this variation would be, as mentioned before: 12 .... B—Kt3 (threat: 13 .... P—Q4); yet, with 13 P—Q5, Kt—K4; 14 Q—K2, White would maintain a strong position.

13 Kt—Q5	Kt×B
14 P×Kt	

White no longer has his two Bishops, but the open KB file is a valuable asset in return.

14	R—KB1
15 R—B2	Kt—K2
16 Kt—KB4	B—Kt5

One defender the less for the critical square at his KB2, against which White will soon concentrate all his forces.

17 QR—KB1	Q—B1

Trying to parry as best he can the threat which has suddenly arisen of 18 Kt—K6.

18 P—KR3	B—Q2
19 Kt—B4	P—Kt3

The bid for freedom, 19 .... B—Kt4, would cost Black a piece after 20 Kt×B, B×Q; 21 Kt×Q, B×R; 22 Kt×Kt ch, K—R1; 23 R×B.

20 P—Kt4
Initiating a powerful attack.

20	K—Kt2
21 P—K5	

This threatens first and foremost: 22 Kt×B, RP×Kt; 23 Kt—R5 ch, P×Kt; 24 R×P ch, R×R; 25 R×R ch, with mate to follow.

21 ...... P—Q4
Proffering a pawn to ease the hostile pressure.

22 Kt×B	RP×Kt
23 P—K4	

Instead of winning the pawn by 23 Kt×QP, Kt×Kt; 24 B×Kt, B—K3, etc., with a measure of relief for the defending forces, White carries on his attack with the utmost energy.

23	P×P
24 Q×P	B—B3
25 Q—K3	

The threat of 26 Kt—R5 ch still obtains.

25	K—R1
26 Kt—R5	

At all cost! Less convincing, though also good, would be 26 Kt—K6.

26 ...... P×Kt
Otherwise 27 Q—R6 is decisive.

27 R×P	R×R
28 R×R	

After the conquest of his KB2, Black is defenceless.

28 ...... Kt—Q4
After 28 .... B—Q4, there would also follow 29 Q—R6 (.... B×R; 30 Q—B6 ch, K—Kt1; 31 B×B ch, and mate in 3).

29 Q—R6   Q—KKt1
30 B×Kt   Q—Kt3
Or 30 .... B×B; 31 Q—B6 ch, followed by mate.

31 R—B8 ch   Resigns.

7

White   *Black*
STEINITZ   VON BARDELEBEN

(Hastings, 1895)

The feature of the following game is how White fastened on a small weakness in the enemy's camp and how, by skilful manœuvring, he prevented him from castling. Never relaxing his grip, he wound up the game with one of the most beautiful and æsthetically satisfying combinations ever devised on the chessboard.

1 P—K4   P—K4
2 Kt—KB3   Kt—QB3
3 B—B4   B—B4
4 P—B3   Kt—B3
5 P—Q4   P×P
6 P×P   B—Kt5 ch
7 Kt—B3

A move already advocated by Greco the Calabrese in 1619, by which White offers to give up a pawn for the attack.

7 ......   P—Q4
The usual and better course here is 7 .... Kt×KP; though Black must not hope to hold the gain of the pawn.

8 P×P
White has come out of the preliminary skirmish with a pawn in the centre. Even though it is isolated, this pawn will prove a tower of strength.

8 ......   KKt×P
9 Castles   B—K3
After this move which, to all appearances, is perfectly sound, Black loses his chance of castling. He should, at all cost, have played 9 .... B×Kt, and then completed his development.

10 B—KKt5   B—K2
11 B×Kt   QB×B
12 Kt×B   Q×Kt
13 B×B   Kt×B
14 R—K1
After this orgy of exchanges, Black finds himself unable to castle. With his next moves he tries to get his King into safety by "artificial castling," but it takes too much time.

14 ......   P—KB3
15 Q—K2   Q—Q2
16 QR—B1   P—B3
17 P—Q5
A fine *vacating sacrifice.* The square Q4 is made available for the Knight, thus greatly intensifying the attack.

17 ......   P×P
18 Kt—Q4   K—B2
Black has almost castled, but not quite.

19 Kt—K6
Threatening 20 R—B7.

19 ......   KR—QB1
20 Q—Kt4   P—KKt3
21 Kt—Kt5 ch K—K1

22 R×Kt ch
An amazing situation! All White's pieces are *en prise,* and Black threatens .... R×R mate. Yet he cannot take the checking Rook, 22 .... Q×R; 23 R×R ch, R×R; 24 Q×R ch, and White remains a piece ahead. The variations resulting from 22 .... K×R show the astounding degree of precision, which was required of White's calculations, before he could venture on the move in the text, e.g. 22 .... K×R; 23 R—K1 ch, K—Q3; 24 Q—Kt4 ch (neither 24 R—K6 ch, K—B4; nor 24 Q—B4 ch, K—B4 would do); 24 .... R—B4 (or 24 .... K—B3; 25 R—B1 mate, or 24 .... K—B2; 25 Kt—K7 ch, K—Kt1; 26 Q—B4 ch, and wins); 25 R—K6 ch, and wins. In this beautiful combination the Rook remains *en prise* for several moves until Black, compelled to capture it, succumbs to a mating finish.

22	K—B1
23 R—B7 ch	K—Kt1
24 R—Kt7 ch	Resigns

Mate in eleven moves can be prevented only at ruinous cost in material, e.g.: 24 .... K—R1; 25 R×P ch, K—Kt1; 26 R—Kt7 ch, K—R1; 27 Q—R4 ch, K×R; 28 Q—R7 ch, K—B1; 29 Q—R8 ch, K—K2; 30 Q—Kt7 ch, K—K1; 31 Q—Kt8 ch, K—K2; 32 Q—B7 ch, K—Q1; 33 Q—B8 ch, Q—K1; 34 Kt—B7 ch, K—Q2; 35 Q—Q6 mate.

8

White	Black
STEINITZ	LASKER

(Match, 1896–7)

In the following game we see the application of that important principle—economy of means. Black, faced with the dilemma either of having an extra piece and submitting to an attack, or of having an extra pawn only, with the superior position, unhesitatingly renounces spurious possessions.

1 P—K4	P—K4
2 Kt—KB3	Kt—QB3
3 B—B4	B—B4
4 P—B3	Kt—B3
5 P—Q4	P×P
6 P×P	B—Kt5 ch

After a passive retreat—6 .... B—Kt3—White would soon exploit his superiority in the centre by 7 P—Q5, Kt—K2; 8 P—K5, Kt—K5 (after 8 .... Kt—Kt5, the same energetic thrust 9 P—Q6 secures White's advantage); 9 .... P×P; 10 P×P, Kt×BP; 11 Q—Kt3, Kt×R (or 11 .... Castles; 12 Kt—Kt5, with a winning attack); 12 B×P ch, K—B1; 13 B—Kt5, forcing the win.

7 Kt—B3	Kt×KP
8 Castles	B×Kt

After 8 .... Kt×Kt; 9 P×Kt, B×P, the high-mettled continuation 10 Q—Kt3 (already indicated in 1619 by the "Calabrese") gives White the better chances.

9 P×B

The *coup juste* is here 9 P—Q5, which prevents Black from freeing his game. White will soon recover the piece so sacrificed.

9 ......   P—Q4

A good move, consolidating Black's position, whereas 9 .... Kt×QBP would be a blunder because of 10 Q—K1 ch, followed by Q×Kt.

10 B—R3

This sacrifice proves to be not quite sound. But after 10 B—Q3, Castles; 11 B×Kt, P×B; 12 Kt—Kt5, Q—Q4, Black would also maintain the advantage.

10	P×B
11 R—K1	B—K3

Giving back the piece of his own free will, relying all the more on his extra pawn. Much more dangerous would be 11 .... P—B4, because of 12 Kt—Q2 (threatening 13 P—B3); 12 .... K—B2; 13 Kt×Kt, P×Kt; 14 R×P, and the black King is not yet in safety.

12 R×Kt	Q—Q4
13 Q—K2	Castles

Black has thus overcome all the difficulties of the opening.

14 Kt—K5	KR—K1
15 Kt×Kt	

He estimates that with Bishops of opposite colours the draw will be easier to achieve.

15	Q×Kt
16 R—K1	R—Kt1

Whilst his Bishop obstructs the open K file, Black now tries to organise an attack on the K side.

17 R—K5	P—QKt3
18 B—B1	P—KKt4

A well-founded sacrifice of a pawn. White would have done better to refuse it.

19 R×P	R×R
20 B×R	R—Kt1
21 P—B4	B—Q4

Threatening 22 .... P—KR3, which would also be available after 22 Q—R5, P—KR3 (instead of 22 .... B×P; 23 Q×BP); 23 Q×RP, Q×Q; 24 B×Q, R×P ch, with advantage to Black.

22 P—Kt3	K—Kt2
23 P—KR3	Q—Kt4
24 K—R2	R—Kt3
25 Q—KB2	P—KB3

Not only driving back the hostile Bishop, but preventing also the irruption 26 R—K5.

26 B—R4	B—B3
27 P—Kt4	Q—Q4

After the regrouping of Queen and Bishop, Black's pressure on the long diagonal becomes evident.

28 Q—B2

Greater resistance was possible after 28 P—B5 (and if then 28 .... R—R3 White replies, not with 29 Q—B2, R×B, etc., but with 29 B—Kt3, Q—B6; 30 Q—K2), for now Black is able to throw another unit into the fight.

28	P—KR4
29 P—Kt5	P×P
30 B×P	

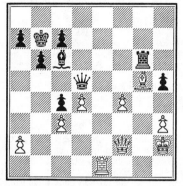

30 ...... P—R5

Blockading the hostile position. If now, e.g. 31 R—KKt1, there follows equally 31 .... R×B (32 R×R, Q—R8 mate, or 32 P×R, Q—Q3 ch).

31 R—KB1	R—Kt1
32 Q—Q2	P—R4
33 P—R4	R—K1

Threatening 34 .... R—K6. Weak would be 33 .... B×P, because of 34 Q—KKt2, forcing the exchange of Queens.

34 P—B5 R—KKt1
Resigns

A *Zugzwang* position, any move by White leading to loss in material.

9

| *White* | *Black* |
| SPIELMANN | DURAS |

(Carlsbad, 1907)

The dangers of a denuded King's field are well illustrated in the following game, in which White, with great ingenuity, gains access to the critical square at Black's KR2.

1 P—K4	P—K4
2 Kt—KB3	Kt—QB3
3 B—B4	B—B4
4 P—B3	Kt—B3
5 P—Q4	P×P
6 P×P	B—Kt5 ch
7 Kt—B3	

This move of Greco's (instead of 7 B—Q2) is rarely seen in modern tournament practice, as it does no more than secure a draw for White.

7	KKt×P
8 Castles	B×Kt
9 P—Q5	

The *Möller attack*, thought out in 1898, strengthens White's chances.

9 ...... B—B3
The only good reply.

| 10 R—K1 | Kt—K2 |
| 11 R×Kt | P—Q3 |

If at once 11 .... Castles, White has the choice between the thrust 12 P—Q6 and the "bayonet attack" 12 P—KKt4.

12 B—Kt5
Here also 12 P—KKt4 is a noteworthy continuation.

12 ...... Castles
Allowing his K position to be broken up. A continuation which has been thoroughly analysed is: 12 .... B×B; 13 Kt×B, Castles; 14 Kt×RP (the only way to maintain the attack, for if 14 Q—R5, P—KR3, and Black has nothing more to fear); 14 .... K×Kt; 15 Q—R5 ch, K—Kt1; 16 R—R4, P—KB4; 17 Q—R7 ch (other continuations such as 17 R—K1 or 17 B—K2 lead to no clear-cut result); 17 .... K—B2; 18 R—R6, R—KKt1; 19 R—K1, Q—B1; 20 B—Kt5 (cutting off the King's line of retreat); 20 .... R—R1; 21 Q×R, P×R; 22 Q—R7 ch, K—B3; 23 R×Kt, Q×R; 24 Q×RP ch, forcing a perpetual check.

13 B×B P×B
14 Kt—R4
The value of this move lies in the fact that the Queen can now reach the critical sector with the utmost rapidity.

14	Kt—Kt3
15 Q—R5	K—R1
16 QR—K1	B—Q2
17 B—Q3	

Preparing the final assault.

17 ...... R—KKt1
Hoping to consolidate his position by 18 .... R—Kt2.

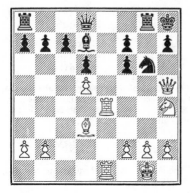

18 R—K7
Unmasking the Bishop, so that after 18 .... Kt×R; White can play 19 Q×P mate.

```
18 ......        R—Kt2
19 B×Kt          P×B
20 Kt×P ch       K—Kt1
```
Or 20 .... R×Kt; 21 Q×P mate.

```
21 R×R ch        Resigns
```
(For after 21 .... K×R; 22 R—K7 ch, and Black has no resource.)

10

White	Black
SCHIFFERS	HARMONIST

(Frankfort, 1887)

An attack often becomes irresistible when the defence has to attend to more than one weakness at the same time.
In the following game White, in addition to the traditional attack on KB7, obtains complete control of the K file, and the resulting pressure becomes overwhelming.

```
1 P—K4          P—K4
2 Kt—KB3        Kt—QB3
3 B—B4          B—B4
4 P—B3          Kt—B3
5 P—Q4          P×P
6 P×P           B—Kt5 ch
7 B—Q2
```
Development by opposition.

```
7 ......         B×B ch
```
The gain of a pawn by 7 .... KKt×P would be illusory, for after 8 B×B, Kt×B;

9 Q—Kt3 (with a double attack on KB7 and QKt4); 9 .... P—Q4; 10 Q×Kt, P×B; 11 Castles, Q—Q4; 12 Kt—R3, White recovers his pawn with a clearly superior position.

```
8 QKt×B          P—Q4
```
With this counter-thrust in the centre—which is very important for Black in nearly all open games—Black relieves the tension to a considerable extent. Not only is his QB now mobile, but the hostile centre is partly eliminated.

```
9 P×P            KKt×P
```
Positional judgment: the pawn which White has maintained in the centre is both *isolated* and *blockaded* by Black's central Knight.
The chances are approximately equal, and the game looks like drifting to a peaceful conclusion.

```
10 Q—Kt3
```
With pressure on the adverse post at Q5. An amusing continuation might arise from 10 Castles, Castles; 11 Kt—K5 (combinative play. Thoughtless would be 11 Q—Kt3 at this juncture; and there would be nothing more than a draw after the quiet continuation 11 R—K1, because of 11 .... QKt—K2 and 12 .... P—QB3); 11 .... Kt×P; 12 Kt—Kt3, Kt×Kt; 13 B×Kt (Q5), Kt×R (falling into the trap, whilst after 13 .... Q—B3 Black obtains an even game); 14 B×P ch, K—R1; 15 Q—R5, with a winning attack.

```
10 ......         QKt—K2
```
Careless would be 10 .... Kt—R4, because of 11 Q—R4 ch, P—B3; 12 B—Q3, Castles; 13 Castles, and White already threatens 14 P—QKt4.

```
11 Castles KR     Castles
12 KR—K1
```
This instant occupation of the open K file serves ulterior motives. Another good continuation is 12 Kt—K4.

```
12 ......         P—QB3
```
A sound defensive move with a three-fold object: (1) to strengthen the post at Q4; (2) to threaten 13 .... P—QKt4 eventually; (3) to give the Queen easy access to the Q side.

```
13 P—QR4
```
Preventing the advance 13 .... P—QKt4, as mentioned above, and giving the white Queen increased mobility.

Another good continuation is again
13 Kt—K4.

13 ......   Q—B2
After 13 .... Q—Kt3, White replies
14 Q—R3, with advantage.

14 QR—B1
With the transparent threat of 15 B×Kt,
Kt×B; 16 Q×Kt. Other energetic con-
tinuations are 14 Kt—K4 or 14 Kt—K5.

14 ......   Kt—B5
Instead of relinquishing the important
post at Q4—unmasking at the same time
a very dangerous diagonal—he should have
defended the position by 14 .... Q—R4,
or even 14 .... Q—B5.
Weak, however, would be 14 .... B—K3,
on account of 15 Kt—Kt5, and if 14 ....
Q—Kt3 then, as before mentioned, 15 Q—R3.

15 Kt—Kt5   Kt (K2)—Kt3
Critical though Black's position has
become, 15 .... Kt—B4 would have provided a more active defence.

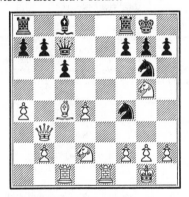

16 R—K8
A beautiful *deflecting sacrifice*.

16 ......   R×R
Or 16 .... B—K3; 17 R×R, R×R;
18 Kt×B, Kt×Kt; 19 B×Kt, P×B;
20 Q×P ch, and White has won an important pawn.

17 B×P ch   K—R1
Or 17 .... K—B1; 18 Kt×P ch, K—K2;
19 R—K1 ch, B—K3; 20 R×B ch, and
White wins.

18 B×R   Kt—K7 ch
With the passing satisfaction of winning
an adverse Rook, after which White initiates
the final assault.

19 K—R1   Kt×R
20 Kt—B7 ch   K—Kt1
21 Kt—R6 dbl ch   K—B1
22 Q—Kt8 ch   K—K2
23 B×Kt   P×B
24 Q×P ch   K—Q1
25 Q—B8 ch   K—Q2
26 Kt—K4
The reserve cavalry threatens 27 Kt—B5
mate.

26 ......   Q—Q1
27 Q—Q6 ch   K—K1
28 Kt—B6 ch   Resigns.

11

White	Black
HOFFMANN	VON PETROFF

(Warsaw, 1844)

*The main feature of the following out-
standing game is the simultaneous onslaught
of both adversaries on KB7.*
*Black's manœuvres culminate in a magnifi-
cent Queen sacrifice, followed by a relentless
King-hunt.*

1 P—K4   P—K4
2 Kt—KB3   Kt—QB3
3 B—B4   B—B4
4 P—B3   Kt—B3
5 P—Q4   P×P
6 P—K5
This intermediary manœuvre (instead of
the usual recapture by 6 P×P) contains
some practical chances.

6 ......   Kt—K5
The energetic counter-thrust in the centre,
6 .... P—Q4; contesting territory is preferable to the superficial move in the text.

7 B—Q5
Looking for adventure. By playing
simply 7 P×P, B—Kt5 ch; 8 B—Q2, Kt×B;
9 QKt×Kt, etc., White could have enjoyed
a peaceful life.

7 ......   Kt×KBP
Forced, but forcible also.

8 K×Kt   P×P dis ch
9 K—Kt3
The retreat to K1 was more reasonable.
At Kt3 the King enjoys a sense of false
security. Faulty, however, would be 9 B—K3,

because of 9 .... B×B ch; 10 K×B, P×P;
and if 11 B×P ch, not 11 .... K×B;
12 Q—Kt3 ch, followed by Q×P (Kt2),
but 11 .... K—K2; and Black wins
material.

9	P×P
10 B×P	Kt—K2
11 Kt—Kt5	

The lure of the combination. White also
gives free rein to his gifts of imagination
instead of continuing prudently with
11 P—KR3 (and if 11 .... Kt—B4 ch;
12 K—R2), with a watchful defence.

11	Kt×B
12 Kt×BP	

Here is the crux of White's combination.
However, he allows only for the continuation
12 .... K×Kt; 13 Q×Kt ch, K—K1,
although even then he could not very well
play 14 Q×B, on account of 14 ....
Q—Kt4 ch; 15 K—B2, R—B1 ch; 16 K—K1,
Q×P, etc. White's reasoning, when he
played his 11th move, was at fault, as
Black's stroke of genius on the next move
clearly demonstrates.

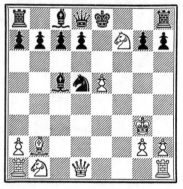

12	Castles

Black gives up a whole Queen, with the
sole object of controlling the open KB file
and thus cutting off the hostile King's
retreat.

13 Kt×Q

Or e.g. 13 Kt—R6 ch, P×Kt; 14 Q×Kt ch,
R—B2; 15 Q×B, P—Kt4 ch; 16 K—R3,
P—Q3 dis. ch; and wins.

Or, again, 13 Q×Kt, R×Kt; 14 P—KR3
(if 14 P—KR4, B—B7 ch, followed by
15 .... Q×P mate); 14 .... Q—Kt4 ch;
15 K—R2, Q×B5 ch; 16 P—Kt3, Q—B7 ch;
17 Q—Kt2, Q×Q ch; 18 K×Q, R—B7 ch;
19 K—Kt1, R×B dis ch; and Black remains
with an extra piece.

13	B—B7 ch

The sequel is a classic example of a King-
hunt.

14 K—R3	P—Q3 dis ch
15 P—K6	Kt—B5 ch
16 K—Kt4	Kt×KP

Threatening mate in two by 17 ....
R—B5 ch and 18 .... R—R5.

17 P—Kt3	Kt×Kt dis ch
18 K—R4	R—B5 ch
19 K—Kt5	Kt—K3 ch
20 K—R5	P—Kt3 ch
21 K—R6	R—R5 ch
22 P×R	B—K6 mate

12

White	Black
SCHUMOFF	VON JÄNISCH

(St. Petersburg, 1845)

*The next game illustrates how certain
manœuvres merely waste energy (e.g. 7 P×Kt,
8 Q—K2 ch, 12 Q—R5, 14 Q—Kt5 ch), and
help the adverse development. In the end
the white King's field is denuded of defenders,
with the result that might be expected.*

1 P—K4	P—K4
2 Kt—KB3	Kt—QB3
3 B—B4	B—B4
4 P—B3	Kt—B3
5 P—Q4	P×P
6 P—K5	P—Q4

This good move frees Black's game.

7 P×Kt

This exchange helps Black's mobilisation.
After the usual continuations 7 B—QKt5 or
7 B—K2, Black settles down in the centre
by 7 .... Kt—K5.

7	P×B
8 Q—K2 ch	

Having lost a pawn in the scramble, White
tries to engineer an attack and neglects
simpler measures, such as 8 KBP×P or
8 QBP×P.

8	B—K3
9 P×KtP	

If 9 Kt—Kt5, Q×P.

9	R—KKt1
10 P×P	

Relatively best is 10 B—Kt5. The

attempt 10 Kt—Kt5 (threatening 11 Kt×B, P×Kt; 12 Q—R5 ch, followed by Q×B) would again be abortive, e.g.: 10 .... Q—Q4; 11 Kt×RP, Castles ; 12 Kt—B6, Q×P, etc.

10	Kt×P
11 Kt×Kt	B×Kt
12 Q—R5	

This sally by the Queen, which, single-handed, carries on the fight, makes matters worse for White.

The continuation indicated was: 12 Castles, Q—B3; 13 Kt—B3, Q×P; 14 P—KKt3, with, after 14 .... Castles, some advantage still to Black.

| 12 ...... | Q—B3 |
| 13 Castles | R×P |

He could also unconcernedly have played 13 .... Castles (for then 14 B—Kt5 would be of no value because of 14 .... Q×P), but the text move shows up the weakness of White's manœuvres.

14 Q—Kt5 ch
The least evil would be 14 Kt—B3.

| 14 ...... | P—B3 |
| 15 Q×KtP | |

The white Queen's hour of triumph; Black is definitely prevented from castling. But now her own King succumbs to a well-prepared assault.

15 ...... R×P ch
A *break-up sacrifice*.

16 K×R	Q—Kt3 ch
17 K—R1	B—Q4 ch
18 P—B3	B×P ch

And mate next move.

13

| White | Black |
| 1st FUSILIERS | BOMBAY |

(Bombay, 1853)

1 P—K4	P—K4
2 Kt—KB3	Kt—QB3
3 B—B4	B—B4
4 P—B3	Kt—B3
5 P—Q4	P×P
6 P—K5	P—Q4
7 B—QKt5	

Skilfully evading a premature engage-

ment. Weak would be 7 P×Kt, P×B, etc.; but 7 B—K2 is playable.

| 7 ...... | Kt—K5 |
| 8 B×Kt ch | |

After 8 Kt×P, a solid continuation would be 8 .... B—Q2.

Against 8 P×P, Black would eschew the tempting 8 .... B—Kt5 ch (9 K—B1, threatening 10 Q—R4) in favour of 8 .... B—Kt3; with an evenly balanced position.

| 8 ...... | P×B |
| 9 P×P | B—Kt3 |

If 9 .... B—Kt5 ch; then, as indicated above, 10 K—B1, threatening 11 Q—R4.

10 Castles B—Kt5
This leads to more lively play than would arise from 10 .... Castles; 11 P—KR3, etc.

| 11 B—K3 | Castles |
| 12 Q—B2 | |

White must resort to incisive methods. Neither 12 QKt—Q2, Kt×Kt; 13 Q×Kt, B×Kt; 14 P×B, Q—R5, etc., nor 12 P—KR3, B—KR4; 13 P—KKt4, B—Kt3 would be comforting for White.

12	B×Kt
13 P×B	Kt—Kt4
14 Q—KB5	P—B3
15 Q—Kt4	P—KR3
16 P—B4	P—KB4
17 Q—Kt2	Kt—K3
18 R—Q1	Q—R5
19 Q—Kt3	Q—R4
20 Kt—B3	KR—K1
21 R—Q2	Kt—B1
22 Kt—K2	R—K3
23 Q—Kt2	R—Kt3
24 Kt—Kt3	Q—R5
25 K—R1	

From the 14th move onwards White has effected cool-headed manœuvres, which, besides consolidating his position, have created counter-threats.

25 ...... Kt—K3
Or 25 .... Q—Kt5; 26 P—KR3, etc., or 25 .... Q—Q1; 26 Q—R3, showing that the ensuing loss of a pawn could not be avoided.

26 Kt×P	R×Q
27 Kt×Q	R—Kt5
28 Kt—Kt2	R—KB1
29 P—KR3	R (Kt5)×P

The loss of the exchange is forced. After 29 .... R—Kt3; 30 Kt—R4, K—R2;

31 P—B5, Black's position becomes even more serious.

30 Kt× R	Kt× Kt
31 K—R2	Kt—Kt3
32 K—Kt3	K—B2
33 P—Kt4	K—K3
34 R—KKt1	R—B2
35 P—KR4	P—QR4
36 P—R3	P× P
37 P× P	Kt—K2
38 K—R3	K—Q2
39 P—R5	K—K3
40 R—Kt4	R—B6 ch
41 K—Kt2	R—B2
42 R—Q1	K—Q2
43 R—KKt1	Kt—B4
44 K—R3	K—K2
45 R—B4	K—K1

If 45 .... K—B1, for the "over-protection" of the KKtP, White still obtains a favourable liquidation by 46 P—K6, R—B3; 47 R—Kt6, etc.

46 R× Kt
Decisive, for both R and K penetrate into the hostile position.

46	R× R
47 R× P	R× P ch
48 K—Kt4	R—R8
49 K—B5	R—Q8
50 K—K6	K—B1
51 B× P	R—KR8
52 R—Kt6 dis ch	R× B
53 R× R	

Thanks to far-seeing strategy, White has again won the exchange, and all is plain sailing in the ensuing R v B ending.

53	B× P
54 R—R3	B—Kt7
55 P—B4	P—Q5
56 P—B5	B—B6
57 P—B6	Resigns.

14

White	Black
SCHUMOFF	KOLISCH

(St. Petersburg, 1862)

As in game 12, White gives here insufficient attention to his own safety. His evolutions tend to divert his forces from the essential sector, which is his King's field and the open KKt file.

1 P—K4	P—K4
2 Kt—KB3	Kt—QB3
3 B—B4	B—B4
4 Castles	Kt—B3

By attacking the KP Black speeds up castling. After 4 .... P—Q3 White plays 5 P—B3, so as to reply to 5 .... B—KKt5 with the counter-sally 6 Q—Kt3, or better still, with 6 P—Q4, P× P; 7 Q—Kt3.

5 P—Q4
If 5 P—B3, then, without much danger, 5 .... Kt× P; but instead of the bold move in the text, White can continue quietly with 5 P—Q3 or 5 Kt—B3 (*Italian Four Knights' Game*).

5 ......   B× P
Best, because if 5 .... QKt× P; 6 Kt× P, and if 5 .... P× P; 6 P—K5, with manifold complications (*Max Lange Attack*).

6 Kt× B   Kt× Kt
Again after 6 .... P× Kt; 7 P—K5, etc., is to White's advantage.

7 P—B4
A less flashy continuation is 7 B—KKt5.

7	P—Q3
8 P× P	P× P
9 B—Kt5	Q—K2

Preparing to castle on the Q side. After 9 .... B—K3, White has a good reply in 10 Kt—R3.

10 P—QKt4
He unnecessarily fears 10 .... Q—B4, and weakens his position. A normal course would have been:
10 Kt—B3, e.g. (*a*) 10 .... P—B3; 11 Kt—K2, B—Kt5; 12 P—B3, ridding himself of troublesome hostile pieces; or
(*b*) 10 .... B—K3; 11 B—Q3, Castles QR; 12 K—R1, with equal chances;
(*c*) 10 .... Q—B4 (a tempting move, which is brilliantly refuted); 11 B× P ch, K× B; 12 Q—R5 ch, K—K3; 13 B× Kt, P× B; 14 Kt—Q5, and White wins.

10 ......   B—K3
11 B× Kt
Here again 11 B—Q3 was preferable, and even to a greater degree on the next move, for after the exchanges which now ensue, Black's centre becomes more compact.

11	P× B
12 B× B	P× B
13 Q—R5 ch	Q—B2
14 Q—R4	Castles QR
15 Kt—R3	P—KB4

Black energetically assumes the initiative.

16 Q—B2   Q—R4
17 QR—K1

Preventing 17 .... Kt—K7 ch, and thus threatening 18 P×P, P×P; 19 P—B3, Kt—B3; 20 Q×P ch—but Black refuses to wait, and reinforces his pawns on the K side.

17 ......   P—B5
18 P—B3   Kt—B3
19 P—Kt5

Thanks to his control of the Q file, and presently of the KKt file as well, Black maintains the superior position, as he would do against any other continuation.

19 ......   Kt—Kt1
20 Q×RP   P—Kt3

The tempting bait of a pawn has allowed Black to deflect the hostile pieces from the field of action.

21 Q—R4   KR—Kt1
22 R—Q1

This opposition is too optimistic, and he should at all events have played 22 R—B2.

22 ......   R×P ch

An *irruptive sacrifice* with some beautiful features.

23 K×R   Q—K7 ch
24 K—R1

Or 24 R—B2, R—Kt1 ch; 25 K—R1, Q×R; 26 Q—B2, Q—B6 ch, followed by mate, or 24 K—R3, R—Kt1 (threatening mate); 25 R—Q8 ch, R×R (not 25 .... K×R, because of 26 Q—Q1 ch, with the exchange of Queens); 26 Q—B4, R—Q6 ch, and wins.

24 ......   R—Q7
Resigns.

15

White	Black
TAUBENHAUS	BURN

(Nottingham, 1886)

In the following game Black, by an energetic as well as methodical advance of his QP, obtains on the Q file a base for decisive action.

1 P—K4   P—K4
2 Kt—KB3   Kt—QB3
3 B—B4   B—B4
4 P—Q3

Instead of advancing this pawn to its fourth (with or without the preparatory

P—B3), White chooses a quiet continuation, which is sometimes called *Giuoco Pianissimo*.

4 ......   P—Q3
5 P—B3

In this variation also, the text move has its uses: in the case of a pin by 5 .... B—KKt5 it prevents the dangerous 6 .... Kt—Q5; and in addition it gives the white Queen access to the Queen's wing. On the other hand, it deprives the QKt of its natural outlet at QB3, which is why some strategists have a preference for 5 Kt—B3.

5 ......   Kt—B3
6 B—K3   B—Kt3
7 Q—K2   Kt—K2

This manœuvre is the first step towards Black's counter-thrust in the centre, ... P—Q4, with which move he will assume the initiative.

8 QKt—Q2   Kt—Kt3
9 P—KR3   P—B3
10 B—Kt3   Castles
11 P—Kt4

The sequel will show that this move, unless made to reinforce an attack, only creates a weakness (KB3).

A simple continuation such as 11 Castles KR, followed by KR—Q1 and Kt—B1, was called for.

11 ......   P—Q4

A normal reaction. The demonstration on the wing is answered by the thrust in the centre, which, being well prepared, rapidly gains territory.

12 P×P   Kt×QP
13 B×Kt

Already threatened with the loss of a pawn by 13 .... KKt—B5, White decides to give up the "two Bishops." Indeed, if 13 B—B2, there follows 13 .... KKt—B5; 14 Q—B1, P—KB4; and Black definitely dominates the field.

13 ......   P×B
14 Kt—B1

Intimidated by the impending .... P—Q5, White manœuvres aimlessly instead of seeking to simplify his task by 14 B×B, Q×B; 15 Kt—Kt3, Kt—B5; 16 Q—Q2, P—B3; 17 Castles QR, and White's position, though by no means comfortable, could be held.

14 ......   P—Q5
15 B—Q2   P×P
16 P×P   B—Q2

Positional judgment. In addition to the dynamic advantage of his two active Bishops,

Black exerts an enduring pressure against White's retarded pawn at his Q3.

17 Kt—Kt3

If 17 R—Q1, B—R5; and if 17 B—K3, B—R4; revealing the various weaknesses in White's camp.

17	B—Kt4
18 P—B4	B—B3
19 Castles KR	P—B3

One must admire the methodical and deliberate manner in which Black sets to work. Another way of protecting his KP was 19 .... R—K1.

20 Kt—B5	Q—Q2
21 P—KR4	

If 21 B—K3, then not B×Kt; 22 Q×B, Q×P; 23 Q×P, but, quite unperturbed, 21 .... KR—Q1; and if 21 KR—Q1, then 21 .... B—R5.

Therefore, refusing to consider the retreat 21 Kt—K1, White seeks salvation in a desperate enterprise.

21	QR—Q1
22 P—R5	

If 22 Kt—K1, P—K5.

22	Q×P

Black now reaps the first fruits of his fine positional play.

23 Q×Q	R×Q
24 P×Kt	B×Kt
25 B—Kt4	R—K1
26 P×P ch	K×P
27 P—B5	B—B2
28 Kt—Q6	R—KR1
29 Kt—B7	

Or 29 K—R2, K—Kt3 dis. ch; 30 K—Kt3, B—K7 dis. ch; winning the exchange and the game.

29	R—Q5
30 Kt×R	R×P ch
31 K—R2	P—K5 dis ch
32 K—R3	P—KKt4
Resigns.	

16

White	Black
BIRD	ENGLISCH

(London, 1883)

In the lively game which follows, White operates on a secondary battlefield (in this case the left wing); but he does this so cleverly that he succeeds in cutting a way for his forces into the very centre of the hostile fortress.

The final phase—in which Rooks and Knights run amok—abounds in unexpected turns.

1 P—K4	P—K4
2 Kt—KB3	Kt—QB3
3 B—B4	B—B4
4 P—B3	Kt—B3
5 P—QKt4	

This lateral demonstration, instead of the accepted continuations 5 P—Q3 or 5P—Q4, was at all times a favourite idea with that bold and impetuous master-player, H. E. Bird.

5	B—Kt3
6 P—Q3	P—Q3

An energetic counter would be 6 .... P—Q4; 7 P×P, KKt×P, freeing his centre but neglecting to protect his KP. A curious continuation occurred in a game Horwitz-Staunton 1851 as follows: 8 P—Kt5, QKt—K2; 9 Kt×P, Castles; 10 B—Kt2, B—K3; 11 Castles, K—R1; 12 P—QR4, P—KB3; 13 Kt—B3, Kt—Kt3; 14 B—R3, R—K1; 15 Q—Kt3, Kt (Kt3)—B5; 16 R—R2, P—QR3; 17 P×P, P×P; 18 B—B1, QR—Kt1; 19 Q—B2, B—Kt5; 20 KB×Kt, Kt—K7 ch; 21 K—R1, Q×B; 22 P—B4, Q×Kt; 23 P—R3, B×BP; 24 Kt—Q2, Kt—Kt6 ch; 25 K—R2; Black mates in four. (A *semi-smothered* mate.)

7 Castles	Castles
8 B—KKt5	B—K3
9 QKt—Q2	Q—K2
10 P—QR4	P—QR3
11 P—R5	B—R2
12 K—R1	P—R3
13 B—R4	QR—Q1

Methodically preparing to open the Q file

by 14 .... P—Q4, which causes White to redouble his efforts on the Q side.

14 P—Kt5   B×B
15 Kt×B

As after 15 P×B, Kt—Kt1; 16 R—QKt1, QKt—Q2; 17 P×P, P×P; 18 R—Kt7, B—Kt1, etc., White's position would suffer from the chronic weakness of his isolated Q side pawns, White decides to give up a pawn for the time being, for the sake of obtaining freedom of action on the left wing.

15 ......   P×P
16 Kt—K3   B×Kt
17 P×B   Q—K3

Clearly premature would be 17 .... P—Kt4, on account of 18 Kt×KtP.

18 Q—Kt1

Intense activity now begins on the Queen's wing, which now has become the main battlefield.

18 ......   P—Kt4
19 B—Kt3   Kt—QR2
20 P—B4

Enters a new and clever actor. Black cannot reply with 20 .... P×P, because of 21 Q×P.

20 ......   P—B3
21 P—B5   Kt—R4
22 P—R6

He continues, by repeated thrusts, to disorganize the hostile pawn formation.

22 ......   P×RP
23 R×P   Q—Q2
24 P—Q4   Kt×B ch
25 P×Kt   Kt—B1
26 P×QP   P—B3
27 R—B1

Not only has White recovered his pawn, but he has assumed the initiative as well.

27 ......   Kt×P
28 R (B1)×P   Kt—K1
29 Q×P   P—Kt5
30 Kt—R4   P×P
31 P×P   Q×P
32 Kt—B5   Q×P
33 R—K6

Over-refinement. By simply playing 33 Kt×P ch, K—R2; 34 Q—KR5, White could have overcome all resistance. For instance: 34 .... Kt—Kt2; 35 Q—R4, etc.; or 34 .... Q—Kt3; 35 R—R7 ch, Kt—Kt2; 36 R×Kt ch, K×R (36 .... Q×R; 37 Kt—B5 dis. ch); 37 R—B7 ch, and wins.

Again: 34 .... R—Q2; 35 Kt—B7 dis. ch, K—Kt2 (or 35 .... K—Kt1; 36 Q—R8 ch, etc.); 36 Q—R6 ch, K×Kt; 37 R×P ch, Kt×R (or 37 .... K—K2; 38 Q×R ch, K—Q1; 39 R—R8 ch, K—B2; 40 Q—B5, ch and mate next move); 38 R×Kt ch, with mate to follow.

33 ......   R—Q8 ch
34 K—R2   Q—Kt8
35 Q×Q   R×Q

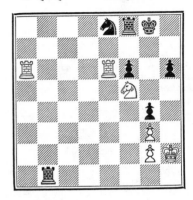

An exciting state of affairs.

36 R—R7

White's domination appears to be complete, but Black will not remain inactive.

An unfortunate attempt would be 36 Kt×P ch, K—Kt2; 37 Kt×P, because of 37 .... R—R1 ch, with mate to follow, whereas, after the move in the text it is White who threatens a mate by 37 Kt×P ch, K—R1; 38 R (K6)—K7.

36 ......   R—Kt4
37 Kt×P ch   K—R1
38 Kt×P   R—Kt4
39 R×Kt

Too optimistic. A terrible blunder would be 39 K—R3, because of 39 .... R—R4 mate. White, however, should have played 39 Kt—B2, keeping his adversary on the run.

39 ......   R—R4 ch
40 K—Kt1   R×R
41 Kt×P   R—R8 ch
42 K×R

A compulsory capture, for if 42 K—B2, R—KB1, and Black would win.

This *stalemate combination* is most instructive.

Bird reported that everyone present, except White, was much amused.

42	R—K8 ch
43 K—R2	R—R8 ch
44 K × R	Stalemate

17

| White | Black |
| DUBOIS | STEINITZ |

(London, 1862)

The feature of the following game is Black's counter-attack on the KR file. It is a classic example of the dangers of castling, under certain conditions, when the adverse King is still in the centre and has the option, if expedient, of castling on the opposite wing.

1 P—K4	P—K4
2 Kt—KB3	Kt—QB3
3 B—B4	B—B4
4 Castles	Kt—B3
5 P—Q3	P—Q3
6 B—KKt5	

By pinning the KKt before Black has castled, and especially when the white King is already located on the critical wing, White lays himself open to a violent counter-attack. Better is 6 B—K3, now or on the next move.

6	P—KR3
7 B—R4	P—KKt4
8 B—KKt3	P—KR4

Black is already master of the field. He threatens to win the Bishop by 9 .... P—R5.

9 P—KR4

After 9 P—KR3, P—R5; 10 B—R2, P—Kt5, Black also has the advantage.

After 9 Kt × KtP, an ingenious continuation arises: 9 .... P—R5; 10 Kt × P, P × B (this sacrifice of the Queen is sound); 11 Kt × Q (against 11 Kt × R, Black continues the attack with 11 .... B—KKt5; 12 Q—Q2, Q—K2, threatening .... Q—R2); 11 .... B—KKt5; 12 Q—Q2 (relatively best is to give back the Queen by 12 Kt—B3); 12 .... Kt—Q5 (threatening 13 .... Kt—K7 ch; 14 K—R1, R × P mate); 13 Kt—B3 (or e.g. 13 P—KR3, Kt—K7 ch; 14 K—R1, R × P ch; 15 P × R, B—B6 mate); 13 .... Kt—B6 ch; 14 P × Kt, B × P (threatening 15 .... P × P mate); 15 P × R, R—R8 mate.

| 9 ...... | B—KKt5 |
| 10 P—B3 | |

Or 10 P × P, P—R5; 11 B—R2, Kt—R2; and Black's attack increases in virulence.

10	Q—Q2
11 P—Q4	KP × P
12 P—K5	P × KP
13 B × P	Kt × B
14 Kt × Kt	Q—B4

Black's attack persists, although White has succeeded in clearing the field.

15 Kt × B

If 15 Q—R4 ch, K—B1.

| 15 ...... | P × Kt |
| 16 B—Q3 | |

If 16 P × P, Castles QR.

16	Q—Q4
17 P—Kt4	Castles QR
18 P—QB4	

Against 18 P × B, Black plays, not 18 .... QP × P; 19 B—B2, but 18 .... R × P; 19 P—QB4, QR—R1; 20 P—B3, P—Kt6; and White can no longer prevent mate by .... R—R8. It is now evident how powerfully Black's 17th move speeded up the destructive attack on the KR file.

18	Q—B3
19 P × B	R × P
20 P—B3	QR—R1

With the threat of 21 .... P—Kt6; 22 B—B5 ch, Q—K3; 23 B—R3 (or 23 B × Q ch, P × B, with unavoidable mate); 23 .... R × B; 24 P × R, Q × RP; and the white King is doomed.

| 21 P × P | Q—K1 |

Threatening mate in two by 22 .... Q—K6 ch.

| 22 Q—K2 | Q—K6 ch |
| 23 Q × Q | P × Q |

Still depriving the black King of the flight square at his KB2.

24 P—Kt3	R—R8 ch
25 K—Kt2	R (R1)—R7 ch
26 K—B3	R × R ch
27 B × R	R—B7 ch
28 K × P	R × B

After the harvest, the forces on either side are equal, but White with his restricted position, to say nothing of his sapless pawns, is lost.

29 P—R4	K—Q2
30 K—Q3	Kt × P
31 K—B3	Kt—K6
32 R—R2	

A desperate effort.

32	R × Kt
33 R—Q2 ch	K—B3
34 R—K2	R—B8 ch
35 K—Q2	R—B7 ch
36 K × Kt	R × R ch
37 K × R	P—B4

Resigns.

18

White	Black
MASON	WINAWER

(Vienna, 1882)

How to penetrate into the enemy camp? The manner in which White solves this problem in the following famous game is worthy of a genius.

1 P—K4	P—K4
2 Kt—KB3	Kt—QB3
3 B—B4	B—B4
4 P—Q3	P—Q3
5 B—K3	B—Kt3
6 QKt—Q2	P—KR3
7 Kt—B1	

Rather than to indicate by 7 Castles, the ultimate location of his King, White does some useful regrouping behind the lines.

7	Kt—B3
8 P—KR3	Kt—K2
9 Kt—Kt3	P—B3
10 B—Kt3	

A preventive retreat. Black cannot now play the counter-thrust in the centre 10 .... P—Q4, because of 11 Kt × P.

| 10 ...... | B × B |

Another plan to realise the above-named thrust would be 10 .... Kt—Kt3, followed by 11 .... P—Q4.

11 P × B	Q—Kt3
12 Q—Q2	P—QR4
13 P—B3	P—R5
14 B—Q1	B—K3
15 Castles	Q—B2
16 Kt—R4	P—QKt4
17 B—B2	

If 17 P—Q4, P—Q4, with the double threat 18 .... KP × P and 18 .... QP × P.

17	P—B4
18 QKt—B5	B × Kt
19 Kt × B	Kt × Kt
20 R × Kt	Kt—Q2
21 QR—KB1	P—B3

Closing the K file, but at the cost of weakening the K side. It is clear now that Black's 10 .... B × B, by the opening of the KB file, has in the end benefited White only.

| 22 B—Q1 | |

A mobile Bishop.

| 22 ...... | P—R6 |
| 23 B—R5 ch | K—K2 |

Black's King is in only comparative security in the middle of the board, in spite of a solid rampart of pawns.

24 P—QKt3	KR—KB1
25 KR—B3	Kt—Kt3
26 R—Kt3	K—Q1
27 B—Kt4	Q—K2
28 B—K2	

With the threat of 29 P—Q4, and the subsequent action of the Bishop (against QKt5) and of the Queen (on the Q file).

28	K—B2
29 P—Q4	P—B5
30 R—Kt1	

This change of front is effected with surprising rapidity.

| 30 ...... | P—Kt4 |

To restore the black Queen's mobility.

| 31 P × BP | P × BP |
| 32 R—QKt4 | |

Deservedly winning a pawn.

32	Q—K3
33 P—Q5	Q—B1
34 B × P	Kt—R5

With the threat of recovering the QBP by 35 .... K—Q1.

| 35 B—Kt5 | Kt—B4 |
| 36 Q—K2 | |

Threatening death and destruction in the enemy ranks by 37 Q—R5. On the whole, White's pawn majority does not amount to much. His advantage really lies in the fact that the enemy forces lack cohesion: a travelling King, an inactive QR, and holes in the pawn formation.

| 36 ...... | P—B4 |
| 37 P × P | P—K5 |

In order to make possible 38 .... Q × P, which at the moment would be a gross mistake on account of 37 .... Q × P; 38 R—B3, and wins.

| 38 B—B6 | R—QKt1 |

Or 38 .... R—R2; 39 Q—Kt5 (threatening 40 Q—Kt6 mate); 39 .... Q—Kt1;

40 Q×Q ch, R×Q; 41 R×R, K×R;
42 P—R4 (breaking up the hostile front);
42 .... R—KKt2; 43 P—B6, R—KB2;
44 P×P, P×P; 45 R×P, R×P; 46 R—Kt8 ch,
K—B2; 47 R—QR8, followed by R×P,
with the decisive gain of another pawn.

39 Q—R5   R—B3
Does this mean consolidation? White's
master-stroke in reply answers the question.

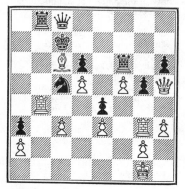

40 R×KtP
An *irruptive sacrifice.*

40 ......   P×R
41 Q—R7 ch   Kt—Q2
42 B×Kt   Q—Kt1
Or .... 42 .... Q×B; 43 R—B4 ch,
K—Q1; 44 Q—R8 ch, recovering a Rook
and maintaining a decisive attack.

43 R—Kt7 ch
This additional point in the combination
is one of the finest conceptions in the
literature of the game.
Technically speaking, the motifs of *deflection* (43 .... R×R; 44 Q×Q), of *disorganisation* (43 .... K—Q1; 44 R×R ch), and
disjunction by a double check (43 .... K×R;
44 B—B8 db. ch) form part and parcel of
the whole.

43 ......   K×R
44 B—B8 dbl ch   K—R1
Or 44 .... K×B; 45 Q×Q ch, K—B2;
46 Q—Kt7 ch, followed by .... Q×R.
The text move is a last attempt at a
desperate but short-lived resistance.

45 Q×Q   R×P
46 Q—Q8   R×P
47 Q—Q7   R—Kt8 ch
48 K—R2   R—Q7
49 Q—B6 ch   K—Kt1

50 Q×P   QR—Kt7
51 B—K6   K—B2
52 Q—B4 ch   K—Kt3
53 B—Q5   P—Kt5
54 P×P   R—KB7
55 Q—B6 ch   K—R2
56 Q—B7 ch   Resigns.

19

White	Black
BUCKLE	HARRWITZ

(London, 1846)

*The course of the next game is as follows:
tranquil mobilisation leads to a skirmish in
the centre from which weaknesses result in
both pawn formations. The gain of a pawn is
effected by White in a most astute manner.
After persistent liquidation, there arises a
Kt end-game and later, on the 38th move,
a pawn-ending with an equal number (four)
of pawns on either side, in which White's
distant passed pawn plays a decisive part:
Black's agony lasts only ten moves.*

1 P—K4   P—K4
2 Kt—KB3   Kt—QB3
3 B—B4   B—B4
4 Castles   Kt—B3
5 Kt—B3
Other good continuations are 5 P—Q3 or
5 R—K1 (5 .... Kt—KKt5; 6 P—Q4),
whilst the sacrifice of a pawn either by
5 P—B3, Kt×P or by 5 P—Q4, B×P is
not very clear.

5 ......   P—Q3
6 P—KR3   Castles
7 P—Q3   B—K3
8 B—Kt3   Kt—K2
9 Kt—K2
Both players try to improve their game
by quiet developing manœuvres.

9 ......   Kt—Kt3
10 Kt—Kt3   P—B3
11 P—B3   P—Q4
12 P—Q4
This counter-stroke imparts an original
note to the contest.

12 ......   P×KP
13 P×B   P×Kt
14 Q×P
After the skirmish in the centre, the white

Queen is brought into the struggle with effect.

| 14 ...... | B×B |
| 15 P×B | Kt—Q4 |

To avoid the pin 16 B—Kt5.

16 Kt—B5
An important outpost.

16 ...... P—Kt3
Instead of voluntarily weakening his Q side pawns, Black had the choice between simplification by 16 .... Kt—R5, etc., or a regrouping of forces by 16 .... Q—B3, to be followed by 17 .... P—Kt3; 18 P×P, P×P; 19 R×R, R×R, etc., with chances for both sides.

| 17 P×P | Q×P |

If now 17 .... P×P; 18 R×R, Q×R; 19 P—B4, KKt—K2 (19 .... KKt—B5; 20 B×Kt, Kt×B; 21 Q×P, winning a pawn as in continuation in the text); 20 Kt×Kt ch, Kt×Kt; 21 B—K3, Q—Kt2; 22 R—Q1, and White has the initiative.

18 P—B4 Kt (Q4)—B5
Playing for a counter-attack at all costs, but wisdom dictated 18 .... Kt (Q4)—K2.

| 19 B×Kt | Kt×B |
| 20 KR—Q1 | |

After 20 Kt—K7 ch, K—R1; 21 Kt×P, P—B3 the white Knight is "in the air," and so White decides to capture Black's weak QBP. If 20 Q×P, Q×P.

20 ...... Q—B2
If 20 .... K—R1; 21 R—Q7. The move in the text prevents one evil, but brings forth another.

21 Q×P	KR—B1
22 Q×Q	R×Q
23 Kt—Q6	

Having gained a pawn, White must now show real mastery in order to turn this small advantage into a win.

23	Kt—K7 ch
24 K—B1	Kt—Q5
25 P—QKt4	P—B4
26 P—B5	R—Kt1
27 R—R4	

A move combining attack with defence.

27	P—Kt3
28 KR—R1	Kt—B7
29 R×P	R×R
30 R×R	Kt×P

If 30 .... R×P; 31 P—B6, and the pawn

will queen. White now cleverly forces another liquidation.

| 31 R—Kt7 | R×R |

Or 31 .... Kt—B3; 32 R×R ch, Kt×R; 33 P—QKt4, Kt—R3; 34 P—B6, etc.
The resulting Kt ending appears to be very difficult to win, but the trend of events is in favour of White.

32 Kt×R	K—B2
33 K—K2	K—K2
34 K—Q2	K—Q2
35 Kt—R5	Kt—R3
36 Kt—Kt3	K—B3
37 K—B3	Kt×P
38 Kt×Kt	K×Kt

The pawn ending thus reached is won for White because of his "distant passed pawn."

| 39 P—R4 | P—R3 |
| 40 P—B3 | P—Kt4 |

If Black plays a waiting move such as 40 .... K—Kt4, Black will still have to give way after 41 P—QKt4.

41 P—R5	P—K5
42 P×P	P×P
43 P—Kt4	K—Q4
44 P—Kt4	K—K4
45 P—Kt5	K—B5
46 P—Kt6	P—K6
47 P—Kt7	K—B6
48 P—Kt8 (Q)	Resigns.

20

| *White* | *Black* |
| TCHIGORIN | TARRASCH |

(Monte Carlo, 1902)

To engineer a King's field attack and to conduct it to a victorious finish by means of unexpected threats and, when necessary, occasional sacrifices, is the prerogative of the great masters.
The following game is a brilliant illustration of such an attack.

1 P—K4	P—K4
2 Kt—KB3	Kt—QB3
3 B—B4	B—B4
4 Kt—B3	Kt—B3

This can be called the *Italian Four Knights'* *Game.*

5 P—Q3   P—Q3
6 B—K3
A solid continuation.

6 ......   B—Kt3
Better than 6 .... B × B; 7 P × B, because
then the doubling of White's KP is more
than compensated by the compactness of
his centre and his prospects on the KB file.

7 Q—Q2
A useful post. (Of less value would be
7 Q—K2, for after 7 .... B—Kt5 the
Queen would be none too comfortable
there.)

7 ......   B—K3
After 7 .... Castles, White has the choice
—a question of temperament—between the
symmetrical 8 Castles KR and the more
boisterous 8 Castles QR.

8 B—QKt5
The only unflagging continuation. For,
after 8 B—Kt3, Black could simplify the
game by 8 .... QB × B; 9 RP × B, B × B;
10 P × B, P—Q4; 11 P × P, Kt × P; 12 Kt × Kt,
Q × Kt, etc., with an even game.

8 ......   Castles
9 B × Kt   P × B
10 P—Q4   B—R4
11 Q—Q3   Q—Kt1
This demonstration prompts White to
give up the attacked pawn, because neither
12 R—QKt1, B × P; nor 12 P × P, Q × P; is
playable for White. And if now 12 Castles
QR, Black does not continue with 12 ....
B × Kt; 13 Q × B, Kt × P; 14 Q × P, etc., but
much more incisively 12 .... Q—Kt2;
13 P × P, P × P; 14 Kt × P, QR—Kt1, and
Black has the initiative.

12 Castles KR   Q × P
This excursion by the Queen will allow
White—at the cost of further sacrifices—to
regroup his forces for the attack.

13 B—Q2   B × Kt
14 B × B   Q—Kt4
15 P × P   B—B5
This hankering after worldly possessions
will lead to no good. Simpler was 15 ....
Q × Q; 16 P × Q, Kt—Q2; and White's
advantage—if any—would be very small.

16 Q—K3   Kt—Kt5
17 Q—Kt5   Kt × KP
18 Kt—Q4
Preserving his forces for the frontal attack
which he has prepared. If, on the other
hand, 18 Kt × Kt, Black with 18 ....

P—B3 obtains, at one stroke, a very good
game.

18 ......   P—B3
19 Q—Kt3   Q—R3
20 Kt—B5   Kt—Kt3
21 P—KR4   B—K3
To accept the offer of the exchange by
21 .... B × R; 22 R × B, R—B2; 23 P—R5
would expose Black to many dangers.

22 Kt—Q4   B—Q2
23 P—R5   Kt—K2
24 P—B4   P—QB4
25 Kt—B3   Q—B5
26 Kt—R4
Defending directly the Bishop and indirectly the threatened KP (for if 26 ....
Q × KP; 27 QR—K1 wins a piece).

26 ......   Q—K3
In order to continue with 27 .... Q—Kt5.

27 P—B5   Q—B2
28 P—R6   K—R1
29 P × P ch   Q × P
30 Q—R2   R—B2
31 R—B3   R—KKt1
32 QR—KB1   Q—Kt4
33 B—Kt2
Making for more fertile fields.

33 ......   B—Kt4
34 B—B1   Q—Kt5
35 R—K1   R (Kt1)—Kt2
Black being in difficulties, his choice of
moves is restricted, whilst White is able to
improve his position. Better would have
been 35 .... B—B3.

36 B—R6   R—Kt1
37 B—B4   R (B2)—Kt2
38 B—R6   R—B2
39 B—Q2   B—B3
40 B—R4   Q—Kt4
A mistake would be 40 .... Q—Kt6,
because of 41 Kt—Kt6 ch, R × Kt; 42 P × R,
and White has won the exchange.

41 R—B2   Q—R4
42 R—B3   R—Kt5
An ill-fated attempt at counter-attack.

43 R—KR3
At last the decisive regrouping is completed, and the threat of 44 Kt—Kt6 ch can
no longer be parried.

43 ......   R (B2)—Kt2
If 43 .... K—Kt1, there follows 44 Kt—B3
and the Queen is "mated."

44 Kt—Kt6 ch   P × Kt
45 P × P   Resigns.

21

White	Black
BOGOLJUBOW	RÉTI

(Göteborg, 1920)

It will be seen in the following game that Black, by measures both wise and patient, throws off the hostile yoke (12 .... K—R1; and 14 .... R—KKt1), himself gains territory (13 .... B—B5 and 22 .... B—B5), and finally takes up the offensive (27 .... P—KB4). It is, therefore, the power of sound manœuvring which we shall see illustrated.

1 P—K4	P—K4
2 Kt—KB3	Kt—QB3
3 B—B4	B—B4
4 P—Q3	Kt—B3
5 Kt—B3	P—Q3
6 B—K3	B—Kt3
7 P—KR3	

Instead of this waiting move, the most effective plan here is 7 Q—Q2, in preparation for Castles QR.

7	B—K3
8 B—QKt5	

Leads to greater complications than 8 B—Kt3.

8	Castles
9 B×Kt	

This exchange makes the black centre more compact. White should have delayed it by first playing 9 B—Kt5.

9	P×B
10 B—Kt5	Q—K2
11 Castles	P—KR3
12 B—R4	K—R1

Methodically preparing the unpinning of the Knight by .... R—KKt1 and then .... P—KKt4. At this stage 12 .... P—KKt4 would have been premature, because of 13 Kt×KtP.

13 P—Q4	B—B5
14 R—K1	R—KKt1
15 P×P	P×P
16 B—Kt3	QR—Q1
17 Q—B1	Kt—Q2
18 Kt—Q1	P—B3
19 Kt—K3	B—B2

A sound manœuvre. For after 19 .... B—K3; 20 Kt—B5, B×Kt; 21 P×B, the games would tend to equalise, whereas now Black can rely on his Bishops. (An old motto says: "The future belongs to him who has the Bishops.")

20 Kt—B5

Although this move maintains White's initiative for some time to come, certain strategic weaknesses in his position will gradually make themselves felt, namely, the restricted Bishop, his weak KB2, the Queen forced back behind the lines, and his adversary's control of the open Q file.

20	Q—B1

The Queen escapes whilst parrying the threat 21 Kt×RP.

21 P—B3

As this move—intending to prepare a demonstration on the Q side—weakens the position in the centre (Q3), it would have been preferable to play 21 P—Kt4 (preventing 21 .... Kt—B4), although even then Black would obtain the better game by 21 .... P—B4 (not 21 .... Q×P, on account of 22 Kt×RP); 22 P—B3, K—R2, followed by .... P—KKt3.

21	Kt—B4

This threatens 22 .... Kt—Q6, and at the same time ties the adverse KR to the protection of the KP.

22 Q—B2

White assumes the defensive. The violent attempt 22 KKt×P, P×Kt; 23 B×P (threatening 24 Q×P mate) would fail, because Black would reply, not 23 .... K—R2; 24 B×KtP, R×B; 25 Q×P ch, K—Kt1; 26 Q—R4, etc., but 23 .... B—Kt3; 24 Q×P ch, B—R2, etc., a sufficient defence.

22	B—B5
23 Kt—Q2	

The only way of guarding the pawn, for if 23 KR—Q1, R×R ch, winning either the KP (24 Q×R, Kt×P) or the QRP (24 R×R, B×P).

23	B—Q6
24 Q—B1	

If 24 Q—Q1, B×P.

24	P—Kt3

At the right moment the opponent's only active piece is driven back.

25 Kt—R4	B—R3

A *vacating* manœuvre: the Knight is enabled to settle on the dominant square at Q6.

26 Q—B2	Kt—Q6
27 KR—Q1	P—KB4

With the persuasive threat 28 .... P—B5.

28 P—R4

A desperate attempt at salvation, for if 28 R—KB1, there follows 28 .... P—B5; 29 B—R2, Kt×BP; 30 R×Kt, B×R ch; 31 K×B, Q—B4 ch; 32 K—K1, Q—K6 ch; 33 K—Q1, Q—B7; 34 Kt(R4)—B3, B—K7 ch; 35 K—B1, B×Kt; 36 P×B, Q×B, and wins.

28	P—B5
29 P—R5	B—B4
30 K—R2	

The loss of a piece cannot be avoided: 30 P—Kt4, B—K2.

30	P×B ch
31 P×P	Q—B7

The threat is 32 .... Kt—K8; 33 R×Kt, R×Kt.

32 R—KB1	Kt—K8

Embarras de richesses! Black wins the exchange as well: 33 R×Q, Kt×Q; and both the white Rooks are attacked.

33 QR×Kt	B×R
34 R×B	Q×Kt
And wins.	

22

White	Black
CANAL	P. JOHNER

(Carlsbad, 1929)

The manner in which White, in the following game, enforces the opening of a file to further his attack is most attractive.

1 P—K4	P—K4
2 Kt—KB3	Kt—QB3
3 B—B4	B—B4
4 P—Q3	Kt—B3
5 Kt—B3	P—Q3
6 B—KKt5	

In conjunction with the four subsequent moves this, the *Canal attack*, affords practical chances.

6	P—KR3

Trying, without delay, to get rid of the uncomfortable pin.

Other suitable counter-measures against the threatened 7 Kt—Q5, are 6 .... B—K3; and 6 .... Kt—QR4.

7 B×Kt	

After 7 B—R4, P—KKt4; 8 B—KKt3, B—KKt5, the initiative would pass over to Black.

7	Q×B
8 Kt—Q5	Q—Q1

If 8 .... Q—Kt3, White would avoid the continuation 9 Kt×Pch, K—Q1; 10 Kt×R, Q×KtP, etc., and play—eliminating all danger to himself—9 R—KKt1, B—Kt3; 10 P—B3, with the predominance in the centre.

9 P—B3	Kt—K2

The idea of getting rid of the hostile QKt is sound. An instructive *faux-pas* (which occurred in a game Canal-Becker from the same tournament) is 9 .... B—K3, with the sequel 10 P—Q4, P×P; 11 P×P, B—Kt3; 12 Kt×B, RP×Kt; 13 P—Q5, Kt—R4; 14 B—Q3, B—Kt5; 15 P—QKt4, winning a piece and the game.

10 P—Q4	P×P
11 Kt×P	Kt×Kt

A more useful counter still, at this stage, is 11 .... P—QB3.

12 B×Kt	Castles
13 Q—Q3	

With the option of castling on either side.

13	Q—B3
14 B—Kt3	

Conserving this efficient piece, whereas after 14 Castles KR, B×Kt; 15 P×B, B—K3; 16 B×B (or 16 B×P, QR—Kt1, followed by .... R×P); 16 .... P×B, there would be no fight left in the game.

14	R—K1
15 Castles KR	B—K3
16 B—B2	P—KKt3

A precautionary measure which, however, weakens the King's field.

17 K—R1	QR—Q1

Intending either to open the Q file by 18 .... P—Q4, or to simplify the game by 18 .... B×Kt; 19 P×B, P—B4 (20 P×P, P×P or 20 P—Q5, B—B1). But his adversary's advance on the next move no longer allows him any thought of counter-action.

18 P—KB4	B—Q2

In reply to 18 .... P—Q4, White is already threatening 19 P—K5.

19 P—B5	P—KKt4

Hoping to keep the critical files closed.

20 Kt—K6	

By this *temporary sacrifice* White clears the KB file. Black's acceptance is compulsory, as otherwise there would follow: 20 .... R—QB1; 21 Kt×B, P×Kt;

22 Q×B, or if 20 .... B×Kt; 21 P×B, Q×KP; 22 B—Kt3, and wins.

| 20 ...... | P×Kt |
| 21 P×P | Q—Kt3 |

Again, if 21 .... Q×KP; 22 B—Kt3.

| 22 P×B | QR×P |
| 23 R—B5 | |

Thanks to the threat of 24 R×B, which prevents the opposition of a Rook by 23 .... R—KB1 (whilst 23 .... R—B2 is not feasible because of 25 B—Kt3), White succeeds in doubling Rooks on the open file.

| 23 ...... | QR—K2 |
| 24 QR—KB1 | |

Steadfast play. A mistake would be 24 Q—Q5 ch, K—Kt2; 25 Q×KtP, on account of 25 .... Q×R; 26 P×Q, R—K8 ch, followed by mate. On the other hand, if 24 P—K5, Q—Kt2 (not 24 .... R×P, as White replies 25 R×R, Q×Q; 26 R×R ch, and wins).

| 24 ...... | K—Kt2 |

If 24 .... R—K4; 25 R—B6, followed by 26 B—Kt3 ch, and if 24 .... R×P; 25 Q—Q5 ch, R (K5)—K3; 26 R—B6, and wins.

25 P—K5
The time is ripe for this advance, the threat being 26 R—B7 ch, Q×R; 27 Q—R7 ch, K—B1; 28 Q—R8 mate.

| 25 ...... | R—KR1 |
| 26 P—K6 | Q×P |

Or 26 .... R×P; 27 R—B7 ch, Q×R; 28 R×Q ch, K×R; 29 B—Kt3, with a convincing gain in material.

| 27 R—B6 | Resigns |

Because of 27 .... Q×R; 28 R×Q, K×R; 29 Q—Kt6 ch, K—K4; 30 Q—B5 mate.

23

White   Black

CAPABLANCA   ELISKASES

(Moscow, 1936)

The secret of successful liquidations is, in the last instance, one of pawn management.

The player who has succeeded in preserving dynamic resources in his pawn structure (as, for example, the greater number of reserve moves or—as is the case in the following game—the possibility of rupturing the enemy front as White does by 48 P—B5) maintains the advantage to the end.

1 P—K4	P—K4
2 Kt—KB3	Kt—QB3
3 B—B4	B—B4
4 Kt—B3	Kt—B3
5 P—Q3	P—Q3
6 B—KKt5	P—KR3
7 B×Kt	Q×B
8 Kt—Q5	Q—Q1
9 P—B3	

As can be seen, White has by his preceding move vacated the square at QB3 without any loss of time, and now he has in view a gain of territory in the centre by 10 P—Q4, or eventually by P—QKt4.

| 9 ...... | Kt—K2 |

Seeking at once to clear up the question of the centre. Other playable replies are 9 .... P—R3 (or even 9 .... P—QR4) or 9 .... B—Kt3 (a "preventive retreat") or 9 .... Castles, simplest of all.

10 Kt—K3
This retreat presages a quiet and patient struggle for position, instead of bringing about, as in the preceding game, a restless and complicated contest by 10 P—Q4, Kt×Kt; 11 B×Kt, P×P; 12 Kt×P, Castles, etc.

| 10 ...... | B—K3 |

Playing for the greatest possible simplification, but more logical would have been 10 .... Castles.

11 B×B
He does not fear the phantom of simplifications, for there will remain some small weaknesses for him to attack.

| 11 ...... | P×B |
| 12 Q—Kt3 | |

Claiming the initiative.

| 12 ...... | Q—B1 |
| 13 P—Q4 | |

A misconception would be 13 Kt×P, for Black would reply, not with 13 .... P×Kt; 14 Q—Kt5 ch, followed by Q×B, but first with 13 .... B×Kt.

| 13 ...... | P×P |
| 14 Kt×P | B×Kt |

Black's last four moves were compulsory. If, for example, 14 .... P—K4; 15 Kt—K6.

| 15 P×B | |
| 16 Castles KR | Castles |

By playing 16 R—QB1, at once White would have made it still more difficult for Black to free himself.

16 ......   Q—Q2
17 QR—B1
If 17 Q×P, KR—Kt1; 18 Q—R6,
R×P, etc., whilst now the threat 18 Q×P
(and if 18 .... KR—Kt1; 19 Q×BP) is
serious.

17 ......   QR—Kt1
The alternative 17 .... P—B3 would
weaken Black's pawn formation for the
end-game.

18 R—B3
He continues the concentration of his
forces rather than initiate a direct attack by
18 P—B4.

18 ......   P—Q4
Taking advantage of the respite thus
afforded by "starting something" in the
centre. But there are dangers in the altera-
tion in the pawn formation which this
attempt brings in its wake. A non-committal
manœuvre would be 18 .... K—R1.

19 Q—B2
Combining attack (QBP) with defence
(KP). Both 19 P—K5 (19 .... Kt—B3)
and 19 Kt—Kt4 (19 .... R—B5; 20 R—Kt3,
K—R2, etc.) would lack precision.

19 ......   P—B3
20 P—K5   R—B5
A false alarm, easily overcome. But
Black's Q side being thoroughly cramped,
he wishes to simulate some activity on the
opposite wing.

21 Q—Q1   QR—KB1
22 P—B3
Methodically preparing P—KKt3 and
P—KB4.

22 ......   Q—Q1
23 P—KKt3   KR—B2
24 P—B4   Kt—B4
25 Kt×Kt   R×Kt
26 P—KR4
In the "heavy artillery" ending, which
now follows, it is clear that White controls
more territory, but to turn this into a win
will necessitate protracted manœuvres.
The move in the text prevents 26 ....
P—KKt4, which now would be refuted by
27 RP×P, P×P; 28 Q—Kt4, etc., with
a winning game for White.

26 ......   P—KKt3
27 K—Kt2   Q—K2
28 P—R3   Q—Kt2
29 QR—B3
Again anticipating, just in time, Black's

counter-thrust 29 .... P—KKt4 (30 BP×P,
R×R; 31 R×R, etc.).   Black now resigns
himself to purely passive strategy.

29 ......   Q—K2
30 Q—B2   K—Kt2
31 P—KKt4
White, on the other hand, seeks to exploit
his pawn majority on the K side, that of
Black on the Q side being practically
blocked.

31 ......   KR—B2
32 K—R3   Q—Q2
33 P—Kt4   R—KKt1
34 R—KKt1   K—R1
35 Q—Q2   R—R2
36 Q—KB2   P—KR4
37 P×P   R×P
38 R—Kt5   Q—R2
39 Q—Kt3   Q—R3
40 Q—Kt4   R—Kt2
41 R—Kt3   K—R2
42 R—Kt2   K—R1
43 K—Kt3   K—R2
44 R—KR2   R—K2
45 R—R3   K—Kt2
This plausible-looking move allows White
to "liquidate" in a manner as elegant as it is
decisive.   Comparatively best was 45 ....
R—K1.

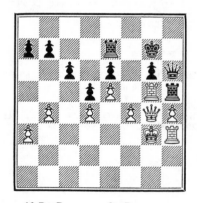

46 R×R   Q×R
47 Q×Q   P×Q
48 P—B5
The break-through.

48 ......   P×P
49 K—B4   R—K3
50 K×P   R—Kt3
51 P—K6   R—Kt5
52 K—K5   R—K5 ch
53 K—Q6   R×QP
54 R—K3   Resigns.

2. EVANS GAMBIT

24

White   Black
DUFRESNE   **HARRWITZ**

(Berlin, 1848)

The centre shaken (Q5 and K5), the black King's fastness toppling under a frontal assault (on the KKt file)—all this interspersed with numerous sacrifices—we have here a true Evans Gambit, an opening which someone floridly described as "a gift of the gods to a languishing chess-world."

1 P—K4	P—K4
2 Kt—KB3	Kt—QB3
3 B—B4	B—B4
4 P—QKt4	

Conceived—about 1826—by Captain W. D. Evans, this brilliant idea seeks to gain a decisive *tempo* for the formation of a powerful centre. "Imported" to the Continent by McDonnell, this "novelty" had as its best protagonists de la Bourdonnais the impetuous, Morphy the unforgettable, and later on Tchigorin the profound.

Fallen into disuse owing to Lasker's discoveries, it is still found in some contemporary games of Dr. Tartakower and C. H. O'D. Alexander.

4	B×P
5 P—B3	B—B4

Besides 5 .... B—R4, this retreat is the only reasonable one, whereas 5 .... B—K2 and 5 .... B—Q3 only make Black's task more difficult.

6 Castles
A restless continuation is 6 P—Q4, P×P; 7 Castles.

6	P—Q3
7 P—Q4	P×P
8 P×P	B—Kt3

The "normal position."

9 B—Kt2
One of the best continuations, the long diagonal being here full of promise for the future.

9	Kt—B3

After the more restrained 9 .... KKt—K2, White continues with 10 Kt—Kt5 or 10 P—Q5.

10 Q—B2
Clearly not 10 QKt—Q2, B—Kt5, nor at once 10 P—K5, P×P; 11 P×P, Q×Q; 12 R×Q, Kt—KKt5, etc.

The move in the text fulfils therefore a number of tasks, such as avoiding the exchange of Queens as well as the counterpin, protecting the threatened KP, and occupying a useful post of observation.

10	Castles
11 P—K5	P×P

Or 11 .... P—Q4; 12 P×Kt, P×B; 13 P×P, and the position of Black's King is compromised.

12 P×P	Kt—Q4

The hope of "neutralising" the Q file will be cruelly deceived. However, after 12 .... Kt—KKt5; 13 Q—K4 (threatening 14 P—K6) White's attack prevails.

13 R—Q1	B—K3
14 B×Kt	B×B
15 Kt—B3	Kt—K2

Or 15 .... Kt—Kt5; 16 Q—R4, P—QR4; 17 P—QR3, and wins.

16 Kt—KKt5
Beginning of the direct attack on the King.

16	Kt—Kt3

Against 16 .... P—Kt3 White would continue 17 KKt—K4, B×Kt; 18 Kt×B, Q—B1; 19 Kt—B6 ch, a victorious exploitation of the "hole" at KB6.

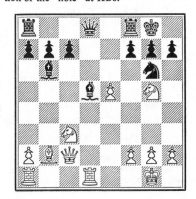

17 Kt×RP	K×Kt
18 Kt×B	Q—Kt4
19 R—Q3	

Initiating a frontal attack in the grand manner.

19	P—QB3
20 R—R3 ch	K—Kt1
21 R—KKt3	Q—R5

A more stubborn defence was 21 .... Q—R3, for now White can let off some more fireworks.

22 Kt—B6 ch	P×Kt
23 R×Kt ch	P×R

Or 23 .... K—R1; 24 R—Kt3.

24 Q×P ch	K—R1
25 P×P	R—B2

A sad necessity in order to parry the double threat 26 Q—Kt7 mate and 26 P—B7 dis ch. Thus the *unmasking of the long diagonal* will serve as the theme of the course of future events.

26 Q×R	R—KKt1

With the counter-threat 27 .... Q×BP, followed by mate.

27 K—R1

Well parried, for now if 27 .... R×P; 28 Q—K8 ch, K—R2 (28 .... R—Kt1; 29 P—B7 dis ch); 29 Q—K7 ch, K—R3 (29 .... K—Kt1; 30 P—B7 ch); 30 B—B1 ch, and wins.
A mistake would be 27 P—Kt3 (27 .... R×P ch) or 27 Q—K8 (27 .... Q×BP ch, followed by mate).

27	Q—KKt5
28 R—KKt1	B×P

Obviously not 28 .... B—Q5 (29 B×B, Q×B; 30 Q—R5 mate). But after the text move a fresh surprise decides the contest.

29 Q—K8	K—R2
30 P—B7	Resigns.

25

White	Black
BIRD	DE RIVIÈRE

(London, 1858)

An interesting feature of the following game is the nonchalance with which White, on two occasions, allows and even challenges

the exchange of Queens, relying, with good reason, on the asset of the open Q file, which asset, in fact, proves decisive.

1 P—K4	P—K4
2 Kt—KB3	Kt—QB3
3 B—B4	B—B4
4 P—QKt4	B×P
5 P—B3	B—B4
6 Castles	P—Q3
7 P—Q4	P×P
8 P×P	B—Kt3
9 P—KR3	

White is in no hurry. This preventive measure forestalls the pin by 9 .... B—Kt5, which would threaten White's handsome centre.

9	Kt—B3

After 9 .... KKt—K2 an imaginative line of play is available in 10 Kt—Kt5, P—Q4 (10 .... Castles; 11 Q—R5); 11 P×P, Kt—R4; 12 P—Q6, Kt×B; 13 Q—R4 ch, P—B3; 14 Q×Kt, Kt—Q4; 15 R—K1 ch, K—B1; 16 R×K7, and White is very active.

10 Kt—B3	Castles

One would think that Black is now out of all dangers, yet his troubles are only just beginning. That is why 10 .... P—KR3 would have been justified.

11 B—KKt5

In accordance with the precept that "a threat is stronger than its execution," this pin, which eventually threatens 12 P—K5, is more serious for Black than immediate action, e.g. 11 P—K5, P×P; 12 P×P, Kt—Q2; 13 P—K6, P×P; 14 B×P ch, K—R1; 15 Kt—KKt5, KKt—K4; 16 Q—R5, P—KR3, and White's attack hangs fire.

11	Kt—K2

This attempt to relieve the pin has its drawbacks. The counter-measure 11 .... P—KR3 was indicated.

12 P—K5

The break-through.

12	P×P

If at once 12 .... Kt—Q2; 13 Kt—Q5 wins.

13 P×P	Kt—Q2

A serious disappointment. Black cannot exchange Queens because, after 13 .... Q×Q; 14 QR×Q he loses a piece.

14 P—K6

Now 14 Kt—Q5 would be useless on

account of 14 .... B—B4, whereas the advance in the text throws the enemy camp into disorder.

14 ......   P×P
15 B×P ch   K—R1
16 Kt—Q5   Kt—KB3

If now 16 .... B—B4, then simply 17 KB×Kt, B×B (or 17 .... Q×B; 18 Kt×Kt, winning a piece); 18 R—K1, R—K1; 19 Q—B2, B—Q3; 20 Kt×Kt, B×Kt; 21 R×B, R×R; 22 Q—QB5, turning the pin to good account.

17 B×Kt   P×B
18 B×B   R×B

Foreseeing no danger, Black holds on to the loot. He should have resigned himself to simplification by 18 .... Q×Kt; 19 Q×Q, Kt×Q; 20 B×P, QR—Q1; and although all his pawns are weak, he has a defendable game.

19 Kt—B4

A fresh disappointment for Black, who, although a pawn ahead, is offered the exchange of Queens.

19 ......   Q×Q

After 19 .... Q—K1; 20 Kt—K6, this Knight's dominating position would seriously influence events.

20 QR×Q   QR—Q1
21 Kt—K6   R×R
22 R×R   R—K1
23 R—Q7

The occupation of the seventh rank is more than an equivalent for the lost pawn. We see here a confirmation of the rule that "the opening up of lines benefits him who has the better development."

23 ......   Kt—Q4

To this ingenious attempt at liberation (24 R×Kt, R×Kt) an even more ingenious reply. If 23 .... P—QB4, White does not answer covetously 24 R×P, P—B5, etc., but solidly 24 Kt—Q2.

24 Kt—Q8

Keeping the King in chancery. If 24 Kt—Kt7, R—K2.

24 ......   Kt—B5
25 Kt—B7 ch   K—Kt1
26 Kt—R6 ch   K—R1
27 Kt—R4

The reserve cavalry is now thrown in, and Black's Rook should not now have left its base. He should have regrouped his forces

by 27 .... Kt—Kt3, although even then his position would have remained difficult.

27 ......   R—K8 ch
28 K—R2   B×P

After 28 .... R—K1 there follows 29 Kt (R4)—B5, with a winning attack.

White mates in five (29 R—Q8 ch, R—K1; 30 R—R ch, K—Kt2; 31 Kt (R4)—B5 ch, K—Kt3; 32 R—Kt8 ch, K—R4; 33 P—Kt4 mate.)

26

White   Black

MORPHY   LÖWENTHAL

(London, 1859)

The following game demonstrates, more clearly than could mere words, the attacking value of the open file.

1 P—K4   P—K4
2 Kt—KB3   Kt—QB3
3 B—B4   B—B4
4 P—QKt4

In the hands of Morphy this move, played in many games against strong amateurs, produced dazzling results.

His opponent here was a master of the first rank.

4 ......   B×P
5 P—B3   B—B4
6 Castles   P—Q3
7 P—Q4   P×P
8 P×P   B—Kt3
9 P—Q5

Although this move, for the time being, closes the *Italian Diagonal*, it has a disorganising effect on Black's game.

9 ......   Kt—K4

This manœuvre only helps to speed up White's action. The *coup juste* is 9 .... Kt—R4, a frequent continuation being 10 B—Kt2, Kt—K2 (if 10 .... Kt×B; 11 Q—R4 ch, followed by Q×Kt); 11 B—Q3, Castles; 12 Kt—B3, Kt—Kt3, and there are breakers ahead for either side.

10 Kt×Kt   P×Kt
11 B—Kt2   K—Q2

Guarding the KP with a counter-threat, eventually, of 12 .... Q—Kt5.

If 11 .... P—KB3, the sacrificial continuation by White of 12 B×P, P×B; 13 Q—R5 ch, K—B1; 14 Q×KP, Q—B3, etc., is unsound. His best line of play in that case is 12 K—R1, Kt—K2; 13 P—B4, with better chances.

12 B—Kt5 ch
If instead of the text move 12 Q—R5, B—Q5.

12 ......   B—Q2
13 B×B ch   K×B
14 Q—Kt4 ch
By the simplest means White not only recovers his pawn, but wins one as well without giving up his attack.

14......   P—B4
Or 14 .... K—K1; 15 Q×P, Q—B3; 16 B×P, and wins. If, on the other hand, 14 .... K—Q3 (here or on the next move), then 15 Kt—Q2 settles Black's fate.

15 Q×P ch   K—K1
16 B×P
White proceeds to direct action in preference to effecting the liquidation: 16 Q×KP, Q×Q; 17 B×Q, K—B2, etc.

16 ......   Kt—R3
17 Q—B4   K—Q2
Hoping to connect the Rooks by this artificial castling.

18 Kt—Q2
A blunder would be 18 Kt—B3, as Black wins a piece by 18 .... QR—K1.

18 ......   QR—K1
19 Kt—B4
Combining defence (of the Bishop) with attack (20 P—Q6, P×P; 21 QR—Q1, etc.).

19 ......   B—B4
Trying to strengthen his Q3, for if 19 .... K—B1; 20 QR—B1 vivifies the attack.

20 QR—Q1
White could effect much by 20 B×BP, KR—B1 (not 20 .... Q×P, because of 21 Kt—K5 ch; R×Kt; 22 B×R, etc.); 21 Q—K5 (or 21 Q—Kt3, Q×P; 22 Q×P ch, Kt—B2, and the tables are turned); 21 .... Kt—Kt5; 22 Q×Q ch, R×Q; 23 B—Kt3, R×KP, etc.—but he prefers not to relax his grip.

20 ......   B—Q3
21 B×B   P×B
22 R—Kt1
Here and on the following move White effects a lightning change of target for his heavy artillery.

22 ......   P—QKt3
23 KR—B1   Q—B3
24 Q—K3   Kt—Kt5
If 24 .... R—QKt1; 25 P—K5.

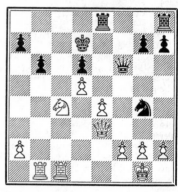

25 Kt×P ch
A brilliant sacrifice, which is to be complemented by an even more generous offer.

25 ......   P×Kt
26 R—B7 ch   K—Q1
Shrinking from the precipice: 26 .... K×R; 27 Q×P ch, K—Q2; 28 Q—R7 ch, followed by 29 R—Kt8 mate.

27 Q×P   Q×P ch
28 Q×Q   Kt×Q
29 R—R7
Recovering his piece, thanks to the threat 30 R—Kt8 mate, and maintaining two extra pawns with a dominating position.

29 ......   Kt—R6 ch
30 P×Kt   K—B1
31 K—B2
And wins
For after 31 .... KR—B1 ch; 32 K—K3, etc., Black is helpless, whilst 31 .... R×P is not possible, as 32 R—R8 ch wins a Rook.

27

White	Black
KOLISCH	PAULSEN

(Bristol, 1861)

The first part of the following game (up to Black's 17th move) consists mainly in consolidating manœuvres on either side.

We then see how a localised contest—conducted on what appears to be a sector of secondary importance—unexpectedly becomes the principal theme of the game, thanks in the main to Black's beautiful pawn sacrifice (19 .... P—B6) and to the co-ordination of his minor pieces.

1 P—K4	P—K4
2 Kt—KB3	Kt—QB3
3 B—B4	B—B4
4 P—QKt4	B × P
5 P—B3	B—R4
6 P—Q4	P × P
7 Castles	P—Q3
8 P × P	B—Kt3
9 P—Q5	

The chief protagonist of this move (instead of 9 B—Kt2 or 9 Kt—B3) was Anderssen.

9 ...... Kt—R4

This manœuvre, if effected without delay, does not represent loss of time, as White's Bishop must react sooner or later, and Black can find the necessary breathing space to consolidate his position.

10 B—Kt2 Kt—K2

Attending to his development. 10 .... Kt × B; 11 Q—R4 ch, B—Q2; 12 Q × Kt would only help White to a sound disposition of his forces.

By the text move Black shows that he has no fear of 11 B × P, because of 11 .... R—KKt1; and Black would have the initiative.

11 B—Q3	Castles
12 Kt—B3	Kt—Kt3
13 Kt—K2	

After the violent initial skirmishes, the play is now characterised by subtle manœuvres.

This "positional" aspect of the *Evans Gambit* shows its wide resources.

13 ...... P—QB4

Following up the advantage which he has acquired on the Q side.

14 Q—Q2 P—B3

Restricting the range of the adverse QB on the long diagonal.

14 .... P—B5 would be useless against 15 B—B2.

15 K—R1 B—Q2

An alternative line of play on Black's Q side would be 15 .... B—B2; 16 QR—B1, R—Kt1; 17 Kt—Kt3, P—Kt4; 18 Kt—B5, P—B5; 19 B—K2, etc., with chances on both sides.

16 QR—B1 P—QR3

17 Kt—K1

He continues his preparations for the advance of his KBP, but more in keeping with the requirements of the situation would have been 17 Kt—Kt3, B—Kt4; 18 Kt—B5, P—B5; 19 B—K2, etc.

17	B—Kt4
18 P—B4	P—B5
19 B—Kt1	P—B6

A very deep sacrifice of a pawn. It not only vacates a square in order to let in an important unit (the QKt), but it also entangles the enemy forces, with the additional hope of turning the open QB file to account.

20 R × P

Clearly not 20 Kt × P (20 .... B × R) nor 20 Q × P (20 .... B × Kt) nor finally 20 B × P (20 .... Kt—B5, followed by .... Kt—K6, winning the exchange).

20	Kt—B5
21 Q—B1	R—B1

This reinforces the outpost position taken up by the QKt, and threatens, *inter alia*, 22 .... B—R4; 23 R—QB2, Kt—Q7, etc.

22 B—Q3 B—K6

A decisive irruption.

23 Q—B2 Kt—Q7

The complement of Black's preceding move. Black's control of the weak squares, which he ultimately turns into material advantage, is very remarkable.

24 R—Kt1	R × R
25 Q × R	Q—Kt3
26 B—B1	B × R
27 Kt × B	B × B
28 Kt × B	Kt × KP

Resigns

E.g. 29 Q—B4, R—K1, etc., or 29 Q—B2, Q—Q5 (threatening 30 .... Q × Kt; 31 Q × Q, Kt—B7 mate); 30 Kt—R3, R—K1; 31 B—Kt2, Q × Kt; 32 Q × Q, Kt—B7 ch; 33 Kt × Kt, R—K8 ch, with mate to follow.

28

White	*Black*
BLACKBURNE	STEINITZ

(London, 1862)

This game illustrates the triumph of patient defence in the face of all dangers.

1 P—K4	P—K4
2 Kt—KB3	Kt—QB3
3 B—B4	B—B4
4 P—QKt4	B × P
5 P—B3	B—B4
6 P—Q4	

More incisive than 6 Castles, P—Q3; 7 P—Q4.

6	P × P
7 Castles	P—Q3

Approaching the "normal position," because if 7 . . . . P × P, White refrains from 8 Q—Q5, Q—K2 (guarding the two threatened points), but plays 8 B × P ch, K × B; 9 Q—Q5 ch, K—K1; 10 Q × B, and White has a fine attacking game.

8 P × P	B—Kt3
9 Kt—B3	

An effective, purely developing, move, instead of 9 B—Kt2 or 9 P—Q5, which we have seen before. An unsound try would be: 9 Q—Kt3, Kt—R4; 10 B × P ch, K—B1; 11 Q—Q5, Kt—KB3; and White's Queen can no longer defend his volatile Bishop.

9	B—Kt5

More usual is (or rather, was, at a time when the *Evans Gambit* was still fashionable) 9 . . . . Kt—R4, after which the *Göring Attack*, 10 B—Kt5, P—KB3; 11 B—K3 secures White's initiative for a long time to come.

10 B—QKt5	

Now the QP is again defended, and in addition there arises the threat 11 P—Q5, P—QR3; 12 B—R4.

10	K—B1

An original parry. After 10 . . . . B—Q2; 11 P—K5, White gains more territory.

11 B × Kt	

Having effectively prevented Black from castling, he should not have relieved his opponent's position by exchanges. The proper continuation here or on the next move is 11 B—K3.

11	P × B
12 B—R3	

With the passing threat 13 P—K5, whilst his Bishop could have continued to render valuable services on its original diagonal by 12 B—K3.

12	B × Kt
13 P × B	Q—Kt4 ch
14 K—R1	Kt—K2

15 Kt—K2	Kt—Kt3
16 KR—Kt1	Q—B3
17 Q—Q3	K—Kt1

Making for KR2, not having castled. If instead 17 . . . . Kt—B5; 18 Kt × Kt, Q × Kt; 19 R—Kt4, Q—R3 (or 19 . . . . Q—B3; 20 P—K5); 20 P—K5, and White's pressure becomes well defined.

18 B—B1	P—KR3
19 P—B4	K—R2
20 P—B5	

White has regained the initiative by clever manœuvring. 20 P—K5 is also very strong.

20	Kt—K2
21 B—Kt2	P—Q4

The contest for central territory, here and in the sequel, is very bitter.

22 P—B3	QR—Q1
23 Kt—B4	

With the promising threat 24 Kt—R5, but, by playing 23 Kt—Kt3, he could have added the threat of 24 P—K5 (thanks to the protection of the pawn at B5).

23	KR—Kt1

A stubborn defence. A very complicated continuation is 23 . . . . P × P; 24 P × P, B × P; 25 Kt—R5, B × B; 26 Kt × Q ch, B × Kt; 27 Q—QR3, B × R; 28 Q × Kt, B—B3; 29 Q × KBP, KR—K1; 30 Q × P, R × P; 31 R × P ch, B × R; 32 Q × R, and White's chances should prevail.

24 Kt—R5	

There is no time for the preparatory 24 R—Kt4, on account of 24 . . . . P × P; 25 P × P, B × P.

24	Q—R5
25 P—B6	Q × Kt

If 25 . . . . KtP × P; 26 P—K5 dis ch.

26 P × Kt	R—Q2
27 P × P dis ch	P—Kt3
28 QR—K1	R—K1
29 R—K5	Q—R5
30 R—B5	

Beautiful as this move is, Black finds a sufficient counter.

Insufficient also was 30 R—K6, QR × KP; 31 QR × KtP, P × R; 32 Q × P ch, K—R1; 33 P—Q6, P × P; 34 P—Q5 dis ch, B—Q5; 35 B × B ch, Q × B; 36 Q × P ch, R—R2; 37 Q—Kt6, R × P ch; 38 K × R, Q—R5 ch; 39 K—Kt2, R—K7 ch, and mate follows.

30	Q × P (K2)

Evidently not 30 . . . . QR × KP; 31 R × P ch, R × R; 32 Q × P ch, K—R1;

33 Q×R, Q—K2; 34 R—Kt8 ch, R×R; 35 Q×Q, and White wins.

| 31 P×P | R (Q2)—Q1 |
| 32 B—R3 | |

If, as a last chance, 32 P—Q5, Black wins after 32 .... B×R; 33 Q—B3, B—Q5; 34 Q×B, Q—K8 ch; 35 K—Kt2, R—K7 ch; 36 K—R3, Q—B8 ch.

| 32 ...... | Q—K3 |
| 33 R—B4 | P—B4 |

Closing down.

| 34 R—R4 | P—KR4 |
| 35 B—Kt2 | R—Q4 |

Obstruction.

| 36 Q—B2 | Q—K7 |

Irruption. Disorganised, and weakened at various points, White must give way.

37 Q—Kt3	Q—Kt4
38 Q—B3	R—K7
39 P—B4	R×P
40 Q—B3	

Just before the end one last and interesting threat, 41 Q×P ch, and wins.

| 40 ...... | Q—Q4 |
| Resigns. | |

29

| White | Black |
| KOLISCH | ANDERSSEN |

(Paris, 1860)

With the King still on his original square, there is always a chance of painful surprises, as will be seen in the following game.

1 P—K4	P—K4
2 Kt—KB3	Kt—QB3
3 B—B4	B—B4
4 P—QKt4	B×P
5 P—B3	B—R4

This retreat is more sensible than 5 .... B—B4, because now the Bishop is out of reach.

6 P—Q4

This is more energetic than 6 Castles, after which Black has a slightly wider choice of continuations, namely:

(a) 6 .... P—Q3; 7 P—Q4, B—Q2 (the

Sanders-Alapin Defence, the alternative being to lead back into the normal position by 7 .... P×P; 8 P×P, B—Kt3); 8 Q—Kt3, Q—K2, etc.

(b) 6 .... Kt—B3; 7 P—Q4, Castles; 8 Kt×P, Kt×KP, etc., leading to very complicated play.

(c) 6 .... Q—B3 (the *Steinitz Defence*). See Game No. 30.

| 6 ...... | P×P |
| 7 Castles | P×P |

In this, the *Compromised Defence*, Black has for the moment three extra pawns, but he is exposed to a particularly violent attack. The alternative continuations are:

(a) 7 .... B—Kt3; 8 P×P (8 Q—Kt3, Kt—R4); 8 .... P—Q3, reaching the normal position.

(b) 7 .... P—Q3; 8 Q—Kt3 (the *Waller Attack*), which is very irksome for Black after 8 .... Q—B3; 9 P—K5, P(Q3)×P; 10 R—K1, B—Q2; 11 B—KKt5, etc.

(c) 7 .... Kt—B3; 8 B—R3, P—Q3; 9 P—K5, and Black's plight is even worse.

(d) 7 .... KKt—K2; 8 P×P, with a persistent attack.

(e) 7 .... P—QKt4; 8 B×P, P×P; 9 B—R3, and White dominates the situation.

(f) 7 .... P—Q6, which is best illustrated by the following game (Anderssen-Dufresne, *Berlin*, 1853): 8 Q—Kt3, Q—B3; 9 P—K5, Q—Kt3; 10 R—K1, KKt—K2; 11 B—R3, P—Kt4; 12 Q×P, R—QKt1; 13 Q—R4, B—Kt3; 14 QKt—Q2, B—Kt2; 15 Kt—K4, Q—B4; 16 B×P, Q—R4; 17 Kt—B6 ch, P×Kt; 18 P×P, R—Kt1; 19 QR—Q1 (meditating an extraordinary combination, instead of contenting himself with the sound but ordinary 19 B—K4); 19 .... Q×Kt (he is incredulous, but also after 19 .... R—Kt5; 20 P—B4, etc., or 19 .... Q—Kt5; 20 Q×Q, R×Q; 21 B—KB5, White has the last word); 20 R×Kt ch, Kt×R (if 20 .... K—Q1; 21 R×P ch, K—B1; 22 R—Q8 ch, forcing the win); 21 Q×P ch, K×Q; 22 B—B5 db ch, K—K1; 23 B—Q7 ch, K—B1; 24 B×Kt mate. A combination second to none in the literature of the game.

| 8 Q—Kt3 | Q—B3 |

After 8 .... Q—K2 the continuation 9 B—R3, P—Q3; 10 P—K5 is sufficiently convincing.

| 9 P—K5 | Q—Kt3 |

If 9 .... Kt×P, there follows 10 R—K1, P—Q3; 11 Kt×Kt, P×Kt; 12 Q—R4 ch, winning a piece.

| 10 Kt×P | P—Kt4 |

This attempt to deflect the hostile attack

meets with little success, nor is 10 ....
B×Kt; 11 Q×B, P—Kt3; 12 P—K6, etc.,
in any way comforting. The relatively
best continuation is 10 .... KKt—K2;
11 B—R3, Castles; 12 Kt—Q5, although
here also Black has no easy task.

11 Kt×P   R—Kt1
12 Q—K3

With this adroit manœuvre White parries
first of all the threat 12 .... P—QR3,
whilst maintaining the initiative.

12 ......   KKt—K2
13 Q—K2

Threatening to capture the hostile Queen,
on a full board, by 14 Kt—R4.

13 ......   Q—R4
14 B—R3   B—Kt2

After 14 .... P—QR3, White plays with
advantage 15 Kt—Q6 ch, P×Kt; 16 P×P.

15 QR—Q1   Kt—B4

As 15 .... Castles is not feasible on
account of 16 R×P, Black tries to regroup
his Knights (threatening 16 .... QKt—K2,
followed by .... B×Kt), but his cramped
position invites trouble.

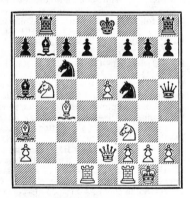

16 R×P

A *King-hunt* sacrifice.

16 ......   K×R
17 P—K6 ch   K—B1

If 17 .... P×P, then, very simply,
18 Q×P ch, K—Q1; 19 R—Q1 ch, QKt—Q5;
20 QKt×Kt.

18 P×P   B—R1
19 Kt×P ch

Another beautiful move, which deprives
the hostile King of a flight square at his
QKt2.

19 ......   Kt×Kt

Or 19 .... K—Kt2; 20 Kt×Kt, and if
20 .... K×Kt; 21 Kt—K5 ch, winning
the Queen.

20 Q—K6 ch   K—Q1

Not 20 .... K—Kt2, because of mate
after 21 Q—R6, or, better still, 21 B—R6.

21 R—Q1 ch   Kt—Q3
22 R×Kt ch

Events now take their course with elemental force, but 22 B×Kt, is quicker.

22 ......   P×R
23 Q×P ch   K—B1
24 B—K6 ch   K—Kt2
25 B—Q5 ch   Q×B

Grievous but necessary, for if 25 ....
K—B1; 26 P—B8(Q) ch, R×Q; 27 Q×KR ch,
K—B2; 28 Q—K7 ch, and mate next move.

26 Q×Q ch   K—R3
27 Q—B4 ch   K—Kt2
28 Q—K4 ch   Kt—B3
29 Kt—K5   K—R3
30 Q—B4 ch   K—R2
31 B—B5 ch   R—Kt3
32 B×R ch

The harvest.

32 ......   B×B
33 Kt×Kt ch   B×Kt
34 Q×B   Resigns.

30

White	Black
TCHIGORIN	STEINITZ

(Match by cable, 1890–1)

*In the following game—which for some
months kept the chess-world on tenterhooks—
we see a clash between an attacking player,
relying on the resources of the imagination,
and a defender who believes in the power of
resistance of the inert mass, but who is
handicapped on this occasion by an unfortunate choice of variation (6 .... Q—B3).*

1 P—K4   P—K4
2 Kt—KB3   Kt—QB3
3 B—B4   B—B4
4 P—QKt4   B×P
5 P—B3   B—R4
6 Castles   Q—B3

The *Steinitz Defence*—a favourite of the
then champion—renders Black's task far
more onerous than the usual 6 .... P—Q3.

7 P—Q4   Kt—R3

He already has no natural moves at his disposal and must resort to baroque strategy. Here he cannot reply with 7 .... P—Q3 (8 P—Q5, followed by 9 Q—R4 ch, winning a piece), nor with 7 .... P×P (8 P—K5, Q—Kt3; 9 P×P, with a powerful centre).

The reply 7 .... P—KR3 is slow, as is seen in the following game, Gunsberg-Steinitz (from their match, *New York*, 1891):

8 Q—R4, B—Kt3; 9 B—QKt5, KKt—K2; 10 B—R3, P×P; 11 P—K5, Q—Kt3; 12 P×P, Kt—Q4; 13 R—K1, Kt—B5; 14 P—Kt3, Q—Kt5; 15 QKt—Q2, Kt—R6 ch; 16 K—Kt2, Kt—Kt4; 17 B—Kt2, Kt—K2; 18 B—K2, Kt—K3; 19 K—R1, Q—B4; 20 Kt—R4, Q×BP (falling into a terrible trap, but after the only permissible move, 20 .... Q—R2, Black also remains in a bad way); 21 Kt—K4, and Black resigns, for after 22 B—KB1, his Queen is lost on a full board.

8 B—KKt5

This sally emphasizes the unfortunate position of Black's Queen. He cannot very well reply with 8 .... Q—Kt3, because of 9 P—Q5, Kt—QKt1; 10 B×Kt, P×B; 11 Kt×P, and White has the advantage both in material and in position.

8 ......   Q—Q3
9 P—Q5   Kt—Q1
10 Q—R4   B—Kt3
11 Kt—R3

Each of White's moves tells, as is often the case in open games, in which it is possible to work with direct threats. At the moment the threat is 12 Kt—Kt5, Q—Kt3; 13 B×Kt, followed by 14 KKt×P.

11 ......   P—QB3

This weakening of his Q3 will play an important part in the course of the game. But after 11 .... P—R3 White could still play (apart from the good continuation in the text, 12 B—K2) 12 Kt—Kt5, P×Kt; 13 Q×R, P×B; 14 Q×B, Castles; 15 B×Kt, P—QB3; 16 Q×KtP, etc.

12 B—K2   B—B2
13 Kt—B4   Q—B1
14 P—Q6

A pretty *deflecting sacrifice* which allows White to gain important territory on the extreme left wing.

14 ......   B×P
15 Kt—Kt6   R—QKt1

16 Q×RP   Kt—K3
17 B—B1   Kt—Kt1

Here is what one was pleased to call a *Steinitz position*, with so many pieces encumbering the first rank.

Black's position—neither developed, nor, properly speaking, susceptible of development—is of course theoretically lost. The great Russian champion now proceeds to prove that it is lost in practice as well.

18 B—R3

Revealing the meaning of the beautiful retrograde manœuvre contained in White's preceding move.

18 ......   P—QB4

Needless to say, Black cannot now reply 18 .... B×B, because of 19 Q×R, and he is compelled further to weaken his position in the centre (Q4).

A plastic illustration of the fact that one weakness leads to another.

19 QR—Q1   Kt—B3
20 B—B4

With the threat 21 B×Kt, BP×B; 22 B×P.

20 ......   B—B2

Still more unfortunate would be the acceptance of the "Greek gift" by 20 .... Kt×P, on account of 21 Kt×B, R×Kt; 22 Q×KtP, R—B3; 23 Kt×P, with the incisive threat of 24 Q×P mate.

21 Kt—Q5   B—Q3

Or 21 .... Kt×Kt; 22 P×Kt, Kt—B5; 23 P—Q6, B×P; 24 B×P, B×B; 25 Q×R, K—Q1; 26 Kt×P, and wins.

22 Kt—R4

Whilst his adversary is condemned to inactivity, White is able further to reinforce his position.

22 ......   Kt×Kt
23 Kt—B5

This beautiful intermediary manœuvre ensures for White a quick and bountiful harvest.

23 ......   P—KKt3
24 Kt×B ch   Q×Kt
25 B×Kt   Q—B2
26 B×Kt   BP×B
27 B×P   R—R1

Or 27 .... P—Q4; 28 P×P, P×P; 29 R×P, and the deadly threat 30 B—Q6 persists. Black cannot save the exchange, and is reduced in the sequel to a painful agony.

28 Q×R	Q×B
29 Q—R4	K—Q1
30 R—Q2	K—B2
31 R—Kt1	R—Q1
32 R—Kt5	Q—B3
33 Q—Kt4	P—Q3
34 P—QR4	Q—K1
35 R—Kt6	Q—B1
36 Q—R5	P—Q4

Or 36 .... K—Kt1; 37 R (Q2)—Kt2, P—Q4; 38 R—R6, threatening 39 R—R8 mate.

37 P×P	K—Kt1
38 P—Q6	Resigns.

31

White	Black
ST. PETERSBURG	VIENNA

(1898)

There are players who, when attacked, become disconcerted; such appears to be White's case in the following game. White apparently thought that attack was his own prerogative, but suddenly (after the sacrifice, 18 .... Kt × P) he saw himself severely manhandled.

1 P—K4	P—K4
2 Kt—KB3	Kt—QB3
3 B—B4	B—B4
4 P—QKt4	B×P
5 P—B3	B—R4
6 Castles	P—Q3
7 P—Q4	B—Kt3

An important decision. Instead of the classic reply 7 .... P×P, which might be looked upon as almost compulsory, Black declares his intention immediately to give back the gambit pawn, in order to obtain the superior end-game after 8 P×P, P×P; 9 Q×Q ch, Kt×Q; 10 Kt×P, Kt—KB3, thanks to the weakness of White's Q side pawns.

This, the *Lasker Defence*, is applicable also after 6 P—Q4, instead of the text move 6 Castles, namely 6 P—Q4, P—Q3 (see Game No. 32).

8 P—QR4
The struggle for the initiative. Let us examine alternative attempts:
(a) 8 P×P, P×P; 9 Q—Kt3 (the exchange of Queens, as mentioned before, turns out badly for White); 9 .... Q—B3 10 B—KKt5, Q—Kt3; and Black's defence is adequate.
(b) 8 Q—Kt3, Q—B3; and Black holds his own.
(c) 8 B—R3, P×P; 9 P×P, B—Kt5; and Black counter-attacks.

8 ......   Kt—B3
Black hopes thus to complete his mobilisation whilst holding the pawn.

9 B—QKt5   P—QR3
A necessary measure. If 9 .... Castles, or 9 .... B—Q2; 10 B×Kt, followed by 11 P—R5, wins a piece.

10 B×Kt ch	P×B
11 P—R5	B—R2
12 Q—R4	

With this sally, which indirectly guards his threatened KP whilst attacking Black's QBP, White seeks to maintain the initiative. After 12 P×P, the telling continuation of a game Tchigorin-Lasker (*St. Petersburg Quadrangular Tournament, 1895–6*) was as follows: 12 .... Kt×P (a pawn for a pawn!); 13 Q—K2, P—Q4; 14 Kt—Q4, Kt×QBP (a fresh surprise); 15 Kt×Kt, B×Kt; 16 Q—Q3, P—QB4; 17 Q—Kt3, B—K3; 18 B—Kt5, Q—Q2; 19 QR—B1, P—KB3; 20 P×P, P×P; 21 B—B4, KR—Kt1; 22 Q—B3, Castles; 23 KR—K1, P—B5; 24 Q—K2, B—KB4; 25 Q—R2, R×P ch (a cruel predicament); 26 K—R1, R×P; and White resigns.

12 ......   P×P
At the right moment Black clears the centre.

13 P×P	B—Q2
14 P—K5	Kt—Q4
15 B—R3	

If 15 P×P, Black plays, not 15 .... P×P (16 R—K1 ch), but 15 .... Castles; 16 P×P, Q×P; and although the balance in material is re-established, Black stands better (two Bishops, more advanced development, centralised Knight).

15 ......   Castles
16 Q—B4
Again, if 16 P×P (here or on the next move), then not 16 .... P×P; 17 B×P, etc., but 16 .... K—R1, trying to assume the initiative.

16 ......   Kt—B5
17 K—R1
In order to reply to 17 .... P—Q4 by

18 Q—B1, without having to fear a "family check" by 18 .... Kt—K7.

17	B—K3
18 Q—B1	

Not 18 Q×BP, on account of 18 .... B—Q4. As the text move gives rise to a powerful counter-attack, he should have submitted to 18 P—Q5, Kt×QP; 19 Q×BP, etc.

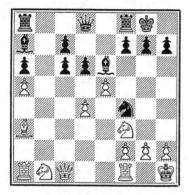

18	Kt×P

A far-seeing sacrifice.

19 K×Kt	B—Q4
20 K—Kt3	P—KB4

The activities of this new arrival are speedily decisive.

21 QKt—Q2

Or 21 Q—Kt5, P—B5 ch; 22 K—Kt4, B×Kt ch, and wins.

21	P—B5 ch
22 K—Kt2	Q—Kt4 ch
23 K—R1	Q—R4
24 Q—B3	

Trying in vain to hold both threatened points (Kt at KB3 and P at Q4).

If 24 K—Kt2, Q—Kt5 ch; and if 24 Q—Q1, B×P; 25 R—B1, B×P, with a harvest of four pawns (plus the attack) for a piece.

24	B×P

This fresh surprise is final.

25 Q—Q3

Or 25 Q×B, B×Kt ch; 26 Kt×B, Q×Kt ch; 27 K—Kt1, R—B4; 28 KR—K1, Q—R6, forcing White to capitulate.

25	B×R
26 R×B	Q×P
27 R—KKt1	QR—Kt1
28 R—Kt2	Q—R4
29 K—Kt1	B×Kt
30 Kt×B	Q—Q4
31 Q—B3	R—Kt8 ch
32 Kt—K1	Q—Q5

The *coup de grâce* (33 Q×Q, R×Kt mate).

33 B—Kt2	P—B4
Resigns.	

32

White	Black
ALEXANDER	TYLOR

(Hastings, 1935–6)

The brilliant young British master proves in this game that, in spite of all defences ancient and modern, the Evans Gambit is not defunct.

1 P—K4	P—K4
2 Kt—KB3	Kt—QB3
3 B—B4	B—B4
4 P—QKt4	B×P
5 P—B3	B—R4
6 P—Q4	P—Q3

This defence, which seeks to render the *Evans Gambit* innocuous, was analysed as early as 1898 by Alapin.

7 Q—Kt3

White cannot afford to let the initiative slip from his grasp. The following continuation leads nowhere: 7 P—Q5, QKt—K2; 8 Q—R4 ch, P—B3, and the black KB is guarded. Nor is 7 Q—R4, P×P more promising. On the other hand, if 7 Castles, B—Kt3, and all is well for Black (*Lasker's Defence*).

The most promising line of play, however, is 7 P×P, P×P; 8 Q—Kt3 (avoiding of course the exchange of Queens); 8 .... Q—B3 (or 8 .... Q—K2; 9 P—QR4, etc., or 8 .... Q—Q2; 9 Castles, with R—Q1 to follow); 9 B—KKt5, Q—Kt3; 10 QKt—Q2, B—Kt3; 11 P—KR4, Kt—B3; 12 B—Q5, and White will regain his pawn with advantage.

7	Q—Q2

The only defence, for if 7 .... Q—K2 (or 7 .... Q—B3), there follows 8 P—Q5, Kt—Q5; 9 Kt×Kt, P×Kt; 10 Q—Kt5 ch, winning a piece. The meaning of White's preceding move (7 Q—Kt3) is now clear: the hostile Queen now occupies an awkward post, and hinders the action of her own QB.

8 P×P

After 8 Castles, the sequel would again be 8 .... B—Kt3 (threatening 9 .... Kt—R4); but a continuation seriously to be considered is 8 P—QR4, anticipating that reply, e.g. 8 P—QR4, B—Kt3; 9 P—R5, Kt×RP 10 R×Kt (with this sacrifice White wishes to maintain, and even to speed up, his attack); 10 .... B×R; 11 P×P, Kt—R3 (an original move suggested by Alexander in 1932); 12 P—K6 (of less value would be 12 B×Kt, P×B; 13 P×P, Castles; and if 14 Kt—K5, Q—K1); 12 .... P×P; 13 Kt—Kt5, P—B3; 14 Castles, Q—K2; 15 B×P, and White has by no means shot his bolt.

8 ......   B—Kt3

Returning the gambit pawn, in the spirit of this defence. If, instead, 8 .... P×P; 9 Castles, with R—Q1 and B—R3 to follow. Still less to be recommended is 8 .... Kt×P; 9 Kt×Kt, P×Kt; 10 B×P ch, Q×B; 11 Q—Kt5 ch, followed by Q×B, to White's advantage.

9 QKt—Q2   Kt—R3
10 Castles   Castles
11 P×P

This allows Black more chances of freeing himself than would 11 B—R3.

11 ......   Q×P
12 B—Q5

But now 12 B—R3 would be useless after 12 .... B—QB4.

12 ......   Kt—R4
13 Q—Kt4   Q—Kt3
14 Kt—K5   Q—R4
15 QKt—B3   P—B3
16 B—R3

In spite of appearances, this move leads to nothing, and the immediate retreat 16 B—Kt3 was indicated.

16 ......   R—K1
17 B—Kt3   P—B4

More simple would be 17 .... Kt×B; 18 P×Kt, P—QB4.

18 Q—Kt5   R×Kt
19 Kt×R   Q×Kt
20 B—Q5

An amusing try would be 20 QR—Q1, threatening 21 Q×B.

20 ......   P—B5

This counter-trap (21 B×P ch, Kt×B; guarding the Queen) loses a piece in the end. A close defence by 20 .... Q—K2 was essential.

21 B—Kt4   B—K3

Now Black is caught in his own snare, for if 21 .... Kt—B3; 22 B×Kt wins.

22 B×Kt   Kt—Kt5

A desperate measure, easily mastered.

23 P—Kt3   QB×B
24 P×B   B×P ch
25 R×B   Kt×R
26 K×Kt   Q—B4 ch
27 K—Kt1   Resigns.

33

White   Black
LILLE   PARIS

(1897)

Although the opening in the following game is treated in a quiet manner, White comes out with a prospective passed pawn on the QR file. In trying to ward off this danger Black must "nolens volens" allow a white Rook to penetrate to the seventh with damaging results. The ending is rich in piquant turns.

1 P—K4   P—K4
2 Kt—KB3   Kt—QB3
3 B—B4   B—B4
4 P—QKt4   B—Kt3

Hoping to obtain a quiet game by thus declining the gambit. The counter-thrust 4 .... P—Q4, however, is bad, as after 5 P×P, Kt×P; 6 B—R3, White has the better of it.

5 P—QR4

Now White feels that he is committed to this course, and so continues the offensive on the extreme left wing. A peaceful alternative, however, can be considered, namely: 5 P—B3, Kt—B3; 6 Q—Kt3, Castles; 7 P—Q3, P—Q3; 8 B—KKt5, Q—K2, etc., with an equal game, reminiscent of a variation of the *Giuoco Piano.*

5 ......   P—QR3

Anticipating the threat of 6 P—R5, B—Q5; 7 P—B3. To this effect 5 .... P—QR4 is less tractable on account of 6 P—Kt5, Kt—Q5; 7 Kt×Kt (if 7 Kt×P, Q—Kt4); 7 .... B×Kt; 8 P—QB3, B—Kt3; 9 P—Q4, Q—B3; 10 B—K3, and White has the better game. Equally, after 5 .... Kt×P; 6 P—R5, B—B4; 7 P—B3, Kt—QB3; 8 Castles, etc., White has the advantage.

6 P—B3
A prudent measure.

6 ...... P—Q3
7 Q—Kt3
This interlude maintains the initiative for White.

If, instead, White were to play, superficially, 7 P—Q3, Kt—B3; 8 Castles, Black has some chances of controlling the game after 8 .... Kt—K2, followed by .... P—B3 and .... P—Q4.

7 ...... Q—K2
8 P—R5 B—R2
9 P—Kt5 P×P
Still more awkward would be 9 .... Kt—Q1; 10 P—Kt6, P×P; 11 P×P, B—Kt1, and Black's Q side remains hemmed in.

10 B×P Kt—B3
If 10 .... B—Q2; 11 P—R6, P×P; 12 R×P, initiating some pressure, whilst after the text move 11 P—R6 can be followed without danger by 11 .... Castles.

11 Castles Castles
If 11 .... Kt×P, we have 12 B×Kt ch, P×B; 13 Q—R4, with a double threat against the adverse Knight and QBP.

12 B×Kt P×B
13 P—Q3
Thus the initial phase of the game ends with a slight advantage to White. Although his passed pawn looks inoffensive enough, it may have to be reckoned with later on.

13 ...... P—R3
14 B—K3 B—K3
15 P—B4 P—B4
16 Kt—B3 Kt—R2
He aims at a K side attack. The wise plan would have been to concentrate forces on the opposing wing, commencing with 16 .... KR—Kt1, etc.

17 Kt—Q2 P—QB3
18 P—B4 P×P
Here Black could have played 18 .... P—B3. But his next move shows that he has more ambitious plans.

19 R×P P—B4
20 P×P B×KBP
21 Kt(B3)—K4 Kt—Kt4
22 R—K1 Kt×Kt
23 P×Kt
Closing the K file in order to turn his artillery to account on the neighbouring KB file.

23 ...... B—K3
24 R(K1)—KB1 R×R
25 B×R R—KB1
26 Q—Kt3 B—Kt1
27 R—Kt1
This lightning change of target is remarkable. Threat: 28 R×B, R×R; 29 B×P. Evidently 27 B×RP would be a blunder because of 27 .... R×R ch; 28 K×R (or 28 Kt×R, B×P); 28 .... Q—B3 ch; 29 B—B4, P—Q4, and Black wins.

27 ...... Q—B3
Guarding the threatened KRP, laying a little trap (28 B×QP, Q—Q5 ch, winning) and even creating a threat, which however proves ephemeral.

28 P—R4 B—QB2
In the belief that there is now a real threat against the hostile Bishop, but in reality only furthering White's plans. But in any event, Black's position has become critical, e.g.: 28 .... Q×B; 29 Q×Q, R×Q; 30 R×B ch, R—B1; 31 R—Kt6 (liquidation here leads to nothing after 31 R×R ch, K×R; 32 P—R6, B—B1; 33 P—R7, B—Kt2; 34 Kt—Kt1, K—K2; 35 Kt—B3, K—Q2; 36 Kt—R4, K—B2, etc.); 31 .... R—R1; 32 R×P, R×P; 33 R×QP, and White has gained appreciable material.

29 P—R6
A quicksilver pawn. If 29 .... Q×B; 30 Q×Q, R×Q; 31 P—R7, R—B1; 32 R—Kt7, R—R1; 33 R×B, and White's advantage is assured.

29 ...... R—Kt1
30 P—R7
This trusty pawn continues on the march. Black cannot reply 30 .... R×R ch; 31 Kt×R, Q—B1, because of 32 B×RP.

30 ...... R—R1
31 R—Kt7
Well calculated! The three-fold point being: the intermediary manœuvre 33 Kt—Kt3, after the demise of the passed pawn (the black Queen is deflected from KKt2), then 34 B×RP (a threat of mate), and finally the astounding activity of the white Knight after 38 Kt×P.

31 ...... Q—R8 ch
32 K—R2 R×P
33 Kt—Kt3 Q—R6
34 B×RP P—Q4
35 R×B R×R

36 Q×R   P×B
37 KP×P   P×P
After 37 .... B×P; 38 Q—Kt8 ch,
followed by 39 P×B, White remains with
an extra piece.

38 Kt×P   B—B2
39 P×P   Q—K6
Not 39.... B×P, because of 40 Q—Q8 ch.
Now White could not continue 40 P—Q6,
on account of 40 .... Q—B5 ch, etc. He,
however, finds a way of galvanising his
forces into decisive action.

40 Kt—Q7   Q—Q5
41 Q—Q8 ch   K—R2
Or 41 .... K—Kt2; 42 Q—B8 ch,
K—Kt3; 43 P—R5 ch, and wins.

42 Q—K7   Q—B5 ch
43 K—R3   Q—B4 ch
44 K—Kt3   P—R4
45 Kt—K5   K—Kt1
46 Q×B ch
A forcible liquidation.

46 ......   Resigns.

34

White   Black
TARTAKOWER   RUBINSTEIN

(The Hague, 1921)

*The more active position of White's pieces
enable him on the 28th move to effect material
gain (B and Kt against R). On the 51st
move he is a whole Knight to the good. Yet
it is only by means of problem-like manœuvres
that he succeeds in enforcing a win.*

1 P—K4   P—K4
2 Kt—KB3   Kt—QB3
3 B—B4   B—B4
4 P—QKt4   B—Kt3
5 B—Kt2
With the double function of attacking the
adverse KP and of guarding his own QR
against eventualities.

5 ......   P—Q3
A more active defence arises from 5 ....
Kt—B3, e.g.: 6 P—QR4, KKt×P, or
6 P—Kt5, Kt—QR4; 7 Kt×P, Castles, etc.,
with complications.

6 P—QR4   P—QR3
7 P—Kt5
An interesting skirmish, by means of
which White maintains the initiative.

7 ......   P×P
Less sound is 7 .... Kt—R4; 8 B—K2.

8 P×P   R×R
9 B×R   Kt—Q5
Here also 9 .... Kt—R4 would have
unduly decentralised the Knight. There is
more justification in 9 .... Kt—Kt1,
returning later to the fray *via* Q2.

10 Kt×Kt
The exchange by 10 B×Kt also has
points, but White reckons that he will
shortly be able to bring the QB back into
play.

10 ......   P×Kt
11 P—QB3
Instead of playing non-committal moves
such as 11 P—Q3 or 11 Castles, White at
once eliminates the troublesome hostile
outpost.

11 ......   Kt—B3
He speeds up his development, whilst
11 .... P×P; 12 Kt×P would only help
that of his adversary.

12 Castles   Castles
13 P—Q3   P—Q4
Black, in a clever manner, works for
emancipation.

14 KP×P   Kt×P
15 Q—B3
But White maintains the initiative by
bringing his Queen into active play.

15 ......   Kt—B3
16 P×P   B×P
17 Kt—B3   Kt—Kt5
18 Kt—Q5   B×B
19 R×B   Kt—K4
20 Q—Kt3   R—K1
21 P—R3   P—QB3
22 P×P   P×P
23 Kt—K3   P—Kt3
More careful would have been 23 ....
B—Q2, for now the white Rook enters the
enemy camp.

24 R—R8   P—R4
Hoping, in good time, to drive the white
Queen from her excellent post of observa-
tion.

A mistake would be 24 .... Kt×P
(25 R×B, Q×R; 26 B×Kt) or 24 ....
Q—B2 (25 P—Q4). Similarly, 24 ....
Q—K2 would call forth 25 P—Q4. For all

these reasons, 24 .... Q—Q2 would have been the least evil.

| 25 B—R6 | P—R5 |
| 26 Q×Kt | |

By this *liquidating sacrifice* White will win two pieces for a Rook.

26	R×Q
27 R×B	Q×R
28 B×Q	

The resulting end-game, Rook against two minor pieces, does not frequently occur in master practice. It results here in an instructive and stubborn fight.

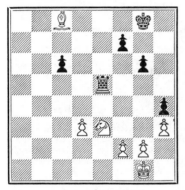

28	R—QR4
29 K—B1	R—R7
30 B—Kt7	R—Q7
31 B—R6	

It goes without saying that White will as far as possible avoid pawn exchanges, each pawn representing chances for the future.

31	K—Kt2
32 K—K1	R—Kt7
33 Kt—Q1	R—Kt8
34 K—K2	P—KB4
35 P—Q4	K—B3
36 B—Q3	R—Kt5
37 K—K3	P—Kt4

After 37 .... P—B5 ch; 38 K×P (38 K—K4, P—B4); 38 .... R×P ch; 39 K—K3, White can turn his pawn majority on the K side to account, whilst keeping Black's passed but isolated pawn on the Q side under restraint.

38 B—K2	R—Kt6 ch
39 K—Q2	R—Kt5
40 K—B3	R—R5
41 Kt—Kt2	R—R8
42 B—B3	P—Kt5

A double pitfall: if 43 P×P, P—R6, etc., and if 43 B×BP, R—B8 ch.

43 B—Q1	K—Kt4
44 K—B2	P×P
45 P×P	K—B5
46 Kt—Q3 ch	K—K5
47 Kt—B5 ch	

A tactical finesse which not only saves the threatened pawn (47 .... K×P; 48 Kt—Kt3 ch), but also keeps the hostile King at bay (47 .... K—Q4; 48 B—B3 ch, K—B5; 49 B—K2 ch, K—Q4; 50 K—B3, etc.).

47	K—B5
48 K—Q2	R—R7 ch
49 K—B3	R—R8
50 B—R4	R×B

An ingenious expedient, but an insufficient one. However, after 50 .... R—R8; 51 Kt—Q3 ch, K—Kt4; 52 B×P, R×P; 53 P—Q5, K—B3; 54 P—Q6, etc., White wins also.

51 Kt×R	K—B6
52 K—Q2	K×P
53 Kt—B5	

And White won

After 53 .... K—Kt6; 54 K—K2, Black exceeded the time limit. His game was, however, lost in any event, as follows: 54 .... K×P (or 54 .... P—B5; 55 Kt—Q3, P—B6 ch; 56 K—K3, etc.); 55 K—B3, K—R7; 56 Kt—K6, K—Kt8; 57 Kt—B4, K—B8; 58 K—K3, K—Kt8 (or 58 .... K—K8; 59 Kt—Kt2 ch, etc.); 59 K—K2 (holding the hostile King); 59 .... K—R8; 60 K—B1, K—R7; 61 K—B2, K—R8 (or 61 .... P—R6; 62 Kt—R5, K—R8; 63 Kt—Kt3 ch, etc.); 62 Kt—Kt6, P—R6 (or 62 .... K—R7; 63 K—B3, P—R6; 64 Kt—B4, etc.); 63 Kt—B4, K—R7 (or 63 .... P—R7; 64 K—B1, P—B4; 65 Kt—R3, followed by mate); 64 Kt—R5, K—R8; 65 Kt—Kt3 ch, K—R7; 66 Kt×P, K—R8; 67 Kt—K3, K—R7 (or 67 .... P—R7; 68 Kt—B1, with mate to follow); 68 Kt—Kt4 ch, K—R8; 69 K—B1, P—B4; 70 P×P, P—R7; 71 Kt—B2 mate.

35

White	Black
WHITAKER	THOMAS
(U.S.A.)	(Great Britain)

(Cable Match, 1930)

This is a contest full of unexpected turns, in which the victory goes to the stronger nerves.

1 P—K4	P—K4
2 Kt—KB3	Kt—QB3
3 B—B4	B—B4
4 P—QKt4	B—Kt3
5 P—Kt5	

A "fancy" continuation.

5	Kt—R4

Less good is 5 .... Kt—Q5, because of
6 Kt×Kt, B×Kt; 7 P—QB3, B—Kt3;
8 P—Q4, etc.

6 Kt×P
White intensifies the struggle in the battle
zone, instead of adopting the wise retreat
6 B—K2.

6	Kt—R3

An interesting alternative is 6 ....
Q—Kt4, with a double attack on the hostile
Kt and KKtP.

7 P—Q4	P—Q3
8 B×Kt	P×Kt

Now White's Bishops are both attacked.

9 B×P	R—KKt1
10 B×P ch	K×B
11 B×P	B—Kt5

The crucial moment. A mistake would
be 11 .... R×P, on account of 12 Q—B3 ch.
The best here is 11 .... Q—Kt4, and
although White has four pawns for a piece,
Black has the initiative.

12 Q—Q3	P—B4

Here again 12 .... Q—Kt4 has its points.

13 Kt—B3	P×P
14 Kt—Q5	Q—K1
15 Q—KKt3	

In spite of the powerful threat 16 Q—B4 ch,
K—K3; 17 Q—B6 ch, K—Q2; 18 Q—Q6 ch,
etc., the move in the text can be mastered.
The simplest was 15 B×P, B×B; 16 Q×B.

15	Kt—B5
16 Q—B4 ch	K—K3

Clearly not 16 .... K—Kt3; 17 Q—B6 ch,
K—R4; 18 Kt—B4 mate.

17 P—KR3
Waste of time. Nor was anything to be
gained by 17 Q—B6 ch, K—Q2, but a continuation could be played, e.g. 17 Kt×B,
P×Kt; 18 B×P.

17	B—R4 ch

Henceforth Black will dictate the course
of events.

18 P—B3
The immediate flight of the white King by
18 K—B1 was not without drawbacks.

18	B×P ch
19 K—B1	

Or 19 Kt×B, Kt×B, threatening 20 ....
Kt—Q6 ch

19	Kt—Q7 ch
20 Q×Kt	

By this temporary sacrifice of the Queen,
White hopes—mistakenly, as it turns out—
to redeem the situation. 20 K—Kt1 would
be unfortunate because of the pretty sequel
20 .... Kt—B6 ch; 21 K—B1, Q×P mate.

20	Q×P ch

A most important intermediary check.

21 K—Kt1	B×Q
22 Kt—B7 ch	K×B
23 Kt×Q	B—KB6

The simplest way.

White resigns
A subtle and attractive continuation could
have been 23 .... B—K7; 24 Kt—R3,
R×P ch; 25 K×R, R—Kt1 ch; 26 K—R2,
B—B5 mate.

3. TWO KNIGHTS' DEFENCE

36

White	Black
VON DER LASA	MAYET

(Berlin, 1839)

Named the Fegatello Attack, *the variation shown in this game, in which the black King is, from the first, driven from pillar to post, is one of the curiosities of the openings.*

1 P—K4	P—K4
2 Kt—KB3	Kt—QB3
3 B—B4	Kt—B3

In the Two Knights' Defence, Black is in a much better position to fight for the initiative than after 3 .... B—B4.

4 Kt—Kt5
This impulsive enterprise can easily bring about changes in the *rôle* of the aggressor.

4 ...... P—Q4
The only way of parrying the attack on the critical point KB2, but a sufficient one. Other, and very ingenious, attempts can be refuted, e.g. 4 .... Kt × P (by 5 B × P ch, K—K2; 6 P—Q4, etc.) and 4 .... B—B4 (by 5 P—Q4, B × P; 6 Kt × BP, etc.).

5 P × P Kt × P
Giving rise to serious repercussions.

6 Kt × BP
The *Fegatello Attack.* Brilliant as this conception undoubtedly is, the following alternative is more convincing: 6 P—Q4, P × P; 7 Castles, B—K3; 8 R—K1, Q—Q2; 9 Kt × BP, K × Kt; 10 Q—B3 ch, K—Kt1; 11 R × B, and wins.

6 ...... K × Kt
7 Q—B3 ch K—K3
He must defend his capture, because after 7 .... K—K1; 8 B × Kt, Q—B3; 9 B × Kt ch, P × B; 10 Q × Q, P × Q; 11 P—Q3, White would be a valuable pawn ahead.

8 Kt—B3 Kt—K2
Against 8 .... Kt—Kt5 White increases the pressure by 9 Q—K4, P—B3; 10 P—QR3, Kt—R3; 11 P—Q4, Kt—B2; 12 B—B4,

K—B2; 13 B × P, B—K2; 14 Castles QR, and White has the upper hand.

9 P—Q4
Another continuation worthy of consideration is 9 Castles, P—B3; 10 R—K1.

9 ...... P—QKt4
Apart from this interesting attempt to slow down the attack, the following two methods of defence have been tried: (a) 9 .... P—B3; 10 B—KKt5, etc.; and (b) 9 .... P—KR3; 10 Castles, P—B3; 11 R—K1, etc. White has in either case good practical chances.

10 Kt × P P—B3
Not, of course, 10 .... Kt—Kt3, as 11 B × Kt ch wins. But he should at once have played 10 .... B—Kt2.

11 Kt—B3 Q—Kt3
This diversion is not as good as it looks; on the other hand, 11 .... B—Kt2; 12 Kt—K4 multiplies White's threats.

12 P × P	B—Kt2
13 Kt—K4	

This new sacrifice, calculated to a nicety, breaks down Black's resistance.

13	Q—Kt5 ch
14 B—Q2	Q × B

At the moment Black is two pieces ahead, but White dominates the play.

15 Q—Kt4 ch K × P
If 15 .... K—B2; 16 Kt—Q6 ch, and if 15 .... Kt—B4; 16 Kt—Kt5 ch, followed by Q × Q.

16 P—B4 ch K—Q5
Or 16 .... Kt × P; 17 B × Kt ch, K × Kt; 18 B—Q6 dis ch, K—Q4; 19 Castles ch, followed by mate.

17 P—B3 ch	Kt × P
18 B × Kt ch	K × Kt
19 P—B5 dis ch	K—Q4
20 Castles ch	K—B4
21 P—Kt4 ch	K—Kt4
22 P—R4 ch	Resigns

37

White	Black
WAYTE	WILLIAMS

(About 1853)

*In this game the opening skirmishes quickly
lead to a final assault, conducted by Black
with superb élan.*

1 P—K4	P—K4
2 Kt—KB3	Kt—QB3
3 B—B4	Kt—B3
4 Kt—Kt5	P—Q4
5 P×P	Kt—QR4

The only entirely satisfactory move. After
5 .... Kt—Q5 (the *Fritz Variation*) White,
according to modern research, obtains a
clear advantage after 6 P—QB3, P—Kt4;
7 B—B1, Kt × P; 8 Kt—K4, etc.

6 B—Kt5 ch   P—B3
Black disdains to regain his pawn by
6 .... B—Q2 in order to accelerate his
development.

7 P×P	P×P
8 Q—B3	

Instead of retiring the threatened Bishop
at once, White tries to complicate matters.
But in any event the initiative now passes to
Black.

8 ......   Q—Kt3
He evidently can play neither 8 ....
P×B (9 Q×R) nor 8 .... P—K5 (9 Kt×KP,
Q—K2; 10 B—Q3, etc.). But 8 ....
Q—B2 is even more effective than the text
move, guarding as it does both the QBP
and the KP.

9 B—R4
After 9 B—K2, Black's best reply, as in
the text, is 9 .... B—KKt5.

9	B—KKt5
10 Q—KKt3	B—QB4

Offering another pawn instead of adopting
the more peaceful continuation 10 ....
P—KR3; 11 Kt—KR3 (11 Q×P ch, K—Q2;
12 Kt×P, R—K1; 13 Q×R ch, K×Q;
14 Kt×R, Q—R3; 15 P—KB3, B—KB4;
and although White has two Rooks for the
Queen, his situation is critical). 11 ....
B—Q3; 12 Castles, Castles (QR); with an
even game.

11 Castles
He thinks in the first place of his King's
safety, instead of embarking on adventure
by 11 Q×P ch.

11 ......   Castles KR
12 B—Kt3
Here again 12 Q×P would be of doubtful
value. After 12 .... B×P ch; 13 K—R1
(not, in any case, 13 R×B, QR—K1, winning); 13 .... QR—K1; 14 Q—B4, P—KR3,
etc., Black has the advantage.

12	P—KR3
13 Kt—KB3	Kt×B
14 RP×Kt	P—K5
15 Kt—K5	B—K7
16 R—K1	Kt—R4
17 Kt—Q7	

Or 17 Q—R4, P—Kt4 (forcing the
adverse Queen away from the defence of
her KB2); 18 Q×KP, B×P ch; 19 K—R1,
B×R; 20 Q×B (attacking two pieces);
20 .... Q—B7; 21 Kt—QB3, KR—K1,
and Black wins.

17	Q—Q1
18 Q—K5	

The subsequent episodes, in which several
pieces remain *en prise* at the same time, are
most interesting.

18	Q×Kt
19 R×B	Q—Kt5

This sally is very ruthless. After 19 ....
Q—Q4; 20 KR×P, Black would have no
compensation for the loss of two pawns.

20 KR×P
Or 20 Kt—B3, Kt—B5; 21 P—Kt3,
Kt×R ch; 22 Kt×Kt, Q×Kt; 23 Q×B,
P—B4; 24 Q×QBP, P—B5, and Black has,
in addition to the exchange, a very strong
attack.

Another instructive line of play is
20 Q×P, Kt—B5; 21 K—B1, Q×R ch;
22 Q×Q, Kt×Q; 23 K×Kt (as a matter of
accountancy, White has a small advantage
of two pawns for the exchange; but,
dynamically, the more active play of Black's
pieces will decide the game in his favour);
23 .... KR—K1 ch; 24 K—B1, R—K3;
25 P—Q3, QR—K1; 26 B—Q2, R—K7;
27 B—K3, R × P, and Black wins.

20 ......   Kt—B5
Very pretty! It is clear that the Knight
cannot be captured because of 21 ....
Q—Q8 ch.

21 P—Kt3   B—Q3
The culmination of the preceding man-
œuvres. This beautiful stroke forces White's
Queen to relinquish the over-protection of
the critical square K1 (e.g. 22 Q×B,
Q—Q8 ch; or 22 P—R3, Q×P).

Resigns.

38

White	Black
STEINITZ	TCHIGORIN

(Match by cable, 1890-1)

There is no need to emphasise the dangers which beset a position insufficiently developed. The following game is, in this respect, a dreadful example.

1 P—K4	P—K4
2 Kt—KB3	Kt—QB3
3 B—B4	Kt—B3
4 Kt—Kt5	P—Q4
5 P×P	Kt—QR4
6 B—Kt5 ch	P—B3
7 P×P	P×P
8 B—K2	

Undoubtedly the best retreat, but the initiative remains with Black.

| 8 ...... | P—KR3 |

Black must of course drive back the intruder without delay, for if 8 .... B—QB4; 9Kt—QB3, P—KR3; 10KKt—K4, etc., and if 8 .... Kt—Q4 (*Villeneuve's Variation*); 9 P—Q4, with advantage to White.

9 Kt—KR3

This *bizarre* retreat, favoured by Steinitz, is cruelly refuted in the present game. 9 Kt—KB3 was indicated.

| 9 ...... | B—QB4 |

Here, as later on, 9 .... B×Kt; 10 P×B would only lighten White's task.

| 10 P—Q3 | Castles |
| 11 Kt—B3 | |

Would White avoid trouble by castling in his turn? No—the sequel could be 11 Castles, Kt—Kt2; 12 K—R1, P—Kt4; 13 P—QB3, B—Kt3; 14 B—K3, Kt—Q4, and Black is in a commanding position.

| 11 ...... | Kt—Q4 |

Taking up a strong central position, while vacating the KB file for the advance of the pawn.

12 Kt—R4

After 12 Kt×Kt, P×Kt, Black's centre would be more powerful than ever. But needless to say, the eccentric position of his Knights is not in White's favour.

Thus one evil begets another, and, instead of rational development, White must have recourse to artificial manœuvres.

| 12 ...... | B—Q3 |
| 13 Kt—Kt1 | |

In the "Steinitz manner." But on this occasion his retrograde evolutions are not crowned with success.

He could not, however, play 13 Castles, because of 13 .... Q—R5, and both white Knights are in jeopardy.

| 13 ...... | P—KB4 |
| 14 P—QB3 | B—Q2 |

Black is able to complete his development at leisure. The threat—a positional one— is 15 .... P—B4, blockading the square Q5 and enabling the Knight to return into play via QB3.

15 P—Q4	P—K5
16 P—QB4	Kt—K2
17 Kt—QB3	B—K3
18 P—QKt3	B—Kt5
19 B—Kt2	P—B5

To be followed by 20 .... Kt—B4.

20 Q—B2

This sacrifice of a pawn for the sake of a hypothetical attack is brilliantly refuted.

It would have been better to submit to a laborious defence by 20 P—QR3, B×Kt ch; 21 B×B, R—Kt1; 22 R—Kt1, etc.

| 20 ...... | Q×P |
| 21 K—B1 | |

At this stage also 21 P—QR3 had its points.

| 21 ...... | P—B6 |

A break-through.

In the subsequent hand-to-hand fighting both adversaries pursue well-defined objectives. But Black's plan proves to be the more profound.

22 P×P	P×P
23 B×P	B—KB4
24 Kt—K4	B×Kt
25 Q—K2	

After 25 B×B, Black terminates the game in an artistic manner, e.g. 25 .... R×P ch; 26 Q×R, Q×KB; 27 Kt—B3, R—KB1; 28 K—Kt2, Kt—Kt3, threatening 29 .... R×Kt; 30 Q×R, Kt—R5 ch. (*Diagram. See p. 48.*)

| 25 ...... | B×B |

Allowing the capture of his Queen, but at a price. (A Rook, two pieces, to say nothing of the attack.)

If 25 .... B—B6; 26 R—Q1.

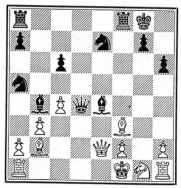

Position after 25 Q—K2

26 Q—K6 ch	K—R2
27 B × Q	B × R
28 Q—R3 ch	Kt—B4

Black's active forces are to the fore.

29 B—K5	QR—K1
30 B—B4	Kt—Q5
31 Q—Q3 ch	B—K5

Very prettily Black "liquidates" and turns to account the value of his Rooks on the open lines.

32 Q × Kt	R × B
33 P—B3	QR—KB1
34 Q × P	P—B4
35 Q—QB7	Kt—B3
36 P—QR3	R × P ch
37 Kt × R	R × Kt ch
38 K—Kt1	B—Q7
Resigns.	

39

| *White* | *Black* |
| BECKER | VIDMAR |

(Carlsbad, 1929)

Once an attacking position is obtained, any hesitation may prove fatal.
The loss of this game is entirely due to Black's neglect of this precept.

1 P—K4	P—K4
2 Kt—KB3	Kt—QB3
3 B—B4	Kt—B3
4 Kt—Kt5	P—Q4
5 P × P	Kt—QR4
6 B—Kt5 ch	P—B3
7 P × P	P × P
8 B—K2	

Here 8 B—Q3 was played in a game Castaldi-Keres (*Stockholm*, 1937), and led to the curious sequel: 8 .... Kt—Q4 (more useful than 8 .... P—KR3; 9 Kt—K4, because, after the text move, Black's KKt will take a very active part in subsequent events. Very good also is 8 .... Kt—Kt5; and, after the retreat of the threatened white Knight, 9 .... P—KB4); 9 Kt—K4, P—KB4; 10 Kt—Kt3, Kt—KB5; 11 B—B1, B—B4; 12 P—QB3, B—Kt3; 13 P—Q4, Kt—Kt3; 14 B—Q3, Castles (preferring to keep the game open, instead of closing the lines by 14 .... P—K5; 15 B—K2, etc.); 15 P—Kt4, Kt—Kt2; 16 B—B4 ch, K—R1; 17 P—Q5 (after which the storm breaks unexpectedly); 17 .... Kt—Q3; 18 B—Kt3, P—B5; 19 Kt—B1, Kt—K5, and White resigns.

| 8 ...... | P—KR3 |
| 9 Kt—KB3 | P—K5 |

Black gains territory in return for the pawn he has lost.

| 10 Kt—K5 | Q—B2 |

Continuing the persecution of the hostile KKt. Black could also first play 10 .... B—Q3, after which White's best line is 11 P—Q4, as in the text.

11 P—Q4

After 11 P—KB4, which lays bare a vital diagonal 11 .... B—QB4; 12 P—B3, Kt—Kt2, etc., is to be recommended.

| 11 ...... | B—Q3 |

A more straightforward idea is 11 .... P × P e.p.; 12 Kt × QP, B—Q3, etc., but Black would not, from choice, give up his outpost pawn, whilst he hopes to drive off sooner or later the enemy's outpost Knight.

12 B—Q2

An interesting interlude by which White declares his readiness to give back the extra pawn eventually, in the interest of his development.

Another, and very old, continuation is 12 P—KB4, Castles; 13 Castles, P—B4; 14 P—B3, with two-edged play.

| 12 ...... | Castles |

Not to be recommended would be the immediate recovery of the pawn by 12 .... B × Kt; 13 P × B, Q × P, on account of 14 B—QB3, Q—B2; 15 Castles, etc., or 14 .... Q—KKt4; 15 Q—Q6, etc., to White's advantage. If, on the other hand, Black voluntarily gives up territory by 12 .... Kt—Kt2, there follows 13 B—QB3.

13 Kt—R3

White pursues an active policy instead of centralising by 13 Castles. By the text move he prevents 13 .... P—B4 (because of 14 Kt—Kt5), nor does he fear the continuation 13 .... B×QKt; 14 P×B, P—B4; 15 P—QB3, R—Q1; 16 Q—R4, etc.

13 ...... B—K3

14 Castles

After this move White already threatens 15 B×Kt, Q×B; 16 QKt—B4, etc., with extensive liquidation.

14 ...... Kt—Kt2

He is compelled to give up territory, for if 14 .... B×KKt; 15 P×B, Q×P; 16 B—QB3, Q—B2 (or 16 .... Q—KKt4; 17 Q—Q6, threatening Q—B7); 17 Q—Q2, Kt—Kt2; 18 B×Kt, P×B; 19 Q×P. Black is lost.

15 K—R1

After 15 P—KB4, P—B4; 16 Kt—Kt5, Q—Kt3, Black's chances begin to improve. Similarly, 15 QKt—B4, QB×Kt; 16 B×B P—B4 is in favour of Black.

15 ...... QR—Q1

A critical moment. Black plays with fire —he thinks he can quietly go on improving his position, whereas he should at once eliminate the hostile outpost and recover his pawn, e.g. 15 .... B×KKt; 16 P×B, Q×P; 17 B—QB3, Q—KB4; and the fight is still very open.

16 QKt—B4 QB×Kt

17 Kt×B B×P

As 17 .... B—K2 would lose still more space, Black takes a chance.

18 P—KKt3

Fearless play.

18 ...... B×P

19 P×B Q×P

Hoping for a perpetual check, but White's next move destroys the illusion.

20 B—B4

And White won on account of his extra piece.

40

White	Black
SPIELMANN	ELISKASES

(Match, 1936)

In this game we find two open files already occupied on the 21st move by Black's Rooks. As could be expected, this dynamic advantage very quickly leads to decisive operations.

1 P—K4	P—K4
2 Kt—KB3	Kt—QB3
3 B—B4	Kt—B3
4 Kt—Kt5	P—Q4
5 P×P	Kt—QR4
6 B—Kt5 ch	P—B3
7 P×P	P×P
8 B—K2	P—KR3
9 Kt—KB3	P—K5
10 Kt—K5	Q—B2
11 P—Q4	P×P e. p.

Aiming as far as possible at an open battle.

12 Kt×QP B—Q3

After this, White is still unable to castle.

13 Kt—R3

In order to reply to 13 .... P—B4 with 14 Kt—Kt5, whereas 13 B—K3, P—B4 would favour Black. But the best line is to castle as quickly as possible, e.g. 13 P—KR3, Castles; 14 Castles, B—KB4; 15 R—K1, QR—Q1; 16 B—B1, and White tries, somehow, to consolidate his position.

13 ...... B—R3

Accurately played. For if 13 .... Castles, at once White gains space after 14 P—QKt4, Kt—Kt2; 15 Kt—B4, etc. But now, if White plays 14 P—QKt4, Kt—B5 maintains and even improves Black's position.

14 P—KKt3 Castles KR

15 Castles QR—Q1

16 B—K3

In view of the latent pressure exercised by the adverse Rook on the Q file, it would have been better for White to have played 16 B—Q2, although even then his position remains difficult.

16 ...... Kt—Q4

17 B—B5 B×B

After 17 Q—B1, KR—K1 Black still has the superior game.

18 Kt×B *(Diagram. See p. 50.)*

18 ...... Kt—B6

A beautiful conception, the point being the unmasking of the open Q file.

19 Kt×B Q—K4

Although Black has one piece less and the KKt is *en prise*, he now recovers the whole of his material with advantage.

20 Q—K1

The sacrifice of the Queen is useless, e.g. 20 P×Kt, R×Q; 21 B×R, on account of 21 .... Q×P; 22 B—K2, Q×Kt, and Black has a clear advantage.

Position after 18 Kt × B

20 ......   Kt × B ch
21 K—R1
Or 21 K—Kt2, Q—Q4 ch; 22 P—B3,
KR—K1; 23 R—Q1, Kt—B5 ch; 24 P × Kt,
R × Q; 25 R × Q, R—K7 ch, followed by
.... R × R, and Black remains the exchange
ahead.

21 ......   KR—K1
Complete mastery. But neither 21 ....
Q—Q4 ch; 22 P—B3, KR—K1; 23 R—Q1
(if 23 .... Kt × P ch; 24 Q × Kt) nor 21 ....
Q—R4; 22 P—KB3, KR—K1; 23 Q—B2,
R—Q7; 24 QR—Q1 (mastering the attack)
would lead to anything.

22 R—Q1   Q—R4
Threatening 23 .... Q—B6 mate. (We
see how the weakness created by White's
14th move has brought retribution.)

23 P—R4
Clearly not 23 P—KB3, on account of
23 .... R × R; 24 Q × R, Kt × P ch.

23 ......   Q—Kt5
24 K—Kt2
In the hope of coming through almost
unscathed, after 24 .... Kt—B5 ch;
25 K—Kt1, R × Q; 26 R × R ch, K—R2;
27 R × R, etc. But a fresh hammer-blow
puts an end to his expectations.

24 ......   Kt × P
25 P × Kt   R—K7 ch
An essential check.

26 R—B2   R × R ch
27 Q × R   Q × R
        Resigns

41

White	Black
SALWE	MARSHALL

(Vienna, 1908)

*To know how to conduct an attack on the
hostile King's field, and how to create breaches
there, is part and parcel of the attacking
player's equipment. A rarer gift is to be
able to foresee where the opponent is going to
castle and to weaken that side beforehand.
Black does this here on his 12th move ....
B—Kt5 ch, by which, for ulterior purposes,
he deliberately provokes a weakening of
White's Q3.*

1 P—K4	P—K4
2 Kt—KB3	Kt—QB3
3 B—B4	Kt—B3
4 Kt—Kt5	P—Q4
5 P × P	Kt—QR4
6 P—Q3	

One of Morphy's ideas. He gives back
the pawn and strengthens the centre.

6	P—KR3
7 Kt—KB3	P—K5
8 Q—K2	Kt × B

Of course not 8 .... B—QB4 at once
because of 9 P × P, as the white Queen
indirectly defends the KB.

9 P × Kt	B—QB4

Strategically, Black occupies an important
diagonal, whilst tactically he prevents
10 Kt—Q4, which would be playable in
reply to either 9 .... B—K2 or 9 ....
B—Q3.

10 KKt—Q2
By this retrograde manœuvre White tries
to consolidate his position without his
interior lines being weakened, as would
be the case after 10 P—KR3, Castles;
11 Kt—R2, P—K6; 12 B × P, B × B;
13 P × B, Kt—K5, or after 10 P—B3,
Castles; 11 Kt—Q4, B—KKt5, etc., with
advantage to Black.

10	Castles
11 Kt—Kt3	B—Kt5

By this intermediate move Black maintains
the initiative. After 11 .... B—Q3;
12 Kt—B3, R—K1; 13 P—KR3, B—QKt5;
14 Castles, etc., White would have consolidated his position and remained a pawn
ahead.

12 Q—B1
This modest retirement is necessary,
because if 12 Q—Q2, there follows 12 ....
P—K6; 13 P × P, B × P.

| 12 ...... | B—Kt5 ch |

Again an intermediary manœuvre, without which White would have a chance of consolidation, e.g. 12 .... B—Q3; 13 P—KR3, B—R4; 14 P—Kt4, B—Kt3; 15 Kt—B3, etc.

This innovation of Marshall's has changed the whole trend of this opening.

| 13 P—B3 |

Plausible, but not good. The weakness at Q3 will make itself felt later.

As, however, 13 B—Q2 cannot be recommended on account of 13 .... B × B ch; 14 QKt × B, R—K1; 15 P—KR3, P—K6, etc., he should have resigned himself to 13 Kt—B3, obtaining some counter-chances after 13 .... B × Kt ch; 14 P × B, P—QKt4; 15 P—KR3, B—R4; 16 P—Kt4, B—Kt3; 17 B—R3, R—K1; 18 Castles, etc.

| 13 ...... | B—K2 |

Here 13 .... B—Q3 can also be played.

14 P—KR3	B—R4
15 P—Kt4	B—Kt3
16 B—K3	Kt—Q2

Reculer pour mieux sauter! This manœuvre infuses new energy into the attack.

| 17 QKt—Q2 | Kt—K4 |
| 18 Castles | P—Kt4 |

Thus the compact mass of adverse pawns will be demolished.

| 19 P × P | Kt—Q6 ch |

This Knight's very powerful position will have a trenchant effect on the course of events.

| 20 K—Kt1 | Q × P |
| 21 K—R1 | |

A little better would have been 21 P—KB4, at once.

21	Q × P
22 P—KB4	P—QR4
23 QR—Kt1	

If 23 P—B5, P—R5, and Black scores first.

23	P—KB4
24 Kt—Q4	Q—R5
25 P—Kt3	

This drives off the hostile Queen, but another important square (QB3) is weakened.

25	Q—Q2
26 P × P	B × P
27 Q—Kt2	P—B4

Dislodging White's only well-posted piece.

| 28 Kt × B | Q × Kt |
| 29 Q × P | |

White has won the local engagement around the advanced KP, but the following beautiful *riposte* demonstrates that Black still holds the strategical lead—which is here the attack against the King's weakened position.

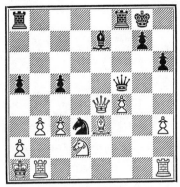

| 29 ...... | B—B3 |

A *temporary sacrifice* of the Queen (30 Q × Q, B × P ch) is offered.

30 Q—B4 ch	K—R1
31 Kt—K4	QR—K1
32 Kt × B	R × Kt
33 B—B1	

Or 33 B—Q2, R—K7.

| 33 ...... | KR—K3 |

Instead of 33 .... R—K7, or 33 .... Kt—K8, both of which formidable threats Black keeps in reserve.

| 34 B—R3 | R—K7 |
| 35 KR—Q1 | Kt—K8 |

The final assault. This Knight has decidedly been the hero of the piece.

36 B × P	Kt—B7 ch
37 K—Kt2	Kt—Kt5 dis ch
Resigns.	

42

| *White* | *Black* |
| HERMANN | CHAROUSEK |

(Budapest, 1896)

Once Black, in this game, has penetrated into the enemy's lines of defence, his attack carries with it fire and destruction. The end comes by means of sparkling combinations, based on a variety of discovered checks.

1 P—K4	P—K4
2 Kt—KB3	Kt—QB3
3 B—B4	Kt—B3
4 Kt—B3	

Leading to a placid continuation, unlike those arising from 4 Kt—Kt5 or 4 P—Q4.

| 4 ...... | Kt × P |

Initiating a lively contest in the central zone, in preference to 4 .... B—B4; 5 P—Q3, P—Q3, which leads into the *Italian Four Knights' Game.*

5 Kt × Kt

Far better than the counter-sacrifice 5 B × P ch, K × B; 6 Kt × Kt, P—Q4, to Black's advantage, e.g. 7 QKt—Kt5 ch, K—Kt1; 8 P—Q3, P—KR3, driving off the intruder, or 7 KKt—Kt5 ch, K—K1; 8 Q—B3, Q—K2, countering White's intentions.

| 5 ...... | P—Q4 |
| 6 B × P | |

Forfeiting the "two Bishops" instead of playing 6 B—Kt5 or 6 B—Q3 (best).

| 6 ...... | Q × B |
| 7 Kt—B3 | Q—Q1 |

On her initial square the Queen is least in the way of the development of her own pieces, whereas 7 .... Q—K3 would block the QB and leave the Queen more exposed to attack.

| 8 Castles | B—Q3 |
| 9 P—Q3 | Castles |

Preferring to complete his mobilisation instead of immediately effecting the pin 9 .... B—KKt5.

10 P—KR3

He prevents the pin mentioned above, but at the cost of weakening his King's field.

10	P—B4
11 R—K1	B—Q2
12 Q—K2	Q—K1
13 B—K3	

By playing 13 B—Q2, he would complete his mobilisation, without presenting his adversary with an attacking *tempo.*

| 13 ...... | Q—Kt3 |
| 14 K—R1 | |

Parrying, at all events, the threat 14 .... P—B5; 15 B—Q2, B × P.

| 14 ...... | P—B5 |
| 15 B—Q2 | Kt—Q5 |

In order to eliminate the KKt, the most

valuable defender of White's King's field.

16 Kt × Kt

He underestimates the danger. But after 16 Q—Q1, Q—R3 White's position also remains critical. A mistake would be 16 Kt × P, because of 16 .... B × Kt; 17 Q × B, Kt × P; 18 Q—Q5 ch, Q—B2, and Black ends up by winning the exchange.

| 16 ...... | P × Kt |
| 17 Kt—K4 | P—B6 |

The break-through.

18 P × P	B × P
19 R—KKt1	Q—R4
20 R—Kt5	Q—R5
21 K—Kt1	

A desperate attempt to avoid, by the King's flight, the damaging results of a discovered check, e.g. 21 Q—K1, B—Kt5 dis ch; 22 K—Kt1, Q—R7 ch; 23 K—B1, Q—R8 ch; 24 K—K2, B × P mate.

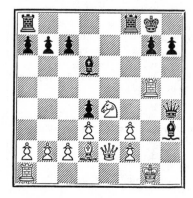

| 21 ...... | B—R7 ch |

After this magnificent offer of a Bishop (a *King's field combination*), Black's King cannot escape. If 22 K × B, there follows 22 .... B—B8 dis ch, winning the Queen.

| 22 K—R1 | B—B8 |

Continuing in the same brilliant vein. The object of the move is to cut off the hostile King's line of retreat. If now 23 Q × B, B—Kt6 dis ch forces the win.

| 23 Q—Q1 | B—K7 |

The finishing stroke.

Resigns
(24 Q × B, B—Kt6 dis ch; 25 K—Kt1, Q—R7 ch; 26 K—B1, Q—R8 mate.

43

White	Black
TARTAKOWER	RÉTI

(Match, 1920)

The well-known sacrifice at KB7 has won many games. The combination in the following game contains some special finesses.

1 P—K4	P—K4
2 Kt—KB3	Kt—QB3
3 B—B4	Kt—B3
4 Kt—B3	Kt × P
5 Kt × Kt	P—Q4
6 B—Q3	

Preserving the Bishop. Less good is 6 B—Kt5, because of 6 .... P×Kt; 7 Kt×P, Q—Kt4, with many possibilities, such as 8 Kt×Kt, Q×B, or 8 P—Q4, Q×P, with advantage to Black.

6	P×Kt

Better than complicating matters by 6 .... P—B4, although it wins back the piece, because after 7 Kt—B3, P—K5; 8 B—QKt5, P×Kt; 9 Q×P, etc., the disposition of White's forces is greatly superior.

7 B×P	B—Q3
8 P—Q4	

White hastens to stir up trouble in the central zone. After the non-committal 8 Castles, Black can already secure the initiative after 8 .... B—KKt5, followed by .... P—B4.

8	P×P

The alternative 8 .... Kt×P occurs in the next game.

9 B×Kt ch	

The only continuation which secures for White, for the time being, the domination of the centre, whereas after 9 Kt×P, Castles; 10 B×Kt (not at once 10 Castles, Kt×Kt; 11 Q×Kt, B×P ch, and wins); 10 .... P×B; 11 Castles, Q—R5, Black has the upper hand.

9	P×B
10 Q×P	Castles
11 Castles	

Castling on the Q side after 11 B—K3 would be more risky..

11	B—KB4
12 P—QKt3	P—B4

Liquidation by 12 .... QB×P; 13 B—Kt2, Q—B3; 14 Q×Q, P×Q; 15 B×P, etc., would be in White's favour.

13 Q—B3	Q—Q2
14 B—R3	Q—Kt4

Not 14 .... Q—B3, on account of

15 Kt—Q4 (e.g. 15 .... B×P ch; 16 K—R1, Q—KR3; 17 Kt×B, and wins).

15 KR—K1	KR—K1
16 Kt—K5	R—K3

Disillusionment would follow 16 .... B×Kt; 17 R×B, R×R; 18 Q×R, B×P, on account of 19 B—Kt2, and wins.

17 Kt×P	

Unexpectedly winning a pawn. Incidentally, White avoids a trap: 17 Q—B3 (attacking R and B), QR—K1; 18 Q×B, B×Kt, and the tables are turned.

17	QR—K1

Neither 17 .... K×Kt; 18 Q—B3, etc., nor 17 .... R×R ch; 18 R×R, R—K1; 19 Kt—K5 is to Black's advantage.

18 R×R	R×R
19 B—Kt2	B—B1

Not 19 .... K×Kt; 20 Q×P ch, K—K1; 21 Q—Kt8 ch, B—B1; 22 B—Kt7, and wins, and still less 19 .... R—B3, because of 20 Kt—R6 ch.

20 Kt—Kt5	R—KKt3
21 Q—B3	Q—Q2

An arduous defence. However, after 21 .... R×Kt; there follows 22 Q—Q5 ch, K—R1; 23 Q—Q8, P—KR3; 24 Q×B ch, K—R2; 25 P—KR4.

22 R—Q1	R—Q3
23 R×R	Q×R
24 P—KR4	P—KR3

Or 24 .... B×P; 25 Q—B7 ch, K—R1; 26 Kt—K6, and wins. The best defence would have been 24 .... Q—Q2, but after 25 Q—K2, P—KR3; 26 Kt—B3, etc., White has a comfortable advantage.

25 Q×B	P×Kt
26 P×P	Q—Q8 ch
27 K—R2	Q—R4 ch
28 K—Kt3	B—Q3 ch
29 B—K5	Q—K7
30 B×B	P×B
31 P—Kt6	Resigns.

44

White	Black
TARTAKOWER	ATKINS

(London, 1922)

The elemental power of Rooks commanding open lines is well illustrated in this beautiful game.

1	P—K4	P—K4
2	Kt—KB3	Kt—QB3
3	B—B4	Kt—B3
4	Kt—B3	Kt×P
5	Kt×Kt	P—Q4
6	B—Q3	P×Kt
7	B×P	B—Q3
8	P—Q4	Kt×P
9	Kt×Kt	P×Kt
10	Q×P	Castles
11	B—K3	

Not 11 Castles, on account of 11 ....
B×P ch. But now White puts his trust in
his cluster of forces in the centre.

| 11 | ...... | Q—K2 |

Preventing 12 Castles KR, as 12 ....
B—K4 would be awkward for White.

| 12 | Castles QR | R—K1 |
| 13 | B—Q5 | |

As this helps Black's counter-play (14 ....
P—B3), the best course was 13 B—B3, with
level chances. A magnificent trap would be
13 KR—K1, Q×B; 14 B—R6, B—B5 ch;
15 K—Kt1, and wins. But Black coolly
replies 13 .... B—K3, obtaining the better
game.

| 13 | ...... | B—K4 |
| 14 | Q—QR4 | P—B3 |

Gradually Black obtains the initiative.

| 15 | B—B3 | B—K3 |
| 16 | K—Kt1 | P—QR4 |

A strong move, threatening 17 ....
Q—Kt5.

17	B—Q4	B—Q3
18	B—Kt6	B—QKt5
19	P—B3	R—R3
20	B—K3	B—B4 ch
21	K—R1	P—QKt4
22	Q—Kt3	B—Q3
23	P—QR4	

Instead of further compromising his
position, he should have resorted to the
patient manœuvre 23 R—Q2.

| 23 | ...... | R—Kt1 |

Now Black definitely has the better game.

24	R—Q2	B—K3
25	Q—Q1	B—K4
26	B—Q4	B—KB5
27	B—K3	B×B
28	P×B	P—Kt5

The decisive advance, forcibly opening up
the position.

| 29 | P×P | QR—Kt3 |

Black conducts the attack with superb
élan. Both the following lines would have
been premature: 29 .... R×P or 29 Q×P
(because of 30 R—Q8 ch) and 29 .... P×P,
on account of 30 P—QKt3, again closing
up the critical R file.

| 30 | R—Q6 | |

The following variation loses beautifully:
30 P×P, R—R3; 31 P—QKt4, R×RP;
32 P×R, Q—R6 ch, followed by mate.

| 30 | ...... | R×P |

Threatening not only 31 .... R×P,
but also 31 .... B—Kt6, followed by
R×P ch.

31	B×P	R×P
32	B—Kt5	R—R7 ch
33	K—Kt1	

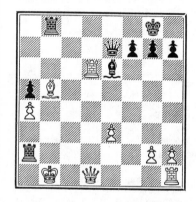

| 33 | ...... | R×RP |
| 34 | K—B2 | |

The white King attempts to escape. If
34 Q×R, Q×R, the Bishop is lost.

34	......	R—R7 ch
35	K—B3	R—B1 ch
36	B—B6	R×B ch

This curious *break-through sacrifice* is a
crowning touch to a powerfully conducted
game.

37	R×R	Q—Kt5 ch
38	K—Q3	Q—Kt4 ch
39	K—Q4	Q×R
40	K—K5	Q—B4 ch
41	K—B4	Q—B4 ch
42	K—Kt3	Q—B7 mate

45

White	Black
TAUBENHAUS	SCHALLOPP

(Manchester, 1890)

Although the force of resistance, inherent in any inert mass, may make it possible to hold a slightly weakened King's field, such is not the case when two or more weaknesses occur in the position (as, for instance, two open diagonals, or a diagonal and a file, both denuded of defenders).

1 P—K4	P—K4
2 Kt—KB3	Kt—QB3
3 B—B4	Kt—B3
4 P—Q4	

Energetic and wise.

4	P×P
5 Kt—Kt5	

But this is an escapade too restless to inspire confidence. The *coup juste* is 5 Castles.

5	Kt—K4

Another possibility, which keeps in check all White's intentions, is 5 .... P—Q4; 6 P×P, Q—K2 ch, followed by 7 .... Kt—K4.

6 B—Kt3

A variation which quickly leads into calm waters is 6 Q×P, Kt×B; 7 Q×QKt, P—Q4; 8 P×P, Q×P, offering to exchange Queens.

6	P—KR3
7 P—KB4	P×Kt
8 P×Kt	Kt×P
9 Castles	

White overestimates his threats against KB7, and does not pay sufficient attention to the dangers which beset his own King's field, now in the direct line of fire.

A curious variation, leading to a speedy draw, arises here: 9 B×P ch, K×B; 10 Q—B3 ch, K—Kt1; 11 Castles, P—Q4; 12 Q—B7 ch, K—R2; 13 Q—R5 ch, with perpetual check.

9	P—Q4
10 P×P e.p.	Q×P

Providing his own King with a good *flight* square, and threatening mate at the same time. Black has already full command of the board.

11 B×P ch	K—Q1
12 P—KKt3	

Still more damaging to his own game would be 12 P—KR3, allowing a *decoy sacrifice* by 12 .... B×P.

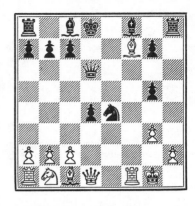

12	B—Q2

Proceeding quietly—but with set purpose —to occupy the long white diagonal. No less to the point would be 12 .... P—Q6, clearing at once the auxiliary black diagonal.

A curious game, Kan-Löwenfisch (*Leningrad*, 1933), went as follows: 12 .... P—Q6; 13 Q—K1 (or 13 Q×P, Q×Q; 14 P×Q, B—B4 ch; 15 K—Kt2, B—R6 ch, and wins); 13 .... Q—Kt3 ch; 14 B—K3, B—QB4; 15 R—B3, B—KKt5; 16 B×B, Q×B ch; 17 R—K3, B—K7, and White resigns, for if 18 Q—QB1, P—Q7. The triumph of the diagonal could find no better illustration.

13 Q—Q3	B—B3
14 Kt—Q2	

A barren hope of relieving the hostile pressure, but the position could hardly be held at this stage, e.g. 14 Kt—R3, Q—R3; 15 Q×P ch, B—Q3; and Black wins.

14	Kt×Kt
15 B×Kt	B—K2
16 QR—K1	R×P

A *sacrifice for space* (17 K×R, Q—R3 ch; and mate in two).

17 R—B5	R×B

A *deflecting sacrifice.*

18 Q×R	Q×P ch
19 K—B1	Q—R6 ch
20 K—K2	Q—Kt5 ch
21 K—B1	Q×R ch
Resigns.	

46

White	Black
HARKSEN	BOGOLJUBOW

(Played by correspondence, 1930)

In this game a counter-sacrifice, wholly unexpected and upsetting the whole outlook of the position, deserves whole-hearted admiration.

1 P—K4	P—K4
2 Kt—KB3	Kt—QB3
3 B—B4	Kt—B3
4 P—Q4	P×P
5 Castles	Kt×P

He wants to clear up the situation and to avoid the complications of the thoroughly analysed *Max Lange Attack* (5 .... B—B4).

Cautious, but cramped, are the alternative defences arising from 5 .... P—Q3 or 5 .... B—K2.

6 R—K1	P—Q4
7 B×P	

With this temporary sacrifice, White recovers his pawn and maintains his pressure on the centre.

7	Q×B
8 Kt—B3	Q—QR4

The best reply, although other Q moves, 8 .... Q—KR4; 8 .... Q—Q1; and 8 .... Q—B5, have been very closely studied. The last-named occurred in a brilliant game, Dadian of Mingrelia-Mitcham (*Zugridi*, 1892), as follows: 8 .... Q—B5; 9R×Kt ch (the strongest line here is 9 Kt×Kt, B—K3; 10 P—QKt3, Q—Q4; 11 B—Kt5, etc.); 9 .... B—K3; 10 B—Kt5 (more prudent would be 10 Kt×P, Castles QR; 11 B—K3, etc., as after the text move Black had the disagreeable reply 10 .... Q—B4); 10 .... B—B4; 11 Kt—Q2, Q—R3; 12 Kt—Kt3, B—Kt3; 13 Kt—Q5, P—R3; 14 Kt—B5, Q—Kt4; 15 R×B ch, K—B1 (or 15 .... P×R; 16 Q—R5 ch, K—B1; 17 Kt×P ch, K—Kt1; 18 Kt—B6 ch, P×Kt; 19 Q—Kt6 mate); 16 Kt—Q7 ch, K—Kt1; 17 Q—Kt4, P—KR4; White mates in three.

9 Kt×Kt

In accordance with the principle that "the threat is more powerful than its execution," this is much stronger than 9 R×Kt ch, B—K3; 10 Kt×P, Castles, and suddenly Black has the attack. Still less to be commended for White is the unstable 9 Kt×P, as is demonstrated in a game Euwe-Réti (*Match, 1920*), as follows: 9 Kt×P, Kt×Kt; 10 Q×Kt, P—KB4;

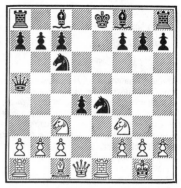

Position after 8 .... Q—QR4

11 B—Kt5, Q—B4; 12 Q—Q8 ch, K—B2; 13 Kt×Kt, P×Kt; 14 QR—Q1 (if 14 R×P, B—B4); 14 .... B—Q3 (a first sacrifice of a Rook); 15 Q×R, Q×B; 16 P—KB4 (if 16 Q×P, B—KB4); 16 .... Q—R5; 17 R×P, B—KR6 (sacrificing his other Rook); 18 Q×R, B—B4 ch; 19 K—R1, B×P ch (he has no more Rooks to give up, so it is the turn of the Bishops); 20 K×B, Q—Kt5 ch, and White resigns, as mate in at most two moves is unavoidable. A minor "Immortal."

9	B—K3
10 QKt—Kt5	

The intermediary manœuvre 10 B—Q2 is to be recommended at this point.

10	Castles
11 Kt×B	P×Kt
12 R×P	Q—KB4

By giving back the pawn, Black has evaded the attack.

An interesting idea here is 12 .... B—K2, with, if possible, ... B—B3.

13 Q—K2	P—KR3

An attempted simplification by 13 .... P—Q6; 14 P×P, Q×P is refuted by a very strong counter-stroke: 15 B—Kt5, Q×Q; 16 R×Q, and White has the upper hand.

14 B—Q2

Development under the enemy's fire. If 14 Kt—R4, then—very prettily—14 .... P—Q6 (or 14 P—QR3, P—KKt4).

14	Q×P

Accepting the challenge.

15 R—QB1	Q×P

More timorous natures would prefer 15 .... Q—R5, but as, after 16 KR×Kt,

P×R; 17 Q—K6 ch, K—Kt2; 18 Kt—K5, R—Q3; 19 Q—K8, White also has a very strong attack, Black wishes at least to increase his material gains.

16 KR×Kt
Only by this *sacrifice of the exchange* can White keep up the attack.

16 ......   P×R
17 Q—K6 ch
Against the plausible 17 Kt—K5, Black defends himself energetically by 17 .... R—K1; 18 Q—R6 ch, Q—Kt2, etc.

17 ......   K—Kt1
18 Q—K4   P—Q6
Parrying the threat 19 R—Kt1, and making the most of his passed pawns.

19 Kt—K5
Here 19 Q×P would be useless on account of 19 .... B—Q3.

19 ......   K—R1
A very subtle defence. Fatal would clearly be 19 .... Q×B; 20 R—Kt1 ch.

20 Kt×BP
Neither 20 Q×BP ch, Q—Kt2, etc., nor 20 Kt×QP, Q—Kt4, etc., is satisfactory. But against the very threatening text move, Black has a beautiful reply at his disposal.

20 ......   Q—Kt2
21 R—B3
To all appearances a terrible threat (22 R—Kt3), but here again the latent defensive power inherent, in principle, in any normal position allows Black to master the situation.
White's best continuation is 21 Q—QR4.

21 ......   B—B4
Effecting the liaison between his forces, temporarily at the cost of a piece.

22 R×B   KR—K1
23 Q—QKt4
Essential, for if 23 Q—QR4, there follows 23 .... Q—Kt8 ch; 24 R—B1, Q×R ch; 25 B×Q, R—K8 mate.

23 ......   Q×Q
And as Black soon recovers his piece, he remains the exchange ahead, and wins.
E.g.: 24 Kt×Q, R—K7; 25 R×P, R×B; 26 P—Kt3, R—Q3; 27 P—QR3, K—Kt1; 28 R×KtP, R—Q8 ch; 29 K—Kt2, P—Q7.

47

White	Black
CANAL	P. JOHNER

(Trieste, 1923)

The harrying of the black King in the following game—both before and after he has castled—is remarkable in its power and perseverance.

1 P—K4	P—K4
2 Kt—KB3	Kt—QB3
3 B—B4	Kt—B3
4 P—Q4	P×P
5 Castles	Kt×P
6 R—K1	P—Q4
7 Kt—B3	

Canal's own invention, this new move (in place of 7 B×P, Q×B; 8 Kt—B3) leads to sparkling play.

7 ......   P×B
Exhaustive analysis has shown that the acceptance of the sacrifice by 7 ....: P×Kt would cause Black many difficulties after 8 B×P, but that by playing 7 .... B—K3 Black can overcome the momentum of the attack.

8 R×Kt ch
After 8 Kt×Kt, B—K2 is a very good reply.

8 ......   B—K3
Or 8 .... B—K2; 9 Kt×P, P—B4; 10 R—B4, and the number of weak points in Black's position grows.

9 Kt×P   Kt×Kt
10 R×Kt   Q—B1
Artificial play. An easier defence could be expected from 10 .... B—Q3, even though White, by 11 B—B4, etc., recovers his pawn with the slightly superior position.

11 B—Kt5
A fine attacking move, which prevents both 11 .... P—KB3 (12 B×P, P×B; 13 Q—R5 ch, etc.) and 11 .... B—K2 (12 B×B, K×B; 13 Q—R5, etc.).

11 ......   B—Q3
12 Kt—K4   Castles
This prevents above all 13 R×B, and appears to make the black King secure. But White, scorning merely to recover his pawn after 13 Kt×B, P×Kt; 14 R×QP, starts a storming attack.

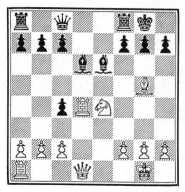

13 Kt—B6 ch
A *break-up sacrifice*.

13 ......   P×Kt
Compulsory, as otherwise: 13 .... K—R1;
14 Q—R5, B—KB4; 15 R—R4, P—KR3;
16 B×P, B—Kt3; 17 Q—Kt5, and there
is the threat of 18 B×P db ch, K×B;
19 R—R7 mate.

14 B×P   B—K4
In view of the threatened 15 Q—R5,
Black decides to return the extra piece and
to seek salvation in a simplified position
with Bishops of opposite colours. If, e.g.
14 .... P—KR3, White wins after 15 Q—R5,
K—R2; 16 R—R4, B—B5; 17 B—Kt5, etc.

15 B×B   P—KB3
16 B—Kt3   R—Q1
A more stubborn resistance would be
offered by 16 .... R—B2.

17 B—R4   P—QB4
18 R×R ch   Q×R
19 Q—B3
The attack against the many weak points
in Black's position increases in vehemence.

19 ......   K—Kt2
Or 19 .... B—Q4; 20 Q—Kt4 ch,
K—B2; 21 Q—B5, K—Kt2; 22 R—Q1,
and wins.

20 Q×KtP ch
By playing 20 B×P ch, Q×B; 21 Q×P ch,
B—B2; 22 Q×R, Q×P, White could
have secured the exchange, but not without
affording his opponent some counter-
chances.

20 ......   B—B2
21 Q—B3   R—Kt1
22 R—Q1   Q—Kt3
23 Q—Kt3 ch   B—Kt3

Or 23 .... K—R3; 24 R—Q6, Q×P;
25 Q—Kt5 mate.

24 R—Q7 ch
The entry of the Rook on the seventh
marks the beginning of the end. A mistake
would be 24 R—Q6, Q×P; 25 B×P ch, on
account of 25 .... Q×B.

24 ......   K—Kt1
25 B×P   R—Kt2
26 R—Q8 ch   K—B2
27 Q—B4
Decisive! (27 .... Q×B; 28 R—B8 ch).

27 ......   Q—K3
28 B—B3 dis ch   Q—B4
If 28 .... B—B4 instead of the text move,
then simply 29 P—KKt4.

29 Q×P ch   Q—K3
Or 29 .... K—K2; 30 R—Q5, and wins.

30 R—B8 ch   Resigns.

48

White   *Black*

TCHIGORIN   CHAROUSEK

(Budapest, 1896)

*In the following game the black King, not
having castled, is the object of many attacks.
Black's unsuccessful but varied attempts to
bring the King into safety form an interesting
feature of the play.*

1 P—K4   P—K4
2 Kt—KB3   Kt—QB3
3 B—B4   Kt—B3
4 P—Q4   P×P
5 Castles
The thrust 5 P—K5 would be premature
by reason of the counter-stroke 5 ....
P—Q4.

5 ......   B—B4
Permitting the well-known *Max Lange
Attack*. This position can also, by an inver-
sion of moves, arise from various other
openings such as the *Giuoco Piano*, the
Scotch Gambit, the *Centre Gambit*, etc.

6 P—K5   P—Q4
Against 6 .... Kt—KKt5 the best reply
is 7 P—B3.

7 P×Kt

After 7 B—QKt5, Kt—K5; 8 Kt×P, B—Q2, etc., the positions tend to equalisation. Now, however, it is war to the knife.

7	P×B
8 R—K1 ch	B—K3

After 8 .... K—B1, White obtains an overwhelming position after 9 B—KKt5, P×P; 10 B—R6 ch, K—Kt1; 11 Kt—B3, B—KKt5; 12 Kt—K4, etc.

9 Kt—Kt5   Q—Q4

Plainly neither 9 .... Q×P (10 Kt×B P×Kt; 11 Q—R5 ch, followed by Q×B) nor 9 .... Castles (10 R×B, P×R; 11 P—B7 ch, K—R1; 12 Q—R5, P—KR3; 13 Q—Kt6, and wins).

Against the peculiar defence 9 .... P—KKt3; White brings a fresh battery into the fray by 10 Q—B3.

10 Kt—QB3	Q—B4
11 QKt—K4	

Too impetuous would be 11 P—KKt4, Q—Kt3; 12 QKt—K4, B—Kt3, etc

11 ......   B—Kt3

Trying to hold on to the pawn, instead of returning it voluntarily by 11 .... Castles QR.

Against 11 .... B—KB1 White would try to disorganise the hostile defence by a temporary sacrifice 12 Kt×BP, K×Kt; 13 Kt—Kt5 ch.

12 Kt—Kt3

White's attack would have more substance after 12 P×P, R—KKt1; 13 P—KKt4, etc.

12	Q—Kt3
13 Kt×B	P×Kt
14 R×P ch	K—Q2
15 Kt—R5	

A clever defence of the Rook. If 15 Q—K2, QR—K1.

15 ......   KR—K1

Not .... QR—K1, otherwise he would lose a *tempo* after 16 Kt—B4, Q—B2; 17 P×P.

16 Kt—B4	Q—B2
17 Q—B3	

Very prettily White maintains the attack.

17 ......   QR—Q1

But, by good play, Black works for the time when his King will be able to leave the danger zone. But the time is not yet for

17 .... R×R; in view of 18 Q—Q5 ch, K—K1; 19 Kt×R, etc.

18 B—Q2   P×P

Here again 18 .... R×R would be too uncomfortable after 19 Q—Q5 ch, K—K1; 20 Q×KR ch, Q×Q; 21 Kt×Q, R—Q2; 22 P×P, K—B2; 23 R—K1, R—K2; 24 R—K4, etc.

19 QR—K1   R×R

Thinking—but erroneously—that the right moment for simplification has arrived.

By interpolating the manœuvre 19 .... Kt—K4, Black could, with advantage, have interrupted the co-ordination of the hostile forces, namely: 20 Q—Q5 ch, K—B1; 21 R×R, Q×R; 22 Q—K4, Q—Q2, etc., and he has consolidated his position.

20 Kt×R	R—K1
21 Kt—Kt5	

Instead of 21 Q—Q5 ch, K—B1, etc., White finds ways and means of reviving the attack.

21	R×R ch
22 B×R	Q—K2
23 Q—B5 ch	K—Q1
24 B—Q2	

Attacking and defending at the same time.

24	Q—K7
25 Q×P ch	Kt—K2
26 P—KR4	P—Q6
27 Kt—B7 ch	K—B1

Or 27 .... K—K1; 28 Kt—K5, B×P ch; 29 K—R2, and now the threat is 30 Q—B7 ch, K—Q1; 31 Q—B8 mate.

28 Q—R8 ch	K—Q2
29 Q—Q8 ch	K—K3

Or 29 .... K—B3; 30 Q—K8 ch, K—Q4; 31 Q—Q7 ch.

30 Kt—Kt5 ch	K—B4
31 Q—KB8 ch	Resigns

(31 .... K—Kt5; 32 Q—B4 ch, K—R4; 33 Kt—K4.)

49

White	*Black*
TCHIGORIN	TEICHMANN

(London, 1899)

In this game we see a frontal attack, carried out alternately on the K and KB files until the defender's resources are exhausted.

1 P—K4	P—K4
2 Kt—KB3	Kt—QB3
3 B—B4	Kt—B3
4 P—Q4	P×P
5 Castles	B—B4
6 P—K5	P—Q4
7 P×Kt	P×B
8 R—K1 ch	B—K3
9 Kt—Kt5	Q—Q4
10 Kt—QB3	Q—B4
11 QKt—K4	B—Kt3
12 P×P	

At the right moment.

12	KR—Kt1
13 P—KKt4	

As can easily be seen, this pawn is taboo,
e.g. 13 .... Q×KtP ch; 14 Q×Q, B×Q;
15 Kt—B6 db ch, and wins.

13	Q—Kt3

If 13 .... Q—K4, then, without misgivings, 14 P—B4, P—Q6 dis ch; 15 K—B1,
etc.

14 Kt×B	P×Kt
15 B—Kt5	

This useful sally keeps the attack going
and, in addition, prevents 15 .... Castles;
whilst threatening 16 Kt—B6 ch.

15	R×P

If 15 .... P—KR3, White still plays
16 Q—B3, on the score of the sequel:
16 .... P×B; 17 Kt—B6 ch, K—B2;
18 R×P (an orgy of sacrifices); 18 ....
K×R; 19 R—K1 ch, Kt—K4; 20 Q—Q5 ch,
K×Kt; 21 Q×Kt ch, K—B2; 22 Q—K7
mate.
Nor is 15 .... P—Q6 a valid reply:
16 P×P, P×P; 17 Q×P, R×P; 18 QR—Q1,
etc.

16 Q—B3	P—K4

The King's flight would be no remedy,
e.g.: 16 .... K—Q2; 17 Kt—B6 ch, K—B1;
18 R×P (in order to succeed, White must
treat the position in the grand manner);
18 .... Q×B; 19 R×Kt, P×R; 20 Q×P,
R—QKt1; 21 R—K1, and wins.

17 Kt—B6 ch	K—B2
18 P—KR4	P—KR3
19 Kt—K4 dis ch	K—K3

Nolens volens, the black King remains
confined to the centre, for after 19 ....
K—Kt1; 20 P—R5, White would secure
the win more easily than in the line of play
actually adopted.

20 P—R5	Q—B2

Hoping, in vain, to exchange Queens.

But after 20 .... Q—R2; 21 Kt—B6,
matters would be even worse for Black.

21 B—B6	KR—Kt1
22 Q—B5 ch	K—Q4
23 P—Kt3	

White revives the attack with the utmost
skill.

23	R×P ch
24 Q×R	R—KKt1
25 P×P ch	K×P
26 B—Kt5	

At the cost of a piece, he closes down the
hostile base of operations, in order to obtain
full control of the rest of the field.

26	P×B
27 Q—Kt3	Kt—R4

If, in order to avoid the threatened mate
(28 Q—Kt3 mate), the King continues his
travels, there follows 27 .... K—Kt5;
28 KR—Kt1 ch, K—R5; 29 Q—Q3, etc.

28 Q×KP	Resigns.

50

White	Black
MIESES	TEICHMANN

(St. Petersburg, 1909)

*Few attacks are found to run smoothly
from beginning to end; they often need
reviving at the right moment. But if the
main action slows down instead, the consequences may easily be very disagreeable.*

1 P—K4	P—K4
2 Kt—KB3	Kt—QB3
3 B—B4	Kt—B3
4 P—Q4	P×P
5 Castles	B—B4
6 P—K5	P—Q4
7 P×Kt	P×B
8 R—K1 ch	

Initiating the pressure on the open K file.
8 P×P would be premature (8 ....
R—KKt1; 9 B—Kt5, P—B3, etc.).

8	B—K3
9 P×P	

This leads to a different development of
the contest than 9 Kt—Kt5, but Black is
faced with difficult problems in either case.

9 ......   R—KKt1
10 B—Kt5   B—K2

The only sound defence. After 10 ....
Q—Q4; 11 Kt—B3, Q—B4; 12 Kt—K4,
B—K2; 13 B × B, K × B; 14 Kt × P, Kt × Kt;
15 Q × Kt, White has by far the best of it.

11 B × B   K × B

Trying to maintain his QP. But 11 ....
Q × B is certainly more natural.

12 QKt—Q2

This routine move develops a piece, but
allows Black to consolidate his position.
It therefore slows down the attack, which,
on the contrary, could have been intensified
by 12 R—K4, with the clear intention of
capturing the troublesome QP.

12 ......   Q—Q4

Henceforth Black steadily gains more and
more territory.

13 P—QKt3   P × P
14 Kt × KtP   QR—Q1
15 Q—K2   P—Q6

By this temporary counter-sacrifice of a
pawn, Black prevents his opponent from
making use, after 16 QR—Q1, of the Q file
as an auxiliary base of operations.

16 P × P   R × P
17 P—Q4   K—B1

It would be futile to mass the artillery on
the KKt file by 17 .... R—KKt1, as
18 P—Kt3 would easily refute this manœuvre.

18 QR—B1   R—Kt3

"Over-protecting" the Bishop and allowing the King increased freedom.

19 R—B3   P—QR4

By this turning movement on the extreme
flank, Black forces matters.

20 Q—Q2   P—R5
21 Kt—B5   Kt × P

In a most consistent manner, Black has
succeeded in concentrating the full weight
of the battle on this point, which he has at
last conquered.
The end is ruthless.

22 Kt × B ch   R × Kt
23 Kt × Kt   Q × Kt
24 Q—B1   R × R ch
25 Q × R   Q × R
          Resigns

51

White   Black
MARSHALL   TARRASCH

(Hamburg, 1910)

*The most admirable feature in this im-
portant game is the manner in which White
keeps the whole board under control: consolidation on the right wing (15 B—R6),
break through on the left (23 P—QR4), and
decisive sacrifice in the centre (28 R × Kt ch).*

1 P—K4   P—K4
2 P—Q4

The *Centre Gambit*, which can lead into
a good many closely related openings.

2 ......   P × P
3 Kt—KB3   Kt—QB3
4 B—QB4   B—B4
5 Castles   Kt—B3
6 P—K5   P—Q4
7 P × Kt   P × B
8 R—K1 ch   B—K3
9 Kt—Kt5   Q—Q4
10 Kt—QB3   Q—B4
11 QKt—K4   Castles QR

Looked upon, until the present game was
played, as the best defence, this continuation
is refuted here in a most ingenious manner.

12 KKt × B

If 12 P—KKt4, the continuation is 12 ....
Q—K4; 13 P—B4, P—Q6 dis ch, in favour
of Black.

12 ......   P × Kt
13 P—KKt4   Q—K4
14 P × P   KR—Kt1
15 B—R6

A move of paramount importance. White
will now maintain this advanced post with
the utmost tenacity, thus preventing the
danger of a counter-attack on the KKt file
from becoming an actuality.
Clumsy would be 15 Kt—Kt5 (15 ....
Q × P; 16 Kt × KP, Q × P ch; 17 Q × Q,
R × Q ch; 18 K—B1, R—Q4, etc.) or
15 Kt × B, Q × Kt; 16 R × P, R × P; and the
attack passes altogether to Black.

15 ......   P—Q6

After 15 .... B—K2, the energetic sally
16 Q—B3 reinforces the attack.

16 P—B3   B—Q3

Instead of voluntarily giving up territory,
he could try to win some himself by 16 ....
P—Q7; 17 R—K2, B—Kt3, etc. But by
playing the simple 18 K—Kt2, White retains
the upper hand.

17 P—B4	Q—Q4
18 Q—B3	B—K2
19 P—Kt5	Q—KB4

A sharper counter-plan would be 19 ....
R—Q2, making room for the Knight. But
still White has the best of it.

20 Kt—Kt3	Q—B2

Black should try to obtain some control
by 20 .... Q—R6, in preference to the
passive defence in the text.

21 Q—Kt4

Without delay White's crack battalions
occupy the most prominent positions.

21	QR—K1

Indirect protection for the threatened KP
(22 Q × P ch, Q × Q; 23 R × Q, B—B4 ch).

22 R—K4

Aiming in two directions, horizontally
(QBP) and vertically (doubling Rooks), this
decisive reinforcement gives a fresh impetus
to White's action.

22	P—Kt4

If 22 .... Kt—R4; 23 QR—K1.

23 P—QR4

Renewed energy.

23 ...:....	P—R3
24 P × P	P × P
25 K—Kt2	Kt—Q1
26 Q—B3	Q—Kt3

Or 26 .... B—B4; 27 R—K5.

27 R—Q4	P—B3

Black's last hope is the defensive power
of his Knight, but the *elimination sacrifice*
which now follows upsets all his plans.

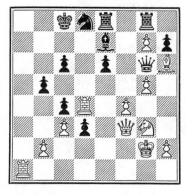

28 R × Kt ch   Resigns.
(28 .... K × R; 29 Q × BP.)

4. HUNGARIAN DEFENCE

52

White	Black
LEONHARDT	HROMADKA

(Pistyan, 1912)

The amusing tactical turn, which results in the capture of the venturesome black Queen, overshadows the more important strategic idea (the fight for the open Q file) which this game illustrates.

1 P—K4	P—K4
2 Kt—KB3	Kt—QB3
3 B—B4	B—K2

The *Hungarian Defence*, which gives Black a cramped but playable game.

4 P—Q4	P—Q3

The whole future course of the game depends on this move. By playing freely 4 .... P×P; 5 Kt×P (if 5 P—B3, Kt—R4); 5 .... P—Q3, Black can avoid the blockade of the centre.

5 P—Q5

Accepting the invitation to give the game a close character. Waiting moves, such as 5 P—B3 or 5 P—KR3, are also playable.

If 5 P×P, then the quiet 5 .... P×P, but not 5 .... Kt×P, because of 6 Kt×Kt, P×Kt; 7 Q—R5, and wins, as was shown, in a telling manner, in a game Eisinger-Naegeli, *Willingen*, 1936: 7 .... P—KKt3; 8 Q×KP, Kt—B3; 9 B—KR6, R—KKt1; 10 Q—Kt5 ch, Q—Q2 (otherwise 11 Q—Kt3); 11 Kt—B3, P—B3; 12 Q—Kt3, B—B4; 13 R—Q1, Q—B2; 14 B—KKt5, Q—K2; 15 B×P ch (a brilliant conception), 15 .... Q×B; 16 R—Q8 ch (the point), 16 .... K—K2; 17 R×R, Q×Q; 18 RP×Q, K—B2; 19 R—R8, and Black resigns, being the exchange and two pawns to the bad.

5	Kt—Kt1
6 B—Q3	

A necessary retreat, not only to make way for the QBP, but also to prevent a lateral offensive by 6 .... P—KB4.

6	Kt—KB3

He could still have tried the energetic counter-thrust 6 .... P—KB4; 7 P×P,

Kt—KB3; 8 Kt—B3, P—B3; 9 P×P, Kt×P, with complications.

Quite useless, however, would be 6 .... P—QB3; 7 P—B4, etc.

7 P—B4	QKt—Q2
8 Kt—B3	

If first 8 P—KR3, Black eliminates the hostile KB by 8 .... Kt—B4.

8	Castles

Or 8 .... Kt—B1; 9 P—KR3, P—KR3; 10 Kt—R2, P—KKt4 (preventing 11 P—B4); 11 Kt—Kt4, and White has the initiative.

9 P—KR3

Not yet 9 B—K3, on account of 9 .... Kt—Kt5; 10 B—Q2, Kt—B4; 11 B—B2, P—B4, and Black has freed his game.

9	Kt—B4
10 B—B2	P—QR4

Trying (by preventing 11 P—QKt4) to establish on the Q side some sort of observation post at QB4.

11 B—K3	P—QKt3
12 P—KKt4	

Before attempting to operate on the Q side, White wishes to restrict his opponent's mobility on the K side.

12	K—R1
13 P—R3	B—Q2

With the object of continuing with 14 .... P—R5 (which would blockade two pawns on White's extreme left), but White does not remain idle.

14 P—Kt4	P×P
15 P×P	Kt—R3
16 R—QKt1	

By the interlude of his last four moves, White has succeeded in dislodging Black's outpost Knight, and has rendered his own pawn phalanx more compact.

16	Kt—KKt1

In order to follow this up with P—Kt3 and P—KB4, starting an engagement on the K side, which incites White to get busy on the opposite wing.

17 B—R4   B × B
18 Q × B   Kt—B4
Foreseen by White when he played his
17th move, this manœuvre leads to nothing.

19 Q—B2   Kt—Q2
20 Kt—K2   R—R6
If 20 .... P—Kt3; 21 Kt—Kt3, and the
advance, eventually, of .... P—KB4 is
permanently out of the question. That is
why Black abandons his ambitions on the
K side and turns his attention to the Q side,
where, for the time being, he feels himself
strong.

21 Castles   Q—R1
22 K—Kt2
In order to mobilise the Bishop and, after
23 B—Q2, followed by B—B3 and R—QR1,
to "have it out" on the critical Q file.

22 ......   R—R7
23 R—Kt2   R × R
24 Q × R   Q—R3
Hoping, by attacking the adverse QBP, to
obtain the necessary time for bringing up
reserves by 25 .... R—R1, which would
ensure the domination of the important open
QR file. But White, very astutely, finds a
way to frustrate his opponent's intentions.

25 P—Kt5   Q—R5
The Queen wanders too far into the
enemy lines. Had Black suspected the deep
and astute trap which is coming, he would
have played 25 .... Q—Kt2, but even then
White, after 26 R—QR1, R—R1; 27 R—R4
would conquer the disputed QR file, thus
securing an important positional advantage.

26 R—QR1   Q × BP
27 Kt—Kt3   Q—Q6
Or, for example, 27 .... Kt—B4;
28 Kt—Q2, Q—Q6 (or else 28 .... Kt—Q6;
29 Kt × Q, Kt × Q; 30 Kt × Kt, with an
extra piece); 29 R—R3, winning the Queen
on a practically full board.

28 R—R3
Or 28 Kt—Q2, followed by 29 R—R3,
but White gives the black Queen another
respite.

28 ......   Q—Q8
29 Kt—Q2
Closing the trap!

29 ......   Kt—B4
30 B × Kt   KtP × B
31 R—R1   Resigns

53

White	Black
TARRASCH	TAUBENHAUS

(Ostend, 1905)

*Here is a game which well illustrates the
means by which the "scientific school" has
secured its successes. In spite of simplification, a small positional advantage is gained
and maintained. Only on the 28th move is
this advantage translated into a gain in
material, small but sufficient to win.*

1 P—K4   P—K4
2 Kt—KB3   Kt—QB3
3 B—B4   Kt—B3
4 P—Q4   P × P
5 Castles   P—Q3
6 Kt × P   B—K2
7 Kt—QB3   Castles
8 P—KR3
A sound waiting move.

8 ......   Kt × Kt
He loses patience. The temporary sacri-
fice 8 .... Kt × P would be disadvantageous
because of 9 QKt × Kt, P—Q4; 10 Kt × Kt,
P × Kt; 11 B—Q3, P × Kt; 12 B × P, etc.
Steadiest is the preparatory move 8 ....
R—K1, e.g. 9 B—B4, Kt × Kt (not 9 ....
Kt—Q2; 10 B × P ch, K × B; 11 Kt—K6,
K × Kt; 12 Q—Q5 ch, K—B3; 13 Q—B5
mate); 10 Q × Kt, B—K3, seeking far-
reaching simplification.

9 Q × Kt   B—K3
10 B × B
White does not fear exchanges, but
10 B—Q3 is also good.

10 ......   P × B
11 P—K5
Or else Black plays 11 .... P—Q4.

11 ......   Kt—Q2
12 P × P   P × P
Now Black's two centre pawns are rather
exposed, and the course of White's future
play is based on this small advantage.

13 B—K3
Strengthening first of all his own KBP.

13 ......   P—Q4
14 KR—K1   R—B4
15 Kt—K2   B—Q3
If 15 .... B—B3; 16 Q—QKt4.

16 Q—Q2	Kt—K4
17 Kt—Q4	Kt—B5
18 Q—Q3	R—K4
19 Kt—B3	R—R4
20 P—QKt3	Kt—K4
21 Kt × Kt	B × Kt
22 B—Q4	

Both opponents seek simplification.

22	B × B
23 Q × B	R—R3

But Black has not succeeded in eliminating his own weakness at K3.

24 P—QB4

A clever *undermining* operation.

24	P × P
25 Q × BP	Q—Q4

Continued liquidation. If 25 .... Q—B3; 26 QR—Q1, R—K1; 27 R—Q7, with telling effect.

26 Q × Q	P × Q
27 R—K7	

The *seventh rank*!

27 ......   R—KB1

He gives up the pawn which cannot be held (for if 27 .... R—Kt1; 28 R—Q7, R—R4; 29 R—Q1, etc.), but hopes for a Rook ending, in which the advantage of one pawn is often insufficient.

28 R × P	R—B2
29 R—Kt8 ch	R—B1
30 R × R ch	K × R

And here is the Rook ending for which both sides were striving. Black's misfortune is that White has an extra pawn on either wing, whereas his own isolated pawn is easily controlled.

31 R—Q1	R—R3
32 P—QR4	R—Q3
33 R—QB1	R—Q2

The attempt to assume the offensive by 33 .... P—Q5 leads to nothing after 34 K—B1, P—Q6; 35 R—B8 ch, K—K2; 36 K—K1, and Black's position is still weaker.

34 K—B1	R—Kt2
35 R—B3	K—K2
36 K—K2	K—Q3
37 K—Q3	R—KB2
38 P—B3	R—Kt2
39 K—B2	R—K2
40 K—Q2	R—Kt2
41 K—Q3	R—K2

The white King's triangular manœuvre should be noticed. It has resulted in a displacement of the black Rook. Better, however, would have been 41 .... R—Kt1.

42 P—QKt4   R—K8

This attempt to turn the enemy position comes one move too late, but Black can no longer rely on passive strategy. The rest is most instructive.

43 P—Kt5	R—KKt8
44 R—B6 ch	K—K4
45 R—QR6	R × P

The balance in material is momentarily re-established, and if now 46 R × P, Black could still hold out with 46 .... R—Kt6.

46 P—B4 ch

This timely *finesse* reduces Black's counterchances.

46	K × P
47 R × P	K—K4
48 P—Kt6	K—Q3
49 P—R5	R—Kt6 ch
50 K—B2	R—Kt7 ch
51 K—Kt3	R—Kt8
52 P—Kt7	Resigns.

5. RUY LOPEZ

54

White	Black
LASKER	BLACKBURNE

(London, 1899)

In the following game the preliminary sparring (moves 8–21) is characterised by desperate pawn skirmishes.

The real battle begins with a double pawn sacrifice (22 .... P—Kt4), which gives Black the mastery over the KKt and KR files, on which he stages an impressive regrouping of forces (28 .... R—KR1). His powerful strategy culminates in the sacrifice of a Rook (31 .... R—R8 ch), the sequel to which is the loss by White of his Queen.

1 P—K4	P—K4
2 Kt—KB3	Kt—QB3
3 B—Kt5	P—Q3

The *Steinitz Defence*, which gives Black a cramped but playable game.

4 P—Q4

Creating tension in the centre. The play would be simplified by 4 B×Kt ch, P×B; 5 P—Q4, P×P; 6 Kt×P, B—Q2; 7 Castles, Kt—B3; 8 Kt—QB3, B—K2, etc., but then neither 9 P—B4, Castles nor 9 B—Kt5, Castles nor 9 Q—B3, P—B4, etc., hold any terrors for Black.

4 ...... B—Q2

If, impulsively, 4 .... P×P, then 5 Q×P, B—Q2; 6 B×Kt, B×B; 7 B—Kt5, P—B3; 8 B—R4, etc., would give White a lasting positional advantage, chiefly owing to his Queen's centralised position.

5 P—Q5

Blocking the centre is not to be recommended. He should continue his development with 5 Kt—B3, reserving the option of castling on either side.

5	Kt—Kt1
6 B—Q3	B—K2
7 Kt—B3	

As the advanced infantryman will soon need strong support, the continuation 7 P—B4 followed by Kt—B3 would be more logical.

7	Kt—KB3
8 Kt—K2	P—B3

A routine player would have castled here and submitted to White's positional superiority. Being an imaginative player, Black prefers to put the whole battlefield on fire.

9 P—B4	Kt—R3
10 Kt—Kt3	

Here again 10 Kt—B3 would be better adapted to keep watch on the important points K4, Q5 and QKt5.

10	Kt—B4
11 B—B2	P—QKt4
12 P—Kt4	

White is not satisfied with the defensive 12 P—Kt3, but himself "starts something" on the Q side.

12	Kt—Kt2
13 QP×P	B×P
14 P×P	B×KtP
15 P—QR4	B—Q2
16 Castles	P—Kt3
17 P—R3	

If 17 B—R6, Kt—Kt5, but now Black resolutely prevents any inroad into his own territory.

As, however, the text move weakens the King's field, it would have been better, for instance, to continue with 17 P—R5 (threatening 18 P—R6); 17 .... P—QR3; 18 B—Kt3, with various threats.

17 ...... P—KR4

The beginning of an attack, conducted by Black with extraordinary virtuosity.

18 B—K3 P—R4

Keeping both wings in mind. By the text move he contests the square QB4.

19 P—Kt5	R—QB1
20 R—B1	Kt—B4

With renewed pressure against the adverse KP.

21 Kt—Q2	P—R5
22 Kt—K2	(*Diagram. See p. 67.*)

22 ...... P—Kt4

A *line clearance* sacrifice.

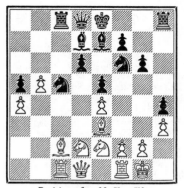

Position after 22 Kt—K2

23 B×P
Accepting the sacrifice in preference to the timorous continuations 23 K—R1, P—Kt5, etc., or 23 P—B3, Kt—R4, followed by .... Kt—B5, and Black still succeeds in opening the KKt file.

23	R—KKt1
24 B×P	B×RP
25 B—KKt3	

Closing up one of the open files (KKt), and not suspecting the possibility of danger on the other.

| 25 ...... | B—K3 |
| 26 R—K1 | |

If 16 P—B3, Kt—R4.

26	Kt—Kt5
27 Kt—B1	B—Kt4
28 R—Kt1	R—KR1

Black's intentions are taking shape.

| 29 Kt—B3 | B—KB5 |
| 30 Kt—Q5 | Q—Kt4 |

Threatening 31 .... Q—R3.

31 P—B3

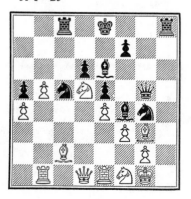

Too late, for now Black is in a position to win the adverse Queen by a brilliant sacrifice.

31	R—R8 ch
32 K×R	B×B
33 Kt×B	

If 33 P×Kt, Q—R5 ch; 34 K—Kt1, B—B7 mate.

33	Kt—B7 ch
34 K—Kt1	Kt×Q
35 Kt—B5	B×Kt (B4)
36 P×B	Q—Q7

The final link in Black's combination, without which White might have obtained almost an equivalent (Rook, Bishop, pawn) for his Queen.

37 KR×Kt	Q×B
38 QR—B1	Q×BP
39 Kt—Kt6	R—Q1
40 Kt—B4	Kt—Kt2
41 Kt—K3	Q—B5
42 K—B2	Q×RP
43 R—B7	Kt—B4
44 R—KR1	R—Q2
45 R—B8 ch	K—K2
46 R (R1)—R8	Q—Q5
Resigns.	

55

| *White* | *Black* |
| TARRASCH | MARCO |

(Dresden, 1892)

This game created enormous interest for the Ruy Lopez Opening showing as it does how much latent dynamic power is inherent in the White formation.

It illustrates one of the deepest traps to be found in the theory of the openings.

1 P—K4	P—K4
2 Kt—KB3	Kt—QB3
3 B—Kt5	P—Q3
4 P—Q4	B—Q2
5 Castles	

It is clear that White cannot win a pawn by 5 B×Kt, B×B; 6 P×P, P×P; 7 Q×Q ch, R×Q; 8 Kt×P, because Black recovers it by 8 .... B×P.

A good modern continuation is 5 Kt—B3, Kt—B3; 6 B×Kt, B×B; 7 Q—Q3, the *Showalter Attack*, which defends the KP and prepares for castling, eventually, on the Q side.

5 ......   Kt—B3
6 Kt—B3   B—K2

There is, as yet, no need for Black to eliminate the tension of the centre pawns by 6 .... P×P; 7 Kt×P, etc., for if White here again pursues the will o' the wisp of winning a pawn by 7 B×Kt, B×B; 8 P×P, P×P; 9 Kt×P, Black recovers his pawn by 9 .... B×P, without any disadvantage.

7 R—K1
After this *over-protection* of the KP, Black should have resigned himself to a clearance in the centre.

7 ......   Castles
After this plausible but *heedless* move, matters rapidly come to a head. He should have played 7 .... P×P; 8 Kt×P, Castles, the *normal position of the Steinitz Defence*, in which Black's game, though cramped, is tenable.

8 B×Kt   B×B
After 8 .... P×B; 9 P×P, Black has lost an important pawn without any compensation.

9 P×P   P×P
10 Q×Q
Not yet 10 Kt×P, because 10 .... Q×Q; 11 Kt×Q, B×P, etc., would actually be in Black's favour.

10 ......   QR×Q
An insoluble problem for Black. If 10 .... B×Q; 11 Kt×P, Black, deprived of a valuable pawn, would be at a manifest disadvantage.
If 10 .... KR×Q, there follows 11 Kt×P, B×P; 12 Kt×B, Kt×Kt; 13 Kt—Q3 (a terrible blunder would be 13 R×Kt, on the score of 13 .... R—Q8 ch, with mate to follow); 13 .... P—KB4; 14 P—KB3, B—B4 ch; 15 K—B1, R×Kt (compulsory, as otherwise a piece is lost); 16 P×R, and White has won the exchange.

11 Kt×P   B×P
After 11 .... Kt×P; 12 Kt×B, White wins, not a pawn, but a clear piece.

12 Kt×B   Kt×Kt
13 Kt—Q3
Again not, precipitately, 13 R×Kt, because of 13 .... R—Q8 ch, and mate follows.
It can be seen that Black, with his eighth move, had foreseen many things, but the astute manœuvre in the text upsets all his calculations.

13 ......   P—KB4
Black defends his assets as long as he can.

14 P—KB3   B—B4 ch
15 Kt×B
If 15 K—B1, B—Kt3; 16 P×Kt, P×P, with check! (here we see that it was not indifferent which black Rook recaptures the Queen on the tenth move); 17 Kt—B4, P—K6; 18 P—KKt3, P—Kt4, and—without particular damage—Black regains his piece.

15 ......   Kt×Kt
16 B—Kt5
This final assault, which wins a piece or the exchange, is full of *finesse*.

16 ......   R—Q4
Still trying to save his minor piece; after any other move, White's reply 17 B—K7 is still more convincing.

17 B—K7   R—K1
18 P—QB4
The final point: White wins the exchange and the game.

56

White   Black
TARRASCH   **LASKER**
(Match, 1908)

This game illustrates in a superb manner the dire consequences of allowing an important piece to stray from the main battlefiedl (19 Q×RP). Black's subsequent action is powerful and ruthless.

1 P—K4   P—K4
2 Kt—KB3   Kt—QB3
3 B—Kt5   Kt—B3
4 Castles
After 4 Kt—B3, B—Kt5, we have the *Spanish Four Knights' Game*.

4 ......   P—Q3
Black leads back into the *Steinitz Defence*. The order of the moves is an improvement, as it avoids the dangerous *Showalter Attack* which occurs after 3 .... P—Q3.

5 P—Q4   B—Q2
The maintenance of the centre by 5 .... Kt—Q2 is also possible.

6 Kt—B3	B—K2
7 R—K1	P×P

At this stage, as demonstrated in the preceding game, it is essential to give up the centre.

8 Kt×P	Castles

In this, the *normal position of the Steinitz Defence*, Black occupies a "hedgehog" formation. All his minor pieces are in a state of expectant defence. White has now a large choice of good continuations, but none likely to upset Black's defensive formation.

9 Kt×Kt
Simplification.

9	B×Kt

A good reply is 9 .... P×Kt; 10 B—Q3, R—Kt1; 11 P—QKt3, Kt—Kt5; and Black fights for the initiative.

10 B×B	P×B
11 Kt—K2	

White, by this adroit manœuvre, strengthens his K side. Incidentally, he tempts his adversary to make the mistake of playing 11 .... Kt×P, after which White gains a decisive advantage by 12 Kt—Q4.

11	Q—Q2
12 Kt—Kt3	KR—K1
13 P—Kt3	QR—Q1

If at once 13 .... Kt—Kt5; 14 Kt—B5, B—B3; 15 Q×Kt, B×R; 16 Kt—R6 ch wins the Queen.

14 B—Kt2	Kt—Kt5

An active defence which needed careful examination. For instance, if now 15 P—KR3, the pretty rejoinder 15 .... B—B3 tries to gain territory; and again, if 15 Kt—B5, Black can play 15 .... B—B3; 16 Q×Kt, B×B, as his Queen is now guarded.

15 B×P
Hoping to crush the hostile formation, while winning a pawn somewhere.

15	Kt×BP

Instead of 15 .... K×B; 16 Kt—B5 ch, K—R1; 17 Q×Kt, etc., the black Knight sells its life dearly.

The aspect and venue of the contest change with kaleidoscopic rapidity.

16 K×Kt	K×B
17 Kt—B5 ch	K—R1
18 Q—Q4 ch	P—B3
19 Q×RP	

In the end White has won a pawn, but there are several "buts": (i) the pawn so won takes as yet no part in the *mêlée*; (ii) in order to win it, the white Queen has had to stray far from home; and (iii) her own King is in a parlous state.

19	B—B1

With the menace, 20 .... R×P; 21 R×R, Q×Kt ch; 22 K—K3, B—R3 ch; 23 K—Q3, P—Q4, and wins. As can be seen, Black has in one fell swoop taken command of the game.

20 Q—Q4	R—K4

Defends his KBP and, at the same time, threatens 21 .... P—Q4.

21 QR—Q1	QR—K1
22 Q—B3	Q—B2
23 Kt—Kt3	

Not only to defend the KP, but also in order to prevent 23 .... Q—R4.

23	B—R3
24 Q—B3	P—Q4

Conquest of the K file. The milestones in this enterprise will be: a very important intermediary check (25 .... B—K6 ch), the trebling of the major pieces (27 .... Q—K3), securing the outpost (by 29 .... P—B5 and 30 .... P—Q5), and, as a climax, the manœuvre (41 .... B—Kt4).

25 P×P	B—K6 ch
26 K—B1	P×P
27 R—Q3	Q—K3

An imposing array of forces on the open K file.

28 R—K2
Useless would be 28 QR×B, R×R; 29 R×R, Q×R; 30 Q×BP ch, K—Kt1, and White has to capitulate.

28	P—KB4
29 R—Q1	P—B5
30 Kt—R1	P—Q5
31 Kt—B2	Q—QR3
32 Kt—Q3	R—KKt4

As Black's heavy artillery has several files at its disposal, his pressure soon proves irresistible.

33 R—R1	Q—R3
34 K—K1	

Flight of the King! If 34 P—KR3, R—Kt6; 35 Q—Q5, P—B6 (a false hope would be 35 .... Q×P, Black's reply being 36 Q×P ch, etc., and not 36 P×Q, R—Kt8 mate).

If 34 Q—R3, Q×Q; 35 P×Q, R—Kt8 mate.

34	Q×P
35 K—Q1	Q—Kt8 ch
36 Kt—K1	R (Kt4)—K4

By this fresh regrouping Black threatens, if nothing else, 37 .... P—Q6; 38 P×P, B—Q5. The remainder of the play is stirring.

37 Q—B6	R (K4)—K3
38 Q×P	R (K1)—K2
39 Q—Q8 ch	K—Kt2
40 P—R4	P—B6

A *vacating sacrifice*, followed by a most telling *unmasking manœuvre*.

41 P×P	B—Kt4
Resigns.	

57

White	Black
SCHLECHTER	LASKER

(Match, 1910)

Two features are worthy of special admiration in the following fine game: White's skill in exploiting the weak points in the adverse position, finally turning positional into material advantage; and Black's desperate ingenuity in discovering a drawing chance in, to all appearances, a hopelessly lost position.

1 P—K4	P—K4
2 Kt—KB3	Kt—QB3
3 B—Kt5	Kt—B3
4 Castles	P—Q3
5 P—Q4	B—Q2
6 R—K1	P×P
7 Kt×P	B—K2
8 Kt—QB3	Castles
9 B×Kt	

This simplification is far from pointless: the black pawn formation is slightly damaged and the white KKt remains in a fine central position.

9	P×B

As a compensation, Black wishes to render his pawn centre more compact, whilst preserving the "two Bishops."

10 B—Kt5	

A sensible pin! However, this Bishop could also be developed to advantage by 10 B—B4 or 10 P—QKt3, R—K1; 11 B—Kt2.

10	R—K1

The interpolation 10 .... R—Kt1; 11 P—QKt3, and then only 11 .... R—K1, has its points. One way or another Black has now in view 11 .... Kt×P; 12 B×B, Kt×Kt, etc.

11 Q—B3	

Another good way of bringing the Queen into play is 11 Q—Q3.

11	P—KR3

In connection with the next move, this is a commendable means of relieving the pressure. A mistake would be 11 .... Kt—Kt5; 12 B×B, Q×B; 13 Kt×P, etc., by which White would win a pawn.

12 B—R4	Kt—R2
13 B×B	Q×B
14 QR—Q1	Kt—B1
15 P—KR3	Kt—Kt3
16 Q—Kt3	Q—Kt4

Playing for an end-game without Queens, in which White's advantage would only be minute.

17 Q×Q	P×Q
18 P—B3	P—B3
19 K—B2	K—B2
20 KKt—K2	P—R4
21 P—QKt3	KR—QKt1
22 Kt—B1	B—K3
23 Kt—Q3	P—QB4
24 Kt—Kt2	

Cleverly preventing the undoubling of the hostile QBP by 24 .... P—B5.

24	Kt—K4
25 Kt—Q5	R—Kt2
26 R—K3	Kt—B3
27 R—B3	

An enterprising Rook!

27	P—Kt3
28 P—QR4	P—B4
29 Kt—K3	R—K1
30 Kt (K3)—B4	

With the threat 31 R×P.

30	R—R2
31 R—K1	B×Kt
32 Kt×B	K—B3
33 Kt—K3	Kt—K4
34 P×P	P×P
35 P—Kt3	R—KR1
36 P—B4	

Very prettily, White obtains a valuable

asset (a passed pawn) on the extreme K wing, and has now a concrete advantage.

36	P×P
37 Kt—Q5 ch	K—B2
38 Kt×KBP	R—Kt2
39 K—Kt2	P—B5

White's 41st move will refute this attempt to obtain counter-chances, and incidentally show up the weaknesses in Black's position.

40 P×P	R—Kt5
41 P—B5	R×QRP
42 P×P	P×P
43 R—B7 ch	K—B3
44 Kt—Q5 ch	K—Kt4
45 P—R4 ch	K—R3
46 Kt—K7	

Every one of White's moves reaches the mark.

46	R—KB1
47 R—Q1	R—B2

Giving up a pawn of his own free will, because 47 .... Kt—B5 is useless against 48 K—B2, to be followed by R—Q4.

48 R×P ch	K—R2
49 R—K6	Kt—Kt3
50 R×Kt	R×Kt
51 R (Kt6)—QB6	R×R
52 R×R ch	K—Kt3
53 R—B6 ch	K—B2
54 K—B3	

After ingenious liquidations, a difficult Rook ending is now reached.

White's intention is to play the King to B4 after 55 P—B4. More incisive, however, would be at once 54 P—B4, as this passed pawn could become a dangerous weapon.

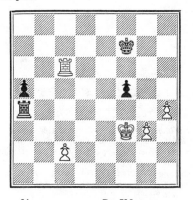

54	R—K5

By this admirable manœuvre Black gives up a second pawn, in order to occupy more effective posts. The following plausible continuation would not be sufficient: 54 .... R—R8; 55 R—QR6, P—R5; 56 K—B4, R—B8 ch; 57 K—Kt5, R—B6; 58 R×P, R×P ch; 59 K×P, and wins.

55 R—B5	K—B3
56 R×P	R—B5

Black's deep conception is revealed! The position of his Rook makes up for the two missing pawns.

57 R—R6 ch	K—K4
58 R—R5 ch	K—B3
59 R—R6 ch	K—K4
60 R—R5 ch	K—B3
61 R—R2	K—K4
62 R—Kt2	R—B6 ch
63 K—Kt2	K—B3
64 K—R3	R—B3

He avoids the trap 64 .... P—B5; 65 R—Kt3, R×P; 66 R—KB3, and White would win.

65 R—Kt8

In view of 65 P—R5, K—Kt4, White gives back one pawn in order to render his Rook more active, but it is not sufficient to ensure victory.

65	R×P
66 R—Kt6 ch	K—Kt2
67 P—R5	R—B5

Cutting off the white King.

68 P—R6 ch	K—R2
69 R—KB6	R—R5
	Drawn

58

White	Black
PRZEPIORKA	RÉTI

(San Remo, 1911)

That it can have serious consequences voluntarily to cede too much territory to an aggressive adversary can be seen in the following lively game.

1 P—K4	P—K4
2 Kt—KB3	Kt—QB3
3 B—Kt5	Kt—B3
4 Castles	P—Q3
5 Kt—B3	B—K2
6 P—Q4	B—Q2
7 R—K1	P×P
8 Kt×P	Castles
9 P—QKt3	

A slow but sound continuation.

9 ......   R—K1

If Black resorts to exchanges, 9 ....
Kt×Kt; 10 Q×Kt, B×B; 11 Kt×B,
Kt—Q2 (threatening 12 .... B—B3), then
White can create some *lasting* weaknesses
in Black's position after 12 Q—B4, P—B3;
13 Kt—Q4.

10 B—Kt2   B—KB1

He continues to build up "behind the
front" a durable system of defences.

11 P—B3

Instead of this passive procedure, he could
have tried to obtain some initiative by
11 Kt×Kt, P×Kt; 12 B—Q3, P—Kt3;
13 P—B4, etc.

11 ......   P—KKt3

This *counter-fianchetto* is intended to ease
the opposing Bishop's pressure on the long
black diagonal.

12 B—KB1

Again giving up territory; he should have
resigned himself to the exchange 12 B×Kt
or 12 Kt×Kt.

12 ......   B—Kt2
13 Kt(Q4)—K2

In view of the threat 13 .... Kt×Kt;
14 Q×Kt, Kt×P, etc., White decides on
a fresh retrograde manœuvre.

13 ......   Kt—KR4

The beginning of a successful counter-
offensive.

14 Q—Q2   Q—R5
15 Kt—Q1   Kt—K4

Avoiding the exchange of Bishops and
introducing a new fighting unit into the
battle zone.

16 P—QB4

In order to be able to play 17 Kt—B2,
which, however, would now be disadvantageous after 16 Kt—B2, Kt×P ch;
17 P×Kt, B×B.
But as Black finds a brilliant refutation
of the plausible move in the text, he should
have looked for some other means of
"patching up" his position, such as, for
instance, 16 B—B3.

16 ......   Kt—Q6

Emphasising in an artistic manner the
weakness of the "ingress square" at Q6.

17 Q×Kt   Q×R
18 Kt(Q1)—B3   Q—R5

Having fairly and squarely won the

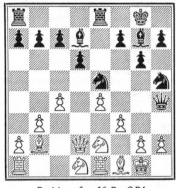

Position after 16 P—QB4

exchange, the black Queen returns to her
post of observation.   White's is a lost cause.

19 P—B5   B—QB3
20 Kt—Q4

Or 20 P×P, QR—Q1. There is no hope
of White gaining the initiative, and so
20 P—Kt3 would have been better.

20 ......   B—K4
21 P—Kt3   B×KtP

White's fortress is collapsing.

22 P×B   Q×P ch
23 B—Kt2

This gives rise to a fresh and cruel surprise.   After 23 K—R1, Kt—B5; 24 Q—Q2,
R—K4, Black also scores a point.

23 ......   Q×B ch
24 K×Q   Kt—B5 ch
25 K—Kt3   Kt×Q
Resigns.

59

	White	Black
	KOSTICH	SELESNIEFF

(Göteborg, 1920)

*Without going as far as some writers on
military matters, who claim that the ideal
manner of conducting a war is to win merely
by manœuvres without any actual fighting, it
must be admitted that the most interesting
feature of the present game is that it was
so won.*

*First we see a reconnoitring manœuvre by
the white Queen, then a turning movement*

by the QR on the K side (QR—Q1—Q3—KR3—KR6—KR8 ch), causing decisive damage to the black forces (loss of Queen and pawns).

1 P—K4	P—K4
2 Kt—KB3	Kt—QB3
3 B—Kt5	Kt—B3
4 Castles	P—Q3
5 P—Q4	B—Q2
6 Kt—B3	B—K2
7 R—K1	P×P
8 Kt×P	Castles
9 KKt—K2	

There is justification for this move, avoiding, as it does, exchanges which would alleviate the difficulties of the second player.

9	Kt—K4

Eliminating the "Spanish Bishop," but thereby Black creates weaknesses in his own camp. The most active defence is 9 .... P—QR3; 10 B—Q3, Kt—KKt5; 11 P—KR3, KKt—K4, or 11 Kt—Kt3, B—B3, etc., with equal chances.

10 Kt—Kt3	B×B
11 Kt×B	KKt—Q2

If he tries a different regrouping "behind the front" by 11 .... R—K1; 12 P—Kt3, B—B1; 13 B—Kt2, White still shows a superiority in space.

12 B—Q2	Kt—QB3

Parrying the *positional threat* of 13 B—R5, P—QKt3; 14 B—B3, with some disarrangement of Black's Q side.

13 B—B3	B—B3
14 Q—Q2	P—QR3
15 B×B	Kt×B
16 Kt—Q4	Kt×Kt
17 Q×Kt	Kt—Q2

Hoping to achieve an exchange of Queens by 18 .... Q—B3, equalising the position.
The astute manœuvre which foils this plan strikes a new note in a contest which seemed to have arrived at a standstill.

18 Q—B3	P—KKt3

If 18 .... R—B1, then 19 Kt—B5 would prevent 19 .... Q—B3, because of the loss of the exchange.

19 QR—Q1	R—K1

By this and the following moves Black tries to stop the disturbing advance by White of 20 P—K5.

20 P—B4	P—KB3
21 P—KR4	

In spite of reduced material, White initiates a lively and joyous attack.

21	Kt—B4

Preventing White's gain of a pawn by 22 Q—Kt3 ch, followed by Q×P.

22 P—R5	Q—K2
23 P×P	P×P
24 P—Kt4	Kt—K3
25 P—B5	

The break-through. The gain of a pawn is only temporary, but the gaps produced in the enemy's position are permanent.

25	Kt—Kt2

Neither 25 .... P×P; 26 P×P, nor 25 .... Kt—B1; 26 P×P, Kt×P (or 26 .... Q—K4; 27 Q—Kt3 ch); 27 Kt—R5, etc., is playable for Black.

26 P×P	Q—K4
27 Q—K3	Q—KKt4
28 Q—Kt3 ch	Kt—K3
29 Kt—B5	Q×P
30 R—Q3	

The turning movement now undertaken will prove successful.

30	K—B1
31 R—R3	P—Q4

An ingenious counter-attempt. If now 32 Q×P, QR—Q1, Black obtains fresh opportunities. White, however, without taking any notice, carries on with his strategic action.

32 R—R6	Q—Kt4
33 Q—KR3	P×P
34 R—R8 ch	

Winning by force the Queen for Rook and Knight.

34	K—B2
35 Q—R7 ch	Kt—Kt2
36 Kt—R6 ch	Q×Kt

He cannot play 36 .... K—K3, because of 37 Q×P ch, K—Q2 (or 37 .... Q—K4; 38 Q—B4 ch, etc.); 38 R—Q1 ch, with an early mate.

37 Q×Q	R×R
38 Q—B4	KR—K1
39 Q×QBP ch	R—K2
40 Q—B4 ch	K—B1
41 R×P	

Now Black's last dangerous pawn has disappeared. Nevertheless, the end-game still requires much *finesse* (on the part of White).

41	......	QR—K1
42	Q—B5	K—B2
43	Q—Q5 ch	K—B1
44	R—R4	R—QB2
45	R—R8 ch	K—K2
46	R—R7	K—B1
47	Q—Q6 ch	R (K1)—K2
48	Q × P ch	K—Kt1
49	R—R4	R—K8 ch
50	K—R2	R—KB2
51	Q—Q8 ch	R—K1
52	Q—Q5	R—K3
53	P—B4	R (K3)—K2
54	P—R4	R—Q2
55	Q—K4	R—B4
56	P—R5	K—B2
57	R—R7	K—B3
58	Q—R4 ch	K—K4

Or 58 .... K—B2; 59 Q—Kt4, K—B3;
60 R—R6 ch, K—K4 (or 60 .... K—B2;
61 Q—Kt6 ch, etc., as in the text);
61 Q—K2 ch, K—B5; 62 P—Kt3 ch,
K—Kt4; 63 Q—K3 ch, K—Kt5; 64 R—R4
mate.

59	Q—Kt3 ch	K—B3
60	R—R6 ch	K—B2
61	Q—Kt6 ch	K—Kt1
62	R—R4	R—K2
63	Q—Q6	K—B2
64	R—R7	R (B4)—K4
65	P—Kt5	P × P
66	P × P	R (K2)—K3
67	Q—B7 ch	R—K2
68	Q—B4 ch	K—Kt3
69	Q—Q3 ch	K—B2
70	Q—Kt3	K—B3
71	Q—B4 ch	Resigns

For if 71 .... K—K3; 72 Q—R6 ch, or
if 71 .... K—Kt3; 72 R—R6 mate.

60

White	Black
NEUMANN	KOLISCH

(Paris, 1867)

*Here is a game from long ago, which yet
makes a very modern impression. The
masterly way in which Black handles his two
Bishops is particularly noteworthy.*

1	P—K4	P—K4
2	Kt—KB3	Kt—QB3
3	B—Kt5	Kt—B3
4	Castles	B—K2

In avoiding the complications of the
4 .... Kt × P variation, the text move (as
does 4 .... P—Q3) leads back into the
Steinitz Defence.

5	Kt—B3	P—Q3
6	B × Kt ch	

The immediate 6 P—Q4 is more lively.
After the exchange in the text, White's
position is far less *plastic*.

6	......	P × B
7	P—Q4	P × P
8	Kt × P	B—Q2
9	P—B4	

An ambitious advance. Several continuations are playable here, e.g. 9 B—Kt5 or
9 P—QKt3, followed by B—Kt2 or 9 Q—Q3
or 9 Q—B3, which latter variation is both
sound and energetic. (Threat: 10 P—K5.)

9	......	Castles
10	Q—Q3	

Here again 10 Q—B3 has its *raison d'être*.

10	......	R—Kt1
11	P—QKt3	P—B4
12	Kt—B3	

This Knight's development at K2 would
be more flexible, as from there the Knight
could move to Kt3 (defending the KP) and
also to Q5 via KB4 (after P—B5 eventually).

12	......	B—B3

One of Black's "two Bishops" already
occupies an observation post.

13	R—K1	R—K1
14	Kt—Q5	

This is too precipitate. The accumulation of forces by 14 B—Kt2 is indicated.

14	......	Kt × Kt
15	P × Kt	B—B3

A beautiful intermediary manœuvre which,
enabling the second Bishop to get into
action, secures the initiative for Black.

16	R × R ch	

After 16 P × B, R × R ch; 17 Kt × R,
B × R; 18 P—B3 (threatening 19 Kt—B2);
18 .... Q—B3; 19 B—Q2, P—Q4; 20 Kt—B2
(or 20 Q × P, B × P, etc.); 20 .... P—B5,
White's game would collapse.

16	......	B × R
17	R—Kt1	B—Q2

To be followed by 18 .... Q—QB1 and
.... B—B4, for which reason White cannot
very well play 18 P—B4.

18 B—Q2	Q—QB1
19 R—K1	

In order to follow this up with 20 B—B3, without permitting Black's 20 .... B—K2. But it is more urgent to play 19 B—B3 at once, with the probable continuation 19 .... B—B4; 20 Q—Q2, B—K2; 21 R—K1, Q—Q2; 22 P—KR3, P—KR4, etc., when the white Queen would be more comfortably placed at Q2 than, as in the actual game, at QB4.

19	B—B4
20 Q—B4	

The only way to protect his QBP.

20	Q—Q2
21 P—B3	R—K1

Black resolutely plays for liquidation, after which the "two Bishops" will have gained in power.

22 P—KR3	R × R ch
23 Kt × R	Q—K1
24 P—KKt4	

Otherwise the counter-threats 24 .... P—KR4 and .... P—R5 would block up White's K side.

24	B—Q2
25 P—QR4	P—B3

Arguing correctly that his two Bishops will deploy their full powers on an open board.

26 K—B1

In order to give his Queen mobility without having to fear the hostile Queen's irruption at K2.

26	P—KR3
27 Q—R6	P × P
28 Q × QP	P—Q5

Black gives up a pawn in order to turn the power of his Bishops to still greater account. For if now 29 Q × BP, Q—K5; 30 P × P, KB × P, Black has full control of the highways of the chessboard.

29 P—B4	B—B3
30 Q × BP	Q—K5
31 Q—Q6	

Anticipating the threat 31 .... P—Q6.

31 ...... B—R5

Strong as this diversion appears to be, it enables the hostile Queen to occupy the important defensive square at White's K5. The waiting and preparatory move 31 .... K—R2 is logical.

32 Q—Kt8 ch	K—R2
33 Q—K5	

A life and death struggle!

33	Q—R8 ch
34 K—K2	B—K5

Finely played! It is more important to prevent perpetual check (35 Q—B5 ch, etc.) than to safeguard the QP.

35 Q × P   P—B4

Initiating a deeply conceived plan, which necessitates the prevention of any diagonal check by White.

36 P × P

If White had fully comprehended the dangers of his position, he would have played 36 Q—K3, with a much more stubborn defence.

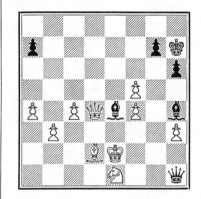

36	Q—R7 ch
37 K—Q1	B × Kt

A very beautiful turn! If 38 B × B, Q—B7 mate, and if 38 Q × B (without check! This is the hidden meaning of Black's 35th move), then 38 .... Q × B mate.

38 K × B   Q—R8 ch

In the short and sharp struggles which ensue, Black produces the maximum effect with the minimum of means.

39 K—K2	Q—B6 ch
40 K—K1	B—Q6

A waiting move, with a double threat of mate at K7 or at K8.

Resigns
(41 Q—B2, Q—R8 ch.)
A classic!

61

White	*Black*
CAPABLANCA	BERNSTEIN

(San Sebastian, 1911)

Besides its high artistic and sportive qualities, the value of the following game is enhanced by its historical interest. It is the first encounter between the new star from overseas and a leading European master.

1 P—K4	P—K4
2 Kt—KB3	Kt—QB3
3 B—Kt5	Kt—B3
4 Castles	B—K2
5 Kt—B3	P—Q3
6 B × Kt ch	P × B
7 P—Q4	P × P
8 Kt × P	B—Q2
9 B—Kt5	

He seeks, above all, rational and straight-forward development of his pieces. However, as it ultimately leads to the exchange of this Bishop, some strategists prefer a more expectative development such as 9 P—QKt3, followed by B—Kt2.

9	Castles
10 R—K1	P—KR3

A good method of relieving the pin. After 10 .... Kt—K1; 11 B × B, Q × B; 12 Q—Q3, the position of the black pieces remains cramped.

11 B—R4	Kt—R2
12 B × B	Q × B
13 Q—Q3	QR—Kt1
14 P—QKt3	Kt—Kt4
15 QR—Q1	

The game would take a more violent course after 15 P—B4.

15	Q—K4

Preventing not only 16 P—B4, but also the preparatory 16 P—Kt3 (on account of 16 .... Q × Kt; 17 Q × Q, Kt—B6 ch; 18 K—Kt2, Kt × Q; 19 R × Kt, KR—K1, and Black has a very good game).

But as this committing of the Queen in the front line is over-hasty, a waiting policy by 15 .... KR—K1 would have been more rational.

16 Q—K3	Kt—K3
17 Kt (B3)—K2	Q—QR4
18 Kt—B5	Kt—B4
19 QKt—Q4	

In order to preserve a Knight on important outpost duties at KB5. In addition, there is the by no means obvious threat 20 QKt × P,

B × QKt; 21 Kt—K7 ch, followed by Kt × B, and wins. Nor has White any longer to fear 19 .... Q × P, because his QBP is now guarded, and 20 R—R1, Q—Kt7; 21 KR—Kt1 wins the opposing Queen.

19	K—R2
20 P—KKt4	QR—K1
21 P—KB3	Kt—K3
22 Kt—K2	

Calculation or intuition? Two qualities for which the Cuban master is justly famous.

22	Q × P

He accepts the challenge, although experience has many a time demonstrated the danger of such enterprises. A more cautious course would have been 22 .... Q—Kt3, by which Black would have obtained the exchange of Queens, conceding White but a small positional advantage.

23 Kt (K2)—Kt3

Calmly giving up a second pawn.

23	Q × BP

More prudent would have been 23 .... Q—R4, in order to exchange Queens after 24 .... Q—Kt3, remaining with an extra pawn in reserve.

24 R—QB1

With the obvious intention of preventing 24 .... Q—B4.

24	Q—Kt7
25 Kt—R5	

The attack, which has now taken definite shape, is conducted by White with extreme virtuosity.

25	R—KR1

A defence which could have been tried, in spite of apparent dangers, is 25 .... P—Kt4.

26 R—K2	Q—K4
27 P—B4	Q—Kt4

Now that the black Queen is cut off from the critical sector, the hurricane breaks.

28 Kt (B5) × KtP

A temporary sacrifice which, although easily seen, necessitated careful preparation, not lacking in elegant points.

28	Kt—B4

If 28 .... Kt × Kt; 29 Kt—B6 ch, K—Kt3; 30 Kt × B, P—B3; 31 P—K5 (the break-through); 31 .... K—B2; 32 Kt × P, R—K2; 33 Kt—K4, and Black has no defence. In any event, 28 .... Q—Kt3 eliminating the Queens would have been better than the move in the text, which leaves the denuded King to his fate.

29 Kt × R	B × Kt
30 Q—QB3	

The triumphant diagonal.

30	P—B3
31 Kt × P ch	K—Kt3
32 Kt—R5	R—Kt1
33 P—B5 ch	K—Kt4
34 Q—K3 ch	K—R5
35 Q—Kt3 ch	

And mates next move.

62

White	Black
DE VERE	STEINITZ

(Dundee, 1867)

In this game we see a homeless King—set upon from all sides—succumb finally to a beautiful and rapidly conclusive sacrifice.

1 P—K4	P—K4
2 Kt—KB3	Kt—QB3
3 B—Kt5	Kt—B3

At one time Dr. Lasker used to be the great protagonist of this active (if not too active) defence.

4 Castles

White disdains to protect his KP either by 4 Q—K2 or more modestly by 4 P—Q3, relying on the superior development which its capture would give him.

4	Kt × P

Challenging thunder and lightning on the K file in preference to adopting a more staid line of defence by 4 .... P—Q3 (5 P—Q4, B—Q2, etc. = *Steinitz Defence*) or 4 .... B—K2, or even 4 .... B—B4.

5 R—K1

Even more vigorous is 5 P—Q4, strengthening the pressure on the centre files. The defence against 5 Q—K2 presents no difficulties, e.g. 5 .... Kt—Q3; 6 B × Kt, QP × B; 7 Kt × P, B—K2; 8 R—K1, B—K3; 9 P—Q4, Kt—B4 (not yet 9 .... Castles; 10 Kt × KBP); 10 P—QB3, Castles; with an equal game.

5	Kt—Q3
6 Kt × P	

Or 6 B × Kt, QP × B; 7 Kt × P, B—K2, followed by .... Castles.

6	Kt × Kt

Instead of this impulsive reply, which tries to eliminate the terrible threat 7 Kt × Kt dis ch, the cool-headed 6 .... B—K2 is the *coup juste.*

7 R × Kt ch	B—K2
8 P—Q4	P—KB3

An unsuccessful attempt to confiscate the opposing KB, which badly weakens the black King's battlements.

As, on the other hand, 8 .... Castles; 9 B—Q3 would leave the white pieces with good attacking positions, simplification by 8 .... Kt × B; 9 R × Kt is the only resource.

9 R—K1	Kt × B

Again after 9 .... Castles; 10 B—Q3, White's pressure would be intensified.

10 Q—R5 ch	P—Kt3
11 Q × Kt	P—B3

After 11 .... Castles, Black's position would be no less awkward.

12 Q—Kt3	P—Q4
13 P—QB4	

This fight for the important diagonal QR2—KKt8 marks an essential stage on the way to success.

13	K—B2

He resorts to artificial castling, because after 13 .... Castles; 14 P × P, P × P; 15 Kt—B3, Black could not protect his QP and KB.

14 Kt—B3

If now 14 P × P, Q × P; 15 Q × Q, P × Q; 16 Kt—B3, B—QKt5, and Black achieves equality.

14	P × P

If 14 .... B—K3; 15 Q × P.

15 Q × P ch	K—Kt2
16 P—Q5	P × P
17 Kt × P	B—B1

But not 17 .... R—K1, because 18 Kt—B7, nor 17 .... B—Q3, after which Black's position remains precarious. (*Diagram. See* p. 78.)

18 Kt × P

A far-sighted sacrifice, which breaks up the black King's citadel.

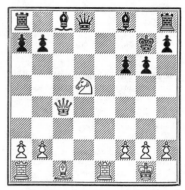

Position after 17 .... B—B1

18 ......   Q×Kt
Or 18 .... K×Kt; 19 Q—B3 ch, followed
by Q×R.

19 B—Q2   P—QKt4
20 Q—Q5   P—Kt5
The terrible threat 21 B—B3 is past, but
at the cost of multiple weaknesses.

21 QR—B1
Instead of rushing for his prey by 21 Q×R,
B—QB4; etc., White in a telling manner
increases the pressure still more. (Threat:
22 R—B7 ch.)

21 ......   Q—B2
22 Q×R   B—K3
23 Q—K4   B×P
24 Q—K5 ch   K—Kt1
25 R—B7
This irruption on the 7th marks the end
of Black's resistance.

25 ......   Q—Q4
26 Q×Q ch   B×Q
27 R—K8   Resigns
(27 .... B—B2; 28 R—R8, K—Kt2;
29 R (R8)×P.) A beautiful game.

63

White	Black
JANOWSKI	BURN

(Cologne, 1898)

*We have here a beautiful example of self-
possession which succeeds in overcoming all
his opponent's powerful and astute attempts—
the haughty Rook (14 R—Kt5), the unmask-*

*ing of the Bishop on the long black diagonal
(19 Kt—B5), the offer of the Queen sacrifice
(20 Q—R4)—all are brought to naught.*

1 P—K4   P—K4
2 Kt—KB3   Kt—QB3
3 B—Kt5   Kt—B3
4 Castles   Kt×P
5 R—K1   Kt—Q3
6 Kt×P   B—K2
By this sound defence—which covers the
K file and prepares for castling—Black
maintains the balance.

7 B—Q3
This desire to preserve the two Bishops is
understandable, but a more natural continuation is 7 Kt—QB3, Castles; 8 P—Q4,
which allows the deployment of the white
forces in a reasoned manner.
An example of this line of play is found
in a game De Vere-Minchin (*London*, 1871):
7 Kt—QB3, Castles; 8 P—Q4, B—B3;
9 B—Q3, P—KR3 (if 9 .... Kt×P;
10 B×P ch); 10 Kt—Q5, Kt—K1; 11 Q—Kt4,
P—Q3; 12 Q—K4, P—KKt3; 13 Kt×KBP
(a break-up sacrifice); 13 .... R×Kt;
14 Q×P ch, K—B1; 15 B×P ch, B—Kt2;
16 Q—R7, Kt—K2; 17 Q—R8 ch, Kt—Kt1;
18 B—R7, and Black resigns.

7 ......   Kt×Kt
After the more restrained defence 7 ....
Castles; 8 Kt—B3, Kt—K1; 9 Kt—Q5, etc.,
White would have an easier time.

8 R×Kt   Castles
9 Kt—B3   P—QB3
Slowly but surely Black is completing the
deployment of his forces.

10 P—QKt3
But White also has to go slow in resolving
the problem of the Queen's Bishop's development.

10 ......   Kt—K1
11 B—Kt2   P—Q4
12 Q—R5
Here 12 Q—B3 is preferable to this
sudden sally; but one way or another
Black's position is already consolidated.

12 ......   Kt—B3
13 Q—R4   B—K3
14 R—Kt5
A turbulent Rook. The negative object
of the move is to stop 14 .... Kt—K5;
15 R×P ch, etc. Its positive aim is shown
in the next note.
If 14 QR—K1, then already 14 ....
P—KR3.

14 ......   P—KKt3

Fearlessly parrying the threat 15 Kt×P, B×Kt; 16 R×P ch, K×R; 17 Q×P mate.

Now it might be thought that White will be able to go *berserk* on the wide-open long diagonal, but the sequel will show the power of resistance inherent in a concentrated if fixed position.

15 Q—R6

Now White's threat is far less ambitious. He intends, by a multiple sacrifice, to obtain a draw by perpetual check, as follows: 16 B×P, BP×B; 17 R×P ch, P×R (or 17 .... K—B2); 18 Q×P ch, K—R1; 19 Q—R6 ch (if 19 Kt×P, R—B2); 19 .... K—Kt1 (instead of 19 .... Kt—R2; 20 Kt×P dis ch, B—B3; 21 Kt×B, R×Kt, etc.); 20 Q—Kt6 ch, etc.

15 ......   P—Q5

This temporary closure of the wide-open diagonal is most important. The following continuation would only be a compromise: 15 .... Kt—Kt5; 16 R×Kt, B×R; 17 Kt×P, P—B3; 18 B×KtP, P×B; 19 Q×P ch, K—R1; 20 Q—R6 ch, and there is nothing left but to conclude peace.

16 Kt—K2   Kt—Kt5

After this, events take a dramatic course.

17 R×Kt   B×R
18 Kt×P   B—Kt4
19 Kt—B5

The first snare: if 19 .... B×Q; 20 Kt×B mate.

19 ......   B—B3
20 Q—R4

The second snare, based on the same picturesque idea, but finding a simple refutation.

20 ......   B×B
21 Kt—K7 ch   K—Kt2
Resigns

An entertaining game.

64

White   Black
SHOWALTER   PILLSBURY
(Match, 1897)

Every manœuvre in chess—be it in attack or defence—should have, as far as possible, a basic idea. In this game, White's main idea is the exploitation of the fact that Black's QB is shut in on both sides.

Thus Black is playing up to the end without his Q side pieces, and White takes advantage of this circumstance by bringing about a series of brilliant combinations.

1 P—K4   P—K4
2 Kt—KB3   Kt—QB3
3 B—Kt5   Kt—B3
4 Castles   Kt×P

This "Berlin" Knight is very enterprising.

5 P—Q4

This advance is more energetic than 5 R—K1 or 5 Q—K2.

5 ......   Kt—Q3

There is too much risk attached to 5 .... P×P (because of 6 R—K1), while 5 .... P—QR3 means loss of time (6 B×Kt, QP×B; 7 R—K1, etc.). The most solid continuation is 5 .... B—K2.

6 B—R4

An original retreat. The classical continuation is 6 B×Kt, whilst the modern line is 6 P×P, Kt×B; 7 P—QR4, and White recovers his piece (the *Magdeburg Attack*).

6 ......   P×P

Intent on gain. The more solid line is 6 .... P—K5; 7 R—K1, B—K2; 8 Kt—K5, Castles, with equalisation.

7 P—B3

In "gambit style."

7 ......   P×P

Even after the more prudent 7 .... B—K2; 8 P×P, etc., White's pressure more than makes up for the missing pawn.

8 Kt×P   B—K2
9 Kt—Q5   Castles
10 R—K1   B—B3

If 10 .... Kt—B4; 11 P—KKt4. But 10 .... R—K1; 11 B—B4, B—B1 is not without its troubles.

11 B—B4

A direct threat: 12 Kt×P, Q×Kt; 13 QB×Kt.

11 ......   Kt—K1

A crucial moment. If left alone, Black will consolidate his position (12 .... P—Q3), but the attacker will not remain idle. (*Diagram. See p. 80.*)

12 R×Kt

An eliminating sacrifice.

12 ......   Q×R

Or 12 .... R×R; 13 B×P, trying to "mate" the Queen. But White now regains

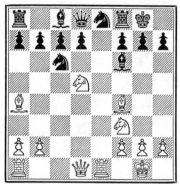

Position after 11 .... Kt—K1

with heavy interest the material engaged in this encounter.

| 13 Kt×P | Q—K5 |
| 14 B—Q6 | |

All goes well with White: now both adverse Rooks are attacked, and the black QP remains blockaded.

14	R—Kt1
15 B—B2	Q—KKt5
16 B×R	K×B
17 Q—Q6 ch	

The final assault.

| 17 ...... | B—K2 |
| 18 R—K1 | |

An episode of great beauty (18 .... B×Q; 19 R—K8 mate).

| 18 ...... | P—KKt3 |

A necessary if undesirable measure. If 18 .... P—B3; 19 B—Kt3, Kt—K4; 20 Q—Q5 (the most effective); 20 .... Kt×Kt ch (or 20 .... B—Kt5; 21 R×Kt, and wins); 21 K—R1, forcing surrender.

| 19 Q—Q2 | Q—R4 |
| 20 Kt—Q5 | B—Q1 |

If, trying to evade the threat 21 Kt×B, Kt×Kt; 22 Q—Q6, Black plays 20 .... B—Q3, the same reply by White, 21 Q—B3, settles matters.

21 Q—B3	P—B3
22 Kt×P	B—R4
Mate in 5	

(Beginning with 23 Kt×QP ch.)

65

| *White* | *Black* |
| HALPRIN | PILLSBURY |

(Munich, 1900)

Aptly named "the most beautiful tournament draw," this game unrolls before our eyes a very kaleidoscope of threats and counter-threats, in order to end up—as do so many hotly contested fights on the chessboard—in a draw.

1 P—K4	P—K4
2 Kt—KB3	Kt—QB3
3 B—Kt5	Kt—B3
4 Castles	Kt×P
5 P—Q4	Kt—Q3
6 P×P	

This seeming sacrifice, in which the piece is recovered almost at once, is the idea of a German amateur, L'Hermet, of Magdeburg. It is not inferior to the usual 6 Kt—B3 or 6 B—R4, but gives White no tangible advantage.

| 6 ...... | Kt×B |
| 7 P—QR4 | |

Not 7 P—B4, P—Q3; to Black's advantage.

| 7 ...... | P—Q3 |

Neither 7 .... Kt(Kt4)—Q5; nor 7 .... Kt—Q3; is any better for Black.

| 8 P—K6 | |

The exploits begin.
Far more prosaic would be the continuation 8 P×Kt, Kt×P; 9 R—K1, B—K2; 10 Kt×Kt, P×Kt; 11 Q×Q ch, K×Q; 12 R×P, B—Q3, etc., with an even game.

| 8 ...... | P×P |

Or 8 .... B×.P; 9 P×Kt, Kt—K4; 10 Kt—Q4, B—Q2; 11 Kt—QB3, B—K2; and here again the contest shows signs of slackening.

| 9 P×Kt | Kt—K2 |
| 10 Kt—B3 | |

Calmly proceeding with his development. Another continuation could be 10 B—Kt5, Q—Q2; 11 Kt—B3.

| 10 ...... | Kt—Kt3 |
| 11 Kt—Kt5 | |

An expedition with far-reaching consequences. The sequel can be looked upon as a beautiful problem evolved in practical play.

11	......	B—K2
12	Q—R5	B×Kt
13	B×B	Q—Q2
14	P—Kt6	

By this important thrust the cohesion of the black pawns is seriously disturbed. If at once 14 Kt—Q5, Black's reply is 14 .... Castles.

| 14 | ...... | BP×P |
| 15 | Kt—Q5 | |

By this sacrifice the K file is laid open.

| 15 | ...... | P×Kt |

If, in order to parry 16 Kt×P, Black plays 15 .... Q—B3, White wins with the following pretty continuation: 16 Kt—K7, Q×P; 17 QR—B1, and wins.

| 16 | KR—K1 ch | K—B1 |

Of course not 16 .... K—B2; 17 R—K7 ch.

17 R—R3

The subsidiary idea underlying White's 7th move now becomes clear. The threat is 18 R—B3 ch, K—Kt1; 19 R—K7, Q—B3 (19 .... Kt×R; 20 Q—B7 mate); 20 R—B8 ch, K×R; 21 Q—B3 ch, with mate in three to follow.

| 17 | ...... | Kt—K4 |
| 18 | R×Kt | |

An *eliminating sacrifice*. White is intent on removing all obstacles from his path.

| 18 | ...... | P×R |
| 19 | R—B3 ch | K—Kt1 |

Has the black King at last reached safety?

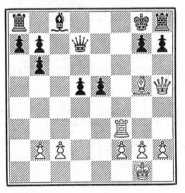

20 B—R6

By this new manifestation of the combinative spirit, White still holds his adversary on the *qui-vive*.

| 20 | ...... | Q—K2 |

By this discreet manœuvre Black tries to escape the stranglehold, and incidentally he prevents a perpetual check by 20 .... P×B; 21 R—Kt3 ch, K—B1 (21 .... Q—Kt2; 22 Q—K8 mate); 22 R—B3 ch, etc.

He cannot play 20 .... Q—K3; 21 Q—Kt5, Q—Q2 (or 21 .... Q×B; 22 Q—Q8 mate); 22 B×P, and wins, nor 20 .... P—Kt3; 21 R—B8 mate.

21 B×P

A break-up sacrifice which demolishes the main rampart. But not 21 R—KKt3, P—Kt3.

| 21 | ...... | K×B |

It is clear that 21 .... Q×B; 22 Q—K8 ch will not answer, nor would 21 .... B—Kt5; 22 Q×B, P—KR4 (22 .... Q×B; 23 Q—K6 ch); 23 Q—Kt6, Q×B; 24 Q—K6 ch, K—R2; 25 R—B7, and White has the advantage; nor, finally, 21 .... B—Q2; 22 B×R, P—K5 (or 22 .... K×B; 23 R—B7, and wins); 23 B—B6, Q—B2; 24 Q—Kt5 ch, Q—Kt3 (or 24 .... K—B1; 25 B—Kt7 ch, and wins); 25 Q×P ch, Q—B2; 26 R—Kt3 ch, K—B1; 27 Q—Q6 ch, K—K1; 28 R—Kt8 ch, Q×R; 29 Q—K7 mate.

After the text move, Black is a Rook and a Bishop ahead, but there is nothing he can do.

22	R—Kt3 ch	K—B1
23	R—B3 ch	K—Kt2
24	R—Kt3 ch	K—B1
25	R—B3 ch	K—Kt1
	Draw	

(By perpetual check.)

66

| *White* | *Black* |
| TARRASCH | LASKER |

(Match, 1908)

Although the doctor from Nuremberg lost the match, he shows in the following scientific game that methodical play can often get the better of even the greatest tacticians.

1	P—K4	P—K4
2	Kt—KB3	Kt—QB3
3	B—Kt5	Kt—B3
4	Castles	Kt×P
5	P—Q4	B—K2

A prudent and proper course.

6 Q—K2

Amplifying White's pressure. Less efficacious is 6 R—K1, Kt—Q3, etc., or, impulsively, 6 P—Q5, Kt—Q3, etc., or again 6 P×P, Castles; 7 Q—Q5, Kt—B4, and Black succeeds in slowing down White's action.

6 ......   Kt—Q3

Not 6 .... P—Q4; 7 Kt×P, etc., nor 6 .... P—B4; 7 P×P, Castles; 8 Kt—B3, Kt×Kt; 9 P×Kt, and, after the clearance, White is in a dominating position.

7 B×Kt   KtP×B

More astute than 7 .... QP×B, after which the open Q file might become of use to White.

8 P×P   Kt—Kt2

Although Black's position is cramped, it can be held.

9 Kt—B3

This quiet developing move surpasses in natural energy all other attempts such as 9 P—B4 or 9 P—QKt3 or 9 Kt—Q4, and finally 9 B—K3.

9 ......   Castles
10 R—K1

Preventing the undoubling of the black pawns, because of 10 .... P—Q4; 11 P×P e. p., B×P (forced). Another good way of preventing Black's advance of the QP to its fourth is 10 Kt—Q4.

10 ......   Kt—B4

Neither 10 .... R—K1; 11 Q—B4, etc., nor—as aforesaid—10 .... P—Q4; 11 P×P e. p., B×P; 12 Q—B4, etc., is tempting for Black.

11 Kt—Q4   Kt—K3
12 B—K3   Kt×Kt
13 B×Kt   P—QB4

If at once 13 .... P—Q4, then 14 Q—K3, followed by Kt—R4, irremediably blockades Black's QB4. The importance of the intermediate manœuvre in the text, which constitutes the *Rio de Janeiro Variation*, stands out clearly. Black first secures the control of his QB4 before starting operations in the centre.

14 B—K3   P—Q4

Now or never!

15 P×P e. p.   B×P

Positional judgment: in spite of "weak squares" on the Q side, his two Bishops on long diagonals should enable him to hold his own.

16 Kt—K4

Still more methodical is 16 QR—Q1 (as played in a later game of the same match). But even then the chances are about equal after 16 .... Q—R5; 17 P—KR3, B—Kt2, etc.

16 ......   B—Kt2

One of the extremely infrequent cases, where the great tactician Dr. Lasker fails to provide in good time against his opponent's intentions, which he should have done by 16 .... B×P ch; 17 K×B, Q—R5 ch; 18 K—Kt1, Q×Kt.

It is true the text move contains a nasty trap (17 Kt×P, B×Kt; 18 B×B, Q—Kt4, and wins), but—and Black has failed to see the true inner meaning of the fact—White will not only undouble the opposing pawns, but will not hesitate to allow Bishops of opposite colours, as he thereby creates easy and lasting objects of attack in the black camp.

17 Kt×B   P×Kt
18 QR—Q1

The direct and positive manœuvres begin, The sequel is a methodical demonstration of the highest order.

18 ......   Q—B3

Similarly, if 18 .... Q—Kt3; 19 P—QB4, blockading Black's backward pawn.

19 P—QB4   KR—K1
20 Q—Kt4   B—B3

Stopping 21 Q—Q7, but also threatening 21 .... Q×P.

21 R—K2   R—K5
22 Q—Kt3   Q—K3

An astute defence. (Threats: 23 .... R—Kt5 or 23 .... Q×P.)

23 P—KR3

Parrying first and foremost 23 .... R—Kt5. Evidently nothing comes of 23 R×P, Q×P, etc., for if after the text move 23 .... Q×P; White's reply is 24 B—R6, P—Kt3; 25 R×R, Q×R; 26 R×P, R—K1; 27 K—R2, and Black cannot get free.

23 ......   R—Q1
24 KR—Q2   R—K4
25 B—R6

If 25 .... Q×B; 26 Q×R, etc. Very prettily White turns his *positional advantage* into one of *material* under most favourable conditions. Less good would be, at once, 25 B—B4, R—K8 ch, etc.

25	Q—Kt3
26 B—B4	R—K3
27 B × P	Q—R4

With the counter-threat of 28 ....
R—Kt3.

28 Q—Kt4

Beautiful simplicity in the means employed! For after 28 B—B4, Q × R ch; 29 R × Q, R × R ch; 30 K—R2, R (K3)—K8, and there would again be breakers ahead for White.

28	Q × Q
29 P × Q	R—K5
30 B × P	R × R
31 R × R	P—KR4
32 R—Q6	

The final stroke, by which White is able to preserve his superiority in material, e.g. 32 .... B—Kt2; 33 R—Q8 ch, K—R2; 34 R—Q7, B—B3; 35 R—B7, B—K1; 36 B × P, etc., which is why

Black resigns.

67

White	Black
MARSHALL	LASKER

(Match, 1907)

A temporary sacrifice (13 .... P × P), which ultimately stands revealed as a most profound exchange combination, is the feature of this game, and lays the foundation of Black's victory.

1 P—K4	P—K4
2 Kt—KB3	Kt—QB3
3 B—Kt5	Kt—B3

As mentioned before, Dr. Lasker, during the greater part of his career, remained faithful to this type of *active defence*.

4 P—Q4

This, the *Barry Continuation*, is very ingenious and quite defendable. The most efficacious continuation at this point is 4 Castles.

| 4 ...... | P × P |

Eliminating the dangerous pawn which, after 4 .... Kt × KP; 5 P—Q5, might become troublesome.

5 Castles

Or 5 P—K5, Kt—K5; 6 Castles, B—K2, returning to the variation in the text.

| 5 ...... | B—K2 |

Of less value is 5 .... P—Q3; 6 Kt × P, B—Q2; 7 B × Kt, P × B; 8 Q—B3, threatening 9 P—K5.

6 P—K5

Trying to increase the pressure in the centre, whereas, after 6 Kt × P, Castles; 7 Kt—QB3, Kt × Kt; 8 Q × Kt, P—Q3, etc., the heat of battle subsides.

6	Kt—K5
7 Kt × P	Castles

A wise measure. Far more febrile was the continuation of a game Bird-Steinitz, which was played in their early days: 5 P—K5, Kt—K5; 6 Kt × P, B—K2; 7 Castles, Kt × Kt; 8 Q × Kt, Kt—B4; 9 P—KB4, P—QKt3 (preparing a pretty trap, into which Black himself falls); 10 P—B5, Kt—Kt6; 11 Q—K4 (not 11 RP × Kt, B—B4); 11 .... Kt × R; 12 P—B6, B—B4 ch; 13 K—R1, QR—Kt1; 14 P—K6 (breaking through); 14 .... KR—Kt1 (neither 14 .... P × P; 15 Q × P ch, etc., nor 14 .... Castles; 15 P—K7); 15 Q × P, R—B1; 16 P × BP ch, R × P; 17 R—K1 ch, B—K2; 18 Q—Kt8 ch, R—B1; 19 P—B7 mate. Bravo!

| 8 Kt—B5 | P—Q4 |

Clearly not 8 .... QKt × P; 9 Q—Q5.

9 B × Kt

He need not have given up his "two Bishops." A reasoned continuation could be 9 Kt × B ch, Kt × Kt; 10 P—KB3, Kt—QB4; 11 P—QKt4, Kt—K3; 12 P—KB4, P—KB4, and the close position tends to re-establish equality.

9	P × B
10 Kt × B ch	Q × Kt
11 R—K1	

An indirect protection of the threatened KP (for if 11 .... Q × P; 12 P—KB3), which, however, weakens KB2. This is accentuated by Black's rejoinder, as neither 11 B—B4, P—B3 nor 11 P—KB3, Q—B4 ch is playable. The best continuation would be 11 Q—Q4.

11	Q—R5
12 B—K3	

The immediate continuation 12 P—KB3 displays more staidness, to which Black's reply is not 12 .... Q—B7 ch; 13 K—R1, Kt—B4; 14 B—K3, etc., but 12 .... Kt—Kt4.

| 12 ...... | P—B3 |
| 13 P—KB3 | |

Had White foreseen Black's reply, he would have played 13 Kt—Q2 or 13 P—KKt3.

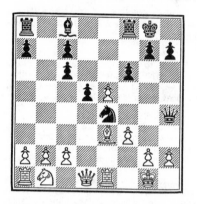

| 13 ...... | P × P |

A deep conception, worthy of this important occasion. (The first game in this match for the World Championship.)

| 14 P × Kt | |

Or 14 P—KKt3, Kt × P; 15 P × Kt, Q × P ch; 16 K—R1, R × P, with ineluctable threats.

| 14 ...... | P—Q5 |
| 15 P—KKt3 | |

Or 15 B—Q2, Q—B7 ch; 16 K—R1, B—Kt5 (a pseudo-sacrifice, as the Bishop cannot be captured by reason of a mate in two); 17 Q—B1, R—B3, etc., with a winning attack.

| 15 ...... | Q—B3 |
| 16 B × P | |

Restoring the loot of his own free will, for here also 16 B—Q2, Q—B7 ch; 17 K—R1, B—R6; 18 R—Kt1, B—B8 (threatening 19 .... B—K7 and 20 .... B—B6 ch) would rapidly lead to a loss for White.

| 16 ...... | P × B |
| 17 R—B1 | Q × R ch |

The moment for shrewd liquidation has arrived.

| 18 Q × Q | R × Q ch |
| 19 K × R | R—Kt1 |

An instructive moment. Instead of the plausible, but far less effective, moves 19 .... B—R3 ch or 19 .... B—R6 ch, the black Rook plays a lone hand.

| 20 P—Kt3 | R—Kt4 |

The command of the 4th rank is frequently very effective.

21 P—B4	R—KR4
22 K—Kt1	P—B4
23 Kt—Q2	K—B2
24 R—B1 ch	K—K2
25 P—QR3	R—R3
26 P—KR4	R—R3
27 R—R1	B—Kt5
28 K—B2	K—K3
29 P—R4	K—K4

The decisive factor in this position is the greater activities of Black's pieces, especially of his King.

30 K—Kt2	R—KB3
31 R—K1	P—Q6
32 R—KB1	K—Q5
33 R × R	P × R

In this ending—Knight and pawns against Bishop and pawns—White becomes a victim of *Zugzwang*.

34 K—B2	P—B3
35 P—QR5	P—QR3
36 Kt—B1	

Or 36 K—K1, K—K6; etc.—a sad case!

36	K × P
37 K—K1	B—K7
38 Kt—Q2 ch	K—K6
39 Kt—Kt1	P—B4
40 Kt—Q2	P—R4
41 Kt—Kt1	K—B6
Resigns.	

68

| White | Black |
| PILLSBURY | POLLOCK |

(Hastings, 1895)

The unique feature of the following game is the unusual number of successive positional pawn sacrifices. From the 25th to the 40th move White works with a unit less. The contest is carried on without Queens, but the white King shows an astonishing versatility.

1 P—K4	P—K4
2 Kt—KB3	Kt—QB3
3 B—Kt5	P—QR3

The *Morphy Defence*, the mysteries of which the experts are still trying to fathom.

4 B—R4	Kt—B3
5 Castles	Kt × P

By this "open defence" (instead of the "closed defence" by 5 .... B—K2 or other expedients), Black at once claims his share of the initiative.

6 P—Q4	

Introducing a fresh protagonist, in order to undermine the K file. Direct methods such as 6 R—K1, Kt—B4 or also 6 Q—K2, Kt—B4, etc., lead only to swift equalisation.

6	P—QKt4
7 B—Kt3	P—Q4
8 P × P	

Less ambitious is 8 Kt × P, Kt × Kt; 9 P × Kt, B—Kt2, etc.

8	B—K3

Black relies on the grouping of his pieces in the centre. The defence of the QP by 8 .... Kt—K2 is more artificial (9 P—QR4, R—QKt1; 10 P × P, P × P; 11 Kt—Q4, etc.).

9 P—B3	

This manœuvre has the double object of reinforcing Q4 and preserving the "Spanish Bishop" in case of 9 .... Kt—R4; 10 B—B2 or 9 .... Kt—B4; 11 B—B2.

9	B—K2

After this cautious move, we reach the "normal position" of the open defence, in which White has a wide choice of more or less venomous continuations (10 R—K1, 10 QKt—Q2, 10 Q—K2, 10 B—K3, 10 B—KB4, or even 10 Kt—Q4, which sacrifices the KP without any particular justification).

10 R—K1	

In preparation for 11 Kt—Q4.

10	Castles
11 Kt—Q4	Kt × Kt

This not only avoids the heartbreak of the *Tarrasch Trap* (11 .... Q—Q2; 12 Kt × B, followed by 13 R × Kt, and wins), but also the manifold complications of the *Breslau Variation*: 11 .... Kt × KP; 12 P—B3, B—Q3; 13 P × Kt, B—KKt5; 14 Q—Q2, Q—R5. The ultimate consequences of the sacrifice of a piece offered by Black are not yet entirely elucidated.

12 P × Kt	B—KB4

He reserves a flight square for the Knight in case of need. This is usually effected by 12 .... P—R3, after which also White remains master of the field (13 P—B3, Kt—Kt4; 14 Kt—B3, etc.).

13 P—B3	Kt—Kt4
14 Kt—B3	P—QB3
15 P—Kt4	

Not content with the tranquil 15 B—K3, White seeks a speedy and striking decision.

15	B—B1
16 P—B4	P—Kt5

The struggle for K5.

17 Kt—R4	Kt—K5
18 P—B5	B—Kt4
19 Q—B3	B × B
20 QR × B	Q—R5
21 R—K2	

Renouncing the more circumspect defence by 21 R—K3.

21	Kt—Kt4
22 Q—Kt3	

Essential, as can be seen: 22 Q—Kt2, Kt—R6 ch; 23 K—R1, Kt—B5.

22	Q × Q ch
23 P × Q	Kt—B6 ch
24 K—B2	Kt × QP

There goes a good pawn! But White (possibly already on his 21st move) has seen much farther ahead. The pressure which he is now able to exercise in all directions is more than sufficient compensation for the loss of material.

25 R—Q2	Kt × B
26 P × Kt	B—Kt2

Or 26 .... B—Q2; 27 Kt—Kt6, QR—Q1; 28 Kt × B, R × Kt; 29 R × BP, etc., to White's advantage.

27 Kt—B5	B—B1
28 K—K3	

Illustrating here and in the sequel Steinitz's maxim: "The King is a strong piece." But if 28 Kt—Q3, Black, with 28 .... P—Kt3, would obtain some play on the K side.

28	P—KR4
29 K—B4	P—Kt3
30 K—Kt5	K—Kt2
31 P—B6 ch	K—R2
32 Kt—Q3	B × P

Still remaining a pawn ahead.

33 R × P	KR—K1
34 R—B7	K—Kt1
35 K—R6	B—B6

Making for the enemy King.

36 R—K7	K—B1

He could have tried another line of defence by 36 .... R × R; 37 P × R, R—K1.

37 R×R ch   R×R
38 K—Kt5
He comes back to guard his KP.

38 ......   B—K5
39 K—B4   R—B1
Black overestimates his resources. He
should have tried merely to hold his own by
39 ...... P—Kt4 ch; 40 K×P, B×Kt;
41 R×B, R×P ch; 42 K—B4, R—K3, etc.

40 Kt×P   R—B4
41 Kt×RP   R—Kt4
42 K—K3
Now the King goes to work in the centre.
If 42 P—QKt4, R—Kt3, recovering his
pawn.

42 ......   R×P ch
43 K—Q4   R×KKtP
Again Black is a pawn ahead, without
detriment, however, to White's chances.

44 Kt—B5   P—R5
45 P—Kt4   P—R6
46 R—QR2   K—Kt1
47 R—R8 ch   K—R2
48 P—K6
Breaking through the front.

48 ......   P×P
49 Kt×B   P×Kt
50 P—B7   R—KB6
51 P—B8 (Q)   R×Q
52 R×R
The student can see how, in this ending,
one *tempo* one way or the other will decide
the issue.

52 ......   P—Kt4
53 K×P   P—Kt5
54 R—B1   P—K4
55 P—Kt5   P—Kt6
56 R—KR1   Resigns.

69

White   *Black*

ALEKHINE   RUBINSTEIN

(Vilna, 1912)

*The eliminating sacrifice effected by Black
in this game (19 .... R×Kt) illustrates the
importance to the King's safety of the
"Knight defender." This elimination causes
the whole of the King's field position to
collapse.*

1 P—K4   P—K4
2 Kt—KB3   Kt—QB3
3 B—Kt5   P—QR3
4 B—R4   Kt—B3
5 Castles   Kt×P
6 P—Q4   P—QKt4
7 B—Kt3   P—Q4
8 P×P   B—K3
9 P—B3   B—K2
10 QKt—Q2
In a laudable endeavour to get rid of the
opposing Knight outpost.

10 ......   Kt—B4
Or 10 .... Kt×Kt; 11 B×Kt, Kt—R4;
12 Kt—Q4, to be followed by P—KB4,
with a fine attacking position for White.
The best course for Black is 10 .... Castles,
awaiting events with equanimity.

11 B—B2
Preserving the "attacking Bishop," but
also very good is 11 Kt—Q4.

11 ......   B—Kt5
If 11 .... P—Q5, taking advantage of the
opportunity of eliminating his weak pawn,
then 12 Kt—K4 improves White's prospects.

12 P—KR3
The most reasonable course here is
12 R—K1, guarding the threatened KP.

12 ......   B—R4
13 Q—K1
Here again 13 R—K1 ensured a very good
game for White, e.g.: 13 .... Q—Q2;
14 Kt—Kt3, etc., or 13 .... P—Q5;
14 Kt—Kt3, etc.

13 ......   Kt—K3
14 Kt—R2   B—Kt3
This preventive manœuvre anticipates
White's intention to gain territory by
15 P—KB4.

15 B×B   BP×B
Far-seeing strategy! Black recognises that
the KB and not the KR file will be needed
as a base for action.

16 Kt—Kt3
Or 16 P—KB4, P—Q5.

16 ......   P—Kt4
17 B—K3   Castles
18 Kt—B3   Q—Q2
19 Q—Q2
In threatening to capture the KKt pawn,
White pays insufficient attention to the scope
of his opponent's threats.

A better course is 19 KKt—Q4 (19 ....
Kt×P; 20 B×P), seeking to establish
equality.

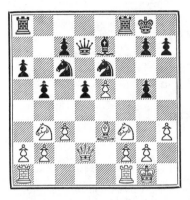

19 ......   R×Kt
A move with manifold virtues: it eliminates a piece essential for White's defence,
gains some pawns for the exchange and,
in addition, disrupts the hostile King's field.

20 P×R	Kt×P
21 Q—K2	R—KB1
22 Kt—Q2	Kt—Kt3
23 KR—K1	B—Q3
24 P—KB4	

Or 24 Q—B1, Kt (K3)—B5.

24	Kt (K3)×P
25 Q—B1	Kt×P ch

Now Black has won a third pawn for the
exchange, to say nothing of his attack. In
these circumstances White is irrevocably
lost.

26 K—R1	P—KKt5
27 Q—K2	Q—B4
Resigns.	

70

White	*Black*
BOTVINNIK	EUWE

(Leningrad, 1934)

*A contest between heavy-weights, in which
threat and parry are harmoniously balanced.
A game characteristic of the style of several
contemporary masters.*

1 P—K4	P—K4
2 Kt—KB3	Kt—QB3
3 B—Kt5	P—QR3
4 B—R4	Kt—B3
5 Castles	Kt×P
6 P—Q4	P—QKt4
7 B—Kt3	P—Q4
8 P×P	B—K3
9 P—B3	B—K2
10 QKt—Q2	Castles

Black refuses to react restlessly by 10 ....
Kt×Kt or 10 .... Kt—B4, and calmly
awaits events. For he need not fear the
complications arising from 11 Kt×Kt,
P×Kt; 12 B×B, P×Kt; 13 B—Q5, Kt×P;
14 B×R (or 14 B×P, Kt×B ch; 15 Q×Kt,
Castles; the games are even); 14 .... Q×B;
15 P—KKt3, Q—B1, with advantage to
Black.

11 Q—K2
By this, the *Thomas Attack*, White continues the local struggle which is engaged
around K4 in a more acute manner than
would be the case after 11 R—K1 or
11 B—B2 (11 .... Kt×Kt; 12 Q×Kt,
P—B3; 13 P×P, B×P, with even chances).

11	Kt—B4

Evading the issue, as simplification by
11 .... Kt×Kt; 12 Q×Kt is awkward for
Black. The best course, however, is to
hold the besieged point as long as possible
by 11 .... B—KB4 (12 R—Q1, Kt—R4;
13 Kt—Q4, B—Kt3; 14 Kt×Kt, B×Kt,
etc.).

12 Kt—Q4
But not 12 B—B2, because of 12 ....
P—Q5, and Black frees his game.

12	Kt×B

After 12 .... Kt×Kt; 13 P×Kt, Black
cannot free his game with 13 .... Kt—Kt2;
14 P—B4, nor with 13 .... Kt—Q2;
14 P—B4, etc., nor finally by 13 ....
Kt×B; 14 Kt×Kt, etc. His best move,
however, would have been 12 .... Q—Q2.

13 QKt×Kt
If 13 Kt×QKt, Kt×B.

13	Q—Q2
14 Kt×Kt	Q×Kt
15 B—K3	

Taking definite possession of an important
diagonal, aiming at Q4 and QB5, the main
objects of White's strategy.
Less methodical would be the assault
15 P—KB4, B—KB4; 16 Kt—Q4, B—B4;
17 B—K3, B×Kt; 18 P×B, Q—KKt3, and
the chances are equal.

| 15 ...... | B—KB4 |
| 16 KR—Q1 | |

Of course not 16 P—Kt4, Q—KKt3.

16	KR—Q1
17 P—B3	B—KB1
18 Q—KB2	

Instead of incisive measures such as 18 P—Kt4, White seeks above all to control as much territory as possible.

| 18 ...... | P—QR4 |

Black cannot afford to remain inactive— it would spell disaster.

| 19 R—Q2 | P—Kt5 |

With great skill, Black transfers the centre of gravity to the extreme Q wing.

20 R—QB1	Q—R5
21 Kt—Q4	B—Kt3
22 P—QKt3	Q—K1
23 P × P	B × P
24 KR—Q1	P—QB4
25 Kt—B2	B × Kt
26 R × B	P—Q5
27 B—Kt5	R—Q4
28 P—B4	

After a period of skirmishes (from the 20th to the 28th move), let us assess the position. Virtually, Black has an advantage on the Q side, where he has a passed pawn, supported but immobilised. Potentially, White has chances on the K side, where his KP exercises a powerful influence. The chances are therefore even.

28	P—R5
29 Q—B3	P × P
30 P × P	R—Q2
31 P—B5	

He takes advantage of a tactical opportunity (31 .... Q × P; 32 Q × R ch) to begin a war of movement.

| 31 ...... | KR—R2 |

Trying to turn the enemy lines.

32 Q—Kt3	R—R8
33 QR—B1	R × R
34 R × R	K—R1

He had to prevent 35 B—B6.

35 R—B1	R—R3
36 P—R3	Q—R1
37 K—R2	Q—K1

The foolhardy enterprise 37 .... R—R8; 38 R × R, Q × R; 39 B—B6, P × B; 40 P × P would be fatal for Black.

38 R—B3	B—R4
39 B—B4	B—B2
40 R—B1	R—R1
41 R—K1	Q—B3
42 P—K6	

This pawn becomes the principal actor in the drama.

42	B × B
43 Q × B	P × P
44 P × P	R—K1
45 P—K7	P—R3
46 Q—B5	

More astute than 46 Q—B8 ch, K—R2; 47 Q—B5 ch, K—Kt1, etc., for now there is every chance of Black's missing his way.

| 46 ...... | Q—Q3 ch |
| 47 K—R1 | K—Kt1 |

He not only avoids the fearful trap 47 .... R × P; 48 Q—KB8 ch, and wins, but also the tempting continuation 47 .... P—Q6; 48 R—K6, Q—Kt1 (not 48 .... Q—Q2; 49 R × P, with check, nor 48 .... Q—Q5; 49 Q—B8 ch); 49 Q × QP.

48 R—K6	Q—Q2
49 Q—K5	
Draw	

(49 .... P—Q6; 50 R—Q6, Q × P; 51 Q × Q, R × Q; 52 R × QP.)

A very fine game.

71

| White | Black |
| YATES | GUNSBERG |

(Chester, 1914)

The time spent in effecting a pawn capture of doubtful value often allows the enemy pressure to become irresistible.

This is the painful lesson to be learnt from the very beautiful game which follows.

1 P—K4	P—K4
2 Kt—KB3	Kt—QB3
3 B—Kt5	P—QR3
4 B—R4	Kt—B3
5 Castles	Kt × P
6 P—Q4	P—QKt4
7 B—Kt3	P—Q4
8 P × P	B—K3
9 P—QB3	B—K2
10 B—K3	

In order to carry on with 11 QKt—Q2, without encumbering the Queen's Bishop's diagonal.

10 ......   Castles
11 QKt—Q2   Kt × Kt
He voluntarily gives up his outpost, because its reinforcement by 11 .... P—B4 gives rise to the *Breyer Attack*, 12 P × P e. p., Kt × P (B3); 13 Kt—Kt5, which is very dangerous for Black.

12 Q × Kt   Kt—R4
13 B—B2
The attacking Bishop, the "Spanish Bishop," is to be preserved: after 13 QR—Q1, Kt × B; 14 P × Kt, P—QB3, etc., as also after 13 Kt—Q4, Kt × B, the chances even up.

13 ......   Kt—B5
14 Q—Q3   P—Kt3
15 B—R6
Bold play! After the more prosaic 15 B—B1, B—KB4; 16 Q—K2, B × B; 17 Q × B, the tension disappears rapidly.

15 ......   Kt × KtP
Nolens volens, Black accepts the offer, as after 15 .... R—K1; 16 P—QKt3, he would also have a very difficult stand, but he now has the consolation of some small compensation in material.

16 Q—K2   R—K1
17 Kt—Q4
If he recovers his pawn by 17 B × P, RP × B; 18 Q × Kt, he has to give up the "two Bishops" and to allow sundry weaknesses in his own camp, and so he rightly decides not to allow his impetus to be slackened.

17 ......   Kt—B5
More conformable would be 17 .... P—QB4; and if 18 Kt—B3, Q—Q2; in order not to leave the Knight in its strong central post.

18 P—B4   B—Q2
19 QR—K1
Embarking on a perfectly diabolical enterprise on the K file.

19 ......   P—QB4
Had Black foreseen his opponent's elegant reply, he would have preferred to seek, with 19 .... P—KB4, a slowing-down of the contest.

20 P—K6
An explosive pawn.

20 ......   B—KB3
Many dangers would lurk in 20 .... P × Kt; 21 Q—Kt4.

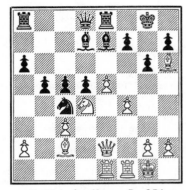

Position after 19 .... P—QB4

21 Q—Kt4   P × Kt
22 P—B5
Instead of adopting the uncertain continuation 22 P × B, R × R; 23 R × R, Kt—K6, etc., White throws all his forces into the attack.
The threat is: 23 KBP × P, BP × P; 24 B × P.

22 ......   P—Q6
23 B × P   B × KP
Giving back the piece, but his terrible adversary soon exacts two-fold retribution.

24 P × B   Q—Kt3 ch
25 K—R1   Resigns
For after 25 .... R × P; 26 R × R, Q × R; 27 Q × Q, P × Q; 28 R × B, the remaining Bishop is also lost.

72

White	Black
ALEKHINE	EUWE

(Match, 1935)

A most tense struggle, in which the interest never flags, in spite of one or two missed opportunities, due perhaps to the importance of the occasion.

1 P—K4   P—K4
2 Kt—KB3   Kt—QB3
3 B—Kt5   P—QR3
4 B—R4   Kt—B3
5 Castles   Kt × P
A favourite variation of the Dutch champion.

6 P—Q4	P—QKt4
7 B—Kt3	P—Q4
8 P×P	B—K3
9 P—B3	B—K2

Here is the *normal position*.

10 P—QR4

An interlude full of vitality, but not devoid of risk.

10 ...... P—Kt5

Much more enterprising than 10 ....
R—QKt1; 11 P×P, P×P; 12 B—K3, and
White has the additional asset of the open
QR file.

After 10 .... Kt—R4, the energetic continuation in a game Ahues-Monticelli, *San
Remo*, 1930, was as follows: 11 P×P, P×P;
12 B—B2, Castles; 13 Kt—Q4, Kt—B5;
14 R×R, Q×R; 15 P—B3, Kt—B4;
16 P—QKt4, Kt—R3; 17 P—B4, P—QB4
(better is 17 .... B—Q2); 18 Kt×B,
P×Kt; 19 Q—R5, resigns (for if 19 ....
P—Kt3; 20 B×P, and if 19 .... P—R3;
20 Q—Kt6).

11 Kt—Q4

By this *pawn sacrifice* White hopes to
obtain a decisive advantage on the K file,
now opened, but encumbered with black
pieces. A less turbulent continuation could
be 11 R—K1, Kt—B4; 12 B—B2, etc.

11 ...... QKt×P
12 P—KB4

Rushing to the attack. If 12 Q—K2
(preventing 12 .... Kt—B5, and threatening 13 P—B3), then 12 .... Kt—Kt3.

12 ...... Kt—B5

This move, instead of gaining, loses territory, which Black could have avoided by
interpolating 12 .... B—Kt5; 13 Q—B2,
P—QB4, etc.

13 P—B5

A disappointing variation would be:
13 Kt×B, P×Kt; 14 B×Kt, P×B;
15 Q—R5, P—Kt3; 16 Q—K5, because
of 16 .... B—B4 ch; 17 K—R1, Kt—B7 ch;
18 R×Kt, Q—Q8 ch, followed by mate.

13 ...... B—QB1
14 Q—K1

Of no value would be 14 Kt—B6,
B—B4 ch, but by playing 14 Q—K2, he
could have strengthened his threat of
15 B×Kt.

14 ...... B—Kt2
15 P×P P—B4

This energetic advance costs White a
pawn.

16 P—B6

As 16 P×P is inadmissible on account of
16 .... B×P; 17 Q—Q1, Q—B3, etc., and
as to retire the Knight would lose the
QKtP (e.g. 16 Kt—B2, P×P; 17 Kt×P,
Q—Kt3 ch, and wins), White tries to
enlarge his field of action.

16 ...... B×P
17 Kt—B5 Castles
18 P×P R—K1

Good and simple is also 18 .... Q—B2.

19 Q—Kt4 Q—B1
20 B×Kt P—QR4

An *intermediary manœuvre* of the
greatest importance. For if now, e.g.
21 Q—Kt3, there follows 21 .... P×B;
22 Q—QR3 (or 22 Q×P, B—R3, winning
the exchange); 22 .... Q—B3, and Black
dictates the course of events.

21 Q—R3 P×B
22 Kt—B3 Kt×P

He is content with a gain of material
instead of seeking a swift decision by 22 ....
Kt×Kt; 23 P×Kt, R—K7; 24 R—R2,
QB×P; 25 R×R, B×R, etc., the reason
being presumably shortness of time.

23 B—K3 Q—B3
24 R—B3 Kt—Q6
25 QR—KB1 R×B

Thinking that harvest time has come, but
more convincing is 25 .... R—K4 (threat:
26 .... R×Kt, etc.). As, however, the
sacrifice of the exchange is but temporary
and any exchanges favour Black's chances,
the text move should also lead to success.

26 Kt×R B—Q5

Against 26 .... Q—Kt3, which also is
powerful, White would have to defend himself as best he can by returning the exchange:
27 R×B.

27 Q—K7

Averting the worst, for if 27 QKt—Q1,
R—K1, and wins easily.

27 ...... Kt—K4
28 K—R1 Kt×R

After the optimistic 28 .... R—K1, there
would be an unpleasant surprise with
29 R×P, and the tables are turned!

29 R×Kt	R—KB1
30 P—R3	

Safety first! White avoids a plausible move in 30 Kt—B5, Black's staggering reply being 30 .... Q×R, etc.

30	B×Kt

This exchange, with which Black gives up the advantage of the "two Bishops," makes White's task of saving the game considerably less arduous. Much more *compelling* is 30 .... Q—QKt3.

31 Q×KB	Q—K3
32 R—Kt3	R—K1
33 Q—Kt5	Q—K4
34 Q×Q	R×Q
35 R—Kt4	R—K6
36 K—Kt1	

Not yet 36 R×P, e.g. 36 .... R×P ch; 37 K—Kt1, R—Kt6; 38 R—B7, R×P ch; 39 K—B1, R×P; 40 Kt—Kt5, B—R3; 41 R—R7, B×Kt ch; 42 P×B, P—Kt4; 43 R×RP, K—Kt2, with an easy win.

36	R—Q6
37 R×P	R—Q7
38 P—QKt4	R×P ch
39 K—B1	R—Kt7
40 R—Q4	

Not 40 R—B7, R×P; 41 Kt—Q5, R—Kt8 ch; 42 K—B2, P—Kt4, etc., and still less 40 P×P, B—R3; 41 Kt—Kt5, R×Kt, and wins.

40	P—Kt3

More effective would be 40 .... P—R4.

41 P×P	

The passed pawn becomes a valuable asset. A mistake, however, would be 41 P—Kt5, B—Kt7 ch, followed by .... B×P.

41	R—B7
42 Kt—Kt5	K—Kt2
43 K—K1	R—B4
44 R—Q6	B—B3
45 P—R6	

More chances of a draw arise, paradoxically, from 45 R—Q4, B×Kt; 46 P×B, R×P; 47 R—QR4, the Rook thus being posted *behind* the passed pawn.

45	B×Kt
46 P—R7	B—B3
47 R×B	R—QR4
48 R—B7	

See preceding note—the lateral protection of the pawn renders the Rook far less agile.

48	R×P (R5)
49 K—Q2	

Better first 49 P—R4, preventing Black's next move.

49	P—Kt4
50 K—B3	P—R4

A more methodical exploitation of the black mass of pawns consists in 50 .... P—R3, followed by .... K—Kt3; .... P—B4 and .... K—R4, etc.

51 K—Kt3	R—R8
52 K—B4	P—Kt5
53 P×P	P×P
54 K—Q4	K—Kt3

The crisis.

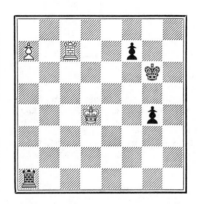

55 K—K5	

Curiously enough, 55 K—K3 affords White better chances of a draw (e.g. 55 .... P—B4; 56 K—B4, R—R5 ch; 57 K—Kt3, R—R6 ch; 58 K—B4, etc.).

55	P—B3 ch

By first "cutting off" the adverse King by 55 .... R—R5, Black would have had victory within his grasp. Now the fighting dies down.

56 K—B4	R—R5 ch
57 K—Kt3	P—B4

Or 57 .... K—Kt4; 58 R—Kt7 ch, K—B4; 59 K—R4, draw.

58 K—R4	K—B3
59 R—QKt7	

Draw.

73

White	Black
LASKER	RUBINSTEIN

(St. Petersburg, 1914)

There are Rook endings in which an advantage of one or even two pawns is not sufficient to ensure victory.

But here is an end-game, apparently simple and, after Black's 58th move, with equal material on either side, in which a seemingly unimportant feature turns the scale in White's favour.

1 P—K4	P—K4
2 Kt—KB3	Kt—QB3
3 B—Kt5	P—QR3
4 B—R4	Kt—B3
5 Castles	Kt × P
6 P—Q4	P—QKt4
7 B—Kt3	P—Q4
8 P × P	B—K3
9 P—B3	B—QB4

Avoiding the normal position of the open defence by 9 .... B—K2, Black decides to open out.

10 QKt—Q2
If 10 Q—Q3, Black avoids 10 .... Castles (because of 11 QKt—Q2, and he must give way in the centre), and plays 10 .... B—Kt3, so that he can reply to 11 QKt—Q2 by 11 .... Kt—B4, followed by 12 .... Kt × B, simplifying matters.

10	Castles
11 B—B2	Kt × Kt
12 Q × Kt	

After 12 B × Kt, the same reply by Black as in the text would have more vigour.

12	P—B3

This opening of the file weakens Black's base too much. Better would be 12 .... R—K1.

13 P × P   R × P
By playing 13 .... Q × P, Black would at any rate have prevented the reply in the text.

14 Kt—Q4
Simple and good. Against the more complicated 14 Kt—Kt5, Black has a satisfactory guard in 14 .... B—B4.

14	Kt × Kt

Relinquishing to his adversary the trump card of the open QB file, on which he will be able to exercise a lasting pressure.

15 P × Kt   B—Kt3
He would have obtained a larger share of the play by 15 .... B—Q3, etc.

16 P—QR4	R—Kt1
17 P × P	P × P
18 Q—B3	Q—Q3
19 B—K3	

Preventing 19 .... P—B4.

19	B—KB4
20 KR—B1	B × B
21 R × B	

A great end-game player, Dr. Lasker will know how to influence the whole future course of the game by his pressure on the QB file.

21	R—K1
22 QR—QB1	KR—K3
23 P—R3	R—K5
24 Q—Q2	QR—K3
25 R—B6	Q—Q2
26 R × R	Q × R
27 Q—Q3	Q—K1
28 Q—B3	K—B2
29 Q—Q3	K—Kt1
30 Q—B3	Q—K3
31 R—R1	Q—K1
32 K—B1	P—R3
33 Q—Q3	K—B2
34 R—B1	K—Kt1

The whole of this part of the game from move 27 to move 34 is characterised by waiting manœuvres.

35 Q—Kt3   Q—B2
36 R—Q1
It is clear that he cannot play 36 Q × KtP, on account of 36 .... R × B.

36	P—B3
37 P—B3	Q—B3
38 Q—Q3	R—K2
39 B—B2	Q—Q3
40 Q—B2	K—B2
41 R—B1	R—K3
42 Q—B5 ch	R—B3
43 Q—K5	

Obtaining either liquidation, scientifically prepared, or a gain in territory.

43	R—K3

He cannot play either 43 .... Q—Q2 (44 B—Kt3, etc.) nor, of course, 43 .... Q × Q (44 P × Q), and wins.

44 Q × Q	R × Q
45 K—K2	K—K2
46 K—Q3	R—Kt3
47 P—KKt3	R—B3
48 P—B4	K—Q2

If 48 .... P—Kt4; 49 B—K3.

49	R—K1	R—B1
50	R—QR1	P—R4

Threatening 51 .... P—R5.

51	B—K3	P—Kt3
52	R—KB1	K—Q3
53	P—KKt4	

The situation becomes clear: Black's pawn majority on the Q side is depreciated, but White is in a position to exploit his majority on the K side.

53	......	P×P
54	P×P	P—B4

More patient would be 54 .... K—K3.

55	P×P ch	B×P
56	B×B ch	K×B

In this seemingly dreary ending, White succeeds in producing a small masterpiece.

57	P—B5	P×P
58	P×P	R—B3
59	R—B4	

Placing his adversary under *Zugzwang*.

59	......	P—Kt5

If 59 .... K—Q3; 60 K—Q4, etc., and if 59 .... P—Q5; 60 K—K4, etc.

60	P—Kt3	R—B2

Or 60 .... R—B1; 61 P—B6, R—B2; 62 R—B1, K—Q3; 63 K—Q4, K—K3; 64 R—QR1, and wins.

61	P—B6	K—Q3
62	K—Q4	K—K3
63	R—B2	K—Q3

Liquidation by 63 .... R×P; 64 R×R ch, K×R; 65 K×P, etc., would produce a "book win" for White.

64	R—QR2	

A turning manœuvre.

64	......	R—B2
65	R—R6 ch	K—Q2
66	R—Kt6	Resigns.

74

White	Black
BURN	TARRASCH

(Ostend, 1907)

After lengthy consolidating manœuvres on either side, White succeeds in winning a well-merited pawn, after which Black's resistance quickly collapses. On the whole, a game won in simple but eloquent fashion.

1	P—K4	P—K4
2	Kt—KB3	Kt—QB3
3	B—Kt5	P—QR3
4	B—R4	Kt—B3
5	Castles	Kt×P
6	P—Q4	P—QKt4
7	B—Kt3	P—Q4
8	P—QR4	

White introduces an interesting interlude, instead of the classic move 8 P×P.

8	......	R—QKt1

After this instinctive reply, White obtains control of the QR file.

Useless would be 8 .... P—Kt5, as 9 P—R5 would disorganise his pawn formation, but the correct reply—unknown at the time this game was played—is 8 .... QKt×P; 9 Kt×Kt, P×Kt, with well-balanced positions. (This theoretical discovery enabled Schlechter to draw his championship match with Dr. Lasker in 1910.)

9	RP×P	RP×P
10	P×P	B—K3
11	P—B3	

Reminiscent of the classical line of development, this position yet ensures White's superiority, thanks to his control of the open QR file.

11	......	B—QB4

After 11 .... B—K2 a curious continuation occurred in a game, Romanowski-Flamberg (played in *Triberg*, 1915, in the Tournament for Interned Russians, organised by the British Chess Federation), namely: 12 B—K3, Castles; 13 R—R6, Q—Q2; 14 Kt—Q4, QKt×P; 15 Kt×B, P×Kt; 16 R×P, and Black resigned.

12	Q—Q3	

The simplest is 12 QKt—Q2, Castles; 13 B—B2.

12	......	B—Kt3

If 12 .... Castles; 13 QKt—Q2, whereas, after the text move, White has to cope with the threat 13 .... Kt—B4, followed by Kt×B.

13	B—B2	

Similarly, if 13 B—K3, there follows 13 .... Kt—B4; not of course 13 Q×KtP, on account of 13 .... B×P ch.

13	......	Castles
14	B—B4	

Well thought-out development! The hasty measure 14 QKt—Q2 would lose a pawn after 14 .... B—KB4; 15 Q—K2, Kt×QBP; 16 P×Kt, B×B.

14 ......   B—KB4
15 Q—K2   R—K1
16 B—Q3

Making a pretence of attacking Black's QKtP, but in reality striving at last to bring out his QKt.

16 ......   Kt—Q3
If 16 .... P—Kt5; 17 P—B4.

17 B×B   Kt×B
18 Q—Q3   Q—Q2
19 QKt—Q2

A belated completion of White's concentric development, but all the more effective.

19 ......   Kt (B4)—K2
20 KR—K1   Kt—Kt3
21 B—Kt3   Kt—R4
22 P—Kt3

Simple moves by White, which constrain Black's attacking propensities, show that his development is far more natural.

22 ......   P—Kt5
Evidently not 22 .... P—QB3 (23 P—K6), but 22 .... QR—Q1 also would prove troublesome for Black after 23 Kt—Q4, etc.

23 P—B4
Decisive. There is a double threat not only to win a pawn by 24 P×P, but also a piece by 24 P—B5.

23 ......   Kt—Kt2
Played in the hope of recovering his pawn; otherwise he would have preferred, after all, to give up the exchange for a pawn by 23 .... P—QB3; 24 P—K6, etc.

24 P×P   KR—Q1
25 P—Q6   B—B4
Or 25 .... P×P; 26 Kt—B4.

26 Kt—B4   P×P
27 P×P   Q—B3
The QP can still not be taken: if 27 .... Kt×P; 28 Kt×Kt, B×Kt; 29 B×B, Q×B; 30 R—K8 ch, Kt—B1 (30 .... R×R; 31 Q×Q); 31 Q×Q, R×Q; 32 R×R.

28 QR—Q1   R—Q2
This prevents 29 P—Q7, but loses the exchange. However, after 28 .... R—R1; 29 P—Q7, there is no defence.

29 KKt—K5   Kt×Kt
30 Kt×Kt   Resigns

75

White	Black
MARÓCZY	BERGER

(Vienna, 1908)

One plausible but unfortunate move by the King (10 K—B1, instead of 10 K—R1), and a débâcle becomes inevitable.

1 P—K4   P—K4
2 Kt—KB3   Kt—QB3
3 B—Kt5   P—QR3
4 B—R4   Kt—B3
5 Castles   Kt×P
6 P—Q4   P×P
Instead of the classical 6 .... P—QKt4, Black takes the risk of opening the K file.

7 R—K1   P—Q4
8 Kt×P
With the double threat of 9 P—KB3 and 9 Kt×Kt.

8 ......   B—Q3
Staging a sacrificial variation. This most ingenious, if not quite correct, turn was thought out in 1906 by experts in Riga, and is therefore called the *Riga Variation*.

9 Kt×Kt   B×P ch
10 K—B1
A false step! Acceptance of the sacrifice, it is true, would quickly lead to a draw by perpetual check (10 K×B, Q—R5 ch; 11 K—Kt1, Q×P ch; 12 K—R1, Q—R5 ch, etc.), but by fearlessly playing 10 K—R1 White could gradually overcome the fury of the attack, as follows: 10 .... Q—R5; 11 R×Kt (essential); 11 .... P×R; 12 Q—Q8 ch (down to earth again!); 12 .... Q×Q; 13 Kt×Q dis ch, K×Kt; 14 K×B, and although a correct estimate is difficult to form, White has the material advantage, and his pieces will play a predominant part in the middle game.

10 ......   Q—R5
He threatens mate. Nor need he fear the liquidation given in the preceding note (in the event of 10 K—R1), as his KB is not now *en prise*.

11 B—K3
By playing 11 Kt—Q4 dis ch, he could have a defensive *tempo* of no little importance.

11 ......   Castles
12 Kt—Q4   B—Kt5
13 Kt—KB3
At last bringing back a defender to

the critical sector. After 13 P—KB3,
Kt—Kt6 ch; 14 K—B2, B—R4, the white
king would remain in a trap.

| 13 ...... | Q—R4 |
| 14 Kt—B3 | QR—Q1 |

Defending and attacking at the same time.
This Rook is to play an important part in
coming events.

| 15 Q—Q3 | B×Kt |
| 16 P×B | Q×P |

Threatening 17 .... Kt—Kt6 mate.

17 Kt×Kt	P×Kt
18 Q—B3	Q—R6 ch
19 K—K2	Q—Kt5 ch
20 K—B1	R—Q4
21 B—Kt3	R—KR4

With the unanswerable threat of 22 ....
B—K4 and 23 .... R—R8 mate.

| 22 P—B4 | P×P e p |
| Resigns | |

(23 Q—Q2, Q—R6 ch; 24 K—B2,
Q—Kt7 mate.)

76

| White | Black |
| *SCHLECHTER* | *SALWE* |

(St. Petersburg, 1909)

*The "fireworks" which White produces in
the following game are most remarkable, in
that they result from purely positional play,
after a quiet and uneventful development.*

1 P—K4	P—K4
2 Kt—KB3	Kt—QB3
3 B—Kt5	P—QR3
4 B—R4	Kt—B3

Premature would be 4 .... P—QKt4;
5 B—Kt3, Kt—B3 (if 5 .... Kt—R4;
6 B×P ch); 6 Kt—Kt5, P—Q4; 7 P×P,
Kt×P; 8 Kt×BP (the *Spanish Fegatello*);
8 .... K×Kt; 9 Q—B3 ch, K—K3;
10 Kt—B3, Kt—K2 (if 10 .... Kt—Kt5;
11 P—QR3, winning back the piece without
delay); 11 P—Q4, etc., with a ruthless attack.

| 5 Castles | B—K2 |

Compared to the "open defence," of
which we have seen examples in the preceding games, this, the "closed defence,"
imparts an entirely different character to
the game.

Here again 5 .... P—QKt4; 6 B—Kt3,
B—K2 would be over-hasty, as White now
has an opportunity for a wing attack by
7 P—QR4.

| 6 R—K1 | P—QKt4 |

As can easily be ascertained, he cannot
play 6 .... Castles, as he would then lose
a pawn without any compensation by
7 B×Kt, QP×B; 8 Kt×P. But 6 ....
P—Q3 is playable.

| 7 B—Kt3 | P—Q3 |
| 8 P—B3 | |

Not only in order to prepare the advance
P—Q4 eventually, but also—and principally
—to preserve the "Spanish Bishop."

8	Kt—QR4
9 B—B2	P—B4
10 P—Q3	

Instead of this, 10 P—Q4 looks more
energetic, but there is method in the text
move: the QKt is to be brought into play
via Q2—B1—K3, before bringing pressure
to bear on the centre by 20 P—Q4.

| 10 ...... | Kt—B3 |

An alternative plan is 10 .... Castles, to
be followed, in due course, by .... Kt—K1
and .... P—B4.

11 QKt—Q2
After another waiting move such as
11 P—KR3, Black could already obtain the
initiative by 11 .... Castles; 12 QKt—Q2,
P—Q4, etc.

| 11 ...... | Castles |

Even here 11 .... P—Q4 could be played,
but Black does not as yet wish to commit
himself.

12 Kt—B1
After 12 Q—K2, Black would not at once
play 12 .... P—Q4 (13 P×P, followed by
14 Kt×P, and White wins a pawn), but, as
a preliminary, 12 .... R—K1.

| 12 ...... | Q—B2 |

This move, as would 12 .... R—K1,
indirectly guards the KP, and has the intention of preparing the thrust .... P—Q4,
this move being the normal reaction against
White's expectative 10 P—Q3.

13 B—Kt5
Tactically the text move prevents 13 ....
P—Q4; in view of 14 B×Kt.

| 13 ...... | Kt—K1 |

Or 13 .... R—Q1; 14 Kt—K3 and, again
just in time, 14 .... P—Q4 is prevented.

14 Kt—K3	B × B
15 Kt × B	Kt—K2
16 P—QR4	R—QKt1
17 P × P	P × P
18 Q—Q2	P—R3
19 Kt—B3	B—K3
20 P—Q4	

The opening up of the centre at last!

20	Kt—KB3
21 R—R6	R—R1
22 P × KP	

Ingenious as this offer of the exchange undoubtedly is, Black could have rendered it nugatory by 22 .... Kt × P; 23 B × Kt, R × R, etc.

22	R × R
23 P × Kt	P × P

Now, however, the black King's compromised position is in White's favour.

24 Kt—Q5	B × Kt
25 P × B	K—Kt2
26 Kt—R4	

Threatening 27 R × Kt.

26	R—K1
27 P—R3	Q—Q1
28 R—K3	Kt—Kt3
29 Kt—B5 ch	K—B1

Try as he may, the black King is unable to leave the danger zone.

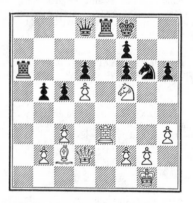

30 R—K6
A brilliant unmasking manœuvre.

30 ......　　　　　R × R
Not 30.... P × R; because of mate in two.

31 P × R
The check can wait, as Black can play neither 31 .... P × P; nor even 31 ....

Q—K1 (in each case on account of 32 Q × P ch).

31	P—Q4
32 Q × P ch	K—K1
33 P × P ch	K × P
34 Q—R7 ch	K—K3
35 Q × Kt	R—R7

Fighting now for a lost cause.

36 P—QKt4
A pretty defence by displacement, which increases White's control of territory.

36 ......　　　　　P × P
If 36 .... R × B; 37 Kt—Kt7 ch, followed by Q × R.

37 Kt—Q4 ch　　　K—Q2
A tragi-comedy would be 37 .... K—K4; 38 Q—Kt3 mate.

38 B—B5 ch　　　Resigns.

77

White	*Black*
ALEKHINE	ELISKASES

(Podjebrad, 1936)

In this game we can ascertain that, para-doxical as it may seem, the advance of the QP in two stages (10 P—Q3 and 16 P—Q4) can prove more energetic than the double step (10 P—Q4).

1 P—K4	P—K4
2 Kt—KB3	Kt—QB3
3 B—Kt5	P—QR3
4 B—R4	Kt—B3
5 Castles	B—K2

This closed treatment of the *Ruy Lopez* forms a link between old-time conceptions (combinative play, war of movement, sacrifices) and the modern outlook (positional play, trench warfare, manœuvring).

6 R—K1	P—QKt4
7 B—Kt3	P—Q3
8 P—B3	Kt—QR4
9 B—B2	P—B4
10 P—Q3	

If a great player decided on this rather passive-looking move, in preference to the immediate thrust 10 P—Q4, it must be on account of its latent potentialities.

10 ......   Kt—B3
Having outgrown its usefulness on the
edge of the board, the Knight returns to co-
operate in the centre. Thus the over-
protection of the KP will already allow the
thrust 11 .... P—Q4; 12 P×P, Q×P, etc.

11 QKt—Q2   Castles
This is sounder than 11 .... P—Q4, after
all, for 12 P×P, Q×P; 13 P—Q4 would be
troublesome for Black.

12 Kt—B1   R—K1
With this indirect defence of his KP,
Black continues his preparations for the
coming thrust P—Q4.

13 Kt—K3   P—Q4
Showing at any rate a spirit of consistency. One might think that Black's
emancipation is proceeding apace.

14 P×P   Kt×P
15 Kt×Kt   Q×Kt
16 P—Q4
This belated opening up of the centre
proves powerful.

16 ......   KP×P
17 B—K4   Q—Q2
18 P×P   B—B3
Thinking there is still time for manœuvring, whereas he should at once complete his mobilisation by 18 .... B—Kt2.

19 B—Kt5
A decisive conquest of territory.

19 ......   R×B
He is practically compelled to give up the
exchange, as, after 19 .... B×B; 20 Kt×B,
P—R3; 21 Q—R5, his position would be
most precarious.

20 R×R   B×P
21 Kt×B   Kt×Kt
22 Q—R5
White's attack is fast gaining in vigour.

22 ......   B—Kt2
It goes without saying that the reply to
22 .... P—R3 would be the sacrifice
23 B×P, P×B; 24 Q×RP, etc.

23 R—R4   Q—B4
24 B—K3
A very effective retreating manœuvre,
which, after the exchange of Queens, leads
to a won end-game, e.g.: 24 .... Q×Q;
25 R×Q, Kt—B7; 26 R—Q1, Kt×B;
27 P×Kt.

24 ......   R—Q1
In avoiding the Scylla of a lost ending,
Black falls into the Charybdis of a nasty
surprise. In his optimism he only reckoned
with 25 Q×Q, Kt×Q; 26 R—R5, P—Kt3,
etc., when, with his Rook on an open file,
he could still struggle on.

25 R×Kt
A crushing blow—Black resigns.

78

White	Black
CAPABLANCA	*VIDMAR*

(New York, 1927)

*A temporary sacrifice (16 KKt×P) infuses
fresh energy into the fight—in spite of all the
immediate and ulterior simplifying manœuvres which occur in this game.*

1 P—K4	P—K4
2 Kt—KB3	Kt—QB3
3 B—Kt5	P—QR3
4 B—R4	Kt—B3
5 Castles	B—K2
6 R—K1	P—QKt4
7 B—Kt3	P—Q3
8 P—B3	Kt—QR4
9 B—B2	P—B4
10 P—Q4	

Energetic as this advance appears to be,
it still leaves many arduous problems in the
centre for White to solve.

10 ......   Q—B2
It must be conceded that Black, by his
last three moves, has established a well-
balanced position with counter-chances on
the Q side (*Tchigorin's System*).

11 QKt—Q2
A purely developing move, which is
adopted more frequently than 11 P—QR4
or 11 P—KR3.
Against 11 P—Q5 Black could initiate an
immediate counter-action on the Q side by
11 .... B—Q2, followed by .... P—Kt5,
etc.

11 ......   Castles
By playing at once 11 .... Kt—B3 or,
more effectively still, 11 .... B—Kt5, Black
—by his pressure on Q4—could challenge
his opponent to a decision in the centre

12 P—KR3

Seeing that Black has not put his whole energy into the localised fight around Q4, White seizes the opportunity of making a sound precautionary move, instead of speeding up the development of his pieces by 12 Kt—B1.

12 ......   Kt—B3

Insisting on having it out in the centre. An attempt to transfer the centre of gravity of the contest to the open QB file (12 .... BP×P; 13 P×P, B—Q2; 14 Kt—B1, KR—B1) would be countered by 15 B—Q3.

13 P—Q5

The crucial point. As White does not wish to simplify matters too much by 13 P×KP, P×P, etc., and as 13 Kt—B1 would mean a speculative sacrifice of a pawn after 13 .... BP×P; 14 P×P, QKt×P; 15 Kt×Kt, P×Kt, etc., White decides to close up the centre.

13 ......   Kt—Q1

The retreat 13 .... Kt—Kt1 would be more laborious.

14 P—QR4

Instead of 14 Kt—B1, continuing the Knight's peregrinations, White interpolates an interesting episode.

14 ......   P—Kt5

He abandons the square at QB4 to his adversary, in preference to giving up to him the open QR file by 14 .... R—Kt1; 15 P×P, P×P, etc.

15 Kt—B4   P—QR4

Had Black foreseen his opponent's beautiful reply, he would have anticipated it by 15 .... Kt—Kt2, upon which White would complete the development of his forces by 16 B—Kt5.

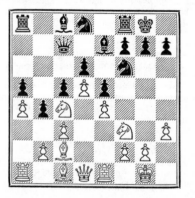

16 KKt×P

A temporary sacrifice, as elegant as it is unexpected. Its object is the purely positional one of effecting exchanges favourable to White.

16 ......   B—R3
17 B—Kt3   P×Kt
18 P—Q6   B×P
19 Q×B

And not 19 Kt×B, because of 19 .... P—B5.

19 ......   Q×Q
20 Kt×Q   Kt—Kt2
21 Kt×Kt   B×Kt
22 P×P   BP×P

Here, however, 22 .... RP×P would afford more chances of counter-action.

23 P—B3

Securing his base.

23 ......   KR—Q1
24 B—K3

After the considerable clearance of the battlefield, White can show a substantial positional advantage in his two well-placed Bishops.

24 ......   P—R3
25 KR—Q1   B—B3
26 QR—B1   B—K1
27 K—B2   R×R
28 R×R   R—B1

Curiously enough, although posted on an open file, this Rook has no future there.

29 P—Kt4

A methodical blockade.

29 ......   B—Q2

If 29 .... Kt—Q2; 30 R—Q5.

30 B—Kt6   B—K3
31 B×B   P×B
32 R—Q8 ch

Cleverly conceived liquidation. In the duel of the Bishop against the Knight, the latter will not be swift enough.

32 ......   R×R
33 B×R   Kt—Q2
34 B×P   Kt—B4
35 P—Kt3

A final *finesse*, deflecting the Knight's itinerary.

35 ......   Kt×KtP
36 B×P   Kt—Q5
37 P—R5   Resigns

37 .... Kt—B3; 38 P—R6, followed by B—B5 and P—R7.)

A game of discreet but telling manœuvres.

79

White	Black
ALEKHINE	FINE

(Hastings, 1937)

We see here a purely positional pawn sacrifice (14 Q × B), borne of unbounded trust in the dynamic possibilities of the position. The results are surprisingly crushing.

1	P—K4	P—K4
2	Kt—KB3	Kt—QB3
3	B—Kt5	P—QR3
4	B—R4	Kt—B3
5	Castles	B—K2
6	R—K1	P—QKt4
7	B—Kt3	P—Q3
8	P—B3	Kt—QR4
9	B—B2	P—B4
10	P—Q4	Q—B2
11	QKt—Q2	

A Knight with a future.

11	......	Castles
12	Kt—B1	

With a pawn sacrifice in view, which will vitalise the position to a greater degree than would either 12 P—Q5 or 12 P—KR3.

12	......	B—Kt5

In quest of loot; it would have been more prudent to play 12 .... Kt—B3 or 12 .... BP × P; 13 P × P, Kt—B3.

13	Kt—K3	

Here again White had a solid continuation in 13 P—Q5, but he prefers to embark on bigger and bolder plans.

13	......	B × Kt
14	Q × B	

Complementary to the two preceding moves. Otherwise, 14 P × B is also playable.

14	......	BP × P
15	Kt—B5	

Establishing an outpost, thanks to the absence of the hostile QB.

15	......	P × P
16	Q × P	

The white Queen continues to take the most active part in the struggle. It is clear that Black cannot play 16 .... Q × Q, because of the intermediate 17 Kt × B ch, winning a piece.

16	......	KR—B1
17	Q—KKt3	B—B1

Again, if 17 .... P—Kt3; 18 B—Q3, preserving the "two Bishops." And if 17 .... Kt—R4; 18 Q—Kt4.

18	B—Q3	Kt—B3
19	B—Kt5	Kt—K1
20	QR—B1	

Still more useful would have been, at once, 20 QR—Q1, e.g. 20 .... P—Kt3; 21 B—Kt1, Q—Kt2; 22 Kt—R6 ch, etc., with advantage to White.

20	......	Q—Kt2

Threatening large-scale simplification by 21 .... Kt—Kt5. The expedition 20 .... Q—R4 turns out badly, because of 21 Kt—R6 ch, K—R1 (21 .... P × Kt; 22 B—Q2 dis ch); 22 Kt × P ch, K—Kt1; 23 Kt—R6 ch, K—R1; 24 Q—B3, Kt—B2; 25 Q—B7, Kt—K2 (or 25 .... P × Kt; 26 B—B6 ch, followed by mate); 26 Q—Kt8 ch, Kt × Q; 27 Kt—B7 smothered mate!

21	P—QR3	P—Kt3

Seeking to relieve the stranglehold, for now White must declare his intentions at once, because of the threat 22 .... P × Kt; 23 B—B6 dis ch, B—Kt2, etc.

22	Kt—R6 ch	B × Kt
23	B × B	Kt—Q5
24	QR—Q1	P—Kt5

Black's activities on the Q side are becoming disquieting.

25	P—B4	

For which reason White must hasten to open lines of attack.

25	......	P × BP
26	Q × P	P × P
27	P × P	R—B6
28	Q—B2	Kt—K3

After 28 .... Kt—QB3, White would increase the scope of his temporarily blocked KB by 29 P—K5, P × P; 30 B—K4, etc.

29	P—QR4	QR—B1
30	R—KB1	KR—B2

Not so much an error of judgment as a lack of confidence in his own means of defence.

More resourceful would have been 30 .... QR—B2, leaving the other Rook within the enemy's camp and forcing him to look after his KB.

31	R—Kt1	

Henceforth White is master of the field.

31	......	Q—B3

If 31 .... Q—R2; 32 B—K3.

32 P—R5   Kt—B4

Otherwise there follows 33 R—Kt6.

33 B—QB4   Q—Q2
34 Q—R2

This fine manœuvre makes White's attack unanswerable.

34 ......   Kt×P

The defence by 34 .... Kt—K3 is illusory, on account of the splendid turn, 35 B × Kt, Q × B; 36 Q × Q, P × Q; 37 R—B8 mate.

35 R×P   Q×R
36 B×Q ch   R×B
37 Q—K6

The final point. White wins another piece.

37 ......   Resigns.

80

White   *Black*

RAUZER   RIUMIN

(Leningrad, 1936)

The manner in which White turns to account his attack on the opposing King's field is as original as it is instructive.

1 P—K4   P—K4
2 Kt—KB3   Kt—QB3
3 B—Kt5   P—QR3
4 B—R4   Kt—B3
5 Castles   B—K2
6 R—K1   P—QKt4
7 B—Kt3   P—Q3
8 P—B3   Kt—QR4
9 B—B2   P—B4
10 P—Q4

An impetuous advance, undertaken by White in the full consciousness of the responsibilities which the desire for an immediate initiative brings in its train.

10 ......   Q—B2
11 QKt—Q2   Kt—B3

Instead of the non-committal 11 .... Castles, Black starts a local engagement around the enemy QP.

A doubtful counter-measure would be 11 .... BP×P; 12 P×P, Kt—B3; 13 P—Q5,

Kt—QKt5; 14 B—Kt1, P—QR4; 15 Kt—B1, and while Black's action on the open QB file would soon reach a dead-end, White's play on the K side would be full of promise.

However, Black has a perfectly sound continuation here in 11 .... B—Kt5, which would have the same object as the move in the text, namely, that of exercising pressure on White's centre.

12 P—QR4

An interesting interlude. Other continuations which have to be considered are:

(*a*) 12 P—Q5, locking the centre, but preparing, after Kt—B1, P—KR3, P—KKt4, Kt—Kt3, K—R2, R—KKt1, etc., a slow but enduring K side attack.

(*b*) 12 P × KP, P × P, simplifying the game.

(*c*) 12 Kt—B1, offering a temporary sacrifice of a pawn by 12 .... BP×P; 13 P×P, QKt×P; 14 Kt×Kt, P×Kt; 15 B—Kt5, and White will soon regain his pawn with the better game.

(*d*) 12 P—KR3, Castles; 13 Kt—B1. But now the pawn sacrifice is of doubtful value, as Black would be able, without too much inconvenience, to conserve his extra pawn.

12 ......   R—QKt1

Or 12 .... P—Kt5; 13 Kt—B4, threatening 14 P—R5, to White's advantage.

13 P × KtP   P × KtP
14 P × BP

Instead of the moves mentioned before (14 P—Q5 or 14 Kt—B1), White decides on this simplification in the centre, hoping to liven up the game after Kt—B1—K3, by posting this Knight at Q5, or, as in the game, at KB5.

14 ......   P×P
15 Kt—B1   B—K3
16 Kt—K3   Castles
17 Kt—Kt5   KR—Q1
18 Q—B3   R—Q3

He underrates the enemy's plan, adumbrated in the preceding note. Otherwise he would have rendered both critical squares inaccessible by 18 .... P—R3; 19 Kt×B, P×Kt, with equal chances.

19 Kt—B5

Too dangerous a scout to be left unchallenged.

19 ......   B×Kt
20 P×B

Instead of allowing the tension to be

relaxed by 20 Q×B, Q—Q2, etc., White
infuses new energy into the game.

20	P—R3
21 Kt—K4	Kt×Kt
22 B×Kt	B—B3
23 B—K3	Kt—K2
24 P—QKt4	

Widening the scope of the QB.

24	P—B5
25 P—Kt3	R—Q2
26 R—R7	Q—Q1
27 R×R	Q×R
28 P—R4	K—R1

Thinking that there is no assault by
pawns to be feared.

29 P—Kt4
As Black is unable to play 29 .... B×P,
on the score of 30 Q—R3, B—B3; 31 P—Kt5,
winning the Bishop, the White pawn phalanx
acquires, thanks to this tactical detail, a
formidable impetus.

| 29 ...... | Kt—Kt1 |

Affording a retreat for the threatened
Bishop.

30 P—Kt5
The assault continues.

30	B—K2
31 R—Q1	Q—B2
32 P—B6	

The assault strikes home.

| 32 ...... | B×BP |

A sad necessity, for if 32 .... P×BP;
33 Q—B5, K—Kt2; 34 P×RP ch, K—B1;
35 P—R7, K—Kt2; 36 P—R8 (Q) ch, K×Q;
37 Q—R7 mate.

33 P×B	Kt×P
34 B—B2	R—Q1
35 B×P	

This fresh spitefulness had to be calculated to a nicety.

35	R×R ch
36 B×R	P—K5
37 B—B4	

But not 37 Q—B5, because of 37 ....
Q—Q3; 38 B—K2, P×B. Now it is all
over.

| 37 ...... | Q—Q1 |
| 38 Q—K2 | Resigns. |

81

| *White* | *Black* |
| KERES | RESHEVSKY |

(Stockholm, 1937)

*The following game has been named the
"Jewel of the Stockholm Olympiad of 1937."
Black makes sustained efforts to prevail, first
on the QB file and then on the K file; but
White—sure of his ground—demonstrates in
the end, first by the temporary sacrifice
22 Kt—KB5 and then by the real sacrifice
29 B×KtP, that the main battlefield is the
K side.*

1 P—K4	P—K4
2 Kt—KB3	Kt—QB3
3 B—Kt5	P—QR3
4 B—R4	Kt—B3
5 Castles	B—K2
6 R—K1	P—QKt4
7 B—Kt3	P—Q3
8 P—B3	Kt—QR4
9 B—B2	P—B4
10 P—Q4	Q—B2
11 P—QR4	

This interlude, in place of the more usual
11 QKt—Q2, carries the threat of 12 RP×P,
RP×P; 13 P—QKt4.

| 11 ...... | P—Kt5 |

A playable continuation is 11 ....
R—QKt1, for if White were greedily to
snatch a pawn by 12 RP×P, RP×P;
13 P×KP, P×P; 14 Kt×P, Q×Kt;
15 R×Kt, then Black, with 15 .... Kt—Kt5,
would suddenly be able to counter-attack.

12 P×KtP
After 12 QKt—Q2, Castles, the games are
even.

| 12 ...... | P×KtP |
| 13 P—R3 | |

It is necessary to prevent the troublesome
sortie 13 .... B—Kt5, for Black would
obtain the initiative after 13 P—QKt3,
B—Kt5; 14 P—Q5, Castles; 15 B—Q3 (or
15 QKt—Q2, KR—B1); 15 .... Kt—Q2.

| 13 ...... | Castles |

If at this stage 13 .... Kt—Q2 (aimed
against 14 B—Kt5), then 14 P—QKt3,
B—Kt2; 15 B—Kt2 would enable White to
exert pressure in the centre.

14 QKt—Q2
Of little value here would be 14 B—Kt5,
on account of 14 .... R—K1; 15 QKt—Q2,
Kt—Q2, easily coping with the pin.

14 ......   B—K3

More ambitious than 14 .... B—Q2.
The idea is to provoke 15 P—Q5, B—Q2,
after which the threats in the centre would
no longer obtain.

15 Kt—B1   KR—B1
16 Kt—K3

Arriving just in time to rescue the exposed
KB.

16 ......   P—Kt3

Preparing a more enterprising use of the
KKt than would be 16 .... Kt—K1. If
at once 16 .... Kt—R4, then 17 P—Q5,
B—Q2; 18 Kt×P, winning a pawn.

17 P—QKt3   Kt—R4
18 B—Kt2   B—B3
19 QR—B1

The hostile pressure on the open QB file
is mastered at last. White now threatens
20 P×P, P×P; 21 Kt—Q5, B×Kt; 22 P×B,
winning the opposing KP.

19 ......   P×P

Thus the skirmish around Q4 terminates
in White's favour. If 19 .... Kt—KB5;
20 Kt—Q5.

20 Kt×P

Avoiding the trap 20 B×P, B×KtP.

20 ......   Q—Q2

Threatening the sacrifice 21 .... B×RP;
22 P×B, Q×KRP; 23 Q—B3, Q×Q;
24 Kt×Q, B×B.

21 R—Kt1

Now White's QB is no longer "in the air."

21 ......   R—B4

Who has the initiative?

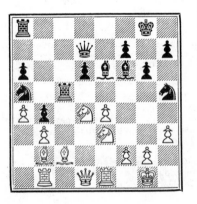

22 Kt (Q4)—B5

Thanks to this temporary sacrifice, the
game assumes a fresh and energetic turn.
White threatens 23 Kt×P.

22 ......   B×Kt

After 22 .... P×Kt, White has the choice
of two good continuations, as follows:
23 P×P or 23 Q×Kt, P×P (23 .... P—B5;
24 P—K5); 24 Q—R6, B×B; 25 B×P,
P—B4; 26 B×R, etc.

23 P×B

But not 23 Kt×B, because of 23 ....
R×B.

23 ......   B×B
24 R×B   R—K1
25 B—Q3

Another good continuation would be, at
once, 25 Q—Kt4, with the double threat
26 P×P and Q×P.

25 ......   Q—B3
26 Q—Kt4   Q—Kt3

He could have attempted 26 .... R—B6;
27 Q×P, R×B; 28 Q×Kt, Kt—B5;
29 Q—Kt4, R—K5, etc. But White has
a better continuation in 27 R—B2, R×Kt;
28 KR×R, R×R; 29 B×R, Q×B;
30 Q—Q4, etc.; or again, 27 R—Q1, R×B;
28 R×R, Q—B8 ch; 29 Kt—Q1, R—K8 ch;
30 K—R2, R×Kt; 31 Q×R, Q×R;
32 R×P, etc.

And if 26 .... R—B8; 27 QR—K2.

27 QR—K2   QR—K4

Or 27 .... Kt—KKt2; 28 Kt—Q5, R×R;
29 Kt—B6 ch, K—R1; 30 R×R, KKt×P;
31 R—K8 ch, K—Kt2; 32 Q—Kt5, with
a double mating threat 33 R—Kt8 or
33 Kt—R5.

28 P×P   RP×P
29 B×KtP

A correct sacrifice.

29 ......   P×B
30 Q×P ch   K—R1

After 30 .... Kt—Kt2 there follows
prettily 31 Kt—B5, Q—B2; 32 Kt×Kt,
Q×Kt; 33 Q×R ch, and wins.

The best defence would be 30 ....
K—B1, upon which White—far from
remaining satisfied with a perpetual check—
would still play for a win with 31 Kt—Q5,
Q—B4; 32 R×R, R×R; 33 R×R, P×R;
34 Q—B5 ch, K—Kt1; 35 Q×P, and
Black's position is still most precarious in
spite of his extra piece.

31 Kt—B5
There is no defence against this hammer-blow.

| 31 ...... | R (K1)—K3 |

After 31 .... R × R, White mates in three.

32	Q × Kt ch	K—Kt1
33	Q—Kt5 ch	K—B1
34	Q—Kt7 ch	K—K1
35	Kt × P ch	

A most elegant finish!

| 35 ...... | Resigns. |

82

White	Black
AITKEN	RESHEVSKY

(Stockholm, 1937)

During the whole course of this game White seeks and scorns danger, without, however, succeeding in breaking down a tenacious and inventive defence.

1	P—K4	P—K4
2	Kt—KB3	Kt—QB3
3	B—Kt5	P—QR3
4	B—R4	Kt—B3
5	Castles	B—K2
6	R—K1	P—QKt4
7	B—Kt3	P—Q3
8	P—B3	Kt—QR4
9	B—B2	P—B4
10	P—Q4	Q—B2
11	P—KR3	

If 11 QKt—Q2 is more incisive, 11 P—QR4 bolder, and 11 P—Q5 more circumspect, the move in the text is perfectly sound.

| 11 ...... | Castles |

A noncommittal reply, which is the most widely used.   Other possible continuations are 11 .... B—Q2, followed by .... R—QB1, bearing on the Q side, or 11 .... Kt—B3 on the centre, or even 11 .... P—Kt4 on the K side.

| 12 | QKt—Q2 | Kt—B3 |
| 13 | P—Q5 | |

He decides to block the centre, in order to concentrate on the K side.   Other playable lines are 13 P—QR4 or 13 Kt—B1, with the positional sacrifice of a pawn.

| 13 ...... | Kt—Q1 |

A playable alternative is 13 .... Kt—Kt1.

| 14 | Kt—B1 | |

Without interpolating the interesting episode 14 P—QR4, White unwaveringly pursues the object he has set himself by the preceding move: a direct K side attack.

| 14 ...... | Kt—K1 |

Black's counter-play aims at effecting the counter-thrust .... P—B4.

| 15 | P—KKt4 | |

Preventing, as it does, the enemy threat, this move is more energetic than 15 Kt—Kt3.

| 15 ...... | P—Kt3 |
| 16 | B—R6 | |

Or at once 16 Kt—Kt3.

| 16 ...... | Kt—KKt2 |
| 17 | Kt—Kt3 | P—B3 |

There is a great deal of resistance in the "hedgehog position" which Black has adopted.

| 18 | K—R1 | |

More cautious than 18 K—R2.

| 18 ...... | Kt—B2 |
| 19 | B—K3 | |

The retreat 19 B—Q2 is also not without its uses.

| 19 ...... | K—R1 |
| 20 | R—KKt1 | |

This trench warfare demands lengthy preparations.

20	B—Q2
21	Q—K2	P—B5
22	Kt—Q2	

Another resilient retreat would be 22 Kt—R2.   If 22 Kt—R4, P—B4.

22	R—KKt1
23	R—Kt2	QR—KB1
24	P—B3	

The impetuous advance 24 P—B4 would only benefit Black, who, after 24 .... P × P; 25 B × P, Kt—K4, would have a Knight established on a strong square.

| 24 ...... | Q—B1 |

As for Black, he still seeks to advance his BP, in order to clear up matters, and he succeeds in doing so.

| 25 | QR—KKt1 | P—B4 |

Changing over from trench warfare to a war of movement.

26 Kt × KBP

A brilliant conception. Instead of indulging in an exhaustive liquidation, commencing with 26 KtP × P, etc., White, by this positional sacrifice of a piece for two pawns, seeks to gain the initiative.

| 26 ...... | P × Kt |
| 27 KP × P | Kt × P |

He hastens to give back the piece, as otherwise the white pawn-mass would become overwhelming, e.g. 27 .... Kt—K1; 28 Kt—K4, etc.

28 P × Kt	B × P
29 R × R ch	R × R
30 R × R ch	K × R
31 Q—Kt2 ch	K—B1
32 B × B	Q × B

Here is the grand liquidation after all. Black relies on the many weak points which will remain in the white camp.

33 Kt—K4

But the radiation of this Knight makes up for all weaknesses—White stands better.

33	P—KR4
34 K—R2	Q—R2
35 Q—Q2	Kt—R1
36 B—Kt5	Q—B4
37 B × B ch	K × B
38 Q—KB2	

After 38 Q—Kt5 ch, Q × Q; 39 Kt × Q, Kt—B2, etc., Black's King would be better placed for future events, whereas, with the Queens on the board, the ending is still full of life. Mr. Aitken seems to be an expert in the art of "living dangerously."

38	Kt—B2
39 Q—R7 ch	K—B1
40 Q—Kt8 ch	

Clearly not 40 Q × P, Q × BP, to Black's advantage.

40	K—Kt2
41 K—Kt2	Q—B5
42 Q—R7	Q—B8

Each Queen is set on doing as much damage as possible.

43 Kt × P

If 43 Q—B2, Q—Q8.

43	Q—Q7 ch
44 K—B1	Q × QP
45 Kt—K4	P—R5
46 Q—B2	Q—Q8 ch
47 K—Kt2	Q—Q1
48 Q—R7	Q—Q6
49 Q—B2	Q—Kt8
50 Q × P	

It must be conceded that in this duel of the two Amazons each player courageously seizes upon every chance.

50	Q × P ch
51 K—Kt3	K—B1
52 Q—B6	Q—B8
53 Q × RP	Q—Kt8 ch
54 K—R4	Q—K6
55 Q—B8 ch	K—Kt2
56 Q—Kt4 ch	K—B1
57 Q—B8 ch	

Although White might have tried with 57 Q—B5, etc., to exploit the advantage he has acquired, he considers Black's resources to be sufficient to obtain a draw, and therefore himself puts an end to hostilities.

| 57 ...... | K—Kt2 |

Draw.

83

White	Black
TEICHMANN	SCHLECHTER

(Carlsbad, 1911)

Here we have one of the finest examples of what the "Spanish Bishop" can achieve in the so-called "close defence" of the Ruy Lopez.

1 P—K4	P—K4
2 Kt—KB3	Kt—QB3
3 B—Kt5	P—QR3
4 B—R4	Kt—B3
5 Castles	B—K2
6 R—K1	P—QKt4
7 B—Kt3	P—Q3
8 P—B3	Castles

In preference to deciding at once on manœuvres on a wing by 8 .... Kt—QR4 or 8 .... B—Kt5, Black preserves the option of carrying out operations in the centre.

9 P—Q3

Besides this quiet continuation, White can well play more impetuously 9 P—Q4, or prepare for this advance by 9 P—KR3.

| 9 ...... | Kt—QR4 |

He decides after all on lateral manœuvres, instead of bearing on the centre by 9 .... B—K3 (10 B × B, P × B, etc.), or by 9 .... B—Kt2 (10 QKt—Q2, P—Q4, etc.).

10 B—B2	P—B4
11 QKt—Q2	Q—B2
12 Kt—B1	Kt—B3
13 Kt—K3	

Preventing Black's 13 .... P—Q4. The same object could be achieved by 13 B—Kt5, only it would lead to the elimination of the Bishops after 13 .... Kt—K1.

| 13 ...... | B—Kt2 |

Or 13 .... B—K3; 14 Kt—Kt5. However, Black's QB has a restricted field of action on its new post.

14 Kt—B5

An important outpost.

| 14 ...... | KR—K1 |

As 14 .... P—R3 would seriously weaken the King's field, Black elaborates a rather artificial manœuvre for the regrouping of his KR and KKt.

| 15 B—Kt5 | Kt—Q2 |

As mentioned previously, this withdrawal of the defending Knight from its responsible post is not without drawbacks. As a preliminary measure, 15 .... P—R3 has its points.

16 B—Kt3

This reoccupation of a valuable diagonal is energetic and strategically sound.

| 16 ...... | Kt—B1 |
| 17 B—Q5 | |

With the direct threat of winning the exchange by 18 B × Kt.

| 17 ...... | Kt—Kt3 |

This abandonment of a good defensive post will have serious consequences. The defence 17 .... B × B; 18 Kt × B, Kt—Q1, etc., shows more cohesion.

| 18 B × B | KKt × B |

Against 18 .... QKt × B White has the same reply as in the text.

19 B × P ch

A disrupting sacrifice.

| 19 ...... | K × B |
| 20 Kt—Kt5 ch | K—Kt1 |

The King is in trouble. Black can play neither 20 .... K—Kt3; 21 Kt—K6, etc., nor 20 .... K—B3; 21 Kt × P ch, etc., and least of all 20 .... K—B1; 21 Kt—K6 ch.

21 Q—R5	Kt × Kt
22 Q × P ch	K—B1
23 Q × Kt ch	K—Kt1

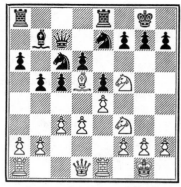

Position after 18 .... KKt × B

Or 23 .... K—K2; 24 Q—K6 ch, forcing mate (24 .... K—B1; 25 Kt—R7), or winning the Queen (24 .... K—Q1; 25 Kt—B7 ch).

24 Q—Kt6

This waiting move ensures the win for White. If at once 24 R—K3, then 24 .... P—Kt3; 25 Q × P ch, Q—Kt2.

| 24 ...... | Q—Q2 |

After 24 .... Q—K2; White has a mate in two.

25 R—K3

The decisive reinforcement. Black resigns.

84

| *White* | *Black* |
| WAINWRIGHT | ATKINS |

(Oxford, 1910)

Besides the catastrophe which occurs on the KKt file, the feature of this game is the by-play on the neighbouring files, the KB file (38 .... P—B6) and the KR file (45 .... R—R6 ch).

1 P—K4	P—K4
2 Kt—KB3	Kt—QB3
3 B—Kt5	P—QR3
4 B—R4	Kt—B3
5 Castles	B—K2
6 R—K1	P—Q3

More reserved, but not less playable than the more usual 6 .... P—QKt4; 7 B—Kt3, and only now 7 .... P—Q3.

7 P—B3
Playable also is 7 P—Q4, B—Q2, or else
7 B×Kt ch, P×B; 8 P—Q4, P×P; but,
dynamically, it is not particularly effective.

7 ......   Castles
8 P—KR3
The text move is intended to safeguard
his inner lines before launching out with
P—Q4.

8 ......   P—QKt4
More straightforward strategy would be
a regrouping behind the lines by 8 ....
B—Q2; 9 P—Q4, Q—K1, etc., or 8 ....
Kt—Q2; 9 P—Q4, B—B3, etc.

9 B—Kt3
More effective than 9 B—B2, for now the
Bishop still remains in active service (controlling Q5), and is not driven away by
9 .... Kt—QR4, which incidentally would
also deflect a hostile unit from the battlefield.

9 ......   K—R1
A waiting move. He could also work in
the centre by 9 .... B—K3; but the most
usual procedure is 9 .... Kt—QR4;
10 B—B2, P—B4; 11 P—Q4, Q—B2;
12 QKt—Q2, Kt—B3; etc., with equal
chances.

10 P—QR4
White decides on a well-known sub-
sidiary manœuvre as a preliminary to P—Q4.
There is nothing in 10 Kt—Kt5, Q—K1.

10 ......   R—QKt1
11 P×P   P×P
12 P—Q4   Q—K1
Anticipating the threat 13 P—Q5. To
this end it would be unwise to abandon the
centre by 12 .... P×P; 13 P×P, P—Q4;
14 P—K5, Kt—K5; 15 Kt—B3, Kt×Kt;
16 P×Kt, and White has the whip hand.

13 QKt—Q2   Kt—Kt1
14 Kt—B1   P—Kt3
15 B—Q5
This threat of winning a pawn by
16 B×Kt, Q×Kt; 17 P×P is easily parried.

15 ......   B—B3
16 Kt—Kt3
A more vigorous plan would be
16 P—KKt4, followed by Kt—Kt3.

16 ......   B—KKt2
17 B—K3   P—B3
18 P×P
Favouring his opponent with the open

KB file without any particular necessity.
The diversion 18 Q—Kt3 would have been
sound.

18 ......   BP×P
19 Kt—Q2   B—K3
20 B—Kt3   B×B
21 Kt×B   Kt—Q1
During the next phase Black allows his
opponent to worry the Q side, while in the
meantime he gradually concentrates his own
forces on the K side.

22 Kt—QR5   Kt—K3
23 Q—Q2   Q—Q2
24 P—Kt4   R—B2
25 Kt—Kt3   Kt—B5
The occupation of this "strong point"
marks an important stage in the development of Black's attack.

26 K—R2   P—R4
27 KR—Q1   QR—KB1
28 Kt—K2
Or 28 B×Kt, P×B; 29 Kt—B1, P—Kt4;
30 P—B3, P—Kt5, and Black still obtains
an open file.

28 ......   P—Kt4
Firmness of purpose.

29 B×Kt   KtP×B
Now the open KKt file speaks for itself.

30 P—B3   Kt—B3
31 Q—Q3   B—R3
32 R—R5   R—QKt1
33 R—R7   R—KKt2
34 R—Q2   R(Kt1)—Kt1
35 Kt(K2)—B1
Prudence demanded 35 Kt—Kt1.

35 ......   R—Kt6
36 R(R7)—R2
White is at a loss what to do. Even
after 36 R—KB2 there would follow 36 ....
Q—Kt2 (threatening 37 .... R×RP ch);
37 Q—B1, Kt×P; 38 P×Kt, P—B6, etc.

36 ......   Q—Kt2
This trebling of the heavy artillery contains the telling threat 37 .... R×RP ch
(38 K×R, Q—Kt6 mate or 38 P×R,
Q—Kt8 mate).

37 Q—B1
Parrying the threat mentioned above, but
allowing another to take its place. (*Diagram.
See p. 107.*)

See p. 107.

37 ......   Kt×P
Breaking up the enemy front.

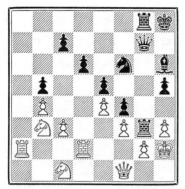

Position after 37 Q—B1

38	P × Kt	P—B6
39	R—KB2	B—B5
40	K—R1	P × P ch
41	R × P	R × P ch
42	K—Kt1	B—K6 ch

Bearing down from all sides on the opposing King.

43	QR—B2	R—Kt6
44	K—R2	

Or, equally, 44 K—R1, B × R.

44	......	B × R
45	R × B	R—R6 ch

And mate next move. (46 K × R, Q—Kt6 mate or 46 Q × R, Q—Kt8 mate.) A beautiful finish.

85

White	*Black*
ALEXANDER	KERES

(Hastings, 1937–8)

A game rich in strategic contents. A great fight, the draw being agreed only after all attacking resources on either side have become exhausted.

1	P—K4	P—K4
2	Kt—KB3	Kt—QB3
3	B—Kt5	P—QR3
4	B—R4	Kt—B3
5	Castles	B—K2
6	R—K1	P—QKt4
7	B—Kt3	P—Q3
8	P—B3	Castles
9	P—KR3	

Restrained energy. If at once 9 P—Q4, B—Kt5.

| 9 | ...... | Kt—QR4 |

Taking advantage of the breathing space to initiate a lateral offensive known as *Tchigorin's Plan.*

10	B—B2	P—B4
11	P—Q4	Q—B2
12	QKt—Q2	Kt—B3

Calling for a decision in the centre.

| 13 | P—Q5 | Kt—QR4 |

In his restricted position Black tries to vary the programme; that is why he avoids 13 .... Kt—Q1 and 13 .... Kt—Kt1, although these continuations are well as more rational.

| 14 | P—QKt3 | |

White takes precautionary measures on the Q side, before getting to work on the other wing. If 14 Kt—B1, P—B5, etc., whereas now, if 14 .... P—B5; 15 P—QKt4, Kt—Kt2; 16 P—QR4, etc.

14	......	B—Q2
15	Kt—B1	Kt—Kt2
16	P—B4	

If 16 Kt—K3 at once, then 16 .... P—B5; 17 P—QKt4, P—QR4, disrupting the Q side.

| 16 | ...... | KR—Kt1 |

Better would be, first, 16 .... P × P; 17 P × P, KR—Kt1, as now White succeeds in turning the square at QB4 into a "live point" (18 QKt × P).

| 17 | Kt—K3 | P × P |

The advance 17 .... P—Kt5 would only anticipate White's intention to close the Q side so as to operate on the K side with all possible energy.

| 18 | QKt × P | B—KB1 |

Not yet 18 .... Kt—QR4, on account of 19 KKt × P.

| 19 | P—QR4 | |

He decides on this move, which weakens the QKtP, in order to prevent 19 .... B—Kt4, and to maintain a Knight on a good observation post at QB4.

Thus White has the best of the local skirmish on the Q side.

19	......	Kt—QR4
20	KKt—Q2	P—Kt3
21	P—KKt4	

In a twinkling the fight is transferred to

the other wing. However, a more methodical execution of this plan would have been 21 Kt×Kt, Q×Kt; 22 Kt—B4, Q—B2; 23 P—B4.

21 ......   P—R4
Starting a counter-attack at the right moment.

22 Kt×Kt
Similarly, if at once 22 Q—B3, then 22 .... Kt—R2; 23 Q—Kt3 (or 23 P×P, Kt—Kt4, etc., or 23 B—Kt2, B—R3, etc.); 23 .... P×P; 24 P×P, B—R3 would keep White occupied.

22 ......   Q×Kt
23 Q—B3
Clearly not 23 Kt—B4, on account of 23 .... Q—B6, with a double objective, White's QR and KRP.

23 ......   Kt—R2
24 R—B1
The Rook abandons a favourable post in order to eliminate the Knight's pin. If 24 R—K2, B—Kt4, and if 24 P×P, Kt—Kt4. More to the point is 24 Q—Kt3, at once.

24 ......   Q—Q1
25 Q—Kt3   P×P
26 P×P   Q—Kt4
27 P—B3
Compulsory modesty. If 27 B—Q1 (to be followed by 28 Kt—B4 and P—B4), then, quite simply, 27 .... Q—B5, coping with the hostile threats.

27 ......   Q—K6 ch
If, instead, 27 .... Q—B5; 28 Q—B2, there is the above-mentioned threat 29 Kt—B4. As, however, the excursion in the text is not without risk, 27 .... P—B4 (and if 28 Kt—B4, P—B5) is playable.

28 K—Kt2   Q—B6
29 R—R2
In the ensuing phase, White carefully consolidates his Q side, while on the K side—where White has the run of the open KR file—matters take on a threatening aspect for the black King.

29 ......   B—K2
30 Kt—Kt1
Not 30 Kt—B4, R×P; 31 B×R, Q×KB, and wins.

30 ......   Q—Kt5
31 R—KR1   Kt—B1
32 B—Q2

Not yet 32 Q—R2, P—B3; 33 Q—R8 ch, K—B2; 34 R—R7 ch, Kt×R; 35 Q×Kt ch, K—K1; 36 Q—Kt8 ch, B—B1; 37 B—R6, K—K2; 38 Q—R7 ch, K—Q1; 39 B×B, P—B5 (preventing 40 B×P); 40 R—Kt2, Q—K8, and Black's now unfettered Queen secures a perpetual check.

32 ......   Q—Q5
33 R—K1
He alters his plans. The text move wins the Queen, but 33 Q—R2, according to the line of play indicated in the preceding note (improved by the diversion of the black Queen) would have won the game!

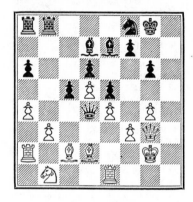

33 ......   P—B5
Forced, in view of the threat 34 B—B3.

34 B—K3   P×P
35 B×Q   P×R
36 B—R1
Not 36 Kt—B3, P×B; 37 Kt×P, R—Kt7. More useful than the text move, however, would be 36 B—B3.

36 ......   P×Kt (Q)
37 R×Q   R×R
38 B×R   P—Kt4
An important move, which blockades the K side and provides the black Knight with *strong points* (notably at KB5). 38 .... B×RP would be weak because of 39 P—B4, P—B3; 40 P—Kt5 breaking down Black's defences.

39 B—B2
White is reduced to a laborious defence. If Q—K1, Black plays—not 39 .... B×RP; 40 Q—Kt4, B—Kt4; 41 B×P, etc.—but 39 .... R—Kt1; 40 B—B2, B—Q1; and the black forces get into action.

39	R—B1
40 Q—B2	Kt—Kt3
41 Q—Q2	K—Kt2

In order to have in reserve a turning movement by the Rook (via KR1). Otherwise the immediate attack 41 .... Kt—B5 ch; 42 K—B1, B—Q1, etc., would be possible.

42 B—B3	Kt—B5 ch
43 K—B1	B—Q1

Black looks for complications in preference to the immediate draw by 43 .... R—KR1; 44 K—Kt1 (forced); 44 .... Kt—R6 ch; 45 K—B1, Kt—B5, etc.

44 Q—K3	K—B3
45 B—Kt3	R—Kt1
46 Q—R7	R×B
47 Q×B	R—Kt8 ch
48 B—K1	B—R4
49 Q×QP ch	K—Kt2
50 Q×P ch	K—B1

There was the try 50 .... K—Kt3; 51 Q—B5 ch, K—R3.

51 Q—R8 ch	K—K2
52 Q—K5 ch	Draw

An equitable solution, as either player would lose in trying to force a win, e.g. 52 .... K—Q2; 53 Q—B5 ch, and now he neither can play 53 .... K—Q3 (54 P—K5 ch, winning the Rook), nor 53 .... K—B2 (54 P—Q6 ch, winning the Bishop), nor, finally, 53 .... K—Q1 (54 Q×KtP ch, winning the Knight).

86

White	*Black*
CAPABLANCA	BOGOLJUBOW

(London, 1922)

An historic occasion, in that Señor Capablanca, the then champion of the world, meets for the first time one of the finest representatives of the neo-romantic school, an exciting game, in which the theatres of war change with extreme rapidity. The fine ending is worthy of a great game.

1 P—K4	P—K4
2 Kt—KB3	Kt—QB3
3 B—Kt5	P—QR3
4 B—R4	Kt—B3
5 Castles	B—K2
6 R—K1	P—QKt4
7 B—Kt3	P—Q3
8 P—B3	Castles
9 P—Q4	P×P

More consistent is the immediate sally 9 .... B—Kt5, e.g. 10 P—Q5, Kt—QR4; 11 B—B2, P—B3, and Black's counterchances are not to be despised.

10 P×P	B—Kt5
11 B—K3	

Methodical, but by playing 11 Kt—B3 (e.g. 11 .... B×Kt; 12 P×B, etc., with a reinforced centre, or 11 .... Kt—QR4; 12 B—B2, etc.; or again, 11 .... R—K1; 12 Kt—K2, B—KB1; 13 Kt—Kt3, etc.), White would increase the greater suppleness of his game, due to Black's ninth move.

11	Kt—QR4
12 B—B2	Kt—B5
13 B—B1	

Loss of time, which, however, is soon to bring a gain in space.

13	P—B4
14 P—QKt3	Kt—QR4
15 B—Kt2	

If 15 P—Q5, Kt—Q2; 16 B—Kt2, B—B3, holding his own.

15	Kt—B3
16 P—Q5	Kt—Kt5
17 QKt—Q2	Kt×B
18 Q×Kt	R—K1
19 Q—Q3	

Relieving the QKt of its guardianship of the point KB3.

19	P—R3

If 19 .... Kt—Q2; 20 P—K5, B×Kt; 21 Kt×B, P×P; 22 Kt×P.

20 Kt—B1	Kt—Q2
21 P—KR3	

Now 21 P—K5, B×Kt; 22 Q×B, P×P, etc., would not be advantageous for White.

21	B—R4

This desire to preserve his two Bishops does not conform to the needs of a dangerous situation. By playing 21 .... B×Kt; 22 Q×B, B—B3, Black could hope for equality.

22 Kt (B3)—Q2	

Preparing for vast operations on the K side.

22	B—B3
23 B×B	Q×B
24 P—QR4	

Multilateral action. If at once 24 Q—K3 (in preparation for 25 P—B4), then 24 .... P—Kt4.

24	P—B5
25 P × BP	Kt—B4
26 Q—K3	P × RP

Creating for himself the asset of a supported passed pawn.

27 P—B4

A double threat: 28 P—K5 or 28 P—B5, cutting off the adverse Bishop.

27 ......   Q—K2

If now 28 P—B5, P—B3 saves the threatened Bishop in the nick of time. But White will, at any rate, succeed in forcing it out of play.

28 P—Kt4	B—Kt3
29 P—B5	B—R2
30 Kt—KKt3	Q—K4

Black prepares a counter-action which will lead to numerous exchanges.

31 K—Kt2

More useful would be 31 K—B2.

| 31 ...... | QR—Kt1 |
| 32 QR—Kt1 | P—B3 |

At once 32 .... R—Kt7 is more to the point.

33 Kt—B3	R—Kt7 ch
34 R × R	Q × R ch
35 R—K2	Q—Kt6
36 Kt—Q4	

Far less dynamic would be 36 Kt—Q2, guarding the QBP, but assigning to this Knight a far more modest part.

36 ......   Q × Q

Both sides desire an end-game. Too risky would be 36 .... Q × P; 37 Kt—K6, with very strong pressure in the centre (not 37 R—QB2, Q × P).

37 R × Q	R—Kt1
38 R—QB3	K—B2
39 K—B3	R—Kt7
40 Kt (Kt3)—K2	B—Kt1

One more move—K—K1—and all the black forces could usefully participate in the fight, which would even up the respective chances of the contestants.

41 Kt—K6

A *dislodging manœuvre.*

41 ......   Kt—Kt6

The Knight has to leave its favourable post. The exchange would be fatal: 41 .... Kt × Kt; 42 QP × Kt ch, etc. No less damaging would be the gain of a pawn by

41 .... Kt × P; 42 K × Kt, R × Kt ch; 43 K—Q4, R—Q7 ch; 44 R—Q3, R × R ch; 45 K × R, and White wins easily.

42 P—B5

The birth of a passed pawn for White.

42	P × P
43 Kt × BP	Kt—Q7 ch
44 K—B2	

Not 44 K—K3, P—R6.

44	K—K2
45 K—K1	Kt—Kt8
46 K—Q3	P—R6

An exciting pawn race. But by playing 46 .... K—Q3; 47 Kt × P (R4), R—Kt5; 48 Kt (R4)—B3, Kt × Kt; 49 Kt × Kt, B—B2; 50 K—Q2, P—Kt3, Black could still put up a fight.

| 47 P—Q6 ch | K—Q1 |
| 48 Kt—Q4 | |

With the decisive threat 49 Kt—B6 ch, followed by 50 P—Q7 ch.

48	R—Kt3
49 Kt(Q4)—K6 ch	B × Kt
50 P × B	R—Kt1
51 P—K7 ch	K—K1
52 Kt × P	Resigns

After 52 .... P—R7 the simple sequel is 53 Kt × R, P—R8 (Q); 54 P—Q7 ch, with an early mate, and if 52 .... R—R1 or 52 .... R—Kt2; 53 Kt—B7 ch.

87

| White | Black |
| CAPABLANCA | MARSHALL |

(New York, 1918)

The most interesting feature of the following game is the cool and collected manner in which White weathers the storm which shakes his position after 15 .... Kt × P, and how he gradually recovers ground and finishes brilliantly.

1 P—K4	P—K4
2 Kt—KB3	Kt—QB3
3 B—Kt5	P—QR3
4 B—R4	Kt—B3
5 Castles	B—K2
6 R—K1	P—QKt4
7 B—Kt3	Castles
8 P—B3	P—Q4

By this pawn sacrifice (instead of the solid

and sound 8 .... P—Q3) Black tries to obtain the initiative.

```
 9 P×P          Kt×P
10 Kt×P         Kt×Kt
11 R×Kt         Kt—B3
```
The threats 12 .... B—Q3 and .... Kt—Kt5 have now become actual.

```
12 R—K1
```
The most rational defence is 12 P—Q4, B—Q3; 13 R—K2 (over-protecting KB2).

```
12 ......        B—Q3
13 P—KR3         Kt—Kt5
```
A pretty sacrifice, but another plan of attack would be 13 .... B—Kt2; 14 P—Q4, Q—Q2, followed by .... Q—B3 or .... QR—K1.

```
14 Q—B3
```
Well parried; the Queen also pursues aggressive aims. It would be fatal to accept the sacrifice, on account of 14 P×Kt, Q—R5; 15 P—Kt3, KB×P; 16 P×B, Q×P ch; 17 K—B1, B×P, and wins.

```
14 ......         Q—R5
15 P—Q4
```
A beautiful but unfortunate idea would be 15 R—K8, as Black would play 15 .... B—Kt2, and not 15 .... R×R, etc.

```
15 ......          Kt×P
```
The storm breaks.

```
16 R—K2
```
The only saving clause. If 16 Q×Kt, Black plays, not at once 16 .... B—Kt6 (because of 17 Q×P ch, followed by mate), but first an intermediate check 16 .... B—R7 ch; 17 K—B1, B—Kt6; 18 Q—K2 (18 Q×P ch is not feasible at this point, by reason of 18 .... R×Q, with check!); 18 .... B×P; 19 P×B, QR—K1, and White's position must collapse.

```
16 ......          B—KKt5
```
Another good continuation of the attack would be 16 .... Kt—Kt5. But a direct sacrifice either by .... Kt×P ch or by 16 .... B×P would prove insufficient.

```
17 P×B
```
Not 17 Q×Kt, because of 17 .... B—Kt6; 18 Q—B1, B×R; 19 Q×B, QR—K1, and wins.

```
17 ......          B—R7 ch
18 K—B1           B—Kt6
```
The answer to 18 .... Kt—R8 is 19 B—K3.

```
19 R×Kt
```
Another way of avoiding the mate is 19 K—K1.

```
19 ......          Q—R8 ch
20 K—K2           B×R
```
Here 20 .... Q×B offers Black better chances.

```
21 B—Q2
```
From this point Black's pressure grows steadily less.

```
21 ......          B—R5
22 Q—R3           QR—K1 ch
23 K—Q3           Q—B8 ch
24 K—B2
```
A secure harbourage.

```
24 ......          B—B7
25 Q—B3           Q—Kt8
26 B—Q5
```
Gaining space.

```
26 ......          P—B4
27 P×P            B×P
28 P—Kt4          B—Q3
29 P—R4
```
Rescue of the Rook.

```
29 ......          P—QR4
```
This advance is too abrupt. 29 .... R—B1 is more vigorous.

```
30 P×KtP          P×P
31 R—R6           P×P
32 Kt×P           B—Kt5
33 P—Kt6
```
This pawn speedily enforces the win.

```
33 ......          B×Kt
34 B×B            P—R3
35 P—Kt7          R—K6
```
White mates in 5
(By 36 B×P ch, etc.)

88

White	Black
LASKER	*TEICHMANN*

(St. Petersburg, 1909)

It is every player's ambition to win his games without obvious mistakes on his opponent's part. White realises this ideal here in an exceptionally energetic manner.

1	P—K4	P—K4
2	Kt—KB3	Kt—QB3
3	B—Kt5	P—QR3
4	B—R4	Kt—B3
5	Castles	B—K2
6	Q—K2	

This, the *Worrall Attack*, much favoured by some British masters, is another method of protecting White's KP, and has the same effect as 6 R—K1, namely, to threaten the gain of a pawn.

| 6 | ...... | P—QKt4 |

A more independent line of play than 6 .... P—Q3; 7 P—B3, Castles; 8 P—Q4. After 6 .... Castles, White wins a pawn by 7 B×Kt and 8 Kt×P, and, finally, if 6 .... B—B4; Black in effect gives away a *tempo*.

| 7 | B—Kt3 | P—Q3 |

A bolder but in no way more commendable continuation here is 7 .... Castles; 8 P—B3 (very good is also 8 P—QR4); 8 .... P—Q4 (sacrificing a pawn instead of 8 .... P—Q3); 9 P×P, Kt×P; 10 Kt×P (accepting the offer, although 10 P—Q4, with equal chances, is more cautious); 10 .... Kt—B5, etc.

| 8 | P—B3 | Castles |

Awaiting events, instead of trying to guide their course by 8 .... Kt—QR4; 9 B—B2, P—B4; 10 P—Q4, Q—B2, etc.

| 9 | P—Q4 | |

White stirs up the centre without losing time over the preliminary measure 9 P—KR3.

| 9 | ...... | P×P |

He abandons the centre. A more spontaneous continuation would be 9 .... B—Kt5; 10 R—Q1 (another plan would be to close the Q file by 10 P—Q5, Kt—QR4; 11 B—B2, etc.); 10 .... Q—B1; 11 P—KR3, B—R4, with equal chances.

| 10 | P×P | B—Kt5 |
| 11 | R—Q1 | |

This re-grouping of Rook and Queen is part of the idea of this variation; the KR gets into active play more quickly than usual.

| 11 | ...... | P—Q4 |

Not satisfied with waiting moves such as 11 .... R—K1 or 11 .... Q—B1, Black tries to obtain some say in the centre.

| 12 | P—K5 | |

More dynamic than 12 P×P.

12	......	Kt—K5
13	Kt—B3	Kt×Kt
14	P×Kt	P—B3

A dangerous course, as, in principle, any opening up of the game benefits the better-developed side. A rational reply would be 14 .... Q—Q2.

| 15 | P—KR3 | B—R4 |
| 16 | P—Kt4 | |

The struggle livens up and soon becomes embittered.

| 16 | ...... | B—B2 |

He deliberately provokes White's next move, but 16 .... B—Kt3 would have been less complicated.

| 17 | P—K6 | |

Striking root in the enemy camp.

17	......	B—Kt3
18	Kt—R4	Kt—R4
19	Kt×B	P×Kt
20	B—B2	P—KB4
21	K—R1	B—Q3
22	P×P	Q—R5

If 22 .... P×P; 23 Q—R5. We are witnessing a race between the two Queens as to which shall be the first to penetrate into the enemy lines.

| 23 | Q—B3 | |

Attack and defence at the same time.

| 23 | ...... | P×P |
| 24 | R—KKt1 | |

Threatening 25 B—Kt5.

24	......	P—B5
25	R—Kt4	Q—R3
26	P—K7	

Better than the lifeless 26 R—Kt6, Q—R5, etc., this disrupting advance brings about a speedy decision.

| 26 | ...... | B×P |
| 27 | B×P | Q—K3 |

Protecting the QP and hoping to be able to play the defensive 28 .... B—B3.

| 28 | R×P ch | |

A very elegant turn.

| 28 | ...... | Resigns |

(28 .... K×R; 29 R—Kt1 ch, K—B2 [29 .... K—B3; 30 B—K5 mate]; 30 Q—R5 ch, followed by mate.)

89

White	Black
ALEKHINE	MONTICELLI

(San Remo, 1930)

By means of manœuvres both energetic (9 P—QR4) and profound (22 Kt—K1, soon followed by P—KB4), White obtains complete control of the board.

Black's propitiatory sacrifice of a piece for two pawns proves insufficient, and so Black's mistake at the end of the game (33 .... R—K5) does nothing to mar the exemplary strategy employed by White throughout this contest.

1 P—K4	P—K4
2 Kt—KB3	Kt—QB3
3 B—Kt5	P—QR3
4 B—R4	Kt—B3
5 Castles	B—K2
6 Q—K2	P—QKt4
7 B—Kt3	P—Q3
8 P—B3	

The P—QR4 variation is applicable at this stage.

8	Castles
9 P—QR4	

Instead of the immediate 9 P—Q4, White interpolates an important episode which widens his sphere of control.

| 9 ...... | R—Kt1 |

Relinquishing the QR file.

He could have played 9 .... B—Kt5 (10 P—R3, B—R4; 11 P—Kt4, B—Kt3; 12 P—Q3, or 10 P×P, P×P; 11 R×R, Q×R; 12 Q×P, Kt×P, etc.).

10 P×P	P×P
11 P—Q4	P×P

Giving up the centre as well, for he must provide against 12 P—Q5, winning the Knight. It can be seen that the by-play introduced by White's ninth move is already bearing fruit.

| 12 P×P | |

Here 12 Kt×P, Kt×Kt; 13 P×Kt, R—K1 would merely have eased Black's position.

12	B—Kt5
13 R—Q1	P—Q4

Trying to deprive the white pawn centre of its flexibility. After the preparatory move 13 .... R—K1 White maintains his superiority in the centre by 14 B—K3, B—KB1 (not 14 .... KKt×P, because of

15 B—Q5); 15 P—R3, B×Kt; 16 Q×B, etc. After 13 .... Q—Q2 White continues his rational development by 14 Kt—B3. For all these reasons, an attempt at simplification by 13 .... R—R1 is Black's wisest course.

| 14 P—K5 | |

Tension in the centre, in preference to the simplifying exchange 14 P×P.

14	Kt—K5
15 Kt—B3	Kt×Kt
16 P×Kt	Q—Q2

Much more solid than 16 .... P—B3.

17 P—R3	B—KB4
18 R—R6	K—R1

A choice of evils. But as 18 .... R—R1; 19 R×R, R×R; 20 Q×P would cost a pawn, Black's relatively best defence would have been 18....Kt—Q1.

| 19 Kt—Kt5 | |

Inciting Black's next move, which will later on prove to have weakened the black King's defences. The *vacating manœuvre* 19 Kt—K1, to be followed by P—KKt4 and P—KB4, is also playable.

19	P—R3
20 P—Kt4	B—Kt3

Trying to conserve his two Bishops.

21 Kt—B3	Kt—Q1
22 Kt—K1	

This fine *vacating manœuvre* brings renewed energy into the contest.

22	P—QB3
23 Kt—Q3	

If at once 23 P—KB4, Black holds his own after 23 .... P—KB4.

| 23 ...... | Kt—K3 |

But if now 23 .... P—KB4; 24 Kt—B4, B—R2; 25 P—K6, etc., White maintains his superiority.

| 24 P—KB4 | |

In view of the imposing array of white pawns, Black has to take some decisive step.

24	P—KB4
25 P×P e.p.	B×P
26 P—B5	Kt×P
27 P×Kt	B×P ch
28 K—Kt2	QR—K1
29 Q—B3	B—B2

By his *propitiating sacrifice* of a piece for two pawns, Black has tried to change the aspect of the fight. But White succeeds in maintaining his advantage.

30 Kt—B4	B—K4
31 B—R3	R—KKt1
32 B—B5	

The three black pawns on the Q side are now in chancery.

| 32 ...... | B—Kt1 |
| 33 B—KB2 | |

Having skilfully consolidated his base, White intends to realise some decisive threats by 34 B—B2, etc. The game is virtually won for him.

| 33 ...... | R—K5 |

A blunder such as happens fairly frequently in lost positions. The continuation could have been 33 .... Q—Kt2; 34 R—R2, Q—B2 (34 .... R—K5; 35 Kt—Q3, etc.); 35 Kt—Q3 (or 35 B—Kt3), Q—R7 ch; 36 K—B1, R—K5; 37 Q—Kt2, and Black is lost.

| 34 Q×R | Resigns. |

90

| *White* | *Black* |
| THOMAS | RUBINSTEIN |

(Hastings, 1922)

The battle for the open Q file in this game, especially on Black's 27th and 30th moves, is waged in the grand manner.

1 P—K4	P—K4
2 Kt—KB3	Kt—QB3
3 B—Kt5	P—QR3
4 B—R4	Kt—B3
5 Q—K2	

A "pseudo-Worrall" which is far less effective than 5 Castles, B—K2; 6 Q—K2, because now Black has wider opportunities for his KB.

| 5 ...... | P—QKt4 |

More restricted would be 5 .... B—K2; 6 P—B3, P—QKt4; 7 B—B2, etc., or 5 .... P—Q3; 6 P—B3, etc. But if at once 5 .... B—B4; 6 B×Kt, QP×B; 7 Kt×P, Q—Q5; 8 Kt—Q3, B—R2; 9 Kt—B3, etc., and Black has lost a pawn without sufficient compensation.

| 6 B—Kt3 | B—B4 |
| 7 P—B3 | |

The interlude 7 P—QR4, R—QKt1 (but not 7 .... P—Kt5, on account of 8 B×P ch, K×B; 9 Q—B4 ch, followed by Q×B); 8 P×P, P×P, etc., secures the QR file for White, but allows Black the control of the neighbouring QKt file.

7	Castles
8 Castles	P—Q3
9 P—Q3	Kt—K2

Black tries to secure fresh positions by 9 .... B—KKt5, but abandons what he holds, for the text move gives up the control of his Q5. This procedure is not without risk.

| 10 B—Kt5 | |

Instinctively White refuses to be content with the simple and good continuation 10 B—K3, followed by QKt—Q2, and without any trouble, P—Q4. This important thrust could have been effected at once, e.g. 10 P—Q4, P×P; 11 P×P, B—Kt3; 12 P—K5, KKt—Q4; 13 B—Kt5, Q—Q2; 14 R—K1, and the chances in these fighting variations turn in favour of White.

10	Kt—Kt3
11 Kt—R4	Kt×Kt
12 B×QKt	P—R3

Sounding the attack!

13 K—R1	P—Kt4
14 B—Kt3	K—Kt2
15 Kt—Q2	Q—K2
16 B—B2	B—Q2
17 KR—K1	QR—K1
18 P—QR4	

Overestimating his resources—although his position is rather cramped—he opens the QR file, without the certainty of retaining it under his control.

Better would have been 18 P—B3, followed by B—B2.

18	KR—R1
19 P×P	P×P
20 Kt—B1	P—R4

He permanently assumes the initiative.

21 P—B3	P—R5
22 B—B2	B×B
23 Q×B	P—KKt5
24 P×P	

After this move Black's attack will be far more ruthless than if White had played 24 K—Kt1 (parrying the threat 24 .... P—Kt6).

24	Kt × KtP
25 Q—B3	P—R6
26 P—KKt3	

Evidently not 26 P × P, R × P.

26	Q—Kt4
27 Kt—K3	R—R1
28 Kt × Kt	B × Kt
29 Q—B2	R × R
30 R × R	R—R1
31 R—QKt1	

Clearly not 31 R × R, on account of 31 .... Q—B8 ch; 32 Q—Kt1, B—B6 mate. A little better, however, would be at once 31 R—KB1.

31	P—Kt5
32 B—Kt3	P—KB3
33 P—B4	

Against the plausible 33 B—Q5 would follow 33 .... P × P; 34 B × R (or 34 P × P, R—QKt1; 35 R—R1, R—Kt7; 36 Q × R, Q—K6, threatening mate); 34 .... P—B7; 35 Q × P, Q—K6, with the win in sight.

33	P—KB4
34 K—Kt1	P × P
35 R—KB1	

Seeking, at the cost of a pawn, some counter-play on the newly-opened KB file. Otherwise Black would have taken charge of it after 35 P × P, R—KB1.

| 35 ...... | P—K6 |

Coolly demonstrating that White's action will consist of a single check.

| 36 Q—B7 ch | K—R1 |
| 37 Q—Q5 | |

He tries to drive the hostile Rook from its open file.

| 37 ...... | P—B3 |

A subtle deflecting sacrifice of a pawn, which is also meant to gain time.

| 38 Q × BP | |

Or 38 Q × QP, P—K7; 39 R—B8 ch, K—Kt2, and wins.

38	R—QB1
39 Q—K4	P—K7
40 R—K1	P—Q4

A beautiful final turn, which serves to deflect the opposing Queen (41 Q × QP, Q—K6 ch), or alternatively, to force a way for his own Rook.

| 41 P × P | R—B8 |
| Resigns. | |

91

White	Black
THOMAS	SPIELMANN

(Carlsbad, 1923)

It is interesting to note how White, in the following game, gradually gains territory— keeping up a permanent pressure on the weak points in his opponent's position—until Black, in desperation, embarks on a doubtful combination which leads to his downfall.

1 P—K4	P—K4
2 Kt—KB3	Kt—QB3
3 B—Kt5	P—QR3
4 B—R4	Kt—B3
5 Q—K2	P—QKt4
6 B—Kt3	B—B4
7 P—B3	P—Q3
8 Castles	Castles
9 P—Q3	

If, in order to achieve P—Q4, White were to try 9 P—KR3, Q—K2; 10 R—Q1, B—Kt3, he would find that 11 P—Q4 is still impossible.

| 9 ...... | B—KKt5 |

Here 9 .... B—K3; 10 B × B, P × B; 11 B—K3, etc., would not be favourable for Black.

| 10 B—K3 | |

Of little use would be 10 B—Kt5, P—R3; 11 B—KR4, P—Kt4; 12 B—Kt3, Kt—KR4, etc., whereas now White's set plan is to effect the thrust P—Q4, for instance after 10 .... B × B; 11 P × B, Q—K2; 12 QKt—Q2, etc.

10	Q—K2
11 QKt—Q2	Kt—Q1
12 P—KR3	B—R4
13 B × B	

At this stage 13 P—Q4 would still assist Black's counter-play after 13 .... P × P; 14 P × P, B—QKt5, whilst the text move creates a permanent weakness in Black's position.

13	P × B
14 Q—K3	Q—Q3
15 Kt—R4	

With the tactical threat of occupying a strong point by 16 Kt—B5, and the strategical idea of broadening his base of action by 16 P—KB4.

White has the better game.

| 15 ...... | Kt—K3 |

Countering the far-reaching threat. For

if 15 .... B—Kt3; 16 P—KB4, P×P;
17 R×P, R—K1; 18 Kt×B, RP×Kt;
19 QR—KB1, White's pressure goes on
increasing.

16 Kt—B5	Q—Q1
17 Kt—B3	B×Kt
18 Q×B	P—Kt3
19 Kt—Kt3	Kt—B5

An active defence.

20 QR—Q1	Q—K2
21 Kt—K2	

With the utmost coolness, White deals
with Black's attempts at liberation.

21	Kt (B3)—R4
22 Kt×Kt	Kt×Kt
23 K—R2	QR—Q1
24 P—Kt3	Kt—K3
25 Q—K3	R—Q3

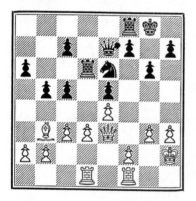

26 P—KB4
Formation of a chain of pawns in the
centre, which intensifies White's grip on the
course of events.

26	P×P
27 P×P	KR—Q1
28 P—B5	

Passing into enemy territory with speedy
results.

28	Kt—Kt4

Whilst guarding the fateful KBP, Black
hopes to engineer an effective counter-
demonstration.

29 Q×P
Thanks to a tactical *pointe*, White has at
last the weak QBP, and that without either

losing his own backward QP or having to
fear retaliation.

It is quite an art to exploit enemy weaknesses whilst masking your own.

The value of the text move is enhanced
by the fact that White avoids two 'tempting
continuations in 29 P—K5 (countered by
29 .... P—B5; 30 QP×P, R×R; 31 R×R,
R×R; 32 B×R, KKtP×P, etc.) and
29 P—KR4 (refuted by 29 .... Q—K4 ch;
30 K—Kt2, P—B5, etc.).

29	Kt×P

Threatened with 30 P—B6, Black seeks
salvation in a trap (30 P×Kt, R—Q7 ch,
winning the Queen).

30 Q—K3
A fresh pin, and this time a permanent
one.

30	Q—K4 ch
31 K—Kt2	P×P
32 P×Kt	R—Kt3 ch
33 K—R1	R×R
34 R×R	P×P

Or 34 .... P—B5; 35 R—Q8 ch, K—Kt2;
36 Q—Q4, Q×Q; 37 P×Q, P—B6;
38 R—Q7, R—B3; 39 K—Kt1, and wins
easily. Black's chief misfortune lies in the
fact that the energetic-looking 34 ....
R—Kt6 is lamentably refuted by 35 Q×R ch,
Q×Q; 36 R—KKt1.

35 R—KB1	R—Kt2
36 Q—B4	Q—K1
37 Q×BP	P—K6
38 B×P ch	

The art of liquidation.

38	R×B
39 Q×R ch	Q×Q
40 R×Q	K×R
41 K—Kt2	

The beginning of the end.

41	K—B3
42 K—B3	K—Kt4
43 P—Kt3	K—B4
44 K×P	K—K4
45 P—B4	P×P
46 P×P	P—QR4
47 P—QR4	P—R3
48 P—R4	P—R4
49 K—Q3	K—Q3
50 K—Q4	K—B3
51 P—B5	Resigns.

92

White	Black
YATES	RUBINSTEIN

(Budapest, 1926)

Although this game is one of the shortest ever played in an international masters' tournament, it contains some points of strategic interest. Black underestimates the power of a pin (11 B—Kt5), and collapses suddenly.

1 P—K4	P—K4
2 Kt—KB3	Kt—QB3
3 B—Kt5	P—QR3
4 B—R4	Kt—B3
5 Q—K2	P—QKt4
6 B—Kt3	B—B4

Hoping to prevent, as far as possible, the advance P—Q4 by White.

7 P—B3	Castles
8 Castles	P—Q3
9 R—Q1	

Instead of the usual 9 P—Q3, White conceives the bold plan of enforcing the thrust P—Q4 as quickly as possible without providing by 9 P—KR3 against the pin 9 .... B—KKt5.

| 9 ...... | Q—K2 |

He deliberately allows the advance in question to be made, thinking only of its weak points, and not realising the full extent of the threat. If he objected to 9 .... B—KKt5; 10 P—KR3, B×Kt; 11 Q×B, etc., he could at least have minimised the hostile threat by 9 .... R—K1; 10 P—Q4, P×P; 11 P×P, R×P; 12 B×P ch, K—B1, etc.

10 P—Q4
Now this works.

| 10 ...... | B—Kt3 |

With the threat 11 .... P×P; 12 P×P, Q×P, etc., but White is not waiting for this.

| 11 B—Kt5 | Kt—Q1 |

This further unconcern is to have fatal consequences. If, however, 11 .... P×P, White has the intermediary manœuvre 12 B—Q5, B—Q2; 13 P×P, etc. Black should without delay have loosened White's grip by 11.... P—R3.

| 12 Kt—R4 | Kt—K3 |

If now 12 .... P—R3, there follows 13 Kt—Kt6, winning the exchange; and if 12 .... P—Kt3; 13 Q—B3, K—Kt2;

14 Kt—B5 ch, P×Kt; 15 P×P, B—Kt2; 16 Q—Kt3, and wins. The best defence would have been 12 .... K—R1.

| 13 Kt—B5 | Q—K1 |

Black's position is already tottering. If 13 .... Q—Q1; 14 KB×Kt, P×B; 15 Kt×KtP, K×Kt; 16 P×P, with a winning attack. And if 13 .... Q—Q2 (the lesser evil); 14 QB×Kt, P×B; 15 R—Q3, etc.

After the text move there is a catastrophe.

14 B×KKt	P×B
15 B×Kt	Resigns

For after 15 .... P×B; 16 Q—Kt4 ch, Black has only the choice between mate and losing the Queen by 16 .... Q—Kt3; 17 Kt—K7 ch.

93

White	Black
ANDERSSEN	STEINITZ

(Vienna, 1873)

From quiet unenterprising to passive play is but a step. What the consequences can be—helplessness of the Queen, persecution of the King—is shown in the following game.

1 P—K4	P—K4
2 Kt—KB3	Kt—QB3
3 B—Kt5	P—QR3
4 B—R4	Kt—B3
5 P—Q3	

This ancient continuation was much favoured by the masters of former days. Assuredly it is not a move of an attacking character; but if White is allowed to complete his development unmolested, his game will gradually and increasingly become aggressive.

| 5 ...... | P—Q3 |

If 5 .... B—B4 (one would, of course, avoid 6 B×Kt, QP×B; 7 Kt×P, because of 7 .... Q—Q5, etc.) the best reply is 6 B—K3.

Similarly, after 5 .... P—QKt4; 6 B—Kt3, B—B4; 7 B—K3 keeps Black's aspirations in check.

6 B×Kt ch
As this exchange has at least as many drawbacks as advantages, a more patient

strategy would dictate 6 Kt—B3, or else
6 P—B3.

6	P × B
7 P—KR3	

Another precautionary measure. If
7 B—Kt5, P—B4.

7	P—Kt3

Opening up a promising diagonal for
the KB.

8 Kt—B3

A more flexible continuation would be
8 P—B3, aiming at the centre.

8	B—KKt2
9 B—K3	R—QKt1

Is this to be the file of the future?

10 P—QKt3	P—B4

Blockading White's Q4.

11 Q—Q2	P—R3
12 P—KKt4	Kt—Kt1

Commencing a lengthy but fruitful pil-
grimage towards Q5.

13 Castles QR

Having gained a partial success with his
two preceding moves, namely, by preventing
Black's castling and by starting an attack on
the K side, White now overestimates the
solidity of his Q side.

Better would have been 13 Kt—K2,
Kt—K2; 14 Kt—Kt3, Kt—B3; 15 P—B3,
etc., effecting a useful regrouping of his
forces.

13	Kt—K2
14 Kt—K2	Kt—B3
15 Q—B3	

If 15 P—B3, then 15 .... P—QR4, with
the concrete object of further weakening
White's King's field. But as the manœuvre
in the text is too slow, the following continuation is preferable: 15 Kt—Kt3, Kt—Q5;
16 B × Kt (not 16 Kt × Kt, BP × Kt, winning
the incarcerated Bishop); 16 .... BP × B;
17 P—B4, with a defendable game.

15	Kt—Q5
16 KKt—Kt1	

In order not to allow the hostile pressure—
already great—to increase, White has to have
recourse to artificial retreating manœuvres.
The following continuation would only have
led to trouble: 16 B × Kt, BP × B; 17 Q—B6 ch,
B—Q2; 18 Q × RP, R—R1; 19 Q—B4,
R × P, etc.

16	Castles

Taking advantage of the right tactical
moment in order to castle.

17 Kt—Kt3	B—K3
18 KKt—K2	Q—Q2
19 B × Kt	BP × B
20 Q—Kt2	

Poor lady! Black's advantage is definite.

20	P—QR4
21 K—Q2	

The King's flight.

21	P—Q4

Opening up the centre.

22 P—KB3	Q—K2
23 QR—KB1	

He prefers to keep his King in the centre,
rather than to expose him to fresh molestations after 23 K—K1, Q—Kt5 ch; 24 K—B2,
P × P; 25 QP × P, P—KB4.

23	Q—Kt5 ch
24 K—Q1	P—R5
25 R—R2	P—QB4

Initiating a very energetic action.

26 Kt—B1	P—B5
27 P—R3	Q—K2
28 P—Kt4	P—B6
29 Q—R1	Q—Kt4

Having "entombed" the white Queen by
the clever manœuvres of his last five moves,
Black proceeds to exact penalties on the
other wing.

30 QR—B2	P—B4
31 KP × BP	P × P
32 P—R4	Q—Kt3
33 Kt × P	B × Kt
34 P × B	R × BP
35 Kt—K2	

White stubbornly defends a lost cause.

35	QR—KB1
36 Q—R2	Q—B2
37 R—R3	K—R2
38 Kt—Kt1	B—B3
39 K—K2	R—KKt1
40 K—B1	B—K2
41 Kt—K2	R—R4
42 P—B4	

Or 42 R (B2)—R2, R × P; 43 R × R,
B × R; 44 R × B, Q × P ch; 45 K—K1,
R—Kt7, and White is lost; or again,
42 Kt—Kt1, R × P; 43 R × R, B × R;
44 R—Kt2, R × R; 45 K × R, Q—Kt3 ch;
46 K—B1, Q—Kt6, with an early mate.

| 42 ...... | B × RP |
| 43 QR—B3 | P—K5 |

The break-through.

44 P × P	Q—Kt3
45 Kt—Kt3	B × Kt
Resigns	

(46 QR × B, Q × P, etc.) A ruthless game.

94

| White | Black |
| STEINITZ | BLACKBURNE |

(London, 1876)

In this game we are shown how to weaken the black squares in the enemy camp (14 .... P—Kt3). How to exploit such weaknesses is even more difficult. Here it is achieved by White in a scintillating manner.

1 P—K4	P—K4
2 Kt—KB3	Kt—QB3
3 B—Kt5	P—QR3
4 B—R4	Kt—B3
5 P—Q3	P—Q3
6 P—B3	

Quiet but energetic strategy. After 6 Kt—B3 or 6 Castles, Black could eliminate the "Spanish Bishop" by 6 .... P—QKt4; 7 B—Kt3, Kt—QR4, followed by 8 .... Kt × B, etc.

| 6 ...... | B—K2 |

Some players prefer 6 .... P—KKt3, followed by .... B—Kt2, etc.

7 P—KR3

Useful as is this manœuvre, White could also get his pieces into action at once by 7 QKt—Q2, Castles; 8 Kt—B1, P—QKt4 (or at once 8 .... B—K3; 9 Kt—Kt3, etc.; 9 B—B2, P—Q4; 10 Q—K2, B—K3; 11 Kt—K3, etc.).

It is to be noted that the white QKt, in this variation, effects a clever itinerary "behind the front," which would not be possible after 7 Castles.

| 7 ...... | Castles |
| 8 Q—K2 | Kt—K1 |

As the intended 9 .... P—B4 is going to be prevented, a better plan would be 8 .... P—QKt4; 9 B—B2, P—Q4, with play in the centre.

| 9 P—KKt4 | P—QKt4 |
| 10 B—B2 | B—Kt2 |

This Bishop would co-operate more effectively after 10 .... B—K3.

| 11 QKt—Q2 | Q—Q2 |
| 12 Kt—B1 | |

This regrouping behind the front is characteristic of this variation.

| 12 ...... | Kt—Q1 |
| 13 Kt—K3 | Kt—K3 |

Over-hasty. More cautious would be 13 .... P—Kt3; and although White can try to roll up the K side, there is now a Bishop (Black's KB) which can keep the black squares under observation.

| 14 Kt—B5 | P—Kt3 |

Black underestimates the effect of the text move, as regards the *black square complex* in his camp and its deterioration.

15 Kt × B ch	Q × Kt
16 B—K3	Kt (K1)—Kt2
17 Castles QR	

The ideal of "flexibility" caused White to refrain from castling prematurely on the seventh move, and to reserve for himself the option of castling on either side.

| 17 ...... | P—QB4 |
| 18 P—Q4 | |

At last the opening up of the centre.

18	KP × P
19 P × P	P—B5
20 P—Q5	Kt—B2
21 Q—Q2	

Not at once 21 B—Q4, on account of 21 .... Kt × P.

| 21 ...... | P—QR4 |
| 22 B—Q4 | |

The influence of this Bishop, now established on the long diagonal, leaves its mark on the further course of the game.

| 22 ...... | P—B3 |
| 23 Q—R6 | P—Kt5 |

In order to drive off the terrible QB by KKt—Kt4; but White is in no mood to wait.

24 P—Kt5

The first breach.

| 24 ...... | P—B4 |

Or 24 .... P × P; 25 Kt × P, Kt (Kt2)—K1; 26 KR—Kt1, Kt—Kt4; 27 Kt × P, Kt × B; 28 R × P ch, Kt—Kt2; 29 R × Kt, R × P; 30 Kt—B6 ch, and wins.

| 25 B—B6 | Q—B2 |
| 26 P × P | |

26 ......   PxP
Or 26 .... KKt×P; 27 B×Kt, P×B;
28 P—Kt6, Q×KtP (28 .... P×P;
29 Q—R8 mate, or 28 .... Q×B; 29 Q×P
mate); 29 KR—Kt1, R×B; 30 Kt—R4,
and wins.

27 P—Kt6
The break-through. A furious onslaught.

27 ......   Q×P
Or 27 .... Q×B; 28 Q×P mate, or
27 .... P×P; 28 Kt—Kt5, and Black is
lost.

28 B×Kt
A beautiful final point (28 .... Q×B;
29 KR—Kt1). Black cannot avoid the loss
of a piece.

28 ......   Q×Q ch
29 B×Q   R—B3
30 KR—Kt1 ch   R—Kt3
31 B×P
Increasing his advantage. Black could
resign here.

31 ......   K—B2
32 B×R ch   P×B
33 Kt—Kt5 ch   K—Kt1
34 KR—K1   Resigns.

95

White	Black
STEINITZ	TCHIGORIN

(Second match, Havana, 1892)

*This famous game well illustrates the power
of the open KR file, when occupied by a Rook
on the alert, and ready to swoop down on the
hostile King's position.*

1 P—K4	P—K4
2 Kt—KB3	Kt—QB3
3 B—Kt5	Kt—B3
4 P—Q3	

Here is the "old" line of development
applied against the *Berlin Defence*.

4	P—Q3
5 P—B3	P—KKt3
6 QKt—Q2	

Much sounder than the superficial
6 Castles, as it retains the option of castling
on the opposite wing with the attendant
assault by pawns against the King's field.

6	B—Kt2
7 Kt—B1	Castles
8 B—R4	

He even forfeits a *tempo* (compared with
the *Morphy Defence*, 3 .... P—QR3;
4 B—R4), for no other purpose than to
consolidate his base before seeking adventure. Otherwise moves such as 8 Kt—K3
or 8 Kt—Kt3, or even the preparatory
8 P—KR3, are quite playable, although
answered in all three cases by an offensive
in the centre with 8 .... P—Q4.

8 ......   Kt—Q2
Seeing that his opponent is in no apparent
hurry, Black thinks that he also can afford
leisurely manœuvres. But here, more than
ever, 8 .... P—Q4 was the rational course,
followed by 9 Q—K2, Q—Q3; 10 P—KR3,
P×P; 11 P×P, Kt—QKt5; 12 B—QKt5,
P—QR3; 13 B—QB4, P—QKt4, and the
outlook has changed to Black's advantage.

9 Kt—K3	Kt—B4
10 B—B2	

Safeguarding his "attacking Bishop" for
future events.

10	Kt—K3
11 P—KR4	

Starting an offensive which is characteristic of this type of position: opening up of
the KR file against the opposing K side
fianchetto, needless to say in connection
with castling on the opposite wing.

11 ......   Kt—K2
Belatedly preparing some counter-action
in the centre—which he could have already
effected, without preparation, on the eighth
move. 11 .... P—KR4 would be useless,
because of 12 P—KKt4.

12 P—R5	P—Q4
13 RP×P	BP×P

More cautious would be 13 .... RP×P.

14 P×P	Kt×P
15 Kt×Kt	Q×Kt
16 B—Kt3	Q—B3
17 Q—K2	B—Q2
18 B—K3	K—R1
19 Castles QR	

Connection between the Rooks is established; the battle is in full swing.

19	QR—K1

In order to continue with .... Kt—Q5; eventually.

20 Q—B1
Now 20 .... Kt—Q5 would be refuted by 21 R×P ch, followed by mate in a few moves.

20	P—QR4
21 P—Q4	

Initiating a combination which is as deep as it is brilliant. The main idea is to obtain command of the long black diagonal.

21	P×P
22 Kt×P	B×Kt

Compulsory. He must part with the defending KB, for again, if 22 .... Kt×Kt, there follows 23 R×P ch.

23 R×B
White's intentions are gradually being revealed. His QB is here more valuable than the Rook.

23	Kt×R

Hoping, after 24 B×Kt ch, R—B3, etc., to build up a defence around the threatened King. Against 23 .... P—R4, White has a telling reply in 24 B—R4, winning a piece. The lesser evil would therefore have been 23 .... R—K2.

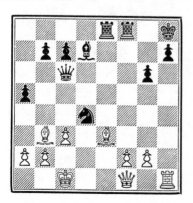

24 R×P ch
The awakening of the lion. The ensuing King-hunt is convincing.

24	K×R
25 Q—R1 ch	K—Kt2
26 B—R6 ch	K—B3
27 Q—R4 ch	K—K4
28 Q×Kt ch	Resigns

(If 28 .... K—B4 there is a mate by 29 Q—B4, or even by 29 P—Kt4.)

96

White	Black
DURAS	SWIDERSKI

(Vienna, 1908)

Having conquered the KKt file, White— slowly but surely—concentrates all his batteries there, supported by an active Bishop, whilst Black's lethargic Bishop remains passive too long.

1 P—K4	P—K4
2 Kt—KB3	Kt—QB3
3 B—Kt5	P—QR3
4 B—R4	Kt—B3
5 P—Q3	

Here is a modern master employing an ancient continuation. By his next move, however, he attempts to infuse new life into it.

5	P—Q3

A solid reply. He could, instead, try to incommode his adversary by 5 .... P—QKt4; 6 B—Kt3, B—B4; 7 B—K3, P—Q3, etc.

6 P—B4
Unlike the classic continuation 6 P—B3, this, the *Duras Attack*, strives not only to prevent 6 .... P—QKt4, but also to blockade Black's Q4. Its drawback is the weakening of his own Q4.

6	B—K2

The counter-action 6 .... P—KKt3 (e.g. 7 Kt—B3, B—Kt2, or 7 P—Q4, B—Q2) is rational and playable.

7 P—KR3
In order to prevent the pin 7 .... B—Kt5, etc. Another continuation could be: 7 Kt—B3, Castles; 8 P—Q4.

| 7 ...... | Castles |

8 Kt—B3

More precise is, first, 8 B—K3 (watching Q4 and preparing for P—Q4 eventually), for now Black could have tried to alter the course of things by 8 .... Kt—Q5.

| 8 ...... | Kt—Q2 |

A less artifiical development is 8 .... B—K3.

| 9 B—K3 | B—B3 |

It would be too risky to try 9 .... P—B4; 10 P × P, R × P; 11 P—Q4, and the opening of lines would favour White, who has the better development. That is why Black prefers to keep the game closed.

10 B × Kt	P × B
11 P—KKt4	P—B4
12 Q—Q2	Kt—Kt1

Aiming at Q5 via QB3, where, however, an inglorious fate is awaiting it.

More concise would be 12 .... P—B3, preventing, first of all, access to his Q4, and giving rise to all sorts of other projects.

13 Castles QR

Unmolested by his adversary, White has achieved a sound and powerful grouping of his forces.

13	Kt—B3
14 Kt—Q5	Kt—Q5
15 Kt × Kt	BP × Kt
16 Kt × B ch	Q × Kt

Or 16 .... P × Kt; 17 B—R6, R—K1; 18 P—B4, K—R1; 19 P—KB5, R—KKt1; 20 QR—Kt1, and White can start a telling attack.

| 17 B—Kt5 | Q—K3 |
| 18 P—B4 | |

He succeeds in hemming in his opponent's position.

| 18 ...... | P—KB3 |

A plausible move, which, however, facilitates the opening of the KKt file. With greater coolness 18 .... B—Kt2 or 18 .... P—QB3 could have been played.

| 19 P—KB5 | Q—K2 |
| 20 B—R4 | P—B3 |

Or 20 .... P—R3; 21 B—B2, P—B3; 22 P—KR4, and White still obtains an open file on the critical sector. He should have played 20 .... B—Kt2, in order to connect the two Rooks.

| 21 P—Kt5 | |

Direct hostilities are beginning.

21	K—R1
22 P × P	P × P
23 QR—Kt1	B—Kt2

A Bishop with no future.

| 24 Q—R6 | R—B2 |
| 25 R—Kt6 | |

Preventing 25 .... R—KKt1, and gaining a *tempo* for the doubling of his Rooks.

25	QR—KB1
26 KR—Kt1	P—Q4
27 B—K1	

Skilful regrouping.

27	P × BP
28 P × P	P—B4
29 R (Kt6)—Kt4	B—B3
30 Q—R4	Q—Kt2
31 Q—Kt3	

This trebling of the major pieces (threatening 32 R—Kt8 ch) settles matters.

Very strong would also be 31 B—Q2, e.g. 31 .... R—QKt1; 32 P—Kt3, P—QR4; 33 Q—Kt3, Q—R1; 34 B—R6, and Black is defenceless against the threat 35 B—Kt7 ch.

| 31 ...... | Q—R1 |
| 32 B—Q2 | Resigns |

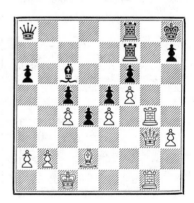

The concentration of the white forces on the open file is imposing.

A piquant finish could be: 32 .... B × P; 33 B—R6, B × P; 34 B—Kt7 ch, R × B (or 34 .... K—Kt1; 35 B × P dis ch, B—Kt3; 36 R × B ch, etc.); 35 R × R, B—Kt3; 36 R × P ch, K × R; 37 Q × B ch, with mate to follow.

97

White	Black
MASON	JANOWSKI

(Monte Carlo, 1902)

Here is a game noteworthy for the depth of its conception.

White treats the opening rather tamely (7 B×Kt ch), upon which Black tries to enliven the struggle by castling on the Q side, a most unusual occurrence in the Ruy Lopez (except in the exchange variation).

This adventure results in the gain of a pawn by White (24 Kt×P). There follows a lengthy period of manœuvring, during which White gradually gains the initiative (45 Q—R4), and winds up with one of the most startling combinations in modern chess (49 Kt—Q4).

In the resulting end-game the white Knight prevails over the black Bishop.

1	P—K4	P—K4
2	Kt—KB3	Kt—QB3
3	B—Kt5	P—QR3
4	B—R4	Kt—B3
5	Castles	B—K2
6	Kt—B3	

A quiet continuation. More flexible is the defence of the KP by 6 R—K1 or 6 Q—K2 (*the Worrall Attack*), with the option of playing P—QB3.

Playable also is the quiet line 6 P—Q3 (the *Deferred Anderssen Continuation*) or 6 P—B3, leaving the KP *en prise* (for after 6 P—B3, Kt×P; 7 Q—K2, Kt—B3; 8 B×Kt, QP×B; 9 Kt×P, Castles; 10 P—Q4, White would have a very good game).

| 6 | ...... | P—Q3 |

A reserved reply. 6 .... P—QKt4; 7 B—Kt3, P—Q3 is more comprehensive.

7 B×Kt ch

A wise decision, for after 7 P—Q4 there follows 7 .... P—QKt4; 8 B—Kt3 (or 8 P×P, P×P, with equalisation); 8 .... QKt×P; 9 Kt×Kt, P×Kt; 10 Q×P, P—B4, followed by .... P—B5, winning a piece. This opening trap occurs in several variations of the *Ruy Lopez*.

| 7 | ...... | P×B |
| 8 | P—Q4 | P×P |

Instead of abandoning the centre, he could have maintained it by 8 .... Kt—Q2 (Tchigorin's move).

| 9 | Kt×P | B—Q2 |
| 10 | P—QKt3 | |

He decides on a slow development, as no direct enterprise at this stage would lead to a concrete result, e.g.:

(*a*) 10 B—Kt5, Castles; 11 R—K1, P—R3; 12 B—R4, Kt—R2; 13 B×B, Q×B, with a well-equalised game.

(*b*) 10 P—B4, Castles, etc.

(*c*) 10 Q—B3 (threatens 11 P—K5); 10 .... P—B4; 11 Kt—B5, B×Kt; 12 Q×B, Castles, with equal chances.

| 10 | ...... | Q—Kt1 |

Instead of the obvious 10 .... Castles, Black indulges in a highly artificial manœuvre.

| 11 | B—Kt2 | Q—Kt2 |
| 12 | R—K1 | Castles QR |

A most infrequent case of castling on the Q side for Black in the *Ruy Lopez*, but the originality of this plan does not signify its soundness. Castles KR is better.

| 13 | Q—Q3 | KR—K1 |

In order to continue 14 .... P—B4; 15 Kt—B5, B—B1, without interrupting communications between his Rooks.

14 P—QKt4

With this pretty offer of a pawn White insists on his rights to the initiative on the Q side.

| 14 | ...... | B—B1 |

Too dangerous would be 14 .... Q×P; 15 QR—Kt1, as well as 14 .... P—B4; 15 Kt—Kt3 (if 15 P×P, then not 15 .... Q×B; 16 P—B6, etc., but 15 .... P×P; 16 Kt—Kt3, B—K3; 17 Q—B3, P—B5, etc.); 15 .... P×P; 16 Kt—Q5, and White dominates the position.

| 15 | QR—Kt1 | P—Q4 |

Trying to open up his game. The alternative would be 15 .... P—B4; 16 P×P, P×P; 17 B—R3, Q—R2; 18 Kt—Kt3, B—K3; 19 Q—K3, with advantage to White.

16	P—K5	Kt—Kt5
17	Kt—B3	P—Kt3
18	P—KR3	B—KB4
19	Q—Q2	Kt—R3

Clearly not 19 .... B—R3; 20 Q—Q1, and the black Knight has no retreat.

20	P—R3	Kt—Kt1
21	Kt—Q4	B—K3
22	Kt—R4	Kt—R3
23	Q—B3	Kt—B4

Voluntarily giving up the pawn, because after 23 .... B—Q2; 24 Kt—Kt3 White conquers the dominating square QB5.

24 Kt×P	R—Q2
25 Kt—Q4	Kt×Kt
26 Q×Kt	B—KB4

In the lengthy sequence of manœuvres which follows, Black tries in vain to turn his two Bishops to account.

27 QR—B1	Q—B3
28 Kt—B3	P—KR4
29 Kt—K2	B—R3
30 P—KB4	B—B1
31 Q—B2	B—K3
32 Kt—Q4	Q—Kt3
33 R—Kt1	B—KB4
34 B—B3	

Instead of liquidating by 34 Kt×B, Q×Q ch; 35 K×Q, P×Kt, etc., White considers his centralised Knight more precious than an opposing Bishop.

34	B—K5
35 P—QR4	P—QB3
36 P—R5	Q—R2
37 R—Kt2	

Avoiding exchanges by 37 Kt×P, Q×Q ch; 38 K×Q, B×BP.

| 37 ...... | R—Kt2 |
| 38 KR—Kt1 | |

Even here White prefers to do battle rather than to adopt the slow continuation 38 Kt×P, Q×Q ch; 39 K×Q, K—Q2; 40 Kt—Q4, KR—Kt1; 41 KR—QKt1, P—R5, and Black has still some fight left, although he is two pawns down.

38	K—Q2
39 K—R1	KR—Kt1
40 Q—K1	

The unpinning of the Knight could have been effected more cautiously by 40 Q—Q2, for after the text move Black had a counter-combination by 40 .... KB×P, e.g. 41 B×B, Q×Kt, etc., or 41 Kt×P, K×Kt; 42 B×B, Q—Q5, etc.

| 40 ...... | B—K2 |
| 41 Kt—Kt3 | |

A trap, e.g. 41 .... KB×P; 42 B×B, R×B; 43 Kt—B5 ch, Q×Kt; 44 R×R, and White has won the exchange.

41	R—Kt4
42 B—Q4	Q—Kt2
43 B—B5	B×B
44 P×B	R—Kt5

Not without danger would be 44 .... B×P, on account of 45 Kt—Q4.

45 Q—R4

The beginning of a turning movement in the grand manner.

45	K—B1
46 Q—B6	Q—Q2
47 K—R2	Q—K3

Better would be 47 .... K—B2.

48 Q—R8 ch   K—Q2

After 48 .... K—B2 White has the same brilliant reply.

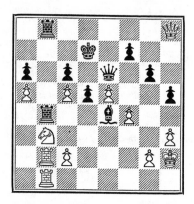

49 Kt—Q4

A liquidating sacrifice. It was of course foreseen by White on his preceding move.

49 ......   R×R

If 49 .... R×Kt; 50 R—Kt7 ch, followed by mate, and if 49 .... R×Q; 50 R×R, etc.

50 Q×R

The point! The black Queen will find herself in an ambush and be lost.

50	R×Q
51 R×R	K—B2
52 Kt×Q ch	K×R
53 Kt—Q4	

There follows an ending in which the Knight's dominating position is the deciding factor.

53	K—B2
54 P—Kt4	P—R5
55 P—B3	K—Q2
56 K—Kt1	K—B2
57 K—B2	K—Q2
58 P—B5	P×P
59 P×P	K—B2
60 K—K3	B—Kt7
61 Kt—B3	B×P
62 Kt×P	B—Kt5
63 K—B4	B—K7
64 Kt—B3	B×Kt
65 K×B	Resigns

98

White	Black
H. WOLF	PRZEPIORKA

(Pistyan, 1922)

Although White's attack in this game seems to develop in slow motion, in the end it leads to the beautiful solution of a positional problem.

1 P—K4	P—K4
2 Kt—KB3	Kt—QB3
3 B—Kt5	P—QR3
4 B—R4	Kt—B3
5 Castles	B—K2
6 Kt—B3	

A species of *Four Knights' Game*, in which however White's KB is the better developed.

| 6 ...... | P—QKt4 |

More enterprising than 6 .... P—Q3.

| 7 B—Kt3 | P—Q3 |
| 8 P—Q3 | |

If at this point 8 P—QR4, P—Kt5; 9 Kt—Q5, Kt—QR4, and Black contests the initiative. The try 8 B—Q5 would lead only to wholesale exchanges and equality.

| 8 ...... | Kt—QR4 |

The elimination of the adverse KB eases Black's game.

| 9 Kt—K2 | Kt × B |
| 10 RP × Kt | P—B4 |

If 10 .... Castles; 11 P—QKt4.

11 B—Q2	Castles
12 Kt—Kt3	Q—B2
13 Q—K2	R—K1
14 P—R3	B—B1
15 Kt—R4	P—Q4

It can be seen that Black also has aggressive plans. But prudence demanded 15 .... P—Kt3, followed by B—KKt2.

| 16 B—Kt5 | |

Henceforth the threat of undermining the black King's position dictates the course of events.

16	Q—B3
17 Q—B3	P × P
18 P × P	R—K3
19 QR—Q1	B—Kt2
20 KR—K1	P—B5

This attempt at counter-play is not sustained enough. He should take advantage of the opportunity of playing 20 .... P—Kt3.

| 21 KKt—B5 | R—B1 |
| 22 P × P | P × P |

If 22 .... Q × BP, White, in the temporary absence of Black's Queen, can get in the combination 23 Kt—R6 ch, P × Kt; 24 B × Kt, and wins.

23 R—K2	P—QR4
24 P—B3	Kt—Q2
25 KR—Q2	

With assets such as the dominating position of the KKt at KB5 and the possession of the only open file, White has a won game.

| 25 ...... | Kt—B4 |
| 26 R—Q8 | |

Threatening (for instance, after 26 .... Kt—Q6) to win the exchange by 27 Kt—K7 ch.

| 26 ...... | R—K1 |
| 27 R (Q8)—Q6 | |

Now White himself gives up the exchange. The true inwardness of White's preceding move stands revealed. The Rook's irruption on the eighth rank was a feint, the object being to deflect the hostile Rook from the sixth rank.

| 27 ...... | B × R |

After 27 .... Q—B2 the *battery* 28 Q—Kt4 is decisive.

| 28 R × B | Q—B2 |

As White cannot now play 29 Kt × P (because of 29 .... Q × R), and as Black has in view the consolidating continuation 29 .... R—K3, his game, saving the unforeseen, seems tenable.

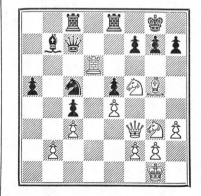

| 29 B—B6 | |

But here is the unexpected, which transforms the position into a beautiful problem.

29 ......   R—K3
Not 29 .... P × B, in view of 30 Q—Kt4 ch,
followed by mate at KKt7, nor 29 ....
P—Kt3, on account of 30 Kt—R6 ch,
K—B1; 31 B—Kt7 ch (an impressive point);
31 .... K × B; 32 Q—B6 ch, K—B1 (or
32 .... K × Kt; 33 Kt—B5 ch, K—R4;
34 Q—R4 mate); 33 KKt—B5, P × Kt;
34 Kt × P, with mate to follow.

30 Q—Kt4   P—Kt3
31 Q—Kt5   R × B
Compulsory, in view of the threat 32 Q—R6.

32 Q × R   Kt—K3
White mates in three.
(33 Kt—R6 ch, K—B1; 34 R × Kt, and
35 Q—R8 mate.)

99

White	Black
MORPHY	LÖWENTHAL

(Match, 1858)

*The following game illustrates superiority
in territory better than any theoretical
dissertation.*

1 P—K4   P—K4
2 Kt—KB3   Kt—QB3
3 B—Kt5   P—QR3
4 B—R4   Kt—B3
5 P—Q4
More vigorous is 5 Castles, but Morphy
always liked to open up the game as soon
as possible.

5 ......   P × P
Foolhardy would be 5 .... Kt × KP,
because of 6 Q—K2, P—B4; 7 P—Q5, etc.

6 P—K5
There is no more than equality in 6 Castles,
B—K2; 7 P—K5, Kt—K5, etc. 6 Q—K2
offers most practical chances.

6 ......   Kt—K5
7 Castles   Kt—B4
The most rational line of play is 7 ....
B—K2, in order to castle as soon as possible
in answer to 8 Kt × P. If 8 R—K1,
Kt—B4; 9 B × Kt, QP × B; 10 Kt × P,
Kt—K3; 11 Kt—B5, Q × Q; 12 R × Q,
B—Q1, etc., a simplified ending is the result.

8 B × Kt   QP × B
9 Kt × P   Kt—K3
Or 9 .... B—K2; 10 P—KB4, launching
an attack.

10 Kt × Kt   B × Kt
11 Q—K2   B—QB4
More active than 11 .... B—K2.

12 Kt—B3   Q—K2
13 Kt—K4   P—R3
Castles on either side would be bad, on
account of 14 B—Kt5.

14 B—K3   B × B
15 Q × B   B—B4
16 Kt—Kt3   B × P
Greed prevails, but prudence demands
here for preference 16 .... Q—K3, blockading KB4, and preventing White's pawn
attack.

17 P—B4   P—KKt3
Again he cannot castle. If 17 ....
Castles QR; 18 Q—R7, and if 17 ....
Castles KR; 18 P—B5, threatening 19 P—B6,
as well as the gain of the Bishop by 19 KR—B1,
B—R5; 20 P—Kt3, B—Kt4; 21 P—QR4.
As the text move fails to solve the positional
problem in a satisfactory manner, Black
should have cut the Gordian knot by 17 ....
P—KB4, even though White remains with
the superior position after 18 KR—B1,
B—K5; 19 Kt × B, P × Kt; 20 Q × P, etc.

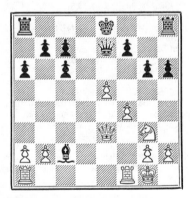

18 P—K6
With this neat dagger thrust White
threatens 19 Q—QB3, attacking both the
QB and the KR. The play is typical of
Morphy.

18 ......   B—B4
If 18 .... Castles KR; 19 P—B5, with a

speedy win. And if 18 .... B—R5;
19 Q—Q4.

19 Kt×B	P×Kt
20 P×P ch	K×P
21 Q—KR3	

In the sequel one must admire how the
maximum effect is obtained with the minimum of means. Again the real, the profound Morphy.

21	Q—B3
22 QR—K1	KR—K1
23 R—K5	

Occupation of the *strong point*. As Black
cannot reply with 23 .... R×R; 24 P×R,
Q×P; 25 R×P ch, etc., he must allow the
doubling of the hostile Rooks.

23	K—Kt3
24 KR—K1	R×R
25 R×R	R—Q1
26 Q—Kt3 ch	K—R2
27 P—KR3	

It is strange that, although a pawn down,
White should be able to play waiting moves
without relaxing his domination of territory.

27	R—Q2
28 Q—K3	P—Kt3
29 K—R2	P—B4
30 Q—K2	Q—Kt3
31 R—K6	Q—Kt2
32 Q—R5	R—Q4

And not 32 .... R—B2; 33 R×P ch.

33 P—QKt3
Reaching a curious case of *Zugzwang* on
an open board.

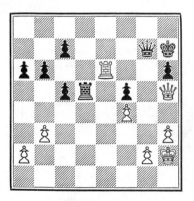

33	P—Kt4

Or 33 .... P—R4; 34 P—QR4, and all
four black pawns are blockaded.

34 R×P	R—Q3

Black tries to free his game at the cost of
a pawn. If 34 .... P—B5; 35 P×P, P×P;
36 R—QB6, P—B6; 37 P—R4, R—R4;
38 Q—Q1, R—R2; 39 Q—Q5, with a won
game for White.

35 Q×BP ch	Q—Kt3
36 Q×Q ch	K×Q
37 R—R5	R—Kt3

Or 37 .... P—B3; 38 P—QR4, P×P;
39 R×RP, R—Q5; 40 R—B4, with an easy
win. White's ending on the K side plays
itself.

38 P—KKt4	P—B3
39 K—Kt3	P—R4
40 R—R7	P×P
41 P×P	K—B3
42 P—B5	K—K4
43 R—K7 ch	K—Q3
44 P—B6	R—Kt1
45 P—Kt5	R—KB1
46 K—B4	P—B5
47 P×P	P×P
48 K—B5	P—B6
49 R—K3	

And wins.

100

White	*Black*
YATES	REY ARDID

(Barcelona, 1929)

*In a desperate contest such as the following,
the initiative remains in the end with the
player who has first succeeded in seizing an
open file.*

1 P—K4	P—K4
2 Kt—KB3	Kt—QB3
3 B—Kt5	P—QR3
4 B—R4	Kt—B3
5 Castles	B—B4

The *Möller Defence*, which the great
Danish theorist evolved in 1903, tries to
exploit for Black the "Italian diagonal,"
with sustained pressure against White's KB2.

6 P—B3
A methodical continuation. The temporary sacrifice 6 Kt×P yields only equality
after 6 .... Kt×Kt; 7 P—Q4, Kt×P;
8 R—K1, B—K2; 9 R×Kt, Kt—Kt3;
10 P—QB4, P—Kt3, etc.

6 ......   B—R2

Black builds up his plan of defence on this preventive retreat.

7 P—Q4   KKt × P

The future of Black's game depends on the solidity of this outpost.

8 Q—K2   P—B4
9 P × P   Castles
10 B—B2

As this move (as does also 10 QKt—Q2) allows the strong reply 10 .... P—Q4, he should have played 10 B—Kt3 ch, K—R1; 11 B—Q5, and White has a slight advantage.

10 ......   P—Q4
11 P × P e. p.   Kt × QP
12 QKt—Q2   R—K1

The occupation of the open K file now constitutes an undeniable asset in Black's favour.

13 B—Kt3 ch   K—R1
14 Q—Q3   Q—B3
15 Kt—B4

White experiences difficulties in completing his development.

15 ......   Kt × Kt
16 Q × Kt   B—K3
17 Q—B4   B × B
18 P × B   B—Kt3
19 Q—Kt3

He goes on manœuvring instead of continuing his mobilisation, if but modestly, by 19 B—Q2.

19 ......   P—R3

The extended development by 20 B—Kt5 had to be prevented.

20 R—R4

Will this Rook prevail against the well-equipped hostile fortress? It would have been wiser to relieve the enemy pressure by 20 B—→K3 (e.g. 20 .... B × B; 21 P × B, QR—B1; 22 Kt—Q4, etc.).

20 ......   R—K7
21 R—R4   QR—K1
22 Q—R3

The threat 23 B × P looks very strong, but Black has a parry in a fine *intermediary manœuvre*.

22 ......   QR—K5
23 R—R5

Clearly not 23 B × P, R × R, etc., and still less 23 R × R, P × R; 24 Kt—Kt5, Q × P ch; 25 R × Q, R—K8 mate.

23 ......   P—B5

This faithful pawn not only defends itself, but chokes the opposing Bishop.

24 R—KB5

Is it emancipation at last? The struggle becomes fast and furious.

24 ......   Q—Q3

With the unanswerable threat 25 .... R × BP. Thus the basic idea of the *Möller Defence* has been realised.

25 K—R1   R × BP
26 R—Kt1

The only refuge. If 26 R × R, Q—Q8 ch; 27 Kt—Kt1, Q × Kt ch; 28 K × Q, R—K8 mate.

26 ......   KR—K7
27 R—B7

A desperate venture. If 27 R—B1, Kt—Q1; 28 Kt—Kt5, R—K8; 29 P—Kt3, R × R ch; 30 Q × R, P × Kt, and wins.

27 ......   B × R
28 Q—B5

The last cartridge.

28 ......   B—B4

Defence (against 29 R—B8 ch) and attack (29 .... R—K8 ch) at the same time.

29 P—R4   Q—Q8 ch
    Resigns
(30 K—R2, R × P ch; 31 K × R, Q—K7 ch, etc.)

101

White	Black
CAPABLANCA	MILNER-BARRY

(Margate, 1935)

It is a special art to fasten on the weak points in risky variations—and such is, after all, the "Möller Defence."

Señor Capablanca was ever known as an iconoclast of "variations."

1 P—K4   P—K4
2 Kt—KB3   Kt—QB3
3 B—Kt5   P—QR3
4 B—R4   Kt—B3
5 Castles   B—B4

The basis of the *Möller Defence* is assuredly less scientific than that of the *closed defence* 5 .... B—K2 or the *open defence* 5 .... Kt×P. The British master P. S. Milner-Barry has sacrificed many a valuable point on the shrine of experimental theory. It is the player's loss, but the theory's gain.

6 P—B3	B—R2
7 P—Q4	Kt×KP
8 R—K1	

The entry of the Rook into the lists proves more forceful than that of the Queen by 8 Q—K2.

8	P—B4
9 QKt—Q2	

Concentric play.

An ingenious idea here consists in the sacrifice of the exchange by 9 R×Kt, P×R; 10 B—KKt5, Kt—K2; 11 Kt×P, Castles; 12 B—Kt3 ch, but by replying no less ingeniously with 12 .... P—Q4, Black holds his own.

9	Castles

He underestimates his adversary's resources and, in particular, the white King's Rook's potential activities. He should have resigned himself to 9 .... Kt×Kt.

10 Kt×Kt	P×Kt
11 B—KKt5	

A far-seeing intermediary manœuvre.

11	Q—K1
12 R×P	P—Q3

If 12 .... P—Q4; 13 R×P.

13 P×P	Q—Kt3
14 R—KB4	

Sound strategy! Not only the counter-threat of 14 .... R×Kt is eliminated, but also all chances of Black obtaining some counter-play on the semi-open KB file vanish.

14	R×R
15 B×R	B—Kt5

What can he do? If 15 .... P—Kt4; 16 Q—Q5 ch, etc.; if 15 .... P×P; 16 B×Kt, etc.; and if 15 .... Kt×P; 16 B×Kt, P×B; 17 Q—Q8 ch, K—B2; 18 Kt×P ch.

16 Q—Kt3 ch	Q—B2

With a faint chance of salvation after 17 Q×P, R—Kt1; 18 Q×Kt, Q×B, etc. But the fine and incisive manœuvre which now follows puts an end to all resistance.

17 Kt—Kt5	Q×Q
18 B×Q ch	Resigns.

102

White	Black
LASKER	STEINITZ

(Return match, Moscow, 1896)

A game in which the Queens have been exchanged need by no means take a dull and arid course.

In the following struggle, Black cleverly unmasks his opponent's weak points whilst masking his own. The vertical co-operation of the black Rooks is most instructive.

1 P—K4	P—K4
2 Kt—KB3	Kt—QB3
3 B—Kt5	P—QR3
4 B—R4	P—Q3

The *Steinitz Defence Deferred* is sound and lasting.

5 P—Q4	

This straightforward move is the strongest against the Steinitz defence proper (3 .... P—Q3; 4 P—Q4). Here, curiously enough, it proves to be the least energetic.

5	B—Q2

A rather anxious reply. By boldly playing 5 .... P—QKt4; 6 B—Kt3, Kt×P (but not 6 .... P×P, on account of 7 B—Kt5, followed by 8 Kt×P); 7 Kt×Kt, P×Kt, Black could have given the game an incisive character, as follows:

(*a*) 8 Q×P (a cruel mistake); 8 .... P—QB4; 9 Q—Q5 (gladly attacking two objects, Black's QR and KBP); 9 .... B—K3; 10 Q—B6 ch, B—Q2; 11 Q—Q5, P—B5, winning a piece for two pawns. This opening trap is called "Noah's Ark," and has even occurred in master play.

(*b*) 8 B—Q5, R—Kt1; 9 B—B6 ch (or at once 9 Q×P, B—Q2; 10 P—QR3, with approximately even games); 9 .... B—Q2; 10 B×B ch, Q×B; 11 Q×P, etc., with a simplified position tending to equality.

(*c*) 8 P—QB3 (in gambit style, trying to liven up the game); 8 .... B—Kt2 (after 8 .... P×P, White would at the least have a forced draw by 9 Q—Q5, B—K3; 10 Q—B6 ch, B—Q2; 11 Q—Q5, etc.); 9 P×P, Kt—B3, with chances for both sides.

6 B—Kt3	

Releasing his hold without necessity. He could have kept up the tension by 6 P—B3, after which Black could have continued straightforwardly by 6 .... Kt—B3, or more insidiously by 6 .... KKt—K2, followed by .... Kt—Kt3; .... B—K2, etc., or finally by 6 .... P—KKt3, followed by 7 .... B—Kt2, etc., with a playable game.

6 ......   B—K2
Of course not 6 .... Kt—B3; 7 B—Kt5, etc.

7 P × P	P × P
8 Q—Q5	B—K3
9 Q × Q ch	R × Q
10 B × B	P × B
11 P—B3	

White's plan, initiated by his sixth move, is now clear: elimination of the Queens and creation of a doubled pawn in the hostile camp. But, for once, Dr. Lasker, the great end-game player, is at fault; he overlooks that a genuine end-game is still very far off.

Black already commands the open Q file, and will soon operate on the KB file as well.

| 11 ...... | Kt—B3 |
| 12 QKt—Q2 | B—B4 |

And here is, in addition, a diagonal which will be under Black's management.

| 13 P—QKt4 | B—R2 |
| 14 P—QR4 | P—QKt4 |

Cutting short White's designs on the extreme Queen's wing.

15 K—K2

Useless would be 15 P × P, P × P; 16 R—R6, B—Kt3 (or 16 Kt × P, B × P ch).

15 ......   B—Kt3

Evading the threat 16 P × P, P × P; 17 Kt × P.

16 P × P	P × P
17 Kt—K1	R—KB1
18 P—B3	R—B2
19 Kt—Kt3	

A very natural desire to let the inactive Bishop into the open. Yet it is a tactical inadvertence by which Black will be enabled to turn his positional advantage into one of material. 19 R—B1 is necessary as a preliminary measure.

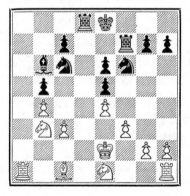

19 ......   Kt × KP

Gain of a pawn of which the protection is illusory (20 P × Kt, R—B7 mate). The rest is a question of technique.

| 20 B—Kt2 | Kt—Q3 |

Threatens not only 21 .... Kt—B5, but also the break-through (even against 21 Kt—Q2) by 21 .... P—K5, etc.

21 R—KB1	Kt—B5
22 B—B1	Kt—K2
23 B—Kt5	Kt—Q4

Well calculated. This sacrifice of the exchange enables Black to take the hostile King under the concentrated fire of four batteries.

24 B × R	Kt—B5 ch
25 K—Q1	R—Q2 ch
26 K—B2	

Or 26 K—B1, Kt—K7 ch, etc.

26	Kt—K6 ch
27 K—Kt2	Kt × R
28 B—Kt5	Kt—K6
29 B × Kt	P × B

After a few exchanges, Black remains with only an extra pawn, but with the same overwhelming positional advantage.

| 30 R—B1 | P—K4 |
| Resigns | |

Practically a *Zugzwang* position for White, while Black can further intensify the pressure by 31 .... R—Q3 and .... R—Kt3 or R3.

103

| *White* | *Black* |
| CAPABLANCA | MARSHALL |

(Match, 1909)

The historical interest of this game lies in the introduction of a new variation (5 .... P—B4), which caused White a great deal of trouble.

Having recognised the value of this line of play, which had then passed unnoticed, Capablanca revived it eighteen years later in the Budapest tournament of 1928, thus creating the "Siesta Gambit."

1 P—K4	P—K4
2 Kt—KB3	Kt—QB3
3 B—Kt5	P—QR3
4 B—R4	P—Q3
5 P—B3	P—B4

Reminiscent of the *Schliemann Defence*

(3 .... P—KB4), without its attendant risks.
Less imaginative, but equally playable, are
the following continuations:

(*a*) 5 .... B—Q2, consolidating the inner
lines.

(*b*) 5 .... Kt—B3, a purely developing
move.

6 P×P

A normal reply. A line of play leading—
by sacrificial play along the edge of a precipice—to a theoretical draw is 6 P—Q4.
(See No. 105, Réti-Capablanca.)

    6 ......   B×P

Bad would be, at once, 6 .... P—K5;
7 Kt—Q4.

7 P—Q4   P—K5

Trying to establish an effective outpost.
Neither 7 .... P×P; 8 Kt×P, etc., nor
7 .... P—QKt4; 8 B—Kt3, etc., is favourable to Black.

8 Q—K2

The battle is joined in the centre. Against
8 Kt—Kt5; 8 .... P—Q4 is a consolidating
reply. 8 P—Q5 results in skirmishes which
lead to a draw. The *intermediary* manœuvre 8 B—KKt5 is shown in game No. 104,
A. Steiner-Capablanca.

    8 ......   B—K2
    9 KKt—Q2   Kt—B3
    10 P—KR3

White's mobilisation is slow, but he hopes
sooner or later to undermine Black's
advanced positions.

    10 ......   P—Q4

In the meantime Black strengthens his
central formation.

    11 Kt—B1   P—QKt4

This episode is less to the point than
11 .... Castles.

    12 B—B2   Kt—QR4
    13 Kt—K3   B—Kt3
    14 Kt—Q2   Castles
    15 P—QKt4

Having consolidated his base, White now
undertakes an offensive on the wing.

    15 ......   Kt—B5
    16 QKt×Kt   QP×Kt

After 16 .... KtP×Kt; 17 P—QR4,
White would have a definite majority on the
Q side, with an easy game. As it is, the
black KP is now exposed.

    17 P—QR4   Kt—Q4
    18 Kt×Kt   Q×Kt
    19 P×P

If 19 B—K3, P—QR4 disintegrates White's
Q side.

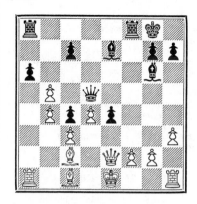

    19 ......   P—K6

Easing the position in the centre.

    20 Castles   R×P
    21 R×R   P×R ch
    22 Q×P   R—KB1
    23 Q—K2   B×B
    24 Q×QB   P×P
    25 B—K3   B—Q3

White's pawn structure on the Q side is
superior, but Black's pieces are more active.
The chances are becoming even.

    26 B—B2   Q—Kt4
    27 Q—K4

Preventing 27 .... Q—B5.

    27 ......   P—R3

Here 27 .... Q—Q7 leads to nothing, on
account of 28 B—K1 (or even 28 Q—K3,
as the exchange of Queens would favour
White).

    28 R—K1

After 28 R—R8, Q—B8 ch; 29 B—K1,
R×R; 30 Q×R ch, K—R2; 31 Q—K4 ch,
P—Kt3, etc., White's position would be
none too comfortable.

    28 ......   R×B

A clever liquidation.

    29 K×R   B—Kt6 ch
    30 K—Kt1   B×R
    31 Q×B   Drawn

In this game Marshall did honour to the
fine opening which he himself evolved.

104

White	Black
A. STEINER	CAPABLANCA

(Budapest, 1928)

The following game is of theoretical interest, as being, so to speak, the official consecration of this particular variation, which, incidentally, has derived its name from the fact that the 1928 tournament in Budapest was also called the "Siesta Tournament."

The contest itself is of great interest. The manner in which Black first of all nullifies his opponent's aspirations in the opening and then, after the exchange of Queens, slowly and gradually extends his domination of territory until it results in material gain, marks the great technician as well as the artist.

1 P—K4	P—K4
2 Kt—KB3	Kt—QB3
3 B—Kt5	P—QR3
4 B—R4	P—Q3
5 P—B3	P—B4
6 P×P	B×P
7 P—Q4	P—K5

It is clear that Black's game will remain powerful if he can maintain this advanced post.

8 B—KKt5	B—K2
9 Kt—R4	B—K3

A consolidating retreat, which parries all dangers.

10 B×B	Kt×B

Much inferior would be 10 .... Q×B; 11 P—Q5, Q×Kt; 12 P×Kt, P—QKt4; 13 B—Kt3, P—K6; 14 Castles, etc.

11 Q—R5 ch	P—Kt3
12 Q—R6	

Instead of this exaggerated optimism, sane strategy by 12 Q—K2, P—Q4; 13 Castles was called for.

12	Kt—KKt1

By this original retrograde manœuvre, Black reorganises his forces.

13 Q—B4	

After 13 Q—Kt7, there would have been no need for Black to resort to a sacrificial continuation by 13 .... Q×Kt; 14 B×Kt ch, P×B; 15 Q×R, Castles; for the simple line 13 .... Q—B3; 14 Q×BP, KKt—K2 secures the better chances for Black.

13	Kt—B3
14 Kt—Q2	Castles

Energetic as well as rational.

15 Castles KR	

He also hastens to bring his King into safety, before which 15 QKt×P would be too risky, e.g. 15 .... Kt×Kt; 16 Q×Kt, R—K1; 17 Castles QR (or 17 Castles KR, B—B5, winning the exchange); 17 .... Q—Kt4 ch; 18 R—Q2, P—Q4, and wins.

15	P—Q4

Threatening to win the KKt by 16 .... Kt—KR4.

16 Q—Kt5	

For if 16 P—KKt3, parrying the above-mentioned threat, 16 .... Kt—KKt5 now wins the Queen. After the text move White threatens to force a perpetual check by 17 KKt×P, P×Kt; 18 Q×P ch, K—R1; 19 Q—R6 ch, K—Kt1 (19 .... Kt—R2; 20 Q×B); 20 Q—Kt6 ch.

16	Kt—KR4
17 Q×Q	Kt×Q

And not 17 .... QR×Q; 18 B×Kt, P×B; 19 P—KKt3, etc., for Black desires to avoid any weakening of his pawn formation for the end-game.

18 P—KKt3	

Because of the threat 18 .... P—KKt4.

18	B—R6
19 Kt—Kt2	Kt—K3
20 B—Kt3	P—B3
21 B—Q1	

Better would be, either now or on the next move, P—KB4. The following exchange will only increase Black's offensive powers:

21	QR—K1
22 B×Kt	P×B
23 P—KB4	P—R5

Very cleverly getting rid of his isolated pawn.

24 KR—K1	P×P
25 P×P	B×Kt
26 K×B	R—K2
27 Kt—B1	R—Kt2

The threat 28 .... Kt×P ch forces a fresh displacement of the hostile King.

28 K—R1	P—KR4

Another battering-ram aimed at White's defences (by 29 .... P—R5).

29 P—B4	

For which reason White tries to worry his adversary on another sector of the front.

29	Kt × QP
30 KR—Q1	Kt—B6
31 P × P	P—R5

Simpler would be, first, 31 .... P × P; 32 QR × P, P—R5, for now White grasps the counter-chance which the text move affords him.

32 P—Q6	P × P
33 K—Kt2	Kt—R5 ch
34 K—Kt1	P—Kt7

This new and premature advance renders Black's task more difficult. A mistake would also be 34 .... R × P; 35 P—Q7. But the preparatory 34 .... K—R2 would be very strong, e.g. 35 QR—B1, R × P; 36 P—Q7, R—B7; 37 Kt × P (37 P—Q8 (Q) leads to a mate in two); 37 .... R—Kt7 ch; 38 K—R1 (or 38 K—B1, R—B2 ch; 39 K—K1, Kt—B6 mate); 38 .... R (Kt2) × Kt; 39 R—B3, Kt—B6; 40 R × Kt, P × R, followed by 41 .... R—R6 mate.

| 35 Kt—R2 | R × P |

A diabolical pitfall, which White, however, avoids.

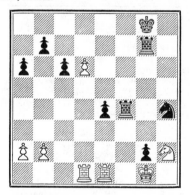

36 R—Q4

Gaining a *tempo* by the threat of 37 P—Q7, which enables him to bring his other Rook into play. Premature would be, at once, 36 P—Q7, R—B8 ch; 37 Kt × R (or 37 .... R × R; 38 P × R (Q) db ch, K × Q; 39 R × P, remaining with two extra pawns); 37 .... Kt—B6 ch; 38 K—B2, P—Kt8 (Q) ch; 39 K—K2, R—Kt7 mate.

36	R—Q2
37 R—K1	Kt—B4
38 KR × P	R × R
39 R × R	R × P
40 Kt—B3	R—Kt3
41 R—K5	Kt—Q3
42 R—K2	K—B1
43 R × P	R—B3

After 43 .... R × R ch; 44 K × R, the ensuing Knight ending would hold out little promise.

44 Kt—K5	K—K2
45 R—KB2	R—K3
46 Kt—Q3	R—K6
47 Kt—B4	Kt—B5
48 P—Kt3	Kt—K4
49 Kt—Kt2	R—QB6
50 R—K2	K—Q3
51 K—B1	R—B8 ch

A cunning check, for if now 52 Kt—K1, Kt—Q6 brings about a general liquidation, and if 52 R—K1, Kt—Q6; 53 R × R, Kt × R wins another pawn.

52 K—B2	Kt—Q6 ch
53 K—K3	Kt—Kt5
54 P—R3	

Else there follows 54 .... R—QR8; 55 P—R4, R—QKt8.

| 54 ...... | R—B6 ch |
| 55 K—Q4 | R—B7 |

A pretty resource.

| 56 R—K1 | P—B4 ch |

Winning a second pawn and—in spite of White's heroic resistance—the game.

57 K—K4	R × Kt
58 P × Kt	R—Kt5 ch
59 K—Q3	P × P

More effective than 59 .... R × P; 60 K—B3, etc. But in either case the Rook ending leaves White without hope.

White resigned in a few more moves.

105

| White | Black |
| RÉTI | CAPABLANCA |

(Berlin, 1928)

The preceding game marked the birth of a variation. This one confirms its value by subjecting White to a terrible débâcle.

1 P—K4	P—K4
2 Kt—KB3	Kt—QB3
3 B—Kt5	P—QR3
4 B—R4	P—Q3
5 P—B3	P—B4

The *Siesta Gambit* at work.

6 P—Q4
Trying an upheaval of the centre.

6 ......   BP × P
After 6 .... KP × P; 7 B × Kt ch, P × B;
8 Kt × P, White would have the best of it.

7 Kt—Kt5
The crucial moment. An automatic draw
would be brought about (as shown in the
first instance by Maróczy) by 7 Kt × P,
P × Kt; 8 Q—R5 ch, K—K2; 9 B—Kt5 ch,
Kt—B3; 10 B × Kt, P × B; 11 P × P,
Q—Q4 (ingeniously maintaining his gain, for
if now 12 P × Kt ch, P × P, White's Bishop is
pinned); 12 B—R4, K—K3; 13 B × Kt,
P × B; 14 Q—K8 ch, K—B4; 15 Q—R5 ch,
K—K3; 16 Q—K8 ch, with perpetual check.
This draw by a sacrifice is reminiscent of the
Möller Attack in the *Giuoco Piano.*

7 ......   P × P
An interesting idea, due to the Russian
master Znosko-Borovsky, is 7 .... P—Q4;
8 P × P, B—QB4.

8 Kt × KP
Simplification by 8 B × Kt, P × B; 9 Q × P
is essential here.

8 ......   Kt—B3
9 B—KKt5   B—K2
10 Q × P
Heedless. But even after 10 B × Kt ch,
P × B; 11 Q × P, Castles, Black has an
advantage in territory, thanks to his open
KB file. The best, therefore, would be
10 B × Kt, B × B; 11 Q—R5 ch, P—Kt3
(or else 11 .... K—B1); 12 Q—Q5, and the
chances are approximately even.

10 ......   P—Kt4
11 Kt × Kt ch   P × Kt
Now there are three white pieces *en prise.*

12 Q—Q5   KtP × B
Black, with two opposing Bishops liable
to capture, makes a wise selection, for if
12 .... BP × B; 13 B—Kt3 saves the piece.

13 B—R6
Trying to force a way into the enemy
camp, as after 13 Q × Kt ch, B—Q2, Black
wins.

13 ......   Q—Q2
The *coup juste,* which defends the threat-
ened Knight and vacates a square for the
King, parrying the threat of a perpetual
check.
A terrible blunder would be 13 ....
B—Q2; 14 Q—R5 mate.

14 Castles   B—Kt2
15 B—Kt7   Castles

After this reply events crowd fast on one
another.

16 B × R   Kt—K4
Putting down his trumps.

17 Q—Q1
Or, for instance, 17 Q—Q4, Kt—B6 ch;
18 P × Kt, R—Kt1 ch; 19 K—R1, B × P mate.

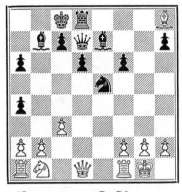

17 ......   B—B6
A *break-up sacrifice.*

18 P × B
Or 18 Q—Q4, R—Kt1; 19 P—KKt3,
Q—R6, etc.
Now White hopes to survive after the
continuation 18 .... R—Kt1 ch; 19 K—R1,
Q—R6; 20 R—Kt1, R × R; 21 Q × R,
Q × BP ch; 22 Q—Kt2, etc.

18 ......   Q—R6
Black's last four moves were hammer-
blows.

Resigns
(For the double threat 19 .... R—Kt1 ch
and 19 .... Kt × P ch cannot be parried.)

106

White   Black
ALEKHINE   KOLTANOWSKI
(London, 1932)

*After an opening on accepted lines, White,
in this game, at first merely tries to maintain
his positional advantage by precautionary
measures (19 P—QR3 and 20 P—KR3),
putting his trust in the dynamic resources
occasioned thereby.*
The resulting sacrifice (22 Kt × QBP) is of

an unusual nature. After the break-up of Black's Q side, White's entry on the K side is all the more effective.

1 P—K4	P—K4
2 Kt—KB3	Kt—QB3
3 B—Kt5	P—QR3
4 B—R4	P—Q3
5 B × Kt ch	

In this line of play, which might be termed the *Exchange Variation Deferred*, White tries to solve the problem of the opening by sheer simplicity.

5	P × B
6 P—Q4	P × P

Thus giving up the centre shows less tenacity than its maintenance by 6 .... P—B3; e.g. 7 B—K3, Kt—K2; 8 Kt—B3, B—K3 (this regrouping is more flexible than either 8 .... Kt—Kt3; 9 Q—Q2, B—K2; 10 Castles QR, or 8 .... P—Kt3; 9 Q—Q2, B—Kt2; 10 B—R6, etc.); 9 Q—Q2, Kt—B1; 10 Castles QR (after 10 Castles KR, the struggle soon slows down); 10 .... Kt—Kt3; 11 P—QKt3, B—K2, and Black's defence is solid.

7 Kt × P

This is more effective than 7 Q × P, Kt—B3; 8 Castles, B—K2, with an even game.

7	B—Q2

After 7 .... P—QB4; 8 Kt—KB3, Black's Q4 is materially weakened, and White threatens to advance P—K5 eventually.

8 Castles

Unassumingly completing the development of his K side. More ambitious appears to be 8 Kt—QB3, Kt—B3; 9 Q—B3 (threat: 10 P—K5), but by the immediate countermeasures 9 .... P—B4; 10 Kt—B5, B × Kt; 11 P × B (if not quite peaceably 11 Q × B); 11 .... B—K2; 12 Q—B6 ch, Kt—Q2; 13 Kt—Q5, R—R2 (making everything safe); 14 Castles, Castles, etc., Black restores the balance.

8	P—Kt3

Playable, but it requires more circumspection than the normal development by 8 .... Kt—B3; 9 Kt—QB3, B—K2, etc., with equal chances.

9 Kt—QB3	B—Kt2
10 R—K1	

Preventing the straightforward 10 .... Kt—B3 (which would be answered by 11 P—K5).

If 10 B—K3, Kt—B3; 11 P—KR3 (11 Q—Q2, Kt—Kt5); 11 .... Castles; 12 Q—Q2, R—K1; 13 B—Kt5, Q—Kt1 (now two white pawns are attacked); 14 B × Kt, B × B, and Black has two Bishops.

10	Kt—K2
11 B—B4	

Following up the idea of his sixth move: to exert pressure on K5, preparing at the same time to post a battery—Queen and Bishop—on a black diagonal.

11	Castles
12 Q—Q2	P—QB4
13 Kt—Kt3	

Simpler would be 13 KKt—K2, but at all events not 13 Kt—B3, because of 12 .... B—Kt5.

13	Kt—B3
14 B—R6	

A positional exchange—in the result Black, deprived of his defensive KB, will remain weak on the *black square complex*.

14	B—K3
15 B × B	K × B
16 Kt—Q5	P—B3
17 QR—Q1	R—QKt1
18 Q—B3	Q—B1
19 P—QR3	

Having achieved a positional superiority by virtue of his pressure on the long black diagonal and on the Q file, White is mainly concerned in preventing liberating measures by Black (such as 19 .... Kt—Kt5).

19	Q—Kt2
20 P—R3	

Another modest-looking move. But it may prove essential (flight square for the King!) in some sub-variation of the important events now in course of preparation.

20	R—B2
21 R—K3	Q—Kt4

The crisis. In view of his adversary's threatening preparations he should, for better or for worse, have resigned himself to simplification by 21 .... B × Kt. This would eliminate an important unit, and after the probable continuation 22 P × B, Kt—Q5; 23 Kt × Kt, P × Kt; 24 R × P, Q × P (an eye for an eye, a pawn for a pawn!); 25 Q—Q2, Q—R8 ch, Black could hope to hold his own, although White has some positional advantage.

The move in the text is intended to threaten 22 .... P—B5, but the Queen strays too far away from the main battlefield.

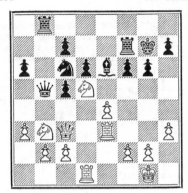

22 Kt×P (B7)
A *break-up sacrifice*, many moves deep.

22 ......　　　　R×Kt
23 R×P
White, with two pawns for his piece, and threatening the very heart of the enemy position, need not fear the future.

23 ......　　　　B—B5
Amongst various possible replies, all of which had to be taken into consideration by White, the following may be noted:
23 .... Kt—Q1; 24 R—B3, R—B2; 25 Kt×P, Q—K1; 26 QR×P, and White without slackening his attack already has four pawns for his piece.
Or 23 .... Kt—Q5; 24 Kt×Kt, and wins.
Or 23 .... Q—B5; 24 Kt×P, etc.
Or 23 .... B×Kt; 24 Q×P ch, K—R3; 25 R×B, Q—R5; 26 R×Kt, recovering his piece in decisive fashion.
Or 23 .... P—B5; 24 R×B, P×Kt; 25 Q×BP ch, K—R3; 26 R×KtP, etc.
Or 23 .... R—K1; 24 Kt×P, Kt—Q1; 25 P—QKt4, meeting all threats.
Or 23 .... K—B2; 24 R—B3, K—K2; 25 P—QR4, Q—Kt3; 26 R×B ch, K×R; 27 Kt×P ch, K—Q3; 28 Q×P ch, K×Kt; 29 R—B3 ch, K—Kt5; 30 Q—Q6 ch, K—R4; 31 Q—Q5 ch, K×P; 32 R—R3 ch, K—Kt5; 33 P—B3 mate.
Or, finally, 23 .... B—B2; 24 R×P, Kt—Q5 (or 24 .... K—Kt1; 25 Kt×P, Q×P; 26 Kt×P, etc.); 25 Kt×Kt, P×Kt; 26 Q×R, K×R; 27 R—B3 ch, and wins.

24 P—QR4
A manifold *deflecting sacrifice* (Bishop, Knight or QBP).

24 ......　　　　Q×P
25 Kt×P　　　　Q—Kt4
26 Q×P ch　　　K—Kt1
27 Kt—Q7
The hero of the piece.

27 ......　　　　R—Q1
If 27 .... QR—QB1; 28 R—KB3, etc., and if 27 .... R—K1; 28 Q—QB3, and wins.

28 R—KB3
Indirectly guarding the Knight.

28 ......　　　　Q—Kt5
Intending to threaten 29 .... KR×Kt.

29 P—B3　　　　Q—Kt4
30 Kt—K5
The *coup de grâce.*

30 ......　　　　R(Q1)—QB1
31 Kt×Kt　　　　Resigns
(31 .... R×Kt; 32 R—Q8 ch, R×R; 33 Q×R, K—Kt2; 34 Q—B8 mate.)

107

White	Black
KERES	ALEKHINE

(Margate, 1937)

In this game Black gets into early difficulties about castling, which he finally effects at the cost of a pawn and a general deterioration of his position. After that, things go quickly downhill for Black against White's finely incisive play.

At the end of the game, and in a lost position, we have the very exceptional occurrence of an oversight by Dr. Alekhine.

1 P—K4	P—K4
2 Kt—KB3	Kt—QB3
3 B—Kt5	P—QR3
4 B—R4	P—Q3
5 P—B4	

White tries incisive methods. The text move, reminiscent of the *Duras Variation* (3 .... P—QR3; 4 B—R4, Kt—B3; 5 P—Q3, P—Q3; 6 P—B4), tries to blockade the square at Q5 and to prevent 5 .... P—QKt4.

5 ......　　　　B—Q2
In affecting this measure, which sooner or later becomes necessary, he reserves the option of various possibilities on the K side, 6 .... Kt—B3, or 6 .... B—K2, or 6 .... P—KKt3. In a curious game, Böök-Andersen, *Warsaw*, 1935, the counter-thrust 5 .... P—B4 was tried and found wanting.

The game went on: 6 P—Q4, BP×P; 7 Kt×P (this sacrifice, which only produces a draw after 5 P—B3, P—B4, proves decisive in this position); 7 .... P×Kt; 8 Q—R5 ch, K—K2; 9 B×Kt, Q×P (after 9 .... P×B; 10 B—Kt5 ch, Kt—B3; 11 P×P, Black, not having in this case the astute defence 11 .... Q—Q4, again forfeits the piece); 10 Q—K8 ch, K—Q3 (now after 11 Q×KB ch, Kt—K2; 12 Q×R, B—Kt5, etc., Black would win); 11 B—K3, Q×BP (not 11 .... Q×KtP; 12 P—B5 mate); 12 Kt—B3, B—Kt5; 13 R—Q1 ch, and Black resigns.

6 Kt—B3   P—KKt3
After 6 .... Kt—B3 White could more easily obtain a lasting pressure in the centre by 7 P—Q4, B—K2; 8 Castles, etc.

7 P—Q4
In preference to methodical preparations by 7 P—Q3, B—Kt2; 8 B—K3, etc., White seeks an immediate upheaval in the centre.

7 ......   B—Kt2
8 B—K3   Kt—B3
More rational is 8 .... KKt—K2, leaving the wing Bishop with a free horizon.

9 P×P   P×P
He avoids—much to his detriment—the simplification 9 .... QKt×P; 10 Kt×Kt, P×Kt, for if then 11 B—B5, Black could hold his own by 11 .... B×B; 12 Q×B ch, Q—Q2, etc.

10 B—B5
Now, however, Black's inability to castle on the K side is a real drawback.

10 ......   Kt—KR4
This attempt to obtain the initiative is easily refuted, and he should therefore have tried to free his position by 10 .... Kt—KKt1, followed by .... KKt—K2.

11 Kt—Q5
Countering Black's intention to play his KKt to his K3 via KB5.

11 ......   Kt—B5
12 Kt×Kt   P×Kt
13 P—K5
Offering a pawn—a deep conception.

13 ......   P—KKt4
Although acceptance by 13 .... Kt×P; 14 Kt×Kt, B×Kt; 15 Q—K2 would leave White with a clear-cut attack, it would have been preferable to the text move, which in no way eases Black's position.

14 Q—Q5   KB—B1
If—intent on his own schemes—14 .... P—Kt5, there follows the sparkling 15 P—K6, QB×P (15 .... P×P; 16 Q—R5 mate); 16 B×Kt ch, P×B; 17 Q×P ch, B—Q2; 18 Q—K4 ch, B—K3; 19 R—Q1, Q—B1; 20 Q—B6 ch, B—Q2; 21 R×B, Q×R; 22 Q×R ch, and wins.

15 B×B   R×B
16 Castles QR   Q—K2
17 B×Kt
Stopping Black from castling on the Q side as well.

17 ......   B×B
18 Q—Q3   B—Q2
This makes castling possible at last, but at the price of a pawn. More steady in any case would be 18 .... P—R3, keeping as far as possible his patrimony intact.

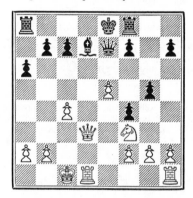

19 Kt×P
This Knight cannot, of course, be captured.

19 ......   Castles
20 Kt—B3
A wise decision, for if 20 Kt×RP, R—R1; 21 Kt—B6, B—Kt5, and Black wins the exchange.

20 ......   P—KB3
21 P×P   R×P
22 KR—K1
White has an overwhelming position.

22 ......   Q—Kt5
A mistake, of course, in a bad position, and leading to a *débâcle*. But if 22 .... Q—Kt2; 23 Q—Q4, threatening 24 Q—R7, or eventually Kt—K5.

23 Q×B ch   Resigns.

108

White	Black
WINAWER	ENGLISCH

(London, 1883)

The art of penetrating into the enemy fastness is tellingly illustrated in the following game. The fact that the plan, once conceived, takes a long time to carry out only emphasises the difficulties of the problem in hand.

1 P—K4	P—K4
2 Kt—KB3	Kt—QB3
3 B—Kt5	P—QR3
4 B×Kt	

The "exchange variation," which seeks to solve the puzzle of the opening by simplification.

4	QP×B

A more artificial continuation is 4 .... KtP×B, for now Black sees a compensation for his doubled pawn in the open Q file and the mobility of his QB.

5 Castles

As is well known, the gain of a pawn by 5 Kt×P is illusory, on account of 5 .... Q—Q5, or, more vigorously still, 5 .... Q—Kt4.

5	B—KKt5

Playing for the initiative.

6 P—KR3	B×Kt

But already abandoning the quest; and yet the attempt 6 .... P—KR4; 7 P—Q3 (clearly not 7 P×B, P×P; 8 Kt×P, Q—R5; 9 P—KB4, P—Kt6, forcing mate); 7 .... Q—B3, etc., is to be commended.

7 Q×B	Q—Q3
8 P—Q3	

The game assumes a quiet course, even though the contestants will castle on opposite wings.

8	P—B3
9 Kt—Q2	Castles
10 Kt—B4	Q—K3
11 Q—Kt3	P—KKt4
12 P—QR4	P—Kt3

It is necessary to avoid a blockade by 13 P—R5, whereas now, after 13 P—R5, P—Kt4 the Q side files would remain closed.

13 B—K3	Kt—K2
14 P—KB3	Kt—Kt3
15 Q—K1	P—QR4
16 Q—B3	B—Kt5
17 Q—Kt3	Q—K2
18 P—Kt3	P—R4
19 K—Kt2	P—R5
20 P—Kt4	

White also sees to it that his castled position remains safely closed.

20	KR—K1
21 K—R2	Kt—B1
22 P—B3	B—B4
23 QR—Q1	Kt—K3
24 Q—B2	B×B
25 Kt×B	Q—B4
26 Kt—B5	R—Q2
27 R—Q2	KR—Q1
28 KR—Q1	Kt—B5

Not unskilfully, Black has established this strong point without, however, supporting its pressure by the aid of some other piece.

29 P—Q4

Just in time, White transforms the weakness of the backward pawn into a powerful lever in the centre.

29	Q—B5
30 P—Q5	

On the strength of a tactical *finesse*, this advance is more disturbing for Black than 30 P—Kt3, Q—B2, etc.

30	P×P

This impatient haste to eliminate his doubled pawn is easy to understand, but first 30 .... K—Kt1 also has its points.

31 P×P	K—Kt1

Threatening 32 .... R×P, which at this point would still be premature because of 31 .... R×P; 32 Kt—K7 ch (or if 31 .... Kt×QP; 32 R×Kt, R×R; 33 Kt—K7 ch, etc.).

32 Q—K4

An ingenious defence, whereas after 32 P—Q6, P×P; 33 Kt×QP, R×Kt; 34 R×R, R×R; 35 R×R, Q—B8 Black's threats would be very powerful.

32	Q×Q

If 32 .... Q—B4; 33 P—B4, Q—Kt5; 34 Q—B2, etc., but 32 .... Q—Kt6 would have been playable.

After the exchange of Queens the impetus on either side seems to have died down, and a long period of "war of attrition" now sets in.

33 P×Q	K—Kt2
34 R—KB2	P—B3
35 P—B4	P—B4
36 Kt—K3	R—K1
37 R—QR1	R—KB1
38 R—R3	R—B1
39 R—Kt3	

Mountain artillery.

39	R—KB1
40 Kt—B2	R—QR1
41 K—Kt1	R—K1
42 K—B1	R—QR1
43 R (B2)—B3	R—K1
44 Kt—K3	R—KB1
45 Kt—B5	R—K1
46 R—Kt5	

Whilst Black is condemned to complete passivity behind his cramped lines, White's pieces display a surprising activity. He now threatens not only 47 KR—QKt3, but also 47 P—Kt4 (47 .... RP×P; 48 P—R5 or 47 .... BP×P; 48 P—B5).

46	K—R2

Enabling him to reply to 47 KR—QKt3 by 47 .... R—QKt1.

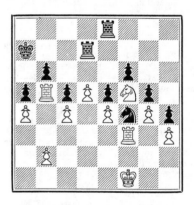

47 P—Kt4
A sacrifice which disintegrates the enemy bulwarks. The sequel is dramatic.

47	RP×P

In the problemist's parlance, a "mirror variation"—47 .... BP×P; 48 P—B5.

48 P—R5	R—QKt1

Trying to patch up the breach. After 48 .... P×P; 49 R×P ch, K—Kt3; 50 R—Kt5 ch, K—B2; 51 R×P ch K—Q1; 52 R—QKt3, the end would be swift.

49 R—QKt3	R—QB2
50 R—Kt1	R—Q2

Or 50 .... Kt×RP; 51 R—R1, threatening 52 P×P db ch, K—Kt2; 53 Kt—Q6 mate.

51 R—R1	R (Kt1)—Kt2
52 P×P dbl ch	K—Kt1
53 R—R6	R—Q1
54 R×BP	Kt×RP

The last gasp.

55 R (B5)—R5	K—B1
56 P—B5	P—Kt6
57 P—B6	P—Kt7
58 R—R8 ch	

Or—as a "dual"—58 Kt—K7 ch, followed by 59 R—R8 mate.

58	R—Kt1
59 Kt—K7 mate	

109

White	Black
LASKER	STEINITZ

(Match, 1894)

A game which is impressive, not only in the singleness of purpose with which Black carries out the main ideas underlying the defence (pressure on the open Q file and co-operation of the two Bishops), but also by the economy of means employed (break-up sacrifice, 18 .... P—B5; overwhelming advance, 34 .... P—B4; and quite particularly the Knight v. Bishop ending, with its almost geometrical aspect). Such games demonstrate that the absence of Queens need not deprive the play of life and movement.

1 P—K4	P—K4
2 Kt—KB3	Kt—QB3
3 B—Kt5	P—QR3
4 B×Kt	QP×B
5 P—Q4	

Logical play, for only in the end-game can White turn his extra pawn on the K side to account.

5	P×P

Accepting the challenge of "having it out in the centre." An interesting idea (due to the former U.S. champion, Marshall) is 5 .... B—KKt5; 6 P×P (alternatively 6 B—K3); 6 .... Q×Q ch; 7 K×Q, Castles ch; 8 K—K1 (best); 8 .... R—K1, and Black recovers his pawn.

6 Q×P

If 6 Kt×P, P—QB4, and the exchange of Queens will be effected in circumstances less favourable for White. Now, by the early exchange of Queens White would like, so to speak, to eliminate the whole phase of the middle game and rapidly enter upon the end-game.

6 ......   Q×Q
7 Kt×Q   P—QB4

The most active continuation. Playable also is 7 .... B—Q2 at once, followed by .... Castles QR. If 7 .... Kt—B3; 8 Kt—Q2.

8 Kt—K2   B—Q2
9 QKt—B3

Instead of this simple development, a more astute mobilisation results from 9 P—QKt3, e.g. 9 .... B—B3; 10 P—KB3, B—K2; 11 B—Kt2, and White covers the whole of the territory. Or 9 .... P—B5; 10 P×P, B—K3; 11 Kt—Q2, and White holds on to his pawn.

9 ......   Castles

After his rapid and straightforward development, Black has already overcome all the difficulties of the opening.

10 B—B4   B—B3
11 Castles KR   Kt—B3
12 P—B3

Thus White's majority in the centre is held for a long time to come.

12 ......   B—K2
13 Kt—Kt3   P—KKt3
14 KR—K1   Kt—Q2
15 Kt—Q1   Kt—Kt3
16 Kt—B1

With the idea of controlling his Q2, but all this regrouping behind the front demonstrates that all is not well with White.

16 ......   R—Q2
17 B—K3   KR—Q1

Black has massed his troops on the critical sector and, in the sequel, will demonstrate that, in spite of the exchange of Queens, the end-game is not yet, and the play shows the sacrifices and other conceptions germane to the middle game.

18 P—QKt3   P—B5

A fine pawn sacrifice, which devaluates the hostile pawn mass.

19 B×Kt   P×B
20 P×P   B—Kt5
21 P—B3   B—B4 ch
22 K—R1   R—Q6
23 R—B1   P—QR4

If at once 23 .... P—B4; 24 Kt—Kt2.

24 Kt (Q1)—K3

Making for Q5. He should have tried to perturb his adversary with 24 Kt—Kt2.

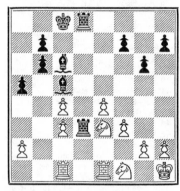

24 ......   P—B4

A magnificent conception, breaking down the King's defences.

25 P×P

Or 25 Kt—Q5, P×P; 26 P×P, with new weaknesses in White's position.

25 ......   P×P
26 P—KR3

If 26 Kt×P, R×KBP; 27 Kt—K7 ch (27 P×R, B×P mate—triumph of the *two Bishops*); 27 .... B×Kt; 28 P×R, B×P ch; 29 K—Kt1, B—B4 ch; 30 Kt—K3, R—Q7, and wins.

26 ......   R—Kt1

Upholding the mating threat (if 27 Kt×P, R×KBP; 28 P×B, B×P ch; 29 K—R2, B—Kt8 mate), and stressing the fact that, in addition to the oblique pressure (on the long white diagonal), there is now vertical pressure (on the open KKt file).

27 Kt—Q5   B×Kt
28 P×B   R×QP
29 KR—Q1   R×R
30 R×R   P—B5

This resplendent pawn blockades, on its own, not only the adverse Knight but the whole trio of white pawns on the K side.

31 K—R2

If 31 Kt—R2, P—R4; 32 R—Q5, R—K1, etc., and if 31 Kt—Q2, R—Q1.

31 ......   R—K1
32 P—QR4   K—B2

As the end-game approaches, the King sets out towards concrete objectives.

33	P—R4	K—B3
34	P—B4	B—Kt5
35	K—R3	R—K8

Masterly liquidation. In the ensuing ending, Bishop against Knight, Black holds the trump cards.

36	R×R	B×R
37	K—Kt4	K—B4
38	K×P	K×P
39	K—K4	

If 39 P—R5, then 39 .... P—Kt4; 40 P×P (or 40 Kt—K3 ch, K—Q6, threatening 41 .... B—Q7); 40 .... P—R5, and, with giant strides, the pawns make for the queening squares.

39	......	B×P
40	P—Kt3	B—Q1
41	Kt—K3 ch	K—Kt5
42	K—Q3	K×P
43	K—B2	K—Kt5
44	P—B4	K—B4
45	P—B5	K—Q3
46	P—Kt4	P—Kt4
47	Kt—Q1	K—K4
48	Kt—B3	P—Kt5
49	Kt—R4	K—Q5
50	Kt—Kt2	P—Kt4
51	K—Kt3	B—K2
52	P—Kt5	P—R5 ch
53	Kt×P	P×Kt ch
54	K×P	K—K4
55	K—Kt3	K×P

Resigns.

110

White   *Black*

LASKER   CAPABLANCA

(St. Petersburg, 1914)

A magnificent game, in which White attains the greatest possible effect with the utmost economy of means.

His twelfth move, P—B5, may be said to effect in itself a blockade of the whole of Black's position.

1	P—K4	P—K4
2	Kt—KB3	Kt—QB3
3	B—Kt5	P—QR3
4	B×Kt	

Lasker's speciality.

4	......	QP×B
5	P—Q4	P×P
6	Q×P	Q×Q
7	Kt×Q	B—Q3
8	Kt—QB3	

A purely developing move. If, more actively, 8 P—KB4, P—B3; while, against quiet moves such as 8 Castles, 8 B—K3, Black can, without inconvenience, reply 8 .... Kt—K2.

8	......	Kt—K2
9	Castles	Castles

Black could, with greater flexibility, have played 9 .... B—Q2, leaving his adversary in doubt as to the side on which he might castle.

10 P—B4

Partly showing his cards.

10	......	R—K1

With the threat, 11 .... B—QB4; 12 B—K3, Kt—Q4, etc., but simpler would be 10 .... B—QB4 at once.

11 Kt—Kt3

Already preventing the above-mentioned development of the KB and virtually threatening 12 P—K5.

11	......	P—B3

Resigning himself to a cramped game. However, if 11 .... P—KB4; 12 P—K5, B—Kt5; 13 Kt—K2, Kt—Kt3 did not appear desirable to him (on account of White's passed KP), Black should have taken the advantage of the opportunity of bringing his QB into the firing line by 11 .... B—K3.

12 P—B5

A bold advance—its good points (restriction of Black's QB and blockade of his Knight, extended range of his own QB) more than counter-balance its drawback (exposed KP). There follows a ferocious fight.

12	......	P—QKt3
13	B—B4	

He deprives his opponent of his only actively placed piece.

13	......	B—Kt2

The following continuation promises a little more freedom of action: 13 .... B×B; 14 R×B, P—B4; 15 R—Q1, B—Kt2, etc.

14 B×B

Inconsistent as this move may appear—it undoubles the adverse pawns—yet it increases the number of weaknesses in Black's position.

| 14 ...... | P × B |
| 15 Kt—Q4 | QR—Q1 |

As if under the spell of his opponent's will, Black restricts himself to too passive a defence. By playing 15 .... B—B1 (in order to prevent 16 Kt—K6) and then .... R—R2, Black could more or less count on some modest scope of activity.

16 Kt—K6

Intrusion. A Knight at K6 spells trouble.

16	R—Q2
17 QR—Q1	Kt—B1
18 R—B2	P—QKt4
19 R (B2)—Q2	R (Q2)—K2
20 P—QKt4	

Prevents Black from freeing his Bishop by 20 .... P—B4.

20 ......   K—B2

Caught, as he is, in a spider's web, Black would have done better to break free by 20 .... R × Kt; 21 P × R, R × P, etc., even at the cost of the exchange. A win for White would then be by no means certain.

21 P—QR3	B—R1
22 K—B2	R—R2
23 P—Kt4	P—R3
24 R—Q3	P—QR4

This counter-attempt adds to Black's difficulties. Here again 24 .... R × Kt would have been relatively the best expedient.

25 P—KR4	P × P
26 P × P	R (R2)—K2
27 K—B3	R—Kt1
28 K—B4	P—Kt3
29 R—Kt3	

Preparing QR—KKt1 and P—Kt5.

| 29 ...... | P—Kt4 ch |
| 30 K—B3 | Kt—Kt3 |

Better than this "trappy" move, at any rate, would be 30 .... P × P; 31 R—R3, P—Q4, etc.

31 P × P

White obtains a valuable asset by opening the KR file. 31 R × P, Kt—B5 would have allowed Black some counter-chances after .... Kt—K4 ch, etc.

31	RP × P
32 R—R3	R—Q2
33 K—Kt3	

He leaves the long white diagonal with a view to 34 P—K5.

33 ......   K—K1

Parrying—but only for the time being—the threatened advance of the KP.

34 QR—KR1

In order to win the Bishop by 35 R—R8.

34 ......   B—Kt2

35 P—K5

After this *vacating sacrifice* events move fast.

35	QP × P
36 Kt—K4	Kt—Q4
37 Kt (K6)—B5	B—B1

Compulsion. If 37 .... R—QB2; 38 Kt × B, R × Kt; 39 Kt—Q6 ch.

38 Kt × R	B × Kt
39 R—R7	R—B1
40 R—R1	K—Q1
41 R—R8 ch	B—B1
42 Kt—B5	Resigns

There is nothing to be done against the three threats: 43 R—Q7 ch, or 43 Kt—Kt7 ch, or 43 Kt—K6 ch. If, for instance, 42 .... Kt—Kt3; 43 R—Kt8, winning the Knight, and if 42 .... Kt—K2; 43 Kt—K6 ch, and wins.

111

| *White* | *Black* |
| FAKTOR | RUBINSTEIN |

(Lodz, 1916)

We recognise here the true meaning of the saying that "Before the end-game"—which White here would like to bring to pass by the exchange of Queens—"the gods have instituted the Middle Game"—in which Black busily creates weak points in the enemy camp.

1	P—K4	P—K4
2	Kt—KB3	Kt—QB3
3	B—Kt5	P—QR3
4	B × Kt	QP × B
5	P—Q4	P × P
6	Q × P	Q × Q
7	Kt × Q	B—Q3
8	P—KB4	P—B3
9	B—K3	Kt—K2
10	Kt—Q2	Kt—Kt3
11	P—KKt3	P—QB4
12	KKt—B3	P—Kt3
13	Castles KR	B—Kt2
14	KR—K1	Castles QR
15	B—B2	KR—K1

The mobilisation on either side being now completed, Black proceeds to lay siege to the exposed point in the opposing lines.

16	R—K2	R—Q2
17	QR—K1	QR—K2
18	P—KR4	P—KR4
19	P—B4	P—R4
20	P—R4	K—Q2
21	K—B1	B—B3
22	P—Kt3	K—B1
23	R—K3	B—Q2

Seeking a more favourable field of action.

24	K—Kt2	P—B3
25	QKt—Kt1	B—B2
26	Kt—B3	Kt—R1
27	R—Q3	Kt—B2
28	R (K1)—Q1	B—Kt5
29	R (Q1)—Q2	Kt—R3
30	B—Kt1	B—Kt1
31	B—B2	B—K3
32	R—Q1	B—KB2
33	B—Kt1	B—Kt3

White has long been reduced to a waiting policy, and now Black has succeeded in finding suitable employment for his QB.

34	Kt—Q2	Kt—B2
35	R—K1	B—KR2
36	K—B3	Kt—R3
37	B—B2	Kt—Kt5
38	B—Kt1	P—KKt4

After Black's lengthy and slow preparations, the struggle now proceeds at an accelerated pace.

39	R—K2	P × BP
40	P × P	R—Kt1
41	R—K1	R (K2)—KKt2
42	Kt—K2	P—B4

Forcibly piercing both the KB and the K files, for if now 43 P—K5, there follows the *break-up sacrifice* 43 .... B × P; 44 P × B, Kt × P ch; 45 K—K3, P—B5 ch; 46 Kt × P, R—Kt6 ch, and wins.

Thus a tactical *finesse* crowns Black's methodical preparations.

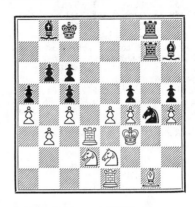

43	P × P	B (R2) × P
44	Kt—K4	

Or 44 R—B3, R—K1; 45 R (B3)—B1, resuming operations on the now open K file.

44	......	B × Kt ch

As soon as a white Knight shows signs of usefulness, it is ruthlessly eliminated, Black gaining material into the bargain (the KBP).

45	K × B	R—K1 ch
46	K—B3	R—KB2
47	R (Q3)—Q1	

Of no use would be 47 R—KB1, because of 47 .... B × P; 48 Kt × B, R × Kt ch; 49 K × R, R—B1 ch, followed by .... R × R, and Black still has won a vital pawn.

47	......	R (K1)—B1
48	R—KB1	B × P
49	Kt × B	R × Kt ch
50	K—Kt2	R × R
51	R × R	R × R
52	K × R	Kt—R3

In this ending the Knight must still hasten to accomplish an urgent task, for if the white King could reach K4 in time, Black's extra pawn, doubled and threatened, could hardly be exploited.

53	K—K2	Kt—B4
54	B—B2	Kt—Q5 ch
55	K—Q3	Kt × P
56	B—K3	

By restricting the opposing Knight, White recovers one of his pawns, but the resulting ending is won for Black.

56	K—Q2
57 K—B3	Kt—Q5
58 B×Kt	P×B ch
59 K×P	K—Q3
60 K—Q3	K—K4

Aiming at both sides.

A deceptive continuation—most instructive for the beginner—is as follows: 60 .... K—B4; 61 K—B3, P—Kt4 (or 61 .... K—Q3; 62 K—Q4, etc., holding his own); 62 BP×P, P×P; 63 P×P, K×P; 64 K—Kt3, K—B4; 65 K—R4, K—Q5; 66 K×P, K—K5; 67 K—Kt4, K—B5; 68 K—B3, K—Kt5; 69 K—Q2, K×P; 70 K—K2, K—Kt6; 71 K—B1, and—miraculously—White achieves the draw.

| 61 K—B3 | P—B4 |

Resigns.

(62 K—Q3, K—B5, etc.)

112

| White | Black |
| CAPABLANCA | JANOWSKI |

(St. Petersburg, 1914)

This game is notable for the exceedingly elegant manner in which White carries out an assault by pawns against a seemingly impregnable position.

1 P—K4	P—K4
2 Kt—KB3	Kt—QB3
3 B—Kt5	P—QR3
4 B×Kt	QP×B
5 Kt—B3	

A sound developing move, which leaves White free as regards future decisions in the centre.

| 5 ...... | B—QB4 |

After 5 .... B—QKt5; 6 Kt—K2, etc., or 5 .... B—KKt5; 6 P—KR3, etc., or 5 .... Kt—B3; 6 Kt×P, etc., or, finally, 5 .... B—Q3; 6 P—Q4, etc., White obtains the mastery in the centre.

Best is 5 .... P—B3, building up, from the first, a protective rampart in the centre, e.g. 6 Kt×P (an unsound sacrifice); 6 .... P×Kt; 7 Q—R5 ch, K—K2, etc., or 6 P—Q3, P—QB4, blocking the game, or 6 P—Q4, P×P; 7 Q×P, Q×Q; 8 Kt×Q, P—QB4; 9 KKt—K2, B—K3, followed by .... Castles QR, and Black has a good development.

| 6 P—Q3 | |

If 6 Kt×P, then not so much 6 .... B×P ch; 7 K×B, Q—Q5 ch; 8 K—K1, Q×Kt; 9 P—Q4, as 6 .... Q—Q5; 7 Kt—Q3, B—R2, and White, in spite of his extra pawn, has a difficult position.

| 6 ...... | B—KKt5 |

Here again 6 .... P—B3 would be more solid.

| 7 B—K3 | B×B |

If 7 .... B—Q3; 8 P—Q4.

| 8 P×B | Q—K2 |

There is not sufficient substance in Black's counter-plans. More wieldy would be 8 .... Kt—K2; 9 Castles, Castles, etc. Incidentally, a better place for the Queen would be at Q3.

| 9 Castles | Castles |

At this stage 9 .... Kt—B3, followed by .... Castles KR would be strategically sounder.

| 10 Q—K1 | Kt—R3 |

Here 10 .... Kt—B3 is preferable to the tortuous development in the text.

| 11 R—Kt1 | |

Marking the start of an attack.

11	P—B3
12 P—Kt4	Kt—B2
13 P—QR4	B×Kt
14 R×B	P—QKt3
15 P—Kt5	BP×P
16 P×P	P—QR4
17 Kt—Q5	Q—B4
18 P—B4	Kt—Kt4
19 R—B2	Kt—K3
20 Q—B3	R—Q2
21 R—Q1	K—Kt2

He remains in the danger zone. Flight to the other wing by 21 .... K—Q1 is to be preferred.

| 22 P—Q4 | |

This well-prepared advance gains much space.

| 22 ...... | Q—Q3 |

Compulsory, for if 22 .... Q—B1; 23 P×P.

23 R—B2	P×P
24 P×P	Kt—B5
25 P—B5	

A devastating advance. It is noteworthy that the whole phalanx of four white pawns co-operates in the attack.

25	Kt×Kt
26 P×Kt	Q×QP
27 P—B6 ch	K—Kt1
28 P×R	Q×QP
29 P—Q5	R—K1
30 P—Q6	P×P
31 Q—B6	

And White wins.

113

White	Black
DURAS	ALEKHINE

(Mannheim, 1914)

A grand battle of tactics.

1 P—K4	P—K4
2 Kt—KB3	Kt—QB3
3 B—Kt5	P—QR3
4 B×Kt	KtP×B

Unusual and interesting, but hardly as rational as 4 .... QP×B, which opens up Black's game.

5 P—Q4	P×P

If 5 .... Kt—B3; 6 B—Kt5.

6 Q×P	Q—B3

After the less incisive 6 .... P—Q3, there follows 7 Castles, Q—K2 (if 7 .... Kt—B3; 8 P—K5); 8 Kt—B3, Kt—B3; 9 R—K1, and Black is still restricted in his development.

7 Castles

Agreeing to simplification, whereas the more turbulent continuation 7 P—K5, Q—Kt3; 8 Castles, Q×P; 9 Kt—B3 would have given him a fine attacking position for the pawn he has lost.

7	Q×Q
8 Kt×Q	R—Kt1
9 Kt—Kt3	

If 6 P—QKt3, P—QB4; 10 Kt—K2, P—B5, with practical chances for Black.

9	Kt—K2
10 B—Q2	Kt—Kt3
11 B—B3	Kt—B5

Strategy of pin-pricks.

12 R—K1	B—K2
13 QKt—Q2	

If 13 B×P, R—Kt1, and if 13 P—Kt3, Kt—K3.

13	Castles
14 Kt—B4	

The mobilisation is completed, and manœuvring begins.

14	R—K1
15 Kt (B4)—R5	

Whilst this move restrains the opposing Q wing for some time to come, the QKt drifts too far away. The simplest would be 15 P—Kt3, Kt—K3; 16 QR—Q1.

15	B—B1
16 QR—Q1	P—QB4

In order to move his QP at last, which White will still try to prevent with his next two moves.

17 P—K5	Kt—K3
18 Kt—B4	P—R3
19 P—KR4	

Unnecessary finessing.

19	B—K2
20 P—Kt3	P—Kt4

An energetic advance.

21 P×P	P×P
22 Kt (Kt3)—R5	

As Black is exerting pressure on the K side, White tries to balance matters on the other wing.

22	K—R2

Making for his KKt3, in order to participate in the battle.

23 K—Kt2	K—Kt3
24 R—KR1	Kt—Q5

An *amplifying sacrifice*, by which Black tries to enlarge the scope of his operations.

25 B×Kt	P×B
26 R×P	B—Kt5
27 Kt—Kt3	

Evading the threat 27 .... B×Kt; 28 Kt×B, R×KtP, and three more white pawns would be *en prise*.

27	P—Q4

Attacking furiously.

28 Kt—K3

Not 28 P×P e. p., B—Kt2 ch; 29 P—B3, P×P; 30 Kt×P, R—K7 ch; 31 K—B1, B×P, etc., nor, of course, 28 R×P, B—Kt2.

28	P—QB4
29 R×P	

A judicious sacrifice of the exchange for two pawns, making an end to the furious activities of the two Bishops.

| 29 ..... | B—Kt2 |
| 30 P—QB4 | R × P |

Recovering a pawn—the balance of power again inclines towards Black.

31 P—R3

Instead of simply 31 R—Q1, White wishes to clear up the situation.

| 31 ..... | B × P |

Compulsory, as well as compelling. The hand-to-hand fight is most exciting.

32 Kt—R5

The counter-stroke. If 32 P × B, B × R ch; 33 P × B, QR × Kt; 34 R—Q1, R—K5; 35 P—Q6, R—Q5; 36 R × R, P × R; 37 P—Q7, R—Kt1; 38 Kt—B4, K—B3, and Black wins.

| 32 ..... | B × R ch |
| 33 P × B | |

Now Black faces the multiple threat 34 P × B, or 34 Kt—B6, or (after 33 .... R × KtP) 34 Kt (R5)—B4.

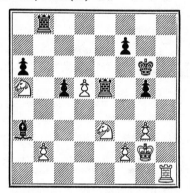

| 33 ..... | R × Kt |

A fine *riposte*. The skirmishes of the last five moves recall the thrust and parry of two brilliant fencers.

| 34 P × R | R × P ch |
| 35 K—B3 | P—B4 |

And not 35 .... R—Q7; 36 Kt—B4.

36 P—Kt4

Not 36 Kt—B4, P—Kt5 ch; 37 K—B4, R—Kt5.

36	P × P ch
37 K—K4	R—Kt5 ch
38 K—Q3	B—Kt7
39 P—Q6	B—B3
40 R—KB1	P—Kt6

A race between opposing pawns.

| 41 P—Q7 | R—Kt1 |
| 42 R—Q1 | |

Or 42 Kt—B6, P—Kt7; 43 R—KKt1 (or 43 R × B ch, K × R; 44 Kt × R, K—K2, and wins); 43 .... R—Kt3; 44 P—Q8 (Q), B × Q; 45 Kt × B, R—Q3 ch; 46 K—B4, R × Kt; 47 R × P, K—B4, and Black still wins.

42	P—Kt7
43 K—K2	R—Kt7 ch
44 K—B3	R—Q7

Conquest of the vital file and pawn.

45 R—KKt1	R × P
46 R × P	R—Q6
47 R—QB2	R—B6
48 R × R	B × R
49 Kt—B4	P—R4
50 Kt—Kt6	B—Kt5
Resigns.	

114

| *White* | *Black* |
| ENGLISCH | STEINITZ |

(London, 1883)

The reader who recognises that logic, justice and science can never be insipid or boring will find much hidden beauty in the following orderly game.

1 P—K4	P—K4
2 Kt—KB3	Kt—QB3
3 B—Kt5	P—KKt3

Unless White succeeds quickly in breaking down the barricades of this *Fianchetto Defence*, they will prove powerful.

4 P—Q4

That is why the text move is better than dilatory measures such as 4 P—B3 or 4 Castles, or again 4 Kt—B3.

| 4 ..... | P × P |
| 5 Kt × P | |

At this point the interlude 5 B—Kt5 (thought out in 1898 by that profound master Pillsbury) renders Black's defence most arduous, e.g. 5 .... P—B3; 6 B—KR4, B—Kt2; 7 Castles, etc., or 5 .... B—K2; 6 B × B, Q × B; 7 Castles, with advantage to White.

| 5 ..... | B—Kt2 |
| 6 B—K3 | |

Trying to establish a cluster of pieces in

the centre. If 6 Kt × Kt, then hardly 6 ....
KtP × Kt; 7 B—QB4, etc., with an active
game for White, but rather, fearlessly, 6 ....
QP × Kt; 7 Q × Q ch, K × Q, etc., with equal
chances.

6	Kt—B3
7 Kt—QB3	Castles
8 Castles	

A more "responsible" plan would be
8 P—B3 (not only to *overprotect* the KP, but
also to prevent 8 .... Kt—KKt5); 8 ....
P—KR3; 9 Q—Q2, K—R2; 10 Castles QR,
which, as the Kings have castled on opposite
wings, would lead to a tense battle.

| 8 ...... | Kt—K2 |

Black prepares a counter-offensive in the
centre, in preference to the purely defensive
plan 8 .... P—KR3; 9 P—B3, K—R2,
etc., or the more *expectative* 8 .... R—K1;
9 P—B3, etc.

Nothing comes of 9 P—K5, Kt—K1 or
9 B—Kt5, P—KR3, etc., but a useful
measure would be 9 P—KR3.

| 9 Q—Q2 | P—Q4 |

If 9 .... Kt—Kt5; 10 B—KB4.

| 10 P × P | Kt (K2) × P |
| 11 Kt × Kt | Q × Kt |

If 11 .... Kt × Kt; 12 B—KR6, and
Black's best Bishop must go.

| 12 B—K2 | |

White has shown little ambition in the
opening, and is already reduced to defensive
measures. The "strategic initiative" has
passed over to Black, who will hold on to it
until the end.

| 12 ...... | Kt—Kt5 |

Unmasking his wing Bishop.

| 13 B × Kt | B × B |
| 14 Kt—Kt3 | Q × Q |

He willingly acquiesces in exchanges.

15 Kt × Q	QR—Q1
16 P—QB3	KR—K1
17 Kt—Kt3	P—Kt3
18 P—KR3	B—K3
19 KR—Q1	P—QB4

Restraining both of White's minor pieces.

20 B—Kt5	P—B3
21 B—B4	K—B2
22 P—B3	P—KKt4
23 R × R	R × R
24 B—K3	P—KR3
25 R—K1	P—B4
26 P—KB4	B—B3
27 P—Kt3	P—QR4
28 Kt—B1	P—R5
29 P—R3	B—B5

The restriction of the Knight continues.

| 30 K—B2 | P × P |
| 31 B × BP | B—KKt4 |

The beauty of this move—which gives up
the two Bishops and seems to leave too little
material on the board—lies in its simplicity.
In principle it is essential to weigh up carefully such exchanges, which modify the
position of the pawns. Black here has
made all the necessary calculations.

| 32 B × B | |

If 32 K—K3, Black does not at once play
32 .... R—K1 ch; 33 K—B2, R × R;
34 K × R, etc., with a tenable game for
White, but 32 .... K—Kt3, improving his
position while White can do nothing to
improve his own.

| 32 ...... | P × B |
| 33 K—K3 | |

Essential in order to prevent the irruption
of the hostile look on his second rank.

| 33 ...... | K—B3 |

The approach of the King will play a
decisive part in the ultimate phase of the
contest.

| 34 P—KR4 | |

In his blockaded position White has no
good move. For instance, if 34 R—R1,
K—K4.

34	P × P
35 P × P	R—K1 ch
36 K—B2	R × R
37 K × R	K—K4
38 Kt—K2	

If 38 P—R5, K—B3, followed by ....
K—Kt4 and .... K × P, etc.

| 38 ...... | B × Kt |
| 39 K × B | K—B5 |

And here is the duel of the Kings.
Although normally the *distant passed pawn*
wins, in this case Black will be able to confiscate the adverse pawn without losing his
own.

| 40 P—B4 | |

Or 40 P—R5, K—Kt4; 41 K—B3, K × P;
42 K—B4, K—Kt3, and wins.

| 40 ...... | K—Kt5 |
| 41 K—K3 | P—B5 ch |

Evidently not 41 .... K × P; 42 K—B4.

| 42 K—K4 | |

Or 42 K—B2, K × P, etc. But now it is
no longer a case of capturing the opposing

pawn, but the queening of his own, which wins, by a length, the race to the queening square.

42	......	P—B6
43	K—K3	K—Kt6
	Resigns	

A hard-fought battle.

115

| *White* | *Black* |
| TARRASCH | ALEKHINE |

(Carlsbad, 1923)

Another beautiful game which runs an orderly course. It furnishes a very instructive example of the blockade of a pawn.

Rendered backward in a manner both discreet and skilful, White's pawn at QB2 finds itself blockaded not only vertically (by Black's Rook at QB1), but also diagonally (by the Bishop at KKt2). Its fall on the thirtieth move is, justly, followed by the loss of the game.

1	P—K4	P—K4
2	Kt—KB3	Kt—QB3
3	B—Kt5	P—KKt3
4	P—Q4	Kt × P

By this modernised treatment (instead of 4 .... P × P; 5 B—KKt5), the *Fianchetto Defence* becomes playable.

| 5 | Kt × Kt | P × Kt |
| 6 | Q × P | Q—B3 |

White is now in a dilemma: exchange of Queens with simplification, or the taking of risks.

7 Q—Q3

Artificial, but as neither 7 Q × Q nor 7 B—K3 gives White anything tangible, the restrictive continuation 7 P—K5, Q—Kt3; 8 Q × Q, RP × Q; 9 B—KB4, etc., offers the best practical chances.

7	......	B—Kt2
8	Kt—B3	P—B3
9	B—QB4	Kt—K2
10	B—K3	

More to the point 10 P—QR4, preventing Black's next move.

10	......	P—QKt4
11	B—Kt3	P—QR4
12	P—QR4	

Too uncompromising, but even after the flexible—and more cautious—12 P—QR3, Black obtains some initiative by 12 .... B—QR3.

12	......	P—Kt5
13	Kt—Q1	Castles
14	Castles	P—Q4

This forces (on account of the threat 15 .... B—QR3) an exchange in the centre, which means the opening of the QB file.

15	P × P	B—QR3
16	B—QB4	B × B
17	Q × B	P × P
18	Q—Q3	P—Q5
19	B—Q2	QR—B1

This completes the walling up of White's QBP, and its capture is already threatened by 20 .... Q—B4, which White's next move, however, prevents for the time being.

20	R—K1	R—B2
21	P—QKt3	KR—B1
22	R—QB1	Q—B4
23	R—K4	

Or 23 Kt—Kt2, R × P, with a definite advantage for Black.

23	......	Kt—Q4
24	Kt—Kt2	Kt—B6
25	B × Kt	

Compulsory. If 25 KR—K1, Q × Q; 26 P × Q (Kt × Q, Kt—R7); 26 .... Kt—K7 ch, and Black wins.

25	......	R × B
26	Q—K2	B—R3
27	P—Kt4	Q—B3
28	R—K8 ch	R × R
29	Q × R ch	K—Kt2
30	R—B1	R × BP

Not only has the besieged pawn at last fallen, but the consequences are decisive.

31 Kt—Q3   Q—B6

Far stronger than 31 .... Q—K3; 32 Q × Q, P × Q.

32 Kt—K5

This counter-attack offers the best chance of salvation, for if 32 Q—K5 ch, K—Kt1; 33 Q × QP, R—Q7; 34 Kt—K5, R × Q; 35 Kt × Q, R—Q6, followed by R × P.

32	......	Q—Q4
33	Kt—Q7	Q—Q3
34	R—Q1	

Threatens 35 R × P, Q × R; 36 Q—B8 mate.

| 34 ...... | B—K6 |

With this beautiful problem-like move (35 P × B, Q × P ch), Black calls the hostile Rook to order.

| 35 R—KB1 | B—Kt4 |
| 36 Q—K5 ch | |

If 36 R—Q1, again, then 36 .... B—K2.

36	Q × Q
37 Kt × Q	B—B5
38 Kt—B4	P—Q6
39 R—Q1	R—B6

Setting up house within the enemy lines.

| 40 Kt × P | |

The moral satisfaction of regaining his pawn is marred by a serious displacement of the Knight.

| 40 ...... | K—B3 |

The entry into the lists of the King decides the issue.

41 P—R4	K—K4
42 K—Kt2	K—Q5
43 K—B3	B—B2
44 Kt—B4	R × P

A rich harvest!

| 45 Kt—K3 | R—B6 |

Clearly not yet 45 .... R—R6, because of 46 Kt—B2 ch.

46 R—QKt1	B—R4
47 Kt—Q1	R—R6
48 Kt—K3	R × P
49 P—Kt5	R—R6
50 R—Kt1	P—Kt6
51 R—Kt4 ch	K—B4

Not 51 .... K—B6, in view of 52 R—B4 ch.

52 R—B4 ch	K—Kt4
53 R—B8	R—R8
54 R—Kt8 ch	B—Kt3

A beautiful final point. If now 55 Kt—Q5, there follows 55 .... P—Q7; 56 R × B ch, K—B4, etc.

Resigns.

116

White   *Black*
JANOWSKI   TRENCHARD
(Vienna, 1898)

An interesting illustration of the ills attendant upon the inability to castle. In this case the black King drags himself laboriously to QR1, there to perish ingloriously.

1 P—K4	P—K4
2 Kt—KB3	Kt—QB3
3 B—Kt5	P—B4

The *Schliemann Defence*. With this counter-gambit Black attempts to seize the initiative. There are, however, many pitfalls and difficulties in the way.

| 4 P—Q3 | |

Simple and good. There are more complications after 4 P—Q4, BP × P, etc., and more trouble after 4 P × P, P—K5, etc. Another rational move is 4 Kt—B3.

| 4 ...... | P × P |

There is more life in 4 .... Kt—B3, or even 4 .... P—Q3, though White can, in either case, reply with 5 P × P.

5 P × P	P—Q3
6 Kt—B3	Kt—B3
7 B—Kt5	

Another strong continuation is 7 Q—Q3, B—Kt5; 8 P—QR3, followed by B—QB4.

| 7 ...... | B—K2 |
| 8 B—QB4 | |

And now Black is definitely prevented from castling on the K side. If 8 Q—Q3, B—K3.

| 8 ...... | Kt—QR4 |

A fruitless deflection of the Knight. A painstaking counter-plan would be 8 .... B—Kt5; 9 Q—Q3, Q—Q2, making 10 .... B—K3 possible.

| 9 Q—K2 | B—Kt5 |
| 10 Castles QR | Q—B1 |

If 10 .... Q—Q2, remaining exposed to the action of the Rook, then 11 P—KR3, B—R4; 12 B—Kt5 ch (instead of 12 P—KKt4, Kt × B; 13 Q × Kt, B—B2); 12 .... P—B3 (12 .... Kt—B3; 13 P—KKt4, followed by 14 Kt × P); 13 B—QR4, etc., with persistent threats.

| 11 P—KR3 | Kt × B |

He hopes for effective simplification by 12 Q × Kt, B—K3; 13 Q—Kt5 ch, B—Q2; (best) 14 Q—Kt3, B—K3, and at last castling on the K side is possible. Fatal would be 11 .... B—K3, on account of 12 B × B, Q × B; 13 Q—Kt5 ch, Kt—B3; 14 Q × KtP, and wins. As both 11 .... B—R4; 12 B—Kt5 ch, etc., and 11 .... B × Kt; 12 P × B, etc., would hardly favour Black's chances, his best play is 11 .... B—Q2, intending 12 .... Kt × B; 13 Q × Kt, B—K3, etc.

12 P×B

This adventitious KtP becomes a powerful asset in White's game.

12	Kt—Kt3
13 B×Kt	B×B
14 P—Kt5	B—K2
15 P—Kt6	P—KR3
16 Q—Kt5 ch	Q—Q2
17 Q—Kt3	B—B3

Parrying the double threat 18 Q—B7 ch and 18 Kt×P.

18 P—R4   P—QR4

A compulsory weakening of his position. As Black's attempts to enforce his castling on the K side have failed, and castling on the Q side would henceforth be unfavourable, Black's cause is virtually lost.

19 Kt—QKt5

Threatening 20 Kt×QP ch.

| 19 ...... | Kt—B1 |
| 20 P—Kt4 | |

On account of Black's KRP being pinned, there is a threat of 21 P—Kt5, B—Q1; 22 P×P, etc.

| 20 ...... | R—B1 |
| 21 R—R5 | |

Threat: 22 KKt×P.

| 21 ...... | Q—B3 |

If 21 .... Q×P; 22 Kt×BP ch, etc.

22 Q—K6 ch

Having harried the black pieces sufficiently, White now centres his attention on the opposing King.

| 22 ...... | Kt—K2 |

If 22 .... B—K2; 23 KKt×P, P×Kt; 24 Q×Q ch, P×Q; 25 Kt×P mate.

23 P—Kt5

A "rolling up" sacrifice. Once the KR file is open, the investment of the opposing forces will be effected without much trouble.

| 23 ...... | P×P |
| 24 QR—R1 | K—Q1 |

Beginning of the King's flight. If 24 .... Q×KP; 25 Kt×BP ch, K—Q1; 26 Q×QP ch, K—B1; 27 Kt×R, with a double threat of mate by 28 Q—B7 or 28 Kt—Kt6.

| 25 R—R8 | Q—K1 |

The inner lines are still fairly safe, but the outside ring of defences is tottering.

26 Kt×QP

A *break-up sacrifice.*

26	P×Kt
27 Q×P ch	K—B1
28 Q—B5 ch	K—Kt1
29 Kt×KP	

The point of the sacrifice, the threat now being 30 R×R, Q×R; 31 Kt—Q7 mate.

| 29 ...... | B×Kt |
| 30 Q×B ch | K—R2 |

Or 30 .... K—B1; 31 Q×KtP, etc.

31 Q×P ch	K—Kt1
32 Q—K5 ch	K—R2
33 Q—Q4 ch	K—Kt1

Slightly more resistance offers 33 .... K—R3.

34 Q×P   Kt×P

A desperate attempt at salvation. If 34 .... R—Kt1; 35 R×R, Kt×R; 36 R—R7, Q—B1; 37 Q—K5 ch, K—R2; 38 Q—Q4 ch, K—Kt1; 39 R—Q7, and wins.

35 QR—R7

A conclusive reply.

| 35 ...... | R—R2 |

More stubborn would be 35 .... Q—QB1.

36 R×R   Q×R

Or 36 .... Kt×R; 37 R—R8.

| 37 Q—B7 ch | K—R1 |
| 38 R—Q7 | Resigns |

The tomb of the Pharaoh. Mr. Trenchard became the victim in this game of a hazardous variation, which he has been one of the first to introduce into master practice.

117

| *White* | *Black* |
| PILLSBURY | TARRASCH |

(Monte Carlo, 1903)

A memorable game between the two leaders in the tournament. Instead of the careful play one might expect, both players throw caution to the winds, and from the beginning wallow in a welter of complications, in which Black succeeds in having the last word.

Aptly named "a battle of giants," this game shows an extremely long and heroic defence on the part of White, even after he has lost a piece.

1 P—K4   P—K4
2 Kt—KB3   Kt—QB3
3 B—Kt5   P—B4
4 Kt—B3

The most logical reply, calm and energetic at the same time.

4 ......   Kt—B3

Contesting the centre, whereas after 4 ....
P×P; 5 QKt×P, he would lose his hold
there, with a hostile piece established in the
middle of the board. A game Brinckmann-
Kieninger, *Ludwigshafen,* 1932, continued
after 4 .... P×P; 5 QKt×P as follows:
5 .... Kt—B3 (if 5 .... P—Q4; 6 Kt×P);
6 Kt×Kt ch, P×Kt; 7 P—Q4, P—K5;
8 Kt—Kt5 (8 Kt—R4, Q—K2); 8 ....
B—Kt5 ch (a vacating check); 9 P—B3,
P×Kt (better would be 9 .... Castles);
10 Q—R5 ch, K—B1; 11 B×KtP, (decisive)
11 .... Kt—K2; 12 B—QB4, P—Q4;
13 B×P, Resigns.

5 P×P

Less good is 5 Q—K2, because of 5 ....
Kt—Q5, with complications.

5 ......   P—K5

A close struggle ensues around this pawn.
Less consistent would be 5 .... B—B4;
6 Castles; 7 Kt×P, Kt×Kt; 8 P—Q4,
and White has a dominating position.

6 Q—K2

He could besiege, or even undermine,
Black's KP by 6 Kt—Kt5, P—Q4; 7 P—Q3,
B×P; 8 P×P, P×P; 9 Q—K2.

6 ......   Q—K2

He immediately occupies the critical K file,
whereas after 6 .... P—Q4; 7 P—Q3 White
could proceed there with his work of dissolution.

7 B×Kt

Necessary, for if at once 7 Kt—Kt5 (or
7 Kt—KR4), there follows 7 .... Kt—Q5.

7 ......   KtP×B
8 Kt—KR4   P—Q4
9 P—Q4   P—QR4

Preparing for the intensified action of his
QB, which is to make up for his lost pawn.

10 B—Kt5   B—R3

A necessary measure.

11 B×Kt   Q×B
12 Q—R5 ch   K—Q2

Instead of the pusillanimous 12 ....
Q—B2, Black has to play *va-banque.*

12 Kt—Kt6

But White also has to take the doubtful
course of material gain at the cost of
his development. There would, indeed, be
little attraction in 13 Castles QR, B—K2;
14 P—KKt3, Q—Kt4 ch; 15 Q × Q, B × Q ch;
16 K—Kt1, QR—KB1; 17 QR—Kt1,
KR—Kt1, etc., and Black prepares to
recover his pawn.

13 ......   Q×QP

Forced. If 13 .... R—KKt1; 14 Kt—K5
ch.

14 Kt×R

For the time being, White is a whole Rook
ahead, but his King is in difficulties.

14 ......   B—B4
15 Q—R4   R×Kt
16 R—Q1   Q—Kt5

More effective than either 16 .... Q—B5
or 16 .... Q—K4.

17 Q—Kt4

A very promising counter-action. He
cannot play 17 Q × KP, because of 17 ....
R—K1.

17 ......   K—Q1
18 Q×KtP   R—K1
19 Q—B6 ch   K—Q2
20 P—QR3   Q—Kt3

Avoiding the trap 20 .... Q×KtP;
21 Kt×QP.

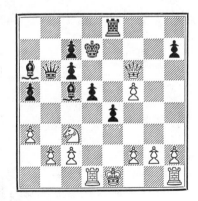

21 R—Q2

If 21 K—Q2, B—Q5.

21 ....   P—K6
22 P×P   B×KP
23 Kt×P

If 23 K—Q1, Q×P. In his precarious
position White decides not only to give back
the exchange but to give up a piece as well.

23	B × R ch
24 K × B	Q—B7 ch
25 K—Q1	

Clearly not 25 K—B1, R—K8 ch;
26 R × R, Q × R mate.

25	Q—K7 ch

A necessary interim check; he protects his
own Bishop and then proceeds to win the
piece.

26 K—B1	P × Kt
27 R—Q1	P—B3
28 Q—R4	Q × P
29 Q × P ch	R—K2
30 Q—R4	Q—K5
31 Q—R8	Q × P
32 Q—R8	B—B1
33 Q—R7 ch	K—K1
34 Q × P	Q—B5 ch
35 K—Kt1	Q × P
36 Q—B5	

Although he only has a pawn for a
Bishop, White hopes to reduce the number
of hostile pawns and so to neutralise Black's
advantage.

36	B—Kt2
37 P—Kt4	Q—K7
38 R—R1	R—KB2
39 R—R8 ch	K—Q2
40 R—R6	R—B8 ch
41 K—Kt2	Q—K2
42 Q—Q4	R—K8
43 R—R5	

In order to prevent the exchange of
Queens by 43 .... Q—K4.

43	K—B2
44 Q—B4 ch	K—Kt3
45 Q—Q4 ch	P—B4

The effect of this move is to disjoint the
white trio of pawns.

46 P × P ch	Q × P
47 R—R6 ch	B—B3
48 Q—B6	Q—Kt4 ch
49 K—B3	Q—B5 ch
50 K—Kt2	Q—Kt4 ch
51 K—B3	Q—B5 ch
52 K—Kt2	Q—Kt4 ch
53 K—B3	

The repetition of moves is intended to
gain time. The rule concerning the draw by
repetition of moves was not then in force.

53	R—K6 ch
54 K—Q2	R—K7 ch
55 K—Q1	R—K1
56 K—Q2	Q—K7 ch
57 K—B1	Q—K8 ch
58 K—Kt2	Q—K4 ch

At last, by the exchange of Queens, Black
takes an important step forward.

59 Q × Q	R × Q
60 R—R4	

Trying to eliminate Black's last pawn by
61 P—B4, which would lead to a "book"
draw.

60	R—K5
61 R—R8	K—B4
62 R—QB8	R—K1
63 R—B7	K—Q3
64 R—KR7	B—Kt4
65 K—B3	B—R5
66 R—R2	R—K5
67 R—Kt2	K—B4
68 R—R2	R—K6 ch
69 K—Kt2	B—Kt4
70 R—R8	R—K7
71 R—B8 ch	K—Q5
72 K—Kt3	B—B5 ch
73 K—Kt2	B—Q6
74 K—Kt3	B—B4
75 R—B7	R—K1
76 P—B3 ch	

This advance, which Black has been at
such pains to enforce, diminishes the
cohesion of the white forces. If 76 K—Kt2,
R—QB1, etc.

76	K—Q6
77 R—B5	R—Kt1 ch
78 K—R4	B—K5
79 R—B7	K—B7
80 R—B6	B—Q6

Black goes methodically to work, in
preference to 80 .... P—Q5, etc.

81 R—B5	B—B5
82 K—R5	K × P
83 P—R4	

A last throw. If 83 .... K—Q5;
84 R × P ch, K × R (instead of 84 ....
B × R) stalemate.

83	R—R1 ch
Resigns.	

118

White	Black
CAPABLANCA	BLACKBURNE

(St. Petersburg, 1914)

*Black has underestimated the danger of
the open KKt file, and finds himself unable to
bring up the necessary reinforcements in
time.*

1 P—K4	P—K4
2 Kt—KB3	Kt—QB3
3 B—Kt5	Kt—Q5

This, *Bird's Defence*, appeals to many attacking players, and demands very careful play on the part of White.

4 Kt × Kt

Besides this simple continuation, which seeks to take advantage of Black's doubled pawn, the flexible retreat 4 B—B4 is to be recommended.

| 4 .... | P × Kt |
| 5 Castles | P—KKt3 |

The continuation 5 .... B—B4; 6 P—Q3, Kt—K2; 7 Kt—Q2, Castles, etc., is also acceptable.

6 P—Q3	B—Kt2
7 Kt—Q2	Kt—K2
8 P—KB4	P—QB3

In view of the offensive manifestly intended by Black, he would have saved an important *tempo* by 8 .... P—QR3.

| 9 B—B4 | P—Q4 |
| 10 B—Kt3 | |

More astute than making matters easier for Black by first exchanging 10 P × P, etc.

10	Castles
11 Kt—B3	P—QB4
12 P—K5	P—QKt4

The utmost self-possession is needed by White against this assault by pawns.

13 P—B3	P—B5
14 B—B2	QP × P
15 KtP × P	Q—R4

An unnecessary diversion.

| 16 B—Q2 | B—Kt5 |
| 17 P—Q4 | |

White has now a remarkable chain of pawns.

| 17 ...... | Q—Kt3 |
| 18 R—Kt1 | |

The initiative now passes to White.

| 18 ...... | P—QR3 |

For if 18 .... P—QR4; 19 P—QR4.

19 P—KR3	B—B4
20 P—Kt4	B × B
21 Q × B	P—B4

He tries to stem the coming onslaught. If, for instance, 21 .... Q—K3; 22 Kt—Kt5, and White effects even more vigorously the overwhelming advance 23 P—B5.

22 K—R2

Final preparations.

| 22 ...... | Kt—B3 |

Yet another defender leaves the critical sector. More useful would be 22 .... K—R1.

| 23 R—Kt1 | Kt—Q1 |

Strengthening the inner lines by 23 .... R—R2 would be preferable.

| 24 P × P | R × P |

If 24 .... P × P; 25 Kt—R4, Q—K3; 26 R—Kt5, and wins.

| 25 Kt—R4 | R—R4 |

If 25 .... R—B2; 26 P—B5.

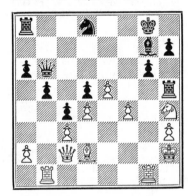

26 Kt × P

A break-up sacrifice.

| 26 ...... | P × Kt |

Compulsory acceptance. If 26 .... Q—K3; 27 P—B5, R × P; 28 Q × R, and wins.

| 27 R × KKtP | Q—Kt1 |

To be able to reply to 28 QR—Kt1 by 28 .... R—QR2, but White now demonstrates that the time is ripe for the final assault. 27 .... Q—B2 offered slightly better defensive chances.

28 R × B ch

"Once more into the breach . . ."

28	K × R
29 R—Kt1 ch	K—B1
30 Q—Kt6	

The *coup de grâce*.

| 30 ...... | R × P ch |

A rancorous check.

| 31 K × R | Resigns. |

119

White	Black
MAYET	ANDERSSEN

(London, 1851)

In the following short game, the opening of the KR file at the cost of a piece allows Black to wall in the hostile King.

1 P—K4	P—K4
2 Kt—KB3	Kt—QB3
3 B—Kt5	B—B4

A very old move, recommended by an early European chess author, Luana (1497), which seeks to exploit the "Italian counter-diagonal."

4 P—B3
More active than 4 Castles, KKt—K2. In any event, not 4 Kt×P, because of 4 .... Q—Kt4.

| 4 ...... | Kt—B3 |

More flexible is 4 .... KKt—K2.

5 B×Kt
If 5 P—Q4, P×P; 6 P×P, B—Kt5 ch, etc. In order to avoid this relieving check, however, 5 Castles is better.

| 5 ...... | QP×B |
| 6 Castles | B—KKt5 |

Already claiming the initiative.

| 7 P—KR3 | P—KR4 |

A correct sacrifice, which White should have declined by 8 P—Q3.

| 8 P×B | P×P |
| 9 Kt×P | P—Kt6 |

Decisive.

| 10 P—Q4 | Kt×P |

With the fine threat 11 .... R—R8 ch.

| 11 Q—Kt4 | B×P |

One hammer-stroke after another.

12 Q×Kt
Or 12 P×B, P×P ch; 13 R×P, R—R8 ch; 14 K×R, Kt×R ch; 15 K—Kt1, Kt×Q; 16 Kt×Kt, Q×P ch; 17 Kt—K3, P—KB4, and Black must win.

| 12 ...... | B×P ch |
| 13 R×B | Q—Q8 ch |

And Black mates in 3.

120

White	Black
ZUKERTORT	ANDERSSEN

(Breslau, 1865)

One of the many tragedies which, from time to time, are enacted around the ominous square KB2.

1 P—K4	P—K4
2 Kt—KB3	Kt—QB3
3 B—Kt5	KKt—K2

The *Cozio Defence*, which variation embarrasses Black's game more than any other, and which has no longer any adherents.

4 P—B3
The most energetic line of play is 4 Kt—B3, P—KKt3; 5 P—Q4, P×P; 6 Kt—Q5, B—Kt2; 7 B—Kt5, P—KR3; 8 B—B6, etc.
Less good is 4 P—Q4 at once, because of 4 .... P×P; 5 Kt×P, P—Q4, and Black frees his game.

| 4 ...... | P—Q3 |

Here 4 .... P—Q4; 5 Kt×P, P×P is indicated.

| 5 P—Q4 | B—Q2 |
| 6 Castles | Kt—Kt3 |

In his obstructed position, Black cannot afford the time for such evolutions. Better is 6 .... P—KKt3.

| 7 Kt—Kt5 | P—KR3 |

A fatal weakening of the position. But after 7 .... B—K2; 8 Q—R5, White still has the better of it.

8 Kt×P	K×Kt
9 B—B4 ch	K—K2
10 Q—R5	Q—K1

Falling into the abyss. He should at least have played 10 .... B—K1.

11 B—Kt5 ch
Or even 11 Q—Kt5 ch, P×Q; 12 B×P ch, with a beautiful *diagonal mate*.

| 11 ...... | P×B |
| 12 Q×P mate. | |

121

White	Black
NAGY	MALMGREN

(Correspondence Championship, 1938)

The correspondence player contributes largely to theoretical research in chess.

In this smart little game, White finds hidden resources in the position, and instead of the long drawn-out battle which so often results from this opening, the fight is over before it has properly begun.

1 P—K4	P—K4
2 Kt—KB3	Kt—QB3
3 B—Kt5	P—QR3
4 B—R4	Kt—B3
5 Castles	Kt × P
6 P—Q4	P—QKt4
7 B—Kt3	P—Q4
8 P × P	B—K3
9 P—B3	B—K2
10 B—KB4	

Instead of the other continuations, 10 QKt—Q2, or 10 R—K1, or 10 Q—K2, or 10 P—QR4, or 10 Kt—Q4, or finally, 10 B—K3, White chooses a telling reply, which allows the QKt to move to Q2 without shutting in the QB, and brings this Bishop into the heat of battle.

10	P—Kt4

If 10 .... Castles; 11 Kt—Q4.

11 B—K3
Having fulfilled the mission of weakening the enemy.

11	P—KKt5
12 KKt—Q2	

A brilliant *finesse*. After 12 Kt—Q4,

QKt × P; 13 Kt × B, P × Kt; 14 B—Q4, Q—Q3, etc., the fight becomes wild.

12	Kt—B4

Not 12 .... QKt × P; 13 B—Q4.

13 P—KB4
Less promising would be 13 Q—K2, B—B4; 14 R—Q1, Kt—R4; 15 Kt—B1, Kt × B; 16 P × Kt, P—QB3, etc., with an even game.

13	B—B4

If 13 .... Kt × B; 14 Kt × Kt, vacating the square for the other Knight with control of Q4.

14 B—B2	B × B
15 Q × B	P—Q5

Trying to clear up matters in the centre.

16 B—B2	P × P

Necessary is 16 .... P—Q6, although even then, after 17 Q—Q1 this pawn and the KKtP would provide easy targets for White.

17 Q × BP
The transfer of the centre of gravity from the K file to the Q file and now to the QB file is original.

17	Q—Q6

The lesser evil is 17 .... P—Kt5; 18 Q—B4 (if 18 Q—B2, Kt—Q5, etc.; and if 18 Q—B1, Q—Q4, etc.); 18 .... Kt—R4; 19 Q × KtP, etc.

18 R—B1	Resigns.

For a piece is lost.

6. SCOTCH GAME AND SCOTCH GAMBIT

122

White	Black
EDINBURGH	LONDON

(1824–26)

The following game already reflects the general character of the Scotch Game, an opening new at the time. The course of play, although perhaps calmer than is the case in most open games, allows White to make the most of some small weaknesses in Black's position.

After the 32nd move the respective Rooks on either side penetrate into the enemy lines, and the battle assumes epic proportions.

1	P—K4	P—K4
2	Kt—KB3	Kt—QB3
3	P—Q4	Kt × P

The correct continuation is 3 .... P × P. Against the truculent 3 .... P—Q4, White maintains the initiative by 4 B—QKt5.

4 Kt × Kt

Good enough, but a vigorous reply is 4 Kt × P, as illustrated in a curious manner by the game Cochrane-Staunton, *London*, 1842, as follows: 4 Kt × P, Kt—K3; 5 B—QB4, P—QB3 (with the ingenuous counter-threat 6 .... Q—R4 ch, followed by .... Q × Kt); 6 Kt × BP, K × Kt; 7 B × Kt ch, K × B; 8 Castles, K—B2 (a return ticket!); 9 B—K3, Kt—K2; 10 P—KB4, P—Q4; 11 P—B5, K—Kt1; 12 P—QB4, P—QKt4; (trying to cut the Gordian knot); 13 P × KtP, BP × P; 14 Kt—B3, B—Kt2; 15 P—K5, P—Kt5; 16 P—B6 (threat: 17 P—B7 mate); 16 .... P × P; 17 P × P, Kt—Kt3 (or 17 .... P × Kt; 18 P—B7 ch, K—Kt2; 19 B—Q4 ch, and wins); 18 P—B7 ch, K—Kt2; 19 Q—Q4 ch, and wins.

4	......	P × Kt
5	Q × P	Kt—K2

If he tries to contest the white Queen's important post by 5 .... Q—B3, the continuation would be 6 P—K5, Q—QKt3; 7 B—K3, Q × Q; 8 B × Q, and White's position remains superior.

6	B—QB4	Kt—B3
7	Q—Q5	Q—B3
8	Kt—B3	B—Kt5

Speeding up the development of the K side. If 8 .... Kt—Kt5; 9 Q—Q1, B—B4; 10 Castles, Castles; 11 P—QR3; Kt—B3; 12 Kt—Q5, Q—Q1; 13 Q—R5, White has the better position.

9	B—Q2	P—Q3

Here 9 .... Castles would· be more in conformity with his preceding move.

10	B—QKt5	B—Q2
11	Q—B4	B—QB4

Parries the threat 12 B × Kt.

12	Castles KR	Castles KR
13	Q—Q3	Kt—K4

A skilful easing up of the struggle, whereas the plausible 13 .... Kt—Kt5 would lead to 14 Kt—Q5, Kt × Q; 15 Kt × Q ch, P × Kt; 16 B × Kt, etc., or 14 .... Kt × Kt; 15 B × B, etc., with a clear advantage to White.

14	Q—Kt3	B × B
15	Kt × B	P—B3

Repelling the hostile Knight, but weakening the QP in the process.

16	Kt—B3	Kt—B5
17	B—Kt5	Q—Kt3
18	P—Kt3	P—B3

The London team tries to solve Black's difficult problem in the best possible manner.

19	B—B1	Q × Q
20	P × Q	B—Q5

Another very clever manœuvre.

21	P × Kt	B × Kt
22	R—Kt1	P—QKt3
23	R—Q1	QR—K1

Disdaining a passive resistance by 23 .... QR—Q1, Black tries to create points of attack.

24	R—Kt3	

At the right moment White enforces the

retirement of the Bishop, for if 24 ....
B—K4; 25 P—B4, and wins.

24	B—R4
25 P—KB3	P—KB4
26 P×P	R—K7
27 P—Kt4	R×BP
28 B—B4	R×BP
29 B×P	R—K1
30 R—R3	

White, above all, wants to immobilise the
hostile Bishop. If now 30 .... R—K8 ch;
31 R×R, B×R; 32 R×P, winning a pawn.
Nor would 30 .... R—B6 help Black, on
account of 31 R—R4, maintaining the
pressure. Finally, after 30 .... R—K7;
31 P—Kt5, R(B5)—B7; 32 P—Kt4, R×P;
33 R×R, R×R; 34 B—B4, White is by far
the more active. The desire to prevent
31 P—Kt5 explains Black's next move.

30	P—KR3
31 B—B7	R—K2
32 R—Q8 ch	K—R2

Or 32 .... K—B2; 33 B—Q6 (threat:
34 R—B8 mate); 33 .... R—K1;
34 R—Q7 ch, with a definite advantage
to White.

| 33 R—QB8 | R—B8 ch |

The immediate doubling of Rooks by
33 .... R—B7 would have been rational,
but Black has no inkling of the astonishing
sacrifice which White has in view.

34 K—R2	R(K2)—K8
35 K—R3	R—R8 ch
36 B—R2	B—B6

In continuance of his plausible plan,
Black threatens 37 .... B—K4.

37 P—B4	B—Q7
38 P—Kt3	B—R4
39 R—K3	R—B7

It looks as if the black Rooks were to
triumph. But appearances are deceptive.

| 40 P—Kt5 | |

Vacating a flight square for his King, but
with the immediate threat of 41 P—Kt6
mate.

40	R(R8)×B ch
41 K—Kt4	P—R4 ch
42 K—B3	R(R7)—B7 ch
43 K—K4	P—Kt3
44 R—B7 ch	K—Kt1
45 K—K5	

Continuing the brilliant conception. The
King gets under way to mate his opponent.

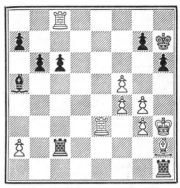

Position after 39 .... R—B7

45	R—B4 ch
46 K—B6	R×P ch
47 K×P	R—B1
48 R—Kt7 ch	K—R1
49 K—R6	

Nothing would be gained by 49 QR—K7,
because of 49 .... B—B6, and Black's
extra piece would begin to tell. That is
why the white King must continue his surprising evolutions.

| 49 ...... | B—Kt5 |
| 50 R—K6 | R—B4 |

Parrying the mate in two.

51 R—R7 ch	K—Kt1
52 R—Kt6 ch	K—B1
53 R×BP	R—B4

An exciting moment. If 53 ....
K—Kt1, there follows the victorious advance
54 P—Kt6, P—R5; 55 R—Kt7 ch (but
ueither 55 P—Kt7, R—R4 ch nor 55 P—Kt4,
QR×P, etc.); 55 .... K—R1; 56 R×RP,
P×P; 57 P—Kt7 ch, K—Kt1; 58 R—B8 ch,
R—B1; 59 P×R (Q) ch, B×Q ch;
60 R—Kt7 ch, K—R1; 61 R×B mate.

54 R—B6 ch	K—K1
55 P—Kt6	R—QB6
56 P—Kt4	

Closing the door.

| 56 ...... | B—B1 ch |
| 57 R×B ch | |

The death-blow.

57	K×R
58 P—Kt7 ch	K—B2
59 R—R8	R—B3 ch
60 K—R7	Resigns

123

White   *Black*
TCHIGORIN   SCHIFFERS
(Match, 1880–1)

*In this beautiful game—which well illus-
trates the attacking resources inherent in the
Scotch Game—there are memorable happenings on the K file: continuous pinning, the
sacrifice of the exchange, followed by that of
the Queen, irruption, eruption. . . .*

1 P—K4	P—K4
2 Kt—KB3	Kt—QB3
3 P—Q4	P × P
4 Kt × P	B—B4

An ancient continuation. The more
modern defence is 4 .... Kt—B3. After
4 .... Q—R5 (Steinitz's idea), the following
is White's best reply: 5 Kt—Kt5 (if
5 Kt—KB3, Q—R4, with equalisation);
5 .... Q × KP ch; 6 B—K3, and the pawn
won by White will bring him no happiness
on account of his backward development.
After 4 .... KKt—K2, there occurred
a curious continuation in a game won
by Hopkins, *London*, 1936, as follows:
5 Kt—QB3, P—KKt3 (5 .... P—Q3 is
necessary); 6 B—KKt5, B—Kt2; 7 Kt—Q5
(a splendid *coup*, threatening 8 Kt × QKt
and 9 B × Kt); 7 .... B × Kt (or 7 ....
QKt × Kt; 8 B × Kt, "mating" the Queen);
8 Q × B (a *deflecting sacrifice*); 8 ....
Kt × Q; 9 Kt—B6 ch, K—B1; 10 B—R6
mate.

5 B—K3   Q—B3
Attacking the adverse Knight, and at the
same time providing against the threat
6 Kt × Kt, followed by 7 B × B.

6 P—QB3
This sound supporting move preserves
White's good position in the centre.

6 ......   KKt—K2
7 B—QB4
A salient moment. Zukertort's favourite
7 B—K2 gives no more than a draw, neither
does Blackburne's 7 B—QKt5. An interesting manœuvre is Dr. Meitner's 7 Kt—B2.
Louis Paulsen's preference was for 7 Q—Q2,
which is shown in the following game,
Paulsen-Bier, *Nuremberg*, 1883: 7 Q—Q2,
Kt—Q1 (7 .... P—Q4 is preferable);
8 P—KB4, P—Q3; 9 B—Q3, Kt—K3;
10 P—K5 (already a decisive inroad);
10 .... P × P; 11 Kt × Kt, B × B;
12 B—Kt5 ch (unmasking the Q file);
12 .... Kt—B3; 13 Kt × BP ch, K—B1;

14 Q × B, R—QKt1; 15 Q—B5 ch, Q—K2;
16 Q × Q ch, and Black, a piece to the bad,
resigned.

7 ......   P—Q3
Resigning himself to restricted defence,
instead of trying to free his game by 7 ....
Kt—K4; 8 B—K2, Q—Kt3 (making a show
of attacking two opposing pawns at the
same time); 9 Castles, P—Q4, etc., and
instead of grasping a doubtful pawn,
Black tries to obtain freedom.

8 P—B4   Q—Kt3
He tries to keep his opponent occupied by
his double attack on White's KP and KKtP.
After the simple development 8 .... Castles;
9 Castles, White's advantage becomes more
definite.

9 Castles
Weak would be 9 Q—B3, B—KKt5;
10 Q—Kt3, Q × P. White could, it is true,
guard both threatened points with 9 Q—B2.
But an attacking player such as was, at all
times, the great Russian Tchigorin, would
never hesitate to give up a sick pawn for
the sake of an attack.

9 ......   Q × P
Accepting the gift, but now White's
pressure on the wide-open central file will
persist. Incidentally, after 9 .... Castles;
10 Kt—Q2, the problem of the opening is
far from being solved for Black.

10 R—K1   Q—Kt3
If 10 .... Castles; 11 B—Q3, Q—Q4;
12 P—B4.

11 Kt × Kt	B × B ch
12 R × B	P × Kt
13 Q—K2	Q—B3
14 Kt—Q2	

White has ample time to bring up his
reserves.

14	P—Q4
15 B—Q3	B—K3
16 R—KB1	P—Kt3

Necessary, for if 16 .... Castles;
17 P—B5, Kt × P; 18 B × Kt, B × B;
19 P—KKt4, White wins a piece.

17 Kt—Kt3   Castles KR
18 P—KKt4
He begins to wall up the opposing forces.
(Threat: 19 P—B5.)

18 ......   QR—K1
19 Kt—B5   P—Q5
More self-possessed would be 19 ....
B—B1, awaiting events.

20 P—Kt5   Q—R1
Poor lady! If 20 .... Q—Kt2; 21 Kt × B,
P × Kt; 22 R × P, P × P; 23 B—B4, etc.

21 R × B
The execution begins.

21 ......   P × R
22 Q × P ch   K—Kt2
23 R—K1
A deeply thought-out preparation. The
basic idea of White's strategy (frontal
pressure) is to be revived.

23 ......   P × P
After any move by the Knight there
follows 24 Q—Q7 ch, and if 23 .... R × P;
24 Q—K5 ch.

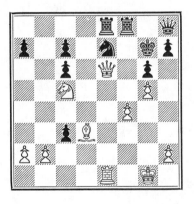

24 Q × Kt ch
A Queen sacrifice, which leads to a mate.

24 ......   R × Q
25 R × R ch   K—Kt1
Or 25 .... R—B2; 26 Kt—K6 ch,
K—Kt1; 27 R—K8 ch, R—B1; 28 R × R
mate.

26 B—B4 ch   R—B2
27 R—K8 ch   K—Kt2
28 Kt—K6 mate
Without being altogether a smothered
mate, this is certainly a notable finish.

124

White   *Black*
BLACKBURNE   VAN VLIET
                 AND MANLOVE

(London, 1893)

*The salient feature of this fine game is the
clever manner in which the consultants
gradually succeed in wresting more and more
territory from their great opponent, the end-
game in particular being of classic beauty.*

1 P—K4   P—K4
2 Kt—KB3   Kt—QB3
3 P—Q4   P × P
4 Kt × P   B—B4
5 B—K3   Q—B3
6 P—QB3   KKt—K2
7 B—QKt5
This favourite move of Blackburne's
(which above all prevents 7 .... P—Q4,
because of 8 P × P, Kt × P; 9 Kt × Kt, etc.),
brought him, in the course of his glorious
career, many notable successes. The more
remarkable is the resistance which he
encounters here.

7 ......   P—QR3
Instead of the ordinary continuation,
leading to approximate equality, 7 ....
Castles; 8 Castles, P—Q3, etc., the allies
strike out on their own, with scant respect
for the authorities.

8 B—R4   P—QKt4
9 B—Kt3   Kt—R4
10 Castles   P—Q3
11 Kt—Q2   Kt × B
Elimination of the "Scotch Bishop," as
troublesome, at times, for Black as is the
"Spanish Bishop."

12 Q × Kt   Castles
13 P—KB4
An ordinary attacking move, but first the
indirect strengthening of Q4 by 13 QR—Q1
would be preferable.

13 ......   Kt—B3
Black's use of the Knights in this game
bears the hallmark of originality. Already
the allies are directing events.

14 QKt—B3   Kt—R4
15 Q—B2   Kt—B5
16 B—B1
A painful retreat, but after 16 Q—B2,
Kt × B; 17 Q × Kt, R—K1, etc., the contest
between Black's Bishops and the white
Knights would be very promising for Black.

16 ......   B—KKt5
An indirect attack on White's Q4.

17 P—QKt3
Instead of this plausible move, which costs a pawn and ultimately the game, White should have eliminated the pin by 17 K—R1, e.g. 17 .... QB×Kt; 18 Kt×B, Kt—K6; 19 B×Kt, B×B; 20 P—KKt3, and, although Black still has most of the play, the games tend to equalise.

17 ......   QB×Kt
Already decisive. The localised contest around White's QB has ended in Black's favour.

18 R×B   B×Kt ch
19 K—R1
Saving, at any rate, the exchange.

19 ......   Kt—K6
20 Q—Q3
Having lost a pawn, White tries to set up the strongest possible defence, with chances of counter-attack as the game progresses. After 20 B×Kt, B×B; 21 R×B, Q×KBP; 22 R—B3, Q—K4; 23 R—B5, Q—K3, and, as his KP is very weak, there would be no satisfaction for White.

20 ......   B×P
21 R—Kt1   Kt—Kt5
This manœuvre is far superior to 21 .... B—Q5; 22 B×Kt, B×B; 23 Q×B, QR—K1; 24 R—K1, and, thanks to his central nucleus, White can fight on.

22 Q×B   Kt—B7 ch
23 K—Kt1   Q×Q
24 R×Q   Kt×P
25 R×P   QR—B1
Well calculated. The opposition of the Rooks discomfits the hostile intruder.

26 R—K7   KR—K1
27 R×R ch   R×R
28 B—Kt2   R—QB1
29 R—K1   P—B4
Maintaining the Knight in the enemy zone.

30 R—K2   K—B2
31 P—KKt4   P—Kt3
32 K—Kt2   K—K3
33 K—B3   P—Q4
34 P—Kt5   P—Kt5
Both sides strive to create strong points. In the ensuing *technical phase* the allies show up well against their great adversary.

35 K—K3   P—QR4
36 K—Q3   R—B4
37 B—Q4   R—B3
38 R—QB2   K—Q2
Accepting the challenge of a duel between Knight and Bishop.

39 R×R   K×R
40 B—Kt7   Kt—B4 ch
41 K—K3   Kt—K3
42 B—K5   K—B4
43 B—B6
Or 43 K—Q3, P—Q5; 44 B—Kt8, K—Q4, etc.

43 ......   P—Q5 ch
44 K—B3
The King prefers to remain the guardian of the KBP.

44 ......   K—Kt4
45 B—K5   K—B4
46 B—Kt8   K—Q4
47 B—R7
The Bishop has to leave the useful diagonal. If 47 B—K5, Kt×P ch, etc.

47 ......   P—Q6
48 K—K3   Kt×BP
The beginning of the end.

49 B—Kt6   P—R5
50 B—Q8
Not 50 P×P, K—B5, etc., nor 50 K×Kt, P—Q7.

50 ......   P×P
51 P×P   Kt—K3
52 B—Kt6   Kt—B4
Well thought out, for in the King's end-game Black's passed pawn ensures victory.

53 B×Kt   K×B
54 K×P   K—Q4
55 K—K3   K—K4
56 P—R3   P—B5 ch
And Black wins.

125

White   *Black*
BLACKBURNE   WARD
(London, 1907)

Whereas in the following game Black's Queen, in capturing a Rook, gets into difficulties, in White's case a similar capture is effected by a nimble Knight, which is soon back in the firing line, and with deadly effect. A lively game.

1 P—K4	P—K4
2 Kt—KB3	Kt—QB3
3 P—Q4	P × P
4 Kt × P	B—B4
5 B—K3	Q—B3
6 Kt—Kt5	

Instead of the supporting move 6 P—QB3, White undertakes a cavalcade—conceived in 1904 by the Russian master B. Blumenfeld—which transforms the *positional* course of the game into an acutely contested battle.

6	B × B
7 P × B	Q—R5 ch

A tempting adventure, but the most prudent line of play is 7 .... Q—Q1; 8 Kt—QB3, KKt—K2, and Black has nothing to fear.

8 P—Kt3	Q × KP

Ambitious, but here also the return of the Queen to Q1 would have been to the point.

9 QKt—B3	

Or at once 9 Kt × P ch, K—Q1; 10 Kt × R, Kt—B3; 11 Q—Q6, Q × R; 12 Kt—Q2 (if 12 Kt—B3, Q—B6); 12 .... Kt—K1, and Black has consolidated his game.

9	Q × R
10 Kt × P ch	K—Q1
11 Q—Q6	Kt—B3

Restoring the communication between the forces, whereas after 11 .... R—Kt1 White would continue in the "grand style" by 12 Q—B8 ch, K × Kt; 13 Kt—Kt5 ch, K—Kt3; 14 P—QR4 (threat: 15 P—R5 ch, Kt × P; 16 Q—Q8 ch); 14 .... P—QR4; 15 Q—Q6, KKt—K2; 16 P—QKt4, with a whirlwind attack.

12 Kt × R	Kt—K1

Most vigorous would be 12 .... Q—B6; 12 Kt—B7, Q × KP ch, and Black has an equal share in the play.

13 Q—B4	

Preventing henceforth 13 .... Q—B6, White can, at leisure, complete his mobilisation and impose his will on his adversary.

13	P—B3
14 Castles	Kt—K4

With a view to 15 .... Q—B6.

15 Kt—Q5	Q × P

As 15 .... Q—B6 would no longer be useful, allowing 16 Q—QR4, Kt—B3; 17 B—Kt5, etc., Black goes out for plunder.

16 B—Kt5	

Intending 17 Q—QR4, Kt—B3 (17 .... P—QR3; 18 Q—R5 ch); 18 B × Kt, QP × B (18 .... KtP × B; 19 Q—R5 ch); 19 Kt × P dis ch, and wins.

16	Kt—B3

Black is compelled to give up territory. If, e.g. 16 .... Kt—Q3; 17 Kt × BP, and if 16 .... R—B1; 17 Q—QKt4.

17 Kt (R8)—B7	Q—R3

An illusory hope of obtaining an endgame with an extra pawn after 18 Q × Q, P × Q; 19 Kt × Kt, R × Kt, etc.

18 Kt—K6 ch	

An *unmasking* sacrifice.

18	P × Kt
19 Kt—Kt6 dis ch	

The point, whereas 19 Kt × P dis ch, K—K2, etc., leads to nothing.

19	K—K2
20 Kt × B ch	K—B1
21 Q—B3	

More astute than at once 21 Q—K4, P—B4.

21	Kt—K4
22 Q—K4	

Adroit manœuvring. If 22 Q × P, Q × P ch; 23 K—Kt1, Q—B4, and Black can still hold out.

22	Q—Kt3

If 22 .... P—QR4; 23 Q—Q4, and Black is still at bay.

23 Q—Kt4 ch	Resigns

(23 .... K—B2; 24 Q—K7 ch, K—Kt1; 25 B × Kt, etc.)

A vigorous game.

126

White	Black
SPIELMANN	TARRASCH

(Breslau, 1912)

Another game in which castling on opposite sides leads to a fast and furious battle. As usual, the player who first succeeds in breaking through the opposing defences wins.

1 P—K4	P—K4
2 Kt—KB3	Kt—QB3
3 P—Q4	P × P
4 Kt × P	B—B4
5 B—K3	

With the well-known threat of 6 Kt × Kt, followed by B × B.

The incisive refutation of 5 Kt—B5 is 5 .... P—Q4; 6 Kt × P ch, K—B1; 7 Kt—R5, Q—R5; 8 Kt—Kt3, Kt—B3; 9 B—K2, Kt—K4; 10 P—KR3, R—KKt1, etc., to Black's advantage.

If 5 Kt × Kt, Q—B3; simplifying, and if 5 Kt—Kt3, B—Kt3, and Black is in no danger.

5	B—Kt3

A sound idea.

6 Kt—QB3	

He attends to the development of his pieces in preference to rounding off Black's position by exchanges: 6 Kt × Kt, KtP × Kt; 7 B × B, RP × B, etc.

6	P—Q3

Or 6 .... KKt—K2; 7 B—QB4 (preventing 7 .... P—Q4); 7 .... Castles; 8 Castles, Kt—K4; 9 B—Kt3, and White maintains his position.

7 B—K2	

Restrained energy. Less good is either 7 B—QKt5, KKt—K2 or 7 B—QB4, Kt—B3, etc., or again, 7 Kt—Q5, Kt—B3, which would relieve the tension by exchanges.

7	Kt—B3
8 Q—Q2	

Without spending any time on preventive measures such as 8 P—KR3, White gets his interior lines in motion. Lifeless would be 8 Castles, Castles, etc.

8	Kt—KKt5

A well-known stratagem, intended to deprive the opponent of one of his Bishops.

9 B × Kt	B × B
10 P—KR3	

A more artificial way to drive back the intruder would be 10 P—B3, particularly so as this pawn might soon have a dynamic mission to fulfil (P—KB4), instead of playing a purely static *rôle* (P—KB3).

Other playable moves are 10 P—KB4 at once or 10 Kt—Q5.

10	B—Q2
11 Kt—Q5	Castles
12 Castles QR	

White's treatment of the opening has been exemplary. By castling on the opposite side, he enters upon a violent struggle.

12	B—K3

In place of this regrouping of forces, he had better chances of a draw by 12 .... B × Kt; 13 B × B, Kt × B; 14 Q × Kt, B—K3, etc.

13 B—Kt5	

Taking advantage of the fact that Black cannot reply 13 .... P—B3, White disorganises the hostile positions.

13	Q—Kt1

For if 13 .... Q—Q2 or 13 .... Q—K1, then, with even greater effect, 14 Kt—B6 ch, P × Kt; 15 B × P, Kt—K2; 16 Q—R6, forcing the mate, and if 13 .... Q—B1; 14 Kt × Kt is final.

14 Kt—B6 ch	

Immobilising Black's K side, this sacrifice —whether accepted or not—is decisive.

14	K—R1
15 Kt × Kt	P × Kt (QB3)
16 Q—B4	

Intending 17 Q—R4, P—KR3; 18 B × P, which is final. This forces the opponent to take heroic measures.

16	Q—Q1
17 Kt × P	

He is content to win the exchange and a pawn, instead of being thoroughly ruthless by 17 Q—R4, P—KR3; 18 B × P, P × Kt (or 18 .... Q × Kt; 19 B—Kt5 dis ch); 19 B × R dis ch, K—Kt1; 20 B—R6 (threat of 21 Q—Kt3 ch); 20 .... K—R2; 21 B—Kt5 dis ch, K—Kt2; 22 Q—R6 ch, K—Kt1; 23 B × P, Q × B; 24 Q × Q, and Black is lost without appeal.

17	P—B3
18 Kt × R	Q × Kt

With the Queen and two Bishops on the board, he obtains more counter-play than by 18 .... P × B; 19 Kt × B, P × Q; 20 Kt × Q, R × Kt; 21 R—Q2, etc.

19 Q—R4 ch	K—Kt1
20 B—Q2	Q—B1
21 P—R3	

As White has succeeded in maintaining his substantial advantage in material, one might think that there is no more to be said, but Black still has some arrows in his quiver.

21	Q—R3
22 P—KB4	Q—B5

With the double threat of 23 .... Q × P

and 23 .... Q—R7; 24 B—B3, B—K6 ch, followed by 25 .... Q—R8 mate.

23 Q—Kt3
If 23 QR—K1, Black plays 23 .... B—Q5, and not 23 .... Q—R7; 24 B—B3.

23	Q×P
24 KR—K1	Q—B4
25 P—Kt3	P—B4
26 Q—R4	B—Q4
27 P—KKt4	

The final assault.

27	Q—Q2
28 B—B3	Q—B2
29 P—Kt5	

A break-through.

29 ...... P×P
He must willy nilly allow the KKt file to be opened. If 29 .... B—B6; 30 P×P, and if 29 .... P—B4; 30 P—Kt6.

30 Q×P B—B6
A despairing attempt, for if 30 .... B—K3; 31 R×B.

31 R—K7 Resigns.

127

White	Black
NIMZOWITSCH	TARRASCH

(San Sebastian, 1911)

The following game, which very soon enters upon the end-game phase, skipping, so to speak, the middle game, is impressive in its almost geometrical character, reserving to the very end, in a King and pawns ending, a most thrilling surprise.

1 P—K4	P—K4
2 Kt—KB3	Kt—QB3
3 P—Q4	P×P
4 Kt×P	Kt—B3

The modern defence, which tends to avoid fluctuation and thereby the pitfalls of the opening.

5 Kt×Kt
An impatient continuation, instead of 5 Kt—QB3 with greater expectations.
An amusing draw occurs after 5 P—K5, Kt×P; 6 Q—K2, Q—K2; 7 Kt—B5,

Q—K3 (or 7 .... Q—Kt5 ch); 8 Kt—Q4, Q—K2, etc.

5 ...... KtP×Kt
6 B—Q3
Logical play. If 6 Kt—Q2, B—B4, seeking to assume the initiative.

6 ...... P—Q4
More straightforward than 6 .... P—Q3.

7 P×P
If 7 Kt—Q2, B—QB4, and if 7 P—K5, Kt—Kt5.

7 ...... P×P
8 Castles
The tension would be relieved after 8 B—Kt5 ch, B—Q2; 9 B×B ch, Q×B; 10 Castles, B—K2, etc.

8 ...... B—K2
9 P—QB4
White tries, in too dogmatic a fashion, to reduce the number of pawns. 9 Kt—B3, Castles; 10 B—KKt5, P—B3, etc., would lead to equality.

9 ...... Castles
Of doubtful value would be 9 .... P—Q5; 10 P—QKt4. In spite of its energetic appearance, White's last move only enabled all the hostile minor pieces to get into action.

10 P×P	Kt×P
11 B—K4	B—K3
12 Kt—B3	

Trying to speed up his backward development, but his pawns lose contact with each other.

12	Kt×Kt
13 P×Kt	Q×Q
14 R×Q	QR—Q1

Now it is Black who—with good reasons— seeks exchanges.

15 B—K3	P—QB4
16 B—B3	

More to the point would be 16 P—KR3, but he tries to make things complicated for his opponent.

16	R×R ch
17 R×R	R—Kt1

Occupying a more favourable file than that occupied by White's Rook. If 17 .... B×P; 18 R—Q7, easily recovering his pawn. (Not 18 R—R1, R—Kt1; 19 B—K4, R—Kt7, etc.)

18 P—KR3   R—Kt7
19 B—Q5
The first attempt to save the loss of a pawn.

19 ......   B × B
20 R × B   R × RP
21 P—QB4
The first disillusionment. If 21 B × P, R—R4, and wins.

21 ......   R—R8 ch
22 K—R2   R—R4
Clearly not 22 .... R—R7, as White could play 23 B × P.

23 P—B4
With one pawn less, White cannot afford to remain inactive.

23 ......   P—B3
24 K—Kt3   K—B2
25 K—B3   P—QR3
26 P—R4   R—R5
Having secured his weak points (the Bishop by the King's proximity and the QRP by moving it), Black can go on simplifying.

27 B × P   R × P
28 B × B   K × B
A Rook-ending is now reached, which at first sight promises a drawn result, but some *rare finessing* is yet to enliven the game.

29 R—KR5   P—R3
30 R—R5   R—B3
31 K—Kt4   R—Kt3
Now if 32 K—B5, R—Kt4 ch wins. A far more convincing way to prevent the white King getting into the game than 31 .... P—Kt3, which allows liquidation by 32 P—R5.

32 P—B5   K—B2
33 K—R5
Barring a miracle, White thinks himself safe, but the miracle occurs.

33 ......   P—Kt3 ch
Accurately thought out. The result hangs by a thread.

34 K × P
Or 34 P × P ch, K—Kt2; 35 R—R2, R—Kt4 ch; 36 K—Kt4, P—R4 ch; 37 K—B3, P—R4, followed by .... K × P, and Black's advantage is definite.

34 ......   P × P
35 R × BP   R—Kt1
The point being to force the exchange of

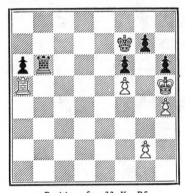

Position after 33 K—R5

Rooks after 36 K—R5, as in the text, or also after 36 K—R7.

36 K—R5   R—Kt4
37 K—Kt4
Trying to get into the "square."

37 ......   R × R
38 K × R   P—R4
39 K—K4   P—B4 ch
A beautiful final point.

Resigns
If 40 K—Q3, P—B5; 41 K—B4, K—Kt3; etc., and wins easily.

128

White	Black
NIMZOWITSCH	RUBINSTEIN

(Vilna, 1912)

The interesting feature here is how Rubinstein discovers—one might almost say creates—a weak point in his adversary's position and how he fastens on it, never to let go, until the game is won.

1 P—K4   P—K4
2 Kt—KB3   Kt—QB3
3 P—Q4   P × P
4 Kt × P   Kt—B3
5 Kt—QB3
Simple and good. The same position can occur in the *Scotch Four Knights' Game* after 1 P—K4, P—K4; 2 Kt—KB3, Kt—QB3; 3 Kt—B3, Kt—B3; 4 P—Q4, P × P (instead of 4 .... B—Kt5); 5 Kt × P, etc.

5 ...... B—Kt5

This pin is more menacing than either 5 .... B—B4 or 5 .... P—KKt3.

6 Kt×Kt

If 6 B—KKt5, P—KR3, and if 6 B—QB4, Castles.

6 ...... KtP×Kt
7 B—Q3

Premature would be 7 P—K5, because of 7 Q—K2, putting the adventurous pawn "on the spot."

7 ...... Castles

It is also possible to play, much more incisively, 7 .... P—Q4. More restrained is 7 .... P—Q3.

8 Castles   P—Q4
9 P×P   P×P
10 B—KKt5   P—B3

An important decision. Less rational is for Black to renounce his good KB by 10 .... B×Kt; 11 P×B, P—KR3; 12 B—R4, and White's pressure persists.

The defence of the threatened QP by a piece, 10 .... B—K3, occurred in an exhibition game Alekhine-Lasker, *Moscow*, 1914, and led to a surprising continuation, as follows: 11 Q—B3, B—K2; 12 KR—K1 (if 12 Q—Kt3, Kt—R4, with a free game); 12 .... P—KR3; 13 B×P, P×B; 14 R×B, P×R; 15 Q—Kt3 ch, K—R1; 16 Q—Kt6, Q—K1; 17 Q×P ch, draw (by perpetual check).

11 Kt—K2

Instead of this regrouping, an increased pressure by 11 Q—B3 occurred in a game Romanovski-Capablanca, *Moscow*, 1935, with the following remarkable continuation: 11 .... B—K2; 12 KR—K1, R—Kt1; 13 QR—Kt1, P—KR3; 14 B×P, P×B; 15 Q—K3 (threatening both Q×B and Q×KRP); 15 .... B—Q3; 16 Q×KRP, R—Kt5 (the only sound defence); 17 Q—Kt5 ch, K—R1; 18 Q—R6 ch, K—Kt1; 19 Q—Kt5 ch, draw (by perpetual check).

11 ...... R—K1

Emphasising the pressure on the open K file, especially against the junction K5.

From the wide repertory of possible replies (11 .... B—QB4, or 11 .... B—Q3, or 11 .... Q—Q3, or 11 .... B—Kt5, or again 11 .... P—KR3), Black decides on the one with the greatest initiative.

12 Kt—Q4   Q—Q3

Useful unpinning.

13 B—R4

More astute than 13 Q—B3, Kt—K5; 14 B—K3, Q—Kt3, and Black takes the lead.

13 ...... Kt—K5
14 P—QB3   B—QB4
15 P—B3

If 15 Q—R5, R—K4.

Simplification by 15 B×Kt, R×B, etc., or 15 B—Kt3, Kt×B; 16 RP×Kt, etc., would undoubtedly give Black a more comfortable game.

15 ...... Q—R3

An elegant reply.

16 P×Kt

Acquiescing to liquidations, which, however, will expose the weaknesses in his position. But after 16 B—Kt3 or 16 B—KB2, Black would have retained the advantage of the initiative.

16 ...... Q×B
17 P×P   P×P

There is no hurry to win a pawn by 17 .... B×Kt ch; 18 P×B, Q×QP ch; 19 K—R1, Q×QP, by which the game would lose in plasticity. Maintenance of the pressure gives Black richer and more varied chances.

18 B—B5   P—Kt3
19 B×B   QR×B
20 R—B2   R—K5
21 P—KKt3   Q—K2

Now, frontal pressure on the K file has become the theme of Black's strategy.

22 Q—Q2   P—B4
23 R—Q1   R—K6
24 K—Kt2   Q—K5 ch
25 K—Kt1   B—Kt3

Preventing the advance of White's QKtP, thanks to the converging pressure of his Rooks against the QBP.

26 R—B4   Q—K2
27 K—Kt2   R—B5

Threatening 28 .... B×Kt, followed by 29 .... R—K7 ch.

28 Kt×P

A despairing sacrifice. If 28 K—B2, R—K5, with an increase in Black's attacking resources.

28 ......   R—K7 ch
29 K—R1   Q—K3

And wins.

A clear-cut victory.

129

White   *Black*

SPIELMANN   LASKER

(Moscow, 1935)

*It is rare indeed that a King's peregrinations
—of the type undertaken by the black monarch
in this game—end without a catastrophe.*

1 P—K4	P—K4
2 Kt—KB3	Kt—QB3
3 P—Q4	P×P
4 Kt×P	Kt—B3
5 Kt—QB3	B—Kt5
6 Kt×Kt	KtP×Kt
7 B—Q3	P—Q4

A trenchant reply. But the more reserved
7 .... P—Q3 has hidden resources, as is
shown in the game Rometti-Gromer,
Toulouse, 1937; 7 .... P—Q3; 8 Castles,
Q—K2; 9 B—Q2, B—Q2; 10 R—K1 (the
preventive measure 10 P—KR3 is indicated);
10 .... Kt—Kt5; 11 B—K2, Kt×BP;
12 Q—B1 (for if 12 K×Kt, B—B4 ch;
13 K—Kt3, Q—B3, and wins); 12 ....
Kt—Kt5; 13 B×Kt, B×B; 14 Kt—Q5,
B×B; 15 Q×B, Q—Q2 (not 15 ....
P×Kt; 16 P×P, B—K3; 17 P×B, etc.);
16 Q—Kt5, P×Kt; 17 Q×KtP, Castles
QR, and White resigns.

8 P×P

If 8 P—K5, Kt—Kt5, and Black's KP
becomes a target.

8 ......   Q—K2 ch

By this intermediary check Black obtains
an early exchange of Queens, which seems to
promise a peaceful ending. But Lasker,
who was a great specialist in the queenless
game, prefers this to the usual variation
8 .... P×P; 9 B—KKt5, etc.

9 Q—K2   Q×Q ch
10 K×Q

Unpinning the Knight and at the same
time mobilising the KR. The text move
shows more vigour than 10 B×Q, B×Kt ch;
11 P×B, P×P, etc., tending to a draw.

10 ......   P×P

Black also shows a fighting spirit, the
move in the text being more bellicose than
10 .... B×Kt; 11 P×B, Kt×P; 12 B—Q2,
etc., with an approximately even game.

11 Kt—Kt5

Suddenly the fight flares up.

11 ......   K—Q1

If 11 .... B—R4; 12 B—KB4, and Black
is prevented from castling.

12 R—Q1	P—B3
13 P—QB3	R—K1 ch
14 K—B1	B—B1
15 Kt—Q4	K—B2
16 B—B4 ch	K—Kt3

An heroic decision. More prosaic is,
clearly, 16 .... B—Q3; 17 B×B ch, K×B;
18 Kt—B5 ch, B×Kt; 19 B×B, and the
consequence might easily be a dull draw.

17 P—QR4   P—QR4
18 P—QKt4

In the sequel White succeeds in creating
dangerous mating nets, in spite of the
absence of Queens.

18 ......   P×P

For instance, if 18 .... B—Q2; 19 P×P ch,
R×P (not 19 .... K×P; 20 B—B7 mate,
nor 19 .... K—B4; 20 Kt—Kt3 mate);
20 KR—Kt1 ch, K—R2; 21 B—B7, and
wins.

19 P—R5 ch

This pawn is taboo, for if 19 .... R×P;
20 R×R, K×R; 21 B—B7 ch, K—R5;
22 R—R1 mate.

19 ......   K—Kt2
20 P×P   Kt—K5

Black tries in vain to organise some
counter-demonstrations. If 20 .... B×P;
21 KR—Kt1, P—B4; 22 Kt—B2, etc., and
if 20 .... B—Q2; 21 KR—Kt1, preparing
for 22 P—Kt5.

21 Kt×P   P—Kt4

Only a counter-thrust can minimise the
crisis. To accept the sacrifice would be
fatal: 21 .... K×Kt; 22 QR—B1 ch,
K—Q2 (or 22 .... K—Kt2; 23 R—B7 ch,
K—Kt1; 24 R—K7 dis ch, followed by
mate); 23 B—Kt5 ch, K—K2; 24 R—B7 ch,
K—Q1; 25 R×P ch, and wins.

22 B×Kt   R×B
23 Kt—Q8 ch   K—R3
24 B×P

This temporarily wins a second pawn, but
it allows the opponent some breathing space,
for the consolidation of his position.

The win was obtainable, in a blaze of
glory, by 24 R×P, R×B; 25 P—Kt5 ch,
K—R2; 26 R—B1, with fatal threats, or
24 .... B×P; 25 B×P, and the struggle is
hopeless for Black.

24 ......   B—K3

Supporting the passed QP, which will
become a strong counter-asset.

25 Kt—B6   B—Kt2

Turning the Bishop to account on the long diagonal is much better than 25 .... B×P; 26 QR—Kt1, etc.

26 QR—B1   R—QB5
27 B—K3

He still seeks complications. It would have been wiser to have played for the endgame by 27 R×R, P×R; 28 Kt—Q4, B×Kt; 29 R×B, K—Kt4; 30 B—Q2, etc., as now White's victory is by no means assured, in spite of his two extra pawns, by reason of the Bishops of opposite colours.

27 ......   K—Kt4
28 Kt—R7 ch   K×P
29 B—Kt6   R—B6
30 R—Kt1 ch   R—Kt6
31 Kt—B6 ch   K—R5
32 B—Q4

White sees that, in spite of the black King's exposed position, there is no possibility of applying the final sanctions, and so he decides on liquidation.

32 ......   R×R
33 R×R   B×B
34 Kt×B   R—R3

Neither 34 .... R×P; 35 R—R1 ch, K—Kt5; 36 Kt—B6 ch, etc., nor, evidently, 34 .... K×P; 35 R—R1 ch, followed by R×R, is admissible here.

35 R—R1 ch   K—Kt5
36 K—K2   B—Q2
37 Kt—B2 ch

Too hesitating. He should have fortified his position by 37 K—Q3, R×P; 38 Kt—B2 ch, K—Kt4; 39 R×R ch, K×R; 40 K—Q4, with every chance of a win, or 37 .... B—R5; 38 R—QB1, R×P; 39 Kt—B6 ch, B×Kt; 40 R×B, R—R7; 41 R—B6, with good practical chances.

37 ......   K—B6
38 Kt—K3   B—Kt4 ch
39 K—K1   P—Q5

Against expectations, Black has now taken the lead.

40 R—B1 ch

The plausible 40 Kt—Q5 ch would even lose: 40 .... K—Kt7; 41 R—Q1; R—K3 ch; 42 K—Q2, R—K7 mate.

40 ......   K—Q6
41 R—Q1 ch   K—B6

But 41 .... K—K5 would be useless, because of 42 Kt—B2, P—Q6; 43 P—B3 ch

(an important check); 43 .... K—K4 (or 43 .... K—B5; 44 Kt—Q4); 44 Kt—Kt4, R—Q3; 45 P—R6, etc.

Draw.

A grand fight.

SCOTCH GAMBIT

130

White	Black
VON BILGUER	VON DER LASA

(Berlin, 1838)

A curious feature of this game is the repeated change in the main field of battle. Beginning, as a real gambit should, with an attack on KB7, the play is suddenly transferred to the Q side, where a powerful action results in the blockading move 18 P—Kt6, only, soon after, to display its full weight on the open K file (20 KR—K1), forcing a lightning decision.

The game shows to what remarkable heights chess science and strategy could rise a hundred years ago.

1 P—K4   P—K4
2 Kt—KB3   Kt—QB3
3 P—Q4   P×P
4 B—QB4

The *Scotch Gambit* in which White—at the cost of a pawn—seeks to give the play an accelerated rhythm.

Against 4 P—B3, Black's best plan is to lead into the *Danish Gambit Declined* by 4 .... P—Q4; 5 KP×P, Q×P; 6 P×P, etc.

Against 4 B—QKt5 (which Blackburne humorously called the "Mac Lopez") the counter-development 4 .... B—B4; followed by .... KKt—K2; and .... Castles; can be recommended.

4 ......   B—Kt5 ch
5 P—B3   P×P
6 Castles

In real gambit style!

6 ......   P—Q3

He grows cautious; it would be too risky to accept the second pawn by 6 .... P×P (the "compromised defence of the Scotch Gambit"); 7 B×P, Kt—B3; 8 Kt—Kt5, Castles; 9 P—K5, P—Q4; 10 P×Kt, P×B; 11 Q—R5, P—KR3; 12 Kt—K4, etc., with advantage to White.

Awkward, too, for the defence, would be

6 .... Q—B3; 7 P—K5, P×P; 8 B×P, Q—Kt3; 9 B—Q3, etc., as well as 6 .... P—B7; 7 Q×P, P—Q3; 8 P—QR3, B—R4; 9 P—QKt4, B—Kt3; 10 B—Kt2, etc., and White is master of the field.

7 P—QR3
Initiating a remarkable action on the Q side.

| 7 ...... | B—R4 |
| 8 P—QKt4 | B—Kt3 |

Or 8 .... P—B7; 9 Q×P, B—Kt3; 10 Q—Kt3, etc., with a continuation similar to that in the text.

| 9 Q—Kt3 | Q—B3 |

Against the more reserved 9 .... Q—K2, White also obtains the upper hand by 10 Kt×P, B—K3; 11 Kt—Q5, B×Kt; 12 P×B, etc.

10 B—KKt5
More enterprising still than 10 Kt×P.

10	Q—Kt3
11 Kt×P	B—K3
12 Kt—Q5	P—KR3
13 B—Q2	B×Kt

A leap into the abyss would be 13 .... Q×P; 14 KR—K1, followed by 15 Kt×B and 16 B×B, with destruction. But as the text move opens the fateful K file for his adversary, Black should have defended himself by 13 .... KKt—K2.

14 P×B
Far more conclusive than 14 B×B.

| 14 ...... | QKt—K2 |
| 15 P—QR4 | |

An important interpolation.

| 15 ...... | P—R3 |

It is clear that Black cannot open yet another file for his opponent by 15 .... P—QR4; 16 P×P, B×P, as 17 Q×P wins.

| 16 P—R5 | B—R2 |
| 17 P—Kt5 | Kt—KB3 |

Hastening to establish communications between his Rooks after 18 P×P, P×P; 19 Q—Kt7, Castles KR; etc., but White's intentions prove to be far more sinister.

18 P—Kt6
An *effective* blockade.

| 18 ...... | P×P |

After 18 .... B—Kt1; 19 KR—K1 still keeps Black in fetters.

19 P×P	Kt—K5
20 KR—K1	Kt×B
21 Kt×Kt	B—Kt1

This aspect of a blockade is a rare occurrence.

22 Q—K3
A frontal assault of overwhelming intensity. After 22 B—Kt5 ch, K—Q1 or 22 R—K3, K—Q1, Black's resistance would be prolonged.

| 22 ...... | Q—B3 |
| 23 Kt—K4 | |

The final manœuvre.

| 23 ...... | Q—B4 |

Or 23 .... Q—K4; 24 P—B4.

| 24 Kt—Kt3 | Q—B3 |
| 25 Kt—B5 | |

Thus, in the skirmish between the Knight and the Queen, the former has gained a *tempo*.

| 25 ...... | Resigns. |

131

| White | Black |
| STAUNTON | VON JÄNISCH |

(Brussels, 1853)

"Simple means—convincing results" might be the motto of this game, which is typical of Staunton at his best.

1 P—K4	P—K4
2 Kt—KB3	Kt—QB3
3 P—Q4	P×P
4 B—QB4	B—B4

A judicious reply.

5 Castles
Phlegmatic play. After 5 P—B3, Black has the choice of several continuations, e.g.:
(a) 5 .... P×P (accepting the gift); 6 Kt×P, P—Q3; 7 Q—Kt3, Q—Q2; 8 Kt—Q5, KKt—K2; 9 Q—B3, Castles; 10 Castles, with even chances.
(b) 5 .... P—Q6 (giving back the pawn); 6 Q×P, Q—K2; 7 B—K3, Kt—B3; 8 QKt—Q2, and White has developed his game without hindrance.
(c) 5 .... P—Q3; 6 P×P, B—Kt3;

7 Castles, Kt—B3, reaching a position in the *Giuoco Piano.*

(*d*) 5 .... Kt—B3; 6 P×P, B—Kt5 ch, another *Giuoco Piano* position.

5	P—Q3

A "Max Lange Attack" could result from 5 .... Kt—B3, e.g. 7 P—K5, P—Q4, but it was little known at the time this game was played.

Against 5 .... KKt—K2 an incisive continuation occurred in a game Staunton-Mayet, *London*, 1851: 6 Kt—Kt5, P—Q4; 7 P×P, Kt—K4 (better, 7 .... Kt—R4); 8 B—Kt3, P—KR3; 9 Kt—K4, B—Kt3; 10 P—KR3, Kt×P (a fatal capture); 11 Q—R5 (an amusing turn, winning one of the Knights); 11 .... Castles (if 11 .... P—Kt4; 12 B×Kt); 12 Q×Kt, B—K3; 13 B×P, resigns.

6 P—B3

True to the gambit style, which underlies this variation. A useless expedition would be 6 B—KKt5, KKt—K2; 7 P—B3, B—KKt5; 8 B—Kt5, P×P; 9 Kt×P, Castles, and Black has succeeded in consolidating his position.

6	P×P

Instead of this hazardous capture, 6 .... Kt—B3; 7 P×P, B—Kt3, etc., or also 6 .... B—KKt5 would have led into a quite playable variant of the *Giuoco Piano.*

7 Kt×P   B—K3

Black's position is already unsatisfactory, and neither the text move nor other continuations such as 7 .... Kt—B3; 8 B—KKt5, etc., or 7 .... P—KR3; 8 Q—Kt3, etc., or 7 .... B—KKt5; 8 Q—Kt3, could prevent White from taking advantage of his opponent's twisted central position in a most instructive manner.

8 B×B	P×B
9 Q—Kt3	Q—B1
10 B—K3	

Not at once 10 Kt—KKt5, because of 10 .... Kt—Q5.

10	B×B
11 P×B	Kt—B3
12 Kt—KKt5	Kt—Q1
13 QR—B1	

A useful intercalation on the Q side. (Threat: 14 Kt—Kt5.)

13	P—QR3
14 Kt—R4	

Threatening 15 Kt—Kt6, winning the exchange, as Black cannot reply 14 .... R—QKt1, for then 15 Kt—Kt6, "mating" the Queen.

14	Q—Q2
15 P—K5	

Rupture of the front.

15	P—R3

If 15 .... P×P; 16 Kt—B5, and if at once 15 .... P—Kt4; 16 P×Kt, P×Kt; 17 Q—B2, winning.

16 Kt—KB3	P—QKt4

A desperate counter-attempt, for the least possible evil would have been 16 .... Kt—Q4.

17 P×Kt	P×Kt
18 Q—B2	P×P

Black has, at the moment, two extra pawns, but the helpless position of his King will soon tell against him.

19 Q—Kt6 ch	K—K2

Again choosing of two evils the greater, but after 19 .... Q—B2; 20 Q×Q ch, Kt×Q; 21 R×P, Castles, White's advantage is quite definite.

20 Kt—K5

An *unmasking sacrifice.*

20	QP×Kt
21 Q×P ch	Resigns

With the depressing choice between two mating aspects: 21 .... K—K1; 22 Q×R ch, K—K2; 23 Q—B8 mate, or 21 .... K—Q3; 22 KR—Q1 mate.

132

White	Black
BLACKBURNE	GIFFORD

(The Hague, 1874)

A beautiful sacrifice of the Queen, drawing the opposing King into a mating net—a feast for the eye and a treat for the mind.

1 P—K4	P—K4
2 Kt—KB3	Kt—QB3
3 P—Q4	P×P
4 B—QB4	B—B4
5 Kt—Kt5	

An optimistic jaunt.

5 ......   Kt—R3
6 Q—R5
Spineless would be the transaction:
6 Kt×BP, Kt×Kt; 7 B×Kt ch, K×B;
8 Q—R5 ch, P—Kt3; 9 Q×B, because of
the counter-thrust 9 .... P—Q4, whereby
Black obtains the initiative.

6 ......   Q—K2
Against 6 .... Q—B3 White could play
7 P—B4, as in the text.

7 P—B4
Exchanges by 7 Kt×BP, Kt×Kt;
8 B×Kt ch, K×B; 9 Q×B, P—Q3, etc.,
would not be profitable as yet. Alternatively, 7 Castles, P—Q3; 8 P—KR3,
B—Q2; 9 P—B4, Castles QR, and Black
has nothing more to fear.

7 ......   Castles
Assigning to his King a rather storm-swept
domicile. In the sense of the preceding
note the following continuation would have
been reasonable: 7 .... P—Q3; 8 P—KR3,
B—Q2; 9 Castles, Castles QR, etc.

8 Castles   P—Q3
9 P—B5
With a fourfold object: preventing both
9 .... B—KKt5 and 9 .... B—K3,
threatening a break-through by 10 P—B6,
and extending the range of his own QB.
These advantages outweigh the drawback of
his K5 becoming weak.

9 ......   P—Q6 dis ch
A little better would be 9 .... Kt—K4 at
once.

10 K—R1   P×P
11 Kt—QB3   Kt—K4
12 Kt—Q5
The final assault begins.

12 ......   Q—Q1
13 P—B6
Breaking through.

13 ......   Kt—Kt3
If 13 .... Kt×B; 14 Kt—K7 ch, K—R1;
15 P×P ch, K×P; 16 Kt—K6 ch (the
simplest); 16 .... B×Kt (or 16 ....
P×Kt; 17 Q×Kt ch, K—R1; 18 R×R ch,
followed by mate); 17 Q×Kt ch, K—R1;
18 Q—B6 mate.

14 P×P   K×P
It looks as if Black now threatens the
capture of the hostile Queen by 15 ....
B—KKt5.

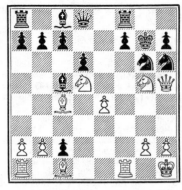

15 Q×Kt (R6) ch
This *King hunt sacrifice*, which lures the
King on a journey from which there is no
return, is one of great beauty.

15 ......   K×Q
16 Kt—K6 dis ch
Demonstrating the potential force of a
discovered check.
Another continuation, also winning—but
how much less precise and elegant!—is
16 Kt×BP db ch, K—Kt2; 17 B—R6 ch,
K—Kt1; 18 Kt×Q, R×Kt; 19 Kt×P dis ch,
K—K1; 20 Kt×R, etc.

16 ......   K—R4
17 B—K2 ch   K—R5
18 R—B4 ch
A deflecting sacrifice.
A more brutal execution would be
18 P—Kt3 ch, K—R6; 19 KKt—B4 ch,
Kt×Kt; 20 Kt×Kt mate.

18 ......   Kt×R
19 P—Kt3 ch   K—R6
20 KKt×Kt mate
An æsthetically most satisfying game.

133

White	Black
LICHTENHEIN	MORPHY

(New York, 1857)

The way of an eagle.

1 P—K4   P—K4
2 Kt—KB3   Kt—QB3
3 P—Q4   P×P
4 B—QB4   Kt—B3

By an inversion of moves, a modern variation of the *Two Knights' Defence* is now reached.

5 P—K5
A premature thrust. He should have played 5 Castles. After the impulsive expedition 5 Kt—Kt5, Black has an adequate defence by 5 .... P—Q4; 6 P × P, Q—K2 ch, followed by .... Kt—K4.

5 ......   P—Q4
This central thrust secures the initiative for Black.

6 B—QKt5
After 6 P × Kt, P × B; 7 Q—K2 ch, B—K3; 8 P × P, B × P; 9 Kt—Kt5, Q—Q4, Black has the better game.

6 ......   Kt—K5
Far more powerful than 6 .... Kt—Q2; 7 B × Kt, P × B; 8 P—K6, and Black steers for trouble.

7 Kt × P
Here again 7 Castles is preferable.

7 ......   B—Q2
Defence and counter-threat.

8 Kt × Kt
Instead of this move, which helps to strengthen Black's centre, the lateral manœuvre 8 Kt—Kt3 would have given White more equal chances.

8 ......   P × Kt
9 B—Q3   B—QB4
10 B × Kt
Thinking to avoid all trouble, whereas, in reality, trouble now begins. After 10 Castles, Black would continue with 10 .... Q—R5, as in the game.

10 ......   Q—R5
We must admire Morphy's genius, which imparts to the whole subsequent course of the game a wholly ruthless energy.

11 Q—K2
Not 11 P—KKt3, Q × B ch, followed by .... Q × R, nor 11 B—K3, B × B, and wins.
But even after 11 Castles, P × B, followed by .... Castles QR, Black's cause would prevail.

11 ......   P × B
12 B—K3
Plausible and fatal. If White did not wish to weaken his position by 12 P—KKt3, he should at least have sought salvation in castling.

12 ......   B—Kt5
An intermediary manœuvre.

13 Q—B4
If 13 Q—Q2, R—Q1, and wins. Only by 13 P—KKt3 could he avoid the worst.

13 ......   B × B
14 P—Kt3
Or 14 Q × QBP ch, B—Q2; 15 Q × R ch, K—K2; 16 P—KKt3, Q—Kt5; 17 Q × R, B × P ch; 18 K × B, Q—B6 ch; 19 K—Kt1, B—R6, forcing the mate. Or 14 Castles, B—Kt3; 15 Q × QBP ch, K—K2, and Black remains a piece ahead.

14 ......   Q—Q1
15 P × B
Allowing Black to demonstrate the grand conception, initiated on Black's ninth move.

15 ......   Q—Q8 ch
16 K—B2   Q—B6 ch
17 K—Kt1   B—R6
The death sentence.
As he cannot come to his King's rescue, White has nothing left but a few rancorous checks.

18 Q × QBP ch   K—B1
19 Q × R ch   K—K2
      Resigns.

7. FOUR KNIGHTS'
AND THREE KNIGHTS' GAME

134

White	Black
PAULSEN	MORPHY

(New York, 1857)

Although this game is adorned by one of the most famous Queen sacrifices in the literature of the game, it also illustrates quite a number of additional tactical and strategic points: a temporary sacrifice, operations on open files, exploitation of a hole (Q3), breaking up of the King's defences, irruption on the seventh rank, etc.

Historically, this game spread Morphy's fame to Europe and presaged his coming triumphs on the old continent.

1 P—K4	P—K4
2 Kt—KB3	Kt—QB3
3 Kt—B3	

A forerunner of the modern style, Louis Paulsen prefers a quiet and solid opening, whereas the general tendency of his time was to play the gambits—King's, Scotch, Evans, etc.

3	Kt—B3
4 B—Kt5	

The *Spanish Four Knights*, the most scientific of all. Playable also is 4 B—B4, the *Italian*, and 4 P—Q4, the *Scotch Four Knights*.

Less pugnacious is the restricted development 4 B—K2, and Gunsberg's original suggestion 4 P—QR3, which is best answered by 4 .... B—B4, claiming the initiative.

4	B—B4

A more stimulating reply than the symmetrical 4 .... B—Kt5.

5 Castles	

This continuation, storing up energy, is better than hitting out at once with 5 Kt×P (5 .... Kt×Kt; 6 P—Q4) or than 5 P—Q3, renouncing any offensive in the centre.

5	Castles

After the more timid 5 .... P—Q3, the initiative for a long time to come remains with White after 6 P—Q4, P×P; 7 Kt×P, B—Q2; 8 Kt—B5, Castles; 9 B—Kt5, etc.

6 Kt×P	

This *temporary sacrifice* (6 .... Kt×Kt; 7 P—Q4) is not without risks for White, as his great adversary immediately tries to demonstrate. After 6 B×Kt, QP×B; 7 Kt×P, R—K1; 8 Kt—Q3, B—Q5, etc., the game has lost some of its plasticity, and after 6 P—Q3, P—Q3; 7 B—Kt5, Kt—K2, etc., leads to a slowing down of operations.

6	R—K1

Aiming at the full development of his forces. After 6 .... B—Q5; 7 Kt—B3, B×Kt; 8 QP×B, Kt×P; 9 R—K1, P—Q4; 10 P—B4, Kt—B3; 11 B—Kt5, White has command of the central files. If 6 .... Kt—Q5; 7 B—B4.

7 Kt×Kt	

A careful defence is 7 Kt—B3, Kt×P; 8 P—Q4, Kt×Kt; 9 P×Kt, B—B1, and the position tends to equality.

7	QP×Kt
8 B—B4	

An immediate and full retreat shows more prudence by 8 B—K2, Kt×P; 9 Kt×Kt, R×Kt; 10 P—Q3, R—K1; 11 P—QB3, with 12 P—Q4 to follow.

8	P—QKt4

Not yet 8 .... Kt×P, on account of 9 Kt×Kt, R×Kt; 10 B×P ch, for if 10 .... K×B; 11 Q—Q3 ch, followed by Q×R.

An interesting idea here is 8 .... Kt—Kt5 with 9 P—KR3, Kt×P; 10 B×P ch, K—R1, and Black has the last word.

9 B—K2	Kt×P
10 Kt×Kt	R×Kt
11 B—B3	

He is hypnotised by Black's weakness at

his QB6. More self-control is shown by 11 P—Q3, R—K3; 12 P—QB3, to be followed by 13 P—Q4.

11 ......   R—K3
12 P—B3
An error of judgment. He underrates the dangers of the hole at Q3. After 12 P—Q3, White's game could be defended.

12 ......   Q—Q6
13 P—QKt4   B—Kt3
14 P—QR4
A clever plan. Beaten in the first skirmish, White wants to make up leeway in the second, and to release, by turning manœuvres, the pressure established by Black's Queen.

14 ......   P×P
Necessary, because of the threat 15 P—R5. If 14 .... P—QR3; 15 P×P, Q×KtP (evidently not 15 .... RP×P, nor 15 .... BP×P); 16 P—Q4, breaking the charm.

15 Q×P   B—Q2
16 R—R2
Intending 17 Q—B2, but the immediate opposition of the Queen by Q—R6 is essential.

16 ......   QR—K1
A crushing concentration. (Threat: 17 .... Q×R ch.

17 Q—R6
Too late.

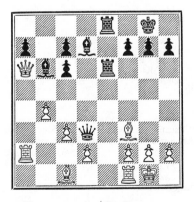

17 ......   Q×B
A splendid sacrifice of the Queen, which breaks the hostile King's defence.

18 P×Q   R—Kt3 ch
19 K—R1   B—R6
20 R—Q1

Clearly neither 20 P—Q4, B—Kt7 ch; 21 K—Kt1, B×P mate, nor 20 R—Kt1, B—Kt7 ch; 21 R×B, R—K8 ch, followed by mate in two. Relatively better would have been 20 Q—Q3.

20 ......   B—Kt7 ch
21 K—Kt1   B×P dis ch
22 K—B1   B—Kt7 ch
Morphy has his whole plan cut and dried in his mind. Another method is 22 .... R—Kt7, with a view to .... R×P and .... R—R8 mate.

23 K—Kt1   B—R6 dis ch
24 K—R1   B×P
25 Q—B1
The only chance of prolonging the game for a little while.

25 ......   B×Q
26 R×B   R—K7
27 R—R1   R—R3
28 P—Q4   B—K6
    Resigns
(29 B×B, R (R3)×P ch; 30 K—Kt1, R—Kt7 mate.)

135

White	Black
PAULSEN	GÖRING

(Leipzig, 1877)

A feature of this game is the gain of a piece by means of stratagems as skilful as they are astute.

1 P—K4   P—K4
2 Kt—KB3   Kt—QB3
3 Kt—B3   Kt—B3
4 B—Kt5   B—Kt5
The most plausible continuation. Playable also are 4 .... B—K2 or 4 .... P—Q3, leading into the *Ruy Lopez*.

A painful loss of time is 4 .... P—QR3, as White can then play 5 B×Kt, QP×B;

6 Kt × P, and Black will find it difficult to recover his pawn.

5 Castles
Calmly continuing his mobilisation. The escapade 5 Kt—Q5 is useless, because Black, after 5 .... Kt × Kt; 6 P × Kt, P—K5; 7 P × Kt, QP × P, recovers his piece with advantage.
If 5 P—Q3, the reply 5 .... Kt—Q5 is serviceable.

5 ......   Castles
Again, if prematurely 5 .... P—Q3; 6 Kt—Q5 is promising.

6 B × Kt
This apparently simplifying liquidation is not without guile. As, however, the preservation of the two Bishops is preferred on principle, the "academic" continuation remains 6 P—Q3.

6 ......   QP × B
After 6 .... KtP × B, White obtains an advantage in territory by 7 Kt × P, Q—K1; 8 Kt—Q3 (more efficacious than either 8 Kt—B3 or 8 Kt—Kt4); 8 .... B × Kt; 9 QP × B, Q × P; 10 R—K1, etc.

7 P—Q3
Having to some extent to decentralise the adverse pawn mass on the Q side, White now forces his adversary to think about his threatened KP. Equality only would result from 7 Kt × P, R—K1; 8 Kt—Q3, B × Kt; 9 QP × B, Kt × P; 10 Q—B3, Kt—Q3; 11 B—B4, Q—B3, etc.

7 ......   B—Kt5
A critical point. From amongst a number of possibilities, Black selects the most active defence.

8 P—KR3   B—KR4
9 K—R1
Besides this skilful preparatory move, 9 B—Kt5 also is good. On the other hand, 9 P—Kt4 would be faulty, because of the break-up sacrifice 9 .... Kt × KtP; 10 P × Kt, B × P, etc.

9 ......   Q—K2
He recognises that the over-protection of the KP has become necessary.
The same object is served by 9 .... Q—Q3, and if 10 P—Kt4, B—Kt3, etc.

10 R—KKt1
Not only with the tactical object of soon making P—KKt4 possible, without having to fear a possible sacrifice, but also with the strategic plan in view of utilising the KKt file as a powerful base of action.

10 ......   QR—Q1
With the transparent threat of winning a pawn (e.g. after 11 B—K3) by 11 .... KB × Kt; 12 P × B, Kt × P.
The simplification 10 .... KB × Kt would have allowed Black, on this or the next move, to get rid of a tenacious combatant.

11 Q—K2   P—KR3
12 Kt—Q1   B—B4
13 P—KKt4   B—KKt3
14 Kt—R4   K—R2
He cannot play 14 .... Kt × KP, because of the intermediary capture by White, 15 Kt × B.

15 B—K3   Kt—Q2
If 15 .... Kt—Kt1; 16 Kt—B5 forces open the KKt file by 16 .... B × Kt; 17 KtP × B, etc.

16 Kt—B5
A genuine outpost.

16 ......   Q—K3
17 R—Kt3
White's far-reaching plans are beginning to take shape.

17 ......   R—KR1
Black would obtain a more stubborn defence by 17 .... P—B3.

18 B × B   Kt × B
19 QKt—K3
Reinforcing the position he has established.

19 ......   Q—B3
Vacating the square for the Knight, but here again 19 .... P—B3 has its points.

20 QR—KKt1   Kt—K3
In order, at least, to prevent White's P—Kt5.

21 Q—Q2
Aiming at both flanks.

21 ......   Kt—Kt4

Faltering strategy. It is true, there is nothing in 21 .... Kt—B5, where the Knight would occupy a "strong" but "dead" point; but the regrouping by 21 .... QR—K1 would be good, not only to protect the KP indirectly, but also to vacate a possible flight square for the Queen (at Q1).

22 Q—R5

By this skilful diversion, White not only attacks the QRP and QBP, but (e.g. in the event of 22 .... R—QB1; 23 Kt—B4) the KP also.

22 ......   Kt—K3

He wishes to reply to 23 Kt—B4 with 23 .... P—B4, but the overloaded position of the black pieces in the royal corner is likely to bring about a catastrophe.

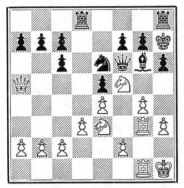

23 P—Kt5

A vacating thrust.

23 ......   Kt × P

Or 23 .... P × P; 24 Kt—Kt4, winning the Queen in a curious manner.

24 P—KR4   B × Kt

Despair, for again, if 24 .... Kt—K3; 25 Kt—Kt4 wins.

25 P × Kt   B × P ch

A piece is lost. The rest, which requires no comment, is played by White with the utmost energy.

26	P × B	P × P
27	Kt—Kt4	K—Kt1 dis ch
28	K—Kt2	Q—Kt3
29	Q × KP	P—B3
30	Q—K6 ch	K—B1
31	R—K1	R—K1
32	Kt—K5	Q × P ch
33	R × Q	R × Q
34	Kt—Kt6 ch	Resigns

136

White	*Black*
NIMZOWITSCH	LEONHARDT

(San Sebastian, 1911)

This game contains a remarkable and most cruel trap, by means of which the black Queen is caught in the middle of the board.

1	P—K4	P—K4
2	Kt—KB3	Kt—QB3
3	Kt—B3	Kt—B3
4	B—Kt5	B—Kt5
5	Castles	Castles
6	B × Kt	

And here we see Nimzowitsch—a modern, not to say hyper-modern, player *par excellence*—indulging in an almost archaic continuation!

6	......	QP × B
7	P—Q3	B—Kt5
8	P—KR3	B—KR4
9	B—Kt5	

With the threat 10 P—Kt4, B—Kt3; 11 Kt × P, whilst if he optimistically plays 9 P—Kt4 at once, the routine sacrifice 9 .... Kt × KtP; 10 P × Kt, B × P; 11 K—Kt2, P—KB4, etc., would be fatal to White.

| 9 | ...... | Q—Q3 |
| 10 | B × Kt | |

Simplicity of means! It will avail Black nothing to have two Bishops against two Knights, as his QB will be driven out of play, whilst the depreciation of the black pawns on the Q side will mean an appreciable advantage for White, should it come to an end-game.

| 10 | ...... | Q × B |

If 10 .... QB × Kt; 11 Q × B, Q × B; 12 Q × Q, P × Q; 13 Kt—K2, the white pawns' superiority would be still more marked.

| 11 | P—Kt4 | B—Kt3 |
| 12 | K—Kt2 | QR—Q1 |

With the obvious threat 13 .... B × Kt; 14 P × B, B × P.

| 13 | Q—Q2 | B × Kt |

Otherwise the itinerary Kt—Q1—K3 might bring the Queen's Knight to B5 and turn it into a potent outpost.

14	P × B	P—B4
15	Kt—Q2	Q—K2
16	Kt—B4	P—Kt3
17	Kt—K3	P—KB3
18	R—KKt1	Q—Q2
19	K—R2	K—R1
20	R—Kt3	

As can be seen, the scheme of White's

preparations on the K side is identical with that illustrated in the preceding game.

20 ......   Q—Kt4

As Black sees no danger—on account of the reduced material—on the castled position, he wishes to involve his adversary on the opposite wing.

21 Q—K1

The Queen in a long-distance duel.

21	Q—R5
22 Q—QB1	R—Q2
23 P—R4	B—B2
24 P—QB4	B—K3
25 Q—Kt2	P—QR4
26 QR—KKt1	Q—B3

He sees trouble ahead, after all, on the K side, and brings back his Queen post-haste to the fold.

27 R (Kt1)—Kt2   Q—Q3

In order to continue on her way *viâ* K2, or to obtain, by the excursion 28 .... Q—Q5, a line on his opponent's intentions. The struggle appears to be without salient points.

28 Q—B1

Dodging an awkward visitor—what could be more natural?

And yet this move is due to a truly diabolical inspiration!

28 ......   Q—Q5

Nothing could be more tempting than to occupy an influential post. But it would have been wiser to follow a purely defensive policy by 28 .... Q—K2, and give up all ambitious dreams.

29 Kt—Q5

Caging the bird. The Queen's capture by

30 P—QB3 is imminent. Note how both white Rooks co-operate in this exploit.

29 ......   R×Kt

He succeeds in saving the Queen, but at what price! (A clear Rook.)

| 30 P—QB3 | Q×QP |
| 31 KP×R | |

But not 31 R×Q, R×R, and there is some fight left, whereas now the rest is silence.

31	Q×P (B5)
32 P×B	Q×KP
33 Q—B2	P—B5
34 Q—B5	Q×Q
35 P×Q	

And White wins.

137

White	Black
TARRASCH	JANOWSKI

(Ostend, 1907)

In the variation illustrated by this game, the opening of the KB file is the basic idea. Here Dr. Tarrasch scores one of his finest successes.

1 P—K4	P—K4
2 Kt—KB3	Kt—QB3
3 Kt—B3	Kt—B3
4 B—Kt5	B—Kt5
5 Castles	Castles
6 P—Q3	P—Q3

Maintaining the symmetry. But if the activities of White's QKt are feared, the continuation 6 .... B×Kt; 7 P×B, P—Q3 is perfectly valid.

7 B—Kt5

The sign of the pin! Less incisive would be other continuations such as 7 Kt—K2, or 7 B×Kt, P×B; 8 Kt—K2, or 7 Kt—Q5, or, in a waiting mood, 7 P—KR3.

7 ......   Kt—K2

End of the symmetry. Fatal would be 7 .... B—Kt5, by reason of the piquant continuation 8 Kt—Q5, Kt—Q5; 9 Kt×B, Kt×B; 10 Kt—Q5, Kt—Q5; 11 Q—Q2, and White has a decided advantage, as Black cannot continue to copy White's moves, e.g.: 11 .... Q—Q2; 12 B×Kt,

B × Kt; 13 Kt—K7 ch, K—R1; 14 B × P ch,
K × B; 15 Q—Kt5 ch, K—R1; 16 Q—B6
mate.

8 Kt—KR4
Already signifying his intention of opening
the KB file by P—KB4.

Less good is 8 B × Kt, P × B; 9 Kt—KR4,
as then Black succeeds, just in time, in consolidating his position after 9 .... P—B3;
10 B—B4, Kt—Kt3; 11 K♦ × Kt, RP × Kt;
12 P—B4, B—B4 ch; 13 K—R1, K—Kt2;
14 Q—B3, Q—K2, etc.

After the preventive retreat 8 B—QB4,
a game Mattison-Kostitch, *Bardiov*, 1926,
had the following trenchant continuation:
8 B—QB4, P—B3; 9 Kt—K2, Kt—Kt3
(more consistent would be 9 .... P—Q4);
10 P—B3, B—R4; 11 Kt—R4, Kt × Kt;
12 B × QKt, P—KR3 (an error of judgment.
This was the last chance of seeking counter-
play in the centre by 12 .... P—Q4);
13 P—B4 (he is not afraid of ghosts); 13 ....
P × P; 14 Kt × P, P—QKt4 (if 14 ....
P—KKt4; 15 Kt—R5, with a winning
attack); 15 B—QKt3, Q—Kt3 ch; 16 P—Q4,
B—KKt5 (if 16 .... P—Kt4; 17 Kt—Kt6);
17 Q—Q2, P—Kt4 (anything loses);
18 Kt—Kt6, P × B; 19 R × Kt, and Black
resigns.

8 ......   P—B3
Preparing counter-operations in the centre.
After 8 .... Kt—Kt3; 9 Kt × Kt, RP × Kt;
10 Kt—Q5, B—QB4; 11 Kt × Kt ch, P × Kt;
12 B—KR6, and White has the better game.

9 B—QB4   B—Kt5
A fruitless attempt to impede White's
P—KB4. Nor would other moves succeed,
such as 9 .... B—K3, or 9 .... Kt—K1,
nor 9 .... Kt—Kt3 (10 Kt × Kt, P × Kt;
11 P—B4, etc.); or finally, 9 .... P—Q4
(10 B—Kt3, Q—Q3; 11 P—B4, etc.).

Therefore the best means of preventing
the expansion of White's game is 9 ....
K—R1, unpinning the KBP, after which
10 P—B4, P × P; 11 B × Kt, P × B; 12 R × P,
Kt—Kt3; 13 Kt × Kt ch, BP × Kt affords
Black a comfortable game. White's best
course, in that case, is to bring about equality
by 10 B × Kt, P × B; 11 Q—R5, Kt—Kt3,
etc.

10 P—B3   B—K3
11 B × Kt   P × B
12 B × B   P × B
13 P—B4

This advance, which vitalises the KB file,
is the key to this variation.

13 ......   Kt—Kt3
14 Kt × Kt   P × Kt
15 Q—Kt4

Although the black King's defences appear
to be adequate, the frontal attack, initiated
by the text move, wins all along the line.
What follows is a masterpiece of clarity and
conciseness in chess.

15 ......   Q—K1
Or 15 .... K—B2; 14 P × P, QP × P;
15 R—B3, and the black King's position
remains precarious. After the text move,
White's KBP becomes a battering-ram.

16 P—B5   P × P
17 P × P   B × Kt
18 P × B   K—Kt2
19 R—B3   R—R1

If 19 .... P—KKt4; 20 P—KR4, which
the move in the text is to prevent.

20 P × P   Q—K2
As 20 .... Q × P is not feasible, on
account of 21 Q—Q7 ch, Black's position,
with a powerful wedge driven into his game,
gradually becomes hopeless.

21 P—KR4   P—Q4
22 QR—KB1   QR—KB1
23 P—R5   R—R3
24 QR—B2   KR—R1
25 Q—B5

Vacating the KKt file for the triumphant
advance of the "third Musketeer."

25 ......   Q—Q3
26 P—Kt4   Q—K2

Hoping to control the critical square
KKt4.

27 P—Kt5
A decisive advance.

27	P × P
28 Q × R ch	R × Q
29 R × R	Q × R

There is nothing left. If 29 .... Q—B4;
30 P—Q4, P × P; 31 QR—B7 ch, K—R3;
32 R—R7 (or R—R8) mate.

30 P—R6 ch	K × RP
31 R × Q	K × P
32 K—Kt2	P—K5
33 P × P	P × P
34 K—Kt3	Resigns.

138

| *White* | *Black* |
| CAPABLANCA | H. STEINER |

(Exhibition of Living Chess,
Los Angeles, 1933)

*A very spectacular game. The KB file,
opened early, demonstrates its full power.*

1 P—K4	P—K4
2 Kt—KB3	Kt—QB3
3 B—Kt5	Kt—B3
4 Kt—B3	B—Kt5
5 Castles	Castles
6 P—Q3	P—Q3
7 B—Kt5	B × Kt
8 P × B	Kt—K2

Better is Dr. Metger's continuation 8 ....
Q—K2.

9 Kt—R4
More energetic than 9 B × Kt, P × B, and
certainly more *à propos* than 9 B—QB4
(9 .... Kt—Kt3; 10 Kt—R4, Kt—B5;
11 B × QKt, P × B; 12 Kt—B3, B—K3,
with a consolidated position).

9 ......   P—B3
After 9 .... Kt—Kt3; 10 Kt × Kt,
RP × Kt; 11 P—KB4, or 10 .... BP × Kt;
11 B—B4 ch, K—R1; 12 P—B4, White will
have the supremacy on the critical sector.

10 B—QB4   B—K3
This move detracts from, instead of
adding to, the stability of the black King's
position.
Against 10 .... P—Q4, the strongest line
is 11 B—Kt3.
Or 10 .... Kt—Kt3; 11 Kt × Kt
RP × Kt; 12 P—B4, with an attack.
For all these reasons, the waiting move

10 .... K—R1 (intending eventually to continue 11 .... Kt—Kt3; 12 Kt × Kt ch,
BP × Kt) is to be recommended.

11 B × Kt	P × B
12 B × B	P × B
13 Q—Kt4 ch	

The King hunt begins.

13 ......   K—B2
The King defending his pawn.

14 P—KB4
A well-known scheme.

14 ......   R—KKt1
Or 14 .... Kt—Kt3; 15 P—B5.

15 Q—R5 ch   K—Kt2
The fact that the King has to keep defending a pawn can lead to no good.

16 P × P
Opening the critical file.

16 ......   QP × P
Clearly not 16 .... BP × P; 17 R—B7 ch.
After the text move, Black prepares to consolidate his game either by 17 .... Kt—Kt3,
or by 17 .... Q—Kt3 ch, followed by
QR—KB1. Therefore the logic of events
prescribes a violent solution.

17 R × P
A *denuding sacrifice.*

17 ......   K × R
18 R—B1 ch   Kt—B4
Sad, but necessary.

19 Kt × Kt
This elegant refusal to secure an extra
piece amounts, in a way, to a *negative
sacrifice.*

It is an admirable point of the initial sacrifice, for after 19 P × Kt, K—K2, Black's game would become defendable. Now, however, the black King's flight square at K2 is taboo.

| 19 ...... | P × Kt |
| 20 R × P ch | |

In the ensuing short ending, the greatest possible effect is obtained with the smallest possible means.

20	K—K2
21 Q—B7 ch	K—Q3
22 R—B6 ch	K—B4

After 22 .... Q × R; 23 Q × Q ch, K—Q2; 24 Q—B7 ch, K—Q3; 25 Q × RP, White's victory is assured, on account of his two connected passed pawns.

But now, short of a miracle, Black hopes to hold his own, e.g. 23 Q—B4 ch, K—Kt3; 24 Q—Kt4 ch, K—R3; 25 Q—B4 ch, K—Kt3, and the black King has found a far more solid stronghold on the Q side than the one which he had on the opposite wing.

23 Q × KtP
And here is the miracle! A waiting move, leaving a Rook *en prise*, again breaks down the defences. There is a double threat of mate, by 24 Q—Kt4, or, more prosaically, by 24 R × P.

| 23 ...... | Q—Kt3 |

A vain attempt to improvise a defence.

24 R × P ch
A sacrifice in the problem-manner.

| 24 ...... | Q × R |
| 25 Q—Kt4 mate | |

A very beautiful finish.

139

| *White* | *Black* |
| SPIELMANN | RUBINSTEIN |

(Carlsbad, 1911)

In this magnificent contest, the manner in which White elaborates his K side attack is no less worthy of praise than its execution.

1 P—K4	P—K4
2 Kt—KB3	Kt—QB3
3 Kt—B3	Kt—B3
4 B—Kt5	B—Kt5
5 Castles	Castles
6 P—Q3	P—Q3
7 B—Kt5	B × Kt
8 P × B	Q—K2

Introducing ingenious regroupings (.... Kt—Q1—K3; and .... R—Q1) which increase the security of Black's position. This system, due to Metger, gives better results in practice than for instance 8 .... Kt—K2 or 8 .... P—KR3; 9 B—KR4, B—Kt5, etc.

9 R—K1
Preparing the offensive in the centre by 10 P—Q4, by over-protecting the KP.
A "peace at any price" continuation would be 9 KB × Kt, P × B; 10 P—KR3, etc.

| 9 ...... | Kt—Q1 |

The first regrouping.

| 10 P—Q4 | Kt—K3 |

He could quite well play 10 .... B—Kt5 first.

11 B—QB1
"East or west, home's best."

| 11 ...... | P—B3 |

The most vigorous continuation is the thrust 11 .... P—B4, e.g. 12 P—Q5 (disappointing would be 12 P × KP, P × P; 13 Kt × P, on account of 13 .... Kt—B2, winning a piece); 12 .... Kt—B2; 13 B—Q3, B—Kt5; 14 P—KR3, B—R4, and Black holds his own.

12 B—B1
Intending entirely fresh activities after P—Kt3. The potential effect of the two Bishops, to all appearances on the retired list, is remarkable.

| 12 ...... | R—Q1 |

The second regrouping. 12 .... Q—B2 would show less initiative.

13 P—Kt3
Increasing the scope of White's game.

| 13 ...... | Q—B2 |

More decided would be 13 .... P—B4.

14 Kt—R4
White could have prevented the ensuing central thrust by 14 B—KKt2.

14 ......   P—Q4
In quest of emancipation.

15 P—KB4
If 15 KP×P, KKt×P, and Black has
a target.

15 ......   P×BP
Helping White's intentions. 15 ....
KKt×P would have served.

16 P—K5
The infantry to the fore.

16 ......   Kt—K5
17 P×P   P—KB4
An unsuccessful attempt to close the
position.

18 P×P e. p.
But not 18 Kt×P, Kt×KBP.

18 ......   Kt×P (B3)
19 P—B5
White remains master of the battlefield.

19 ......   Kt—B1
20 Q—B3   Q—B2
21 B—Q3   B—Q2
22 B—KB4   R—K1
23 B—K5   P—B4
24 K—R1   P—B5
25 B—K2   B—B3
Threatening 26 .... R×B; 27 P×R,
P—Q5. But 25 .... R×B; 26 P×R,
B—B3; 27 Q—Kt2, P—Q5; 28 B—B3, etc.,
leads to no immediate result.

26 Q—B4   Kt (B1)—Q2
27 B—B3   R—K2
28 R—K2
This preparation to double Rooks on an
entirely different file (KKt) is interesting.

28 ......   R—KB1
If 28 .... QR—K1, then equally
29 R—KKt1, whereas the text move
intends a regrouping of Rook and Queen.

29 R—KKt1   Q—K1
30 R (K2)—Kt2   R (B1)—B2
In order to threaten 31 .... Kt×B, but
White is able to intensify the pressure on
KKt7.

31 Q—R6   K—B1
A critical juncture. If White fails to
effect a breach in the hostile fortress, he will
have to retreat.

32 Kt—Kt6 ch
A *penetrating sacrifice.*

32 ......   P×Kt
33 Q—R8 ch   Kt—Kt1
34 B—Q6
A decisive pin. He is in no hurry to
produce his trumps on the KKt file, as the
threat of 35 R×P remains.

34 ......   Q—Q1
With a view to 35 .... Kt—B3, whereas
34 .... Kt—B3 at once loses because of
35 P×P.

35 R×P   Kt—B3
36 R×Kt
A *complementary sacrifice,* shoring up
White's prospects.

36 ......   R×R
Not 36 .... P×R; 37 R×Kt mate, nor
36 .... Q—K1; 37 Q×P mate.

37 R×P
Even more convincing than 37 Q×P ch.

37 ......   Resigns.

140

White	Black
TARRASCH	RUBINSTEIN

(Mährisch-Ostrau, 1923)

*A feature of this fine game is the persistent
manner in which Black strives for and secures
the initiative, by skilfully and repeatedly
breaking through on various files.*

1 P—K4	P—K4
2 Kt—KB3	Kt—QB3
3 Kt—B3	Kt—B3
4 B—Kt5	B—Kt5
5 Castles	Castles
6 P—Q3	P—Q3
7 B—Kt5	B × Kt
8 P × B	Q—K2

The *Metger Variation*—both solid and ingenious.

9 R—K1	Kt—Q1
10 P—Q4	B—Kt5

Black throws all his troops into the critical sector. It is more enterprising, but it also carries more responsibility.

11 P—KR3

Challenging the pinning Bishop's intentions—a sound principle which eliminates future dangers.

11	B—R4

More risky would be 11 .... B × Kt; 12 Q × B.

12 P—Kt4

White also has ambitions.

12	B—Kt3
13 P—Q5	

More consistent would be 13 Kt—R4. Alternative possibilities are 13 B—Q3, strengthening the position, or the preparatory 13 R—Kt1.

13	P—B3

Seeking at once to obtain the initiative.

14 B—QB4

More rational would be 14 B—Q3, immediately. Even 14 B—KB1 is not without its points.

14	R—B1

Threatening to win a pawn by 15 .... P × P; 16 B × P, R × P.

15 P × P

Rounding off Black's pawn centre, but after 15 R—K3, P × P; 16 B × P, Kt—K3, Black has the freer game.

15	P × P
16 B—Q3	Kt—K3
17 B—QB1	

If 17 B—R4, Kt—B5, and Black takes the lead.

17	Kt—B4
18 Kt—Q2	

Overestimating the strength of his castled position, he denudes it of defending forces. Better, at once, 18 B—R3.

18	P—KR4

Black's offensive begins.

19 B—R3	Kt—K3
20 Kt—B4	P—B4
21 B—QB1	P × P
22 P × P	Kt—R2
23 K—Kt2	Kt (R2)—Kt4
24 P—B3	QR—Q1
25 Kt—Kt2	

The crisis is near. White would welcome the opportunity of closing the centre by 26 P—QB4. But if, with that end in view, he plays 25 Kt—K3, the reply 25 .... Kt—B5 ch would disorganise the royal encampment.

As, however, the text move fails to effect its purpose and serves only to get the Knight out of play, the courageous 25 K—Kt3 would have been best.

25	P—Q4
26 P × P	R × P
27 P—QB4	R—Q5
28 B—K3	

For if 28 R × P, Q—B3, with multifarious threats.

28	R—Q3
29 Q—K2	P—K5

Another break-through.

30 P × P	Kt × P
31 Q—B3	Kt (K5)—Kt4
32 Q—Kt3	Q—Kt2 ch

The conquest of the long diagonal is Black's first token of victory.

33 K—B1	R—Kt3

If 33 .... R—Q2; 34 QR—Kt1.

34 Kt—R4	B × B ch
35 P × B	

35 ......   P—B4

A third and decisive break-through. It
is to be noted that Black's strategy, in this
game, consists in the clearing of the files:
QB (by 13 .... P—B3), KR (by 18 ....
P—KR4), Q (by 25 .... P—Q4), K (by
29 .... P—K5), and now, finally, the KB
file.

36 B×Kt

If 36 Kt×R, P—B5.

36 ......   P×P dis ch
37 K—Kt1   Kt×B
38 Kt×R   Kt—B6 ch
39 K—B2   Kt×R dis ch
   Resigns

For if 40 K×Kt, Q—R8 ch, followed by
Q×R, and if 40 K—K2, R—K1 ch;
41 K—Q2, Kt—B6 ch, followed by ....
Q×Kt, and in either case Black's advantage
in material is conclusive.

An impressive game.

141

White	Black
MARÓCZY	BOGOLJUBOW

(London, 1922)

*A remarkable feature of the following game
is the way in which Black conducts operations
on the open K file. His play, a combination
of finesse and energy, is truly artistic.*

1 P—K4   P—K4
2 Kt—KB3   Kt—QB3
3 Kt—B3   Kt—B3
4 B—Kt5   B—Kt5
5 Castles   Castles
6 P—Q3   P—Q3
7 Kt—K2

He prefers manœuvring to a concrete
measure such as 7 B—Kt5.

7 ......   B—QB4

A preventive retreat. He tries to enliven
the play in preference to 7 .... Kt—K2;
8 P—B3, B—R4; 9 Kt—Kt3, P—B3;
10 B—R4, Kt—Kt3, etc. Far more bind-
ing—and even dangerous—is the attempt
to seize the initiative by 7 .... B—Kt5 or
7 .... Kt—KR4.

8 P—B3   B—Kt3

Continuing his strategy of preventive
retreats, this time aiming at White's intended
P—Q4.

9 Kt—Kt3

After this regrouping, which over-protects
the KP, the advance of the QP is again on
the agenda.

9 ......   K—R1

Another—and very deep—preventive
measure, the object of which is to reply to
10 B—Kt5 by 10 .... P—KR3; 11 B—KR4,
R—KKt1, followed by .... P—KKt4,
without having to fear White's sacrifice of
a Knight for two pawns and the attack.

10 B—K3

He changes his plans. Instead of the pin
10 B—Kt5, or of the advance 10 P—Q4,
White wants to become sole master of the
centre. It would, however, have been better
to prepare for the text move by 10 P—KR3.

10 ......   Kt—KKt5

Of little use would be 10 .... B×B;
11 P×B, because then White would have
a reinforced centre, and also a base of
action in the open KB file.

11 B×B   RP×B
12 P—Q4   P—B3

A more orthodox defence of the threatened
KP would be 12 .... Q—K2.

13 P—KR3

As the black KKt could not for ever stay
at its exposed post, the text move only helps
it to depart, not without a weakening, as
yet imperceptible, of White's King's field.
More useful is 13 Q—Q2.

13 ......   Kt—R3

The "Knight errant."

14 B×Kt

Otherwise Black's QKt, proceeding via
K2, Kt3 to KB5, might cause White some
disagreeable surprises.

14 ......   P×B
15 R—K1   B—K3

Marking the beginning of Black's counter-
offensive.

16 P—R3   Q—K2
17 Q—Q3   R—KKt1
18 Kt—B5

Too passive would be 18 Kt—R2,
P—KKt4; 19 P—B3, and that is why White
himself calls for hand-to-hand fighting.

18 ......   B×Kt

The simple can be profound! If 18 ....
Kt×Kt; 19 P×Kt, B—B2, Black loses
a tempo for the necessary retreat, whereas,

after the move in the text, Black can at once realise the opening of the KKt file.

19 P × B	P—Kt3
20 P × KtP	R × KtP
21 Kt—R4	R—Kt4

If 21 .... R—Kt2; 22 Kt—B5, the game is to a great extent simplified. But now this bold Rook can operate on three files.

22 P—KB4	R—R4
23 Kt—B3	R—KKt1
24 QP × P	QP × P
25 P × P	R × RP
26 P—K6	

Creating a valuable asset. A cruel deception would be 26 P × P, Q × BP; 27 Q—Q4, by reason of 27 .... R × Kt.

26	Kt—Kt5

Strengthening the attack in a brilliant manner, as the pressure on the KKt file is not discontinued, but merely veiled. (Threat: 27 .... R—R8 ch.) Less intense would be 26 .... Q—Kt2; 27 R—K2, and White has a defence.

27 Q—Q7	

Seeking the exchange of Queens, for, clearly, neither 27 P × R, Kt—K4 dis ch, nor even 27 Q—B5, R × Kt; 28 Q × R, Q—B4 ch; 29 K—R1, R—Kt4 is acceptable.

Relatively best would be 27 Q—Q4, after which, however, 27 .... Q—Kt2; 28 R—K2, R × Kt tips the scales in Black's favour.

27	Q—B4 ch
28 Q—Q4	

After 28 Kt—Q4, Black has the same eloquent rejoinder 28 .... Q—KR4, etc.

28	Q—KR4

With the deadly threat of 29 .... R—R8 mate.

29 K—B1	

Flight of the King! For if 29 P × R, Kt—K4 dis ch; 30 K—B1, Q × Kt ch; 31 Q—B2, Q × P ch; 32 K—K2, Q—Q6 mate.

29	R—Kt6

This move, quietly powerful, threatens not only 30 .... Q—R8 ch; 31 Q—Kt1, R × Kt ch; 32 P × R, Kt—R7 ch, etc., but also 30 .... R × P; 31 K × R, Kt—K4 dis ch, and wins.

30 R—K2	

There is no saving clause, e.g. 30 Q—Kt1, R × Kt ch; 31 P × R, Kt—R7 ch, etc., or

again 30 Q—K4, R × Kt ch, etc., or, finally, continuing the King's flight 30 K—K2, R × P ch, etc.

30	R × Kt ch

Winning a piece in elegant fashion, for if 31 P × R, Q—R8 ch; 32 Q—Kt1, Kt—R7 ch, winning the Queen.

31 K—K1	Kt—K4
Resigns	

As Black remains a piece ahead.

142

White	*Black*
STERK	MARSHALL

(Pistyan, 1912)

A fine game, in which White refutes an over-hasty advance by Black (6 .... P—Q4) in a manner both brilliant and energetic.

1 P—K4	P—K4
2 Kt—KB3	Kt—QB3
3 Kt—B3	Kt—B3
4 B—Kt5	B—Kt5
5 Castles	Castles
6 P—Q3	P—Q4

Instead of the ordinary routine continuation 6 .... P—Q3 (or 6 .... B × Kt; P × B, P—Q3), Black tries something new.

This idea can safely be effected in the following manner: 6 .... B × Kt; 7 P × B, and then only 7 .... P—Q4 (the *Svenonius Variation*), e.g. 8 B × Kt, P × B; 9 Kt × P, Q—Q3; 10 B—B4, R—K1, and Black, in return for his pawn, has sufficient compensation in the superior disposition of his pieces.

The attempt in the text, a "pseudo Svenonius," has the drawback that it allows White's QKt to participate in the course of events.

7 Kt × QP	

A powerful move.

7	Kt × Kt
8 P × Kt	Q × P
9 B—QB4	

Undermining the hostile position, whilst improving his own. Spineless would be 9 B × Kt, P × B; 10 Q—K2, R—K1, and Black is out of danger.

9	Q—Q3
10 P—B3	B—QB4
11 P—QKt4	B—Kt3
12 P—QR4	

Keeping the enemy on the run.

| 12 ...... | P—QR4 |

After 12 .... P—QR3; would follow 13 B—R3, with the threat 14 P—Kt5.

| 13 P—Kt5 | Kt—K2 |
| 14 Kt—Kt5 | |

White's every move tells.

| 14 ...... | Q—Kt3 |

After 14 .... P—R3; 15 B—R3 marks White's superiority, e.g.: 15 .... B—QB4; 16 Kt×P, R×Kt; 17 Q—B3, B—B4 (or 17 .... B—K3; 18 KB×B, Q×B; 19 Q×P, etc.); 18 B×B, Q×B; 19 P—Kt4, etc., or 15 .... Q—B3; 16 Kt—K4, Q—R5; 17 P—Kt3, Q—R6; 18 P—Q4 (not 18 B×Kt, B—Kt5, followed by .... B—B6); 18 .... R—K1; 19 Q—B3, etc.

| 15 Q—K2 | B—KB4 |

An attempt to confuse matters. If 15 .... P—R3; 16 Q×P (not 16 Kt—B3, nor 16 Kt—K4, because of 16 .... B—Kt5, with gain in territory).

| 16 P—Kt4 | |

Played with much self-possession. 16 Q×P shows far less ambition.

16	P—R3
17 P×B	Kt×P
18 K—R1	P×Kt

Now Black has, for the moment, actually won a pawn, but White's pressure on the KKt file quickly becomes decisive.

| 19 R—KKt1 | P—Kt5 |
| 20 B—R3 | |

Over-hasty would be 20 R×P, by reason of 20 .... Q—R4, e.g. 21 B—R3 (of course not 21 R×P ch, Kt×R, guarding his Queen, nor 21 B—K3, B×B; 22 P×B, Kt—Kt6 ch, winning his opponent's); 21 .... B×P; and Black has taken the lead.

| 20 ...... | Kt—R3 |

An heroic decision to give up the exchange. But if 20 .... KR—K1; 21 R×P, Q—R4; 22 QR—KKt1 (threat: R×P ch); 22 .... K—R1 (with the counter-threat 23 .... Kt—R3); 23 Q—K4, P—KB3 (if 23 .... B×P; 24 R—Kt5); 24 B—B7, Q×B; 25 Q×Kt, with a winning attack.

21 B×R	R×B
22 R—Kt2	R—K1
23 P—B3	

A decisive stratagem, for if 23 .... P×P; 24 Q×BP, Q—B4; 25 Q×P, etc.

23	Q—Kt4
24 R—K1	Q—K2
25 P×P	

The KKt file, it is true, is now closed, but the KKtP becomes a battering-ram.

25	Q—R6
26 P—Kt5	Kt—B4
27 P—Kt6	

An irresistible advance.

27	R—K2
28 Q—R5	Kt—R3
29 Q×Kt	

A fine conclusion.   Resigns.

143

| *White* | *Black* |
| BERNSTEIN | RUBINSTEIN |

(Vilna, 1912)

A remarkable feature of this game is that Black gives up two pawns, without any prospect of immediate sanctions, and yet gets within an ace of winning the game—a far from commonplace adventure.

1 P—K4	P—K4
2 Kt—KB3	Kt—QB3
3 Kt—B3	Kt—B3
4 B—Kt5	Kt—Q5

One of those glorious moves by Black, which demonstrate that the second player, even in one of the most scientific openings, need not abandon all dreams of a counter-offensive.

The text move was played in a game Elson-Delmar, *Philadelphia*, 1875, and then in *Monte Carlo*, 1902, in a game Maróczy-Marshall. Later on it became the basis of a system adopted successfully by Rubinstein. Omniscient theory recognises the soundness of this, the "Rubinstein-Marshall Variation."

| 5 B—B4 | |

Black experiences the most difficulties after 5 B—R4, e.g. 5 .... B—B4; 6 Kt×P,

Castles; 7 Kt—Q3 (very sound also is the retreat 7 Kt—B3; but if 7 P—Q3, P—Q4, etc., and if 7 Castles, P—Q3, followed by 8 .... B—KKt5, to Black's advantage); 7 .... B—Kt3; 8 Kt—B4, P—Q4; 9 P—Q3, and White, without much damage, maintains an extra pawn.

If, however, White should prefer to avoid all kinds of surprises, he is able to simplify matters by 5 Kt×Kt, P×Kt; 6 P—K5, P×Kt; 7 P×Kt, Q×P (it would be too risky to win a pawn by 7 .... P×QP ch; 8 B×P, Q×P; 9 Castles, B—K2; 10 B—Q3, with a fine attack); 8 QP×P, Q—K4 ch; 9 Q—K2, Q×Q ch; 10 B×Q, P—Q4, and the time is ripe for peace negotiations. This line of play has deprived the Rubinstein-Marshall of its potentialities.

      5 ......   B—B4

True to the spirit of the variation, Black continues in gambit style, declaring his willingness to sacrifice a pawn for the sake of rapid development.

The great Labourdonnais' constant advice was: "Bring out your pieces." The following curious game, Jowett-McDonald, *London*, 1885, illustrates the consequence of neglecting this precept: 5 .... Kt×P; 6 B×P ch (instead of 6 Kt×Kt, P—Q4), 6 .... K×B; 7 QKt×Kt, Kt×Kt ch (better is 7 .... P—Q3); 8 Q×Kt ch, K—Kt1; 9 Kt—Kt5 (a beautiful conclusion; there is a double threat of mate by 10 Q—B7 or 10 Q—Q5); Black resigns.

      6 Kt×P

Accepting the Greek gift. Against 6 P—Q3, Black can reply with 6 .... P—Q3; 7 Kt—QR4, B—Kt3, etc., or 6 .... Q—K2; or even, giving up a pawn, 6 .... P—Q4.

      6 ......   Q—K2

More urgent than 6 .... Castles.

      7 Kt—B3

Against 7 Kt—Q3 there is the same energetic reply 7 .... P—Q4. Deficient would be 7 B×P ch, K—B1, or 7 Kt×BP, P—Q4; 8 Kt×P, Q×P ch; 9 Kt—K3, B—KKt5.

      7 ......   P—Q4

In the grand manner.

      8 B×P

Not without drawbacks would also be 8 Kt×P, KKt×Kt (better than 8 .... Q×P ch; 9 Kt—K3, etc.); 9 B×Kt, P—QB3, etc.

      8 ......   B—KKt5

A troublesome pin, whereas nothing results for Black from 8 .... Kt×B; 9 QKt×Kt, Q×P ch; 10 Kt—K3, B—KKt5; 11 P—Q3.

      9 P—Q3   P—B3
    10 B—Kt3   Kt—Q2

Firm strategy.

    11 B—Kt5

Or 11 P—KR3, B×Kt; 12 P×B, Kt—K4; 13 P—B4, Q—R5; 14 P×Kt, Kt×B, and wins.

    11 ......   Q—Q3

He prefers not to relieve the tension, although the transaction 11 .... Kt×Kt ch; 12 P×Kt, Q×B; 13 P×B, Kt—K4; 14 P—KR3, Q—B5 would have left him with a strong attacking position.

    12 Kt—QKt1

Regrouping on account of the threatened point at KB3.

    12 ......   Q—Kt3
    13 B—K3   B×Kt
    14 P×B   Q—Kt7

After this very promising irruption, it seems as if only a miracle could save White.

    15 K—Q2

Flight of the King. If 15 R—B1, Kt×KBP ch; 16 K—K2, B×B; 17 K×B, Kt×P, with continued molestation.

    15 ......   Kt×P ch

Recovering, at any rate, a pawn. After 16 K—K2, B×B; 17 K×B, Black has nothing concrete.

    16 K—B1   R—Q1
    17 P—KR3

With a view to 18 Q—B1. If at once 17 Q—B1, Q×Q ch; 18 R×Q, Kt×P.

    17 ......   B×B ch
    18 P×B   KKt—K4

The reserve cavalry. If 18 .... Q—B7; 19 Kt—Q2.

    19 Q—B1   Q—Kt4

He finds a way of molesting the adverse King even in his new stronghold.

    20 Q—K2

Not 20 Q—B2, R×P.

    20 ......   Kt—Q5

This piquant turn forces the repetition of moves.

21 Q—Q2
Again not 21 Q—B2, Kt × B ch; 22 RP × Kt, R × P.

| 21 ...... | QKt—B6 |
| 22 Q—K2 | Kt—Q5 |

Draw.
A "fighting draw."

144

White	Black
ED. LASKER	ENGLUND

(Scheveningen, 1913)

In the following brilliant game, Black's King, driven from pillar to post, seems at last to have found peace, when a Queen's sacrifice shatters his illusions, forcing a most elegant "diagonal mate."

1 P—K4	P—K4
2 Kt—KB3	Kt—QB3
3 Kt—B3	Kt—B3
4 B—Kt5	Kt—Q5
5 Kt × P	

Accepting the challenge.

| 5 ...... | Q—K2 |

A logical reply. After 5 .... B—Kt5; 6 B—Q3, Q—K2; 7 Kt—Kt4, White can already think of maintaining his gain. And after 5 .... B—B4; 6 B—K2, keeps his extra pawn without any disadvantage.

6 Kt—B3
Against the impetuous 6 P—B4, Black comes out well after 6 .... Kt × B; 7 Kt × Kt, P—Q3; 8 Kt—KB3, Q × P ch; 9 K—B2, Kt—Kt5 ch; 10 K—Kt3, Q—Kt3, etc.

| 6 ...... | Kt × P |

This capture is the cause of all subsequent trouble. By playing 6 .... Kt × B; 7 Kt × Kt, Q × P ch; 8 Q—K2, Q × Q ch; 9 K × Q, Kt—Q4; 10 R—K1 (or 10 P—B4, P—QR3); 10 .... P—Q3, etc., Black would have obtained at least an equal game.

7 Castles
White's advantage in development will soon be convincing.

| 7 ...... | Kt × Kt |
| 8 QP × Kt | Kt × Kt ch |

He should have played 8 .... Kt—K3, obstructing the critical file.

| 9 Q × Kt | Q—B4 |

And now he should, at all cost, have tried 9 .... P—QB3; 10 B—Q3, P—Q4; 11 B—KB4, B—K3, etc., or 10 B—KB4, P—Q4 (not 10 .... P × B; 11 KR—K1, etc., nor 10 .... P—Q3; 11 B × P ch); 11 B—Q3 (11 Q × P would be unsound, because of 11 .... P × B, etc.); 11 .... B—K3, and Black seeks to establish a line of defence.

| 10 R—K1 ch | B—K2 |
| 11 B—Q3 | P—Q4 |

After 11 .... P—Q3 the same reply, 12 B—K3, would be even more conclusive.

| 12 B—K3 | Q—Q3 |

Or 12 .... Q—B3; 13 B—Q4.

| 13 B—KB4 | Q—KB3 |

Harassed, Black is already obliged to leave a corpse on the way. For if 13 .... Q—B4; 14 P—QKt4, etc. After 13 .... Q—QB3; 14 Q—K2, with a double threat at K7 and QKt5, and if 13 .... Q—Q2; 14 Q—Kt3, with a double threat, this time against KKt7 and QB2.

14 Q × P
Very elegant! White leaves his QB *en prise*, as after 14 .... Q × B there would follow 15 B—Kt5 ch, P—B3 (15 .... K—B1; 16 Q—Q8 ch, B × Q; 17 R—K8 mate); 16 B × P ch, P × B; 17 Q × QBP ch, K—B1; 18 Q × R, etc., with a winning attack.

| 14 ...... | P—B3 |

He cannot risk taking the Bishop, and can no longer hope to re-establish equality.

| 15 Q—K4 | B—K3 |

Black at last brings his QB out, but his position has many vulnerable points.

| 16 R—K3 | B—QB4 |

Now or never he should have tried 16 .... Castles QR.

17 B—K5	Q—R3
18 R—Kt3	B—KB1
19 R—Q1	Castles

Castling into the lion's mouth.

20 Q × P ch
A *clearance sacrifice*, leading to an attractive mate.

| 20 ...... | P × Q |
| 21 B—R6 mate | |

145

White	Black
BOGOLJUBOW	RUBINSTEIN

(Match, 1920)

*In the following game all the white pieces
develop a remarkable dynamic force.*

1 P—K4	P—K4
2 Kt—KB3	Kt—QB3
3 Kt—B3	Kt—B3
4 B—Kt5	Kt—Q5
5 Kt × P	Kt × P

The only correct reply is 5 .... Q—K2.

6 Kt × Kt	Kt × B
7 Kt × BP	

The contest is of a hazardous character.

7	Q—K2

If 7 .... K × Kt; 8 Q—R5 ch, followed
by Q × Kt.

8 Kt × R	Q × Kt ch
9 K—B1	

The first surprise. After 9 Q—K2,
Q × Q ch; 10 K × Q, P—Q4, etc., Black
would have an easy task.

9	Kt—Q5

Or 9 .... P—KKt3; 10 P—Q3, Q—K4;
11 Q—B3, Q × Kt; 12 B—Kt5, Kt—Q5;
13 R—K1 ch, Kt—K3; 14 P—B3, and
White holds the reins.

10 P—KR4

The second surprise. Not only does
White's King obtain a flight square, if it
should be wanted, but his KRP becomes
a trenchant weapon, whilst his "motorised"
KR threatens to get into action via R3.

10	P—QKt4

He refrains from playing 10 .... P—Q4,
in order to be able, later on, to obstruct the
open K file by .... Kt—K3.

11 P—Q3

More conformable than 11 R—R3,
B—K2, etc., or 11 P—QB3, B—Kt2, etc.
Here again the following expedition would
be unfavourable: 11 Q—R5 ch, P—Kt3;
12 Q × P, on account of 12 .... Q—K7 ch;
13 K—Kt1, Q—K8 ch; 14 K—R2, B—Q3 ch,
etc.

11	Q—B4
12 B—Kt5	

Supported by the advanced KRP, the
white Bishop is now comfortably settled in
the hostile camp.

If now 12 .... P—KR3, he replies, not
13 Q—R5 ch, P—Kt3, etc., but simply
13 B—K3, followed by 14 P—R5 and
15 Kt—Kt6, saving the Knight.

12	P—Kt3
13 Q—Q2	B—KKt2

At last the venturesome Knight is to be
caught. But meanwhile the white Rooks
are gaining in power.

14 R—K1 ch	Kt—K3

Or 14 .... K—B1; 15 P—R5, B × Kt;
16 P × P, Q × KtP; 17 Q—B4 ch, K—Kt1;
18 R—R6, and wins.

15 P—R5

An unsettling advance.

15	P × P

After 15 .... B × Kt; 16 P × P, Q × P;
17 R—R6, Q—B4; 18 P—KKt4, Q—B2;
19 Q—Kt4, R—Kt1; 20 Q—K4, B—Kt2;
21 R × P, B × Q; 22 R × B ch, Q—B1
(22 .... Kt—B1; 23 R × B ch); 23 R × Q ch,
K × R; 24 B—R6 ch, and 25 R × B, and
White remains two pawns to the good.

16 R × P	B × Kt

Or 16 .... P—KR3; 17 R × P, B × R;
18 B × B, Q—R2; 19 Q—Kt5, Q × Kt;
20 Q—R5 ch, K—K2; 21 B—Kt5 ch, winning
the Queen.

After the text move Black has become the
stronger in material; but the disorganised
position of his pieces will cause his ruin.

17 Q—Kt4

The Queen enters into the fray by means
of very fine manœuvres.

17	P—B4

After 17 .... P—Q3; 18 P—Kt4, and if
17 .... K—B2; 18 Q—K7 ch, K—Kt1;
19 R × Kt, P × R; 20 B—R6, and wins.

18 Q—KR4	K—B2

In order to reply to 19 R × P ch by 19 ....
B—Kt2, but White has far more ambitious
plans in view. (*Diagram. See p. 188.*)

19 B—Q8	Q—Kt3
20 R—R6	Q × R

A desperate decision, for if 20 ....
Q—B4; 21 P—KKt4, etc.

21 Q × Q	Kt × B
22 Q—R5 ch	Resigns.

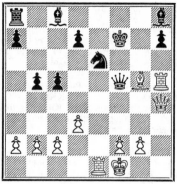

Position after 18 .... K—B2

THREE KNIGHTS' GAME

146

White	Black
ROSENTHAL	STEINITZ

(Vienna, 1873)

A full-bodied game! If one feature, more than another, deserves notice, it is the skilful manner in which Black turns to account the latent power of his two Bishops. The white forces are continually forced to retreat, with corresponding loss in territory.

1 P—K4	P—K4
2 Kt—QB3	Kt—QB3
3 Kt—B3	P—KKt3

He avoids symmetry in preference to the well-trodden paths of the Four Knights' Game.

Apart from this archaic continuation and the modern treatment by the early sortie 3 .... B—Kt5, other lines have been tried, such as the reserved 3 .... B—K2; the obtuse 3 .... KKt—K2; and even the chancy counter-gambit 3 .... P—B4 (of which the following is a frightful example: 4 P—Q4, BP×P; 5 KKt×P, Kt—B3; 6 B—QB4, P—Q4; 7 Kt×QP, KKt×Kt; 8 Q—R5 ch, P—Kt3; 9 Kt×P, Kt—B3; 10 B—B7 ch, K×B; 11 Kt—K5 db ch, K—K3; 12 Q—B7 ch, K—Q3; 13 Kt—B4 mate).

4 P—Q4
Quite listless would be 4 B—Kt5, B—Kt2,

5 Castles, KKt—K2; 6 P—Q3, Castles, and Black, with .... P—Q4 or .... P—KB4, begins to take the lead.

4 ......   P×P
Instead of this impulsive reply, 4 .... B—Kt2; 5 P×P, Kt×P; 6 Kt×Kt, B×Kt, with a complicated game, is worth trying.

5 Kt×P
He allows his adversary to complete his development in peace. In a game played in London, 1883, between the same opponents, White obtained a clearly superior position after 5 Kt—Q5, B—Kt2; 6 B—KKt5, P—B3; 7 B—KB4, P—Q3; 8 Kt×P, etc.

5	B—Kt2
6 B—K3	

White rightly prefers to maintain a piece in the centre, rather than to strengthen the adverse pawn centre by 6 Kt×Kt, KtP×Kt, etc.

6 ......   KKt—K2
By this development on inner lines (instead of 6 .... Kt—B3, or, more accurately, 6 .... P—Q3; 7 Q—Q2, Kt—B3, etc.), Black avoids blocking this KB as well as the advance, eventually, of his KBP.

7 B—QB4
White concentrates on the rapid mobilisation of his K side. A more pugnacious continuation is 7 Q—Q2, Castles; 8 Castles KR, etc.

7 ......   P—Q3
As 7 .... P—Q4 is still impossible, Black makes the more modest advance in the text, without, however, giving up the hope of utilising his QP later on in a more ambitious manner.

8 Castles	Castles
9 P—B4	Kt—R4
10 B—Q3	P—Q4
11 P×P	

Not 11 P—K5, P—QB4, followed by the *fork* 12 .... P—Q5.

11	Kt×P
12 Kt×Kt	Q×Kt
13 P—B3	

A necessary defensive measure. It can be seen how important a part Black's KB plays on the long diagonal.

13 ......   R—Q1
Threatening 14 .... P—QB4.

14 Q—B2

In order to play 15 B—K4, in answer to 14 .... P—QB4.

14	Kt—B5
15 B×Kt	Q×B

A new threat: 16 .... B×Kt; 17 B×B, R×B.

16 Q—B2	P—QB4
17 Kt—B3	P—Kt3
18 Kt—K5	Q—K3
19 Q—B3	B—QR3
20 KR—K1	P—B3

Driving away White's only well-developed piece.

21 Kt—Kt4

Not 21 Q—B6, Q×Q; 22 Kt×Q, R—Q3; 23 Kt—K7 ch, K—B2; 24 B—B2, R—K1, and wins, nor 21 Kt—B6, KR—QB1, etc.

21	P—R4
22 Kt—B2	Q—B2

Black has a definite positional advantage in that he controls all the important lines.

23 P—B5

This restless attempt only aggravates the situation. As he cannot yet play 23 QR—Q1 (23 .... B—Kt2, followed, by 24 .... Q×P), he should have been content to play 23 P—QKt3.

23	P—KKt4
24 QR—Q1	B—Kt2

The "two Bishops"!

25 Q—Kt3   R—Q4

A fertile reinforcing manœuvre. A blunder would be 25 .... Q×P; 26 R×R ch, R×R; 27 Q—B7.

26 R×R	Q×R
27 R—Q1	

The Q file conquered—but at the cost of a pawn.

27	Q×BP
28 Q—B7	B—Q4
29 P—QKt3	R—K1
30 P—B4	B—B2
31 B—B1	

Not 31 R—Q7, R×B; 32 R×B, R—K8 mate.

31 ......   R—K7

The *seventh rank*! The whole game is characterised by Black's firm and profound strategy.

32 R—B1   Q—B7

Besides the gain of a pawn, this threatens to win a piece by 33 .... R×Kt.

33 Q—Kt3   Q×RP

And Black wins.

147

White	Black
SCHLECHTER	MARSHALL

(Ostend, 1905)

In this game White obtains by simple—one could say discreet—means, results on the KB file which usually demand a fierce attack.

1 P—K4	P—K4
2 Kt—KB3	Kt—QB3
3 Kt—B3	B—Kt5

An enterprising *sortie*.

4 B—B4

Countering with a quiet, purely developing move.

Instead of this *Italian Three Knights' Game*, the *Spanish* version is applicable by 4 B—Kt5, KKt—K2 (or else 4 .... Kt—B3, back to the *Four Knights*); 5 P—Q4, P×P; 6 Kt×P, Castles; 7 Castles, etc., with an even game.

4	Kt—B3
5 Castles	P—Q3

A false speculation would be, clearly, 5 .... B×Kt; 6 QP×B, Kt×P, on account of 7 B×P ch, K×B; 8 Q—Q5 ch, followed by Q×KKt.

More elastic than the continuation in the text is 5 .... Castles, e.g. 6 P—Q3, B—K2; 7 P—KR3, P—Q3, and Black has a strong defence.

6 Kt—Q5

A vigorous idea would be 6 P—Q4, P×P; 7 Kt—Q5, Kt×Kt; 8 P×Kt, Kt—K2; 9 B—Kt5 ch, etc., with a number of inconveniences for Black.

6	B—QB4
7 P—Q3	B—KKt5
8 P—B3	

With a threefold mission: to prevent 8 .... Kt—Q5; to prepare a Q side demonstration; and to provide an outlet for the Queen.

8	Q—Q2
9 P—Kt4	B—Kt3
10 P—QR4	P—QR3
11 B—K3	

The following: 11 Kt × B, P × Kt; 12 B—K3, Q—B2, yields nothing worth while.

| 11 ...... | Kt × Kt |

If at once 11 .... B × B, then 12 Kt × B.

| 12 B × Kt | |

White maintains a quiet, though potentially lively, game in preference to creating a dead centre at Q5 by 12 P × Kt, Kt—K2, etc.

| 12 ...... | B × B |
| 13 P × B | |

The factor of the open KB file, which White has created, is as yet only in embryo.

| 13 ...... | Castles KR |
| 14 P—R5 | |

With the object, after 15 Q—R4, of obtaining some advantage in the pawn structure on the Q side.

14	Kt—Q1
15 P—R3	P—B3
16 B—Kt3	B—K3
17 R—R2	B × B
18 Q × B	Q—K3
19 P—B4	Q—R3

As this attempted attack is easily mastered, its net result is to deflect the Queen from the critical sector.

More solid would be at once 19 .... P—B3.

| 20 R—K2 | R—K1 |

In view of the potential threat of 21 P—B5, P × P; 22 Kt × P.

| 21 Q—B3 | R—QB1 |
| 22 Q—K1 | |

An astute manœuvre. (Threat: 23 Kt—R4.)

| 22 ...... | R—B2 |

Trying at least to fortify his second rank. The continuation 22 .... P—KKt4; 23 Q—Kt3, etc., is too risky.

| 23 Kt—R4 | P—KKt3 |
| 24 Kt—B3 | |

Schlechter's art of manœuvring is shown here in all its suppleness.

24	P—B3
25 Kt—R2	R—KB1
26 Kt—Kt4	Q—Kt2

Thinking he can hold out. A possible line would be 26 .... Q—Kt4; 27 Q—Kt3 (threatening 28 Kt × BP ch); 27 .... K—Kt2; 28 P—R4, Q—R4; 29 QR—KB2, and in spite of many dangers, Black has sufficient means of defence.

27 Q—R4

Having created a weak point (KB6) in the enemy camp, White now concentrates all his forces on that portion of the front.

27	K—R1
28 QR—KB2	P—KKt4
29 Q—R5	QR—B2

The disputed pawn is arithmetically but not positionally defendable.

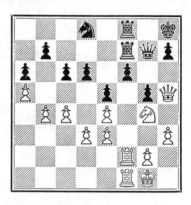

30 Kt × BP

Pretty play.

| 30 ...... | Kt—K3 |

If 30 .... R × Kt; 31 R × R, R × R; 32 Q—K8 ch, winning the exchange and the game.

| 31 Kt × P | Q × Kt |

He has nothing better. If 31 .... R × R; 32 Kt—B6 dis ch, with mate to follow; and if 31 .... Kt—B5; 32 R × Kt.

32 Q × Q ch	R × Q
33 R × R ch	Kt × R
34 R × Kt ch	K—Kt2
35 R—Q8	K—B3
36 R × P ch	Resigns

For after 36 .... K—K2; 37 R—Kt6, a fourth pawn is lost (KKt or QKt), and that is too much!

148

White	Black
LEONHARDT	TARRASCH

(Hamburg, 1910)

In the following game the black forces, especially the black Rooks, become disconnected, and the magnificent and fruitful evolutions carried out by the ideally placed white troops provide an object lesson in the art of concentration.

1 P—K4	P—K4
2 Kt—KB3	Kt—QB3
3 Kt—B3	B—Kt5
4 Kt—Q5	B—R4

After 4 .... B—B4, White would continue calmly but confidently 5 B—B4, P—Q3; 6 P—B3, in preparation for the important advance P—Q4.

After 4 .... B—K2, this advance can be effected at once: 5 P—Q4, P×P (5 .... P—Q3; 6 B—QKt5, etc.); 6 Kt×P, Kt×Kt; 7 Q×Kt, and White stands well.

The most initiative continuation is 4 .... Kt—B3.

5 B—B4

He aims at the rapid development of his K side, whereas 5 P—B3, Kt—B3; 6 P—Q4, P×P relieves the tension.

5	P—Q3

After 5 .... Kt—B3; 6 Castles, Kt×P; 7 P—Q4, White has an attack in compensation for his pawn.

6 Castles	Kt—B3
7 P—Q3	

Too impulsive would be 7 P—Q4, B—KKt5; 8 P—B3, P×P; 9 B—KKt5, Kt—K4, and Black's counter-play is not to be despised.

7	P—KR3

The fear of the pin 8 B—KKt5 being quite justified, the immediate exchange 7 .... Kt×Kt would also be to the point, e.g. 8 P×Kt (more energetic than 8 B×Kt, Castles, etc.); 8 .... Kt—K2; 9 P—Q4, P—KB3, etc., with a playable game.

8 P—B3	Kt×Kt

If 8 .... Castles; 9 P—QR4, P—R3; 10 P—QKt4, B—Kt3; 11 Kt×B, P×Kt; 12 Q—Kt3, and White holds the best trumps.

9 P×Kt

More insistent than 9 B×Kt.

9	Kt—K2
10 P—Q4	

This success in the centre secures for White the command of the K file.

10	P×P

For, if 10 .... P—K5; 11 Kt—Q2, P—KB4; 12 Q—R4 ch, P—B3; 13 P×P, P×P; 14 P—Q5, B—Q2; 15 P×P, QB×P; 16 B—Kt5, and Black's position is cracking on all sides.

11 Q—R4 ch	P—B3
12 P×BP	KtP×P
13 Kt×P	B—Q2
14 R—K1	

Again threatening 15 Kt×P.

14	K—B1

Proceeding towards artificial castling. If 14 .... P—QB4; 15 Kt—B6, e.g. 15 .... B×Kt; 16 Q×B ch, K—B1; 17 Q—B3, etc., or 15 .... R—QB1; 16 Kt×Q, B×Q; 17 Kt×P, and wins, or 15 .... Castles; 16 Q×B, B×Kt; 17 Q×Q, KR×Q; 18 R×Kt, and wins, or 15 .... Q—B2; 16 R×Kt ch, and wins.

15 B—B4

He spies another vulnerable spot (pawn at Q6), nor does he fear 15 .... P—QB4; 16 Q—R3, B—B2 (16 .... P×Kt; 17 B×QP); 17 Kt—Kt5, B×Kt; 18 B×B, etc., with a considerable positional advantage for White.

15	B—B2
16 Q—R3	Kt—B1
17 R—K3	

Effecting the doubling of Rooks on the open K file: what could be more clear-cut or more energetic?

17	K—Kt1
18 QR—K1	P—Q4

He tries to intercept the most threatening diagonal, but thereby calls up other hostile dynamic forces. There is, however, nothing better.

19 B×B	Q×B

The calm before the storm. (*Diagram. See p. 192.*)

20 R—K8 ch

A beautiful *irruptive sacrifice* of the exchange, which holds magical points.

20	B×R
21 R×B ch	K—R2
22 B—Q3 ch	P—B4

A variation, many moves deep, arises

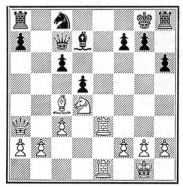

Position after 19 .... Q × B

not 25 .... P × Kt; 26 B × P mate, nor
25 .... Kt—Kt3; 26 Q—Kt7 mate; and if
25 .... P—B3; 26 Q × P ch, K—Kt1;
27 Q × P ch, K—B1; 28 Q × P ch, etc.,
winning easily); 26 Q × BP ch, K—R1;
27 Kt—R4 (more elegant than the despoil-
ing continuation 27 Q—B8 ch, K—R2;
28 Q × P ch, K—Kt1; 29 Q × P ch, etc.);
27 .... Q—K8 ch; 28 B—B1, Kt—K2;
29 Q × Kt, Q × Q; 30 Kt × P ch, followed by
Kt × Q, etc., with an overwhelming advantage in material.

23 R × R ch	K × R
24 Q—B8 ch	K—R2
25 B × P ch	P—Kt3
26 B × P ch	

With this magnificent "point," White puts
the crowning touch on his combination.

| 26 ...... | Resigns |

(26 .... K × B; 27 Q—B5 ch, K—Kt2;
28 Kt—K6 ch.)

from 22 .... P—Kt3, e.g. 23 R × R ch,
K × R; 24 Q—B8 ch, K—R2; 25 Kt—B5
(a splendid turn); 25 .... Q—K4 (evidently

8. PONZIANI'S OPENING

149

White	Black
FALKBEER	*SCHURIG*

(Leipzig, 1850)

A game in which the errors are instructive. The weakening of the diagonals around the disabled black King leads to a catastrophe, which is consummated by means of a brilliant sacrifice of the Queen.

1 P—K4	P—K4
2 Kt—KB3	Kt—QB3
3 P—B3	

A preparatory move, which affords Black a respite of one *tempo*. He can take advantage of this "pause" in a number of ways.

3	P—B4

A violent reply, indicated by Ponziani himself in 1782.

4 P—Q4

A well-known principle: against a wing attack, a counter-thrust in the centre.

4	P×QP

More lucid is 4 .... P—Q3, and more trenchant 4 .... BP×P; 5 Kt×P, Q—B3.

5 P—K5

Ingenious. Instead of adopting the true gambit style, one could continue: 5 KP×P, P—Q4; 6 Kt×P, Kt—B3; 7 B—Q3, etc.

5	P×P
6 Kt×P	B—Kt5
7 B—QB4	

This occupation of the *denuded diagonal* must override all other considerations.

7	B×Kt ch

An over-hasty exchange. 7 .... Kt—R4 is more rational.

8 P×B	P—Q3

If now 8 .... Kt—R4, there follows 9 B×Kt, R×B; 10 Q—Q5, with a double attack on the adverse KR and Knight.

If Black lacks the nerve to play 8 .... KKt—K2, awaiting events, the straightforward continuation 8 .... P—Q4; 9 B×P, Q—K2, etc., provides a better defence than the text move.

9 Q—Kt3	Kt×P

He is already resigned to giving up a piece for two pawns, instead of defending his possessions by 9 .... KKt—K2 (and if 10 B—B7 ch, K—B1).

In any event, 9 .... Kt—R4 is useless, by reason of 10 Q—R4 ch, P—B3; 11 B×Kt, R×B; 12 P×P, and Black's position is desperate.

10 Kt×Kt	P×Kt
11 B—B7 ch	

Magnanimous. He demonstrates that, even without 11 B×Kt, his mobile forces (Queen, two Bishops and later on a Rook) can ensure the win.

11	K—K2

But not 11 .... K—B1; 12 B×Kt, R×B; 13 B—R3 ch, K—K1; 14 Q×R ch, etc., with a rich harvest for White.

12 B—R3 ch	K—B3

The black King is now in comparative safety, but the black Queen will be incommoded.

13 R—Q1	B—Q2
14 P—KB4	

The blockade continues.

14	P—K5

Or 14 .... P—KKt3; 15 P×P ch, K—Kt2; 16 Castles (not yet 16 P—K6, Q—R5 ch); 16 .... Q—QB1; 17 P—K6, B—B3; 18 Q—B4, Kt—B3; 19 B—K7, and Black has no resource.

15 Q—Q5

Threatening to assimilate the Bishop. Being master of the situation, White could also have continued, in a convincing manner, with 15 B×Kt, R×B; 16 Q—Q5, etc., or with preparatory measures 15 Q—B4 or 15 B—R5.

15	Kt—K2

For if 15 .... B—B3; 16 Q—K6 mate, and if 15 .... Kt—R3; 16 B—R5, P—KKt3; 17 Q—K5 ch, K—B2; 18 B—K2, Q—K1; 19 R×B ch (an *eliminating sacrifice*); 19 .... Q×R; 20 B—B4 ch, and wins.

16 Q—B4

If 16 Q×B, Black plays—not 16 ....

Q × Q; 17 R × Q, K × B; 18 R × Kt ch, etc.
—but 16 .... K × B, and Black has at least
saved his piece.

16 ......   R—KB1
Or first 16 .... P—QKt4; 17 Q—Kt3.

17 B—R5   P—KKt3
18 B—K2   Q—K1
19 B—B5
Too prosaic a continuation would be:
19 Q—Q4 ch, K—B2; 20 Q × B, etc.
White seems to have a game of "cat and
mouse" and to have taken upon himself the
obligation to go in only for a direct King's
field attack. In any case, matters are now
getting serious. The actual threat is:
20 B—Q4 mate.

19 ......   B—K3
After 19 .... K—Kt2 White could play,
not only 20 Q—Q4 ch, followed by Q × B,
but even, aiming high, 20 B—Q4 ch,
K—R3; 21 R—Q3, P × R; 22 Q × QP,
P—KKt4; 23 Q—R3 ch, followed by mate.

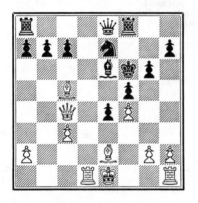

20 Q × B ch
This splendid sacrifice of the Queen keeps
the adverse King within the danger zone.

20 ......   K × Q
21 B—B4 ch   Kt—Q4
For if 21 .... K—B3; 22 B—Q4 mate.

22 R × Kt   K—B2
Permitting the discharge of a double check.
By playing 22 .... K—B3; 23 B—Q4 ch,
K—K2; 24 R—K5 ch, K—Q2; 25 R × Q,
KR × R, Black could have avoided the mate,
but not the loss of the game.

23 R—Q7 db ch   K—B3
White mates in two.

150

White   Black
WAYTE   RANKEN

(About 1885)

*One of many fine games played between
the two reverend gentlemen, but a particularly
thrilling one.*
*The practical chances afforded by the early
sacrifice of a piece in this opening (5 ....
B—B4) are exploited here by the aggressor
in an admirable manner.*

1 P—K4   P—K4
2 Kt—KB3   Kt—QB3
3 P—B3   Kt—B3
Emphasising the fact that the natural
defence of White's threatened KP by the
QKt is not available here.

4 P—Q4   Kt × KP
He accepts the challenge. Other continuations have fewer adherents:
(a) 4 .... P × P; 5 P—K5, etc.
(b) 4 .... P—Q4; 5 B—QKt5, etc.
(c) 4 .... P—Q3; 5 B—K3, B—K2 (but
not 5 .... KKt × P; 6 P—Q5, followed by
Q—R4 ch and Q × KKt, an *opening trap*);
6 P—Q5, Kt—QKt1; 7 QKt—Q2, etc., and
White has the freer game.

5 P—Q5   B—B4
A bold sacrifice! More logical, however,
is 5 .... Kt—Kt1.
After 5 .... Kt—K2 the amusing continuation of a game Bachmann-Kunstmann,
Augsburg, 1899, ran as follows: 6 Kt × P,
Kt—Kt3; 7 B—Q3, Kt × KBP; 8 B × Kt,
Kt × Q (or 8 .... Q—B3; 9 Q—K2, Kt × R;
10 B × P ch, K—Q1; 11 Kt—B6 ch, followed by mate); 9 B × P ch, K—K2;
10 B—Kt5 ch, K—Q3; 11 Kt—B4 ch,
K—B4; 12 QKt—R3, (threat: 13 P—Kt4
mate); 12 .... Kt × KtP (or 12 ....
P—QR4; 13 B × Q, remaining a piece
ahead); 13 B—K3 mate.

6 P × Kt
Compulsory courage, for if he refuses the
offer, Black, after 6 B—K3, B × B; 7 P × B,
Kt—Kt1, etc., has the better game.

6 ......   B × P ch
If 6 .... Kt × KBP; 7 Q—Q5.

7 K—K2   P—Q4
He does not count the dead, for, after
7 .... KtP × P; 8 Q—R4, P—KB4;
9 QKt—Q2, etc., Black's attack dies away.

8 P×P	B×P
9 Q—R4 ch	P—B3
10 QKt—Q2	P—B4
11 Kt×Kt	BP×Kt
12 K×B	

If 12 Kt×P, B—Kt3, and now 13 Kt×P is inadmissible because 13 .... Q—Q2 wins the Knight.

12	Castles
13 B—K3	P×Kt
14 P—KKt3	

After 14 P×P, P—K5, White's troubles are only beginning.

14	Q—B1
15 B—B5	R—B3
16 R—Q1	P—QR4
17 R—Q2	B—R3

With two pawns and an enduring pressure for his pieces, Black does not fear exchanges.

18 B×B	Q×B
19 R—K1	P—K5
20 P—QR3	

He underestimates the danger, and goes to work too methodically. By at once playing 20 P—QKt4, White would be better able to weather the storm, e.g. 20 .... Q—B5; 21 Q—Kt3, etc., or 20 .... Q—B1; 21 P×P, etc., or, finally, 20 .... P×P; 21 Q×Q, R×Q; 22 P×P, with a simplified position.

20	Q—B1

An ultra-rapid change of objective.

21 K—Kt1	Q—R6
22 P—QKt4	R—K1

He abandons the Q side and proclaims the central zone as the main battlefield.

23 Q×RP	P—R4

A turning movement.

24 Q—R6	

If 24 B—B2, Black still plays 24 .... P—R5.

24	P—R5
25 Q—B1	Q—Kt5
26 Q—B2	

Or 26 B—B2, P×P; 27 P×P, R—R3, with 28 .... Q—R4 to follow.

26	R—Kt3

If at once 26 .... P×P; 27 Q×KtP.

27 P—Kt5	

A desperate attempt! But the only possible defence would be 27 K—R1, and after 27 .... P×P; 28 Q×KtP.

27	RP×P
28 RP×P	

If now 28 Q×KtP, Q—B4, winning the Queen.

28	R—R3

Encircling the King and threatening 29 .... R—R6, followed by .... R×P, which White's next move is intended to prevent.

29 B—K3	R—R6
30 B—B4	Q—R4

Threatening to turn White's extreme right wing.

31 Q—R2	

The only resource.

31	R×Q
32 R×R	Q—Kt3
33 P—Kt6	

The last trump.

33	P—K6

A *deflecting sacrifice.*

34 R×P	R×R
35 B×R	Q×P ch
36 K—R1	Q—K8 ch
37 B—Kt1	Q×P

And Black wins.

151

White	Black
POLLMÄCHER	ANDERSSEN

(Leipzig, 1855)

In the following stirring game we see once again that the position of the castled King on the Q side presents more vulnerable points than "normal" castling.

The accumulation of "mines" and "countermines" is certainly quite out of the ordinary.

1 P—K4	P—K4
2 Kt—KB3	Kt—QB3
3 P—B3	P—Q4

The most logical reply (for after 4 P×P, Q×P the black Queen cannot be driven away by 5 Kt—B3), and the most enterprising as well.

4 B—Kt5	P×P
5 Kt×P	Q—Q4

After 5 .... Q—Kt4 there follows equally 6 Q—R4. A cautious defence is 5 .... B—Q2.

6 Q—R4

Defending directly the KB and indirectly the KKt, for if 6 .... Q × Kt; 7 B × Kt ch wins.

```
6 ......          Kt—K2
7 P—KB4          P × P e. p.
```

After 7 .... B—Q2; 8 Kt × B, K × Kt; 9 Castles, Kt—B4; 10 P—QKt4 (parrying the threat of 10 .... B—B4 ch; 11 K—R1, Kt—Kt6 ch; 12 P × Kt, Q—R4 mate); 10 .... B—Q3; 11 Kt—R3, etc., White has most of the trumps.

8 Kt × P (B3)   Q—R4

The most rational continuation is 8 .... P—QR3; 9 B—K2, Kt—Kt3; 10 Castles, P—Kt4, etc., freeing his forces.

9 Castles   B—Kt5

Or, less expansively, 9 .... B—K3; 10 P—Q4, Castles; 11 P—B4, B—Kt5; 12 P—Q5, Kt—B4 (13 P × Kt, B—B4 ch; 14 K—R1, Kt—Kt6 mate); 13 B—B4, and White's very strong centre ensures him the better game.

```
10 P—Q4          Castles
11 B—KB4          K—Kt1
```

Here 11 .... P—QR3 would be to the point, e.g. 12 B—Q3, Kt—Q4; 13 B—Kt3, B—Q3, etc., or 12 KB × P, P × B; 13 Q × P ch, K—Q2, etc.

```
12 QKt—Q2          P—QR3
13 B—Q3          Kt—Q4
14 B—Kt3          B—Q3
15 Kt—K4
```

An important actor in the coming drama.

```
15 ......          B × B
16 P × B          Kt—K6
```

A tempting expedition, but 16 .... Kt—Kt3, strengthening the black King's defences, would have been better.

17 Kt—B5

A nonchalant reply, which shows no disinclination to give up the exchange by 17 .... Kt × R; 18 R × Kt for the sake of the attack.

```
17 ......          R—Q3
```

Parrying the potential threat, 18 Kt × P ch, P × Kt; 19 Q × Kt, etc., without, however, eliminating further surprises.

18 Kt × P

A *break-up sacrifice.*

```
18 ......          R—R3
```

Seeking salvation in a furious counter-attack. If 18 .... K × Kt; 19 B × P ch.

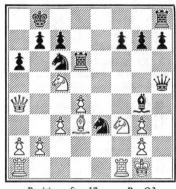

Position after 17 .... R—Q3

19 Kt—R4

Damming the critical KR file.

```
19 ......          Q—Q4
```

Laying a fresh *mine,* 20 .... R × Kt; 21 P × R, Q × P mate.

20 Kt—B5

The *counter-mine.* If .... R × Kt; 21 B—K4.

```
20 ......          R—K1
```

Resuscitating the threat, 21 .... R × Kt; but in the meantime White has prepared a direct assault on the hostile fortress.

```
21 Kt × P ch          K—B1
22 Kt—B5
```

Returning to the starting point, with a real threat, for if now 22 .... R × Kt; 23 Q—R8 ch, Kt—Kt1; 24 Q × Q, Kt × Q; 25 P × R, and wins.

```
22 ......          K—Q1
23 QR—K1
```

Most ingeniously he parries the threat, 23 .... R × Kt, after which there follows 24 Q—R8 ch, B—B1; 25 R × Kt, R × R; 26 P × R, and Black cannot continue with 26 .... R—Kt6, on account of 27 B—K4. If, on the other hand, 23 .... Kt × R, the sequel is 24 Q—R8 ch, B—B1; 25 R × R ch, K × R; 26 Q × B ch, Kt—Q1; 27 B × Kt, and White remains with a telling advantage in material.

```
23 ......          B—B1
24 Q—R8          P—Kt3
```

To prevent 25 Kt—Kt7 ch, K—Q2; 26 R × Kt, R × R; 27 B—B5 ch, etc., but the white Bishop now puts in an appearance on the opposite wing.

25 B—R6   Kt—R2

A desperate attempt, which, however, allows White to effect a far-reaching liquidation.

26 Q × Q ch

Instead of 26 Q × Kt, in order to have done with alarums and excursions.

26 ......   Kt × Q
27 B × B   Kt × B
28 Kt—Kt7 ch   K—Q2
29 R × P ch   Resigns.

152

White   *Black*

TCHIGORIN   STEINITZ

(Vienna, 1898)

Deprived of his normal rampart by a fine temporary sacrifice (22 B × P ch), the black King wanders over the Q side without finding a suitable refuge.

1 P—K4   P—K4
2 Kt—KB3   Kt—QB3
3 P—B3   P—Q4
4 Q—R4

Although less natural than the developing move 4 B—Kt5, the text move is not without guile.

4 ......   P—B3

Steinitz's speciality. Weakening is 4 .... P × P; 5 Kt × P, Q—Q4; 6 Kt × Kt, P × Kt; 7 B—B4.

If 4 .... Q—Q3; 5 B—Kt5, and if 4 .... B—Q2; 5 P × P, Kt—Q5; 6 Q—Q1, Kt × Kt ch; 7 Q × Kt, P—KB4; 8 B—B4, B—Q3; 9 P—Q3, and it is hard to see where Black can find compensation for the pawn given up (*Caro's Sacrifice*). A far more audacious manner of sacrificing a pawn for development is 4 .... Kt—B3; 5 Kt × P, B—Q3, etc. (*Leonhardt's sacrifice*).

5 B—Kt5   P × P

Forcing exchanges, but at the price of a pawn. A more massive continuation would be: 5 .... Kt—K2; 6 P × P, Q × P; 7 P—Q4, B—Q2; 8 B—K3, P × P; 9 P × P, etc., with an even game.

6 B × Kt ch   P × B
7 Q × P ch   B—Q2
8 Q × KP   Kt—K2

Up to the present White has controlled the game, but Black will now have something to say.

9 ......   B—B3

The passive continuation, 9 .... P × P; 10 Kt × P, P—QB4; 11 Kt—K6, B × Kt; 12 Q × B, Q—Q4; 13 Q—K2, etc., would leave White with a definite and lasting advantage in space.

10 Q—K2   P—K5

This pawn now becomes a bone of contention.

11 KKt—Q2   Q—Q4
12 Castles   Castles

Bringing the King into provisional safety. No good comes of 12 .... P—K6; 13 P × P, nor of 12 .... B—Kt4; 13 P—QB4, B—R3; 14 P × Q, B × Q; 15 R—K1, B—R4; 16 Kt × P, Castles; 17 P—Q6, P × P; 18 QKt—B3, and White has kept this pawn with advantage.

13 R—K1   P—B4
14 P—B3

A well-known stratagem, undermining the opposing outpost.

14 ......   R—K1
15 P × P   P × P
16 Kt—R3

A miscalculation would be 16 Kt × P, Kt—B4. Similarly, 16 Q × P, Q × Q; 17 Kt × Q, would lose the exchange, thus: 17 .... Kt—Kt1; 18 QKt—Q2, Kt—B3; 19 Kt × Kt, R × R ch, etc.

16 ......   Kt—B4
17 Kt—B2   P—KR4

The time is not ripe for 17 .... B—Kt4, on account of 18 P—B4, Kt × P; 19 Q—Kt4 ch (the intermediary check which the text move is to eliminate); 19 .... B—Q2; 20 P × Q, B × Q; 21 Kt × Kt, B—QB4; 22 Kt—Kt3, and White remains a piece ahead.

18 Kt—B1

Consolidation.

18 ......   Kt—R5

Seeing its efforts round K6 frustrated, the Knight seeks other employment. If 18 .... B—Q3; 19 P—B4.

19 B—B4   Kt—Kt3

The momentarily unguarded state of this piece is to be brilliantly exploited by White.

20 Q—R6 ch   K—Kt1

Evidently not 20 .... B—Kt2; 21 Q × Kt.

21 KKt—K3   Q—K3

Had Black foreseen the crushing reply, he

would have taken refuge in an end-game by
21 .... Q—QKt4; 22 Q×Q ch, B×Q;
23 B—Kt3, etc.

After 21 .... Q—Q2 there follows
22 P—Q5, Kt×B; 23 P×B, Q—B1;
24 Q—Kt5 ch, K—R1; 25 P—QKt4, with
increasing difficulties for Black.

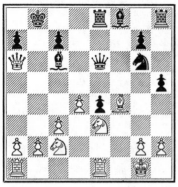

22 B×P ch

A temporary sacrifice, which destroys the
black King's already sparse barricades.

22 ......   K×B
23 P—Q5   B×P
24 Q—R5 ch

This oblique check is the point of the
sacrifice, whereas if 24 Q×P ch, B—Kt2.

24 ......   Q—Kt3

Pinning the KKt. If 24 .... K—Q3;
25 Kt×B, Q×Kt; 26 QR—Q1 wins, and if
24 .... K—B3; 25 Kt—Q4 ch.

25 Q×B   B—Q3
26 Kt—Q4   Kt—B5

If 26 .... P—R3; 27 Q—B7 ch, K—Kt1
(if 27 .... R—K2, then, not blindly
28 Q×Kt, B×P ch, followed by .... Q×Q,
but 28 Kt—Q5 ch. Again, if 27 ....
Kt—K2; 28 Kt—Q5 ch, and wins);
28 Kt—B4, Q—B2; 29 Q×Kt, B×P ch;
30 K—R1, Q×Kt; 31 K×B, and White is
a piece ahead.

27 Kt—Kt5 ch   K—Q2
28 Q—B5 ch   K—Q1
29 Kt×B   Q×Kt
30 Kt—B4   Q—QB3
31 Q×Kt   Q×Kt
32 QR—Q1 ch   K—B1
33 R—Q4   Q—B4
34 R×P   KR—B1
35 Q—K3   R×R
36 Q×R

Avoiding a painful let-down: 36 R—Q8 ch,
K—Kt2; 37 Q×Q, R—K8 mate!

36 ......   P—R4
37 Q—K3   Q—B4

A last hope—38 .... Q—B8 mate.

38 P—KR3   P—Kt4
39 R—B4 ch   K—Kt2
40 R—B5   Q—Q2
41 Q—K4 ch   K—Kt3
42 R—Q5   Q—B3
43 Q—Q4 ch   K—Kt2
44 R×RP   Resigns.

153

White	Black
BERNE	PARIS

(1921)

*An inactive white Queen against an active
and troublesome black Queen—the results of
this difference in the employment of the chief
piece on either side can be seen with great
clarity in the following game.*

1 P—K4   P—K4
2 Kt—KB3   Kt—QB3
3 P—B3   P—Q4
4 Q—R4   Kt—B3

Played in a spirit of absolute independence, this move (of Leonhardt's) plainly
envisages the sacrifice of one or even two
pawns.

5 Kt×P   B—Q3

Finely played, and promoting the quickest
possible development of the K side.

6 Kt×Kt

Or 6 P×P, B×Kt; 7 P×Kt, Castles, and
Black leads the way.

6 ......   P×Kt
7 P—Q3

White notices that the "consistent" continuation 7 Q×P ch, B—Q2; 8 Q—R6,
P×P; 9 B—Kt5, Castles; 10 B×B, Q×B,
etc., would only serve Black's interests.
Relatively best would be 7 P—Q4, P×P;
8 B—QR6, etc.

After 7 P—K5, a game Fink-Alekhine,
Pasadena, 1932, had the following harrowing
continuation: 7 .... B×P; 8 P—Q4,
B—Q3; 9 Q×P ch (worse than ever at this
stage); 9 .... B—Q2; 10 Q—R6, Castles;
11 B—K2, R—K1; 12 Kt—Q2 (if 12 Castles,

R—Kt1, threatening 13 .... R—Kt3;
14 Q—Q3, B—Kt4); 12 .... R—Kt1 (again
threatening 13 .... B—Kt4); 13 P—QR4
(if 13 Castles, Kt—Kt5); 13 .... Q—K2;
14 Kt—B1 (if 14 K—B1, again 14 ....
B—Kt4; 15 B×B, Q—K8 mate. If 14 Q—Q3,
B—KB4, and so 14 K—Q1 would be
relatively the best); 14 .... B—Kt4, and
White resigns.

7 ......   Castles
8 B—Kt5
He is forced still to adjourn his K side
development because, if 8 B—K2, R—K1,
White could not hope for a peaceful life.

8 ......   P—KR3
9 B×Kt   Q×B
10 B—K2
If 10 Q×BP, R—Kt1, or 10 Kt—Q2,
R—Kt1, restricting White to a wearisome
defence.

10 ......   Q—Kt4
With the double threat 11 .... Q×P and
11 .... Q—B8 ch, etc. Less good would
be 10 .... R—Kt1, on account of 11 Q—B2.

11 Kt—Q2
A definite mistake would be 11 Castles,
because of 11 .... B—KR6; 12 B—B3,
Q—B5, and wins.

11 ......   Q×P
12 B—B3   Q—R6
13 Castles
White has almost redressed the balance,
but his Queen's inactivity gives Black fresh
chances of attack, as his next move will
show.

13 ......   B—B5
14 B—K2   Q—R5
Attacking the valuable KBP, and preventing at the same time the reply 15 P×P, on
account of 15 .... B×Kt ch, with the gain
of the white Queen.

15 Q—Q4   R—K1
16 K—B2
Trying to shake off the pin and laying
a trap at the same time. More straightforward play, however, would be 16 KR—Kt1,
B—K4; 17 Q—K3, awaiting events.

16 ......   P×P
He avoids a catastrophe which, after
16 .... B×Kt; 17 R×B, P×P; 18 P×P,
R×P, would arise from 19 Q—Q8 ch,
Q×Q; 20 R×Q ch, K—R2; 21 B—Q3,
and White wins.

17 P×P
If 17 Kt×P, P—KB4 would win a piece.
Or 17 KR—Kt1, P×P ch; 18 B×P, B—Kt4,
and Black, with an extra pawn, seeks to
liquidate.

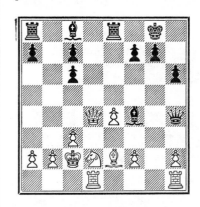

17 ......   B—B4
The black QB gets into action in a most
elegant manner.

18 Q—B5   B—Kt3
19 P—B3   B×Kt
20 K×B
He has no option, for if 20 R×B,
B×P ch; 21 P×B, Q×P ch, followed by
.... Q×R.

20 ......   QR—Q1 ch
21 K—K3
If 21 K—B1, Q—B5 ch; 22 K—B2,
B×P ch; 23 P×B, Q×P ch; 24 B—Q3,
R×B; 25 R×R, Q×R.

21 ......   R×R
22 B×R
After 22 R×R, there is the same reply,
22 .... B×P.

22 ......   B×P
The ice-breaker.

23 K—Q2   R—Q1 ch
24 K—K2
Or 24 K—K3, R—Q6 ch; 25 K—K2,
Q—B5, fashioning a rapid mate.

24 ......   B×P ch
A beautiful final stroke.

Resigns
If 25 K×B, R—Q6 ch; 26 K—K2,
Q—K5 ch; 27 K—B2, R—Q7 ch; 28 K—Kt3,
Q×R, etc.

9. PHILIDOR'S DEFENCE

154

White	Black
ATWOOD	WILSON

(London, 1798)

The Art of Sacrifice!—The following game indicates that in this respect the Ancients had nothing to learn from the Moderns.

Contemporaries of Philidor—who, however, was able to give them considerable odds —the contestants are representative of the best class of players of their day.

1 P—K4	P—K4
2 Kt—KB3	P—Q3

Philidor's dogma.

3 P—Q4

The most trenchant continuation. A good developing move is 3 B—B4. The preparatory and therefore slower 3 P—B3 occurred in a game Schulder-Boden (about 1865), and led to the following tempestuous continuation: 3 P—B3, P—KB4; 4 B—B4, Kt—KB3; 5 P—Q4, P×KP; 6 P×P, P×Kt; 7 P×Kt, Q×P; 8 P×P, Kt—B3 (Black is already much ahead in development); 9 P—B4, B—Q2; 10 B—K3, Castles; 11 Kt—Q2, R—K1; 12 Q—B3, B—B4; 13 Castles QR (thinking himself now safe from all danger); 13 .... P—Q4; 14 B×QP, Q×P ch (a most beautiful Q sacrifice, leading to a "diagonal cross-mate"); 15 P×Q, B—R6 mate.

3 ...... P—KB4

This classical continuation is known under the name of *Philidor's Counter-attack*.

4 QP×P

A lively continuation, which is in no way inferior to other possible moves:

(*a*) 4 KP×P, P—K5; 5 Kt—Kt5, B×P; 6 Kt—QB3, Kt—KB3; 7 P—B3, etc.

(*b*) 4 B—QB4, BP×P; 5 Kt—Kt5, Kt—KR3; 6 Castles, etc.

(*c*) 4 Kt—B3 (preferred by modern players, as combining the defence of the KP with the useful development of a piece); 4 .... BP×P (or 4 .... Kt—KB3); 5 QKt×P (if 5 KKt×P, Kt—KB3); 5 .... P—Q4; 6 Kt×P, etc.

4	BP×P
5 Kt—Kt5	P—Q4
6 P—K6	

Driving an uncomfortable wedge into the hostile position.

6 ...... Kt—KR3

To prevent 7 Kt—B7, etc. If 6 .... B—B4; 7 Kt—QB3, to the best advantage.

7 Kt—QB3	P—B3
8 KKt×KP	

A very early example of the *positional sacrifice*, which is esteemed so highly at the present day.

8 ...... P×Kt

Instead of accepting the sacrifice, a cautious line of play would be 8 .... Kt—B4; 9 Kt—KKt5, Q—B3; 10 B—Q3, P—KR3. If 8 .... B×P; 9 B×Kt.

9 Q—R5 ch	P—Kt3
10 Q—K5	R—Kt1
11 B×Kt	B×B
12 R—Q1	Q—K2

The crisis. A more active defence results from 12 .... Q—Kt4.

13 B—B4

Defence of the advanced pawn. Or 13 Kt×P, B×P; 14 Kt—B6 ch, K—B1; 15 Kt×R, B×Kt, with the exchange of Queens.

13	P—QKt4
14 B—Kt3	P—R4

This furious counter-attack affords White a respite of a *tempo*, which he utilises in masterly fashion. 14 .... B—KKt2 would therefore have been better.

15 Kt×KP

Well calculated. Apparently Black only expected 15 P—QR3, after which 15 .... B—KKt2 would still have been possible.

15 ...... P—R5

Obstinacy, but if 15 .... B—KKt2; 16 Kt—Q6 ch, K—Q1 (or 16 .... K—B1;

17 Q—B4 ch, Q—B3; 18 Kt×B, Q×Q;
19 R—Q8 mate); 17 Q—QB5 (illustrating
the principle that the threat is stronger than
its execution, this quiet move is more effective
than 17 Kt—B7 db ch or 17 Kt—B5 dis ch);
17 .... Kt—Q2 (a desperate attempt, for
if 17 .... K—B2; 18 Kt×P ch, etc.; if
17 .... QB×P; 18 Kt—B5 dis ch; and if
17 .... B—Q2; 18 Q—Kt6 mate); 18 Q×BP,
R—Kt1; 19 Kt×B, and wins without
appeal.

16 Kt—B6 ch
More conclusive still than 16 Kt—Q6 ch.

16	K—B1
17 Kt×R	K×Kt
18 R—Q8 ch	

A beautiful *deflecting sacrifice*, and the
crowning glory.

| 18 ...... | Q×R |

Or 18 .... B—B1; 19 R×B ch, Q×R
(19 .... K×R; 20 Q—R8 mate); 20 P—K7
dis ch, P×B; 21 Q—R8 ch, K×Q; 22 P×Q
(Q) mate.

| 19 P—K7 dis ch | Resigns. |

155

White	Black
STAUNTON AND	MORPHY AND
OWEN	BARNES

(London, 1858)

*The capture by the Queen of a Rook in the
corner is known to be very dangerous. It is
particularly interesting and instructive to see
how Black, in this game, turns this event to
good account.*

1 P—K4	P—K4
2 Kt—KB3	P—Q3
3 P—Q4	P—KB4
4 QP×P	BP×P
5 Kt—Kt5	P—Q4
6 P—K6	Kt—KR3
7 Kt—QB3	P—B3
8 KKt×KP	P×Kt

Self-reliance.

9 Q—R5 ch	P—Kt3
10 Q—K5	R—Kt1
11 B×Kt	B×B
12 R—Q1	Q—Kt4

And it is again a case of self-reliance to
allow the hostile Queen to penetrate into
the black position. A passive defence would
be 12 .... Q—K2.

13 Q—B7
For Black to have permitted this intrusion,
which threatens 14 Q×B ch, as well as a
mate on the move, is proof of steady nerves
or most accurate calculation.

| 13 ...... | B×P |
| 14 Q×KtP | |

Following the itinerary which events pre-
scribe. If 14 Kt×P, Q—K2.

| 14 ...... | P—K6 |

Continuing an active defence. There is
a fine threat of 15 .... P×P ch and 16 ....
Q—K6 mate.

15 P—B3
White deems 15 P×P, Q×P ch; 16 B—
K2, etc., to be too hazardous.

| 15 ...... | Q—K2 |
| 16 Q×R | |

The capture of a Rook—at the cost of
a Queen's embarrassment—is a well-known
theme of chess tactics.

| 16 ...... | K—B2 |

Black's problem—not an easy one—is to
keep the opposing Queen in chancery.
  Thus, if at once 16 .... B—KB5;
17 B—R6, K—B2; 18 Q—Kt7, etc.

| 17 Kt—K4 | B—KB5 |
| 18 B—K2 | K—Kt2 |

Not yet 18 .... Q—B2, by reason of
19 P—KKt3, B—K4; 20 Kt—Kt5 ch.

19 Castles
First 19 P—KKt3 is better, although the
white allies desire to castle as soon as
possible.

| 19 ...... | Q—QB2 |

At last the threat of winning the Queen
becomes effective (20 .... Kt—Q2), and
added to it is a subsidiary threat: 20 ....
B×P ch.

20 Kt—B5
A counter-attempt, which allows the

Queen to escape, but leaves a disabled King. If 20 P—KKt3, Kt—Q2; 21 Q×R ch, K×Q; 22 P×B, Q×P, and White's two Rooks would not make up for the Queen, as his King's position shows signs of breaking up.

| 20 ...... | B×P ch |
| 21 K—R1 | B—B1 |

Preventing 22 Q—Kt7.

22 R—Q4

Barring 22 .... Q—B5.

| 22 ...... | B—Kt6 |

With the threat of 23 .... Q—K4.

| 23 R—K4 | K—R1 |
| 24 R—Q1 | |

Against 24 R×P the same reply by Black, 24 .... Q—KKt2, would be immediately decisive.

| 24 ...... | Q—KKt2 |
| 25 R—KR4 | |

Still preventing the deadly 25 .... Q—R3 ch in an ingenious manner.

| 25 ...... | B×R |
| 26 Q×Kt | |

Relief of the Queen, but at a disastrous cost. The conclusion is still full of interest.

26	B—R3
27 Q—R2	B×B
28 R—Q7	Q—R3

Attack and defence. If now 29 Q—K5 ch, the counter-check 29 .... B—B3 dis ch is decisive. A mistake, however, would be 28 .... Q—B3, because of 29 Kt—K4, Q—K3; 30 R×P ch, K×R; 31 Kt—Kt5 ch, followed by Kt×Q.

29 Kt—K4

With the threat of 30 Kt—B6, which Black, however, parries in a manner as unexpected as it is conclusive.

29	B—B5
30 Kt—B6	P—K7
31 R—K7	

Fighting to the last round.

31	Q—B8 ch
32 Q—Kt1	Q×Q ch
33 K×Q	P—K8 (Q) ch
34 R×Q	B×R
Resigns.	

156

| White | Black |
| ANDERSSEN | PAULSEN |

(Vienna, 1873)

Quiet and steady evolutions lead gradually to the final assault, of which the details (34 Kt (K4)—B6 ch and 37 R×B ch) are the more scintillating. One of those games in which the contestants castle on opposite wings, keeping the tension at high pitch by continuous manœuvring. For once Black's two Knights prove to be more agile and effective than the opposing two Bishops.

1 P—K4	P—K4
2 Kt—KB3	P—Q3
3 P—Q4	P×P

This abandonment of the centre is by no means compulsory. The counter-attempt 3 .... B—Kt5, however, is still less substantial, as is shown in the following famous game, Morphy—the Duke of Brunswick and Count Isouard de Vauvenargues, *Paris, 1858:* 4 P×P, B×Kt (forced); 5 Q×B, P×P; 6 B—QB4, Kt—KB3 (better, 6 .... Q—B3); 7 Q—QKt3 (a double threat); 7 .... Q—K2 (if 7 .... Q—Q2; 8 Q×P, Q—B3; 9 B—QKt5); 8 Kt—B3 (disdaining 8 Q×P, on account of 8 .... Q—Kt5 ch, exchanging Queens); 8 .... P—B3; 9 B—KKt5, P—Kt4; 10 Kt×P, P×Kt; 11 B×KtP ch, QKt—Q2; 12 Castles QR, R—Q1 (if 12 .... Castles; 13 B—R6 ch, followed by mate); 13 R×Kt, R×R; 14 R—Q1, Q—K3 (or 14 .... Q—Kt5; 15 B×Kt, Q×Q; 16 B×R mate); 15 B×R ch, Kt×B; 16 Q—Kt8 ch (a sparkling finish); 16 .... Kt×Q; 17 R—Q8 mate.

| 4 Q×P | Kt—QB3 |

If, in preparation for this move, 4 .... B—Q2, then 5 B—KB4, Kt—QB3; 6 Q—Q2 secures for White a superior disposition of forces.

5 B—QKt5	B—Q2
6 B×Kt	B×B
7 B—Kt5	

Developing the Q side at top speed.

| 7 ...... | Kt—B3 |

Best. If 7 .... Q—K2; 8 Q×KtP, and if 7 .... P—B3; 8 B—R4, Kt—R3; 9 Kt—B3, etc., Black's development is effected in a far more artificial manner.

| 8 Kt—B3 | B—K2 |
| 9 Castles QR | |

The mobilisation on either side being almost completed, it can be established that

White, with a powerful piece and a useful pawn in the centre, has an advantage in territory.

9 ......   Castles

A sound precautionary measure would have been 9 .... P—KR3.

10 KR—K1

Emphasising his advantage in the centre. A possible development could be 10 P—KR4, P—KR3; 11 Kt—Q5 (consistent play); 11 .... P×B; 12 Kt×B ch, Q×Kt; 13 P×P, Kt×P; 14 R—R5, Q—K3; 15 QR—R1, P—B4; 16 Kt—K5 (superb); 16 .... P×Kt; 17 P—Kt6, forcing mate. (Alekhine v. van Mindeno, Holland 1938).

10 ......   R—K1

If here 10 .... P—KR3, then, safely, 11 B—R4, for 11 .... Kt×P; 12 R×Kt would cost Black a piece.

11 K—Kt1   B—Q2

Besides ceding territory, this move encumbers the Q file. The tentative move 11 .... P—KR3 has its points, e.g. 12 B—R4, Kt—R4, etc., or 12 B—K3, Kt—Kt5, or 12 B—B1, Kt—Q2, etc., with a defendable position.

12 B×Kt   B×B
13 P—K5

A fine break-through.

13 ......   B—K2
14 Kt—Q5   B—KB1

But not 14 .... P×P; 15 Kt×B ch, R×Kt; 16 R×P, P—QB4; 17 Q—Q6, and wins.

15 P×P   P×P

If 15 .... B×P; 16 Kt×P, neatly winning a pawn.

16 R×R   B×R
17 Kt—Q2

The battlefield being now cleared, it can be seen that White has succeeded in inflicting on his opponent a grave weakness at Q6.

In the coming duel between the two white Knights and the two black Bishops, the former possess easy targets.

17 ......   B—B3
18 Kt—K4   P—B4

This weakening move is intended to eliminate the potential threat of 19 Kt (K4)—B6 ch, P×Kt (a prudent course would be 19 .. ♝. K—R1, and if 20 Q—KR4, P×Kt; 21 Kt×P, P—KR3, etc.); 20 Kt×P ch, K—R1; 21 Kt—K8 dis ch, K—Kt1; 22 R—Q3, etc.

19 Kt (K4)—B3   Q—Q2
20 P—QR3   Q—KB2
21 P—R3   P—QR3
22 P—KKt4

After a few preparatory moves the assault begins.

22 ......   R—K1
23 P—B4   R—K3
24 P—Kt5   P—Kt4
25 P—KR4   R—K1
26 Q—Q3   R—Kt1
27 P—R5   P—R4
28 P—Kt4

White, very decidedly, stops any adverse expansion on the Q side, but his threats on the other wing remain in force.

28 ......   P×P
29 P×P   Q×P

This eliminates an awkward opponent (in view of the potential P—R6), but not without opening new and important lines.

30 Q×BP   Q—B2
31 Q—Q3   B—Q2

The threat 32 R—R1 has to be parried.

32 Kt—K4   Q—B4

He hastens to occupy the dangerous diagonal sector, in order to eliminate the potential threat of 33 Kt (K4)—B6 ch, P×Kt; 34 Kt×P ch, K—R1; 35 R—R1, P—R3; 36 Q—Q4, B—Kt2; 37 Q×P, R—Q1; 38 Q—Q3, B—KB1 (or 38 .... B×Kt; 39 R×P ch, etc.); 39 R—Q1, and wins.

After 32 .... B—B4, and equally after 32 .... Q—Kt3, the sacrifice 33 Kt (K4)—B6 has decisive results.

33 R—R1   R—K1

Calling forth the storm. Better is 33 .... K—R1.

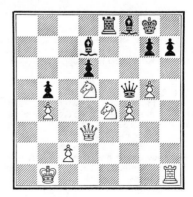

34 Kt (K4)—B6 ch

This sacrifice, which has been "in the air" for a long time, has, at this stage, some additional and attractive points.

34	P×Kt
35 Kt×P ch	K—B2
36 R×P ch	B—Kt2

If 36 .... K—Kt3; 37 R×B.

37 R×B ch

A fresh surprise.

37	K×R
38 Kt×R ch	K—B1
39 Q×Q ch	B×Q
40 Kt×P	

And White wins.

157

| White | Black |
| ADAMS | TORRE |

(New Orleans, 1920)

A game from the youth of the Mexican genius, in which he succumbs to a truly miraculous concatenation of circumstances.

1 P—K4	P—K4
2 Kt—KB3	P—Q3
3 P—Q4	P×P
4 Q×P	Kt—QB3

Or, without hastening to attack the Queen, but first attending to the development of his K side: 4 .... Kt—KB3; 5 Kt—B3, B—K2; 6 B—K3, Castles; 7 Castles, Kt—B3; 8 Q—Q2, and White has a better all-round development.

5 B—QKt5

He prefers to exchange one of his Bishops rather than to let his Queen relinquish her useful post of observation, otherwise 5 Q—K3 would also be acceptable.

| 5 ...... | B—Q2 |
| 6 B×Kt | B×B |

This is more promising than 6 .... P×B, which, without necessity, weakens the pawn formation on the Q side.

7 Kt—B3

Here and on the next move B—Kt5, with a view to castling on the Q side, is also playable.

| 7 ...... | Kt—B3 |
| 8 Castles | |

Rapidly completing the first stage of his mobilisation.

| 8 ...... | B—K2 |

The *fianchetto* development cannot here be effected, e.g. 8 .... P—KKt3; 9 B—Kt5, B—Kt2; 10 Kt—Q5, B×Kt; 11 P×B, Castles; 12 Q—KR4, etc.

9 Kt—Q5	B×Kt
10 P×B	Castles
11 B—Kt5	P—B3

Here, as in many similar cases, 11 .... P—KR3, forcing a disclosure of the invading Bishop's intentions, is justified. Apart from this consideration, the text move is too abrupt, as the opening-up of the game normally benefits the better-developed side —White in this case.

A consolidating move, such as 11 .... R—K1 (or 11 .... P—KR3; 12 B—R4, R—K1), is called for.

| 12 P—B4 | P×P |
| 13 P×P | P—QR4 |

In order to be able to move his QR. More natural, however, would be 13 .... P—QR3.

14 KR—K1

The opening of the K file begins to tell.

| 14 ...... | R—K1 |

Better, at once, 14 .... Q—Q2, or still 14 .... P—R3, etc.

| 15 R—K2 | R—QB1 |

If .... P—KR3 was to be recommended before, at this stage the move has become essential.

16 QR—K1

Now the threat is 17 B×Kt, forcing the disorganising reply 17 .... P×B. It can be seen that the pin, too long disregarded, has gained in importance.

| 16 ...... | Q—Q2 |

Hoping to maintain the *liaison* between the three major pieces.

| 17 B×Kt | B×B |

Plausible, but fatal, this move gives rise to "fireworks" almost unique in chess literature. 17 .... P×B was necessary, although even then Black remains with the clearly inferior position.

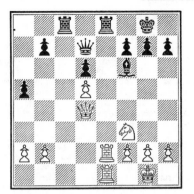

18 Q—KKt4

This magnificent offer of the Queen (an *overload sacrifice*) is intended to deflect one of the supports of the black KR. Black sees now—*post festum*—how useful 11 .... P—KR3 would have been, as now the King would have a flight square.

18 ...... Q—Kt4

The only available square, from which the Queen can guard the KR.

19 Q—QB4

The "brilliancy" continues.

After the very plausible 19 P—QR4, there would follow 19 .... Q × R; 20 R × Q, R—B8 ch, and mate in two.

19 ...... Q—Q2
20 Q—B7

For the third time the Queen is offered in sacrifice, this time in even more thrilling a manner.

20 ...... Q—Kt4

In order to reply to 21 Q × KtP by 21 .... Q × R.

21 P—QR4

This Queen-hunt is transcendent.

21 ...... Q × RP
22 R—K4

An important displacement.

22 ...... Q—Kt4
23 Q × KtP

By this, the fourth offer of the Queen, her rival is denied access to all the intercepting squares (Q2, QKt4, QR5).

Resigns.

158

White	Black
KASHDAN	KOLTANOWSKI

(London, 1932)

An early "débâcle" is a rarity in these days of scientific chess. White begins, marshals his forces, and wins. Castling on opposite sides is the explanation.

1 P—K4	P—K4
2 Kt—KB3	P—Q3
3 P—Q4	P × P

He attempts to simplify the theme of the contest.

4 Kt × P

White's mobile centre (composed of a piece and a pawn) already secures for him an enduring positional advantage.

4	Kt—KB3
5 Kt—QB3	B—K2
6 B—KB4	

Stressing the rapid development of his Q side. By playing 6 B—QB4, Castles; 7 Castles, Kt—B3, etc., we obtain a *Hungarian Defence*. Another plan of development is: 6 B—Q3, Castles; 7 Castles, B—Q2; 8 P—B4, Kt—B3; 9 KKt—K2, etc., or again, 6 B—K2, Castles; 7 Castles, Kt—B3; 8 Kt × Kt, P × Kt; 9 P—QKt3, etc.

6	Castles
7 Q—Q2	R—K1

As this pressure on the semi-open K file can easily be countered, simple development of the minor pieces by 7 .... Kt—B3 or, still more solidly, by 7 .... B—Q2, followed by .... Kt—B3, affords Black an easier game than the text move.

8 Castles

Foreshadowing, by castling on the opposite wing, a fight *á outrance*.

8	B—B1
9 P—B3	

Helping the defence, but as the sequel will show immediately, the attack as well.

9 ...... QKt—Q2

Development on inner lines, for if—in a straightforward manner—9 .... Kt—B3, White obtains the better game after 10 Kt × Kt, P × Kt; 11 P—K5, Kt—R4; 12 B—KKt5, etc.

Therefore a rational continuation would be 9 .... B—Q2, followed by .... Kt—B3, etc.

10 P—KKt4
Encircling strategy.

10 ......   Kt—K4
11 B—K2   P—QR3
He recognises that his only counter-chances are to be found on the Q side. If 11 .... P—B4; 12 KKt—Kt5, and if 11 .... P—Q4; 12 B×Kt, R×B; 13 P—Kt5, Kt—R4; 14 P—B4, etc.

12 P—KR4
Direct action.

12 ......   P—QKt4
To be followed, eventually, by .... Kt—B5 or .... P—Kt5, but as all these lateral aspirations can but arrive too late, he should have tried to obtain breathing-space by 12 .... P—B4.

13 P—R5
To be followed by P—Kt5, whereas, if at once 13 P—Kt5, Kt—R4.

13 ......   B—K3
He helps his opponent's intentions. He should, now or never, have played 13 .... P—B4.

14 Kt×B   P×Kt
15 B×Kt   P×B
Already Black's pawn formation in the centre is pitiable, but—as a Russian proverb has it—"Misfortunes rarely come singly."

16 P—Kt5
Winning a piece without any inconvenience. The game is over before it is properly begun!

16 ......   B—Q3
17 P×Kt   Q×P
18 Q—K3   Q—K2
19 R—Q3   KR—Q1
20 Q—Q2   Resigns.

159

White	Black
YATES	MARCO

(The Hague, 1921)

The counter-attack, which Black, with his King on his original square, is sometimes able to initiate on the KKt file, is beautifully illustrated here.

1 P—K4   P—K4
2 Kt—KB3   P—Q3
3 P—Q4   Kt—Q2
Holding the KP whilst blocking the Q file (for if 3 .... Kt—QB3; 4 P×P, and Black forfeits castling). This line of play—fairly sound and, odd as it may seem, even aggressive—was thought out about 1889 by the American master Major Hanham. The Austro-Rumanian master Georg Marco later on made it his speciality.

4 B—QB4   P—QB3
This supporting move, soon to be followed by .... Q—B2, is a useful complement of the scheme of the *Hanham Variation*. If 4 .... B—K2; 5 P×P, Kt×P (5 .... P×P; 6 Q—Q5, and wins at once); 6 Kt×Kt, P×Kt; 7 Q—R5 is decisive, and if 4 .... KKt—B3; 5 Kt—Kt5, e.g. 5 .... R—KKt1 (or, not less tragically, 5 .... Q—K2; 6 B×P ch, K—Q1; 7 Kt—K6 ch. The lesser evil is therefore 5 .... P—Q4, etc.); 6 B×P ch, K—K2; 7 Kt—K6, "mating" the Queen.

5 Kt—B3
Another good developing move is 5 Castles. Two restless continuations—leading to varied complications—are 5 Kt—Kt5 and 5 P—QR4 (preventing 5 .... P—QKt4).

5 ......   B—K2
6 Castles
Following the "book." More awkward for Black is 6 P×P, P×P (if 6 .... KKt×P; 7 Kt×Kt, P×Kt; 8 Q—R5, etc.); 7 Kt—KKt5, B×Kt (or 7 .... Kt—R3; 8 Kt—K6, P×Kt; 9 B×Kt, Kt—Kt3; 10 Q—R5 ch, etc., with advantage to White); 8 Q—R5 (a double attack); 8 .... P—KKt3 (or 8 .... Q—B3; 9 B×B, Q—Kt3; 10 Q—R4, etc., to White's advantage); 9 Q×B, Q×Q; 10 B×Q, and, with his two Bishops, White has the better chances in the coming end-game.

6 ......   P—KR3
Preventing various escapades by White after 6 .... KKt—B3; 7 Kt—KKt5, but also preparing for a counter-attack.

7 B—K3   KKt—B3
8 B—Kt3
He could face matters more energetically by 8 P—QR4.

8 ......   Q—B2
9 Kt—Q2   P—KKt4
He prevents 10 P—B4, and discloses his own plans—refraining from castling.

10 P—QR4   Kt—B1
11 P—R5

More in keeping with the situation is, at once, 11 Kt—B4, followed by Q—Q2 and KR—Q1, etc.

11 ......   Kt—Kt3
12 R—K1   Kt—B5
13 P—B3

If 13 P—Kt3, Q—Q2; threatening .... Q—R6.

13 ......   R—KKt1
14 Kt—B1   B—K3

Over-hasty would be 14 .... P—Kt5; 15 B × Kt, P × B; 16 P—K5, etc.

15 Kt—Kt3   Q—Q2
16 P—Q5

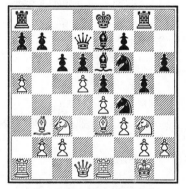

16 ......   B—R6

A *disrupting sacrifice*, giving the black pieces access to White's disorganised position.

17 P × B

Against 17 P—R6 Black maintains a strong K side attack after 17 .... Kt × KtP; 18 RP × P, Q × P; 19 B—R4, Kt × B; 20 P × P, Q—B1; 21 R × Kt, P—R3, etc.

17 ......   Q × P
18 Q—Q2

If 18 R—K2 (with a view to 19 Q—KB1), Black carries on with 18 .... P—Kt5.

18 ......   KKt—R4
19 Q—B2

He underestimates the power of Black's attack. He would attain a certain amount of relief by 19 Kt × Kt, Q × BP (threatens 20 .... Kt—R6 mate); 20 B × Kt, KtP × B dis ch; 21 Kt—Kt3, P × Kt; 22 P—R3, etc., or 19 .... Q × Kt; 20 R—KB1, with defensive resources.

19 ......   P—Kt5
20 K—R1

If 20 Kt × Kt, KtP × P dis ch; 21 Kt—Kt3, B—R5; 22 K—R1, R × Kt; 23 B × Kt, R—Kt7, and wins. And if 20 Q—B1, Kt × Kt.

20 ......   P × BP
21 R—KKt1   B—R5
22 B × Kt   P × B
23 Kt × Kt

A desperate bid for salvation.

23 ......   B × Q
24 R × R ch   K—K2
25 Kt × P   Q—R5
26 R—Kt7   K—B1

If 26 .... Q × Kt, White could hold out with 27 P × P.

27 R × P ch   K × R
28 P × P dis ch K—Kt2
29 Kt—K6 ch   K—R1
30 Kt—Q5   P × P

Or more ruthlessly 30 .... B—Kt6, with mate to follow.

Resigns.

160

White	Black
THOMAS	ALEKHINE

(Hastings, 1934)

A hard-fought game, resulting, after many skirmishes, in an end-game: Knight and three pawns v. Bishop and three pawns. The manner in which the opposing pawns are kept under the strictest restraint by both players is worthy of careful study.

1 P—K4   P—K4
2 Kt—KB3   P—Q3
3 P—Q4   Kt—Q2

The *Hanham Variation* will always attract an aggressive and spontaneous player.

4 Kt—B3   P—QB3
5 B—QB4   B—K2
6 Castles

He does not attempt to eliminate the middle-game by Schlechter's positional manœuvre: 6 P × P, P × P; 7 Kt—KKt5, B × Kt; 8 Q—R5, P—KKt3; 9 Q × B, Q × Q; 10 B × Q, etc.

| 6 ...... | P—KR3 |

A useful preventive measure.

| 7 P×P |

Simple and good.

7	P×P
8 Q—K2	Q—B2
9 B—K3	

Here 9 P—QR4 would prevent 9 .... P—QKt4, but would weaken the Q side.

| 9 ...... | P—QKt4 |

As the plan to castle on the Q side by 9 .... Kt—B1; 10 B—Kt3, Kt—B3; 11 P—KR3, B—K3; 12 QR—Q1, KKt—Q2; 13 P—QR4, would still require artificial manœuvres. Black decides to take to guerrilla warfare.

| 10 B—Kt3 | KKt—B3 |

If at once 10 .... Kt—B4; Black would be faced with awkward problems after 11 B—Q5, P×B; 12 Kt×QP.

| 11 P—QR3 | Kt—B4 |
| 12 B—R2 | Kt—K3 |

The struggle for *strong squares.* The grasping continuation 12 .... QKt×P; 13 Kt×Kt, Kt×Kt would afford Black little comfort on account of 14 B×QRP, P—KB4; 15 B—K3, and Black's position would be too exposed.

| 13 KR—Q1 | Kt—Kt5 |
| 14 Kt—K1 | |

Simpler would be 14 P—R3, but he wishes to complicate matters.

| 14 ...... | Kt—Q5 |
| 15 Q—Q2 | |

With this and the next move, White, with great self-possession, extinguishes the "spark." A complete misapprehension would be 15 B×Kt, P×B, and Black wins a piece by the double threat 16 .... P×Kt and 16 .... Q×P ch; 17 K—B1, Q—R8 mate.

15	Castles
16 P—R3	Kt×B
17 Q×Kt	P—QR4
18 Kt—K2	

Evading the dissolving threat 18 .... P—Kt5.

18	B—QB4
19 Kt×Kt	B×Kt
20 Q—KKt3	Q—K2

Avoiding the terrible pitfall 20 .... B×KtP; 21 QR—Kt1, B—Q5; 22 R×B, and wins.

| 21 P—B3 |

Driving off a dangerous enemy and consolidating his own position.

Black, to be sure, has two Bishops, but White has command of the only open file. The chances tend to equalise.

| 21 ...... | B—Kt3 |
| 22 R—Q2 | B—B2 |

Just in time to oppose the Rooks.

| 23 Kt—B2 |

More to the point than 23 QR—Q1, after which 23 .... P—Kt5 would be possible.

| 23 ...... | R—Q1 |
| 24 QR—Q1 | B—K3 |

He must neutralise the open file and the white King's Bishop's important diagonal.

25 B×B	Q×B
26 R×R ch	R×R
27 R×R ch	B×R

Although a simplified end-game is reached, there are still many problems to be solved.

28 Q—Q3	B—Kt4
29 Kt—K3	P—Kt3
30 K—R2	Q—Kt6

An expedition which must be taken seriously.

31 Q—K2	P—R4
32 P—Kt3	P—KR5
33 P×P	

Countering his opponent's plans by—falling in with them.

33	B×P
34 Kt—Kt4	B—Kt4
35 Kt—K3	

He prevents 35 .... B—B8, and avoids the casual trap 35 Kt×P, B—B5 ch.

35	Q—R7
36 Q—B2	Q—R8
37 K—Kt2	Q—K8
38 Q—Q3	Q—B8
39 Kt—Kt4	Q×KtP
40 Q—Q7	Q×RP

If 40 .... Q×BP; 41 Q—K8 ch, K—Kt2; 42 Kt×P, etc., whereas now the sequel would be 41 Q—K8 ch, Q—B1; 42 Q×KP, Q—K2, etc.

41 Kt×P	Q—K2
42 Q×Q	B×Q
43 Kt×QBP	

Even the end of the ending is furiously contested.

43	B—B3

If 43 .... P—R5; 44 Kt × B, with check!,
K—B1; 45 Kt—Q5, coming back in time,
and wins. Similarly, if 43 .... B—Q1;
44 Kt × B, P—R5; 45 Kt—B6, P—R6;
46 Kt—Kt4.

44 Kt × P	B × P
45 Kt—Kt3	B—K4
46 K—B3	K—B1
47 K—Kt4	K—K2
48 P—B4	B—B6
49 P—R4	K—Q3
50 P—R5	P × P ch
51 K × P	P—Kt5
52 K—Kt5	B—Kt2

Thinking of the defensive.

53 K—B5	K—B3
54 P—K5	K—Q4
55 Kt—R5	B—R3
56 Kt—Kt3	K—B5
57 Kt—R5 ch	K—Q6
58 Kt—Kt3	K—K6

With a hold on both wings, Black has at
last obtained the maximum effectiveness of
his forces.

59 Kt—R1

Alone this problem-move saves the situation (59 .... B × P; 60 Kt—B2 ch).

59	K—Q6
60 Kt—Kt3	K—B7
61 Kt—R5	K—B6
62 K—K4	B—B1
63 P—B5	Draw

After 63 .... P—Kt6; 64 Kt × P, K × Kt,
White will take care not to play 65 P—K6,
P—B3, etc., but will enforce the peace treaty
by 65 P—B6, K—B5; 66 P—K6, P × P;
67 K—K5, etc.

161

White	*Black*
TEICHMANN	NIMZOWITSCH

(San Sebastian, 1911)

*After lengthy manœuvres, Black succeeds in
opening the KR file to his own advantage.*

*Of great theoretical importance, this fine
game is also remarkable for the firm strategy
employed by Black in the middle-game.*

1 P—K4	P—K4
2 Kt—KB3	P—Q3
3 P—Q4	Kt—KB3

Attacking White's KP instead of defending
his own. As immediately afterwards he re-
enters the scheme of the *Hanham Variation*,
he succeeds by this transposition of moves
(3 .... Kt—KB3, followed by 4 ....
QKt—Q2) in effecting a rapid and complete
mobilisation of the K side.

4 Kt—B3

An important decision. If 4 B—QB4,
Kt × P equalises. The continuation 4 P × P
causes Black more anxiety, as was shown in
a game Rellstab-Tylor, *Hastings*, 1930:
4 (P × P) Kt × P; 5 Q—Q5, Kt—B4;
6 B—Kt5, Q—Q2 (artificial, as would also
be 6 .... P—KB3. The simplest line of
play is 6 .... B—K2; 7 P × P, Q × P;
8 Kt—B3, Castles, and White's positional
advantage is only minute; 7 Kt—B3, P × P;
8 B—Kt5, P—QB3 (if 8 .... Kt—B3;
9 Kt × P wins); 9 Q × KP ch, Kt—K3 (if
9 .... Q—K3; 10 Castles QR); 10 R—Q1,
P—B3 (again, 10 .... Q—B2; 11 Q × Q,
Kt × Q; 12 R—Q8 mate); 11 Q—K2,
Q—KB2; 12 B—QB4 (the decisive pin);
12 .... P—Kt4 (if 12 .... P × B; 13 Kt × P,
followed by Kt × Kt); 13 B—Kt3, P—Kt5;
14 Kt—K4, B—R3; 15 Q—K3, Kt—Q2;
16 B × Kt, Q × B; 17 Kt × P ch, K—B2;
18 R × Kt ch, B—K2; 19 Kt—K5 ch, and
Black resigns (19 .... K—B1; 20 Kt—Kt6 ch,
K—B2; 21 R × B ch, etc.).

4	QKt—Q2

Leading into the *Hanham Variation*, which
strives to keep the central files closed. A
more open game results from 4 ....
P × P, with 5 Q × P or 5 Kt × P.

5 B—QB4

The development of the KB by 5 B—K2
is too restricted, and 5 P—QKt3, B—K2;
6 B—Kt2 too artificial.

5	B—K2
6 Castles	

The sacrifice 6 B × P ch is unsound, nor is
6 Kt—KKt5, Castles; 7 B × P ch, R × B;
8 Kt—K6, Q—K1; 9 Kt × BP, Q—Q1;
10 Kt × R, P—QKt3 to be recommended.

6	Castles

A rational move is 6 .... P—KR3,
reserving his decision.

7 Q—K2	P—B3

Less solid is 7 .... P × P, adopted in a
game Tylor-Koltanowski, *Hastings*, 1930, as

follows: 7 .... P×P; 8 Kt×P, R—K1
(fatal; 8 .... Kt—Kt3 was necessary);
9 B×P ch, K×B; 10 Kt—K6, K×Kt;
11 Q—B4 ch, P—Q4; 12 P×P ch, K—B2
(or 12 .... K—Q3; 13 Kt—Kt5 ch, K—K4;
14 R—K1 ch, K—B4; 15 Q—Q3 ch, with
mate in two); 13 P—Q6 dis ch, Kt—Q4 (or
13 .... K—B1; 14 P×P, and the Queen
is "mated"); 14 P×B, and wins.

8 B—KKt5
Other reasonable continuations are
8 B—K3 or 8 P—KR3, followed by B—K3,
but the most sensible is 8 P—QR4.

8	P—KR3
9 B—R4	Kt—R4
10 B—KKt3	

The gain of a pawn by 10 Kt×P would
be illusory, because of 10 .... Kt—B5.

10	Kt×B
11 RP×Kt	P—QKt4
12 B—Q3	

More active would be 12 B—Kt3, and if
12 .... P—QR4; 13 P—R3.

| 12 ...... | P—R3 |
| 13 P—R4 | B—Kt2 |

Consolidation.

14 QR—Q1	Q—B2
15 P×KtP	RP×P
16 P—KKt4	

Rather aimless. Better would be 16 P×P,
P×P, striving for equality.

| 16 ...... | KR—K1 |
| 17 P—Q5 | |

Here again 17 P×P, P×P would be
better policy, but White overestimates the
resources of his position.

| 17 ...... | P—Kt5 |

And not 17 .... P×P; 18 Kt×KtP.

18 P×P	B×P
19 Kt—Kt1	Kt—B4
20 QKt—Q2	Q—B1
21 B—B4	

An astute defence of the threatened pawn,
for if 21 .... Q×P; 22 B×P ch, K×B;
23 Kt×P ch, followed by Q×Q, and wins.

21	P—Kt3
22 P—KKt3	K—Kt2
23 Kt—R2	

The defence of the KKtP, now become
necessary, causes this fresh withdrawal.

| 23 ...... | B—KKt4 |

Methodically gaining territory.

24 P—KB3
Compulsory modesty. If, boldly, 24 P—B4,
P×P; 25 P×P, B—B3; 26 B—Q3, KB×P,
Black gathers a pawn with impunity.

| 24 ...... | Q—B2 |
| 25 KR—K1 | R—R1 |

After the lengthy evolutions which have
taken place so far, the opening of the KR
file now gives the contest a fresh impetus.

26 QKt—B1	P—R4
27 P×P	R×P
28 B—Q5	QR—R1
29 B×B	Q×B
30 Q—B4	Q—Kt3
31 K—Kt2	Kt—K3

Whilst the two adverse Knights are "confined to barracks," the black Knight enjoys
an enviable mobility.

| 32 R—K2 | Kt—Q5 |
| 33 R (K2)—K1 | Q—Kt2 |

In order to reinforce, by 34 .... Q—Q2
(threatening 35 .... R×Kt ch; 36 Kt×R,
Q—R6 ch, followed by .... Q×Kt ch), the
already powerful pressure on the K side.

34 R×Kt
Trying, at the most favourable moment,
violently to alter the course of events. This
sacrifice of the exchange is not without
practical chances, and only Black's most
accurate counter-play will enable him to
keep the upper hand.

| 34 ...... | P×R |
| 35 Kt—Kt4 | |

Or 35 Q×QP ch, B—B3, etc.

35	Q—Kt3
36 P—B4	B—K2
37 R—Q1	P—B4

The beginning of the end.

| 38 Kt—B2 | P×P |
| 39 Q×P ch | |

Clearly not 39 Kt×P, P—Q4.

39	Q×Q
40 R×Q	P—Q4
41 P—Kt4	B—B4

White's every move is countered.

42 R—Q1	R—R5
43 R×P	B×Kt
44 K×B	R×P
45 K—K3	R—QB1
46 K×P	R—B5 ch
47 K—Q3	R (B5)×KBP

And Black wins.

162

White	Black
ALEKHINE	MARCO

(Stockholm, 1912)

A direct K side attack, characterised by the advance of the KBP, and conducted by White with the greatest virtuosity. One of the world champion's early triumphs.

1	P—K4	P—K4
2	Kt—KB3	P—Q3
3	P—Q4	Kt—KB3
4	Kt—B3	QKt—Q2
5	B—QB4	B—K2
6	Castles	Castles
7	Q—K2	P—B3
8	P—QR4	

Energetic play.

| 8 | ...... | P—KR3 |

If 8 .... Q—B2; 9 B—KKt5.

| 9 | B—Kt3 | Q—B2 |

Or 9 .... Kt—R2; 10 B—K3, B—B3; 11 KR—Q1, and White has, in good time, maintained his Q4.

| 10 | P—R3 | |

A well-known manœuvre, which allows 11 B—K3 without permitting the counter-stroke 11 .... Kt—Kt5.

10	......	K—R2
11	B—K3	P—KKt3
12	QR—Q1	K—Kt2
13	Kt—KR2	Kt—KKt1

Instead of this retrograde manœuvre, he should have played 13 .... Kt—R4, which not only provided a better defence, but would even have admitted of some counterplay eventually by .... P—KB4.

14	P—B4	P—B3
15	Q—Kt4	P×QP
16	B×P	Kt—B4

If 16 .... Kt—K4; 17 Q—Kt3.

| 17 | P—B5 | Kt×B |

Leaving one corpse already on the way (the KKtP), for if 17 .... P—KKt4; 18 QB×Kt, P×B; 19 Q—R5, with the cruel threat of 20 Q—Kt6 ch, K—R1; 21 B×Kt, R×B; 22 Q×P mate.

18	Q×P ch	K—R1
19	P×Kt	B—Q2
20	Q—Kt3	

He wishes to play Kt—Kt4, which now would be a tragic blunder because of 20 Kt—Kt4, B—K1, winning the Queen!

20	......	R—B2
21	Kt—Kt4	Q—Q1
22	Kt—K2	R—Kt2
23	Kt—B4	Q—K1
24	Q—R4	Q—B2
25	R—Q3	

Protecting his base, and preferring the maintenance of the threat 26 Kt×RP to its hasty execution.

| 25 | ...... | K—R2 |

If 25 .... P—B4; 26 B×QBP.

| 26 | Kt—Kt6 | |

A most powerful position.

| 26 | ...... | R×Kt |

A decision easy to understand. After 26 .... P—Q4 the sequel could be: 27 R—B4, P—B4; 28 Kt×RP, Kt×Kt; 29 Q×Kt ch, K×Q; 30 R—R4 ch, K—Kt4; 31 B—K3 mate.

| 27 | P×R ch | Q×P |
| 28 | B×BP | |

A telling conclusion.

28	......	B×Kt
29	B×B	R—K1
30	R×P	Q—Kt2
31	B—B6	Kt×B
32	KR×Kt	Resigns.

163

White	Black
BLAKE	WAHLTUCH

(Liverpool, 1923)

After Black has unwisely opened up the game (8 .... P×P and 17 .... P—Q4), White settles the issue by a beautiful sacrifice of the Queen for two minor pieces.

| 1 | P—K4 | P—Q3 |

The so-called *Old-Indian Defence.*

2	P—Q4	Kt—KB3
3	Kt—QB3	QKt—Q2
4	Kt—B3	P—K4

Returning, after a very curious inversion of moves, to the *Hanham Defence* (improved version)!

5 B—QB4	B—K2
6 Castles	Castles
7 R—K1	P—B3
8 B—Kt3	

A preventive retreat in order to reply to 8 .... P—QKt4 by 9 P—Q5, breaking up the hostile pawn chain.

| 8 ...... | P × P |

This belated abandonment of the centre is not compulsory. The continuation 8 .... P—KR3, followed by 9 .... Q—B2, would keep up the pressure in the centre.

9 Q × P
More vigorous than 9 Kt × P.

| 9 ...... | Kt—B4 |

Or 9 .... Q—Kt3; 10 B—Kt5, Q × Q; 11 Kt × Q, and in spite of the exchange of Queens, Black's game, principally on account of the exposed QP, remains inferior.

| 10 P—KR3 | Kt—K3 |

If 10 .... Kt × B; 11 RP × Kt, the anxiety about his QRP would force fresh weaknesses upon Black.

| 11 Q—K3 | Q—B2 |
| 12 B—Q2 | Kt—R4 |

Instead of this impulsive attempt, 12 .... R—Q1 at once would have been preferable, although even then the thrust .... P—Q4 can be effected only with difficulty.

13 Kt—K2
Preventing 13 .... KKt—B5.

13	R—Q1
14 QR—Q1	P—R4
15 P—B4	

A strong move, strengthening the blockade of Q5.

15	P—R3
16 P—Kt4	Kt—B3
17 Kt—Kt3	P—Q4

Seeing that his adversary has built up a formidable attack, ready to start, Black undertakes, at all costs, a counter-action in the centre.

A patient—but at the same time passive—continuation would be 17 .... Kt—R2; 18 Kt—B5, B—B1, etc.

| 18 BP × P | B—B4 |

Anticipating success, for if 19 Q—B3, Q × Kt ch wins, and if 19 P—Q6, Q × P (the simplest); 20 P—K5, B × Q; 21 P × Q, B—B4, and Black will be a valuable pawn ahead.

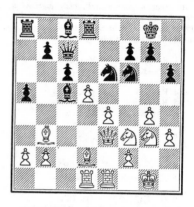

19 P × Kt
Compulsory as well as compelling, this sacrifice of the Queen for two minor pieces contains dangerous threats for Black.

19	B × Q
20 P × P ch	K—R2
21 B × B	Kt × KtP

A desperate counter-sacrifice. If 21 .... R × R; 22 P—B8 (Q), etc.; if 21 .... Kt—Q2; 22 P—K5, etc.; and if 21 .... B—Q2; 22 B—B5, etc.; and if 21 .... P—QKt3 (preventing 22 B—B5); 22 B—KB4, Q—K2; 23 R × R, Q × R; 24 R—Q1, etc., with ample compensations.

| 22 R × R | Q × R |
| 23 B—B5 | |

Harvesting.

23	B—Q2
24 P—B8 (Q)	Q × Q
25 B × Q	R × B
26 P × Kt	R × Kt

And, on balance, Black remains a piece down.

| 27 B—Q1 | Resigns. |

10. PETROFF'S DEFENCE

164

White	Black
(Unknown)	KIESERITZKY

(Paris, about 1846)

In the following game both sides claim the initiative. It will be seen here that dynamic resources are of greater importance than worldly possessions.

1	P—K4	P—K4
2	Kt—KB3	Kt—KB3
3	Kt×P	Kt×P

This capture is illusory, the only correct reply being 3 .... P—Q3, and then, after the white Knight has retired, 4 .... Kt×P. If 3 .... Q—K2; 4 Kt—KB3, to White's advantage. A doubtful sacrifice of a pawn is 3 .... Kt—B3.

4	Q—K2	Q—K2

Compulsory, for if, needlessly, 4 .... Kt—KB3, there follows the thunderclap 5 Kt—B6 dis ch, and wins.

5	Q×Kt	P—Q3

Work for the recovery of the piece begins.

6	P—Q4	P—KB3

Better is, however, 6 .... Kt—Q2, although White, with 7 Kt—QB3, preserves an advantage in development.

7	P—KB4	

Here 7 Kt—QB3 favoured White even more: 7 .... QP×Kt; 8 Kt—Q5, Q—Q3; 9 P×P, P×P; 10 B—KB4, Kt—Q2; 11 Castles, B—K2; 12 B—B4, and if then, sceptically, 12 .... P×B; 13 KR—K1, wins.

7	......	Kt—Q2
8	Kt—QB3	BP×Kt

More astute than 8 .... QP×Kt; after which the amusing sequel of a game quoted by Damiano (in 1512!) was: 8 .... (QP×Kt); 9 Kt—Q5, Q—Q3; 10 QP×P, P×P; 11 P×P, Q—QB3; 12 B—QKt5, Q—B4; 13 B—K3, Q×KB; 14 Kt×P ch, winning the Queen.

9	Kt—Q5	Kt—B3

The saving clause.

10	Kt×Kt ch	P×Kt
11	B—Kt5 ch	

A fresh danger!

11	......	P—B3

12	B×P ch	P×B
13	Q×P ch	K—B2
14	Q×R	B—QKt2

It can be seen that Black's sacrifice of the exchange, initiated by his 11th move, has secured for him a fine counter-attack.

15	Q×P	P×QP dis ch
16	K—B2	R—Kt1

Introducing the trump card of vertical pressure.

17	R—KKt1	Q—K5

A decisive irruption.

18	P—KKt3	Q×QBP ch
19	K—B1	

The King at bay. If 19 K—K1, Q—K5 ch, etc.

19	......	Q—Q8 ch
20	K—B2	Q—B6 ch
21	K—K1	B—Kt2

Clearing a way for the Rook.

22	Q×P	R—K1 ch
23	K—Q2	R—K7 ch

A geometrical demonstration.

24	K—Q1	R—KB7 dis ch
25	K—K1	Q—K7 mate

165

White	Black
BUDAPEST	PARIS

(1842–5 by correspondence)

Emerging from an interesting opening skirmish a pawn to the good, White liquidates cleverly, and shows a remarkable degree of precision in the end-game duel of Knight (and six pawns) against Bishop (and five pawns).

1	P—K4	P—K4
2	Kt—KB3	Kt—KB3
3	Kt×P	P—Q3
4	Kt—KB3	

The only rational move. Other moves by the Knight: 4 Kt—B4 or 4 Kt—Q3, or even 4 Kt×P, can only be looked upon as experiments.

4	......	Kt×P
5	P—Q4	

Energetically occupying the centre.

5	......	P—Q4

Black is equally bent upon keeping a footing in the centre. He even has a trusty piece there, but White's strategy will be directed towards taking advantage of the Knight's exposed position.

6 B—Q3   B—Q3

At a much later date (about 1910), Marshall the Impetuous reintroduced this variation to master practice—but with sundry refinements, based on the positional sacrifice of one, or even two pawns, thus providing one of the most interesting chapters of the Petroff Defence.

A reserved line of play is 6 .... B—K2; an enterprising idea is 6 .... Kt—QB3, but too enterprising would be 6 .... B—Kt5. Too passive, however, would be the voluntary retirement 6 .... Kt—KB3.

7 Castles

Deferring the lateral demonstration, which could be effected at once by 7 P—B4.

7 ......   Castles

Against 7 .... B—KKt5 White could reply, as in the text, with 8 P—B4 or with 8 R—K1, P—KB4; 9 Kt—B3.

8 P—B4

Undermining the base of Black's outpost.

8 ......   B—K3

An important moment. Much more energetic is 8 .... B—KKt5, e.g.:

(*a*) 9 Kt—B3, Kt×Kt; 10 P×Kt, P×P; 11 B×P, Q—B3, with an equalised game.

(*b*) 9 P—B5 (a fruitless blockade); 9 .... B—K2, and Black has nothing to fear.

(*c*) 9 P×P, the most logical reply, but Black answers "in the grand manner": 9 .... P—KB4; 10 Kt—B3, Kt—Q2 (offering a second pawn!); 11 P—KR3, B—R4; 12 Kt×Kt, P×Kt; 13 B×P, Kt—B3, and Black, who will in any event recover one pawn, seizes the initiative.

9 Q—B2

A provocativ measure, intended to weaken the K field. If at once 9 Q—Kt3, P—QKt3; 10 P×P, B×P; 11 Q—B2 (and not 11 Q×B, on account of 11 .... B×P ch); 11 .... Kt—KB3; 12 B—KKt5, P—KR3, etc., Black would be safe from any loss in material.

9 ......   P—KB4
10 Q—Kt3

Now the double threat is effective, for if 10 .... P—QKt3; 11 P×P, B×P; 12 Q×B *with check*, and wins.

10 ......   P×P
11 Q×KtP   P—B3
12 B×Kt

Clearly not 12 Q×R, because of 12 .... Q—B2, shortly winning the adventurous Queen.

12 ......   P×B
13 Kt—Kt5

Everything fits in beautifully.

13 ......   B—KB4

After 13 .... B—Q4, then equally 14 Kt—QB3.

14 Kt—QB3   Q—Q2

Seeking salvation in an arid ending. If 14 .... P—KR3; 15 KKt×P, B×Kt; 16 Kt×B, B×P ch; 17 K×B, Q—R5 ch; 18 K—Kt1, Q×Kt; 19 Q×R, Q—K2; 20 B—Q2, Q—QB2; 21 B—Kt4, R—Q1; 22 B—B5, and Black has no sort of compensation for his vanished Rook.

15 Q×Q   Kt×Q
16 KKt×KP

The pawn in dispute has fallen, and the rest is a question of technique.

16 ......   B—B2
17 R—K1   QR—Kt1
18 R—K2   Kt—Kt3
19 Kt—B5   B—Q3
20 KKt—K4   B—B2
21 Kt—B5

Returning to the fray, for if 21 Kt—Kt3, B—Q6.

21 ......   B—Q6
22 R—K3   B—B7

Black does not like to part with his two Bishops.

23 Kt—K6   R—B2
24 Kt×B   R×Kt
25 R—K2

Preparing an ingenious *sortie* by the Bishop.

25 ......   B—Q6
26 B—B4   B×R
27 B×R   R—K1
28 B×Kt   P×B
29 R—K1

Bringing about a promising ending, whereas 29 Kt×B, R×Kt; 33 R—Kt1, R—Q7, etc., would favour Black.

29 ......   B—R4
30 R×R ch   B×R
31 Kt—K4

Threatening 32 Kt—Q6. In the next phase of the game the Knight proves to be more effective than the Bishop.

31 ......   P—QKt4
32 P—QR3   B—Kt3
33 P—B3   K—B2
34 K—B2   K—K3
35 K—K3   P—R3
36 P—KKt4   K—Q4
37 Kt—B3 ch   K—Q3
38 P—B4

Using his pawn-majority on the K side,

whilst Black's pawn formation on the
Q side is depreciated in view of his doubled
pawns.

38	B—K1
39 P—B5	B—Q2
40 Kt—K4 ch	K—K2

If 40 .... K—Q4; 41 P—B6. Black
now would like to reduce the danger by
41 .... P—Kt3.

41 K—B4
A decisive gain in territory, giving access
to K5.

41	B—K1
42 K—K5	B—B2
43 P—KR4	B—Q4
44 P—Kt5	P×P
45 P×P	B—Kt1
46 P—Kt6	Resigns

For if 46 .... B—Q4; 47 P—B6 ch,
P×P ch; 48 Kt×P, B—K3; 49 P—Kt7,
and Black must give up his Bishop for the
passed pawn.

166

White	*Black*
ANDERSSEN	LÖWENTHAL

(London, 1851)

*An interesting game, in which two leading
tacticians of the good old days adapt their
manœuvres to the exigencies of positional play.*

1 P—K4	P—K4
2 Kt—KB3	Kt—KB3
3 Kt×P	P—Q3
4 Kt—KB3	Kt×P
5 Kt—B3	

A continuation recommended and practised

by Anderssen, whose chief concern was to
develop his pieces as rapidly as possible.

It was taken up later on, and had some
fleeting success at the beginning of this
century.

5 ......   P—Q4
An interesting counter-idea; Black is prepared eventually to sacrifice a pawn in order
to speed up his development.

Loss of time and territory would clearly
result from 5 .... Kt—KB3; 6 P—Q4,
P—Q4; 7 B—Q3. More rational is 5 ....
Kt×Kt, e.g. 6 KtP×Kt, B—K2; 7 P—Q4,
Castles, etc., with an even game, or
6 QP×Kt, B—K2; 7 B—Q3, Castles;
8 Castles, B—Kt5, and Black has nothing
to fear.

6 B—Kt5 ch
His desire to accelerate still further the
development of his pieces is to have the
opposite effect. If 6 B—Q3, P—KB4, etc.
But after the insistent continuation 6 Q—K2,
B—K2 (6 .... P—KB4; 7 P—Q3); 7 Kt×Kt,
P×Kt; 8 Q×P, Castles; and now neither
9 B—K2 nor 9 B—Q3 nor 9 P—Q4, R—K1,
etc., but, boldly, 9 B—B4, and White maintains his pawn with advantage.

6	P—B3
7 B—R4	B—QB4
8 Castles	Castles
9 B—Kt3	B—KKt5
10 P—Q4	B—Q3

Or 10 .... B×Kt; 11 Q×B, B×P;
12 Kt×Kt, P×Kt; 13 Q×P, and—*ceteris
paribus*—White has the theoretical advantage
of two well-placed Bishops.

11 Q—Q3
Skilful unpinning.

11 ......   Kt×Kt
If 11 .... B—KB4 (threatening to win the
exchange by 12 .... Kt—Kt6); 12 Q—K2.

12 P×Kt	Q—B3
13 Kt—K1	

He refrains from exposing his K side, but
at the cost of an appreciable loss of territory.

13	B—KB4
14 Q—B3	Q—Kt3

Black has taken the lead.

15 B—KB4	B—K5
16 Q—Kt3	B×B
17 Q×B	Kt—Q2
18 P—B3	B—B4
19 P—B4	

A bold conception, giving up the threatened pawn at QB2, in order at last to free
his Bishop.

19 ......   P × P

If 19 .... Kt—Kt3, White plays—not 20 P × P, P × P, and his Bishop remains shut in—but 20 P—B5, Kt—Q2; 21 P—B4, etc.

20 B × P	B × P
21 R—B2	B—B4
22 P—Kt4	B—K3
23 B—Q3	Q—B3
24 Q—K4	P—KKt3
25 Kt—Kt2	B—Q4
26 Q—B4	P—KKt4

Instead of playing, timidly, 26 .... Q × Q; 27 Kt × Q, Kt—Kt3, etc., Black himself complicates the position.

27 Q—Q2   K—R1

He now threatens 28 .... Q × QP.

28 B—B2   Kt—B4

An elegant evolution.

29 P—KR4	Kt—K3
30 R—Q1	P × P
31 Q—Q3	Q—Kt2

Black's position would be too strained after 31 .... Kt—Kt4, even though neither 32 P—B4 (32 .... Kt—K5) nor 32 Kt × P (32 .... Kt—R6 ch, followed by .... Q × Kt) would then be playable.

| 32 Kt × P | Kt—B5 |
| 33 Q—B1 | |

He has to prevent 33 .... Kt—R6 ch.

33 ......   B—K3

Planning activity.

Bold would be the transaction 33 .... B × RP; 34 B × P, Q × B; 35 R × B, and as 35 .... Q × Kt is inadmissible on account of 36 R—R2, the position of the disabled black King would be still worse.

| 34 R—R2 | P—KB4 |
| 35 Kt—Kt2 | |

This prevents 35 .... P × P.

| 35 ...... | Kt—Kt3 |
| 36 Q—Q3 | QR—Q1 |

Still not 36 .... P × P; 37 Q × Kt.

Now Black threatens 37 .... P—B4.

37 Q—K3	KR—K1
38 P × P	B × BP
39 B—K4	B × B
40 P × B	Kt—K4

Carrying on his equestrian exercises.

| 41 R—R3 | R—KKt1 |

Cards on the table! The wide-open KKt file is to be the main theatre of war.

| 42 Q—K2 | R—Q3 |
| 43 R—Q2 | |

He still cannot play 43 P × Kt, because of 43 .... R × R ch.

43 ......   Q—Q2

This again prevents 44 P × Kt, and attacks the KR.

44 Q—R5	Kt—Kt5
45 Q—QB5	QR—Kt3
46 Q—B3	Kt—B3

The game of thrust and parry continues.

47 R—K3

If 47 P—Q5, then vigorously 47 .... Q—Kt2, etc.

47 ......   Q—Kt2

A formidable trebling of the major pieces.

48 Q—Kt2   Kt—R4

Threatening a fourth attack on the hostile Knight; White's resistance now crumbles.

49 R—KR3

Or 49 K—R2, Kt—B5; 50 Kt × Kt, R—R3 ch; 51 Kt—R3, Q—Kt8 mate.

49	Kt—B5
50 R—R2	Kt × Kt
51 QR × Kt	P—B4

A thorough disorganisation (52 P—Q5, Q × Q).

52 P—K5   R × R ch

And Black wins

For after the pieces have been exchanged, there follows 55 .... P × P.

167

White	Black
GUNSBERG	*WEISS*

(New York, 1889)

The capture by the white Queen of a distant pawn enables Black to launch a powerful K side attack, first on the KKt and then on the KR file.

Black's decisive sacrifice (21 .... R × P) is a worthy and logical climax.

1 P—K4	P—K4
2 Kt—KB3	Kt—KB3
3 Kt × P	P—Q3
4 Kt—KB3	Kt × P
5 P—Q4	P—Q4

Disclosing his intention to maintain, as

far as possible, his Knight on its exposed outpost position; any other move, such as 5 .... B—K2 or 5 .... B—Kt5, would necessitate its early retreat.

6 B—Q3   Kt—QB3

Reserving the development of the KB at K2 or Q3, and of the QB at KKt5 or K3.

7 Castles   B—K2
8 R—K1

Nothing is gained by 8 P—B4.

8 ......   B—KKt5
9 P—B3

With the double mission of supporting the threatened QP and of increasing the range of White's Queen.

If 9 B×Kt, P×B; 10 R×P, B×Kt; 11 Q×B, Kt×P, with a slight advantage to Black.

If 9 P—B4, Kt—B3; 10 P×P, KKt×P; 11 Kt—B3, Castles; 12 B—K4, B—K3, and White's isolated QP is well and truly stopped.

9 ......   P—B4

Weakening but compulsory.

10 QKt—Q2

A solid continuation. An ingenious idea, due to the Danish analyst Dr. Krause, is 10 P—B4, this *advance by stages* being now more rational because of the more exposed formation of Black's K side.

10 ......   Castles
11 Q—Kt3

Relieving the pin and attacking at the same time. It would be more laborious to effect the unpinning of the Knight by 11 Kt—B1, followed by Kt—Kt3 and P—KR3.

11 ......   K—R1

Parrying at least the most serious threat.

12 Q×KtP

Hazardous! 12 Kt—B1 is required here.

12 ......   R—B3

Defending the QKt with a powerful threat: 13 .... R—Kt1; 14 Q—R6, Kt—Kt5, etc.

13 Q—Kt3   R—Kt1
14 Q—B2   R—KKt3

At express speed Black obtains a concentric K side attack.

15 P—QKt3   B—Q3
16 B—K2

In preparation for 17 Kt—B1.

16 ......   B—KR6
17 B—B1

If 17 P—Kt3, P—KR4, with fresh resources.

17 ......   Q—B3
18 P—Kt3   B×B
19 K×B   R—KB1

Threat of 20 .... P—B5, for if then 21 Kt×Kt, P×Kt; 22 Q×P, P×P, etc., and White is swamped.

20 Kt×Kt

An optimistic decision.

20 ......   BP×Kt

At a stroke, the pressure passes from the KKt to the KB file.

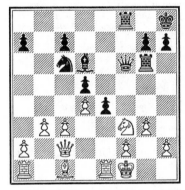

21 Kt—R4   R×P

A superb sacrifice, shattering White's lines of defence.

22 P×R   B×P
23 K—Kt2

There is nothing better. If 23 Kt—Kt2, B×P, etc.

23 ......   B×Kt
24 B—K3   Q—B6 ch
25 K—R2   B—K2
26 K—Kt1   R—B3
27 K—B1   Q—Kt5

In an instructive manner he keeps the opposing King in a trap.

28 Q—Q1

Trying to force a passage for his King.

28 ......   R—B6
29 R—B1   Q—R6 ch
Resigns

For if 30 K—K2, R×B ch; 31 P×R, Q—Kt7 mate, and if 30 K—Kt1, R—B3, to be followed by 31 .... R—Kt3 ch.

168

White	Black
LASKER	PILLSBURY

(St. Petersburg, 1896)

A specimen of the art of attacking. Its three main constituents, creating tension— latent or actual—temperament, and the fullest exploitation of the mobility of pieces, are finely illustrated here.

Pillsbury it was who brought the Petroff Defence back to favour by endowing it with some fresh aggressive turns. Amongst the attacking players of all time he occupies a place of honour.

A remarkable feature of the game is the activity of Black's KKt. After occupying an outpost position, the basic idea of the opening (4 .... Kt×P), and an elastic retirement (12 .... Kt—Kt4), it centralises (14 .... Kt—K3), moves forward magnificently (17 .... KKt×P), to end in a blaze of glory (19 .... Kt×P).

1 P—K4	P—K4
2 Kt—KB3	Kt—KB3
3 Kt×P	P—Q3
4 Kt—KB3	Kt×P
5 P—Q4	P—Q4
6 B—Q3	B—K2

The best means of maintaining the Knight at K5.

7 Castles	Kt—QB3

Black's last two moves can also be played in inverted order.

8 R—K1	B—KKt5
9 P—B3	P—B4
10 Q—Kt3	

A premature lateral attack, which Black refutes by—ignoring it.

10	Castles
11 B—KB4	

No useful purpose is served by "logical" continuations:

(*a*) 11 B×Kt, P×B; 12 R×P, B×Kt; 13 P×B, R×P, etc., with advantage to Black.

(*b*) 11 Q×P, R—B3; 12 Q—Kt3 (evading the threat 12 .... R—Kt1; 13 Q—R6, Kt—Kt5); 12 .... R—Kt1; 13 Q—B2, R—KKt3; 14 B—K2, B—Q3, and Black's counter-attack is in full cry.

(*c*) 11 QKt—Q2, K—R1, with an uneasy *in statu quo* position in the centre. The object of the text move is to throw the QBP into the fray before developing the QKt. Well-founded in principle, this plan encounters tactical difficulties.

11	B×Kt
12 P×B	Kt—Kt4

While White has wasted his time in fruitless demonstrations, Black has conjured up a very real attack on the K side.

13 K—Kt2

The King himself is forced to take a hand in the defence, for 13 B×Kt, B×B; 14 Q×P, R—B3; 15 Q—Kt3, B—B5, etc., would be depressing.

13	Q—Q2

An indirect defence of the QKt and QB pawns, for if 14 Q×KtP, Kt—K3; 15 B—QB1, R—Kt1; 16 Q—R6, R—B3, etc., with a surging attack.

14 Q—B2

He already has to change his plans. If 14 Kt—Q2, Kt—K3; 15 K—Kt3 (neither 15 B—Kt3 nor 15 B—K3 will serve on account of 15 .... P—B5, and after 15 B—K5, Kt×B, followed by 16 .... Kt—B5 ch, winning the other Bishop); 15 .... Kt×B; 16 K×Kt, B—Q3 ch, and wins.

14	Kt—K3
15 B—QB1	

Retreat all along the line.

15	B—Q3

While Black improves his position with every move.

16 Kt—Q2

If 16 B×P, R×B; 17 Q×R, Kt—B5 ch wins.

16	QR—K1
17 Kt—B1	Kt (K3)×P
18 Q—Q1	R×R
19 Q×R	

Thinking his greatest troubles over, whereas they are only beginning.

19	Kt×P

A sacrifice both brilliant and deep.

20 K×Kt	P—B5

Result: blockade. Threat: 21 .... Q—R6 ch.

21 Q—Q1

Allowing the King to make his way *via* K2 towards the better-guarded Q side. This journey can, however, be effected only by giving back the piece.

21	Kt—K4 ch
22 K—K2	

Or 22 K—Kt2, P—B6 ch; 23 K—R1, Q—R6; 24 Kt—K3, Kt—Kt5 (better than

24 .... Kt×B; 25 Q—Kt1, and White can still maintain a stubborn resistance); 25 Q—Kt1, Kt×P, and White is helpless.

22	Q—Kt5 ch
23 K—Q2	Q×Q ch
24 K×Q	Kt×B

On balance, Black, having recovered his piece, has now two extra pawns and an overwhelming position—a just reward for his masterly play.

The rest is a question of technique.

25 K—K2	Kt—K4
26 P—B3	R—K1
27 P—Kt3	Kt—Kt5 dis ch
28 K—Q2	Kt—K6
29 B—Kt2	Kt—Kt7

Preventing 30 R—K1, and threatening to win yet another pawn by 30 .... Kt—R5.

30 P—KR3	B—B4
31 Kt—R2	B—B7
32 P—B4	

In order at least to bring the Knight to K5 via KKt4, for if at once 32 Kt—Kt4, B—K8 ch; 33 K—Q3, P—KR4, driving back the white Knight.

| 32 ...... | P×P |
| 33 P×P | P—KR4 |

Completing the blockade.

Resigns
A splendid game.

169

| White | Black |
| TARRASCH | MARCO |

(Vienna, 1898)

A game of encircling manœuvres, in which White finally succeeds in breaching his opponent's battlements (26 Kt—K6).

Without any tangible mistakes on the part of Black, except that he pins his faith in too passive a defence, this game is one of the best achievements of the winner of this big tournament.

1 P—K4	P—K4
2 Kt—KB3	Kt—KB3
3 Kt×P	P—Q3
4 Kt—KB3	Kt×P
5 P—Q4	B—K2
6 B—Q3	Kt—KB3

Instead of supporting his outpost Knight by 6 .... P—Q4, Black, with the text move, concedes time and territory.

7 Castles	Castles
8 P—KR3	B—K3
9 P—B4	

The beginning of a local skirmish round Q5.

| 9 ...... | P—B3 |
| 10 Kt—Kt5 | |

A fine manœuvre.

| 10 ...... | Kt—R3 |

Rushing—*via* QB2—to the succour of his K3. For if 10 .... P—KR3; 11 Kt×B, P×Kt; 12 Q—K2 (aiming at the weakness at K6, whilst preventing 12 .... P—K4); 12 .... Q—Q2; 13 R—K1, K—B2; 14 Kt—B3, etc., Black's situation, with his King exposed, would remain critical.

| 11 Kt—QB3 | |

If 11 P—B4, Kt—QKt5, and if 11 Kt×B, P×Kt; 12 Q—K2, Kt—B2, and Black has adequate means of defence.

| 11 ...... | Kt—B2 |

Better would be, at this stage, 11 .... P—R3, in order to exchange White's Knight, or to force its retirement prior to the advance of the KBP.

| 12 P—B4 | |

An ambitious pawn.

| 12 ...... | P—KR3 |
| 13 Kt—B3 | |

He preserves his shock troops.

| 13 ...... | Q—B1 |
| 14 Q—B2 | |

Another localised struggle, this time for KB5. Premature would be 14 P—KKt4, and Black could fish in troubled waters by 14 .... B×P; 15 P×B, Q×P ch; 16 K—R1, etc.

| 14 ...... | R—Kt1 |
| 15 P—KB5 | |

Choking his opponent's game.

| 15 ...... | B—Q2 |
| 16 B—B4 | |

With his pieces ideally developed, White has a general, though no specific, threat.

| 16 ...... | P—QKt4 |

The counter-play which Black seeks to obtain requires too much time before it can achieve any concrete result.

17 P—QKt3	P—B4
18 P—Q5	P—Kt5
19 Kt—K2	P—QR4
20 P—Kt4	Kt—R2
21 P—KR4	

White's three musketeers become threatening.

21	Q—Q1

Obtaining at least a postponement of the hostile KKtP's advance.

22 B—Kt3	P—R5
23 K—R1	R—R1
24 QR—K1	Kt—K1

In order, at last, to mobilise his KB. But the cramped position of Black's forces brings retribution. Better would be 24 .... R—K1, followed by .... B—KB1.

25 Kt—B4	B—KB3

Or, e.g. 25 .... P—B3; 26 Kt—K1, B × Kt; 27 BP × P, P—B4 (the only move to save the KKt); 28 KB × P, and White is set for victory.

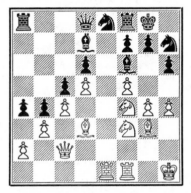

26 Kt—K6	

A very beautiful turn. If 26 .... P × Kt; 27 BP × P, P × P; 28 P × P, B—B1 (the only move to avoid the loss of two pieces); 29 B × Kt ch, K—R1; 30 P—Kt5, etc., with a speedy decision, which is why Black prefers to give up the exchange.

26	P × P
27 P × P	Q—Kt3
28 Kt × R	K × Kt
29 P—Kt5	

By this beautiful pawn sacrifice, White gains access to the enemy fortress. On the other hand, centralisation by 29 Q—K2, Q—Q1, etc., would have led to nothing.

29	P × P
30 P × P	Kt × P
31 Q—KR2	

Threatening only 32 Q—R8 mate.

31	K—Kt1
32 Kt × Kt	B × Kt
33 P—B6	

A fine *unmasking* advance.

33	P—Kt3
34 B × KtP	Resigns

170

White   *Black*

JANOWSKI   MARSHALL

(Match, Biarritz, 1912)

A win by Black, if only from the point of view of the sense of justice, which is inherent in the game of chess, has about it something comforting.

When such a win is effected by a whole series of problem-like moves, leading to a Queen sacrifice (12 .... Q × Kt) reminiscent of the famous Four Knights'—Paulsen-Morphy—it discloses the inexhaustible fund of æsthetic joy which chess contains.

1 P—K4	P—K4
2 Kt—KB3	Kt—KB3
3 Kt × P	P—Q3
4 Kt—KB3	Kt × P
5 P—Q4	P—Q4
6 B—Q3	B—Q3

An ancient idea, which the American champion took up with the addition of several bold innovations, and which he preferred to the everyday continuations 6 .... B—K2 and 6 .... Kt—QB3.

An over-hasty idea is 6 .... B—Kt5, after which the following bewildering sequel occurred in a game Thomas—A. R. B. Thomas, *Hastings*, 1937–8: 7 Castles, P—KB4 (7 .... Kt—QB3; 8 R—K1, P—B4; 9 P—B4, etc.); 8 P—B4, Kt—QB3; 9 Kt—B3 (more complicated than 9 P × P); 9 .... B × Kt; 10 P × B, QKt × P (what an affray! like a swarm of bees in the middle of the board); 11 P × Kt, QP × KP; 12 B × P, P × B; 13 R—K1, Kt—K3 (not 13 .... Kt—B6 ch; 14 Q × Kt); 14 Q—Kt4, K—B2; 15 Kt × P, B—K2; 16 B—B4, B—B3; 17 QR—Q1 (in spite of equal material, Black is lost); 17 .... P—KR4 (if 17 .... Q—QB1; 18 B × P, Q × B; 19 Kt—Q6 ch, etc., or 18 .... Kt × B; 19 R—Q7 ch, etc.); 18 Q—B5, P—KKt3; 19 Kt—Kt5 ch (a beautiful final stroke). Black resigns, for if 19 .... Kt×Kt; 20 R—Q7 ch, gaining the hostile Queen with check. A fine game by Sir George Thomas.

7 P—B4

More impatient than, first, 7 Castles, Castles; 8 P—B4, B—KKt5, with complications.

7 ...... Castles

Keeping up the tension, in preference to simplification by 7 .... B—Kt5 ch; 8 QKt—Q2, Kt×Kt; 9 B×Kt, Q—K2 ch; 10 Q—K2, Q×Q ch; 11 K×Q, B×B; 12 K×B, B—B3, etc.

8 P×P

Instead of this optimistic capture, a reinforcing move such as 8 Castles or 8 Kt—B3 is indicated.

8 ...... B—Kt5 ch
9 K—B1

The logical complement of the two preceding moves, which, however, demonstrates that they were premature. If 9 QKt—Q2, Kt×Kt; 10 B×Kt, R—K1 ch, and Black has a definite pull.

9 ...... Q×P
10 Q—B2 R—K1
11 Kt—B3

He appears to expect only 11 .... B×Kt; 12 P×B, when his centre would be rounded off nicely, and compensate him for the loss of castling.

11 ...... Kt×Kt
12 P×Kt

He rejoices in view of the threats 13 P×B and 13 B×P ch, but the position holds some magnificent resources.

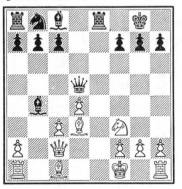

12 ...... Q×Kt

A bolt from the blue. This Queen's sacrifice had to be calculated far beyond its main variation, 13 P×Q, B—R6 ch; 14

K—Kt1, R—K8 ch; 15 B—B1, R×B mate, for the position holds many and varied possibilities for White.

13 P×B

Hoping to win a pawn after all, although it would have been better for him to lose one by 13 P—KR3, threatening 13 .... Q—Q4; 14 P×B, Q×P; 15 B—Kt2, Q×P; 16 B×P ch, K—R1; 17 B—Q3, with even chances.

13 ...... Kt—B3

A splendid continuation which, so to speak, changes his original idea (a disorganising sacrifice) to a new plan (an irruptive sacrifice).

14 B—Kt2

Here again 14 P—KR3 is better, or at least 14 B—Q2.

14 ...... Kt×KtP

Cards on the table! Of no value, evidently, would be 14 .... Q—R4; 15 P—QR3, etc.

15 B×P ch K—R1
16 P×Q

Accepting the challenge, for if, e.g. 16 Q—B4, B—R6; 17 R—KKt1, K×B; 18 P×B, Kt—Q6; 19 Q—B2, Q×RP ch; 20 R—Kt2, R—K5 (if 20 .... P—KKt3, then, not 21 K—Kt1, Kt—B5, etc., but 21 Q—B3, with the threat 22 P—Q5); 21 K—Kt1 (if 21 R—Q1, the same answer applies, 21 .... QR—K1); 21 .... QR—K1, and wins.

16 ...... B—R6 ch
17 K—Kt1 Kt×Q
18 B×Kt R—K7

After this irruption, the attack is in full swing.

19 R—QB1 QR—K1
20 B—B3 R (K1)—K6

Most ingenious, but simpler would be, as pointed out by Captain the Hon. A. J. Lowther, 9 .... R×B; 10 R×R, (10 R—K1, R×R ch; 11 B×R, R—B3;) 10 .... R—K3; etc.

21 B—Kt4

If 21 B—K4, R×QB, and if 21 P×R, R—Kt7 ch; 22 K—B1, R×B dis ch, followed by .... R×R ch and .... R×R.

21 ...... R×P (B6)
22 B—Q1 R—B3

Elegant to the end (23 B×R, R—Kt3 ch, followed by mate).

Resigns.

171

White	Black
CAPABLANCA	KOSTITCH

(Match, Havana, 1919)

This "war of attrition" contains numerous instructive moments.

1	P—K4	P—K4
2	Kt—KB3	Kt—KB3
3	Kt × P	P—Q3
4	Kt—KB3	Kt × P
5	Q—K2	

In spite of its apparent simplicity, the text move is in no way inferior to 5 P—Q4, for it immediately seeks to undermine the enemy outpost. Frequently this continuation (prepared by that great apostle of simplification, Dr. Lasker) leads to the exchange of Queens, without, however, affording Black complete emancipation.

5	......	Q—K2

Compulsory, because of 6 P—Q3.

6 P—Q3

Dislodgement! Another plan could be: 6 P—Q4, Kt—QB3; 7 B—K3, B—Q2 (7 .... B—Kt5 is more aggressive); 8 QKt—Q2, Castles; 9 P—Q5, Kt × Kt; 10 K × Kt, Kt—Kt1; 11 B × P, P—QKt3 (suicide, but after 11 .... Q × Q; 12 B × Q, P—QKt3; 13 B × Kt, and White is a pawn ahead); 12 Q—R6 ch, Kt × Q; 13 B × Kt mate.

6	......	KKt—B3
7	B—Kt5	

With the awkward threat of spoiling Black's pawn formation by 8 B × Kt, P × B, etc.

7	......	Q × Q ch

The exchange fails to bring Black the desired relief. But 7 .... B—Kt5 or 7 .... Kt—B3 would also have their drawbacks. Relatively best is 7 .... B—K3; 8 Kt—B3, P—B3, and Black holds his own.

8	B × Q	B—K2
9	Kt—B3	B—Q2

He must prevent the diversion 10 Kt—Kt5.

10 Castles KR

A more rapid development of the artillery on the centre files would result from 10 Castles QR, but White wants to get to work solidly if slowly.

10	......	Castles
11	KR—K1	Kt—B3
12	P—Q4	KR—K1

A stubborn battle commences for the only open file.

13	B—Kt5	P—QR3
14	B—QR4	P—Kt4
15	B—Kt3	Kt—QR4
16	R—K3	P—B3
17	QR—K1	K—B1
18	B—KB4	

The threat is (e.g. after 18 .... Kt—R4) 19 R × B, R × R; 20 B × QP, R—K1; 21 R × R, R × R; 22 Kt—K5, and White must win.

18	......	Kt—Kt2
19	P—KR3	P—R3
20	B—R2	B—Q1
21	R × R ch	B × R
22	P—QR4	

Having conquered the open K file, White begins to take an interest in other sectors.

22	......	P—B4
23	Kt—K4	Kt × Kt

If, first, 23 .... P—B5, then—also first— 24 Kt × QP, P × B; 25 Kt × Kt, etc., to White's advantage.

24 B—Q5

Very skilful, this intermediary manœuvre.

24	......	R—R2
25	B × KKt	B—K2
26	P × KtP	P × KtP
27	P × P	P × P
28	B—Kt8	R—R1
29	B—Kt3	R—R2
30	B—Kt8	

A repetition of moves to gain time "on the clock."

30	......	R—R1
31	B—Kt3	R—R2
32	Kt—K5	Kt—Q1
33	P—Kt3	Kt—K3
34	B—Q5	Kt—Q5
35	P—QB3	Kt—B4
36	B—R2	P—Kt5
37	P—Kt4	Kt—Q3
38	P—QB4	R—R6
39	R—K3	Kt—B1
40	B—Kt7	Kt—R2
41	B—Q5	P—B3
42	Kt—B3	Kt—B3
43	Kt—R4	Kt—Q5
44	Kt—B5	

Black's every attempt is frustrated.

44	Kt × Kt
45 P × Kt	B—Q2
46 B—K4	R—R3
47 R—Q3	B—B3
48 B × B	R × B
49 K—Kt2	

Now that the battlefield is cleared, manœuvring will be superseded by active advances.

Black's disadvantage consists in the fact that he has two weaknesses at his QB4 and KKt2, whereas White is vulnerable only at his QKt3.

49	R—R3
50 K—B3	R—R7
51 B—Kt3	K—K1

A more stubborn resistance is offered by 51 .... R—R2, guarding his second rank, and .... K—B2, to be followed by .... P—Kt3, relieving the blockade.

52 B—B4	R—R6
53 B—K3	R—R8
54 K—Kt4	R—R2

In chess, as in life, the right perception often comes too late.

55 K—R5	K—B2
56 R—Q5	R—R6

Seeking salvation in counter-play, for if 56 .... R—B2; 57 P—R4 (relying on *Zugzwang*); 57 .... B—B1; 58 R—Q8, B—K2; 59 R—QR8, and Black must, one way or another, let go.

57 R—Q7	K—K1
58 R—Q3	K—B2
59 P—R4	R—R7
60 R—Q5	R—R4
61 R—Q7	K—K1
62 R—Q3	K—B2
63 R—Q5	

Señor Capablanca has composed a *Zugzwang Symphony*! If 63 .... K—K1; 64 K—Kt6, and if 63 .... B—B1; 64 R—Q7 ch, B—K2; 67 R—B7, and still the black King has to give up the control of his KKt3!

63	R—R6
64 B × BP	B × B
65 R × B	R × P

Numerically even, but the active position of White's King and Rook decides the day.

66 R—B7 ch	K—B1
67 K—Kt6	R—KB6
68 R—B7 ch	K—K1
69 R × KtP	R—B5
70 P—R5	R × QBP
71 K × RP	K—B1
72 R—Kt7	R—Kt5
73 P—B3	

Challenging a decision.

73	R—Kt4
74 R × P	K—B2

Clearly not 74 .... R × P; 75 K—Kt6, R—Kt4 ch; 76 K × P, winning at once.

75 R—Kt4	

In a subtle manner White frees his King.

75	R × P
76 P—B4	R—R4
77 R—Kt7 ch	K—B1
78 R—Kt7	P—B4
79 K—Kt6	R—R3 ch
80 K × P	R—R4 ch
81 K—Kt4	R—R3
82 K—Kt5	R—QB3
83 P—B5	K—Kt1
84 P—B6	R—B8
85 R—Kt7 ch	K—B1
86 P—R6	Resigns

A victory of logic and nerves.

172

White	Black
PARIS	BERNE

(By correspondence 1921–2)

This lively game shows very clearly that, all things being equal, the attacker has the better practical chances.

1 P—K4	P—K4
2 Kt—KB3	Kt—KB3
3 P—Q4	

Steinitz's recommendation.

3	P × P

After 3 .... Kt × P, the continuation 4 B—Q3, P—Q4; 5 Kt × P, B—Q3; 6 Castles, Castles; 7 P—QB4 compels Black to break the symmetry, ensuring White's superiority, e.g.:

(a) 7 .... P—QB3; 8 Q—B2, with advantage to White.

(b) 7 .... P—QB4 (trying to keep up imitation to the end); 8 P × QP, P × P; 9 B × Kt, B × Kt; 10 B × P ch, and White is first in bringing in the harvest.

(c) 7 .... Kt—QB3 (this attempt to rely on counter-play by pieces is due to C. H. O'D. Alexander, who tried it not without success on various occasions); 8 P—B4 (the only move by which White can keep up his prerogative); 8 .... Kt × P (or 8 .... P—B3;

9 Kt×Kt, P×Kt; 10 P—QB5, B—K2;
11 P—B5, etc., with advantage to White);
9 B×Kt, B×Kt; 10 B×P ch, K×B;
11 P×B, and White is at the helm.

It may be mentioned that 3 .... P—Q3
brings about a well-known position of the
Philidor Defence.

4 P—K5

Again, 4 B—QB4 leads into a variation
of the *King's Bishop's Opening.*

4 ......   Kt—K5
5 Q×P

Much more artificial would be 5 Q—K2,
B—Kt5 ch; 6 K—Q1.

5 ......   P—Q4
6 P×P e. p.   Kt×QP
7 B—Q3

Against 7 B—Kt5, a fine retort is 7 ....
Kt—B3 (better than 7 .... P—KB3;
8 B—KB4, Kt—B3; 9 Q—Q2); 8 Q—B3
(or 8 Q—K3 ch, B—K2); 8 .... P—B3;
9 B—KB4, B—Kt5, etc., with equal chances.

7 ......   Kt—B3
8 Q—KB4   B—K2
9 Castles   B—K3
10 Kt—B3   Castles
11 P—QKt3   B—B3

Here 11 .... Kt—K1, with 12 ....
B—Q3 to follow, is preferable.

12 B—Kt2   Q—B1
13 QR—Q1   B—Kt5
14 KR—K1   QB×Kt
15 Q×QB   Kt—Kt5
16 R—K3

Threatening 17 B×P ch, K×B; 18 Q—R5
ch, K—Kt1; 19 R—R3, etc.

16 ......   Kt×B
Should this spell salvation?

17 Kt—Q5

A very fine idea, by which White secures
at least a draw.

17 ......   Kt×B
18 Kt×B ch   K—R1

In case of 18 .... P×Kt; 19 Q×BP, the
sequel could be:

(a) 19 .... Q—Kt5 (erroneous); 20 R—Q4
(but not at once 20 R—Kt3, on account of
20 .... Q×R, followed by .... Kt×R,
and White must take recourse to a perpetual check); 20 .... Q—Kt3; 21 R—Kt3,
KR—K1; 22 K—B1, R—K3; 23 Q—B4,
QR—K1; 24 Q—B1, and White wins.

(b) 19 .... Kt—B4 (sagacious);
20 R—Kt3 ch (if 20 R—Q5, R—Q1); 20 ....
Kt×R; 21 Q—Kt5 ch, K—R1; 22 Q—P6 ch,
etc., with perpetual check.

19 R—Q5

Saving the threatened Rook and preventing the counter 19 .... Q—B4.

19 ......   P—KR3
20 P—KKt4   Q—Q1
21 P—Kt5   R—KKt1
22 Q—R5   Q—KB1
23 Kt×R   R—K1
24 Kt×P   P×Kt
25 Q×P ch   K—Kt1
26 Q×Q ch   Resigns

The QKt is cut off and white's passed
pawn wins easily.

173

White	Black
JANOWSKI	PILLSBURY

(London, 1899)

*A game remarkable chiefly for the fierceness
with which both contestants play for a win,
ever creating new complications and disdaining
measures of safety.*

*Finally, White's astute 39 B—B6, and this
Bishop's activity on the long diagonal, decide
the issue.*

1 P—K4   P—K4
2 Kt—QB3   Kt—KB3
3 Kt—B3   B—Kt5

Instead of the *Four Knights' Game* (3 ....
Kt—B3), Black plays the *Russian Three
Knights' Game,* and assumes greater lia-
bilities.

4 Kt×P

As Black will soon, and without difficulty, recover his pawn, the continuations 4 Kt—Q5 or 4 B—B4 are to be recommended.

4 ......   Castles

He is in no hurry to win back his pawn, which he could do by 4 .... Q—K2 (and not 4 .... B×Kt; 5 QP×B, Kt×P, because of 6 Q—K2).

5 B—K2

A wise decision. 5 P—Q3 would be dangerous, because of 5 .... P—Q4, sounding the attack.

5 ......   P—Q3

More useful than 5 .... R—K1; 6 Kt—Q3, B×Kt; 7 QP×B, Kt×P; 8 Castles, and White is slightly ahead in development.

6 Kt—B3	B×Kt
7 QP×B	Kt×P
8 Castles	Kt—Q2
9 R—K1	QKt—B3

Black has established the *liaison* between his forces and has achieved equality.

10 B—Q3	Kt—B4
11 B—KKt5	P—KR3
12 B—R4	B—Kt5
13 P—KR3	Kt×B
14 Q×Kt	B×Kt
15 Q×B	P—KKt4

This weakening of the King's field is compulsory, in order to avoid greater ills. But as the material is much reduced, Black has good hopes of minimising the risks of this advance.

16 B—Kt3	Kt—Q2
17 Q—B5	

A manœuvre which restricts Black's position (by preventing 17 .... P—KB4) and furthers his own mobility (allowing the advance of his KBP).

Nothing good would come of 17 Q×P, R—Kt1; 18 Q×RP, R×P, etc.

17	K—Kt2
18 QR—Q1	R—K1
19 P—KB4	R×R ch
20 R×R	Kt—B1
21 P—KR4	

Ingenious.

21	Q—Q2

If 21 .... P×RP; 22 B—B2, P—B4; 23 Q—Kt4 ch, and White has the upper hand.

22 Q—Q3	P×RP
23 B×P	Kt—Kt3
24 B—B2	P—KB4

Obstreperous! But neither 24 .... Kt×P

(25 Q—Q4 ch) nor 24 .... P—QB4 (25 B×P) is playable.

25 P—B4	K—R2

Seriously threatening 26 .... Kt×P.

26 Q—KB3	R—KKt1
27 K—R2	P—Kt3

Much more comfortable, if equality were his aim, would be 27 .... Q—B3, etc., but he has far more ambitious intentions.

28 P—KKt3	P—QR4
29 Q—Q5	

Fighting for territory.

29	R—KB1
30 B—Q4	

The Bishop covers vast territory, and as there is a concrete threat of 31 B—B3, followed by Q—Q4 and eventually R—K6, Black sees himself compelled to take precautionary measures.

30	Q—B2
31 Q—B6	R—KKt1
32 Q—Q5	

Changing his mind. For now Black, by himself exchanging Queens, would undouble White's pawns and leave his remaining two pieces in a dominating position.

32	R—KB1
33 P—R4	

Powerful strategy! Black's pieces are under *Zugzwang* in the middle of the board, e.g. 33 .... Q—Q2; 34 P—B5, etc., and if 33 .... K—Kt1; 34 R—K6.

33	P—R4
34 P—Kt3	P—R5

Alea jacta est! The contest takes a new turn by the clearance of the KKt file. But better would be 34 .... Q×Q; 35 P×Q, and only now 35 .... P—R5.

35 Q—B3	K—R3

He must prevent 36 Q—R5 ch, K—Kt1; 37 P×P, etc. If 35 .... P×P ch; 36 K×P, K—Kt1 (36 .... R—KKt1; 37 Q—R5 mate); 37 Q—R5, etc., working now on three files (KR, KKt, K).

36 P×P

Well and truly captured, for if 36 .... Kt×RP; 37 Q—Kt3, and the end is near.

36	R—KKt1
37 R—KKt1	

The pressure on the KKt file proves decisive.

37	Kt—B1

Indeed, if 37 .... Kt×RP; 38 Q—R3, Q—R4; 39 R×R, and White wins as he likes.

38 R—Kt5   Kt—K3
Is it safety?

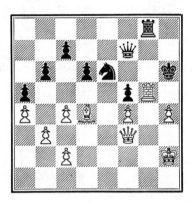

39 B—B6
A magnificent manœuvre, based on the

motif of the interdependence of squares
(39 .... Q × B; 40 Q—R5 mate).

39 ......   Kt—Kt2
If 39 .... Kt × R; 40 BP × Kt ch, K—R2
(or 40 .... K—Kt3; 41 P—R5 ch, K—R2;
42 Q × P ch, etc.); 41 Q × P ch, R—Kt3;
42 P—R5, and wins.

40 Q—Q5
The remainder is very incisive.

40 ......   Q—K1
41 Q—Kt2   Q—B2
42 B × Kt ch   R × B
43 R × R   Q × R
44 Q—Kt5 ch
The final "point."

44 ......   K—R2
45 Q × P ch   K—R1
46 Q—R5 ch   K—Kt1
47 Q—KKt5   Resigns.

11. GRECO'S COUNTER-GAMBIT

174

White   *Black*

MAYET   HANSTEIN

(Berlin, 1837)

Regardless of the safety of his King (as already shown by his second move), Black's play leads to a raging and tearing fight (13 B×P).

1 P—K4   P—K4
2 Kt—KB3   P—KB4

Intending to reply to 3 P×P with 3 .... P—K5, but White has a far more troublesome continuation.

3 Kt×P

With the direct threat 4 Q—R5 ch, etc.

3 ......   Q—B3

Attack and defence at the same time.

4 P—Q4   P—Q3
5 Kt—B4   P×P
6 Kt—B3

A new actor appears on the scene, threatening 7 Kt×KP or 7 Kt—Q5. Against 6 Kt—K3 one can recommend 6 .... Kt—B3; 7 Kt—Q5, Q—B2, etc.

6 ......   Kt—K2

Cumbersome. 6 .... P—B3 would also be awkward because of 7 P—Q5. But the defence could be strengthened by 6 .... Q—Kt3.

7 P—Q5

A mistake would be 7 Kt×KP, on account of 7 .... Q—K3; 8 Q—K2, P—Q4.

7 ......   Q—Kt3
8 P—KR3   P—KR4

To be able to play 9 .... B—B4 without having to fear 9 P—KKt4.

9 B—B4   B—B4

At once 9 .... P—R3 would be more prudent, for after the text move White could also have played 10 Kt—Kt5, e.g. 10 .... Kt—R3; 11 QKt×QP ch, P×Kt; 12 Kt×P ch, etc., or 10 .... K—Q1; 11 Kt×BP, K×Kt; 12 Kt×P, etc., bringing fire and sword to the black King's position.

10 Q—Q4   P—R3
11 P—QR4

Preventing 11 .... P—Kt4.

11 ......   Kt—Q2
12 Castles   QKt—B3

This plausible move allows the storm to break. If 12 .... Q—B3; 13 Kt×P, and if 12 .... Castles; 13 Q—R7, followed by 14 P—QKt4, etc. The black King should therefore have sought safety on the opposite wing, 12 .... K—B2.

13 B×P

A telling sacrifice. The black King's defences now tumble like a house of cards.

13 ......   P×B
14 Kt×P ch   K—Q2
15 Kt×KtP

Obtaining a third pawn—to say nothing of cumulative threats—for the piece sacrificed.

15 ......   Kt—B1

To minimise the effect of 16 Kt—B5 ch (or first, 16 Q—Kt6).
But the position is no longer tenable, e.g. 15 .... R—B1; 16 Q—R7, R—B2; 17 Kt—B5 ch.

16 P—Q6   K—K1

To be followed up by 17 .... Kt—Q2. If 16 .... Q—B2; 17 Q—K5.

17 Q—K5 ch   K—Q2

A homeless King. If 17 .... K—B2; 18 B—B4 ch.

18 B—Kt5 ch

A beautiful final sacrifice.

18 ......   P×B
19 Q×P ch   K—K3
20 Kt—Q8 mate

175

White   *Black*

SPIELMANN   NIMZOWITSCH

(Semmering, 1926)

Here is a game of the greatest possible interest, from both the theoretical and the sporting point of view.
It was the first occasion on which so hazardous an opening was adopted in an important international tournament, and the

first prize depended on the result. Black was very nearly successful (17 .... Kt—Kt5, instead of 17 .... QR—QB1, as played in the game), and—as is the fate of most pioneers in every field—he became the victim of his own courage.

1 P—K4	P—K4
2 Kt—KB3	P—KB4
3 Kt×P	Q—B3
4 P—Q4	P—Q3

At once 4 .... P×P is playable.

5 Kt—B4	P×P
6 Kt—B3	Q—Kt3

Another idea is 6 .... B—B4, e.g. 7 Kt—K3, P—B3, etc., or 7 Kt—Q5, Q—B2, etc., or 7 Kt—Kt5, Kt—QR3, etc.

7 P—Q5

Of little value. Other attempts, such as 7 Kt—K3, Kt—KB3, etc., or 7 B—B4, Kt—KB3; 8 Kt—K3, B—K2, can easily be met. The best practical chances are afforded by the trenchant continuation 7 P—B3, P×P; 8 Q×P, etc.

7	Kt—KB3
8 B—K3	B—K2
9 Q—Q4	Castles

Having completed his mobilisation on the K side and supported his exposed KP, Black has thus solved the problem of the opening in a satisfactory manner.

10 Kt—Q2   P—B4

Seeking to obtain the initiative, even at the cost of a pawn.

The desire to maintain the defence of the contentious pawn by 10 .... B—B4 would be risky, e.g. 11 P—KR3, P—KR4; 12 Castles, followed by B—K2 and P—KKt4, and the KKt file is in danger.

11 P×P e.p.

If 11 Q—B4, QKt—Q2, followed by .... Kt—K4, with an excellent game for Black.

11	Kt×P
12 Q—B4 ch	K—R1
13 Castles	

Evidently not 13 KKt×P, P—Q4; 14 Kt×P, Q×Kt, and in this affray White has lost a piece.

13	B—Kt5
14 P—B3	P—Q4

Very aptly played. Without imagination, however, would be 14 .... P×P; 15 P×P, B—B4; 16 R—Kt1, and White assumes the offensive.

15 Kt×QP	Kt×Kt
16 Q×KKt	P×P
17 P×P	

A critical moment. White has gained a pawn, but his position is precarious.

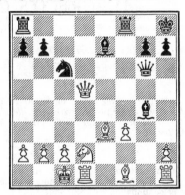

17 ....   QR—B1

In order to threaten (e.g. after 18 P×B) 18 .... Kt—Kt5, but in playing simply 17 .... Kt—Kt5 at once; 18 Q—Kt3, P—QR4 (threatening 19 .... P—R5), Black could have kept his adversary on the *qui-vive*.

If, however, Black is satisfied with an equal game he could achieve this easily, and even elegantly, by 17 .... Q×P ch; 18 K×Q, Kt—Kt5 ch; 19 K—Kt1, Kt×Q, etc.

The text move affords White a breathing-space, of which he will take advantage in an energetic manner.

18 B—Q3

And not 18 P×B, by reason of 18 .... Kt—Kt5; 19 Q—K4, R×P ch; 20 K—Kt1, R×Kt dis ch; etc.

18 ......   B—KB4

Compulsory liquidation.

19 B×B	R×B
20 Q—B4	

Still preventing 20 .... Kt—Kt5.

20	P—Kt4
21 Q—KKt4	Q—B2
22 KR—Kt1	

By skilful manœuvring White has de-vitalised Black's threats and has himself obtained a considerable attack.

22	Kt—Kt5
23 P—B3	Kt×P ch
24 K—Kt1	P—Kt5

Desperate efforts. Worse still would be

24 .... Kt×P ch; 25 P×Kt, R×QBP, because of 26 B—Q4.

25 B—Q4	B—Kt4
26 P—QB4	P—Kt6
27 Kt—K4	Q—Kt3
28 Q×B	

This sacrifice of the Queen is decisive.

28	R×Q
29 R×R	Q—B2
30 Kt—Q6	

Instead of the undefined continuation 30 R×P, Q×R; 31 B×Q ch, K×B, White forces matters in an elegant manner.

| 30 ...... | Q×KBP |

Black's threats are very serious, but it is White's turn to speak.

31 B×P ch	K—Kt1
32 B—K5 dis ch	K—B1
33 R—B5 ch	Resigns.

176

| *White* | *Black* |
| TRIFUNOVIC | APSCHENEEK |

(Stockholm, 1937)

One of those tragedies which are apt to happen when a King, unable to castle, becomes the object of a King-hunt across the board. A modern "Fegatello."

1 P—K4	P—K4
2 Kt—KB3	P—KB4
3 Kt×P	Q—B3
4 Kt—B4	P×P
5 Kt—B3	Q—KKt3
6 P—Q3	

Undermining the enemy outpost.

| 6 ...... | B—Kt5 |

Clearly fatal would be the quest of a pawn by 6 .... P×P; 7 B×P, Q×P; 8 Q—R5 ch, P—Kt3 (or 8 .... K—Q1; 9 B—K4); 9 Q—K5 ch, with 10 B—K4, and wins.

| 7 P×P | Q×P ch |
| 8 Kt—K3 | |

Vacating a good square for the Bishop and guarding the KKtP.

| 8 ...... | B×Kt ch |

Hastening to spoil White's pawn formation before he can play 9 B—Q2.

| 9 P×B | Kt—KB3 |
| 10 B—B4 | |

Preventing Black from castling, and threatening to obtain a decisive advantage after 11 Castles, followed by R—K1.

| 10 ...... | P—B3 |

He hopes to close the critical diagonal by 11 .... P—Q4, which attempt will be brilliantly refuted.

| 11 Castles | P—Q4 |

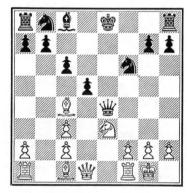

| 12 Kt×P | |

This fine sacrifice opens up the game.

| 12 ...... | Q×B |
| 13 R—K1 ch | |

Far more convincing than 13 Kt—B7 ch, K—B2; 14 Kt×R, Kt—R3.

| 13 ...... | K—B2 |
| 14 Kt×Kt | |

Black's last defending piece disappears.

| 14 ...... | K×Kt |

After 14 .... P×Kt there follows mate in three by 15 Q—R5 ch, etc. Black would last a little longer after 14 .... B—B4.

| 15 Q—Q6 ch | B—B3 |

After 15 .... K—B2 there is a mate in two, and after 15 .... K—B4 a mate in three.

| 16 B—Kt5 ch | |

The black King's helpless position is now obvious.

| 16 ...... | K×B |
| 17 R×B | Kt—Q2 |

Trying at least to prevent the fatal check at K5. If 17 .... K—R4; 18 Q—K5 ch, P—Kt4; 19 Q×R, Q×R; 20 Q×P ch,

winning the Queen (20 .... Q—R3;
21 P—Kt4 ch, or 20 .... K—Kt5;
21 Q—R3 ch).

18 Q × Kt   Q × BP
19 P—B4 ch   K—R4
Or 19 .... K × P; 20 R—B1 ch, K—Kt4;
21 Q—K7 ch, etc.

20 R—K5 ch   K—R3
21 R—R5 ch
Played with *éclat*. Black resigns.

177

White	Black
KOZELEK	ELISKASES

(By correspondence, 1928–9)

*In this game we see a defence of extremely
rare occurrence. But Black succeeds in
grasping the initiative and putting the K file
on fire before White has had time to prepare
for castling. The result is exciting and
decisive.*

1 P—K4   P—K4
2 Kt—KB3   P—Q4
This defence, which might be termed a
Centre Counter Deferred, is not without
vigour.
After 2 .... P—KB3 (the *Damiano
Defence*), the continuation 3 Kt × P, Q—K2;
4 Kt—KB3 ensures for White a considerable advantage in development.

3 P × P
Best. If 3 Kt × P, B—Q3.

3 ......   P—K5
Gaining territory. Black would encounter
much trouble after 3 .... Q × P; 4 Kt—B3,
Q—K3 (preventing 5 B—B4); 5 B—Kt5 ch,
B—Q2; 6 Castles, etc.

4 Q—K2   Kt—KB3
Continuing in Gambit style. After 4 ....
Q × P; 5 Kt—B3, etc., or 4 .... Q—K2;
5 Kt—Q4, Kt—KB3; 6 Kt—QB3, Q—K4;
7 Kt—B3, Q—K2; 8 Kt—KKt5, B—B4;
9 Q—Kt5 ch, etc., White secures a considerable advantage.

5 Q—Kt5 ch
Instead of this unlucky diversion, which
only promotes Black's development, the continuation 5 Kt—B3, B—K2; 6 Kt × P,
Kt × P; 7 Kt—B3, Kt—Kt3, etc., would
have led to a satisfactory position, although
one requiring patience.

5 ......   P—B3
6 P × P   P × P
7 Q—K5 ch   B—K2
8 Kt—Kt5   QKt—Q2
9 Q—B4   Castles
Black has already completed the first stage
of his mobilisation while White is wasting
the energy of two of his pieces around
Black's KP.
Black's actual threat is 10 .... Kt—Q4.

10 Kt × KP
Here again White cannot bring out
another piece, e.g. 10 B—B4, Kt—Q4;
11 B × Kt, B × Kt, followed by .... P × B,
winning a piece.

10 ......   Kt—Q4
11 Q—B3   R—K1
Black has two pawns less, but his position
is dominating.

12 P—Q3   Kt—K4
An ancient *motif*: the *Queen-hunt*.

13 Q—Kt3
A full retreat by 13 Q—Q1 is imperative,
but even then White's position remains precarious after 13 .... B—Kt5 ch, etc.

13 ......   B—R5
Unmasking the vital file without delay.

14 B—Kt5
The only move to save the Queen.

14 ......   B × B
15 Q × B
Salvation of the Queen—perdition of the
King!

15 ......   Q × Q
16 Kt × Q   Kt—B6 db ch
Illustrating once again the power of the
double check.

17 K—Q1   R—K8 mate
Q.E.D.

12. CENTRE GAME AND DANISH GAMBIT

178

White *Black*

FROM   NEUMANN

(Paris, 1867)

The choice of an aggressive opening (as here) does not secure in all circumstances a monopoly of aggressiveness for the first player. It rather tends to make the situation hazardous for both players. The slightest lack of precision or energy, any momentary relaxation, and the rôles of attacker and defender are reversed.

1 P—K4	P—K4
2 P—Q4	P×P
3 B—QB4	Kt—QB3

As White seems in no hurry to recapture the pawn, Black prepares to defend it as far as he can. For this purpose, 3 .... P—QB4 would be of doubtful value (4 Kt—KB3, Kt—QB3; 5 P—B3, with a strong initiative for White). And again, 3 .... B—B4; would be painful for Black (4 B×P ch, K×B; 5 Q—R5 ch, followed by Q×B). After the sally 3 .... Q—R5 White recaptures the pawn by 4 Q×P, protecting the threatened KP.

4 Kt—KB3	B—B4

At this stage 4 .... B—Kt5 ch would be too dangerous, on account of 5 P—B3, P×P; 6 Castles, P×P (the *Compromised Scotch Gambit*. More prudent, without, however, being more favourable, is 6 .... P—Q3 or 6 .... Q—B3); 7 B×P, Kt—B3; 8 Kt—Kt5, Castles; 9 P—K5, and Black's troubles are only beginning.

5 P—B3	Kt—B3

Let us develop! If, instead, 5 .... P×P; 6 Kt×P, P—Q3; 7 Q—Kt3, White's attack more than compensates for the pawn given up.

6 Castles

Heedless. With 6 P×P, B—Kt5 ch, White could have led into a sound variation of the *Giuoco Piano*.

6	Kt×P
7 P×P	P—Q4

Thanks to this interpolation, Black holds his own in the centre. The immediate retreat 7 .... B—K2 would be weak, on account of 8 P—Q5, with advantage to White.

8 R—K1	B—K2

By masking the K file, Black is able to maintain his extra pawn.

But if 8 .... B—Kt3, White advantageously recovers the piece after 9 B×P, Q×B; 10 Kt—B3, Q—QR4; 11 R×Kt ch.

9 B—Q3	P—B4
10 Kt—K5	Castles.

Safety first! Inferior would be 10 .... QKt×P, not only in view of 11 Q—R4 ch, Kt—B3; 12 Kt×Kt, Q—Q2; 13 B—QKt5, etc., but also because of 11 B×Kt, QP×B; 12 Q—R5 ch, P—Kt3; 13 Kt×P, etc.

11 Kt×Kt	P×Kt
12 Q—K2	B—Q3
13 P—B3	

White has now a bad game, and this move, which weakens the King's field, does not improve matters.

13	Q—R5
14 P—KKt3	

Or 14 P×Kt, B×P ch; 15 K—B1 (15 .... K—R1; 16 B—Kt6 dis ch, etc.); 15 .... P×P dis ch, and wins, or again, 14 P—KR3, Q—Kt6, etc.

The text move gives rise to a sacrifice which breaks up the King's field. (*Diagram. See p. 232.*)

14	Kt×P
15 P×Kt	Q×KtP ch
16 K—R1	B—Q2

He completes his mobilisation without allowing himself to be hurried. It would have been premature to have played 16 .... R—B3, e.g. 17 Q—K8 ch, B—B1; 18 Q—K2, R—Kt3; 19 R—B1, B—Q2 (or else 19 .... B—Q3; 20 Q—K8 ch, B—B1; 21 Q—K2, with a repetition of moves); 20 Q—R2, and White repels the attack!

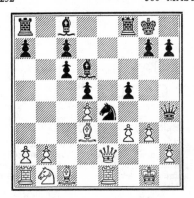

Position after 14 P—KKt3

17 B—K3	R—B3
18 R—Q1	R—Kt3
Resigns.	

179

White	Black
WINAWER	RIEMANN

(Berlin, 1881)

The most difficult part of an attack is the preliminary and laborious building up, after which the most beautiful variation appears only as the logical consequence of the preparatory work.

This is seen in this fine game; White opens the QR file by 20 P—Kt5 and 21 P—R5, and completes the co-ordination of his troops by castling as late as the 24th move.

1 P—K4	P—K4
2 P—Q4	P×P
3 Q×P	Kt—QB3
4 Q—K3	B—Kt5 ch
5 P—B3	

The simplest is 5 B—Q2, for if then 5 .... B×B ch; 6 Kt×B, which helps White's development.

5	B—R4

A better continuation is 5 .... B—K2, remaining at hand for the defence of the K side.

6 Q—Kt3	Q—B3

Playable also is 6 .... Kt—B3, after which 7 Q×KtP would be very hazardous because of 7 .... R—KKt1; 8 Q—R6, Q—K2, and Black assumes the offensive.

7 B—KB4	P—Q3
8 B—QKt5	B—Q2
9 Kt—Q2	P—KR3
10 Kt—B4	B—Kt3
11 P—KR4	

Preventing 11 .... P—Kt4.

11	KKt—K2
12 Kt—B3	Kt—Kt3
13 Kt×B	RP×Kt
14 B—K3	QKt—K4
15 B—K2	

Conserving the potential advantage of two well-posted Bishops.

15	B—B3
16 Kt—Q2	Castles QR
17 P—R5	Kt—B1
18 P—R4	

The signal for the attack.

18	Q—K2
19 P—Kt4	P—B3
20 P—Kt5	

The immediate advance of the neighbouring RP would be far less effective, e.g. 20 P—R5, P—QKt4; 21 P—R6, P—QKt3, and White cannot force open a file for his Rooks.

20	B—K1
21 P—R5	P×P
22 R×P	P—QKt3
23 R—R7	

Threatening 24 B×KtP.

23	Kt (K4)—Q2
24 Castles	

"Better late than never."

24	Kt—K3
25 KR—R1	

The arrival of the second Rook in the critical sector already threatens 26 R—R8 ch, Kt—Kt1 (26 .... K—Kt2; 27 R—R7 mate); 27 KR—R7 (with the threat 28 B×KtP); 27 .... B—Q2; 28 Kt—B4, and Black is lost.

25	Kt (K3)—B4
26 B—Kt4	Kt—K3
27 Kt—B4	Q—B2

Black's position is now hopelessly cramped.

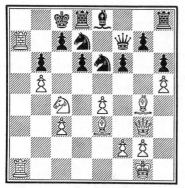

28 Q×P

An unexpected and brilliant sacrifice of the Queen, which Black cannot accept by reason of 28 .... P×Q; 29 Kt×QP ch, K—Kt1; 30 R—Kt7 mate.

On the other hand, White now threatens 29 B×Kt, followed by 30 Q×P mate.

An insufficient parry would be 28 .... Kt (Q2)—B4; (29 R—R8 ch, K—Kt2; 30 R—R7 mate) or 28 .... Kt—Kt1 (29 B×Kt ch).

28	P—KB4
29 R—R8 ch	Kt—Kt1
30 Kt×P ch	

And mate next move.

180

| White | Black |
| WINAWER | STEINITZ |

(Nuremberg, 1896)

This masterly game is an object-lesson in the technique of the attack.

The main factors it illustrates are as follows: Castling on the opposite side to the adversary, in order to render the contest as incisive as possible (7 Castles). Offer of the sacrifice of the KP, which opens files or diagonals (8 B—B4). Direct threat against the weak point KB7 (10 Q—B4). Soon afterwards the other critical square in the hostile camp, KR7, is also attacked (13 B—Q3). Exploiting the KR file (14 P—KR4). A fine "eliminating sacrifice" (16 R×Kt). A deflecting manœuvre, to bring away a hostile defensive piece (17 B—K4). Trenchant action of the two Bishops on two adjacent diagonals.

Opening of the KR file (19 P×P). The decisive threat (21 R×P ch, P×R; 22 Q×P mate) which enforces resignation.

1 P—K4	P—K4
2 P—Q4	P×P
3 Q×P	Kt—QB3
4 Q—K3	Kt—B3

Bold as it looks, this move is well worth playing, as is demonstrated by the following beautiful variation: 5 P—K5 (unwisely accepting the challenge); 5 .... Kt—KKt5; 6 Q—K4 (or 6 Q—K2, P—Q3, etc.); 6 .... P—Q4; 7 P×P e.p. dis ch, B—K3; 8 P×P, Q—Q8 ch; 9 K×Q, Kt×P ch, followed by .... Kt×Q, to Black's advantage.

| 5 Kt—QB3 | B—Kt5 |

More enterprising than 5 .... B—K2, whilst 5 .... Kt—QKt5 is of no value because of 6 Q—K2, followed by P—QR3.

| 6 B—Q2 | Castles |
| 7 Castles | R—K1 |

Threatening to win a pawn by 8 .... B×Kt; 9 B×B, R×P, etc.

| 8 B—B4 | |

Giving up, with good cause, the defence of the threatened pawn.

If 8 B—Q3 or 8 P—B3, then 8 .... P—Q4, with advantage to Black, and if 8 Q—Kt3, then—without fear—8 .... Kt×P; 9 Kt×Kt, R×Kt, and White no longer has sufficient compensation for the sacrificed pawn.

| 8 ...... | B×Kt |

Steinitz's dictum that "a sacrifice is best refuted by its acceptance" is here put to the test.

But much more prudent would be 8 .... P—Q3, followed by .... B—K3.

| 9 B×B | Kt×P |

It is clear that 9 .... R×P would be answered by 10 B×Kt.

| 10 Q—B4 | |

In exchange for his pawn White now has a direct attack on KB7 as well as the combined action of the well-posted "two Bishops."

10	Kt—B3
11 Kt—B3	P—Q3
12 Kt—Kt5	B—K3
13 B—Q3	P—KR3
14 P—KR4	Kt—Q4
15 B—R7 ch	K—R1

Not 15 .... K—B1, on the score of 16 Kt×B ch, R×Kt; 17 R×Kt.

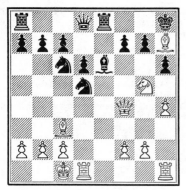

16 R×Kt

Eliminating, by this sacrifice, a trouble-some defender.

16 ......   B×R
17 B—K4

This retreat loses no time, as not only is the enemy Bishop attacked, but Black has also to attend to the threat 18 Kt×P ch, B×Kt; 19 Q×P ch, followed by mate.

17 ......   P—B3

There is more resistance in the following defence: 17 .... R×B (giving back the exchange); 18 Kt×R (as his own Queen is attacked, 18 Kt×P ch would be clumsy on account of 18 .... K—Kt1); 18 .... Kt—K4 (closing the long black diagonal).

But White has a brilliant rejoinder in 19 Kt×P, Q×Kt (or 19 .... P×Kt; 20 R—Q1, regaining the piece with advant-age); 20 B×Kt, Q—QB3; 21 R—Q1, B×RP (better, however, would be 21 .... B—K5; 22 P—QB3); 22 R—Q6, winning by force.

18 B×B   BP×Kt
19 P×P   Kt—K4
20 P—Kt6   Resigns

Because of the unanswerable threat 21 R×P ch, P×R; 22 Q×P mate.

181

White   Black
TARTAKOWER   RESHEVSKY
(Stockholm, 1937)

In the following game, Black succeeds in warding off with the greatest sang-froid his adversary's repeated assaults, whilst main- *taining a small advantage in material. He then proceeds, in spite of the power of resist-ance inherent in every position, to overcome all obstacles of force, time and space, and thus to exploit his advantage.*

The game is a good illustration of the style and strength of the present generation of grand masters.

1 P—K4   P—K4
2 P—Q4   P×P
3 Q×P   Kt—QB3
4 Q—K3   Kt—B3
5 Kt—QB3   B—Kt5

This pin (instead of the more reserved 5 .... B—K2) sets up an indirect pressure against the adverse KP (see Black's seventh move).

6 B—Q2   Castles
7 Castles   R—K1
8 B—B4   P—Q3

Instead of accepting the "Greek gift" (8 .... B×Kt; 9 B×B, Kt×P), the dangers of which were illustrated in the preceding game, Black wisely proceeds with his development.

9 Kt—B3   B—K3
10 B×B   R×B
11 Kt—KKt5   R—K1
12 P—B4

Abrupt, but necessary, for if 12 P—B3, P—Q4, whilst after the text move, 12 .... P—Q4 would be answered by 13 P—K5, P—Q5; 14 Q—R3, P×Kt; 15 B×P, etc., with a very strong attack for White.

12 ......   P—KR3
13 P—KR4   Q—B1

Again Black wisely refrains from taking the proffered piece, because after 13 .... P×Kt; 14 RP×P, B×Kt; 15 B×B, Kt×P; 16 Q—R3 (which manœuvre the text move is intended to forestall); 16 .... K—B1; 17 B×P ch, K—K2 (or 17 .... K×B; 18 Q—R6 ch, followed by mate); 18 KR—K1, Black's position would collapse.

14 Q—B3   K—B1

Even now acceptance of the sacrifice would be premature, e.g. 14 .... P×Kt; 15 RP×P, B×Kt; 16 B×B, Kt×P; 17 Q—R5, etc.

If 14 .... Q—Kt5; 15 Kt—Q5, Q×Q; 16 Kt×Q, Kt×Kt; 17 P×Kt, and White has eliminated the weakness at K4.

By the text move, providing a flight-square for the KKt, Black now threatens to con-fiscate the hostile Knight.

15 Kt—Q5

The best practical chance for White consisted in the *de facto* sacrifice of the piece by 15 KR—K1 (over-protecting the critical pawn); 15 .... P×Kt (or else 16 Kt—R3, with a good game); 16 RP×P, Kt—KKt1; 17 Q—R5, and White's attack must be taken seriously.

15	Kt×Kt

Instead of winning a piece by 15 .... B×B ch; 16 R×B, P×Kt—which would allow White to maintain his attack—Black decides on a line of play which brings him in a good pawn for the end-game.

16 P×Kt	Kt—Q5
17 Q—Q3	Kt—K7 ch
18 K—Kt1	B×B
19 R×B	

If 19 Q×B, P×Kt could be played without any risk.

19	Kt×P
20 Kt—R7 ch	K—Kt1
21 Kt—B6 ch	P×Kt
22 Q—Kt3 ch	Kt—Kt3
23 P—R5	Q—B4

Better than 23 .... K—Kt2; 24 P×Kt, P×P; 25 Q—B4, etc. In spite of being, in -this case, two pawns down, White would exercise a serious pressure.

24 P×Kt	P×P
25 R—B2	Q—Kt4
26 Q—QB3	Q—K4

Forcing the exchange of Queens. If 27 Q×P, Q—K8 ch, and if 27 Q—Q2, Q—K6.

27 R (B2)×P	Q×Q
28 P×Q	K—Kt2
29 R—B2	R—KB1
30 R—K2	QR—K1
31 KR—K1	R×R
32 R×R	R—B8 ch

In the ensuing Rook ending, Black is not only a pawn ahead, but his pawn formation is more compact. Nevertheless, he has no easy task to win.

33 K—Kt2	K—B2
34 P—B4	P—KR4
35 K—B3	P—KKt4
36 P—B5	

The only way to obtain some counter-play.

36	P×P
37 K—B4	P—Kt5

Or 37 .... P—Kt3; 38 K—Kt5, R—B3; 39 R—K5, R—Kt3; 40 K—R6 (with the threat: K—Kt7 and K×BP); 40 .... P—B3; 41 P×P, R×P; 42 R×KtP approximately redressing the balance.

38 K×P	P—Kt6
39 K—Q4	P—R5

After 39 .... R—B7; 40 K—K3, R×R ch; 41 K×R, K—B3; 42 K—B3, etc., and White's position could be held.

40 P—B4	P—Kt3
41 P—R4	R—B7
42 R—K4	

At this stage 42 K—K3 offers no hope of salvation, whereas the continuation in the text is still full of subtle points.

42	R×P
43 R×P	R—QR7
44 R—Kt4	P—Kt7

After 44 .... R×P; 45 R×P, P—Kt4; 46 K—B5, White avoids the loss of a second pawn (46 .... R×P ch; 47 K×P, or 46 .... P×P; 47 K—B6).

45 P—R5

The only resource.

45	P×P
46 K—B3	

After 46 K—B5, R—QB7; 47 K—Kt5 (47 K—B6, R×P ch); 47 .... P—R5; 48 K—Kt4, P—R4 ch; 49 K—R3, K—K2, Black's superiority in material becomes too strong.

46	P—R5
47 P—B5	K—B3
48 R—Kt8	

Threatening 49 P—Q6, P×P; 50 P—B6.

48	K—K4
49 R—Kt5 ch	

After 49 P—Q6, P×P; 50 P—B6, Black has the counter 50 .... R—R8; 51 R×P, R—QB8 ch; 52 R—QB2 (or 52 K—Kt4, R×P; 53 K×P, P—Q4, the hostile King being cut off, the passed pawn wins without difficulty); 52 .... R×R ch; 53 K×R, K—K3 (essential, in order to be "in the square" of the adverse pawn); 54 K—B3, P—Q4; 55 K—Kt4 (55 K—Q4, P—R6); 55 .... K—Q3; 56 K×P, K×P, and wins without difficulty.

49 ......   K—B3

If 49 .... K—B5; 50 P—Q6 (e.g.: 50 ....
P×P; 51 P×P, K×R; 52 P—Q7, P—Kt8 (Q);
53 P—Q8 (Q) ch, K—B5; 54 Q—B6 ch,
K—Kt6; 55 Q—Kt7 ch, K—R7; 56 Q—R8 ch,
K—Kt7; 57 Q—Kt8 ch, followed by Q×R,
the game would be drawn).

50 R—Kt8

If, instead, 50 P—Q6, P×P; 51 P×P,
Black can play neither 51 .... K×R;
52 P—Q7, with a draw as shown above, nor
even 51 .... K—K3; 52 R—Kt6 ch,
K—Q2; 53 K—Kt4, P—R4 ch; 54 K×P,
P—R6; 55 K—R4, with a certain draw.

But he can continue with 51 .... P—R4;
52 P—Q7, K—K2; 53 R—Kt7 ch, K—Q1;
54 K—B4, R—Q7; 55 K—B5 (or 55 K—B3,
P—R6); 55 .... P—R6; 56 K—B6, P—R7,
and Black wins.

50 ......   K—B2
51 R—Kt4   P—R4

As now the white King cannot approach,
Black's victory is getting nearer.

52 P—B6   K—K2
53 R—Kt6   K—B2
54 R—Kt4   R—B7
55 P—Q6   P—R6

A race to the respective queening squares,
but Black arrives with a check, and this
decides the contest.

56 P×P   P—R7
57 P—B8 (Q)   P—R8 (Q) ch
58 K—B4   R—B7 ch
59 K—Kt5   Q—B8 ch
60 K—R4   R—R7 ch
61 K—Kt3   Q—Kt8 ch
62 K—B3   R—B7 ch
63 K—Q4   P—Kt8 (Q) ch
        Resigns.

182

White   *Black*
MIESES   ALEKHINE

(Scheveningen, 1913)

*It is easily overlooked that the accepted
relative valuation of the pieces (e.g. the
Queen is worth more than a Rook, two
Knights are stronger than a Rook, a Rook is*
*stronger than a Bishop, a Bishop is equal to
a Knight, etc.) is only valid in theory. The
peculiarities of a position can and do change
all that.*

*In this game the sacrifice of the Queen for
a Rook, Knight and pawn (11 .... Kt×Kt)
is based, in the main, on the increased activity
which Black will obtain from his pieces.*

1 P—K4   P—K4
2 P—Q4   P×P
3 Q×P   Kt—QB3
4 Q—K3   B—K2
5 B—Q2

After 5 Q—KKt3, Black would avoid the
artificial defence 5 .... B—B3 (6 Kt—QB3,
with a good game for White), and would
boldly play 5 .... Kt—B3, e.g. 6 Q×KtP,
R—KKt1; 7 Q—R6, R—Kt3; 8 Q—K3,
Kt×P, with advantage to Black, or 6 B—Q2,
Kt—KR4; 7 Q—KB3, P—KKt3, and Black
stands very well.

5 ......   Kt—B3
6 Kt—QB3   Castles
7 Castles   P—Q4

As White cannot reply with 8 P—K5
(8 .... Kt—KKt5, followed by ....
Kt×KP), the text move frees Black's game.

8 P×P   Kt×P
9 Q—Kt3

Simplification here would lead to a dull
game, e.g. 9 Kt×Kt, Q×Kt; 10 B—Kt4,
Q—K3 (unsound would be 10 .... Q×RP;
11 B×B, Kt×B; 12 Q×Kt, B—Kt5, by
reason of 13 Q—R3); 11 Q×Q, B×Q;
12 B×B, Kt×B, with an even game.

9 ......   B—R5

A terrible blunder would be 9 ....
Kt×Kt; 10 B×Kt (with the two-fold threat
Q×P mate and R×Q); 10 .... B—Kt4 ch;
11 P—B4, and wins. It is easy to see why
Black wishes to drive the hostile Queen
from her advantageous post.

10 Q—B3   B—K3
11 B—K3

Had White foreseen the incisive reply now
impending, he would have preferred to continue his development by 11 Kt—R3 (e.g.
11 .... Kt—K4; 12 Q—K4, Kt—KKt5;
13 P—B3, Kt—B7; 14 Kt×Kt, B×Kt,
with equality). (*Diagram. See p. 237.*)

11 ......   Kt×Kt

A fine example of a *positional sacrifice*
(one which produces no immediate or
calculable results).

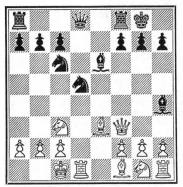

Position after 11 B—K3

12 R×Q	Kt×P ch
13 K—Kt1	QR×R
14 B—K2	

After 14 P—B3, B—QKt6; 15 B—K2, B—B3, the white King's position is precarious, even though the black Knight cannot get out.

14	Kt (R7)—Kt5
15 Kt—R3	KR—K1
16 Kt—B4	B—B4
17 R—QB1	P—KKt3
18 P—Kt4	

White's aggressive measures are not justified in this position. He should have sought to simplify by 18 B—Kt5, etc.

18	B—K5
19 Q—R3	B—B3
20 B—B3	B×B
21 Q×B	Kt—K4
22 Q—K2	

Or 22 Q—Kt2, Kt—B5.

| 22 ...... | P—B4 |

A new champion enters the lists. White cannot reply with 23 B×P, because of 23 .... Kt (K4)—Q6.

23 R—Kt1	P—B5
24 P—R4	Kt—Q4
25 Kt×Kt	R×Kt
26 P—B4	

Or 26 R—Q1, R—Kt4; 27 B—Q4, R—K3, threatening 28 .... Kt—Q6, and Black maintains the initiative.

| 26 ...... | Kt—Q6 |

A very pretty stroke. After 27 P×Kt, Black's reply would not be 27 .... R×P; 28 R—Kt3, B—Q5; 29 Q×R, P×Q; 30 B×B, etc., but 27 .... P×P; 28 Q—Q2, R—QKt4, and Black's pressure is very powerful.

| 27 Q—B3 | R—QKt4 |
| 28 P×Kt | |

White is compelled to accept this fresh sacrifice, and he has now a Queen for a Rook, but Black's attack is not to be gainsaid.

28	R×P ch
29 K—B1	P×P
30 K—Q1	R—QB1
31 P—Kt5	

A better defence was 31 R—Kt2. Black is now able to weave a mating net.

| 31 ...... | R (B1)—B7 |

Threatening mate in two.

32 K—K1	R—Kt8 ch
33 Q—Q1	B—B6 ch
Resigns	

Equally final would have been 33 .... R—K7 ch.

183

| *White* | *Black* |
| MASON | SCHLECHTER |

(Paris, 1900)

In this short but expressive game, we can but admire the simplicity of means used by the victor.

One might say that he uses no means at all, no stratagems or other refinements, and that he succeeds in overcoming all resistance merely by virtue of the law that "one weakness begets another."

1 P—K4	P—K4
2 P—Q4	P×P
3 Q×P	Kt—QB3
4 Q—K3	Kt—B3
5 B—K2	

Development on the Q side (5 Kt—QB3 or 5 B—Q2) is more in the spirit of the opening, since the idea underlying White's second move is to establish pressure on the Q file.

| 5 ...... | Q—K2 |

Well countered! Black not only prevents 6 P—K5, but is now attacking the hostile KP.

If, instead, 5 .... B—K2, the 6 P—K5 (6 .... Kt—Q4; 7 Q—K4) is in White's favour. If, passively, 5 .... P—Q3, White obtains a normal development after 6 B—Q2, B—K2; 7 Kt—QB3, Castles; 8 Castles, etc.

6 Kt—QB3
Against 6 P—QB3, Black would reply
with even more vigour 6 .... P—Q4.

| 6 ...... | P—Q4 |

Opening up the game.

7 P×P	Kt—QKt5
8 B—Q3	KKt×P
9 Kt×Kt	Kt×Kt
10 Q×Q ch	B×Q

In this simplified position, Black has a
small but distinct advantage in development.

11 P—QB4
A weakening move, which contributes
nothing to White's development.
If he play first 11 P—QR3, B—K3, and
again 12 P—QB4, Kt—Kt3; 13 P—QKt3,
his pawn-formation on the Q side would
suffer.
The most suitable continuation is therefore 11 B—Q2.

11	Kt—Kt5
12 B—Kt1	B—K3
13 P—QR3	Kt—B3
14 B—B4	

If 14 B—Q3, Kt—K4, and if 14 P—QKt3,
Kt—Q5.

14	B—B3
15 B—R2	Castles QR
16 Kt—K2	

If 16 R—Kt1, B—B4, and if 16 B—B1,
Kt—Q5, with fresh troubles for Black, who
therefore sees himself already compelled to
give up a pawn.

| 16 ...... | B×KtP |
| 17 QR—Kt1 | B—B3 |

He could win a second pawn by 17 ....
KB×P, but he rightly sees that this weak
pawn will fall sooner or later, and decides,
therefore, to maintain his KB on the
dominating diagonal.

18 Castles	Kt—Q5
19 Kt×Kt	R×Kt
20 B—K3	R—Q6
21 B—B1	KR—Q1
22 B—Kt2	B×B
23 R×B	R×P
24 KR—Kt1	R (R6)—Q6

He threatens mate, and allows his
opponent no counter-chances.

| 25 B—Kt3 | R—Q7 |
| 26 B—B2 | R×B |

Well-judged liquidation.

| 27 R×R | B—B4 |
| | Resigns. |

DANISH GAMBIT

184

| White | Black |
| PERLIS | BLACKBURNE |

(Ostend, 1907)

*Black conducts the attack in this game with
the youthful abandon peculiar to his style,
and makes use of its multiple resources in
a way that savours of magic.*

*The phase of the game from the 11th to
the 24th move abounds in surprising turns.
The rapid and astute way in which Black
finally drives home his advantage (30 ....
P—Q4; 33 .... P—Q5 ch; 34 .... P×Kt)
is equally remarkable. To sum up: an artistic
performance.*

1 P—K4	P—K4
2 P—Q4	P×P
3 P—QB3	

The *Danish Gambit*.

| 3 ...... | P—Q4 |

Contesting the centre in preference to
accepting the gambit.

| 4 KP×P | Q×P |
| 5 P×P | Kt—QB3 |

Focussing his attention on the isolated QP.

| 6 Kt—KB3 | B—Kt5 |
| 7 B—K2 | Kt—B3 |

Here the novice should avoid the frightful
blunder 7 .... B×Kt; 8 B×B, Q×QP;
9 B×Kt ch, and Black loses the Queen.

8 Castles
Better is 8 Kt—B3, and if either 8 ....
B—Kt5 or even 8 .... Q—QR4; 9 Castles.
If 8 .... Q—KR4; 9 P—KR3.

| 8 ...... | B—Q3 |

Black preserves the option of castling on
either wing.

9 Kt—B3	Q—KR4
10 R—K1	Castles KR
11 P—KR3	

Now that White is definitely threatened
with 11 .... B×Kt, followed by .... Q×P,
it is for him a choice of evils, namely either
the text move or 11 P—KKt3, which equally
weakens the King's position, or 11 Kt—K5,
which loses material by reason of 11 ....
Kt×Kt; 12 P×Kt, B×P; 13 P—KR3 (or
13 B×B, B×P ch, followed by .... Kt×B,
with an advantage of two pawns); 13 ....
B×B; 14 Q×B, Q×Q, etc., and Black has
the better game.

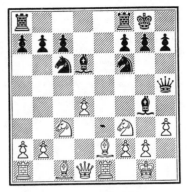

11 ......   QR—Q1
The beginning of a grand combination.

12 P × B	Kt × KtP
13 B—KKt5	B—R7 ch
14 K—B1	B—K4
15 B—Q3	

If 15 B × R, there is the beautiful continuation 15 .... Q—R8 ch; 16 Kt—Kt1, Kt—R7 mate.

| 15 ...... | R × P |
| 16 Kt × B | |

If 16 Kt × R, Kt × Kt, cutting off the King's retreat, but clearly not 16 .... Q—R8 ch; 17 K—K2, Kt × Kt ch; 18 K—Q2, etc.

16 ......   R—K1
Another quiet move, but how powerful! It needs, however, a great deal of self-possession to make such a move when, temporarily, two pieces down. Of far less value would be the plausible continuation 16 .... QKt × Kt, as White would not reply with 17 B × P ch, K × B; 18 Q × R, Kt—R7 ch; 19 K—Kt1, Kt (R7)—B6 ch; 20 P × Kt, Kt × P ch, followed by .... Kt × Q, but with 17 R × Kt, R × B; 18 Q × R, Kt × R; 19 Q—Kt3, Q—R8 ch; 20 K—K2, Q × R; 21 Q × Kt, Q × P ch; 22 K—B3, and the fight would still be an open one.

17 R—K4	R × R
18 B × R	QKt × Kt
19 B—B4	Kt—Kt3
20 B—Kt3	Q—R8 ch
21 K—K2	Q × P
22 Q—R1	

Seeking to relieve his position, for if 22 Q—Q5, Kt—B3; 23 K—Q3, R × B, etc., and if 22 Q—Q7, R × B ch, and, finally, if 22 K—Q3, R—Q1 ch, etc. But the strongest resistance would result from 22 Q—Q4, Kt—B3; 23 K—Q3.

22	Q × Q
23 R × Q	P—KB4
24 K—B3	

This attempt to maintain the extra piece (24 .... P × B; 25 K × Kt) comes to naught, and Black ultimately remains two pawns ahead.

24	Kt (Kt5)—K4 ch
25 K—Kt2	P × B
26 Kt × P	Kt—B2
27 R—K1	

With the threat of 28 Kt—B6 ch.

27	R—K2
28 P—B3	Kt—Q3
29 B × Kt	P × B
30 R—Q1	P—Q4

Very pretty! Not only would it be unsafe to take the pawn (31 R × P, Kt—B5 ch), but the pawn itself is to play the biggest part in the final struggle.

31 Kt—B3	R—Q2
32 K—B2	Kt—K2
33 K—K3	P—Q5 ch
34 K—K4	

Not 34 R × P, Kt—B4 ch, but he could have held out longer with 34 K—K2. Now a fresh *finesse* puts an end to the fight.

| 34 ...... | P × Kt |
| | Resigns |

Because of 35 R × R, P—B7; 36 R—B7, Kt—B3, and there is nothing left for White.

185

| *White* | *Black* |
| MIESES | WOLF |

(Monte Carlo, 1903)

In the following skirmishing conflict Black succeeded in establishing equality. But then he took too little notice of his opponent's intentions, a proceeding at all times likely to prove fatal in attack or defence.

1 P—K4	P—K4
2 P—Q4	P × P
3 P—QB3	P—Q4
4 KP × P	

Correct play; the ill effects of the needless 4 P—K5 are splendidly illustrated in the following brevity, Mieses-Rubinstein, *Prague*, 1908:

4 P—K5, P×P; 5 Kt—KB3, P×P;
6 B×P, Kt—KR3; 7 Kt—B3, B—K3;
8 B—Q3, B—K2; 9 Q—B2, Kt—B3;
10 P—QR3 (White is forced on the defensive,
and has therefore no compensation at all
for his two pawns); 10 .... Q—Q2;
11 B—QB1, Kt—B4; 12 Q—R4, Castles KR;
13 Q—KB4, P—B3; 14 P—Kt4, P×P;
15 Kt×KP, Kt×Kt; 16 Q×QKt, B—B3,
and White resigns.

4	Q×P
5 P×P	Kt—QB3
6 Kt—KB3	B—Kt5
7 B—K2	Castles
8 Kt—B3	

Against 8 .... Q—KR4 White would
equally play 9 B—K3, in order to reinforce
his position in the centre.

8	Q—QR4
9 B—K3	B—QB4
10 Castles	Kt—B3

Black recognises that it would be futile
to win a pawn at this juncture, e.g. 10 ....
B×Kt; 11 B×B, Kt×P; 12 B×Kt, B×B;
13 Q—Kt3, Q—Kt3; 14 Q×P, Kt—R3;
15 Q—QB4, Q—B4; 16 Q—Kt3, Q—Kt3;
17 Q×Q, and White has a strong initiative.

11 Q—Kt3
White seeks to attack, and troubles little
about a pawn.

11	Kt×P
12 B×Kt	B×B
13 Kt×B	R×Kt
14 Q×P	

Recovering his pawn, but allowing the
adversary to strengthen his game.

A bold continuation would be 14 B—B4,
R—B1; 15 Kt—Kt5, R—Q2; 16 P—QR4,
with sustained aggressiveness.

14	Q—KKt4
15 B×B ch	Q×B
16 QR—B1	R—Q2
17 Q—Kt3	Kt—R4

Embarking upon a counter-attack with insufficient forces. It would have been better to
hold the balance between attack and defence,
by playing 17 .... Q—R4; 18 Kt—Kt5,
P—QR3; 19 Kt—R7 ch, K—Kt1; 20 Kt—B6
ch, K—R1, or 18 Kt—R4, Q—Q4;
19 Q—QR3, K—Kt1, etc.

18 P—KR3	Q—Kt3
19 Kt—R4	Q—Q6

Trying for simplification.

20 R—B3	Q—Q4
21 Q—R3	Kt—B5

In the belief that the text move would not
only eliminate the counter-threat 22 R—B5,
but also create the double threat of 22 ....
Q×P mate and 22 .... Kt—K7 ch.

He thus falls into a melancholy trap,
which he could have avoided by 21 ....
K—Kt1; 22 R—B5, Q—B2; 23 R—R5,
P—QR3, and, although White's attack is
still strong, Black is not defenceless.

22 Kt—Kt6 ch   Resigns.

186

<table>
<tr><td>White</td><td>Black</td></tr>
<tr><td>NYHOLM</td><td>RÉTI</td></tr>
</table>

(Baden, 1914)

*When either one side or the other omits to
castle, there is no doubt that the game
assumes an artificial character. In addition,
the omission to castle can bring in its wake
many dangers, as can be seen here.*

1 P—K4	P—K4
2 P—Q4	P×P
3 P—QB3	P×P
4 B—QB4	P—Q4

As in all open games (1 P—K4, P—K4),
this move means for Black the emancipation
of his game.

Other methods of declining the third
pawn (such as 4 .... B—Kt5; or 4 ....
P—B7; or 4 .... P—Q3; or 4 ....
Kt—QB3; or, finally, 4 .... Kt—KB3)
are far less effective.

5 B×P
After 5 KP×P, closing the Bishop's
diagonal, Black can develop without difficulty, e.g.: 5 .... P×P; 6 B×P, Kt—KB3;
7 Kt—KB3, B—Q3; 8 Castles, Castles;
9 Kt—B3, B—KKt5; 10 R—K1, QKt—Q2;
and White has no adequate compensation
for the missing pawn.

5	P×P
6 QB×P	Kt—KB3
7 Kt—KB3	

The following stratagem would be insufficient: 7 B×P ch, K×B; 8 Q×Q, on the
score of 8 .... B—Kt5 ch; 9 Q—Q2,
B×Q ch; 10 Kt×B, P—B4, followed by

.... B—K3 and .... R—Q1; and Black's
pawn majority on the Q side will tell in the
end-game.

7 ......   B—Kt5 ch
8 K—B1

Or 8 Kt—B3, Kt × B; 9 P × Kt, Q—K2 ch,
and the simplification of the play is in
Black's favour.

After the text move, however, White's
position is disorganised.

8 ......   Castles

Evading the threats of 9 Q—R4 ch or
(after 8 .... P—B3) 9 B × KBP ch, K × B;
10 Q—Kt3 ch, followed by Q × B.

Henceforth Black will have the initiative.

9 Q—Kt3   Kt—B3

Very subtle indeed! If now White were
to be tempted by the lure of a piece to be
won, the sequel would be: 10 B × QKt,
P × B; 11 Q × B, R—Kt1; 12 Q—Q4
(12 Q × R, B—R3 ch); 12 .... R × B;
13 Q × R, Q—Q8 ch; 14 Kt—K1, B—R3 ch;
15 K—Kt1, Q × Kt mate.

10 Kt—B3	Q—K2
11 P—QR3	B—Q3
12 R—K1	Kt—K4

The manner in which Black now proceeds
to gain more and more territory is instructive.

13 Kt × Kt	B × Kt
14 B—B4	P—B3
15 P—KR4	P—QKt4
16 B—K2	B—K3
17 Q—B2	Q—B4
18 R—B1	KR—Q1
19 P—Kt3	P—QR4
20 Q—Kt1	R—Q7

In effecting this occupation of the seventh
rank, Black had to make exact calculations
regarding the effect of a "discovery" by the
white Knight (21 Kt—Q5 or 21 Kt × P).

21 Kt—Q5	R × QB
22 Q × R	

This loses a piece, Black's rejoinder being
most ingenious, but after 22 Kt × Kt ch,
B × Kt; 23 Q × R, B × Q; 24 R × Q, P—R5;
25 R × BP, P—Kt5; 26 P × P, P—R6,
White's cause is equally lost.

22	Q × Kt
23 P × Q	B × Q
24 R—B2	B × QP
Resigns.	

187

White	Black
ZUKERTORT	MUNK

(Berlin, 1870)

*Here is an example of a trap in the opening
(9 Kt—Q5). But the game is chiefly remarkable for the energetic way in which White
makes use of his extra piece and quickly
nullifies his opponent's superiority in pawns.*

1 P—K4	P—K4
2 P—Q4	P × P
3 P—QB3	P × P
4 B—QB4	

Instead of this munificence, which constitutes the *Danish Gambit* proper, White
can very well continue with 4 Kt × P (4 ....
B—B4; 5 B—QB4, etc., with an enduring
attack).

4	P × P
5 B × P	B—Kt5 ch

Not as promising as it looks.

It may be noted that Black, with 5 ....
P—Q4, could obtain the variation of the
opening shown in the preceding game, and
which could be termed the "Danish Gambit
half-declined."

6 Kt—QB3   Kt—QB3

In developing the QKt, Black at the same
time guards his Bishop-errant. If, however, 6 .... Kt—KB3; 7 B × P ch, K × B;
8 Q—Kt3 ch, followed by .... Q × B; and
if 6 .... Q—K2; 7 Q—B2, followed by
Castles.

7 Kt—B3   Kt—B3

A routine development, but even after
a reasoned continuation, such as 7 ....
P—Q3; 8 Q—Kt3, Kt—R3; 9 Castles,
Castles; 10 Kt—Q5, etc., White would
have an imposing attack.

8 Castles   P—Q3
9 Kt—Q5

This constitutes an "Opening-trap" into
which Black falls—possibly with his eyes
open.

9 ......   Kt × Kt

Better is, in any event, 9 .... Castles;
10 Kt × Kt ch, P × Kt; 11 Kt—R4, Kt—R4;
12 B—K2, and, precarious though Black's
position is, there is, as yet, no immediate
danger.

10 P × Kt   Castles

After any move by the QKt, White wins
a piece by 11 Q—R4 ch.

Now Black's only hope is to obtain an equivalent for the lost Knight in three passed pawns, but White's well-placed "two Bishops" are too powerful an asset.

11	P×Kt	P×P
12	Q—Q4	Q—B3
13	Q×Q	

By this exchange Black loses his last chance of counter-action, which he might still have had after 13 B×P ch, Q×B; 14 Q×B, B—R3, etc.

13	......	P×Q
14	B×P	P—Q4
15	B—Q3	P—KR3

Clearly not 15 .... P—B4; 16 Kt—Kt5, P—KR3; 17 B—R7 mate.

16 P—Kt4

The remainder is played *fortissimo*.

16	......	B×P
17	Kt—K5	B—KR6
18	K—R1	KR—B1
19	R—Kt1 ch	K—B1
20	B—R7	K—K1
21	R—Kt8 ch	B—B1
22	R×B ch	K×R
23	R—KKt1	Resigns.

188

White	*Black*
MIESES	MARSHALL

(Monte Carlo, 1903)

White's main idea in the Danish Gambit is to provide free diagonals for the Bishops. If—as in the following ruthless little game—there are also open files for the Rooks, the attack soon becomes irresistible.

1	P—K4	P—K4
2	P—Q4	P×P
3	P—QB3	P×P
4	B—QB4	P×P
5	B×P	P—Q3

A much sounder defence than 5 .... B—Kt5 ch.

6 Kt—K2

6 Kt—KB3 is certainly more straight-forward, but the most energetic continuation is 6 P—B4, e.g.: 6 .... Kt—Q2; 7 Kt—KB3, Kt—B4; 8 Kt—Kt5, Kt—KR3;

9 Castles, and White dictates the course of events.

To be considered also is 6 Q—Kt3.

6	......	Kt—QB3
7	Castles	B—K3
8	B—Q5	

An effective anchorage. 8 B×B, P×B; 9 Q—Kt3 leads to nothing because of 9 .... Q—B1.

8	......	Kt—B3
9	Q—Kt3	Q—B1
10	Kt—B4	Kt—Q1

In place of this cramped defence, one can recommend 10 .... B×B; 11 P×B, Kt—K4; 12 R—K1, B—K2; 13 B×Kt, P×B; 14 R×P, Q—Q2; 15 Q—Kt3 (or 15 Q×P, Castles, etc.); 15 .... Castles QR, and Black can cope with any eventuality.

11 B×Kt

The first step towards disorganising the hostile position.

11	......	P×B
12	Kt—R5	P—B3
13	R—K1	B—K2
14	Q—KB3	R—KKt1
15	Kt×P ch	B×Kt
16	Q×B	P×B

He should not have allowed the K file to be opened. Comparatively best would have been 16 .... Q—Q2; 17 Kt—B3, Q—K2, etc.

17	P×P	R—Kt3
18	Q—R8 ch	K—Q2
19	Kt—B3	

The reserve cavalry enter: the battle is won.

| 19 | ...... | B×P |

Or 19 .... B—R6; 20 Q—K8 ch, K—B2; 21 QR—B1, K—Kt1 (21 .... B×P; 22 Kt—R4 dis ch); 22 Kt—Kt5, Q—Q2; 23 R—K7, and wins.

20	Q—K8 ch	K—B2
21	Kt×B ch	K—Kt1

To all appearances the black King has at last found comparative security, but now White's artillery brings about a triumphant finale.

22	QR—B1	Kt—B3
23	R×Kt	

A *clearance sacrifice*.

23	......	P×R
24	R—Kt1 mate.	

189

White	Black
MIESES	TCHIGORIN

(Hanover, 1902)

The exciting vicissitudes of this instructive game, can be divided into three phases, from the point of view of Black:

Stopping the enemy's first onslaught; building up a close but defendable position; watching all openings and, at the right moment, launching the counter-attack.

1 P—K4	P—K4
2 P—Q4	P×P
3 P—QB3	P×P
4 B—QB4	P×P
5 B×P	Q—K2

This defence is not without logical foundation. The Queen surveys the critical sector, prepares for castling on the Q side, and in addition threatens to win one of the Bishops by 6 .... Q—Kt5 ch.

6 Kt—QB3	P—QB3
7 Q—B2	P—Q3

Suicidal would be 7 .... P—Q4; 8 B×P, P×B; 9 Kt×P, and wins.

8 Castles	
9 B—K2	B—K3

At the cross-roads. Instead of giving up territory, the imaginative 9 Kt—Q5 maintains the initiative.

9	Kt—Q2
10 Kt—B3	Kt—B4

Not 10 .... Castles, as yet, because 11 Q—R4, and White gets going.

11 R—Q4	Castles
12 KR—Q1	Q—B2

Slowly but surely Black proceeds with his development. 12 .... Kt—B3 would be premature, on account of 13 P—K5.

13 Kt—QR4	Kt—Q2
14 R (Q1)—Q3	KKt—B3
15 R—B3	B—K2

The "hedgehog" position, which Black has obtained, is cramped but solid, his pawns being particularly strong in the defence of the King's position.

16 R—Kt4

With the threat of 17 B—R6, which is, however, prevented by Black's next move.

16	Kt—QKt1
17 Kt—Q4	P—Q4

This counter-thrust in the centre provokes the crisis.

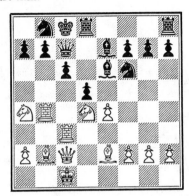

18 Kt×P

Being already two pawns to the bad, and threatened with the loss of a third, White, by the offer of the Knight, tries to alter the normal course of things.

18	Kt×Kt
19 B—R6	Q—B5 ch

As neither 19 .... K—Kt1; 20 R×Kt, nor 19 .... K—Q2; 20 R×P, nor 19 .... P×B; 20 R×Kt, nor 19 .... Kt×R; 20 R×Q ch, nor, finally, 19 .... B—Q2; 20 B×P ch, is admissible, the "relieving check" in the text is the only move, which, however, saves the situation and refutes the hostile combination.

20 R—K3

Or 20 K—Kt1, B×R; 21 R×Kt ch, K—Kt1, and the whole of White's game collapses.

20	B×R
21 Q×Kt ch	Q—B2
22 B×P ch	K—Kt1
23 B—K5	

His final trump.

23	Q×B
24 R—QKt3	Q—B2
	Resigns.

13. BISHOP'S OPENING

190

White	Black
BOWDLER	CONWAY

(London, 1788)

*A forerunner of the "Immortal Game."
White gives up the two Rooks in their corners
and all his pieces except Queen and Bishop,
and drives a successful King hunt to its logical
conclusion.*

1 P—K4	P—K4
2 B—B4	

The *truth*—as it was known in those far-off days.

2	B—B4

This symmetrical variation is called the *Classical Defence*.

3 P—Q3	

A quiet continuation. 3 Kt—QB3 leads back into the *Vienna Game*, and 3 Kt—KB3, Kt—QB3 into the *Giuoco Piano*.

3	P—QB3

Pawn strategy. But after an active development by 3 .... Kt—KB3; 4 Q—K2 (preventing 4 .... P—Q4); 4 .... Castles, Black has a very good game.

4 Q—K2	P—Q3

If, instead, 4 .... Kt—B3, White is already able to play 5 P—B4, and to obtain the initiative after 5 .... P×P; 6 P—K5, etc., or 5 .... P—Q3; 6 Kt—KB3, etc. As Black, by his last move, has renounced expansion in the centre, the preceding move has robbed his QKt of its natural development at QB3.

5 P—B4	

Intensifying the struggle. 5 Kt—QB3 first would be sound and strong. It will be noticed that the players of the Philidor era preferred, in the opening, to pay attention to pawns rather than pieces.

5	P×P
6 B×P	Q—Kt3

A double attack against White's KKt and QKtP. How can it be parried?

7 Q—B3	

By not defending either point, but staging an astute *unmasking combination*.

7	Q×P

Starting his Queen on an expedition which, in the end, will prove ill-fated. Similarly, if 7 .... B×Kt; 8 B×P ch, etc. But by first of all blocking up the KB file by 7 .... Kt—B3, Black could have maintained his threats. It is true, however, that the wondrous consequences of the continuation in the text were hard to foresee.

8 B×P ch	

An ambush.

8	K—Q2

Clearly not 8 .... K×B, because of the recoil 9 B—K5 dis ch. Playable would be 8 .... K—B1; 9 Kt—K2, Kt—B3.

9 Kt—K2	Q×R

A spirit of consistency. Or 9 .... Kt—B3; 10 K—Q2, Q×R.

10 K—Q2	

In order to play 11 R—KB1, to be followed by QKt—B3, relying both on his attack and on the difficulties the black Queen will experience in getting clear of this "wasps'·nest."

10	B—Kt5 ch

He stresses his advantage in material instead of trying to consolidate his gains, either by 10 .... Kt—B3 or 10 .... Q—B3.

11 QKt—B3	

Sensation! He gives up another Rook rather than allow Black to redress the balance by 11 P—B3, Q—Kt7 ch; 12 K—K3, Kt—B3; 13 P×B, K—B2; 14 P—KR3, R—B1, etc., or by 11 K—B1, Q—B3, etc.

11	B×Kt ch

By playing 11 .... Q×R at once Black would still maintain his KB in its defensive functions.

12 Kt×B	Q×R
13 Q—Kt4 ch	

The final assault.

13	K—B2
14 Q×P	

At once 14 Q—Kt3 would be powerful.

14	Kt—Q2
15 Q—Kt3	

And not 15 Q×R, because of 15 ....
Q×P ch, followed by .... KKt—B3, and
Black takes his revenge by imprisoning the
Queen.

15	P—Kt3

An illusory refuge. Or, e.g. 15 ....
Kt—K2; 16 B×P ch, K—Q1; 17 B—B7
mate. Or 15 .... Kt—K4; 16 B×Kt,
P×B; 17 Q×P ch, etc., with improved
chances for White. But 15 .... P—Kt4
would give the black King more breathing
space than the move in the text.

16 Kt—Kt5 ch
A beautiful surprise, which spreads a
mating net around the black King.

16	P×Kt
17 B×P ch	K—Kt2

An amusing detail: 17 .... K—B3;
18 B—Q5 mate.

18 B—Q5 ch	K—R3
19 P—Q4	

Opening the door by this turn of the key.

19	P—Kt5

There is no saving clause.

20 B×P	K—Kt4
21 P—B4 ch	K×B

White mates in two.
A turbulent game.

191

White	Black
McDONNELL	DE LA BOURDONNAIS

(Match, 1834)

*After a formidable opening contest of
"thrust-and-parry" (moves 9–21), Black
emerges a piece down, but with a mass of
pawns on the K side which proves more
powerful than his adversary's on the other
wing.*

*This "battle of pawns" is one of the most
thrilling ever witnessed on the chessboard.*

1 P—K4	P—K4
2 B—B4	B—B4
3 P—QB3	

The so-called classical attack.

3	Q—K2

Preventing 4 P—Q4, and threatening at
the same time 4 .... B×P ch; 5 K×B,
Q—B4 ch, followed by .... Q×B.

The most rational continuation, however,
would be an intensified development on the
K side by 3 .... Kt—KB3; 4 P—Q4, P×P;
5 P—K5, P—Q4; 6 P×Kt, P×B; 7 Q—R5,
Castles (correct!); 8   Q×B,   R—K1 ch;
9 Kt—K2, P—Q6, etc., winning back the
piece with equal chances.

4 Kt—B3
The timid 4 P—Q3 would give up any
idea of expansion in the centre. With the
text move White promotes the rapid development of his pieces.

4	P—Q3
5 Castles	B—Kt3

A *preventive retreat*—an idea adopted on
many occasions by the great strategists of
modern times.

6 P—Q4   Kt—KB3
With the idea of completing the initial
stage of his mobilisation, rather than of
really threatening to capture the KP—for
the opening of the K file would be fraught
with danger.

It is seen that Black's third move was
a useful one, as he can hold the point K4.

7 Kt—R3
This *eccentric development* is necessary,
for 7 QKt—Q2 would obstruct his QB and
7 B—K3 would encumber the K file. The
sortie 7 B—Kt5 would lack weight, for, if
effected *before* Black's .... Castles KR, it
would call for 7 .... P—KR3; 8 B—R4,
P—Kt4; 9 B—Kt3, QKt—Q2, ruthlessly
unpinning the Knight.

7	B—Kt5

But this counter-pin, effected *after* his
opponent has castled on the critical wing, is
to be recommended, as it would not be to
White's advantage to disturb his King's
field by 8 P—R3, B—KR4; 9 P—KKt4.

8 Kt—B2	QKt—Q2
9 Q—Q3	

Although this move unpins the Knight
and guards the KP, it produces—owing to
the Queen's unnatural position—some weird
complications in the centre. More expedient
would be 9 R—K1.

9	P—Q4

The counter-action begins.

10 P × QP	P—K5
11 Q—Q2	P × Kt
12 R—K1	Kt—K5
13 Q—B4	P—KB4
14 P × P	P—Kt4

He does not make it easy for White to recover his piece.

15 Q—K3	Kt—K4

A strategy of "pin pricks."

16 B—Kt5 ch	P—B3
17 P × B	Kt × KtP
18 Q—K2	P × B
19 P—B3	

Retaliation.

19	Kt (Kt5)—B3
20 P × Kt	Kt × KP
21 Q × P ch	

If 21 Q—R5 ch, Q—B2; 22 Q × KtP, R—KKt1.

21	Q—Q2
22 Q × Q ch	K × Q
23 P—B4	

A fresh phase. White has now an extra pawn (doubled), but the position of Black's minor pieces, especially of his well-supported Knight, is more aggressive, and the formation of the respective cluster of pawns makes the time factor more important than the material factor. Who will get there first?

23	QR—K1
24 P—B5	B—Q1
25 P—Q6	

A threatening outlook, but the black king will firmly withstand all assaults.

25	P—B5
26 P—Kt4	KR—B1
27 R—B1	P—KR4
28 Kt—R3	

If 28 P—KR4, Kt—Kt6, etc.

| 28 ...... | B—B3 |
| 29 B—Kt2 | P—Kt5 |

With great virtuosity he brings his KBP through a difficult stage of his journey (if 30 R × P, B × P ch).

30 Kt—B4	P—B6
31 Kt—K5 ch	B × Kt
32 P × B	

Chain against chain. But Black's is the more incisive.

32	P—R5
33 QR—Q1	P—B7 ch
34 K—R1	P—R6

With an outflanking threat of 35 .... P—Kt6.

| 35 R—Q3 | R—KKt1 |
| 36 P—Kt5 | |

No longer able to cope with his adversary's plans, he tries to make his own threats effective.

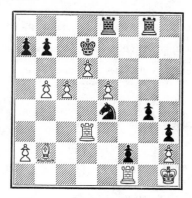

| 36 ...... | P—Kt6 |

The last act of the drama.

| 37 P × P | R × KtP |

A beautiful "point," instead of 37 .... Kt × P ch; 38 R × Kt, R × R; 39 R × P, etc., and the rôles are reversed.

| 38 R—Q4 | QR—KKt1 |

The winning retort. Threat: 39 .... R—Kt8 ch.

| 39 P—K6 ch | |

A stubborn fight. If 39 .... K × P; 40 R × Kt, with check.

| 39 ...... | K—Q1 |
| 40 QR—Q1 | P—R7 |

A fresh surprise. Black's two passed pawns co-operate powerfully in the attack. If now 41 K × P, R—Kt7 ch; 42 K—R1 (42 K—R3, R (Kt1)—Kt6 ch, with mate to follow); 42 .... R (Kt7)—Kt4, with fatal threats.

| 41 P—K7 ch | K—Q2 |
| 42 P—B6 ch | |

"All men on deck!"

42	P × P
43 P × P ch	K × P
44 P—K8 (Q) ch	

A peace offering in the hope of deflecting

the storm, otherwise there follows 44 ....
R—Kt8 ch; 45 K × P, R (Kt1)—Kt7 ch;
46 K—R3, Kt—Kt4 ch, followed by mate.

44	R × Q
45 K × P	R—K3

With the incisive threat of 46 .... R—R3
mate.

46 R—B1 ch	K—Kt4
47 P—R4 ch	K—Kt5

Not 47 .... K × P; 48 R—B4 ch, followed
by R × Kt.

48 B—B3 ch	R × B
49 R × R	K × R
50 P—Q7	R—Q3
51 K—Kt2	R × P
52 R—B1 ch	K—Q6
53 K—B1	

His last illusion disappears, for after
53 R—Q1 ch there follows 53 .... K—K7;
54 R × R, P—B8 (Q) ch, etc.

53	K—K6
Resigns	

A very beautiful game.

192

White	*Black*
DE LA BOURDONNAIS	McDONNELL

(Match, 1834)

*The most striking feature in the following
eventful game is the destruction of White's
particularly strong centre, whilst the finish—
with the white King at bay in the corner and
faced with a forced mate—is not without its
humour.*

1 P—K4	P—K4
2 B—B4	B—B4
3 Q—K2	

A supporting move, indicated as early as
1561 by Ruy Lopez, with the ingenuous
threat of 4 B × P ch.

3	Kt—KB3

Besides this purely developing move, the
replies 3 .... P—Q3 and 3 .... P—QB3
are useful.

4 P—Q3
A wise procedure. Strategy lacking in

foresight would prompt 4 B × P ch, K × B;
5 Q—B4 ch, P—Q4; 6 Q × B, Kt × P, with
advantage to Black.

With the text move White reserves the
option of developing his K side by
4 Kt—KB3 or 4 P—B4.

4	Kt—B3
5 P—QB3	Kt—K2

Premature would be 5 .... Castles, on
account of 6 B—KKt5, and if, impulsively,
5 .... P—KR3; 6 P—KR4, etc.

6 P—B4
Having consolidated his base, White now
challenges the centre.

6	P × P
7 P—Q4	B—Kt3
8 B × P	

With a strong pawn centre, White has
satisfactorily solved the problem of the
opening—but Black, without losing faith,
is looking for some weakness in the enemy
camp.

8	P—Q3
9 B—Q3	Kt—Kt3
10 B—K3	Castles
11 P—KR3	R—K1

An indication of Black's idea to exert
pressure on the semi-open K file, although,
for the moment, White's KP can be
adequately defended.

12 Kt—Q2   Q—K2
Black's pressure continues. It is in itself
an achievement for Black to have some
counter-play at this stage, or at least some
definite objective.

13 Castles   P—B4
Undermining the hostile centre.

14 K—Kt1   P × P
15 P × P
Although White's centre is still very
strong, it has now to be self-supporting.

15	P—QR4
16 KKt—B3	B—Q2
17 P—KKt4	

A waiting policy in the centre—attack on
the wing—such is White's motto.

17	P—R3
18 QR—Kt1	P—R5

Nor does Black remain inactive,

19 P—Kt5	P×P
20 B×P	P—R6
21 P—Kt3	B—B3
22 R—Kt4	

Of course not 22 P—Q5, B×P, e.g. 23 P×B, Q×Q; 24 B×Q, R×B, etc.; or 23 B×Kt, Q×B, with the sudden threat of 24 .... Q—Kt7 mate.

The necessity for the *artificial manœuvre* in the text demonstrates that White's centre has only hypothetical power and mobility. It is continually exposed to attack, and there is no threat at all of a break-through.

22	B—R4

An eliminating manœuvre.

23 P—R4	B×Kt
24 Kt×B	R—R4
25 P—R5	

On the principle that "a threat is more powerful than its execution."

25	R×B

Compulsory and compelling. This sacrifice of the exchange completely alters the picture.

26 R×R	Kt—B5
27 Q—B3	Kt×B
28 P—Q5	

If 28 Q×Kt, Kt×KP, and wins. White, in trying to redress the balance, must continue his artificial evolutions.

28	Kt×QP

A trenchant reply, e.g. 29 P×Kt, Q×R, etc.; or 29 R×Kt, B×R; 30 P×B, Q—K4; 31 Kt—B4, Q—B6, etc.

29 KR—Kt1	

The sequel will show that White's threats amount only to one check. The crisis is near.

29	Kt—B6 ch
30 K—R1	

If 30 K—B2, Q×R; 31 R×Q, Kt—K8 ch, and wins.

30	B×P
31 R×P ch	K—R1
32 Q—Kt3	

Threatening mate in two by 33 R—Kt8 ch or 33 R—R7 ch. If 32 Kt×B, Kt×Kt.

32	B—Kt3

A manœuvre with two objectives: closing White's base of action (the KKt file), and unmasking his own artillery.

33 P×B	Q—K8 ch

An original finish.

Position after 32 Q—Kt3

34 R×Q	R×R ch
35 Q×R	Kt×Q
36 R—R7 ch	K—Kt1
37 P×P ch	K×R
38 P—B8 (Q)	Kt—B7 mate

193

White	Black
The Rev. G. A. MacDONNELL	BODEN

(London, 1865)

Combinations are sometimes surprisingly duplicated! The sacrifice of Black's Queen (20 .... Q×Kt), disintegrating the opposing King's position, reminds us of two other famous games, namely, Paulsen-Morphy, played in 1857 (Four Knights' Game, No. 154), and Janowski-Marshall, played in 1912 (Petroff's Defence, No. 170).

The subsequent "points" in the present combination vary its execution.

1 P—K4	P—K4
2 B—B4	B—B4
3 P—QKt4	

A fancy opening, the invention of the Scotch master himself.

3	B×P

Or 3 .... B—Kt3; 4 P—QR4 (if not 4 B—Kt2, P—Q3, or 4 Kt—KB3, P—Q3; 5 P—Q4, etc.); 4 .... P—QR4; 5 P—Kt5, Kt—KB3; 6 P—Q3, and White has a strong game.

4 P—QB3	

After 4 P—B4 (*MacDonnell's Double*

Gambit) Black's best plan, instead of acceptance by 4 .... P×P; 5 Kt—KB3, etc., is to advance in the centre by 4 .... P—Q4; 5 KP×P, P—K5; 6 Kt—K2, Kt—KB3, etc.

| 4 ...... | B—B4 |
| 5 P—Q4 | |

White tries to outflank the enemy in preference to reverting to the *Evans Gambit* formation by 5 Kt—B3, Kt—QB3; 6 P—Q4, etc.

5	P×P
6 P×P	B—Kt5 ch
7 K—B1	

Threatening 8 Q—Kt3 or 8 B×P ch, K×B; 9 Q—Kt3 ch, followed by Q×B.

| 7 ...... | B—R4 |

If 7 .... B—K2; 8 Q—Kt3. But 7 .... Kt—QB3 brings another piece into the lists, e.g. 8 Q—Kt3, Q—K2, etc., or 8 P—Q5, Kt—K4, etc.

| 8 Q—R5 | |

To be considered is the continuation 8 B×P ch, K×B; 9 Q—R5 ch, P—Kt3; 10 Q×B, also dislodging the hostile King.

| 8 ...... | P—Q4 |

The only possible parry.

| 9 B×P | Q—K2 |
| 10 B—R3 | Kt—KB3 |

Black always finds the right answer.

11 B×P ch	Q×B
12 Q×B	Kt—B3
13 Q—R4	Kt×KP

Re-establishing the numerical balance, but dynamically Black's chances are superior.

| 14 Kt—KB3 | B—Q2 |

Threatening 15 .... Kt—K4, and preparing to castle on the Q side, his only chance.

| 15 QKt—Q2 | Kt×Kt ch |
| 16 Kt×Kt | Castles QR |

This contains the astute threat 17 .... Kt×P; 18 Q×P (18 Q×Kt, B—Kt4 ch, winning the Queen); 18 .... B—Kt4 ch; 19 K—K1 (or 19 K—Kt1, Kt—K7 ch); Q—K1 ch; 20 K—Q1, B—R5 ch; 21 K—B1, Kt—K7 ch; 22 K—Kt1, Q—Kt3 ch, forcing the mate.

| 17 R—QKt1 | Q—Q4 |

Throwing the whole weight of the Queen into the fray, in preference to spasmodic enterprises such as 17 .... Kt×P; 18 Q×P, B—Kt4 ch, etc., or 17 .... Q×P; 18 Q—Kt5, P—QKt3, etc.

18 Kt—B3	B—B4
19 R—Q1	KR—K1
20 B—B5	

In order to guard, as far as possible, the pawns at Q4 and QR2. He expects only 20 .... P—QKt3 (which would be telling enough), but Black has prepared a far more ingenious and skilful scheme to settle the issue.

White's battered position is already beyond repair. If, for instance, 20 Q—Kt3, Q×Q; 21 P×Q, B—B7 wins a vital pawn, and if 20 P—R4, B—Kt5, etc.

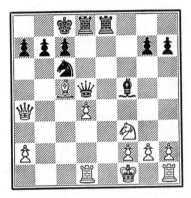

| 20 ...... | Q×Kt |

A *break-up sacrifice* of the Queen.

| 21 P×Q | B—R6 ch |
| 22 K—Kt1 | R—K3 |

Threatening a fatal check.

| 23 Q—B2 | |

Watching the fateful square (KKt6), but another and diabolical machination puts an end to all resistance.

| 23 ...... | R×P |

Most elegant.

| 24 B×R | |

Or 24 R×R, R—K8 mate, or 24 R—Kt1, Kt—K4; 25 R—Kt3, R—Q8 ch (dual 25 .... R—Kt3 ch); 26 Q×R, R—Kt3 mate.

| 24 ...... | Kt×B |
| Resigns | |

White is unable to control all three *focal points* at the same time: KKt6, KB3, K1. Thus, if 25 R×Kt, R—K8 mate, and if 25 Q—Q3, R—Kt3 ch; 26 Q×R, Kt×P mate.

194

White	Black
FRANZ	MAYET

(Berlin, 1858)

A singular game, in which White, after winning a Queen for a Rook, cannot prevent subsequent losses; later on with even two Queens against Black's four pieces he cannot escape defeat! A spectacular contest.

1 P—K4	P—K4
2 B—B4	Kt—KB3

This is the active defence which first tarnished the reputation of this opening and caused it to disappear almost altogether from the modern repertory.

3 Kt—KB3
An identical position occurs in *Petroff's Defence* after 1 P—K4, P—K4; 2 Kt—KB3, Kt—KB3, and now 3 B—B4, instead of the accepted continuations 3 Kt×P or 3 P—Q4 or 3 Kt—B3.

3	Kt×P
4 Kt×P	

This recovers the pawn but allows Black to obtain a footing in the centre (4 .... P—Q4).

Bolder is the sacrifice of a pawn for the sake of a prospective attack by 4 Kt—B3, as in the following game won by Dadian of Mingrelia: 4 (Kt—B3) Kt×Kt (if 4 .... Kt—B4; 5 Kt×P, Black would meet troubles of another kind); 5 QP×Kt, P—KB3; 6 Castles (not yet 6 Kt×P, Q—K2); 6 .... P—Q3; 7 Kt—R4 (threat of 8 Q—R5 ch); 7 .... P—KKt3; 8 P—B4, P—KR4; 9 Kt—B3, Q—B3; 10 P×P, P×P; 11 B—Kt5, Q—Kt3 ch; 12 K—R1, Q—Q3, (all goes well, thinks Black), 13 Kt×P, (a bolt from the blue), Q×Q; 14 B—B7 mate.

4	P—Q4

Throwing back the Bishop, and hoping later on to get rid of the Knight as well.

5 B—Kt3	B—K3
6 Castles	B—Q3
7 P—Q4	Q—B3

Here again 7 .... P—KB3 would be faulty on account of 8 Q—R5 ch, P—Kt3 (8 .... K—K2; 9 Kt—Q3, etc.); 9 Kt×P, B—B2; 10 B×P, etc. The simplest would be 7 .... Castles.

8 P—KB4
Guarding the outpost and threatening

9 P—B5, which incites Black to take immediate counter-measures.

8	P—B4

Meaning to reply to 9 P—B5 by 9 .... P×P; 10 P×B, Q×Kt, etc. A passive and more cautious course would be 8 .... P—B3; 9 P—B5, B—QB1.

9 B—R4 ch
Far more troublesome than 9 P—B3 because of 9 .... Kt—B3; with the threat 10 .... P×P; 11 P×P, Kt×P.

9	K—K2

Forfeiting castling with a good grace, for if 9 .... Kt—Q2 10 P—B5, P×P; 11 P×B, Q×Kt; 12 P×Kt ch, winning a piece.
The most rational continuation, however, is 9 .... B—Q2.

10 P—B4
Instead of being content with the solid 10 P—B3, White throws his forces into the turmoil.

10	QP×P

If 10 .... BP×P; 11 P×P, B×P; 12 Kt—QB3, etc., White has the advantage.

11 Q—B2	B—B4

With the counter-threat of 12 .... Kt—Kt6. If 11 .... B—Q4; 12 R—K1, winning a piece, e.g. 12 .... Q—B4; 13 Kt—QB3, etc., or 12 .... B×Kt; 13 R×Kt, etc.

12 Q×P
Here again White could have maintained a pressure by 12 P—KKt4 or 12 R—K1, e.g. 12 .... B×Kt; 13 R×Kt, etc., or 12 .... Kt—Kt6; 13 Kt—Kt4 dis ch, etc.

12	P×P
13 Q—Kt5	P—QKt3
14 R—K1	B—B4
15 P—QKt4	

Both sides display much imagination.

15	P—QR3
16 Q—B4	P—QKt4
17 Q—Q5	B×P
18 R×Kt	B×R
19 Q×B	R—QB1

Intrepid play. The following alternatives would lead to nothing: 20 Kt—Kt4 dis ch, Q—K3, or 20 Kt—B6 dis ch, K—Q1, etc.

20 Q—Kt7 ch
Winning the adverse Queen by force. The continuation 20 B—Q2 (or 20 B—R3 or 20 B—Kt2) is playable.

20	K—Q1
21 Kt×P ch	Q×Kt
·22 Q×Q	R×B ch
23 K—B2	Kt—Q2
24 B—Kt3	

Or 24 Q—Kt8 ch, B—B1; 25 B—Kt3, K—B2, and White still has to cope with difficulties.

| 24 ...... | K—B2 |
| 25 Q×P | B—B4 |

Although Black has, in fact, only a Rook for a Queen, he never relaxes his threats.

26 P—B5

Better is 26 B—K6 at once.

26	R—K1
27 B—K6	R—K2
28 Q—Kt3 ch	K—Kt2
29 Q—Q3	K—Kt3
30 P—QR4	Kt—K4
31 P—R5 ch	K—B2
32 Q—K4	P—Q6 dis ch
33 K—Kt3	B—Q3
34 Q—R8	Kt—B3 dis ch
35 K—R4	B—K4
36 Q—B8 ch	K—Q3
37 Kt—Q2	B×R

By hard work Black has doubled the compensation for his lost Queen, but now White's passed KBP is showing enterprise.

38 Kt—K4 ch	K—K4
39 P—B6	R×B
40 P—B7	R—R3 ch
41 K—Kt5	R—Kt3 ch
42 K—R5	K×Kt
43 P—B8 (Q)	

The balance of power between two Queens and two Rooks, Bishop and Knight does not tell the whole tale. Black's passed and advanced QP represents a permanent asset.

| 43 ...... | B—K4 |

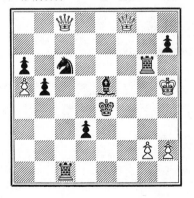

44 Q—B3 ch

A cursory glance at the position makes it hard to believe that the two white Queens cannot, between them, engineer a perpetual check.

44	K—Q5
45 Q (B8)—B5	R—B6
46 Q (B3)—K4 ch	K—B4
47 Q—B8 ch	K—Q3
48 Q—B2 ch	R—Q5
49 Q—B8 ch	B—Q3
50 Q—B2	P—Q7

The charter of victory.

51 Q×Kt ch	K×Q
52 Q×R	R—B4 ch
53 K—R6	R—Q4
54 Q—Kt6 ch	K—Q2
55 Q—Kt7 ch	K—K3
56 Q—B8 ch	K—K4
57 Q—R8 ch	K—B5
58 Q—B6 ch	K—K5
59 Q—B3 ch	K—Q5
60 K×P	K—B5
61 Q—K4 ch	K—Q5
62 Q—B2 ch	K—Q4
63 Q—KB5 ch	B—K4
64 Q—B3 ch	K—B5
65 Q—Q1	

A Queen's agony.

65	R—Q6
66 P—R4	B—B6
67 P—R5	R—K6
68 Q—B1 ch	K—Kt6
69 Q—Q1 ch	K—Kt7
Resigns.	

195

White   *Black*

MIESES   **RUBINSTEIN**

(Breslau, 1912)

"A draw is a result after all," says a chess author. And indeed, a game such as the following—full of unexpected turns—has its own artistic and sporting value.

1 P—K4	P—K4
2 B—B4	Kt—KB3
3 P—Q4	

An intrepid advance.

| 3 ...... | P×P |

After 3 .... Kt×P; 4 P×P (threatening

5 Q—Q5); 4 .... Kt—B4; 5 P—B4,
White has the initiative.

4 Kt—KB3
An identical position can be reached *via*
the *Petroff Defence*: 1 P—K4, P—K4;
2 Kt—KB3, Kt—KB3; 3 P—Q4 (*Steinitz's
Continuation*); 3 .... P×P; 4 B—QB4, etc.
Of no value would be 4 P—K5, P—Q4;
5 B—Kt3, Kt—K5, etc.

4 ......   Kt×P
Producing serious complications.
The following could not be recommended:
4 .... B—Kt5 ch; 5 P—B3, P×P; 6 P×P,
etc.; or 4 .... B—B4 reverting to a variation
of the *Scotch Gambit*. But the most
reasoned course is to lead into an academic
continuation of the *Two Knights' Defence*
by 4 .... Kt—B3 (5 Castles, the *Max Lange
Attack*).

5 Q×P
After 5 Castles, B—K2; 6 R—K1, P—Q4,
Black has freed his game.

5 ......   Kt—KB3
Neither 5 .... Kt—Q3 nor 5 .... Kt—B4
is desirable.

6 B—KKt5
White's superior development compensates for the pawn he has given up.

6 ......   B—K2
7 Kt—B3   Kt—B3
Another line of defence is 7 .... P—B3;
8 Castles QR, P—Q4, etc., or 7 .... Castles;
8 Castles QR, P—B3, etc.

8 Q—R4   P—Q3
9 Castles QR
Linear pressure.

9 ......   B—K3
Castling would be far more dangerous
because of 10 B—Q3, with latent threats.

10 B—Q3
Still preventing Black from castling. If
10 KR—K1, B×B; 11 B×Kt, B—K3,
again closing the K file.

10 ......   Q—Q2
Keeping .... Castles QR in reserve.
Preparatory measures such as 10 ....
P—QR3 or 10 .... P—KR3 would only
mean loss of time, calling for the reply
11 KR—K1.

11 B—Kt5
This manœuvring to and fro by the Bishop

has its reasons. Here it prevents 11 ....
Castles QR, after which would follow
12 Kt—K5, Q—K1; 13 Kt×Kt, P×Kt;
14 B—R6 ch, K—Q2; 15 Kt—R4 (threatening mate), and the King hunt has only
begun.

11 ......   Castles KR
12 Kt—Q4
Preventing above all 12 .... B—B4
(13 Kt×B, Q×Kt; 14 B—Q3, followed by
15 B×Kt, and wins). Ineffective would be
12 Kt—K5, Q—K1.

12 ......   P—QR3
13 B—Q3
Returning to the all-important diagonal.

13 ......   Kt—K4
Besides containing a slight pitfall, the
text move is intended at last to get rid of
the adverse KB.

14 P—B4
Keeping his adversary on the alert. After
14 KR—K1, the reply 14 .... P—B4
would be still more efficacious.
The following, intending to win a pawn,
but losing a piece instead, is a mistake:
14 B×P ch, Kt×B; 15 B×B, Kt—Kt3,
and Black wins.

14 ......   Kt×B ch
15 R×Kt   P—B4
In order to be able to place his QB
at KB4, for if at once 15 .... B—B4;
16 R—K3, QR—K1; 17 R×B, R×R;
18 B×Kt, P×B; 19 Kt—Q5, and Black is
at bay.

16 R—Kt3
Seeing that his opponent is not amenable,
White intensifies his attack. If now 16 ....
P×Kt; 17 B×Kt, B×B; 18 Q×B, P—KKt3;
19 Q×P, etc.

16 ......   K—R1
17 Kt—B3
If 17 Kt×B, P×Kt; 18 R—R3, R—B2,
and White's attack is finely mastered.

17 ......   Kt—Kt1
In order also to eliminate the other Bishop,
which is so troublesome for Black. White
must exchange, in view of the threat 18 ....
P—KB3.

18 B×B   Q×B
19 Kt—KKt5   Kt—R3
If 19 .... Kt—B3; 20 Kt×P, and wins;
and if 19 .... P—R3, Black's Knight will
remain locked out for a long time to come,

although White has at the moment no decisive attack at his disposal.

20 R—K1
Preventing 20 .... P—B3.

20 ...... Q—Q2
21 R(Kt3)—K3 KR—K1
The sequel will show that 21 QR—K1 had some points in its favour.

22 QKt—K4 B—B4
At last Black succeeds in occupying the coveted diagonal. The crisis is at hand.

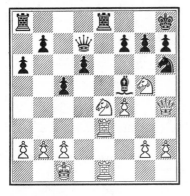

23 Kt—B6
This *break-up sacrifice* was so to speak "in the air" ever since Black's 19th move, but now it is reinforced by the unmasking of the K file. The thrilling play hereafter offers an attractive illustration of well-balanced attack and defence—both perfectly conducted.

23 ...... P×Kt
24 Q×Kt B—Kt3
25 Kt×P
This sacrifice, a sequel to the preceding one (23 Kt—B6), shows its real significance only on White's next move. Without this possibility White would have had to retire and agree to exchanges, bringing Black, with his extra pawn, nearer to victory.

25 ...... B×Kt
26 R—KKt3
A magnificent point. White's linear pressure culminates in a double threat of mate (27 Q—Kt7 or 27 Q×P).

26 ...... R×R ch
27 K—Q2 R—K7 ch
A pretty resource which saves Black from defeat.

28 K—Q1
White cannot take the Rook, otherwise 28 .... Q—K3 ch, followed by 29 .... R—KKt1, parries all threats. And if 28 K—B1, then not hastily 28 .... R×P ch; 29 K—Q1, but calmly 28 .... R—K8 ch, continuing his series of checks.

28 ...... R—K8 ch
Drawn by perpetual check.

196

White Black
CHAROUSEK SCHALLOPP
(Cologne, 1898)

In the following elegant game White engineers a win out of practically "nothing." His exploitation of an increasing pressure on the open KB file is an object lesson in logic.

1 P—K4 P—K4
2 B—B4 Kt—KB3
3 P—Q3
An ultra-solid continuation.

3 ...... B—B4
Black also resorts to the quietest reply. The following leads to greater commitments: 3 .... P—Q4; 4 P×P, Kt×P; 5 Kt—KB3, Kt—QB3; 6 Castles, B—KKt5; 7 R—K1, and White will take advantage of the isolated weakness of the black KP. If 3 .... P—B3; 4 Q—K2 (delaying the projected advance 4 .... P—Q4); 4 .... B—K2; 5 P—B4, P—Q3 (5 .... P—Q4 is now hazardous); 6 Kt—KB3, and White has a lasting initiative.
Against 3 .... Kt—B3; 4 Kt—KB3 leads to a peaceful variation of the *Two Knights' Defence*. The advance 4 P—B4 can be mastered by 4 .... P×P; 5 B×P, P—Q4; 6 P×P, Kt×P, etc., with equality. After 4 Kt—QB3 we obtain:
(a) After 4 .... B—Kt5, a *Vienna Game*.
(b) After 4 .... B—B4; 5 Kt—B3, a *Giuoco Piano*.
(c) After 4 .... B—B4; 5 P—B4, P—Q3; 6 Kt—B3, a *King's Gambit Declined*.
(d) After 4 .... B—K2; 5 Kt—B3 (or 5 KKt—K2); 5 .... P—Q3, etc., a *Hungarian Defence*.

4 Kt—QB3 P—Q3
5 B—K3
Lifeless would be 5 Kt—R4, B—Kt3;

6 Kt×B, RP×Kt, and Black has some compensation for the elimination of his controlling Bishop (an open QR file, a compact mass of pawns on the Q side, a general simplification of the contest).

5 ......   B×B

Presenting his adversary with an as yet invisible asset in the open KB file. An easier continuation is 5 .... B—Kt3, or even 5 .... Kt—B3, as after 6 B×B, P×B, Black's pressure on the Q file would compensate him for his doubled QBP.

6 P×B   P—B3
7 Q—K2   Castles
8 Kt—B3   P—QKt4
9 B—Kt3   P—QR4
10 P—QR4

Very readily White blocks up the Q side, so as to devote the more energy to the opposite wing, where the open KB file furnishes him with an ideal base of action.

10 ......   P—Kt5
11 Kt—QKt1

More useful than 11 Kt—Q1.

11 ......   QKt—Q2
12 QKt—Q2   Kt—B4
13 Castles KR   Kt×B
14 Kt×Kt   B—R3
15 Q—K1

Evading the threat 15 .... Kt×P.

15 ......   Kt—K1
16 Q—Kt3   P—Kt3
17 R—B2   Kt—Kt2
18 QR—KB1   P—KB4

Restless play, which only precipitates events to his detriment. Better is 18 .... Q—K2.

19 Kt—R4

This parries the threat 19 .... P×P, and attacks the KBP a fourth time, whereas it is effectively defended but twice (on account of a potential pin on the KKt file).

19 ......   P—B5
20 P×P   P×P
21 R×P

Winning the pawn fairly and squarely, as the fork .... P—Kt4 is not applicable now or on the next move.

21 ......   R×R
22 Q×R   Q—B2

For if 22 .... P—Kt4; 23 Q—B7 ch, K—R1; 24 Kt—B5, etc. And if 22 .... Q—K2, then fearlessly 23 QKt×P, e.g. (a) 23 .... P—Kt4; 24 Kt×P, Q—Q2;

25 Q—B6 (not 25 Q×KtP, Q×Kt; 26 Kt—B5, Q—B2; 27 Kt—R6 ch, K—R1; 28 R—B7, because of 28 .... Q—B4 ch, exchanging Queens); 25 .... P×Kt (or 25 .... Q×Kt; 26 Q—B7 ch, K—R1; 27 Q—B8 ch, R×Q; 28 R×R mate); 26 Kt—K7 ch, K—R1; 27 Q—B8 ch, followed by mate; or (b) 23 .... B×P; 24 QKt×P, etc.

23 Kt—QB5

An elegant manœuvre. But not 23 QKt×P, on account of 23 .... Kt—R4; 24 Q—Kt5, B×P, etc.

23 ......   Kt—R4
24 Kt×B   Q—Kt3 ch
25 Q—B2   Q×Q ch
26 K×Q   R×Kt
27 K—K3

It is hard to imagine that this position should lead to an easy and rapid win.

27 ......   K—Kt2
28 Kt—B3   Kt—B3

Or 28 .... P—R3; 29 Kt—Q4, etc.

29 Kt—Kt5   P—R3
30 Kt—K6 ch   K—B2
31 Kt—B5

A *deflecting sacrifice*.
In a twinkling Black's game collapses.

31 ......   P×Kt

Or 31 .... R—R2 (parries 32 Kt—Q7); 32 P—K5, P×Kt (32 .... P×P; 33 Kt—K4, winning the Knight); 33 R×Kt ch, followed by R×BP, and wins.

32 P—K5   K—K3
33 R×Kt ch   K×P
34 R×KtP   Resigns

Black is without resource in this Rook ending.

197

White	Black
SCHULTEN	HORWITZ

(London, 1846)

We complete our panorama of the Bishop's Opening with a beautiful game from former days We see here that the splendour of chess combinations knows no time, people or places (see the unexpected sacrifice of the Queen on the 15th move), and that an aggressive temperament will always find points of attack even in a peaceful opening, and also with Black.

1 P—K4	P—K4
2 B—B4	Kt—KB3
3 Kt—QB3	

Black could now lead into an inoffensive variation of the *Vienna Game* (1 P—K4, P—K4; 2 Kt—QB3, Kt—KB3; 3 B—B4, Kt×P, etc.; see game No. 202, Tartakower-Spielmann). 3 P—B4 shows misplaced energy, e.g. 3 .... P—Q4; 4 P×QP, P—K5 (in the manner of Falkbeer).

3 ......   P—QKt4

A "fancy" move, by which Black reveals his intention to forsake the beaten track.

4 B×P	B—B4
5 P—Q3	P—B3
6 B—QB4	Q—Kt3
7 Q—K2	

Another playable defence of the KBP is 7 Q—Q2, with a view to freeing his game by 8 Kt—R4 and Kt×B.

7 ......   P—Q4

Another act of violence.

8 P×P	Castles
9 Kt—K4	

Rapid development by 9 Kt—B3, followed by Castles, is indicated. The slow and artificial manœuvre in the text will justly lose a pawn.

9	Kt×Kt
10 P×Kt	B×P ch

A little surprise—but instructive.

11 Q×B	Q—Kt5 ch
12 B—Q2	

The wrong development. With 12 Q—Q2,

Q×B; 13 Q—Q3 White could have avoided loss and might have redressed the balance, thanks to his extra pawn.

12 ......   Q×B

Attacking two pawns, of which White will naturally protect the more important.

13 Q—B3

A little better would be 13 Q—K3.

13 ......   P—KB4

He disdains re-establishing numerical equality by 13 .... Q×BP, on the principle of "striking the iron whilst it is hot," and, incidentally, the text move brings two more pieces into play.

14 P×KBP	B×P
15 Q—QKt3	

Taking to flight in the most plausible but unfortunate manner, in face of the by no means fatal threat of 15 .... B×P. With 15 Q—K2, Q×BP; 16 B—B3, etc., White could hold out.

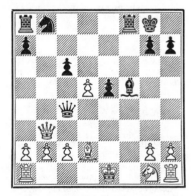

15 ......   Q—B8 ch

A sacrifice of surpassing beauty. The adverse King is drawn by this "magnet" sacrifice into a *défilé* (the KB file), where he will fall a victim to the automatic fire of a Rook-Bishop battery.

16 K×Q	B—Q6 db ch
17 K—K1	R—B8 mate

An "ever-green" amongst games.

14. VIENNA GAME AND VIENNA GAMBIT

198

White	Black
PAULSEN	ROSENTHAL

(Vienna, 1873)

In the fine positional contest which follows, Paulsen—the forerunner of Mieses and Spielmann in his predilection for the Vienna Opening—shows how tension can increase slowly but surely, until it finds its natural release in a break-through (21 P—R5), and even in sacrifices (26 Q × P).

1 P—K4	P—K4
2 Kt—QB3	

The strength of this move—paradoxically —is that it threatens nothing.

2	Kt—QB3
3 P—KKt3	

As Black's 3 .... P—Q4 is unwanted at the moment, this "long term" development of the KB is quite commendable.

3	B—B4
4 B—Kt2	

In an open game, and at a time when chess went through its "heroic period," White applies a principle which was later on to be brought to the fore by the masters of "hyper-modern" chess, Breyer, Réti, Nimzowitsch, Bogoljubow, and up to a point by Alekhine and others, namely, *control of the centre instead of its occupation.*

4	P—Q3

Over-cautious players would play first 4 .... P—QR3, in order to preserve the active KB against 5 Kt—R4.

5 P—Q3	Kt—B3
6 KKt—K2	

The positional manoeuvre 6 Kt—R4 can be applied here, but 6 Kt—Q5 is artificial, and the sequel 6 .... B—Kt5; 7 P—KB3, B—K3 is slightly in Black's favour.

6	B—KKt5

Not sufficiently weighty would be the counter-offensive 6 .... Kt—KKt5; 7 Castles, P—KR4; 8 P—KR3, Kt—R3;

9 Kt—Q5, B—K3; 10 P—B3, and White assumes the initiative. The text move is intended to create a weakness at White's KR3, but the simplest would be 6 .... B—Q2; 7 Castles, Q—B1, to be followed by the positional manoeuvre 8 .... B—KR6.

7 P—KR3	B—Q2
8 Kt—R4	

Eliminating the adverse KB, a troublesome controller of an important diagonal. Or 8 Castles, Q—B1; 9 K—R2, P—KR4, and Black has a counter-attack of sorts.

8	B—Kt3

Viewed differently, Black could have played 8 .... Q—B1; 10 Kt × × B, PKt, preventing White's Castles KR.

9 Kt × B	RP × Kt
10 P—KB4	

Pleasing strategy: without having castled, White strikes out in the centre.

10	P × P
11 Kt × P	Q—K2
12 P—B4	

Preventing 12 .... P—Q4.

12	Q—K4
13 Castles	Castles QR
14 Kt—K2	Kt—Q5
15 B—B4	Kt × Kt ch
16 Q × Kt	Q—KR4
17 P—KKt4	Q—Kt3
18 P—QR4	P—R4

An understandable desire to obtain some counter-play. Passive measures such as 18 .... QR—K1 or 18 .... B—B3 would be answered by 19 P—R5.

19 P—Kt5	Kt—R2
20 Q—K3	P—KB3

The question is: who will get there first?

21 P—R5	

He loses no time in defending the KKtP by 21 P—R4 (allowing 21 .... P × P; 22 P × P, P—R5, etc.). White, by the rolling-up manoeuvre in the text, starts to apply sanctions.

21 ......   Kt×P
22 K—R2

Eliminating the threat 22 .... Kt×P ch, and securing his prospects on the other wing.

22 ......   P×P

If 22 .... P—Kt4; 23 P—R6, P—Kt3; 24 P—R7, K—Kt2; 25 P—K5 dis ch (the KB wakes up); 25 .... B—B3; 26 B×B ch, K×B; 27 B×Kt, Q×B (or 27 .... P×B; 28 Q—B3 ch, etc.); 28 Q—K4 ch, and wins.

23 R×P

This Rook acts powerfully in two directions: main threat, 24 R—R8 mate; and if 23 .... B—B3; 24 B×Kt, P×B; 25 R×P, etc.

23 ......   P—Kt3
24 R—R7   B—B3
25 P—B5

Breaking up the hostile front.

25 ......   KtP×P

Of course, not 25 .... QP×P; 26 R×P ch, etc. But does the text move mean consolidation?

26 Q×P

Brilliant and decisive! (26 .... P×Q; 27 R×P ch, K—Kt1; 28 R×P dis ch, K—B1; 29 R×Q, with an easy win.)

26 ......   Q—K1
27 Q—R5

White's entry into the lists has been most effective.

27 ......   Kt—K3
28 R—B1   P—Kt4
29 Q—R6 ch   K—Q2
30 R×P

Precise up to the end.

30 ......   P×B
31 R×QP ch   Resigns.

199

White	*Black*
MIESES	ASZTALOS

(Kaschau, 1918)

Black's aggressive strategy is very instructive, and demonstrates that the King's fianchetto in an open game is not without risk.

1 P—K4   P—K4
2 Kt—QB3   Kt—KB3
3 P—KKt3

Very good, if slow, against 2 .... Kt—QB3; this move is awkward here, where the adversary has duly prepared a counter-action in the centre.

3 ......   P—Q4

Black's well-known bid for freedom. Less ambitious are other continuations, such as 3 .... B—B4; 4 B—Kt2, Castles; 5 KKt—K2, etc., or 3 .... Kt—B3; 4 B—Kt2, P—Q3; 5 P—Q3, B—K2; 6 KKt—K2, Castles; 7 P—KR3, Kt—K1; 8 P—KKt4, etc.

4 P×P   Kt×P
5 B—Kt2

Not 5 Kt×Kt, Q×Kt, and Black's Queen gets powerfully into action; or 5 KKt—K2 (concerned about his QB3); 5 .... B—KKt5; 6 B—Kt2, Kt×Kt; 7 KtP×Kt, Kt—B3; 8 P—Q4, Q—B3, etc., with advantage to Black.

5 ......   B—K3

On the lines of the preceding note, the enterprising turn 5 .... Kt×Kt; 6 KtP×Kt, B—QB4; 7 Kt—K2, Kt—B3; 8 Castles, Castles, etc., has its points.

6 KKt—K2   Kt—QB3
7 P—Q3

If, less modestly, 7 P—Q4, there follows 7 .... Kt×Kt; 8 B×Kt ch (or 8 P×Kt, B—Q4, with a clear advantage for Black); 8 .... P×B; 9 P×Kt, Q—Q4; 10 R—KKt1, R—Q1, and Black has a fine game. Similarly, if 7 Castles, B—K2; 8 P—Q4 (better, 8 P—Q3); 8 .... Kt×Kt; 9 P×Kt, B—Q4, and White must either give up the KB—guardian of the castled King—or obstruct it by 10 P—B3.

7 ......   B—K2
8 Castles

A precarious lodging. A waiting move, such as 8 P—KR3, was indicated.

8 ......   P—KR4

Sounding the attack. The bellicose character of the subsequent play is indicated by the advance in the text, whereas, had he also castled, Black might have already called a peace conference.

9 P—KR3

A well-known stratagem, intending to reply to 9 .... P—R5 by 10 P—KKt4, keeping the files closed.

9 ......   Q—Q2
10 K—R2   P—B4
11 P—Q4

Trying to obtain a strong supporting square (at Q4 or KB4). If 11 B—K3, P—R5, etc., and if 11 P—KR4, P—KKt4; 12 B×P, B×B; 13 P×B, P—R5, etc., breaking through the enemy front. Therefore the lesser evil for White would have been simplification by 11 Kt×Kt, B×Kt; 12 B×B, Q×B, etc.

11 ......   P—K5
12 Kt—B4   Kt×KKt
13 B×Kt   Castles QR
14 P—B3

In his precarious situation White tries at least to bring his KB back to life.

14 ......   P—R5

A disintegrating advance, which had to be calculated to a nicety.

15 P—Q5

He hopes to redress the balance after 15 .... B×P; 16 Kt×B, Q×Kt; 17 Q×Q, R×Q; 18 BP×P, etc. But Black does not allow himself to be tempted away from his action on the wing.

15 ......   P×P ch
16 K—R1

If 16 B×P, P—B5; 17 B×P, B×KP; 18 P×Kt, B×B db ch, and wins.

16 ......   P—KKt4

Continuing on the same strategic lines, which are both imaginative and energetic.

17 B×P (Kt3)   P—B5
18 P×Kt

Still more disastrous for White would be 18 P×B, Q×P, etc.

18 ......   Q×P

The "point" and the basis of all of Black's calculations, for he will regain his piece at once, thanks to the intermediate attack on White's Queen.

19 Q—K1   P×B
20 Q×KtP   B—Q3
21 Q—K1   B×KRP

The decisive breach.

22 Kt×P   B—B4 ch
23 K—Kt1   B—R7 ch
24 K—B2   Q×P ch
        Resigns

(25 Q—K2, B×Kt.)

A game played by Black with sustained energy.

200

White   Black
MIESES   JANOWSKI

(Paris, 1900)

The fact that White, in this game, leaves his Queen "en prise" for six consecutive moves makes it unique in chess literature. It is the culmination of his far-seeing and powerful strategy.

1 P—K4   P—K4
2 Kt—QB3   Kt—QB3
3 B—B4

In this, the *Vienna Game* proper, Black has little to fear.

3 ......   B—B4

But 3 .... Kt—B3 is more reassuring.

4 P—Q3

Here is a good opportunity to play 4 Q—Kt4, of which a telling example, Mieses-Tchigorin, *Ostend*, 1906, ran as follows: 4 (Q—Kt4) Q—B3 (better would be 4 .... P—KKt3; 5 Q—Kt3, P—Q3, etc., or 4 .... K—B1; 5 Q—Kt3, P—Q3, etc.); 5 Kt—Q5 (well-calculated); 5 .... Q×P ch; 6 K—Q1, K—B1; 7 Kt—R3, Q—Q5; 8 P—Q3 (threatening to win the Queen by 9 P—B3); 8 .... P—Q3 (or 8 .... B—Kt3; 9 R—B1, etc.); 9 Q—R4, B×Kt; 10 Q×B, Kt—R4; 11 R—B1 (deep play), Kt×B; 12 Q—Q7, P—KB3; 13 Kt×KBP (brilliant); 13 .... Q—B7 (not 13 .... Kt×Kt; 14 R×Kt ch, P×R; 15 B—R6 ch, K—Kt1; 16 Q—Kt7 mate, nor even 13 .... P×Kt; 14 R×P ch, etc.); 14 R×Q, B×R; 15 Kt—R5, Resigns.

4 ......   P—Q3

After 4 .... Kt—B3; 5 B—KKt5, White obtains a fine initiative.

5 P—B4   Kt—B3
6 P—B5   Kt—QR4

Valueless. More useful would be 6 .... Kt—Q5, e.g. 7 B—Kt5, P—B3; 8 P—QR3, P—QKt4; 9 B—R2, Q—Kt3, with counter-chances.

7 Q—B3

An energetic course, conforming to the idea of the preceding move, namely, to lay stress on K side operations. Without backbone would be 7 B—Kt3, Kt×B; 8 RP×Kt, with a free game for Black.

7 ......   P—B3

He tries to even up matters by play in the

centre, namely, 8 .... P—QKt4; 9 B—Kt3, Kt×B; 10 RP×Kt, P—Q4. There is for Black nothing good in 7 .... Kt×B; 8 P×Kt.

8 P—KKt4   P—KR3

After 8 .... Kt—Q2, hoping to stem his adversary's onslaught (9 .... Q—R5 ch), there follows 9 P—Kt5, Kt×B; 10 P×Kt, Kt—Kt3; 11 P—Kt3, B—Kt5 (or 11 .... B—Q5; 12 KKt—K2); 12 P—QR3, B×Kt ch; 13 Q×B, Q—K2; 14 Kt—B3, etc., and White still exerts a multilateral pressure.

9 P—KR4	P—QKt4
10 B—Kt3	Kt×B
11 RP×Kt	P—KR4
12 P×P	

The policy of the open door! After 12 P—Kt5, Kt—Q2, the critical zone remains closed (13 P—B6, P—Kt3, etc., or 13 P—Kt6, P—B3, etc.).

12	Kt×RP

If 12 .... R×P; 13 B—Kt5.

13 KKt—K2	Q—Kt3
14 Kt—Kt3	

A struggle for *strategic points*. We see once more that the opening of lines benefits the better-developed side.

14	Kt—B3
15 B—Kt5	B—Kt2
16 P—R5	

A quick-silver pawn. Threat: 17 P—R6.

16	Kt—R2
17 B—Q2	Castles QR

Hoping, at one stroke, to have displaced the centre of gravity, but White shows that the K side is still the main theatre.

18 P—R6

The pivot.

18	P—Kt3

If 18 .... P×P; 19 R×KRP, and the opponent's critical corner is dead. Evidently, not 18 .... KR—Kt1; 19 P×P, R×P; 20 P—B6, Kt×P; 21 Kt—B5, R—Kt8 ch; 22 R×R, B×R; 23 B—Kt5, and wins, nor 18 .... QR—Kt1; 19 K—K2, maintaining his threats.

19 Castles	KR—Kt1

Or 19 .... B—B7; 20 QKt—K2. A little better is 19 .... QR—Kt1.

20 P×P	P×P
21 QR—B1	K—Kt1
22 Q—B7	R—R1

He even thinks of laying a trap. Or

22 .... Q—B2; 23 Q×Q ch, K×Q; 24 R—B7 ch, R—Q2; 25 KR—B1, R—Q1; 26 R—Kt7, R×R; 27 P×R, R—KKt1; 28 R—B7 ch, K—Kt1; 29 B—R6 (threat of 30 R—B8 ch); 29 .... P—Q4; 30 P×P, P×P; 31 Kt×KtP, and Black has no resource.

23 Q×P	QR—Kt1

Will he win a piece?

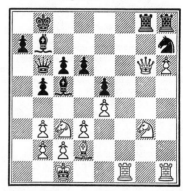

24 Q—Kt7

Offering the Queen. For if 24 .... R×Q; 25 P×R, R—Kt1; 26 R×Kt, P—Q4; 27 R—R8, Q—Q1; 28 QR—R1, K—B2; 29 Kt—B5, B—QB1; 30 R×R, Q×R; 31 R—R8, and wins.

24	B—B1
25 Kt—B5	B×Kt
26 R×B	B—Kt5

Again, if 26 .... R×Q; 27 P×R, R—Kt1; 28 R×Kt, P—Q4; 29 R—R8, Q—Q1; 30 QR—R5, K—B2; 31 B—Kt5, Q—K1; 32 B—B5, followed by R×R, and R—R8, and wins.

27 K—Kt1	B×Kt
28 P×B	Kt—B1
29 KR—KB1	Kt—Kt3
30 Q—Q7	

After being *en prise* six times!

30	R—Q1
31 Q—K6	Kt—B5

If 31 .... Kt—B1; 32 R×Kt, etc.

32 B×Kt	P×B
33 QR×BP	

Balance: two extra pawns and a dominating position.

33	Q—B4
34 R—B7	Q—Kt4

Prevents 35 Q—K7, but there follows another surprise.

35 R—B8   Q—QB4
36 Q—K7   Resigns.

201

White	Black
MIESES	FRITZ

(Düsseldorf, 1908)

A great specialist in this opening, Mieses has, with it, obtained many sparkling victories; here is one of his defeats, and a painful one. Black took advantage of a counter-chance with remarkable consistency.

1 P—K4   P—K4
2 Kt—QB3   Kt—QB3
3 B—B4   Kt—B3
This leads to a far easier game than 3 ....
B—B4.

4 P—Q3   B—Kt5
In order to free his game by 5 .... P—Q4.
After 4 .... B—B4, there are a number of safe continuations for White, e.g.: 5 Kt—B3 (back to the *Giuoco Pianissimo*); 5 P—B4 (*King's Gambit Declined*); 5 B—K3; or 5 B—KKt5.

5 B—KKt5
A sound continuation. Too innocuous would be 5 Kt—K2, P—Q4; 6 P×P, Kt×P; 7 B×Kt (or 7 Castles, B—K3; 8 Kt×Kt, B×Kt; 9 B×B, Q×B; 10 P—KB4, Castles QR, and Black has a very good game); 7 .... Q×B; 8 Castles, Q—R4, and Black has overcome the pitfalls of the opening.

5 ......   P—KR3
6 B×Kt   B×Kt ch
By this intermediary exchange, a dangerous combatant is eliminated, whereas after 6 ....
Q×B; 7 Kt—K2, P—Q3; 8 Castles, B—K3; 9 Kt—Q5 (the despised Knight!); 9 .... B×Kt; 10 B×B, B—B4; 11 P—B3, Castles KR; 12 K—R1 (preparing the advance of the KBP); 12 .... Kt—K2; 13 B—Kt3, Kt—Kt3; 14 P—KB4, White has the initiative.

7 P×B   Q×B
8 Kt—K2   Kt—K2
A similar line of play occurs after 8 ....
P—Q3; 9 Castles, P—KKt4; 10 P—Q4, P—KR4, and the issue is uncertain.

9 Castles   P—KKt4
It is important to prevent 10 P—B4, etc.

10 Kt—Kt3
This tentative manœuvring by White only wakens up the latent hostile forces.
More purposeful would be 10 P—Q4, e.g.
10 .... P—Q3; 11 R—Kt1 (still immobilising the enemy QB); 11 .... Kt—Kt3; 12 Q—Q3, Castles; 13 P—B3, and White's consolidating measures have been effective.

10 ......   P—KR4
In view of White's intention to settle down comfortably in the critical zone by 11 Kt—R5, Black renders this more awkward by means of a pawn sacrifice.

11 Kt×P
Otherwise 11 .... P—R5, with expansion.

11 ......   Q—KR3
Now the KR file has become alive—to Black's benefit!

12 P—Kt4
A compulsory weakening of the position.

12 ......   Kt—Kt3
Scenting an attack.

13 Q—B3   Kt—B5
14 P—KR3   P—Q3
15 QR—Kt1   P—QB3
16 Kt×Kt
More patient, however, would be 16 K—R2, to be followed by R—KR1, as the lines about to be opened (KKt and KR) will help Black.

16 ......   KtP×Kt
17 K—Kt2   K—K2
A case in which the King is perfectly safe in the middle of the board.

18 R—KR1   P—Kt4
19 B—Kt3   Q—Kt4
20 P—Q4
If 20 Q—K2 (with 21 P—B3 in view), then 20 .... P—KB4, etc.

20 ......   R—R5
21 P×P   P×P
22 Q—Q3
Dreaming of aggression on the Q file after 23 QR—Q1, but his opponent refuses to wait. 22 Q—K2 would provide a more stubborn resistance, e.g. 22 .... B×P; 23 P×B, R×P ch; 24 K—B1 (an amusing mate results from 24 K—B3, R—Kt6 ch; 25 P×R, Q×P); 24 .... R—KKt1; 25 K—K1, and White still holds out.

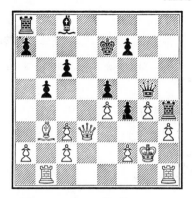

22 ...... B×P
After this sacrifice, the white King's position is ablaze.

23 K—B1
Not 23 P×B, Q×P ch; 24 K—B1, R×R mate.

23 ...... R—Q1
Exacting a price for the white Queen's safety. White—instead of winning a piece—actually loses one.

24 B—Q5	P×B
25 P×P	P—B6
26 Q×KtP	B×P ch
27 K—K1	R—K5 ch
28 K—Q1	R—K7
29 Q—Q3	P—K5
30 Q—Q4	QR×P
Resigns.	

202

| *White* | *Black* |
| TARTAKOWER | SPIELMANN |

(Ostend, 1907)

After bringing a mettlesome pawn to the 7th rank (11 P×P ch), all White had to do in the following game was to let the logic of events guide him in the choice of dynamic continuations (such as 22 B—R6, then 23 B—Kt7, etc.).

1 P—K4	P—K4
2 Kt—QB3	Kt—KB3
3 B—B4	Kt×P

An answer not devoid of commitments. If 3 .... Kt—B3; 4 P—B4, Kt×P;

5 Kt—B3, etc., with a fine attack. The most rational continuation for Black is therefore 3 .... B—B4; 4 P—Q3, P—Q3; 5 P—B4, Kt—B3 (or even 5 .... B—K3; 6 P—B5, B×B; 7 P×B, QKt—Q2; 8 Q—B3, P—B3, etc., with counter-play in the centre); 6 Kt—B3, etc., reaching the *normal position* of the *King's Gambit Declined*. After 3 .... B—Kt5 the continuation in a friendly game, Alekhine-Euwe, *The Hague*, 1921, was as follows: 4 P—B4, P×P; 5 P—K5, Q—K2; 6 Q—K2, Kt—Kt1; 7 Kt—Q5, Q—R5 ch; 8 K—Q1, B—R4; 9 Kt—KB3, Q—R4; 10 Kt—B6 ch (bolt from the blue), P×Kt; 11 P×P dis ch, K—Q1; 12 R—K1, Resigns.

4 Q—R5
The correct reply. Neither 4 Kt×Kt, P—Q4, etc., nor 4 B×P ch, K×B; 5 Kt×Kt, P—Q4, etc., would favour White's chances.

4 ...... Kt—Q3
5 B—Kt3
Lively play. 5 Q×KP ch, Q—K2; 6 Q×Q ch, B×Q, etc., could only equalise.

5 ...... Kt—B3
More solid is 5 .... B—K2, still giving back the pawn of his own free will (6 Q×KP), but speeding up his chance of castling (e.g. if 6 Kt—Kt5, Castles, etc., or if 6 Kt—B3, Kt—B3; 7 Kt×P, Castles, etc.).

6 Kt—Kt5
Accepting the challenge and initiating a clash of arms full of unexpected turns. If 6 P—Q3, P—KKt3, White already loses some valuable territory.

6 ...... P—KKt3
Compulsory, for if 6 .... Kt×Kt; 7 Q×P mate.

7 Q—B3 Kt—B4
Not hazarding the "poker variant," 7 .... P—B4; 8 Q—Q5, Q—K2; 9 Kt×P ch, K—Q1; 10 Kt×R, P—Kt3, etc., Black tries to elude the danger in another way.

8 P—Kt4 P—QR3
Or 8 .... Kt—R3; 9 P—Q4, threatening 10 B×Kt.

9 P×Kt P×Kt
10 P×P Q—K2
Forced, because of 10 .... P—B3; 11 P—Kt7, B×P; 12 Q—R5 ch, K—K2; 13 Q—B7 ch, K—Q3; 14 Q×B, and wins.

11 P×P ch
Quo non ascendam? Well guarded by the

KB, this advanced passed pawn strongly influences events and imparts to the game a particularly original character.

11	......	K—Q1
12	P—Q3	Kt—Q5
13	Q—R5	B—Kt2

If 13 .... Kt×B, then—not 14 B—Kt5, Kt×R; 15 B×Q ch, B×B, etc. (Black thus obtains three pieces for the Queen)—but 14 BP×Kt, with the threat eventually of 15 B—Kt5.

| 14 | Kt—B3 | R—R3 |

An active defence.

| 15 | Kt×Kt |

An active attack, without fearing the opening of the K file, which sooner or later must fall under White's domination.

| 15 | ...... | P×Kt dis ch |
| 16 | K—B1 |

More plausible would be 16 K—Q1, but then Black would defend himself by the sacrifice of the exchange: 16 .... R—K3; and White's QR would remain out of action, whereas now both the white Rooks find important work to do, one on the K file and the other on the KKt file.

16	......	R—KKt3
17	B—Q2	P—Q3
18	R—K1	B—Kt5

An ingenious reply.

| 19 | R×Q | B×Q |
| 20 | R—K1 |

The only square, as after 20 R—K4, B—B6, or 20 R—K6, R×R; 21 B×R, K—K2, Black recovers his pawn—and what a pawn!—with an equal game.

| 20 | ...... | B—B6 |

This looks very threatening. If 20 .... B—Kt5; 21 P—KR3, and clearly not 20 .... R—B3; 21 B—Kt5.

| 21 | KR—Kt1 | B—K4 |

Obstructing at least the more dangerous file. After 21 .... R×R ch; 22 K×R, P—R3, there follows 23 R—K6.

| 22 | B—R6 |

An *indirect irruption*. Now Black would like to give up the exchange if only to eliminate the obsession of the advanced pawn.

| 22 | ...... | K—K2 |
| 23 | B—Kt7 |

Continuing its mysterious zig-zag evolutions.

| 23 | ...... | R—Q1 |
| 24 | B×B |

Showing his hand at last. He prefers the gain of a second pawn with an intensified action of his QR to the gain of the *exchange* by 24 P—B8 (Q) ch, R×Q; 25 B×R ch, K×B, etc.

24	......	P×B
25	R×P ch	K—B1
26	R—Kt3

Without pausing for 26 R×P, White presses the pursuit of the disorganised enemy.

His aim is to outflank the adverse King on the right wing (KKt or eventually KR file).

26	......	B—B3
27	R (K5)—Kt5	R (Q1)—Q3
28	R—R5	R×R

If 28 .... P—R3; 29 R×RP, forcing, as already adumbrated, the entry into the hostile fortress.

| 29 | RP×R | P—R3 |
| 30 | P—Kt4 |

Still the same objective (31 P—Kt5, P×P; 32 R—R8 ch).

| 30 | ...... | B—B6 |
| 31 | R×KtP |

Now the pawn has fallen, like a ripe fruit, into White's hands.

31	......	P—Kt3
32	R—K5	R—Q1
33	P—Kt5	P—R4
34	P—Kt6	Resigns.

203

| *White* | *Black* |
| BLACKBURNE | HANHAM |

(New York, 1889)

A fine example of Blackburne's skill. The manner in which he outflanks the opposing forces is both original and instructive.

| 1 | P—K4 | P—K4 |
| 2 | Kt—QB3 | B—B4 |

Besides the academic replies 2 .... Kt—QB3 or 2 .... Kt—KB3, this also is playable. But 2 .... B—Kt5 is too enterprising, and 2 .... P—Q3 too passive. Against the speculative 2 .... P—KB4,

White can play 3 P × P, Kt—KB3; 4 P—KKt4, etc., a *King's Gambit Accepted* with the colours reversed, and in addition a good extra move (Kt—QB3).

3 P—B4

A violent measure. Disappointing would be 3 Kt—R4, B × P ch; 4 K × B, Q—R5 ch, etc. The best is 3 Kt—B3, as, for instance, in a game Réti-N., *Vienna*, 1913, which went as follows: 3 (Kt—B3) Kt—QB3 (reverting to the *Three Knights' Game*; after 3 .... P—Q3, White obtains the superior development by 4 P—Q4, P × P; 5 Kt × P, Kt—KB3; 6 B—K2, etc.); 4 Kt × P, Kt × Kt; 5 P—Q4, B × P (or 5 .... B—Q3; 6 P × Kt, B × P; 7 P—B4, B × Kt ch; 8 P × B, etc., with advantage to White); 6 Q × B, Q—B3 (threat: 7 .... Kt—B6 ch); 7 Kt—Kt5, K—Q1 (fatal; 7 .... P—B3 is necessary, after which 8 Kt—B7 ch loses, but 8 Kt—Q6 ch would maintain White's superiority); 8 Q—B5, and the double threat of 9 Q—B8 mate and 9 Q × P ch is so strong that Black resigned.

3	P—Q3

An enterprising line is 3 .... Kt—QB3, e.g. 4 P × P (4 Kt—B3 is more substantial); 4 .... P—Q3; 5 P × P, Q × P, etc., and Black has more than an equivalent for his pawn.

4 Kt—B3	Kt—KB3

More efficacious than 4 .... Kt—QB3, which leaves White a wider choice of moves (5 B—B4, 5 B—Kt5, 5 Kt—QR4).

5 B—B4	P—B3

Instead of the usual 5 .... Kt—B3, Black looks for complications.

6 P—Q3

He maintains as far as possible the *tension of the centre pawns.* 6 P × P, P × P; 7 Q—K2 (7 Kt × P, Q—Q5); 7 .... QKt—Q2, etc., would only facilitate Black's task.

6	Q—K2

Intending 7 .... P × P; 8 B × P, P—Q4; but White has no difficulty in mastering this intended expansion in the centre. If 6 .... B—KKt5; 7 P × P, P × P; 8 B × P ch, K × B; 9 Kt × P ch, followed by Kt × B, and White is two pawns ahead. The best continuation is 6 .... QKt—Q2, e.g. 7 Q—K2, P—QKt4; 8 B—Kt3, P—QR4; 9 P—QR3, Q—Kt3, etc.

7 Q—K2	P—QKt4
8 B—Kt3	P—QR4
9 P—QR4	

More trenchant than 9 P—QR3.

9	P—Kt5
10 Kt—Q1	B—R3

This is of no immediate use. Better would be 10 .... B—Kt5

11 P × P	P × P
12 B—Kt5	QKt—Q2
13 Kt—K3	B × Kt

He eliminates an awkward customer. The threat was 14 Kt—B5, or against 13 .... P—Kt3; 14 Kt—Kt4.

14 Q × B	Kt—B4

Weakening his mobile bases. An unsuccessful attempt would be 14 .... Kt—Kt5; as after 15 Q—K2, P—B3; 16 B—Q2, White dominates the highways. The proper course would be effected by 14 .... P—R3; 15 B—R4, P—Kt4; 16 B—Kt3, and although White's position remains superior, Black has means of resistance.

15 Kt—Q2

Systematic consolidation and unmasking the critical KB file.

15	Q—R2

Seeking salvation in tactical expedients. The lesser evil would be 15 .... Kt—K3.

16 Q—Kt3

Avoiding the shoals: 16 B × Kt, Kt × P ch; etc., and definitely assuming the initiative.

16	KKt—Q2
17 B—K3	

Re-establishing a lasting pin.

17	P—Kt3
18 Castles KR	Castles KR
19 Q—B2	

Initiating the final assault in a most astute manner.

19	K—Kt2
20 Q—R4	P—B3

A feeble barricade.

21 Q—R6 ch

Not 21 B—R6 ch, K—R1; 22 B × R, Kt × B dis ch.

21	K—R1
22 R—B3	QR—K1

To be able to reply to 23 R—R3, with 23 .... R—K2; but White has a far more expeditious means of settling matters.

23 Q × P ch

And mate in 3.

204

White	Black
STEINITZ	NEUMANN

(Dundee, 1867)

When this game was played, the extravagant move 4 P—Q4, instead of the supposedly forced 4 Kt—B3, was at first thought to be due to an oversight on the part of the then champion Steinitz, for the resulting King hunt is truly alarming. In many subsequent games, however, he proved the virility of this paradoxical continuation, which supports, even in the opening stages, his theory of: the King— a strong piece.

1 P—K4	P—K4
2 Kt—QB3	Kt—QB3
3 P—B4	P × P

We now have a kind of *King's Gambit Deferred* (1 P—K4, P—K4; 2 P—KB4, P × P; 3 Kt—QB3, Kt—QB3), but more prudent is 3 .... B—B4; e.g. 4 P × P, P—Q3; 5 P × P, Q × P; and, for his pawn, Black has taken the lead.

4 P—Q4	

Sensational!

4	Q—R5 ch
5 K—K2	P—Q3

He already sees that his task is not as easy as it looks, and that he must set to work with deliberation. After 5 .... P—Q4; 6 P × P, B—Kt5 ch; 7 Kt—B3, etc., Black's momentary pressure would drop to zero.

6 Kt—B3	

Beginning to recover territory.

6	B—Kt5
7 B × P	B × Kt ch

He is glad to displace the King still further, but a more pressing strategy would demand 7 .... P—B4. If 7 .... Q—B3; 8 K—K3.

8 K × B	KKt—K2

Or, e.g. 8 .... Kt—B3; 9 B—QKt5, Castles; 10 B × Kt, P × B; 11 Q—Q3, Q—R4 ch; 12 K—B2, B—K2; 13 KR—KB1, Q—R4; 14 K—Kt1, and having artificially castled at last, White has the better game.

9 B—K2	Castles
10 B—K3	

Evading the threat 10 .... Kt—K4 ch; 11 P × Kt, P × P; and Black recovers his piece with advantage. If 10 P—KKt3, Q—B3; with the double threat of 11 .... P—KKt4; and 11 .... Kt × P ch.

10	Q—B3 ch

He tries to keep the opposing King in chancery for, otherwise, there follows 11 P—KKt3 and K—Kt2, and White is out of all danger.

11 K—Kt3	P—Q4
12 B—Kt4 ch	

Not at once 12 P—K5, Kt—B4 ch.

12	K—Kt1
13 P—K5	Q—Kt3

With the threat of 14 .... P—KR4. But 13 .... Kt—B4 ch is a little better.

14 K—B2	

The King makes his escape.

14	P—KR4
15 B—R3	P—B3

He still has dreams of attack.

16 P × P	Q × BP ch
17 Q—B3	

He brings the adversary back to earth.

17	Q × Q ch

Clearly not 17 .... Kt × P; 18 Q × Q, P × Q; 19 B × Kt. But also after 17 .... Q—Kt3; 18 KR—QB1, Kt—Kt5; 19 Q—K2, Q—B3 ch; 20 K—Kt1, the only result would be the furthering of White's intentions. After the exchange of Queens, the grouping of the white forces proves superior.

18 P × Q	P—KKt3
19 Kt—K2	Kt—B4
20 B × Kt	

Bringing about an almost even and practically symmetrical position in which White will be the first to attack weaknesses in the opposing formation (Q5 and KR5).

20	P × B
21 P—B3	B—Q3
22 B—B4	K—B1

Even if Black first occupies the open KKt file by 22 .... KR—Kt1; he would have to relinquish it again after 23 KR—Kt1 (e.g. 23 .... K—B1; 24 B × B, etc., or 23 .... B × B; 24 Kt × B, etc.).

The finish is impressive.

23 KR—KKt1	K—Q2
24 R—Kt7 ch	

One objective is achieved. All goes according to plan.

24	Kt—K2
25 QR—KKt1	K—K3
26 B × B	R × B
27 Kt—B4 ch	K—B3

Or 27 .... K—Q2; 28 R—B7, to be
followed by 29 QR—Kt7.

28 Kt—Q3
Conquest of the *strong point* at K5.

28 ......   R—Kt3
29 P—Kt3   R—KR3
30 Kt—K5   R—R3
31 P—QR4
Or already here: 31 Kt—Q7 ch, K—K3;
32 Kt—B5 ch, followed by Kt×R.

31 ......   R—R4
Or 31 .... P—Kt3; 32 R—B7 ch, K—K3;
33 QR—Kt7, Kt—Kt3 (a last attempt);
34 R×P, Kt×Kt; 35 QR—K7 ch, K—B3;
36 R×Kt, K—Kt4; 37 R—QB7, with an
easy win.

32 P—Kt4   R—R3
33 Kt—Q7 ch   Resigns
A deeply-conceived victory.

VIENNA GAMBIT
205

White	Black
CORZO	CAPABLANCA

(Match, Havana, 1900)

*As Morphy, at the age of twelve, had
already many achievements to his credit, so
did Capablanca, in the following exhilarating
game, give proof of his youthful genius.*

*By winning this match, Capablanca, at the
age of twelve, became champion of Cuba.*

1 P—K4   P—K4
2 Kt—QB3   Kt—QB3
3 P—B4   P×P
4 Kt—B3   P—KKt4
The *classical defence.*

5 P—KR4   P—Kt5
6 Kt—KKt5
The chances of this, the *Hamppe-Allgaier
Gambit,* are, in practical play, considerable.

6 ......   P—KR3
7 Kt×P   K×Kt
8 P—Q4
More sustained is 8 B—B4 ch, as in a
game Tartakower-Berman, *Paris,* 1934
(a horrifying example): 8 (B—B4 ch) K—K1
(or, just as superficially, 8 .... K—Kt2;
9 Q×P ch, K—R2; 10 Q—B5 ch, K—Kt2;

11 Q—B7 mate; only 8 .... P—Q4
9 B×P ch, K—K1, etc., is therefore playable); 9 Q×P, Kt—K4; 10 Q—R5 ch,
K—K2; 11 Q×Kt mate. An interesting
attempt, in place of the text move, is
8 Q×P, as in an entertaining game,
Krejcik-N., *Vienna,* 1922, as follows:
8 (Q×P) B—Q3; 9 B—B4 ch, K—B1;
10 P—Q4, Kt×P (if 10 .... Kt—B3;
11 Q—Kt6); 11 B×P, Kt×P ch; 12 K—Q2,
Kt×R; 13 B×B ch, P×B; 14 R—B1 ch,
Kt—B3; 15 Q—Kt6, Resigns.

8 ......   P—Q4
The most incisive. A playable defence is
also 8 .... P—B6 (9 B—B4 ch, P—Q4;
10 B×P ch, K—K1; 11 P×P, B—K2, etc.);
or 8 .... Kt—B3.
A less stubborn defence is 8 .... P—Q3;
9 B×P, B—Kt2; 10 B—B4 ch, K—Kt3;
11 P—K5, etc.

9 P×P
Or, e.g. 9 B×P, B—Kt5; 10 P—K5
(10 B—QKt5, KKt—K2); 10 .... Kt—K3;
11 B—K2, Q—Q2; 12 Castles, K—Kt2; and
Black succeeds in consolidating his position.
Black's refutation of the text move is very
effective.

9 ......   Q—K2 ch
10 K—B2
Not 10 K—Q2, Q—K6 mate. And if
10 B—K2, P—B6, etc., or 10 Q—K2, Kt×P.

10 ......   P—Kt6 ch
11 K—Kt1
White's King is in a trap. Black's
problem is how to take advantage of the fact.

11 ......   Kt×P
A far-seeing manœuvre.

12 Q × Kt
If 12 B × P, Kt—B4.

| 12 ...... | Q—B4 |
| 13 Kt—K2 | |

He can neither play 13 Q × Q, B × Q ch,
with mate to follow, nor 13 B—K3, P × B;
14 Q × R, P—K7 dis ch, etc.

| 13 ...... | Q—Kt3 |

A beautiful point with tangible results: an
immediate threat, 14 .... B—QB4; and a
distant threat of the QR obtaining control
of a file after the exchange of Queens.

14 Q × Q	RP × Q
15 Kt—Q4	B—QB4
16 P—B3	R—R5

The final point of the combination.

| 17 B—K2 | B × Kt ch |
| 18 P × B | R × QP |

And, on balance, a valuable extra pawn
for Black.

| 19 P—Kt3 | Kt—B3 |

Neither now, nor on the next move,
19 .... R × P; 20 B—B4.

20 B—Kt2
Combinative, but 20 B—B3 is better.

20	R—Q7
21 B—R5 ch	Kt × B
22 B × R	P—B6

A *vacating advance.*

| 23 P × P | Kt—B5 |
| 24 B—K5 | |

There is no salvation, e.g. 24 P—R5,
R—Kt7 ch; 25 K—B1, R—B7 ch; 26 K—K1,
Kt—Kt7 ch; 27 K—Q1, Kt—K6 ch; 28 K—B1,
R—B7 ch; 29 K—Kt1, B—B4; and wins.

24	R—Kt7 ch
25 K—B1	R—B7 ch
26 K—K1	Kt—Q6 ch
Resigns.	

206

| White | Black |
| MILNER-BARRY | ALEXANDER |

(Cambridge, 1932)

*A game of threats and counter-threats,
sacrifices and counter-sacrifices, tensions and
counter-tensions; such, in short, as real
gambit players, ancient and modern, are
wont to play!*
A feast for the eye and mind.

1 P—K4	P—K4
2 Kt—QB3	Kt—QB3
3 P—B4	P × P
4 Kt—B3	P—KKt4

There is nothing better than this *classic
defence.* After 4 .... B—Kt5, the impressive continuation of a game won in his
early days by Steinitz, was as follows: 5 Kt—
Q5, B—R4; 6 Kt × P, P—Q3; 7 P—B3,
B—KKt5; 8 B—Kt5, K—B1 (preparing for
—a miscalculation?); 9 Castles, Kt—K4
(here it is); 10 Kt × Kt (a first surprise),
B × Q; 11 KKt—Kt6 ch (the second surprise); 11 .... BP × Kt (after 11 ....
RP × Kt, the same thunderous reply);
12 Kt × P mate.

| 5 P—Q4 | |

The Pierce Gambit offering the KKt, as in
the famous *Muzio Gambit,* is not to be taken
lightly.

| 5 ...... | P—Kt5 |

Accepting the challenge, for after 5 ....
B—Kt2; 6 P—Q5, Kt—K4; 7 P—Q6, etc.,
White has the advantage. 5 .... P—Q3
6 P—Q5 is also in White's favour.

| 6 B—B4 | P × Kt |
| 7 Castles | P—Q4 |

Necessary emancipation. If 7 .... B—Kt2;
8 B × P, B × P ch; 9 K—R1, White has
enduring chances.

| 8 KP × P | B—KKt5 |
| 9 R—K1 ch | |

But 9 Q—K1 ch is better and affords equal
opportunities. A bold but insufficient idea
is the Queen sacrifice: 9 P × Kt, P—B7 ch;
10 R × P, B × Q; 11 P × P, B—KKt5;
12 B—Kt5 ch, B—Q2, etc.

| 9 ...... | KKt—K2 |
| 10 P × P | |

More astute would be, first, 10 Kt—K4,
B—Kt2 (10 .... P—B7 ch; 11 K × P, B × Q;
12 Kt—B6 mate); 11 P × P.

| 10 ...... | B—R6 |
| 11 B × P | R—Kt1 ch |

The counter-pressure begins.

12 B—Kt3	Kt—R4
13 B—Kt5 ch	P—B3
14 Kt—K4	B—Kt2
15 K—R1	

If 15 P × P, Q × P ch, and White, in view
of the piece which he has given up, could
not think of agreeing to an exchange of
Queens.

15	Q×P
16 P—QB4	Q—Q2

But not 16 .... Q×QP; 17 Q—K2, Q—Q2; 18 QR—Q1, Q—K3; 19 Q—Q2, B—K4 (19 .... K—B1; 20 Q—Q8 ch, R×Q; 21 R×R mate); 20 Kt—Kt5, etc., and thus Black would have opened the Q file for his opponent's benefit.

17 P—Q5

Seeking to obtain fresh resources.

17	K—B1
18 P—Q6	Kt—B4
19 Kt—B5	Kt×B ch
20 P×Kt	Q—B4
21 P—Q7	

This looks very alarming.

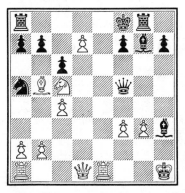

21	B—Q5

An ingenious reply, fulfilling many functions: (i) masking the Q file, (ii) unmasking his own KKt file, (iii) deflecting the adverse Queen eventually (22 Q×B, Q×P ch), (iv) attacking the Knight, (v) cutting off the King's flight as long as this Bishop remains safe.

22 Kt×P

Still seeking safety in artificial manœuvres (22 .... Kt×Kt; 23 B×P, with renewed threats of 24 R—K8 ch and 24 Q×B).

22 ...... Q—R4

Against this, Black is able to take calm and clear-cut measures. Threat: 23 .... B—B8 mate. It is to be noted that the adverse Bishop remains *en prise* all the time, but nobody cares, other events being of greater importance.

23 R—K8 ch	R×R
24 P×R (Q) ch	K×Q
25 Q—K2 ch	K—B1
26 Kt×Kt	

Or 26 Q—R2, Q×P ch.

26	B—Kt5 dis ch
Resigns	

Just in time to avoid being mated on the next move.

The young opponents have dared, in our scientific era, to play one of the most dangerous gambits in a masters' tournament, and it may well be said that the game does credit to winner and loser alike.

207

White	Black
VON JAENISCH	STAUNTON

(Match, London, 1851)

A fighting game which does credit to both players.

The win of Rook, Bishop, Knight and pawn against Queen is technically both interesting and instructive.

1 P—K4	P—K4
2 Kt—QB3	Kt—KB3
3 P—B4	

The resources of the *Vienna Gambit Proper* are many and varied.

3 ...... P—Q4

Only this counter-thrust in the centre can hold the position. After 3 .... P×P, a ruthless continuation could be: 4 P—K5, Q—K2; 5 Q—K2, Kt—Kt1 (a melancholy return); 6 Kt—B3, P—Q3 (plausible, but fatal; better would be 6 .... P—Q4; 7 Kt×P, Q—Q1); 7 Kt—Q5, Q—Q1; 8 P×P dis ch (if 8 Kt×P ch, K—Q2); 8 .... B—K3; (if 8 .... K—Q2; 9 Kt—K5 ch); 9 Kt×P ch, K—Q2; 10 Kt—K5 ch, K—B1; 11 Kt×B, P×Kt; 12 Q—B4 ch, Kt—B3; 13 Q×Kt ch, P×Q; 14 B—R6 ch, K—Kt1; 15 Kt×P mate.

After 3 .... P—Q3, the continuation, no less ruthless, could be: 4 Kt—B3, QKt—Q2; 5 B—B4, B—K2; 6 B×P ch, K×B; 7 Kt—Kt5 ch, K—Kt3; 8 P—B5 ch, K×Kt (or 8 .... K—R3; 9 Kt—B7 mate); 9 P—Q3 dis ch, K—R5; 10 Q—B3, followed by 11 Q—R3 mate.

Finally, after 3 .... Kt—B3, White obtains a substantial advantage in territory by 4 P×P, QKt×P; 5 P—Q4, Kt—Kt3; 6 P—K5, Kt—Kt1; 7 Kt—B3, etc.

4 P×QP P—K5

By an inversion of moves the game reverts

to *Falkbeer's Counter Gambit.* After 4 ....
Kt×P; 5 Kt×Kt, Q×Kt; 6 P×P, Kt—B3;
7 Kt—B3, B—KKt5; 8 B—K2, etc., White
has a vigorous game.

    5 P—Q4
If 5 P—Q3, B—QKt5; 6 P×P, Kt×KP;
7 Q—Q4, Q—K2, and White's game is not
without anxious moments.
If 5 B—Kt5 ch, P—B3; 6 P×P, P×P,
etc., and Black has the initiative. Similarly,
5 B—B4, B—QB4; is embarrassing for White.
For all these reasons it would be best at
once to besiege the advanced black pawn by
5 Q—K2.

5	B—QKt5
6 B—B4	Kt×P
7 B×Kt	Q×B
8 Kt—K2	B—Kt5
9 Castles	B×QKt
10 Kt×B	

Ingenious, but Black meets all dangers
quite unperturbed.

10	Q—Q2
11 Q—K1	P—KB4

An unprofitable adventure would be
11 .... Q×P ch; 12 B—K3, Q—B5;
13 Q—Kt3, P—KB4; 14 P—KR3, followed
by Q×P, etc.

12 B—K3	Castles
13 Q—R4	R—B3
14 P—KR3	R—KR3
15 Q—B2	B—R4
16 P—KKt4	

This violence is necessary as, otherwise,
Black retains a valuable asset in his supported passed pawn.

16	B—B2
17 P—KR4	B—B5
18 KR—K1	P×P
19 Kt×P	B—Q4
20 P—B5	R—QKt3

Black finds the correct reply to White's
every attempt.

21 B—Kt5	Kt—R3

Safer than 21 .... R×P; 22 Kt—B5.

    22 P—B4
More solid would be 22 P—B3, followed
by Kt—Kt3.

22	B×P
23 Kt—B5	P—Kt6

A good reply, as White cannot defend
three pawns at the same time (KBP, QP and
QKtP).

    24 Q×P
For 24 Q—B4, Kt×Kt; 25 P×Kt, R×P,
or 24 Kt×Q, P×Q ch; 25 K×P, R×P ch,
etc.

24	Q×P
25 R—K5	Q—Kt3
26 P—Kt3	B—B2
27 Kt—Q7	

White prefers to take his chance, as after
27 Kt×Kt, R×Kt the Bishops of opposite
colours are no compensation for his lost
pawn.

27	R—Q3
28 P—R5	Q×P
29 Kt—B6 ch	

He wins the Queen, but at too high
a price. If 29 B—K7, R—KKt3.

29	P×Kt
30 B×P dis ch	Q—Kt3
31 R—KKt5	R×B
32 K—R2	R—K1
33 R—KKt1	Q×R
34 Q×Q ch	R—Kt3
35 Q—Q2	P—B3
36 R×R ch	B×R

The contest of *ideas* has come to an end;
now *technique* has its say. In point of
material values, the Rook, Bishop, Knight
and pawn are superior to the Queen. But
her mobility maintains to the end practical
chances of obtaining a perpetual check.

    37 Q—Kt5
If 37 P—Q5, R—Q1; 38 P—Q6, R—Q2,
etc.

37	Kt—B2
38 Q—QR5	Kt—Kt4
39 P—Q5	P—Kt3
40 Q—Q2	R—Q1
41 P—R4	R×P
42 Q—B4	

Having lost the first round (moves 37–41),
White does not despair, but maintains his
efforts to reduce the number of adverse
pawns.

42	Kt—Q3
43 Q—B6	R—Q7 ch
44 K—Kt1	R—Q8 ch
45 K—R2	R—Q7 ch
46 K—Kt1	R—Q8 ch
47 K—R2	R—Q4
48 Q—Q8 ch	Kt—K1
49 Q—K7	R—Q7 ch
50 K—Kt1	R—Q6
51 P—Kt4	R—Q5
52 P—Kt5	P×P
53 P×P	R—Q4
54 Q—K6 ch	B—B2
55 Q—Kt4 ch	K—B1
56 Q—Kt4 ch	Kt—Q3

57 Q—R3	K—K1
58 Q×P	R×P

Here is the second round (moves 42–58), which ends up even, each combatant having confiscated a pawn.

59 Q—B7	R—Kt8 ch
60 K—R2	R—Kt7 ch
61 K—Kt1	Kt—B5
62 Q—B6 ch	K—K2
63 Q—K4 ch	B—K3
64 Q×P ch	K—Q3

In the third round (moves 59–64) White has even succeeded in winning back a unit, but in the final and decisive phase Black's extra pawn must tell.

65 Q—KKt7	P—Kt4
66 Q—B8 ch	K—Q4
67 Q—Q8 ch	K—B3
68 Q—K8 ch	B—Q2
69 Q—K4 ch	K—B2
70 Q—Q4	B—B3
71 Q—B5	K—Kt2
72 K—B1	R—Q7
73 K—K1	R—Q2
74 K—K2	R—Q7 ch
75 K—K1	R—Q4
76 Q—B8	Kt—K4
77 Q—Kt7 ch	K—R3
78 Q—QB7	P—Kt5

A step forward, but hardly earned.

79 Q—B8 ch	K—Kt4
80 Q—Kt8 ch	K—B5
81 Q—Kt6	P—Kt6
82 K—K2	B—Kt4
83 Q—B7 ch	K—Kt5 dis ch
84 K—K3	R—B4
85 Q—Q8	Kt—Q6
86 Q—Q4 ch	B—B5
87 K—Q2	P—Kt7
88 Q—B3 ch	K—R5
89 K—B2	B—Kt6 ch
90 K—Kt1	B—R7 ch

Avoiding a last trap: 90 .... R×Q; stalemate!

91 K×B	R×Q
Resigns.	

208

White	Black
TCHIGORIN	CARO

(Vienna, 1898)

The white King's peregrinations in the following game are nothing short of amazing, and make it unique in the annals of master chess.

1 P—K4	P—K4
2 Kt—QB3	Kt—KB3
3 P—B4	P—Q4
4 P—Q3	

An archaic continuation, recommended particularly by Steinitz.

4	B—QKt5

Playing a kind of *Ruy Lopez* with the colours reversed (and in which consequently the "defence" has an extra move thrown in).

After 4 .... P—Q5, White can play 5 QKt—K2, or even 5 Kt—Kt1, with a compact game.

After 4 .... QP×P; 5 BP×P, Kt—Kt5; 6 Kt×P (if 6 P—Q4, P—K6); 6 .... Kt×KP; 7 P—Q4, Kt—Kt3; 8 B—Q3, etc., White has the better chances.

After 4 .... KP×P, White obtains a well-balanced position by 5 P×P, B—QKt5; 6 B×P, Kt×P; 7 B—Q2, etc.

Finally, for 4 .... Kt—B3, see the following game, Steinitz-Lasker.

5 P×KP	Kt×P

A "correct" sacrifice in the sense that it ensures the draw by perpetual check.

If 5 .... Kt—Kt5; 6 P—Q4 (e.g. 6 .... P×P; 7 B—QB4, P—K6; 8 Q—B3, etc.), White has an attacking position.

6 P×Kt	Q—R5 ch
7 K—K2	

If 7 K—Q2, P—Q5, recovering the piece, and if 7 P—Kt3, Q×KP ch; 8 Q—K2, Q×R; 9 Kt—B3, B—Kt5; and wins.

7	B×Kt
8 P×B	B—Kt5 ch
9 Kt—B3	P×P
10 Q—Q4	

In a most astute manner he maintains his extra piece. If now 10 .... P×Kt ch; 11 P×P, and the adverse Bishop is held in a horizontal pin.

10	B—R4

Insisting on regaining what is his due.

11 K—K3

The only correct reply. If 11 K—Q1, P×Kt (giving up the Queen for the moment); 12 Q×Q, P×P dis ch; 13 Q×B, P×R (Q), and wins.

If 11 K—Q2, Q—Kt5 (the Knight is virtually pinned, as after 12 Kt—K1 or 12 Kt—Kt1, there follows 12 .... Q—Q8 ch); 12 P—KR3, Q—B5 ch; 13 K—K1, Q—Kt6 ch, followed at last by 14 .... P×Kt; with advantage to Black. Finally, if 11 B—K3, P×Kt ch; 12 P×P, Q—K2, etc., with equalisation.

11 ......   B × Kt

A find! If now 12 P × B, Q—K8 ch; 13 K—B4 (13 B—K2, Q × R); 13 .... Q—R5 ch; 14 K—K3 (14 K—B5, P—Kt3 mate); 14 .... Q—K8 ch, etc., White obtains a perpetual check. An astonishing example of the *duplication of stratagems*: the same idea occurs, with the colours reversed, in the *Siesta Variation* of the *Ruy Lopez*: 1 P—K4, P—K4; 2 Kt—KB3, Kt—QB3; 3 B—Kt5, P—QR3; 4 B—R4, P—Q3; 5 P—B3, P—B4; 6 P—Q4, BP × P; 7 Kt × P, P × Kt; 8 Q—R5 ch, K—K2; 9 B—Kt5 ch, Kt—B3; 10 B × Kt, P × B; 11 P × P, Q—Q4; 12 B—R4, K—K3; 13 B × Kt, P × B; 14 Q—K8 ch, K—B4; 15 Q—R5 ch, K—K3; 16 Q—K8, with perpetual check.

12 B—Kt5 ch

A sworn enemy of drawn games, the great Russian master plays *va banque*, although this decision is fraught with many hazards. But "there is nothing new under the sun." A game Steinitz-Blackburne, *London*, 1876, ran an identical course up to the move in the text.

12 ......   P—B3
13 P × B   Q—R3 ch

If at once 13 .... P × B; 14 Q × KP, as happened in the Steinitz-Blackburne game mentioned above.

14 K × P   Q—Kt3 ch
15 K—K3   P × B
16 B—R3   Kt—B3
17 Q—Q5   Q × P
18 QR—QB1   Q—B4
19 KR—K1

An indirect defence of the KP (19 .... Q × KP ch; 20 K—B2).

19 ......   R—Q1
20 Q × P

Re-establishing the balance in material.

20 ......   P—QR3
21 Q—Kt1

Definitely not 21 Q × KtP, R—Q6 ch, etc.

21 ......   Q—Kt4 ch
22 P—B4   Q—Kt7
23 B—Q6   Q—R6 ch

Embarking on a series of checks, intended to keep the adverse King on the edge of a precipice. If 23 .... R × B; 24 P × R, Castles, White consolidates his position by 25 Q—K4. If 23 .... Kt—R4; 24 P—B4, etc. But 23 .... Kt—K2 affords Black fresh resources.

24 K—K4   P—B4 ch
25 K—Q5   Q—Kt7 ch
26 K—B4   P—Kt4 ch
27 K—Q3   Q—B6 ch
28 K—B2   Q—B7 ch
29 K—Kt3   R—QB1

With the potential threat of 30 .... Kt—R4 ch; 31 K—Kt4, R—B5 ch, followed by 32 R—R5 mate.

If at once 29 .... Kt—R4 ch; 30 K—Kt4, Kt—B5; 31 Q × P, Q—Kt7 ch; 32 K—B5, Q—B7 ch; 33 K—Q5, Q—Q7 ch; 34 K—B6, Q—Kt7 ch; 35 K—B7, and the white King prevails.

30 R—B2   Q × BP

Or 30 .... Kt—R4 ch; 31 K—Kt2, Kt—B5 ch; 32 K—R1, and White's King at last is in safety.

31 K—Kt2   Kt—R4
32 K—R1   Q—B5
33 P—K6

Applying the closure.

33 ......   Kt—B3

With the counter-threat of 34 .... Kt—Q5.

34 Q—Q1   P—KR4
35 R—Kt1   R—R2

Or 35 .... Q × KP; 36 R—K2, and wins. Or 35 .... Kt—Q5; 36 P × Kt, Q × R; 37 Q × Q, R × Q; 38 R × P, and White still must win.

36 R × P

The *coup-de-grâce* (36 .... R × R; 37 Q × P ch).

36 ......   Resigns.

209

White	Black
STEINITZ	LASKER

(London, 1899)

A striking feature of the following fine game is Black's "double sacrifice" (15 .... Kt × P and 16 .... B × P ch), followed by a "quiet move" (17 .... P—KB3), the logical result of ultra-rapid and concentric development.

1 P—K4   P—K4
2 Kt—QB3   Kt—KB3
3 P—B4   P—Q4
4 P—Q3

Adopting once again his favourite continuation—tricky, but slow—the former champion sees it refuted by an adversary of the very first rank.

4	......	Kt—B3
5	BP × P	QKt × P
6	P—Q4	Kt—Kt3

Remaining on the critical wing. Another plan, leading to an even game, is: 6 .... Kt—B3; 7 P—K5, Kt—K5; 8 Kt × Kt, P × Kt; 9 B—K3, B—K2; 10 B—QB4, Castles, etc.

7 P × P

But now the continuation given in the preceding note does not ease matters in the centre as does the text move.

| 7 | ...... | Kt × P |
| 8 | Kt × Kt | Q × Kt |

The black Queen occupies a powerful square, whence it cannot very well be driven away (9 P—B4 would weaken White's position).

9	Kt—B3	B—Kt5
10	B—K2	Castles
11	P—B3	B—Q3

Already Black's forces have obtained a development.

12 Castles   KR—K1

Premature would be 12 .... Q—KR4; 13 P—KR3, B × P; 14 Kt—K5, etc. The text move contains no direct threats, but it can eventually be followed by 13 .... P—KB3; and 14 .... Kt—R5.

13 P—KR3

Less impulsive would be 13 B—Q2.

| 13 | ...... | B—Q2 |
| 14 | Kt—Kt5 | |

Here again 14 B—Q2 is indicated.

| 14 | ...... | Kt—R5 |
| 15 | Kt—B3 | |

The lesser evil is 15 B—B3

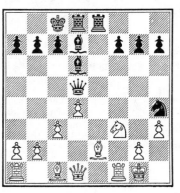

15 ...... Kt × P

A *break-up sacrifice*, of which the chief beauty lies in the fact that it requires a complementary sacrifice on the next move.

16 K × Kt   B × P ch

Taking the last defence by storm. If now 17 K × B, there follows 17 .... Q—B4 ch; 18 K—Kt2, Q—Kt5 ch; 19 K—R1 (19 K—B2, Q—Kt6 mate); 19 .... Q—R6 ch; 20 K—Kt1, Q—Kt6 ch; 21 K—R1, R—K5 (threat: 22 .... R—R5 ch; 23 Kt × R, Q—R7 mate); 22 B—KKt5, QR—K1 (with the threat of 23 .... Q—R6 ch; 24 K—Kt1, R—Kt5 ch; 25 K—B2, Q—Kt6 mate; less powerful would be 22 .... R—Kt5; 23 R—B2, Q × R; 24 Q—KB1, etc.); 23 Kt—K5, B × Kt; 24 P × B, Q × B; 25 R—B2, R—R5 ch; 26 R—R2, R × R ch; 27 K × R, Q × P ch, followed by .... Q × B, and Black remains with three extra pawns.

17 K—B2   P—KB3

Whereas after 17 .... B × R; 18 B × B, etc., White could still offer a stubborn resistance, the text move brings into play Black's additional trump: an assault by pawns.

| 18 | R—KKt1 | P—KKt4 |
| 19 | B × P | |

In view of the threat 19 .... P—Kt5, White tries to avoid the worst by voluntarily giving back the piece.

| 19 | ...... | P × B |
| 20 | R × P | Q—K3 |

Numerically the games are even, but dynamically Black's forces, including the *two Bishops*, are overwhelming.

| 21 | Q—Q3 | B—B5 |
| 22 | R—R1 | |

He is under the unfortunate necessity of giving up the exchange in order to bring the "reserve Rook" into play. E.g.: 22 R—Kt7, B—B4; 23 Q—Kt5, P—QR3; 24 Q—K6 ch, and wins. Again: 22 R—QR5, B—K6 ch; 23 K—K1, K—Kt1, etc., and White plays without his QR.

22	......	B × R
23	Kt × B	Q—B3 ch
24	B—B3	B—B4
25	Kt × P	Q—KKt3
26	Q—Kt5	P—B3
27	Q—R5	R—K2
28	R—R5	

There is nothing better, e.g. 28 Q × P, R × Kt; 29 Q—R8 ch, K—B2; 30 Q—R5 ch, K—Q2, etc.

28	B—Kt5
29 R—KKt5	Q—B7 ch
30 K—Kt3	B × B
Resigns.	

210

| White | Black |
| HROMADKA | SCHREIBER |

(Munich, 1936)

A beautiful game in the modern style, in which the strategy of the blockade, helped by a first sacrifice of the exchange (17 R × B), followed near the end by another (27 R—Kt6), is entirely successful.

1 P—K4	P—K4
2 Kt—QB3	Kt—KB3
3 P—B4	P—Q4
4 P × KP	

The most energetic continuation.

| 4 ...... | Kt × P |
| 5 Q—B3 | |

An old continuation favoured by Paulsen, but the usual 5 Kt—B3 is more natural.

An instructive *opening trap* is 5 P—Q3, after which the plausible 5 .... Q—R5 ch; 6 P—Kt3, Kt × P; 7 Kt—B3, Q—R4; 8 R—KKt1 leads to Black's discomfiture; but the rational continuation 5 .... Kt × Kt; 6 P × Kt, P—Q5; 7 Kt—B3, P—QB4 leaves Black with a very comfortable game.

| 5 ...... | P—KB4 |

Not without commitments. But Black would derive scant comfort from 5 .... Kt × Kt; 6 QP × Kt, etc. An astute, if temporary, defence of the attacked Knight is provided by 5 .... Kt—QB3; e.g. 6 B—Kt5 (if, unsuspectingly, 6 Kt × Kt, there follows 6 .... Kt—Q5; 7 Q—Q3, P × Kt; 8 Q × P, B—KB4, etc., and White's game is wrecked!—another, and very instructive, *opening trap*); 6 .... Kt × Kt; 7 KtP × Kt, B—K2 (a more confused transaction is: 7 .... Q—R5 ch; 8 P—Kt3, Q—K5 ch; 9 Q × Q, P × Q, etc.); 8 P—Q4, Castles; 9 B—Q3, P—B3 (challenging a decision); 10 Q—R5, P—KKt3; 11 B × P (*sacrifice for a draw*, if 11 Q—R6, R—B2, to Black's advantage); 11 .... P × B; 12 Q × P ch, K—R1; 13 Q—R6 ch, K—Kt1; 14 Q—Kt6 ch, with perpetual check. Hromadka-Lasker, *Märisch-Ostrau*, 1923.

| 6 P—Q3 | |

He decides to rid himself of the intruding Knight without delay, as after 6 KKt—K2, Kt—QB3; 7 P—Q4, Kt—Kt5; 8 K—Q1, P—B4, Black takes the lead.

| 6 ...... | Kt × Kt |
| 7 P × Kt | P—Q5 |

More enterprising than 7 .... B—K2; 8 P—Q4, which would round off White's game nicely.

| 8 Q—Kt3 | |

This very ingenious continuation in the gambit style improves White's chances, which would be far less propitious after 8 B—K2, Kt—B3, etc., to say nothing of 8 P × P, Q × P, etc. Other *disentangling manœuvres* are also very good, as for instance 8 Q—B4, Kt—B3; 9 Kt—B3, etc., or 8 Q—B2, P × P; 9 P—Q4, etc.

| 8 ...... | Kt—B3 |
| 9 B—K2 | Q—Q4 |

If 9 .... B—K3; 10 R—Kt1.

| 10 B—B4 | |

Methodical play. Another conception is 10 B—B3, Q × KP ch; 11 Q × Q ch, Kt × Q; 12 P × P, Kt × B ch; 13 Kt × Kt, with a fine centre, or 10 .... Q—B4; 11 Kt—K2, Kt × P; 12 Castles, and White gives up worldly possessions for an attack.

10	B—K3
11 P—B4	B—Kt5 ch
12 K—B2	

The game being a closed one, the King is perfectly safe here.

| 12 ...... | Q—Q2 |
| 13 R—Kt1 | Castles QR |

He hopes to mount an attack on the K side, but 13 .... Castles KR affords greater resistance.

| 14 B—B3 | B—B4 |
| 15 R—Kt5 | P—QKt3 |

Or 15 .... B—Kt3; 16 P—B5, Kt × P; 17 P × B, Kt × B; 18 P × P, and wins.

| 16 Kt—K2 | P—QR3 |

Forcing the issue, but White's reply is eloquent. A more reserved continuation is 16 .... B—K2; 17 P—KR4, KR—Kt1; 18 KR—QKt1, but here also White assumes the initiative. (*Diagram. See p. 273.*)

| 17 R × B | |

A fine *positional sacrifice.*

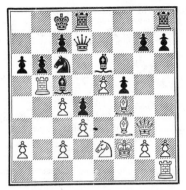

Position after 16 .... P—QR3

17	P×R
18 R—QKt1	QR—Kt1
19 P—KR4	

An important move, preventing 19 .... P—Kt4, and foreshadowing White's plan of establishing a *blockade*.

| 19 ...... | Kt—Q1 |

He thinks he can oppose the enemy's aspirations by peaceful means, for the ruthless effort 19 .... P—Kt4; 20 P×P, P—R3; 21 P—Kt6, P—KR4 would require too much self-denial. But shutting the stable door after the horse is gone is nothing unusual.

| 20 B—Kt5 | Q—R5 |
| 21 R—Kt2 | Kt—B2 |

If 21 .... Q—R6; 22 B—B1.

| 22 Kt—B4 | |

The Knight is out to eliminate Black's best defensive piece.

22	Q—K1
23 Kt×B	Q×Kt
24 B—Q5	Q—KKt3
25 P—K6	Kt—Q3
26 Q—K5	

In order to be able to play 27 B—K7 without exchanging Queens.

The *blockade* of Black's position is worthy of note.

| 26 ...... | R—K1 |
| 27 R—Kt6 | |

A beautiful final stroke, intended to eliminate Black's last defender.

| 27 ...... | Resigns. |

211

| White | Black |
| SPIELMANN | MARÓCZY |

(Teplitz-Schönau, 1922)

A great specialist in the Vienna Game, Spielmann succeeds here in engineering a frontal attack at the cost of a pawn.

The skilful marshalling of his forces (16 Q—QB1; 17 R—R3—Kt3) leads to the direct onslaught (19 B×P), the final phase being both interesting and attractive.

1 P—K4	P—K4
2 Kt—QB3	Kt—KB3
3 P—B4	P—Q4
4 P×KP	Kt×P
5 Kt—B3	

The most rational continuation.

| 5 ...... | B—K2 |

Recommended by that player of genius, Breyer. The text move combines present consolidation with the future galvanisation of the KB file (7 .... P—KB4). Far less sound are other moves by the KB, such as 5 .... B—QKt5 (6 Q—K2) or 5 .... B—QB4; 6 P—Q4, B—QKt5 (7 Q—Q3, P—QB4; 8 B—Q2, etc.).

After 5 .... B—KKt5; the following impressive continuation is from a game Spielmann - Flamberg, *Mannheim*, 1914: 6 Q—K2 (with the two-fold threat of 7 Kt×Kt and 7 Q—Kt5 ch); 6 .... Kt—B4; (the best is 6 .... Kt×Kt); 7 P—Q4 (a bold conception), 7 .... B×Kt; 8 Q×B, Q—R5 ch; 9 P—Kt3 (a *real sacrifice* of a pawn); 9 .... Q×QP; 10 B—K3, Q×P (more prudent would be 10 .... Q—QKt5); 11 Castles, P—QB3; 12 Kt×P, P×Kt; 13 R×P, Q—K3 (or 13 .... Q—K5; 14 B—Kt5 ch, Kt—B3; 15 B×Kt, Q×Q; 16 B×Kt ch, P×B; 17 R—K1 ch, B—K2; 18 R×B ch, K—B1; 19 R×P dis ch, K—Kt1; 20 R×R mate); 14 B—QB4, Q—K5; 15 B×Kt, Resigns.

| 6 P—Q4 | |

Best. The adverse Knight, as will be seen, can be dislodged later on. If 6 P—Q3, Kt×Kt; 7 P×Kt, Castles, followed by 8 .... P—KB3, with counter-chances. If 6 Q—K2, P—KB4, holding his own, and after 6 B—K2, Castles; 7 Castles, Kt—QB3, Black already has the initiative.

| 6 ...... | Castles |

Insufficient would be combinative play by 6 .... B—R5 ch; 7 P—Kt3, Kt×P; 8 P×Kt, B×P ch. Finally, if 6 .... B—QKt5; 7 Q—Q3.

7 B—Q3   P—KB4
8 P×P e.p.   Kt×P

A less thorny road towards equalisation is 8 .... B×P; 9 Castles, Kt—B3, etc., or, even more lucidly, 8 .... Kt×Kt; 9 P×Kt, B×P; 10 Castles, Kt—B3, etc.

9 Castles   Kt—B3

After 9 .... B—KKt5; 10 Q—K1, P—B4; 11 Kt—K5, etc., White has the advantage.

10 B—KKt5   B—KKt5

The preparation for a pawn sacrifice (by 13 .... Kt×P).

11 Q—K1   P—KR3

First unpinning! The alternative, 11 .... B×Kt; 12 R×B, Kt×P, would be immediately fatal by reason of 13 R—R3, P—KR3; 14 B×P, P×B; 15 Q—Kt3 ch, and wins.

12 B—Q2

Too hazardous would be 12 B×P, but the safest retreat is 12 B—K3.

12 ......   B×Kt
13 R×B   Kt×P

Beginning of the *danse macabre*.

14 R—Kt3

Not 14 R—R3, on account of 14 .... B—B4; 15 K—R1, Kt—Kt5.

14 ......   B—B4
15 K—R1   R—K1
16 Q—QB1

With the powerful threat of 17 B×P. But the sacrifice of a Rook by 16 R×P ch results only in a draw by perpetual check: 16 .... K×R; 17 Q—Kt3 ch, K—R1; 18 B×P, Q—Q2; 19 Q—R4, Kt—R2, etc.

16 ......   Kt—R4

This strategy of pinpricks is the only plausible one. If 16 .... Kt—K5; 17 Kt×Kt, P×Kt; 18 B—B4 ch, K—R2; 19 B—B3, Kt—B4; 20 R—R3, P—K6; 21 B—Q3, and White has a won game.

17 R—R3

Not 17 R—Kt6, because of 17 .... Q—R5; 18 B×P, R—K3, etc. The soundest would be 17 R—Kt4 (17 .... Kt—KB3 or 17 .... Q—Q2; 18 R—Kt6), but White wishes first to fathom his opponent's intentions.

17 ......   Kt—KB3
18 R—Kt3   Q—Q2

This makes matters worse instead of better. He should have played 18 .... Kt—R4, and if — looking for gain — 19 R—Kt4, then 19 .... Q—Q2; 20 R—Kt6, R—K3, and he has a defence.

19 B×P   Kt—Kt5

This is the reply on which Black had built all his hopes.

20 Q—B4

Defending (against 20 .... Kt—B7 ch) and attacking (the KKt) at the same time.

20 ......   Kt—K7

If 20 .... Kt×B; 21 Q×KKt. The text move is a despairing trap (21 Kt×Kt, Kt—B7 ch, and Black wins!).

21 Q×Kt   Kt×R ch
22 Q×Kt   Resigns

A fighting game.

212

White	Black
KAN	BOTVINNIK

(Moscow, 1935)

In the following game Black causes his own ruin by kidnapping two pawns on the QB file (11 .... B×P and 21 .... Q×P), as his opponent soon has three adjacent open files (QR, QKt and QB) on which to operate.

1 P—K4   P—K4
2 Kt—QB3   Kt—KB3
3 P—B4   P—Q4
4 P×KP   Kt×P
5 Kt—B3   Kt—QB3
6 Q—K2

A grave disappointment would result from a quiet developing continuation by 6 B—K2, e.g. 6 .... B—QB4 (threat: 7 .... Kt—B7, "mating" the Queen); 7 P—Q4, Kt×QP (a cruel surprise); 8 KKt×Kt, Q—R5 ch; 9 P—Kt3, Kt×P; 10 Kt—B3, B—B7 ch (more trouble); 11 K×B, Kt—K5 db ch; 12 K—K3, Q—R3 ch (more convincing even than 12 .... Q—B7 ch); 13 K—Q4, P—B4 ch; 14 K×QP, Q—B3 ch; 15 K—B4, B—K3 ch, and wins.

The most solid is therefore 6 B—Kt5, although the continuation 6 .... B—K2; 7 Castles, Castles; 8 P—Q4, P—B4, etc., has no trenchant results. Similarly, after 6 P—Q3, Kt×Kt; 7 P×Kt, B—K2, and Black completes his development without trouble.

Not without risks is 6 P—Q4, B—KKt5; 7 B—QKt5, B—Kt5; 8 B×Kt ch, P×B; 9 Q—Q3, B—KB4, etc.

6 ......   B—KB4

Bringing his pieces out. If 6 .... B—KKt5, then — fearlessly — 7 Kt×Kt, Kt—Q5 (this tempting interlude costs a piece. Relatively best is 7 .... P×Kt; 8 Q×P, B×Kt; 9 P×B, Q—Q5, etc.); 8 Q—Q3, B×Kt; 9 Kt—B3 (not at once 9 P×B, P×Kt; 10 Q×P, Q—R5 ch; 11 Q×Q, Kt×KBP ch, etc., followed by .... Kt×Q, and the tables are turned); 9 .... B—B4; 10 P×B, Q—K2; 11 P—B4, and White wins. Hasenfuss-Sigurdsson, *Folkestone*, 1933.

7 Q—Kt5

An optimistic sally, which—succeeds! Caution dictates 7 P—Q3.

7 ......   Kt—B4

Instinctively, Black wants to protect his two pawns (QP and QKtP).

A reply which meets the case is at once 7 .... P—QR3, and then if 8 Q×KtP or 8 Q×QP, Kt—Kt5, which shows that the white Queen has entered the fray without due preparation.

8 P—Q4	P—QR3
9 Q—K2	Kt—K5
10 Q—K3	

White has restored the balance, and now maintains the superior grouping of his forces (a good centre, open KB file, etc.).

The *pawn sacrifice* is basically sound.

10	Kt×Kt
11 P×Kt	B×P

Accepting the Greek gift.

12 Q—B2	B—KB4
13 Kt—R4	B—K3
14 B—Q3	

Well developed at the price of a pawn, this Bishop is becoming very active.

14	Q—Q2
15 Castles	Kt—R4
16 Kt—B5	Castles

Or 16 .... P—KKt3; 17 Kt—R4, with fresh targets.

17 Q—K2	Q—B3
18 R—Kt1	P—R3
19 B—Q2	Kt—B5
20 Kt—K3	Kt×Kt
21 B×Kt	Q×P

Having had, at all times, a difficult game, Black has at least secured an advantage in material.

As against this, the new open file will soon make itself felt.

22 KR—B1	Q—R4
23 Q—QB2	

The final assault.

23	P—QB3
24 B—Q2	Q—B2
25 Q—R4	

All White's forces are co-operating. The two-fold threat now is 26 KB×P and 26 B—R5.

25	R—Q2

There is no saving clause.

26 B×QRP	Resigns.

15. KING'S GAMBIT AND KING'S GAMBIT DECLINED

213

White	Black
KIESERITZKY	CALVI

(Paris, 1847)

In the following pretty game—which well reflects the lively style of the period—the most attractive feature is White's struggle for expansion on the K file (17 B—K6, then 23 P—K6, and finally, 26 Kt—K4).

1 P—K4	P—K4
2 P—KB4	P×P
3 Kt—KB3	P—KKt4

The *classical defence.*

4 P—KR4

The most energetic reply.

| 4 ...... | P—Kt5 |
| 5 Kt—K5 | |

Known as the *Kieseritzky Gambit*, this *gambetto grande* was already known in the sixteenth century.

5 ......   P—KR4

An ancient idea which scorns the consolidation of the inner lines, which is obtained chiefly by developing the pieces 5 .... B—Kt2 or 5 .... Kt—QB3 or 5 .... Kt—KB3 or 5 .... P—Q4, followed by .... Kt—KB3.

| 6 B—B4 | R—R2 |

A painstaking Rook! The dangers of the artificial manœuvre 6 .... Kt—KR3 are well illustrated in a game Lafon l'Aisné-Roussereau, *Paris*, 1680—a Kieseritzky two centuries before his time!: 7 P—Q4, P—Q3; 8 Kt—Q3, Q—K2; 9 Kt—B3, B—B4; 10 B×P, Kt×RP; 11 Q—Q2, Kt—Kt3; 12 Castles QR, P—QB3; 13 KR—B1, B—K3; 14 B—KKt5, Q×B (an ingenious, if insufficient, expedient); 15 Q×Q, B—R3; 16 Q×B, R×Q; 17 B×B, P×B; 18 R—B6, K—Q2 (or 18 .... K—K2; 19 QR—B1, etc.); 19 Kt—B4, Kt×Kt; 20 R×R, Resigns.

| 7 P—Q4 | P—Q3 |

Or first, 7 .... P—B6; 8 P×P, P—Q3;

9 Kt—Q3, etc. The attempt 7 .... B—K2 would only stimulate the white forces, e.g. 8 B×P, B×P ch; 9 P—Kt3, B—Kt4; 10 R×P (the awakening of the white KR); 10 .... R×R; 11 B×P ch, K—B1; 12 B×R, B×B; 13 Kt—Kt6 ch, K—Kt2; 14 Kt×B, and White wins easily.

8 Kt—Q3	P—B6
9 P×P	P—QB3
10 Kt—B4	

Preventing both 10 .... P—Q4 and 10 .... B—K3.

10 ......   Kt—K2

Less cumbersome would be 10 .... Kt—B3. The QKt could later on be developed via Q2 to Kt3, and the KB could find employment by .... B—R3 and eventually .... B×Kt.

| 11 Kt—B3 | Kt—Q2 |
| 12 K—B2 | R—R1 |

Or first, 12 .... B—Kt2; 13 Q—Q3, and now only 13 .... R—R1, in view of the threat 14 P—K5.

| 13 Q—Q3 | B—Kt2 |
| 14 B—Q2 | K—B1 |

The King relinquishes the critical K file, but remains in the danger zone. An ill-fated enterprise would be 14 .... Q—Kt3; 15 B—K3, Q×KtP; 16 QR—QKt1, Q—R6; 17 Kt—Kt5, Q×Q; 18 Kt×P ch, K—B1; 19 P×Q, etc., and White has a big advantage.

| 15 QR—K1 | Q—Kt3 |
| 16 B—K3 | Q—B2 |

Here again 16 .... Q×KtP would be too risky.

17 B—K6

A pretty episode.

17 ......   P—Kt4

Hoping that the moment is favourabe for a counter-action on the Q side. Or atl once, 17 .... Kt—QKt3; 18 B—Kt3, but neither 17 .... Kt—QB4 nor 17 .... Kt—K4, by reason of 18 P×Kt, P×B; 19 P×P, and wins.

18 P—Kt4	Kt—QKt3
19 B—Kt3	P—R4
20 P—R3	P—R5
21 B—R2	B—Kt2

Rather than to hope for things to happen in the distant future, he should have played 21 .... B—Q2.

22 P—K5
Piercing the front.

22 ...... P—Q4
He tries to keep the lines closed, for if, e.g. 22 .... P×P; 23 P×P, B×P (or 23 .... R—Q1; 24 B—Q4, etc.); 24 B—Q4, B×B ch; 25 Q×B, R—KR2; 26 Q—B6, and wins.

23 P—K6
Energetic play.

23	B—B1
24 B—B1	Q—Q3
25 P×P	K×P

A decisive mistake, allowing the hostile Knight to get powerfully into play. Better would be the intermediary measure 25 .... B—B4, although Black's position would still be uneasy after 26 Q—Q2, K×P; 27 QKt—K2, etc.

26 Kt—K4	Q—B2
27 Kt—Kt5 ch	K—Kt1
28 R×Kt	

A sacrifice which has the double task of eliminating a defending piece and of speeding up the concentration of his own forces.

28	Q×R
29 R—K1	Q—B3

He tries in vain to establish some counter-scheme. For if 29 .... Q—Q1; 30 Kt—Kt6, R—KR3; 31 Kt—K7 ch, K—B1; 32 Kt—R7 ch, R×Kt; 33 Q×R, B×P ch; 34 K—B1, and Black has no resource.

30 R—K8 ch	B—B1
31 Kt—Kt6	B—KB4

Or 31 .... K—Kt2; 32 Kt×B, R×Kt; 33 Q—R7 mate, or 32 .... B—KB4; 33 KKt—K6 ch, K—Kt3; 34 Kt—B4 ch, K—Kt2; 35 R×KR, R×R; 36 Q—Q2, etc.

32 Q×B
Winning a piece.

32	Q×Q
33 Kt—K7 ch	K—Kt2
34 Kt×Q ch	K—B3
35 R—K6 ch	

Weaving a mating net.

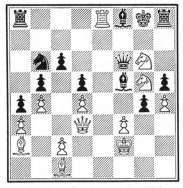

Position after 31 .... B—KB4

35 ...... K×Kt
36 B—Kt1
And White mates in two.

214

White	*Black*
ROSANES	ANDERSSEN

(Breslau, 1863)

A classic, showing how mind can triumph over matter.

Held fast as in a vice, the white King has no escape after Black's sacrifice of a Rook (12 .... K—B1, gaining time) and later of the Queen (20 .... Q—B8 ch, gain in space).

1 P—K4	P—K4
2 P—KB4	P×P
3 Kt—KB3	P—KKt4
4 P—KR4	P—Kt5
5 Kt—K5	Kt—KB3

An active defence.

6 B—B4
As this immediate action against KB7 is easily met, 6 P—Q4 is more useful.

6 ...... P—Q4
7 P×P B—Q3
Continuing to show an active spirit, although 7 .... B—Kt2; 8 P—Q4, Kt—R4; 9 Kt—QB3, Castles, etc., would be sounder.

8 P—Q4 Kt—R4
Maintaining the same spirit: not only does the text move guard the gambit pawn, but

it indicates Black's future line of play on the critical sector. If 9 Castles, Q×P, and, in reply to other moves, 9 .... Kt—Kt6.

9 B—Kt5 ch
He gets entangled in an expedition, which neglects the safety of his own King. If 9 Kt×KtP, Kt—Kt6, etc. The best, in spite of all apparent dangers, is 9 Castles, e.g. 9 .... Q×P; 10 Q—K1, Q×Q; 11 R×Q, K—B1; 12 Kt—QB3, etc.

9 ......   P—B3
Preparing for sacrifices in material, in order to speed up his action on the sector which he recognises as the most important. Otherwise, 9 .... K—B1 is playable.

10 P×P   P×P
11 Kt×QBP   Kt×Kt
If 11 .... Q—Q2; 12 Kt×P wins.

12 B×Kt ch   K—B1
Great play! But 12 .... B—Q2; 13 B×B ch, Q×B; 14 Castles, etc., would deprive Black's attack of all vitality, and so he prefers to give up his QR for nothing more than an attacking *tempo*.

13 B×R   Kt—Kt6
14 R—R2
Better is 14 K—B2.

14 ......   B—KB4
15 B—Q5   K—Kt2
16 Kt—B3   R—K1 ch
17 K—B2   Q—Kt3
Threatening 18 .... B—K4.

18 Kt—R4
Or 18 P—R4, B—K4; 19 Kt—Kt5, P—QR3, etc.

18 ......   Q—R3
Threatening mate in four by 19 .... Q—K7 ch, etc.

19 Kt—B3
If 19 P—B4, Q×Kt; 20 Q×Q, R—K7 ch; 21 K—Kt1, R—K8 ch; 22 K—B2, R—B8 mate.

19 ......   B—K4
A great fight for the diagonal, which is but weakly defended by White's QP.
If now 20 P×B, Q—Kt3 ch; 21 K—K1, Q—Kt8 ch; 22 K—Q2, Q—K6 mate.

20 P—R4
Intending, after 20 .... Q—Kt3; to play 21 Kt—Kt5, P—QR3; 22 P—B3, etc., but Black is disinclined to wait, and announces mate in 4.

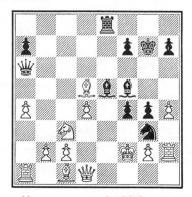

20 ......   Q—B8 ch
A splendid sacrifice of the Queen, of which the object is to deflect the opposing Queen from the protection of Q4.

21 Q×Q   B×P ch
22 B—K3   R×B
A quiet preparation for the mate on the next move.

23 K—Kt1
Or 23 Kt—Kt5, R—K7 mate. There could be no more impressive demonstration of the power of a double check.

23 ......   R—K8 mate.

215

White	Black
MARSHALL	VON SCHEVE

(Monte Carlo, 1904)

How to play the rôle of the aggressor although the exchange down! In the end the vital white forces triumph over the amorphous conglomeration of the opposing pieces.

1	P—K4	P—K4
2	P—KB4	P×P
3	Kt—KB3	P—KKt4
4	P—KR4	P—Kt5
5	Kt—K5	Kt—KB3
6	B—B4	P—Q4
7	P×P	B—Q3
8	Castles	

An unexpected sacrifice which gains an invaluable *tempo* for the attack.
Invented by the U.S.A. amateur, Professor

Isaac Rice, at the beginning of this century, the *Rice Gambit* offers numerous practical chances.

8	B × Kt
9 R—K1	Q—K2
10 P—B3	

Not yet 10 P—Q4, on account of 10 .... B × P ch; 11 K—B1, B—K4.

10	P—B6

He takes advantage of the breathing space in order to win the exchange in quite an astute manner. Unfavourable for Black would be 10 .... Q—B4 ch; 11 P—Q4, Q × B; 12 R × B ch, followed by B × P, etc. But Black's counter-chances are best exploited by 10 .... Kt—R4; 11 P—Q4, Kt—Q2; 12 P × B, Kt × P (12 .... Q—B4 ch; 13 Q—Q4); 13 P—QKt3, Castles; 14 B—R3, Kt—B6 ch; 15 P × Kt, Q × P, etc.

11 P—Q4	Kt—K5

With the brazen threat of 12 .... P—B7 ch.

12 R × Kt	B—R7 ch
13 K × B	Q × R
14 P—KKt3	Castles
15 B—Q3	

He prefers—for the sake of the attack—to give up a pawn, rather than to win one by 15 B—B4, B—B4; 16 B × P, Kt—Q2, after which Black would soon obtain the initiative.

15	Q × P (Q4)
16 P—B4	Q—KR4

Evidently not 16 .... Q × QP; 17 B × P ch. But his base would be better guarded by 16 .... Q—Q1; 17 B—R6, R—K1; 18 Kt—B3, P—QB3.

17 Kt—B3	P—QB3
18 Kt—K4	P—KB4
19 Kt—Q6	P—B5

In order to reply to 20 B × P by 20 .... R × B; 21 Kt × B (21 P × R, Q × P ch, etc.); 21 .... Kt—Q2, with a turn of the tide.

20 Q—K1	P × P ch
21 Q × P	Kt—Q2
22 B—Kt5	P—B7

He hopes to play 23 .... R—B6, with pressure on the KB file, which hope, however, is not to be fulfilled. But if 22 .... Kt—B3; 23 R—K1, White has the greater control of territory.

23 B—B5	Kt—Kt3
24 Kt × B	QR × Kt

Not 24 .... R × B; 25 Kt—K7 ch, with

Kt × R to follow. But now White is able to initiate the final assault.

25 B—K6 ch	R—B2

A Bishop can take only one Rook at a time, thinks Black. If 25 .... K—R1; 26 Q—K5 ch, followed by mate. A more stubborn resistance would result from 25 .... K—Kt2; 26 Q—K5 ch, K—Kt3, etc.

26 R—KB1	R—K1
27 B × R ch	Q × B
28 Q × KtP	Q—Kt3
29 R × P	Kt × P

The balance in material is re-established; but in effect White's threats dominate the position.

A little better would be 29 .... R—K5; 30 Q—B3, Kt—Q2, etc., but White retains the advantage.

30 P—R5	R—K5

Falling into the abyss. But Black's downfall could not be avoided, e.g. 30 .... Q—Kt2; 31 Q—B4, R—KB1; 32 B—B6, etc.

31 B—R6	

A very beautiful final turn.

31	Resigns.

216

White	Black
STOLTZ	SÆMISCH

(Swinemünde, 1932)

Here is a Kieseritzky Gambit treated in the modern manner. Instead of seeking fulminating attacks, White himself brings about the exchange of Queens and succeeds in manœuvring his adversary, in spite of simplifications, into an untenable position.

1 P—K4	P—K4
2 P—KB4	P × P
3 Kt—KB3	P—KKt4
4 P—KR4	P—Kt5
5 Kt—K5	Kt—KB3
6 P—Q4	

With good reasons he refrains from an immediate attack by 6 B—B4, the effect of which would be neutralised by 6 .... P—Q4.

6	P—Q3
7 Kt—Q3	Kt×P
8 B×P	

White is still a pawn to the bad, but his development is effected in a more rational manner.

8	Q—K2
9 Q—K2	B—Kt2
10 P—B3	P—KR4

Here 10 .... B—B4 is to be preferred.

11 Kt—Q2

An important stage! White has no fear of simplification.

If, however, he dallies with 11 P—KKt3, P—Q4; 12 B—Kt2, P—KB4; 13 Kt—Q2, B—K3, Black's impetus begins to be felt.

| 11 ...... | Kt×Kt |

He could easily have played 11 .... P—KB4, instead of agreeing so readily to the exchange of Queens.

| 12 K×Kt | Q×Q ch |
| 13 B×Q | B—B4 |

Better is 13 .... B—K3.

14 KR—KB1

Exercising pressure, and that very skilfully, on the KB file, whereas the more plausible-looking continuation 14 QR—K1 would have no success after 14 .... Castles.

| 14 ...... | Kt—Q2 |

Here again 14 .... Castles would be better.

15 Kt—Kt4

By this manœuvre the threat 16 QB×P, P×B; 17 R×B, etc., becomes actual.

| 15 ...... | Kt—B3 |

The difficulties of Black's game are becoming evident. If 15 .... Castles QR; 16 QB×P. If 15 .... B—K3; 16 P—Q5, etc. Finally, if 15 .... B—K5; 16 QR—K1.

16 B—Kt5 ch

And here is an *unmasking manœuvre* which will at last turn the central file to account. A bitter disappointment would result from 16 QB×P, Kt—K5 ch; 17 K—K1, Kt×B.

| 16 ...... | B—Q2 |

A serious mistake would be 16 .... P—B3; 17 Kt×P, R—Q1; 18 B—Kt5, etc. Relatively best would be 16 .... K—B1; 17 B×P ch, P×B; 18 R×B, and White's advantage is not, as yet, overpowering.

17 QR—K1 ch

By this very important intermediary check White interrupts the connection between the black Rooks, the co-operation of the white forces meanwhile remaining perfect.

| 17 ...... | K—Q1 |

Greater promise of security is afforded by 17 .... K—B1.

18 B—Kt5

A fine and decisive manœuvre. The unmasking of the adjacent files (K and KB) was effected without loss of time.

| 18 ...... | B×B |
| 19 R×Kt | |

The finishing stroke.

| 19 ...... | Resigns |

After 19 .... B×R; 20 B×B ch, K—Q2; 21 R—K7 ch, K—Q1; 22 Kt—Q5, P—B3; 23 R×BP dis ch, K—K1; 24 R—K7 ch, K—Q1; 25 R—R7 dis ch, followed by R×R ch.

Having, of his own free will, played the *King's Gambit* on three occasions, Stoltz, besides winning the tournament, had the satisfaction of scoring $2\frac{1}{2}$ points with this opening.

217

| White | Black |
| The Rev. G. A. MacDONNELL | ANDERSSEN |

(London, 1862)

In the following turbulent game, White succeeds in recovering the piece he has sacrificed, but by a prodigious effort Black manages to engineer a perpetual check.

1 P—K4	P—K4
2 P—KB4	P×P
3 Kt—KB3	P—KKt4
4 P—KR4	P—Kt5
5 Kt—Kt5	

Courting destruction! The *Allgaier Gambit* belongs to the past.

5	P—KR3
6 Kt×P	K×Kt
7 B—B4 ch	

The most plausible, but this gambit can be played in two other and different ways:

(a) The archaic aspect: e.g. Thorold-G. A. MacDonnell, about 1870: 7 Q×P, Kt—KB3; 8 Q×BP, B—Q3; 9 B—B4 ch (if 9 P—K5, B×P; 10 Q×B, R—K1, and wins, and if 9 Q—B3, Kt—B3; 10 P—B3, Kt—K4, etc., with a considerable advantage to Black); 9 .... K—Kt2; 10 Q—B2, R—B1; 11 Castles, Kt—Kt5; 12 Q—Q4 ch, B—K4; 13 Q—Q5, R×R ch; 14 K×R (or 14 B×R, Q×P, etc.; now Black is able to mate in 8); 14 .... Q—B3 ch; 15 K—K2, Q—B7 ch; 16 K—Q1, Q—Kt8 ch; 17 K—K2, Q×P ch; 18 K—K1, B—Kt6 ch; 19 K—Q1, Q—B6 ch; 20 B—K2, Q—R8 ch, and mate next move.

(b) Modern aspect: H. Delaire-N., 7 P—Q4, P—Q4 (playable is also 7 .... P—B6; 8 B—B4 ch, P—Q4; 9 B×P ch, K—Kt2, etc.); 8 B×P, B—K2 (best is 8 .... Kt—KB3, e.g. 9 P—K5, Kt—R4; 10 B—Q3, K—Kt2, etc., or 9 Kt—B3, B—Kt5; 10 B—K2, Kt—B3, etc.); 9 P—KKt3, Kt—KB3; 10 Kt—B3, P—KR4; 11 Q—Q3, P×P; 12 Kt×P, B—KB4; 13 Kt—Kt5 ch, K—Kt3; 14 Q×B ch (a *magnet sacrifice*); 14 .... K×Q; 15 B—Q3 ch, Kt—K5; 16 B×Kt ch, K—B3; 17 B—K5 mate.

| 7 ...... | P—Q4 |
| 8 B×P ch | K—K1 |

If 8 .... B—K3; 9 B×B ch, K×B; 10 Q×P ch, etc. The safest is 8 .... K—Kt2; 9 P—Q4, P—B6; 10 P×P, Kt—KB3, etc.

| 9 P—Q4 | P—B3 |

Little good results from 9 .... P—B6; 10 P×P. The most rational is 9 .... Kt—KB3; 10 Kt—B3, B—Kt5; 11 B×BP, Kt×B; 12 P×Kt, Q×P; 13 Castles, B×Kt; 14 P×B, Kt—B3, with equal chances.

| 10 B—Kt3 | B—K2 |

As now 10 .... Kt—B3 no longer has a double objective in the adverse KB and KP, it would be advantageously answered by 11 Castles, etc. That is why Black adopts a different line of defence, aiming at the blocking of the dangerous K and KB files.

| 11 Castles | P—B6 |
| 12 P×P | P—Kt6 |

After 12 .... P×P; 13 Q×P, Q×P ch; 14 K—R1, Kt—B3; 15 Kt—B3, etc., Black's wide-open position is unpromising. But it is the weight of the white centre which will tell heavily against Black.

| 13 P—KB4 | Kt—B3 |
| 14 P—B5 | |

If at once 14 P—K5, then, not 14 .... B—KKt5; 15 Q—Q3, etc., but 14 .... Kt—Kt5.

14	P—KR4
15 P—K5	Kt—Kt5
16 P—B6	Kt—B7

On the principle that "attack is the best defence."

| 17 Q—Q2 | B—KR6 |
| 18 R—K1 | Kt—R3 |

If 18 .... B—KB1; 19 Q—Kt5.

| 19 P×B | Q×KP |

Having given back the piece, Black can breathe more freely and think of castling on the Q side, which would favour his chances.

| 20 Q—Kt5 | |

Preventing .... Castles QR, and giving, by the exchange of Queens, a fresh turn to the game.

20	Q×Q
21 B×Q	B—Kt5
22 B—B6	

By first playing 22 K—Kt2, White could have avoided many dangers.

| 22 ...... | B—B6 |

Black threatens a pretty mate in two by 23 .... Kt—R6 ch; 24 K—B1, P—Kt7.

| 23 B—K6 | Kt—B2 |

The reserve Knight approaches the critical corner post haste.

24 Kt—Q2	Kt×B
25 Kt×B	Kt—B5
26 B×R	

Accepting a peaceful but original ending, for if 26 Kt—Kt5, R—KKt1.

| 26 ...... | Kt (B7)—R6 ch |
| 27 K—R1 | |

By no means 27 K—B1, P—Kt7 mate.

| 27 ...... | Kt—B7 ch |

Perpetual check.

218

| White | Black |
| SCHLECHTER | TCHIGORIN |

(Vienna, 1903)

The splendour of the following game consists—paradoxically—in the entire absence of splendour! Black succeeds in suppressing each and every attempt by White, whose proper rôle in this opening is to be ferocious, to initiate an attack.

Black's outstanding defensive powers make up for the lack of all outward show.

1 P—K4	P—K4
2 P—KB4	P × P
3 Kt—KB3	P—KKt4
4 B—B4	

Less incisive, but more elegant than 4 P—KR4.

| 4 ...... | P—Kt5 |

Played with a good deal of self-possession; the usual precautionary measure is 4 .... B—Kt2.

5 Castles

This has been played for 400 years, and still is sensational. To sacrifice a clear piece in the opening, not so much for an attack as to obtain attacking chances (the open KB file), is certainly, if successful, an achievement.

Sound or not, the *Muzio Gambit* will always hold a place of honour in the theory of the openings.

5	P × Kt
6 Q × P	

The *Double Muzio*, 6 B × P ch, is unsound, e.g. 6 .... K × B; 7 Q × P, P—Q3; 8 Q × P ch, Kt—B3; 9 P—Q4, Kt—B3; 10 Kt—B3, B—Kt2, and Black is able to consolidate his position.

| 6 ...... | Q—K2 |

A very old idea, brought to honour by a modern mind. The accepted continuation 6 .... Q—B3 allows White a very wide choice of promising continuations, particularly 7 P—K5 (giving up another pawn in order to increase the resources of the attack; or 7 P—B3, or even 7 P—QKt3, Q × R; 8 Kt—B3, etc.); 7 .... Q × P; 8 P—Q3, B—R3; 9 Kt—B3, Kt—K2; 10 P—Q2, QKt—B3; 11 QR—K1, Q—B4 (better than 11 .... Q—B4 ch; 12 K—R1, K—Q1; 13 QB × P, etc.); 12 Kt—Q5, K—Q1; 13 Q—K2 (Lean's attack; if 13 B—B3, R—K1, etc.); 13 .... Q—K3 (best, for if, e.g. 13 .... Kt × Kt; 14 B × Kt, Q × B; 15 B—B3, and wins); 14 Q—B2 (if 14 Kt × Kt, then not 14 .... Q × Kt; 15 Q—R5, Q—Kt4; 16 Q × P, R—B1; 17 Q × RP, etc., but 14 .... Q × Q; 15 Kt × Kt ch, KtP × Kt; 16 R × Q, P—Q4, etc.); 14 .... Q—B4 (if 14 .... Q—Kt5; 15 P—KR3, Q—Kt3; 16 B × P, with the better game); 15 Q—K2, Q—K3; drawn game.

7 P—Q4

Parrying the threat: 7 .... Q—B4 ch, followed by .... Q × B. A more complicated idea would be 7 P—QKt3, B—Kt2; 8 Kt—B3, etc. But 7 Q × P, speeding up

the attack, has not sufficient weight behind it, e.g. 7 .... Q—B4 ch; 8 P—Q4, Q × P ch; 9 B—K3, Q × B; 10 Q—K5 ch, Q—K3; 11 Q × R, Q—KKt3, and Black's defence is sound.

7	Kt—QB3
8 Q × P	

Acquiescing in pacification. Too slow would be 8 P—B3, B—R3, etc., but the following bold continuation affords the most practical chances: 8 Kt—B3, Kt × P; 9 Q—Q3, Kt—K3; 10 Kt—Q5, Q—B4 ch; 11 K—R1, etc.

| 8 ...... | B—R3 |

After 8 .... Kt × P; 9 B × P ch, Q × B; 10 Q—K5 ch, Q—K2; 11 Q × R, there are chances for both sides, while after the move in the text White has to go in for a far more prosaic continuation.

9 Q × P ch	Q × Q
10 B × Q ch	K—Q1
11 P—B3	B × B
12 R × B	Kt—R3
13 B—R5	P—Q3
14 R—B1	

Positional judgment: with two pawns for his piece, a good centre and the open KB file, White's position is not without compensation.

| 14 ...... | K—K2 |

Not yet 14 .... B—Kt5, by reason of 15 B × B, Kt × B; 16 R—B7, etc.

15 P—KR3	B—Q2
16 Kt—Q2	QR—KB1
17 Kt—B4	Kt—Q1

Both sides proceed to regroup their forces.

18 Kt—K3	P—B3
19 P—KKt4	Kt—K3
20 Kt—B5 ch	Kt × Kt
21 KP × Kt	

Or 21 KtP × Kt, Kt—Kt2; 22 B—K2, P—Q4, breaking the hostile pawn chain.

21	Kt—Kt2
22 P—B6 ch	

If 22 QR—K1 ch, K—B3.

The text move is White's best practical chance.

22	R × P
23 R × R	K × R
24 R—B1 ch	K—Kt4

A bold reply, maintaining and increasing Black's advantage. Of course not 24 .... K—K2 (25 R—B7 ch, followed by .... R × Kt), and if 24 .... K—K3; 25 R—K1 ch,

K—Q4 (or else again 25 .... K—B3; 26 R—B1 ch, etc.); 26 B—B7 ch, B—K3; 27 B×B ch, Kt×B; 28 P—B4 ch, recovering his piece.

| 25 R—B7 | Kt×B |
| 26 R×B | |

White has fought valiantly, but his opponent's extra piece now weighs heavily in the balance.

| 26 ...... | Kt—B5 |
| 27 K—R2 | K—R5 |

If at once 27 .... P—KR4; 28 K—Kt3. But after the text move the white King is firmly held, and Black need not worry about his own scattered pawns.

| 28 R×KtP | P—KR4 |
| Resigns | |

A chivalrous decision—but it is justified because of 29 P×P, Kt×P (R4); 30 R×P, R—K1, etc.

Winner of the Gambit Tournament, Vienna, 1903, Tchigorin displayed much *élan* with the white, and great steadiness with the black pieces.

219

| *White* | *Black* |
| RÉTI | FLAMBERG |

(Abbazia, 1912)

A very exciting game! Although the Queens are exchanged early, the contest is magnificently tense up to the very last.

1 P—K4	P—K4
2 P—KB4	P×P
3 Kt—KB3	P—KKt4
4 B—B4	P—Kt5
5 Castles	P—Q4

The modern tendency on the part of Black to emancipate his game before accepting the sacrifice.

6 P×P

Also after 6 B×P the attack is maintained, e.g. 6 .... P×Kt; 7 Q×P, P—QB3; 8 Q×P, Kt—B3; 9 Kt—B3, B—K2; 10 P—K5, P×B; 11 P×Kt, etc., or 6 .... P—QB3; 7 B×KBP ch, K×B; 8 Kt—K5 ch, K—K1; 9 P—Q4, etc.

| 6 ...... | P×Kt |
| 7 Q×P | B—Q3 |

8 P—Q4

The attack can also be sustained by 8 P—Q3, Kt—K2; 9 B×P, B×B; 10 Q×B,

Castles; 11 Kt—B3, Kt—Kt3; 12 Q—Kt3, Kt—Q2; 13 QR—K1, etc.

| 8 ...... | Q—B3 |

Seeking to exchange Queens, but a more stubborn resistance results from 8 .... Kt—K2; 9 B×P, B×B; 10 Q×B, Castles; 11 Kt—Q2, Kt—Kt3; 12 Q—Kt3, K—Kt2 (rendering the KBP mobile); 13 QR—K1, Kt—Q2; 14 Kt—K4, P—KB4; 15 Kt—Kt3, Kt—B3 (sacrificing without regret the litigious pawn, but adding to the number of the defenders of Black's K position; if, however, 15 .... Kt—Kt3; 16 Kt—R5 ch, K—R1; 17 Q—R6, R—KKt1; 18 P—Q6, Q—B1; 19 R—K8, Q×R; 20 Kt—B6, and Black is lost—Réti v. Freyman in the same tournament); 16 Kt×P ch, B×Kt; 17 R×B, Q—Q3 (threat: 18 .... Kt—Kt5); 18 P—KR3, QR—K1; 19 R—K5, Kt×P; 20 Q—Kt5, R×R; 21 R×R, Kt—Kt3; 22 B—Kt3, Q×P ch; 23 R—K3, R—B5; 24 Q—Kt3, R—K5, and Black wins—Réti-Auerbach in the same tournament.

| 9 Q—K4 ch | Q—K2 |
| 10 Kt—B3 | |

A fine surprise! With a profound insight into the position, White does not fear to enter into a simplified phase of the contest.

| 10 ...... | Kt—Q2 |

If 10 .... Kt—KB3; 11 Q—Q3.

11 B×P	Q×Q
12 Kt×Q	B×B
13 R×B	P—KB4

An attempt to free his game, for if 13 .... Kt—K2; 14 P—Q6.

14 R×P

White already has three pawns for his piece and, as the sequel will show, a lasting attack.

| 14 ...... | Kt—K2 |

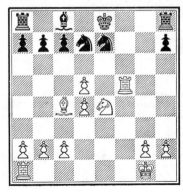

15 R—K1
An elegant reply.

15 ......   Kt—QKt3
After 15 .... Kt × R; 16 Kt—Q6 db ch,
K—B1 (16 .... K—Q1; 17 Kt—B7 mate);
17 R—K8 ch, K—Kt2; 18 Kt × Kt ch,
K—B3; 19 R × R, K × Kt; 20 B—Q3 ch,
K—B3; 21 R × P, White, with a dominating
position, has four pawns for the piece. And
if 15 .... R—B1; 16 R—R5.

16 B—Kt5 ch   K—Q1
17 R—K5   Kt—Kt3
18 Kt—Kt5
Largesse again! The key to White's victory is his complete mastery over the open
K file.

18 ......   Kt × R
19 R × Kt
Threatening 20 Kt—B7 mate, and even
after 19 .... R—B1; 20 Kt—B7 ch, R × Kt;
21 R—K8 mate.

19 ......   B—Q2
20 Kt—B7 ch   K—B1
21 Kt × R   B × B
22 R—R5   B—B5
23 R × P   B × QP
24 P—KR4
Forward! This pawn will cost Black
a piece.

24 ......   B—K5
25 R—Kt7   B × BP
26 P—R5   P—R4
27 P—R6   P—R5
28 P—R7   B × P
29 R × B   Kt—B5
30 Kt—B7   R—R3
31 P—KKt4   Kt × P
32 R—R8 ch   K—Q2
33 Kt—K5 ch   K—K3
34 P—Kt5   Kt—Q8
Arriving too late; but if 34 .... K—B4;
35 P—Kt6, R × P ch; 36 Kt × R, K × Kt;
37 R—QB8, P—B3; 38 R—B7, etc.

35 R—KB8
Cutting off the black King.

35 ......   Kt—K6
36 K—B2
If at once 36 P—Kt6, Kt—B4, whereas
after the move in the text 36 .... Kt—B4 is
not permissible on account of 37 R—K8 ch.

36 ......   Kt—Q4
37 P—Kt6   Resigns
If 37 .... Kt—B3; 38 P—Kt7, followed
by R × Kt ch, and if 37 .... Kt—K2;
38 P—Kt7, followed by R—K8.

220

White	Black
McDONNELL	DE LA BOURDONNAIS

(Match, 1834)

*Furor Hibernicus. In the following set
battle, the storming of the black fortress is
carried out with incomparable* élan.

1 P—K4   P—K4
2 P—KB4   P × P
3 Kt—KB3   P—KKt4
4 B—B4   P—Kt5
5 Kt—B3
Instead of 5 Castles, which is the *Muzio
Gambit* proper, the text move, which contains some resources peculiar to itself, was
adopted several times in this match. It is
therefore quite properly called *McDonnell's
Attack.*
Another violent line of play is 5 P—Q4,
P × Kt, etc., *Ghulam Khassim's Attack.* Altogether too prodigal is the *Wild Muzio:*
5 B × P ch, K × B; 6 Kt—K5 ch, K—K1
(best); 7 Q × P, Kt—KB3; 8 Q × P, P—Q3;
9 Kt—KB3, R—Kt1; 10 Castles, R—Kt5;
11 Q—K3, R × P, etc., holding his own.

5 ......   P × Kt
Or first, 5 .... P—Q4; 6 B × P, P × Kt;
7 Q × P, Kt—KB3; 8 Q × P, and White
carries on his attack without respite.

6 Castles
Varying the programme, for the obvious
continuation (which McDonnell adopted
several times in the match) is 6 Q × P, as
played in a game Marshall-Maróczy (*Vienna
Gambit Tournament*, 1903), which went thus:
6 .... P—Q4 (not 6 .... Q—B3; 7 Kt—Q5,
etc., nor 6 .... B—R3; 7 P—Q4, etc., nor
again 6 .... Kt—QB3; 7 Q × P, etc., but
6 .... P—Q3, the most compact defence,
e.g. 7 P—Q4, B—K3; 8 Kt—Q5, P—QB3,
etc., or 7 Castles, B—K3; 8 Kt—Q5,
P—QB3, etc., holding his own well);
7 Kt × P (more efficacious than 7 B × P);
7 .... P—QB3; 8 Kt × P, Q—B3; 9 P—B3
(not 9 Castles, Q—Q5 ch, followed by ....
Q × B); 9 .... B—R3; 10 P—Q4, Kt—K2;
11 Castles, Castles; 12 Kt—Q5 (pretty);
12 .... Kt × Kt; 13 Q × Q, Kt × Q; 14 B × B,
QKt—Q2; 15 B × R, K × B; 16 P—K5,
Resigns (16 .... Kt—Q4; 17 B × Kt, P × B;
18 P—K6, etc.).

6 ......   P—QB3
If 6 .... P × P; 7 R × P, etc. but a more

useful defensive measure would again be
6 .... P—Q3, with .... B—K3, etc.

7 Q × P   Q—B3
A better line is 7 .... B—R3.

8 P—K5
The storm breaks.

8 ......   Q × P
9 B × P ch
An old *motif*, with some special points.

9 ......   K × B
10 P—Q4
Putting the Bishop into action at high
speed. It is quite clear that, being in a
minority of two pieces, the attacker must
rely on the speed of his troops to restore
the balance.

10 ......   Q × P ch
11 B—K3
The point of points!

11 ......   Q—Kt2
12 B × BP   Kt—B3
Trying to barricade the KB file, for if
12 .... K—K1; 13 QR—K1 ch, followed
by 14 B—K5.

13 Kt—K4
There is much subtlety in White's conduct
of the attack. Much less convincing would
be 13 B—K5, B—K2; 14 Kt—K4, R—Kt1,
etc.

13 ......   B—K2
14 B—Kt5   R—Kt1
There is nothing better.

15 Q—R5 ch   Q—Kt3
16 Kt—Q6 ch
Very attractive play.

16 ......   K—K3
If 16 .... B × Kt; 17 R × Kt ch, followed
by R × Q. But now the black King will be
driven from pillar to post.

17 QR—K1 ch   K × Kt
Or 17 .... K—Q4; 18 P—B4 ch, K—B4
(18 .... K—Q5; 19 B—K3 ch, followed
by mate); 19 B—K3 db ch, K—Kt5;
20 Q—B5 ch, K—R5; 21 P—Kt3 mate.

18 B—B4 mate.

221

White	Black
DE LA	COCHRANE
BOURDONNAIS	

(Paris, 1821)

*One of those games which demonstrate that
a King's Gambit is a very hazardous undertaking, in which the safety of White's own
King is by no means assured.*

1 P—K4   P—K4
2 P—KB4   P × P
3 Kt—KB3   P—KKt4
4 B—B4   P—Kt5
5 Kt—K5
The *Salvio Gambit*, in which White
refrains from sacrificing a piece (by 5 Castles,
or otherwise), but in which the defender
obtains dangerous counter-chances.

5 ......   Q—R5 ch
Naturally! This move is already mentioned by Polerio in the 16th century, who
bases his quotation on the games between
the Portuguese Stacharia and the Spaniard
Avalos.

6 K—B1   P—B6
Introduced into master practice by
Cochrane himself, this move is the strongest
continuation in this position, which in olden
times was of frequent occurrence and much
discussed. Here are two further examples
of this variation: l'Abbé Roman-Jean-
Jacques Rousseau, *Môtiers Travers*, 1770:
6 .... Kt—KR3; 7 P—Q4, P—Q3; 8 Kt—Q3,
P—B6; 9 P—KKt3, Q—R6 ch; 10 K—B2,
Q—Kt7 ch; 11 K—K3 (on this occasion
the King is well equipped for flight); 11 ....
Kt—Kt1; 12 Kt—B4, B—R3; 13 B—B1,
Q × R; 14 B—Kt5 ch, P—B3; 15 B × P ch,
P × B; 16 Q × Q, Resigns. (The great phil-
osopher fell a victim here to a well-known
variation.) The modern aspect: Itze-Reinlé,
Murau, 1925: 6 .... B—Kt2 (a new
attempt); 7 Kt × BP, P—Q4 (freedom at all
costs); 8 B × P, B—Q5; 9 Q—K1, P—Kt6;
10 P—KR3, P—B6 (he could have plotted
against the Queen by 10 .... B—Kt5,
threatening 11 .... B—B7, but he prefers,
with the text move, to hatch a conspiracy
against the King); 11 Kt × R (his last
carousal); 11 .... B × RP (threatens 12 ....
B × P mate); 12 R × B, Q × R (dreadful);
13 P × Q, P—Kt7 mate.

7 P—KKt3
After 7 P × P, there is an expressive continuation by 7 .... P × P; 8 Q × P, Kt—KB3;

9 Kt×BP, P—Q4; 10 B×P, B—R6 ch; 11 K—Kt1, Q—K8 ch; 12 Q—B1, Q×Q mate. Best is 7 P—Q4.

| 7 ...... | Q—R6 ch |
| 8 K—B2 | |

The heedless King's peregrinations commence; or 8 K—K1, Q—Kt7; 9 R—B1, Q×P.

8	Q—Kt7 ch
9 K—K3	B—R3 ch
10 K—Q3	P—Q4
11 B×P	Kt—R3
12 P—B3	P—QB3
13 B×KBP ch	K—K2
14 B—Kt3	

This routine move loses an important *defensive tempo*, which he could have put to better use by playing 14 Q—B1 at once.

14	Kt—B4 ch
15 K—B2	Kt×P
16 Q—B1	B—B4

Forcing the gate.

17 Q×Q	Kt—B7 dis ch
18 P—Q3	P×Q
19 R—Kt1	R—Q1
20 B×B	Kt×B
21 R×P	Kt×P
22 Kt×Kt	B×Kt ch
23 K—B1	

Homeless!

23	KR—B1
24 Kt—Q2	Kt—B4
25 B—Q1	

If 25 R—B2, Kt×P.

| 25 ...... | Kt—K6 |
| 26 KR—Kt1 | B—B8 |

But not at once 26 .... R—B7, by reason of 27 R—K1. Black's offensive, though easy to conceive, still needs a sure and energetic hand.

27 P—Kt3
If 27 B×P, then, not 27 .... Kt×B; 28 R×B, etc., but implacably 27 .... R—B7.

| 27 ...... | R—B7 |

Irruption.

| 28 R×B | Kt×R |
| 29 Kt×Kt | R×B ch |

Coup-de-grâce.

| 30 K×R | R×Kt ch |

And Black wins.

222

| White | Black |
| ANDERSSEN | NEUMANN |

(Berlin, 1865)

The following game is picturesque, on account of the mines and counter-mines in which it abounds.

1 P—K4	P—K4
2 P—KB4	P×P
3 Kt—KB3	P—KKt4
4 B—B4	B—Kt2

The most cautious continuation.

5 P—Q4
Or, disclosing his intentions at once, 5 P—KR4 (*Philidor's Gambit*), or, more solidly, 5 Castles (*Hanstein's Gambit*).

| 5 ...... | P—Q3 |
| 6 P—KR4 | |

Deciding on violence.

| 6 ...... | P—KR3 |
| 7 Q—Q3 | |

Or at once 7 P×P, P×P; 8 R×R, B×R, and only now 9 Q—Q3 (a trap); 9 .... P—Kt5; 10 P—K5, P×Kt (10 .... B—Kt2 or 10 .... K—B1 is necessary); 11 Q—R7, and White recovers his material with advantage. Other continuations: 7 Kt—B3, Kt—QB3, etc., or 7 P—B3, P—Kt5, etc., are in favour of Black.

| 7 ...... | Kt—QB3 |

After 7 .... P—Kt5 White would obtain the concerted action of his forces after 8 Kt—Kt1, Q—B3; 9 P—B3, P—KR4; 10 Kt—QR3, Kt—K2; 11 Kt—K2, etc.

8 P×P
Showing his hand.
Useless would be 8 Q—Kt3, mainly because of 8 .... P—Kt5.

8	P×P
9 R×R	B×R
10 P—K5	

With the transparent menace (e.g. after 10 .... P×P or 10 .... P—Kt5) of 11 Q—R7, with a threefold attack against the KB, KKt and KBP.

10	B—Kt2
11 Q—R7	K—B1
12 Kt—B3	

Or 12 Q—R5, Q—K2, and Black has sufficient means of defence.

12 ......   Kt—R3

With the blatant threat of 13 .... B—B4, kidnapping the Queen. If 12 .... P—Kt5; 13 Q—R5.

13 B—Q3   Kt—QKt5
14 B—K4

Trying to harden the centre even at the cost of lost time, for if, e.g. 14 B—Q2, P—Kt5; 15 Kt—KKt1, Q—R5 ch; 16 K—B1, P×P; 17 P×P, B×P, etc.

14 ......   P—Q4
15 B—Q3   P—Kt5
16 Kt—KKt1   Q—R5 ch
17 K—B1   Kt×B
18 Q×QKt   P—B6

Black has done some good work: repulse of the Queen, seizing the initiative, and now, with the text move, entry into the enemy lines.

19 P×P   P—Kt6
20 B—K3   Q—R8
21 Q—K2

But White also has fairly well restored the situation.

21 ......   B—R6 ch
22 K—K1

Flight of the King from the devastated areas.

22 ......   Kt—B4
23 K—Q2   P—B4

Here is the forcible means of overthrowing the somnolent centre, whereas the cautious line 23 .... P—QB3; would renounce all ambition.

24 Kt×P   P×P
25 B—Kt5   R—K1
26 B—B6   B—R3 ch
27 K—Q3   Kt—K6

The harrying continues.

28 K×P   Kt×Kt
29 K×Kt   B—K3 ch
30 K—Q4   R—B1
31 P—Kt3   Q—R4
32 P—QB4   P—Kt4
33 P—B5   P—Kt5

To prevent 34 P—Kt4.

34 P—R3

He tries in vain to break the ring which surrounds his King. If 34 R—Q1, B—Kt4, eliminating the hostile outpost (Bishop at B6).

34 ......   R—Kt1
35 Q—R6

Leaving the base on an illusory expedition. Better, at all events, would be 35 P—B6.

35 ......   Q—R7

Calculated to a nicety.

36 Q—K2

Return of the prodigal. If 36 Q—Q6 ch, K—Kt1; 37 Q×R ch, K—R2; 38 Q—R8 ch, K—Kt3; 39 Q—Kt8 ch, K—R4; 40 R—Q1, Q—Kt7 ch; 41 K—K4 (or 41 K—Q3, Q—B6 ch; 42 K—K2, Q—K6 ch; 43 K—B1, Q—B7 mate); 41 .... Q—B7 ch; 42 R—Q3 (42 K—Q4, Q—B6 ch; 43 K—K4, Q—K6 mate); 42 .... B—B4 ch; 43 K—Q5 (43 K×B or 43 K—Q4, Q×R mate); 43 .... Q×R ch; 44 K—B6, Q—Q2 mate.

36 ......   P×P
37 P—B6   R—Kt5 ch
38 K—B5   R×P
39 R—Q1

Or 39 P—B7, B—K6 ch; 40 K any, R—Kt3 mate.

39 ......   K—Kt1
40 R—Q8 ch

The last cartridge; if Black now plays mechanically 40 .... K—R2, he is himself mated by 41 Q—K4 ch, etc.

40 ......   B—B1 ch
    Resigns.

223

White	Black
THOROLD	*WAYTE*

(London, 1866)

In the following, White fondly imagines that he has an attack on the K file—until Black starts attacking in real earnest on the adjacent B file.

1 P—K4	P—K4
2 P—KB4	P×P
3 Kt—KB3	P—KKt4
4 B—B4	B—Kt2
5 Castles	P—Q3
6 P—Q4	P—KR3
7 P—B3	

Creating some additional resources. If 7 P—KKt3, P—Kt5; 8 Kt—R4, P—B6, to Black's advantage.

7	P—QB3

If, instead, 7 .... B—K3; 8 B×B, P×B; 9 Q—Kt3, Q—B1; 10 P—Kt3, and White has a promising game. If, in preparation, 7 .... Q—K2, then 8 Kt—R3, P—R3; 9 P—KKt3, P—Kt5; 10 Kt—R4, P—B6; 11 B—B4, B—K3; 12 Kt—B5, etc., maintains a vigorous initiative for White. If 7 .... Kt—K2; 8 P—KKt3, P—Kt5; 9 Kt—R4, P—B6; 10 Kt—R3 (the tempting sacrifice 10 Kt×P, P×Kt; 11 Q×P, Castles; 12 B×P ch, K—R1; 13 Q—R5, Kt—Kt1, etc., is less clear); 10 .... Castles; 11 B—B4, P—R3 (11 .... P—Q4; 12 Kt—Kt5); 12 Q—Q2, etc., White has a fine game. The most useful continuation is 7 .... Kt—QB3, eventually castling on the Q side after 8 Q—Kt3, Q—K2; 9 Kt—R3, Kt—B3, etc. Or 8 P—KKt3, P—Kt5; 9 Kt—R4, P—B6; 10 Kt—Q2, preparing to sacrifice (a lively continuation which affords practical chances without having recourse to a sacrifice is 10 Q—Kt3, Q—K2; 11 Kt—B5, B×Kt; 12 P×B, etc.); 10 .... B—B3; 11 QKt×P, P×Kt; 12 Q×P, etc., with practical chances.

8 Q—Kt3	

Or 8 P—KKt3, P—Kt5; 9 Kt—R4, P—B6; 10 Kt—Q2, intending to sacrifice this Knight at KB3.

8	Q—K2
9 P—Kt3	

The stratagem which is to break the spell of the maleficent pawns.

9	P—Kt5
10 Kt—R4	P—B6
11 B—B4	P—Kt4
12 B—Q3	B—B3
13 Kt—B5	

The only move, as, with the Queen away and the KB file encumbered, the sacrifice 13 Kt×P, P×Kt; 14 R×P would be of no value.

13	B×Kt
14 P×B	P—Q4
15 Kt—Q2	Q—Q2
16 KR—K1 ch	

In the next phase White tries to create a base of action on the K file.

16	Kt—K2
17 B—K5	B×B
18 P×B	Castles
19 P—K6	P×P
20 R×P	K—Kt2
21 QR—K1	

More patient would be, first, 21 K—B2, e.g. 21 .... Kt×P; 22 B×Kt, R×B; 23 QR—K1.

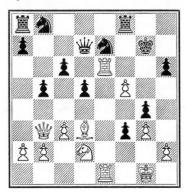

21	P—B7 ch

Utterly changing the aspect of the battle.

22 K×P	Kt×P
23 K—Kt2	Q—KB2

In a trice the centre of gravity is transferred from the K file to the KB file!

24 QR—K5	Kt—Q2

Well parried! If now 25 B×Kt, Kt×R; 26 R×Kt, Q—B3 wins, which is why White prefers to give up the exchange.

25 R×Kt	Q×KR
26 Q—B2	R×R
27 B×R	Q—K7 ch
28 K—Kt1	Kt—K4
Resigns	

If the King takes to flight by 29 K—R1 to evade the threat 29 .... Q×Kt; 30 Q×Q, Kt—B6 ch, there follows 29 .... Kt—B5; 30 Kt×Kt, Q—B8 mate.

224

White	Black
The Rev. G. A. MacDONNELL	BIRD

(About 1870)

In the furious attack which follows, mind triumphs over matter.

1 P—K4	P—K4
2 P—KB4	P × P
3 Kt—KB3	B—K2

Although reduced to the ranks of irregular openings, the *Cunningham Gambit* is not without finesse.

4 B—B4
Best.

4	B—R5 ch
5 K—B1	

The chances of the *Wild Cunningham*— 5 P—Kt3, P × P; 6 Castles, P × P ch; 7 K—R1—are deceptive.

5 ......   P—Q4
If, more conservatively, 5 .... P—Q3; 6 P—Q4, B—Kt5; 7 Kt—B3 (after 7 B × P, Q—B3; 8 B—K3, Kt—K2 the games would be even); 7 .... Kt—KB3; 8 B × P, White, having without difficulty regained his pawn, has the best of it.

6 B × P   Kt—KB3
A temporary sacrifice (7 Kt × B, Kt × B).

7 Kt—B3	Castles
8 Kt × B	

This transaction fails to come up to expectations. Stronger is 8 P—Q4, e.g. 8 .... P—B3; 9 B—Kt3, B—Kt5; 10 B × P, Kt—R4; 11 Q—Q2, B × Kt; 12 P × B, and White's strong centre is an asset in any enterprise.

8	Kt × B
9 Kt × Kt	Q × KKt
10 Kt × P	

A futile rush for material possessions.

10	Kt—B3
11 Kt × R	Kt—Q5

Preventing 12 Q—K1, on account of 12 .... Q × Q ch; 13 K × Q, Kt × P ch, followed by .... Kt × R.
Black's chances are already superior.

12 P—Q3	P—B6
13 P—KKt3	

Or, e.g. 13 B—K3, P × P ch; 14 K × P, B—Kt5, and wins.

13 ......   Q—R6 ch
The beginning of the King-hunt.

14 K—B2	Q—Kt7 ch
15 K—K3	Kt × P ch
16 K—B4	P—KB4
17 P—K5	P—KR3

Threatening 18 .... P—Kt4 mate.

18 P—KR4	P—Kt4 ch
19 P × P	P × P ch
20 K × P	Q × P ch
21 K—R5	Q—Kt5 ch
22 K—R6	K—B2

A beautiful final stroke, quiet and compelling.

Resigns.

225

White	Black
RUBINSTEIN	YATES

(Hastings, 1922)

In the following fighting draw the fortunes of war vary, for Black, having satisfactorily solved the problem of the opening (deferred protection of the gambit pawn by 8 .... P—KKt4), ventures later on a doubtful enterprise (15 .... Q × KtP), and then finds salvation as if by a miracle (21 .... Q × R ch). An original contest.

1 P—K4	P—K4
2 P—KB4	P × P
3 Kt—KB3	Kt—KB3

The *modern defence*, which prepares for a clearance in the centre, enjoys an increasing reputation. Less precise is 3 .... P—Q4 at once because of 4 P × P, Kt—KB3 (4 .... Q × P; 5 Kt—B3, etc.); 5 B—B4 (instead of reverting to the continuation in the text by 5 Kt—B3); 5 .... B—Q3 (or 5 .... Kt × P; 6 B × Kt, Q × B; 7 Kt—B3, etc., and White is better); 6 Q—K2 ch, and White has secured a slight advantage in the opening.

4 Kt—B3	P—Q4
5 P × P	

If 5 P—K5, Kt—R4, etc.

5 ......   Kt × P
6 Kt × Kt
Trying to find the solution in simplicity. The following continuations would hardly be in White's favour: 6 B—B4, Kt × Kt; 7 KtP × Kt, B—Q3; 8 P—Q4, Castles, etc.; or 6 B—Kt5 ch, P—B3; 7 Q—K2 ch, B—K3, etc.; or 6 B—K2, Kt × Kt; 7 KtP × Kt, B—K2; 8 P—Q4, Castles; 9 Castles, Kt—B3; etc.; and, finally, 6 P—Q4, B—QKt5; 7 B—Q2, Q—K2 ch; 8 K—B2, Kt—K6; etc.

6	Q × Kt
7 P—Q4	B—K2

The "point" of Black's defence: the gambit pawn is now *indirectly protected* (8 B × P, Q—K5 ch, followed by .... Q × B).

Less good would be to *guard it directly* by
7 .... B—Q3 (8 P—B4, Q—K3 ch; 9 K—B2,
etc.); or to leave it *unguarded* by 7 ....
B—Kt5 (8 B×P, etc.).

8 B—Q3

A lively line is 8 P—B4, Q—K5 ch;
9 K—B2, etc., or 8 .... Q—R4 ch;
9 B—Q2, etc., or 8 .... Q—KR4; 9 B×P,
Castles; 10 B—K2, B—Kt5 ch; 11 K—B2,
etc., with equalisation.

The least restrained continuation is
8 B—K2, P—KKt4; 9 Castles, with manifold prospects for White.

8 ......   P—KKt4

Threat: 9 .... P—Kt5 and .... Q×KtP.

9 Q—K2

If 9 P—B4, Q—Q3.

9 ......   B—KB4

Opposing a possible threat of 10 B—K4.

10 B×B   Q×B
11 P—KKt4

Inviting 11 .... Q×KtP, upon which
12 R—KKt1 would at last give White the
attack for which he is looking.

The truculent measure in the text is
intended to repress the threatening mass of
pawns, but the following shows more steadiness: 11 B—Q2, Kt—B3 (not 11 .... Q×P;
12 R—QB1, etc., nor 11 .... P—Kt5;
12 Kt—K5, etc.); 12 Castles QR.

11 ......   Q—Q2

With this astute retreat Black asserts his
superiority, which would be far less palpable
after 11 .... Q—K3; 12 Q×Q, P×Q;
13 P—KR4, etc.

12 B—Q2

He rightly avoids 12 Kt×P, Kt—B3;
13 P—B3, Castles QR, and Black dominates
the situation.

12 ......   Kt—B3
13 Castles QR   Castles QR
14 P—KR4   P—B3
15 P—B4   Q×KtP

Having come out of the opening with
flying colours, Black now needlessly embarks
upon a hazardous expedition. He should,
by 15 .... P—KR4, have stressed the rôle
of his mobile chain of pawns.

16 P×P   P×P
17 P—Q5   Kt—Kt5
18 Q×B   Kt—Q6 ch
19 K—B2   Q×Kt
20 Q—K6 ch   K—Kt1
21 R—R3

Intent upon capturing the errant Knight,
but Black finds a skilful and imaginative
expedient to save himself from defeat.

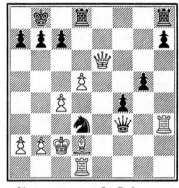

21 ......   Q×R ch
22 K×Q   Kt—B7 ch
23 K—K1   Kt×R
24 Q×Kt   P—KR4

Black's advanced and united passed pawns
compensate his material deficit.

25 B—B3   P—Kt5
26 Q—R4   KR—Kt1
27 Q×RP   P—Kt6
28 B—Q4   QR—K1 ch
29 K—Q2   QR—KB1
30 P—Q6

An adroit measure.

30 ......   P×P
31 Q—R6   K—R1
32 Q×QP   R—Q1
33 Q—B5   R×B ch

Eliminating a dangerous piece.

34 Q×R   P—Kt7

If 34 .... P—B6; 35 Q—Q5, R—KB1;
36 Q—Q6, etc.

35 Q—Kt1   R—Kt6

An exciting finish.

36 P—Kt4   P—R3
37 K—K2   P—B6 ch
      Draw

(38 K—B2, R—R6; 39 Q—Q1, R—R8;
40 Q—Q8 ch, K—R2; 41 Q—Q4 ch, etc.,
with perpetual check.)

226

White   *Black*
STOLTZ   RELLSTAB
(Swinemünde, 1932)

*The course of the following game, in the
modern manner, runs on orderly lines.*

It demonstrates that even in the ultra-open

game, the King's Gambit, it is possible to renounce violent attacks and to rely simply on positional advantages such as a superior development, an open, radioactive file, a pair of Bishops.

1 P—K4	P—K4
2 P—KB4	P×P
3 Kt—KB3	Kt—KB3

The *modern defence* might be called prosaic, for it seeks to lead the course of events back to the normal.

| 4 Kt—B3 | P—Q4 |

Now or never.

5 P×P	Kt×P
6 Kt×Kt	Q×Kt
7 P—Q4	Kt—B3

Here 7 . . . . B—K2; indirectly defends the gambit pawn.

| 8 B×P | B—Kt5 |

Or, less pretentiously, 8 . . . . B—Q3; 9 B×B, Q×B.

| 9 B×P | |

After 9 P—B3, Castles, Black reaches all his objectives.

| 9 . . . . . . | B×Kt |

Trying to make up for his inability to castle and for the temporary loss of a pawn, by disorganising the enemy base.

If 9 . . . . R—B1, then, not 10 B—KB4, Q—K5 ch; 11 Q—K2, B×Kt; 12 P×B, followed by Q×Q ch and Kt×P, with advantage to Black, but 10 B—Kt3, and if 10 . . . . Kt—Kt5; 11 P—B3.

Therefore the best course is 9 . . . . K—Q2; 10 B—Kt3, R—K1 ch; 11 K—B2, K—B1, etc., effecting *artificial castling* with prospects of evening up matters.

10 Q×B	Q×Q
11 P×Q	R—B1
12 B—KB4	Kt×P
13 Castles	

With this surprising reply, White takes the initiative.

| 13 . . . . . . | B—B4 |

Clearly not 13 . . . . R×P ch; 14 K—Kt1, etc., nor 13 . . . . Kt×QBP; 14 B—Kt5 ch, etc.

| 14 B—K5 | |

Every move tells.

| 14 . . . . . . | Kt—K3 |
| 15 B—Kt5 ch | |

Bringing the enemy camp into disarray.

15	K—B1
16 B—Q7	R—R1
17 B×Kt	R—K1

Or 17 . . . . P×B; 18 R—Q7.

| 18 R—Q5 | |

A very subtle *intermediary manœuvre,* which deflects the opposing Bishop.

| 18 . . . . . . | B—K6 ch |
| 19 K—Kt1 | P×B |

If 19 . . . . R×B; 20 R—Q8 ch, winning at least the exchange.

| 20 R—Q7 | |

This incursion having succeeded, Black's position, at one stroke, becomes untenable.

| 20 . . . . . . | R—KKt1 |

If 20 . . . . R—K2; 21 B—Q6, and if 20 . . . . B—R3; 21 R×QKtP.

| 21 B—Q6 ch | Resigns. |

227

| *White* | *Black* |
| ANDERSSEN | KIESERITZKY |

(London, 1851)

Universally known as "The Immortal Game," this magnificent example of Anderssen's combinative powers is still without a peer in the annals of chess.

"Every amateur should know it," proclaims Steinitz; *"and admire it,"* adds Tarrasch; *"but also criticise,"* claims Réti, whose objections, however, proved erroneous.

1 P—K4	P—K4
2 P—KB4	P×P
3 B—B4	

The *Bishop's Gambit* is less imaginative but more tenacious than 3 Kt—KB3.

| 3 . . . . . . | Q—R5 ch |

A reflex check, a stillborn manœuvre.

| 4 K—B1 | P—QKt4 |

The *Bryan Counter-Gambit.* Instead of this lateral demonstration intended to sectionalize the attacker's impetus, many other schemes are available, e.g.:

(a) Archaic Continuation: 4 . . . . P—KKt4 (the *classical defence*); 5 Kt—QB3, B—Kt2; 6 P—Q4, Kt—K2; 7 P—KKt3 (*McDonnell's Attack*); 7 . . . . P×P; 8 K—Kt2, etc., to White's advantage.

(b) Semi-modern: 4 . . . . P—Q4; 5 B×P, P—KKt4, etc. (See the next game, Jackson-Lawrence.)

(c) Modernised: Goldwater-Treystman (*New York,* 1936): 4 . . . . Kt—KB3; 5 Kt—KB3 (if 5 Kt—QB3, Kt—Kt5); 5 . . . . Q—R4; 6 P—Q3 (more energetic is 6 Kt—B3, P—Q3; 7 P—Q4, etc.); 6 . . . . P—KKt4; 7 Kt—B3, P—Q3; 8 Q—K1, P—Kt5; 9 P—K5, P×Kt; 10 P×Kt dis ch, K—Q1;

11 QB×P (disastrous; better is 11 B—Q5); 11 .... P×P ch; 12 K×P, R—Kt1 ch; 13 B—Kt3, B—R6 ch; 14 K—Kt1, P—Q4 (decisive); 15 B×P (or 15 Kt×P, B—B4 ch; 16 Kt—K3, Q—B6, etc.); 15 .... B—B4 ch; White resigns.

    5 B×P   Kt—KB3
    6 Kt—KB3

Hastening to drive the Queen away, for if 6 Kt—QB3, Kt—Kt5; 7 Kt—R3, Kt—B3, and Black has prospects of a counter-attack: e.g. 8 Kt—Q5, Kt—Q5; 9 Kt×P ch, K—Q1; 10 Kt×R, P—B6; 11 P—Q3, P—B3; 12 B—QB4, P—Q4; 13 B×P, B—Q3; 14 Q—K1, P×P ch; 15 K×P, Q×Kt ch (drawing the King into a mating net); 16 K×Q, Kt—K6 dis ch; 17 K—R4, Kt—B6 ch; 18 K—R5, B—Kt5 mate: Schulten-Kieseritzky.

    6 ......   Q—R3

Easier would be 6 .... Q—R4 and .... P—Kt4.

    7 P—Q3   Kt—R4

Here again 7 .... P—Kt4 is a more natural way of defending the gambit pawn.

    8 Kt—R4

A subtle guard against 8 .... Kt—Kt6 ch, but 8 K—Kt1 (or 8 K—B2) would be a blunder on account of 8 .... Q—Kt3 ch, followed by .... Q×B.

    8 ......   Q—Kt4

This simultaneous attack on two pieces proves illusory. Better would be 8 .... P—KKt4; 9 Kt—B5, Q—KKt3.

    9 Kt—B5   P—QB3

In order at last to free the QP and to rid himself of the adverse KKt. There is nothing in 9 .... P—Kt3, because of 10 P—KR4, Q—B3; 11 Kt—B3, and White maintains his advanced posts.

    10 R—Kt1

This very profound sacrifice pursues without respite the active policy inaugurated by White's 8th move. The sequel is forced.

    10 ......   P×B
    11 P—KKt4   Kt—KB3
    12 P—KR4   Q—Kt3
    13 P—R5   Q—Kt4
    14 Q—B3

Threatening to win the encircled Queen by 15 B×P.

    14 ......   Kt—Kt1
    15 B×P   Q—B3
    16 Kt—B3

Here 16 P—K5 would lead to nothing after 16 .... Q—B3, whereas now White

has forged two fresh threats in 17 Kt—Q5 and 17 Kt×P.

    16 ......   B—B4

Black seeks salvation in a counter-attack. Steadier, however, would be 16 .... B—Kt2.

    17 Kt—Q5

A grandiose conception, giving up both Rooks when already one piece down. If 17 P—Q4, then, not 17 .... B×P; 18 Kt—Q6 ch, etc., but 17 .... B—K2; trying to hold his own.

    17 ......   Q×P

Nearing the climax.

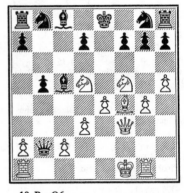

    18 B—Q6

And here is the "immortal" sacrifice. If 18 B—K3, then, not 18 .... Q×R ch; 19 K—Kt2, etc., nor 18 .... Q×BP; 19 R—B1, Q×P ch; 20 K—Kt2, etc., but 18 .... Q—R6, with a stubborn resistance.

    18 ......   Q×R ch

After 18 .... B×B, White mates in four.

    19 K—K2   B×R

If 19 .... Q×R (relinquishing the control of his KKt2), White mates in two.

A slight chance of a draw is afforded by 19 .... Q—Kt7, etc.

    20 P—K5

With a renewed threat of mate in two by 21 Kt×P ch, K—Q1; 22 B—B7 mate.

    20 ......   Kt—QR3

In spite of many dangers, an obstinate resistance could result from 20 .... B—R3, e.g.: 21 Kt—B7 ch, K—Q1; 22 Kt×B (22 Q×R, Q—B6); 22 .... B—Kt3 (to prevent 23 B—B7 ch); 23 Q×R, Q—B6; 24 Q×Kt ch, Q—B1; 25 Q×Q ch, K×Q; 26 B—B8, P—R3 (best); 27 Kt—Q6 ch, K—Q1; 28 Kt×P ch, K—K1; 29 Kt×R, K×B; 30 Kt—Kt6 ch, K—B2; 31 P—B3,

K—K3; 32 P—Q4, and White, with a valuable extra pawn, would win. But one sees that, after so many brilliant turns, the game might have had a more or less arid finish.

21 Kt × P ch   K—Q1
22 Q—B6 ch
A last exploit!

22 ......   Kt × Q
23 B—K7 mate
A forced mate by three minor pieces against the *full* array of the black forces!

228

White	Black
E. M. JACKSON	T. F. LAWRENCE

(London, 1897)

In the following game, played in the true spirit of the gambit, an orgy of sacrificial combinations by White secures for him a well-deserved victory against a powerful opponent.

1 P—K4	P—K4
2 P—KB4	P × P
3 B—B4	P—Q4
4 B × P	Q—R5 ch
5 K—B1	P—KKt4

Combining the modern idea (3 .... P—Q4) with the classical tradition.

Of no value is 5 .... B—Q3 (6 Q—K2, P—KB3; 7 P—Q4, etc.) or 5 .... Kt—K2 (6 Kt—QB3, P—KKt4; 7 Kt—B3, Q—R4; 8 P—KR4, etc.), but the move most likely to free his game is 5 .... Kt—KB3 (e.g. 6 Kt—QB3, B—QKt5; 7 B—Kt3, Kt—B3; 8 Kt—B3, Q—R4, etc.).

6 Kt—KB3

This direct attack could be deferred and the game continued by 6 P—Q4 or 6 Q—B3, or — most effectually — by 6 P—KKt3 (*Tchigorin's Attack*).

6 ......   Q—R4
7 P—KR4   B—Kt2
He avoids the plausible 7 .... P—KR3 (8 B × P ch, Q × B; 9 Kt—K5, Q—Kt2; 10 Q—R5 ch, etc.—*Sanders's Attack*).

8 K—B2   P—Kt5
9 Kt—Kt5   Kt—KR3
10 P—Q3   Castles
A preparatory measure, 10 .... P—QB3 (11 B—Kt3, Castles, etc.), is to be recommended.

11 QB × P
A bold conception. He avoids wasting time on measures of secondary importance, for if 11 Kt—QB3, P—B3; 12 B—Kt3, P—Kt6 ch; 13 K—K1, B—Kt5; 14 Q—Q2, P—B6, etc.

11 ......   B × P
12 Kt—Q2   B × R
13 Q × B
A *positional sacrifice* of the exchange. In return for the exchange, so gracefully given up, White dominates the *long black diagonal* completely denuded of its natural defenders.

13 ......   Kt—Q2
14 Kt—B4
Instead of the commonplace 14 QB × P, Kt—Kt3; 15 B—QKt3, B—K3, etc., White, in a subtle manner, weaves fresh webs around the hostile position.

14 ......   P—B3
Having neglected this useful measure on the 10th, 11th, and again on the 13th move, Black decides to carry it out at a tactically inopportune moment.

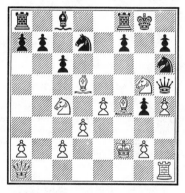

15 Kt—K6
A beautiful stroke, which turns to account the momentary inactivity of Black's QB.

15 ......   P—Kt6 ch
Rejecting 15 .... P × B (16 Q—Kt7 mate) as well as 15 .... P × Kt (16 B × P ch, Kt—B2; 17 Kt—Q6, etc.), Black tries for counter-chances.

16 K—K1
Of course not 16 K × P, Q—Kt5 ch, etc., nor 16 B × P, P × Kt, *with check.*

16 ......   P × Kt
17 B × P ch   R—B2
After 17 .... Kt—B2, White has the same reply as in the text.

18 R—R3   Kt—K4
Ingenious, but inadequate.

19 R × P ch   Kt—Kt3
20 B × R ch   Kt × B
21 Q—B6

Threatening (e.g. after 21 .... B—Q2)
22 Kt—K5, Kt × Kt; 23 B × Kt, Q—R3;
24 Q—R8 ch, K—B2; 25 R—B3 ch, K—K2;
26 B—B6 ch, K—K3; 27 Q × R, Q—B8 ch;
28 K—B2, Q × P ch; 29 K—Kt1, and White
wins.

21 ......   B—Kt5
22 Kt—K3   B—Q2
23 Kt—B5   B × Kt
24 P × B   R—K1 ch
25 B—K3   Q—R3

A last gasp.

26 P × Kt   R × B ch
27 K—B2

The triumphant "point."

27 ......   Kt—Q3

Despair! If 27 .... R × R; 28 P × Kt ch.

28 P × P dbl ch   K × P
29 Q × Q ch   Resigns.

A beautiful game.

229

White   *Black*
SPIELMANN   BOGOLJUBOW
(Carlsbad, 1923)

*In the following game, Black's frontal attack
is conducted with great skill; a noteworthy
feature is the energy he displays on the
adjacent K and KB files.*

1 P—K4   P—K4
2 P—KB4   P × P
3 B—B4   Kt—KB3

A modern line of defence, which, however,
is more effective against White's 3 Kt—KB3.
If 3 .... P—KB4; 4 Q—K2, and if 3 ....
Kt—QB3; 4 P—Q4. Finally, if 3 ....
Kt—K2; 4 Kt—QB3, P—QB3; 5 Q—K2,
with a clear advantage to White.

4 Kt—QB3

If 4 P—K5, P—Q4.

4 ......   P—B3

Seeing that 4 .... P—Q4 remains inadmissible, Black adopts an old continuation
called the *Chinese Variation*, because it was
played in a correspondence game, Shanghai-
Chefoo, about 1824. It aims, eventually, at
a lateral offensive.

If 4 .... B—Kt5; 5 P—K5, P—Q4;
6 B—Kt5 ch (and not passively 6 B—Kt3,
Kt—K5, etc.); 6 .... P—B3; 7 P × Kt,

P × B; 8 Q—K2 ch, etc., and White has the
better game.

Finally, if 4 .... Kt—B3; 5 Kt—B3,
B—Kt5; 6 Kt—Q5, and White holds his
own.

5 P—Q4

Better would be 5 B—Kt3. But the most
stubborn continuation is 5 Q—B3, Q—K2;
6 KKt—K2, P—QKt4; 7 B × P, P × B;
8 P—K5, Q × P; 9 Q × R. B—B4; 10 P—Q4,
B × P; 11 B × P, etc., with advantage to
White. Or 5 Q—B3, P—Q4; 6 P × P,
B—Q3; 7 P—Q3, B—KKt5; 8 Q—B2,
etc., and White has the better game.

5 ......   B—Kt5

Reviving the threat against White's KP.
But 5 .... P—QKt4 would be of no
value, because of 6 B—Q3.

6 Q—B3   P—Q4

Black goes squarely to work. After
6 .... Castles; 7 B × P, Kt × P; 8 Kt—K2,
White could manage to consolidate his
position.

7 P × P   Castles

Foreshadowing intensified action on the
open K file.

8 Kt—K2

Blocking the critical file as best he can;
8 P × P, Kt × P would further Black's
development.

8 ......   P × P

Thus Black's fourth move shows a good
return.

9 B—Q3   B—Kt5
10 Q × BP   B × Kt

By this seemingly premature exchange,
White will in the end be prevented from
castling, for if 11 B × B, R—K1, and White
still cannot castle.

11 K × B   Kt—B3
12 B—K3   R—K1
13 KR—KB1

In order to effect artificial castling by
R—B3, followed by K—B1.

13 ......   Q—K2

Threatening, eventually, 14 .... Kt × P;
15 Q × QKt, B—B4, etc.

14 R—B3   QR—Q1
15 K—B1   R—Q3
16 Q—R4

Or 16 K—Kt1, R—K3 (an imposing
array of heavy artillery); 17 B—B2, B × Kt;
18 P × B, Kt—K5, and Black has a dominating position.

| 16 ...... | B × Kt |
| 17 B—KKt5 | |

A fierce attempt to obtain some practical chances, for if 17 P × B, Kt—K5; 18 Q × Q, R × Q; 19 B × Kt, P × B; 20 R—B2, Kt—R4, and the ending would be hopeless for White owing to his many weaknesses.

| 17 ...... | B × QP |

Superb, and calculated to a nicety.

18 B × Kt

White has no choice, otherwise there follows 18 .... P—KR3; 19 B × P, Kt—K5 breaking up all attacks and remaining with an extra piece.

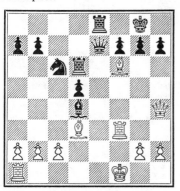

| 18 ...... | Q × B |

A temporary sacrifice of the Queen.

19 Q × P ch

Evidently not 19 R × Q, R × R ch, etc.

| 19 ...... | K—B1 |
| Resigns | |

A wise decision. For if—

(a) 20 R × Q, R × R ch; 21 B—B5, R—R3, a pretty manœuvre, winning the Queen.

(b) 20 Q—R8 ch, K—K2; 21 Q—R5, P—KKt3; 22 R—K1 ch, R—K3; 23 R × Q, R × QR ch; 24 K × R, K × R dis ch, recovering the Queen and remaining with an extra piece.

230

| *White* | *Black* |
| TARTAKOWER | CAPABLANCA |

(New York, 1924)

An abortive attempt to take the second player by surprise. "You cannot give a world champion the odds of a pawn" was the summary judgment of a contemporary critic.

Technically, a noteworthy feature of the game is the fertile use made by Black of intermediary manœuvres (6 .... B—Kt5 ch; 9 .... Kt—Q4; 13 .... P—QKt4).

1 P—K4	P—K4
2 P—KB4	P × P
3 B—K2	

The *Restricted Bishop's Gambit*, the resources of which must not be underestimated.

3 ......   P—Q4

The most incisive reply. Far less useful is 3 .... Q—R5 ch; 4 K—B1, etc., or 3 .... P—KKt4; 4 P—Q4, P—Q3; 5 P—KR4, etc., or 3 .... Kt—K2; 4 P—Q4, or again, 3 .... Kt—QB3; 4 P—Q4, or, finally, 3 .... P—KB4; 4 P—K5, P—Q3; 5 P—Q4, etc.

| 4 P × P | Kt—KB3 |

More restful than 4 .... Q × P; 5 B—B3, etc.

5 P—B4

A more solid continuation is 5 Kt—KB3.

5 ......   P—B3

He now either recovers his pawn or obtains an advantage in development.

| 6 P—Q4 | B—Kt5 ch |

A very subtle *intermediary check*. After 6 .... P × P; 7 B × P, P × P; 8 B × P, B—Kt5 ch; 9 Kt—B3, Castles; 10 Kt—K2, B—Kt5; 11 Castles, QKt—Q2; 12 Q—Kt3, etc., White would have the last word.

7 K—B1

He is afraid of ghosts. If 7 Kt—B3, then 7 .... Kt—K5; would certainly have caused damage. But the simple 7 B—Q2, would maintain the balance, e.g. 7 .... Kt—K5; 8 Kt—KB3, or 7 .... B × B ch; 8 Q × B, etc.

| 7 ...... | P × P |
| 8 B × P | |

More consistent would be 8 P—B5.

8 ......   P × P

The great expert in simplification finds the right continuation. If 8 .... Castles; 9 P—B5, with complications.

9 B × Kt

Sancta simplicitas. White's hallucination consists in thinking that his great opponent loses a piece by a check on the Q side (9 .... R × B; 10 Q—R4 ch, followed by .... Q × B), whereas it is a case of a well-calculated enterprise. He should therefore have made the best of 9 B × BP, Castles; etc., with the white position slightly disarranged, but defendable.

9 . . . . . .   Kt—Q4

A very fine *intermediary manœuvre*, which not only saves the piece, but marks the beginning of hostilities against the opposing King.

10 K—B2

If 10 B—B4, Q—B3, and White cannot play 11 P—KKt3, on account of 11 . . . . Kt—K6 ch.

10 . . . . . .   R × B
11 B × P   Castles
12 Kt—KB3

He underestimates the power of the hostile KKt, and will have to pay the price. With 12 B × Kt, Q × B; 13 Kt—QB3, etc., White could still have hoped to organise a defence.

12 . . . . . .   Kt—B3

The principal actor which ensures Black's dynamic superiority.

13 Kt—B3   P—QKt4

Completing his development under fire! White could not embark on 14 B × P, B × Kt; etc., nor 14 Kt × P, Kt—K5 ch; 15 K—Kt1, B—Kt5, etc.

14 B—Q3   Kt—Kt5 ch
15 K—Kt1   B—Kt2
16 B—B5   QB × Kt
17 P × B

If 17 Q × B, Q × P ch. But after the text move the white King's asylum is in jeopardy.

17 . . . . . .   Kt—K6
18 B × P ch   K—R1

And not 18 . . . . K × B, etc., because of 19 Q—Q3 ch, followed by . . . . Q × Kt, and White's game is free.

19 Q—Q3   B × Kt
20 P × B   Kt—Q4
21 B—K4   Kt—B5
22 Q—Q2   Q—R5

There is nothing in 22 . . . . Q—Kt4 ch; 23 K—B1, etc.

23 K—B1   P—B4
24 B—B6   R—B3

White's game now rapidly goes downhill.

25 P—Q5   R—Q1
26 R—Q1   R × B
27 P × R   R × Q
28 R × R   Kt—K3
29 R—Q6   Q—B5 ch
30 K—Kt2   Q—K7 ch
Resigns.

231

White	*Black*
SPIELMANN	MÖLLER

(Göteborg, 1920)

A very beautiful sacrifice of the Queen— White's forces meanwhile displaying a prodigious activity—gives this game a character of its own.

Named "the Knight of the King's Gambit," the master Spielmann celebrates here a well-merited triumph.

1 P—K4   P—K4
2 P—KB4   P × P
3 Q—B3

The *Hungarian Gambit*, introduced into master practice by Charousek and Breyer, two of the most original and independent minds amongst chess players of all time.

Another continuation of paradoxical appearance is 3 Kt—QB3, as played in a game by correspondence in 1934, Keres-Toldsepp: 3 (Kt—QB3) B—Kt5 (the best is here 3 . . . . Q—R5 ch at once, 4 K—K2, P—Q4; 5 Kt × P, B—Kt5 ch; 6 Kt—B3, etc.); 4 Kt—Q5, Q—R5 ch; 5 K—K2 (in the Steinitz manner); 5 . . . . B—Q3; 6 Kt—KB3, Q—Kt5; 7 P—Q4, Kt—K2; 8 Kt—B3, P—QKt3; 9 K—B2, Kt—Kt3; 10 B—K2, B—K2; 11 P—KKt3, P × P ch; 12 P × P, B—Kt2 (he should first have played 12 . . . . P—Q3); 13 Kt—KKt5, Resigns (his Queen is lost).

3 . . . . . .   Kt—QB3

Best! If 3 . . . . Q—R5 ch; 4 P—Kt3, P × P; 5 P × P, Q—B3; 6 Kt—B3, Q × Q; 7 Kt × Q, and White's advantage in development will tell notwithstanding the absence of Queens. If 3 . . . . P—Q4; 4 P × P, Kt—KB3; 5 Kt—B3, etc., White has the best of it.

4 P—B3

If 4 Kt—K2, P—Q4, etc. The simplest is 4 Q × P.

4 ......   Kt—B3

Preparing the disintegrating advance of the QP. Premature would be 4 .... P—Q4; 5 P×P, Kt—K4; 6 B—Kt5 ch, P—B3; 7 Q—K2, Q—K2; 8 P—Q4, and White takes the lead.

```
5 P—Q4          P—Q4
6 P—K5          Kt—K5
7 B—Kt5
```

If 7 B×P, B—K2, followed by .... Castles and .... P—KB3, and Black controls some commanding squares.

7 ......   Q—R5 ch

Instead of following the classic scheme of the *King's Gambit*, Black should have tried to get counter-play for his pieces by 7 .... B—K2, etc.

8 K—B1   P—Kt4

Winning the exchange by 8 .... Kt—Kt6 ch would lead to a sad situation for Black after 9 P×Kt, Q×R; 10 B×P, etc.

Now Black threatens both 9 .... B—KKt5 and 9 .... P—Kt5; 10 Q×BP, B—R3.

9 Kt—Q2

A most ingenious conception! If 9 P—KKt3, P×P; 10 P×P, Kt×P ch, etc., or 10 K—Kt2, B—R6 ch; 11 Kt×B, P—Kt5, and wins.

9 ......   B—KKt5

If 9 .... P—Kt5, then not 10 Q×BP, B—R3; 11 P—KKt3, B×Q; 12 P×Q, B×Kt, etc., but 10 Q—K2, avoiding the worst.

```
10 Kt×Kt          B×Q
11 Kt×B          Q—R3
12 Kt—B6 ch      K—Q1
13 P—KR4         B—K2
14 Kt×KtP
```

Harrying the enemy.

```
14 ......          Q—Kt3
15 Kt×QP
```

Another pawn captured literally "in passing."

```
15 ......          B×Kt
16 P×B           Q—B7
```

Trying to assert himself, but this new expedition proves disastrous.

```
17 B—K2          Kt—K2
18 Kt×KBP
```

The mopping up continues.

18 ......   P—QB4

If 18 .... Kt—B4, then equally 19 R—R3, and if 18 .... Q—B4; 19 B—Q3, for 19 .... Q×KtP is inadmissible by reason of 20 Kt—K6 ch.

Sounder than the violent attempt in the text is 18 .... P—QB3.

```
19 R—R3          P×P
```

Fatal. Flight by 19 .... Q—B4 or 19 .... Q—R5 is essential.

```
20 R—Q3          K—Q2
```

If now 20 .... Q—R5; 21 R×P ch.

Playable would be 20 .... Kt—B4; 21 B—Q1, Kt—K6 ch (21 .... Kt—Kt6 ch; 22 K—K1); 22 B×Kt, Q×KtP; 23 R×P ch, and White has a *positional* as well as a *numerical* advantage.

21 B—Q1

An original capture of the Queen.

```
21 ......          Q×R ch
22 Kt×Q          P×P
23 P×P            KR—Q1
24 B—K2           Kt—B4
25 B—B4           K—B2
```

In search of an asylum. If 25 .... K—B1; 26 B—Kt4.

```
26 R—Kt1          P—Kt3
27 P—K6 dis ch    K—B1
28 Kt—K5
```

A beautiful final stroke.

28 ......   Resigns.

KING'S GAMBIT DECLINED

232

White	Black
RUBINSTEIN	HROMADKA

(Mährisch-Ostrau, 1923)

The brilliant tactics in the following impressive game are reminiscent of Morphy. But on closer examination we can also enjoy the high strategy of the moderns—firm, profound and multilateral—adapted to the exigencies of the open game.

```
1 P—K4          P—K4
2 P—KB4
```

And so, in this technocratic age, we see the *King's Gambit* still being played.

2 ......   B—B4

But also that it is preferable not to accept it. If 2 .... Kt—KB3; 3 Kt—KB3, Kt×P; 4 P×P, Kt—Kt4; 5 P—Q4, etc., assuming the initiative. The most independent line of play is 2 .... P—Q4 (3 KP×P, P—K5: *Falkbeer's Counter Gambit*).

3 Kt—KB3   P—Q3
4 Kt—B3

The same position can arise from a *Vienna Opening.*

4 ......   Kt—KB3

If, first, 4 .... Kt—QB3; 5 B—Kt5 is strong.

5 B—B4

White's last two moves are often played in inverted order: 4 B—B4, Kt—KB3; 5 Kt—B3, Kt—B3; and now 6 P—Q3 is hardly active enough, e.g. Tchigorin-Burn, *Ostend*, 1906: 6 (P—Q3), Castles; 7 Q—K2, R—K1; 8 P—B5, P—Q4; 9 B—Kt3, B×P; 10 B—Kt5, P×P; 11 P×P, B×P; 12 Q—B4, Q—Q4; 13 Q—Kt5, B—B7 ch; White resigns —a *débâcle*).

5 ......   Kt—B3

The alternative is 5 .... P—B3.

6 P—Q3   B—KKt5

More solid is here (or on the next move) 6 .... B—K3. If 6 .... Castles; 7 P—B5, in White's favour.

7 P—KR3

Initiating a bold and ingenious plan. But as Black could have evaded it, the most telling move is 7 Kt—QR4.

7 ......   B×Kt
8 Q×B   Kt—Q5

The fighting becomes fast and furious. More prudent is 8 .... P×P.

9 Q—Kt3

Alea jacta est. 9 Q—Q1 would be pusillanimous, and Black would obtain the initiative after 9 .... P—B3, followed by .... P—QKt4.

9 ......   Q—K2

The crucial point. He wishes to bring his King into safety by .... Castles QR, as the acceptance of the Greek gift would be damaging, e.g. 9 .... Kt×P ch; 10 K—Q1, Kt×R; 11 Q×P, K—Q2 (or 11 .... R—KB1; 12 P×P, P×P; 13 Kt—Kt5, B—K2; 14 R—B1, etc., with overpowering threats); 12 P×P, P×P; 13 R—B1, B—K2; 14 B—Kt5, and White's attack gains in impetus.

Bad is also 9 .... Castles; 10 P×P, P×P; 11 B—KKt5, Kt×P ch; 12 K—Q1, etc. But he could have avoided all trouble by 9 .... P×P.

10 P×P   P×P
11 K—Q1   P—B3

Sounder than 11 .... Castles QR; 12 R—B1.

12 P—QR4

The counter-thrust 12 .... P—QKt4 must be prevented.

12 ......   R—KKt1
13 R—B1

Initiating a lasting pressure on the KB file. 13 B—KKt5 would not be good, because of 13 .... P—KR3.

13 ......   P—KR3

Instead of this over-cautious measure, he should play 13 .... Castles, for White's threats of 14 B—KKt5 (P—KR3; 15 B×Kt, P×B; 16 Q—R2, P—KR4, etc.) and 14 Q—R4 (14 .... P—KR3; 15 QB×P, R—R1, etc.) are ephemeral.

14 Kt—K2   Castles

Simpler would be 14 .... Kt×Kt; 15 K×Kt, Castles.

15 Kt×Kt   B×Kt
16 P—B3   B—Kt3

If 16 .... Kt×P; 17 Q—Kt4 ch.

17 P—R5   B—B2
18 B—K3   K—Kt1
19 K—B2   K—R1

Protects the QRP, by which the threat of 20 .... Kt×P becomes real.

20 R—B3

High strategy, based on bilateral objectives. The threat of Q—B2 thus gains in power, for White pressure will be, not only *diagonal* (towards QR7), but also *vertical* (towards KB6).

Much less intensive would be 20 Q—B2 at once, as after 20 .... B—Kt1 neither 21 B×KRP, P×B; 22 Q×Kt, R×P, etc., nor 21 P—KKt4, R—R1, etc., would lead to anything.

20 ......   Kt—Q4

A morbid ingenuity. Steadiness dictates 20 .... B—Kt1; 21 Q—B2, R—Q2, consolidating his base.

21 B—Kt1

He refuses to allow his opponent to fish in troubled waters after 21 P×Kt, P—K5; 22 B—B4, P×R, etc.

21 ......   Kt—B5

He continues to play with fire. Better would be atonement by 21 .... Kt—B3.

22 Q—B2   B—Kt1
23 P—KKt3

Skilfully conquering the KB file.

23 ......   Kt×RP
24 R×P   Q—Q3

Hopeless would be liquidation by 24 ....

Kt × Q; 25 R × Q, KR—B1; 26 R × KKtP, etc. But now, after any normal move by the threatened Queen, Black will wish to play for Bishops of opposite colours.

25 Q—Kt6

A thunderbolt.

25 ......   R—Q2

If 25 .... P × Q; 26 P × P dis ch, B—R2; 27 R × B ch, K—Kt1; 28 KR × P ch, K—B1; 29 B—R6, and wins.

26 B—B5   R × R

If 26 .... Q—B2; 27 Q × Q, R × Q; 28 R × R, B × R; 29 B × R, and wins.

27 B × Q   R—B7 ch
28 Q × R

Simplest, as White remains with an extra piece.

28 ......   Kt × Q
29 B—B5   Resigns.

233

White   Black
SPIELMANN   SCHLECHTER
(Ostend, 1906)

In the following game an elegant Queen sacrifice for two minor pieces changes the whole aspect of the game, without, however, leading to a definite conclusion.

1 P—K4   P—K4
2 B—B4   Kt—KB3
3 P—Q3   B—B4
4 Kt—QB3   P—Q3
5 P—B4

By a skilful transposition of moves, White has avoided the risks of the *King's Gambit Accepted*. Here he need not fear 5 .... Kt—Kt5; 6 P—B5, Kt—B7; 7 Q—R5, and White has the more enduring chances.

5 ......   Kt—B3
6 Kt—B3   B—KKt5

Here 6 .... B—K3 is more solid.

7 Kt—QR4

More effective than 7 P—KR3.

7 ......   P × P

Let us examine Black's choice of moves:
(a) 7 .... B × Kt; 8 Q × B, Kt—Q5; 9 Q—Kt3 (9 Q—Q1, P—QKt4; 10 B × BP ch, K × B; 11 Kt × B, P × Kt; 12 P × P, with a fine attack); 9 .... Kt × P ch; 10 K—Q1, Kt × R; 11 P × P, with considerable complications.
(b) 7 .... Kt—Q5; 8 Kt × B, P × Kt; 9 P—B3 (9 P × P, Kt—Q2); 9 .... Kt × Kt ch; 10 P × Kt, B—R4; 11 Q—K2, Q—Q3; 12 P × P (if 12 P—B5, P—KKt3); 12 .... Q × KP; 13 P—B4, Q—K2; 14 Q—Kt2, etc., with advantage to White.
(c) 7 .... Castles; 8 Kt × B, P × Kt; 9 P—B3, etc.
(d) 7 .... Kt—Q2; 8 Kt × B, Kt × Kt; 9 Castles, etc.
(e) 7 .... P—QR3; 8 Kt × B, P × Kt; 9 P—QR4, etc.
(f) 7 .... Q—K2 (in preparation for .... Castles QR); 8 Kt × B, P × Kt; 9 Castles, etc., with equal chances, so that this would be the best course to take.

8 Kt × B   P × Kt
9 B × P   Kt—KR4
10 B—K3

The two active Bishops on an unobstructed field give White the advantage.

10 ......   Castles

After the immediate attempt 10 .... Kt—K4; the catastrophic sequel could be 11 Kt × Kt (*à la Légal*); 11 .... B × Q; 12 B × P ch, K—K2; 13 B × P ch, K—B3; 14 Castles ch, K × Kt (14 .... K—Kt4; 15 B—K3 ch, K—R5; 16 QR × B, Q—K2; 17 Kt—B3 ch, K—Kt5; 18 K—B2, threatening 19 P—R3 mate); 15 R—B5 mate.

11 Castles   Kt—K4

Here again this attempt should fail, but after 11 .... P—QKt3; 12 B—Q5, Q—Q3; 13 Q—Q2, White remains master of the field. (*Diagram. See p. 300.*)

12 Kt × Kt

This Queen sacrifice brings a more than satisfactory return.

12 ......   B × Q
13 Kt × P   R × Kt

If 13 .... Q—R5; 14 Kt—Q8 dis ch, R—B2; 15 R × R, etc., and if 13 .... Q—K2; 14 B—KKt5.

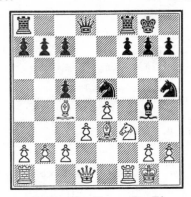

Position after 11 .... Kt—K4

14 B × R ch
He selects a more peaceful continuation, which enables his adversary more or less to hold the position.

Far more dynamic would be 14 R × R, K—R1; 15 R × B, P—QKt3; 16 P—K5, subjecting Black to the pressure of a numerous host.

14	K—R1
15 QR × B	Kt—B3
16 B × P	P—QKt3
17 B—B2	

Although stronger numerically (thanks to his two extra pawns), White yet has no forcible line of play at his disposal.

17	Kt—Kt5
18 B—Q5	P—B3
19 B—K6	

Futile would be 19 KB × P, R—B1; 20 B—Q5, R × P.

19	Kt × B
20 R × Kt	Q—Q5
21 P—B3	Q—K6
22 K—B1	

If 22 R—KB1, R—KB1; 23 P—KKt3, P—Kt3, etc., and White's conquest of the KB file is in doubt.

22	P—Kt3
23 R—B3	Q—R3
24 P—KR3	R—K1
25 B—Q7	R—KB1
26 B—Kt4	K—Kt2
27 P—Q4	Q—K6
28 R × R	K × R

In this ending the white King is in too open a position, and so the Queen can hold her own.

29 B—B3
Or 29 R—K1, Q—Q7; 30 R—K2, Q—B8 ch; 31 K—B2, Q—B5 ch; 32 B—B3, and the white forces are still reduced to inactivity.

| 29 ...... | K—K2 |
| 30 P—K5 | |

          Draw.

234

White	Black
TARTAKOWER	SCHLECHTER

(St. Petersburg, 1909)

In this game the numerous—if easy— sacrifices by White illustrate the multifarious dangers of the black King's castled position, weakened as it is at various points, such as his KB2 (14 Kt × P), the focal point at his KB3 (16 R × Kt), and his exposed KR3 (19 B × P), etc.

1 P—K4	P—K4
2 P—KB4	B—B4
3 Kt—KB3	P—Q3
4 P × P	

In conjunction with White's next move, this, the *Marshall Attack*, is realised with even greater precision by playing, first, 4 P—B3, e.g.:

(a) 4 .... Kt—KB3; 5 P × P, P × P (not 5 .... Kt × P; 6 Q—R4 ch); 6 Kt × P, etc., as in the text.

(b) 4 .... B—KKt5; 5 P × P, P × P; 6 Q—R4 ch, B—Q2; 7 Q—B2, etc.

(c) 4 .... P—B4; 5 BP × P (but not 5 KP × P, Q—K2; 6 B—B4, Kt—KB3, etc.); 5 .... QP × P (not 5 .... BP × P; 6 Q—R4 ch, followed by Q × KP); 6 P—Q4, etc.

(d) 4 .... Kt—QB3; 5 B—Kt5, B—Q2; 6 P—Q4, etc.

(e) 4 .... B—Kt3; 5 B—Q3, Kt—QB3; 6 B—B2, etc.

| 4 ...... | P × P |
| 5 P—B3 | Kt—KB3 |

Black has a choice of moves here, e.g.:

(a) 5 .... Q—K2; 6 P—Q4.

(b) 5 .... B—KKt5; 6 Q—R4 ch (an adroit check); 6 .... B—Q2; 7 Q—B2, and White will have the better game.

(c) 5 .... P—B4; 6 P—Q4 (less good is 6 P × P, B × P; 7 P—Q4, P P; 8 P × P, B—Kt3); 6 .... KP P; 7 B—B4, BP × P; 8 Kt—K5, Kt—KB3; 9 Kt—B7, Q—K2; 10 Kt × R, and White must win.

(d) 5 .... Kt—QB3; 6 B—Kt5 (less sound
is 6 P—QKt4, B—Kt3; 7 B—Kt5, Kt—B3;
8 Kt × P, Castles, etc., with sacrifices loom-
ing ahead); 6 .... Kt—B3; 7 Kt × P,
Castles; 8 Kt—B3, Kt × P; 9 P—Q4, B—Q3;
10 Castles, etc., with good prospects for
White.

6 Kt × P

An alternative plan is 6 P—Q4, P × P;
7 P—K5, etc.

6 ......   Castles

Or 6 .... Q—K2; 7 P—Q4, B—Q3;
8 Kt—B3, Kt × P; 9 B—K2, Castles;
10 Castles, P—QB4; 11 QKt—Q2, and
White has a slight advantage in space.
A blunder would be 6 .... Kt × P;
7 Q—R4 ch, followed by Q × Kt.

7 P—Q4   B—Q3
8 Kt—B3

A wise retreat. White seeks the conquest
of the centre, and not merely the gain of
a pawn. If 8 Kt—Q2, B × Kt; 9 P × B,
Kt—Kt5, etc., and if 8 B—Q3, B × Kt;
9 P × B, Kt × P; 10 B × Kt, Q—R5 ch;
11 K—B1, Q × B, with advantage to Black.

8 ......   Kt × P
9 B—Q3   R—K1

After 9 .... Kt—KB3; 10 Castles,
B—KKt5; 11 QKt—Q2, P—B4; 12 Q—B2,
etc., White has the greater mobility.

10 Castles   P—KR3

But here the fear of ghosts causes Black to
weaken his King's field. He could have
maintained his outpost at K5 by calling up
his reserve cavalry by 10 .... Kt—Q2,
followed by .... QKt—B3. For if then
11 B × Kt, R × B; 12 Kt—Kt5, R—K2;
13 Q—R5, P—KR3; 14 Kt × P, Q—K1,
Black can withstand any storm. White
would therefore have replied to 10 ....
Kt—Q2; by 11 QKt—Q2.

11 QKt—Q2   Kt—KB3
12 Kt—B4

Fighting for the strategic point K5.

12 ......   P—B4

Undermining the hostile centre.

13 Kt (B3)—K5   P × P

If 13 .... B—K3; 14 Kt × B, Q × Kt;
15 B × P, etc.

14 Kt × P

A *break-up sacrifice*.

14 ......   K × Kt
15 Q—R5 ch   K—Kt1

If 15 .... K—B1; 16 B × P.

Position after 13 .... P × P

16 R × Kt

A fresh surprise.

16 ......   R—K8 ch

Not 16 .... Q × R; 17 Q × R ch, etc., nor
16 .... P × R; 17 Q—Kt6 ch, etc.

17 R—B1   R × R ch
18 B × R   B—B1
19 B × P   Q—B3

Or 19 .... P × B; 20 Q—Kt6 ch, B—Kt2;
21 Kt—Q6, Q—B3; 22 B—B4 ch, K—R1;
23 Kt—B7 ch, K—Kt1; 24 Kt—Kt5 dis ch.

20 B—Kt5   Q—B4
21 Kt—Q6

This fresh sacrifice allows White to riddle
the hostile position before the consolidating
move .... B—K3.

21 ......   B × Kt
22 B—B4 ch   B—K3
23 R—KB1

Winning the Queen by force, for if 23 ....
Q—K5; 24 Q—K8 ch, K—R2; 25 B × B,
etc., and if 23 .... Q—K4; 24 Q—K8 ch,
K—R2; 25 B—Q3 ch, wins.

23 ......   Q × R ch
24 B × Q   Kt—Q2
25 B—Q3   Kt—B1
26 P × P   B—KB2
27 Q—B3   Kt—K3
28 B—K3   R—Kt1
29 P—KKt4

A new and decisive wave of the attack.

29 ......   P—KKt4
30 Q—B6   B—B1
31 B—R7 ch

The sixth sacrifice.

31 ......   K × B
32 Q × B ch   Kt—Kt2
33 B × P   Resigns.

235

White	Black
ROSANES	ANDERSSEN

(Breslau, 1862)

The opening phase of the following game illustrates the basic idea of the Falkbeer Counter Gambit, which is the speeding up of Black's pressure on the K file, even at the cost of sacrifices. Later on there is a fine attack—crowned by a beautiful sacrifice of the Queen—against the castled King on the Q side.

   1 P—K4   P—K4
   2 P—KB4   P—Q4
With this counter-thrust in the centre, Black foreshadows the coming struggle for the initiative.

   3 P×QP   P—K5
The *Counter Gambit par excellence*! If 3 .... P×P; 4 Q—B3, and if 3 .... P—QB3; 4 Kt—QB3, and White retains the advantage of the first move.

   4 B—Kt5 ch
A compromising check, as by maintaining his extra pawn White will afford his opponent a chance of an easy attack. The soundest procedure is to undermine the opposing outpost at once by 4 P—Q3. Less consistent are other continuations, e.g. 4 Kt—QB3, Kt—KB3; 5 P—Q3, B—QKt5; 6 P×P (if 6 B—Q2, P—K6; 7 B×P, Castles, and the attack makes up for the two pawns lost); 6 .... Kt×P; 7 Q—Q4, Q—K2; 8 B—K2, Castles, and Black has most of the play. Or 4 Q—K2, Kt—KB3; 5 P—Q3, B—QB4 (if 5 .... Q×P; 6 Kt—QB3, B—QKt5; 7 B—Q2, B×Kt; 8 B×B, etc., with advantage to White); 6 P×P, Castles; 7 Kt—QB3, R—K1, and Black's resources are not to be despised, although he is in a minority of two pawns.

   4 ......   P—B3
If 4 .... B—Q2; 5 Q—K2, and White is better off.

   5 P×P   Kt×P
The most sustained line of play.

   6 Kt—QB3
The only consolidating move is 6 P—Q3.

   6 ......   Kt—B3
   7 Q—K2
If 7 KKt—K2, Q—Kt3.

   7 ......   B—QB4
   8 Kt×P   Castles
Black's aggressive plan stands out clearly. He does not worry about his two pawns as long as he has the attack.

   9 B×Kt   P×B
 10 P—Q3   R—K1
 11 B—Q2   Kt×Kt
 12 P×Kt   B—B4
 13 P—K5   Q—Kt3
Co-operation! If 13 .... B×P; 14 Q—B4.

 14 Castles
The only way of defending the two threatened points (Kt and QKtP). Black's difficulties are only beginning.

 14 ......   B—Q5
 15 P—B3   QR—Kt1
 16 P—QKt3
After 16 P—QKt4 a pretty variation would be 16 .... Q—R4; 17 B—K1, Q—R6 ch; 18 Q—Kt2, QR×P, etc.

 16 ......   KR—Q1
He paves the way—by cutting off the Q file—for a most beautiful combination.

 17 Kt—B3
After 17 P×B, Q×QP, there is no resource against Black's threatened 18 .... Q—R8 mate.

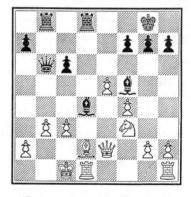

 17 ......   Q×P
Sacrifice of the Queen for only one pawn. White is lost.

 18 P×Q   R×P
 19 B—K1   B—K6 ch
And mate next move.

236

White	Black
SPIELMANN	TARRASCH

(Mährisch-Ostrau, 1923)

In the following fine game, Black leaves a piece "en prise" as early as the eighth move (8 .... Castles), in order to gain an important tempo for his attack.

The way in which this attack unfolds on the adjacent K and KB files, and later on the KKt file as well, is most impressive.

1 P—K4	P—K4
2 P—KB4	P—Q4
3 KP×P	P—K5
4 P—Q3	

Immediately undermining the adverse outpost.

4 ......   Kt—KB3

If 4 .... Q×P; 5 Q—K2, to White's advantage. But if 4 .... P×P, then not so much 5 Q×P (5 .... Kt—KB3; 6 Kt—QB3, B—QB4, etc.), as 5 B×P (e.g. 5 .... Q×P; 6 Kt—QB3, Q—K3 ch; 7 KKt—K2, Kt—KB3; 8 Castles, Q—Kt3 ch; 9 K—R1, and White has the superior mechanism).

5 P×P

Another plan is to continue the siege of the advance pawn by 5 Kt—QB3 or 5 Q—K2.

5 ......   Kt×KP

With the threat of 6 .... Q—R5 ch.

6 Kt—KB3

The frontal attack by 6 Q—K2 is easily mastered after 6 .... Q×P; 7 Kt—Q2 (7 Kt—QB3, B—QKt5); 7 .... P—KB4; 8 P—KKt4, Kt—QB3 (an intermediary manœuvre, far more useful than 8 .... B—K2; 9 B—Kt2, etc.); 9 P—B3, B—K2; 10 B—Kt2 (threatening to win a piece by 11 P×P); 10 .... Q—B2 (10 .... B—R5 ch; 11 K—Q1); 11 Kt×Kt, P×Kt; 12 B×P, B—R5 ch; 13 K—B1, Castles, and Black obtains the attack.

6 ......   B—QB4

Black's main asset is his domination of the open diagonal. If 6 .... B—KB4; 7 B—K3.

7 Q—K2

After the plausible 7 B—Q3, Black continues in sacrificial style: 7 .... Castles; 8 B×Kt, R—K1; etc., with a winning attack.

7 ......   B—B4

A challenging *sortie*. Other continuations have proved unsound, e.g.:

(a) 7 .... B—B7 ch; 8 K—Q1, Q×P ch; 9 KKt—Q2, P—KB4; 10 Kt—B3, etc.

(b) 7 .... P—B4; 8 B—K3, etc.

(c) 7 .... Q×P; 8 KKt—Q2, P—B4; 9 QKt—B3, Q—K3; 10 KKt×Kt, P×Kt; 11 Q×P, etc.

(d) 7 .... Castles; 8 Q×Kt, R—K1; 9 Kt—K5, P—KB3; 10 B—Q3, and wins.

8 P—KKt4

An impulsive move, which will have untoward consequences. He should have recognised the futility of any attempt at gain and sought equalisation by 8 Kt—B3.

8 ......   Castles

A brilliant retort.

9 P×B   R—K1

The first move of a formidable frontal attack.

10 B—Kt2

If 10 Kt—K5, Q—R5 ch, and if 10 Q—Kt2, Q×P; 11 B—K2, Kt—QB3; 12 Kt—B3, Q×BP, with overwhelming pressure.

10	Kt—B7
11 Kt—K5	Kt×R
12 B×Kt	Kt—Q2

Not at once 12 .... P—KB3, on account of 12 .... P—KB3; 13 P—Q6, e.g. 13 .... P×Kt; 14 Q—B4 ch, followed by Q×B, or 13 .... P×P; 14 B—Q5 ch, K—B1; 15 Q—R5, etc.

13 Kt—QB3	P—KB3
14 Kt—K4	

Or, e.g. 14 B—Q2, P×Kt; 15 Castles, P×P; 16 Q—B4, B—Q3, and his advantage in material is safeguarded.

14	P×Kt
15 Kt×B	Kt×Kt
16 P×P	Q—R5 ch
17 K—B1	

Or 17 K—Q1, Q—Q5 ch, followed by .... Q×KP.

17 ......   R—KB1

Shifting the attack.

18 K—Kt1

Or 18 Q—B3, Q—B5 ch; 19 K—Kt1, Q×BP, etc., or 18 P—B6, QR—K1, etc., or, finally, 18 P—K6, R×P ch; 19 K—Kt1, QR—KB1; 20 B—K3, Kt—K5, forcing the decision.

18 ......   Q—Q5 ch
More precise than 18 .... R × P.

19 B—K3
Or 19 Q—K3, Q—Q8 ch.

19	Q × KP
20 R—K1	Kt—Q2
21 Q—B4	K—R1
22 B—K4	QR—K1
23 B—Q4	Q—B5
24 R—K2	Kt—B3

Of course not 24 .... R × B; 25 R × R,
Q × R; 26 B × P ch.

25 B × Kt   P × B
Black's pressure on the K and KB files
has resulted in the opening of the KKt file
with decisive results.

26 P—KR3
Or, e.g. 26 R—K1, R—Kt1 ch; 27 K—R1,
Q—B6 ch; 28 B × Q, R × R ch, with mate to
follow.

26 ......   R—Kt1 ch
          Resigns
(27 K—R1, Q—KB8 ch, followed by
mate.)

237

White	Black
TCHIGORIN	WALBRODT

(Nuremberg, 1896)

*Loss or sacrifice of a piece? The manner
in which White demonstrates that 5 Q—K2
is a sacrifice—and a sound one at that—is
very pleasing.*

1 P—K4	P—K4
2 P—KB4	P—Q4
3 Kt—KB3	

A solid continuation.

3	QP × P
4 Kt × P	B—Q3

Other more or less ingenious tries are:
(a) 4 .... Kt—Q2; 5 P—Q4, P × P e.p.;
6 Kt × QP, etc.
(b) 4 .... Kt—QB3; 5 B—Kt5, Kt—B3;
6 Q—K2, etc.
(c) 4 .... Kt—KB3; 5 P—Q4, P × P e.p.;
6 B × P, etc.

5 Q—K2
A deep conception! 5 P—Q4, P × P e.p.;
6 B × P, etc., would be playable.
Very bellicose is 5 B—B4, as in Anderssen-
Schallopp, *Berlin*, 1864: 5 (B—B4) B × Kt;
6 P × B, Q—Q5 (instead of hunting for
pawns, he should play 6 .... Kt—QB3;
7 Q—K2, B—B4; 8 B—Kt5, Kt—K2,
etc.); 7 Q—K2, Q × KP; 8 P—Q4, Q × QP;
9 Kt—B3, Kt—KB3; 10 B—K3, Q—Q1;
11 Castles, P—KR3; 12 B—B5, QKt—Q2
(plausible, but fatal); 13 Q × P ch, Kt × Q;
14 B × P mate.

5	Q—K2
6 Q × P	P—KB3
7 P—Q4	P × Kt

A meticulous player would prefer 7 ....
B × Kt.

8 BP × P   P—B3
If, hoping for counter-play, 8 ....
Kt—KB3, there follows 9 Q—K2, Castles;
10 P × B, Q × P; 11 Q—B4 ch, B—K3;
12 Q—B5, and White, having recovered his
material, has an extra pawn.

9 B—QB4	B—B2
10 Castles	B—K3
11 B—KKt5	

Maintaining the attack very prettily.

11 ......   Q × B
If 11 .... Q—Q2; 13 Kt—Q2.

12 B × B   Kt—KR3
After 12 .... Kt—K2; 13 Kt—B3,
White's game also remains superior.

13 B—B8	Kt—Q2
14 B × P	K—K2
15 B × P	QR—KB1

He already has four pawns for his piece,
with a clear advantage.

16 Kt—B3	R × R ch
17 R × R	R—KB1
18 Kt—Q5 ch	K—Q1
19 Kt—B4	R—K1
20 Q—Q5	Q—K2
21 B—Kt5	

A *vacating manœuvre*. White's pieces
develop astonishing power.

21	P—Kt4
22 Q—R8 ch	B—Kt1
23 Kt—Q5	Q—K3
24 B × Kt	K × B
25 Q—Kt7 ch	

And wins. (25 .... K—Q1; 26 Q × B ch,
Q—B1; 27 Q—Q6 ch, Q—Q2; 28 Q × Q ch,
K × Q; 29 Kt—B6 ch, etc.)

BOOK II

SEMI-OPEN GAMES

16. FRENCH DEFENCE

238

White *Black*
FALKBEER ST. AMANT
(Birmingham, 1858)

The first object of a player, be he master or amateur, is to castle as soon as possible, unless he has some other and more complicated aim in view. The failure to do this is the cause, in the following game, of an instructive débâcle.

1 P—K4	P—K3
2 P—Q4	P—Q4
3 P×P	P×P

The *Exchange Variation*. If not the best solution of the problem of the centre, it is at least clear-cut and definite, and as it tends towards a draw, is to be recommended against a stronger player.

4 B—K3
Here 4 Kt—KB3 or 4 B—Q3 are more usual.

4	Kt—KB3
5 P—QB4	B—K2
6 Kt—QB3	Castles
7 Q—Kt3	

Whilst Black has already castled, White is unwisely busying himself on the Q side.

7	P—B3
8 B—Q3	P—QKt3

"Defence by displacement"; moreover, Black can now mobilise his QB.

9 KKt—K2
9 Kt—B3, followed by Castles KR, would have been more solid.

9	B—K3
10 P—KR3	

Quite legitimate: countering 10 .... Kt—Kt5.

10	P—B4
11 P—Kt4	

But this is a wild charge. He can no longer castle on the K side with any safety, whilst Castles QR would be more than risky in view of Black's advanced Q side pawns. The best course was liquidation by 11 Kt—B4, QP×P; 12 B×P, B×B; 13 Q×B, P×P; 14 Q×P, Q×Q; 15 B×Q, and the position looks like becoming equalised.

11	Kt—B3

Increasing the pressure against the hostile QP (thus, if 12 QP×P, we have the "fork" 12 .... P—Q5, winning a piece), and threatening 12 .... QP×P; 13 B×P, Kt—QR4, and wins.

12 BP×P
With this move White hopes to initiate a saving manœuvre, but he will find that Black has seen one move further.

12	KKt×QP
13 Q—B2	P×P
14 B×P	Kt (Q4)—Kt5
15 Q—Q2	

As in the end this move costs a piece, it would in any event have been better to play 15 B×P ch, K—R1; 16 Q—K4, and White tries, as best he can, to guard his two threatened Bishops (e.g. 16 .... Kt×B; 17 Kt×Kt, B—B5; 18 Kt—B6, etc.).

But, with an anxious King in the centre and his pieces in jeopardy, White has the inferior position.

15	Kt (B3)×B
16 Kt×Kt	Q×Kt
17 B×P ch	K×B
18 Q×Q	Kt—B7 ch

The complications of the last three moves, culminating in a "family check" (K, Q and R), well illustrate the power of a Knight astutely handled.

19 K—Q2	Kt×Q
20 P—B4	QR—Q1
21 QR—KB1	B—B5
22 R—B2	B—B4

And Black wins.

239

White *Black*
GRAU NIMZOWITSCH
(San Remo, 1930)

When the adversaries castle on opposite sides, the result is usually an exceptionally violent battle. In this style of game, the chief trump card is the opening of a file.

In the following game, the castled position on the K side for once proves the more vulnerable.

1 P—K4	P—K3
2 P—Q4	P—Q4
3 P×P	P×P
4 B—Q3	Kt—QB3

An asymmetrical variation. The idea is not to allow White to dictate events, but to avoid symmetry, waiting for an opportunity of seizing the initiative.

The academic development is: 4 .... B—Q3; 5 Kt—KB3, Kt—KB3; 6 Castles, Castles, etc., with even prospects.

5 P—QB3	B—Q3
6 Kt—B3	

If 6 Kt—K2, then 6 .... Q—R5.

6	KKt—K2
7 Q—B2	

As White does not intend to castle on the Q side, this move can be looked upon only as a serious loss of time. The loss of the game can be attributed to it. A good line of play is 7 Castles, B—KKt5; 8 R—K1, Q—Q2; 9 QKt—Q2, and if 9 .... Castles QR; 10 P—QKt4, and White's attack is the first off the mark.

7	B—KKt5
8 QKt—Q2	Q—Q2
9 Castles	P—B3

Sounding the attack.

10 R—K1	P—KKt4
11 P—KR3	

As in many similar cases, this move only serves to weaken the King's field, providing the adversary's impetuous attack with an objective.

11	B—K3
12 Kt—B1	Castles QR
13 P—QKt4	

A belated move to counter-attack, but of no avail against the great strategist Nimzowitsch.

13	QR—Kt1
14 P—QR4	Kt—Q1

In order to reply to 15 B—Kt5 by 15 .... P—B3. "Do not shrink from any move which consolidates the position": this was Nimzowitsch's motto.

15 P—Kt5	P—KR4
16 KKt—R2	R—Kt2
17 P—R5	K—Kt1
18 B—R3	B×B
19 R×B	P—R5

If at once 19 .... P—Kt5; 20 P—R4. The text move therefore prepares—thanks to White's 11th move—the opening of the KKt file, after which Black's offensive becomes irresistible.

20 P—Kt6	KR—Kt1
21 P—R6	BP×P
22 P×P	

Having thrust forward his infantry in a desperate assault, White aims at QR7, which, for this reason, Black's next move seeks to fortify.

22	QKt—B3
23 B—Kt5	P—Kt5
24 P×P	B×P
25 Q—Q2	Q—Q3
26 R—R2	B—K7

By this fine combination, Black wins the Bishop, a fitting culmination of his powerful strategy, for if 27 Q×B, R×P ch; 28 K—R1, R—Kt8 mate.

White resigns.

240

White	Black
BIRD	MASON

(New York, 1876)

Here is a beautiful game played in the lively style of long ago. Without attempting to obtain, in the opening phase, any convincing advantage, White succeeds—after much manœuvring—in breaking into the enemy camp (25 Q×P), and, once established near the hostile batteries, he initiates, by the intuitive sacrifice of his Queen against Rook and Knight, such a symphony of threats, irruptions, interruptions, cavalcades, etc., that the enemy in the end succumbs.

1 P—K4	P—K3
2 P—Q4	P—Q4
3 Kt—QB3	Kt—KB3
4 P×P	

Simplification akin to that which is sometimes played on the third move.

4	P×P
5 Kt—B3	B—Q3
6 B—Q3	Castles
7 Castles	P—KR3

Preventing the pin by 8 B—KKt5, and preparing the enterprising continuation 8 .... Kt—QB3, instead of the more passive 8 .... P—B3.

8 R—K1	Kt—B3
9 Kt—QKt5	B—QKt5
10 P—B3	B—R4
11 Kt—R3	B—Kt5
12 Kt—B2	Q—Q2
13 P—Kt4	B—Kt3
14 P—KR3	B—KR4
15 Kt—K3	

Not yet 15 P—Kt4, because of 15 ....

KKt×P; 16 P×Kt, Q×P ch, followed by
.... Q×Kt, and Black would win two
pawns in this skirmish.

15	KR—K1
16 P—Kt5	Kt—K2
17 P—Kt4	B—Kt3
18 Kt—K5	Q—B1
19 P—QR4	P—B3
20 P×P	P×P
21 B—R3	Kt—K5
22 Q—B2	

Apart from defending the QBP, this manœuvre contains aggressive intentions on the
diagonal QKt—KR7 (e.g. after K—Kt2 and
P—B3).

22	Kt—Kt4

Hastening, before it is too late, to organise
a counter-thrust.

23 B×Kt	R×B
24 B×B	P×B
25 Q×P	

Instead of protecting his threatened KRP,
White seeks to penetrate into the enemy
camp.

After 25 K—Kt2, Q—B1, the continuation 26 Q×P would be a blunder, on
account of 26 .... R×Kt, and wins.

25	Kt×P ch
26 K—R2	Kt—B5
27 Q—B5	Kt—K3

A disappointment was in store for Black,
had he tried the following continuation:
27 .... Q×Q; 28 Kt×Q, R—K3;
29 KKt×P, etc., or 28 .... R—QB2;
29 P—R5 (but not in this case 29 KKt×P,
on the score of 29 .... K—B1; 30 Kt—K5,
R×P).

28 Kt—Kt2	Q—B2
29 P—R5	

The beginning of a far-sighted combination.

29	B×RP
30 R×B	R—KB1

After 30 .... Q×R, White plays, not
31 Kt×P, Q—B2 ch, but 31 Kt—Kt6, with
an emphatic advantage.

But now, instead of yielding territory,
White embarks upon a very curious positional sacrifice, relying on the dominating
position of his pieces.

31 R—R6	R×Q
32 P×R	Kt—Q1
33 Kt—KB4	Q—B1
34 Kt (B4)—Kt6	

The first surprise! Black cannot now
play 34 .... R×Kt; 35 R×R, Q×R, by
reason of 36 R—K8 ch, followed by mate.

Position after 30 .... R—KB1

34	R—K1
35 Kt×P	

The second surprise! If 35 .... R×R;
36 KKt—K7 ch, regaining the Queen and
remaining a piece ahead. And if 35 ....
Kt×Kt; 36 R×R ch, Q×R; 37 R×Kt
(threatening 38 R—B8, Q×R; 39 Kt—K7 ch,
and wins).

Black should, however, have chosen this
continuation, but with 37 .... K—R2, but
he thinks that the text move will give him
ample returns.

35	Q—B2 ch
36 Kt (B6)—K5	Q×P
37 R—K3	Q—Q7

The third surprise! If 37 .... Q×P;
38 Kt—B3 wins. Black's game is going
from bad to worse.

38 K—Kt2	Q×P
39 P—B6	

He cannot play 39 Kt—B3, in view of the
threat of 39 .... Q—Kt5 ch.

39	P×P
40 R×BP	Kt—K3
41 R—KKt3	Kt—Kt4
42 Kt—Kt4	K—Kt2
43 Kt—B4	

The work of the white Knights is remarkable.

43	Q—K5 ch
44 K—R2	Kt—R2

Not 44 .... Kt—B6 ch; 45 R×Kt,
Q×R; 46 Kt—R5 ch, followed by R×Q.

45 Kt—R5 ch	K—R1
46 R×P	Q—B7
47 Kt (R5)—B6	R—K2
48 K—Kt2	P—Q5
49 Kt—K5	

Decisive, because of the threat 50 R—Kt8 mate.

| 49 ...... | Q—B1 |
| 50 Kt—Kt6 ch | Resigns. |

241

| *White* | *Black* |
| BLACKBURNE | SCHWARZ |

(Berlin, 1881)

The opening of the KR file not infrequently leads to large-scale combinations.

The piquant feature of this game is that White quietly castles on the K side without any apparent intention of embarking on any startling operations on that wing.

After the KR file has become open (after Black's tempting but unnecessary exchange 14 .... Kt × Kt), the mobilisation of the white Rooks on that file becomes the objective of White's strategy and leads to a sparkling termination.

1 P—K4	P—K3
2 P—Q4	P—Q4
3 Kt—QB3	Kt—KB3
4 P × P	P × P
5 Kt—B3	B—Q3
6 B—Q3	P—B3
7 Castles	Castles
8 Kt—K2	

In this peaceful and nearly symmetrical opening, White has yet managed to have one additional piece in play, which piece, the QKt, the text move is intended to transfer to the main battlefield.

8	B—KKt5
9 Kt—Kt3	Q—B2
10 B—K3	QKt—Q2
11 Q—Q2	

White is willing to let his K side pawns be doubled and isolated (by 11 .... QB × Kt; 12 P × B), for then he would be able to start a serious attack on the open KKt file by K—R1 and R—KKt1.

| 11 ...... | KR—K1 |
| 12 QR—K1 | Kt—K5 |

Preferring the "open battle" to continuing "trench warfare" by 12 .... Kt—B1.

13 Q—B1	B × KKt
14 P × B	Kt × Kt
15 RP × Kt	B × P

This proffered sacrifice explains the meaning of the two preceding exchanges. If it is accepted (16 P × B, Q × P ch; 17 K—R1), Black would have at least a draw by perpetual check, and, in case of non-acceptance, he has gained a pawn.

16 K—Kt2

White now proceeds to demonstrate that his opponent's combination has only served, by the opening of the KR file, to give White the opportunity of a persistent attack.

16	B—Q3
17 R—R1	Kt—B1
18 R—R3	P—KKt3

In face of the threat of the doubled Rooks, Black is forced to move one of the King's field pawns, which weakens the black King's defences.

If 18 .... P—KR3, there follows 19 QR—R1, and then the sacrifice 20 B × P, with devastating effect.

19 QR—R1	QR—Q1
20 B—KKt5	R—Q2
21 P—QB4	

With this fresh thrust, White threatens either to win the exchange (22 P × P, P × P; 23 B—Kt5) or to conquer valuable territory (e.g. 21 .... R—B1; 22 P—B5, B—K2; 23 B—KB4, Q—R4; 24 B—K5, etc.).

21	P × P
22 B × BP	P—KR4
23 R—R4	P—Kt4
24 B—Kt3	Kt—K3
25 B—B6	Kt—B5 ch

Hoping to bar the threatening irruption 26 Q—R6.

If, with the same object in view, 25 .... B—B5; there follows 26 Q—B2 K—B1; 27 R × P, and wins.

25 .... B—B1; offers more resistance.

26 Q × Kt

This beautiful Queen sacrifice eliminates a troublesome defender.

26	B × Q
27 R × P	P × R
28 R × P	Resigns.

242

White	Black
TARRASCH	MIESES

(Match, Berlin, 1916)

In this short but expressive game, it will be noticed that, at the critical moment, Black's King's field is guarded by only one piece (a Knight, which, to make matters worse, is pinned), whilst White has succeeded in concentrating no less than four pieces (Queen, Rook and two Bishops) for the final onslaught. It is not surprising that an attack against a fortress so poorly defended should succeed. We may add that, in spite of its apparent simplicity, the game is noteworthy for the economy of means employed.

1 P—Q4	P—K3
2 P—K4	P—Q4
3 Kt—QB3	P × P
4 Kt × P	Kt—Q2
5 Kt—KB3	KKt—B3
6 B—Q3	

Maintaining a piece in the centre. Thus White can claim a slight advantage in territory.

6	B—K2
7 Castles	Kt × Kt
8 B × Kt	Kt—B3
9 B—Q3	P—QKt3
10 Kt—K5	

A very strong outpost.

| 10 ...... | Castles |

Or 10 .... B—Kt2; 11 B—Kt5 ch, K—B1; 12 P—QB4, and Black, having had to forgo castling, is a sick man.

White will now demonstrate the advantage of the *two Bishops.*

| 11 Kt—B6 | Q—Q3 |
| 12 Q—B3 | |

Without wasting time, White brings his Queen into play by the threat: 13 Kt × B ch, Q × Kt; 14 Q × R.

12	B—Q2
13 Kt × B ch	Q × Kt
14 B—KKt5	QR—B1

Unconscious of danger! It was necessary to play 14 .... P—KR3.

15 KR—K1

An important preparatory move. If 15 Q—R3 at once, 15 .... P—K4.

| 15 ...... | KR—K1 |
| 16 Q—R3 | |

The decisive attack against KR7.

| 16 ...... | Q—Q3 |

Black cannot now avoid loss of material. 16 .... P—KR3 would come too late, because of the sacrifice 17 B × P, P × B; 18 Q × RP, followed by R—K3, or 17 .... P—K4; 18 Q—Kt3, Kt—R4; 19 Q—B3, etc.

| 17 B × Kt | P × B |
| 18 Q—R6 | |

In order to prevent the King from escaping—an instructive turn, which the beginner would do well to note.

18	P—KB4
19 R—K3	Q × P
20 P—QB3	

The *coup de grâce,* for Black's Queen can no longer prevent the mate at her KKt2.

| 20 ...... | Resigns. |

243

White	Black
BOGOLJUBOW	ALEKHINE

(Match, 1929)

This game is an object lesson on how to gain a slight positional advantage in the opening and, what is more difficult, on how to maintain it. It shows, incidentally, that such an advantage, even if maintained, may at times need freshening up (26 R—B6). Then comes the most difficult problem of all, a problem solved here in masterly fashion— how to turn the advantage into a win.

1 P—K4	P—K3
2 P—Q4	P—Q4
3 Kt—QB3	Kt—KB3
4 B—Kt5	P × P
5 Kt × P	B—K2
6 B × Kt	P × B

More solid is 6 .... B × B.

| 7 Kt—KB3 | P—KB4 |
| 8 Kt—B3 | |

White threatens (e.g. after 8 .... Kt—Q2) to play 9 P—Q5, to advantage, and Black's next move is practically forced.

8	P—QB3
9 P—KKt3	Kt—Q2
10 B—Kt2	

White's development has left his forces more active, and he will hold on to this advantage throughout this long and exciting game.

10	Q—B2
11 Q—K2	P—Kt4
12 Kt—K5	B—Kt2
13 Castles QR	Kt—Kt3

After 13 .... Kt—B3 White would keep up the pressure by 14 KR—K1, R—KB1; 15 K—Kt1, Castles; 16 Kt×KBP, R×Kt; 17 Q×P ch, followed by Q×R. But if White plays 14 KR—K1, after the move in the text Black frees his game by 14 .... B—B3.

14 Q—R5	R—KB1
15 P—B4	P—Kt5
16 Kt—K2	Kt—Q4
17 B×Kt	BP×B
18 K—Kt1	P—QR4
19 P—Kt4	P×P
20 P—B5	P×P
21 Q×P (B5)	

Having, by the last two pretty moves, disconnected Black's centre pawns, White is able to use his pair of Knights much more freely than his opponent.

21	P—R5
22 KR—K1	P—R6
23 P—Kt3	B—B1
24 Q×RP	B—K3
25 Q—Q3	Castles
26 P—B3	

Thus the QB file will be opened to White's advantage (26 .... P×P; 27 R—QB1).

26	K—Kt2
27 R—QB1	Q—Kt3
28 P×P	B×P
29 R—B6	

This intermediary manœuvre enables White to double Rooks, whereas after 29 R—B1, R—B1 White's action would be at a standstill.

29	Q—R4
30 KR—QB1	R—B1
31 Kt—KB4	B—Q3

A trap! After 32 R×B, R×R ch; 33 K×R, Q—K8 ch; 34 K—B2, R—B1 ch;

35 R—B6, R×R ch; 36 Kt×R, K×R, Black has equalised.

But White declines to deviate from his plan of attack.

| 32 Kt×B | P×Kt |
| 33 Q—R7 ch | |

This invasion of the enemy camp proves decisive.

33	R—B2
34 R×R ch	B×R
35 Q—Q7	Q—Kt3
36 Kt—Q3	R—Q1

After 36 .... R—B3 White decides the issue as follows: 37 Kt—B5 ch, K—Kt1; 38 Kt—R6 ch, or 37 .... K—R2; 38 Kt—R4, or, finally, 37 .... K—R1; 38 Q—R4 ch, Q—R2; 39 Q—B6 ch, K—Kt1; 40 Q—K8 ch, followed by mate.

| 37 R×B ch | |

The total liquidation, which this move evokes, had to be calculated very far ahead.

37	Q×R
38 Kt—B5 ch	K—Kt3
39 Q×Q ch	K×Q
40 Kt×P ch	K—Q2
41 Kt×R	K×Kt
42 P—Kt4	

The duel of the Kings, though unequal, is still quite instructive.

42	K—Q2
43 K—B2	K—B3
44 K—Kt3	K—Kt4
45 K×P	K—B5
46 P—Kt5	

A sacrifice to gain space.

46	K×KtP
47 K—Kt3	K—R4
48 P—QR4	K—R3
49 K—Kt4	K—Kt3
50 P—R5 ch	K—B3
51 K—R4	Resigns.

244

| White | Black |
| EUWE | FLOHR |

(Match, Carlsbad, 1932)

A wise pedagogue has written somewhere that the first strategic object in chess should be to castle. In this game White, by scientific manœuvres, succeeds in preventing his opponent from castling. After Black's King has sought security on the adjacent square at KB1, White proceeds to demonstrate that there too he is vulnerable.

1 P—K4	P—K3
2 P—Q4	P—Q4
3 Kt—QB3	Kt—KB3
4 B—KKt5	P×P
5 Kt×P	B—K2
6 B×Kt	P×B

In another game of the same match, Flohr tried the more solid 6 .... B×B, and drew the game.

7 Q—Q2	P—KB4

An urgently needed counter-measure, as after 7 .... Kt—Q2; 8 P—QB4, P—KB4; 9 Kt—QB3, White exerts increased pressure in the centre.

8 Kt—QB3	P—QB3

To prevent the eventual break-through by P—Q5, etc.

9 Castles	Kt—Q2
10 P—KKt3	P—Kt3
11 B—Kt2	B—Kt2

Black has a "hedgehog position," cramped but defensible.

12 Kt—R3	

Instead of the simple development 12 Kt—B3, White is intent on keeping up a continued domination of the long diagonal by his KB.

12	Q—B2

By playing 12 .... Kt—B3; 13 KR—K1, Q—Q3, Black could have castled on the Q side, with better chances of equalising the game.

13 Q—K2	

Still preventing Black's .... Castles QR, because of 14 P—Q5.

13	Kt—B3
14 KR—K1	K—B1

Black has no option but to give up all thoughts of castling, for if 14 .... Castles KR; 15 Kt—B4, and if 14 .... Castles QR; 15 Kt—KKt5 (15 .... QR—B1; 16 Kt×BP, R×Kt; 17 Q×P ch, followed by Q×R).

15 Kt—KKt5	

Threatens, above all, 16 Q×P.

15	Q—Q3
16 P—B4	P—KR3
17 Kt—B3	Kt—Q4
18 Kt—K5	R—R2

No good would come of 18 .... Kt×Kt;

19 P×Kt, Q—R6 ch; 20 K—Q2, because after 20 .... Q×P; 21 R—QR1, Q—Kt7; 22 KR—QKt1, the venturesome Queen is lost.

19 B×Kt	BP×B
20 P—KKt4	

The beginning of a decisive frontal attack.

20	P×P
21 Q×P	P—KR4
22 Q—B3	P—R3
23 P—B5	B—Kt4 ch
24 K—Kt1	K—K2
25 P×P	P×P
26 R—Kt1	B—R3

Compulsory, e.g. 26 .... B—KB3; 27 Kt—Kt6 ch, K—B2; 28 QR—KB1, Q—Q1; 29 Kt—K5 ch, and wins.

27 QR—KB1	

With the devastating threat: 28 Q—B6 ch, K—K1; 29 R—Kt8 ch.

27	Q—Kt5
28 P—QR3	Resigns

Because of—

(a) 28 .... Q—Q3; 29 Q—B6 ch, K—K1; 30 R—Kt8 ch, etc.

(b) 28 .... Q—R4; 29 Q—B7 ch, R×Q; 30 R×R ch, with mate to follow.

(c) 28 .... Q×QP; 29 Q—B6, K—Q3; 30 Kt—B7 ch, K—B4; 31 Q—K7 ch, and mate next move.

245

White	Black
STEINITZ	WINAWER

(Paris, 1867)

The most dangerous thing for Black to do, already one move behind as the second player, is to neglect his King's safety and to deprive him of his natural guardians (the Bishop at K2 and the Knight at KB3). Even in closed games débâcles can result such as we have seen in open games—especially in the Gambits: Evans', Danish and King's Gambits.

1 P—K4	P—K3
2 P—Q4	P—Q4
3 Kt—QB3	B—Kt5

Reinforcing the threat to White's KP by pinning the supporting Knight and forcing White at once to declare his policy in the centre. This makes up for the fact that Black will ultimately lose a *tempo* by withdrawing the Bishop (to Q3 or K2), unless he exchanges it for the Knight, a procedure hardly to be recommended at the beginning of a game.

4 P×P
A wise decision. The exchange variation has, at this point, a greater justification in that White has in the meantime developed a piece (Knight at QB3) against a doubtfully placed Bishop (at QKt5).

4	P×P
5 B—Q3	

Reserving the choice of developing the KKt at B3 or K2, thus lending elasticity to White's play.

5	B—K3

A non-productive move; he should strive for a more extended development of his QB, e.g. 5 .... Kt—KB3; 6 Kt—K2, B—Kt5, etc.

6 Kt—B3	P—KR3

Preventing 7 Kt—Kt5 or 7 B—Kt5, but the safeguarding of his King is still further delayed. The best continuation is 6 .... Kt—QB3 (restraining the hostile KKt); 7 Castles, Kt—B3, etc.

7 Castles	B×Kt

Consistent, but not compulsory, this exchange will deprive the black King of one of his natural guardians. To employ modern terminology, Black, by the absence of his KB, will find himself weak on the "black square complex" on the K side. This will stand out clearly after his 15th move.

8 P×B	Kt—Q2
9 R—Kt1	Kt—Kt3

The idea of moving this developed Knight away from the central zone, merely to guard the QKtP, cannot be sound. Undoubtedly better was to post the Rook at Kt1.

10 Kt—K5	Kt—K2
11 P—KB4	B—B4
12 B×B	Kt×B
13 B—R3	Kt—Q3

Away from their usual lines of development, the two Knights play a pitiful rôle. 13 .... Kt—K6 would be disappointing, on account of 14 Q—R5, P—Kt3; 15 Kt×KtP, P×Kt; 16 Q—K5 ch, K—Q2; 17 Q×Kt, and, without bettering his position, Black has lost a pawn.

14 P—B5	Kt—K5
15 P—B6	P—Kt3

Hoping to keep the position closed. If 15 .... Kt×KBP; 16 Q—K1 (threat: 17 Kt—B6 dis ch); 16 .... Q—B1 (or 16 .... Kt—K5; 17 Kt×P, etc.); 17 Kt—Kt6 dis ch, and wins.
And if 15 .... P×P; 16 Q—R5, etc.

16 Q—Kt4	Q—B1

Faced by the terrible threat of 17 Q×P, P×Q; 18 P—B7 mate, Black only partially meets the case with the move in the text.
Relatively best was 16 .... R—KKt1, although even then White, by continuing 17 QR—K1 would dominate the board.

17 Q×P
This magnificent Queen sacrifice demonstrates the weakness of the King's position.

17	Q—K3
18 Q—Kt7	Castles
19 Kt×P	

And wins, the painful continuation being:

19	Kt×QBP
20 Kt×QR	R×Kt
21 P—B7	Kt—Q2
22 QR—K1	Kt—K7 ch
23 K—R1	P—B4
24 B×P	Q—K5
25 P—B8 (Q)	Kt×Q
26 KR×Kt	Kt—Kt6 ch
27 Q×Kt	R×R
28 B×R	Resigns.

246

White	Black
ALEKHINE	YATES

(Hastings, 1925-6)

It is one thing to seize an opportunity of winning brilliantly, but quite another to know how and when to "liquidate." It is assuredly no mean achievement to see the win many moves ahead, after several exchanges in an entirely simple and, to all appearances, even position. This is admirably illustrated by the following game.

1 P—Q4	P—K3
2 P—K4	P—Q4
3 Kt—QB3	B—Kt5
4 P×P	P×P
5 B—Q3	Kt—KB3
6 B—Kt5	

More enterprising than 6 Kt—B3 or 6 Kt—K2.

6 ......   Castles
7 Kt—K2

A more imaginative development than the routine move 7 Kt—B3, which would allow the symmetrical counter-pin 7 .... B—Kt5, leading to far less varied play.

7	R—K1
8 Castles	P—B3
9 Kt—Kt3	QKt—Q2
10 Kt—R5	B—K2
11 R—K1	P—KR3
12 B—R4	Kt × Kt
13 B × B	R × B
14 Q × Kt	Kt—B3
15 Q—R4	B—Q2

Intending, now that the Queen is guarded by the other Rook, to embark on a general exchange by 16 .... R × R ch; 17 R × R, Kt—R2, but White, in a most astute manner, cuts across these plans.

16 R—K5

It is a part of Alekhine's outstanding artistry to force his adversary, by the occupation of a dominant post, to effect the exchange of a given piece on a given square.

16	R × R
17 P × R	Kt—R2
18 Q × Q	R × Q
19 P—B4	R—K1
20 K—B2	Kt—B1
21 P—QKt4	

Embarking on what might be termed an attack by the minority, White having, on the Q side, but three pawns to his opponent's four. White's object in this is to render the adverse pawn formation less compact and thereby more vulnerable.

21	Kt—K3
22 P—Kt3	K—B1
23 R—K1	P—KKt3

He fortifies the K side (anticipating a possible thrust 24 P—B5), but the danger now comes from the other wing.

But if, first, 23 .... P—R3, White plays 24 P—QR4, trying to enforce the advance P—Kt5.

24 P—Kt5   Kt—B4

Exchange by 24 .... P × P; 25 Kt × QP would clearly be against Black's interests.

25 P × P	P × P
26 R—QKt1	K—K2
27 R—Kt4	P—KR4
28 Kt—K2	K—Q1
29 R—Kt8 ch	K—K2
30 R × R ch	B × R
31 K—K3	Kt × B
32 P × Kt	

The Knight v. Bishop ending which follows is most instructive. Generally, the Bishop is thought to be slightly superior to the Knight in the end-game. (Dr. Tarrasch used to refer to the player with the Bishop as having the "minor exchange.") But in the present instance the Knight will prove much more agile.

32	P—QB4
33 P—Q4	P—B5

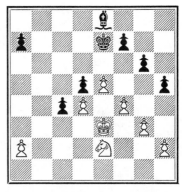

34 P—B5

Having, by his last excellent move (33 P—Q4), caused the immobilisation of the adverse wing, White, with the text move, opens up a victorious way on the K side.

For Black cannot very well reply 34 .... P × P, by reason of 35 Kt—B4, B—B3; 36 Kt × P, etc.

34	P—Kt4
35 P—KR4	P—B3
36 P × P	P × KtP
37 Kt—Kt1	B—Q2
38 P—B6 ch	K—K1
39 Kt—B3	P—Kt5
40 Kt—R4	B—K3
41 Kt—Kt6	B—B2
42 Kt—B4	K—Q2
43 K—K2	P—R4
44 K—K3	

A *Zugzwang* position, by which White wins a pawn. (If 44 .... P—R5; 45 P—R3.)

44	B—Kt1
45 Kt × RP	B—B2
46 Kt—B4	B—Kt1
47 Kt—K2	B—K3
48 K—B4	K—K1
49 K—Kt5	K—B2
50 Kt—B3	

Zugzwang again, forcing access to KKt6 for the white King.

50	K—B1
51 K—Kt6	K—Kt1
52 P—B7 ch	

A *vacating sacrifice* (clearing KB6).

52	K—B1
53 K—B6	B×P
54 P—K6	B—R4
55 Kt×P	B—K1
56 Kt—B3	Resigns.

247

White	Black
CAPABLANCA	ALEKHINE

(Match, Buenos Aires, 1927)

"Multum ex parvo!" In this historical game (the first of the match), a slight lack of precision in the opening on the part of White costs him the initiative, later a pawn, and in consequence the game.

1 P—K4	P—K3
2 P—Q4	P—Q4
3 Kt—QB3	B—Kt5

The choice of this move, previously under-estimated, on such an important occasion shows its inherent vitality.

4 P×P	P×P
5 B—Q3	Kt—QB3
6 Kt—K2	KKt—K2
7 Castles	B—KB4

Black's treatment of the opening is both astute and scientific. Instead of playing the routine move 7 .... Castles, he advant-ageously brings out his QB, thereby pre-serving his choice of castling on either side.

| 8 B×B | Kt×B |
| 9 Q—Q3 | |

Aiming at the K side (10 Q×Kt) as well as the Q side (10 Q—Kt5, winning a pawn at Q5 or QKt7). Black's excellent rejoinder parries both threats.

| 9 ...... | Q—Q2 |
| 10 Kt—Q1 | |

The development of another piece by 10 B—B4 would be more straightforward.

| 10 ...... | Castles KR |

He decides that, after all, 10 .... Castles QR would be too risky. The chances are even for the time being.

11 Kt—K3	Kt×Kt
12 B×Kt	KR—K1
13 Kt—B4	

Again with the threat of winning a pawn by 14 Q—Kt5.

| 13 ...... | B—Q3 |
| 14 KR—K1 | |

In allowing the following escapade (14 .... Kt—Kt5), the Cuban plays with fire. 14 P—QB3 was simple and good.

Bad would be, however, 14 Kt×P, because of 14 .... B×P ch, followed by 15 .... Q×Kt, and the initiative would fall to Black.

| 14 ...... | Kt—Kt5 |
| 15 Q—Kt3 | |

By playing 15 Q—Q2 (15 .... Q—B4; 16 KR—QB1), White could have kept his material intact, but he would still have had a difficult game.

| 15 ...... | Q—B4 |
| 16 QR—B1 | |

This unexpectedly loses a pawn, and after a heroic resistance, the game.

Let us examine alternative continuations:
(a) 16 KR—QB1, B×Kt; 17 Q×Kt, R×B; 18 P×R, B×KP ch; 19 K—R1, B×R; 20 R×B, R—K1, and if now 21 Q×P, then 21 .... Q×P.

(b) 16 R—K2, B×Kt; 17 Q×Kt, Q—R4, with a double attack against Rook and RP.

(c) 16 Kt—Q3, the only way to avoid the loss of a pawn, but 16 .... Kt×Kt would leave White with a doubled isolated pawn on the Q file, which would be a permanent weakness in his game.

| 16 ...... | Kt×BP |
| 17 R×Kt | |

Or 17 Q×Kt, Q×Q; 18 R×Q, B×Kt.

17	Q×Kt
18 P—Kt3	Q—B4
19 QR—K2	P—QKt3
20 Q—Kt5	P—KR4
21 P—KR4	R—K5

With the threat: 22 .... R×RP; 23 P×R, Q—Kt5 ch, followed by mate in three.

| 22 B—Q2 | |

Temporarily giving up a second pawn offers relatively the best chances of salvation.

| 22 ...... | R×QP |

A mistake would be 22 .... R×RP, as 23 R—K8 ch would provide the white King with a flight square at K2.

23	B—B3	R—Q6
24	B—K5	R—Q1
25	B×B	R×B
26	R—K5	Q—B6
27	R×RP	Q×R
28	R—K8 ch	K—R2
29	Q×R ch	Q—Kt3
30	Q—Q1	R—K3

By allowing White to recover his pawn, Black gets his Rook into effective play on the open K file. The ensuing end-game with major pieces is instructive.

31	R—R8	R—K4
32	R×P	P—QB4
33	R—Q7	Q—K3
34	Q—Q3 ch	P—Kt3
35	R—Q8	P—Q5
36	P—R4	R—K8 ch

Here Black could have shortened the game by 36 .... Q—K2; 37 R—QKt8, Q—B2; 38 R—KB8, K—Kt2 (this chasing of the errant Rook is amusing); 39 R—QR8, R—K8 ch; 40 K—any, Q—Kt2, and wins.

37	K—Kt2	Q—B3 ch
38	P—B3	

If 38 Q—B3, R—Kt8 ch, winning the Queen (a well-known device, which the beginner should note). White, forced to leave his King more and more exposed, is lost.

38	......	R—K6
39	Q—Q1	Q—K3
40	P—KKt4	R—K7 ch
41	K—R3	Q—K6
42	Q—KR1	Q—B5
43	P—KR5	R—KB7
	Resigns.	

248

	White	*Black*
	BOGOLJUBOW	BERGER

(Scarborough, 1927)

In the variation selected by White, the main idea is the formation of a chain of pawns in the centre.

One single move, neglectful of this primary object and seeking the illusory gain of a pawn (8 P×P, instead of 8 P—QB3), is the cause of all the subsequent trouble. The skilful way in which the London master exploits this error of judgment is most instructive.

1	P—K4	P—K3
2	P—Q4	P—Q4
3	Kt—QB3	B—Kt5
4	P—K5	

The most forcible continuation.

4	......	Kt—K2

The more usual 4 .... P—QB4; occurs in the next game.

5	B—Q2	P—QB4

Superior to 5 .... Kt—B4; which gives White the better game.

6	Kt—Kt5	

Combinative play, relying on manœuvres by pieces. An alternative method, which is sometimes adopted, 6 P—QR3, B×Kt; 7 P×B, leads to play of much less lively character.

6	......	B×B ch
7	Q×B	Castles
8	P×P	

Renouncing the formation of a pawn-chain. (See introductory comment.)

8	......	Kt—Q2
9	Q—B3	P—QR3
10	Kt—Q6	Q—B2

He calmly proceeds to recover his pawn, whilst preserving the positional superiority resulting from the weaknesses in the hostile pawn-formation, these pawns being either too far advanced (K5) or lacking in mobility.

11	Kt—B3	Q×P

Clearly not 11 .... Kt×BP; because of 12 P—QKt4. The student should always be on the look-out for pins, either vertical, horizontal or diagonal.

12	Q×Q	Kt×Q
13	B—Q3	Kt—B3
14	Castles KR	R—Q1

Threatening .... Kt×P.

15	Kt×B	QR×Kt
16	P—QR3	P—QKt4
17	KR—K1	R—B2
18	QR—Q1	KR—QB1
19	P—B3	Kt—R4
20	Kt—Q4	Kt—B5
21	R—K2	Kt—R5
22	B×Kt	KtP×B

Black's threatened pressure on the half-open QKt file now becomes the main theme of the next phase of the contest.

23 P—B4	P—Kt3
24 P—KKt4	R—Kt2
25 R (Q1)—Q2	R (B1)—Kt1
26 Kt—B6	R—QB1
27 Kt—Q4	R (B1)—Kt1
28 Kt—B6	R—K1
29 P—B5	R—Kt3
30 Kt—Q4	R (K1)—Kt1
31 P×KP	P×P
32 K—B1	Kt×KtP
33 Kt×P	Kt—Q6
34 Kt—B7	R—Kt8 ch
35 K—Kt2	Kt—B5 ch
36 K—B3	Kt×R
37 R×Kt	R (Kt1)—Kt7

Sound play! After the exchange of Rooks, the superiority of Black's remaining Rook over the Knight becomes more pronounced.

38 R×R	R×R
39 P—K6	K—B1
40 Kt×QP	R×P
41 K—K3	P—KR4

Black's passed pawn becomes a tower of strength, whilst White's is easily kept in check.

42 P×P	P×P
43 K—B4	P—R5
44 K—K5	R—K7 ch
45 K—Q6	P—R6
Resigns	

A masterly game on the part of Black.

249

White	Black
ALEKHINE	NIMZOWITSCH

(San Remo, 1930)

The theme of the vertical pin (on the QB file), which results in this game from the skirmishes of the opening, is followed out to the end in a most telling manner.

1 P—K4	P—K3
2 P—Q4	P—Q4
3 Kt—QB3	B—Kt5
4 P—K5	P—QB4
5 B—Q2	Kt—K2
6 Kt—Kt5	

No sooner unpinned, the Knight becomes an active participant in the battle.

6	B×B ch
7 Q×B	Castles
8 P—QB3	

Wisely seizing the opportunity of welding his chain of pawns.

8	P—QKt3

The most rapid as well as the soundest development is 8 .... QKt—B3.

9 P—KB4	B—R3
10 Kt—B3	Q—Q2
11 P—QR4	QKt—B3

From the point of view of driving the Knight away from its challenging post, the most effective manœuvre is 11 .... P—B5 (12 Kt—Q6, Kt—B1 or 12 Kt—R3, Q×P), whereas now White, with a brilliant thrust, will gain additional territory on the critical sector (here the QB file and surroundings).

12 P—QKt4	P×KtP

If 12 .... P—B5; 13 Kt—R3 (with the threat of a fork by 14 P—Kt5); 13 .... Kt—Q1; 14 Kt—B2, and White, having locked the Q side, will proceed to attack on the opposite wing.

13 P×P	B—Kt2
14 Kt—Q6	P—B4
15 P—R5	Kt—B1
16 Kt×B	Q×Kt
17 P—R6	Q—KB2

If 17 .... Q—K2; 18 B—Kt5, and the black QKt must beat an inglorious retreat, as 18 .... Kt×KtP loses a piece (19 R—QKt1).

18 B—Kt5	Kt (B1)—K2
19 Castles KR	P—R3
20 KR—B1	KR—B1
21 R—B2	

The vertical pin on the QB file increases in effectiveness.

21	Q—K1

Hoping to make a stand on QB3, for after 21 .... Kt—Q1; 22 QR—QB1, R×R; 23 R×R, R—B1; 24 B—Q7, R×R; 25 Q×R, White would have obtained full control of the open QB file.

22 QR—QB1	QR—Kt1
23 Q—K3	R—B2

It is essential for Black to double his Rooks in view of the hostile threat 24 Q—R3, followed by 25 Q—R4. But now White executes a most instructive regrouping on the critical file.

24 R—B3	Q—Q2
25 R (B1)—B2	K—B1
26 Q—B1	

The "trebling" is most successfully

achieved, the chief unit, the Queen, being at the rear of the "battery."

26 ......   QR—B1

The black QKt, being pinned both vertically and diagonally, is lost if White can increase his already fourfold attack.

27 B—R4   P—QKt4

In view of the fresh threat of 28 P—Kt5, Black must sacrifice a pawn in order to gain an *approach tempo* for his King.

28 B×P   K—K1
29 B—R4   K—Q1
30 P—R4

Obtaining, on a full board, a *Zugzwang* position.

30 ......   Q—K1
31 P—Kt5   Resigns.

250

White	Black
ALEKHINE	EUWE

(Match, 1935)

There undoubtedly is, in chess, such a thing as the "hypnosis of the error," and it almost looks as if it has been at work in the following game.

On the seventh move Dr. Alekhine, impetuously and almost consciously, tries a new move (7 P—KKt4) which cannot be good—being in contradiction to all the tenets of good play. Unconsciously his opponent, Dr. Euwe, allows this surprise move to get the better of his judgment, and fails to make the immediate

counter-thrust which was indicated (7 .... P—K4, in place of 7 .... P—QKt3). He then directs his King to the sector desired by his adversary (10 .... Castles, instead of 10 .... Q—Q2 and .... Castles QR).

Still later on he seeks safety where it is not to be found (21 .... Q—K5, instead of 21 .... Q—B7 or 27 .... Q—Q4), and thus White's gamble has succeeded.

1	P—K4	P—K3
2	P—Q4	P—Q4
3	Kt—QB3	B—Kt5
4	Kt—K2	P×P
5	P—QR3	B—K2

Black prefers to give up the pawn he has won, because after 5 .... B×Kt ch; 6 Kt×B, P—KB4 (or 6 .... Kt—KB3; 7 B—Kt5, and White regains his pawn, with an excellent game); 7 B—QB4, and White's pressure on the weakened diagonal QR2—KKt8 more than compensates him for the lost pawn.

6	Kt×P	Kt—QB3
7	P—KKt4	

Instead of this hazardous move, wisdom indicated 7 B—K3, over-protecting the pawn at Q4 and affording freedom of action to White's KKt.

7 ......   P—QKt3

The strongest reply here is 7 .... P—K4, e.g. 8 P—Q5, Kt—Q5; 9 KKt—B3 (if 9 Kt×Kt, Q×P); 9 .... Kt—KB3, and Black has the better game.

8	B—Kt2	B—Kt2
9	P—QB3	Kt—B3
10	Kt(K2)—Kt3	Castles

Instead of castling where White has such a concentration of forces, 10 .... Q—Q2, followed by .... Castles QR, would have equalised matters.

11	P—Kt5	Kt×Kt
12	Kt×Kt	K—R1
13	Q—R5	Q—K1
14	Kt—B6	

A beautiful idea.

14 ......   B×Kt

Or 14 .... P×Kt; 15 P×P, Kt—R4 (but not 15 .... B×BP; 16 B—K4, forcing mate); 16 B×B, Kt×B; 17 P×B, Q×P; 18 B—B4, followed by Castles QR, and White has a lasting attack.

15	P×B	P×P
16	Q—R4	Q—Q1
17	B—B4	

The threat is: 18 B×P, Q×B; 19 Q×BP ch K—Kt1; 20 R—KKt1.

| 17 | ...... | P—K4 |
| 18 | B—Kt3 | P—B4 |

Black gives up the pawn in order to free his game.

| 19 | P×P | R—KKt1 |

Threatening 20 .... Q×Q; 21 B×Q, R×B.

| 20 | B—B3 |

The *coup juste*, maintaining White's attack, is 20 Q—R3, whereas now Black, by a fine counter, obtains fresh chances.

| 20 | ..:.... | Q—Q6 |

Unexpected! White cannot reply with 21 B×Kt, because the rejoinder would be, not 21 .... B×B; 22 Q—B6 ch, followed by Q×B, but, much better, 21 .... B—R3.

| 21 | B—K2 | Q—K5 |

Black has lost his hold on the game, and plays for an end-game which turns out unsatisfactorily. He should have kept up his counter-attack, either by 21 .... Q—B7 or 21 .... Q—Q4, with equal chances.

| 22 | Q×Q | P×Q |
| 23 | B—R4 | |

With the deadly threat of 24 B—B6 ch.

23	......	P—KR3
24	Castles	QR—K1
25	B—B6 ch	K—R2
26	P—KB4	P×P e.p.
27	B×P	

He prefers not to win the exchange, as he could have done by 27 B—Q3 ch, because in that case Black would have obtained a passed KBP with some counter-chances.

27	......	Kt—R4
28	B×B	Kt×B
29	R—Q7	

The entry of the Rook on the 7th rank is decisive.

29	......	Kt—B4
30	R×P ch	K—Kt3
31	R×P	Kt—Q6 ch
32	K—Kt1	K—B4
33	R—Q1	

The adverse Knight must first of all be driven away from its advanced post, for, if 33 R×P at once, the reply is 33 .... R—Kt7, etc.

After the text move Black cannot very well play 33 .... K—K5, on account of 34 R—B4 ch, K—K6; 35 R—Q4, etc.

33	......	Kt×KP
34	R—B1 ch	K—K5
35	R×P	Kt—B5
36	R—Q7	K—K6
37	R—K1 ch	K—B6
38	R×R	R×R
39	R—Q4	Kt—K6
40	R—KR4	Kt—B4
41	R—QKt4	Resigns.

251

| *White* | *Black* |
| STEINITZ | McCUTCHEON |

(Simultaneous performance, 25 boards, New York, 1885)

In the following game we have the delectable spectacle of an amateur trying a counter-attack against the world champion. There is, in addition, a certain historical value attached to the game, in that it is more or less the first official example of a famous variation, the "McCutcheon."

1	P—K4	P—K3
2	P—Q4	P—Q4
3	Kt—QB3	Kt—KB3
4	B—Kt5	B—Kt5

This counter-pin, which disdains the adverse threat of 5 P—K5, and seeks to transfer the weight of the battle to White's QB3, is a good example of Black fighting for the initiative.

The idea was conceived by McCutcheon in the early 'seventies, and since then the greatest masters have failed to prove it unsound.

| 5 | P—K5 | P—KR3 |
| 6 | B×Kt | |

Taken aback by the novelty of this line of play, the master player chooses the most plausible, but least effective, continuation.

If it is not desired to retire the threatened Bishop, a good continuation (but by no means a decisive one) is 6 P×Kt, P×B; 7 P×P, R—Kt1; 8 P—KR4 (best), P×P; 9 Q—R5, Q—B3; 10 Kt—B3, etc.

6	......	P×B
7	Kt—B3	P—KB4
8	B—Q3	P—B4
9	P×P	B×P
10	Castles	Kt—B3
11	Q—Q2	Q—K2
12	Q—B4	B—Q2
13	Kt—QKt5	Castles QR
14	P—B4	B—K1

15 KR—B1	K—Kt1
16 P—QR3	P—R3
17 Kt—B3	P×P
18 B×QBP	Kt—Q5

With his last five moves, Black has weathered the storm on the Q side, and now seeks to deprive the white King of his best defender, before himself assuming the offensive.

19 Kt—K2	Kt×KKt ch
20 Q×Kt	►B—B3

Henceforth Black has the initiative.

21 Q—R3	K—R2
22 P—QKt4	B—Kt3
23 Kt—B3	KR—Kt1
24 B—B1	R—Q7
25 Kt—Q1	Q—Kt4

In order to keep on harrying the adverse King by 26 .... Q—B5.

26 R×B

An unsound combination of the kind frequently adopted in difficult situations.

If 26 P—R4 (trying to carry out his attack on the Q side), then, as mentioned before, 26 .... Q—B5.

If 26 Kt—K3, then not only 26 .... Q—B5 or 26 .... P—B5; but even "liquidation" by 26 .... B×Kt; 27 Q×B ch, Q×Q; 28 P×Q, B×P; and wins.

If 26 R—B3 (to strengthen the third rank and threaten 27 R—KKt3), then again 26 .... Q—B5 or 26 .... P—B5. Black has even a combinative continuation at his disposal, namely: 26 .... B—Q5; 27 R—KKt3, Q—B5; 28 R×R, R×P (with the telling threat of 29 .... R×B mate); 29 Kt×R, Q×Kt ch; 30 K—R1, Q—Kt8 mate.

26	P×R
27 Q—QB3	Q—B5
28 Q×P	R×Kt

An *eliminating sacrifice*.

Resigns.

252

White	*Black*
LASKER	MARSHALL

(Match, Philadelphia, 1907)

If, to transcribe a well-known saying, "patience is one of the attributes of genius," Dr. Lasker's qualities in this respect have perhaps never been shown in a manner so constructive and so individual as in the following game.

1 P—K4	P—K3
2 P—Q4	P—Q4
3 Kt—QB3	Kt—KB3
4 B—Kt5	B—Kt5
5 P×P	

A great believer in simplification, Dr. Lasker at once eliminates the tension of the centre pawns, in preference to the supposedly more energetic moves 5 P—K5 or 5Kt—K2.

5	Q×P
6 B×Kt	P×B

If, first, 6 .... B×Kt ch; 7 P×B, and then only 7 .... P×B, White will seek to exploit his superior development by 8 Q—Kt4.

7 Q—Q2

The real Lasker touch. He wishes to keep his pawn chain intact.

7	B×Kt
8 Q×B	Kt—B3
9 Kt—B3	Q—K5 ch
10 K—Q2	

The King starts on his travels. If 10 B—K2, R—KKt1.

10	B—Q2
11 R—K1	Q—B5 ch
12 Q—K3	Q—Q3
13 K—B1	Castles QR
14 R—Q1	KR—Kt1
15 P—KKt3	Kt—Kt5
16 Q—R3	

Here White underestimates the enemy chances, and is more concerned with attacking the hostile QRP than with defending his own.

By playing 16 Q—Kt3, followed by 17 P—QR3, White could have avoided many dangers.

16	B—B3
17 B—Kt2	B—K5

A crucial point. 17 .... B—Q4 (e.g. 18 P—B3, Kt×P ch; 19 K—Q2, Q—B3, etc.) would have set White many problems.

18 Kt—K1	B×B
19 Kt×B	Kt—B3
20 Q×Q	

In the ensuing end-game Dr. Lasker is in his element.

20	R×Q

If 20 .... P×Q; 21 P—Q5.

21 P—QB3	P—K4

Plausible as this aggressive advance may appear, it disturbs the cohesion of Black's three centre pawns and, in particular, it creates a "hole" at Black's QB4 with, later on, damaging consequences.

22 P—Q5	Kt—K2
23 Kt—K3	P—B3
24 P × P	R × P
25 KR—B1	R—K1
26 P—KB4	P × P

Or 26 .... P—K5; 27 P—B5, with advantage to White.
But now the opening of the KB file represents another trump card—for White.

27 R × P	Kt—Kt3
28 R—B3	Kt—K4
29 R—B2	R—R3
30 P—QR3	R—Q1
31 R × R ch	K × R

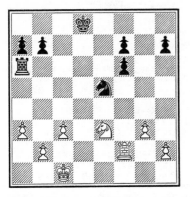

This end-game, with equal forces, is of absorbing interest; in view of the weakness of Black's K side, the problem might be set: White to play and win.

32 K—B2	R—Q3
33 R—B5	Kt—Q2
34 R—KR5	Kt—B1
35 P—B4	

A reminder that White possesses a pawn majority (three against two) on the Q side.

35	K—Q2
36 K—B3	K—K3
37 Kt—Q5	P—QR3
38 P—QR4	R—B3
39 P—R5	

Blockading, unaided, two enemy pawns (QRP and QKtP).

39	R—Q3
40 P—KKt4	R—B3
41 P—Kt3	R—Q3
42 K—Q4	

With the unanswerable threat of 43 R—R6, winning a pawn (the KBP or KRP), whereas if at once 42 R—R6, then 42 .... K—K4.

42	K—Q2
43 R—B5	Kt—K3 ch
44 K—K3	Kt—Kt2
45 Kt × P ch	

The first spoils.

45	K—B3
46 R—B2	R—Q8
47 Kt—Q5	R—QKt8
48 R × P	R × P ch
49 K—K4	Kt—K1

Or 49 .... Kt—K3; 50 K—K5 (50 .... Kt—any; 51 R—B7 mate). It is remarkable that White, with his restricted material, should have succeeded in weaving a mating net.

| 50 R—K7 | P—R4 |

He resists most stubbornly. If 50 .... Kt—Q3 ch; 51 K—Q4, threatening 52 R—B7 mate.

| 51 R × Kt | |

Refusing to fall into the trap: 51 P × P, Kt—Q3 ch; 52 K—K5 (now 52 K—Q4 is no longer feasible, on account of 52 .... Kt—B4 ch); 52 .... Kt × P ch; 53 K—Q4, Kt × P, and the mating net is well and truly destroyed.

51	P × P
52 K—K5	R—KR6
53 R—B8 ch	K—Q2
54 R—B7 ch	K—Q1
55 R × P	R × P
56 K—Q6	R—R3 ch
57 K—B5	R—KKt3
58 Kt—B4	R—B3
59 Kt—Q5	R—KKt3
60 Kt—K7	R—K3
61 Kt—B6 ch	K—B1

A more stubborn defence is 61 .... K—K1. Without detracting from a meritorious performance, it must be mentioned that White, now and on the following move, overlooks (probably he was short of time) that 62 K—Kt6, threatening 63 R—B7 mate, forces immediate surrender.

62 R—Kt7	R—K5
63 K—Q5	R—B5
64 Kt—K5	R—B8
65 R × P	R—QR8
66 P—B5	K—B2
67 R—Kt7 ch	K—B1
68 Kt—B4	R—R7

White announces mate in five, commencing with—69 K—B6.

253

White	Black
EUWE	BOGOLJUBOW

(Budapest, 1921)

Once a solid defence has been built up around the King (whether castled or not), care must be taken to maintain the defensive wall in good repair. Once a breach has been made, the hostile forces crowd in, and the most stubborn defence is of no avail.

1	P—K4	P—K3
2	P—Q4	P—Q4
3	Kt—QB3	Kt—KB3
4	B—Kt5	B—Kt5
5	P—K5	P—KR3
6	B—Q2	B × Kt
7	P × B	Kt—K5
8	Q—Kt4	

Against this frontal attack Black can evidently not reply with 8 .... Castles (9 B × P), nor with 8 .... Kt × B (9 Q × P). He must therefore defend the KKtP either by 8 .... K—B1 (forgoing castling), or, as in the text, by 8 .... P—KKt3, which creates a weakness in the royal battlements.

8	......	P—KKt3
9	P—KR4	

The most energetic continuation. After 9 B—Q3, Black could simplify the game by the elimination, by exchanges, of the chief attacking pieces, e.g. 9 .... Kt × B; 10 K × Kt, Q—Kt4 ch; 11 Q × Q, P × Q, etc.

9	......	P—QB4
10	B—Q3	

Inviting the exchange of the hostile KKt, after which the sacrifice of the white Bishop at KKt6 looms in the distance.

10	......	Kt × B
11	K × Kt	Kt—B3
12	R—R3	Q—R4

Heedless of his own safety. He should have continued with 12 .... P × P; 13 P × P (13 B × P, Kt × P); 13 .... B—Q2, after which the sacrifice 14 B × P would as yet be incorrect by reason of 14 .... Q—R4 ch; 15 P—B3, P × B; 16 Q × KtP ch, K—Q1 (this flight square was vacated in good time by the black Queen); 17 Q—B6 ch, K—B2, and Black is a piece ahead.

13 B × P

After this pretty sacrifice, which opens a breach in the hostile defence, matters take their course with implacable logic.

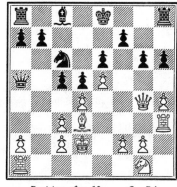

Position after 12 .... Q—R4

13	......	R—B1

Of course, Black can neither accept the sacrifice (13 .... P × B; 14 Q × KtP ch, K—Q1; 15 Q—B6 ch, K—B2; 16 Q × R, remaining the exchange to the good), nor play 13 .... R—KKt1 (14 B × P ch, K × B; 15 R—B3 ch, K—K2; 16 Q × R).

14	R—B3	P × P
15	B × P ch	

White's impetus shows no signs of slackening (15 .... R × B; 16 Q—Kt8 ch).

15	......	K—Q1
16	Q—Kt7	P × P ch
17	K—K1	Q—Kt5
18	B—Kt6	R × R
19	Kt × R	Q—KB5
20	R—Q1	R—Kt1

In order to develop his Q side as best he can, for if at once 20 .... B—Q2; 21 Q—Kt8 ch, K—B2; 22 Q × R, Kt × P; 23 Kt × Kt, Q × Kt ch; 24 K—B1, and Black has no compensation for his Rook.

21 Q—B6 ch

The art of liquidation. Although the forces are equal, White's connected and advanced passed pawns (KB6 and KKt5), which he is about to obtain, will decide the day.

21	......	Q × Q
22	P × Q	B—Q2
23	P—Kt4	K—B2
24	P—Kt5	R—KR1
25	B—Q3	P × P
26	P × P	P—K4

With the threat of a fork by (27 .... P—K5), but this faint hope of salvation is not fulfilled, because the pair of hostile pawns is too far advanced.

27	P—Kt6	B—K3
28	Kt—Kt5	Kt—Q5
29	Kt—R7	Kt—B6 ch
30	K—K2	P—K5
31	P—B7	Kt—Q5 ch
32	K—K3	Kt—B4 ch
33	K—B4	Kt—K2
34	P—Kt7	

A simple confirmation of the fact that connected and far-advanced passed pawns are more than an equivalent for a piece.

34	......	R × Kt
35	P—B8 (Q)	R—R5 ch
36	K—K5	Resigns.

254

White	Black
CHAROUSEK	MARÓCZY

(Budapest, 1897)

The problem of the counter-attack is one of special interest for the second player, for it would be deplorable were he at all times reduced to passive and unenterprising resistance.

A duly prepared and resolutely executed counter-thrust (as here, 17 .... Kt—Q5) is frequently the main object of Black's strategy.

This game offers in addition a notable example of an all-too-enterprising Queen finding herself at bay.

1	P—K4	P—K3
2	P—Q4	P—Q4
3	Kt—QB3	Kt—KB3
4	B—Kt5	B—K2
5	B × Kt	B × B
6	P—K5	B—K2
7	Q—Kt4	Castles
8	B—Q3	P—QB4
9	Q—R3	

As this noisy threat can easily be parried, the only result will be that the Queen will have relinquished a favourable square. The right answer would have been 9 P × P, giving equal chances to either side.

9	......	P—KKt3
10	P × P	Kt—B3
11	P—B4	B × P
12	Kt—B3	P—B3

Fully relying on the solidity of his King position, Black now prepares the counter-offensive, undermining, by way of a beginning, the enemy outpost.

| 13 | Q—R6 | |

Threatening to force at least a perpetual check by means of 14 B × P, P × B; 15 Q × P ch, etc.

13	......	R—B2
14	P × P	Q × P
15	P—KKt3	B—R6

The object of this pretty interlude (16 P × B, Q × Kt ch; 17 K—B2, Q—Kt2, to Black's advantage) is not to win a doubtful pawn at QKt7, but to disorganise the opposing forces.

| 16 | Kt—Q1 | |

He can play neither 16 Castles QR (16 .... Q × Kt) nor 16 R—QKt1 (16 .... B × P; 17 R × B, Q × Kt ch, followed by .... Q × R).

16	......	B—B1
17	Q—R4	Kt—Q5

This counter-thrust lays bare the adverse K side and secures the initiative for Black.

| 18 | Kt × Kt | |

There is little to be said in favour of an exchange by 18 Q × Q, Kt × Kt ch; 19 K—B2, R × Q; 20 K × Kt, because of 20 .... P—K4, etc.

18	......	Q × Kt
19	Q—Kt5	

The white Queen seemingly expects to be able to carry the whole attack on her own shoulders. White's position, however, is difficult, as Black threatens, *inter alia*, 19 .... K—Kt2, followed by 20 .... B—K2; 21 Q—Kt4, P—K4, etc.

Relatively the best is 19 K—Q2, to be followed by 20 P—B3.

| 19 | ...... | B—Q2 |

He calmly concludes his development. If instead, 19 .... K—Kt2, White's defence would be made easier (20 Q—K5 ch, Q × Q ch; 21 P × Q), but now, after 20 Q—K5, Q × Q; 21 P × Q, B—Kt2, Black wins a valuable pawn.

20	P—KR4	B—K2
21	Q—R6	

A sad fate awaits this venturesome Queen. A lesser evil, at all events, would have been 21 Q—K5, even though Black would dominate the board after 21 .... Q × Q; 22 P × Q, R—B6, followed by .... QR—KB1.

21	......	P—K4
22	P—R5	P—KKt4
23	B—Kt6	

A last subterfuge (23 .... P × B; 24 RP × P, and wins).

23	R—Kt2
24 P—B3	Q—Kt3
25 P×KtP	Q—Q1

Threatening to win the Queen by 26 .... B×P.

26 B—B2	B—QB1

Not yet 26 .... B×P, because of 27 Q—Q6.

Resigns.

255

White	*Black*
CAPABLANCA	TARTAKOWER

(Budapest, 1929)

There is an art in obtaining a draw from a critical position, and this art is part and parcel of a chess player's strength.

Psychologically, it is a question not only of nerve, but also of recognising in good time that the situation is serious before it is definitely beyond repair.

Technically, we shall see in this game how Sr. Capablanca, well known as a high exponent of the art of not losing, resolutely effects on the eighteenth move the exchange of Queens and finds salvation in a Rook ending, in which the "co-efficient of the draw" is very high.

1 P—Q4	P—K3
2 P—K4	P—Q4
3 Kt—QB3	Kt—KB3
4 B—Kt5	B—K2
5 P—K5	Kt—K5

Here 5 .... KKt—Q2; is sounder as well as more usual.

6 B×B	Q×B
7 Kt×Kt	P×Kt
8 P—QB3	

Preparing the sally 9 Q—Kt4, which now would be premature because of 8 Q—Kt4, Q—Kt5 ch.

8	Castles
9 Q—Kt4	P—KB4
10 P×P e.p.	Q×P

Owing to the counter-threat of 11 .... Q×P ch, White cannot get rid of the awkward adverse pawn at his K4.

11 Castles	Q—R3 ch
12 K—Kt1	P—K4

Thus Black not only guards his critical pawn (13 Q×P, B—B4), but eliminates another weak pawn of his.

13 Q—Kt3	P×P
14 B—B4 ch	B—K3
15 B×B ch	Q×B
16 P×P	

If 16 R×P, Kt—B3, gaining time, while now Black cannot make this natural developing move 16 .... Kt—B3, because of the fork 17 P—Q5.

16	Kt—R3
17 Kt—R3	Kt—Kt5
18 Q—Kt3	

Practically forcing the exchange of the most important pieces in Black's attack. Disappointing for White would be 18 Q—Q5, Kt×QP; 19 Q—Kt3, P—B3, and Black has the better game. It is clear that 18 P—Kt3 would still further weaken the white King's field.

18	Q×Q

Instead of playing 18 .... Kt—Q4, Black willingly accepts the exchange of Queens, as he hopes to exploit the weaknesses in the white pawn formation.

19 P×Q	QR—Q1
20 KR—K1	Kt—Q6
21 R×P	Kt×BP
22 Kt×Kt	R×Kt

Judged superficially, it seems that the three weaknesses in the White camp remain (at QKt2, QKt3 and Q4), whilst Black has eliminated his own and in addition has the trump card of the Rook on the seventh rank.

But White has seen further and, by a masterly manœuvre, he eliminates this ultimate danger.

23 R—QB1	P—B3
24 R—B2	R×R
25 K×R	K—B2
26 P—QKt4	

A preventive measure. The ensuing duel of the Rooks is instructive.

26	R—Q4

This domination of the fourth rank is useful without being decisive.

27 K—B3	R—KB4
28 R—K2	P—KR4
29 K—B4	P—KKt4
30 P—R3	P—R5
31 P—QKt3	P—R3
32 K—Q3	K—Kt3
33 R—K6 ch	K—R4
34 R—K2	

After 34 R—K7, R—B7; 35 R × P, R × P,
Black would have the advantage.

| 34 ...... | P—Kt5 |
| 35 P × P ch | |

Suicidal would be 35 R—K5, R × R;
36 P × P ch, K × P; 37 P × R, K—B4;
38 K—Q4, P—Kt3, and White loses, as he
has no "reserve moves."

35	K × P
36 R—K7	R—QKt4
37 K—B4	K—Kt6

Draw. (38 R—Kt7 ch, K—B7; 39 R—R7,
K × P; 40 R × RP, etc.)

256

| White | Black |
| ATKINS | BARRY |

(Anglo-American Cable Match, 1907)

*A stirring contest in which Black, harried
without respite, succeeds nearly, but not quite,
in parrying every threat, until finally he can
no longer avoid material loss. Even then he
puts up a grand fight for a lost cause.*

1 P—K4	P—K3
2 P—Q4	P—Q4
3 Kt—QB3	Kt—KB3
4 B—Kt5	B—K2
5 P—K5	KKt—Q2
6 B × B	Q × B
7 Kt—Kt5	Kt—B1

Defending the QBP, but taking the KKt
out of play. It would have been better to
bring it forward with 7 .... Kt—Kt3.

8 P—QB3	P—QR3
9 Kt—QR3	P—QB4
10 Kt—B2	Kt—B3
11 P—KB4	Kt—Q2

Diverting his forces to the Q side. Better
would have been 11 .... B—Q2.

12 Kt—B3	R—QKt1
13 B—K2	P—QKt4
14 Castles	P—Kt3
15 Kt—K3	P—QR4
16 P—KKt4	

By this advance he prepares the advance
P—B5, in order to open the KB file.

16	B—R3
17 P—B5	P—B5
18 Q—Q2	Kt—Kt3
19 P × KP	P × P
20 Kt—Kt2	K—Q2
21 Kt—Kt5	QR—KB1
22 R—B6	

He effects the doubling of his Rooks in
a very advantageous manner, because it
would now be bad for Black to play 22 ....
R × R; 23 P × R, Q × P, on the score of
24 R—KB1, Q—Q1; 25 R—B7 ch, Kt—K2;
26 Q—K3, etc.

22	Kt—Q1
23 QR—KB1	P—R3
24 Kt—B4	

Very well thought out.

24	R × R
25 P × R	Q × P
26 Kt (B4) × KP	Q—K2
27 Kt × Kt	Q × Kt (Kt4)
28 Q × Q	P × Q
29 Kt—B7	R—QKt1
30 B—Q1	P—Kt5
31 Kt × P	

At last White, thanks to elegant manœuvring, has won a pawn and is on the
point of confiscating another; nevertheless,
the technical phase which now follows is
still very difficult.

31	Kt—B1
32 Kt—B7	K—K2
33 Kt—K5	R—Kt3
34 P—Kt5	B—Kt4
35 B—Kt4	B—R3

Evidently neither 35 .... Kt—Q3;
36 Kt × P ch, nor 35 .... Kt—R2; 36 R—B7
ch, is admissible.

36 R—B7 ch	K—K1
37 B—Q7 ch	K—Q1
38 Kt—B6 ch	K—B2
39 B × Kt dis ch	

White liquidates cleverly. 39 B—K8 dis ch,
K—Q3 would lead to nothing.

39	K × B
40 Kt—K7 ch	K—Kt1
41 R—B6	R—Kt2
42 Kt × QP	P × P
43 Kt × P	

Evidently not 43 R × P (43 .... P—B7
and wins), nor 43 P × P (43 .... R—Kt8 ch;
44 K—B2, R—Kt7 ch; 45 K—K3, B—Kt2,
and Black's chances of salvation are on the
increase).

| 43 .... | K—R2 |

44	R—B2	R—R2
45	R—B4	R—QKt2
46	Kt—Q1	P—B6

A pretty stratagem (47 P×P, R—Kt8, winning the Knight).

47	Kt×P	R×P
48	R—B2	R—Kt5
49	R—Q2	R—B5
50	Kt—K2	R—R5
51	K—B2	B×Kt
52	K×B	

Rook-endings in which one side has two extra pawns are nearly always won by the stronger party, and the present example is no exception.

52	......	R—R6
53	K—B2	R—R6
54	K—Kt2	R—R6
55	P—Q5	K—Kt2
56	P—Q6	K—B1
57	P—Q7 ch	K—Q1
58	P—R4	R—QB6
59	K—R2	R—B2
60	K—Kt3	R×P
61	R×R ch	K×R
62	P—R4	K—K3
63	K—Kt4	K—B2

If 63 .... K—K4; 64 P—R5, and wins. Black hopes that, unsuspecting, his opponent may play 64 P—R5, which would bring about a draw after 64 .... P×P ch; 65 K×P, K—Kt2; 66 P—Kt6, K—Kt1, etc. But White shows the necessary circumspection.

64	K—B4	Resigns

The continuation might be 64 .... K—K3; 65 K—K4, K—Q3; 66 K—Q4, K—K3 (if 66 .... K—B3; 67 P—R5 wins); 67 K—B5, and wins easily.

A game which reflects credit on both players.

257

White	*Black*
RELLSTAB	STAHLBERG

(Kemeri, 1937)

It is always risky for Black, in the early part of the game, to declare his intention of making the Q side the main theatre of war, and to accumulate his forces there. One unexpected manœuvre, and the black King's fastness can fall like a house of cards.

1	P—K4	P—K3
2	P—Q4	P—Q4
3	Kt—QB3	Kt—KB3
4	B—Kt5	B—K2
5	P—K5	KKt—Q2
6	B×B	Q×B
7	P—B4	

A very good continuation, reinforcing as it does the advanced post at K5.

7	......	P—QB4

A wise plan is first to play 7 .... P—QKt3.

8	Kt—Kt5	Castles
9	P—B3	

It is now clear that, by his preceding move (8 Kt—Kt5), White wished to gain the time necessary to complete his pawn chain.

He had no thought of the escapade 9 Kt—B7, which would hardly be worth while, as after 9 .... P×P; 10 Kt×R, P—B3, Black has the advantage.

9	......	QKt—B3
10	Kt—B3	P—B3
11	B—Q3	KBP×P
12	BP×P	P×P
13	P×P	Kt—Kt3

Black expects too much from his operations on the Q side. Although after 13 .... Q—Kt5 ch; 14 Q—Q2, Q×Q ch, 15 K×Q, White stands a little better—thanks to his King's active rôle in the centre—Black should have decided on that simplifying line of play.

14	Castles	B—Q2
15	Kt—Q6	

Settling down in the enemy's camp.

15	......	B—K1
16	Q—B2	P—KR3

He should have played 16 .... P—Kt3.

17 Kt—R4

Leading to a solution at once energetic, brilliant and speedy.

17 ......   B—R4

Trying in vain to stem the onslaught. Neither would 17 .... R×R ch; 18 R×R be of any use, as then White has the additional asset of being able to control the open KB file, e.g. 18 .... Q×KKt; 19 B—R7 ch, K—R1; 20 R—B8 mate, or 18 .... Kt×QP; 19 B—R7 ch, K—R1; 20 Kt—Kt6 ch, B×Kt; 21 Q×B, threatening 22 Kt—B7 ch.

Greater resistance results from 17 .... Kt×QP; (e.g. 18. B—R7 ch, K—R1; 19 R×R ch, Q×R), but White would have replied with 18 R×R ch, Q×R (18 .... K×R; 19 Q—B2 ch); 19 Q—B7, with many threats.

18 B—R7 ch   K—R1
19 Kt—Kt6 ch   B×Kt
20 Q×B

A decisive inroad. Black has no defence against the pending 21 Kt—B7 ch.

20 ......   R—B4

Or e.g. 20 .... Kt×QP; 21 Kt—B7 ch, R×Kt; 22 R×R, Q—Kt4; 23 QR—KB1, Q×Q; 24 B×Q, K—Kt1; 25 R×P, etc.

21 R×R

The most convincing move. Black resigns.

258

White   *Black*
ALEKHINE   FAHRNI
(Mannheim, 1914)

This game is of historical interest, as being the first example in tournament practice of the "Chatard-Alekhine Attack" (6. P—KR4, in place of the usual 6 B×B), but it is, in addition, of high artistic merit.

The game illustrates in a telling manner the value of the sacrifice in chess. Notwithstanding White's overwhelming position, it is only by a sacrifice of a piece (18 B×P) that he succeeds in breaking down his opponent's defences.

1 P—K4   P—K3
2 P—Q4   P—Q4
3 Kt—QB3   Kt—KB3
4 B—Kt5   B—K2
5 P—K5   KKt—Q2
6 P—KR4

The *Chatard-Alekhine Attack.*

6 ......   B×B

Accepting—and how mistakenly!—the "Greek gift" of a pawn. A number of defences have been tried at this stage, amongst which the bold 6 .... P—KB3 is particularly interesting. See Game No. 260.

7 P×B   Q×P
8 Kt—R3

After 8 Kt—B3, Q—K2, White's KKt would have little future and be in the way of its own Queen. After the text move it will return to the heat of battle via KB4.

8 ......   Q—K2
9 Kt—B4   Kt—B1

Black's position is already painful. Other moves have been tested, such as 9 .... P—QR3, or 9 .... Kt—QB3, or 9 .... Kt—Kt3; but in all cases White, with 10 Q—Kt4, obtains a very strong attack.

10 Q—Kt4

With the double threat of 11 Q×KtP and 11 KKt×QP, P×Kt; 12 Q×B ch.

10 ......   P—KB4
11 P×P e.p.   P×P
12 Castles

Not yet 12 KKt×P, because of 12 .... P×Kt, with check. But now this becomes a real menace.

12 ......   P—B3
13 R—K1   K—Q1

He leaves the critical file of his own free will. As Black can neither play 13 .... QKt—Q2 (14 Kt×KP) nor 13 .... Kt—R3 (14 B×Kt, P×B; 15 KKt×QP, BP×Kt; 16 Kt×P, Q—KB2; 17 Q—B4, with the double threat of 18 Kt—B7 ch and 18 Kt×P ch), nor, finally, 13 .... B—Q2 (again because of 14 KKt×QP), his Q side remains paralysed.

14 R—R6   P—K4
15 Q—R4   QKt—Q2

He defends his assets as long as he can. After 15 .... P—KB4; 16 Q×Q ch, K×Q; 17 QR×P ch, White would have regained his pawn with a dominating position.

16 B—Q3   P—K5
17 Q—Kt3

Reinstating the threat: 18 KKt×P, P×Kt; 19 Kt×QP, Q—B2; 20 Q—B7 ch, K—K1; 21 B×P, Kt—K3; 22 B—B5, and wins.

17 ......   Q—B2

If Black plays 17 .... Q—Q3, the same sacrifice as in the text would win brilliantly, namely: 18 B×P, P×B; 19 QR×P (threatening to win the Queen by 20 Kt—K6 ch); 19 .... K—B2; 20 KKt—Q5 ch, P×Kt; 21 Kt—Kt5 ch, and wins.

18 B×P
The decisive sacrifice.

```
18 ......        P×B
19 Kt×P         R—KKt1
```
If 19 .... Q—K2, in order to pin White's QKt, White unpins it at once with 20 R—K3 (threat: 21 Kt—B5), and if 19 .... Q×P, then simply 20 Kt×P, Kt×Kt; 21 R×Kt destroys Black's game.

```
20 Q—QR3        Q—Kt2
21 Kt—Q6!
```
An indirect defence of the threatened Rook. (21 .... Q×R; 22 Kt—B7 ch, followed by Kt×Q.)

```
21 ......        Kt—QKt3
22 Kt—K8        Q—KB2
23 Q—Q6 ch      Q—Q2
24 Q×P ch
```
And mate next move.

259

White	Black
BOGOLJUBOW	SPIELMANN

(Vienna, 1922)

Threats provide the chief and most varied weapons in the arsenal of strategic ideas. In the following beautiful game, it will be noticed how the first player obtains an advantage by the co-ordination of threats on both wings (moves 8, 9, 19 and 21 by White).

```
1 P—Q4          P—K3
2 P—K4          P—Q4
3 Kt—QB3        Kt—KB3
4 B—Kt5         B—K2
5 P—K5          KKt—Q2
6 P—KR4         Castles
7 B—Q3
```
This occupation of a live diagonal already foreshadows an eventual sacrifice at KR7.

```
7 ......         P—QB4
8 Kt—R3
```
Black, at this early stage, has to face a real threat in 9 B×P ch, K×B; 10 Q—R5 ch, K—Kt1; 11 B×B, Q×B; 12 Kt—KKt5, forcing mate.

```
8 ......         R—K1
```
Vacating KB1 for the Knight. Another possible defence is 8 .... P—KR3.

9 Kt—Kt5
With the already unanswerable threat of settling the Knight on Q6, thus illustrating the *black square weakness* in the enemy camp.

```
9 ......         P—B4
10 Kt—Q6        P×P
```
Giving up the exchange is compulsory: if 10 .... Q—R4 ch; 11 B—Q2, and if 10 .... R—B1, then, quite simply, 11 Kt×B, B×B; 12 Kt×B, Q×QKt; 13 Q—R5, P—KR3; 14 Kt×P (the most telling); 14 .... R—B2; 15 B×P, and wins.

```
11 Kt×R         Q×Kt
12 B—Kt5
```
Defending the threatened KP. A doubtful defence would be 12 P—KB4, B—Kt5 ch; 13 K—B2, P—KR3, taking advantage of the imprisonment of White's QB.

```
12 ......        B—Kt5 ch
13 B—Q2         Q—K2
14 P—KB4!       Q×P ch
15 Kt—B2        Q—K2
```
Black has now two pawns for the exchange, but his position is tottering.

```
16 P—R3         B×B ch
17 Q×B          Q—B4
18 B—Q3         Kt—QB3
19 P—KKt4!      Kt—Kt3
```
Instead of resorting to passive resistance by 19 .... Kt—B1, he tries to build up a counter-attack.

```
20 Q—K2         Kt—B5
21 P—Kt4!       Q—K2
```
Or 21 .... Q—Kt4; 22 P×P, P×P; 23 Q—R5, P—KR3; 24 R—KKt1, K—B1; 25 Q—Kt6, and the black King, abandoned by his pieces, is lost.

```
22 B×Kt         P×B
23 Q×P          B—Q2
```
Or 23 .... P—KKt3; 24 P×P, P×P; 25 K—Q2, and White's attack quickly becomes irresistible.

```
24 P×P          R—KB1
```
Hoping to obtain some counter-play on the KB file, but White finds a way of overcoming all resistance in a few moves.

```
25 P—Kt5        Kt—Q1
26 P—B6
```
Decisively breaking into the enemy camp.

```
26 ......        P×P
27 Kt—K4        P×P
28 P×P          Resigns.
```

260

White	Black
PANOV	JUDOVITCH

(Tiflis, 1937)

"Sacrifice, lest you be sacrificed!" Guided
by this motto, the two opponents engage in
one of the most curious and desperate contests
of recent years.

1 P—K4	P—K3
2 P—Q4	P—Q4
3 Kt—QB3	Kt—KB3
4 B—Kt5	B—K2
5 P—K5	KKt—Q2
6 P—KR4	P—KB3
7 B—Q3	

In order to preserve the initiative for
himself, White is already obliged to give up
a piece, as after 7 P × P, Kt × P, Black would
have a position full of potentialities.

7	P—QB4

After 7 .... P × B; 8 Q—R5 ch, K—B1
(or 8 .... P—Kt3; 9 B × P ch); 9 R—R3,
etc., the acceptance of the sacrifice turns out
to be in favour of White.

8 Q—R5 ch	K—B1
9 Kt × P	

Seeking a violent solution, in preference to
quietly retreating the Queen after 9 P × P,
Kt × P.

9	P × B

The counter-point! After 9 .... P × Kt;
10 P—K6, White's prospects would be
strengthened.

10 R—R3	P—Kt5

Cleverly anticipating the threat 11 R—B3
ch.

11 Kt—B4	

Or 11 Q × KtP, P × Kt; 12 R—B3 ch,
Kt—B3, and Black, although he has returned
his gains, has the better position.

11	Kt × P

Reciprocal sacrifices!

12 P × Kt	P × R
13 B × P	

Threatening 14 Kt—Kt6 ch. He cannot
play at once 13 Kt—Kt6 ch, because of the
ingenious parry, 13 .... P × Kt; 14 Q × R ch,
K—B2; 15 Q—R7, Q × B; 16 P × Q, P—R7,
and Black wins.

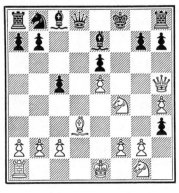

Position after 12 .... P × R

13	R × B

By this fresh counter-sacrifice, Black
eliminates an awkward opponent.

14 Q × R	P—R7

The victorious march of this pawn, which
has succeeded in passing four hostile pawns,
is truly remarkable.

15 K—K2	P—R8 (Q)
16 Kt—Kt6 ch	K—B2
17 Kt—R8 ch	Q × Kt

The simplest course. Being a Queen and
a Bishop ahead, Black can afford this
largesse.

18 Q × Q	Kt—B3
19 Q—R5 ch	K—Kt1
20 Kt—R3	

One more trap. For if now Black were
to gobble up the Rook, White can force a
perpetual check by 21 Q—K8 ch, B—B1;
22 Kt—Kt5, Kt × P; 23 Q—R5, B—Q3,
24 Q—K8 ch, etc.

20	Q × P
21 Q—K8 ch	B—B1
22 Kt—Kt5	Kt × P

This parries 23 Q—B7 ch and, in addition,
threatens 23 .... B—Q2; 24 Q × R, B—Kt4
ch, etc.

23 P—B4	Q—Kt5 ch
24 K—B1	Q × P ch
25 K—Kt1	Q—Kt5 ch
26 K—B1	B—Q2

The *coup de grâce*.

White resigns. (27 Q × R, B—Kt4 ch,
with mate to follow.)

261

White	Black
STEINITZ	VASQUEZ

(Havana, 1888)

In consequence of half-measures on the part of Black, White, in this game, was able to open the dangerous KKt file. As, incidentally, Black lost his support at Q4, allowing free passage to the adverse advanced KP, it is small wonder that White's attack swept over him with cyclonic force.

1 P—K4	P—K3
2 P—Q4	P—Q4
3 Kt—QB3	Kt—KB3
4 P—K5	

Unlike the pin by 4 B—Kt5, or simplification by 4 P × P, the move in the text—Steinitz's own idea—boldly challenges the centre.

4	KKt—Q2
5 P—B4	P—QB4
6 P × P	B × P

Instead of the recapture in the text, or by 6 .... Kt × BP, the intermediate development 6 .... Kt—QB3 materially strengthens the defence.

7 Q—Kt4

The beginning of an attack which might easily become dangerous.

7	Castles
8 Kt—B3	Q—K2

More useful would be at once 7 .... P—B4.

9 B—Q3	P—B4
10 Q—R3	Kt—QB3

A more circumspect line of defence would be 10 .... P—KR3, which enables Black to reply to 11 P—KKt4 by 11 .... P × P; 12 Q × P, R—Q1, followed by .... Kt—B1, and Black makes a strenuous fight of it.

11 P—KKt4

As now Black cannot play 11 .... P × P (12 Q × P ch, K—B2; 13 B—Kt6 mate), the text move brings fire and sword into the enemy camp.

11	P—KKt3
12 P × P	KP × P

Hara-kiri! After 12 .... KtP × P Black's position would be painful but tenable.

13 Kt × P   Q—Kt2

If 13 .... Q—B2; 14 Kt—Kt5, Q × Kt; 15 Q × P mate.

14 B—Q2   P—QKt4

Instead of trying to blockade the adversary's passed pawn by 14 .... Kt—Q1, followed by .... Kt—K3, Black embarks upon an adventure.

He tempts his opponent to play 15 Kt—B7, after which would follow, not 15 .... R—Kt1; 16 Kt—K6, etc., but 15 .... KKt × P; 16 Kt × R, Kt × B ch; 17 P × Kt, Q × P, and the attack goes over to Black. Similarly, after 15 B × KtP, B—Kt2, Black, in spite of being two pawns down, has counter-chances.

15 B—B3

Refusing so suspect a gift, White occupies the long black diagonal to cause further damage.

15 ......   B—Kt2

If 15 .... P—Kt5 (which nevertheless afforded better chances), 16 Kt—B6 ch.

16 P—K6	Kt—B3
17 Kt × Kt ch	R × Kt
18 Castles QR	B—K6 ch
19 K—Kt1	B × P
20 B × BP	

A magnificent *finale*.

20	Q—B1
21 KR—Kt1	P—Kt5

Or 21 .... R × B; 22 R × P ch.

22 KB × P   Resigns

(If 22 .... RP × B; 23 R × P ch, R × R; 24 Q—R8 mate.)

262

White	Black
SCHALLOPP	TARRASCH

(Breslau, 1889)

In the following game we can admire the dogged persistence with which Dr. Tarrasch maintains the initiative, first obtained on the open diagonal (Black's QR2—KKt8), after 19 .... Q × R on the open KB file, and finally, after 24 .... Kt—Q7 on the seventh rank, in the heart of the enemy lines.

1 P—K4	P—K3
2 P—Q4	P—Q4
3 Kt—QB3	Kt—KB3
4 P—K5	KKt—Q2
5 P—B4	P—QB4
6 P × P	Kt × BP
7 Kt—B3	Kt—B3
8 B—K2	Q—Kt3

Establishing a permanent watch on the weakened diagonal QR2—KKt8 (which at present prevents 9 Castles, on account of 9 .... Kt—Q6 dis ch; 10 K—R1, Kt—B7 ch, winning the exchange).

9 QR—Kt1	Kt—Q2
10 B—Q2	P—B3
11 P×P	Kt×P
12 Kt—QR4	Q—B2
13 Castles	

White has succeeded in castling, but not in placing a single piece on an active post.

| 13 ...... | B—Q3 |
| 14 Kt—Kt5 | |

If he plays 14 P—KKt3, to protect the threatened KBP, the position of White's King would become still more vulnerable.

| 14 ...... | Castles |
| 15 P—B4 | |

Seeing himself threatened with 15 .... P—KR3; 16 Kt—R3, P—K4, White wishes to anticipate this hostile action by some energetic measure.

15	P—KR3
16 P—QB5	P×Kt
17 P×B	Q×P
18 P×P	Kt—K5
19 R×R ch	Q×R

As a result of the skirmishes of the last few moves, Black has obtained possession of the open KB file. He has, besides, a well-guarded passed QP, whilst the opposing KKtP is doubled—a chronic weakness.

| 20 B—K3 | Q—KB4 |
| 21 P—R4 | |

Thus the weakness of one pawn (KKt5) leads to other weaknesses.

Too niggardly would be the defence of the threatened pawn by 21 Q—QB1, after which Black's 21 .... Kt—K4 would increase the pressure.

And if 21 Q—KB1, P—K4, with advantage to Black.

| 21 ...... | B—Q2 |
| 22 Kt—B5 | |

Allowing an interesting combination. But after any other move, such as 22 B—Kt4 or 22 B—B3, Black's compact centre and his control of the open KB file ensures his superiority.

| 22 ...... | P—Q5! |
| 23 Kt×B | |

Not 23 B×P, Kt×Kt; 24 B×Kt, Q×B, with check, and Black would have won a piece in this affair.

| 23 ...... | P×B |
| 24 B—B3 | Kt—Q7 |

A decisive irruption.

| 25 R—B1 | Kt—Q5 |
| 26 K—R2 | |

Or 26 B×P, Q—B7 ch; 27 K—R2, Q×RP ch; 28 K—Kt1, Q—B7 ch; 29 K—R2, Kt—K7 (threat: 30 .... Q—R5 mate); 30 Q—K1, Kt×R; 31 Q×Kt (B1), Q—R5 ch; 32 K—Kt1, P—K7, compelling surrender.

26	Q—B5 ch
27 K—R3	Kt (Q7)×B
28 P×Kt	P—K7
Resigns.	

263

| White | Black |
| PILLSBURY | LASKER |

(Nuremberg, 1896)

When the road is blocked, you must force a way through ("break-through sacrifice," 21 P—B5), and if a defender comes up the best thing to do is to deflect him from his path ("deflecting sacrifice," 24 R×Kt). Although such strategy is clear-cut and energetic, it does not always succeed. When it does (as in this beautiful game), it is a feast for eye and mind.

1 P—K4	P—K3
2 P—Q4	P—Q4
3 Kt—QB3	Kt—KB3
4 P—K5	KKt—Q2
5 P—B4	P—QB4
6 P×P	Kt—QB3!

Instead of the immediate recapture by 6 .... B×P or 6 .... Kt×BP, Black—who can afford to wait, as the pawn cannot escape him—makes a sound developing move.

| 7 P—QR3 | Kt×BP |

Another and very interesting line of play occurs after 7 .... B×P; 8 Q—Kt4, Castles, etc.

| 8 P—QKt4 | Kt—Q2 |
| 9 B—Q3 | P—QR4 |

The struggle on the Q side is growing very lively. By this thrust Black intends to reconquer the square at his QB4.

10 P—Kt5	QKt—Kt1
11 Kt—B3	Kt—B4
12 B—K3	QKt—Q2
13 Castles	P—KKt3

If at this point or later .... Kt × B, White strengthens his centre by 14 P × Kt, followed eventually by P—Q4.

14 Kt—K2	B—K2
15 Q—K1	Kt—Kt3
16 KKt—Q4	

The Knight, from its central position, not only overprotects the exposed QKtP, but also aims at the other wing (KB5), and even at the centre (K6).

| 16 ...... | B—Q2 |
| 17 Q—B2 | |

With the threat of winning a pawn by 18 Kt × P (18 .... P × Kt; 19 B × Kt, or 18 .... Kt × Kt; 19 B × Kt), a pretty turn.

| 17 ...... | Kt (Kt3)—R5 |
| 18 QR—Kt1! | |

This move, which deprives the QRP of its protection, is calculated many moves ahead.

| 18 ...... | P—R4 |

With a view to preventing once and for all the thrust P—Kt4, followed by P—B5.

| 19 P—Kt6 | Kt × B |
| 20 P × Kt | B × P |

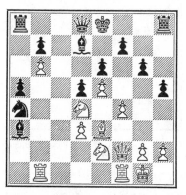

Now Black has won a pawn, but at the cost of dislocating his forces, which fact White now exploits in a manner worthy of a genius.

If 20 .... Kt × P; 21 Kt × P, P × Kt; 22 B × Kt, to White's advantage.

21 P—B5

This elegant sacrifice of a pawn serves a double purpose: (1) It disorganises the hostile chain of pawns. (2) It vacates the square at KB4 to permit the entry of the reserve cavalry.

| 21 ...... | KtP × P |

Or 21 .... KP × P; 22 Kt—B4, B—B3; 23 Kt × B (the simplest); 23 .... P × Kt; 24 P—Kt7, R—QKt1; 25 B—R7, winning the exchange and holding out further threats.

| 22 Kt—B4 | P—R5 |

Preventing the intrusion, 23 Q—Kt3, followed by Q—Kt7.

| 23 R—R1 | B—K2 |

Against 23 .... Q—K2, Black has a victorious counter by 24 Kt × BP, P × Kt; 25 Kt × P, etc.

24 R × Kt!

A *deflecting sacrifice*, which will lead to an *irruptive sacrifice* at K6.

24	B × R
25 QKt × KP	P × Kt
26 Kt × KP	B—Q2

Black has nothing better than to offer his Queen in atonement, for after 26 .... Q—B1; 27 Q × BP, his crumbling defences would become untenable.

| 27 Kt × Q | R × Kt |

Theoretically Black possesses in his Rook and Bishop against the hostile Queen almost an equivalent, but his many weak points must tell against him in the end.

The agony is slow but certain.

28 B—B5	R—QB1
29 B × B	K × B
30 Q—K3	R—B3
31 Q—Kt5 ch	K—B2
32 R—B1	R × R ch
33 Q × R	R—QB1
34 Q—K1	P—R6
35 P × P	R—Kt1 ch
36 K—B2	P—R5
37 Q—Kt4	R—Kt3
38 K—B3	P—R6
39 Q × P	R × P
40 Q—B5	R—K3
41 Q—B7	K—K2
42 K—B4	P—Kt3
43 P—R4	R—QB3
44 Q—Kt8	B—K1

An unfortunate necessity; he must lose another pawn, e.g. 44 .... R—R3; 45 K—Kt5, R—QB3; 46 P—R5, etc.

45	K × P	R—R3
46	Q—B7 ch	K—B1
47	Q—Q8	P—Kt4
48	P—K6	R—R2
49	K—K5	P—Kt5
50	Q—Q6 ch	Resigns.

264

White   *Black*

MARTINOLICH   TARTAKOWER

(Vienna, 1907)

The choice of an enterprising variation (such as in this game, the "Gledhill Attack") does not necessarily confer a monopoly in aggression. Some barely noticed episode (as here, the counter-thrust .... P—KR4-5), a subsidiary manœuvre, some transitory measure, may occur, and the rôles of attacker and defender are reversed.

1	P—K4	P—K3
2	P—Q4	P—Q4
3	Kt—QB3	Kt—KB3
4	P—K5	KKt—Q2
5	Q—Kt4	

The *Gledhill Attack* offers practical chances.

| 5 | ...... | P—KR4 |

In conjunction with his next move Black, by this advance, proceeds without delay to deny the white Queen access to her KKt3.

The usual course is to play 5 .... P—QB4, with the continuation, 6 Kt—B3, P × P; 7 Kt × P, Kt × P; 8 Q—Kt3, Kt—Kt3; 9 KKt—Kt5, Kt—R3; 10 P—KR4, and White has a fine attacking position in return for his pawn.

6	Q—Kt3	P—R5
7	Q—Kt4	P—QB4
8	Kt—B3	P × P
9	Kt—QKt5	

Now that White's KKt3 is controlled by Black, 9 KKt × QP, Kt × P would lose a pawn without any compensation. White must strive to regain his pawn by more *artificial* means.

9	......	Kt—QB3
10	B—KB4	P—R3
11	QKt × P	Kt × Kt
12	Kt × Kt	Q—Kt3

Henceforth Black has the initiative.

13 Castles

After 13 Kt—Kt3, Q—Kt5 ch; 14 P—B3, Kt × P; 15 Q—Kt5, Q—K5 ch, White would be a pawn down with nothing to show for it.

13	......	Kt—B4
14	B—K3	B—Q2
15	K—Kt1	Q—B2
16	P—KB4	R—B1
17	R—B1	Kt—R5

Threatening (say after 18 B—Q3) 18 .... Kt × P; 19 K × Kt, Q—B6 ch; 20 K—Kt1, B—R6, followed by the pitiless mate at QKt7.

18 P—B4

If 18 Kt—Kt3, then still 18 .... Kt × P; 19 K × Kt, Q—B6 ch; 20 K—Kt1, and now simply 20 .... Q × B (not 20 .... B—R6, because of 21 B—Q4).

18	......	Q—Kt3
19	P—QKt3	Q—Kt5
20	B—Q3	P—QKt4!

Helping to shake the white King's defences.

21	P × QP	Kt—B6 ch
22	K—R1	Q—R4
23	R—B2	

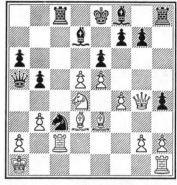

Or 23 B—QKt1, Kt × QP, and Black's attack shows no signs of slackening.

23 ......   Kt × RP!

The work of this Knight is remarkable. White now tries to find salvation in action in the centre, leaving his King to carry on as best he may, for if 24 R × Kt, there follows 24 .... Q—B6 ch, with further damage to the hostile camp.

24	R × R ch	B × R
25	P × P	Kt—Kt5 dis ch
26	K—Kt2	Q—R7 ch
27	K—B1	

White's misfortune is that 27 K—B3 is impossible on account of 27 .... Kt—Q4 mate.

27	Kt × B ch
28 K—Q1	Kt—B7 ch
29 B × Kt	Q × B
30 P × P ch	K × P
31 P—B5	

With the threefold object of masking the Queen, guarding the Knight, and threatening Q—Kt6 ch.
If 31 P—K6 ch, K—Kt1; and the black King is safe (e.g. 32 Kt—B5, B × P; 33 Kt—K7 ch, K—B2, etc.).

| 31 ...... | B—B4! |

Attack and defence (as now Black's King has a good flight square at KB1).

32 Q—Kt6 ch	K—B1
33 Kt—B3	B—Kt2
34 P—K6	B × Kt ch
35 P × B	Q × P ch
36 K—Q2	B—Kt5 ch
37 K—B2	Q—B6 ch
38 K—Kt1	Q—Q6 ch!
39 K—Kt2	B—B6 ch
Resigns	

(40 K—R3, P—Kt5 ch; 41 K—R4, Q—Kt4 mate.)

265

| *White* | *Black* |
| McCONNELL | MORPHY |

(New Orleans, 1850)

If the first player commits himself in the opening to a ruthless advance (as in this game to 3 P—K5, instead of simple development by 3 Kt—QB3, or simplification by 3 P × P), he must in the sequel keep on supporting this advance, failing which the counter-play may have serious consequences.

1 P—K4	P—K3
2 P—Q4	P—Q4
3 P—K5	

The question whether this is a "strong point" or a "dead point" is still being discussed!

| 3 ...... | P—QB4 |

The counter-action begins.

| 4 P—QB3 | |

This strengthening of the pawn chain is to be commended.

| 4 ...... | Kt—QB3 |
| 5 P—KB4 | |

But this widening of the front opens up White's position too much. That is why simple development by 5 Kt—B3 is preferred at this point.

| 5 ...... | Q—Kt3 |
| 6 Kt—B3 | B—Q2 |

A good move, by which Black not only continues to develop his counter-operations on the Q side (culminating in a strong pressure on the QB file by .... R—QB1), but also practically prevents White's most natural development, 7 B—Q3, after which would follow 7 .... P × P; 8 P × P, Kt × QP; 9 Kt × Kt, Q × Kt; and, as there is no reply, 10 B—Kt5 ch, Black would have won a clear pawn.

| 7 P—QR3 | |

White unduly delays the development of his pieces. The best continuation is 7 B—K2, Kt—R3 (threatening ultimately to win the QP by .... Kt—B4); 8 P—QKt3, and White's game is difficult but playable.

7	Kt—R3
8 P—QKt4	P × QP
9 P × P	R—B1
10 B—Kt2	Kt—B4
11 Q—Q3?	

This move allows the youthful but brilliant opponent to decide the game by a compelling sacrifice.
Better would have been 11 Q—Q2, which would at least prevent any sacrifice at QKt4, e.g. 11 .... Kt × KtP; 12 P × Kt, B × P; 13 Kt—B3, etc., or 11 .... B × P; 12 P × B, Kt × KtP; 13 Kt—R3, etc.

11	B × P ch!
12 P × B	Kt × KtP
13 Q—Q2	R—B7

Instead of the ordinary 13 .... Kt—B7 ch; followed by .... Q × B; Black finds an elegant termination, and mates, on the next move—the white Queen!

| 14 Q—Q1 | Kt—K6 |
| Resigns. | |

[Morphy was thirteen years of age when he played this game, which is the only known game in which he adopted the French Defence.]

266

White	Black
PAULSEN	TARRASCH

(Nuremberg, 1888)

Having gained command of the QB file for his Rooks, Black, in this game, exploits this advantage in masterly fashion.

1 P—K4	P—K3
2 P—Q4	P—Q4
3 P—K5	P—QB4
4 P—QB3	Kt—QB3
5 Kt—B3	Q—Kt3

The last three moves of Black were in accordance with the plan to mine the white pawn chain at his Q4.

6 B—Q3

White can afford this development (instead of the more meticulous 6 B—K2), because after 6 .... P×P; 7 P×P, Kt×QP; 8 Kt×Kt, Q×Kt; 9 B—Kt5 ch, the black Queen is lost.

6	P×P

If at once 6 .... B—Q2, then already 7 P×P, B×P; 8 Castles, and White stands better.

7 P×P	B—Q2

Threatening to win the critical pawn at White's Q4, which, however, even if sufficiently guarded, will remain as a chronic weakness in White's position.

8 B—K2

Against 8 B—B2, Black would play 8 .... Kt—Kt5, gaining the initiative.

8	KKt—K2
9 P—QKt3	Kt—B4
10 B—Kt2	B—Kt5 ch

Now White can no longer castle, the alternative being the loss of the QP.

11 K—B1   B—K2

The object of this retreat is to enable Black to reply to 12 P—KKt4 with 12 .... Kt—R5, this Knight thus remaining available for aggressive purposes.

12 P—Kt3	P—QR4
13 P—QR4	R—QB1

The file of the future.

14 B—Kt5	Kt—Kt5
15 B×B ch	

Better at once 15 Kt—B3, as in the next game.

15	K×B
16 Kt—B3	Kt—B3
17 Kt—QKt5	Kt—R2

Winning the localised fight for the square at QKt4.

18 Kt×Kt	Q×Kt
19 Q—Q3	Q—R3

Forcing an end game in which Black, thanks to the fact that his QR is already in play, commands more territory.

20 Q×Q	P×Q
21 K—Kt2	R—B7
22 B—B1	R—QKt1
23 R—QKt1	R—B6
24 B—Q2	R (B6)×P
25 R×R	R×R
26 B×P	R—Kt7
27 B—Q2	

In a clever manner White still saves the situation, for if 27 .... Kt×QP; 28 B—B3.

27	B—Kt5
28 B—B4	P—R3
29 P—Kt4	Kt—K2
30 R—R1	Kt—B3
31 B—B1	R—B7
32 B—R3	R—B5
33 B—Kt2	B—B6
34 B×B	R×B

In the simplified ending, which now follows, the black Rook's greater activity is decisive.

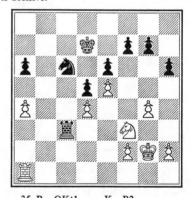

35 R—QKt1	K—B2
36 P—Kt5	R—B5
37 P×P	P×P
38 P—R5	R—R5
39 K—Kt3	R×RP
40 K—Kt4	R—R6
41 R—Q1	R—Kt6
42 P—R4	Kt—K2
43 Kt—K1	Kt—B4
44 Kt—Q3	P—QR4

A mistake would be 44 .... Kt×QP;

45 Kt—B5, R—Kt4 (45 .... R—Kt5;
46 Kt×RP ch, followed by Kt×R);
46 Kt×RP ch, K—Kt3; 47 R×Kt, K×Kt;
48 K—R5, and, in spite of Black's extra
pawn, White would get busy.

45	Kt—B5	R—QB6
46	R—QKt1	Kt×QP
47	Kt—R6 ch	K—Q1
48	R—Kt8 ch	R—B1
49	R—Kt7	K—K1
50	Kt—B7 ch	K—B1
51	Kt—Kt5	Kt×Kt
52	R×Kt	R—R1

And Black wins.

267

White	*Black*
NIMZOWITSCH	TARRASCH

(San Sebastian, 1912)

*One of the curiosities of the theory of the
openings! This game, played twenty-four
years after the preceding one (Paulsen-
Tarrasch), rehabilitated a variation, which
up to that time was thought to be in favour
of Black. A slight improvement by White on
his 15th move caused this reversal of opinion.*

1	P—K4	P—K3
2	P—Q4	P—Q4
3	P—K5	P—QB4
4	P—QB3	Kt—QB3
5	Kt—KB3	Q—Kt3
6	B—Q3	P×P
7	P×P	B—Q2
8	B—K2	KKt—K2
9	P—QKt3	Kt—B4
10	B—Kt2	B—Kt5 ch
11	K—B1	B—K2
12	P—KKt3	P—QR4
13	P—QR4	R—QB1
14	B—Kt5	Kt—Kt5
15	Kt—B3	

Up to this move, we have a repetition—
intentional on the part of both players—of
the Paulsen-Tarrasch game. But the move
in the text (superseding the exchange 15 B×B
ch, K×B; 16 Kt—B3, etc.) furthers the co-
ordination of the white forces.

15	......	Kt—QR3
16	K—Kt2	

"Artificial castling."

16	......	Kt—B2
17	B—K2	B—Kt5
18	Kt—R2	Kt—QR3
19	B—Q3	Kt—K2
20	R—QB1	Kt—B3
21	Kt×B	Kt (R3)×Kt
22	B—Kt1	

After much manœuvring, White has scored
the advantage of the "two Bishops."

22	......	P—R3
23	P—Kt4	Kt—K2
24	R×R ch	B×R
25	Kt—K1	R—B1
26	Kt—Q3	P—B3
27	Kt×Kt	Q×Kt
28	P×P	R×P
29	B—B1	Kt—B3
30	P—Kt5	P×P
31	B×P	R—B1
32	B—K3	Q—K2
33	Q—Kt4	

Combining attack with defence.

33	......	Q—B3
34	R—Kt1	R—R1
35	K—R1	R—R5

If 35 .... R—Kt1, protecting the threat-
ened KKtP, then 36 B—R7. But 35 ....
K—B1 would be more steady (36 R—Kt3,
R—R5).

36	Q—Kt3	R×P

Black can no longer save his KKtP because
of the threat 37 B—Kt5. Black prefers to
give up the exchange for a pawn, which,
however, he will lose in the end.

37	B×R	Kt×B
38	Q×P	Q—B6 ch

He cannot reply with 38 .... Q×P, on
account of 39 Q—R8 ch, K—Q2; 40 R—Kt7
ch, K—Q3; 41 Q—Q8 ch, K—K4; 42 Q—B7
ch, K—B3; 43 R—B7 ch, *finis*.

39	Q—Kt2	Q×Q ch
40	R×Q	Kt×P
41	P—R4	Resigns.

268

White	*Black*
NIMZOWITSCH	LÖWENFISCH

(Carlsbad, 1911)

*The ability to garnish strategic ideas with
concrete points, and to place tactical enterprises in the service of a big general idea,
marks the artist in chess. In the following
valorous game, White's main idea is that of
a blockade, foreshadowed by his third move.*

1 P—K4	P—K3
2 P—Q4	P—Q4
3 P—K5	P—QB4
4 P—QB3	Kt—QB3
5 Kt—B3	P—B3

Instead of maintaining by 5 .... Q—Kt3 the attack on the base of the hostile pawn chain (White's Q4), he tries to undermine its head.

| 6 B—QKt5 | B—Q2 |
| 7 Castles | Q—Kt3 |

If 7 .... KBP×P, White must play neither 8 Kt×P (8 .... Kt×Kt winning a piece) nor even 8 P×KP, but 8 B×Kt, B×B; 9 Kt×P, threatening 10 Q—R5 ch, and the dominating position of his KKt ensures for White a lasting advantage.

| 8 B×Kt | P×B |
| 9 P×KBP! | Kt×P |

It is easy to see that 9 .... KtP×P would strengthen Black's critical square at his K4, and would bring succour to his backward KP. But it would be at the price of a serious delay in the development of his pieces and a weakening of his King's defences.

10 Kt—K5	B—Q3
11 P×P	B×P
12 B—Kt5	Q—Q1
13 B×Kt	Q×B
14 Q—R5 ch	P—Kt3
15 Q—K2	R—Q1
16 Kt—Q2	Castles
17 QR—K1	

Threatening 18 Kt×B, R×Kt; 19 Q×P ch.

17	KR—K1
18 K—R1	B—Q3
19 P—KB4	P—B4

His hope of exploiting his pawn majority in the centre will not materialise.

20 P—B4

This pretty thrust must either immobilise the hostile pawn mass after 20 .... P—Q5; 21 Kt—K4, Q—B1; 22 QKt×B, Q×Kt; 23 Kt—Q3, etc., or, as in the text, win a pawn.

| 20 ...... | B—KB1 |
| 21 P×P | B—B1 |

Clearly not 21 .... P×P, on the score of 22 Kt×B, and wins.

22 Kt—K4	Q—Kt2
23 P×P	B×P
24 Q—R6	K—R1
25 R—Q1	B—Kt1
26 P—QKt3	R—Q5
27 R×R	P×R
28 Q—R5	

Were he to play 28 R—Q1 at once, Black

succeeds by 28 .... R—Q1, in placing a Rook *behind* his passed pawn.

28 ......   R—B1

It goes without saying that Black's Rook must seek some other course of action, so that White still has some awkward problems to solve.

| 29 R—Q1 | R—B7 |
| 30 P—KR3 | |

If 30 R×P, R—B8 ch, followed by mate in two.

30 ......   Q—Kt2

Black tries to complicate matters, as he foresees that his isolated QP sooner or later must fall.

31 R×P

He does it after all.

31 ......   B—B4

A surprise?

32 Q—Q8

The counter - surprise! (But neither 32 Kt×B, Q×P mate, nor 32 Q×B, R×Q; 33 Kt×R, Q—Kt4, to Black's advantage.)

If now Black were to play 32 .... B×R, there would follow 33 Q×B (threatening a discovered mate); 33 .... Q—Kt2; 34 Kt—Kt5 (threat: 35 Q—Q8, followed by Kt—B7 ch); 34 .... R—B1 (34 .... P—KR3; 35 Kt×P mate); 35 K—R2, and although Black has the exchange for two pawns, he is under a strategic blockade and cannot improve his cramped position in any way.

| 32 ...... | B—K2 |
| 33 Q—Q7 | Q—R3 |

With the ingenuous threat of a mate in two.

34 R—Q3	B—B1
35 Kt—B7 ch	B×Kt
36 Q×B	R—B1
37 R—Q7	Resigns.

269

White	Black
NIMZOWITSCH	LEONHARDT

(San Sebastian, 1912)

Amongst the many and varied possible sacrifices, the temporary sacrifice plays an important rôle. In the following game a pawn is so sacrificed, and, as frequently happens, the recovery of the pawn brings with it an increased command of territory.

1	P—K4	P—K3
2	P—Q4	P—Q4
3	P—K5	P—QB4
4	Kt—KB3	Q—Kt3
5	B—Q3	

A positional sacrifice of a pawn in order to speed up his development. 5 P × P, B × P would be premature, in view of Black's troublesome attack on White's KB2.

5	......	P × P

If 5 .... Kt—QB3; 6 P × P, B × P; 7 Castles.

6	Castles	Kt—QB3
7	P—QR3	

With the twofold object of preparing 8 P—QKt4, and of preventing 7 .... Kt—Kt5.
The most prudent course for Black would now be 7 .... P—QR4.

7	......	KKt—K2
8	P—QKt4	Kt—Kt3
9	R—K1	B—K2

Preventing 10 P—KR4, which would be available after 9 .... B—Q2, or 10 .... P—QR3.

10	B—Kt2	P—QR4
11	P—Kt5	P—R5

Artificially isolating White's QKtP. Black need as yet have no fear of 12 P × Kt, because of 12 .... Q × B.

12	QKt—Q2	Kt—R2

The Knight retires in view of the threat 13 P × Kt, Q × B; 14 R—Kt1, followed by 15 P × P, and wins.

13	B × P	

Thus, after careful preparation, White has at last recovered his pawn, with a notable increase of controlled territory.

13	....	B—B4
14	B × B	Q × B
15	P—B4	

Concentrating on the conquest of K4 (and later on Q6 as well).

15	......	P × P
16	Kt—K4	Q—Q4
17	Kt—Q6 ch	K—K2
18	Kt × QBP	Q—B4

Parrying the threat 19 Kt—Kt6, whilst keeping control of Q3. If, instead, 18 .... Q × KtP, White wins by 19 B × Kt and 20 Q—Q6 ch

19	B × Kt	RP × B
20	Q—Q6 ch	Q × Q
21	P × Q ch	Resigns

(E.g. 21 .... K—K1; 22 Kt—Kt6, R—QKt1; 23 Kt—K5, followed by 24 P—Q7 ch. Black's cramped position costs him a piece.)

270

White	Black
NIMZOWITSCH	HÅKANSSON

(Match, Kristianstad, 1922)

This is an extreme example of a blockade, the loser being, in the end, completely walled in. We see how a move containing no immediate or serious threats (3 P—K5) can yet influence the whole course of the game, if the opponent fails to take timely counter-measures.

1	P—K4	P—K3
2	P—Q4	P—Q4
3	P—K5	P—QB4
4	Q—Kt4	

Introduced into tournament practice by Nimzowitsch himself, this spectacular sortie is not to be taken lightly.

4	......	P × P
5	Kt—KB3	Kt—QB3
6	B—Q3	

Weak would be 6 Kt × P, because of 6 .... Kt × P; 7 Q—Kt3, Kt—QB3; 8 Kt—Kt5, P—K4.
For this reason White is in no hurry to recover his pawn, and prefers to accelerate his development.

6	......	P—B4
7	Q—Kt3	KKt—K2
8	Castles	Kt—Kt3
9	P—KR4	Q—B2
10	R—K1	B—Q2

Conceiving the idea of castling on the Q side, which, however, will prove troublesome. According to analyses by the Australian Master, Purdy, the developing move 10 .... B—B4 (vacating a good flight-square for the Knight) improves Black's prospects, e.g. 11 P—R5, Kt—B1, followed by

12 .... P—KKt3, with chances on both sides.

11 P—R3
In itself useful, this move increases in value from the fact that it also prepares the attack against the black King's field, should he castle on the Q side.

11 ......   Castles
If 11 .... P—QR4 first (preventing 12 P—QKt4), Black's castling on the Q side would be still more hazardous, as the protecting line of pawns there would be damaged.

12 P—Kt4	P—QR3
13 P—R5	KKt—K2
14 B—Q2	P—R3
15 P—R4	P—KKt4
16 P—Kt5	P—B5
17 Q—Kt4	Kt—QKt1
18 P—B3	

Obtaining a further advantage for his attack, by opening the QB file.

18	R—K1
19 P×QP	K—Q1

Far from having found sanctuary, the black King must fly towards the centre.

20 R—QB1	Q—Kt3
21 P—R5	Q—R2
22 P—Kt6	Q—R1

With the Queen thus buried alive, Black can hardly hope to save the day.

23 R—B7	Kt—B4
24 Kt—B3	B—K2

Or 24 .... Kt—Kt2; 25 R—QB1, Kt—B3; 26 Kt×QP.
After the text move White forces the win in a brilliant manner.

25 Kt×QP!	Kt×P
26 Kt×Kt	P×Kt
27 Q×B ch	Kt×Q
28 Kt—K6 mate.	(*Quasi-étouffé!*)

271
White   *Black*
KERES   ALEXANDRESCU
(Munich, 1936)

Another example of a black Queen confiscating a pawn (at White's QKt2), thereby rousing up all the vital forces in the enemy camp. Soon after we see the black King, in going to the assistance of his Queen, succumbing in the centre of the board.

1 P—K4	P—K3
2 P—Q4	P—Q4
3 P—K5	P—QB4
4 P×P	Kt—QB3
5 Kt—KB3	B×P
6 B—Q3	KKt—K2
7 B—KB4!	

This challenging move is well thought out.

7 ......   Q—Kt3
Allowing himself to be tempted by the double attack against the hostile KBP and QKtP.

8 Castles   Q×P
Consistent but dangerous.

9 QKt—Q2   Q—Kt3
What is the reason for this anxious flight? It is that, after the plausible 9 .... Castles, there follows: 10 Kt—Kt3, Q—R6; 11 B×P ch (the scheme of this sacrifice is most instructive for the novice); 11 .... K×B; 12 Kt—Kt5 ch, K—Kt3 (or 12 .... K—Kt1; 13 Q—R5, and wins); 13 Q—Q3 ch, Kt—B4; 14 Q—R3, R—R1; 15 Q×R, Kt—R3; 16 P—Kt4, forcing mate by Q—R7.

10 P—B4   P—KR3
Preparing to castle, for if at once 10 .... Castles, the sacrifice indicated in the previous note (11 B×P ch) is decisive.

11 Q—B1   Kt—Kt5
If now 11 .... Castles; 12 Kt—Kt3, threatening yet again a sacrifice by 13 B×P. The manner in which White keeps the enemy King in the middle of the board is most astute.

12 B—K2	B—Q2
13 P—QR3	Kt—R3

If 13 .... QKt—B3, the sequel equally is 14 R—Kt1, and the black Queen has no good retreat, e.g. 14 .... Q—R4; 15 R×P, or 14 .... Q—R3; 15 P×P, Q×B; 16 P×Kt, and both Bishops are threatened.

14 R—Kt1	Q—B3
15 B—Kt3	

A sound waiting move. If 15 P×P, Kt×P, gaining an important defensive *tempo*, thanks to the attack on the Bishop.

15 ......   Kt—B4
Trying to eliminate the dangerous Bishop, though this would have been the most propitious moment for castling on the K side.

16 P×P   P×P
Or 16 .... Q×P; 17 R—Q1, Q—B3; 18 B—Kt5, with increasing pressure.

17 P—K6

A beautiful pawn sacrifice, with the double mission of vacating the square at K5 for the Knight and of breaching the enemy fortress.

17 ......   P×P

If 17 .... B×KP; 18 B—Kt5, winning the Queen; and if 17 .... Q×P; 18 B×Kt, winning material.

18 Kt—K5   Kt×B
19 P×Kt   Q—B2
20 Kt×B   K×Kt

If 20 .... Q×Kt; 21 B×Kt, and wins.

21 Q—Kt2

Threatening 22 Q×P ch or, eventually, 22 Q×P.

21 ......   B—Kt3

After 21 .... KR—KKt1 (which is relatively the best defence), White would play, not 22 Q×P, Q×Q; 23 R×Q ch, Kt—B2, etc., but 22 KR—B1, threatening to win a piece by 23 B×Kt, P×B; 24 Kt—Kt3.

22 Q×P ch   K—Q3
23 Kt—K4 ch!

The black King is now at the mercy of the Rooks. The Knight must be taken, otherwise: 23 .... K—B3; 24 B—Kt5 mate.

23 ......   P×Kt
24 KR—Q1 ch   Resigns.

272

White   *Black*

STEINITZ   LASKER

(Nuremberg, 1896)

In this game we witness a contest between the Amazons. Once the mobilisation is completed the two Queens take the field. But what different aims they pursue! The black Queen leads her troops in a victorious expedition while her rival goes in for distant conquests (pawn at QKt7), which in the end prove to be of no value.

1 P—K4   P—K3
2 P—Q4   P—Q4
3 Kt—Q2   P—QB4
4 QP×P

Best is the continuation 4 KP×P, KP×P; 5 B—Kt5 ch, and White has an advantage in development, albeit a minute one.

4 ......   B×P
5 Kt—Kt3   B—Kt3

Thus Black's KB remains on an effective diagonal, whilst the white QKt is posted off the battlefield.

6 P×P   Kt—KB3!

Far more vigorous than the immediate recapture 6 .... P×P.

7 B—Kt5 ch

After 7 P×P, B×P ch; 8 K—K2, Q×Q ch; 9 K×Q, B×P, Black's game is to be preferred.

Similarly, after 7 P—QB4, P×P; 8 P×P (8 P—B5, B×P; 9 Kt×B, Q—R4 ch, followed by .... Q×Kt); 8 .... Q×P; 9 Q×Q, Kt×Q, Black, with two pieces in play, stands better, his adversary having practically none in active service.

7 ......   B—Q2
8 B×B ch   Q×B
9 P—QB4   P×P
10 P—B5   B—B2
11 Kt—B3   Kt—B3
12 Castles   Castles KR
13 Kt(Kt3)—Q4   Kt×Kt
14 Q×Kt   KR—K1

Positional judgment tells us that Black's passed pawn, although isolated and blockaded, acts as an important pivot in the centre. As, moreover, Black has succeeded in being the first to occupy the open K file, it is only to be expected that he will have a marked preponderance on the K side.

15 B—K3   R—K5
16 Q—Q3   QR—K1
17 KR—Q1   P—KR3
18 P—QR3   Q—Kt5

Black's champion enters the lists.

19 P—Kt4   P—KKt4

Calling forth the threat 20 .... Q—R4, to be followed by 21 .... P—Kt5.

20 Q—B3   Q—B4
21 Q—Q3   Q—Kt3
22 Q—Kt5

This removal of the Queen from the main battlefield does not improve matters, nor can White play 22 Kt—Q2, on account of 22 .... B×P ch; 23 K×B, R—R5 ch, followed by .... Q×Q.

As 22 P—R3 is also of doubtful value because of 22 .... Q—R4 (threatening 23 .... P—Kt5; 24 P×P, R×KKtP, etc.), he should have tried to defend the position as best he could by 22 P—Kt3.

22 ......   Q—R4!
23 Q×P

Hoping to keep his adversary occupied;

but Black has at his disposal a sacrifice as convincing as it is instructive.

23	B × P ch
24 Kt × B	R—R5
25 P—B3	

A beautiful variation arises from 25 Q—B7, namely: 25 .... Kt—Kt5; 26 Q—Q7, R × Kt; 27 Q × R ch, K—R2; 28 P—Kt3, R × P; 29 B × R, Q—R7 ch; 30 K—B1, Q × B mate.

25	R × Kt
26 Q—B7	R—R8 ch
27 K—B2	Q—R5 ch
28 Q—Kt3	

Or 28 K—K2, P—Q5; 29 R × R, R × B ch; 30 K—Q2, Q—B7 ch, followed by mate in four at the latest.

28	Q × Q ch
29 K × Q	R × R
30 R × R	R × B

And Black wins.

273

| White | Black |
| MIESES | MARSHALL |

(Vienna, 1908)

The first essential for an attack is—the will to attack! In this game the inventive mind of the American champion overcomes all obstacles one by one, moving at times over treacherous ground until the final assault begins.

Starting with a sacrifice of his own invention (3 .... P—QB4), and culminating in a splendid onslaught (27 .... P—K6), Marshall's strategy can serve as an object lesson to all attacking players.

1 P—K4	P—K3
2 P—Q4	P—Q4
3 Kt—QB3	P—QB4

Seeking the immediate emancipation of Black's game.

| 4 Kt—B3 | Kt—QB3 |
| 5 B—K3 | |

The wisest course, to slow down Black's impetus, is: 5 KP × P, KP × P; 6 B—K2, etc., with a satisfactory development. White, however, is intent on winning the hostile QBP.

| 5 ...... | Kt—B3 |

Instead of playing 5 .... BP × P, or even 5 .... P—B5, Black prefers to ignore the enemy's threat. He thereby obtains a central superiority in space in exchange for his pawn.

6 KP × P	KP × P
7 P × P	B—K2
8 B—K2	Castles
9 Castles	R—K1
10 P—KR3	B—B4
11 P—R3	P—QR4

Preventing 12 P—QKt4, so that, to all intents and purposes, White's extra pawn remains isolated.

12 Kt—QR4	Q—B2
13 Q—B1	QR—Q1
14 B—Q3	Kt—K5
15 Kt—Q2	Q—K4

Threatening to regain the pawn to some advantage, e.g.: 16 P—KKt4, Kt × Kt; 17 Q × Kt, B × B; 18 Q × B, P—Q5; 19 B—Q2, B × P, etc.

16 R—K1	Q—B3
17 B × Kt	P × B
18 Kt—B1	Q—Kt3

The beginning of the direct attack is announced by the threat of 19 .... QB × P.

| 19 Kt—Kt3 | P—R4 |
| 20 Kt × B | |

An unsuccessful attempt to ease the pressure by exchanges.

| 20 ...... | Q × Kt |
| 21 P—QKt4 | Kt—K4 |

The reserve cavalry! The threat eventually is 22 .... Kt—B6 ch; 23 P × Kt, KP × P. The alternative, 21 .... P × P; 22 P × P, Kt × P, would diverge from the general plan and, after 23 R—Kt1, Kt—Q4; 24 R × P, be to White's advantage.

| 22 B—B4 | Kt—Kt3 |

Now 22 .... Kt—B6 ch would be unsound, on the score of 23 P × Kt, KP × P;

24 K—R2, with an adequate defence for White.

23 B—K3	Kt—R5
24 B—B4	Q—Kt3
25 B—Kt3	B—Kt4

A decisive gain in territory, which will enable a Rook to occupy the "seventh."

26 Q—Kt1	R—Q7
27 Q—Kt3	P—K6

Breaking up the hostile ring of fortifications.

28 Q—B3	P × P ch
29 B × P	B—K6

This *discovery manœuvre* forces the mate. White resigns.

274

White	Black
MORPHY	MEEK

(New York, 1857)

The real Morphy—with his ultra-rapid mobilisation of forces—appears in this short game, in which a rather unfortunate defence conjures up an orgy of aggressive measures.

1 P—K4	P—K3
2 P—Q4	P—QB4

Without sufficient support in the centre, this premature thrust already proves almost fatal. It well illustrates the necessity of playing the usual 2 .... P—Q4 first.

3 P—Q5
An energetic reply.

3	P—K4

Misfortunes seldom come singly. Not only has Black disdained the loss of a *tempo*, but his KP will now serve as a target and allow White to open the K file.

That is why 3 .... Kt—KB3; 4 Kt—QB3, P—Q3, with a cramped but tenable game, would have been preferable.

4 P—KB4
Opening the file!

4	P—Q3
5 Kt—KB3	B—Kt5
6 P × P	B × Kt

This exchange (instead of 6 .... P × P) helps White's development.

7 Q × B	P × P
8 B—Kt5 ch	Kt—Q2
9 Kt—B3	Kt—B3

In answer to 9 .... B—Q3 or 9 .... P—KR3, White would play 10 Q—Kt3.

10 B—Kt5   **B—K2**
Quite naturally he tries to unpin the Knight, for after 10 .... B—Q3; 11 Castles, etc., or 10 .... P—KR3; 11 B × Kt, Q × B; 12 Q × Q (the simplest); 12 .... P × Q; 13 Castles KR, B—K2; 14 P—Q6, B—B1 (or 14 .... B × P; 15 QR—Q1, K—K2; 16 B × Kt, K × B; 17 R × P, and wins); 15 Kt—Q5, etc., and Black's game is beyond redemption.

11 P—Q6
The break through, bringing about a decisive gain in space.

11 ......   **B × P**
Losing a piece; but after 11 .... B—B1; 12 Kt—Q5 (with the double threat of 13 Kt—B7 ch and 13 B × Kt, P × B; 14 Kt × P ch); 12 .... Q—R4 ch; 13 B—Q2, Black loses the Queen in a curious manner.

12 Castles QR
And wins.
(E.g. 12 .... Q—Kt3; 13 B × Kt, P × B; 14 Q × P, attacks both Black's KR and B.)

275

White	Black
TCHIGORIN	LASKER

(London, 1899)

The superiority of the two Bishops over Knight and Bishop (or two Knights) is demonstrated here in a masterly manner.

1 P—K4	P—K3
2 Q—K2	

Instead of the usual 2 P—Q4, the great Russian adopts a continuation of his own invention.

2	Kt—QB3
3 Kt—QB3	

A more energetic continuation is 3 P—KB4.

3	P—K4

Giving the game an open character.

4 P—KKt3	Kt—B3
5 B—Kt2	B—B4
6 P—Q3	P—Q3
7 B—Kt5	

Simpler is 7 B—K3, exchanging Bishop for a Bishop instead of a Knight.

7	P—KR3
8 B×Kt	Q×B
9 Kt—Q5	Q—Q1
10 P—QB3	Kt—K2
11 Kt×Kt	Q×Kt
12 Castles	B—Q2
13 P—KB4	Castles QR
14 Kt—B3	B—B3
15 KR—B1	P—B3

Closing the KB file against hostile intentions.

16 K—Kt1

Against 16 Kt—R4 (threatening 17 Kt—Kt6) Black would play, as in the text, 16 .... KR—K1.

16	KR—K1
17 P—B5	B—R5
18 R—B1	K—Kt1
19 Kt—Q2	P—R3
20 B—B3	B—R2
21 P—R4	R—QB1
22 Kt—B4	R (K1)—Q1
23 Kt—K3	B—K1
24 KR—Q1	B—B2

After all this manœuvring both Black's Bishops are placed on effective diagonals.

25 P—B4   P—B3

This move has manifold uses (see Black's 28th and 29th moves).

26 R—B2	B—Q5
27 R (Q1)—QB1	Q—B2
28 Kt—Q1	Q—R4
29 Kt—B3	P—QKt4!

Extending the range of action of the QB.

30 P—Kt3	R—Q2
31 P×P	RP×P
32 Kt—Q5	K—Kt2
33 P—KKt4	R (Q2)—Q1

A deep calculation. The hostile Knight is forced to unmask the black Queen's Bishop's diagonal.

34 Kt—K7   B×P

Triumph of the Bishops.

35 Kt×R

Or 35 Kt×P, R×Kt; 36 R×R, Q—Kt5; 37 R—B7 ch, K—Kt1; 38 P—R3, Q×P, and White is overwhelmed.

Position after 34 Kt—K7

35	R×Kt
36 Q—Q2	Q—R6
37 R—R1	R—QR1
38 R—R2	B×P ch!

Sweeping away the last obstacles.

39 R×B	Q—Kt6 ch
40 K—B1	R×R
41 Q×R	B—K6 ch
42 Q—Q2	Q×P
Resigns.	

276

White	Black
TARTAKOWER	H. MÜLLER

(Kecskemet, 1927)

The following game shows that simplicity of means does not preclude their being effective.

1 P—K4	P—K3
2 P—KKt3	

Instead of the usual 2 P—Q4, White delays the occupation of the centre. It is a new system introduced by Dr. Tartakower in 1924.

2	P—Q4
3 B—Kt2	P×P
4 Kt—QB3	

Too unenterprising would be 4 B×P, Kt—KB3; 5 B—Kt2, P—B4, with equal chances.

4 ......   Kt—KB3

After 4 .... P—KB4 White would continue in real gambit style with 5 P—B3, P × P; 6 Kt × P, and White's advantage in development, together with the weakening of Black's position, makes up for the lost pawn.

The best course is 4 .... B—Q2; 5 Kt × P, B—B3 (threatening 6 .... P—B4); 6 P—KB3, and there are opportunities for both sides.

5 Kt × P	Kt × Kt
6 B × Kt	Kt—Q2
7 Kt—K2	Kt—B3
8 B—Kt2	

The pressure exercised by the Bishop on the long diagonal ensures for White the superior game.

8	P—K4
9 Castles	P—B3
10 P—Q4	

The opening up of the game must benefit the better-developed side.

10	P × P
11 Kt × P	B—K2
12 P—Kt3	Castles
13 B—Kt2	Q—R4
14 P—QR3	

This prevents both 14 .... B—QB4 (because of the fork by 15 P—QKt4) and the freeing manœuvre 14 .... B—QKt5, followed by .... B—B6, etc.

14 ......   B—KKt5
15 Q—K1   Q—B2

Black should have decided on the exchange of Queens as the lesser evil, although White would have the better game after 15 .... Q × Q; 16 KR × Q.

16 P—R3   B—B1

If 16 .... B—R4; 17 Kt—B5.

17 Q—B3   Kt—K1

Hoping to contest one of the long diagonals, but White's QB will now find even more lucrative employment.

18 P—QR4	B—B3
19 B—R3	Kt—Q3
20 Q—B5	R—Q1
21 QR—Q1	

Threatening 22 Kt × P.

This is an unusual case of a practically complete blockade obtained by White on a full board—a rare occurrence. If 21 .... Kt—K1; 22 Q—B8 mate, or if 21 .... P—QKt3; 22 Q × BP.

21 ......   B × Kt

The most interesting variation is 21 .... B—K2; 22 Kt—Kt5, Kt × Kt; 23 Q × B, Q × Q; 24 B × Q, R—K1; 25 P × Kt, R × B; 26 R—Q8 ch, with mate to follow.

22 Q × B   Resigns

For the vertical pin will cost Black a piece.

17. CARO-KANN DEFENCE

277

White	Black
PILLSBURY	CARO

(Vienna, 1898)

The pawn majority on the Q side—an important factor in end games—can also be of moment in the middle game, as can be seen here.

The advance 16 P—Q5, piercing the front, and the capture 22 B×P, laying bare the QB file, are admirable features of White's strategy.

1 P—K4	P—QB3
2 P—Q4	P—Q4
3 Kt—QB3	P×P
4 Kt×P	Kt—B3

"Development by opposition," which permits the doubling of his KBP. To avoid this drawback, the preparatory manœuvre 4 .... Kt—Q2, followed by .... KKt—B3 (Nimzowitsch's stratagem), has been tried, but its artificiality is well illustrated by the following curious little game Arnold-Böhm, *Munich*, 1932: 4 .... Kt—Q2; 5 Q—K2 (instead of this cruel opening trap, White can very well continue his development with 5 Kt—KB3, KKt—B3; 6 Kt—Kt3, P—K3; 7 B—Q3, etc.); 5 .... KKt—B3 (falling into the abyss); 6 Kt—Q6 mate.

5 Kt×Kt ch
Simplest.

5 ...... KP×Kt
Decentralising. He allows his opponent the majority of pawns on the Q side, but hopes to recoup himself by the greater freedom of his pieces in the middle game.

After centralisation by 5 .... KtP×Kt; 6 P—QB3, then .... B—B4. But by playing 6 Q—Q3, followed by P—KKt3 and B—Kt2, White occupies most important points of observation.

6 Kt—B3
Reserving his decision as to the manner of developing his KB. An adroit plan is 6 P—QB3, B—Q3; 7 B—Q3, Castles; 8 Q—B2, which forces a weakening of Black's King's field (8 .... P—KKt3 or 8 .... P—KR3).

6 ...... B—Q3
7 B—Q3
More enterprising than 7 B—K2. Too procrastinating would be 7 P—KR3, Castles; 8 B—Q3, R—K1 ch; 9 B—K3, B—B5, and Black soon obtains the initiative.

7 ...... B—Kt5
A less ambitious plan is 7 .... Castles; 8 Castles, R—K1; 9 Kt—R4, etc.

8 P—KR3 B—R4
Instead of this impulsive move, 8 .... Q—K2 ch; clearing up the situation was called for.

9 P—KKt4
Conquest of the strategic square KB5.

9	B—Kt3
10 Kt—R4	Kt—Q2
11 Kt—B5	B×Kt
12 B×B	P—KKt3

Heedless. Here again 12 .... Q—K2 ch, followed by .... Castles QR, would anticipate many of White's machinations.

13 Q—K2 ch	Q—K2
14 B×Kt ch	K×B
15 B—K3	QR—K1

In order to play 16 .... B—B5, but White plans direct action. Better would be 15 .... KR—K1.

16 P—Q5
A powerful advance, for if 16 .... P×P; 17 Q—Kt5 ch, and if 16 .... B—B5; 17 P×P ch, etc.

16	P—QB4
17 Q—Kt5 ch	K—B1
18 Castles QR	Q—B2
19 R—Q3	R—K5

With the transparent threat 20 .... R—Kt5. Better would be at once 19 .... P—QR3.

20 R—B3 P—QR3
After 20 .... R—Kt5; 21 Q×R, P×Q; 22 R×Q ch, K×R; 23 R—K1, Black's pawn structure would be deficient, but it would be the lesser evil.

21 Q—Q3   KR—K1
After 21 .... P—B4; 22 P×P, P×P;
23 P—B3, R×B; 24 Q×P ch, K—Kt1;
25 R×R, B—B5; 26 Q—K4, P—B4;
27 Q—K6, etc., White has won a valuable
pawn; and after 21 .... R—R5; 22 K—Kt1,
Black is in an *impasse*.

22 B×P
An important capture, for if 22 ....
B×B; 23 P—Q6, Q—B3; 24 P—Q7 ch,
Q×P; 25 R×B ch, etc.

22 ......   K—Q2
23 B—K3   Q—R4
24 P—R3   P—QKt4
Weakening his base. But if, e.g. 24 ....
B—B5; 25 B×B, R×B; 26 P—Q6, White
forges new threats.

25 R—B6
An attacking move requiring accurate
calculation.

25 ......   B—B5
26 K—Kt1   B×B
27 P×B   R×KP
28 Q—Q4   R—K8 ch
29 K—R2
Convincing! After 29 R×R, R×R ch;
30 K—R2, K—K1, etc., Black could still
hold out.

29 ......   R×R
30 Q—R7 ch   Resigns.

278

White	Black
White	*Black*

TARRASCH   TARTAKOWER

(Teplitz-Schönau, 1922)

*In the following game, it is Black's pawn
minority on the Q side, which ventures on an
offensive, rich in results!*

1 P—K4   P—QB3
2 P—Q4   P—Q4
3 Kt—QB3   P×P
4 Kt×P   Kt—B3
5 Kt×Kt ch   KP×Kt
6 B—QB4
Aggressive play.

6 ......   B—Q3
More expansive than 6 .... B—K2, and

more to the point than 6 .... Kt—Q2.
Weak would be 6 .... B—K3, on account
of 7 B×B, P×B; 8 Kt—B3, followed by
Castles and R—K1.

7 Kt—K2
Instead of this colourless continuation,
7 Q—K2 ch would lead to the withdrawal
7 .... B—K2, or to a simplification by
7 .... Q—K2; 8 Q×Q ch, K×Q; 9 B—K3,
etc., and White's small advantage can, in
the nature of things, be realised only in the
end game.

7 ......   Q—B2
Hindering White's development (8 Castles
or 8 B—B4), and thus giving Black a more
substantial game than the neutral 7 ....
Castles; 8 Castles.

8 B—K3   Castles
9 Q—Q2   Kt—Q2
10 B—Kt3   P—QKt4
This offensive will have lasting results.

11 Kt—Kt3   P—QR4
12 P—QB3   Kt—Kt3
13 Kt—K4   P—R5
14 B—B2
A doubtful transaction would be 14 Kt×B,
P×B; 15 Kt×B, Q×Kt; 16 P—QR3,
Kt—B5; 17 Q—Q1, Kt×KtP; 18 Q×P,
Kt—B5, and Black's Knight occupies a
dominant post.

14 ......   Kt—B5
15 Q—Q3   P—KB4
Parrying the threat of 15 Kt×P ch.

16 Kt×B   Kt×P
And not 16 .... Q×Kt; 17 Castles QR,
after which Black's action becomes purpose-
less.

17 Q—K2   Q×Kt
18 B×P   Q—R6
Maintaining his grip.

19 Castles KR
If 19 B×B, Q×P ch; 20 B—Q2, Kt—Q6
ch, and wins.

19 ......   B×B
20 B—B1   Q×BP
21 B×Kt   Q—Q6
Having emerged from all complications
with an extra pawn, Black does not fear
simplification in spite of Bishops of opposite
colours.

22 Q×Q   B×Q
23 KR—Q1   P—R6
An important intermediary manœuvre, for
otherwise White could nullify the hostile

pawn chain by 24 P—QR3, followed by B—B3 and B—Kt4.

24 B—B3
If 24 R × B, P × B; 25 R—Kt1, R × P; 26 R—Kt3, KR—Q1, with an easy win.

24	B—B5
25 B—Kt4	KR—K1
26 R—K1	R × R ch
27 R × R	

Or 27 B × R, R—R5; 28 P—B3, P—Kt5 (threat: 29 .... B × P; 30 R × B, P—Kt6, etc.); 29 R—Kt1, P—Kt6; 30 P × P, P—R7; 31 R—R1, B × P; 32 B—B3, R—B5; 33 B—Kt2, R—B7, and wins.

27 ...... P—R3
In order to be able to play .... R—R5, but more fruitful would be 27 .... P—B3, with the double object of providing not merely a flight square but also a passage way for the King.

28 R—K3
In order to eliminate the troublesome QRP. But its neighbour will prove still more obnoxious. *Ex ossibus ultor.* But if, passively, 28 R—R1, Black's King would march to Q4 after 28 .... P—B4, securing the advantage.

28 ...... R—R5
29 B × P
If 29 B—B5, P—Kt5, followed by .... B × P.

| 29 ...... | P—Kt5 |
| 30 B—B1 | R × P |

White resigns.
If 31 P—B3, P—Kt6; 32 R—B3, B—Q4, followed by .... P—Kt7.

279

| White | Black |
| ALEKHINE | TARTAKOWER |

(Kecskemet, 1927)

A multiple sacrifice is always impressive. In the following game it is the culmination of skilful manœuvres.

1 P—K4	P—QB3
2 P—Q4	P—Q4
3 Kt—QB3	P × P
4 Kt × P	Kt—B3
5 Kt—Kt3	

An interesting sacrifice is 5 B—Q3, Q × P; 6 Kt—KB3, Q—Q1 (better, 6 .... Q—Kt3); 7 QKt—Kt5, P—KR3 (fatal, but after 7 .... P—K3; 8 Castles, etc., also, Black has a difficult time); 8 Kt × P, K × Kt; 9 B—Kt6 ch, K × B; 10 Q × Q, and wins.

5 ...... P—K4
A premature opening up of the game! The most promising continuation is 5 .... Q—Kt3.

6 Kt—B3
There is little to be said for 6 P × P, Q × Q ch; 7 K × Q, Kt—Kt5, etc. The most concentric is 6 B—K3. An interesting sacrificial idea is: 6 Q—K2, Q × P; 7 Kt—B3, B—Kt5 ch (better, 7 .... Q—Q1); 8 P—B3, B × P ch; 9 P × B, Q × QBP ch; 10 Q—Q2, Q × R; 11 B—B4, B—K3; 12 B × B, P × B; 13 Castles, Kt—Q4; 14 Kt—K4, and Black's Queen is lost.

6 ...... P × P
If 6 .... P—K5; 7 Kt—Kt5, B—KB4; 8 Kt × B, Q—R4 ch; 9 P—B3, Q × Kt; 10 Q—Kt3, Q—Q2; 11 B—QB4, Kt—Q4; 12 Kt × KP, eliminating the dangerous pawn, etc.

7 Kt × P
If 7 Q × P, QKt—Q2, etc.

7 ...... B—QB4
More solid is 7 .... B—K2.

8 Q—K2 ch
A paradoxical-looking move, which gives up the protection of the QP and encumbers the KB. Its justification is the speeding up of castling QR and the possibility of effecting later on a freeing manœuvre (11 Q—B4) without loss of time.
If, however, 8 B—K3, Kt—Q4, etc.

8 ...... B—K2
Or 8 .... Q—K2; 9 B—K3, and White's forces are better placed.

9 B—K3 P—B4
In his desire to prevent White from castling on the Q side, Black creates a weakness for himself at QB4. Better would be 9 .... Castles, although even then White's position remains superior after 10 Castles, Q—R4; 11 K—Kt1, Kt—Q4; 12 Q—B3, etc.

10 Kt (Q4)—B5 Castles
11 Q—B4
A fine manœuvre, which has the effect of attacking the QBP whilst liberating his own KB.

11 ......   R—K1
This indirect defence of the QBP is not
permanent. If 11 .... B—K3; 12 Kt × B ch,
Q × Kt; 13 Q × P, Q × Q; 14 B × Q, R—B1;
15 Castles. Better would be at once 11 ....
P—QKt3.

12 B—Q3   P—QKt3
13 Castles QR   B—R3
He should have played 13 .... QKt—Q2,
blocking the critical Q file. He now becomes
the victim of a magnificent attack.

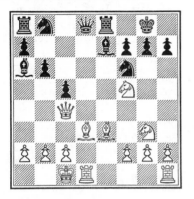

14 Kt—R6 ch
An *unmasking sacrifice*, which must be
accepted, for if 14 .... K—R1; 15 Kt × P ch,
and if 14 .... K—B1; 15 Q × P mate.

14 ......   P × Kt
15 B × P ch
A second sacrifice, which cannot be
declined, e.g. 15 .... K—B1; 16 B × P mate,
or 15 ..,. K—Kt2; 16 Kt—B5 ch, or
15 .... K—R1; 16 Q × KBP, QKt—Q2;
17 Kt—B5, B—KB1; 18 B—Kt6 (threat:
19 R × Kt); 18 .... B—B1; 19 P—KKt4,
etc., with a winning attack. On the other
hand, if 15 .... K × B; 16 Q × P ch.

15 ......   Kt × B
16 Q—Kt4 ch   K—R1
17 R × Q   R × R
A slightly better defence would be provided by 17 .... B × R.

18 Q—K4
The *final point*. The overthrow of the
last line of defences is now a question of
technique.

18 ......   Kt—QB3
19 Q × Kt   B—KB1
20 Kt—B5   B—B5
21 B × RP   B—Q4

22 Q—B7   QR—B1
23 Q—B4   R—B3
24 B × B   R × B
25 Q—K5 ch   Kt—B3
26 Kt—Q6   Resigns.

280

White	Black
SPIELMANN	*HÖNLINGER*

(Match, Vienna, 1929)

*In the following game, we can see very
clearly the various dramatic happenings which
can unfold themselves on an open diagonal.*

1 P—K4   P—QB3
2 P—Q4   P—Q4
3 Kt—QB3   P × P
4 Kt × P   Kt—B3
5 Kt—Kt3   P—K3
He decides to shut in his QB, for the sake
of a better co-ordination in the development
of his forces.

6 Kt—B3   P—B4
7 B—Q3   Kt—B3
Increasing the pressure against Q5.
A more reserved continuation is 7 ....
QKt—Q2; 8 Castles, B—K2; 9 P—B3,
Castles; 10 Kt—K5, and White should
obtain the initiative.
Bad would be 7 .... P × P; 8 Kt × P, as
now 8 .... Q × Kt is inadmissible because of
9 B—Kt5 ch.

8 P × P   B × P
9 P—QR3   Castles
10 Castles   P—QKt3
11 P—Kt4   B—K2
12 B—Kt2   Q—B2
Artificial. He should have tried to even
up matters by 12 .... B—Kt2.

13 P—Kt5   Kt—QR4
14 Kt—K5
If 14 B—K5, then of course not 14 ....
B—Q3 (15 B × B, Q × B; 16 B × P ch), but
14 .... Q—Q1, returning to defend the
home.

14 ......   B—Kt2
15 Kt—Kt4   Q—Q1
16 Kt—K3   Kt—Q4
This attempted attack (17 Kt × Kt, Q × Kt)
will be fiercely repulsed. Steadiness demands
16 .... R—B1, maintaining all the available
personnel on the threatened sector.

17 Q—R5

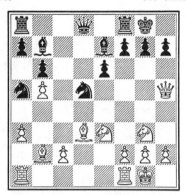

17 ....   P—Kt3

Against 17 .... P—KR3 the attack prevails after 18 B×P, K×B; 19 KKt—B5 ch,
P×Kt; 20 Kt×P ch; and if 17 .... P—B4;
18 KKt×P, P×Kt; 19 Kt×P, White's
poisoned arrows are aimed at the King.

18 Kt—Kt4

Brilliantly returning to the charge (18 ....
P×Q; 19 Kt—R6 mate).

18 ......   B—KB3
19 Kt×B ch   Kt×Kt
20 Q—R6   R—B1

More to the point would be at once
20 .... Q—K2.

21 QR—Q1   Q—K2
22 KR—K1

The harrying tactics continue.

22 ......   Kt—K1
23 Kt—B5   Q—B4

If 23 .... KtP×Kt; 24 B×P; and if
23 .... Q—B2; 24 B—Kt7, winning the
exchange.

24 R—K5

Gaining, by this attack on the Queen,
a decisive tempo.

24 ......   B—Q4
25 Kt—K7 ch   Resigns

(25 .... Q×Kt; 26 Q×RP ch, K×Q;
27 R—R5 ch, K—Kt1; 28 R—R8 mate.)

A very fine game, illustrating the power of
the plunging fire of two Bishops.

281

White	Black
LASKER	*LEE*

(London, 1899)

*The following game proves once again that,
after castling on the Q side, the defending
King is unable to protect the wide King's field
without assistance from his forces.*

1 P—K4   P—QB3
2 P—Q4   P—Q4
3 Kt—QB3   P×P
4 Kt×P   B—B4

One way of solving the problem of the QB.

5 Kt—Kt3

A modern idea is 5 Q—B3. Another is
the offer of a pawn by 5 B—Q3, which is
also playable after 4 .... Kt—B3.

5 ......   B—Kt3
6 Kt—B3   Kt—Q2

If 6 .... P—K3; 7 Kt—K5.

7 P—KR4

Instead of the impetuous continuation in
the text, it is also possible to oppose the
Bishop at once by 7 B—Q3, etc.

7 ......   P—KR3
8 B—Q3

A rational development. In a game
Borges-Silva da Rocha, *Rio de Janeiro*, 1933,
the following truculent continuation was
adopted: 8 B—QB4, P—K3; 9 Q—K2,
B—Q3; 10 Castles, KKt—B3; 11 Kt—K5,
B—R2 (this instinctive reply is a decisive
mistake; he should have played 11 ....
B×Kt; 12 P×B, Kt—Q4, etc.); 12 Kt×KBP
(a bolt from the blue); 12 .... K×Kt;
13 Q×P ch, K—Kt3; 14 P—R5 mate.

If White plays first 8 P—R5, B—R2 and
then only 9 B—Q3, etc., it would only
expose his KRP still more to attack.

8 ......   B×B
9 Q×B   KKt—B3
10 B—Q2

Useless is 10 B—B4, on account of 10 ....
Q—R4 ch; 11 B—Q2, Q—B2. Less reasonable than the development in the text would
be 10 B—K3, P—K3; 11 Castles QR,
Q—R4, etc.

10 ......   P—K3
11 Castles QR   Q—B2

More conformable than 11 .... B—Q3;
after which 12 Kt—K4, Kt×Kt; 13 Q×Kt,
Q—B2; 14 KR—K1 would provide White
with some additional resources.

12 KR—K1   Castles
If 12 .... B—Q3; 13 Kt—B5; whereas, after the move in the text, Black wishes to stress White's weakness at KKt3 with 13 .... B—Q3.

13 Q—Kt3
Escaping from the indirect attack by the adverse QR, for if, e.g. 13 Kt—K4, Kt—B4; 14 Kt×Kt, B×Kt; 15 Q—B3, B—Kt3; 16 P—R4, P—R3, and Black's Q side has an additional and trusty defender. A *positional continuation* could be 13 P—B4, to be followed by B—B3.

13 ......   B—Q3
14 Kt—K2
With the twofold object of escaping capture and preventing the exchange of Bishops after 14 .... B—B5.

14 ......   Kt—Kt5
Or 14 .... Kt—K5; 15 B—K3. Imperceptibly, Black drifts into a sterile action on the K side, without heeding the safety of his own lines. Prudent would be 14 .... Q—Kt3; 15 Q—R4, B—B2 (parrying the threat of 16 B—R5).

15 R—B1   Kt (Q2)—B3
16 Q—R4   K—Kt1
17 P—B4   Q—K2
Better is 17 .... Q—B1.

18 Kt—B3   Q—B2
19 P—KKt3
Again preventing 19 .... B—B5.

19 ......   Q—B1
20 P—QKt4   P—K4
21 P×P   Kt×KP
22 B—K3
Entirely changing the aspect of the contest.

22 ......   Kt×P
Not 22 .... P—QKt3; 23 R×B, etc., nor 22 .... Kt×Kt; 23 Q×P ch, K—B2; 24 B—Kt6 ch, K—Q2; 25 B×R, followed by P—B5, with gain in material.

23 B×P ch   K—B2
24 R—Q4
If 24 .... Kt—K4; 25 Kt×Kt, etc., or 24 .... Kt—Kt3; 25 B×Kt ch, K×B; 26 Q—R5 mate, or 24 .... Q—K3; 25 R—K1, Kt—K4; 26 B—Kt6 ch, K—B1; 27 Q—R8 ch, and wins. Black must therefore play the move in the text, which is what White desires.

24 ......   P—QKt4
25 Kt×P ch   P×Kt
26 Q×P   Kt—R6
27 Q—R5 ch   K—Kt2 dis ch
28 B—B5   B×B
29 P×B   R×R
If 29 .... Q—R1; 30 R—Kt4 ch, K—B3; 31 R—Kt6 ch, etc.

30 Kt×R   Q—Q1
31 P—B6 ch
Beginning of a *danse macabre* in which White, after incidentally recovering his piece, enforces the black King's downfall.

31 ......   K—B1
32 Q—R8 ch   K—B2
33 Q—R7 ch   K—Q3
34 Q×Kt ch   K—Q4
35 R—Q1   Q—Kt3
36 Kt—B3 dis ch   K—K3
37 Q—Q6 ch   K—B4
38 Q—Q3 ch   K—Kt5
39 Kt—K5 ch   Resigns
(Mate in two e.g.: 39 .... K—R6; 40 R—R1 ch, etc., or 39 .... K—R4; 40 Q—B3 ch, etc.)
A great struggle.

282

White	Black
YATES	RÉTI

(New York, 1924)

This game illustrates that, on the K side also, the defending King cannot hope to hold the more restricted K field without the assistance of one or two trusty pieces.

1 P—K4   P—QB3
2 P—Q4   P—Q4
3 Kt—QB3   P×P
4 Kt×P   B—B4
5 Kt—Kt3   B—Kt3
6 Kt—B3   Kt—Q2
7 P—B3
Instead of one of the more usual continuations, White selects a quiet move, reserving his energy for the later phase of the contest.

7 ......   KKt—B3
8 B—QB4   P—K3
9 Q—K2   B—K2
More imagination is shown by 9 .... Q—B2, with .... Castles QR to follow.

10 Castles   Castles
11 R—K1
Threatening 12 B × P, etc.

11 ......   Kt—Q4
A more straightforward parry is 11 ....
K—R1.

12 B—Kt3   P—QR4
As all these wing manœuvres fail to fulfil
their object, 12 .... Q—B2 at once
(13 P—B4, KKt—Kt3) would have been
wiser.

13 P—QR3   Q—B2
14 P—B4   Kt—B5
15 B × Kt   Q × B
16 QR—Q1   B—B3
17 B—B2
Now that all the white pieces are concentrated on the K side, he wants to eliminate
an important defender.

17 ......   KR—Q1
He would free his game better by 17 ....
B × B; 18 Q × B, but he appears to have
unbounded faith in the solidity of his
formation.

18 B × B   RP × B
19 Kt—K4   Kt—Kt3
20 P—QKt3   B—K2
21 R—Q3
A profound conception.

21 ......   B × P
Fatal greed! He should have played
21 .... Q—B2.

22 Kt—K5
A glut of threats. Very strong would also
be 22 KKt—Kt5, R—KB1; 23 P—Kt3,
Q—B2; 24 Q—Kt4, to be followed by
Q—R4.

22 ......   Q—R5
Fleeing before the threat 23 R—KB3.
An attempt to save himself, which would
not be available after 22 KKt—Kt5, is
22 .... R × P; 23 R × R, Q × KKt;
24 KR—Q1, B—K2; 25 Q—K3, etc.

23 R—R3   Q—K2
Still hoping to hold out. If now 24 Q—Kt4
(to be followed by Kt—Kt5 and Q—R4),
then 24 .... R × P. But White finds a
magnificent way of avoiding this awkward
corner.

24 Kt—Kt5
A beautiful final manœuvre, which breaks
down all opposition, for if 24 .... Q × Kt;

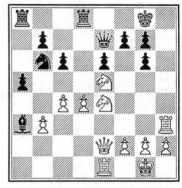

Position after 23 .... Q—K2

25 R—R8 ch., etc., and if 24 .... R—KB1;
25 Q—Kt4, with the threat of 26 Q—R4, or
even 26 R—R8 ch.

24 ......   Resigns.

283

White	Black
MONTICELLI	FINE

(Syracuse, U.S.A., 1934)

*The following game contains beautiful
sacrifices in the Morphy style. They are,
however, prepared scientifically and not
made intuitively—the ideal of the modern
player.*

1 P—K4   P—QB3
2 P—Q4   P—Q4
3 Kt—QB3   P × P
4 Kt × P   B—B4
5 Kt—Kt3   B—Kt3
6 Kt—B3
An accepted continuation, exercising
pressure on K5.

6 ......   P—K3
More cautious is first of all 6 ....
Kt—Q2 (preventing 7 Kt—K5, by reason of
7 .... Kt × Kt; 8 P × Kt, Q—R4 ch, followed by .... Q × KP ch), for now White
could have obtained some advantage in
space after 7 Kt—K5.

7 B—QB4
This Bishop has no future. Apart from

the outpost manœuvre 7 Kt—K5, an intelligent continuation would be to oppose the Bishop by 7 B—Q3.

The most energetic is 7 P—KR4, P—KR3; 8 Kt—K5, which continuation occurred in a game Horowitz-Gudju, *Prague*, 1931, with an inversion of moves, e.g.: 8 .... B—R2; 9 B—QB4, Kt—Q2; 10 Q—K2, KKt—B3 (a decisive mistake; 10 .... Kt×Kt is necessary); 11 Kt×KBP, B—Kt5 ch (11 .... K×Kt; 12 Q×P ch, K—Kt3; 13 P—R5 mate); 12 P—B3, and Black resigned in a few moves.

7	Kt—B3
8 Q—K2	QKt—Q2
9 Kt—K5	Kt×Kt

A clear-cut decision.

10 P×Kt
After 10 Q×Kt, B×P, there is the loss of a pawn without compensation.

10 ...... Kt—Q2
Threatening to win the KP by 11 .... Q—R4 ch.

11 P—B4
He weakens his base. The unpretentious continuation 11 Castles is called for.

| 11 ...... | B—QB4 |
| 12 B—Kt3 | |

Better would be 12 P—B3, Q—Kt3; 13 P—Kt4, driving the adverse KB from the troublesome diagonal, or 12 .... P—Kt4; 13 B—Q3, B×B (clearly not 13 .... Kt×P; 14 Q×Kt, Q×B; 15 Q×B, winning a piece); 14 Q×B, Q—Kt3; 15 Kt—K4, and White is not without resources.

| 12 ...... | P—QR4 |
| 13 P—QR4 | |

Leading to simplification would be 13 P—B3, P—R5; 14 B—B2.

13 ...... Q—Kt3
Seizing the initiative.

| 14 B—Q2 | Castles QR |
| 15 Kt—B1 | |

After 15 Castles, B—Kt5, there is no gainsaying Black's positional advantage.

15 ...... B—Kt5
Simple and strong.

16 Castles Kt—B4
Black's threats are becoming concrete.

17 Q—K3
Plausible, but had White foreseen the splendour of Black's impending evolutions, he would have tried to defend himself as best

he could with 17 B—K3. In any event, his position is already compromised, e.g. neither 17 K—Kt1 (17 .... Kt×B) nor 17 B×B (17 .... Kt×B ch; 18 P×Kt, R×R ch; 19 K×R, Q×B, etc.) can very well be played.

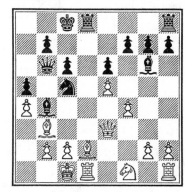

17 ...... R—Q6
An *intercepting sacrifice.*

18 P×R
Compulsory, e.g. 18 Q—K2, R×KB; 19 P×R, Kt×P mate.

18 ...... Kt×B ch
19 K—B2
After 19 K—Kt1, Kt×B ch; 20 R×Kt, Q×Q; 21 Kt×Q, B×R, Black remains with an extra piece.

19 ...... B—QB4
Intimating that the hostile Queen must retreat, after which White's King rapidly succumbs to the co-operation of Black's three pieces, Knight, KB and Queen.

20 Q—R3	Kt—Q5 ch
21 K—B1	Q—Kt6
Resigns	

(E.g. 22 Kt—K3, Q×QP, with a fourfold threat of mate.)

284

| White | Black |
| NIMZOWITSCH | CAPABLANCA |

(New York, 1927)

A "blockade game," and the best of its kind! Inexorable logic directs the course of events.

1 P—K4	P—QB3
2 P—Q4	P—Q4
3 P—K5	

Reminiscent of a variation of the *French Defence*, with, however, two points of difference: in the present case Black's QB can be developed before playing .... P—K3, which is a distinct advantage; secondly, Black's QBP, which in the nature of things must ultimately move to its fourth, does so here in two moves instead of one. On striking a balance, the advance in the text is more in favour of Black than is the similar thrust in the French Defence.

3	B—B4
4 B—Q3	

Eliminating a troublesome opponent, but at the price of a *weakening of his white squares*. Other continuations are: 4 Kt—K2, followed by Kt—Kt3; or 4 P—KB4, followed by Kt—KB3; or 4 Kt—QB3; or especially the *bayonet attack* by 4 P—KKt4, e.g. 4 .... B—Kt3; 5 P—K6, etc.; or 4 .... B—Q2; 5 B—Q3, Q—Kt3; 6 P—QB3, P—K3; 7 Kt—K2, P—QB4; 8 Kt—Q2, Kt—QB3; 9 Kt—B3, P×P; 10 P×P, and White has the superior mechanism.

4	B×B

Not 4 .... B—Kt3; 5 P—K6.

5 Q×B	P—K3

If 5 .... Q—R4 ch, then not 6 P—B3, Q—R3; 7 Q×Q, Kt×Q, with an excellent game for Black, but 6 Kt—Q2, Q—R3; 7 P—QB4, P—K3; 8 Kt—K2, B—Kt5; 9 P—QKt3, etc., avoids a sterile exchange of Queens.

6 Kt—QB3	

Seeking unfettered play for his pieces. Commonplace development would turn out in favour of Black, e.g.:

(*a*) 6 Kt—KB3, Q—Kt3; 7 Castles (if 7 P—B3, Q—R3, making White's castling illusory); 7 .... P—QB4 (if now 7 .... Q—R3, or 7 .... Q—Kt4; 8 Q—Kt3); 8 P—B3, Kt—QB3, and Black has the initiative.

(*b*) 6 Kt—K2, Q—Kt3; 7 Castles, P—QB4 (very good is also 7 .... Q—R3 or 7 .... Q—Kt4); 8 P—QB3, Kt—QB3, and Black takes the lead.

(*c*) 6 P—KB4, Kt—KR3, preventing the awkward thrust 7 P—B5.

6	Q—Kt3

It can be seen that after White's third move Black's counter-play runs on obvious lines, ... Q—Kt3, then .... P—QB4 and .... Kt—QB3, undermining the base (Q4) of the hostile *chain of pawns*.

7 KKt—K2	P—QB4

Not 7 .... Q—R3; 8 Q—Kt3.

8 P×P	

The point of White's sixth move. He does not seek to maintain a *sterile chain of pawns*.

8	B×P
9 Castles	

Against 9 Q—Kt3 the continuation could also have been 9 .... Kt—K2 (10 Q×P, R—Kt1; 11 Q×P, R×P, etc.).

9	Kt—K2
10 Kt—R4	Q—B3
11 Kt×B	Q×Kt
12 B—K3	Q—B2
13 P—KB4	Kt—B4
14 P—B3	

Limiting, without however eliminating, Black's pressure on the QB file, which will provide the theme of future manœuvres.

14	Kt—B3
15 QR—Q1	

Evidently not 15 B—B5, Kt×P, etc.

15	P—KKt3

Without hastening to castle, Black first strengthens his outpost at KB4.

16 P—KKt4	

Restless. Better is 16 B—B2.

16	Kt×B
17 Q×Kt	P—KR4
18 P—Kt5	Castles KR
19 Kt—Q4	Q—Kt3
20 R—B2	KR—B1

The file of the future.

21 P—QR3	R—B2
22 R—Q3	Kt—R4

Before playing .... Kt—K2, Black deliberately indulges in alarums and excursions on the Q side.

23 R—K2	R—K1

Preventing the rupture of his front by 24 P—B5, KP×P; 25 P—K6, P×P; 26 Q×P ch, Q×Q; 27 R×Q, K—Kt2; 28 Kt—B3, etc.

24 K—Kt2	Kt—B3
25 KR—Q2	R (K1)—QB1
26 R—K2	Kt—K2
27 KR—Q2	R—B5

The turning-point! Whilst White is condemned to inactivity, the Black pieces increase their *radius of action*.

28 Q—R3   K—Kt2
29 R—KB2   P—R4
30 R—K2

The white Rooks are reduced to the status of humble guardians of Q4 and KB4. Relatively better is 30 Q—K3, although even then Black intensifies his operations by 30 .... Q—R3, followed by .... P—Kt4.

30 ......   Kt—B4

Profiting from the *tactical moment* when White's KBP is left unguarded.

31 Kt×Kt ch   KtP×Kt
32 Q—B3

For if 32 Q×RP, R—KR1; 33 Q—B3, R—R5, etc., in the forthcoming duel of the respective heavy artillery, the strategic points will be QB4 and K4.

32 ......   K—Kt3
33 KR—Q2   R—K5
34 R—Q4   R—B5
35 Q—B2   Q—Kt4
36 K—Kt3   R (B5)×R
37 P×R

If 37. R×R, R—K7.

37 ......   Q—B5
38 K—Kt2

The only mobile piece in this *progressive blockade*.

38 ......   P—Kt4
39 K—Kt1   P—Kt5
40 P×P   P×P
41 K—Kt2   Q—B8
42 K—Kt3   Q—KR8

Here is the *Zugzwang*.

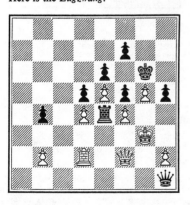

43 R—Q3

Not 43 R—K2, R×R; 44 Q×R, Q—Kt8 ch, followed by .... Q×QP, nor 43 Q—Kt2, R—K6 ch; 44 K—R4, Q×Q; 45 R×Q,

R—KB6, etc., nor 43 Q—B3, Q—Kt8 ch, etc., nor 43 K—R4, R—K8, etc.

43 ......   R—K8
44 R—KB3

The chief threat is 44 .... R—KB8. If 44 P—R3, R—Kt8 ch; 45 K—R4, R—Kt5 mate.

44 ......   R—Q8
45 P—Kt3

If 45 R—Kt3, R—KB8; and if 45 K—R4, R×P.

45 ......   R—QB8
46 R—K3

Or, e.g. 46 K—R4, R—B7; 47 Q×R, Q×R; 48 P—R3, Q×P mate.

46 ......   R—KB8

Resigns.

285

White	Black
TORRE	*FINE*

(Monterey, 1934)

A noteworthy feature of the following game is the skilful precision with which Black makes the most of the latent energy of his QB on the long diagonal.

1 P—K4   P—QB3
2 P—Q4   P—Q4
3 P—KB3

The object of this move is to maintain a flexible centre, even at the cost of a pawn. The continuation in the text can also be played one move later after 3 Kt—QB3, P×P; and now, instead of the normal 4 Kt×P, the bolder 4 P—B3 (*Milner-Barry's Gambit*); 4 .... P—K4 (4 .... P×P; 5 Kt×P, B—Kt5; 6 B—QB4, with a strong attack); 5 QP×P, Q×Q ch; 6 Kt×Q, P×P, etc. An alternative is 4 B—QB4, Kt—B3; 5 P—B3, P—K6; 6 B×P, B—B4; 7 KKt—K2, P—K3, with equal chances.

3 ......   P—K3

Best, as after 3 .... P×P; 4 P×P, P—K4; 5 Kt—KB3, P×P; 6 B—QB4, White obtains, by this gambit turn, a fruitful attack.

4 Kt—B3

In answer to 4 B—K3, Black still abstains

from accepting the gift by 4 .... P×P (on account of 5 Kt—Q2, P×P; 6 KKt×P, etc., with a promising attack), and tries to obtain equality after 4 .... Q—Kt3; 5 B—Q3, P—QB4 (5 .... Q×KtP; 6 Kt—Q2); 6 KP×P, KP×P; 7 P×P, B×P; 8 B×B, Q×B; 9 Q—Q2, Kt—QB3, etc.

4 ......   Kt—B3

A purely developing move, in preference to hasty measures such as 4 .... P×P (5 P×P) or 4 .... B—Kt5 (5 P—K5) or 4 .... P—QB4 (5 KP×P).

5 B—K3

Or at once 5 P—K5, KKt—Q2; 6 P—B4, P—QB4; 7 Kt—B3, Kt—QB3, etc., reverting to a controversial variation of the *French Defence*.

5 ......   B—K2

An unassuming continuation, but after 5 .... B—Kt5; 6 P—K5, KKt—Q2; 7 P—B4, P—QB4; 8 Kt—B3, Kt—QB3; 9 Q—Q2, etc., Black's KB is more committed than in the continuation actually adopted.

If 5 .... Q—Kt3; 6 Q—Q2, Black can neither play 6 .... Q×KtP; 7 R—Kt1, etc., nor 6 .... P—B4; 7 Kt—R4, etc. Too provocative would be 5 .... QKt—Q2; 6 P—K5, Kt—KKt1, etc. But by playing 5 .... P×P; 6 P×P, B—Kt5, White would be faced with a number of problems.

6 P—K5   KKt—Q2
7 P—B4   P—QB4
8 Kt—B3   Kt—QB3
9 B—Kt5

Leading to a barren exchange. Better is 9 Q—Q2.

9 ......   Q—Kt3
10 Castles   Castles

Thanks to the compactness of his position, Black's game is preferable.

11 K—R1   P—QR3
12 B×Kt   P×B
13 Kt—QR4

Instead of this artificial measure, a more straightforward defence of the threatened QKtP is 13 R—QKt1.

13 ......   Q—R4
14 P—B3   P×P
15 P×P   P—QB4

Again!

16 R—B1   P—B5
17 P—KKt4

In view of Black's great superiority on the Q side, White would like to get a direct attack going. By thus weakening his base, however, he signs his death warrant.

17 ......   P—B3
18 R—KB2   P×P
19 BP×P   B—Kt2
20 Q—B2

Better is 20 K—Kt2.

20 ......   B—QB3
21 Kt—B3   Kt—B4

A very fine means of asserting himself. If 22 P×Kt, P—Q5; 23 B×P, B×Kt ch, etc.

22 QR—B1

Avoiding, at any rate, the loss of the exchange (by 22 .... Kt—Q6) and succouring the KKt.

22 ......   Kt—Q6
23 R—Kt2

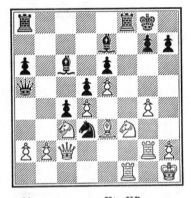

23 ......   Kt×KP

Matters are becoming serious. White loses not only a pawn, but also some important points of support.

24 P×Kt   P—Q5
25 Kt—K4   P×B
26 K—Kt1

Slightly greater resistance would be afforded by 26 R—K2.

26 ......   Q—Q4

Definite conquest of the long diagonal.

27 Kt—B3   Q—Q6

Forcing the exchange of Queens—on account of the sick KKt—after which the power of the black pawn phalanx is decisive.

28 Q×Q   P×Q
29 R—Kt3   P—K7
   Resigns.

286

White	*Black*
SULTAN KHAN	FLOHR

(London, 1932)

The trench warfare—resulting from the tranquil treatment of this opening—ends with the attrition of Black's force, although at one time he appeared to have the initiative. A fine example of the profound and imaginative play of the talented Indian champion.

1 P—K4	P—QB3
2 P—Q4	P—Q4
3 P×P	

A simplifying continuation which—instead of seeking to render the centre mobile (3 Kt—QB3) or flexible (3 P—KB3) or rigid (3 P—K5)—eliminates all tension, and makes both players' tasks more simple.

3	P×P
4 B—Q3	

If, nonchalantly, first 4 P—QB3, then 4 .... B—B4, comfortably solves Black's awkward problem of the QB.

The modern continuation 4 P—QB4 brings back the tension of the pawns in the centre.

4	Kt—QB3

The double threat (5 .... Kt×P and 5 .... Kt—Kt5) incites White to reply 5 P—QB3, whereas after 4 .... Kt—KB3 White would have the alternative 5 Kt—QB3.

5 P—QB3	Kt—B3

After 5 .... P—K4 (6 P×P, Kt×P; 7 Q—K2, Q—K2; 8 B—Kt5 ch, etc.) Black's game would be too open, and after 5 .... P—K3 (6 B—KB4, B—Q3; 7 B×B, Q×B; 8 Kt—B3, etc.) it would be too restricted. But by playing 5 .... Q—B2 (6 Kt—K2, P—K3; 7 B—KB4, B—Q3; 8 B×B, Q×B; 9 Kt—Q2, Kt—B3; 10 Kt—B3, Castles; 11 Castles, P—K4) the liberating thrust .... P—K4 gradually becomes possible.

6 B—KB4	

After 6 P—KR3, the thrust .... P—K4 becomes practicable. Slightly artificial is 6 Kt—K2, e.g. 6 .... B—Kt5; 7 P—B3, B—R4; 8 Kt—B4, B—Kt3, etc., or 7 Q—Kt3, Kt—QR4; 8 Q—R4 ch, B—Q2; 9 Q—B2, Q—Kt3, to be followed by 10 .... B—Kt4 and simplification. The most natural continuation is 6 Kt—B3, B—Kt5; 7 Castles,

etc., setting rapidly to work on the semi-open K file (pressure on K5), whilst Black seeks counter-chances on the QB file.

6	B—Kt5

He tries to solve the problem of the QB, for if 6 .... P—K3; 7 Kt—B3, etc. Best, however, is 6 .... P—KKt3 (7 P—KR3, B—Kt2; 8 Kt—B3, Castles; 9 Castles, P—QR3; 10 R—K1, P—QKt4, with chances to either side).

7 P—B3	

Here 7 Q—Kt3 (7 .... Q—B1) or 7 Kt—K2 (7 .... Q—Q2) would be quite safe. But the most natural move is again 7 Kt—B3 (e.g. 7 .... P—K3; 8 QKt—Q2, B—Q3; 9 B×B, Q×B; 10 Castles, Castles; 11 Q—B2, KR—K1; 12 QR—K1, with the threat of 13 Kt—K5).

7	B—R4
8 Kt—K2	P—K3
9 Kt—Q2	B—Q3
10 B—Kt3	Q—B2
11 Kt—Kt3	B—Kt3

As all the dangerous Bishops will now be eliminated, Black has satisfactorily solved the difficulties of the opening. A stubborn —if simplified—*positional struggle* now follows.

12 R—QB1	QB×B
13 Q×B	Castles KR
14 B×B	Q×B
15 Castles	KR—K1
16 Kt—Kt3	P—KKt3
17 QR—K1	QR—B1

He gives up all idea of advancing the KP and concentrates on the semi-open QB file.

18 R—K2	Kt—Kt1
19 P—QR4	

A picturesque episode. Its tactical object is to prevent .... QKt—Q2—Kt3—B5.

19	KKt—Q2
20 P—R5	Q—R3
21 Q×Q	P×Q
22 R—R1	R—B2
23 Kt—QB1	KR—QB1
24 Kt—Q3	R—Kt2
25 R—R3	Kt—QB3
26 Kt—KB1	R—Kt4
27 P—QKt4	Kt—Q1
28 Kt—K3	R (Kt4)—Kt1
29 K—B2	Kt—Kt2
30 Kt—QB5	Kt (Q2)×Kt
31 KtP×Kt	

The birth of a passed pawn—an important asset.

31	Kt—Q1
32 P—KB4	Kt—B3
33 Kt—Kt4	R—Kt8
34 Kt—K5	Kt × Kt
35 BP × Kt	K—B1
36 K—K3	KR—Kt1
37 R—KB2	K—K2
38 R—B2	K—Q2
39 R (R3)—R2	KR—Kt6
40 K—Q3	R—Q8 ch
41 R—Q2	R—QB8
42 R (R2)—B2	R (B8)—QKt8
43 R—B2	K—K2
44 P—B6	

The will to win.

44	R—Kt1
45 P—B4	R (Kt8)—Kt6 ch
46 R—B3	P × P ch
47 K × P	R (Kt6)—Kt5 ch

At the cross-roads. If 47 .... R × R ch; 48 K × R, R—QB1, seemingly winning a pawn, then 49 P—Q5, P × P; 50 R—B6, followed by K—Q4, etc., marks White's advantage.

48 K—Q3	R—QB1

If 48 .... R—Q1; 49 P—B7

49 K—K3	R—Kt4
50 R—R2	R—B1

He wants to entrust the King with the task of keeping watch over the adverse passed pawn.

51 P—Kt4	K—Q1
52 P—B7 ch	K—B1

He deems the regrouping to be successfully accomplished.

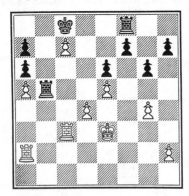

53 R—KB2
A brilliant thought. Even in this simplified position he manages to find sacrificial combinations.

53	R × P
54 R—QB6	

Threat of 55 R × KP.

54	R—R6 ch
55 K—K4	K—Q2
56 R × P ch	K × R
57 R × R	K × P
58 R—B7 ch	K—Q1
59 R × KRP	

After all his turmoil the numerical balance remains undisturbed, but the domination of the seventh rank and the compact formation of White's pawns rapidly decide the game in his favour.

59	P—Kt4
60 R—KKt7	R—R6
61 R × KtP	R × P
62 R—Kt8 ch	K—B2
63 R—Kt6	P—R4
64 R × P	K—Kt2
65 R—KB6	R—KKt7
66 P—K6	R × P ch
67 K—Q5	K—B2
68 R—B7 ch	K—Q1
69 R × P	R—R5
70 K—B5	Resigns.

287

White	*Black*
ALEKHINE	WINTER

(London, 1932)

The attack in the following game is very difficult, conducted as it is practically without any qualitative superiority in material. That it succeeds is due to the transcendental skill displayed here by Alekhine.

1 P—K4	P—QB3
2 P—Q4	P—Q4
3 P × P	P × P
4 P—QB4	

The *modern attack*, which, however, is not new, and was adopted already in a game Réti-Duras, *Vienna*, 1908.

4	Kt—KB3
5 Kt—QB3	Kt—B3

The crucial moment. If 5 .... P—K3, White can at once adopt a blockading strategy by 6 P—B5, and play for an end game with a majority of pawns on the Q side.
Against 5 .... P—KKt3 White plays

neither 6 B—Kt5, Kt—K5, etc., nor 6 P—B5, B—Kt2, but with good effect 6 Q—Kt3, e.g. 6 .... B—Kt2 (deciding on the positional sacrifice of a pawn); 7 P×P, Castles; 8 B—K2, followed by B—B3, etc., to White's advantage.

That is why the best course is to revert to a well-known variant of the *Queen's Gambit Accepted* by 5 .... P×P; 6 B×P, P—K3; 7 Kt—B3, P—QR3; 8 P—QR4, Kt—B3, etc.

6 Kt—B3
The *Caro-Kann* rectangle. If 6 P×P, Kt×P; 7 B—QB4, B—K3, holding his own.

6 ......   B—Kt5
If 6 .... B—B4 or 6 .... B—K3, or even 6 .... P—K3, the blockading advance 7 P—B5 is already justified.

A tense struggle arises from 6 .... P—KKt3, and a simplified contest from 6 .... P×P; 7 B×P, P—K3, etc.

7 P×P
An interesting idea, eventually sacrificing a pawn, is 7 B—K2, e.g. 7 .... P×P; 8 P—Q5, etc., or 7 .... P—K3; 8 P—B5.

7 ......   KKt×P
8 B—QKt5
Threatening 9 Q—R4. But if at once 8 Q—Kt3, the continuation 8 .... B×Kt; 9 P×B, P—K3; 10 Q×P, Kt×P; 11 B—Kt5 ch, Kt×B; 12 Q—B6 ch, K—K2; 13 Q×QKt, Kt×Kt; 14 P×Kt, Q—Q4 restores the balance.

8 ......   Q—R4
Trying to parry the threat by a hazardous counter - stroke. After 8 .... R—B1; 9 P—KR3, B×Kt; 10 Q×B, P—K3; 11 Castles, White is slightly ahead in development. On the other hand, if 8 .... P—K3, then 9 Q—R4, followed by 10 Kt—K5. The simplest is therefore 8 .... B×Kt, followed by 9 .... P—K3.

9 Q—Kt3
The *coup juste*.

9 ......   B×Kt
10 P×B   Kt×Kt
One worry the less.

11 P×Kt
A wise procedure. Against the trap 11 B×Kt ch, P×B; 12 Q—Kt7, the highly amusing continuation of a game Nimzowitsch—Alekhine, *Bled*, 1931, was: 12 .... Kt—Q4 dis ch (the unforeseen counter-trap); 13 B—Q2, Q—Kt3 (shutting in the venturesome Queen); 14 Q×R ch, K—Q2; 15 Castles KR, Kt—B2, and Black wins.

11 ......   P—K3
If 11 .... Castles; 12 P—Q5, R×P; 13 Q×R, Q×P ch; 14 K—K2, Q×R; 15 B×Kt, and wins.

12 P—Q5   P×P
13 Castles   Castles
If 13 .... B—K2; 14 R—K1.

14 B×Kt   P×B
15 R—Kt1   Q—B2
After 15 .... K—Q2 the attack continues with 16 P—QB4.

16 Q—R4   R—Q2
17 B—Q2
Threatening 18 Q—R6 ch, K—Q1; 19 P—QB4, with a view to B—R5.

17 ......   B—B4
18 P—QB4   K—Q1
The *flight of the King* is the best defence, for if 18 .... P×P; 19 Q—R6 ch, K—Q1; 20 B—R5, B—Kt3; 21 R×B, etc., or 18 .... B—Kt3; 19 P—B5, B×P; 20 Q—R6 ch, etc.

19 B—R5   B—Kt3
20 B×B   P×B
21 Q—R8 ch   Q—B1
22 Q—R3
Keeping up the threats in spite of increasingly reduced material 22 Q×Q ch, K×Q; 23 R×P, P×P, etc., yields nothing.

22 ......   Q—Kt1
23 P×P   P×P
The decisive mistake. After 23 .... R×P a stubborn resistance would still be possible, e.g. 24 KR—K1, R—K1, etc., or 24 R—Kt4, P—QKt4, etc.

The best course after 23 .... R×P would therefore be 24 KR—Q1.

24 R—Kt4
Threatening R—QR4—R8. The parry quoted above, 24 .... P—QKt4, is no longer effective on account of 25 Q—R5 ch, Q—B2; 26 Q×P.

24 ......   Q—Q3
25 R—K1   R—B2
26 Q—Kt3   R—K1
27 R—Q1   R—K4
28 R×KtP   R—B3
29 R×R   R—Kt4 ch
30 K—R1   Q×R
31 R—K1   Q—B3
Black is compelled to leave the King to his fate, e.g. 31 .... Q—B2; 32 Q—K3, etc.

32 Q—Kt8 ch   K—Q2
33 P—B4
An intermediary *finesse*, which clinches matters.

| 33 ...... | R—Kt3 |
| 34 Q—K8 ch | K—B2 |

Or 34 .... K—Q3; 35 R—QB1.

35 R—B1 ch	K—Kt3
36 R—Kt1 ch	K—B4
37 Q—Kt5 ch	Resigns

(37 .... K—Q5; 38 R—Q1 ch, K—K5; 39 Q×P ch; and if 37 .... K—Q3; 38 Q—Kt6 ch, K—Q2; 39 Q—R7 ch, forcing mate or the gain of the Queen.)

288

| White | Black |
| DAKE | ALEKHINE |

(Pasadena, 1932)

In the following game an interesting idea (15 .... R—R2) is refuted by an unexpected combination (24 Kt—Kt5).

1 P—K4	P—QB3
2 P—Q4	P—Q4
3 P×P	P×P
4 P—QB4	

A favourite continuation of Alekhine's is applied against himself.

4	Kt—KB3
5 Kt—QB3	Kt—B3
6 Kt—B3	

In the *Four Knights' Variation* of the *Caro-Kann* Black has a wide but difficult choice of moves.

| 6 ...... | B—K3 |

A novelty without a future. In this variation the development of the QB is an arduous problem. If 6 .... B—B4; 7 P—B5, and if 6 .... B—Kt5; 7 P×P, KKt×P; 8 B—QKt5, etc., in favour of White.

The most level-headed course is therefore 6 .... P—K3, for if then 7 P×P, P×P, the play of the pieces slows down. On the other hand, if 7 P—B5, White's pawn play will require the utmost precision. Various variations of the *Queen's Gambit Accepted* can be evoked by 6 .... P×P; 7 B×P, P—K3, etc., and the outlines of a *King's Indian Defence* obtrude themselves after 6 .... P—KKt3.

| 7 P—B5 | |

Strategy of the *blockade*.

7	P—KKt3
8 B—QKt5	B—Kt2
9 Kt—K5	Q—B1
10 Q—R4	B—Q2
11 Castles	Castles
12 B—KB4	

He tries to maintain his hold on the strong point K5.

| 12 ...... | P—QR3 |

Dangerous though it may appear, Black should have tried to minimise the adverse pressure by playing 12 .... Kt—KR4 at once.

13 B×Kt	P×B
14 KR—K1	Kt—R4
15 B—Q2	

Thus White remains master of his K5, and he now threatens 16 QKt×P.

15	R—R2
16 R—K2	B—K1
17 QR—K1	P—B4
18 Kt—B3	Kt—B3

The continuation of the scheme, initiated by Black on his 15th move and embodying a fairly hazardous pawn sacrifice. If 18 .... B—B3; 19 B—Kt5.

| 19 R×P | R×R |
| 20 R×R | P—B5 |

The sacrifice of a pawn now brings another in its wake, Black's hope being to obtain compensating pressure on the KB file. If 20 .... Kt—K5; 21 B—B4, and White controls all important lines of communications.

21 B×P	Kt—K5
22 B—K5	B—R3
23 Kt×Kt	P×Kt

Now, more than ever, Black looks like realising some serious counter-play on the K side, but a sensational surprise is to play havoc with Alekhine's conceptions.

| 24 Kt—Kt5 | Q—B4 |

If 24 .... B×Kt; 25 R—Kt7 ch, K—R1; 26 R—QB7 dis ch.

25 Q—Kt3 ch	B—B2
26 Kt×B	R×Kt
27 R×R	Q×R
28 Q—Kt8 ch	

Better than 28 Q×Q ch, K×Q; 29 K—B1, K—K3; etc., which would allow Black to construct a relatively sound line of defence.

| 28 ...... | Q—B1 |

After 28 .... B—B1; 29 B—Q6, White would achieve a general liquidation of the piece, and, with two extra pawns, victory would be virtually his.

29 P—Q5

The "centre-forward" pierces the front and goes in to Queen.

29	P—K6
30 P—B4	Q×Q
31 B×Q	K—B2

Trying the impossible. The white pawn formation on the Q side is irresistible.

32 P×P	K—K1
33 P—QKt4	K—Q1
34 P—QR4	K—B1
35 B—Q6	P—Kt4
36 P—Kt3	P×P
37 P×P	B—Kt2
38 K—B1	Resigns.

289

White	Black
BOTVINNIK	FLOHR

(Match, 1933)

While it is generally admitted that two Bishops are superior to two Knights, it is not always easy to demonstrate the fact.

The lucid and consistent manner in which Black here exploits this advantage stamps his performance as masterly. The finish is most original: a sacrifice of a piece in the ultimate phase of the game—a rare occurrence.

1 P—K4	P—QB3
2 P—Q4	P—Q4
3 P×P	P×P
4 P—QB4	Kt—KB3
5 Kt—QB3	Kt—B3
6 B—Kt5	

Direct action, threatening to win a pawn by 7 B×Kt and 8 P×P. The value of this *Nordic Attack*, much analysed by Leningrad experts, is not overpowering. It was recommended in 1911 by the Danish theoretician Dr. Krause.

6	P×P

The soundest is 6 .... P—K3.

Against 6 .... Q—Kt3, the continuation of a game Botvinnik-Spielmann, *Moscow*, 1935, a dreadful example, was: 7 P×P (not 7 P—B5, Q × KtP; 8 KKt—K2, B—B4, with the threat .... Kt—QKt5; safest is 7 Q—Q2); 7 .... Q×KtP (ruinous; with 7 .... QKt×P; 8 B—K3, P—K4; 9 P×P e.p., B—B4, etc., Black, at the cost of a pawn, obtains considerable counter-chances);

8 R—B1, Kt—QKt5 (or—the lesser evil— 8 .... Kt—Q1; 9 B—QB4, threatening 10 Kt—Kt5); 9 Kt—R4, Q × RP; 10 B—QB4, B—Kt5; 11 Kt—KB3 (not 11 P—B3, Q×P); 11 .... Q—R6; 12 R—B3, and Black resigns, as the Queen can be saved only at the cost of a piece.

7 P—Q5	Kt—K4

A more stubborn contest arises from 7 .... Kt—QR4, etc.

8 Q—Q4	

Now, thanks to the attack on the QKt, the Queen gets into play without loss of time.

8	Kt—Q6 ch
9 B×Kt	P×B
10 B×Kt	

But this hasty exchange nullifies his previous efforts, for it facilitates his opponent's development. In a subsequent game in the same match 10 Kt—B3 was played, considerably enhancing White's prospects.

10	KP×B

He decided to "decentralise" and even to liberate the adverse QP, and all for the sake of obtaining free play for his pieces.

11 Q×QP	B—Q3

As long as the hostile passed pawn remains blocked, there is no danger.

12 KKt—K2	Castles
13 Castles KR	R—K1
14 QR—Q1	B—KKt5

There is now a set battle of Bishops *v.* Knights.

15 R—Q2	P—QR3

He limits more and more the activity of the opposing Knights.

16 Kt—Kt3	QR—B1
17 P—KR3	B—Q2
18 KR—Q1	P—KKt3

Delimitation on the other wing.

19 R—K2	R×R

He willingly agrees to simplification.

20 KKt×R	P—B4
21 Kt—Q4	Q—K2
22 Q—Q2	R—K1
23 Kt—B3	Q—B3
24 R—K1	R×R ch
25 Kt×R	P—QKt4
26 P—R3	K—Kt2
27 Kt—B3	B—QB1
28 K—B1	B—Kt2
29 P—QKt4	K—B1
30 K—K2	

Plausible as this move appears, the right

course, for tactical reasons difficult to fore-see, is 30 K—K1.

30 ......   P—QR4
Leading to beautiful lines of play in an ending which promised to remain constricted and dry.

31 Q—Q4
For 31 Kt×P, B—R3 would be in Black's favour.

31 ......   Q×Q
32 Kt×Q   P×P
33 QKt×P
Or 33 P×P, KB×P; 34 KKt×KtP, B—R3; 35 K—Q1 (35 K—K3, B—B4 ch); 35 .... KB×Kt; 36 Kt×B, B—B8, winning a valuable pawn.

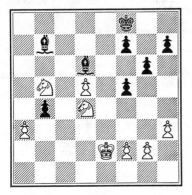

33 ......   P×P
This unexpected sacrifice of a piece is very accurately calculated.

34 Kt×B   P—R7
35 Kt—B2   B—R3 ch
36 K—K3   K—K2
Recovering the piece.

37 Kt×P
Keeping the adverse King away. Capturing the other pawn would not improve matters.

37 ......   K×Kt
38 K—Q4   B—B8
39 P—R4   B×P
40 K—B5
A tragi-comic situation. White's passed pawn cannot be used to advantage.

40 ......   P—B5
          Resigns
(41 K—Q4, K—B3, etc.)

290

White	Black
LÖWENFISCH	*NIMZOWITSCH*

(Vilna, 1912)

Here both sides invade enemy territory. But while the white Queen's only object seems to be an unfortunate pawn (16 Q × P), Black's QKt and QB, settled inside the opposite lines, succeed in destroying the co-operation of the white forces.

1 P—K4   P—QB3
2 P—QB4
Although called "modern," this continuation was adopted in many an ancient game. The object is to blockade the square at Q5. The same position occurs after 1 P—QB4, P—QB3; 2 P—K4.

2 ......   P—K3
A sedate reply. A trenchant continuation is 2 .... P—Q4; e.g. 3 KP×P, P×P; 4 P×P (or 4 P—Q4, the *Panoff Attack*); 4 .... Kt—KB3 (or 4 .... Q×P; 5 Kt—QB3, Q—QR4, as in the *Centre Counter Defence*); 5 B—Kt5 ch, QKt—Q2; 6 Kt—QB3, P—QR3; 7 B—K2, Kt—Kt3, and Black recovers his pawn without damage.

3 Kt—KB3
Stressing the rapid deployment of the K side forces. After 3 P—Q4, P—Q4; 4 BP×P, KP×P; 5 P×P, P×P; 6 Kt—QB3, Kt—KB3; 7 Kt—B3, B—K2; 8 B—Q3, Castles; 9 Castles, B—KKt5, etc., as played already in 1843 in the twentieth game of the Staunton—St. Amant match in Paris!

3 ......   P—Q4
4 KP×P   KP×P
5 P×P   P×P
He declines to speculate, by 5 .... Q×P; 6 Kt—B3, Q—Q1; 7 P—Q4, on the isolation of the QP, which in this position would be a powerful weapon.

6 B—Kt5 ch   Kt—B3
7 Castles   B—Q3
Instead of the modest routine development 7 .... Kt—B3; 8 R—K1 ch, B—K2, etc., Black has in view a more flexible deployment of his forces.

8 P—Q4   Kt—K2
9 B—Kt5
Here the pin is ineffective. After 9 P—KR3, Castles; 10 Kt—B3 (or 10 B—Q3, Kt—Kt5); 10 .... B—KB4; 11 B—Q3, Q—Q2, etc., Black would have disputed the control of the vital diagonal.

9	P—B3
10 B—KR4	Castles
11 QKt—Q2	

If 11 P—KR3, Kt—B4, which is why White allows his Knight to be pinned.

11	B—KKt5

Relying on the mobile grouping of his forces, Black relinquishes the defence of his base.

12 B×Kt

More solid, but also less active, would be 12 B—K2.

12	Kt×B

After 12 .... P×B, he would suffer from a chronic weakness at his QB3.

13 Q—Kt3

An optimistic *sortie*. Better is 13 P—KR3.

13	B—Kt5
14 Kt—K5	

He has designs on the ill-famed QKtP, but underestimates the increasing resources of his opponent's game.

After 14 P—QR3, KB×Kt; 15 Kt×B, Kt×P; 16 Q×KtP, R—Kt1; 17 Q×RP, Kt—K7 ch; 18 K—R1, R×P, etc., Black dominates the board. If 14 Q—Q3, Q—Q2.

14	Kt×Kt
15 Q×B	Kt—Q6
16 Q×P	B—K7
17 KR—Kt1	

Saving the exchange, but at the cost of a very serious dislocation of his position.

17	R—B1
18 Kt—B1	

Or 18 Q×RP, R—B7.

18	P—Kt4

By this recrudescence of energy—courageously accepting the risks—Black forces a decision in his favour.

19 B—Kt3	P—B4
20 B—K5	R—KB2
21 Q—R6	

Intending 22 Kt—Kt3.

21	P—B5

Decisive. Of no value would be 21 .... Kt×B; 22 Q×B, etc., or 21 .... Kt—B5; 22 Q—R6, etc.

22 R—K1

A desperate bid for salvation. If 22 P—B3, R—B7.

22	Kt×R
23 Q×B	

Hoping, in case of 23 .... Kt—B7; 24 Q—R5, etc., to take advantage of the breaches in the adverse King's field.

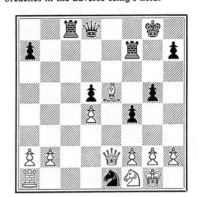

23	Kt×P

Ruthless. But in spite of the deep rents in his position, White still offers a stubborn resistance.

24 Kt—Q2	Kt—R5
25 Kt—B3	Kt—Kt3
26 K—R1	P—Kt5
27 Kt—Q2	Q—Q2
28 R—KKt1	R—B7

Convincing. If 29 R×P, P—B6, etc.; and if 29 Q—Q3, Q—B4, etc.

29 P—KR3	P—Kt6

White resigns.

291

White	Black
TARRASCH	RÉTI

(Vienna, 1922)

In the following magnificent game, the most striking feature is the impressive march of the white King from KKt1 to KB7, in order to "mate" his luckless adversary.

1 P—K4	P—QB3
2 Kt—QB3	

This move (as also 2 Kt—KB3) is dictated by the modern tendency to avoid the beaten track.

| 2 ...... | P—Q4 |
| 3 Kt—B3 | Kt—B3 |

Quite useless would be 3 .... P—Q5 (4 Kt—K2, P—QB4; 5 Kt—Kt3, etc.). If 3 .... B—Kt5; 4 P—KR3, B—R4 (or 4 .... B×Kt; 5 Q×B, P—K3; 6 P—QKt3, with a clear advantage to White); 5 P×P, P×P; 6 P—KKt4, B—Kt3; 7 Kt—K5, and White has the initiative.

After 3 .... P×P, the painful continuation of a game Lasker-Raadsheer (from a simultaneous performance in Holland) was as follows: 4 Kt×P, B—B4 (better, 4 .... Kt—B3; 5 Kt×Kt ch, KP×Kt, etc., or 5 Kt—Kt3, P—B4, etc.); 5 Kt—Kt3, B—Kt3; 6 P—KR4, P—KR3 (better, 6 .... P—B3); 7 Kt—K5, B—R2 (or 7 .... Q—Q3; 8 P—Q4, etc.); 8 Q—R5, P—KKt3 (if 8 .... Q—Q4; 9 B—B4); 9 B—B4 (pretty, for if 9 .... P×Q; 10 B×P mate); 9 .... P—K3; 10 Q—K2, B—Kt2 (plausible, but fatal); 11 Kt×KBP, resigns.

4 P×P

He decides on a "clean-up" in the centre, in preference to complications by 4 P—K5, Kt—K5; 5 P—Q3, Kt×Kt; 6 P×Kt, P—K3, etc.

4	P×P
5 P—Q4	B—Kt5
6 P—KR3	B×Kt

After 6 .... B—R4; 7 P—KKt4, B—Kt3; 8 Kt—K5, followed by P—KR4, and White's initiative would become troublesome.

7 Q×B	P—K3
8 B—Q3	Kt—B3
9 B—K3	B—K2

If 9 .... Q—Kt3; 10 Castles KR, Q×KtP; 11 Kt—Kt5, etc.; or 10 .... Kt×P; 11 Q—B4, B—B4; 12 Kt—R4, winning a piece.

| 10 Castles KR | Castles |
| 11 P—R3 | |

To prevent 11 .... Kt—QKt5.

| 11 ...... | P—QR3 |

But in the case of Black this move has attacking tendencies.

12 Kt—K2	P—QKt4
13 B—KB4	Q—Kt3
14 P—B3	Kt—QR4
15 QR—Q1	Kt—B5
16 B—B1	Q—B3

Trying to put the other Knight into play by .... Kt—K5, followed by .... P—B4.

| 17 Kt—Kt3 | P—QR4 |
| 18 KR—K1 | |

Having neutralised Black's efforts on the Q side, White turns his attention to the centre with a powerful threat, 19 Kt—B5.

| 18 ...... | P—Kt5 |

Too much wrapped up in his own schemes, Black omits to cut across his opponent's intentions by 18 .... R—R2 (or 18 .... KR—K1).

| 19 RP×P | P×P |
| 20 Kt—B5 | |

Seizing the initiative.

| 20 ...... | P×Kt |

He has nothing better, e.g. 20 .... B—Q3; 21 B×Kt, P×Kt; 22 B—B1, etc.; or 20 .... B—Q1; 21 Kt—R6 ch, K—R1; 22 Kt—Kt4, etc.; or 20 .... KR—K1; 21 Kt×B ch, R×Kt; 22 B—Kt5, Kt×P; 23 B×Kt, P×B; 24 B×P ch, K×B; 25 Q×BP, with a winning attack; or, finally, 20 .... Q—B2; 21 Kt×B ch, Q×Kt; 22 B×Kt, P×B; 23 P—Q5, etc., with a definite advantage to White.

21 R×B	P×P
22 P×P	P—Kt3
23 B—R6	Kt—Kt7

Artificial. Better is 23 .... KR—K1.

| 24 R—Kt1 | Kt×B |
| 25 Q×Kt | |

Incautious would be the gain of the exchange by 25 B×R, because of 25 .... Q×P; 26 R—K3, R—R8, etc.

| 25 ...... | KR—Kt1 |

If 25 .... KR—K1; 26 QR—Kt7.

26 R×R ch	R×R
27 Q—Kt3	R—Q1
28 Q—K5	R—R1
29 R—B7	

Forcing the exchange of Queens, on account of the threat 30 Q—K7. There follows a problem-like ending extending over twenty moves!

29	Q—K3
30 Q×Q	P×Q
31 R—Kt7 ch	K—R1
32 R—K7	K—Kt1

Clearly not 32 .... Kt—Kt1; 33 B—Kt7 mate.

| 33 P—B3 | |

Remarkably subtle. If 33 R×KP, K—B2, etc., the black King escapes, and Black obtains counter-chances on account of the weakness of White's QB3. If at once 33 K—R2, Kt—K5.

33 ......   Kt—K1
34 K—R2

An imposing journey begins.

34 ......   Kt—Q3
35 R—Kt7 ch   K—R1
36 R—Q7

Forcing the Knight to a decision.

36 ......   Kt—Kt4
37 K—Kt3

All this is splendidly timed.

37 ......   Kt×BP
38 K—B4   Kt—Kt4
39 K—K5   R—K1
40 K—B6

A terrible threat: 41 K—B7, R—KKt1;
42 R—Q8. Black capitulated at this stage
on account of 40 .... K—Kt1; 41 R—Kt7
ch, K—R1; 42 R—Kt7, Kt—Q3; 43 R—Q7,
Kt—Kt4; 44 K—B7, R—KKt1; 45 R—Q8,
Kt—Q3 ch; 46 R×Kt, P—Kt4; 47 R—Q8,
R×R; 48 B—Kt7 mate.

292

White	Black
White	*Black*
MILNER-BARRY	TARTAKOWER

(London, 1932)

*In the following game White scores a
brilliant win, his manœuvres combining skill
with the utmost energy.*

1 P—K4   P—QB3
2 P—Q4   Kt—B3

An experiment which lacks the elasticity
of *Alekhine's Defence*, 1 P—K4, Kt—KB3;
2 P—K5, Kt—Q4; 3 P—QB4, Kt—Kt3,
etc., or the activity deployed in the centre by
the *Sicilian Defence*, 1 P—K4, P—QB4;
2 Kt—KB3, Kt—KB3; 3 P—K5, Kt—Q4;
4 P—B4, Kt—B2, etc.

3 P—K5

A straightforward line of play. Less good
is the defence of a pawn by 3 B—Q3,
because of 3 .... P—Q3; 4 Kt—KB3,
P—K4 (this important thrust is possible
here, for if 5 P×P, P×P; 6 Kt×P, Q—R4
ch, followed by .... Q×Kt); 5 Kt—B3,
Q—B2, and Black has reverted to a perfectly
playable *Philidor Defence, Hanham Variation*. Very good, however, is the defence of
the pawn by 3 Kt—QB3, e.g. 3 .... P—Q4;

4 P—K5, etc., or 3 .... P—Q3; 4 P—B3 (or
more violently, 4 P—B4); 4 .... Q—B2
(trying to effect the thrust 5 .... P—K4, but
White prevents this also); 5 P—K5, with a
gain in space.

3 ......   Kt—Q4
4 P—QB4   Kt—B2
5 Kt—QB3   P—Q3
6 P—B4

Instead of this variation *on a wide front*,
6 P×P affords an easy game.

6 ......   P×P
7 BP×P   P—KKt3

He procrastinates instead of proceeding at
once to undermine the enemy outpost by
7 .... P—K3, followed by .... P—QB4.

8 Kt—B3   B—Kt2
9 B—K3   P—B3
10 P×P   P×P

Preferring to shut in his KB, rather than
to create by 10 .... B×P a lasting weakness
at his K2.

11 Q—Q2   Castles
12 Castles   B—K3
13 B—R6   B×B
14 Q×B   Q—Q2
15 B—Q3   Kt (Kt1)—R3
16 P—KR4

A well-known stratagem.

16 ......   Kt—Kt5
17 B—K2   Q—B2

Playing with fire, as White's energetic
reply demonstrates. Better is 17 ....
Q—Kt2 at once.

18 KR—B1

In order to refute 18 .... B×P by
19 Kt—KKt5.

18 ......   Q—Kt2
19 Q×Q ch   K×Q
20 P—R3   Kt (Kt5)—R3
21 P—Q5   P×P
22 P×P   B—Q2
23 Kt—Q4   QR—B1
24 K—Kt1   Kt—B4
25 B—B3

This ideally placed Bishop will exert a
dominating influence. The advance P—Q6
will remain as a potential threat.

25 ......   QR—Q1
26 KR—K1

Very strong.

26 ......   KR—K1

Although there is as yet no definite danger,

it would be too onerous for Black to allow his opponent the freedom of the open K file. If e.g. 26 .... R—B2; 27 P—QKt4, Kt—R5; 28 Kt×Kt, B×Kt; 29 P—Q6, R×P (29 .... B×R; 30 P×Kt, etc.); 30 Kt—B5 ch, White wins the exchange.

27 R×R　　　　R×R

If 27 .... Kt×R; 28 P—QKt4, Kt—R3 (clearly not 28 .... Kt—R5; 29 Kt×Kt, B×Kt; 30 Kt—K6 ch, and wins); 29 KKt—Kt5, B×Kt; 30 Kt×B, R—R1; 31 P—Q6, a triumphal advance; and if 27 .... B×R; 28 P—QKt4, Kt—R5; 29 Kt×Kt, B×Kt; 30 P—Q6, etc.

28 P—QKt4　　　Kt—R5

Or 28 .... QKt—R3; 29 P—Q6, winning the QKtP.

29 Kt×Kt　　　B×Kt
30 R—QB1

A striking example of how the occupation of an open file can lead to victory.

30 ......　　　　Kt—Kt4

This gives White the opportunity of winning a piece in a most astute manner. But it is evident that after any other move (30 .... Kt—R3 or 30 .... Kt—R1, to say

nothing of 30 .... R—QB1 or 30 .... R—K2), the advance 31 P—Q6 secures for White gain in material. After 30 .... Kt—R3, White also wins material by 31 P—Kt5, Kt—Kt1; 32 R—B4, R—K8 ch; 33 K—Kt2, B—Q8; 34 R—B1, B×B; 35 R×R, B×QP; 36 R—K8, Kt—Q2; 37 R—K7 ch, followed by R×Kt, and White is a Rook ahead.

31 Kt—K6 ch　　K—R3
32 Kt—B5　　　Kt×P ch
33 K—Kt2　　　Kt—B7
34 Kt×B　　　　Kt×P
35 R—B7　　　　P—QKt4
36 Kt—B5　　　R—K4
37 P—Q6

To wind up, White forces the win in the most elegant manner.

37 ......　　　　R×Kt
38 P—Q7

The point! Whereas 38 R×R would be catastrophic, on account of 38 .... Kt—Q6 ch, followed by .... Kt×R.

38 ......　　　　Kt—Q6 ch
39 K—Kt1　　　R×R
40 P—Q8 (Q)　　R—B8 ch
41 K—R2　　　　Resigns.

18. THE SICILIAN DEFENCE

293

White	Black
McDONNELL	DE LA BOURDONNAIS

(Match, 1834)

In the following game, a game of a monumental character, White succeeds in establishing a vast and unbroken chain of pawns, ranging originally from QKt2—K5. Under the shelter of this screen, he prepares and establishes a blockade—in the true sense of the word—of the opposing King's field. The decisive break-through is then only a question of time.

1 P—K4   P—QB4
2 P—KB4
A very fashionable continuation in former times. Subsequently it fell into disuse when if was found that the position becomes too exposed thereby.

2 ......   P—K3
Leading to a variation of the *French Defence*. Another plan, which treats the centre with more discretion, is 2 .... P—Q3, soon to be followed by .... P—KKt3 and .... B—Kt2, etc.

3 Kt—KB3   P—Q4
4 P—K5
He prefers complications to the liquidating continuation 4 P×P, P×P; 5 P—Q4, Kt—QB3; 6 B—Kt5, etc.

4 ......   Kt—QB3
5 P—B3
A supporting move. White's main idea in this variant is to maintain a chain of pawns in the centre.
Less consistent is 5 B—Kt5, and spineless would be 5 P—Q3, followed by B—K2 or 5 P—KKt3, followed by B—Kt2.

5 ......   P—B3
An important decision. In a subsequent game of the same match, the continuation was 5 .... P—B4; 6 B—Q3, B—K2; 7 B—B2, Q—Kt3; 8 Castles, etc. Other continuations are 5 .... Kt—R3 and 5 .... Q—Kt3.

6 Kt—R3
An ingenious manœuvre originated by McDonnell. Another line of play is

6 B—Q3, Kt—R3; 7 B—B2, Q—Kt3; 8 Castles, etc.

6 ......   Kt—R3
7 Kt—B2
Not at once 7 P—Q4, because of 7 .... P×P and 8 .... B×Kt.

7 ......   B—K2
Another game of the same match continued 7 .... Q—Kt3; 8 P—Q4, QBP×P; 9 BP×P, B—Kt5 ch (or 9 .... B—Q2; 10 P—KR4, R—B1; 11 B—K2, etc.); 10 Kt×B, Q×Kt ch; 11 K—B2, Castles; 12 P—QR3, Q—Kt3, etc.

8 P—Q4   Castles
9 B—Q3   P—B5
Driving off the KB from an effective diagonal. But he thereby renounces any counter-action on the Q side.

10 B—K2   B—Q2
11 Castles   P—QKt4
The pawn's progress has no objective of any value.

12 Kt—K3   P—R4
13 K—R1   P×P
If 13 .... P—B4; 14 R—KKt1, followed by P—KKt4, and White obtains an open file for his evolutions.

14 BP×P   Kt—B4
15 P—KKt4
Foreshadowing ambitious plans.

15 ......   Kt×Kt
16 B×Kt   B—K1
In order to harry the adverse King, boldly denuded of supporting forces, from K5 *via* KKt3.

17 Q—Q2   B—Kt3
18 Kt—Kt5   B×Kt
Or 18 .... Q—Q2; 19 P—KR4, P—R3; 20 P—R5, cutting across the black Queen's Bishop's plans (e.g. 20 .... B—K1; 21 Kt—R3, etc., or 20 .... B×Kt; 21 P×B, B×B; 22 Q×B, etc.).

19 B×B   Q—Q2
A little better would be the interpolation 19 .... B—K5 ch; 20 K—Kt1, Q—Q2, etc.

20 P—KR4   P—Kt5
He hopes to achieve something on the Q side, but he should play for simplification

by 20 .... R×R ch; 21 R×R, R—KB1, etc.

21 K—R2	P×P
22 P×P	P—R5
23 P—R5	B—K5
24 P—R6	

Driving a powerful wedge into the enemy's lines.

24	P—Kt3
25 B—B6	QR—Kt1
26 B—Kt7	Q—K2
27 K—Kt3	R×R
28 R×R	P—R6
29 B—B6	Kt—R4

Unable to be of assistance on the K side (29 .... Kt—Q1; 30 R—B8 ch), the trusty Knight seeks other, and very aggressive, ways of being useful.

| 30 B—Q1 | Kt—Kt6 |

Ingenious, as the capture 31 P×Kt would not be without danger.

31 Q—KB2	Kt—B8
32 B—R4	Kt—Q6
33 Q—B1	P—Kt4

He hopes to be able to follow this up with 34 .... Kt—B5, after which the white patrols (Rook and QB) would be taken unawares. It is clear that Black refuses to remain inactive, yet every pawn move necessarily weakens his case.

| 34 B—B2 | Kt—B4 |

Else 35 B×Kt, B×B; 36 Q—B1, followed by Q×KtP, and if 34 .... Kt—B5; 35 B×B, P×B; 36 Q×P.

35 P×Kt

Entering upon the last—and very picturesque—phase of the contest. Curiously enough, the presence of Bishops of opposite colours, instead of lightening the task of the defence, makes it more difficult because White's Bishop becomes impregnable.

35	B×B
36 P—B6	B—R5
37 P—B7	R—K1
38 Q—B1	

Decisive, as Black's chief bastion (KKtP) now falls.

38	Q×P
39 Q×KtP	B—B7
40 B—B8 dis ch	B—Kt3
41 B×P	

White not only wins a pawn, but, more important still, his Bishop again becomes mobile.

| 41 ...... | Q—Q2 |
| 42 B—Q6 | P—Q5 |

A desperate attempt.

| 43 Q—B4 | Q—B1 |
| 44 Q×P | |

A rich harvest.

| 44 ...... | Q—B3 |

Or e.g. 44 .... Q—Kt2; 45 Q×P, Q—R8; 46 Q×P ch, R×Q; 47 R—B8 mate.

| 45 Q—R7 | |

And White wins.

294

| White | Black |
| ST. AMANT | STAUNTON |

(Match, 1843)

In both this and the preceding game the line of play selected is the ancient variation 2 P—KB4, but in the present case the white chain of pawns is weak at its middle base (Q4). In order to mask this weakness, White has recourse to haphazard manœuvres (P—Q5), but finds that Black's operations on the K side are far more effective.

1 P—K4	P—QB4
2 P—KB4	P—K3
3 Kt—KB3	Kt—QB3
4 P—B3	P—Q4
5 P—K5	Q—Kt3

Instead of opening the K side by 5 .... P—B3 or closing it by 5 .... P—B4, Black, with the text move, embarks on a vast and lasting offensive, which emphasises the hazards of White's second move.

| 6 B—Q3 | |

As White will experience difficulty in maintaining his Bishop on this handsome diagonal, 6 B—K2, followed by Castles, is a rational alternative.

6 ...... B—Q2
7 B—B2
Not yet 7 Castles, P—B5 dis ch.

7 ...... R—B1
8 Castles Kt—R3
9 P—KR3 B—K2
10 K—R2
White attends to "improvements" on the K side, as the development of the other wing is fraught with difficulties. But 10 P—QKt3 would be more useful.

10 ...... P—B4
It will be noticed that Black is in no hurry to castle.

11 P—R3 P—R4
Preventing 12 P—QKt4.

12 P—QR4
He now hopes to utilise the liberated square at QKt5.

12 ...... Kt—B2
13 P—Q4
Compulsory at last, in view of the eventuality of 13 .... P—Kt4.

13 ...... P—R3
14 R—K1 P—Kt3
Eliminating the threat 15 B×P, P×B; 16 P—K6.

15 Kt—R3 P×P
16 Kt×P Kt×Kt
17 P×Kt
Clearly not 17 Q×Kt, Q×Q; 18 P×Q, B×Kt, winning a piece. The weakness of the point Q4 now becomes chronic.

17 ...... P—Kt4
Without delay Black now starts a war of movement on the K side, where he is master.

18 Kt—Kt5 B×Kt
19 P×B
Although safe for the moment, his pawn is an additional vulnerable point in White's position.

19 ...... R—B5
A try-on. 19 .... P×P at once is sound.

20 B—Q3 R—QB1
Not 20 .... R×P; 21 B—K3, etc., but 20 .... R—Kt5 also is dangerous.

21 B—K2 P×P
22 R—B1 Kt—Kt4
23 B×P Kt—K5
24 R—B1 R×R
25 Q×R K—Q2
One of the cases in which the King, not

having castled, feels perfectly comfortable in the centre.

26 Q—K3 B—Kt4
27 B—Q3 R—KKt1
28 B×Kt QP×B
The object of this move is not only to increase the cohesion of his pawns, but also to prevent the irruption of the white Rook on the KB file which would occur after 28 .... BP×B; 29 B×B, etc.

29 B×B P×B
The four massed pawns are impressive.

30 Q—QKt3
Defending the pawn at QKt5 and indirectly the QP also, in the hope eventually of effecting the advance P—Q5.

30 ...... P—Kt5
31 R—Q1
If 31 P—Q5, Q—Q5.

31 ...... P×P
32 Q×P Q—Q1
33 P—Q5
Thus he prevents 33 .... R—R1 (34 P×P dis ch).

33 ...... K—B1
The King steals away.

34 Q—B3 ch K—Kt1
35 P—Q6 P—B5
36 Q—B5
He still hopes to effect the advance 37 P—Kt6, which would tip the balance in his favour. But 36 R—QB1 is better.

36 ...... P—K6
A decisive advance.

37 Q—B2
A precipitate retreat, which is enforced by Black's threat, 37 .... Q—R5 ch; 38 K—Kt1, Q—B7 ch, followed by mate.

37 ...... Q—R5 ch
38 K—Kt1 R—QB1
Driving the Queen away from her aggressive post before administering the death-blow.

39 Q—K2
The Queen is confined to the second rank, or otherwise there follows 39 .... Q—B7 ch, or 39 P—Q7, R×Q; 40 P—Q8 (Q) ch, Q×Q; 41 R×Q ch, K—B2; 42 R—Q1, R×P, and Black wins.

39 ...... R—R1
And Black wins.

295

White	Black
ANDERSSEN	WYVILL

(London, 1851)

In the following game we witness how evil begets evil. Having delayed the advance .... P—Q4; too long, Black later on has to face many worries around that point. In trying to save a pawn (13 .... B×Kt), he allows the opposing QB to occupy the devastated long diagonal, which proves to be suicidal.

1 P—K4   P—QB4
2 B—B4
An archaic continuation (already indicated by Cozzio in 1766), and much favoured by Anderssen.

2 ......   P—K3
A logical reply, cutting the Bishop's diagonal and preparing .... P—Q4, etc.

3 Kt—QB3
Or e.g. 3 Q—K2, Kt—QB3; 4 P—QB3, P—QR3; 5 P—QR4, P—QKt3, etc.

3 ......   P—QR3
An intermezzo of some value, because the positional threat 4 .... P—QKt4; 5 B—K2 (5 B—Kt3, P—B5, and wins); 5 .... B—Kt2 necessitates some counter-measure on the part of Black so that the text move implies at all events no loss of time.
After 3 .... Kt—QB3 at once 4 Kt—B3, Kt—B3; 5 P—Q3, P—Q4 (or 5 .... Kt—QR4; 6 Castles, Kt×B; 7 P×Kt, P—Q3, etc., or, more reservedly, at once 5 .... P—Q3); 6 P×P, P×P; 7 B—QKt5, B—Q2 (the most solid); 8 Castles, B—K2, etc., the games tend to equalise.

4 P—QR4   Kt—QB3
Premature would be 4 .... Kt—KB3 (5 P—K5) and 4 .... Kt—K2 (5 P—Q4).

5 P—Q3
Or, in order to speed up castling, 5 Kt—B3, Kt—B3; 6 Castles (alternatively, 6 P—Q3, P—Q4; 7 P×P, P×P; 8 B—K2, etc.; but premature would be 6 P—K5, Kt—KKt5; 7 Q—K2, Q—B2, and White loses the KP); 6 .... P—Q4; 7 P×P, P×P; 8 R—K1 ch, B—K2; 9 B—B1, Castles, and Black has a very good game.

5 ......   P—KKt3
If 5 .... Kt—B3; 6 B—KKt5, but more to the point than the text move is 5 .... KKt—K2, with a view to 6 .... P—Q4.

6 KKt—K2
A more flexible development than 6 Kt—KB3, which would obstruct the KBP.

6 ......   B—Kt2
7 Castles   KKt—K2
Here again if 7 .... Kt—B3; 8 B—KKt5.

8 P—B4   Castles
9 B—Q2   P—Q4
"Better late than never," thinks Black, but now 9 .... P—Q3 is preferable.

10 B—Kt3
Astute play! Black's position remains tied up, whereas 10 P×P, P×P; 11 B—Kt3, B—K3; would free it at one stroke.

10 ......   Kt—Q5
If 10 .... P×P, White plays 11 P×P, maintaining his hold on the centre, but not 11 Kt×P, B×P, etc.

11 Kt×Kt   B×Kt ch
12 K—R1   B—Q2
A faulty speculation, which, for the time being, abandons the control of Q4. But if 12 .... P×P; 13 Kt×P, B×P; 14 R—QKt1, B—Q5; 15 P—B3, B—Kt2; 16 Kt×P, P—Kt3; 17 Q—B3, R—Kt1; 18 Kt—K4, B—Kt2; 19 Q—K2, with the better chances. The most level-headed procedure is 12 .... P—Kt3, followed by .... B—QKt2.

13 P×P   B×Kt
He gives up the principal defender of the black square zones (especially the long diagonal), which is tantamount to suicide. He should be content to put up as stubborn a defence as possible by 13 .... P×P; 14 Kt×P, KB×P; 15 R—QKt1, B—Kt2; 16 Kt×Kt ch, Q×Kt; 17 B—Q5, B—QB3; 18 B×B, P×B; 19 Q—B3, Q—Q2, etc.

14 B×B   P×P
He underestimates the loophole which is now at White's disposal, and which gives White the absolute mastery of the long diagonal. 14 .... Kt×P is therefore essential, although White has a definite positional advantage after 15 B—Q2, B—B3; 16 Q—Kt4, etc.

15 B—B6
Eluding the threat 15 .... P—Q5, and himself threatening (e.g. after 15 .... B—B3) 16 R—K1, R—K1; 17 Q—K2, etc.

15 ......   B—K3
16 P—B5
In connection with the following sacrifice

of the exchange, this thrust demolishes the black King's triangular rampart. A neat turn.

16 ......   B × P
17 R × B   P × R
18 Q—R5   Q—Q3

With a last hope that after 19 Q—Kt5 ch (an ingenuous check); 19 .... Kt—Kt3; 20 P—R4, Q—B5, all might yet be well.

19 Q—R6   Resigns.

296

White	Black
ANDERSSEN	WYVILL

(London, 1851)

Most skilfully combining the defence of his King's field with aggressive tendencies on the Q side, Black, by a strongly conceived pawn sacrifice (28 .... Kt—K6) succeeds in opening up the Q side, where he launches a strong and persevering attack.

1 P—K4   P—QB4
2 P—Q4

Opening up the centre. A less thorny path to this end is 2 Kt—KB3, and after 2 .... Kt—QB3 or 2 .... P—K3, or also 2 .... P—Q3; 3 P—Q4, P × P; 4 Kt × P, etc.

2 ......   P × P

If 2 .... P—K3; 3 P—Q5.

3 Kt—KB3

A simplifying continuation is 3 Q × P, Kt—QB3; 4 Q—K3.

3 ......   Kt—QB3

He makes no attempt to conserve his gain, which he could do—but only at the expense of his development—by 3 .... Q—R4 ch; 4 P—B3 (4 B—Q2, Q—Kt3); 4 .... P × P; 5 Kt × P, etc.

4 Kt × P   P—K3

Or first 4 .... Kt—B3; 5 Kt—QB3, and only now 5 .... P—K3.

5 B—K3

He defends his KKt in good time, leaving it to the other Bishop to guard his KP, but after this manœuvre neither Bishop will be altogether comfortable. The most rational is 5 Kt—QB3.

5 ......   Kt—B3
6 B—Q3   B—K2

He first of all completes his K side development and does not allow himself to be tempted by the violent variant 6 .... P—Q4; 7 Kt—Q2, P—K4; 8 Kt—K2, P—Q5; 9 B—KKt5, and Black would only have wasted his energy.

7 Castles   Castles
8 Kt—Q2   P—Q4

Emancipation!

9 Kt × Kt   P × Kt
10 P—K5   Kt—Q2

The contest takes on a closed character, recalling a variation of the *French Defence*, but Black has this advantage, that the white QB is not particularly effective where he is.

11 P—KB4   P—KB4

Resolutely closing a dangerous diagonal.

12 R—B3

Black is well able to cope with this attack.

12 ......   P—B4

The beginning of the counter-action.

13 R—R3   R—B2

In order to reply to 14 Q—R5 by 14 .... P—Kt3.

14 P—QKt3   P—Kt3
15 Kt—B3   Kt—Kt3

Self-possessed strategy. The black King's fortress being sufficiently guarded, the Knight gives up the *rôle* of a defender and sets out to seek his fortune on other parts of the board.

16 B—B2   P—Q5
17 B—R4   Kt—Q4
18 Q—Q2   P—QR4
19 B × B   R × B
20 Kt—Kt5

After much trouble the white Knight has at last conquered a strong square, whence, however, he has as yet no serious threats. The same cannot be said of the next move by his black rival.

20 ......   Kt—K6
21 Q—B2   B—Kt2
22 B—B1   Kt—Kt5
23 Q—R4   Q—Q2
24 R—Q1   R—QB1
25 B—K2   P—R4

Compulsory, for if 25 .... Kt—K6; 26 R × Kt.

26 R—Kt3   Q—K1

Eluding the threat 27 P—KR3 (Kt—K6; 28 R×Kt), but guarding the KKtP against eventualities.

27 R—Q2

Not yet 27 R—R3, on account of 27 .... Kt—K6, attacking the QR. But now the threat 28 P—KR3, Kt—K6; 29 B×P (P×B; 30 Kt×P dis ch, K—R2; 31 Q—B6, etc.) is becoming real.

27 ......   R—Kt2

Reinforcing the critical file.

28 P—B3

He thinks he can force events (for if 28 .... P×P; 29 R×P, etc., or 28 .... R—Q1; 29 Kt×P), but Black's advanced QP will sell his life dearly; or e.g. 28 B—B4, B—Q4; 29 B×B, P×B.

28 ......   Kt—K6

Returning to the charge and, in addition, threatening 29 .... P×P; 30 R—Q6, P—B7, or 30 R—Q3, Kt—Q4; 31 B—B3, P—B7.

29 P×P

Acceptance of the proffered pawn opens the flood-gates for his adversary. On the other hand, the more cautious 29 P—B4, closing the files, leaves Black with a sure and lasting asset in his supported passed pawn.

29 ......   P×P
30 R×P   R—B8 ch
31 K—B2   Kt—Q4
32 KR—Q3   Q—B3

At one stroke, Black throws all his forces into the fray.

33 R—Q2

Over cautious. The defensive 33 B—B3 is indicated.

33 ......   Q—Kt3
34 B—B4

With the fine threat of 35 Kt×P.

34 ......   R—B7

Creating an interesting *imbroglio*.

35 K—K1

Not now 35 Kt×P (35 .... R×R ch), nor 35 Kt—B3 (35 .... R×R ch; 36 Kt×R, Q×R ch, etc.). If 35 K—K2, Q×R; 36 R×R, Kt×P ch, etc., and if 35 R×R, Q×R ch; 36 K—Kt3, Q—K6 ch; 37 Kt—B3, Kt—B6, etc. Therefore the best defence would be 35. K—Kt3 (R×R; 36 R×R, Q—K6 ch; 37 Kt—B3, etc.).

35 ......   R×R
36 R×R   Q—Kt8 ch

A persuasive irruption.

37 B—B1   R—QB2
38 R—Q1   R—B7
39 Q—Kt3   B—R3
40 Q—KB3   B×B
41 Resigns.

297

White	Black
MORPHY	ANDERSSEN

(Match, 1858)

An historical game: an over-bold attempt by Black in the opening (7 .... P—B4), conceived and worked out by Anderssen in the course of a Parisian ramble. By not making sufficient allowance for the first player's latent energy, he allows the genius of his adversary not only to break up his defences by a sacrifice, but also to undermine his morale for the rest of the match.

1 P—K4   P—QB4
2 P—Q4   P×P
3 Kt—KB3   Kt—QB3
4 Kt×P   P—K3
5 Kt—Kt5

Without any delay (5 Kt—QB3 or 5 B—K2 or 5 B—K3) Morphy hits out, and his assault succeeds.

5 ......   P—Q3

He allows his mental balance to be shaken, and creates a serious weakness in his own camp. Morphy himself played 5 .... P—QR3 at this stage in a game against Lowenthal, but the strongest is 5 .... Kt—B3, for now 6 Kt—Q6 ch would be a futile check, e.g. 6 .... B×Kt; 7 Q×Kt, Kt×P, etc., or 6 QKt—B3, B—Kt5, and Black obtains a perfectly satisfactory game.

6 B—KB4   P—K4

Instead of thus weakening his Q4, he could have evolved a line of defence by 6 .... Kt—K4; 7 B×Kt, P×B; 8 Q×Q ch, K×Q, etc.

7 B—K3   P—B4

To dare to embark on a counter-attack in such an exposed position is to challenge the logic of things. The defensive measure 7 .... P—QR3 is clearly necessary.

8 QKt—B3   P—B5

The crucial mistake, turning a tottering position into a desperate one.

If 8 .... P×P; 9 QKt×P, P—Q4; 10 Q×P.

If 8 .... P—QR3; 9 Kt—Q5, P×Kt; 10 B—Kt6, to be followed by 11 Kt—B7 ch and Kt×R.

If 8 .... Kt—B3; 9 B—Kt5, P—QR3 (relatively best); 10 B×Kt, P×B; 11 Q—R5 ch, K—Q2; 12 Q×P ch, K—K1; 13 Q—R5 ch, K—Q2; 14 Kt—R3, and, on balance, White has won a valuable pawn.

Therefore the least evil is 8 .... B—K3; e.g. 9 P×P, B×BP; 10 Kt—Q5, R—B1; 11 P—QB3, P—QR3; 12 KKt—B7 ch, K—Q2 (not 12 .... R×Kt; 13 B—Kt6, nor 12 .... K—B2; 13 B—QB4); 13 B—Kt6, Kt—B3, and Black struggles to defend himself.

9 Kt—Q5

The miracle of the sacrifice.

9 ......   P×B
10 KKt—B7 ch   K—B2
11 Q—B3 ch

The simple continuation, however, is 11 Kt×R, P×P ch; 12 K×P, Q—R5 ch; 13 P—Kt3, Q×P; 14 B—Kt2, etc.

11 ......   Kt—B3
12 B—B4   Kt—Q5
13 Kt×Kt   P—Q4

Well parried! Any other move loses forthwith:

(a) 13 .... B—K3; 14 B×B ch, Kt×B; 15 Kt—Q5 dis ch, etc.

(b) 13 ..... Kt—K3; 14 Kt—Kt4 dis ch, etc.

(c) 13 .... K—Kt3; 14 Q—R5 ch, K×Kt; 15 P×P, etc.

(d) 13 .... K—K2; 14 QKt—Q5 ch, K—Q2; 15 Q—B7 ch, B—K2 (or 15 .... K—B3; 16 Kt—Kt4 ch, etc.); 16 P×P, R—B1; 17 P×Kt, R×Q; 18 B—Kt5 mate.

14 B×P ch   K—Kt3

But now, having cleared the air to some extent by his preceding move, Black should have retraced his steps by 14 .... K—K2; e.g. 15 Q—R5, P×Kt; 16 Q—B7 ch, K—Q3; 17 Kt×R, Kt×P ch (if 17 .... Q—K2; 18 Castles QR); 18 K—K2, Q—K2 (18 .... Kt×R; 19 B×P); 19 Q×Q ch, B×Q; 20 QR—QB1, Kt—Q5 ch; 21 K×P, B—Q2; 22 R—B7 (or 22 B×P, R—QKt1; 23 B—Q5, R×P, etc.); 22 .... R×Kt; 23 R×P, B—B3; 24 B×B, Kt×B; 25 R—QB1, Kt—Q1; 26 R—Q1 ch, K—K3; 27 R—B7, R—Kt1; 28 P—QKt3, and the struggle is still very stubborn.

Also better than the ill-fated move in the text, which does not allow for White's magnificent *riposte*, would be the indirect exchange of Queens by 14 .... Q×B; 15 Kt×Q dis ch, Kt×Q ch; 16 P×Kt, P×P ch; 17 K×P, B—B4 ch; 18 K—K2, R—QKt1. With two Bishops against two Knights, Black might find some consolation for the loss of a pawn.

15 Q—R5 ch

A fresh surprise.

15 ......   K×Kt

Pharaoh's tomb.

16 P×P   Kt×P ch

A longer resistance arises from 16 .... Q×Kt:

(a) 17 Castles ch, Kt—B4 (17 .... K—K2; 18 R—B7 ch); 18 R×Kt ch, B×R; 19 Q×B ch, K—K2; 20 Q—K6 ch, K—Q1; 21 B×P, Q×P (not 21 .... Q×B; 22 R—Q1 ch, nor 21 .... Q—Q3; 22 Q×Q, B×Q; 23 B×R, remaining with three extra pawns); 22 B×R, B—B4, and the struggle still continues; or

(b) 17 P×Kt (the right way); 17 .... B—Kt5 ch (or 17 .... K—K2; 18 Castles QR, etc., or 17 .... P—KKt3; 18 Q—R4 ch, K—Kt2; 19 Castles KR, etc.); 18 P—B3, B×P ch; 19 K—K2, K—K2; 20 KR—KB1, etc., clearing the way.

17 K—K2   Resigns

(For now, after 17 .... Q×Kt; 18 KR—B1 ch, K—K2; 19 R—B7 ch, K—Q3; 20 R×Q, K×R; 21 R—QB1, another black piece is lost.)

298

White	Black
PILLSBURY	MIESES

(Paris, 1900)

In the following game it is pleasing to see Black's QP, isolated but well-centralised at Q4, render yeoman service in counter-acting White's advantage of "the move." It goes without saying that, in doing so, this pawn eschews a purely static rôle (by remaining inactive at Q4) and assumes "dynamic" tasks, as manifested by the fine advances 11 .... P—Q5, and even 15 .... P—Q6.

1 P—K4   P—QB4
2 Kt—KB3

The *classical continuation*, by which White

seeks to develop his game according to general principles: bring out your minor pieces, occupy the centre, open lines of attack!

| 2 . . . . . . | P—K3 |
| 3 P—Q4 | P × P |

Almost forced. Yet Marshall has demonstrated in many important games that the self-willed counter-thrust 3 . . . . P—Q4 is all but sound.

| 4 Kt × P | Kt—KB3 |
| 5 Kt—QB3 | |

Evidently not 5 P—K5, Q—R4 ch, followed by . . . . Q × KP. Less straightforward would be 5 Kt—Q2 or 5 B—Q3, either continuation permitting 5 . . . . P—Q4 without further difficulties.

| 5 . . . . . . | Kt—B3 |

And now we have the *Sicilian Four Knights' Game*. More awkward is the immediate *sortie* 5 . . . . B—Kt5. A sound, if expectative, line of play is the well-known *Scheveningen Variant*: 5 . . . . P—Q3; followed by . . . . B—K2; and . . . . Castles; presenting an example of an opening with a *restricted centre* (pawns at K3 and Q3).

6 KKt—Kt5

The so-called *main variation* of the *Sicilian Defence*, which has lately fallen into disuse. By exchanging, 6 Kt × Kt, KtP × Kt, the opponent's centre becomes very strong.

Sound but tranquil continuations are the preventive 6 P—QR3 (6 . . . . P—QR3; 7 B—K2, B—K2), and the positional 6 P—KKt3, followed by B—Kt2.

Finally, an enterprising line, sacrificing one or even two pawns, is 6 B—K2, e.g. 6 . . . . B—Kt5; 7 Castles, B × Kt (wiser is 7 . . . . Castles); 8 P × B, Kt × P; 9 B—B3, Kt × QBP (prudence calls for 9 . . . . P—Q4; 10 Kt × Kt, P × Kt; 11 B × Kt, P × B, etc., with chances of equalisation); 10 Q—Q3, and White dominates the field.

| 6 . . . . . . | B—Kt5 |
| 7 P—QR3 | |

After 7 Kt—Q6 ch, K—K2; 8 B—KB4, Q—R4; Black cleverly shakes off his opponent's hold.

Against 7 B—KB4, Black replies, in the grand style: 7 . . . . Kt × P; 8 Kt—B7 ch, K—B1; as in a game Reggio—Tarrasch, *Monte Carlo*, 1902: 9 Kt × R, Q—B3; 10 Q—B3, Kt × Kt; 11 B—Q2, Kt—Q5; 12 Q—Q3 (12 Q × Q, Kt × P mate); 12 . . . . Q—K4 ch; 13 B—K3, Kt—R5 dis ch; 14 P—B3, Kt × KtP; 15 Q—Kt1 (or 15 Q—Q2, B × P; 16 Q × B, Kt—B6 ch; winning the Queen); 15 . . . . B × P mate.

| 7 . . . . . . | B × Kt ch |
| 8 Kt × B | P—Q4 |

A trenchant advance; or first, 8 . . . . Castles; 9 B—Q3, P—Q4; 10 P × P, P × P; 11 Castles, etc.

| 9 P × P | P × P |

Accepting the famous *isolated QP*. If 9 . . . . Kt × P; 10 Kt × Kt, Q × Kt; 11 Q × Q, P × Q; 12 B—Q3, etc., White, after this simplification, has a small but enduring positional advantage.

10 B—KKt5

Instead of this pawn hunt, the rational continuation is 10 B—Q3, Castles; 11 Castles, P—KR3; 12 P—R3 (if 12 Kt—K2, Kt—K5); 12 . . . . B—K3; 13 B—KB4, etc.

| 10 . . . . . . | Castles |

Better than 10 . . . . B—K3, which provides White with an easy mark.

11 B—K2

The gain of a pawn by 11 B × Kt, Q × B; 12 Q × P would be bad, as Black would initiate a devastating attack on the K and Q files.

11	P—Q5
12 Kt—K4	Q—R4 ch
13 P—Kt4	Q—K4
14 Kt × Kt ch	P × Kt
15 B—R6	

Expecting 15 . . . . R—K1, after which 16 K—B1, followed by B—Q3, would restore the balance.

| 15 . . . . . . | P—Q6 |

This piercing of the critical sector is well worth the exchange.

| 16 P × P | Kt—Q5 |
| 17 B × R | |

If 17 B—K3, Kt—B7 ch.

| 17 . . . . . . | K × B |

A disappointment would be 17 . . . . B—Kt5; 18 B—Q6.

18 R—R2	B—K3
19 R—Q2	R—K1
20 Castles	B—Kt6
21 Q—Kt1	B—Q4

A very important *retrograde manœuvre*.

22 B—Q1

Is it consolidation?

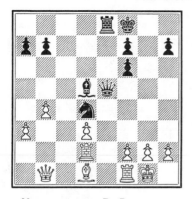

22 ......   B × P

A recuperative sacrifice.

It is to be noted that Black, hoping for more, disdains an elegant draw by 22 .... Q—Kt4; 23 P—B4, Kt—K7 ch; 24 R × Kt, R × R; 25 P × Q, R × P ch; 26 K—R1, R—B7 dis ch; 27 K—Kt1, R—Kt7 ch, etc., with perpetual check.

23 K × B

The game would take a very bad turn for White after 23 P—B4, Q—K6 ch; 24 KR—B2, B—R6; 25 R—K2, Kt—B6 ch; 26 K—R1, Q × KR, forcing an early mate.

    23 ......   Q—Kt4 ch
    24 K—R1   Q × R
    25 B—Kt4   Q—B5
    26 R—Kt1

The only means of reinforcing the King's bodyguard. After 26 B—R5, Kt—B6; 27 B × Kt, Q × B ch; 28 K—Kt1, R—K4, the white King, denuded of defenders, would succumb. Alternatively, 26 P—R3, P—B4; 27 B—Q1 (27 B—R5, Q—R5); 27 .... R—K3, and wins.

    26 ......   P—B4
    27 B—R5   Kt—B6

If 27 .... R—K3; 28 Q—QB1.

    28 B × Kt   Q × B ch
    29 R—Kt2   R—K7

Intending to reply to 30 Q—Kt1 with 30 .... R—Q7, and to 30 Q—Q1 with 30 .... R × P; 31 Q × Q, R × Q, etc., with a conclusive advantage. As the text move contains no threat, White takes advantage of the breathing-space to put in a word himself.

Black could have tried for a win by 29 .... R—Q1.

30 Q—QB1

The saving clause, calling attention to the fact that the black King's keep also is not too well guarded.

    30 ......   Q × QP
    31 Q—B5 ch

Draw by perpetual check.

(31 .... R—K2; 32 Q—B8 ch, R—K1; 33 Q—B5 ch, etc.)

A hard-fought game.

299

White	Black
GRIFFITH	HAMMOND

(Richmond, 1912)

In the hard fight given below, Black succeeds—by suppressing, so to speak, the phase of the middle game—in bringing about an ending, not without, however, leaving some weak points in his position, notably at Q3 and KR3. In the ensuing Rook end game—which, as is well known, has the highest co-efficient of a draw—White's final triumph is one of logic and perseverance.

    1 P—Q4   P—QB4
    2 P—K4

A Sicilianised *Benoni.*

    2 ......   P × P
    3 Kt—KB3   Kt—QB3
    4 Kt × P   Kt—B3
    5 Kt—QB3   P—K4

Instead of the academic 5 .... P—K3 or 5 .... P—Q3, Black by this fancy move calls for an immediate settlement in the centre.

6 KKt—Kt5

Trying at once to exploit the "hole" at Q6. If 6 Kt—B5, P—Q3, and Black gets rid of the invader.

    6 ......   P—QR3

If instead 6 .... P—Q3; 7 B—Kt5, P—QR3; 8 B × Kt, P × B; 9 Kt—R3, P—Kt4; 10 Kt—Q5, and White, besides damaging the hostile position, has succeeded in conquering, thanks to the absence of the opposing KKt, the strategic point Q5. On the other hand, if 6 .... B—Kt5, then not 7 Kt—Q6 ch, K—K2; 8 Kt—B5 ch, K—B1; 9 B—Q2, P—Q4, etc., but, scientifically, 7 P—QR3, B × Kt ch; 8 Kt × B, and White has two important assets: the *two Bishops* and a steady pressure on Black's QP.

| 7 Kt—Q6 ch | B×Kt |
| 8 Q×B | Q—K2 |

Leading to extensive liquidation; only the exercise of outstanding virtuosity will make a win possible for White.

| 9 Q×Q ch | Kt×Q |

And not 9 .... K×Q, on account of 10 B—KKt5, with the threat of 11 Kt—Q5 ch, whereas now the junction Q5 is well under observation.

10 B—KKt5	P—R3
11 B×Kt	P×B
12 P—KKt3	

A sound idea.

| 12 ...... | Castles |

Entrusting the King with the protection of the KB and KR pawns.

| 13 R—Q1 | K—Kt2 |

More to the point is 13 .... P—B4.

| 14 B—R3 | |

If first 14 P—KR4, then not 14 .... R—Q1; 15 R—Q6, followed by 16 B—R3, and White has a definite hold, but 14 .... P—B4, e.g. 15 B—R3, P×P; 16 B×P (or 16 Kt×P, P—Q4, etc.); 16 .... P—B4; 17 B×B, Kt×B; 18 R—Q7 ch, R—B2; 19 R—Q5, R—K2; 20 R—Q8, Kt—Kt3, and Black stubbornly defends himself.

| 14 ...... | P—Q3 |

Well parried. The duel between the strategist and the tactician becomes very interesting.

15 B×B	Kt×B
16 Kt—Q5	R—R2
17 Kt—K3	R—Q1
18 Kt—B5 ch	K—R2
19 R—Q3	P—Kt3
20 P—KKt4	K—Kt3
21 K—K2	R—B2
22 P—QB3	R—B5
23 P—B3	P—Kt4
24 KR—Q1	R—B3
25 P—Kt3	R—Kt3
26 P—KB4	

A fresh stage.

26	R—B3
27 R—R3	R—R1
28 KR—Q3	

In order to follow this up with R—R5 and KR—R3.

28	P×P
29 K—B3	R—B2
30 K×P	R—Q2
31 R—R5	Kt—K2

Avoiding the worst.

| 32 Kt×Kt ch | |

The following line leads to no decisive result: 32 R×P, R×R; 33 Kt×Kt ch, K—R2; 34 Kt—B5, R—Q7; 35 R×P ch, K—Kt1; 36 R×P, R×QRP, etc.

| 32 ...... | R×Kt |
| 33 R×QP | |

At last a small gain in material, which, however, can be maintained only by very astute play.

| 33 ...... | KR—K1 |
| 34 P—K5 | |

He succeeds in eliminating one battery. After 34 R—Q4, the two black Rooks would remain in full active service.

| 34 ...... | R—K3 |

Black evidently exchanges the more noxious of the two adverse Rooks, for after 34 .... R×P; 35 R×R, R×R; 36 R×P, R—B4; 37 R—Kt6, R×P; 38 R×P, R—B7; 39 P—QR4, R×P; 40 P—R5, R—R7; 41 P—Kt4, etc., Black would have regained his pawn, but with a lost game.

35 R×R	R×R
36 R—B5	P×P ch
37 R×P	R—B3 ch
38 K—Kt3	R—Q3
39 R—QB5	

In this final phase, White's task is far from easy.

39	P—B3
40 P—KR3	R—Q6 ch
41 K—R4	R—Q3
42 P—B4	P×P
43 R×P	

And not 43 P×P, scattering his infantry.

43	P—B4
44 R—B4	P×P
45 P×P	

Far more useful than 45 R×P ch.

45	R—Kt3
46 R—R4	R—Q3
47 P—R3	K—Kt2
48 R—R5	K—Kt3
49 P—Kt4	K—Kt2
50 K—R5	R—K3
51 K—R4	K—B2

Sooner or later the abandonment of his third rank would become necessary, for if 51 .... K—Kt3; 52 P—R4, e.g. 52 .... R—Kt3; 53 P—QKt5, P×P; 54 P×P (threat: 55 R—R6); 54 .... K—Kt2; 55 K—R5, etc., or 52 .... R—Q3; 53 P—QKt5, P×P; 54 P×P, K—Kt2; 55 R—R7 ch, K—Kt1; 56 K—R5, R—Q4 ch; 57 K×P, R×P; 58 R—R8 ch, K—B2; 59 P—Kt5, R—Kt3 ch; 60 K—R7, and wins.

52 R—B5

Improving the Rook's position.

52	R—QKt3
53 K—R5	K—Kt2
54 R—B7 ch	K—Kt1
55 R—QR7	K—R1
56 P—R4	K—Kt1
57 P—R5	R × P

For if 57 .... R—Q3; 58 R—Kt7, followed by R—Kt6.

58 R × P	K—B2

If 58 .... K—Kt2; 59 R—Kt6 ch, winning another pawn.

59 R—R8	K—K2

But now 59 .... K—Kt2, remaining in the "neutral zone," would be more tenacious.

60 P—R6	R—R5

61 P—R7

The decisive advance, as the black King cannot return in time to the "neutral zone."

61	K—B2
62 R—R8	R—R7

A last hope for a miracle: 63 P—R8 (Q), R—R7 mate.

63 K—R4	Resigns.

300

White	*Black*
YATES	HAIDA

(Marienbad, 1925)

In the following beautiful game, a King's field Attack, from small beginnings (10 Q—Kt4) and contending against a big concentration of forces, succeeds brilliantly for the very reason that the large number of defending pieces on a narrow sector prove to be mutually obstructive.

1 P—K4	P—QB4
2 Kt—KB3	P—K3
3 P—Q4	P × P
4 Kt × P	Kt—KB3
5 Kt—QB3	B—Kt5

Accelerating his K side development, an alternative to the main variation 5 .... Kt—B3; 6 KKt—Kt5, B—Kt5, etc.

6 B—Q3

After 6 Kt—Kt5, Black is under no compulsion to revert to the *main variant* by 6 .... Kt—B3, for he can safely play 6 .... Castles; 7 P—QR3, B × Kt ch; 8 Kt × B, P—Q4, etc.

Too thin would be the escapade 6 B—KKt5, B × Kt ch; 7 P × B, Q—R4, and Black wins a pawn.

Very picturesque is the attack 6 P—K5, with three ramifications: 6 .... Kt—K5; 7 Q—Kt4, etc.; or 6 .... Kt—Q4; 7 B—Q2, etc.; or 6 .... Q—R4; 7 P × Kt, etc.

6	Kt—B3

Too precipitate would be 6 .... P—Q4; 7 P—K5, Kt—K5 (after 7 .... KKt—Q2; 8 Q—Kt4, White's attack succeeds rapidly); 8 B × Kt, P × B; 9 Castles, etc., to White's advantage.

The best is *Jaffé's Variation*: 6 .... P—K4; 7 Kt—K2 (better than 7 Kt—B5, Castles, etc.); 7 .... P—Q4; 8 P × P, Kt × P; 9 Castles, etc., with a complicated game.

7 Kt × Kt

If 7 Kt—K2, Kt—K4, etc., and if 7 B—K3, P—Q4, etc.

7	KtP × Kt

Against 7 .... QP × Kt, White would not continue in humdrum fashion 8 Castles (allowing Black to free his game by 8 .... P—K4); but tightens his grip by 8 P—K5, e.g. 8 .... Kt—Q4; 9 B—Q2, etc., or 8 .... Kt—Q2; 9 Q—Kt4, Q—R4; 10 Castles, etc., with sustained pressure.

8 Castles

He should strike while the iron is hot, and play energetically 8 P—K5, Kt—Q4; 9 Q—Kt4, e.g. 9 .... P—Kt3; 10 Castles, B × Kt; 11 P × B, Kt × P; 12 B—R3, etc., or 9 .... Q—R4; 10 Castles, Kt × Kt; 11 Q × P, etc., and White stands much better.

8	Castles

Having castled, Black can hope for consolidation.

9 P—K5	Kt—K1

But now 9 .... Kt—Q4 would be more conformable.

| 10 Q—Kt4 | B—K2 |
| 11 B—KR6 | |

A frontal attack on a well-equipped position.

White could have played 11 Q—R3, first in order to create weaknesses there.

| 11 ...... | P—KB4 |

Relying on his strong armament, Black ventures on this escapade, when he could have shaken the opponent's hold by 11 .... K—R1; forcing the retreat 12 B—K3.

| 12 P×P e.p. | R×P |

And not 12 .... B×P; 13 Q—K4, P—Kt3; 14 B×R, etc.

| 13 B—KKt5 | R—B2 |
| 14 Kt—K4 | P—Kt3 |

There is no need for Black to weaken his King's field, when he could have brought matters to a head in the centre by 14 .... P—Q4; 15 B×B, R×B; 16 Kt—Kt5, Kt—B3, with even chances.

15 QR—K1	P—Q4
16 B×B	R×B
17 Kt—Kt5	P—K4
18 Q—R4	P—K5

Thinking, by this move, to recover at one stroke the whole of the territory previously ceded, he becomes the victim of an astonishing conception. He should first have consolidated his game by 18 .... B—Q2.

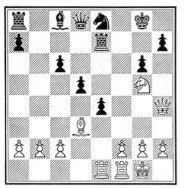

| 19 R×P |

A sacrifice as brilliant as it is sound. A faulty exploitation of the temporary lack of mobility of the adverse KR would be 19 Kt×RP (19 .... B—B4), and similarly, 19 Kt×KP (19 .... P×Kt; 20 R×P, R—Q2, etc.).

| 19 ...... | P×R |
| 20 B—B4 ch | K—B1 |

He has nothing better. If 20 ....

K—R1; 21 Kt—B7 ch, etc., and if 20 .... K—Kt2; 21 Q×P ch, K—B3; 22 Q—R4 (with the decisive threat of 23 Kt—B7 dis ch); 22 .... K—Kt2 (22 .... Q—R4; 23 Kt×P db ch); 23 Kt—B7, with the two-fold threat of 24 Q—R8 mate or 24 Kt×Q.

| 21 Q—R6 ch | R—Kt2 |

Or 21 .... Kt—Kt2; 22 Kt×P ch, K—K1; 23 Kt—B6 ch, K—B1; 24 Q—R8 mate.

22 Kt×P ch	K—K2
23 Q—Kt5 ch	K—Q2
24 R—Q1 ch	Kt—Q3
25 Kt—B6 ch	

Even more forceful than 25 R×Kt ch, K×R; 26 Q×Q ch.

| 25 ...... | K—K2 |

For if 25 .... K—B2; 26 Q—R5 ch, followed by Q×Q.

| 26 Kt×P dis ch | Resigns. |

301

| White | Black |
| *MARCO* | *MAROCZY* |

(Ostend, 1905)

An exceptionally short game, but full of a dramatic under-current! An over-hasty attempt by Black (9 .... P—KKt4) finds a refutation as brilliant as it is logical.

1 P—K4	P—QB4
2 Kt—KB3	P—K3
3 P—Q4	P×P
4 Kt×P	P—QR3

Intending to build up with .... Q—B2 a strong system of defence.

Besides purely developing moves such as 4 .... Kt—QB3 or 4 .... Kt—KB3, the move in the text—conceived by Paulsen—has much in its favour.

| 5 B—K3 | |

Almost a waiting move. A more usual line is 5 Kt—QB3, Q—B2; 6 B—Q3, Kt—KB3; 7 Castles, B—K2; 8 K—R1, P—Q3 (instead of the routine move 8 .... Castles, or 8 .... P—Q4, opening the centre, Black now establishes a *restricted centre*); 9 P—B4, QKt—Q2 (it is to be noted that in the *Paulsen Variation* Black can develop his QKt at QB3 or, as here, at Q2); 10 Q—K2,

P—QKt4, with an even game. In searching for the most efficacious line of play, White can also try 5 P—QB4 (blockading Q5) or 5 P—KKt3 (with a more intense development of his KB), or 5 B—K2 (intending B—B3), without, however, obtaining any real advantage from the opening.

5	Kt—KB3
6 Kt—Q2	

Not 6 P—K5, Q—R4 ch, followed by .... Q×KP, nor 6 Kt—QB3, B—Kt5.

6 ...... P—Q4

He suddenly changes his system, which really calls for 6 .... Q—B2; 7 B—K2, P—Q4 (now in order); 8 KKt—Kt3, Kt—B3 (not 8 .... P×P; 9 P—QB3, B—K2; 10 Q—B2, etc., nor 8 .... Kt×P; 9 Kt×Kt, P×Kt; 10 P—QB3, etc.); 9 P—QB3, B—K2; 10 Q—B2, Castles; 11 Castles KR, R—Q1, and the initiative is still at stake.

7 P—K5	KKt—Q2
8 P—KB4	Kt—QB3
9 P—B3	

White's forces are now ideally posted, e.g. 9 .... B—K2; 10 B—Q3, or 9 .... Kt—B4; 10 P—QKt4, Kt—Q2; 11 B—Q3, and White commands all strategic points.

9 ...... P—KKt4

He imagines that this move will disrupt his opponent's game (e.g. 10 P×P, KKt×P, etc., or 10 P—KKt3, P×P; 11 P×P, Q—R5 ch, etc.), but White's rejoinder is a stunning blow.

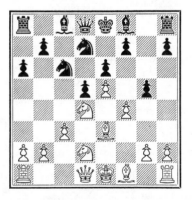

10 Kt×P

A beautiful sacrifice, which discloses the defects in Black's King's field, created by his preceding move.

10	P×Kt
11 Q—R5 ch	K—K2
12 P—B5	

A corollary to his 10th move, threatening not only 13 P—B6 ch, but also — and principally (e.g. after 12 .... P×P, or 12 .... Q—K1) — 13 B×P ch.

12 ...... Kt—B3

Hoping to appease White's fury in case of 13 P×Kt ch, K—Q3, etc. If 12 .... QKt×P; 13 B×P ch, Kt—B3; 14 B×Kt ch, K×B; 15 Q—R4 ch, followed by Q×Q.

13 B—B5 ch Resigns

For if 13 .... K—Q2; 14 Q—B7 ch, Kt—K2 (or 14 .... B—K2; 15 P×Kt, R—K1; 16 P×B, Kt×P; 17 Q×P ch, K—B2; 18 B—Kt6 ch, K—Kt1; 19 Q—K5 ch, followed by mate); 15 P×Kt, P×P; 16 P×Kt, etc.

302

White	Black
MARÓCZY	EUWE

(Scheveningen, 1923)

The principal actor here is White's KP. After contesting the predominance in the centre at K4, it becomes a strong outpost (15 P—K5), penetrates into the opposing lines (26 P—K6), finally reaching the core of Black's resistance (27 P—K7), whence it threatens the very heart of the hostile fortress (KB8). This is the backbone of White's attack.

1 P—K4	P—QB4
2 Kt—KB3	Kt—QB3

A more elastic reply than 2 .... P—K3.

3 P—Q4	P×P
4 Kt×P	Kt—B3

By playing 4 .... P—QR3, followed by .... Q—B2 (or even 4 .... Q—B2; 5 Kt—Kt5, Q—Kt1, subsequently driving off the troublesome Knight), Black can revert to the *Paulsen Variation.*

5 Kt—QB3 P—Q3

More reserved than 5 .... P—K3 (6 KKt—Kt5, B—Kt5, etc.).

6 B—K2

At the cross-roads! As an alternative to the waiting policy adopted here, White can also play the more imaginative 6 P—KKt3, with 7 B—Kt2. Less good is 6 B—QB4 (6 .... P—K3) and 6 Kt×Kt, P×Kt, etc., but a sound modern idea is 6 B—KKt5.

6 ......   P—K3

The well-known *Scheveningen Variation*, which is based on a *restricted centre* (pawns at K3 and Q3), and which eventually borrows from the *Paulsen Variant* the formation, pawn at QR3 and Queen at QB2. Thus, the *Scheveningen Variation* is akin both to the *Paulsen Variation* and the *Dragon Variation*, 6 .... P—KKt3, which used to be applied exclusively at this stage. This line of play has proved to be very flexible, and is much favoured in modern master practice.

7 Castles   B—K2
8 K—R1

This move is important because White, in the interest of the attack, wishes to throw the KBP forward, and therefore anticipates any future and disagreeable pin.

However, 8 P—B4 at once is playable, e.g. 8 .... Q—Kt3; 9 B—K3, Q×P; 10 KKt—Kt5, with the twofold threat of 11 R—Kt1 and 11 Kt—B7 ch.

An interesting *opening trap*.

8 ......   Castles
9 P—B4   Q—B2
10 Kt—Kt3

An ingenious manœuvre, by which White avoids a simplifying exchange at Q4.

Useless would be 10 KKt—Kt5, Q—Kt1; followed by .... P—QR3; and if 10 B—K3, Kt—QR4, followed by .... Kt—B5; depriving White of his pair of Bishops.

But a bold line can be tried: 10 B—B3, P—QR3; 11 P—KKt4 (the *bayonet attack*), 11 .... B—Q2; 12 P—Kt5, Kt—K1; 13 KKt—K2, etc.

10......   P—QR3
11 P—QR4

White has to decide whether it is better to prevent 11 ...∴ P—QKt4; or, allowing this advance, to try to find its refutation. He decides on a preventive measure. An alternative would be: 11 B—K3, P—QKt4; 12 P—QR3, B—Kt2; 13 Q—K1, QR—Q1; 14 R—Q1, K—R1 (not yet 14 .... Kt—QR4; 15 Kt×Kt, Q×Kt; 16 Kt—Q5, and wins); 15 B—B3, Kt—QR4; 16 Kt×Kt, Q×Kt; 17 Q—B2 (threat, 18 B—Kt6); 17 .... Kt—Q2; 18 P—KKt4, and the battle is at its height.

11 ......   P—QKt3

Instead of thus creating a weak point,

Black could seek to solve the problem of the QB by 11 .... B—Q2, followed later on by .... B—K1.

12 B—B3   B—Kt2
13 B—K3   Kt—QKt5

Seeing that his adversary has the supremacy on both wings, Black tries to recoup himself by action in the centre (.... P—Q4).

14 Q—K2   P—Q4

Threatened with 15 Q—B2, Black feels that he must undertake something. Will it be freedom or weakness in the centre?

A waiting policy would dictate 14 .... QR—K1, and if 15 Q—B2, Kt—Q2, etc.

15 P—K5   Kt—K5

A better move is 15 .... Kt—Q2.

16 B×Kt   P×B
17 Q—B2   P—QKt4

If 17 .... B—Q1, White doubles Rooks on the Q file.

18 P×P   P×P
19 Kt—Q4   B—QB3
20 Q—Kt3

The turning-point. The white Queen's itinerary Q1—K2—KB2—KKt3 is significant for the general lay-out of his operations.

20 ......   R×R
21 R×R   R—Kt1

Holding on to his worldly possessions, but 21 .... R—R1, showing his readiness to throw ballast overboard, is a wiser decision.

22 P—B5

White's attack takes a definite shape.

22 ......   P×P
23 Kt×BP

A complement of his 19th move.

23 ......   B—B1
24 B—B4

With the decisive threat of reaping material gain by 25 P—K6.

24 ......   R—R1

Or 24 .... Q—Q2; 25 KKt×P, B×Kt; 26 B—R6, P—B3; 27 P×P, etc.

25 R—QB1   P—Kt3

He has nothing better, e.g. 25 .... Q—Kt2 (or 25 .... Q—Q2); 26 KKt×P, and if 25 .... Q—B1; 26 Kt—R6 ch.

26 P—K6

An *unmasking advance*.

26 ...... Q—Kt2
27 P—K7
Convincing, for if 27 .... B×P; 28 Kt×B ch, Q×Kt; 29 B—Q6, followed by B×Kt.

27 ...... B—Kt2
28 Kt×B K×Kt
Deprived of his most trusted defender, the black Bishop, the King must soon succumb to White's concentric assault.

29 Q—R4 P—B3
30 Q—R6 ch K—Kt1
31 B—Q6 Resigns.

303

White	Black
BOHATYRCHUK	CAPABLANCA

(Moscow, 1925)

In the elegant game which follows, Black demonstrates that, provided it is adequately prepared, the liberating thrust .... P(Q3)—Q4 is productive.

1 P—K4 P—QB4
2 Kt—KB3 Kt—QB3
3 P—Q4 P×P
4 Kt×P Kt—B3
5 Kt—QB3 P—Q3
6 B—K2 P—K3
7 Castles B—K2
8 B—K3
Another method (besides 8 K—R1) of preparing the advance of the KBP, if the bold and immediate advance 8 P—B4 is thought to be too hazardous.

8 ...... Castles
9 P—B4 B—Q2
Preparing for counter-action on the QB file.

10 Kt—Kt3
Instead of manœuvring, a straightforward way of creating an attack is 10 Q—K1, P—QR3; 11 P—QR4, Q—B2; 12 R—Q1 (the bayonet attack 12 P—KKt4 is premature here, e.g. 12 .... Kt×Kt; 13 B×Kt, P—K4, winning a pawn); 12 .... Kt—QR4; 13 Q—Kt3, Kt—B5; 14 B—B1, etc., and he has successfully re-grouped his forces.

10 ...... P—QR3
The *Paulsen Formation* (.... P—QR3,

with .... Q—B2 eventually) is by no means the main idea of the *Scheveningen Variation*, but its very frequent adjunct.

11 P—QR4
If it is not desired to enter into commitments on the Q side, a methodical way of continuing the game is 11 Q—Q2, P—QKt4; 12 P—QR3, R—B1; 13 QR—Q1, etc.

11 ...... Kt—QR4
With the text move Black seizes the initiative on the Q side, and at the same time forestalls the positional threat 12 P—R5.

12 Q—K1
The turning-point in the game. Relying on the prospects of his K side attack, White allows a serious weakening of his Q side. In any event, after 12 Kt×Kt, Q×Kt, or 12 Kt—Q4, R—B1, Black has already surmounted the difficulties of the opening.

12 ...... Kt×Kt
13 P×Kt B—B3
14 B—B3 Q—B2
Not yet 14 .... Q—R4, because of the well-known stratagem 15 Kt—Q5 (Q—Q1; 16 Kt×B ch, Q×Kt; 17 B—Kt6, etc., with the dynamic advantage of *the two Bishops*).

15 R—B1 QR—B1
16 Q—Kt3
Heralding an attack on the K side. If 16 P—QKt4, Q—Q2; with 17 .... P—QKt4 to follow.

16 ...... Q—R4
17 KR—Q1 P—Q4
A vigorous thrust. Black does not fear the spectre of the *isolated pawn*, as this drawback will be more than set off by the increased mobility of his forces.

18 P×P B×P
19 B×B P×B
20 B—Q4 B—B4
21 Q—B2
Better is 21 K—R1, although even then Black maintains the lead after 21 .... B×B; 22 R×B, Kt—K5; 23 Q—K3, KR—K1, etc.

21 ...... Kt—Kt5
He surprisingly gives up the last defence of the isolated pawn for the sake of dynamic prospects, which he has, however, carefully weighed.

22 Q—Q2
If, e.g. 22 Q—B3, the continuation would

not be 22 .... B × B ch; 23 R × B, Q—Kt3; 24 R—Q1, etc., but, more cunningly, 22 .... Q—Kt3; 23 Q × P, Kt—K6 (23 .... KR—Q1; 24 B × B); 24 B × B, R × B; 25 Q—Q4 (25 Q—Q6, R—B3, winning the exchange); 25 .... Kt × R; 26 Kt—Q5, Q—K3, and the unexpected mating threat enables Black to maintain the gain of the exchange.

22 ......   KR—K1
Threatening 23 .... Kt—K6, while White can now reply neither with 23 B × B (23 .... Q × B ch), nor with 23 Kt × P (23 .... B × B ch, etc.).

23 K—R1   Q—Kt5
He continues his clever evolutions, on a terrain strewn with pitfalls.

24 Kt × P
In the mistaken belief that he can at last capture the tantalising pawn. Without being able altogether to redress the balance, he should have simplified matters by 24 B × B, etc.

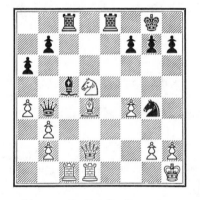

24 ......   Q × B
But not 24 .... Q × Q; 25 R × Q, B × B; 26 R × R, R × R; 27 Kt—K7 ch, K—B1; 28 Kt × R, Kt—B7 ch; 29 K—Kt1, and White wins. There follows an artistic *dénouement*.

25 Kt—K7 ch   K—B1
The decisive "point." But obviously not 25 .... B × Kt; 26 Q × Q, nor 25 .... R × Kt; 26 Q × Q, and wins.

26 Q × Q   B × Q
27 Kt × R   Kt—B7 ch
28 K—Kt1   Kt × R dis ch
Resigns.

304

White	Black
LASKER	PIRC

(Moscow, 1935)

In this stormy game, Black defers castling and neglects his own King's security in order to indulge in routine manœuvres on the Q side. The foolhardiness of this procedure is demonstrated by White with the utmost brilliance (13 R × Kt).

1 P—K4	P—QB4
2 Kt—KB3	Kt—QB3
3 P—Q4	P × P
4 Kt × P	Kt—B3
5 Kt—QB3	P—Q3
6 B—K2	P—K3
7 Castles	P—QR3

Instead of the customary 7 .... B—K2, followed by 8 .... Castles (safety first), Black at once starts manœuvring on the Q side.

8 B—K3	Q—B2
9 P—B4	Kt—QR4

The anticipation of the *Paulsen System* has as yet done no harm; but now he should have contented himself with 9 .... B—K2, consolidating his interior lines. There would follow 10 Q—K1, Kt—QR4; 11 R—Q1, Kt—B5; 12 B—B1, and White's re-grouping of his forces is effectively accomplished. It is in order to prevent this that Black expedites his counter-action on the Q side.

10 P—B5
Straight to the point—the KB file springs into life. If 10 Q—K1, as mentioned above, then 10 .... Kt—B5, forcing the pitiful retreat 11 B—B1, or else the exchange of the important King's Bishop. And if 10 Kt—Kt3, Kt—B5 (not 10 .... Kt × Kt; 11 RP × Kt, etc.); 11 B × Kt, Q × B; 12 P—K5, Kt—K5, etc., with a fierce battle in the centre.

10 ......   Kt—B5
An excess of consistency, which proves to be a decisive error of judgment. He should have kept the position closed by 10 .... P—K4, e.g. 11 Kt—Kt3, Kt—B5; 12 B × Kt, Q × B; 13 Q—B3, P—R3, and in spite of Black's weakness at Q3, which is more or less balanced by the weakness of White's KP, Black's game is tenable.

11 B × Kt	Q × B
12 P × P	P × P

After this plausible recapture, the storm breaks. But also after 12 .... B × P, Black's position is far from enviable.

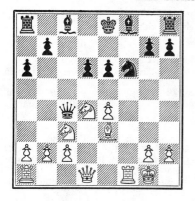

13 R × Kt

After this sacrifice of the exchange, Black's game collapses like a house of cards.

| 13 ...... | P × R |
| 14 Q—R5 ch | K—Q1 |

After 14 .... K—Q2, White wins by 15 Q—B7 ch, B—K2; 16 Kt—B5 (a pretty manœuvre, which needs foresight); 16 .... R—K1; 17 Kt ᐳ P, K ᐳ Kt; 18 Q × R, etc.

The most complicated but also the most artistic win results after 14 .... K—K2 from 15 Kt—B5 ch, with the following ramifications:

(a) 15 .... P × Kt; 16 Kt—Q5 ch, K—Q1 (16 .... K—Q2; 17 Kt—Kt6 ch); 17 B—Kt6 ch, K—Q2; 18 Q—B7 ch, K—B3; 19 Q—B7 ch, K—Kt4; 20 P—R4 ch, Q × P; 21 P—B4 ch, Q ᐳ P; 22 R—R5 mate.

(b) 15 .... K—Q2; 16 Q—B7 ch, K—B3; 17 Kt—Q4 ch, K—Kt3 (17 .... K—B4; 18 Q—B7 ch, K—Kt5; 19 P—R3 mate); 18 Kt—Kt3 dis ch, winning the Queen.

| 15 Q—B7 | B—Q2 |

After 15 .... B—K2 the win is as follows: 16 Kt—B5, Q—B2 (or 16 .... R—K1; 17 B—Kt6 ch, K—Q2; 18 Kt × P, etc.); 17 Kt—QR4 (not at once 17 B—Kt6, Q × B, with check!); 17 .... R—B1; 18 Q × RP, K—K1 (or 18 .... P × Kt; 19 B—Kt6, and wins); 19 B—Kt6, Q—Q2; 20 Q—R5 ch, R—B2; 21 Kt—Kt7 ch, K—B1; 22 Q—R8 mate.

| 16 Q × P ch | K—B2 |
| 17 Q × R | B—R3 |

A last hope of getting some compensation for the exchange after 18 Q × R, B × B ch; 19 K—R1, B × Kt, etc., but White's reply shatters all his illusions.

18 Kt × P ch

Breaking down the last defences.

18	Q × Kt
19 Q × R	B × B ch
20 K—R1	Resigns.

305

| *White* | *Black* |
| LASKER | NAPIER |

(Cambridge Springs, 1904)

The idea of opposing a fianchetto formation (Sicilian, Ruy Lopez, Indian or any other) by a pawn attack on the wing, and by castling on the other side (or, as here, not castling at all), is full of possibilities.

1 P—K4	P—QB4
2 Kt—QB3	Kt—QB3
3 Kt—B3	P—KKt3

This *Fianchetto Defence* (also called the *Dragon Variation*), formerly frequently used at the tournaments, fell into disuse for a time, but has more recently been taken up again with renewed vigour.

4 P—Q4	P × P
5 Kt × P	B—Kt2
6 B—K3	P—Q3
7 P—KR3	

If 7 Q—Q2, with a view to castling on the Q side, then, after 7 .... Kt—B3, he will still have to play 8 P—KR3 or, more artificially, 8 P—B3, in order to prevent 8 .... Kt—KKt5.

| 7 ...... | Kt—B3 |
| 8 P—KKt4 | |

Now White's bold but considered strategic plan is clear. A more non-committal line of play is 8 B—K2, Castles; 9 Q—Q2 (if 9 P—KKt4, P—Q4); 9 .... P—QR3 (more useful is 9 .... B—Q2, to be followed eventually by 10 .... Kt × Kt, and then .... B—B3); 10 R—Q1, Q—B2; 11 P—KKt4, P—QKt4 (instead of this suicidal move, simplification by 11 .... Kt × Kt; 12 B × Kt, B—K3, etc., is indicated); 12 P—Kt5, Kt—Q2; 13 Kt—Q5, and Black resigned (because of 13 .... Q—Kt2; 14 Kt × Kt, Q × Kt; 17 Kt × P ch), Taubenhaus-Smorodsky, *St. Petersburg*, 1914.

| 8 ...... | Castles |

Whatever may be White's machinations, the black King has no choice of domicile.

| 9 P—Kt5 | Kt—K1 |

Simpler would be 9 .... Kt—Q2, e.g.

10 P—KR4, Q—R4; 11 P—B4, Kt×Kt;
12 B×Kt, P—K4, and Black has chances of
equalising the game.

10 P—KR4	Kt—B2
11 P—B4	P—K4
12 Kt(Q4)—K2	P—Q4

With the over-ambitious desire to refute
White's lateral assault by counter-action in
the centre. 12 .... B—Kt5 would be better.

13 KP×P
And not 13 Kt×P, by reason of 13 ....
P×P; 14 B×BP, Kt×Kt; 15 P×Kt,
Kt—Kt5, etc., or 14 Kt×Kt, Q×Kt;
15 B×BP, Q—K2; 16 B—Kt2, Q—Kt5 ch,
etc., or 14 B—B5, R—K1, etc.

| 13 ...... | Kt—Q5 |
| 14 Kt×Kt | |

Not 14 B×Kt, P×B; 15 Kt×P, Kt×P,
etc.; the game is becoming too open for
White's safety.

14 ...... Kt×P
This intermediate move (with which Black
must have reckoned when deciding on his
12th move) to all appearances secures a
clear advantage for Black after 15 Kt×Kt,
P×Kt; 16 B×P, Q×Kt; 17 B×B, Q×R;
18 B×R, Q×P ch, etc.

15 Kt—B5
But with this magnificent parry, White
seems to have got out of the affray with the
gain of a piece.

15 ...... Kt×Kt
Yet Black is equal to the occasion, and
saves his material neatly.

| 16 Q×Q | R×Q |
| 17 Kt—K7 ch | |

One fine turn follows another! If 17 Kt×B,
Kt—Q4; 18 B—Q2, P×P, etc., and if
17 P×Kt, B×Kt.

17 ...... K—R1
Not 17 .... K—B1; 18 B—B5, Kt—K5;
19 B—QR3, Kt—Q3; 20 Kt×B, QR×Kt;
21 Castles, K—K2; 22 B—Kt2, and wins.
But now Black again seems to have the last
word, for if, e.g. 18 Kt×B, Kt—Q4, and if
18 P×Kt, P×P; 19 B—Q4, R—K1, recovering his piece with advantage.

18 P—R5
Thanks to his unexpected advance, the
contest assumes a different aspect. Black
is now threatened with a ruthless King's
field attack, namely: 19 RP×P, BP×P;
20 Kt×P ch, K—Kt1; 21 B—B4 ch,
Kt—Q4; 22 B×Kt ch, R×B; 23 Kt—K7
ch, and wins.

| 18 ...... | R—K1 |
| 19 B—B5 | P×RP |

Other ideas, also full of the unexpected,
and turning in favour of White, are 19 ....
KP×P; 20 P×P, BP×P; 21 B—Q3, etc.,
or again, 19 .... B—B1; 20 RP×P, etc.

20 B—B4
Strengthening his position with an imper-
turbable calm. The transaction 20 P×Kt,
B—B1; 21 B—Kt5, R×Kt; 22 B×R, B×B
would allow Black, by leaving him with
two Bishops, valuable compensation for the
loss of the exchange.

20 ...... P×P
Rightly seeking to improve his chances in
a counter-attack. Neither 20 .... B—B1
nor 20 .... B—K3, nor again 20 ....
Kt—K5 is altogether satisfactory.

21 KB×P
It all works splendidly.

21 ...... Kt—K5
A magnificent counter-effort.

22 B×R	B×P
23 R—QKt1	B—B6 ch
24 K—B1	B—KKt5

And here, after all the preceding vicissitudes, is the culminating point of the game.
Black, momentarily a Rook down, threatens
25 .... R×B or 25 .... Kt×B or 25 ....
Kt—Kt6 ch, or finally 25 .... Kt—Q7 ch.
How can White cope with this multitude of
threats?

25 B×KRP
A decision as surprising at first sight as it
is wise on consideration: he gives back the
Rook in return for a pawn!

25 ...... B×B
Or 25 .... Kt—Kt6 ch; 26 K—B2, B×B
(26 .... Kt×B; 27 R—R4); 27 R×B,
reverting to the continuation in the text.

26 R×B	Kt—Kt6 ch
27 K—Kt2	Kt×R
28 R×P	

The balance in material is still level,
but Black's weak BP is doomed.

28 ...... P—R4
Clearly not 28 .... R—KB1; 29 Kt—Kt6
ch.

29 R—Kt3	B—Kt2
30 R—KR3	Kt—Kt6
31 K—B3	

"The King—a strong piece," as Steinitz used to say.

31	R—R3

Here again, neither 31 .... R—KB1 nor 31 .... B—K4, on account of 32 Kt—Kt6 ch.

32 K × P	Kt—K7 ch
33 K—B5	Kt—B6
34 P—R3	Kt—R5
35 B—K3	Resigns

(There is no reply to P—Kt6, e.g. 35 .... B—B1; 36 B—Q4 ch, B—Kt2; 37 P—Kt6, P—R3; 38 R × P mate.)

A justly celebrated game.

306

White	*Black*
ALEKHINE	BOTVINNIK

(Nottingham, 1936)

The following contest, in spite of its brevity and its drawn result, is no less dramatic than the preceding game. The normal balance of position is maintained through all the various complications, and, strategically, we see once again how a lateral attack is parried by a counter-thrust in the centre (10 P—Kt4, P—Q4).

1 P—K4	P—QB4
2 Kt—KB3	P—Q3

A modern *opening finesse*, which is to lead by a detour to the *Dragon formation*, whereas in the usual way, after 2 .... Kt—QB3; 3 P—Q4, P × P; 4 Kt × P, Kt—B3; 5 Kt—QB3, P—Q3, White can (instead of 6 B—K2, P—KKt3) apply the *Anti-dragon variation* 6 B—KKt5. See Game No. 308, Alekhine-Silva da Rocha.

3 P—Q4	P × P
4 Kt × P	Kt—KB3
5 Kt—QB3	

Against the artificial attempt to cement the centre by 5 P—KB3, the reply is, not feebly 5 .... Kt—B3; 6 P—QB4, P—KKt3; 7 Kt—B3, B—Kt2; 8 B—K3, Castles; 9 Q—Q2, with a better formation for White, but courageously 5 .... P—K4; 6 Kt—Kt5, P—Q4 (in gambit style); 7 P × P, B—QB4 (not

yet 7 .... Kt × P; 8 Q × Kt); 8 P—QB4, Castles, etc., and Black, for the pawn sacrificed, has the initiative.

5	P—KKt3
6 B—K2	

A likely experiment is either 6 B—Kt5 (6 .... B—Kt2; 7 Q—Q2, etc.), or 6 B—Kt5 ch (6 .... B—Q2; 7 B—K3, Castles; 8 P—B3), or finally, 6 P—B3 (6 .... B—Kt2; 7 B—K3, Castles; 8 Q—Q2, Kt—B3; 9 Castles, etc.)

6	B—Kt2
7 B—K3	

Following Lasker's idea as shown in the preceding game. He could also play Castles here or on the next move.

7	Kt—B3
8 Kt—Kt3	

A well-known *consolidating manœuvre*, emanating from the Viennese master J. H. Bauer, which tries to prevent the liberating thrust 8 .... P—Q4. Other possible continuations are 8 P—B4, 8 P—KR3, 8 Q—Q2, or 8 Castles.

8	B—K3

Black is watchful, and fights for the control of his Q4 and of QB5 eventually. However, 8 .... Castles could also be played. But the counter-measure 8 .... Q—R4 would be too abrupt.

9 P—B4

This move is consistent, but carries with it certain commitments.

9	Castles

Coaxing his adversary with this peaceable move, instead of hastening his♦ counteraction by 9 .... Kt—QR4 (in order to initiate a local struggle for the possession of this important square). If 9 .... P—Q4, 10 P—K5.

10 P—Kt4

His answer: *the bayonet attack.* After 10 Castles, Kt—QR4, with a satisfactory game.

10	P—Q4

The only way of maintaining the balance, whereas after 10 .... Kt—QR4; 11 P—Kt5 (not 11 P—B5, B—B5, etc.); 11 .... Kt—K1 (better than 11 .... Kt—Q2; 12 Kt—Q4, to White's advantage); 12 Q—Q2, R—B1; 13 B—Q4, Kt—B5; 14 B × Kt, R × B; 15 Castles QR, and White has the better game.

11 P—B5
Against 11 P—K5, the fine reply 11 ....
P—Q5 frees Black's game.

11	B—B1
12 KP × P	Kt—Kt5
13 P—Q6	

The turning-point of the struggle. The
following lines are of doubtful expediency:
(a) 13 P × P, RP × P; 14 B—B3, Kt × KtP;
15 B × Kt, B × B; 16 Q × B, Kt × P ch;
17 K—K2, Kt × R; 18 R × Kt, B × Kt;
19 P × B, etc., with Rook and two pawns
against two minor pieces.
(b) 13 B—B3, P × P (13 .... P—K3;
14 B—B5); 14 P—Kt5, Kt—K5 (not 14 ....
Kt—Kt5; 15 B—B5, with fresh dangers for
Black).
The imbroglio could not well be worse.

13 ......   Q × P
Not, however, 13 .... KP × P; 14 P—Kt5,
followed by P—B6.

14 B—B5
After 14 Q × Q, P × Q; 15 Castles QR,
P ˃ P, etc., Black would be out of all danger.

14 ......   Q—B5
Surrounded by dangers, Black always finds
the only correct move. Weak would be
14 .... Q. Q ch; 15 R ˃ Q, Kt—B3;
16 P—Kt5, Kt—Q2; 17 P—B6, B—R1;
18 B—R3, R—K1; 19 Kt—Q5, and White
has full command of the situation.

15 R—KB1	Q ˃ RP
16 B · Kt	

White is at the moment a piece ahead, and
in order to keep afloat, Black must—give up
another!

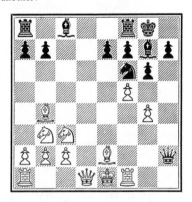

16 ......   Kt × P
The destruction of White's last pawn

defences enables Black to reach the safe
harbour of a perpetual check.

17 B × Kt
Compulsory acceptance! If 17 B—B5,
Q—Kt6 ch; 18 B—B2, B × Kt ch; 19 P × B,
Q × P ch; 20 Q—Q2, Q × Q ch, followed by
.... Kt × B and .... B × P, and Black has
four pawns for his piece.

17 ......   ' Q—Kt6 ch
18 R—B2
Not 18 K—K2, Q × B ch, nor 18 K—Q2,
B—R3 ch.

18 ......   Q—Kt8 ch
Draw.
A notable game between two protagonists
of *imaginative* chess.

307

White	*Black*
RICHTER	ENGELS

(Bad Saarow, 1937)

*This superb contest shows with outstanding
clearness that attacking is an art, and not
merely a matter of technique.*
*The game is full of original and refreshing
ideas, and the decisive sacrifice 23 Kt × RP
leaves a wholly æsthetic impression.*

1 P—K4	P—QB4
2 Kt—KB3	P—Q3
3 B—K2	Kt—QB3
4 P—Q4	P × P
5 Kt × P	Kt—B3
6 Kt—QB3	P—KKt3
7 Castles	B—Kt2
8 B—K3	

The purist prefers here 8 Kt—Kt3, as
illustrated in the beautiful brevity, Alekhine-
Desler, *Hamburg*, 1930: 8 Kt—Kt3, Castles
(more refractory is 8 .... B—K3; 9 P—B4,
Kt—QR4); 9 P—B4, B—Q2 (too passive!
more enterprising is here again 9 ....
B—K3); 10 B—B3, R—B1; 11 K—R1,
P—QR3; 12 P—QR4, Kt—QR4; 13 P—K5
(decisive penetration), Kt—K1; 14 Kt × Kt,
Q × Kt; 15 B × P, R—B2; 16 B—B3, B—Kt4
(he should have played 16 .... B—K3, preventing 17 Kt—Q5), 17 P—QKt4 (a dagger
thrust); 17 ....   Q × KtP; 18 Kt—Q5,
Q—B4 (18 .... Q—R4; 19 B—Q2);
19 P × B, Resigns.   A perfect gem!

8 ...... Castles

Renouncing the advance 8 .... P—Q4, as after 9 P×P, Kt×P (9 .... Kt—QKt5; 10 P—Q6); 10 QKt×Kt, Q×Kt; 11 B—B3, Q—B5; 12 P—B3, Black has not yet solved the problem of the opening.

9 Q—Q2

An important juncture! Instead of preparatory moves such as 9 P—KR3 or 9 P—B3, controlling KKt4, but which are apt to lead to .... P—Q4, White is intent on the speedy concentration of his forces. The alternative is 9 Kt—Kt3, as shown above.

9 ...... Kt—KKt5

Seeking to deprive his opponent of the *two Bishops*. Without any value at this stage would be 9 .... P—Q4, on account of 10 P×P, Kt×P (10 .... Kt—QKt5; 11 P—Q6); 11 QKt×Kt, Q×Kt; 12 B—B3, Q—B5; 13 P—QKt3, Q—R3; 14 Kt×Kt, P×Kt; 15 P—QB3, B—B4; 16 QR—Q1, and White has taken the lead.

The most prudent is 9 .... B—Q2; 10 QR—Q1, with play on the Q side.

10 B×Kt B×B
11 P—B4

Launching an effective K side attack, instead of the purely positional continuation, 11 P—B3, B—Q2; 12 QR—Q1, etc.

11 ...... B—Q2

Retiring in good time from the danger zone, before being cut off by P—B5. If 11 .... Kt—R4; 12 P—QKt3.

12 QR—Q1 R—B1

Instead of this routine move, a more independent idea is 12 .... Q—R4, followed eventually by .... P—B4.

A deceptive simplification would be 12 .... Kt×Kt; 13 B×Kt, B×B ch; 14 Q×B, B—B3, as White could still embark on a bold attack by 15 P—QKt4, Q—Kt3; 16 P—Kt5, B—Q2; 17 Kt—Q5, Q—Q1; 18 P—B5, P—B3 (18 .... B×KtP; 19 P—B6); 19 P×P, P×P; 20 P—B4, etc.

13 Q—B2 Kt—R4
14 P—B5 Kt—B5
15 Kt—Q5

Without losing time by 15 B—B1, White allows his second Bishop to be exchanged. In the resulting duel between *Knights and Bishops* he relies on the dominating position of his cavalry.

15 ...... Kt×B
16 Q×Kt R—K1

The gain of a pawn would be futile (16 .... B×Kt; 17 R×B, R×P), because of

18 Q—R6, with a winning attack (threats: 19 Kt×P ch, Q×Kt; 20 P—B6, etc., or 19 P—K5, with R—KR4 to follow).

Better than the text move is 16 .... B—QB3, in order, at the right moment, to eliminate one of the threatening Knights.

17 Q—B2 P—K3
18 Kt—K3

Premature would still be 18 P×KP, P×P; 19 Q—B7 ch, K—R1, etc., as well as 18 P—B6, P×Kt; 19 P×B, Q—K2; 20 P×P, P—B4, etc.

18 ...... K—R1

Or e.g. 18 .... KP×P; 19 P×P, Q—K2; 20 P×P, BP×P; 21 Kt—Q5, and White still has command of important strategic points.

19 P—B6 B—B1

If 19 .... B—R3; 20 Kt—Kt4.

20 P—K5

A telling pawn sacrifice! The idea is to bring his KKt *via* KB3 into the fray without losing the important pawn at KB6.

20 ...... P×P
21 Kt—B3 Q—B2

Necessary, in view of the threat 22 Kt×P.

22 Kt—Kt5 K—Kt1

Let us examine the other two methods of guarding the KBP:

(a) 22 .... B—Kt4; 23 P—B4, B×P; 24 Kt×B, Q×Kt; 25 Kt×P ch, K—Kt1; 26 Kt×P, and wins.

(b) 22 .... B—B3; 23 Kt—Kt4 (threat: 24 Kt×KP); 23 .... K—Kt1 (or 23 .... P—KR3; 24 Kt×RP, B×Kt; 25 Q—R4, etc.); 24 Kt×RP, Q—Kt3; 25 Q×Q, followed by Kt×B and Kt×P, with an easily won end game.

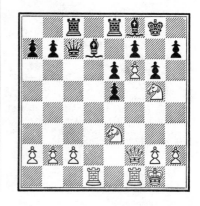

23 Kt × RP
A remarkable sacrifice.

23 ......   K × Kt
After 23 .... B—R3; 24 Kt—Kt4,
B—B5; 25 P—KKt3, and White wins.

24 Q—R4 ch   K—Kt1
Or 24 .... B—R3; 25 Kt—Kt4, etc.

25 R—B3
White is just in time with his final assault
on the KR file.

25 ......   B—Kt2
26 R—R3   K—B1
27 Q—R8 ch
The climax.

27 ......   B × Q
28 R × B mate.

308

White   Black
ALEKHINE   SILVA DA ROCHA
(Montevideo, 1938)

*A remarkable feature of this game is the
cousummate ease with which White—without
any noticeable error on his opponent's part—
succeeds in obtaining an advantage sufficient
to score a win. Dr. Alekhine knew, when
the need arose, not only how to create, but
also how methodically to prepare for, a
winning position.*

1 P—K4   P—QB4
2 Kt—KB3   Kt—QB3
3 P—Q4   P × P
4 Kt × P   Kt—B3
If already here 4 .... P—KKt3, then,
instead of 5 Kt—QB3, B—Kt2; 6 B—K3, etc.,
White can—as demonstrated by Maróczy—
improve his position by 5 P—QB4, e.g.
5.... B—Kt2; 6 B—K3, Kt—B3; 7 Kt—QB3,
P—Q3 (against 7 .... Kt—KKt5, Breyer's
idea, the reply is 8 Q × Kt, Kt × Kt;
9 Castles, Kt—B3; 10 B—Q2); 8 Kt—Kt3,
Castles; 9 P—B3, B—Q2; 10 Q—Q2,
Kt—K1; 11 Castles, and White increasingly
restricts the hostile position.

5 Kt—QB3   P—Q3
A wise precaution. If at once 5 ....
P—KKt3, White renders his opponent s task

difficult by 6 Kt × Kt (instead of the academic
6 B—K2, B—Kt2; 7 Castles, Castles, etc.);
6 .... KtP × Kt (the lesser evil is 6 ....
QP × Kt; 7 Q × Q ch, K × Q; 8 B—QB4,
K—K1; 9 Castles, B—Kt2, etc.); 7 P—K5,
Kt—Kt1; 8 Q—B3, preventing .... P—Q4;
and having therefore the better game.

6 B—KKt5
The turning-point. The text move increases
Black's difficulties, as he cannot now realise
the *Dragon Formation* (although he can play
the *Scheveningen Variation* by 6 .... P—K3).
This *Anti-dragon Variation* is thought so
strong that Black more often than not plays
2 .... P—Q3 in preference to 2 ....
Kt—QB3.

6 ......   B—Q2
The continuation 6 .... P—KKt3;
7 B × Kt, P × B; 8 Q—Q2 is not attractive
for Black, and if 6 .... Q—R4; 7 B—Kt5,
B—Q2; 8 Kt—Kt3, etc.
The most usual continuation is 6 ....
P—K3, as in Richter—Wagner, *Hamburg*,
1932: 7 Kt × Kt (the positional continuation
is 7 Q—Q2, or, in order to prevent 7 ....
Q—R4, the diversion 7 Kt—Kt3); 17 ....
P × Kt; 8 P—K5, P × P (if 8 .... Q—R4,
then not 9 B—Kt5, P × B; 10 P × Kt,
P—Kt5; 11 P × P, B × P; 12 Kt—K4,
Q—K4, etc., in Black's favour, but simply
9 B × Kt, P × B; 10 P × QP, Q—K4 ch;
11 B—K2, B × P; 12 Q—Q3, and White has
the advantage); 9 Q—B3, R—QKt1;
10 R—Q1, Q—B2; 11 Kt—K4, B—Kt5 ch;
12 P—B3, Kt × Kt; 13 B—Q8 (a very fine
intermediary manœuvre, whereas 13 R—Q8
ch, Q × R; 14 B × Q would have unpleasant
consequences for White after 14 .... B × P
ch); 13 .... Q—Kt2; 14 Q × Kt, B—B1
(better 14 .... B—Q2); 15 Q × KP, B—Q2;
16 R—R6 (a fresh surprise); 16 .... P—B3
(after 16 .... Q × P; 17 B—B7, etc., White
still has a decided advantage); 17 B × P,
P × B; 18 Q—R5 ch. Resigns.

7 B—K2
Here 7 B × Kt, KtP × B, etc., would not
be profitable.

7 ......   P—K3
8 Kt—Kt3
By this sound lateral manœuvre, he avoids
any simplification in the centre, whilst stressing the pressure along the semi-open Q file.
If 8 KKt—Kt5, Q—Kt1, etc., and if
8 Q—Q2, P—KR3 (9 B—R4, Kt × P).

8 ......   P—QR3
At this stage, and later on as well, Black
has no great desire to play .... B—K2, for

then White would obtain some positional advantage by simply playing 9 B × Kt, P × B (compulsory); 10 Q—Q2, etc.

9 Castles   P—Kt4
10 P—QR3   Kt—QR4

By this demonstration on the wing, Black abandons the control of the centre. Thus, in trying to avoid small ills (10 .... B—K2; 11 B × Kt, P × B), Black conjures up far greater evils.

11 Kt × Kt   Q × Kt
12 Q—Q4

Surveying the whole board, but preventing 12 .... P—Kt5.

12 ......   B—K2

Bowing to the inevitable.

13 KR—Q1

He calmly proceeds to improve his position, and enlivens the rather arid game with a "little combination," namely: if now 13 .... P—Kt5; 14 B × Kt, B × B; 15 Q × QP, and Black's QB is attacked!

13 ......   Q—B2

Better than giving up space in this manner would be 13 .... R—Q1, threatening 14 .... P—Kt5 (15 B × Kt, B × B, etc.).

14 P—QR4

A most instructive turn. Whereas in many games (e.g. No. 302, Maróczy—Euwe), White anticipates the impetuous advance of the adverse QKtP, White here calmly allows it to be effected in order to refute it afterwards.

14 ......   P—Kt5

As neither 14 .... P × P; 15 Kt × P, etc., nor 14 .... R—QKt1; 15 P × P, P × P; 16 R—R7 is satisfactory, Black tries to complicate matters in order to fish in troubled waters.

15 B × Kt

If at once 15 Q × KtP, R—QKt1; 16 Q—R3, P—Q4, etc., or 16 Q—Q4, P—K4 (instead of 16 .... R × P; 17 Kt—Q5, Q × P; 18 R—Q2, R—Kt8 ch; 19 B—B1, etc.); 17 Q—Q2, R × P; 18 B × P (if 18 B × Kt, P × B; 19 Kt—Q5, Q × P, etc.); 18 .... Castles; 19 B × Kt, B × B, etc., and Black can still cut some capers.

15 ......   P × B
16 Q × KtP   Q—B4

Resigning himself to the loss of a pawn, but seeking, at least, simplification. If now 16 .... R—QKt1; 17 Q—Q4, and if 17 .... R × P; 18 Kt—Q5, Q × P; 19 Kt × P ch, etc.,

nor is 17 .... P—K4; 18 Q—Q2, R × P; 19 B × P satisfactory.

17 Q—Q4

Subtle simplicity. White marks time.

17 ......   R—QKt1

Clearly not 17 .... Castles KR; 18 Q × Q, P × Q; 19 R × B. Relatively better would be 17 .... Q × Q; 18 R × Q.

18 Q × Q   P × Q
19 B × P

He demonstrates that the passed QR pawn possesses diabolic strength.

19 ......   R × P
20 B—Kt5   B × B
21 Kt × B   Castles

Hopeless would be 21 .... R × P; 22 Kt—B7 ch, K—B1; 23 P—R5, etc.

22 P—QB4   R—R1
23 P—R5   R—R3
24 P—Kt3

Not yet 24 R—Q7, R × RP.

24 ......   R—Kt5
25 R—Q7   B—B1
26 R—R7

After this fine exchanging manœuvre' the win becomes easy.

26 ......   R × R
27 Kt × R   R—Kt1

Returning post-haste, but there is no saving clause.

28 P—R6   R—R1
29 Kt—Kt5   B—K2
30 P—R7   B—Q1
31 R—Q1   B—Kt3
32 R—Q7   K—Kt2
33 R—Kt7   Resigns.

309

White .   Black
SPIELMANN   NIMZOWITSCH
(San Sebastian, 1911)

This game is remarkable for the simplicity of means by which Black gains the upper hand. Here the presence of Bishops of opposite colours does not facilitate but aggravates the defender's task, and the disintegrating effect of Black's Bishop is the more effective.

1 P—K4   P—QB4
2 Kt—KB3   Kt—KB3

With this provocative move—which was

first played in an important game in the present tournament and was later on much favoured by Rubinstein—Black proceeds to demonstrate the relativity of Time and Space. A forerunner of *Alekhine's Defence* 1 P—K4, Kt—KB3, this variation scored many successes before being tamed.

3 Kt—B3 P—Q4
More reserved is 3 .... P—Q3, followed by .... P—KKt3.

4 P×P
After 4 P—K5, Black can—besides the sly continuation 4 .... KKt—Q2 (e.g. 5 Kt×P, Kt×P; 6 Kt—K3, Kt×Kt ch; 7 Q×Kt, Kt—B3, etc.)—risk the "leap in the dark" 4 .... Kt—K5, and if 5 Kt—K2 (intending to confiscate the recalcitrant Knight by 6 P—Q3), then 5 .... P—B5.

4 ...... Kt×P
5 B—B4
Non-committal. Feeble is also 5 P—Q4, Kt×Kt; 6 P×Kt, P—K3; 7 B—Q3, B—K2, etc., and, as the position becomes clarified, Black will begin to lay stress on the weaknesses in the white formation. After 5 Kt×Kt, Q×Kt; 6 P—Q4, P—K3, the games are even.

Much more astute is L. Steiner's stratagem: 5 Kt—K5, Kt×Kt; 6 KtP×Kt (if 6 Q—B3, Q—Q4; 7 Q×Kt, Kt—Q2; 8 B—Kt5, P—QR3, and Black has freed his game); 6 .... Q—Q4 (more solid is 6 .... Q—B2, e.g. 7 B—Kt5 ch, Kt—Q2; 8 Q—K2, P—K3; 9 Castles, B—Q3; 10 R—K1, Castles, and Black has an adequate defence); 7 B—Kt5 ch, Kt—Q2 (preferable, in spite of appearing risky, is 7 .... Kt—B3; 8 Kt×Kt, P×Kt; 9 B—K2, Q×KtP; 10 B—B3, Q—Kt3, etc.); 8 Q—K2 (a piquant conception); 8 .... P—QR3 (against 8 .... Q×KtP, the splendid reply 9 Q—Q3, Q×R ch; 10 K—K2, P—K3; 11 B×Kt ch, etc., brilliantly forces the win); 9 B×Kt ch, B×B; 10 Castles, etc., with enduring dynamic assets for White.

Sir George Thomas's stratagem contains the most vitality: 5 B—Kt5 ch, B—Q2; 6 Kt—K5, B×B (trying to cut the Gordian knot, instead of the more complicated continuation 6 .... Kt—QB3 or 6 .... Kt—KB3). If, plausibly, 6 .... Kt×Kt, there follows elegantly 7 Q—B3, P—B3; 8 Q—R5 ch, P—Kt3; 9 Kt×P, K—B2; 10 Kt—K5 db ch, forcing capitulation. (Thomas–Sapira, *Antwerp*, 1932.)

Against the artificial manœuvre 5 Kt—K4, the highly amusing continuation of a game P. Johner–Tartakower, *Berlin*, 1928, was as follows: 5 .... P—K3; 6 P—Q4, P×P; 7 Kt×P, B—K2; 8 B—Kt5 ch, B—Q2;

9 P—QB4, Kt—KB3; 10 Kt—QB3 (still avoiding exchanges for no apparent reason); 10 .... Castles; 11 Castles, Q—B2; 12 Q—K2, Kt—B3; 13 Kt—B3, KR—K1 (an astute manœuvre); 14 B—Kt5, Kt—KKt5; 15 B×B (falling into the trap; but even after the only possible parry, 15 P—KKt3, White's game totters); 15 .... Kt—Q5; White resigns.

5 ...... P—K3
Or at once 5 .... Kt×Kt; 6 KtP×Kt, P—K3, etc. Playable also is 5 .... Kt—Kt3, as the sacrifice 6 B×P ch would be unsound.

6 Castles B—K2
7 P—Q4 Kt×Kt
8 P×Kt Castles
9 Kt—K5 Q—B2
Skilfully applying pressure on the QB file. If 9 .... Kt—Q2; 10 P—B4, Kt—Kt3; 11 B—K2, etc., or 10 .... Kt—B3; 11 B—Kt2, with advantage to White.

10 B—Q3
Not 10 P—B4, P×P; 11 Q—K2 (if 11 P×P, P—B3, winning a piece, and 11 Q×P, B—B4, winning the Queen); 11 .... P×P; and Black has won two pawns with impunity.

10 ...... Kt—B3
11 B—KB4 B—Q3
12 R—K1
To avoid the creation of a weak point at K5. If 12 Kt×Kt, B×B.

12 ...... P×P
13 P×P Kt—Kt5
Instead of the doubtful transaction 12 .... Kt×P; 13 B×P ch, K×B; 14 Q×Kt, etc., Black applies a far simpler method of depriving his adversary of the *two Bishops*.

14 B—Kt3 Kt×B
15 Q×Kt P—QKt3
16 P—QB4
White's *hanging pawns* in the centre will be a source of worry rather than of strength.

16 ...... B—R3
17 QR—B1 QR—B1
18 Q—Kt3 P—B3
19 Q—R4
Or 19 Kt—B3, B×B; 20 RP×B, B×P, with the gain of a vital pawn.

19 ...... P×Kt
20 P×P
Or 20 Q×B, P×P; 21 R×P, B×B; 22 RP×B, R×P; 23 K×R, Q—B2 ch; 24 K—Kt1, Q×R, threatening Q—K6 ch.

20 ...... B—R6
By this piquant interpolation, which leaves White with a *dead point* at K5 (instead of

20 .... KB×P; 21 R×B), Black secures
a palpable positional advantage.

| 21 | Q×KB | B×P |
| 22 | R—K4 | Q—Q2 |

Far more energetic than 23 .... P—QKt4.
Black unpins his Bishop and turns to account
the superior disposition of his forces.

23 P—R3

Obviously not 23 KR×B, R×R; 24 R×R,
Q—Q8 mate. Or 23 Q—Q6, Q×Q (not
23 .... Q—R5; 24 KR×B, R×R;
25 Q×P ch, and wins); 24 P×Q, B×P;
25 R×R, R×R; 26 R—K1, K—B2 (26 ....
B—Q4; 27 B—R4, or 26 .... R—Q1;
27 R—R1); 27 R—R1 (27 B—R4, K—K1,
or 27 R—Q1, B—Q4); 27 .... R—B7, and
Black has a decisive advantage in two united
passed pawns.

23	......	B—Q4
24	R—K2	Q—Kt2
25	P—B4	Q—KB2
26	R (K2)—QB2	R×R
27	R×R	Q—Kt3
28	Q—QB3	

Losing a pawn, but he has nothing better.

| 28 | ...... | B×RP |
| 29 | B—R4 | |

At last White's Bishop is freed at the cost
of a pawn (29 R×B, Q—Kt8 ch, followed
by .... Q×R), but Black's advantage is
already decisive.

29	......	B—Q4
30	B—K7	R—K1
31	B—Q6	Q—K5
32	Q—B7	P—KR3
33	R—B2	Q—K8 ch
34	R—B1	Q—K6 ch
35	R—B2	P—QR4
36	B—K7	Q—K8 ch
37	R—B1	Q—K6 ch
38	R—B2	K—R1

Parrying the subtle threat 39 B—B6.

39	B—Q8	Q—K8 ch
40	R—B1	Q—K6 ch
41	R—B2	Q—K8 ch
42	R—B1	Q—Kt6

Preparing the final assault.

43	R—B2	R—B1
44	Q×P	R×P
45	B—K7	P—R5
46	K—B1	Q×P ch
	Resigns.	

310

White	Black
YATES	NIMZOWITSCH

(Carlsbad, 1929)

*In the following game, White does not
allow himself to be intimidated by his great
adversary, and finds an adequate reply to all
his attempts at violence. A fine example of
an active defence!*

| 1 | P—K4 | P—QB4 |
| 2 | Kt—KB3 | Kt—KB3 |

"*Spécialité de la Maison.*"

3 P—K5

More authoritative, but incurring more
responsibilities than 3 Kt—B3

| 3 | ...... | Kt—Q4 |
| 4 | Kt—B3 | |

This move contains much concealed
energy. After 4 P—B4, these methods lead
to equality, namely: 4 .... Kt—Kt3;
5 P—Q4, P—K3; 6 P—Q5, P—Q3, etc., or
4 .... Kt—B2; 5 P—Q4, P×P; 6 Q·P,
Kt—B3; 7 Q—K4, P—Q4; 8 P·Pe.p.,
Q×P; 9 Kt—B3, Q—Kt3; 10 Q·Q,
RP×Q, etc., or even 4 .... Kt—Kt5;
5 P—Q4, P×P; 6 P—QR3 (if 6 Kt·P,
P—Q3, etc.); 6 .... KKt—B3; 7 B—B4,
P—Q3, etc.

An intensive line of play is 4 P—Q4, P·P;
5 Q·P (or 5 Kt·P, P—K3, etc., with an
even game); 5 .... P—K3; 6 P—B4,
Kt—QB3; 7 Q—K4, etc., exerting pressure.

| 4 | ...... | P—K3 |

Holding his own. If 4 .... Kt×Kt;
5 QP·Kt, etc., to White's advantage. Not
without drawbacks would be digressions by
the Knight: 4 .... Kt—Kt3, or 4 ....
Kt—B2; 5 P—Q4, P·P; 6 Q×P, Kt—B3;
7 Q—K4, etc., or also 4 .... Kt—Kt5;
5 P—Q4, etc.

5 Kt—K4

Instead of this artificial manœuvre, the smoothest continuation is 5 Kt×Kt, P×Kt; 6 P—Q4, P—Q3 (a curious formation, in the shape of a closed fist, of the five pawns in the middle of the board); 7 KP×P, B×P; 8 B—K2, etc., with a slight positional advantage for Black.

5 ......   P—B4

Black fights energetically for the initiative.

6 Kt—B3

If 6 P×P e.p., Kt×P (not 6 .... P×P; 7 Kt—R4); 7 Kt×Kt, Q×Kt, Black has an advantage in space. White has now lost some time, but he has the satisfaction of having disarranged the hostile K side.

6 ......   Kt×Kt

Trusting in the power of resistance of his own position, Black opens up enemy lines.

7 QP×Kt   B—K2
8 B—KB4   Q—Kt3

A demonstration. Of course not 8 .... P—KKt4; 9 Kt×P, B×Kt; 10 Q—R5 ch, etc.

9 P—QKt3   Q—B2
10 B—Q3   P—QKt3
11 Q—K2   P—B5

A promising idea, for which Black chooses the tactical moment when 12 B×QBP cannot be played on account of 12 .... P—QKt4; 13 B×KtP, Q×P ch, followed by .... Q×R ch, etc.

12 P×P

The trebled pawn on the exposed QB file does not present a pretty picture, but, after all is said and done—it is an extra pawn!

12 ......   Kt—B3
13 Castles KR   B—Kt2

More to the point is 13 .... B—R3, to be followed by .... Kt—R4, but Black thinks the recovery of the pawn of only relative importance, and prefers to attack.

14 KR—K1   Castles QR
15 QR—Q1   B—B4

If 15 .... Kt—R4; 16 Kt—Q4.

16 Kt—Q2

Playing for consolidation by 17 Kt—Kt3.

16 ......   P—KKt4

He considers the time ripe for the big *coup*.

17 B—K3   Kt×P

Black exults, having regained a sound

pawn and left his adversary with bad ones.

18 B×B

Not 18 QB×P, Kt—Kt5, with a double threat.

18 ......   Kt—Kt5
19 P—Kt3   Q×B
20 B—K4

Effecting, by this beautiful and unexpected manœuvre, a complete change in the situation.

20 ......   B—R3

The transaction 20 .... B×B; 21 Kt×B, P×Kt; 22 Q×Kt, Q×P; 23 KR×P does not appeal to Black.

21 B—Kt2

The dispossession of the original holder of the long white diagonal is effected in an original manner.

21 ......   K—B2
22 P—KR3   Kt—B3
23 Q—B3

Threatening 24 Kt—Kt3, Q×P; 25 R—Q4, etc.

23 ......   Q—B3
24 Q—K3

He prefers a pitched battle to a partial liquidation by 24 Q×Q ch, P×Q; 25 R×P, Kt—K5; 26 B×Kt, P×B; 27 R×P, P—B4; 28 KR—K1, P—R3, etc., and, although White has "on paper" two extra pawns, the win could hardly be enforced.

24 ......   Kt—K5
25 Kt×Kt   P×Kt
26 Q×KtP   P—Q4

Grimly holding on to the advanced pawn; if, e.g. 26 .... B×P; 27 R×KP, B—Q4; 28 Q—B4 ch, K—B1 (or 28 .... K—Kt2; 29 R—B4, etc., or 28 .... P—Q3; 29 R—R4, etc.); 29 R—R4, P—QR4 (29 .... B×B; 30 R—B4); 30 B×B, P×B; 31 KR—Q4, Q×P; 32 R×P, and Black's disrupted position cannot be defended.

27 P×P   P×P
28 Q—K5 ch   K—B1
29 P—QR4   KR—B1
30 Q—Q4   Q—B5
31 P—R4   Q×Q
32 R×Q

A new phase begins.

32 ......   R—B2

With multiple objects (33 .... QR—B1, or 33 .... KR—Q2, or 33 .... R—B2).

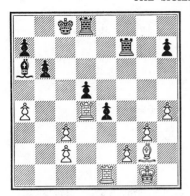

33 P—QB4
An unanticipated resource.

33 ...... QR—B1
Seeking salvation in a counter-attack.
Black would have no real chance after
33 .... B × P; 34 B × P, etc., or after 33 ....
P × P; 34 B—R3 ch, K—B2; 35 R (Q4) × KP,
etc.

34 P × P   R × P
35 B × P   P—R3
36 P—Q6
The rest requires no comments.

36 ......   R—B8 ch
37 R × R   B × R
38 P—Kt4   B—R3
39 B—B5 ch   K—Q1
40 P—KR5   B—K7
41 K—R2   P—R4
42 K—Kt3   R—B3
43 K—B4   Resigns.

311

White   Black
LEONHARDT   RICHMOND
(Hastings, 1904)

*In the struggle for the initiative, Black
renounces castling, leaving his King in the
middle of the board. In the struggle for the
attack, White tries to take advantage of the
adverse King's position by a frontal attack,
giving up a piece in the process. After sur-
mounting many dangers, the defender's success
illustrates the power of resistance inherent in
an inert mass, provided this resistance is
guided by a clear mind and a firm hand.*

1 P—K4   P—QB4
2 Kt—QB3
Followed at once by P—KKt3, and later
on by P—Q3, this *closed treatment* of the
Sicilian Defence is not without guile. If at
once 2 P—KKt3, Black plays 2 .... P—Q4
(which the text move is intended to prevent),
and Black's game is free.

2 ......   Kt—QB3
This symmetrical reply, followed later on
by the symmetrical *counter-fianchetto* ....
P—KKt3, represents the most viable idea
in this difficult chapter.
A different plan, trying to spread out in
the centre, is 2 .... P—K3; 3 P—KKt3,
P—Q4; 4 P × P, P × P; 5 B—Kt2, Kt—KB3;
6 P—Q3, B—K2; 7 KKt—K2, P—Q5 (putting a stop to the threatened thrust 8 P—Q4);
8 Kt—K4, and White has the initiative.

3 KKt—K2   P—KKt3
4 P—KKt3   B—Kt2
5 B—Kt2   P—Q3
6 P—Q3   Kt—Q5
With this move, which, although fitting
into the general scheme, is usually played a
little later, Black indicates his intention of
taking the lead at the earliest opportunity.
Other feasible plans are: (*a*) 6 .... Kt—B3,
in order to castle as soon as possible;
(*b*) 6 .... B—Q2, to be followed by ....
Q—B1, with pressure on the diagonal
QB1—KR6, e.g. 7 Castles, Q—B1; 8 Kt—Q5,
P—KR4, burning his bridges; (*c*) 6 ....
P—K3, with .... KKt—K2 to follow.

7 P—KR3
Or at once 7 Castles, and if 7 .... B—Kt5;
8 P—B3.

7 ......   B—Q2
8 B—K3   P—K3
If 8 .... Q—B1; 9 Kt—B4.

9 Castles   Q—Kt3
Black could also have played 9 ....
Kt—K2 at once, with a view to ....
KKt—B3, strengthening his colonial pos-
sessions at Q5.
Another line of play would be 9 ....
R—Kt1, to be followed by .... P—QKt4,
or even at once 9 .... P—QKt4 (if
10 P—K5, P—Q4).

10 R—Kt1   Kt—K2
11 Q—Q2   P—KR3
This move is equivalent to giving up
castling.

12 P—R3   P—QR4
In order to prevent 13 P—QKt4, but it is

clear that castling on the Q side now becomes undesirable for Black.

| 13 K—R2 | P—R5 |
| 14 P—B4 | |

Hoping to break down the opposite wall of pawns.

| 14 ...... | P—B4 |

A reply which shows spirit.

15 KR—K1

A discreet preparation. It is hard to credit that the K file, now crowded by seven pieces, could be rapidly unmasked.

| 15 ...... | P—R4 |
| 16 P—R4 | Kt—Kt1 |

To be followed by .... Kt—KB3 and .... Kt—Kt5 ch (taking advantage of the hole at KKt5).

| 17 P×P | KtP×P |
| 18 Kt—Q5 | |

A pretty idea, aiming at piercing the K file (if 18 .... P×Kt; 19 Kt×Kt, etc.), but, luckily for Black, at chess—unlike draughts —there is no compulsion to capture.

| 18 ...... | Q—Q1 |
| 19 B×Kt | |

Instead of the sheepish retreat 19 QKt—B3 (upon which Black would have proceeded with his plan by 19 .... R—Kt1, followed by .... Kt—KB3), White reckons on maintaining his position.

| 19 ...... | P×B |
| 20 Q—Kt4 | |

A promising sacrifice. But if 20 Kt—Kt4, R—Kt1, etc., and Black has the advantage.

| 20 ...... | P×Kt |

Black must effect this capture, for if 20 .... B—QB3; 21 Kt×P.

| 21 Kt×P dis ch | Kt—K2 |
| 22 B×P | R—KR3 |

A skilful defence.

23 R—K3

If 23 B×P, R—Kt1 (threat: 24 .... B×Kt); 24 Kt—B6, B×Kt; 25 B×B ch, K—B1; 26 Q×RP, R×P, etc. Better would be at once 23 B—R2.

| 23 ...... | K—B1 |
| 24 B—R2 | Q—B2 |

Preventing 25 Q—B4.

| 25 QR—K1 | R—K1 |
| 26 Kt—Kt5 | Q—Kt3 |

Not 26 .... Q×P ch; 27 R (K3)—K2,

Q—B4; 28 Q×Q, P×Q; 29 Kt—B7, R—B1; 30 R×Kt, R×Kt; 31 R—B7 ch, and wins.

27 Q—B4

A vain attempt, but by playing 27 P—B4 (B×Kt; 28 P×B, Q—Q5, etc.), White would have disavowed his previous policy.

| 27 ...... | P—Q4 |

Short-circuiting his opponent's plans.

28 Q—Kt4	Q×Kt
29 R×Kt	Q×Q
30 R×R ch	B×R
31 P×Q	B×P
32 B×P	B—B2
Resigns	

Black's defence is above all praise.

312

White	Black
WOLF	LASKER

(Mährisch-Ostrau, 1923)

The manner in which Black carves out for himself a chance of counter-play in the centre, culminating in the thrust 13 .... P—Q4, is nothing short of exemplary.

1 P—K4	P—QB4
2 Kt—QB3	Kt—QB3
3 P—KKt3	P—KKt3

This *counter-fianchetto* is more stable than the following schemes:

(a) 3 .... P—K3; 4 B—Kt2, Kt—B3; 5 KKt—K2, P—Q4 (opening the centre); 6 P×P, P×P; 7 P—Q4, etc.

(b) 3 .... Kt—B3; 4 B—Kt2, P—Q3; 5 KKt—K2, P—K4 (blocking up the centre); 6 Castles, P—KR4; 7 P—KR3 (in order to reply to 7 .... P—R5 with 8 P—KKt4); 7 .... P—KKt4; 8 P—Q3, R—KKt1; 9 Kt—Q5, with uncertain issue.

4 B—Kt2	B—Kt2
5 P—Q3	P—Q3
6 KKt—K2	Kt—B3

The motto is "Development before everything."

7 Castles

More to the point is 7 P—KR3, followed by B—K3, Q—Q2, P—KB4, etc., with a nice formation in the centre.

| 7 ...... | Castles |
| 8 P—KR3 | |

If at once 8 B—K3, Kt—KKt5.

8 ...... Kt—K1

Very effectively unmasking the long diagonal. More dilatory is 8 .... B—Q2, which, after 9 B—K3, etc., favours White's prospects.

9 B—K3 Kt—Q5

Hindering White's primary intention of playing 10 P—Q4.

10 K—R2

Too many preparations, although he evidently could not play 10 Q—Q2 at once because of 10 .... B × P. The most energetic would be 10 P—KKt4, with a view to Kt—Kt3 and P—KB4, etc.

10 ...... B—Q2
11 Q—Q2 R—B1
12 Kt—Q1

Here again 12 P—KKt4 would be more incisive.

12 ...... B—QB3
13 Kt—Kt1 P—Q4

This advance, well prepared by the five preceding moves, pulverises the centre.

14 P—QB3 Kt—K3
15 P × P B × QP
16 P—B3 Kt—Q3
17 Kt—B2 Kt—B4
18 Kt—Kt4 Q—Q3
19 Kt—K2 P—KR4
20 Kt—R6 ch Kt × Kt
21 B × Kt P—R5
22 B × B Kt × B
23 Q—B4 P × P ch
24 Q × P P—K4

Threatening 25 .... Kt—R4.

25 K—R1 KR—K1
26 KR—Q1 Q—KB3
27 Q—B2 Kt—K3
28 R—Q2 K—Kt2

Preparing the invasion of the open KR file.

29 K—R2 QR—Q1
30 P—R3 R—KR1
31 R—K1 Kt—Kt4
32 Kt—Kt1

After many heterogeneous attempts, the Knight is to remain on the defensive.

32 ...... Q—B5 ch
33 K—R1

In the hope of regaining territory after 33 .... R—QB1; 34 Q—K3, etc.

33 ...... B × P

His profound manœuvres now culminate in a finely wrought combination.

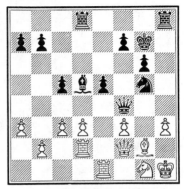

Position after 33 K—R1

34 B × B Kt × P
35 Q—K3

Or 35 Kt × Kt, R × Kt ch; 36 K—Kt2, R—R7 ch.

35 ...... Kt—Kt4 dis ch
Resigns

(36 K—Kt2, R—R7 ch; 37 K—B1, R × R, etc.)

313

White	Black
NIMZOWITSCH	GILG

(Kecskemet, 1927)

By a most astute sacrifice of a pawn (8 P—Q4), White disrupts the central zone, which in the sequel becomes a highway for all kinds of irruptions (e.g. 15 B × P ch), and other violent expeditions (e.g. 20 R × B).

1 P—K4 P—QB4
2 Kt—KB3 Kt—QB3
3 B—Kt5

By way of varying his *répertoire*, White assigns his KB a part infrequently seen in this opening.

3 ...... Q—B2

Black, over-cautious, gives too much thought to the strengthening of his Q3. He should simply continue his development by 3 .... P—Q3 or 3 .... P—KKt3, etc.

4 P—B3   P—QR3
5 B—R4   Kt—B3
6 Q—K2   P—K4
7 Castles   B—K2
8 P—Q4

A very shrewd offer of a pawn.

8 ......   BP×P

Not to be commended is 8 .... Castles;
9 B×Kt, Q×B; 10 P×KP, etc. But it
would be best to refuse the bait, and to keep
K4 under fire by 8 .... P—Q3 (9 P—Q5,
P—QKt4, etc.).

9 P×P   Kt×QP
10 Kt×Kt   P×Kt
11 P—K5   P—Q6

If at once 11 .... Kt—Q4; 12 P—K6, etc.

12 Q—K3

Making for an observation post at KKt3,
(e.g. if 12 .... B—B4; 13 Q—Kt3).

12 ....   Kt—Q4
13 Q—Kt3   P—KKt3

He cannot play the normal 13 ....
Castles, because of 14 B—Kt3 (not yet
14 B—R6, B—B3; 15 P×B, Q×Q;
16 BP×Q, P×B, etc.); 14 .... Q—B3;
15 B×Kt, Q×KB; 16 B—R6, winning the
exchange.

14 B—Kt3   Kt—Kt5

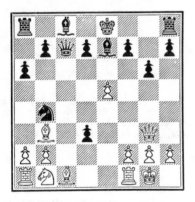

15 B×P ch

Ransacking the hostile fortress.

15 ......   K—Q1

Not 15 .... K×B, on account of
16 P—K6 ch, followed by Q×Q.

16 B—R6

The sequence of sacrifices continues.

16 ......   Kt—B7
17 Kt—B3

Easy, but pretty to look at. If now
17 .... Kt×R; 18 Kt—Q5, Q—B3;
19 B—K3 (weaving a mating net); 19 ....
P—Q3; 20 B—Kt6 ch, K—Q2; 21 P—K6
mate.

17 ......   Kt—Q5

With the desperate counter-threat 18 ....
Kt—K7 ch.

18 Q×QP   Q×P
19 KR—K1   Q—B3
20 R×B

More fireworks.

20 ......   Resigns

To wind up, a double "key": if 20 ....
K×R; 21 Kt—Q5 ch, and if 20 .... Q×R;
21 Q×Kt, etc.

314

White	Black
White	*Black*
KERES	ELISKASES

(Semmering-Baden, 1937)

*In the following game there is a curious
contrast between the early and hesitating
manœuvres on either side and White's precise
and trenchant sacrifice of the exchange.*

1 P—K4   P—QB4
2 Kt—KB3

The old *Sicilian Gambit*, 2 P—QKt4
(which was discussed already in 1623 in an
Italian MS.), has been found wanting. The
continuation is 2 .... P×P; 3 P—QR3 (if
3 P—Q4, P—Q4; 4 P—K5, B—B4, etc., in
favour of Black); 3 .... P—Q4 (awkward
for Black is 3 .... P×P; 4 Kt×P, P—Q4;
5 P×P, Q×P; 6 B—Kt2, etc.); 4 KP×P (or
4 P—K5, Kt—QB3; 5 P—Q4, Q—Kt3;
6 B—K3, B—B4, etc., and Black is active);
4 .... Q×P; 5 B—Kt2, P—K4, etc., with
advantage to Black.

2 ......   P—Q3

We have seen the numerous advantages of
this move, preparing a strong defence with
resctricted centre (leading either to the
Dragon or the *Scheveningen Variations*),
reserving the development of the QKt (at
Q2 or QB3).

Has it then only advantages and no vulnerable points?

3 P—QKt4
Here is the answer! On the strength of one extra developing move, White tries to rejuvenate the *Sicilian Gambit*, which was introduced to tournament practice by Keres himself.

3 ......   P × P
The *Keres Gambit Accepted*! To decline it is of doubtful expediency, e.g. 3 .... Kt—KB3; 4 P × P, Kt × P; 5 P × P, Kt × P (Q3); 6 B—Kt2, etc., with fine initiatory position for White.

4 P—Q4
Unlike the original *Wing Gambit*, the present variation allows White to make straight for the centre, instead of deflecting his impetus to the extreme left wing by 4 P—QR3.

4 ......   Kt—KB3
Intending .... P—Q4.

5 B—Q3
Storing his energy instead of spending it prematurely on 5 P—K5, P × P; 6 Kt × P, etc.

5 ......   P—Q4
After 5 .... B—Kt5; 6 P—QR3 reopens the argument, e.g.: accepting the sacrifice 6 .... P × P; 7 Kt × P, Kt—B3; 8 P—B3, with a fine attack in view; or giving back the pawn, 6 .... Kt—B3; 7 P—Q5, B × Kt (not at once 7 .... Kt—K4, because of the well-known *Queen sacrifice*, 8 Kt × Kt, B × Q; 9 B—Kt5 ch, and wins); 8 P × B, Kt—K4; 9 B—Kt5 ch, QKt—Q2; 10 P × P, and White has the better game.

6 QKt—Q2
If 6 P—K5, Kt—K5.

6 ......   P × P
7 Kt × P   QKt—Q2
More simple would be 7 .... Kt × Kt.

8 QKt—Kt5
A distant expedition, with various unexpected halts. After 8 Castles, the following simplification tends to equalisation: 8 .... Kt × Kt; 9 B × Kt, P—K3; 10 B—Kt2, B—K2; 11 B—Q3, Castles; 12 Kt—K5, Kt × Kt; 13 P × Kt, P—B4, etc.

8 ......   Q—B2
Black's tribulations are beginning. After 8 .... P—KR3, White has the choice between the very promising sacrifice 9 Kt × P, K × Kt; 10 Kt—K5 ch, Kt × Kt; 11 P × Kt, Kt—Q4 (forced); 12 Q—R5 ch, K—Kt1;

13 B—Kt6, B—K3; 14 P—KB4, etc., and the less attractive but still favourable line: 9 Kt—K6, Q—Kt3 (9 .... P × Kt; 10 B—Kt6 mate); 10 Kt × B, etc.

9 P—B4   P—KR3
If 9 .... P × P e.p.; 10 Q—Kt3, P—K3; 11 Kt × BP, K × Kt; 12 Kt—Kt5 ch, White has an incisive attack.

10 Kt—R3   P—KKt4
11 QKt—Kt1
The seeming modesty of the text move disguises a great law, that of the *regeneration of squares*. The Knight finds, *via* K2, etc., fresh sources of energy.

11 ......   B—Kt2
12 Kt—K2   P—K4
13 Kt—Kt3
White's attack takes a new lease of life.

13 ......   Castles
14 Castles   P—K5
After 14 .... P × P; 15 Kt—B5, etc., Black's worries would still be many. Relatively best is 14 .... R—K1.

15 QKt × P   Kt × Kt
16 B × Kt   Q × P
17 B—Q3   Q—Q4
If 17 .... Q—B6; 18 R—Kt1.

18 R—K1   P—Kt5
19 Kt—R4   Kt—Kt3
Recognising that White's QP is still safe from capture, but wiser would be 19 .... Kt—B3, increasing the number of defenders in the blazing sector.

20 R—Kt1   B—Q2
If 20 .... P—QR4; 21 P—QR3. If 20 .... Q × RP; 21 R × P. And if 20 .... B × P; 21 B × P, etc.

21 R—K4   KR—K1
22 R—B4   Q—Q3
23 B—Q2   Kt—Q4

24 R × KKtP

A far-sighted sacrifice of the exchange, eliminating an important centre of resistance.

24	B × R
25 Q × B	Q—KB3

Not 25 .... Kt—B3; 26 Q × B ch, K × Q; 27 Kt—B5 ch, etc.

26 Kt—B5	K—B1
27 Kt × B	Q × Kt
28 Q—R5	

Stronger than at once 28 Q—R4, R—K3, which leaves the black Knight in active service.

28	Kt—B3
29 Q—R4	P—KR4
30 R × P	QR—B1
31 P—KR3	

Safety first. A terrible blunder would be 31 B—B5, because of mate in two by 31 .... R—B8 ch, etc. Or, e.g. 31 R × P, Q—Kt5; 32 Q × Kt, R—B8 ch; 33 B × R, R—K8 ch; 34 B—B1, R × B ch; 35 K × R, Q—Q8 mate.

31	R—B2
32 R—Kt5	

The final assault. Threat: 33 B—Kt4 ch, K—Kt1; 34 R—Kt5, winning the Queen.

32	R—K3

In order to reply to 33 B—Kt4 ch with 33 .... K—K1, but the abandonment of the all-important rank allows of another solution.

33 R × RP	Resigns

(33 .... Kt × R; 34 Q—Q8 ch, R—K1; 35 B—Kt4 ch, etc.)

19. THE CENTRE COUNTER

315

White	Black
MORPHY and	STAUNTON and
BARNES	OWEN

(London, 1858)

The following game shows very clearly how a King's castled position, intact and strong, can step by step become weakened and denuded of its natural defenders.

Already on the 12th move, as an indication of things to come, we see the defending Knight eliminated (12 Kt×Kt ch), then the first and unimportant hole (13 .... P—Kt3), followed shortly afterwards by a far more serious rent in the position (15 .... P—KR4), which, twelve moves later after sustained efforts, White will succeed in breaking asunder (27 Q×RP). Black's attempt to bring up fresh covering forces (30 .... B—Kt3) is refuted by White's brilliant assault (31 P—B5) by which he wins the exchange. The final, purely technical, phase is long but very instructive.

1 P—K4	P—Q4
2 P×P	Q×P
3 Kt—QB3	Q—Q1
4 P—Q4	Kt—KB3
5 B—Q3	Kt—B3
6 B—K3	P—K3

Instead of blocking the Bishop's natural outlet, Black could have played 6 .... B—Kt5, e.g. 7 Kt—B3, P—K3, etc., or again, 7 P—B3, B—R4, followed by .... B—Kt3, bringing this Bishop into active participation.

7 Kt—B3	B—Q3
8 Castles	Castles
9 Q—K2	P—QKt3
10 B—KKt5	

Hostilities have commenced. First of all, Black's KKt is to be disposed of.

10	B—Kt2
11 Kt—K4	B—K2
12 Kt×Kt ch	B×Kt
13 Q—K4	

A sound intermediary manœuvre, by which White causes a small weakening of the hostile King's field, at the same time bringing the white Queen definitely into play.

13	P—Kt3
14 Q—R4	B×B
15 Kt×B	P—KR4

A sad necessity.

16 P—QB3	Q—B3
17 QR—K1	

Quite premature would be 17 P—KKt4, because of 17 .... Q—B5. Nor can White play 17 P—KB4 (with a view to playing 18 P—KKt4), on account of 17 .... Kt×P; 18 P×Kt, Q×P ch, followed by Q×B, recovering his piece with two extra pawns. We perceive that White must proceed very methodically with the development of his attack.

17	Kt—K2
18 P—KB4	Kt—B4
19 Q—R3	KR—K1
20 R—K5	QR—Q1
21 KR—K1	

Threatening 22 B×Kt, KtP×B (forced); 23 Q×RP.

21	Kt—Kt2
22 P—KKt4	

At last White can proceed with his first onslaught, which, however, has to be calculated to a nicety. For if now 22 .... Q×P, there follows 23 R—KB1 (this sacrifice of a second pawn is more convincing than 23 P×P, Kt×P; 24 R—KB1, Q—Q7, etc.); 23 .... Q×KtP ch; 24 Q×Q, P×Q; 25 Kt×BP, R—Q4; 26 B×P, threatening 27 Kt—R6 ch, and Black cannot escape serious loss, e.g. 26 .... R—K2; 27 Kt—R6 ch, K—R1; 28 R—B8 mate.

22	P—B4
23 B—K4	B—R3
24 KtP×P	Kt×P
25 B—B3	P×P

They dare not play 25 .... Kt×P; 26 Q—R7 ch, K—B1, and look for counter-chances in the centre.

26 B×Kt	P×B
27 Q×RP	Q—Kt2

With the ephemeral counter-threat of 28 .... P—B3. A pretty variation would arise from 27 .... Q×P, namely 28 Kt×BP (but not 28 Q—R7 ch, K—B1; 29 Q—R6 ch, K—K2; 30 R×P ch, K—Q2, etc.);

28 .... Q×Kt; 29 R—Kt5 ch, K—B1;
30 Q—R6 ch, K—K2; 31 R—Kt7, R—KKt1;
32 Q×P ch, followed by mate, the white
Rook, itself pinned, pinning the black
Queen!

28 K—B2	Q—B3
29 Q—R4	B—Q6
30 Q—Kt3	B—Kt3

In the vain hope of masking the open
KKt file.

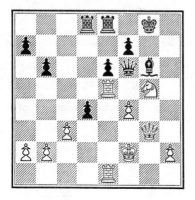

31 P—B5

An *unmasking sacrifice*. As Black cannot
play 31 .... KP×P (32 R×R ch), and he
is threatened with 32 Kt—K4 (e.g. after
31 .... QP×P or 31 .... K—B1), followed
by 33 P×B; he must submit to White's
dictation.

31	B×P
32 Kt—K4 dis ch	Q—Kt3
33 Kt—B6 ch	

Winning the exchange against a pawn, the
result of the hole created at Black's KB3 by
his 13th move, ... P—KKt3. The rest of
the game is characterised by Black's stubborn
resistance.

33	K—B1
34 Q×Q	B×Q
35 Kt×R	K×Kt
36 P—KR4	P—Q6
37 K—K3	

A necessity, in view of the hostile threat
of 37 .... P—Q7; 38 R—Q1, B—B7. After
the text move Black could have played
37 .... P—Q7; 38 R—Q1, R—Q6 ch;
39 K—K2, R—R6; 40 R×P, R×P, but
he prefers to conserve his QP, evidently
underestimating the value of the adverse
passed pawn.

37	K—K2
38 K—Q2	R—Q3
39 R—KKt5	K—B3
40 R—B1 ch	B—B4

If 40 .... K—Kt2; 41 P—R5, K—R3;
42 P×B, K×R; 43 P×P, and wins.

41 R—Kt8	R—Q4
42 P—R5	R—K4
43 R—B2	R—K5
44 R—R2	B—R2
45 R—KR8	K—Kt2
46 R—R8	

Intending to play havoc with the enemy's
Q side, thanks to the threat 47 P—R6 ch.

46	K—R3
47 R×P	R—KB5
48 R—Kt7	P—K4
49 R×P ch	P—B3
50 P—R4	P—K5
51 R—K6	P—K6
52 P—R5	R—B6

And White wins.

316

| White | Black |
| STEINITZ | MONGREDIEN |

(London, 1862)

*The sacrifice of a Rook on an open Rook
file is well known, but in the following splendid
game we have as a preliminary a difficult
manœuvre by the Rook, from KB1 via B3 to
KR3. The value of the sacrifice is enhanced
by the fact that it has to be followed by quiet
positional moves (i.e. without giving checks)
before the last resistance breaks down.*

1 P—K4	P—Q4
2 P×P	Q×P
3 Kt—QB3	Q—Q1
4 P—Q4	P—K3
5 Kt—B3	Kt—KB3
6 B—Q3	B—K2

More solid than 6 .... B—Q3, but
Black's game remains cramped.

| 7 Castles | Castles |
| 8 B—K3 | P—QKt3 |

If first 8 .... QKt—Q2, there still follows
9 Kt—K5, e.g. 9 .... Kt×Kt; 10 P×Kt,
Kt—K1; 11 Q—R5, P—KKt3; 12 Q—R6,
and White gets a footing inside the enemy
lines.

9 Kt—K5   B—Kt2
10 P—B4   QKt—Q2
11 Q—K2   Kt—Q4

After 11 .... Kt×Kt; 12 BP×Kt, the open KB file would favour White's chances.

12 QKt×Kt   P×Kt

Black decides again to close up the Bishop's diagonal, because if 12 .... B×Kt; 13 P—B4, B—Kt2; 14 QR—Q1, the greater control of territory enjoyed by White would become a serious matter.

13 R—B3

Now White's attack takes shape more rapidly than one would expect. The text move already threatens the sacrifice 14 B×P ch, K×B; 15 R—R3 ch, K—Kt1; 16 Q—R5, followed by mate.

13 ......   P—KB4

Against 13 .... Kt—B3 White could proceed with 14 P—KKt4, and against 13 .... P—Kt3 with 14 P—B5.

14 R—R3   P—Kt3
15 P—KKt4   P×P

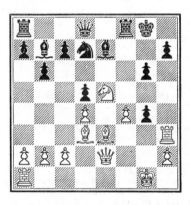

16 R×P

Instead of 16 Q×P, Kt×Kt, followed by 17 .... B—B1; with some counter-play by Black, White breaks down the defence by a Rook sacrifice many moves deep.

16 ......   Kt×Kt
17 BP×Kt   K×R
18 Q×P   R—KKt1

Neither 18 .... R—B4 (19 B×R, P×B; 20 Q×P ch, etc.), nor 18 .... K—K1 (19 Q—R5 ch, K—Kt2; 20 B—R6 ch, K—Kt1; 21 B×P, etc.) can save the situation.

19 Q—R5 ch   K—Kt2
20 Q—R6 ch   K—B2
21 Q—R7 ch   K—K3

Or 21 .... R—Kt2; 22 B×P ch, K—B1; 23 Q—R8 ch, R—Kt1; 24 B—R6 mate.

22 Q—R3 ch   K—B2
23 R—B1 ch   K—K1
24 Q—K6

Again a waiting move (as on the 18th), which completes the encirclement of Black's King.

24 ......   R—Kt2
25 B—Kt5   Q—Q2

Or 25 .... B—B1; 26 Q—B6 ch, B—Q2; 27 Q×P ch, R×Q; 28 B×R mate.

26 B×P ch   R×B
27 Q×R ch   K—Q1
28 R—B8 ch

And White mates next move.

317

White   Black
JOHN   MIESES
(Düsseldorf, 1908)

An inventive mind will nearly always find attacking possibilities in the opposing King's field, when that King has castled on the Q side. Here the most interesting feature lies in the fact that, as soon as the white King has decided on his location, four consecutive pawn moves by Black—each one more convincing than the last—suffice to set the hostile fortress afire.

1 P—K4   P—Q4
2 P×P   Q×P
3 Kt—QB3   Q—QR4
4 B—B4

To be followed by P—Q3. White thinks that this will give him a very solid position, but the more energetic 4 P—Q4 occupies the centre.

4 ......   Kt—KB3
5 P—Q3   P—B3

Anticipating White's next move, Black secures an honourable retreat for his Queen.

6 B—Q2   B—Kt5

Instead of the meticulous 6 .... Q—B2, Black plays the move in the text, because he recognises that no "discovery" by the Knight is to be feared.

| 7 P—B3 | B—B4 |
| 8 Kt—Q5 | |

If 8 Kt—Kt5, Q—Q1, White's Knight must retreat at once, whereas after the text move White has in view the deterioration of the enemy pawn formation.

| 8 ...... | Q—Q1 |
| 9 Kt×Kt ch | KtP×Kt |

Better than 9 .... KP×Kt, because now the black King can fairly safely remain in the centre.

10 Q—K2

Preparing to castle on the Q side, as castling on the other wing appears too risky in view of the open KKt file.

10	Kt—Q2
11 B—B3	Q—B2
12 Castles	P—Kt4

Sounding the attack.

| 13 B—Kt3 | P—QR4 |
| 14 P—QR3 | |

Necessary, in view of the hostile threat of 14 .... P—R5, but now Black succeeds in opening lines of attack.

If 14 P—QR4, P×P, and White cannot play 15 B×P, on account of 15 .... Q—B5 ch, followed by .... Q×B.

14	P—Kt5
15 P×P	P×P
16 B—Q4	

If 16 B×KtP, there follows 16 .... R—R8 ch; 17 K—Q2, Q—B5 ch; 18 K—B3 (compulsory if the QB is to be saved); 18 .... R×R; 19 Q×R, Q—K4 ch; 20 P—Q4 (or 20 K—B4, Kt—Kt3 mate, or 20 K—Q2, B—R3 ch, followed by mate); 20 .... Q—K6 ch; 21 K—B4, B—K3 ch; 22 P—Q5, Kt—Kt3 mate.

| 16 ...... | B—K3 |

Eliminating White's best defensive piece at the cost of a pawn. At this juncture, 16 .... R—R8 ch leads to nothing after 17 K—Q2, etc.

17 B×B	P×B
18 Q×P	B—R3 ch
19 K—Kt1	

If 19 B—K3, Kt—B4, followed by 20 .... B×B ch, and wins.

19	Q—R4
20 P—B3	Q—R5
21 R—K1	

Or 21 Kt—K2, P—Kt6, shutting in the white King. After the move in the text

White himself threatens mate at K7, but Black gets home first.

| 21 ...... | Q—R8 ch |
| 22 K—B2 | P—Kt6 ch |

Pretty and decisive, for if 23 K×P, Q—R5 mate, and if 23 Q×P, Q×R.

Resigns.

318

| White | Black |
| SCHLECHTER | MIESES |

(St. Petersburg, 1909)

The feature of this splendid game is the unusual activity of Black's Queen. As is normal in the Centre Counter Defence, the Queen, as early as the 3rd move, occupies an observation post at QR4, waiting for opportunities which seldom arise. Here, however, of ten moves made in the final and brilliant attack (from 15 .... Kt—Kt5), no less than six were made by this warlike Queen.

1 P—K4	P—Q4
2 P×P	Q×P
3 Kt—QB3	Q—QR4
4 P—Q4	Kt—KB3
5 B—QB4	

In this opening the white KB has little future either here or at Q3; nor is 5 B—Q2, profitable because of 5 .... P—QB3. The best plan is to play 5 Kt—B3, eventually followed by B—K2.

| 5 ...... | Kt—B3 |
| 6 Kt—K2 | B—K3 |

Black speeds up his development in an original manner. He fears neither the doubling of pawns by 7 B×B, P×B, etc., nor a fork by 7 P—Q5 (because of 7 .... Castles; 8 Kt—B4, B×P; 9 Kt×B, P—K3, etc.).

| 7 B—Q3 | Castles |
| 8 Castles | B—B4 |

Making room for the development of the other Bishop.

9 B—K3	B×B
10 Q×B	Kt—QKt5
11 Q—B4	

Willingly giving up his QBP in the hope of obtaining an attack on the open QB file.

For if 11 Q—Q2, Q—KB4; 12 KR—B1, P—K4, the initiative would be Black's.

11	Kt × BP
12 QR—B1	Kt × B
13 P × Kt	P—K3
14 P—K4	R—Q2

With the twofold task of defending the pawn at QB2 as well as (after 15 P—K5, Kt—Kt5) that at KB2.

15 P—QR3

After 15 P—K5, Kt—Kt5; 16 R—B3, Kt—R3, Black would equally have had the best of it (e.g. 17 P—KR3, Kt—B4; 18 P—KKt4, Kt × P; 19 Kt × Kt, R × Kt; 20 Q × R, B—B4, winning the Queen). But 15 P—K5 would at any rate have prevented the black Queen's lightning swoop to the K side.

15 ...... Kt—Kt5

Initiating a smashing attack, whilst threatening to win the exchange by 16 .... Kt—K6.

16 R—B3

Being in a minority of one pawn, he cannot seek the exchange of Queens by 16 Q—Kt5, and must try other methods.

| 16 ...... | Q—KKt4 |
| 17 Kt—Q1 | Q—Q1 |

As the sequel shows, 17 .... B—Q3 at once was better.

18 Kt (Q1)—B3

He should have played 18 Kt—B2, ridding himself of the very troublesome adverse Knight.

18 ...... Q—Kt4

Returning to the attack.

19 Kt—Q1 B—Q3

Bringing another piece into the fight.

20 P—K5

Plausible though it looks, this move allows Black to carry out a superb combination. He should therefore have tried to defend himself as best he could with 20 P—R3.

| 20 ...... | B × KP |
| 21 P × B | Q—R5 |

With the double threat of 22 .... Q × P ch, or (if 22 P—R3) 22 .... Q—K8 ch; 23 R—B1, Q × R ch; 24 K × Q, R × Kt ch; 25 R × R, Kt—K6 ch, followed by .... Kt × Q, and Black, having recovered the pieces sacrificed, remains with two extra pawns.

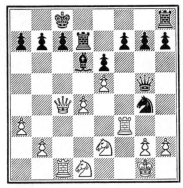

Position after 20 P—K5

| 22 R—KKt3 | Q × P ch |
| 23 K—B1 | R × Kt ch |

Another aspect of the main idea underlying the combination mentioned above—the *Knight fork.*

24 R × R Q × R
Resigns

After 25 Kt × Q, Kt—K6 ch, followed by .... Kt × Q, also after 25 Q × KP ch, P × Q; 26 Kt × Q, Kt × P; 27 R—K1, Kt—Q6; 28 R × P, Kt × P, Black remains with two extra pawns.

319

| White | Black |
| DURAS | SPIELMANN |

(Vienna, 1907)

Most impressive, in the following game, is the fact that White coolly carries on his attack while his own King is threatened with disaster. A duel with rapiers on the edge of a precipice!

1 P—K4	P—Q4
2 P × P	Q × P
3 Kt—QB3	Q—QR4
4 P—Q4	Kt—KB3
5 Kt—B3	B—Kt5
6 B—K2	Kt—B3
7 B—K3	

Foreseeing that Black intends to castle on the Q side in order to increase his pressure against the QP, White conceives an ingenious plan to counter this danger.

Indeed, after the superficial continuation

7 Castles, the continuation of a game W. Cohn—Tartakower, *Ostend*, 1907, was as follows: 7 .... Castles; 8 B—K3, P—K4 (Black's pressure on the Q file affords him an ideal attacking formation); 9 P—Q5, Kt×P; 10 Kt×P, Kt×B; 11 B×B ch, P—B4; 12 Kt×Kt, P×Kt; 13 Q—B3, Kt×B; 14 Q×P, B—Q3, and Black won quickly on account of his extra piece.

| 7 ...... | Castles |
| 8 Kt—Q2 | |

Instead of hastily leading into the continuation shown above (W. Cohn—Tartakower) by 8 Castles, P—K4, White disentangles himself in good time.

| 8 ...... | B×B |
| 9 Q×B | Q—KB4 |

The point of White's strategy is that here Black cannot play 9 .... Kt×P, on account of 10 B×Kt, R×B; 11 Kt—Kt3, and wins.

10 Kt—Kt3	P—K3
11 P—QR3	B—Q3
12 Castles QR	

The games are more or less even, but White has massed more troops opposite the castled King.

| 12 ...... | Kt—Q4 |
| 13 Kt—R4 | P—K4 |

Aggressive play. Files and diagonals, it is true, are being opened, but as his opponent is better developed, this is more likely to benefit him. On the other hand, if 13 .... P—QKt3 there would follow 14 Q—R6 ch, K—Kt1; 15 Kt (R4)—B5, P×Kt; 16 Q×Kt, with the double threat of 17 P×P and 17 Kt—R5.

The more prudent line of play would have been: 13 .... Kt—Kt3, e.g. 14 Kt (R4)—B5, B×Kt; 15 Kt×B, P—K4 (if 15 .... Q—Q4; 16 P—QKt3); 16 P×P, Q×KP, etc., and the contest is considerably simplified.

| 14 P×P | B×KP |
| 15 Kt (R4)—B5 | |

With the threat, now become actual, of 16 Kt×P, K×Kt; 17 Q—Kt5 ch, Kt—Kt3; 18 Kt—B5 ch, K—Kt1; 19 Q×QKt.

15	Kt—Kt3
16 P—QR4	P—QR4
17 P—Kt4	

Higher strategy: his last move having provoked a weakening of the adverse King's field, White initiates a Q side attack, first having diverted the hostile Queen to the K side.

It would still have been unsound to continue with 17 Kt×KtP, K×Kt; 18 Kt—B5 ch, K—Kt1; 19 Q—R6, on account of 19 .... Q—B1.

| 17 ...... | Q—B3 |
| 18 P—QB3 | |

A necessary measure, for if 18 Kt×KtP, B×P ch; 19 K—Kt1, B—R6, and Black scores first.

| 18 ...... | KR—K1 |

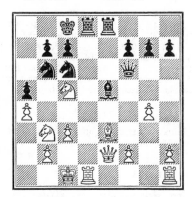

19 Kt×KtP

An uncommon sacrifice in view of the dangers besetting the white King.

19	R×R ch
20 R×R	B×BP
21 Kt (Kt7)—B5	Kt—Kt5

Preventing not only the deadly 22 Q—R6 ch, but also the capture of the exposed Bishop.

22 P—Kt5

Vacating the square KKt4, because if at once 22 Kt×P, B—Q5.

| 22 ...... | Q—K4 |
| 23 Kt×P | P—R4 |

After 23 .... B—Q5, as also after 23 .... Q×Kt, Q—Kt4 ch wins. The object of the text move is to prevent this check (or at least to lessen its effect in the case of 24 P×P e.p., Q×Kt; 25 Q—Kt4 ch, P—B4, etc.), but White is now able to confiscate the troublesome Bishop.

24 P×B	Q×P ch
25 K—Kt1	Q×Kt
26 R—Q8 ch	

A last surprise. If now 26 .... K×R; 27 Kt—Kt7 ch, and if 26 .... R×R; 27 B×Q.

| 26 ...... | Resigns. |

320

White	Black
RUBINSTEIN	*BERNSTEIN*

(San Sebastian, 1911)

An almost miraculous escape in a compromised position is shown in this game.

1 P—K4	P—Q4
2 P × P	Q × P
3 Kt—QB3	Q—QR4
4 P—Q4	Kt—KB3
5 Kt—B3	B—Kt5
6 P—KR3	

At once eliminating the adverse pin.

6 ......   B × Kt

Although this exchange develops White's Queen advantageously, Black fears the retreat 6 .... B—R4, etc. The continuation in a blindfold game, Alekhine—Schroeder, *New York*, 1924, was as follows: 7 P—KKt4, B—Kt3; 8 Kt—K5 (by this outpost manœuvre White is able to threaten both wings); 8 .... QKt—Q2 (after 8 .... P—B3, providing a line of retreat for Black's Queen, White continues with advantage 9 P—KR4); 9 Kt—B4 (a successful Queen-hunt); 9 .... Q—R3; 10 B—B4, Q—K3 ch; 11 Kt—K3, Castles; 12 P—Q5, Q—Kt3; 13 Kt—B4, Q—Kt5; 14 P—R3, Q—B4; 15 B—K3, and Black resigned.

7 Q × B   P—B3

Masking the QKtP, and securing a retreat for the Queen. But Black's game remains cramped.

8 B—Q2	QKt—Q2
9 Castles	P—K3
11 B—QB4	Q—B2
11 KR—K1	Castles
12 B—Kt3	P—KR3

Instead of taking so many precautions, it would have been better to speed up the development of his pieces by 12 .... B—K2, followed by .... Kt—Kt3 and .... R—Q2.

13 K—Kt1	Kt—Kt3
14 Kt—K2	

If 14 B × P, R × B.

14	B—K2
15 P—B4	R—Q2
16 P—QR4	Kt—R1
17 B—B4	B—Q3
18 B—K3	Q—R4

Trying to create an active defence.

19 R—QB1	B—Kt1
20 KR—Q1	Kt—B2
21 Kt—B4	KR—Q1
22 B—Q2	Q—R3
23 B—B3	Q'—Kt3
24 K—R2	Kt—R3
25 Kt—Q3	P—B4

Trying to free his game. Otherwise he is threatened with the following continuation: 26 P—B5, Q—B2; 27 Kt—K5, R—K2; 28 B—B4 (stronger than 28 Kt—B4, Q—Q2, or than 28 Kt × KBP, R × Kt; 29 B × P ch, R (Q1)—Q2), and Black's game remains terribly tangled.

26 P—R5	Q—B2
27 P × P	Kt × P
28 Kt × Kt	R × R
29 R × R	R × R

After 29 .... Q × Kt, White also has a decided advantage.

30 Kt × KP

This pretty interlude wins an important pawn.

30	P × Kt
31 Q × R	Kt—K5
32 B—Kt4	Kt—B4
33 Q—R5	P—QKt3

Black defends the *status quo* with tenacity.

34 B—Q1	Q—K2
35 B—KB3	B—Q3
36 P × P	P × P
37 Q—Kt6	B—K4
38 B—R3	B—B3
39 P—QKt4	Q—Q2

In the knowledge that, after 39 .... Kt—R5; 40 K—Kt3, Q—Q2; 41 Q—K4, things would go from bad to worse, Black embarks upon a desperate enterprise—and saves the situation.

40 P × Kt   Q—Q7 ch

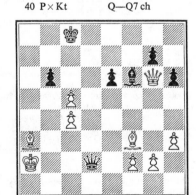

41 K—Kt3

Unfortunate timidity. There was a win after 41 K—Kt1, Q—K8 ch; 42 K—B2, Q—B6 ch (or 42 .... Q × P ch; 43 K—Kt3, Q—K6 ch; 44 K—R4, and wins); 43 K—Q1, Q—Kt6 ch (or 43 .... Q × B; 44 Q—K8 ch, K—B2; 45 Q—B6 ch, K—Q1; 46 Q—Q6 ch, K—B1; 47 B—Kt7 ch, K × B; 48 P—B6 ch, winning the Queen); 44 K—K1 (not 44 Q—B2, Q × B; 45 P × P, Q—Q3 ch; 46 K—K2, Q × P, and Black could count on a draw, because of Bishops of opposite colours); 44 .... B—B6 ch (or 44 .... Q—B6 ch; 45 K—K2, Q × P ch; 46 Q—Q3, Q—R7 ch; 47 K—K3, B—Kt4 ch; 48 K—K4, and Black has no more checks); 45 K—B1, Q × P ch; 46 K—Kt1, and White wins without difficulty.

41 ......   Q—B6 ch

And draws by perpetual check. Namely: 42 K—R4 (not 42 K—R2, Q × P ch; 43 K—Kt1, Q—Kt6 ch; 44 K—B1, B—Kt4 ch, and wins); 42 .... Q—R4 ch (not 42 .... Q × P ch; 43 B—Kt4, P—Kt4 ch; 44 K—R5, B—Q1 ch; 45 K—R6, and wins, because if 45 .... Q—R7 ch; 46 K × P, or 45 .... Q × B; 46 Q × P ch, K—Kt1; 47 Q—Q6 ch, B—B2; 48 Q—B8 ch, followed by mate); 43 K—Kt3, Q—B6 ch, etc.

321

White	*Black*
ED. LASKER	MIESES

(Scheveningen, 1913)

As long as the King remains in his original position, the danger of a catastrophe is always present. This is well illustrated here.

1 P—K4	P—Q4
2 P × P	Kt—KB3
3 P—Q4	Q × P
4 Kt—QB3	Q—QR4
5 Kt—B3	B—B4

Thinking thus to avoid the schemes and intrigues which arise from 5 .... B—Kt5, as shown in the preceding game.

A new idea, with the object of easing the task of the defence, is 5 .... Kt—K5; 6 B—Q2, Kt × B; 7 Q × Kt, B—B4, with a simplified contest.

6 Kt—K5

This outpost manœuvre threatens not only 7 Q—B3, but also 7 P—KKt4.

6 ......   Kt—K5

It would have been wiser to play 6 .... P—B3, parrying the threat of 7 Q—B3 (because of 7 .... B × P, the QKtP now being masked), and reserving, in case of 7 P—KKt4, the honourable retreat 7 .... B—Q2. The variation might run as follows: 6 .... P—B3; 7 B—Q3, B × B; 8 Q × B, QKt—Q2; 9 P—B4, P—K3, and the games are approximately even.

7 Q—B3   Kt—Q3

Black's game remains difficult, although this defensive move guards four points (KB4, QKt2, KB2 and QB5).

If 7 .... Kt × Kt, then not 8 Q × B (8 .... Kt—K5 dis ch; 9 P—B3, Kt—Q3, defending KB2 and QB1), but simply 8 P × Kt, and the Queen's threats against QKt7, KB5 and eventually also against KB7 remain in being.

8 B—Q2

If 8 Kt × P, then not 8 .... Kt × Kt; 9 Q × P, but 8 .... K × Kt; 9 P—KKt4, Kt—B3, and Black obtains counter-chances.

8 ......   P—K3

Evidently neither 8 .... B × P nor 8 .... P—QB3 is sufficient, the first because of 9 Kt—Kt5, Q—Kt3; 10 Kt × Kt ch, followed by 11 Q × P ch, and the second also because of 9 Kt—Kt5, followed by Kt × Kt ch and Q × B.

9 P—KKt4   B—Kt3

This overprotection of the pawn at KB2 is necessary, for after 9 .... B × BP the continuation would be as above.

10 P—KR4   Q—Kt3
11 Castles

Protecting directly the two threatened pawns (at QKt2 and QB2) and indirectly the QP.

11	P—KB3
12 Kt × B	P × Kt
13 B—Q3	Q × P

Discerning that the defence of the threatened sector by 13 .... K—B2 would be futile (e.g. 14 P—R5, P × P; 15 P × P, etc.), Black tries to obtain compensation elsewhere.

14 B × P ch   K—Q2

After 14 .... K—K2, Black's K side remains paralysed, but now the position of the King on the open Q file brings its own punishment.

15 B—K3	Q—Kt5
16 P—R3	Q—QB5
17 Q × KtP	Q—B3
18 B—K4	Resigns.

322

White	Black
WEISS	BLACKBURNE

(New York, 1889)

This game is an object lesson in the art of liquidation. Although White provokes the first exchanges (9 P—Q5), in the hope of gaining some initiative, Black succeeds in exploiting the more active position of his pieces, with a small gain in material on the 25th move.

Although long, this game is most attractive on account of the straightforward simplicity of the means employed.

1 P—K4	P—Q4
2 P×P	Kt—KB3
3 P—Q4	Q×P
4 Kt—QB3	Q—QR4
5 Kt—B3	P—B3

He shows wisdom in providing, in good time, for the possible retreat of his Queen.

6 Kt—K5

The most energetic continuation. After 6 B—K2, B—B4, however, Black equalises without incurring any danger.

6	QKt—Q2

Driving off without delay the hostile Knight from its advanced post. Against 6 .... B—B4 White can continue quietly with 7 B—Q3, or violently with 7 P—KKt4.

7 Kt—B4	Q—Q1

After 7 .... Q—B2 White would develop his pieces rapidly by 8 Q—B3, followed by B—KB4. A tragic mistake would be 7 .... Q—Kt5, on account of 8 P—QR3, capturing the Queen on a full board.

8 B—K2	P—KKt3
9 P—Q5	

Disengaging the centre, thus, does not improve White's chances. He should have continued far more methodically with 9 B—K3, B—Kt2; 10 Q—Q2, Castles; 11 Castles QR.

9	P×P
10 Kt×P	Kt×Kt
11 Q×Kt	B—Kt2
12 P—KR4	

Prudence called for 12 Castles, Castles; with a tendency to equalisation.

12	Castles

Fearlessly castling on the side likely to be attacked, because he foresees that he will be able to nip his adversary's attacking propensities in the bud.

13 P—R5	Kt—B3
14 Q×Q	

Or, e.g. 14 Q—QB5, Q—Q4, and the exchange of Queens is no less favourable to Black.

14	R×Q
15 P×P	RP×P
16 B—Q3	B—K3
17 B—Q2	QR—B1

The greater activity of all the black pieces ensures success. If White, for instance, plays 18 Kt—K3, there follows 18 .... Kt—Kt5; 19 Kt—Q1, Kt—K4; 20 B—K2, B—Q4, with an increasing command of territory.

18 Kt—K5	Kt—Q2
19 Kt×Kt	R×Kt
20 B—QB1	

Unable to play either 20 Castles QR (because of 20 .... R×B) or 20 B—B3, White assumes the defensive.

20	B—B5
21 R—R3	

Or 21 B×B, R×B; 22 P—QB3, R×P, and Black gains material.

21	B×B
22 R×B	R×R
23 P×R	R—B7

The entry of the Rook on the seventh rank wins a pawn by force.

24 R—Kt1	B—Q5
25 B—Q2	R×P

Avoiding the trap 25 .... B×P; 26 K—Q1, and White wins.

Another possibility, in place of the text move, was 25 .... B×P ch, but then there follows not 26 K×B, R×B ch, winning a second pawn (Q6 or KKt7), but 26 K—Q1, R—B4; 27 P—QKt4, R—KR4; 28 K—K2, B—Kt3; 29 R—QB1, and White can still hold on, whereas now Black, with almost geometrical precision, forces a winning Bishop's end game.

26 R×R

Obviously not 26 R—R1, R×B.

26	B × R
27 B—K3	P—R3
28 K—Q2	K—B1
29 K—B2	B—K4
30 K—Kt3	K—K1
31 K—B4	K—Q2
32 K—B5	B—B2
33 P—B3	P—K3
34 P—R4	P—Kt3 ch
35 K—B4	K—B3
36 K—B2	P—B3
37 B—K3	B—Q3
38 B—Q4	P—K4
39 B—K3	P—Kt4 ch

After much labour, a step forward.

40 P × P ch	P × P ch
41 K—Kt3	K—Q4
42 B—B2	P—B4
43 K—B3	P—Kt4
44 P—Kt4	P × P
45 P × P	B—B4
46 B—K1	P—K5
47 P × P ch	K × P
48 B—Q2	B—K6

Careless, however, would be 48 ....
B—K2, on account of 49 B × P, B × B;
50 K—Kt4, forcing the draw.

49 B—K1

"Nothing is lost yet," thinks White, for if
now 49 .... B—B4, again 50 B—Q2, and
if 49 .... K—B6; 50 K—Kt4, eliminating
an irksome pawn. But Black will demonstrate that "it will still work" with the
remaining KKtP.

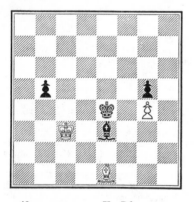

49	K—B6
50 K—Kt4	K × P
51 K × P	K—B6
52 K—B4	P—Kt5
53 K—Q3	

Or 53 B—R4, B—B7, etc.

53	B—B7
54 B—R5	P—Kt6
55 B—B7	P—Kt7
56 B—R2	B—Kt3
57 K—Q2	K—Kt5
Resigns.	

323

| White | Black |
| MORPHY | ANDERSSEN |

(Match, 1858)

*The "positional sacrifice" of a pawn,
mostly effected for the sake of gaining an
advantage in development, has always been
an important weapon in the armoury of the
attacking players of all time.*

1 P—K4	P—Q4
2 P × P	Q × P
3 Kt—QB3	Q—QR4
4 P—Q4	P—K4

Seeking not only to leave the field clear
for both his Bishops, but also to eliminate
the adverse centre. But it is usually the
better-developed side which benefits by the
clearance.

5 P × P

Best for White is 5 Kt—B3, for if then
5 .... P × P; 6 Q × P, White has another
piece in play; and if 5 .... P—K5; 6 Q—K2,
and Black's exposed pawn will shortly fall.

5 ...... Q × P ch

Recovering his pawn without delay. But
by first playing 5 .... B—QKt5, Black
would have caused his adversary more
trouble.

| 6 B—K2 | B—QKt5 |
| 7 Kt—B3 | |

Instead of the defensive 7 B—Q2, the
American champion shows by the move in
the text that he perceives clearly that his
position will give him full value for the pawn
sacrificed.

7	B × Kt ch
8 P × B	Q × P ch
9 B—Q2	Q—B4
10 QR—Kt1	

It will be seen that, for the unit given up,
White has four pieces in play and Black only
one—the Queen, which, moreover is liable
to be the target of fresh attacks.

10	......	Kt—QB3
11	Castles	Kt—B3
12	B—KB4	Castles

Of course not 12 .... Kt—Q4, on account of 13 R—Kt5. By playing 12 .... Q—K2 (13 B—QKt5, Castles), or else 12 .... Q—QR4 (13 R—Kt5, Q × P; 14 B × P, Castles), Black could have maintained his extra pawn, but it would have meant moving his Queen for the sixth time, without, however, her occupying a more propitious square.

That is why he prefers to give back the pawn of his own free will, hoping to ease the hostile pressure.

| 13 | B × P | Kt—Q5 |
| 14 | Q × Kt | Q × B |

If first 14 .... Q × P, with the idea of attacking both Bishops, then 15 B—QB4, and nothing happens.

| 15 | B—Q3 | B—Kt5 |

If 15 .... R—Q1; at once, there follows 16 Q—QR4, and the white Queen's aggressive position creates new threats. If, on the other hand, 15 .... P—KR3; Black's King's field becomes weakened.

| 16 | Kt—Kt5 | KR—Q1 |

If 16 .... B—R4 (in order to strengthen the King's field by 17 .... B—Kt3), there follows 17 Kt—K4, Kt × Kt; 18 Q × Kt (with a double attack on KR7 and QKt7); 18 .... B—Kt3; 19 Q × P, and now White has the extra pawn.

| 17 | Q—Kt4 |

If White plays 17 B × P ch, in the mistaken expectation of gaining a pawn, the sequel is: 17 .... Kt × B; 18 Q × B, Kt × Kt; 19 Q × Kt, Q × P; 20 R × P, Q × RP, and Black has got out of his difficulties very satisfactorily.

| 17 | ...... | B—B1 |

Unfortunate, but necessary if he wishes to avoid the loss of a pawn, for if 17 .... P—QKt3 or 17 .... QR—Kt1, we have, not 18 B × P ch as shown before, but 18 Kt × RP, Kt × Kt; 19 Q × B, now really winning a valuable pawn.

| 18 | KR—K1 | P—QR4 |
| 19 | Q—K7 | Q × Q |

Compulsory, because if 19 .... R—Q2; 20 Q—K8 ch, with mate to follow. In the sequel the white Rook reaches the seventh rank with the usual ravaging effect.

| 20 | R × Q | Kt—Q4 |

If 20 .... R—B1; 21 B—B4, Black's position is already desperate.

| 21 | B × P ch |

Not 21 R × BP, because of 21 .... P—R3.

21	......	K—R1
22	R × BP	Kt—B6
23	R—K1	Kt × P
24	R—B4

The decisive manœuvre, threatening both 25 Kt—B7 ch and 25 R—KR4.

| 24 | ...... | R—R3 |
| 25 | B—Q3 |

And White wins.

324

| White | Black |
| TARRASCH | MIESES |

(Göteborg, 1920)

The player who is ahead in development has no need of complicated positions and ferocious attacks in order to drive home his advantage. In spite of the simplification of means (as is the case in this game after the 12th move), this "potential" advantage can be turned into one of material, requiring in the end nothing more than a technical performance of adequate skill.

1	P—K4	P—Q4
2	P × P	Q × P
3	Kt—QB3	Q—QR4
4	P—Q4	P—K4
5	Kt—B3

Instead of facilitating Black's counter-play by 5 P × P, B—QKt5, White brings another piece into play.

| 5 | ...... | B—QKt5 |
| 6 | B—Q2 | B—Kt5 |

Or 6 .... P × P; 7 Kt × P, Q—K4 ch; 8 Q—K2, and White's advantage will persist even after the exchange of Queens.

| 7 | B—K2 | P × P |

The exchanges now forced upon Black will help his adversary to turn to account the mobility of his pieces, e.g. 7 .... QB × Kt; 8 B × B, P—QB3; 9 P—QR3, B—K2; 10 Kt—Q5, Q—Q1; 11 Kt × B, Q × Kt; 12 B—QKt4, Q—K3; 13 Castles, and White dominates the board.

| 8 | Kt × P | Q—K4 |
| 9 | QKt—Kt5 |

With the threefold mission of guarding the KKt, attacking the adverse KB and threatening the gain of a pawn by 10 Kt × P ch, Q × QKt; 11 KB × B.

Whether he wishes it or not, Black must have recourse to a general liquidation.

9	B × B
10 Q × B	B × B ch
11 K × B	Q × Q ch
12 K × Q	

In this simplified position the sequel must show whether White's advance of five *tempi* (or, to put it more concretely, the advantage of two more mobile pieces) can be transformed into a decisive advantage.

| 12 ...... | Kt—QR3 |
| 13 KR—K1 | Castles |

After 13 .... Kt—K2; 14 K—B3, the black King would remain tied to the centre. But the move in the text gives rise to an original combination by White.

| 14 Kt × P ch | K—Kt1 |
| 15 QKt—B6 ch | |

The point of the preceding move, whereas, after 15 QKt—Kt5, Black wins a Knight by 15 .... P—QB3.

15	P × Kt
16 Kt × P ch	K—B1
17 Kt × R	K × Kt

After auditing the account, we find that the ending of Rook and two Pawns against two Knights is definitely to White's advantage. It only remains for him to exploit this numerical advantage.

| 18 QR—Q1 ch | K—K1 |

After 18 .... K—B1; 19 K—B3, White would threaten to bring his Rook to the eighth and eventually to the seventh rank.

19 K—Q3 dis ch	Kt—K2
20 K—B4	P—R4
21 R—Q3	Kt—Kt1

In view of the threat 22 QR—K3, the Knight must hasten to the help of its companion.

22 QR—K3	Kt—B3
23 P—QKt4	P—B3
24 P—B4	K—B2
25 P—QR4	

Avoiding a subtle trap, namely: 25 P—Kt5, Kt—R4 ch; 26 K—Kt4, Kt—Q4 ch; 27 K × Kt, R—R1 mate.

25	R—QKt1
26 P—B3	R—Q1
27 R—Q3	R × R
28 K × R	K—K1
29 P—R5	K—Q2
30 P—R6	Kt—Q4
31 R—QR1!	Kt—R2

After 31 .... Kt × BP ch; 32 K—K4, Kt × KKtP; 33 P—R7, Black loses a Knight.

| 32 P—Kt3 | P—B3 |
| 33 R—R4 | |

Overprotecting in order to advance the QBP, after which the massed Q side pawns decide the issue.

33	Kt—Kt3
34 R—R5	P—Kt3
35 P—B4	Kt (Kt3)—B1
36 R—R1	Kt—Q3
37 K—Q4	Kt (Q3)—B1
38 K—B5	K—B2

Or 38 .... Kt—Q3; 39 R—Q1, Kt(R2)—B1; 40 R × Kt ch, Kt × R; 41 P—R7, and queens.

| 39 R—K1 | Kt—Kt3 |

Or (to prevent, as long as possible, the entry of the Rook) 39 .... K—Q2; 40 P—Kt5, P × P; 41 P × P, K—B2; 42 R—K6, and wins.

| 40 R—K7 ch | Kt—Q2 ch |
| 41 R × Kt ch | |

A decisive liquidation: White's pawns, passed, united and advanced, prove to be more powerful than a piece.

41	K × R
42 P—Kt5	P × P
43 P × P	Kt—B1
44 P—Kt6	Resigns.

325

| White | Black |
| LEONHARDT | MIESES |

(Prague, 1908)

Here is a game of varying fortunes, White having, on the 4th move, already sacrificed a pawn, which he recovers only on the 31st move. After that comes his triumphant access to richesse, the gain of a pawn on the 32nd move, and of yet another on the 36th. Then comes Black's turn: in a remarkable Rook ending he wins back one pawn, and a second one on move 49, equality is achieved, and it all ends in a peaceful draw.

1 P—K4	P—Q4
2 P × P	Q × P
3 Kt—QB3	Q—QR4
4 P—QKt4	

This *Centre Counter Gambit* is sound without being decisive. Usually White will sooner or later regain his pawn with a good game.

| 4 ...... | Q × KtP |

Declining the gambit would not be satisfactory, e.g.: (a) 4 .... Q—Kt3; 5 Kt—B3, etc.; (b) 4 .... Q—K4 ch; 5 B—K2, P—QB3; 6 Kt—B3, Q—B2; 7 Castles, and White has made four developing moves against one—a very modest one—by Black.

| 5 R—Kt1 | Q—Q3 |

A playable retreat would be 5 .... Q—R4; 6 R—Kt5, Q—R3, after which, however, Black's position would be no less difficult.

| 6 Kt—B3 | |

If 6 Q—B3, then, at all cost, 6 .... P—QB3, and not 6 .... Kt—KB3, because of 7 R × P, B × R; 8 Q × B, and wins. (8 .... Q—B3; 9 B—Kt5.)

| 6 ...... | Kt—KB3 |
| 7 P—Q4 | P—B3 |

Parrying once and for all the threat of Kt—QKt5.

8 B—Q3	P—QKt3
9 Castles	P—K3
10 Q—K2	B—K2
11 Kt—K4	Kt × Kt
12 Q × Kt	Q—Q4

Another and more natural plan of defence is 12 .... Kt—Q2 (and if 13 B—QKt5, B—Kt2).

13 Q—Kt4	B—B3
14 P—B4	Q—Q1
15 B—R3	Kt—Q2
16 KR—K1	Kt—B1

Intending to continue with .... Kt—Kt3 and then .... Kt—K2, and he can castle at last. There is no doubt that White's attack is full compensation for the pawn given up.

17 QR—Q1	Q—B2
18 B—QB1	Kt—Kt3
19 P—KR4	Castles
20 P—R5	Kt—K2
21 Q—K4	P—Kt3
22 B—B4	Q—Q2
23 B—K5	B × B
24 P × B	B—Kt2
25 Q—B4	Q—K1
26 Q—B6	P—KR3

The only way to ward off the formidable menace 27 P—R6, for if 27 .... P × P, then 28 B × P ch, K × B; 29 Kt—Kt5 ch, K—Kt1; 30 Q—R6, forcing mate at KR7; and if 27 .... Q—Q1, then 28 B × P.

| 27 P × P | Kt × P |
| 28 Kt—R4 | Q—Q1 |

Since after 28 .... Kt × Kt; 29 Q × Kt,

Black's King's field would become untenable, he seeks salvation in the exchange of Queens.

29 B × Kt	Q × Q
30 P × Q	P × B
31 R × P	B—B1

Black cannot stop to count the damage, e.g. 31 .... QR—K1; 32 R—Q7, R × R; 33 R—Kt7 ch, K—R1; 34 Kt × P mate.

32 R × P	B—B4
33 Kt × B	P × Kt
34 R—Q7	R—B2
35 R—Q5	R—K1
36 R × BP	

The battle of the four Rooks is interesting From being a pawn down, White is now two. pawns up, but his adversary's Rooks are very active.

36	R—K8 ch
37 K—R2	R—QR8
38 R—K5	R × RP
39 P—B4	R—Q7
40 P—B5	R (Q7)—Q2
41 R—K8 ch	

By playing, here or on the next move, P—Kt4, White could have intensified the pressure.

| 41 ...... | K—R2 |
| 42 R (B6)—K6 | P—KR4 |

Thanks to this thrust, Black succeeds in separating the passed pawns, and makes it possible for his King to attack them successfully.

43 R (K6)—K7	K—R3
44 R × R (Q7)	R × R
45 R—K7	R—Q5
46 R—K8	R—Q2
47 K—Kt3	K—Kt4
48 R—K7	R—Q6 ch
49 K—B2	K × P (B3)
50 R × P	

Draw.

326

| White | Black |
| SCHUMER | THOMAS |

(London, 1912)

Here Black not only succeeds in defending a difficult position, but by will-power and ability he acquires, step by step, decisive territory. One recalls the law of the "balance of position" promulgated many years ago by Steinitz, according to which the inert mass, in a manner of speaking, defends itself.

1 P—K4	P—Q4
2 P×P	Q×P
3 Kt—QB3	Q—QR4
4 P—QKt4	Q×KtP
5 R—Kt1	Q—Q3
6 P—Q4	P—QR3

Whilst preventing White's Kt—QKt5, this move gives Black a freer position than does 6 .... P—QB3.

7 Q—Q3	Kt—QB3
8 Kt—B3	Kt—B3
9 B—K2	P—KKt3
10 Kt—Q1	

Black's counter-threat 10 .... B—B4 is fairly disturbing, e.g. if, instead of the text move, 10 Kt—K4, there follows 10 .... Kt×Kt; 11 Q×Kt, B—B4; 12 Q—R4, Castles QR, and Black has a very good game.

As, however, the manœuvre chosen is a little artificial, it would have been better to continue with 10 B—KKt5, B—B4; 11 Q—Q2.

10	B—B4
11 Q—Kt3	P—QKt4

In moving out of danger this pawn gets ready to support future attacking manœuvres.

12 B—R3	Q—K3

On the strength of his surplus pawn, Black offers exchanges.

13 Q—Kt2	B—R3

Prevents the useful 14 Kt—K3.

14 Kt—B3	Castles KR
15 Castles	Kt—Q4
16 KR—K1	Q—Q2

Evading the threat of 17 KB×P.

17 QR—Q1	

He should have tried to fortify his centre by 17 B—B5. Now Black, by a far-sighted conception, will not only enforce liquidations, but also emerge with a decisive asset on the extreme Q wing.

17	P—Kt5
18 Kt×Kt	P×B
19 Q—Kt3	KR—Kt1
20 Q—B4	B—K3
21 Kt—K5	Q×Kt
22 Q×Kt	Q×Q
23 Kt×Q	R—Kt7
24 P—Q5	B—Q2
25 Kt×P ch	K—B1
26 B—Q3	R×RP

After nine forced moves on the part of his opponent, Black is now possessed of a far-advanced passed pawn.

27 Kt—B6	B—Kt2
28 K—B1	B—B6
29 R—K3	R—Kt7
30 K—K2	P—R7
31 R—QR1	

Necessary in view of the threat 31 .... R—Kt8.

31	R—K1

A last *finesse*. Premature would be 31 .... R×P ch; 32 B×R, B×R, on account of 33 R—QR3.

Now Black threatens: 32 .... R×R ch; 33 P×R (or 33 K×R, R×P, etc., as in the text); 33 .... B—Kt5 ch; 34 K—B2, R—Kt8; 35 R×P, B—K8 ch; 36 K—Kt1, B—R5 dis ch; 37 B—B1, B—K7, and wins.

32 P—B3	R×R ch
33 K×R	R×P
34 B×R	B×R
35 B—Kt3	B—Q5 ch
	Resigns.

327

White	Black
DE RIVIÈRE	DUBOIS

(Paris, 1858)

In this very beautiful game, White, from the first, neglects his development and hankers after worldly possessions: a pawn picked up on the 2nd move, an exchange won on the 11th, are far from sufficient to compensate White for the storm which breaks around his KB2.

1 P—K4	P—Q4
2 P×P	Kt—KB3

He is in no hurry to recapture the pawn, and wishes to create complications.

3 B—Kt5 ch	B—Q2
4 B×B ch	

Thus White will be able to maintain his extra pawn, but at the cost of the development of his pieces. A wise course would have been 4 B—B4.

4	Q×B
5 P—QB4	

The preceding remark applies here also. By giving up the pawn in question White could have maintained the balance, e.g. 5 Kt—QB3, Kt×P; 6 Kt×Kt, Q×Kt; 7 Q—B3, P—QB3; 8 Q×Q, P×Q, etc.

5	P—B3
6 P×P	Kt×P
7 Kt—KB3	P—K4

The gain in territory effected by this advance is manifest. Not only is the way cleared for the development of the KB and the hostile thrust P—Q4 prevented, but the continuation .... P—K5 is foreshadowed.

8 Castles
If 8 P—Q3, Castles; with intensified pressure on the Q file.

| 8 ...... | P—K5 |
| 9 R—K1 | |

After 9 Kt—K1, Castles QR; 10 Kt—QB3, B—Q3, White's situation remains no less critical. In this case Black would concentrate his effort against White's KR2, instead of, as now, against his deserted KB2.

| 9 ...... | Castles |
| 10 Kt—Kt5 | Q—B4 |

Black continues in combinative style in preference to allowing White to recover some ground by 10 .... R—K1; 11 Kt—QB3, etc.

| 11 Kt×BP | B—B4 |
| 12 R—B1 | |

Or 12 Kt×QR, B×P ch; 13 K—R1, B×R (threatening 14 .... Q—B8 mate); 14 Q×B, R×Kt, with an overpowering advantage in position for Black.

| 12 ...... | Kt—KKt5 |

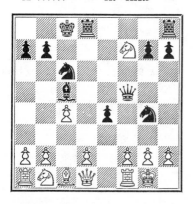

13 Kt×KR
Or 13 Q—K2, QR—B1; 14 Kt×R, Kt×BP; 15 R×Kt (or 15 P—KKt3, Kt—Q5, winning the Queen); 15 .... B×R ch; 16 K—R1, Kt—Q5; 17 Q—B1 (or 17 Q—Q1, B—K8; 18 P—KR3, Q—B8 ch; 19 K—R2, B—Kt6 ch, winning the Queen);

17 .... B—R5; 18 Q×Q ch, R×Q; 19 P—KKt3, R—B8 ch; 20 K—Kt2, R×B; 21 P×B, Kt—B7, followed by .... Kt×R, and Black remains the exchange ahead.

| 13 ...... | Kt×BP |
| 14 Q—K1 | |

After 14 R×Kt, Q×R ch; 15 K—R1, R—B1 (Black plays for the mate, whilst 15 .... R×Kt would give his adversary some breathing space); 16 P—KR3 (or 16 Q—Kt4 ch, K—Q1; 17 Q—Kt5 ch, Kt—K2, etc., or again, 16 P—KKt3, Kt—K4, with .... Kt—B6 to follow); 16 .... B—Q3 (threatening mate after 17 .... Q—B8 ch); 17 Q—Kt1, Q—Kt6; 18 Kt—B3, R—B8, followed by 19 .... Q—R7 mate.

14	R—B1
15 P—Q4	B×P
16 Kt—Q2	

Or 16 B—K3, B×B; 17 Q×B, Kt—R6 ch, with unavoidable mate.

16	Kt—Q6 dis ch
17 K—R1	Kt×Q
18 R×Q	R×R
19 P—KR3	

The forces are equal, but positionally White is paralysed.

19	P—K6
20 Kt—K4	R—B8 ch
21 K—R2	B—K4 ch
22 P—Kt3	Kt—Q5
23 P—KR4	P—KR4

Completing the mating net.

24 Kt—Kt5	Kt (Q8)—B6 ch
25 Kt×Kt	R—B7 ch
26 K—R3	Kt×Kt
Resigns	

None too soon, as he cannot avoid being mated on the next move.

328

| *White* | *Black* |
| MARÓCZY | MENCHIK |

(Carlsbad, 1929)

Frontal attacks against the King's field on an open KKt file are always impressive. Even more ruthless are those on the KR file.

A striking feature in the following game is the minute care with which White prepares the final assault.

1 P—K4	P—Q4
2 P × P	Kt—KB3
3 B—Kt5 ch	B—Q2
4 B—B4	B—Kt5

Black has to resort to long-winded manœuvres in order to recover her pawn.

5 P—KB3	B—B4
6 Kt—B3	QKt—Q2
7 P—Q3	Kt—Kt3
8 KKt—K2	

If 8 B—Kt5 ch, B—Q2, and Black still recovers the pawn. That is why White prefers to carry on with his development.

8	QKt × P
9 Kt × Kt	Kt × Kt
10 Kt—Kt3	B—Kt3
11 P—B4	P—K3
12 Castles	Kt—Kt3

If at once 12 .... B—B4 ch; 13 P—Q4 is troublesome.

13 B—Kt3	B—B4 ch
14 K—R1	Castles

Declaring the King's final domicile, against which White will now launch a lasting attack. A less accommodating plan would have been 14 .... Q—Q2, with .... Castles QR, and Black could herself have tried to become aggressive on the K side.

15 Q—B3	Q—B1

Controlling both QKt2 and KB4, whereas, after 15 .... P—QB3, there follows 16 P—B5, P × P; 17 Kt × P, with increased attacking resources.

16 Kt—K2	

A vacating manœuvre.

16	Kt—Q2
17 P—Kt4	

White's attack becomes more concrete.

17	Kt—B3
18 Kt—Kt3	

Premature would be 18 P—KR4, because of 18 .... P—KR4.

18	P—KR3
19 P—KR3	P—B3
20 B—Q2	Q—Q2
21 QR—K1	QR—Q1
22 R—K2	K—R1
23 R—Kt2	

The massing of troops on the critical sector continues.

23	B—R2
24 P—KR4	Kt—Kt1
25 P—R5	Kt—K2
26 P—B5	P × P

Or 26 .... P—K4; 27 Kt—K4, B—QKt3; 28 P—B6, cleaving a breach in the enemy defences.

27 Kt × P	B × Kt

As Black is threatened with 28 Kt × KtP, K × Kt; 29 Q—B6 ch, K—Kt1; 30 B—B3, B—Q5; 31 B × B, Q × B; 32 B × P ch, R × B; 33 Q × R ch, K—R1; 34 Q × Kt, winning the exchange, Black decides on exchanging the Bishop, which however enables White to turn the open KKt file to account. A similar continuation would arise from 27 .... Kt × Kt; 28 P × Kt, etc.

28 P × B	B—Q5

If, instead, 28 .... P—B3; 29 Q—Kt4, Kt—Q2; 30 P—Q4, followed by R (B1)—Kt1, with a decisive strengthening of the frontal pressure.

And if 28 .... Kt—Q4; 29 P—B6, Kt × P; 30 QB × P, etc.

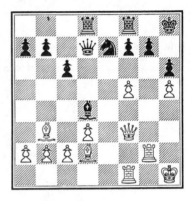

29 P—B6	

A decisive break-through.

29	Kt—Q4

If 29 .... B × BP; 30 QB × P, B × P; 31 B—Q2, B—B3; 32 P—R6, utilising fresh troops.

30 P × P ch	B × P
31 P—B4	Kt—K2
32 R × B	

A break-up sacrifice.

32	K × R
33 Q—B6 ch	K—Kt1
34 R—Kt1 ch	

Immediate threats are needed, for if 34 B—B3, a preparatory measure, then 34 .... Q—R6 ch; 35 K—Kt1, Q—Kt6 ch, etc., with perpetual check.

34	Kt—Kt3
35 R × Kt ch	P × R
36 P—B5 dis ch	R—B2

If 36 .... K—R2; 37 P × P mate.

37 Q × P ch   Resigns

Because 37 .... K—R1; 38 B—B3 ch, R—Kt2; 39 Q × P ch mate; or 37 .... K—B1; 38 B × P ch, R—Kt2; 39 Q—B6 ch, K—K1; 40 Q × R, Q—R6 ch; 41 K—Kt1, and Black has no resource left.

329

White	Black
LASKER	ALEKHINE

(St. Petersburg, 1914)

The chess player knows the joys of the "moral victory" such as is shown in this game, in which Black succeeds in saving an otherwise desperate situation by means of a perpetual check.

1 P—K4	P—Q4
2 P × P	Kt—KB3
3 P—Q4	Kt × P

A more complicated line of play than the so-called main variation of the Centre Counter Defence, which could arise here after 3 .... Q × P; 4 Kt—QB3, Q—QR4, etc.

4 Kt—KB3

If White plays 4 P—QB4, Black can venture on 4 .... Kt—Kt3, or even 4 .... Kt—Kt5 (threatening 5 .... Q × P), but the soundest is 4 .... Kt—KB3.

4	B—Kt5
5 P—B4	Kt—Kt3
6 Kt—B3	

As this routine development allows Black to start an offensive in the centre, the sounder continuation here is 6 B—K2, which preserves a slight initial advantage for White, e.g. 6 .... Kt—B3; 7 P—Q5, B × Kt; 8 B × B; Kt—K4; 9 B—K2, and Black cannot play 9 .... QKt × P because of 10 B × Kt, Kt × B; 11 Q—R4 ch, followed by Q × Kt.

6	P—K4
7 P—B5	

After 7 P × P, Q × Q ch; 8 Kt × Q, Kt—B3; 9 B—B4, Castles; 10 B—K2, B—Kt5 ch; 11 Kt—B3, KR—K1, Black would recover his pawn without trouble and obtain the better development.

7 ......   P × P

If 7 .... Kt—Q4; 8 Q—R4 ch, B—Q2; 9 Q—Kt3 would be to White's advantage, but better here was 7 .... KKt—Q2, maintaining the central pressure (e.g. 8 Q—Kt3, B × Kt; 9 P × B, Kt—QB3, etc.), whereas now the white Queen effectively gets into play.

8 Kt—K4   Kt (Kt3)—Q2

After 8 .... Q—K2; 9 B—Kt5 ch, P—B3; 10 Q—K2, P × B; 11 P × Kt, White has the better chances.

9 Q × P	Q—K2
10 B—QKt5	Kt—B3

If 10 .... P—QB3, White simply plays 11 B—K2, threatening 12 Kt—Q6 ch.

11 B × Kt	P × B
12 Castles	B × Kt
13 P × B	Castles

Both Kings' fields are compromised, but Black's the more seriously of the two.

14 Q—R4	Kt—K4
15 K—Kt2	Q—K3

An original idea, by which the black King is left to his own devices, with a view to a counter-attack. But if 15 .... K—Kt2, White quickly obtains full control of the board after 16 B—K3, followed by QR—B1—B3, etc.

16 Q × RP	Q—B4
17 Q—R8 ch	K—Q2
18 R—Q1 ch	

Winning a Rook, but allowing Black to get in a word. This could have been prevented by 18 Q—R3.

18 ......   K—K3

If 18 .... B—Q3; 19 Q—R3, followed by P × B.

19 Q × R	Q × P ch
20 K—Kt1	

Clearly not 20 K—B1, Q—R8 ch; 21 K—K2, Q × Kt ch, etc.

20 ......   B—K2

Nothing is to be gained by 20 .... Q—Kt5 ch; 21 K—B1, etc. Nor would 20 .... Q × Kt be satisfactory, because of 21 Q—B8 ch, K—B3; 22 B—K3, etc. The text move sets White some awkward problems.

21 Q—Q4	Q—Kt5 ch
22 K—R1	

Submitting to perpetual check, because 22 Kt—Kt3 is not playable on account of 22 .... Kt—B6 ch, and if 22 K—B1, Q—R6 ch; 23 K—K2, Q—R4 ch; 24 K—K3 (or 24 K—B1, R—Q1, with advantage to Black); 24 .... Q—B6 ch; 25 K—Q2, R—Q1; 26 Kt—Q6, P × Kt, with a winning attack.

22	Q—B6 ch
23 K—Kt1	Q—Kt5 ch
24 K—R1	Q—B6 ch

And draws by perpetual check.

20. ALEKHINE'S DEFENCE

330

White	Black
A. STEINER	ALEKHINE

(Budapest, 1921)

The rapid development of Black's QB (6 .... B—B4) is instrumental in winning a pawn on the 9th move, victory being achieved on the 62nd. Black's technique here is beyond praise.

1 P—K4 Kt—KB3
The first conscious employment of this opening in a masters' tournament, although it had been analysed as early as 1811 (in *Allgaier's Lehrbuch*, published in Vienna, and in Alexandre's *Encyclopédie*, Paris, 1837).

2 P—K5 Kt—Q4
A Knight errant! Of little use is 2 .... Kt—Kt1; 3 P—Q4, P—K3; 4 B—Q3, as played in a correspondence game between Berwick and Edinburgh in 1860-1.

3 P—Q4
A sound developing move is 3 Kt—QB3, or even 3 B—B4 (3 .... Kt—Kt3; 4 B—Kt3) as played in a game Anderssen-Pearson (*London*, 1862), but at the odds of a Knight.

3 ...... P—Q3
Without delay Black begins to undermine the advanced post.

4 B—KKt5
Here this Bishop is badly placed; it is ineffective, and remains "in the air." If White wishes neither to simplify (4 P×P) nor to complicate (4 P—KB4 or 4 P—QB4, Kt—Kt3; 5 P—B4), he must aim at the centre by 4 Kt—KB3.

4	P×P
5 P×P	Kt—QB3
6 B—Kt5	B—B4
7 Kt—KB3	

A thoughtless routine move. More to the point is 7 P—QB3 (or 7 P—QR3, to be followed by P—QB4).

| 7 ...... | Kt—Kt5 |
| 8 Kt—R3 | |

Not 8 Kt—Q4, Q×Kt, etc.

| 8 ...... | Q×Q ch |
| 9 R×Q | |

After 9 K×Q, Castles ch; 10 K—B1, B—K5, White's position also is unsatisfactory.

9	Kt×P ch
10 Kt×Kt	B×Kt
11 R—QB1	B—K5

Holding on to his small gain.

12 Kt—Q4	B×P
13 R—KKt1	Castles
14 Kt×Kt	

Winning back, at any rate, one pawn. If 14 Kt—B5, B—K5; 15 B×Kt, B×Kt.

14	B×Kt
15 B×B	P×B
16 R×P	R—Q4

The technical phase begins.

| 17 B—B4 | P—K3 |
| 18 K—K2 | |

Threatening to occupy important posts after 19 KR—QB1, R—Q2; 20 B—K3, etc.

| 18 ...... | B—B4 |

An active defence. If now 19 KR—QB1, B—Kt3, etc., Black himself threatens 19 .... K—Kt2, winning the exchange.

| 19 P—Kt4 | |

An ingenious reply, which simplifies as far as possible the play on either side.

19	B×KtP
20 R×KtP	R—Q2
21 B—K3	P—QR4
22 R—B4	P—R4
23 R—R4	B—B6

Aiming at an important objective.

| 24 R—Kt5 | |

If 24 P—B4, P—KB3.

| 24 ...... | R—Q4 |
| 25 P—B4 | P—KB3 |

"An eye for an eye, a pawn for a pawn."

26 R(Kt5)×P	R×R
27 R×R	P×P
28 P×P	B×P
29 R—R7	

Even this simplified phase is still very complicated.

29	R—Kt4
30 K—B3	R—Kt7

If first 30 .... B—Q3; 31 P—KR4 would become dangerous.

31 R—R5

But now 31 P—KR4, R×P; 32 P—R5, P—R5 would be in favour of Black.

31	B×P
32 R×P	B—Q3
33 K—K4	K—Q2
34 B—Q4	R—Q7
35 B—K3	R—K7
36 K—Q3	R—K8
37 B—Q4	R—QB8
38 B—K3	R—Q8 ch
39 K—K4	R—K8
40 K—Q3	P—K4

He has worked hard for this advance.

41 B—B2	R—KB8
42 B—K3	K—K3
43 K—K4	R—KR8
44 B—B2	R—R7
45 B—K3	R—R5 ch

Capture of one rank.

46 K—Q3	B—Kt5
47 R—R7	P—B4

The mobility of this pawn is the chief token of victory.

48 P—R3	P—B5 ch
49 K—K2	B—Q3
50 R—R8	R—R7 ch
51 K—Q1	R—R6
52 K—Q2	K—Q4
53 R—Q8	P—B6 ch

Convincing (if 54 K—Q3, P—K5 ch).

54 K—K2　　K—K5

The battlefield becomes more and more restricted.

55 R×B

Or 55 B—B1, R—R7 ch, confining the King to the last rank.

55 ......　　R×B ch

After many vicissitudes, here at last is the end game proper.

56 K—B2

Or 56 K—Q1, R—Q6 ch; 57 R×R, K×R; 58 P—R4, P—B7 ch (or first 58 .... P—K5, but not, anxiously, 58 .... K—B5; 59 K—B2, draw!); 59 K—B1, K—B6; 60 P—R5, P—K5; 61 P—R6, P—K6; 62 P—R7, P—K7; 63 P—R8 (Q), P—K8 (R) mate.

56 ......　　R—Q6
57 R—QB6

Fighting to the end!

57	R—Q7 ch
58 K—K1	K—Q6
59 R—Q6 ch	K—B7
60 R—K6	R—Q4
61 K—K2	K—Kt6
62 R—QB6	P—B7

Resigns

(63 P—R4, R—Q8, etc., or 63 R—Kt6 ch, K×P; 64 R—R6 ch, K—Kt7; 65 R—Kt6 ch, K—B1; 66 R—Kt8, R—Q7 ch; 67 K—K1, R—Q5; 68 K—K2, R—K5 ch; 69 K—Q3, K—Q8; 70 R—QB8, R—Q5 ch, followed by .... P—B8 (Q) ch.)

331

White	*Black*
BOGOLJUBOW	TARRASCH

(Breslau, 1925)

Archimedes demanded a point of leverage in order to move the world. Very often a chess player needs but an infinitesimal breach to destroy the whole hostile position.

1 P—K4	Kt—KB3
2 P—K5	Kt—Q4
3 Kt—KB3	P—Q3
4 P—Q4	B—B4

Much more active is 4 .... B—Kt5, which, by pinning the KKt, would continue the undermining of the outpost at White's K5.

5 B—Q3　　B—Kt3

Better is 5 .... B×B.

6 P—B4　　Kt—Kt3

He misses the last chance of effecting the liberating exchange 6 .... B×B.

7 B×B　　RP×B
8 P—K6

Breaching the hostile wall.

8 ......　　P—KB3

Unpleasant too would be the continuation 8 .... P×P; 9 Kt—Kt5, Q—Q2; 10 Q—B3, etc.

9 Q—Q3　　Q—B1

If 9 .... P—KB4; 10 Kt—Kt5.

10 Q×P ch　　K—Q1
11 Q—B7

White now threatens, above all, 12 Kt—R4, followed by Kt—Kt6.

11 ......   Kt × P
In order to reply to 12 Kt—R4 by 12 ....
P—Q4, and if 13 Kt—Kt6, Kt—Q3, winning
the Queen.

12 QKt—Q2
He thus succeeds in eliminating Black's
only active piece.

12 ......   Kt × Kt
13 B × Kt   P—KKt4
Thus the most immediate threat, 14 Kt—R4,
is prevented.

14 P—Q5   P—QB4
He must provide his King with an asylum.
If 14 .... P—B3, there follows 15 R—QB1,
Kt—R3; 16 P × P, P × P; 17 B—R5 ch,
Kt—B2; 18 R × P, and wins.

15 B—B3   P—Kt5
Essential to parry the threat 16 B × P.

16 Kt—R4
The decisive manœuvre.

16 ......   R × Kt
Otherwise the sequel would be 17 Kt—Kt6,
but now the *King hunt* will be merciless.

17 Q × B ch   K—B2
18 Q × P ch   K—Kt3
19 Q × QP ch   K—Kt4
20 P—R4 ch   K—B5
21 Q—B4 ch   K × P
On any other move by the King a mate in
two follows, namely 21 .... K—Kt6;
22 K—Q2, after which 23 R—R3 mate, or
21 .... K—Q6; 22 Castles ch, K—K7;
23 R—K1 mate.

22 Castles ch   Resigns
(23 Q × BP or Q6 mate.)

332

White	Black
ALEKHINE	RESHEVSKY

(Kemeri, 1937)

Besides direct sacrifices, *with immediate
consequences, and* positional sacrifices, *the
results of which are seen much later, there
are* potential sacrifices, *in which Dr. Alekhine
excelled. These yield, so to speak, nothing,
but they are apt to render the contest more
incisive Such, in this game, is the sacrifice
of White's pawn at Q4 (by 7 Kt × P), which
imparts a thrilling vitality to the later course
of the game.*

1 P—K4   Kt—KB3
2 P—K5   Kt—Q4
3 P—Q4   P—Q3
4 Kt—KB3   B—Kt5
5 P—B4
A more violent continuation than 5 B—K2
(5 .... P × P; 6 Kt × P, B × B; 7 Q × B, with
a slight advantage to White).

5 ......   Kt—Kt3
6 B—K2   P × P
Enforcing a decision in the centre.

7 Kt × P
The alternative to sacrificing a pawn would
be the intermediary manœuvre 7 P—B5.

7 ......   B × B
8 Q × B   Q × P
9 Castles
White relies on the fact that he has already
some well-developed pieces, whereas Black's
mobilisation is still halting.

9 ......   QKt—Q2
10 Kt × Kt   Kt × Kt
More facile is 10 .... Q × Kt, e.g.
11 R—Q1, Q—B3, or 11 Q—B3, Castles,
etc., whereas now the black Queen has still
to peregrinate from one wing to another.

11 Kt—B3   P—QB3
Clearly not 11 .... Castles; 12 Kt—Kt5,
Q—Kt3; 13 B—K3, P—QB4; 14 P—QKt4,
and White's attack gains in impetus.

12 B—K3   Q—K4
13 QR—Q1   P—K3
Hoping to master his opponent's Bishop
by 14 .... B—B4.

14 Q—B3   Castles
After 14 .... B—B4; 15 R × Kt, K × R;
16 Q × KBP ch, K—B1 (16 .... B—K2;
17 R—Q1 ch, K—B1; 18 Q × B); 17 B—B4,
R—B1 (17 .... Q—B3; 18 Q—B7 mate);
18 Q × R ch, B × Q; 19 B × Q, White remains
with an extra piece.
If 14 .... B—K2; 15 KR—K1 creates
fresh difficulties for Black. That is why he
now returns the pawn, in the hope of
obtaining an even game.

15 B × P
If 15 Q × P, B—B4.

15 ......   Q—QR4
Driving the Bishop from its ominous post,
for if at once 15 .... Q—KB4; 16 Q—Kt3
threatens 17 R × Kt.

16 B—Q4	Q—KB4
17 Q—Kt3	P—K4
18 B—K3	B—Kt5

Trying at last to let his Bishop participate in the course of events.

19 Kt—R4	B—R4
20 P—B4	

In spite of numerical equality, White is able to maintain a multilateral pressure, the consequence of Black's 10th move (.... Kt×Kt, instead of .... Q×Kt).

20	B—B2
21 P—Kt3	

If 21 P×P, Black refrains from 21 .... Q×P, because of 22 B—B4, Q—QR4; 23 B×B, Q×B; 24 Q×Q ch, K×Q; 25 R×P, etc., but plays 21 .... Q—K3, after which he soon recovers the pawn without exchanging Queens. The object of the text move is to have the Knight guarded against eventualities.

21	P—B3

If 21 .... Q—Kt3; 22 Q—R3, etc. But 21 .... P—K5 affords better counter-chances.

22 P×P	Q—K3

Bad would be 22 .... Q×P, on account of 23 B—B4, Q—QR4; 24 Q×P, the right moment to capture this pawn.

23 P—KR3

A sound waiting move, with a defensive value.

23	KR—Kt1
24 B—Q4	Kt×P
25 Q—QB3	Kt—Q2
26 P—B5	

White's pressure on the Q side now becomes the *leit-motif* of the play.

26	KR—K1
27 P—QKt4	Kt—Kt1
28 Kt—Kt6 ch	B×Kt
29 P×B	

Thus is the diagonal KR2—QKt8 closed since Black's 17th move (17 .... P—K4), laid bare again—like a reopened wound.

29	Q×QRP

An ill-judged pawn hunt, which opens an important file and thus helps the opponent's plan of attack.

Better would be 29 .... R—Q2, even though White would still dominate the situation after 30 P—QR4, KR—Q1; 31 R—Q2 (31 P—Kt5, Q—K5); 31 .... Q—K5; 32 KR—Q1, R—Q4; 33 P—Kt5, etc.

30 Q—KKt3	R—Q2
31 B—B5	Q—B2
32 R—R1	

Preparing for the final assault, based on the converging effect of files and diagonals around the penned-in Knight.

32	Q—Kt3
33 Q—R2	R—K4
34 R—R8	R—Q7

This allows a crushing termination, but also after 34 .... Q—K1; 35 Q—Kt3, Black's position could not be held for any length of time.

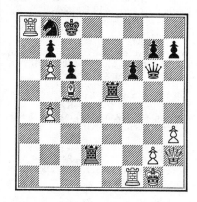

35 R×Kt ch

A *sacrifice* with the effect of a magnet, which leads up to a decisive *break-through* *sacrifice*.

35	K×R
36 Q×R ch	Resigns.

333

White	Black
L. STEINER	KOBLENZ

(Brünn, 1937)

The following game illustrates in a very clear manner the advantages of a superior development. Not only does it enable Black to gain more and more territory, driving the Queen into a corner and confining the adverse King to the middle of the board, but it is organically connected with the pretty sacrifice which decides the issue.

1	P—K4	Kt—KB3
2	P—K5	Kt—Q4
3	P—Q4	P—Q3
4	Kt—KB3	B—Kt5
5	P—KR3	

White wishes to bring his Queen as rapidly as possible into the game, but development by 5 B—K2 would be more useful.

5	......	B×Kt
6	Q×B	P×P
7	P×P	P—K3
8	P—R3	

Premature would be 8 P—B4, Kt—Kt5, but now White actually does threaten 9 P—B4, followed by 10 Q×KtP.

8	......	P—QB3
9	Q—KKt3	

With the twofold mission of immobilising Black's KB by the attack on the KKtP, and of guarding his own exposed KP.

9	......	Kt—Q2
10	Kt—Q2	Kt—K2

Making for KKt3, masking the KKtP, and also attacking the KP.

11	Kt—B3	Kt—KKt3
12	B—Q2	Kt—B4

With the threat 13 .... Kt—K5. Black is seizing the initiative.

13	B—K3	Kt—K5
14	Q—R2	

"Placed on half pay." Against the more plausible-looking move 14 Q—Kt4, there would follow 14 .... Q—R4 ch; 15 P—B3, Q—R5, threatening to win the Queen by 16 .... P—KR4.

14	......	Q—R4 ch
15	P—B3	

Compulsory. If 15 P—Kt4, B×P ch.

15	......	Castles

A mistake would be 15 .... Kt×QBP; 16 B—Q2, B—Kt5; 17 P×Kt, B×BP; 18 R—Q1, and White has won a piece.

16 R—B1

Overprotecting the critical point.

16	......	B—B4

Black is willing to give up a piece in order still more to increase his advantage in development.

17 P—QKt4

Accepting the offer, because, should he refuse it, with 17 B×B, Q×B; 18 R—B2, White still remains at a disadvantage after

18 .... Q—Q4; 19 B—K2, Q—Kt6; 20 B—Q1, Kt×KBP; 21 K×Kt, R×B; 22 R×R, Q×R ch; 23 R—Q2, Q—B4, etc., and Black has a valuable extra pawn.

17	......	Q×RP
18	P×B	Kt×P (QB6)

With the threat of 19 .... Q×R ch; 20 B×Q, R—Q8 mate., Black has an enduring attack and two pawns for his piece.

19	B—K2	Q—Kt7
20	Kt—Kt1	Kt—R7
21	R—Q1	R×R ch
22	B×R	R—Q1

Again threatening an immediate decision by 23 .... Q—B6 ch; 24 K—K2, Q—Q6 ch, etc.

23 P—B4

If 23 Kt—K2, Q—Kt5 ch wins.

23	......	Q—R8
24	B—Q2	Kt—B6
25	B×Kt	Q×QB ch
26	K—B2	

After 26 K—K2, the reply is 26 .... R—Q7 ch, or 26 .... Q—Q7 ch.

26	......	R×B

Having recovered his piece, with a dominating position, Black wins easily.

27	Kt—B3	Q×P ch
28	K—Kt3	R×R
29	Q×R	Q—K6

Winning another pawn.

30	Q—R1	Kt×BP
31	Q—QKt1	Kt—K7 ch
32	K—R2	Q—B5 ch
33	K—R1	Q—B8 ch
34	Q×Q	Kt×Q
35	Kt—Kt5	P—QR4
	Resigns.	

334

White	Black
YATES	KMOCH

(Budapest, 1926)

In a most elegant manner White succeeds in obtaining the key to the black King's position. Equally elegant is his gain of the Queen, forced by a threat of mate.

1 P—K4	Kt—KB3
2 P—K5	Kt—Q4
3 P—Q4	P—Q3
4 P×P	

Trying to avoid the pitfalls of the opening.

| 4 ...... | Q×P |

But Black insists on picking a quarrel, scorning peaceful methods such as 4 .... KP×P.

5 Kt—KB3	B—Kt5
6 B—K2	Kt—QB3
7 Castles	

He proceeds with his straightforward development. A more impulsive continuation is 7 Kt—B3, Castles; 8 Kt×Kt, Q×Kt; 9 B—K3, P—K4; 10 P×P (or 10 Castles, B×Kt; 11 B×B, P—K5; Black still has the initiative); 10 .... B×Kt; 11 P×B (or 11 B×B, Q—R4 ch; 12 B—Q2, Q×P ch, with a big advantage to Black); 11 .... Q—R4 ch; 12 B—Q2, Q×KP, and Black has the lead.

| 7 ...... | Castles |
| 8 P—B3 | |

A wise consolidation. 8 Kt—R3 is also admissible.

| 8 ...... | Kt—B5 |
| 9 B×Kt | |

As can be seen, White has given up his *two Bishops*, for a precept is far from being a dogma. Thus all the white minor pieces are very active.

| 9 ...... | Q×B |
| 10 P—Kt4 | |

The signal to attack, which induces the opponent to put in a word also.

| 10 ...... | P—K4 |

He decided finally to give up a pawn for the sake of his development, for if, calmly, 10 .... P—K3; 11 Q—R4, K—Kt1; 12 Kt—R3 foreshadows a lasting attack. And if 10 .... B×Kt; 11 B×B, Kt—K4, then, simply, 12 B—K2 (threat: Q—R4); 12 .... K—Kt1; 13 Kt—Q2, and the black Knight has to retreat.

| 11 P—Kt3 | |

A skilful counter-measure, whereas, after 11 P—Kt5, B×Kt; 12 B×B, Kt—K2; 13 Q—R4, P—K5; 14 B—K2, K—Kt1, and White's enterprise would be stillborn.

| 11 ...... | Q—R3 |

If 11 .... Q—B4; 12 P—Kt5, etc.

12 Kt×P	Kt×Kt
13 B×B ch	K—Kt1
14 B—B3	P—KB4

Compulsory violence.

| 15 R—K1 | |

After 15 B—Kt2, Kt—Kt5; 16 P—KR3, Kt—B3, this Knight's mission is not yet accomplished.

15	Kt×B ch
16 Q×Kt	P—KKt3
17 Kt—R3	Q—Kt2

If 17 .... B—Q3; 18 Kt—B4, KR—B1; 19 Kt—R5, P—B3; 20 P—Kt5, P—B5; 21 QKtP×P, BP×P; 22 P—B7 ch, K×P; 23 Q×P mate; and if at once 17 .... P—B5; 18 Q×P, Q×Q; 19 P×Q, B—Q3; 20 Kt—B4, B×BP; 21 R—K7, and White will turn his extra pawn to account.

18 Kt—B4	P—KR4
19 Kt—R5	P—B3
20 R—K6	P—R5
21 QR—K1	P×P
22 RP×P	B—Q3
23 Kt—B4	

Returning to the charge, with a diabolical plan in view.

| 23 ...... | B—B2 |

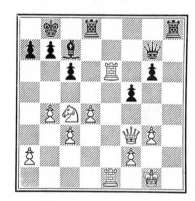

| 24 P—Kt5 | |

Breaking down the barricades. Useless would be 24 R—K7, Q—R3; 25 Q—Kt2, P—B5, etc.

| 24 ...... | P×P |
| 25 Kt—R5 | |

The point of the whole idea. Technically, the momentary deflection of the Bishop is what matters.

25	B×Kt
26 R—K7	R—Q2
27 R×Q	R×R
28 R—K5	

White's advantage in material (Queen against Rook and Bishop), which he will have to stress, is *dynamic superiority*, and he now proceeds to do this with great virtuosity.

| 28 ...... | P—R3 |
| 29 Q—K3 | |

A preparatory measure of extreme discretion. If 29 P—R4, or 29 P—B4, then 29 .... B—B2.

| 29 ...... | R—QB1 |
| 30 P—QB4 | |

A brilliant stratagem.

| 30 ...... | R×P |

If 30 .... B—B2; 31 P×P, B×R; 32 Q×B ch, R—QB2; 33 P—Kt6.

| 31 R—K8 ch | K—R2 |

For if 31 .... R—B1; 32 Q—K5 ch, R—QB2; 33 R×R ch, K×R; 34 Q—K8 mate.

32 P—Q5 dis ch	B—Kt3
33 Q—K5	B—Q5
34 Q—Kt8 ch	K—Kt3
35 P—Q6	Resigns

(The threat is 36 R—K7.)
A splendid achievement.

335

| *White* | *Black* |
| H. WOLF | GRÜNFELD |

(Pistyan, 1922)

Against an attack on the wing, launched prematurely or with insufficient means, the best antidote is counter-action in the centre or on the opposite wing. This game is a good illustration of the method of procedure (14 .... P—Q4).

1 P—K4	Kt—KB3
2 P—K5	Kt—Q4
3 P—Q4	P—Q3
4 P—QB4	Kt—Kt3
5 P×P	

Simple and good. More adventurous spirits do not fear the widening of their front by 5 P—B4. (*The Four Pawns' Attack.*)

5	KP×P
6 B—K3	B—K2
7 B—Q3	QKt—Q2

Bound for KB3, where it is to take the place of its companion in the defence of the K side.

8 Kt—K2	Kt—B3
9 P—KR3	Castles
10 Kt—Q2	

The more natural development is 10 QKt—B3, but White wishes to *over-protect* his QBP in order to release his KB.

| 10 ...... | R—K1 |
| 11 Q—B2 | KKt—Q2 |

He anticipates the enemy attack, and reserves the option of directing this Knight to KB1 for the better protection of the King's field.

| 12 P—KKt4 | |

This truculent enterprise can succeed only when Black has failed to provide for counter-measures. Wisdom demands 12 Castles KR, with an even game.

12	Kt—B1
13 Castles QR	P—B3
14 Kt—KKt3	P—Q4
15 P—Kt5	

Or 15 P—B5, P—QKt3; 16 Kt—Kt3, Kt (B3)—Q2, and Black's counter-attack on the Q side is taking shape.

| 15 ...... | P×P |

Thus Black secures the initiative. On the other hand, after the retreat 15 .... Kt (B3)—Q2 White can without fear proceed with his attack by 16 P×P, P×P; 17 P—KR4, Kt—QKt3; 18 K—Kt1, etc.

| 16 Kt×P | |

After 16 P×Kt, P×B White would incur some loss, namely 17 P×B, P×Q (Q), P×R (Q) ch; 18 P×Q (Q), P×R (Q) ch, winning the exchange, or 17 Q×QP, B×BP, and Black has won a pawn.

16	Kt—Q4
17 P—KR4	Kt—Kt5
18 Q—Kt1	Kt×B ch
19 Q×Kt	Q—Q4

Threatening to win the QRP by 20 .... B—K3.

| 20 P—R3 | |

After 20 K—Kt1, B—K3; 21 P—Kt3 Kt—Q2 (not at once 21 .... P—QR4; 22 Kt—Kt6); 22 P—R5, P—R4, with .... P—R5 to follow, Black's attack prevails.

20	B—K3
21 Kt—Q2	P—QB4

He takes advantage of the right tactical moment (the white Queen being undefended) to open the QB file.

22 Kt—Kt1	P×P
23 Q×P	

Or 23 B×P, QR—B1 ch; 24 Kt—B3, KR—Q1, and Black has command of the situation.

23	KR—B1 ch
24 Kt—B3	Q—Kt6

This lodgment within the enemy lines carries the threat of 25 .... B×RP.

25 Kt—K2

After 25 Kt—R5, in the belief that he would be the first to threaten mate at KKt7, Black would settle matters by 25 .... R×Kt ch; 26 P×R, Q RP ch; 27 K—B2 (27 K—Q2, R—Q1, or 27 K—Kt1, Q—R7 ch; 28 K—B1, B—R6 mate); 27 .... Q—R7 ch; 28 K—Q3, B—B4 ch, etc.

25 ...... B×RP

Although White has fortified his QB3, this sacrifice is successful.

26 P×B	Q P ch
27 K—B2	Q—Kt6 ch
28 K—Q2	

Or 28 K—B1, B—B4; 29 R—Q3 (29 R—Q2, Q—Kt8 mate); 29 .... R—Q1, and wins.

28	R—Q1
29 R—QKt1	Q—B5
30 KR—QB1	R×Q ch
31 Kt×R	R—Q1
32 Kt—K2	Q—R7 ch
33 K—K1	Q—R4 ch
34 K—B1	Q—Q4
35 K—Kt1	

White's King is now safe, but Black's advantage in material is sufficient to win.

35 ...... Q—K5

Threatening 36 .... B—Q4.

36 Kt—KKt3	Q×P
37 Kt—B3	Q—R6
38 R—Kt4	

Not 38 R×P, B—Q4. White now threatens 39 R—KR4.

38	B—Q4
39 R—KR4	Q—Q2
40 Kt—Q4	Kt—Kt3
41 R—R2	Q—Kt5
42 Kt—B5	B—B3
43 P—B3	

To parry the threat 43 .... R—Q8 ch;

44 R×R, Q×R ch; 45 Kt—B1, Kt—K4, followed by .... Kt—B6 ch.

43	Q×BP
44 R—KB2	Q—Kt5
45 K—R2	R—K1

If at once 45 .... Kt—K4; 46 Kt—K7 ch, followed by Kt×B.

46 R—QB3	Kt—K4
47 R—KB4	Q—Q8
48 K—R3	Q—Q4
49 Kt—K4	B—Q2
50 Kt (K4)—Kt3	P—KKt3
Resigns.	

336

White	Black
LASKER	TARRASCH

(Märisch-Ostrau, 1923)

A magnificent game, in which two representatives of the scientific era adapt themselves to the finessing of hyper-modern strategy.

White's exposed centre provides the main battlefield. Tarrasch, the doctrinaire, wins a pawn there, but Lasker, the psychologist, derives from it an ever-increasing tension. His offer of an exchange of Queens, when a pawn down, provides the crowning touch of the contest.

1 P—K4	Kt—KB3
2 P—K5	Kt—Q4
3 P—QB4	Kt—Kt3
4 P—Q4	P—Q3
5 P—B4	

Widening his front, which implies additional commitments. This attempt to refute Black's first move is known as the *main variation.*

5 ...... P×P

If 5 .... P—KB3; 6 B—Q3, threatening 7 Q—R5 ch.

6 BP×P Kt—B3

The attack against White's strong but exposed centre now begins. The attack by 6 .... P—QB4 would be too abrupt, and that by 6 .... P—KKt3 too slow. The historiographer will note that Allgaier's *Lehrbuch*, published in Vienna, 1811 (2nd Edition, 1841), quotes the variation 6 .... B—B4; 7 Kt—KB3, P—K3; 8 B—Q3, B—Kt3; 9 Kt—B3, P—B4, etc.

7 B—K3

Not 7 P—Q5, Kt×KP, but against the preparatory 7 Kt—KB3, B—Kt5.

7 ......   B—B4
8 Kt—QB3

A preventive idea, 8 P—QR3, leads to an artificial and very vulnerable defence after 8 .... P—K3; 9 Kt—KB3, B—Kt5; 10 QKt—Q2, etc. A blunder would be 8 B—Q3, B×B; 9 Q×B, Kt×KP.

8 ......   P—K3

Not 8 .... P—B3; 9 P—K6.

9 Kt—B3

An important moment. More accurate is first 9 B—K2, after which Black has the choice of the following continuations:

(a) *Pinning*: 9 .... B—QKt5; 10 Kt—B3, with a rational development for White.

(b) *A false sortie*: 9 .... Kt—R4; 10 P—QKt3, B—QKt5; 11 Q—Q2, with eventually Q—Kt2 and P—QR3, driving back the intruder.

(c) *An emancipating manœuvre*: 9 .... Kt—Kt5; 10 R—B1, P—B4, etc.

(d) *Undermining forthwith*: 9 .... P—B3.

(e) *Simple development*: 9 .... B—K2; 10 Kt—B3, Castles (or 10 .... P—B3); 11 Castles, P—B3 (see the following game).

(f) *Central pressure*: 9 .... Q—Q2; 10 Kt—B3, Castles (against 10 .... R—Q1, or 10 .... B—KKt5, the best course is not 11 Castles at once, but 11 Q—Q2); 11 Castles (11 Q—Q2, P—B3); 11 .... P—B3, etc., and Black holds his own.

9 ......   B—QKt5

Black could at once have stressed the lack of precision in White's preceding move by 9 .... B—KKt5.

10 B—Q3

Wasted energy, the *coup juste* being 10 B—K2.

10 ......   B—Kt5

The loss of time is more than balanced by Black's pressure in the centre, which secures for him a real advantage.

Useless, however, would be 10 .... B×B; 11 Q×B, etc., as well as 10 .... Kt—R5; 11 Q×Kt, B×B; 12 P—QR3, B×Kt ch; 13 P×B, etc., and White has strengthened his centre.

11 B—K2

He recognises that the attempt to attack by 11 Castles, Kt×QP; 12 B×Kt, KB×Kt; 13 Q×B, Q×B ch; 14 K—R1, Castles QR (not 14 .... Castles KR; 15 Q—R3,

P—KR3; 16 QR—K1, and White achieves his object); 15 QR—Q1, B×Kt; 16 P×B, Q×P (B6) would fail.

11 ......   B×Kt
12 P×B   Q—R5 ch
13 B—B2   Q—B5
14 KR—Kt1   Castles QR

By first playing 14 .... P—KR4; 15 R×P, Castles (or even 15 .... R—Q1), Black could have maintained his objectives in the centre, whereas now White can avert the principal danger at the cost of a distant pawn.

15 R—Kt4   Q×RP
16 R—R4   Q—Kt7
17 B—B1   Q—Kt4
18 Q—B2

Evading the threat 18 .... Kt×KP, etc.

18 ......   P—KR4

If 18 .... P—B3; 19 R—Kt4.

19 R—Q1   Q—R3

But now 19 .... P—B3 would be more energetic.

20 P—R3   B—K2
21 R—R3   B—Kt4
22 Q—K4   P—B3

Better late than never, but now White has brought up reserves.

23 P×P   Q×P

Firmer would be, however, 23 .... B×BP, e.g. 24 Q×P ch, K—Kt1, etc., or 24 B—K3, B—Kt4, etc., or again, 24 B—K2, KR—K1, etc.

24 B—K2   Q—B4

Plausible as it may appear, the exchange of Queens is the decisive mistake. A fighting continuation would be 24 .... Kt—K2, to be followed by .... Kt—B4 or .... Kt—Kt3, and the issue remains open.

25 Q×Q   P×Q
26 B—Q3   P—Kt3
27 Kt—K2

Not 27 R—Kt3, B—R5; 28 R×P, B×B ch; 29 K×B, QKt×P, and Black has a win.

27 ......   P—R5

An exposed pawn. Better would be 27 .... Kt—K2.

28 P—B4   B—B3
29 P—Kt4   K—Kt1

In order to make the threat 30 .... Kt×QP; 31 Kt×Kt, B×Kt; 32 B×B, R×B, without having to fear 33 B×P ch.

30 P—Q5	Kt—K2
31 K—B1	Kt (Kt3)—B1

This move, intending 32 .... P—B3 (if
31 .... P—B3 at once 32 P—Q6), is too
passive. He should try to gain some space
by 31 .... Kt—R5.

32 P—Kt5	P—B3

As is to be expected, this opening of lines
benefits the attack. Better is 32 ....
Kt—Q3, in order to reach K5.

33 KtP × P	P × P
34 R—Kt1 ch	K—R1
35 Kt—Q4	

A powerful manœuvre.

35	B × Kt

After 35 .... P × P; 36 P × P, neither
36 .... Kt × P; 37 Kt—B6, nor 36 ....
R × P; 37 Kt—K6 would be playable for
Black.

36 B × B	R—R2
37 B—K5	Kt—Q3
38 P—B5	Kt—Kt2
39 P—Q6	Kt—Q4
40 R—B1	R—KB1
41 B—R6	Kt—B3
42 B × Kt	

Letting loose his heavy artillery.

42	R × B
43 R—K3	R—B1
44 QR—K1	R (R2)—R1
45 P—Q7	K—Kt1
46 R—K8 ch	K—B2
47 B × Kt	Resigns.

337

White	Black
NAEGELI	MUFFANG

(The Hague, 1928)

In the following game the idea of an inter-
mittent pin, *which forms the basis of Black's
winning combination, is presented in a manner
both eloquent and artistic.*

1 P—K4	Kt—KB3
2 P—K5	Kt—Q4
3 P—QB4	Kt—Kt3
4 P—Q4	P—Q3
5 P—B4	P × P
6 BP × P	Kt—B3
7 B—K3	

If 7 Kt—KB3, B—Kt5, indirectly continuing the attack on White's exposed QP.

7	B—B4
8 Kt—QB3	P—K3
9 B—K2	B—K2
10 Kt—B3	P—B3

By undermining the apex of the hostile
chain of pawns, Black opens the KB file,
which, together with his pressure on the
Q file, will become an important asset to
his plans.

11 Castles	Castles
12 P × P	

By playing 12 Q—K1, White could still
have maintained his outpost at K5 and
avoided the exchange of Queens, e.g. 12 ....
P × P; 13 P × P, etc., or 12 .... Kt—Kt5;
13 Kt—Q1, Kt—B7; 14 Q—B2, Kt × B;
15 Q × Kt, and White has a good game.

12	B × P
13 Q—Q2	Q—K2
14 QR—Q1	QR—Q1
15 P—B5	

In view of the increasing adverse pressure,
White has to have recourse to an *artificial
manœuvre* in order to cover up his weakness
at Q4.

15	Kt—Q4
16 P—QR3	

Better at once 16 B—QB4.

16	K—R1

Safety first!

17 B—QB4	Kt × B
18 Q × Kt	B—Kt5
19 Kt—K2	B × Kt
20 R × B	

Just when Black might be expected to
become anxious for the safety of his threatened KP, the storm breaks.

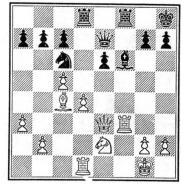

20	B × P

A well-grounded sacrifice. Its value is
enhanced by the fact that the plausible

20 .... Kt—K4, which seems to win the exchange without any trouble, would prove ineffective after 21 R—R3, Kt × B; 22 Q—Q3, and White recovers his piece.

21 R × B   Kt × R
22 Kt × Kt   Q × P

White's Bishop and Knight are "in the air," and provide good targets for the enemy. The position is full of surprising and subtle turns.

23 R × R ch

After 23 Kt × P, the quasi-magical reply 23 .... R × R (24 Q × Q, R—Q8 ch) wins.

23 ......   R × R
24 B—Kt3

Or 24 P—QKt3, P—QKt4, or 24 B × P, R—Q1; 25 Kt—B5, Q × Q ch; 26 Kt × Q, R—K1, and wins (vertical action).

24 ......   R—Q1
Resigns

If 25 Kt—B2, Q × Q ch; 26 Kt × Q, R—Q6, and wins (horizontal action).

338

White	Black
ZNOSKO-BOROVSKI	ALEKHINE

(Paris, 1925)

After his brilliant sacrifice of the Queen, Black still lacks the ultimate key to victory, and must deem himself lucky to achieve the draw. The magnificent fluctuations of this game will remain engraved in the memory.

1 P—K4   Kt—KB3
2 P—K5   Kt—Q4
3 P—QB4   Kt—Kt3
4 P—Q4   P—Q3
5 P—B4   P × P
6 BP × P   Kt—B3
7 B—K3   B—B4
8 Kt—KB3

Threatening 9 P—Q5, and wishing to reserve the choice of development of the QKt either at B3 or (e.g. against 8 .... B—Kt5) at Q2.

8 ......   P—K3

If 8 .... B—Kt5; 9 QKt—Q2 protects, by repercussion, all the white centre pawns. After 8 .... Kt—Kt5 White has yet a third manner of developing the QKt, namely 9 Kt—R3.

9 Kt—B3   Kt—Kt5

A disengaging manœuvre. Nothing is gained by the false alarm 9 .... B—QKt5; 10 B—K2 (but not, as in a preceding game, 10 B—Q3, B—Kt5); 10 .... Castles; 11 Castles, and White has the upper hand.

A sound *alerte*, however, is 9 .... B—KKt5, e.g. 10 B—K2, B × Kt; 11 P × B, Q—R5 ch; 12 B—B2, Q—B5, etc., or 10 P—B5, Kt—Q4; 11 Kt × Kt, Q × Kt; 12 B—K2, Castles; 13 Castles, Q—K5, or 10 Q—Q2, Kt—R4; 11 P—QKt3, and Black continues to harass his adversary.

10 R—B1   P—B4
11 P—QR3

Starting an interesting affray in the centre, which can be delayed by 11 B—K2, B—K2; 12 Castles, Castles; 13 P—QR3, P × P; 14 Kt × P, Kt—B3, etc., with an even game.

11 ......   P × P
12 B—Kt5

Ingenious, but it can be refuted, as his opponent's skilful and imaginative reply demonstrates: as 12 P × Kt, P × Kt; 13 P × P, Kt—Q2, etc., also turns out badly for White, his proper course is 12 Kt × P, e.g. 12 .... Kt—B3; 13 Kt × Kt (13 Kt × B, P × Kt, with an even game); 13 .... Q × Q ch (or also 13 .... P × Kt; 14 B—K2, B—K2; 15 B—B3, Castles, without any damage); 14 R × Q, P × Kt, and the weaknesses on either side balance each other.

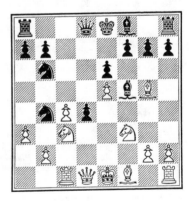

12 ......   P × Kt

A *Queen's sacrifice* in the opening. But Black could play neither 12 .... Q—B2; 13 Kt—Kt5, winning a piece, nor 12 .... B—K2; 13 B × B, Q × B; 14 Kt—QKt5, Kt—B3; 15 Kt—Q6 ch, K—B1; 16 P—B5, Kt—Q4; 17 B—Kt5, etc., with a strong pressure by White.

13 B × Q   R × B

Plausible, but it allows the hostile Queen to excape through the stricken field. A decisive advantage could be obtained by 13 .... P × P; 14 B—Kt5 (best); 14 .... P × R (Q); 15 B × Q, R—Q1, and White's position is tottering.

14 Q—Kt3   P × P
15 Q × P   Kt—R5
16 Q—R1

If 16 Q—Kt3, Kt—B4.

16 ......   Kt—B7 ch
17 R × Kt   B × R

Black, with only Rook, Bishop and pawn for the Queen, dominates the field.

18 Kt—Q4

After 18 B—K2, B—QB4; 19 Q—R2, B—K5; 20 Q—Kt3, B—B3, White is still held in a vice.

18 ......   B—Kt3
19 P—B5

White frees himself very neatly.

19 ......   Kt × P

And not 19 .... B × P; 20 B—Kt5 ch, K—K2; 21 Kt—Kt3.

20 B—Kt5 ch   Kt—Q2
21 Q—B3   P—QR3

Black refuses to play with fire (21 .... B—K2; 22 Q—B7), and insists on clearing up the situation.

22 B × Kt ch   R × B
23 Q—B8 ch   R—Q1
24 Q × P

Played in great style, and worthy of his adversary. Black will now have three fine pieces for the Queen, which, however, exhibits an astonishing vigour.

24 ......   R × Kt
25 Q—B6 ch   R—Q2

Clearly not 25 .... K—Q1; 26 Q—Kt6 ch, nor 25 .... K—K2; 26 Q—B5 ch.

26 Castles

With the big threat of 27 R—Q1.

26 ......   B—Q6
27 R × P

A feat of valour! The draw by 27 Q—B8 ch, R—Q1 (27 .... K—K2; 28 R × P ch); 28 Q—B6 ch no longer satisfies him.

27 ......   B—B4 ch

The wounded lion fights back.

28 K—R1   B—Kt4

Creating a defence, thanks to the QRP.

29 Q × P ch   R—K2

He can play neither 29 .... B—K2; 30 R × B ch, R × R; 31 Q—B8 ch, K—B2; 32 Q × R, etc., nor 29 .... K—Q1; 30 R × R ch, B × R; 31 Q—Q5 (double threat: 32 Q × B, and 32 P—K6); 31 .... R—B1; 32 P—Kt4, and White's cause prevails.

30 R × R ch   B × R
31 Q—B8 ch

This extraordinarily stirring and eventful game is now to end in a draw by perpetual check! Yet White would be justified in trying for a win by 31 P—QR4, e.g. 31 .... B × P; 32 Q × P, winning the QB, or 31 .... B—Q2; 32 Q × P, capturing an important stronghold, or finally and chiefly, by 31 .... R—B1; 32 P—Kt4, etc., mastering Black's counter-action.

31 ......   B—Q1
32 Q—K6 ch   B—K2
33 Q—B8 ch   B—Q1
34 Q—K6 ch

     Draw.

339

White	Black
STOLTZ	*COLLE*

(Bled, 1931)

"He who sows the wind, reaps the whirlwind," a Biblical saying which is well illustrated in the following game.

1 P—K4   Kt—KB3
2 P—K5   Kt—Q4
3 P—QB4   Kt—Kt3
4 P—B5

An incisive idea, of which the object is to bring about an immediate clash of pieces in the centre.

Another interesting continuation (instead of the "normal" 4 P—Q4) is 4 P—QKt3, e.g. 4 .... P—Q3; 5 P × P, KP × P; 6 B—Kt2, or 4 .... P—Kt3; 5 B—Kt2, B—Kt2; 6 P—Q4, with no immediate or definite objectives.

4 ......   Kt—Q4
5 Kt—QB3

More insistent than 5 B—B4, P—K3; 6 P—Q4, P—Q3, etc.

5 ......   Kt × Kt

This exchange is to procure Black freedom of action in the centre, but he could try to maintain himself there by 5 .... P—K3; as in the game Halosar—Becker, *Austro-German Tournament, Berlin*, 1938: 6 B—B4 (or, more solidly, 6 P—Q4, Kt × Kt; 7 P × Kt, P—Q3, etc.); 6 .... Kt × Kt (if 6 .... P—QB3; 7 Kt—K4); 7 KtP × Kt, P—Q4 (rightly refusing the doubtful gift by 7 .... B × P, after which 8 P—Q4 would help White's development); 8 BP × P e.p., P × P; 9 P × P, B × P; 10 P—Q4, Q—B2; 11 Q—K2 (more circumspect would be 11 Q—Q3); 11 .... Kt—Q2; 12 Kt—B3 (plausible, but suicidal); 12 .... P—QKt4; White resigns, as he loses a piece.

6 QP × Kt

After 6 KtP × Kt, P—Q3, Black would have no more worries.

6 ......   Kt—B3

Here again 6 .... P—Q3 promises equality. Another method of eliminating at least one of the enemy scouts is 6 .... P—K3; 7 B—K3, P—QKt3, etc.

7 Kt—B3   P—KKt3

His last chance of playing .... P—Q3.

8 B—QB4   B—Kt2
9 B—B4   Castles
10 Q—Q2   P—Kt3
11 P—KR4   P—KR4
12 Castles QR

White has a formidable position in which one pawn more or less is of no account.

12 ......   P—K3

Greed as exemplified by 12 .... P × P would suffer swift punishment by 13 P—KKt4, P × P; 14 P—R5, P × Kt; 15 P × P, breaking down the battlements.

13 B—KKt5

After the preparatory 13 Q—B2, not 13 .... P—B4 (14 B × P ch), but 13 .... Q—K1.

13 ......   P—B3

Now 13 .... Q—K1 would be refuted by 14 B—B6.

14 P × BP   B × P
15 Q—B2

Announcing the direct attack.

15 ......   Q—K1
16 B—Q3   K—Kt2
17 P—KKt4

Proceeding by violent jerks, instead of methodically, compromising the opposing King's field by 17 Q—Q2.

17 ......   RP × P
18 QR—Kt1   B × B ch

He skilfully keeps the KKt file closed, thus refuting his opponent's combination, whereas 18 .... P × Kt; 19 B × P would lead to a loss.

19 Kt × B   Kt—K4
20 B—K4

Preserving his attacking Bishop he intends to reply to 20 .... R—QKt1 by 21 P—B3, so as to have the "last word" on the critical KKt file. But Black shows himself equal to the situation.

20 ......   B—R3

Giving up the exchange for the sake of the initiative.

21 B × R

White fails to see the danger, and accepts the gift.

21 ......   Kt—Q6 ch

Not at once 21 .... Q × B, because of 22 Q—K4. Black's diabolical plot begins to reveal itself.

22 K—Kt1   Q × B

And now, not 22 .... R × P; 23 Q—R4.

23 P—QB4   Kt—K4
24 Q—B3   R—B4
25 P—B4

Impatiently, White burns his bridges. The more rational continuation would be 25 R—K1(e.g. 25 .... K—Kt1; 26 Kt—K4, B—Kt2; 27 Kt—Kt3, etc.).

25 ......   P × P e.p.
26 R—K1   P—B7

This pawn has become an important asset.

| 27 R×Kt | K—Kt1 |

An excellent rejoinder. Of course, he could not play 27 .... Q×R ch; on account of 28 R—K1 dis ch.

28 R—KB1

Holding on desperately to his loot. But he had a better chance of resistance in 28 QR—K1, P×R (Q) ch; 29 R×Q, etc.

| 28 ...... | Q—Kt7 |
| 29 Q—Q3 | B×P |

He begins to obtain a return for his investments. A terrible blunder would be 29 .... R×R; 30 Q×P ch, followed by mate.

| 30 Q×B | R×R |
| 31 Q—Q3 | |

He only anticipates 31 .... R—K8 ch, after which 32 K—B2, K—B1; 33 Q—Q2, etc., would turn the tables in favour of White. A rude awakening awaits him. But White has no satisfactory continuation, as 31 K—B2 is inadmissible by reason of 31 .... R×P, and if 31 R—B1, R—K8.

| 31 ...... | Q×R ch |

Resigns

A fine battle between two dare-devils.

340

| White | Black |
| YATES | COLLE |

(Hastings, 1926)

A game as brilliant as it is instructive. White engineers a K side attack (14 Kt—R4), widens his base of action (20 P—KB4), finds a target at KR7 and, leaving his own Queen en prise (24 Kt—K7), finishes in a blaze of glory.

1 P—K4	Kt—KB3
2 P—K5	Kt—Q4
3 Kt—QB3	

A sound, unpretentious move, stressing the development of pieces in preference to manœuvres by pawns. Another good move of the same type is 3 B—B4.

| 3 ...... | Kt×Kt |

Against 3 .... P—K3; 4 Q—B3 can be recommended. Similarly, 3 .... P—Q3 is less resolute than the move in the text.

4 KtP×Kt

After 4 QP×Kt, P—Q3, Black frees his game without difficulty.

| 4 ...... | P—Q3 |

At this stage also, this is better than 4 .... P—Q4.

5 Kt—B3

After 5 P—KB4, the simplest continuation is 5 .... P×P; 6 P×P, B—B4. On the other hand, the following continuation might be fancied for White: 5 P×P, KP×P; 6 P—Q4, P—Q4; 7 B—Q3, etc. The position is now reminiscent of the *Exchange Variation* of the *French Defence*, with this difference: the absence of the defending Knight (at KB3) is liable to be awkward for Black.

| 5 ...... | P—KKt3 |

Avoiding the beaten track, Black chooses a slow method of development instead of the usual 5 .... B—Kt5, seeking equality. If 5 .... P×P; 6 Kt×P.

6 P—Q4	B—Kt2
7 B—KB4	Castles
8 B—K2	

More useful here than 8 B—Q3, B—Kt5.

| 8 ...... | Kt—B3 |
| 9 P×P | BP×P |

After 9 .... KP×P, Black's position, with a "hole" at KB3, would be less compact.

| 10 Q—Q2 | Q—B2 |
| 11 Castles KR | |

Premature would be 11 B—KR6, e.g. 11 .... Kt×P; 12 P×Kt, B×B; 13 Q×B, Q—B6 ch, followed by .... Q×R ch.

| 11 ...... | P—Kt3 |

By first playing 11 .... R—K1, Black could reply to 12 B—KR6 by 12 .... B—R1, preserving this guardian of his King's field.

12 B—KR6

A sound *exchanging manœuvre*, which weakens the enemy base.

12	B—Kt2
13 B×B	K×B
14 Kt—R4	Kt—R4
15 QR—K1	QR—B1
16 B—Q3	P—K3

If 16 .... Q×P; 17 Q×Q, R×Q; 18 R×P, and White has advantageously recouped himself on the KP. Or 16 .... KR—K1; 17 Q—Kt5, P—B3; 18 Q—Kt3, Q×P; 19 Kt×P, P×Kt; 20 Q×P ch, K—B1; 21 Q—R6 ch, K—Kt1; 22 B—R7 ch, with an early mate.

17 Q—B4   Q—Q1

Of little use would be 17 .... Q×P, as White would avoid 18 Q×P, KR—Q1; 19 Q—K5 ch, K—Kt1, etc., and play 18 R—K3. Now Black threatens not only 18 .... R×P, but also the fork 18 .... P—KKt4.

18 R—K3

Rendering these two threats illusory, for 18 .... P—KKt4; 19 R—Kt3, and if 18 .... R×P; 19 R—R3.

18 ......   Q—B3
19 Q—Kt4   R—B2

If 19 .... R×P; 20 B×P, R×R; 21 P×R, etc. Thus Black, for the time being, no longer aims at QB6.

20 P—KB4

A serious strengthening of the attack. If at once 20 R—R3, R×P; 21 B×P, R×R; 22 B—Q3 dis ch, K—R1; 23 Q×R, R—KKt1; 24 Kt—B3, R—Kt2, etc., Black has a fine chance of a counter-attack.

20 ......   K—R1
21 R—R3   R×P
22 P—B5

An assault in the grand manner.

22 ......   KtP×P
23 Kt×P   Q—Kt3

Allowing a very beautiful finish. But if 23 .... P×Kt; 24 R×P ch, K×R; 25 R×P, R×B; 26 R×Q, and wins. Or 23 .... R×B; 24 P×R, etc.

24 Kt—K7

Bravo! A spark of genius. Mr. Yates has left a heritage of beautiful and artistic games of which any master might well be proud.

24 ......   Resigns.

341

White   Black

JACKSON   NOTEBOOM

(Scarborough, 1930)

In the following game, the first twenty-five moves are taken up in trench warfare. There then follows the war of movement, of which the break-through at KB6 is the distinctive feature.

On this square occurs the final clash, in which Black thought he could win a piece, *only to find himself thwarted by a very fine combination comprising an unexpected sacrifice of the Queen.*

1 P—K4   Kt—KB3
2 Kt—QB3   P—Q4
3 P×P   Kt×P

It is to be noted that the same position can arise from the *Centre Counter Defence* (1 P—K4, P—Q4; 2 P×P, Kt—KB3; 3 Kt—QB3, Kt×P).

4 B—B4

White wishes to clear up the situation in the centre, in preference to simplification by 4 Kt×Kt, Q×Kt; 5 Q—B3, Q—QB4; 6 Q—B3, P—K4; 7 Kt—B3, Kt—B3; 8 Q×Q, B×Q, etc.

4 ......   B—K3

Threatening 5 .... Kt×Kt, followed by .... B×B. If, however, 4 .... Kt×Kt, then not 5 KtP×Kt, but 5 Q—B3, P—K3; 6 Q×Kt, and White, without doubling his pawns, has obtained a tangible advantage in development.

As, however, the text move is artificial, and the supporting moves 4 .... P—K3 or 4 .... P—QB3 are too passive, the rational course is 4 .... Kt—Kt3; 5 B—Kt3, P—QB4, and Black has rapidly surmounted the difficulties of the opening.

5 B—Kt3   P—KKt3
6 Kt—B3   B—Kt2
7 Castles   Castles
8 R—K1   P—QB3

He prefers to maintain the tension in the centre, as, after simplification by 8 .... Kt×Kt; 9 KtP×Kt, B×B; 10 RP×B, White would still have some superiority in space.

9 Kt—K4   Kt—B2
10 P—Q4   B×B
11 RP×B   Kt—Q2
12 P—B3   P—QR3
13 P—QKt4   Kt—Q4
14 B—Q2   R—K1
15 Q—Kt3   P—R3
16 Kt—B5   Q—B1
17 R—K2   P—Kt3
18 Kt×Kt   Q×Kt
19 QR—K1   P—K3
20 Kt—K5   Q—Kt2
21 Q—B2

During the phase of development starting from his 8th move, White has succeeded in provoking a number of weakening moves (15 .... P—R3; 17 .... P—Kt3; 19 .... P—K3), and now he will bring back his Queen to the K side.

21	QR—B1
22 Q—K4	Kt—B3
23 Q—B3	Kt—R2

Parrying the threat 24 B×P. White, by his next two moves, stresses in another manner the black-square weakness in the opposing camp.

24 Kt—B4	KR—Q1
25 B—B4	B—B1
26 P—R4	P—KR4
27 B—K5	R—Q2
28 Kt—Q2	

Making for KB6, where a goodly battle is about to be fought.

| 28 ...... | B—K2 |
| 29 Kt—K4 | P—B3 |

If 29 .... B×RP; 30 Kt—Q6, winning the exchange. With the text move Black initiates a combination which is brilliantly refuted by his adversary.

More prudent is 29 .... R—B1, which, however, leaves Black's position no less precarious on account of its many "holes."

30 Kt×P ch	B×Kt
31 B×B	R—KB2
32 R×P	QR—B1

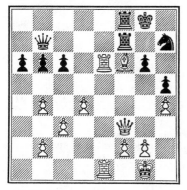

33 B—K5

A brilliant, if temporary, sacrifice of the Queen.

33	R×Q
34 R×P ch	K—B2
35 R—Kt7 ch	K—K3

Or 35 .... K—K1; 36 B—B7 dis ch, followed by mate. But also, after the text move, Black is in desperate straits.

36 R×Q	KR—B2
37 R×P	K—Q2
38 P—B3	Kt—B3
39 R×RP	Resigns.

342

| White | Black |
| NIMZOWITSCH | ALEKHINE |

(Semmering, 1926)

A game which takes a sensational course. In it a great player, too much taken up with his own schemes of attack, becomes the victim of a grand ambush (33 Kt—Kt6 ch) prepared by his astute adversary.

| 1 P—K4 | Kt—KB3 |
| 2 Kt—QB3 | P—Q4 |

A trenchant reply.

3 P—K5

He could clear up matters in the centre by 3 P×P, Kt×P; 4 B—B4 (a sound variation of the *Centre-Counter Defence*), but prefers to intensify the struggle forthwith.

| 3 ...... | KKt—Q2 |

Playable also is the counter-thrust 3 .... P—Q5, e.g. the game Balla—Sterk, *Budapest*, 1921: 4 P×Kt, P×Kt; 5 KtP×P (better than 5 P×KP, Q×KP ch; 6 Q—K2, or than 5 P×KtP, P×P ch; 6 B×P, B×P, etc.); 5 .... KtP×P (less good is 5 .... KP×P; 6 P—Q4, B—K3; 7 B—Q3, P—QB4; 8 Kt—K2, etc., in favour of White); 6 P—Q4, P—K4; 7 B—Q3, Kt—B3; 8 Kt—K2, B—K3; 9 Castles, Q—Q2; 10 B—K3, Castles; 11 Q—B1, R—Kt1; 12 Q—Kt2, R×P ch (a *mirage*! 12 .... B—Q3 is what he should have played); 13 K×R, B—R6 ch; 14 K—Kt1 (refutation! whereas 14 K—R1, Q—Kt5 would have given Black best); 14 .... Q—Kt5 ch; 15 Kt—Kt3, Q—B6; 16 B—K4, resigns.

4 P—B4

Artificial, but after 4 P—Q4 Black can, with 4 .... P—K3, revert to a variation of the *French Defence*, which can have no terrors for him. A difficult decision. A calm temperament would decide on 4 Kt×P, Kt×P; 5 Kt—K3, etc., but a pugnacious spirit would go for 4 P—K6, both of which are shown in the next two games.

4	P—K3
5 Kt—B3	P—QB4
6 P—KKt3	

He revels in hyper-modern ideas ("fantail" deployment, restricted centre).

A far less useful development of the KB would be 6 B—Kt5, P—QR3; 7 B×Kt ch, B×B, and Black already and actually stands better.

6	Kt—QB3
7 B—Kt2	B—K2
8 Castles	Castles
9 P—Q3	Kt—Kt3

More incisive is 9 .... P—B3 at once (and if 10 P×P, B×P, with a fine co-ordination of the black troops).

10 Kt—K2	P—Q5

This not only prevents 11 P—B3, followed by P—Q4, but also and principally vacates an effective square for the travelling KKt.

11 P—KKt4	P—B3
12 P×P	P×P
13 Kt—Kt3	Kt—Q4
14 Q—K2	B—Q3
15 Kt—R4	

Guarding the KBP and preparing the advance 16 P—B5. But the same object could be effected—and more dynamically—by 15 Kt—R5.

15	QKt—K2

Rendering the advance 16 P—B5 illusory.

16 B—Q2

More pertinent would be 16 Kt—K4, e.g. 16 .... P—B4; 17 Kt—Kt5, sounding the attack, or 16 .... Q—B2; 17 Kt×B, Q×Kt; 18 B—Q2, etc., having eliminated an important hostile unit.

16	Q—B2
17 Q—B2	P—B5

He tries at all costs to obtain the initiative.

18 P×P	Kt—K6

For after 19 B×Kt, P×B White cannot play 20 Q×P, because of 20 .... B—B4, but—at chess—capturing is not compulsory!

19 B×Kt	P×B
20 Q—B3	Q×P
21 Kt—·K4	B—B2
22 P—Kt3	

An indirect defence of the QBP (22 .... Q×BP; 23 QR—QB1, followed by R×B). If 22 P—Kt5, Kt—Q4, etc. (not 22 .... P—B4; 23 Kt—B6 ch, etc., nor 22 .... P×P; 23 Kt×P, R×P; 24 Q—R5, etc.).

22	Q—Q5
23 P—B3	Q—Kt3
24 K—R1	Kt—Q4
25 P—B5	

Thus White defends this pawn by advancing it, but leaves his KB4 unguarded. He could have played 25 Q—Kt3.

25	Kt—B5

For the time being Black has the upper hand in the pitched battle.

26 KR—Q1	K—R1
27 B—B1	P×P
28 P×P	B—K4
29 R—K1	

Aiming at the exposed KP, but relinquishing his control of the Q file, which will allow the adverse QB to be liberated. A more promising course is 29 B—B4.

29	B—Q2
30 R×P	B—B3
31 QR—K1	Kt—Q4
32 R—Q3	Kt×P

Black thinks that this incisive combination must break down the core of White's resistance, but he has reckoned without an astute counter-stroke. The correct procedure is 32 .... Kt—B5; 33 KR—K3, and Black has the choice between a repetition of moves by 33 .... Kt—Q4, etc., and 33 .... R—KKt1, seeking fresh chances, in spite of his being a pawn down.

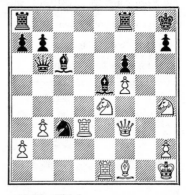

33 Kt—Kt6 ch

With this beautiful sacrifice—incidentally the only saving clause—White turns the tables. Bad would be, for example, 33 R×Kt, B×R; 34 Q×B, Q—B7.

33	P×Kt

Compulsory, as after 33 .... K—Kt2; 34 Q—Kt2 (not 34 Q—Kt4, because of the loophole 34 .... P—KR4); 34 .... K—B2; 35 Kt×B ch, P×Kt; 36 R×Kt, and wins.

34 Q—Kt4

With this magnificent move—one of the finest waiting moves known in chess literature—White decides the day.

The more plausible looking 34 P×P leads to nothing decisive, e.g. 34 .... K—Kt2; 35 Q—R3, R—R1; 36 R—Q7 ch, B×R; 37 Q×B ch, K×P, and, owing to the threat of mate, White has to be content with a perpetual check.

34	R—B2
35 R—R3 ch	K—Kt2
36 B—B4	

A fresh hammer-blow.

| 36 ...... | B—Q4 |

Not 36 .... P—Kt4; 37 R—R7 ch, K×R; 38 Q—R5 ch, etc., nor 36 .... K—B1; 37 B×R, K×B; 38 Q×P ch, etc.

37 P×P	Kt×Kt
38 P×R dis ch	K—B1
39 R×Kt	B×R ch
40 Q×B	K—K2
41 P—B8 (Q) ch	

Clearing the field. In this new phase of the contest, and in spite of much reduced material, White's pressure persists.

| 41 ...... | R×Q |
| 42 Q—Q5 | Q—Q3 |

Not 42 .... Q—B3; 43 R—R7 ch, K—K1; 44 B—Kt5.

43 Q×P ch	K—Q1
44 R—Q3	B—Q5
45 Q—K4	R—K1
46 R×B	Resigns

An eventful and exciting game.

343

| *White* | *Black* |
| TARTAKOWER | COLLE |

(Nice, 1930)

The technique of the attack, when the adversary has castled on the Q side, is well illustrated in this game.

1 P—K4	Kt—KB3
2 Kt—QB3	P—Q4
3 P—K5	KKt—Q2
4 Kt×P	

Leading to interesting operations in the centre.

| 4 ...... | Kt×P |
| 5 Kt—K3 | |

The position of this well-centralised Knight promises an enduring advantage for White, but there is no weak point in Black's game.

| 5 ...... | QKt—B3 |

Against 5 .... P—QB4 a good continuation for White is 6 P—KB4, KKt—B3; 7 B—B4, P—KKt3; 8 Kt—B3, B—Kt2;

9 Castles, etc., and the white forces are well co-ordinated.

| 6 P—QKt3 | |

Lacking in energy would be 6 Kt—B3, Kt×Kt ch; 7 Q×Kt, Q—Q3; 8 B—Kt5, B—Q2, etc.

| 6 ...... | P—KKt4 |

With this "extended fianchetto" Black also wants to prevent the advance P—KB4.

| 7 B—Kt2 | |

If 7 P—KR4, B—Kt2, threatening 8 .... Kt—Q6 ch.

7	B—Kt2
8 P—Q4	Kt—Kt3
9 B—Kt5	Q—Q3
10 Q—Q2	

A *fata morgana* would be 10 B×Kt ch, Q×B; 11 P—Q5, because of the interpolation 11 .... B—B6 ch, and Black saves his piece with advantage.

10	B—Q2
11 Castles	Castles (QR)
12 Kt—K2	Kt—B5

After 12 .... Q—Kt5, White obtains the initiative by 13 Q—Q3.

| 13 Kt×Kt | P×Kt |

More solid is 13 .... Q×Kt, after which the correct reply is 14 P—Q5.

| 14 Kt—B4 | Q—Kt3 |

On account of the weakness of his doubled KBP, Black avoids the exchange of Queens which would occur after 14 .... Q—Kt5 (15 B×Kt, Q×Q ch; 16 R×Q, B×B; 17 P—KB3, etc.).

| 15 P—Q5 | |

If 15 P—KB3, Kt×P.

| 15 ...... | P—B6 |
| 16 P×P | |

The gain of a piece by 16 P×Kt, B×P; 17 Q—R5, P×P; 18 R×R ch, R×R; 19 R—Kt1, Q—R3 ch; 20 K—Kt1, Q×P, etc., would be a delusion, as then Black's attack would prevail.

16	B×B ch
17 K×B	P—QR3
18 B×Kt	B×B
19 Q—B3	

Conserving the QP, for if 19 .... B×P; 20 R×B.

| 19 ...... | B—Kt4 |
| 20 P—Q6 | KP×P |

Not 20 .... BP×P; 21 Kt—K5 dis ch, nor 20 .... B×Kt; 21 P×KP.

21 KR—Kt1   Q—R4

If 21 .... Q—R3; 22 Kt×P ch, followed by Kt×BP, winning the exchange.

22 R—Q5   Q×RP
23 Kt×P ch   K—Kt1
24 Kt×B

Most provoking! Both white Rooks are "in the air," and neither can be taken (24 .... R×R; 25 Q×R ch, or 24 .... Q×R; 25 Q×P ch).

24 ......   P×Kt
25 KR—Q1   R—QB1

If 25 .... Q—R5; 26 R—Q7.

26 R×P   P—QB3

Preventing 27 Q—B6. If 26 .... K—R1; 27 Q—R5 ch, K—Kt1; 28 R×P ch, K×R; 29 Q—Kt5 ch, K—R2; 30 R—Q4, and wins.

27 R—K5

If 27 R—QR5, Q—B2.

27 ......   R—B2

Guarding the second rank. If 27 .... QR—Q1; 28 R×R ch, R×R; 29 R—K7.

28 R—QR5

The right move at the right time. The text move is effected with the gain of a *tempo* (attack on the KR), and, incidentally, Black's .... Q—B2 is now prevented.

28 ......   R—K1
29 Q—Q4

Threatening a *smothered mate*. White's attack proceeds—rigid and rectangular.

29 ......   QR—K2
30 P—KB4

Cutting off the retreat 30 .... Q—B2, and threatening 31 Q—Q6 ch.

30 ......   Q—R3
31 Q—Kt6   Q—Kt2 ch
32 P—B3   Q—B1

Or 32 .... R—K7 ch; 33 K—R3 (the only correct move, for if 33 K—Kt1, Q—Kt3 ch; 34 K—R1, Q—B3, etc.); 33 .... Q—B1 ch (33 .... Q×P; 34 R—Q8 ch); 34 P—Kt4, Q—K2; 35 R—R7, and Black is defenceless.

33 R—R7

A most instructive regrouping, threatening 34 Q—R5 and 35 R—R8 mate. If now 33 .... R—K7 ch; 34 K—R1, Q—K2; 35 Q—R5, etc.

Black resigns.

344

White	Black
SPIELMANN	*LANDAU*

(Match, Amsterdam, 1933)

The following game provides a beautiful example of a blockade, instituted as early as the 4th move (4 P—K6), and maintained so skilfully that Black up to the very end has no chance of liberating his game.

1 P—K4   Kt—KB3
2 Kt—QB3

Besides this defence by a *piece* and the defence by *displacement* (2 P—K5), the defence by a *pawn* (2 P—Q3) is also playable. A curious continuation could be: 2 P—Q3, P—K4 (or 2 .... P—Q4, or the non-committal 2 .... P—B4); 3 P—KB4, B—B4 (better is 3 .... Kt—B3); 4 P×P, Kt×P (consistent, but risky); 5 P×Kt (acceptance of the sacrifice leads to a draw; its refutation can be attempted by 5 Q—Kt4, P—Q4; 6 Q×P, etc.); 5 .... Q—R5 ch; 6 K—Q2 (the only correct reply); 6 .... B×Kt; 7 R×B, Q—B7 ch; 8 B—K2, Q—Q5 ch; 9 B—Q3 Q—B7 ch, with perpetual check.

2 ......   P—Q4
3 P—K5   KKt—Q2
4 P—K6   P×P

Or 4 .... Kt—KB3; 5 P×P ch, K×P; 6 Kt—B3, and the persecution of the black King goes on.

5 P—Q4

Best, however, is 5 Kt—B3, for after the move in the text Black could have restored his chances by giving back the pawn at once, by 5 .... P—K4 (e.g. 6 P×P, P—K3, etc., or 6 Kt×P, P×P; 7 Q×P, P—K4, etc.).

5 ......   Kt—KB3

By neglecting the opportunity shown above of liberating his game by 5 .... P—K4, Black resigns himself to an almost permanent state of misery. Useless also would be 5 .... P—B4 (because of 6 Kt—B3), as well as 5 .... P—KKt3 (again because of 6 Kt—B3).

6 Kt—B3

Against 6 B—KB4 the lateral demonstration 6 .... P—B4 would be more effective than in the actual game.

6 ......   P—B4

Too submissive would be 6 .... P—B3

(7 B—KB4, QKt—Q2; 8 B—Q3, with an effective blockade), and too optimistic 6 .... P—KKt3 (7 Kt—K5, QKt—Q2; 8 P—B4, P—B4; 9 B—K3, B—Kt2; 10 B—Q3, etc., controlling the highways and by-ways).

7 P×P

Here is one pawn "*come home.*" Another continuation, based on an important diagonal, is 7 B—KB4 (if 7 .... Kt—B3; 8 Kt—QKt5).

7......   **Kt—B3**

Or, e.g. 7 .... Q—B2; 8 Kt—QKt5, Q×P; 9 B—K3, Q—Kt5 ch; 10 P—B3, Q—R4; 11 P—QKt4, Q—Q1; 12 B—KB4, Kt—R3; 13 QKt—Q4, and Black's troubles are only beginning.

Relatively best would be 7 .... Q—R4; 8 B—KB4, B—Q2, etc., trying to complete his development under the enemy's fire.

8 B—QKt5

If 8 B—KB4, Q—R4.

8 ......   **B—Q2**
9 Castles   **Q—B2**

If 9 .... P—K4; 10 QKt×P.

10 R—K1   **P—KR3**

Or, e.g. 10 .... P—KKt3; 11 Kt—Kt5, Q—B1; 12 B×Kt, P×B; 13 Q—K2, B—Kt2; 14 B—Q2 (better than the immediate harvest by 14 Kt×KP, B×Kt; 15 Q×B, Q×Q; 16 R×Q, K—Q2; 17 R—K2, QR—QKt1, etc.); 14 .... R—QKt1; 15 QR—Kt1, and White holds on to his prey.

11 B×Kt   **P×B**
12 Kt—K5   **P—Kt4**

In order to develop the KB as best he can. After 12 .... Castles (13 Kt—B7), or 12 .... R—KKt1; 13 Kt—Kt6, Castles; 14 Q—Q3, and the KB remains entombed.

13 Q—Q3   **R—KKt1**
14 P—QKt4   **B—Kt2**

After 14 .... P—QR4; 15 R—Kt1, it is White who obtains a fresh base for action.

15 Q—Kt6 ch   **K—Q1**
16 Q—B7   **B—K1**

As White threatened to win the KP by

17 Kt×B, Black decides to give it up of his own free will, for if 16 .... B—QB1; 17 Kt—Kt4.

17 Q×P   **R—KB1**
18 P—Kt5

Rupturing the front.

18 ......   **Kt—K5**

A desperate attempt (19 Kt×Kt, B×Kt). If 18 .... P×P; 19 Kt×QP, Q×P; 20 R—Q1, Kt—Q2 (hoping for 21 Kt×Kt, Q×P ch; 22 K—R1, Q—B8 ch, followed by mate! If 20 .... B—Q2; 21 Kt×Kt, and if 20 .... Q—Q3; 21 Kt—K3); 21 B—K3, Q—R6 (21 .... Q—Q3; 22 Kt—B6 ch, K—B1; 23 KKt×KP ch); 22 Kt—QKt6, and wins.

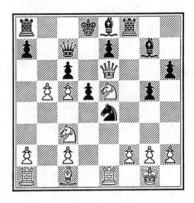

19 R×Kt

This sacrifice, completed by another, is easy to see, but very logical.

19 ......   **P×R**
20 B—B4   **B×Kt**
21 B×B   **Q—Q2**

Despair, for if 21 .... Q—B1; 22 R—Q1 ch, B—Q2; 23 P×P.

22 R—Q1   **P×P**
23 R×Q ch   **B×R**
24 Q×P   **R—KKt1**
25 P—B6   **B—K1**
26 Kt×KtP   **Resigns.**

21. NIMZOWITSCH'S DEFENCE

345

White	Black
WILLIAMS	KENNEDY

(London, 1848)

Here both contestants play for the advance of their KBP, in which both succeed almost at the same time. After the resulting clash, the first to have achieved it (12 .... P—KB4) also reaps the harvest. A very old game employing a very modern defence (1 .... Kt—QB3).

1 P—K4   Kt—QB3
This move was subjected in 1919 to an exhaustive study by Nimzowitsch, and proved to be sound. As in the case of *Alekhine's Defence*, the second player is not afraid of an advance in the centre by hostile pawns, provided his own lines of communication are neither cut nor impaired.

2 P—Q4   P—K4
Inviting his opponent to revert to the *Scotch Opening*, but it leaves him the option of more intense continuations. A more resolute defence results from 2 .... P—Q4.

3 P—Q5
This advance, which blocks the centre, has little substance. But 3 P×P, Kt×P; 4 P—KB4 holds out prospects of a tangible advantage.

3 ......   QKt—K2
4 Kt—KB3
Mechanical development. Ineffective also would be 4 P—Q6, P×P; 5 Q×P, Kt—QB3; 6 Q—Q1, Kt—B3; 7 B—Q3, P—Q4, and Black has a free game. If 4 P—KB4, P×P; 5 B×P, Kt—Kt3, Black exercises firm control of the central square at his K4.
Therefore the plan of campaign 4 B—Q3, followed by KKt—K2, Castles and P—KB4, is to be recommended.

4 ......   Kt—Kt3
5 B—K3
Hoping to restrict the activities of the adverse KB, but Black finds a way of turning this important piece to account.

5	B—Kt5 ch
6 P—B3	B—R4
7 B—Q3	B—Kt3
8 Castles	KKt—K2

Black refrains from obstructing, by 8 .... Kt—B3, the promising advance of his KBP.

| **9 Q—Q2** | P—Q3 |
| **10 P—B4** | |

He vacates the normal square of development of his QKt, but at the cost of valuable time. Besides, as can be seen, White's KB has little breathing space.
Therefore the development of the QKt at QR3 deserves to be taken into consideration.

| **10 ......** | Castles |
| **11 Kt—B3** | B—R4 |

Preventing White from gaining space on the Q side by 12 P—QKt4.

12 Kt—K1
With the object of opening the KB file, which, however, proves of little substance. The pertinent 12 P—QR3 is to be recommended.

12 ......   P—KB4
Carefully prepared, this lateral offensive proves effective. Threat: 13 .... P—B5, winning a piece. Technically this advance represents a natural reaction against the sterile closing of the centre by 3 P—Q5.

13 P—B4
With this counter-thrust, White fights for the initiative, but *si duo faciunt idem, non est idem!* It would be wiser for White to restrict himself to a passive defence by 13 P—B3.

13	BP×P
14 B×KP	B—B4
15 B×B	Kt×B
16 P×P	

A serious mistake, which costs a piece. But in any event, White loses at least a pawn, e.g. 16 K—R1, Kt×B; 17 Q×Kt, Kt×P, etc.

| **16 ......** | Kt×B |
| Resigns | |

(17 Q×Kt, B—Kt3.)

346

White	Black
EUWE	BREYER

(Vienna, 1921)

The following game is bizarre in the opening as well as in the subsequent play. A number of pieces on either side remain unguarded. After a prolonged skirmish Black finally emerges with an extra piece.

1 P—K4	Kt—QB3
2 Kt—QB3	

Instead of resolutely occupying the centre, White proceeds more carefully. Another adaptable continuation is 2 Kt—KB3, inviting Black to revert to an open game, unless he prefers a *King's Fianchetto Defence* by 2 .... P—KKt3, or the *Centre-Counter Defence* by 2 .... P—Q4; 3 P×P, Q×P; 4 Kt—B3, Q—QR4, or again, a *French Defence* by 2 .... P—K3; 3 P—Q4, P—Q4.

2	Kt—B3

He persists in his provocative policy. He could, instead, revert to the *Vienna Game* by 2 .... P—K4, or again, to the *King's Fianchetto* or the *French Defence*.

3 P—Q4	P—K4
4 P×P	

He accepts the challenge, and refrains from bringing about a peaceable variation of the *Scotch Four Knights' Game*, and also from closing the centre by 4 P—Q5, Kt—K2, etc. A pitched battle now follows.

4	QKt×P
5 P—B4	Kt—B3
6 P—K5	

A plausible advance, which gains time— driving back the Knight—as well as space. After 6 B—B4, Black is not obliged to restrict his game by 6 .... P—Q3. He can, on the contrary, produce a counter-threat by 6 .... B—Kt5.

6	Kt—KKt1
7 B—B4	P—Q3

Undermining White's outpost.

8 Kt—B3	B—Kt5
9 Castles	Q—Q2
10 Q—K1	Castles

After a "fancy opening," Black's first strategic object is achieved, but he will now have to surmount a few tactical obstacles.

11 Kt—KKt5	P×P

A rejoinder in the grand style. He cannot,

of course, play 11 .... B—R4, on account of 12 P—K6, but the defences 11 .... B—K3 or 11 .... Kt—R3 are equally burdensome.

12 K—R1

Not yet 12 Kt×BP, Q—Q5 ch, followed by .... Q×B. The simplest would be 12 B—Kt3, e.g. 12 .... P—B3; 13 Kt—B7, Kt—Q5; 14 Kt×QR, B—QB4; 15 K—R1, P×P; 16 B×P, etc., or else 12 .... Kt—Q5; 13 P×P, Kt—R3; 14 B—K3, B—QB4; 15 K—R1, KR—K1; 16 Kt×BP, Kt×B; 17 RP×Kt, B×B; 18 Q×B, Kt×Kt; 19 R×P, etc., or finally, 12 .... Kt—R3; 13 P×P, etc.

12	P—B3
13 Kt—B7	Kt—R4

He takes advantage of the fact that White's KB is unguarded.

14 Kt×QR

Better would be 14 B—Q5, e.g. 14 .... P—B3; 15 Kt×KR, P×B; 16 P×P, threatening 17 Q—R4.

14	Kt×B
15 Q—K4	Kt—Q3
16 Q—Kt4	

White's calculation is as follows: after 16 .... Q×Kt, or also after 16 .... K×Kt, there follows 17 P×P, recovering one of the three hostile pieces (QKt, QB, or KB). If, on the other hand, 16 .... Kt—R3, the sequel is equally 17 P×P, P×P; 18 B—Kt5, B—K2; 19 B×B, Q×B; 20 Kt×P, and White remains the exchange to the good.

16	B—K2

With this discreet parry, which restores co-ordination between the black pieces, the aspect and prospects of the game undergo a radical change.

17 P×P	P×P
18 Kt×P	

As can be seen, White still has a few poisoned arrows in his quiver, but he cannot impose his will. Better would be 18 Kt—B6, P×Kt; 19 Q—R5, etc., trying to fish in troubled waters.

18	Kt×Kt
19 R—B8 ch	B×R
20 Q×B ch	Q—Q1

Black's defence continues to be based on paradoxical moves, whereas 20 .... Kt—Q1 would enable White to regain his piece after 21 B—Kt5, P—KR3; 22 B×Kt, Q×B; 23 Q×P, Kt—B3; 24 Kt—K4, etc.

21 Q×P   Kt—B3

Everything is now defended (Rook, Bishop, and even KP).

22 B—Kt5   R—Kt1

A last *finesse* (23 Q×Kt, R×B). Thus Black is able to maintain his piece.

23 Q—R6   R—Kt3
24 Q—R4   Kt—Q3
25 R—KB1   Kt—B4
26 Q×B   Kt×Q
27 B×Q   Kt(Kt5)—K6

An intermediary manœuvre.

28 R—B3   K×B
29 P—KR3

A final effort to recover his piece after 30 P—KKt4, which Black prevents in a radical manner.

29 ......   R—Kt6
30 R×R   Kt×R ch
     Resigns.

347

White   *Black*

BRINCKMANN   NIMZOWITSCH

(Niendorf, 1927)

If, in the preceding game, the forerunner of hyper-modernism, Breyer, had recourse to balanced manœuvres in order to prevail in a very complicated battle of pieces, in the following game, Nimzowitsch, the father of hyper-modern theory, evolves from the same bizarre opening positional manœuvres resulting in a stubbornly contested battle of pawns.

A fight for squares! With a sure hand, Black dissolves the imbroglio in the centre and demonstrates that his passed pawn at Q6 is a vital force, against which his adversary's at K5 represents mere dead weight.

1 P—K4   Kt—QB3

It goes without saying that Nimzowitsch would not rest content with a theoretical dissertation on this opening without putting it to the searing test of his own tournament practice.

2 Kt—QB3   P—K3
3 P—Q4   P—Q4

Instead of challenging the centre, he could also play for a restricted centre by 3 .... B—Kt5; 4 Kt—B3, P—Q3, etc.

4 P—K5

He seeks to tie up the centre, in preference to simplifying matters by 4 P×P, P×P, which, at one stroke, would liberate the black QB, e.g. 5 Kt—B3, B—KKt5, etc., or 5 B—K3, B—KB4; 6 B—Q3, KKt—K2, and Black has satisfactorily overcome the difficulties of the opening.

4 ......   KKt—K2

If 4 .... QKt—K2; 5 QKt—K2, P—QB4; 6 P—QB3, maintaining his chain of pawns.

5 Kt—B3

Instead of this conventional development, 5 KKt—K2, with P—KKt3, B—Kt2, and Castles, would conform to the needs of the situation.

5 ......   P—QKt3

Solving the arduous problem of the development of his QB, and succeeding at the same time in eliminating its dangerous counterpart.

6 Kt—K2

A mechanical manœuvre. But if, e.g. 6 P—QR3 (intending B—Q3, and Q—K2, with the control of the contested diagonal KB1—QR6), there follows 6 .... P—QR4; 7 B—Q3, B—R3, and Black attains his object.

The best is therefore 6 B—K2.

6 ......   B—R3
7 Kt—Kt3   B×B
8 K×B

The white King forgoes castling. In addition, in consequence of the advance of his KP and of the disappearance of his KB, White's weakness on the white squares will become painfully evident. Black already has the initiative.

8 ......   P—KR4
9 B—Kt5   Q—B1
10 Q—Q3   Kt—Kt3
11 P—B3   P—R5

Black can afford to act in separate detachments.

12 Kt—K2   B—K2
13 P—KR3   B×B
14 Kt×B   QKt—K2
15 K—Kt1   P—KB3

Undermining the hostile pawn chain at its apex (K5), soon to be followed by the undermining of its base (Q4).

16 Kt—B3   Q—Q2

A waiting policy. Premature would be 16 .... P—QB4 (17 Q—Kt5 ch), and even

16 .... Castles (17 P—KKt3, making use of the KR for a flank attack).

17 K—R2   P—QB4
Containing the tactical menace 18 .... Q—B2.

18 P—QB4
The crisis. White also tries to obtain a base of action in the centre, for if 18 KP×P, then, not heedlessly, 18 .... Q—B2 ch, interfering with White's artificial castling.

18 ......   Q—B2
Stressing his threat to win a vital pawn by 19 .... KBP×P.

19 P×QP   P—B5
20 Q—B2   P×QP
21 KR—K1   Castles KR
22 Kt—B3   P×P
23 Kt×KP   Kt×Kt
24 P×Kt
Hoping to obtain a valuable asset in this passed pawn.
If 24 R×Kt, then, without misgivings, 24 .... Kt—B3; 25 Kt×P, Q—Q3; 26 Q×P, Kt×R; 27 P×Kt (or 27 Kt—K7 db ch, K—R1, and wins); 27 .... Q×P ch; 28 P—B4, Q—K3, and Black must win.

24 ......   P—Q5
A well-considered advance.

25 Kt—Kt5   Q—B4
26 Kt—Q6   P—Q6
Continuing his concentric manœuvres. This plan would be frustrated if Black were satisfied with half-measures, e.g. 26 .... P—QKt4; 27 QR—Q1, P—Q6; 28 R×P, R×P; 29 R—Q2, and White is out of danger.

27 Q×P ch   Q×Q
28 Kt×Q   R×P
29 QR—Q1   R—QB1
Intending to play 30 .... QR—B7 in answer to 30 Kt—Q6. If at once 29 .... R—Q1, however, then 30 Kt—Q6 would obstruct the Q file.

30 Kt—K3   R—Q1
31 Kt—B4   Kt—B4
Again preventing 32 Kt—Q6 (32 .... Kt×Kt; 33 R×P, Kt—Kt2; 34 R×R ch, Kt×R; 35 P—K6, Kt×P; 36 R×Kt, R×P); and threatening 32 .... P—QKt4.

32 P—R4   K—B2
33 R—K4
If 33 R—Q2, R—B5.

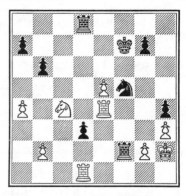

33 ......   R—K7
Extending his zone of influence.

34 R—B4
Not 34 R×R, P×R; 35 R—K1, Kt—Kt6, etc., and still less 34 R×QP, R×KR; 35 R×R, R×Kt, winning a piece.

34 ......   K—K3
35 R—Kt4   P—Q7
An important step forward.

36 R—Kt6 ch   K—B2
37 R—Kt4   R—R3
With the convincing threat of 38 .... P—QKt4, and if 38 Kt×P, R—K8, etc.

38 R—B4   K—K3
39 Kt—Q6   Kt—K6
Resigns.

348

White	Black
KASHDAN	*FLOHR*

(Hamburg, 1930)

A magnificent contest between young representatives of the Old and the New World. Its feature is the subtle end-game play, the winning combination being reminiscent of an end-game study.

1 P—K4   Kt—QB3
2 P—Q4   P—Q4
3 P—K5
This continuation leads to complicated play, but 3 P×P, Q×P; 4 Kt—KB3 is not convincing, as Black can now play 4 .... P—K4.

3 ......   B—B4
Besides this plausible development, Black can play 3 .... P—B3, or the more reserved 3 .... P—K3.

4 P—QB3
Or at once 4 Kt—K2, e.g. 4 .... P—K3 (if 4 .... Kt—Kt5; 5 Kt—R3); 5 Kt—Kt3, B—Kt3; 6 P—KR4, P—KR4; 7 B—K2, B—K2, etc.

4 ......   P—K3
A more ambitious plan is 4 .... P—B3, e.g. 5 P—KB4, B—K5, or 5 Kt—B3, B—Kt5, etc.

5 Kt—K2
More pertinent than 5 B—Q3, KKt—K2; 6 Kt—K2, Q—Q2, etc.

5 ......   KKt—K2
6 Kt—Kt3   B—Kt3
7 B—Q3   Q—Q2
8 Q—B3   P—Kt3
He turns his attention to the Q side.

9 Kt—Q2   Kt—R4
With a view to .... P—QB4, gradually obtaining control of the *white squares* (especially at QB5 and KB4).

10 P—KR4   B × B
11 Q × B   P—QB4
12 P—Kt4
With this violent counter, White fights for the initiative.

12 ......   P × KtP
13 P × P   Kt—B5
Wily play, for acceptance of the proffered pawn would lead to disappointment after 14 Kt × Kt, P × Kt; 15 Q × BP, R—B1, followed by 16 .... Kt—B3.

14 P—R5   R—B1
15 P—R6
Driving a wedge into the enemy lines.

15 ......   P—Kt3
16 Kt—B3   Kt—B4
17 P—R3   Q—R5
With the incidental threat 18 .... B × P ch.

18 R—QKt1   P—R4
19 Kt—K2
With perfect composure, White awaits the storm.

19 ......   P × P
20 P—Kt4
Forcing the gain of a piece, which Black must sacrifice, unless he wishes to abandon

the attack after 20 .... Kt—K2; 21 P × P, Kt—B3; 22 P—Kt5, etc. The sacrifice, however, of a piece for three pawns (of which two are united passed pawns) is promising.

20 ......   P × P
21 P × Kt   KtP × P
22 R—Kt1   P—Kt4
23 Kt—Q2   Kt × Kt
A little better would be at once 23 .... P—Kt5.

24 B × Kt   P—Kt5
25 R—KKt3   R—B5
26 Kt—B1   Q—R2
27 Kt—Kt3
Now the hostile pawn mass is held up.

27 ......   Q—B2
28 K—K2   K—Q2
29 QR—Kt1   R—B7
30 R—Kt8   R × R
31 R × R   B—K2
32 Q—Kt5 ch   Q—B3
33 Q—Kt8   Q—R3 ch
34 K—Q1   R—B1
35 R × R   Q × R
36 Q × Q ch   K × Q
37 K—B2   K—Kt2
38 Kt—B1   K—B3
39 K—Kt3   K—Kt4
40 Kt—R2
The fixed pawns will now be captured ruthlessly, but Black's resistance is still strong.

40 ......   B—R5
41 B—K1   P—B3
42 Kt × P   P × P
43 P × P   B—Kt4
44 Kt—B2   K—B3
45 Kt—Q4 ch   K—Q2
46 K × P   B × P
47 K—Kt3   B—B5
48 Kt—B3   P—R4
49 B—B3
Relieving the Knight in the defence of the all-important KP, for otherwise Black would threaten 49 .... P—R5.

49 ......   B—R3
50 B—Kt4   B—Kt2
51 B—Q6   B—R3
52 K—B3   B—Kt2
53 K—Q3   B—R3
54 K—K2   B—B8
55 K—B1   B—Kt7
56 B—B5   K—B3
57 B—Q4   B—B8
58 K—Kt2
Interrupting for the moment a long and methodical journey.

58 ......   B—B5
59 B—K3

There follows an ending which, for all its clear-cut features, still requires much *finesse*.

59 ......   B × B
60 P × B   P—Q5

Against this astute attempt, White needs to be very cautious.

61 P × P

A mistake would be 61 Kt × P ch, K—Q4; 62 Kt—B3, K—K5; 63 K—B2, P—B5, etc., with a draw in sight.

61 ......   K—Q4
62 K—Kt3   K—K5
63 Kt—Kt5 ch

This problem-like turn, giving up matter (QP) for space (square at KB4), is the only way to victory.

63 ......   K × P
64 K—B4   K—Q4
65 Kt—B3

A little *Zugzwang*.

65 ......   K—B5
66 K—Kt5   K—Q4
67 K—B6   P—B5

Or 67 .... K—K5; 68 Kt—Kt5 ch, K—K6; 69 Kt × P, P—B5; 70 Kt × P, K × Kt; 71 P—K6, P—R5; 72 P—K7, etc., winning by one *tempo*.

68 Kt—R4

Bringing about, in a nicely calculated manner, an end-game with the Queens on the board. Another way to win would be 68 Kt—Kt5, P—R5; 69 Kt × P, P—B6; 70 Kt—B4 ch, K—K5; 71 Kt—R3, K—K6; 72 K—Kt5, etc.

68 ......   K—K5
69 K × P   P—B6
70 Kt × P   K × Kt
71 K—B5   P—R5
72 P—K6   P—R6
73 P—K7   P—R7
74 P—K8 (Q)   K—Kt7

Compulsory, for if 74 .... P—R8 (Q); 75 Q—K4 ch.

75 K—Kt4   Resigns

(For after 75 .... P—R8 (Q), there follow 76 Q—K2 ch, K—Kt8; 77 K—Kt3, with mate to follow.)

349

White   *Black*

MILNER-BARRY   MIESES

(Margate, 1935)

In the following game White, by the positional sacrifice of a pawn (5 P—KB3), obtains a converging pressure on the K side, effects a turning movement against the opposing King's defences (14 P—KR4), and crowns his attack on the critical KR file with a most impressive finish.

1 P—K4   Kt—QB3
2 P—Q4   P—Q4
3 Kt—QB3

Planning to disrupt the centre, instead of simplification by 3 P × P, or mummification by 3 P—K5.

3 ......   P × P
4 P—Q5   Kt—K4

A *faux-pas*. After the circumspect continuation 4 .... Kt—Kt1; 5 Kt × P, P—K3, or 5 B—QB4, Kt—KB3, etc., Black holds his own.

5 P—B3

Without risking this "gambit continuation," White can already obtain a considerable positional advantage by effecting the centralising manœuvre 5 Q—Q4.

5 ......   P × P
Better would be 5 .... P—K6.

6 Kt × P   Kt × Kt ch
7 Q × Kt   Kt—B3
8 B—KB4

Threat: 9 Kt—Kt5.

| 8 ...... | P—QR3 |
| 9 P—KR3 | P—KKt3 |

If 9 .... B—B4; 10 QB × P. The text move
is to further the development of both the
KB and the QB, which White, however, is
going to prevent in no uncertain fashion.

| 10 P—KKt4 | B—Kt2 |
| 11 Castles | |

White already has a decided advantage in
mobility.

| 11 ...... | B—Q2 |

Better, in any case, would be 11 ....
Castles (and if 12 Q—Kt3, Kt—K1).

12 Q—Kt3	R—QB1
13 B—K2	Castles
14 P—KR4	

Heralding the assault.

14	P—B3
15 P—R5	Kt × QP
16 P × P	B × Kt

Trying to check the fatal course of events,
for if 16 .... Kt × B; 17 Q × Kt, BP × P;
18 B—B4 ch, etc., or 16 .... Kt × Kt;
17 P × Kt, etc., or 16 .... BP × P; 17 B—K5,
or finally, 16 .... RP × P; 17 Q—R4,
R—K1; 18 Q—R7 ch, K—B1; 19 B—R6,
etc.

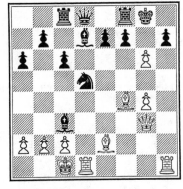

17 Q—R4
A beautiful rejoinder.

| 17 ...... | Kt—B3 |
| 18 P—Kt5 | |

Maintaining his grip.
The jumble of pieces *en prise* is amusing.

| 18 ...... | Q—R4 |
| 19 P × Kt | P—R4 |

A last vain effort to check the impetus of
the attack.

| 20 P × P ch | K × P |
| 21 B × P ch | Resigns. |

22. FIANCHETTO DEFENCES

350

White	Black
PAULSEN	OWEN

(London, 1862)

In this very lively game, Black's violent thrust 4 .... P—KB4 only helps the irruption of the hostile forces. Posted on effective diagonals, White's Bishops prove more useful than his opponent's artillery.

1 P—K4	P—QKt3

"*Fianchetto di Donna,*" which allows White to occupy the centre, but preserves its distant control.

2 P—KKt3	

Instead of this *Counter-Fianchetto,* 2 P—Q4 is very much to the point. A game Tchigorin—Skipworth, *London,* 1883, took the following course: 2 P—Q4, B—Kt2; 3 B—Q3, P—K3 (a will-o'-the-wisp would be 3 .... P—KB4; 4 P×P, B×P; 5 Q—R5 ch, P—Kt3; 6 P×P, Kt—KB3; 7 P×P dis ch, Kt×Q; 8 B—Kt6 mate); 4 Kt—KR3 (or, with less originality, 4 P—QB4, Kt—KB3; 5 Kt—QB3, B—Kt5; 6 Q—K2, etc., or 4 Kt—KB3, P—QB4; 5 P—B3, P—Q3; 6 Castles, Kt—Q2; 7 R—K1, or again, 4 B—K3, P—Kt3; 5 Kt—Q2, B—Kt2; 6 KKt—B3, Kt—K2; 7 Q—K2, etc., always with a powerful instrument in the centre for White); 4 .... Kt—KB3; 5 Kt—B3, B—Kt5; 6 Q—K2, P—KR3; 7 Castles, B×Kt; 8 P×B, P—Q4; 9 P—K5, KKt—Q2; 10 Q—Kt4, K—B1; 11 Kt—B4, Q—K2; 12 R—K1, B—R3; 13 P—B4, B×P (relatively best is 13 .... P—QB3); 14 B×B, P×B; 15 Q—B3, P—QB3; 16 Kt—Kt6 ch, resigns.

2	P—K3

Or at once 2 .... B—Kt2; 3 B—Kt2, P—KB4; 4 P—Q3 (incorrect would be 4 P×P, B×B; 5 Q—R5 ch, P—Kt3; 6 P×P, B—KKt2; 7 P×P dis ch, K—B1; 8 P×Kt (Q) ch, K×Q, and wins); 4 .... Kt—KB3; 5 Kt—QB3, and White retains control of K4.

3 B—Kt2	B—Kt2
4 Kt—QB3	P—KB4

Hazardous. Better is 4 .... P—Q4.

5 KKt—K2	Kt—KB3
6 P—Q3	B—Kt5
7 Castles	B×Kt
8 Kt×B	P×P

More level-headed is 8 .... Castles.

9 Kt×P	

With a serious threat of 10 Kt×Kt ch and B×B, etc.

9	Kt×Kt

Plausible, but depleting the position. However, there is no longer an entirely satisfactory continuation, e.g. 9 .... Q—B1; 10 Kt×Kt ch, P×Kt; 11 Q—R5 ch, K—K2; 12 Q—R6, etc., or 9 .... Kt—B3; 10 B—Kt5, etc., or finally, 9 ....: P—Q4; 10 Kt—Kt5, P—K4 (10 .... Q—K2; 11 Kt×KP, Q×Kt; 12 R—K1); 11 R—K1, with easy targets.

10 Q—R5 ch	

Before recovering his piece, he interpolates the move in the text, which will have important repercussions in the course of the game.

10	P—Kt3
11 Q—K5	Castles
12 P×Kt	Kt—B3
13 Q—B3	P—K4
14 B—R6	R—B2
15 P—B4	

Increasing his range of action in a convincing manner.

15	B—R3
16 P×P	

This *sacrifice of the exchange* is dictated by the logic of events, and is a worthy climax to the preceding manœuvres.

16	B×R
17 R×B	Q—K2

After 17 .... R×R ch; 18 B×R (and if now 18 .... Kt—R4; 19 P—QKt4), the white KB, hitherto obstructed, would get victoriously into play.

18 R×R	Q×R
19 P—K6	

Neatly forcing an entry into the hostile fastness.

19 ......   Q—K2
20 P × P   Kt—K4

If 20 .... Q × QP; 21 P—K5, Q—Q8 ch; 22 K—B2, Kt—Q5; 23 Q—B4 ch (not hastily 23 B × R, Q—K7 ch; 24 K—Kt1, Q—Q8 ch; 25 K—Kt2, etc., with perpetual check); 23 .... K—R1; 24 B × R, and White wins; and if 20 .... Q—B4 ch; 21 Q × Q, P × Q; 22 P—K5, and wins.

21 B—R3

Doing useful work on an *auxiliary diagonal*.

21 ......   P—KKt4

Or, e.g., 21 .... Q—B4 ch; 22 Q × Q, P × Q; 23 B—K6 ch, K—R1 (or 23 .... Kt—B2; 24 B—Kt5); 24 B—Kt5, Kt—B3; 25 B—B6 mate.

The best defence is 21 .... P—B4 (parrying at least the principal threat 22 Q × P), but then 22 B—B4, Kt × P; 23 Q—Q3, R—Q1; 24 Q—Q5 ch, K—Kt2; 25 B—B7, R—QB1; 26 B—Q6, Q—K1; 27 B × Kt, and wins.

22 Q × P   P—Kt5

Allowing a *piquant* finish.

Or 22 .... R—Q1; 23 B—K6 ch, Kt—B2; 24 Q—B3, Q—B4 ch; 25 Q × Q, P × Q; 26 B × P, R × P; 27 B × R, Kt × B; 28 B—B6, remaining with three extra pawns!

23 P—Q8 (Q) ch   Q × Q
24 Q—Kt7 mate.

135

White   *Black*

STEINITZ   MONGREDIEN

(London, 1863)

The feature of the following game is a ferocious attack, such as becomes possible against the King's Fianchetto, *when the defender has castled on that wing and has left the KR file bare. The impetuous advance of White's KRP culminates in a crushing attack on the KR file, with a brilliant—and entirely unexpected—sacrifice of a Rook.*

1 P—K4   P—KKt3

The "*Fianchetto del Re*" which allows White to occupy the centre, in hope of undermining it later on. Similar—and equally cumbersome—play occurs in the *Old Indian Defence*: 1 .... P—Q3, e.g. Hammlisch—N., *Vienna*, 1899: 2 P—Q4, Kt—Q2; 3 B—QB4, P—KKt3; 4 Kt—KB3, B—Kt2; 5 B × P ch, and Black resigns, for if 6 .... K—B3, Q—B3 mate, or 6 .... K—K1; 7 Kt—K6, and the Queen is lost, and if 6 .... K—B1; 7 Kt—K6 ch, forking the King and Queen.

2 P—Q4

Occupation of the centre—what could be more natural? But as the opposing KB will be able to exercise pressure on White's Q4, other continuations are worthy of consideration:

2 Kt—KB3, B—Kt2; 3 B—B4, P—QB4; 4 Castles, Kt—QB3; 5 P—B3, etc.; or
2 P—KB4, B—Kt2; 3 Kt—KB3, P—QB4; 4 B—B4 (or 4 P—Q4, P—Q4; 5 Kt—B3, etc.).

2 ......   B—Kt2
3 P—QB3

At the cross-roads! Although the idea of strengthening the centre is good, it is wiser to attend to immediate development, e.g. 3 Kt—KB3, P—Q3; 4 Kt—B3, Kt—KB3; 5 P—KR3, Castles; 6 B—K3, etc., or 3 P—KB4, P—Q3; 4 P—B3, Kt—KB3; 5 B—Q3, Castles; 6 P—K5, KKt—Q2; 7 Kt—B3, P—QB4; 8 Castles, Q—Kt3; 9 K—R1, etc.

3 ......   P—Kt3

Instead of the slow method of the *double fianchetto*, Black should have freed himself in the centre by 3 .... P—Q4, or even by 3 .... P—K4, etc.

4 B—K3   B—Kt2
5 Kt—Q2   P—Q3
6 KKt—B3   P—K4

If 6 .... P—QB4; 7 P—Q5.

7 P × P   P × P
8 B—QB4   Kt—K2
9 Q—K2   Castles
10 P—KR4

A well-known scheme, which stresses the vulnerability of the *King's Fianchetto*. In order to be fully effective, this attack must be accompanied by the attacker's King withdrawing on to the opposite wing.

10 ......   Kt—Q2

Hastening to replace the Kt on its defensive post at KB3, but even this momentary defection will have painful consequences.

If 10 .... P—KR4; 11 P—KKt4, P × P; 12 Kt—Kt5, etc.

11 P—R5   Kt—KB3
12 P×P
Not 12 Kt×P, Kt×RP.

12 ......   Kt×KtP
It is essential to defend the KP, but the King's field is now very much exposed.

13 Castles QR   P—B4
14 Kt—Kt5   P—QR3
Intending 15 .... P—Kt4, but it is too late. He should have tried, as best he could, to stem the impetus of the enemy attack by 14 .... P—KR3.

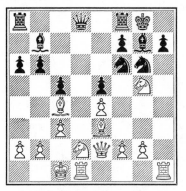

15 Kt×RP
The piece actually to be sacrificed is the

KR. The text move is intended to deflect the defending Knight, after which, thanks to Castles QR, White's reserve Rook at once will be able to step into the breach to replace its sacrificed companion.

15 ......   Kt×Kt
16 R×Kt   K×R
17 Q—R5 ch   K—Kt1
18 R—R1
And not first 18 Q×Kt, permitting the defence 18 .... Q—B3.

18 ......   R—K1
19 Q×Kt   Q—B3
20 B×P ch
The transitory "point" of the whole combination.

20 ......   Q×B
21 R—R8 ch
The final "point," winning the adverse Queen with advantage.

21 ......   K×R
22 Q×Q   Resigns
For after 22 .... QR—Kt1; 23 Q—R5 ch, K—Kt1; 24 Q—Kt6, and White's attack, to say nothing of his advantage in material (Queen and two pawns against two Rooks), decides the issue.
A very fine game.

BOOK III

CLOSED GAMES

23. QUEEN'S GAMBIT ACCEPTED

352

White	Black
DE LA	McDONNELL
BOURDONNAIS	

(Match, 1834)

A game of outstanding merit, in which the principal feature is a positional sacrifice of the Queen for two minor pieces. Black's steady and increasing pressure of all his forces brings in a handsome return in position as well as in material. A triumph for co-ordination!

1 P—Q4	P—Q4
2 P—QB4	P × P

An attempt to refute the gambit by accepting it.

3 P—K4

Too abrupt an advance.

3 ......   P—K4

The correct reply.

4 P—Q5   P—KB4

Another plucky idea is 4 .... Kt—KB3; 5 Kt—QB3, B—QB4; 6 B × P, Kt—Kt5, and Black has the lead.

5 Kt—QB3	Kt—KB3
6 B × P	B—B4

Much less ambitious is 6 .... B—Q3, as played in a game Owen—Boden, *London*, 1867, which continued: 7 Kt—B3, P × P (better here or on the next move 7 .... Castles); 8 Kt—KKt5, B—KB4; 9 Q—R4 ch, QKt—Q2; 10 Kt—K6, Q—K2; 11 Castles, P—QR3; 12 B—KKt5, R—QB1; 13 P—B4, P—R3; 14 B × Kt, Q × B; 15 P × P, B × P; 16 R × B, Q × R; 17 R—KB1, Q—Kt5; 18 B—K2, Q—R5; 19 P—KKt3, B × P; 20 B—R5 ch, and wins.

7 Kt—B3	Q—K2
8 B—Kt5	B × P ch

A successful raid. Of course not 8 .... Castles (9 P—Q6 dis ch) nor 8 .... P × P (9 QKt × P), but the simple counter 8 .... P—KR3 is playable.

9 K—B1

If, sceptically, 9 K × B, then neither 9 .... Q—B4 ch; 10 K—K1, Q × B; 11 Kt × P, Q—Kt5; 12 B × Kt, and wins, nor 9 .... Kt—Kt5 ch; 10 K—K1, Q—B4; 11 Q—K2, etc., but, artistically, 9 .... P × P; 10 B × Kt, Q—B4 ch; 11 K—K1, P × Kt; 12 B—Kt5 ch, P—B3, and Black recovers his piece and seizes the initiative.

9	B—Kt3
10 Q—K2	P—B5
11 R—Q1	B—Kt5
12 P—Q6	

A serious effort to contest the initiative.

12	P × P
13 Kt—Q5	Kt × Kt

Most unexpectedly, Black decides on a rare combination, giving up two pieces for the Queen, with fine prospects.

14 B × Q	Kt—K6 ch
15 K—K1	

After 15 Q × Kt, B × Q; 16 B × P, B × Kt; 17 P × B, B—Q5; 18 P—Kt3, Kt—B3, etc., Black would close his account with a valuable pawn to his credit.

15	K × B
16 Q—Q3	R—Q1

Too niggardly would be 16 .... Kt × R.

17 R—Q2   Kt—B3

Again he scorns the bait 17 .... B—QR4.

18 P—QKt3

If 18 P—QR3, B × Kt; 19 P × B, Kt—Q5; 20 R—B1, QR—B1, etc.

18	B—QR4
19 P—QR3	QR—B1
20 R—Kt1	P—QKt4

This well-prepared sacrifice gains an important *tempo*.

21 B × P	B × Kt
22 P × B	Kt—Q5
23 B—B4	

He closes at least the open QB file, but meanwhile Black's cavalry has overrun the position.

23	Kt × P ch
24 K—B2	Kt × QR

The purely *positional sacrifice* of the Queen

has paid enormous dividends, but White has still something to say.

25	R×P ch	K—B3
26	R—B7 ch	K—Kt3
27	R—Kt7	

If 25 R×QRP, B—Kt3; 28 R—Kt7, Kt×B dis ch.

27	......	Kt(Q7)×B
28	P×Kt	R×P
29	Q—Kt1	

After endless difficulties the Queen has at last obtained some degree of freedom, and now threatens 30 Q—Kt1 ch.

| 29 | ...... | B—Kt3 |

A pretty rejoinder, (30 Q—Kt1 ch, Kt—Kt5 db ch).

| 30 | K—B3 | R—B6 |

The same *motif*.

| 31 | Q—R2 | |

Or, e.g. 31 K—K2, R—B7 ch; 32 K—B3 (32 K—Q3, KR—QB1); 32 .... Kt—Kt7; 33 K—Kt4 (33 Q×R, Kt—K8 ch); 33 .... R—B6, with a mating net.

| 31 | ...... | Kt—B5 dis ch |

Eliminating the threat 32 Q—B7 ch.

| 32 | K—Kt4 | |

For if 32 K—K2, P—B6 ch, and if 32 K—Kt2, R—B7 ch.

| 32 | ...... | R—KKt1 |

Threatening 33 .... P—R4 ch, 34 K—R4, B—Q1; etc., which forces the adversary to throw more ballast overboard.

33	R×B	P×R
34	K—R4	K—B3
35	Q—K2	R—KKt3
36	Q—R5	Kt—K6
	Resigns.	

353

White	Black
DE LA	McDONNELL
BOURDONNAIS	

(Match, 1834)

White prettily demonstrates that the isolated QP is not necessarily a disadvantage.

Here it supports the Knight on outpost duty at K5, and exercises an increasing pressure on the opened K file. A double sacrifice (of the exchange, and then of a Bishop) leads to a ruthless King hunt—a most artistic execution of a well-known theme.

1	P—Q4	P—Q4
2	P—QB4	P×P
3	P—K3	

A cautious move, with, however, some valuable points.

| 3 | ...... | P—K4 |

Energetic. A quiet continuation is 3 .... Kt—KB3; 4 B×P, etc. Bad would be 3 .... P—QKt4; 4 P—QR4, e.g. 4 .... P—QB3; 5 P×P, P×P; 6 Q—B3, and wins. Or 4 .... B—Q2; 5 P×P, B×P; 6 P—QKt3, and White very advantageously recovers the gambit pawn.

| 4 | B×P | |

He allows his QP to be isolated, deeming the resulting compensations to be adequate. Bad would be the liquidation by 4 P×P, Q×Q ch; 5 K×Q, B—K3, and Black has a very good game.

| 4 | ...... | P×P |
| 5 | P×P | Kt—KB3 |

Reserving the option of developing his KB in one of three ways. As it is at present hardly possible to threaten the QP, the most active would be 5 .... B—Q3 now or on the next move. Of no value would be 5 .... B—Kt5 ch; 6 Kt—B3, Kt—KB3; 7 Q—Kt3 (avoiding the blunder 7 B×P ch, K×B; 8 Q—Kt3 ch, Kt—Q4, and Black remains with a piece ahead); 7 .... B×Kt ch; 8 P×B, and White has a reinforced centre and two Bishops.

| 6 | Kt—QB3 | |

Or 6 Kt—KB3, B—Q3. Useless would be 6 Q—Kt3, Q—K2 ch; 7 B—K3, Q—Kt5 ch, with an exchange of Queens.

6	......	B—K2
7	Kt—B3	Castles
8	B—K3	

Or, in order to proceed with the utmost soundness, first 8 P—KR3 (preventing the sallies 8 .... B—KKt5 or 8 .... Kt—Kt5), and then only 9 B—K3.

| 8 | ...... | P—B3 |

To restrain White's QP, but 8 .... B—QKt5, with .... QKt—Q2 or .... Kt—B3, would lead to a freer game.

9	P—KR3	QKt—Q2
10	B—Kt3	Kt—Kt3
11	Castles	KKt—Q4
12	P—QR4	P—QR4
13	Kt—K5	

Boldly seeking adventure.

| 13 | ...... | B—K3 |

A cumbersome defence, although the black QB will now become active. If

13 .... B—KB4; 14 Q—B3. Of little use
would be 13 .... Kt×B; 14 P×Kt, B—B3;
15 Q—R5, Q—K2; 16 R—B3, and again
White's centre is strengthened, and in
addition he has a base of action in the KB
file. If 13 .... P—B3; 14 Kt—Q3, etc.
Therefore 13 .... P—KB4 at once is a valid
scheme.

14 B—B2
Evading multiple exchanges (by 14 ....
Kt×B; 15 P×Kt, B×B; 16 Q×B, Kt—Q4,
etc.), and stressing the high value of the
diagonal QKt1—KR7.

14 ...... P—KB4
15 Q—K2 P—B5
16 B—Q2 Q—K1
17 QR—K1
He threatens to win a pawn by 18 Kt×P.

17 ...... B—B2
18 Q—K4
Entering a phase of threats and direct
action.

18 ...... P—Kt3
Or 18 .... Kt—B3; 19 Q×KBP.

19 B×P Kt×B
20 Q×Kt B—B5
Presenting his bill.

21 Q—R6
At last he unveils his plans. In order to
win material Black has had to weaken and
deplete the King's field.

21 ...... B×R
22 B×P
A complementary sacrifice.

22 ...... P×B
23 Kt×KtP Kt—B1
If 23 .... R—B2; 24 Q—R8 mate.

24 Q—R8 ch
The final assault.

24...... K—B2
25 Q—R7 ch K—B3
26 Kt—B4 B—Q6
Desperation! The object of this move
apart from preventing mate is to reply to 27
Q×B or 27 Kt×B with 27 .... Q—B2.

27 R—K6 ch K—Kt4
28 Q—R6 ch K—B4
29 P—Kt4 mate
Or a *dual* 29 R—K5 mate.

354

White   Black
MARSHALL   JANOWSKI
(Ostend, 1907)

*Here Black tries to play at being a "cave
man." He creates an outpost at K5, places
his KB on a menacing diagonal (7 ....
B—Q3), castles on the opposite wing, and
throws his pawns forward in an illusory
attack (13 .... P—KKt4), only to meet
with a crushing defeat. Not content with a
scientific barrage, White himself embarks on
a fierce counter-attack (13 P—QKt4).*

1 P—Q4 P—Q4
2 P—QB4 P×P
3 P—K3
A favourite continuation of Marshall's.

3 ...... P—K4
4 B×P Kt—QB3
Instead of applying a clear and unpretentious strategy by 4 .... P×P; 5 P×P,
B—Q3, Black indicates by his last move
that he has bolder ambitions.

5 Kt—KB3
Demanding a settlement in the centre.
5 P—Q5, QKt—K2 would unnecessarily
close the main road to traffic.

5 ...... P—K5
He is practically compelled to commit
himself, for after 5 .... P×P; 6 P×P,
B—Kt5; 7 Castles, etc., White's development
is clearly superior.

6 KKt—Q2 P—B4
One boldness leads to another. The
security of the black King is in jeopardy; he

cannot castle on the K side, and his development is neglected. But if 6 .... Kt—B3; 7 Kt—QB3, B—QKt5; 8 Castles, Q—K2; 9 Q—B2, Black is going from bad to worse.

| 7 Castles | B—Q3 |
| 8 Kt—QB3 | |

Hasty would be 8 P—B3, Q—R5; 9 P—KKt3 (or 9 P—B4, P—KKt4); 9 .... B×P; 10 P×B, Q×P ch, with a perpetual check.

| 8 ...... | Q—R5 |
| 9 P—KKt3 | Q—R6 |

If Black were allowed the time, he would obtain a strong attack by .... Kt—KKt5 and eventually .... P—KR4 and KR5.

10 B×Kt

Very skilfully, White vetoes his adversary's intentions.

| 10 ...... | R×B |
| 11 Kt—B4 | |

Eliminating another dangerous piece.

11	B—Q2
12 Kt×B ch	P×Kt
13 P—QKt4	

A robust measure, which nullifies Black's attempts to take the lead. The QKtP, immune from capture (13 .... Kt×KtP; 14 Q—Kt3, and wins), fulfils various functions.

| 13 ...... | P—KKt4 |
| 14 P—B3 | |

Undermining the enemy outpost at exactly the right moment.

| 14 ...... | P×P |
| 15 Q×P | |

If 15 R×P, Castles, with the threat 16 .... P—B5; 17 KP×P, B—Kt5.

| 15 ...... | R—Kt3 |

If 15 .... Castles; 16 Kt—Q5. After 15 .... Kt×KtP, in order to create complications at relatively the most propitious moment, there would follow 16 R—Kt1 (not 16 Q×KtP, B—B3); 16 .... R—QB1; 17 P—K4, P—Kt5; 18 Q—K3, Kt—B3 (18 .... Kt—B7; 19 Q—Q3); 19 P×P dis ch, K—Q1; 20 R×P, and wins.

16 B—R3

Acting upon the principle that "the threat is stronger than its execution," for if at once 16 Kt—Q5, the following imbroglio would occur: 16 .... R—R3; 17 R—B2, Kt—K2; 18 Kt—B7 ch, K—Q1, and the startling counter-threat 19 .... B—B3; 20 Q—K2,

Q×KtP ch; 21 P×Q, R—R8 mate would cost White a piece.

16	Castles
17 QR—B1	K—Kt1
18 Kt—Q5	

Threatening 19 P—Kt5, Kt—R4; 20 B—Kt4, P—Kt3; 21 B×Kt, P×B; 22 Kt—B7, with the double threat of mate by Q—R8 or Kt—R6.

| 18 ...... | R—R3 |
| 19 KR—B2 | R—K1 |

He is anxious about his Knight. If 19 .... P—R3; 20 Kt—Kt6.

20 P—Kt5	Kt—K2
21 Kt×Kt	R×Kt
22 Q—Q5	QR—K3
23 B×P ch	

A thunderbolt. If 23 .... R×B; 24 Q—Kt8 ch.

| 23 ...... | K—R1 |
| 24 R—B7 | Resigns |

A great fight between two great fighters.

355

| White | Black |
| ATKINS | VON BARDELEBEN |

(Hanover, 1902)

White's treatment of the opening is refreshingly original. That it is also effective is shown by the sequel, in which White forces a way into the heart of the hostile position.

1 P—Q4	P—Q4
2 P—QB4	P×P
3 Kt—KB3	

A strong supporting move, introduced by Blackburne: White first prevents the troublesome advance 3 .... P—K4, without compromising his chance of recovering the gambit pawn.

| 3 ...... | Kt—KB3 |

Naturally. If 3 .... P—QKt4; 4 P—K3, P—QB3; 5 P—QR4, Q—Kt3; 6 P×P, P×P; 7 P—QKt3 (not 7 Kt—K5, P—K3; 8 Kt×KBP, K×Kt; 9 Q—B3 ch, Kt—B3; 10 Q×R, B×Kt5 ch, followed by .... Kt—B3); 7 .... P×P; 8 Q×P, P—Kt5; 9 Q—Q5, B—Kt2; 10 B—Kt5 ch, B—B3; 11 Kt—K5, Q×B; 12 Q×P ch, and wins.

Or 3 .... P—QB3; 4 P—K3, P—QKt4;

5 P—QR4, etc., reverting to the line shown above.
If 3 .... P—K3; 4 P—K4, etc., and if 3 .... P—QB4, 4 P—Q5.

4 Kt—B3
Too casual. More insistent is the "modern continuation," 4 P—K3, or the "hyper-modern," 4 Q—R4 ch.

4 ......   B—B4
Trying to prevent P—K4, for as long as he can.
A very imaginative continuation is possible after 4 .... P—QR3, e.g. 5 P—QR4, P—B4 (safer would be 5 .... P—K3; 6 P—K3, P—B4; 7 B × P, etc.); 6 P—Q5 (or, more quietly, 6 P—K3, P—K3; 7 B × P, B—K2; 8 Castles, Castles, etc., with an even game); 6 .... P—K3; 7 P—K4, P × P; 8 P—K5, Kt—K5, etc.
The most precise is 4 .... P—B3; 5 P—QR4, B—B4; 6 P—K3, P—K3; 7 B × P, B—QKt5; 8 Castles, Castles, and Black can hold his own.

5 P—K3   P—K3
6 B × P   QKt—Q2
Evidently not 6 .... B—QKt5 at this stage (7 Q—R4 ch, Kt—B3; 8 Kt—K5, etc.), and if 6 .... P—B3, White no longer needs the counter-measure 7 P—QR4, but he will rather continue with 7 B—Q3.

7 Castles   P—B3
8 P—QR4
He could continue scientifically, 8 B—Q3, or, with more imagination, 8 Q—K2, P—QKt4; 9 B—Kt3, B—QKt5; 10 P—K4, etc. But he prefers to anticipate any expansion of his opponent's game.

8 ......   Kt—Kt3
Diverting the Knight from operations in the centre. Better at once 8 .... B—QKt5.

9 B—Kt3   P—QR4
10 P—R3
If at once 10 Q—K2 (in order to effect the central thrust 11 P—K4), then not 10 .... B—QKt5; 11 P—K4, B × Kt; 12 P × QB, and wins, but 10 .... B—KKt5.

10 ......   B—QKt5
More comfortable than 10 .... B—Q3 (11 Q—K2, etc.).

11 Q—K2   B—Kt3
A *preventive retreat* still hindering 12 P—K4. He could have maintained the struggle for this square by playing 11 .... Kt—K5.

12 Kt—K5
Taking the reins into his own hand.

12 ......   Q—Q3
13 B—Q2   R—Q1
14 QR—Q1   KKt—Q2
More patient would be 14 .... Castles.

15 P—K4
A most ingenious offer of a pawn, which puts life into the game.

15 ......   Kt × Kt
16 P × Kt   Q—K2
For if 16 .... Q × P; 17 P—B4, Q—B2 (17 .... Q—B4 ch; 18 B—K3, winning the Knight); 18 P—B5, with the gain of a piece.

17 P—B4
Threatening 18 P—B5.

17 ......   P—KB4
He tries to cut the Gordian knot, as the following continuation would be disastrous: 17 .... P—R3; 18 P—B5, P × P; 19 P × P, B—R2; 20 P—B6, P × P; 21 R × P, etc.

18 P × P e.p.   P × P
19 QR—K1   B—B2
20 K—R1   Castles
21 B—K3   Kt—B1
22 B—KB2
A beautiful manoeuvre, both discreet and strong, seeking out weaknesses in the hostile position.

22 ......   P—K4
23 B—B2   P × P
24 B—R4   Q—K4
A pretty interlude: if 24 .... B—Q3; 25 P—K5, B × P; 26 Q × B, etc.

25 Q—Kt4 ch   B—Kt3
26 Q × P
Liquidating with decision.

26 ......   B × Kt
27 P × B   Q × Q
If 27 .... Q × BP; 28 B—Kt1, R—Q3; 29 B—R2 ch, B—B2; 30 Q—Kt4 ch, K—R1; 31 B × B, and wins.

28 R × Q   R—Q7
29 B—Kt3 ch   K—Kt2
30 QR—KB1   Kt—Q3
31 P—K5
This move has been impending for some time. The rest needs no commentary.

31 ......   Kt—K5
32 P × P ch   K—R3
33 R—K1   Kt—Kt4
34 R—Kt4   Kt—K5
35 QR × Kt   R—Kt7
36 B—Kt5 ch   K—R4
37 R—K5   Resigns.

356

White	Black
EUWE	FLOHR

(Match, Amsterdam, 1932)

The following game can be divided into three phases: the first (initiated by 11 P—QR4) contains very instructive skirmishes on the Q side; in the second White claims his dues in the centre (20 R—Q1); and in the third White launches a violent attack on the K side (21 KKt—Kt5), brilliantly and relentlessly driven home.

1 P—Q4	P—Q4
2 P—QB4	P×P
3 Kt—KB3	Kt—KB3
4 P—K3	P—B4

Or first 4 .... P—K3; 5 B×P, P—B4 (inadequate would be 5 .... B—Kt5 ch; 6 Kt—B3, Castles; 7 Castles, etc.); 6 Castles, etc., with the same continuation as in the game.

5 B×P	P—K3
6 Castles	Kt—B3

He wants as long as possible to avoid losing a *tempo* by 6 .... B—K2 (7 P×P, Q×Q; 8 R×Q, B×P; 9 Kt—B3, etc., unless White decides on the more compact 7 Q—K2, Castles; 8 R—Q1, etc.).

More original than the text move is 6 .... QKt—Q2 (blocking the Q file and thus avoiding an exchange of Queens, or the awkward opposition of the hostile KR), or, more accurately, 6 .... P—QR3, followed by .... P—QKt4, and then only .... QKt—Q2, etc.

The simplest is 6 .... P×P; 7 P×P, Kt—B3; 8 B—K3 (unless White is willing to risk 8 Q—K2); 8 .... B—K2, and Black is in a good way to free his game.

7 Q—K2

The regrouping of Queen and Rook renders the play more dynamic. Tactically, the text move relies on the fact that the abandonment of the QP is but a *temporary sacrifice* (7 .... P×P; 8 R—Q1, and White advantageously recovers his pawn). Simple development by 7 Kt—B3, however, is also playable.

A peaceful continuation would be 7 P×P, Q×Q; 8 R×Q, B×P, with equality.

| 7 ...... | P—QR3 |

Again, if 7 .... P×P; 8 R—Q1.
White also obtains the superior disposition of forces after 7 .... B—K2; 8 R—Q1, Q—B2; 9 Kt—B3, Castles; 10 P—QR3, etc.

8 R—Q1	P—QKt4
9 P×P	

Or 9 B—Q3, or 9 B—Kt3.

9	Q—B2
10 B—Q3	B×P

Playable is 10 .... Kt—QKt5, depriving his adversary of the two Bishops.

11 P—QR4

Trying to refute Black's 8th move, for which reason he did not try to prevent it by 8 P—QR4. Much less vigorous is 11 QKt—Q2, but a sound, if quiet, continuation is 11 P—QR3 (11 .... B—Kt2; 12 P—QKt4, B—Q3; 13 B—Kt2, and White is slightly better off).

| 11 ...... | P—Kt5 |

Here 11 .... P×P is better fitted to prevent White from getting a grip, e.g. 12 Kt—B3, Kt—QKt5; 13 Kt—K4, B—K2, etc., with an even game, or 12 R×P, Kt—QKt5; 13 B—Kt5 ch, B—Q2; 14 B×B ch, Kt×B; 15 B—Q2, P—QR4; 16 R—QB1, Q—K2, etc., with an artificial *equilibrium*.

12 QKt—Q2

White's perspicacity in deferring the development of this QKt is now clear. Its potentialities either at Kt3 or at QB4 ensure for White a lasting positional advantage.

| 12 ...... | Kt—QR4 |

Preventing 13 Kt—Kt3. If 12 .... Castles; 13 Kt—Kt3, B—K2; 14 B—Q2 (or even 14 P—K4); 14 .... B—Kt2; 15 QR—B1, with the propitious occupation of the QB file.

| 13 P—QKt3 | Kt—Q4 |

It would be better for Black to castle, but he tries to counteract the threat of B—Kt2, followed by QR—B1.

14 B—Kt2	Kt—B6
15 B×Kt	P×B
16 Kt—K4	Kt×P

If 16 .... B—Kt5; 17 B—B2, B—Kt2; 18 KKt—Kt5, with a K side attack.

| 17 QR—Kt1 | Kt—R4 |

If 17 .... R—QKt1; 18 B—B2, Kt—R4; 19 R×R, Q×R; 20 Kt×B, etc.

18 KR—QB1	B—K2
19 R×P	Q—Q1
20 R—Q1	Q—Kt3
21 KKt—Kt5	

Sounding the attack.

| 21 ...... | P—Kt3 |

To prevent 22 Q—R5, whereas if 21 .... P—R3; 22 Q—R5. 21 .... P—B4 would merely be weakening (22 Kt—Kt3, B×Kt; 23 Q—R5 ch, followed by Q×B).

| 22 Q—B3 | Castles |

Not 22 .... P—B4; 23 Kt—Q6 ch, followed by Q × R.

| 23 Kt—B6 ch | B × Kt |
| 24 Q × B | B—Kt2 |

If 24 .... Q—Q1; 25 Kt × RP, K × Kt; 26 B × P ch, P × B; 27 Q × Q, R × Q; 28 R × R, B—Kt2; 29 R—B7 ch, K—R3; 30 R (Q8)—Q7, B—Q4 (if 30 .... R—QB1; 31 R—R7 ch, K—Kt4; 32 P—B4 ch, K—Kt5; 33 R × B, Kt × R; 34 R × Kt); 31 P—B4, and Black must incur further loss.

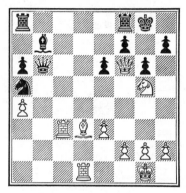

| 25 Kt × RP |

A beautiful sacrifice.

| 25 ...... | KR—Q1 |

If 25 .... K × Kt; 26 B × P ch, K—Kt1 (or 26 .... P × B; 27 R—Q7 ch, etc.); 27 P—K4, with the threat 28 B—R7 ch, K × B; 29 R—R3 ch, etc.

| 26 P—R4 | R—Q2 |

If 26 .... K × Kt; 27 Q × BP ch, K—R1; 28 R—B7.

| 27 P—R5 | Q—Q1 |
| 28 P × P | Resigns. |

357

| White | Black |
| *EUWE* | *ALEKHINE* |

(Return Match, 1937)

The most striking feature in this magnificent game is that the mobility of the white forces is particularly noticeable after the exchange of Queens.

1 P—Q4	P—Q4
2 P—QB4	P × P
3 Kt—KB3	P—QR3

More to the point is 3 .... Kt—KB3.

| 4 P—K3 | Kt—KB3 |

Not 4 .... B—Kt5; 5 B × P, P—K3; 6 Q—Kt3, etc., nor 4 .... P—QKt4; 5 P—QR4, etc.

| 5 B × P | P—K3 |

Not 5 .... B—Kt5; 6 B × P ch, K × B; 7 Kt—K5 ch, etc., nor 5 .... P—QKt4; 6 B—K2.

| 6 Castles | P—B4 |
| 7 Q—K2 | Kt—B3 |

This pressure against the QP is ephemeral. More important is to speed up castling by 7 .... B—K2.

| 8 Kt—B3 |

With counter-pressure against Q5 and K4, whereas 8 R—Q1, another good move, would exert pressure only against Q5. As for the threatened QP, it can be saved, for if 8 .... P × P; 9 R—Q1, P—K4; 10 P × P, White recovers his pawn with some advantage.

| 8 ...... | P—QKt4 |

At this stage, the advance of the QKtP proves more weakening than aggressive. 8 .... B—K2 is necessary.

| 9 B—Kt3 | B—K2 |

Now that Black's Q side is disturbed, this loss of a *tempo* may have serious consequences. For 9 .... P—Kt5, see the following game. If 9 .... P—B5; 10 B—B2, Kt—QKt5; 11 B—Kt1, with latent possibilities. If 9 .... B—Kt2; 10 R—Q1, threatening P—Q5, eventually, favours White's chances.

Therefore the lesser evil is 9 .... P × P, etc.

| 10 P × P |

Simple and strong.

| 10 ...... | B × P |
| 11 P—K4 |

The centre is moving.

| 11 ...... | P—Kt5 |

Or 11 .... Q—B2, a waiting move. Weak would be 11 .... P—K4; 12 B—Q5, as it would lose a pawn. In reply to the text move, Black expects 12 Kt—QR4, B—K2, but White is able to disrupt the centre.

12 P—K5
Deep play.

12 ......   P×Kt
After 12 .... Kt—Q2, White continues advantageously 13 Kt—K4.

13 P×Kt   KtP×P
Against 13 .... Q×P, the same beautiful rejoinder 14 Q—B4 would allow the sequel: 14 .... P×P (or 14 .... Q—K2; 15 B—K3); 15 Q×B, P×R (Q) (or 15 .... P×B (Q); 16 QR×Q, B—Q2; 17 KR—Q1, R—QB1; 18 Kt—K5, with a very pretty win); 16 Q×Kt ch, B—Q2 (or 16 .... K—Q1; 17 R—Q1 ch, or 16 .... K—B1; 17 B—R3 ch, or 16 .... K—K2; 17 Q—B5 ch); 17 Q×R ch, K—K2; 18 B—R3 mate.

14 Q—B4
A powerful diversion, which stresses the fact that Black's pieces on the QB file are loose.

14 ......   Q—Kt3
Protecting both the Knight and the Bishop as, if 14 .... Q—K2; 15 B—K3 wins.

15 Q×BP
He loses no time in recapturing the pawn, as the hostile KBP is now attacked.

15 ......   Kt—Q5
No move here is entirely satisfactory. Thus, e.g. 15 .... Castles; 16 B—R6, R—K1; 17 QR—QB1 wins a piece.

16 Kt×Kt   B×Kt
17 B—R4 ch   K—K2
He must forfeit castling, for if 17 .... B—Q2; 18 B×B ch, K×B; 19 R—Q1, P—K4; 20 B—K3, White wins.

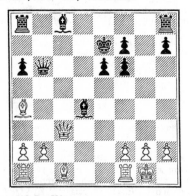

18 B—K3
Pretty play, gaining territory.

18 ......   B×Q
Neither 18 .... B×B; 19 P×B, etc., nor 18 .... R—Q1; 19 QR—Q1, etc., nor, finally, 18 .... P—K4; 19 Q—R3 ch saves the situation.

19 B×Q   B—K4
If 19 .... B×P; 20 B—B5 ch, K—Q1; 21 KR—Q1 ch, K—B2; 22 B—Q6 ch, K—Kt3; 23 QR—Kt1, K—R4; 24 B—B6 wins. After 19 .... B—Kt5; 20 KR—Q1 threatens to win the exchange by 21 B—B6, R—QKt1; 22 B—B7, etc.

20 QR—Q1
Threat: 21 B—B5 ch.

20 ......   K—B1
21 P—B4   B×KtP
22 R—B3
With a threefold threat of 23 R—QKt3 or 23 R—KKt3 or 23 R—Q8 ch, K—Kt2; 24 R—Kt3 ch, etc. White could also win the exchange by 22 B—B6, R—QKt1; 23 B—B7, etc.

22 ......   B—Kt2
23 R—QKt3
Embarras de richesses! There is also an easy win by 23 B—B5 ch, K—Kt2; 24 R—Kt3 ch, K—R3; 25 R—Kt1, etc.

23 ......   B—R6
Desperation, for if 23 .... R—B1; 24 R—Q8 ch, R×R (or 24 .... K—K2; 25 R—Q7 ch, with R×QB to follow); 25 B—B5 ch, followed by mate.

24 R×B
And, with an extra piece, White won on the 41st move in spite of Dr. Alekhine's heroic resistance.

24	R—KKt1
25 R—KKt3	R×R
26 P×R	B—Q4
27 B—Kt3	B×B
28 P×B	K—K1
29 P—QKt4	R—Kt1
30 B—B5	R—B1
31 R—R1	R—B3
32 K—B2	P—B4
33 K—K3	P—B3
34 K—Q4	K—B2
35 K—B4	K—Kt3
36 R—Q1	K—R4
37 R—Q6	R×R
38 B×R	K—Kt5
39 B—K7	K×P
40 B×P	K×BP
41 K—B5	Resigns.

358

White	*Black*
ALEKHINE	BÖÖK

(Margate, 1938)

One of the most wonderful successes in Dr. Alekhine's overflowing honours list!

1 P—Q4	P—Q4
2 P—QB4	P × P
3 Kt—KB3	Kt—KB3
4 P—K3	P—K3
5 B × P	P—B4
6 Castles	Kt—B3
7 Q—K2	P—QR3
8 Kt—B3	P—QKt4
9 B—Kt3	

Identical, up to this move, with the preceding game.

9	P—Kt5
10 P—Q5	

The beginning of a whole series of complications.

10	Kt—QR4

After 10 .... P × P; 11 Kt × P, Kt × Kt; 12 R—Q1, etc., or 10 .... Kt × P; 11 Kt × Kt, P × Kt; 12 R—Q1, B—K3; 13 B—R4, followed by Kt—K5, White has a definite positional advantage. And if 10 .... P × Kt then not 11 B—R4, Q × P, etc., with unnecessary complications, but simply 11 P × Kt, P × P; 12 QB × P, with a greatly intensified development for White.

11 B—R4 ch	B—Q2
12 P × P	P × P

If 12 .... B × B; 13 P × P ch, followed by Kt × B, and Black forfeits castling.

13 R—Q1

A magnificent move, giving up a clear Rook in order to keep up his attack.

13	P × Kt

Black cannot refuse the gifts, for if 13 .... Q—B2; 14 B × B ch, Kt × B; 15 Kt—K4, and White, whose QKt has increased its radius of action, remains master of the situation.

14 R × B

More sacrifices. Obviously 14 Kt—K5 would be useless because of 14 .... B × B, etc., and the advantage would pass over to Black.

14	Kt × R

Black is now a Rook ahead, and will remain so for a long time.

15 Kt—K5	R—R2
16 P × P	

In White's position he can afford to make this quiet move with a view to fresh enterprises.

16	K—K2

A move dictated by instinctive desire to escape at last from the pin (and which threatens 17 .... Kt × Kt). After 16 .... B—Q3, White obtains substantial compensation for his piece by 17 Q—R5 ch, P—Kt3; 18 Kt × P, etc.

17 P—K4

A most disagreeable surprise, for now White has not only prevented 17 .... Kt × Kt (18 B—Kt5 ch, winning the Queen), but has also brought his QB into play (if 17 .... P—R3; 18 Kt—Kt6 ch).

17	Kt—KB3
18 B—KKt5	

Less fruitful would be the development at K3 or QR3, as also at B4.

18	Q—B2
19 B—B4	Q—Kt3

After 19 .... Q—Kt2 there is for White a right and a wrong way to proceed:

(*a*) The wrong way: 20 R—Q1, Q × P (not 20 .... Kt × P; 21 Q × Kt, Q × Q; 22 B—Kt5 mate); 21 Q—Q2, Kt—Q4 (not 21 .... Q—Q4; 22 Q—K3); 22 B—Kt5 ch, K—Q3, etc., with an uncertain issue.

(*b*) The right way: 20 Q—K3, K—Q1 (not 20 .... Q × P; 21 Q × P ch, nor 20 .... Kt × P; 21 B—Kt5 ch, etc.); 21 Q—Q3 ch, K—B1 (if 21 .... K—K2; 22 R—Q1); 22 R—Kt1, Q × P; 23 Kt—B7. The final point! Although all the white pieces are adrift, Black must succumb to the mating threats 24 R—Kt8 mate or 24 Q—Q8 mate.

20 R—Q1	P—Kt3
21 B—KKt5	

Tightening his grip.

21	B—Kt2
22 Kt—Q7	

The sanctions!

22	R × Kt

If 22 .... Q—Kt2; 23 P—K5, and wins.

23 R × R ch	K—B1
24 B × Kt	B × B
25 P—K5	Resigns

(For if 25 .... B—K2; 26 Q—B3 ch, K—Kt2; 27 R × B ch, K—R3; 28 Q—K3 ch, and mate in two.)

359

White	Black
CAPABLANCA	RESHEVSKY

(Nottingham, 1936)

An indifferent opening is followed by a short middle game mainly taken up by the countering of mutual threats. The resulting duel between Knight and Bishop is a superb example of end-game play.

1 P—Q4	P—Q4
2 Kt—KB3	Kt—KB3
3 P—B4	P × P
4 Q—R4 ch	

Here is a "hyper-modern" idea in place of the academic continuation 4 P—K3, or else 4 Kt—B3. The master of to-day is not afraid to let his Queen manœuvre from the very beginning in the rough ground of the Q side.

4	QKt—Q2

The most tenacious. Too passive would be 4 .... P—B3; 5 Q × P (B4), etc., and too accommodating 4 .... B—Q2; 5 Q × BP, P—K3; 6 B—Kt5, etc., whilst the same may be said of 4 .... Q—Q2; 5 Q × BP, Q—B3; 6 Kt—R3, etc.

5 Q × BP	

Hastening to capture a pawn which cannot run away. A stronger continuation is 5 P—KKt3 at once, or else 5 Kt—B3.

5	P—K3
6 P—KKt3	

This move gives the game a purely positional character. The same position occurs, by an inversion of moves, after (a) 1 P—Q4, P—Q4; 2 P—QB4, P—K3; 3 Kt—KB3, Kt—KB3; 4 P—KKt3, P × P; (the *Catalan Gambit*); 5 Q—R4 ch, QKt—Q2; 6 Q × BP (better, first, 6 B—Kt2), etc.

Or (b) 1 P—Q4, Kt—B3; 2 P—QB4, P—K3; 3 P—KKt3, P—Q4; 4 Kt—KB3, P × P; 5 Q—R4 ch, QKt—Q2; 6 Q × BP, etc.

6	P—QR3

Playing for an extended *fianchetto*—a very good idea. Less consistent is 6 .... P—B4 (7 B—Kt2, etc.).

7 B—Kt2	P—QKt4
8 Q—B6	

A vain expedition. Better is 8 Q—B2.

8	R—R2

Very well parried, with an awkward threat in 9 .... B—Kt2.

9 B—B4	

Or 9 B—K3, Kt—Q4; 10 B—Kt5, B—K2; 11 B × B, Q × B; 12 Castles, B—Kt2, followed by .... P—QB4, and Black has satisfactorily freed his game.

9	B—Kt2
10 Q—B1	P—B4
11 P × P	B × P
12 Castles	Castles
13 QKt—Q2	Q—K2

A glance shows that not only is the black Queen better employed than her rival, but also that Black's forces are the more active on the Q side. The Cuban's great art will be employed in gradually overcoming these defects.

14 Kt—Kt3	B—Kt3
15 B—K3	

Striving for simplification.

15	R—B1
16 Q—Q2	Kt—K5
17 Q—Q3	Kt (Q2)—B4
18 Kt × Kt	Kt × Kt
19 Q—Q1	B—R1

More enterprising would be 19 .... B—Q4.

20 R—B1	R (R2)—B2
21 P—Kt3	Kt—Q2

Both players rely on their chances in the end game, and seek exchanges. A sound constructive move would be 21 .... P—B3.

22 R × R	R × R
23 B × B	Kt × B
24 Q—Q4	Kt—Q4
25 R—Q1	P—B3

But now 25 .... R—B1 would be a better parry to the threat of 26 P—K4 Kt—B3; 27 Q—Q8 ch, etc.

26 Kt—K1	B—Kt2
27 B × Kt	P × B

Undoubtedly 27 .... B × B would be wiser here.

28 P—K3	Q—K5
29 P—KR4	P—QR4
30 P—B3	Q × Q

By playing 30 .... Q—K4; 31 K—B2, P—Kt5, etc., Black would retain greater mobility than after the text move.

31 R × Q	R—B8

Aiming, not at an attack, but at a further exchange, which is suicidal. The King should move towards the centre.

32 K—B2	R—R8
33 R—Q2	P—R5
34 Kt—Q3	R—QKt8

Or 34 .... P×P; 35 P×P, R—QKt8; 36 Kt—B5, B—B3; 37 R—R2, and White's mechanism prevails.

35 R—Kt2	R×R ch

Forced, at this stage. The whole subsequent phase is most instructive.

36 Kt×R	B—B3
37 Kt—Q3	P—Kt4

Seeking salvation in a counter-attack.

38 RP×P	BP×P
39 Kt—Kt4	P×P
40 P×P	B—Kt2
41 P—Kt4	

Preventing 41 .... P—R4.

41	K—Kt2
42 K—K2	K—Kt3
43 K—Q3	P—R4

If 43 .... P—Q5; 44 P—K4.

44 P×P ch	K×P
45 K—Q4	K—R5
46 Kt×P	

A well-earned prize.

46	K—Kt6
47 P—B4	P—Kt5

If 47 .... B×Kt; 48 K×B, P—Kt5; 49 P—B5, etc., and White will force the exchange of Queens.

48 P—B5	B—B1
49 K—K5	B—Q2
50 P—K4	

A methodical advance. Over-refined would be 50 Kt—B7, B×P; 51 K×B, K—B6; 52 Kt—Q5, P—Kt6; 53 Kt—B4, K×P; 54 K—K5, P—Kt5, etc., and Black's cause would be saved.

50	B—K1
51 K—Q4	

The continuations 51 P—B6 and 51 P—Kt4 are also playable.

51	K—B6
52 P—K5	P—Kt6
53 Kt—K3	K—B5

A remarkable position. Or 53 .... B—Q2; 54 P—K6, B—B1; 55 P—K7, B—Q2; 56 P—B6, B—K1; 57 Kt—B5, P—Kt7; 58 Kt—R4 ch, K—B5; 59 Kt×P ch, K—B4; 60 Kt—K3 ch, K×P; 61 Kt—Q5 ch, and wins.

54 P—K6	P—Kt7
55 Kt×P ch	K×P
56 K—Q5	K—Kt5
57 Kt—K3 ch	K—B5
58 K—Q4	Resigns.

360

White	Black
GRÜNFELD	TARTAKOWER

(Semmering, 1926)

Simplifications are desired and obtained by Black according to a deliberate and comprehensive plan: he obtains a slight pawn superiority on the Q side, while his Queen, powerfully posted at K5, neutralises White's corresponding advantage on the opposite wing. Greater security for his King, greater mobility of his Queen—these are the factors of Black's victory.

1 P—Q4	P—Q4
2 P—QB4	P×P
3 Kt—KB3	B—Kt5

Sometimes called the *Swedish Variant*, this line of play aims at early counter-action.

4 Kt—K5	

A natural reaction. If 4 P—K4, P—K4, etc., and if 4 P—K3, P—K3; 5 B×P, Kt—Q2 (in order to meet the escapade 6 Q—Kt3 with 6 .... Kt—Kt3, etc., whilst if at once 5 .... Kt—KB3, then 6 Q—Kt3, B×Kt; 7 P×B, P—QKt3; 8 Kt—B3, etc., would exploit weaknesses on the adverse Q side); 6 Kt—B3, KKt—B3, and Black has a good game.

4	B—R4

The best retreat.

5 Kt×QBP	

More coherent is first 5 Kt—QB3, after which would follow, *neither* the unimaginative 5 .... P—K3 (6 P—KKt4, B—Kt3; 7 P—KR4, P—KB3; 8 Q—R4 ch, P—B3; 9 Kt×B, P×Kt; 10 Q×P (B4), etc., to White's advantage);
Nor the hasty 5 .... Kt—Q2 (6 Q—R4, P—QB3; 7 Kt×Kt, Q×Kt; 8 Q×P (B4), P—K3; 9 P—K4, etc., and White has an advantage in space;
But energetically 5 .... P—KB3; 6 Kt×P, P—K3; 7 Q—Kt3, Kt—B3 (8 Q×P, Kt—Kt5); 8 P—K3, R—Kt1, etc.

| 5 ...... | P—K3 |
| 6 Q—Kt3 | Kt—QB3 |

Defence by counter-attack (7 Q×P, Kt×P).

| 7 P—K3 | R—Kt1 |

Black has thus succeeded in securing his Q side without recourse to the weakening .... P—QKt3.

| 8 Kt—B3 | Kt—B3 |
| 9 B—K2 | |

Seeing that the opening has brought him no advantage, White now seeks to reduce the material, which suits Black, who anticipates a favourable end game.

9	B×B
10 Kt×B	B—Kt5 ch
11 Kt—QB3	

Or 11 B—Q2, B×B ch; 12 Kt×B, Castles; 13 Castles, P—K4, and Black already has the initiative.

11	Castles
12 Castles	Kt—Q4
13 Kt×Kt	

More imaginative, but not without commitments, is 13 P—QR3.

| 13 ...... | Q×Kt |
| 14 Q—B2 | P—K4 |

By this important thrust, Black obtains: elimination of the adverse QP, which had control of the centre; the majority of pawns on the Q side; opening of the Q file, where he has the greater opportunities.

15 Kt×P	Kt×Kt
16 P×Kt	Q×KP
17 B—Q2	

A fresh exchange, for if 17 P—QR3, B—Q3; 18 P—KKt3, P—QB4; 19 B—Q2, KR—Q1; 20 B—B3, Q—R4; 21 KR—Q1, B—K4, and Black has the best of it. If 17 R—Q1, KR—Q1, etc.

17	B×B
18 Q×B	KR—Q1
19 Q—B2	R—Q4

In the ensuing heavy artillery duel, Black promptly occupies the most important lines.

20 QR—Q1	QR—Q1
21 R×R	R×R
22 R—Q1	P—KKt3

In this simplified end game, *tactical finessing* will play an important part. Everything depends on one *tempo*. Thus, if White now had a flight square (at KKt3 or KR3), the text move would would not be playable (23 R×R, Q×R; 24 Q×P, Q×P;

25 Q—Kt8 ch, K—Kt2; 26 Q×KtP) and Black must submit to 22 .... R×R ch; 23 Q×R, P—KKt3; 24 Q—Q4, etc., with even chances.

Instead of the text move, 22 .... Q×KtP would be a blunder because of 23 R×R.

| 23 R×R | Q×R |

In the clear-cut ending which follows, Black's dominant position and his majority of pawns on the Q side ensures for him a comfortable if not decisive superiority.

| 24 P—QR3 | |

After 24 P—KKt3, Q×P; 25 Q×P, Q×P; 26 Q—Kt8 ch, K—Kt2; 27 Q×RP, P—QKt4, and Black has a dynamic passed pawn. Or 24 P—QKt3, P—QB4; 25 P—Kt3, P—QKt4, followed already by .... P—B5. Similarly, 24 P—QKt4, P—Kt3; 25 P—KR3, P—QB4, etc., would only serve to increase the speed of Black's QBP.

| 24 ...... | P—QB4 |
| 25 P—R3 | |

After 25 P—KKt3, White would find it much harder to use his additional centre pawn.

| 25 ...... | P—QKt4 |
| 26 P—B4 | |

Too abrupt. More compact would be 26 P—B3, soon to be followed by P—K4.

| 26 ...... | P—B5 |

More astute than 26 .... P—QR4 at once.

| 27 Q—B3 | |

Although this move tries to blockade the adverse pawn mass by preventing .... P—QR4, it lessens his control of the centre. If 27 P—K4, Q—Q5 ch, and if 27 K—R2, P—QR4, etc.

| 27 ...... | Q—K5 |
| 28 K—B2 | P—QR4 |

Another *tactical finesse*, which makes this reinforcement possible, is: 29 Q×RP, Q—B7 ch, followed by .... Q×QKtP, and Black prevails.

| 29 P—KKt4 | P—R3 |
| 30 P—KR4 | Q—R8 |

Skilfully changing the venue, the decision now taking place on the K side instead of the Q side.

| 31 K—Kt3 | |

Or 31 Q×RP, Q×P ch; 32 K—B3, Q—R6 ch; 33 K—B2, Q—R7 ch, followed by .... Q×KtP, and wins.

31	Q—Kt8 ch
32 K—B3	Q—R7
33 P—Kt5	P—R4
34 K—K4	Q×RP
35 Q×RP	Q—R8 ch
36 K—K5	Q—B3
37 Q—R7	

If passively 37 Q—K1, Black wins after 37 .... Q—K3 ch; 38 K—Q4, Q—Kt5; 39 Q—R5, P—R5; 40 Q—Q8 ch, K—R2; 41 Q—B6, Q—Q2 ch, followed by .... P—R6, etc.

37	P—R5
38 P—B5	P×P
39 K×P	Q—B6 ch
40 K—K5	P—R6
41 K—Q4	

Indirectly still preventing 41 .... P—R7 because of 42 Q—Kt8 ch.

41	Q—Kt5 ch
Resigns.	

361

White	Black
GOLOMBEK	*MENCHIK*

(London, 1937)

An interesting and well-contested struggle, of which the outstanding feature is the energy with which White forces an entry into the enemy camp.

1 P—Q4	P—Q4
2 P—QB4	P×P
3 Kt—KB3	P—QR3

A waiting move, which is not without guile.

4 P—K3

If 4 P—QR4, B—Kt5, and, thanks to the interpolation of her 3rd move, Black can more comfortably revert to the *Swedish Variation*, e.g. 5 Kt—K5, B—R4; 6 Kt—QB3, P—K3, as now White cannot play Q—R4.

4	B—Kt5

She reverts to the *Swedish Variation*, having for the time being forestalled the possibility of Kt—K5, etc.

5 B×P	P—K3
6 Q—Kt3	

Too passive would be 6 B—K2 or 6 QKt—Q2, and too nonchalant 6 Kt—B3, or also 6 P—KR3, e.g. 6 .... B—R4; 7 Kt—B3, Kt—KB3; 8 Castles, B—K2 (or

8 .... P—B4, or even 8 .... Kt—B3); 9 Q—K2, Castles; 10 R—Q1, Q—B1, etc., with even chances.

6	R—R2

Black finds an ingenious defence. Other defences would be in favour of White, e.g.: (*a*) 6 .... P—QKt4; 7 Kt—K5, B—KB4; 8 B—K2, threatening B—B3, with a lasting pressure; (*b*) 6 .... B×Kt; 7 P×B, P—QKt4 (or 7 .... R—R2; 8 Kt—B3); 8 B—K2, Kt—KB3; 9 P—QR4, etc.; (*c*) 6 .... Kt—QB3; 7 P—Q5, B×Kt; 8 P×B.

7 Kt—K5	B—R4
8 Castles	Kt—Q2

Better is 8 .... B—Q3, with the development of the K side.

9 P—B4	Kt×Kt
10 BP×Kt	P—QKt4

White having obtained some assets on the K side, Black seeks to gain some initiative on the opposite wing.

11 B—Q3	P—QB4
12 B—K4	R—B2
13 B—Q2	P—B5
14 Q—B2	Q—Q2
15 B—R5	R—B1
16 Kt—Q2	Kt—K2
17 Kt—B3	Kt—B3
18 B—K1	Kt—Kt5

Clearly not 18 .... B—Kt5; 19 B×Kt, and if 18 .... B—K2; 19 P—QR4.

19 B×Kt	B×B
20 P—QR4	

Sound bilateral strategy. He wishes to disrupt the Q side whilst, on the other wing, he has in view the strong manœuvre 21 Kt—Kt5, P—R3; 22 Kt—R3, followed by Kt—B4.

20	B—K2

Parrying the threat. If, to this end, 20 .... P—R3, there follows, as in the text, 21 P×P, P×P; 22 P—Q5.

21 P×P	P×P
22 P—Q5	

A fine advance.

22	B—Kt3

Not 22 .... P×P; 23 B—B5, winning the exchange, and if 22 .... B—B4; 23 Kt—Q4.

23 P—Q6	B×B
24 Q×B	B—Q1
25 Kt—Q4	Castles

At last. If 25 .... B—Kt3; 26 R—R6, B×Kt; 27 Q×B, with the decisive threat 28 R—R7.

26 R—R6   P—B6
27 P—QKt3
If 27 P—QKt4, R—B5.

27 ......   R—B4
28 KR—R1   R—Q4
29 P—QKt4
Preventing 29 .... P—Kt5. The actual threat is 30 R—B6, and the unceremonious capture of the QBP.

29 ......   P—B7
A trap, which at least succeeds in driving the hostile Knight from the field of battle. Against the blunt counter-attempt 29 .... P—B4, White would reply 30 Q—B4, P—Kt4; 31 Q—Kt3, P—B5; 32 Q—R3, R×KP; 33 R—R7, and wins.

30 Kt×BP
Of course, neither 30 Q×P, R×KP, etc., nor—falling into the trap—30 R—B6,

Q×R; 31 Kt×Q, R—Q8 ch; 32 K—B2, R×R; 33 Q×P, P—B3, and Black has a possible defence.

30 ......   P—B3
A vain attempt to break the hold. Better would be 30 .... P—B4; 31 Q—B4, P—Kt4; 32 Q—Kt3, Q—KKt2, etc.

31 R—R7   Q—K1
32 Q—Kt4   P—Kt3
33 Q—R4   R—B2
34 R×R   Q×R
35 R—R8   Q—Q2
If 35 .... Q—B1, then, not 36 Q×P, Q×Q; 37 P×Q, R×P, etc., but 36 Kt—Q4. And if 35 .... R—Q8 ch; 36 K—B2, P×P dis ch; 37 K—Kt3, and wins.

36 Q×P   Resigns
A very lively game.

24. QUEEN'S GAMBIT DECLINED

362

White	Black
ST. AMANT	STAUNTON

(Match, 1843)

In an otherwise almost symmetrical position, White's sway over the open K file enables him to initiate a combination (22 P—Q5) of unusual beauty and effectiveness.

1 P—Q4	P—K3
2 P—QB4	P—Q4
3 P—K3	

White decides on a quiet continuation, because 3 P × P, P × P would free the adverse QB and give Black a pawn majority on the Q side; because an attempted blockade by 3 P—B5 would fail against 3 .... P—QKt3; 4 P—QKt4, P—QR4, etc.; and because he considers that the moves 3 Kt—QB3 or 3 Kt—KB3 (which to-day seem so natural) would conjure up unnecessary risks after 3 .... P × P.

3	Kt—KB3
4 Kt—QB3	P—B4

A sound, liberating move.

5 Kt—B3	Kt—B3
6 P—QR3	

With the definite object of allowing 7 B—Q3, without having to fear 7 .... Kt—QKt5.

6	B—K2

Playable also is 6 .... B—Q3, and if then 7 Kt—QKt5, B—K2, followed by .... P—QR3, repelling the invader.

7 B—Q3	

Another plan is 7 QP × P, B × P; 8 P—QKt4, B—Q3, and White has gained time, but lost territory in the centre.

7	Castles
8 Castles	P—QKt3
9 P—QKt3	B—Kt2
10 P × QP	

He relaxes the *tension in the centre*, if only to shut in Black's QB.

10	KP × P

Simpler would now be 10 .... KKt × P

(e.g. 11 B—Kt2, Kt × Kt; 12 B × Kt, P × P; 13 Kt × P, Kt × Kt; 14 B × Kt, B—KB3, with a well-balanced game), but Black has no desire for simplification.

11 B—Kt2	

If first 11 P × P, P × P, Black has a pair of vigorous hanging pawns in the centre.

11	P × P
12 P × P	

Or 12 KKt × P, Kt × Kt; 13 P × Kt, and the tension would be further reduced, whereas after the text move the eventuality of 13 Kt—K5 remains (and if 13 .... Kt × P; 14 B × P ch, followed by Q × Kt).

12	B—Q3
13 R—K1	

Although the position is again almost symmetrical, White retains the initiative through his occupation of the open K file.

13	P—KR3
14 R—QB1	R—B1
15 R—B2	R—B2
16 QR—K2	P—R3

Black plans an artificial regrouping of forces by .... Q—B1, which, however, is not possible at once, on account of (16 .... Q—B1) 17 Kt—QKt5, R—Q2; 18 B—B5. He could have simplified matters, on this or the next move, by .... R—K2, etc.

17 P—R3	Q—B1
18 Q—Q2	Kt—Q1

Or, e.g. 18 .... Kt—K2; 19 Kt—K5, Kt—B4; 20 Q—B4, Kt—K2; 21 R—K3, preventing 21 .... R × Kt, and launching a fine attack.

19 P—QKt4	Kt—K3

Inviting the crisis. A waiting move such as 19 .... P—QKt4 would be preferable.

20 B—B5	Kt—K5

This hope of cutting the Gordian knot is doomed to disappointment. But after 20 .... R—K2; 21 P—Kt4, etc., Black's position would become precarious.

21 Kt × Kt	P × Kt

If now 22 B × P, B × B; 23 R × B, R—B7, and wins.

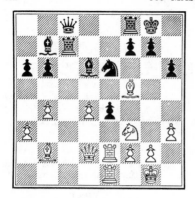

22 P—Q5
A vast and beautiful conception.

22 ......   P×Kt
23 R×Kt
The *preliminary point*, leading to the irruption (23 .... P×R; 24 B×P ch).

23 ......   Q—Q1
24 B—B6
A *transitory point*, bringing about the
downfall of the enemy defences.

24 ......   P×B
25 R×B
The *final point*, regaining the piece—with
increment.

25 ......   K—Kt2
There is nothing else, in view of the threat
26 Q×P. The remainder, with the Queen
for a Rook, is already *res adjudicata*.

26 R×Q   R×R
27 B—K4
And White wins.

363

White	Black
BLACKBURNE	LIPSCHÜTZ

(New York, 1889)

*A fine contest, already foreshadowing the
general character which to-day prevails when
this obstructive variation is played: ambitious
manœuvres by Black on the Q side, whilst
White tries out his creative powers in a K side
attack.*

1 P—Q4	P—Q4
2 P—QB4	P—K3
3 Kt—QB3	Kt—KB3
4 Kt—B3	P—QKt3

One of the oldest aspects of the so-called
Orthodox Defence. Black's QB, shut off
from one side, seeks to develop on the other.

5 B—Kt5	B—K2
6 P—K3	B—Kt2
7 R—B1	

An important supporting move, heralding
White's pressure on the QB file. Introduced
by Blackburne into master practice, this move
has considerably strengthened White's game
in this variation, whereas formerly Black's
chances were considered superior.

7	QKt—Q2
8 P×P	P×P

For if 8 .... Kt×P; 9 Kt×Kt, B×Kt (or
9 .... P×Kt; 10 B×B, Q×B; 11 R×P,
winning a pawn); 10 B×B, Q×B; 11 R×P,
Q—Kt5 ch (or 11 .... B×P; 12 Q—R4, or
11 .... Q—Q3; 12 R—B3, etc.); 12 Q—Q2,
Q×Q ch; 13 Kt×Q, K—Q1; 14 R—B2,
R—QB1 (14 .... B×RP; 15 P—QKt3);
15 R×R ch, K×R; 16 P—QR3, and White
has annexed a vital point.

9 B—Q3	Castles
10 Castles	Kt—K5

Relieving the pin means commitments in
the centre. More to the point is emancipation by 10 .... P—B4.

11 B—KB4
Retaining control of territory and, at the
same time, threatening 12 B×P, Q×B;
13 Kt×Kt.

11	P—QB4

The possibility of this advance is the key
to the whole of this defence.

12 Q—K2
After 12 P×P, P×P, Black's central
pawns would have considerable striking
powers.

12	P—B4

Not 12 .... P—B5, on account of
13 B×Kt, P×B; 14 Kt—Q2, winning a
pawn.

13 KR—Q1
Threatening 14 P×P, with pressure on the
Q file.

13	P—B5

Stressing the *majority of pawns on the
Q side.*

14 B×Kt	BP×B
15 Kt—K5	Kt—B3

Not 15 .... Kt×Kt; 16 P×Kt, nor 15 .... B—Q3; 16 Q—R5, with an attack.

16 P—KKt4	Q—K1

In order to meet 17 P—Kt5 with 17 .... Kt—R4.

17 Q—B1

Skilfully bringing both the Queen and QKt into the firing line.

17	B—Q3
18 P—KR3	R—Q1
19 Q—Kt2	P—QKt4

He considers the situation on the K side sufficiently strengthened, and turns his attention to the other wing.

20 Kt—K2	P—Kt5
21 Kt—Kt3	Kt—Q2
22 Kt×Kt	R×Kt
23 Kt—K2	B×B
24 Kt×B	

In spite of the reduced material, White still has some poisoned arrows in his quiver.

24	QR—KB2

Threat: 25 .... P—Kt4, followed by .... R×P.

25 P—Kt5	R—B4
26 K—R1	P—QR4

Playing his trumps. If 26 .... R×Kt; 27 P×R, R×P; 28 R—K1, Q—B2; 29 R—B2, R—B6; 30 R—K3, maintaining White's advantage.

27 R—KKt1	B—B1
28 Q—Kt3	Q—R5

The crisis.

29 P—Kt3	P×P

Wiser would be 29 .... Q—Kt4.

30 P×P	Q×P
31 R—B7	P—R5

If 31 .... P—Kt3; 32 P—R4.

32 P—Kt6

This final assault is of great beauty.

32	P—R3
33 R×P ch	

A bolt from the blue.

33	K×R
34 Kt—R5 ch	

An original turn, leading to the decisive irruption of the Queen.

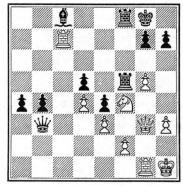

Position after 31 .... P—R5

34	R×Kt

Or 34 .... K—Kt1; 35 Q—B7, etc.

35 Q—B7 ch	K—B3
36 Q—Q6 ch	Resigns.

364

White	*Black*
PILLSBURY	TARRASCH

(Hastings, 1895)

An historical game, which stimulated widespread interest in the Q.G.D. by demonstrating that White can obtain very fine attacking chances.

1 P—Q4	P—Q4
2 P—QB4	P—K3
3 Kt—QB3	Kt—KB3
4 B—Kt5	B—K2
5 Kt—B3	QKt—Q2
6 R—B1	Castles
7 P—K3	P—QKt3

The fashion at the time.

8 P×P	P×P
9 B—Q3	

An attacking post for the Bishop. Later on both 9 B—Kt5 and 9 Q—R4 were tried at this stage. (See next two games.)

9	B—Kt2
10 Castles	P—B4

Black's counter-play on the Q side is taking shape.

11 R—K1
Preparations "behind the front." More promising, however, is 11 Q—K2, Kt—K5; 12 B—KB4, Kt×Kt; 13 P×Kt, P—B5; 14 B—B5, P—Kt3; 15 B×Kt (if 15 B—Kt1, P—QKt4; 16 P—K4, P×P; 17 B×P, B×B; 18 Q×B, Kt—B3; 19 Q—B6, Q—Q4; 20 Q×Q, Kt×Q; 21 B—Q2, KR—B1, and Black's preponderance on the Q side becomes actual); 15 .... Q×B; 16 Kt—K5, Q—K3; 17 B—R6, to White's advantage; or at once 11 Kt—K5.

11 ......   P—B5
At this stage there is much to be said for 11 .... Kt—K5, e.g. 12 B—KB4, Kt×Kt; 13 P×Kt, P—B5; 14 B—B5, P—Kt3; 15 B—Kt1, P—QKt4; 16 P—K4, P×P; 17 B×P, B×B; 18 R×B, Kt—B3; etc.

12 B—Kt1   P—QR3
13 Kt—K5
Pillsbury's idea, with which many resounding successes have been scored.

13 ......   P—Kt4
As 13 .... Kt×Kt; 14 P×Kt, Kt—Q2 (or 14 .... Kt—K1; 15 B×B, Q×B; 16 Kt×P, etc., or 14 .... Kt—K5; 15 B×B, Kt×Kt; 16 B×P ch, and wins); 15 B—B4, Kt—B4; 16 Q—Q2, P—QKt4; 17 QR—Q1, etc., would be awkward for Black, he needs must allow his opponent to erect an imposing structure in the centre.

14 P—B4   R—K1
He wishes to defend the King's field, without having recourse to weakening moves such as .... P—KR3 or .... P—KKt3.

15 Q—B3   Kt—B1
16 Kt—K2
If 16 P—QR3, in order to prevent any gain in space by his adversary, then 16 .... Kt—K5; 17 B×B, R×B; 18 Kt×Kt, P×Kt; 19 B×P (a fatal capture); 19 .... B×B; 20 Q×B, P—B3, winning a piece.

16 ......   Kt—K5
17 B×B   R×B
18 B×Kt   P×B
19 Q—Kt3
If 19 Q—R3, P—B3; 20 Kt—Kt4, B—B1, etc.

19 ......   P—B3
20 Kt—Kt4
Now, thanks to the threat 21 Kt×P ch, White maintains his grip, for if 20 .... P—B4; 21 Kt—R6 ch, K—R1; 22 Kt×P.

20 ......   K—R1
21 P—B5   Q—Q2
22 R—B1
"Taking back," so to speak, his 11th move.

22 ......   R—Q1
23 R—B4   Q—Q3
24 Q—R4   QR—K1
25 Kt—Kt3   B—Q4
26 Kt—B2   Q—B3
Protecting his KP, as well as enabling his QKtP to advance without fear of Kt—QR4 and P—Q5, etc.

27 R—B1
Admirable play.

27 ......   P—Kt5
28 Kt—K2   Q—R5
A false alarm.

29 Kt—Kt4   Kt—Q2
For if 29 .... Q×P; 30 Kt×P.

30 R (B4)—B2   K—Kt1
If 30 .... Q×P; 31 Kt—B4, B—B2; 32 P—Q5 (not 32 Kt—Kt6, B×Kt; 33 P×B, P—R3, with an adequate defence); 32 .... Kt—K4; 33 Kt×P, P×Kt; 34 Q×BP ch, K—Kt1; 35 P—Q6, R—Q2; 36 Kt—K6, and wins.

31 Kt—B1   P—B6
32 P—QKt3   Q—B3
33 P—KR3
In a most astute manner, he prepares a fresh assault.

33 ......   P—QR4
Playing steadily for a decision on the extreme Q wing.

34 Kt—R2   P—R5
35 P—Kt4
In order to open the KKt file.

35 ......   P×P
36 P×P   R—R1
37 P—Kt5   R—R6
Dictated by ambition. Caution demands 37 .... P×P; 38 Q×KtP, Q—B3, etc.

38 Kt—Kt4   B×P
Black's advantage on the Q side is very great, but White has now the lead. Better at once 38 .... K—R1.

39 R—KKt2   K—R1
If 39 .... P×P; 40 Q×P, K—B1; 41 P—B6, etc.

40 P×P   P×P
If 40 .... Kt×P; 41 Kt—K5.

41 Kt×B   R×Kt
42 Kt—R6   R—Kt2
After 42 .... Q—B1 or 42 .... Q—Q4;
43 Q—Kt4 forces mate at KKt8 or KKt7.

43 R×R   K×R
White's attack is giving out, whilst Black
has ponderous threats on the Q side.

44 Q—Kt3 ch
A beautiful surprise!

44 ......   K×Kt
Awaiting the death sentence. But if
44 .... K—B1; 45 Q—KKt8 ch, K—K2;
46 Q×R.

45 K—R1
A waiting move, but the kernel of White's
combination.

45 ......   Q—Q4
Or 45 .... P—B7; 46 R—KKt1, P—B8
(Q); 47 Q—R4 mate.

46 R—KKt1   Q×BP
47 Q—R4 ch   Q—R4
48 Q—B4 ch   Q—Kt4
49 R×Q   P×R
50 Q—Q6 ch
Setting at naught Black's hope of turning
his advanced QBP to account.

50 ......   K—R4
51 Q×Kt   P—B7
Vainly hoping for the miracle: 52 Q—B7
ch, K—R5; 53 Q×R, P—B8 (Q) ch, and
the tables are turned.

52 Q×P mate
A magnificent game endowed with eternal
youth.

365

White	Black
PILLSBURY	MARCO

(Paris, 1900)

*A fine example of the opening, and the
prototype of many others. It well illustrates
Pillsbury's genius for attack.*

1 P—Q4   P—Q4
2 P—QB4   P—K3
3 Kt—QB3   Kt—KB3
4 B—Kt5   B—K2
5 P—K3   Castles
6 Kt—B3   P—QKt3
The *fianchetto* after castling but before
developing the QKt.

7 B—Q3   B—Kt2
8 P×P   P×P
9 Kt—K5
White effects this energetic manœuvre
before castling and moving the QR.

9 ......   QKt—Q2
10 P—B4   P—B4
11 Castles   P—B5
12 B—B2   P—QR3
13 Q—B3   P—Kt4
Parrying 14 Kt×QBP, and proceeding
with his own plan.

14 Q—R3   P—Kt3
Necessary in order to parry the threat
15 Kt×Kt. If 14 .... P—R3; 15 B×P,
etc.

15 P—B5
A fine break-through.

15 ......   P—Kt5
16 P×P   RP×P
17 Q—R4
Singling out Black's weak point (KB6).

17 ......   P×Kt
18 Kt×Kt   Q×Kt
19 R×Kt   P—R4
20 QR—KB1   R—R3
21 B×P
A fresh exploit.

21 ......   P×B
22 R×R ch   B×R
23 R×B ch   K×R
24 Q—R8 ch   K—B2
25 Q—R7 ch   Resigns.

366

White	Black
MARSHALL	KLINE

(New York, 1913)

A brevity in which there is much to admire. The feature of White's play is the logic of its conception, and the economy of means employed in its execution.

1 P—Q4	P—Q4
2 P—QB4	P—K3
3 Kt—QB3	Kt—KB3
4 Kt—B3	B—K2
5 B—Kt5	QKt—Q2
6 P—K3	Castles
7 R—B1	

The *normal position*. Besides the orthodox defence by 7 .... P—QKt3, Black can play 7 .... P—B3; the *Modern Defence*, or 7 .... P—QR3; the *Argentine Defence*, or 7 .... P—KR3; or, a doubtful attempt, 7 .... P—B4.

7	P—QKt3
8 P×P	P×P
9 Q—R4	

A *positional* continuation.

9	B—Kt2

Or 9 .... P—B4, and White proceeds to operate on the Q side (10 Q—B6).

10 B—QR6	B×B
11 Q×B	P—B3

Or 11 .... P—B4; 12 Castles, etc.

12 Castles	Kt—K5
13 B×B	Q×B
14 Q—Kt7	KR—B1
15 Kt×P	Q—Q3
16 R×P	Resigns.

367

White	Black
CAPABLANCA	TARTAKOWER

(London, 1922)

Black succeeds in rehabilitating this strictly orthodox defence (with Queen's Fianchetto), in spite of its bad reputation, by introducing some unexpected turns: the preliminary measure 6 .... P—KR3 (before playing 7 .... P—QKt3) and the sally 9 .... B—K3 (instead of the almost prescribed development of the Bishop at QKt2).

1 P—Q4	Kt—KB3
2 Kt—KB3	P—Q4
3 P—B4	P—K3
4 Kt—B3	B—K2
5 B—Kt5	Castles
6 P—K3	P—KR3

After 6 .... P—QKt3, an energetic line of play for White is found in a game Marshall—Burn, *Paris*, 1900, which went as follows: 7 B—Q3, B—Kt2; 8 P×P, P×P; 9 B×Kt, B×B; 10 P—KR4 (already threatening 11 B×P ch); 10 .... P—Kt3 (if 10 .... P—KR3; 11 P—KKt4, and if 10 .... P—B4; 11 B×P ch, K×B; 12 Kt—Kt5 ch, K—R3; 13 Q—Q3, P—Kt3; 14 P—R5, with fresh threats; best is therefore 10 .... R—K1, with, eventually, ... P—B4); 11 P—R5, R—K1 (or 11 .... P—B4; 12 P×KtP, RP×P; 13 Kt—K5, etc.); 12 P×P, RP×P (better is 12 .... BP×P); 13 Q—B2, Kt—Q2 (too late); 14 B×P, P×B; 15 Q×P ch, B—Kt2 (or 15 .... K—B1; 16 Kt—KKt5, R—K2; 17 Kt—R7 ch, R×Kt; 18 R×R, Q—K1; 19 Q—R6 ch, followed by mate); 16 Kt—KKt5, Q—B3; 17 R—R8 ch, K×R; 18 Q—R7 mate.

7 B—R4   P—QKt3
The delay in playing this component move of the strictly "orthodox" defence has at least the advantage of avoiding the *Marshall Attack*. Black's QKt has not moved yet, and still controls his QR3 and QB3. Known as the *Tartakower Defence*, it is a little disconcerting for White, in his search for a sound and energetic plan.

8 P×P
After any developing move such as 8 B—Q3, or 8 R—B1, or 8 Q—B2, Black can already afford to launch 8 .... P—B4.

8 ......   P×P
Playable also is 8 .... Kt×P; 9 B×B, Kt×B, etc., or 9 B—Kt3, B—Kt2; 10 B—Q3, P—QB4.

9 Q—Kt3
A more compact line of play is 9 B—Q3, P—B4; 10 P×P, P×P, with strong *hanging pawns* in the centre.

9 ......   B—K3
An unusual development of the Bishop (in place of 9 .... B—Kt2).

10 R—Q1   P—B3
In order to bring out the QKt. Playable is, even at once, 10 .... Kt—K5, which White will now try to prevent.

11 Q—B2   Kt—K5

Demonstrating that the Knight can still be unpinned, Black speeds up the rhythm of events.

12 B×B   Q×B
13 Kt×Kt

Accepting the challenge, for after 13 B—Q3, P—KB4, Black has a fortified position in the centre.

13 ......   P×Kt
14 Q×KP

Too passive would be 14 Kt—Q2, P—B4, etc.

14 ......   Q—Kt5 ch
15 Kt—Q2

Or 15 R—Q2, B×P; 16 B—Q3, P—Kt3. Black begins to assert himself on the Q side.

15 ......   Q×KtP

Not 15 .... B×P; 16 P—QKt3.

16 B—Q3   P—Kt3
17 Q—B4   K—Kt2

More astute than 17 .... K—R2; 18 P—KR4, etc.

18 P—KR4   Kt—Q2
19 Kt—K4   Q×RP

He relies on his *phalanx* of passed pawns.

20 P—R5   P—KKt4

And not 20 .... R—R1; 21 P×P, P×P; 22 Q—Q6, Q—Q4; 23 Q—K7 ch, with improved prospects for White.

21 Q—Kt3

Not 21 Kt×P, because of the intermediary check by 21 .... Q—R4 ch, followed by .... Q×Kt.

21 ......   Q—R4 ch
22 K—K2

Establishing the *liaison* between the Rooks.

22 ......   P—KB4

He provokes the sacrifice.

23 Kt×P   P×Kt
24 Q×P ch   K—B2
25 P—R6   R—KKt1
26 Q—R5 ch   K—K2

If instead 26 .... R—Kt3; 27 P—R7, R—R1; 28 R—R1, Q—Q4; 29 P—Kt4, and White's chances are on the up grade.

27 P—R7   R×P

The counter-sacrifice.

28 K—B1

If at once 28 P—R8 (Q), R×Q; 29 Q×R, Q—R7 ch; 30 R—Q2, R×P ch; 31 K×R, Q×R ch, and Black, in addition to two pawns for the exchange, has a violent attack.

28 ......   Q—Q4
29 P—R8 (Q)   R×Q
30 Q×R

Although Black now has only one pawn for the exchange, his attacking position, together with the threatening mass of pawns on the Q side, is such that it requires all of the Cuban's virtuosity to "hold" the position.

30 ......   Q—B6
31 R—Q2   B—Q4

With the threat of 32 .... R×P ch; 33 R×R, Q—Q8 mate.

32 K—K1

The best defence.

32 ......   R—Kt1

Driving the Queen to more propitious regions. More promising is 32 .... R—Kt4, which, incidentally, *overprotects* the isolated KBP.

33 Q—R4 ch

Clearly not 33 R—R7 ch, K—K1, and the Queen is cornered.

33 ......   K—Q3
34 R—B1   B—K3
35 R—B2   P—R4
36 Q—R2 ch   K—K2
37 B—K2   Q—K5
38 K—Q2   P—B4

Necessary, in order to parry White's ingenious threat: 39 P—B3, Q—Q4; 40 B—B4, etc.

39 B—Q3   Q—Kt7
40 Q—R4 ch   Q—Kt4
41 Q×Q ch   R×Q
42 R—QKt1

Threatening 43 P×P, etc.

42 ......   P—KB5

A very strong retort, after which, on White's proposal, the game was given up.

For if now 43 KP×P, R—Q4, etc., to Black's advantage. Best is therefore to give back the exchange as soon as possible by 43 QP×P, Kt×P; 44 R×P, P×P ch; 45 P×P, R—Q4; 46 R×Kt, R×R; 47 R—Kt5, etc., with an automatic draw. Draw.

368

White	*Black*
GRÜNFELD	ALEKHINE

(Carlsbad, 1923)

Black succeeds here in wresting the initiative from his opponent, and in launching a searing offensive. The play, full of beautiful points, both manifest and hidden, is an illustration of Dr. Alekhine's genius for improvisation.

1 P—Q4	Kt—KB3
2 P—QB4	P—K3
3 Kt—KB3	P—Q4
4 Kt—B3	B—K2
5 B—Kt5	QKt—Q2
6 P—K3	Castles
7 R—B1	

The advantage of this basic move is that it renders Black's .... P—B4 more difficult.

7 ......   P—B3

In this, the *normal position of the Queen's Gambit Declined*, Black has a wide choice of moves. He decides on the *modern defence*, which tries to reduce the scope of White's QR.

8 Q—B2

Continuing the *fight for the tempo* (B—Q3 × BP) initiated by his preceding move.

8 ......   P—QR3

Calmly preparing his counter-action (9 .... P × P; 10 B × P, P—QKt4; 11 B—Q3, P—B4, etc.). A premature decision is 8 .... P × P, as illustrated by a game Bogoljubow—Tarrasch, *Hastings*, 1922/3, as follows: 9 B × P, Kt—Q4; 10 B × B, Q × B; 11 Castles, Kt × Kt; 12 Q × Kt, P—QKt3; 13 Q—Q3, R—Q1; 14 Q—K2, P—QB4; 15 B—Kt5, P × P; 16 Kt × P, B—Kt2; 17 R—B7, QR—Kt1; 18 R—Q1, B—Q4; 19 Kt—B6, resigns.

9 P—QR3

Principally to provide fresh employment for his KB. A decision more trenchant is 9 P—QR4, more committal 9 P—B5, more nonchalant 9 B—Q3, and, finally, more simple 9 P × P, KP × P; 10 B—Q3.

9	P—R3
10 B—R4	R—K1
11 B—Q3	P × P

Black has won the *fight for the tempo*.

12 B × P   P—QKt4

More enterprising than 12 .... Kt—Q4; 13 B—Kt3.

13 B—R2   P—B4

At the right moment.

14 R—Q1

Loss of time; better is 14 P × P.

14 ......   P × P

15 Kt × QP

More incisive, but also more hazardous, is 15 P × P.

| 15 ...... | Q—Kt3 |
| 16 B—Kt1 | B—Kt2 |

This possibility alone based on a fine tactical episode—allows Black to complete his development unharmed.

17 Castles

For after 17 KKt × KtP there follows, not 17 .... P × Kt; 18 R × Kt, etc., but 17 .... Q—B3; 18 Kt—Q4, Q × P.

17	QR—B1
18 Q—Q2	Kt—K4
19 B × Kt	B × B
20 Q—B2	P—Kt3
21 Q—K2	Kt—B5
22 B—K4	B—Kt2

Not 22 .... Kt × RP; 23 Q—B3.

23 B × B	Q × B
24 R—B1	P—K4
25 Kt—Kt3	P—K5
26 Kt—Q4	KR—Q1
27 KR—Q1	Kt—K4
28 Kt—R2	Kt—Q6
29 R × R	Q × R
30 P—B3	

In dogmatically proceeding to undermine Black's outpost, he does not allow for the awakening of the latent forces in his opponent's concentric formation.

Better would be 30 Kt—B3, although even then Black's positional advantage is definite.

30 ......   R × Kt

A cataclysm.

31 P × P

Or 31 P × R, B × P ch; 32 K—B1, Kt—B5; 33 Q × KP, Q—B5 ch; 34 K—K1, Kt × P ch; 35 K—Q2, B—K6 ch, and wins.

| 31 ...... | Kt—B5 |
| 32 P × Kt | Q—B5 |

The key to the beautiful combination. White must lose at least a piece.

| 33 Q × Q | R × R ch |
| 34 Q—B1 | B—Q5 ch |

And Black mates next move.

369

White	Black
BOGOLJUBOW	MICHELL

(Margate, 1923)

The pitched battle, announced by White's 17th move (P—K4), causes some weaknesses in his camp. The feature of the game is the admirable manner in which these are exploited by Black.

1	P—Q4	P—Q4
2	P—QB4	P—K3
3	Kt—QB3	Kt—KB3
4	Kt—B3	B—K2
5	B—Kt5	QKt—Q2
6	P—K3	Castles

If 6 .... P—B3; 7 Q—B2 (or 7 R—B1), Kt—K5; 8 Kt × Kt.

| 7 | R—B1 | P—B3 |

As in this *modern defence* Black's QB is blocked in both directions, his strategic aim must be to effect either .... P—QB4 or .... P—K4.

| 8 | Q—B2 | P—KR3 |

Another aspect of the *fight for the tempo.* Playable is 8 .... Kt—K5, etc.

| 9 | B—R4 | P—R3 |
| 10 | P—QR3 | P × P |

Giving up the *fight for the tempo*, which could still be usefully prolonged by 10 .... R—K1.

| 11 | B × P | P—QKt4 |
| 12 | B—R2 | P—B4 |

Seizing the relatively most opportune moment for this liberating advance. If, more passively, 12 .... B—Kt2; 13 B—Kt1, R—K1; 14 Kt—K5, Kt—B1; 15 Castles, etc., White's pressure would become more and more insistent.

| 13 | P × P | B × P |
| 14 | Castles | |

He takes his time. He could have intensified his threats by 14 B—Kt1, Q—Kt3; 15 R—Q1.

| 14 | ...... | B—Kt2 |
| 15 | KR—Q1 | |

White's desire to let both his Rooks join in the fight is comprehensible.

| 15 | ...... | B—K2 |
| 16 | B—Kt1 | P—Kt3 |

Necessary, in view of the threat 17 R × Kt, Q × R; 18 B × Kt. If 16 .... R—K1; 17 Kt—K5.

| 17 | P—K4 | |

If instead, 17 Kt—K5, Q—K1. The text move indicates that White thinks he is progressing.

17	......	K—Kt2
18	B × Kt ch	B × B
19	P—K5	B—K2
20	Kt—Q4	

This momentary masking of the Q file enables Black skilfully to free his game. Clearly White does not wish his KBP to be doubled, but he could have prevented that more comfortably by 20 Q—K2.

| 20 | ...... | Q—Kt3 |
| 21 | Q—K2 | |

An illusion would be 21 KKt × KtP, P × Kt; 22 R × Kt, Q—B3.

21	......	KR—Q1
22	B—K4	B × B
23	Q × B	QR—B1
24	QKt—K2	

Better 24 Kt—B3, but Black already has the better of it.

| 24 | ...... | R × R |
| 25 | R × R | Kt × P |

A very fine conception.

| 26 | Q × Kt ch | B—B3 |
| 27 | Kt × P ch | |

In order to avoid losing a pawn, he must allow some extensive liquidations.

27	......	Q × Kt
28	Q × Q	P × Q
29	R—B7 ch	

By leaving his base, White does not improve his prospects. He could not play 29 R—Kt1, B × P, etc., nor 29 P—QKt3, B—Kt7, etc., but the wisest here or on the next move would be P—KKt3.

29	......	K—Kt1
30	P—KKt4	B × P
31	R—B6	R—Q7
32	R × KP	K—B2
33	R—K3	R—Q8 ch
34	K—Kt2	R—QR8
35	R—B3 ch	K—Kt1
36	Kt—B4	R × P
37	Kt × P	R × R
38	K × R	P—QR4

Although the forces in this Knight *v.* Bishop end game are equal, the dynamic power of Black's united passed pawns is irresistible.

39	K—K4	P—R5
40	K—Q3	K—B2
41	Kt—B4	B—K4
42	Kt—K2	P—R6

This prevents 43 P—B4, on account of

43 .... P—R7, and thus he will with impunity capture the KRP, whereas if at once 42 .... B×P; 43 P—B4, and the Bishop is shut in.

43 Kt—B1	B×P
44 K—B2	K—B3
45 Kt—K2	K—Kt4
46 P—B3	B—K4
47 K—Kt3	P—Kt5

Not 47 .... B—Q3; 48 Kt—B3.

48 K—R2	B—Kt2

Methodical work. Premature would be 48 .... K—R5; 49 P—B4, B—Kt2; 50 P—Kt5, P×P; 51 P×P, K×P; 52 Kt—B1, etc., with a draw in sight.

49 K—Kt3	K—R5
50 Kt—B4	K—Kt6
51 Kt—K6	

After 51 Kt—R5 ch, K×P; 52 Kt×B, K×P, Black would win the Knight for his KRP, and the issue would be settled on the other wing. With the text move, White has a last try for 52 P—Kt5, which is ruthlessly prevented by Black.

51	B—B3
52 Kt—B7	K×P
53 Kt—Q5	B—B6
Resigns	

For after 54 Kt×B, P×Kt; 55 K×RP, K×P; 56 K—Kt3, P—R4, etc., and the K side would now see the decision.

A fine game.

370

White					*Black*

STAHLBERG				MENCHIK

(Lodz, 1938)

A very clear-cut game, in which the woman champion of the world is the victim of diabolical machinations.

1 P—Q4	Kt—KB3
2 P—QB4	P—K3
3 Kt—QB3	P—Q4
4 B—Kt5	QKt—Q2
5 P—K3	B—K2
6 Kt—B3	Castles
7 R—B1	P—B3
8 B—Q3	

Giving up the *fight for the tempo*, in order to complete his K side development as speedily as possible.

8	P×P
9 B×P	Kt—Q4

By this method of unpinning, Black plays for equality. Less easy is a *wing attack*, 9 .... P—Kt4; 10 B—Q3, or, with a similar idea, 9 .... P—KR3; 10 B—R4, P—QKt4; 11 B—Q3, P—R3 (with a view to 12 .... P—B4); 12 P—R4, and Black has difficult problems to solve.

10 B×B	Q×B
11 Castles	

Instead of this lackadaisical continuation, Dr. Alekhine favours the manœuvre 11 Kt—K4, as shown in the following game, Alekhine—Lasker, *Zürich*, 1934: 11 Kt—K4, KKt—B3 (not 11 .... QKt—B3, as he wishes to preserve the option of advancing either the KP or the QBP); 12 Kt—Kt3, P—K4; 13 Castles, P×P; 14 Kt—B5, Q—Q1; 15 Kt (B3)×P, Kt—K4; 16 B—Kt3, B×Kt; 17 Kt×B, Q—Kt3; 18 Q—Q6, Kt (K4)—Q2; 19 KR—Q1, QR—Q1; 20 Q—Kt3, P—Kt3; 21 Q—Kt5, K—R1; 22 Kt—Q6, K—Kt2; 23 P—K4, Kt—KKt1; 24 R—Q3, P—B3; 25 Kt—B5 ch, K—R1; 26 Q×P, resigns.

11	Kt×Kt

If 11 .... KKt—Kt3; 12 B—Kt3.

12 R×Kt	

If 12 P×Kt, P—QB4.

12	P—K4

The turning-point of the contest. Instead of burning her bridges by the text move, Black should have played 12 .... R—Q1, with the idea of regrouping her forces by 13 .... Kt—B1, or of a more efficacious advance of the KP.

13 Q—B2	

An insidious continuation.

A very interesting and much analysed chapter arises from 13 P×P, Kt×P; 14 Kt×Kt, Q×Kt; 15 P—B4, Q—B3 (better than .... Q—K2 or .... Q—K5), and the struggle is, so to speak, three-edged.

13	P×P

This opens the file for White's benefit. More promising would be 13 .... P—K5; 14 Kt—Q2, Kt—B3, etc.

14 P×P	Kt—B3

Protecting, but in a way encumbering the critical sector. Better is 14 .... Kt—Kt3, etc.

15 R—K1	Q—Q3
16 Kt—Kt5	

This escapade sets Black serious problems.

16 ......   Q—B5

A vain effort to restore the situation. Here are some other possibilities: 16 .... P—KR3; 17 Kt×P, etc., or 16 .... Q×P; 17 R—K7, etc., or 16 .... B—Kt5; 17 Q—Kt3, or 16 .... P—KKt3; 17 Q—Kt3, Kt—Q4; 18 B×Kt, P×B; 19 R—B5, etc., or 16 .... B—Q2—the best, for after 17 Q—Kt3, Kt—Kt5, or also after 17 R—B3, P—KKt3; 18 Q—Kt3, Kt—Kt5, Black's game is not without counter-chances.

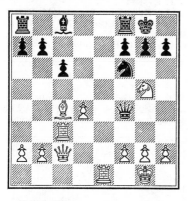

17 Kt×BP

The complications arising from this sacrifice are very exciting.

17 ......   R×Kt

If first 17 .... P—QKt4, then 18 B—Kt3, R×Kt; 19 R—K7, etc.

18 R—B3

Useless would be 18 R—K7, Kt—Q4; 19 R—B3, R×R; 20 R×Q, R—K8 ch; 21 B—B1, Kt×R, etc.; and if 18 Q—Kt3, Kt—Q4.

18 ......   Q—B2

If 18 .... Q—Kt5; 19 R—K8 ch, Kt×R; 20 B×R ch, followed by B—R5. If 18 .... Q—Q3; 19 Q—Kt3, Q—B2; 20 B×R ch, Q×B; 21 R—K8 ch, etc. If 18 .... Q—Kt4; 19 Q—Kt3, Q—Kt3; 20 R—K8 ch, etc.

19 R (B3)—K3

With the principal threat of a mate in two (by 20 R—K8 ch, etc.), besides (e.g. after 19 .... B—Q2, or 19 .... B—Kt5, or 19 .... P—KKt3) 20 R—K7.

19 ......   K—B1

If 19 .... Kt—Q4; 20 B×Kt, P×B; 21 R—K8 ch, winning the Queen.

20 Q×P

Another master-stroke (20 .... Kt×Q; 21 R—K8 mate).

20 ......   B—Kt5

Heroic resistance.

21 Q—R8 ch   Kt—Kt1
22 P—KR3   B—B4

If 22 .... B—Q2; 23 R—K7.

23 B×R   K×B
24 R—KB3   Resigns

Because of the threat 25 P—KKt4, and if 24 .... K—Kt3, then, equally, 25 P—KKt4, B—Q2; 26 Q—R5 mate.

371

White   *Black*
VIDMAR   YATES

(San Remo, 1930)

The gain of several pawns by Black, in spite of attendant dangers, is most original. A hard-fought game, full of subtle points.

1 P—Q4   Kt—KB3
2 P—QB4   P—K3
3 Kt—KB3   P—Q4
4 B—Kt5   QKt—Q2
5 P—K3   B—K2
6 Kt—B3   Castles
7 R—B1   P—B3
8 B—Q3   P—QR3

Preparing for a counter-attack on the Q side.

9 Castles

The simplest. The preventive 9 P—QR4 involves unnecessary commitments. The advance 9 P—B5 lacks proper foundations. The most prosaic is 9 P×P, KP×P; 10 Castles, R—K1; 11 P—KR3, etc.

9 ......   P×P
10 B×P   P—Kt4
11 B—Q3

In order to reply to 11 .... P—Kt5 with 12 Kt—K4, whilst if 11 B—Kt3, P—B4; 12 P—QR4, P—Kt5.

11 ......   P—B4
12 P—QR4

Challenging a decision.

12 ......   P—B5

He counts on the inert but robust mass of his Q side pawns, and refrains from disrupting them by 12 .... P—Kt5, and from dispersing them by 12 .... KtP×P.

13 B—Kt1   Kt—Q4

An eliminating manœuvre. If 13 .... Q—Kt3 (or 13 .... R—Kt1); 14 P×P, P×P; 15 P—K4, etc.

14 B×B   Q×B
15 P×P   Kt×Kt
16 P×Kt   P×P
17 P—K4

White now also tries to assert himself, but the situation in the centre is no longer acute.

17 ......   R—Q1
18 P—K5   B—Kt2
19 Kt—Q2   R—R6

Already aimed at White's weakness at his QB3.

20 P—B4   P—Kt3
21 B—K4   Kt—Kt3
22 B×B   Q×B
23 Q—K1   Kt—Q4
24 Kt—K4   R—R7

As the adverse QBP is overprotected, the Rook amplifies and even changes its target, which now comprises the whole of the seventh rank.

25 Q—R4

Very skilfully, White creates an attack. If 25 R—R1, KR—R1, etc., and if 25 R—Kt1, Kt×QBP.

25 ......   KR—R1
26 R—KB2   K—Kt2
27 QR—B1   Q—K2

Should White's attack fail, the ending is won for Black.

28 Q—Kt3   K—R1
29 Kt—Kt5   K—Kt2
30 Kt—K4   R—R8
31 P—B5

The opening of the KB file becomes an important asset—discounted, however, by the fact that one of the white Rooks is "dead," being pinned.

31 ......   P×P
32 R×P   P—Kt5

A powerful counter-thrust, which takes advantage of the tactical moment when 33 P×P could be refuted by 33 .... KR—R6; 34 Q—Kt5, Q×Q; 35 R×Q, P—B6, and wins.

33 R—B2   R (R1)—R6

On the way to winning a vital pawn.

34 Kt—Q6

Countering, astutely, with the threat 35 Kt—B5 ch.

34 ......   Kt×P

A magnificent reply no less astute, representing, so to speak, a *cross-combination*.

35 Q—Kt4

If 35 Kt—B5 ch, K—B1; 36 Kt×Q, R×R ch; 37 R×R (for if 37 K×R, R—R8 mate); 37 .... Kt—K7 ch; 38 K—B2, Kt×Q; 39 Kt×P ch, BP×Kt; 40 P×Kt, P—Kt6, with an easy win.

35 ......   P—R4
36 Q—B8

Without despairing, White initiates another and very promising action, which Black again masters in a surprising manner.

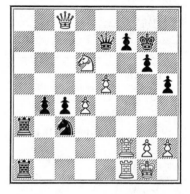

36 ......   Kt—K7 ch

The effect of this very profound offer will be to drive the adverse King into the corner.

37 K—R1

Indeed, if 37 R×Kt, Q—R5 (with the principal threat: 38 .... R×R ch; 39 K×R, R—R8 ch, etc.); 38 P—Kt3 (or 38 R (K2)—KB2, Q×P; 39 Q×P, R×R ch; 40 Q×R, R—R8, and wins the Queen); 38 .... Q×QP ch; 39 R (K2)—KB2 (or 39 K—Kt2, R×R; 40 K×R, R—R8 ch; 41 K—Kt2, Q—Kt8 ch; 42 K—R3, Q—B8 ch; 43 R—Kt2, R—R7, and wins); 39 .... R (R6)—R7, etc.

37 ......   Q—K3
38 Q—Q8

Evidently not 38 R×P ch, Q×R; 39 Kt×Q, R×R mate. And if 38 Q×P,

Q×Q; 39 Kt×Q, R×R ch; 40 R×R,
R—QB6, followed by .... P—Kt6, with a
certain win for Black.

| 38 ...... | R—R1 |

Repelling the invader.

39 Q—Kt5	Kt×P
40 Kt×KBP	Kt—B4
41 Kt—Q6	Kt×Kt
42 P×Kt	P—Kt6
43 P—R3	P—Kt7
44 Q—Kt5	P—B6
45 Q—Kt7 ch	K—Kt1
46 P—Q7	R—Q1
47 Q—Kt4	R×P
48 Q×BP	

By eliminating this pawn, White has
turned the second phase of the battle in his
favour.

48	R×R ch
49 R×R	R—QKt2
50 R—QKt1	R—Kt6
51 Q—B2	R—Kt1
52 Q—B3	

Threatening 53 R×P (not yet 52 R×P,
Q—K8 ch, followed by .... Q—K4 ch and
.... R×R). White fights a losing battle.

52	Q—Kt3
53 Q—B4 ch	K—Kt2
54 Q—B3 ch	K—R2
55 Q—K5	R—Kt2
56 Q—K2	Q—Kt5
57 Q—KB2	Q—B6
58 Q—B1	K—Kt2
59 K—R2	Q—K4 ch
60 K—R1	R—QB2

With the threat of 61 .... Q—K6
(62 R×P, R—B8).

| 61 Q—Q1 | Q—B5 |

Resigns.

372

White   *Black*

CAPABLANCA   ROSSOLIMO

(Paris, 1937)

*Achieving crushing effects from the simplest
means is an art, of which Señor Capablanca
was the high priest.*

1 P—Q4	Kt—KB3
2 P—QB4	P—K3
3 Kt—QB3	P—Q4
4 B—Kt5	B—K2
5 P—K3	Castles
6 Kt—B3	QKt—Q2
7 R—B1	P—B3
8 B—Q3	P—KR3
9 B—R4	P×P
10 B×P	P—QKt4

If 10 .... Kt—Q4; 11 B—Kt3, and if
10 .... P—R3; 11 P—R4, P—QKt4;
12 B—Q3, B—Kt2; 13 Castles, etc., with
advantage to White.

| 11 B—Q3 | P—R3 |

In preparation for 12 .... P—B4.

| 12 P—R4 | |

Trying to force the course of events. If,
more quietly, 12 Castles, P—B4, and if
12 P—K4, Kt×P.

| 12 ...... | P—Kt5 |

After 12 .... B—Kt2; 13 Castles, etc.
White's formation remains preferable. The
best is 12 .... P×P (13 Q×P, R—Kt1;
14 Q—B2, Kt—Q4; 15 B×B, Q×B;
16 Kt×Kt, BP×Kt; 17 Castles, Q—Kt5,
etc.).

| 13 Kt—K4 | |

Disdaining the opportunist continuation
13 B×Kt, followed by Kt—K4.

| 13 ...... | Kt×Kt |

Obtaining substantial exchanges, which,
however, White offsets by lucid strategy.
After 13 .... Q—Kt3; 14 Q—B2, White's
position remains preferable.

14 B×B	Kt×P
15 B×Q	Kt×Q
16 K×Kt	R×B
17 R×P	B—Kt2

He could have simplified more discreetly
by 17 .... P—K4.

18 R—B7	B×Kt ch
19 P×B	Kt—Kt3
20 R—B6	

Not 20 R—Kt7, Kt×P; 21 R×KtP,
Kt—B4, equalising.

| 20 ...... | Kt×P |

After 20 .... Kt—Q4; 21 K—Q2,
P—QR4; 22 R—Q1, White holds all the
trumps.

| 21 K—B2 | |

Not 21 B—B2, Kt×P ch; 22 K—B1,
P—Kt6, etc.

21 ......   KR—Kt1
Or 21 .... KR—QB1; 22 R×R ch,
R×R ch; 23 K—Kt3, Kt—Kt3; 24 B×P,
and, in spite of the reduced material, White's
advantage is definite.

22 R—R1   P—Kt6 ch
23 K—B1
Far more astute than 23 K—Kt1, after
which 23 .... R—Kt5; 24 R×RP, R×R;
25 B×R, P—K4; 26 P×P, R—R5;
27 K—B1, Kt—B4, etc., Black would gain
the *tempo* to create counter-chances.

23 ......   R—Kt5
A more active defence than 23 ....
R—QB1; 24 R×R ch, R×R ch; 25 K—Kt1,
etc.

24 B×P   Kt—Kt3
Parrying the threat 25 R—B4.

25 K—Q2
Positional judgment: White's advantage is
now both *static* (Black's weak QKtP) and
dynamic (greater activity of White's King).

25 ......   P—K4
26 P×P   Kt—B5 ch
27 K—B3   Kt×P (K4)
28 R—B5   R—Kt3
29 B—Q3
This magical turn breaks down all resistance (e.g. 29 .... R—K1; 30 R×Kt, R×R;
31 R—R8 ch, etc.).

29 ......   Resigns.

373
White   *Black*
SCHLECHTER   MARCO
(Monte Carlo, 1904)

*In this game Black persistently tries to
block up the game, first on the Q side, then on
the K side, and finally in the centre. But he
finds his intentions thwarted at every turn,
first by 8 P—B5 (a hazardous advance), then
by the temporary sacrifice 15 B×P (winning
a pawn), and finally the double sacrifice
27 R×B and 28 Kt×P—the break-through.*

1 P—Q4   P—Q4
2 P—QB4   P—K3
3 Kt—QB3   Kt—KB3
4 B—Kt5   B—K2
5 P—K3   Castles
6 Kt—B3   QKt—Q2
7 R—B1   P—QR3
This later became known as the *Swiss*

Defence, sometimes also the *Argentine
Defence.* Its object is (e.g. against the slow
8 P—QR3) to free Black's game swiftly by
8 .... P—KR3; 9 B—R4, P×P; 10 B×P,
P—QKt4; 11 B—K2, B—Kt2; 12 Castles,
P—B4, etc.

8 P—B5
A vain attempt to blockade Black's
position. Simplest here is 8 P×P.

8 ......   P—Kt4
After this timid reply White's plan
succeeds. Over-hasty would be 8 ....
P—K4; 9 P×P, Kt—Kt5; 10 B×B, Q×B;
11 Kt×P, etc. The right method of coping
with White's intentions is 8 .... P—B3;
9 B—Q3, P—QKt3; 10 P—QKt4, P—QR4;
11 P—QR3, RP×P; 12 RP×P, P×P;
13 KtP×P, R—R6; 14 Castles. Q—R4, and
Black has an equal share in the struggle.

9 P—QKt4   P—B3
10 B—Q3   P—QR4
11 P—QR3   R—K1
Now that 11 .... P×P; 12 P×P would
not help to free Black's game, he tries his
luck in the centre.

12 Castles   Kt—R4
Of no value would be 12 .... P—K4;
13 QP×P, Kt—Kt5, because of 14 B—KB4.
That is why Black tries this unpinning
manœuvre on the wing. If, by way of
preparation, 12 .... P—R3, Black's position
remains laborious after 13 B—KB4 (not
13 B—R4, Kt—R4); 13 .... Kt—R4;
14 B—K5. The least evil would therefore
be 12 .... B—Kt2, or first 12 .... P×P;
13 P×P, B—Kt2.

13 B×B   Q×B
14 Kt—K5
A double threat (at QB6 and KR5).

14 ......   Kt×Kt
15 B×P ch
An instructive episode by which White
wins a valuable pawn (if 15 .... K×B;
16 Q×Kt ch, K—Kt1; 17 P×Kt), whereas
after 15 P×Kt, P—Kt3, Black has seen the
worst.

15 ......   K—B1
16 Q×Kt
Not 16 P×Kt, P—Kt3, with the twofold
task of guarding his own Knight and
imprisoning the adverse Bishop.

16 ......   Kt—B5
17 B—Q3
Thanks to this final point, which threatens
an almost smothered mate, White preserves
the spoils.

17	Q—B3
18 B×Kt	KtP×B
19 P—Kt5	

Counteracting Black's intention to keep the position closed by 19 .... P×P; 20 P×P, R—Kt1; 21 R—Kt1, B—Q2, etc.

| 19 ...... | B—Q2 |

After 19 .... P×P; 20 Kt×KtP, soon to be followed by Kt—Q6, White's Knight, anchored on the sixth rank, would exert an overwhelming influence. If 19 .... P—K4, White plays, not 20 QP×P, R×P; 21 Q—R8 ch, K—K2; 22 P×P, B—Kt2; 23 Q—R3, B×P, with good prospects for Black, but 20 KtP×P.

| 20 P×P | B×P |
| 21 R—Kt1 | |

An enduring base of action.

21	P—Kt3
22 Q—R6 ch	K—K2
23 R—Kt6	K—Q2

Or, forcing the exchange of Queens, 23 .... R—R1; 24 Q—B4, Q×Q; 25 P×Q, K—Q2; 26 KR—Kt1, and White still has a won game.

| 24 Q—R3 | |

The threat is eventually 25 P—K4, P×P; 26 P—Q5.

| 24 ...... | Q—Kt4 |

After 24 .... R—R1; 25 Q—Kt3 leads to fresh trouble for Black, e.g. 25 .... Q—K2; 26 KR—Kt1, R—QR2; 27 R×B, K×R; 28 R—Kt6 ch, K—Q2; 29 Kt—Kt5, P—B6 (seeking some counter-chance); 30 Kt×R, P—B7; 31 P—B6 ch (but not 31 R—Kt7 ch, K—K1; 32 Q—Kt8 ch, Q—Q1; 33 R—K7 ch, K×R; 34 Kt—B6 ch, K—B1; 35 Q×Q ch, K—Kt2, and the situation is suddenly reversed); 31 .... K—K1; 32 R—Kt8 ch, Q—Q1; 33 R×Q ch, K×R; 34 Q—Q6 ch, K—K1; 35 Q—B5, and wins.

| 25 KR—Kt1 | R—R1 |
| 26 Q—B3 | P—B4 |

After this the storm breaks, but after 26 .... Q—B4; 27 Q×Q, KtP×Q (if 27 .... KP×Q; 28 Kt×P, winning another pawn); 28 P—R3, etc., Black's cause is lost.

| 27 R×B | |

Brilliant and sound.

| 27 ...... | K×R |
| 28 Kt×P | |

The decisive breach.

| 28 ...... | QR—QKt1 |

Or 28 .... P×Kt; 29 R—Kt6 ch, K—B2; 30 Q×QP, and Black is defenceless.

| 29 Kt—B4 dis ch | |

The only correct "discovery," and the Knight has much to say (Kt×KP ch) in the sequel.

| 29 ...... | K—Q2 |

Or 29 .... K—B2; 30 Kt×P ch, K—Q2; 31 Q—Q5 ch, K—K2; 32 Q—Q6 ch.

| 30 R—Kt7 ch | |

A final touch; White has no need to capture the Rook in order to win.

30	R×R
31 Q×R ch	K—K1
32 P—B6	Resigns

(32 .... Q—Q1; 33 P—B7, etc.)

374

| *White* | *Black* |
| ROSSOLIMO | CUKIERMAN |

(Paris, 1937)

Black plays with fire, by venturing with his Queen within the enemy lines, and loses in a very original manner.

1 P—Q4	P—Q4
2 P—QB4	P—K3
3 Kt—QB3	Kt—KB3
4 B—Kt5	B—K2
5 P—K3	QKt—Q2
6 Kt—B3	Castles
7 R—B1	P—QR3
8 P×P	

This simplifying method (known as the *Carlsbad Variation*) was played a few times in the Capablanca-Alekhine match, and is not without guile.

| 8 ...... | P×P |
| 9 B—Q3 | P—B3 |

Sooner or later necessary, unless it is preferred—

(*a*) To indulge in manœuvres behind the front: 9 .... R—K1; 10 Q—B2, Kt—B1, etc., or

(*b*) To maltreat the Q side by 9 .... P—B4; 10 P×P, Kt×P; 11 Castles, Kt×B (or 11 .... Kt—K3; 12 B—R4, etc.); 12 Q×Kt, B—K3; 13 Kt—Q4, and Black's isolated QP, well and truly stopped, ensures for White a lasting advantage.

10 Q—B2
A sound positional manœuvre. If at once 10 Castles, then Black equalises by 10 .... Kt—K5 (e.g. 11 B×B, Kt×Kt, etc., or 11 B×Kt, B×B, etc., but by no means 11 Kt×Kt, P×Kt; 12 B×B, Q×B, with a *fork*).

10 ......   R—K1
A good plan, vacating the KB square for the QKt. More doubtful would be 10 .... P—R3; 11 B—R4, and the King's defences are none too secure.

11 Castles   Kt—B1
Continuation of the intended plan. An unfortunate attempt would be 11 .... P—R3; 12 B—KB4 (more subtle than 12 B—R4); 12 .... Kt—R4 (in the mistaken belief that he can get rid of the troublesome Bishop); 13 Kt×P (a painful surprise); 13 .... Kt×B (for if 13 .... P×Kt; 14 B—B7, "mating" the Queen); 14 Kt×Kt, and White has won a sound pawn: an opening trap which is well worth knowing, as even experienced masters have at times been caught by it.

12 Kt—K5
Bold play. A *positional plan* would be 12 R—Kt1, to be followed by P—QKt4, P—QR4, P—Kt5, etc., engineering a *minority attack* (two pawns against three). A more dilatory method of carrying out the same general idea is 12 P—QR3 or 12 P—QR4. In reply, Black can play 12 .... Kt—K5, or even 12 .... Kt—R4, etc.

12 ......   B—Q3
Even here, unpinning by 12 .... Kt—K5 could well be effected, e.g. 13 B×B, Q×B; 14 Kt×Kt, P×Kt; 15 B—B4 (for if, unheeding, 15 B×P, there follows 15 .... P—B3; 16 Q—Kt3 ch, B—K3, and Black wins a piece); 15 .... B—K3, etc., with an even game.
Another way of parrying promptly the growing danger is 12 .... Kt—Kt5.

13 P—B4
An imposing edifice, which Black misjudged, thinking he could exploit the weakness at K3.

13 ......   B—K2
14 P—KR3   Kt—R4
More aggressive than 14 .... KKt—Q2.

15 B×B   Q×B
16 R—B3
Guarding the KP against the possible threat of 16 .... P—B3.

16 ......   Q—R5
An optimistic Queen. Note that after 16 .... P—B3; 17 Kt—Kt4, B×Kt; 18 P×B, Black's KKt has no move.

17 P—KKt4
Impressive strategy.

17 ......   P—B3
The return of the Knight 17 .... Kt—B3; is called for.

18 B×P ch
A terrible shock.

18 ......   Kt×B
Compulsory acceptance, for if 18 .... K—R1; 19 Kt—B7 mate.

19 Kt—Kt6
Winning the erring Queen and the game.

375
White	Black
LASKER	CAPABLANCA

(Match, Havana, 1921)

This game is a triumph of logic in chess. In the transition to the middle game, Black succeeds in creating some minute weaknesses in White's position. The remainder of the game is an object lesson in skill and patience, culminating in an end game of rare precision and beauty.

1 P—Q4	P—Q4
2 P—QB4	P—K3
3 Kt—QB3	Kt—KB3
4 B—Kt5	B—K2
5 P—K3	Castles
6 Kt—B3	QKt—Q2
7 Q—B2	

The advantage of this move (introduced by Marshall) is that R—Q1, or even Castles QR, becomes possible. Its drawback is that Black's 7 .... P—B4 may now be more effective than it is against 7 R—B1.

7 ......   P—B4
An incisive reply. More cautious is 7 .... P—B3, e.g. 8 R—Q— (or 8 R—B1, reverting to well-trodden paths); 8 .... R—K1; 9 P—QR3, P—QR3; 10 B—Q3,

P—R3; 11 B—R4, P—QKt4; 12 P×QP, etc., tending to equality.

8 R—Q1

Here 8 Castles, would be too risky (8 .... Q—R4, etc.). After 8 BP×P the best reply is 8 .... Kt×P (not 8 .... KP×P; 9 P×P, Kt×P; 10 B—K2, nor 8 .... BP×P; 9 Kt×P, Kt×P; 10 B×B, Q×B; 11 Kt×Kt, P×Kt; 12 R—B1, Kt—B3; 13 Q—QB5, Q×Q; 14 R×Q, B—K3; 15 B—K2, etc.); 9 B×B, Q×B; 10 Kt×Kt, P×Kt; 11 P×P (better than 11 B—Q3, P×P; 12 Kt×P, Q—Kt5 ch; 13 Q—Q2, Kt—K4, etc.); 11 .... Kt×P; 12 B—K2, B—K3, with an even issue in sight.

| 8 ...... | Q—R4 |
| 9 B—Q3 | P—KR3 |

An important preventive measure against the threat 10 B×P ch, etc.

| 10 B—R4 | BP×P |

The most convenient continuation is 10 .... QP×P; 11 B×P, P—R3 (if 11 .... Kt—Kt3; 12 B—K2, etc., with an advantage in space for White); 12 P×P, Kt×P, and Black has freed his game.

| 11 KP×P | |

More stubborn than 11 KKt×P.

11	P×P
12 B×P	Kt—Kt3
13 B—QKt3	B—Q2
14 Castles	QR—B1
15 Kt—K5	

Staking all on an attack. The sound 15 Q—K2 would prevent Black's next move.

| 15 ...... | B—Kt4 |

Black looks after the free deployment of his forces. Good is also 15 .... KR—Q1, with possibly 16 .... B—K1.

| 16 KR—K1 | QKt—Q4 |
| 17 KB×Kt | |

Simplification. White could retain the initiative by 17 QB×Kt, e.g. 17 .... Kt×B; 18 Kt—Kt6, P×Kt (or 18 .... KR—K1; 19 R×P, etc.); 19 R×P, K—R2; 20 R×B, etc., or 17 .... B×B (best); 18 B×Kt, P×B; 19 Q—B5, etc., with a promising attack.

17	Kt×B
18 B×B	Kt×B
19 Q—Kt3	B—B3
20 Kt×B	P×Kt
21 R—K5	Q—Kt3
22 Q—B2	KR—Q1
23 Kt—K2	

Not, of course, 23 R—QB5, R×P, etc.

| 23 ...... | R—Q4 |
| 24 R×R | |

It would be better to avoid this exchange, which rounds up the adverse pawns, by playing 24 R—K3, e.g. 24 .... Kt—B4; 25 R—QKt3, Q—Q1; 26 R—Kt4, and if 26 .... P—B4; 27 R—B4.

24	BP×R
25 Q—Q2	Kt—B4
26 P—QKt3	

Better, here or on the next move, 26 P—KKt3.

| 26 ...... | P—KR4 |
| 27 P—KR3 | P—R5 |

A blockade is gradually taking shape.

28 Q—Q3	R—B3
29 K—B1	P—Kt3
30 Q—Kt1	

More useful would be 30 Q—Q2.

| 30 ...... | Q—Kt5 |
| 31 K—Kt1 | P—R4 |

A *minority attack.*

| 32 Q—Kt2 | P—R5 |
| 33 Q—Q2 | Q×Q |

Skilful liquidation.

34 R×Q	P×P
35 P×P	R—Kt3
36 R—Q3	

Not 36 R—Kt2, R—Kt5, attacking two isolated pawns.

36	R—R3
37 P—KKt4	P×P e.p.
38 P×P	

After 38 Kt×P 38 .... R—R8 ch; 39 K—Kt2, Kt—Q3; followed by R—QKt8.

| 38 ...... | R—R7 |
| 39 Kt—B3 | R—QB7 |

Threatening 40 .... Kt×QP.

40 Kt—Q1	Kt—K2
41 Kt—K3	R—B8 ch
42 K—B2	Kt—B3
43 Kt—Q1	R—Kt8

Avoiding the trap: 43 .... Kt—Kt5; 44 R—Q2, R—Kt8; 45 Kt—Kt2, R×Kt; 46 R×R, Kt—Q6 ch; 47 K—K2, Kt×R; 48 K—Q2, recovering the piece.

| 44 K—K2 | |

The loss of a pawn is inevitable, e.g. 44 K—K1, Kt—R4, or 44 K—K3, Kt—Kt5.

44	R×P
45 K—K3	R—Kt5
46 Kt—B3	Kt—K2

Threatening to win a second pawn by 47 .... Kt—B4 ch.

47 Kt—K2	Kt—B4 ch
48 K—B2	P—Kt4
49 P—Kt4	Kt—Q3
50 Kt—Kt1	Kt—K5 ch
51 K—B1	R—Kt8 ch
52 K—Kt2	R—Kt7 ch
53 K—B1	R—B7 ch
54 K—K1	R—QR7
55 K—B1	K—Kt2
56 R—K3	K—Kt3
57 R—Q3	P—B3
58 R—K3	K—B2
59 R—Q3	K—K2
60 R—K3	K—Q3
61 R—Q3	R—B7 ch
62 K—K1	R—KKt7
63 K—B1	R—QR7
64 R—K3	P—K4
65 R—Q3	P × P
66 R × P	

If 66 Kt—K2, R—Q7; 67 R × R, Kt × R ch; 68 K—K1, Kt—Kt6, etc., or 67 R × P, Kt—Kt6 ch; 68 K—B2, R × Kt ch; 69 K × Kt, K—K4, followed by 70 .... P—Q5, with an easy win.

66	K—B4
67 R—Q1	P—Q5
68 R—B1 ch	K—Q4
Resigns	

(69 R—Q1, Kt—Kt6 ch; 70 K—K1, R—KKt7, etc.)
An impressive victory.

376

White	Black
ATKINS	RUBINSTEIN

(London, 1922)

The feature of this game is White's skilful conduct of the attack, which, at times hanging by a thread and kept up by problem-like manœuvres, succeeds in the face of many dangers.

1 P—Q4	Kt—KB3
2 Kt—KB3	P—K3
3 P—B4	P—Q4
4 B—Kt5	QKt—Q2
5 P—K3	B—K2
6 Kt—B3	Castles
7 B—Q3	

Speeding up the development of the K side, and spurning ultra-refined stratagems such as 7 R—B2, 7 Q—B2, or 7 P—QR3.

7	P × P

Stressing at once White's loss of a *tempo*. Good is 7 .... P—B4.

8 B × P	P—QR3

Or 8 .... P—QKt3; 9 Castles, B—Kt2; 10 Q—K2, etc., or 8 .... P—B4; 9 Castles, with a concentric development.

9 P—QR4	P—B4

Or 9 .... P—QKt3; 10 Castles, B—Kt2; 11 Q—K2, etc.

10 Castles	Q—R4

Less agitated would be 10 .... P—QKt3; 11 Q—K2, B—Kt2; 12 KR—Q1, Q—B2, etc.

11 Q—K2	P × P
12 P × P	Kt—Kt3
13 B—Q3	R—Q1

In connection with the next two moves, this is a sound stratagem, by which liaison between the various units is established behind the front, whilst initiating a pressure against the opposing isolated QP.

14 KR—Q1	B—Q2
15 Kt—K5	B—K1
16 Q—K3	KKt—Q4
17 Q—Kt3	B × B

He prefers simplification to the complications of 17 .... P—B3; 18 Q—R3.

18 Q × B	Kt × Kt

Here again Black would be exposed to manifold dangers after 18 .... P—B3; 19 Q—R4, P × Kt; 20 Q × P ch.

19 P × Kt	Kt—Q4

For the third time the fork 19 .... P—B3 would lead to disappointment after 20 Q—R4, P × Kt; 21 B × P ch, etc. Too dangerous also would be 19 .... Q × BP; 20 QR—B1, etc. That is why Black prefers to bring his reserve cavalry to the threatened wing, whilst the text move also eliminates the interim threat of 20 Kt × P.

20 Q—R4	

If at once 20 P—QB4, Black consolidates his position by 20 .... P—R3 (not 20 .... Kt—B3; 21 Kt × P).

20	Kt—B3
21 P—QB4	

The attack by 21 Kt—Kt4, Kt × Kt; 22 B × P ch would have no scope after 22 .... K—R1; 23 B—B2 dis ch, Kt—R3, and all is safe.

21	P—R3
22 Q—Kt3	

Preventing 22 .... Q—B6, etc.

22	QR—B1
23 B—B2	B—B3
24 Q—K3	

Preventing 24 .... B—K5, and preparing 25 R—R3 (over-hasty would be 24 R—R3, R×P).

24	P—QKt3
25 R—R3	B—R1
26 Q—B4	

Preparing to evacuate the third rank for the QR, a large-scale manœuvre which must allow for trouble from the other side.

26	P—QKt4

Taking advantage of the tactical moment (when neither 27 RP×P nor 27 BP×P can be played) to provide a retreat for his Queen.

27 R—R3

Ambitious. But neither 27 R—KKt3, K—B1, etc., nor 27 P—B5, QR×P (28 P×R, R×R ch; 29 B×R, Q—K8 mate) would serve White's cause.

27	P×BP

Had Black foreseen his opponent's deep machinations, he would have given up the exchange by 27 .... QR×P; 28 Kt×R, P×Kt.

28 R×P

A brilliant combination.

28	R—B4

An ingenious parry. Fatal would be 28 .... P×R; 29 Q×Kt, also 28 .... Q—Q4; 29 P—B3, etc.

29 R—R3

Avoiding the following shoals:
(a) 29 P×R, R×R ch; 30 B×R, Q—K8 mate.
(b) 29 R—R8 ch, K×R; 30 Kt×P ch, K—Kt1; 31 Kt×R, R—B1; 32 Kt×P, Q—Q4, and Black wins.
(c) 29 R×Kt, R×Kt; 30 Q×R, Q×Q; 31 P×Q, R×R ch; 32 B×R, P×R; 33 B—B2, P×P, etc., to Black's advantage.

29	QR—Q4

Restoring the threat of 30 .... R×P. A false hope would be 29 .... B—K5, as White would not reply 30 B×B, R×Kt, etc., but 30 R—KKt3, R×P; 31 R—Kt1, QR—Q4; 32 P—R3, with the better game.

30 K—B1

The King defends himself, whilst 30 P—Kt3 or 30 P—B3 would be no real help against the threat of 30 .... R×P; 31 R×R, Q—K8 ch.

30	Q—Kt3
31 R—KKt3	R×P

There is no saving clause. If 31 .... K—B1; 32 R×P, K×R; 33 Q—Kt5 ch, K—B1; 34 Q×Kt, Q—B2; 35 P—R4, etc., and White must win.

32 R×R	Q×R
33 Q×Kt	Q—R8 ch
34 K—K2	B—B6 ch

Of five ways of capturing, only one is right.

35 P×B	Resigns.

377

White	Black
BOTVINNIK	VIDMAR

(Nottingham, 1936)

An old strategic motif in a new guise. Three strong points in Black's position (Q5, K6, KB7) are successively demolished on the Pillsbury plan (Kt—K5, followed by P—KB4), laying bare the heart of the hostile fortress. A beautiful game.

1 P—QB4	P—K3
2 Kt—KB3	P—Q4
3 P—Q4	Kt—KB3
4 B—Kt5	B—K2
5 Kt—B3	Castles
6 P—K3	QKt—Q2
7 B—Q3	P—B4
8 Castles	BP×P

He speculates on the isolation of White's QP. A more sober plan—seeking first to develop his own Q side—is 8 .... QP×P; 9 B×P, P—QR3.

9 KP×P	P×P
10 B×P	Kt—Kt3

With the intention of establishing a permanent control of his Q4, but here again 10 .... P—QR3 is the wiser plan.

11 B—Kt3

More effective than 11 B—Q3.

11	B—Q2

Too slow in development. The immediate unpinning on the K side by 11 .... Kt—R4 is more to the point.

12 Q—Q3

Intending to reply to 12 .... KKt—Q4 with 13 B—B2, as after 12 Q—K2, KKt—Q4; 13 B×B, Kt×B; 14 Kt—K5, R—B1, the games would be even.

12 ......   QKt—Q4
13 Kt—K5   B—B3
14 QR—Q1

More ambitious than 14 Kt×B, P×Kt.

14 ......   Kt—QKt5

Instead of this optimistic expedition, he should have consolidated by 14 .... R—B1, and if then 15 Q—R3, Kt×Kt; 16 P×Kt, B—K5.

15 Q—R3   B—Q4

Parrying the new threat of 16 Kt×P, which, however, he could have done more incisively by 15 .... KKt—Q4.

16 Kt×B   QKt×Kt
17 P—B4

As a result of the skirmishes in the centre, White has preserved his outpost and his powerful KB. The text move turns these potential assets into a concrete advantage.

17 ......   R—B1

Or 17 .... P—KKt3; 18 B—R6, R—K1; 19 P—Kt4.

18 P—B5

In a twinkling the KB file has become a powerful base of action.

18 ......   P×P
19 R×P   Q—Q3

This loses irrevocably. A very elegant "losing variation" is 19 .... Kt—QKt5; 20 P—R3, Kt—B3; 21 B×Kt, B×B; 22 Q×P ch, K×Q; 23 R—R5 ch, K—Kt1; 24 Kt—Kt6, B×P ch; 25 K—R1, and Black cannot prevent R—R8 mate. The most stubborn defence is furnished by 19 .... R—B2, after which, however, White increases the pressure by 20 QR—KB1.

20 Kt×P

A well-calculated *disrupting sacrifice*.

20 ......   R×Kt
21 QB×Kt   B×B
22 R×Kt

Recovering his piece with advantage, and more incisively than by 22 B×Kt.

22 ......   Q—B3
23 R—Q6

Ruthless. After 23 R—Q7, R—B1, Black could hold out a little longer.

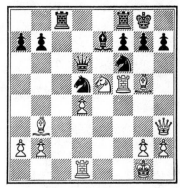

Position after 19 .... Q—Q3

23 ......   Q—K1

Not 23 .... Q×R; 24 Q×R ch, nor 23 .... Q—B2; 24 B×R ch.

24 R—Q7   Resigns.

378

White	*Black*
ALATORZEV	CAPABLANCA

(Moscow, 1935)

Once again, simplicity backed by energy, logic coupled with elegance, and lucidity together with economy of means, have a prodigious cumulative effect.

1 P—Q4   Kt—KB3
2 P—QB4   P—K3
3 Kt—QB3   P—Q4
4 B—Kt5   B—K2

By countering the pin at once, Black is able to reply to 5 P×P by Kt×P, whereas after 4 .... QKt—Q2 White can obtain a favourable variation by 5 P×P, P×P; 6 P—K3 (but not 6 Kt×P, because of the well-known trap 6 .... Kt×Kt; 7 B×Q, B—Kt5 ch, and wins).

5 P—K3   Castles
6 P×P

After this exchange, Black can speedily free his position. 6 Kt—B3 is indicated.

6 ......   Kt×P

He refuses to help the opponent's intentions by 6 .... P×P; 7 B—Q3, etc. Black already begins to take the initiative, stressing his superiority on the Q side.

7 B × B
This fresh exchange is forced.

7 ......   Q × B
An ideal post for the Queen, from which she will support the early advance .... P—QB4.

8 Kt—B3
Inconsistent. His 6th move foreshadowed the occupation of the QB file, and he should now play 8 R—B1 (if then 8 .... Kt × Kt; 9 R × Kt).

8 ......   Kt × Kt
Blocking the QB file to his own advantage, which more than compensates him for the reinforcement of White's centre.

9 P × Kt   P—QKt3
Opening the long diagonal. Every move by Black is lucid, logical and profound.

10 B—K2   B—Kt2
11 Castles   P—QB4
He now has the *strategic initiative*. If, instead, 11 .... Kt—Q2, there follows 12 Kt—Q2, with a view to disputing the benefits of the long diagonal by 13 B—B3.

12 Kt—K5
There would be no compensation for yielding territory by 12 Kt—Q2, because of 12 .... Kt—B3; 13 B—B3, QR—B1, and, within the line of his defences, Black will bring his shock troops to the critical sectors.

12 ......   Kt—B3
This tardy development is not too late, as the opposing Knight must take notice of it.

13 Kt × Kt
Practically forced, as in this case the *Pillsbury Formation* by 13 P—KB4 can be refuted by 13 .... Kt × Kt; 14 BP × Kt, Q—Kt4, etc. After the text move the white King is without his natural protector.

13 ......   B × Kt
14 B—B3   QR—B1
15 P—QR4   P × P
16 BP × P   P—Kt3
Anticipatory caution—he takes advantage of the lull to provide a flight square for his King, before delivering the final assault on the other wing.

17 B × B   R × B
18 Q—Q3
It would avail him nothing to contest the open QB file: 18 Q—Q2, KR—B1; 19 KR—B1, Q—B2, and Black has the last word.

18 ......   Q—Kt2
Tactical meaning: in reply to 19 P—R5, he will play 19 .... P—QKt4. Strategic meaning: occupation of the long diagonal.

19 KR—Kt1   KR—B1
20 P—R3
He still cannot play 20 P—R5, P—QKt4; 21 P—R3 (for if 21 Q × P, Q × Q, etc., or 21 R × P, R—B8 ch, etc.); 21 .... P—QR3, and Black has a well-secured lead.

20 ......   P—QR3
21 Q—R3   R—B7
Marking the decisive stage by this irruption on the *seventh rank*. If, instead, 21 .... Q—B2; 22 Q—Kt3, fixing the hostile QKtP, whilst now, after 22 Q—Kt3, Black regroups his forces by 22 .... KR—B3, followed by .... Q—B2.

22 Q—Q6
An interesting but belated demonstration. Relatively best would be 22 R—QB1.

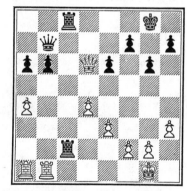

22 ......   R × P
The crowning glory! A splendid sacrifice.

23 Q—Kt3
If 23 K × R, R—B7 ch; 24 K—K1 (or 24 K—Kt3, R × P ch, etc.); 24 .... Q × P; 25 Q—Kt8 ch, K—Kt2; 26 Q—K5 ch, P—B3, cutting short any "spite checks" by the opponent; and if 23 P—Q5, R (B1)—B7 decides. The text move hopes for 23 .... KR—B7; 24 Q × R, R × Q; 25 K × R, and the struggle would only begin.

23 ......   R—K7
      Resigns
One of the finest games of modern times.

379

White	Black
STAHLBERG	AITKEN

(Stockholm, 1937)

In the following game White indulges in too much manœuvring on the Q side, and Black very skilfully takes advantage of the fact by a beautiful diversion on the opposite wing.

1 P—Q4	P—Q4
2 P—QB4	P—K3
3 Kt—KB3	Kt—KB3
4 Kt—B3	B—K2
5 B—Kt5	Castles

Having already provided against the pin by his preceding move, he could have played 5 .... Kt—K5 at once.

6 P—K3	Kt—K5

The *Atkins, or Lasker Variation*, which was frequently played in two important matches Marshall-Lasker (1907) and Marshall-Capablanca (1909), and proved to be sound but barren. Black can also first play 6 .... P—KR3, and if 7 B—R4, only then 7 .... Kt—K5.

7 B×B	Q×B
8 Q—B2	

A more ancient treatment is 8 P×P, Kt×Kt (forced); 9 P×Kt, P×P; 10 Q—Kt3, after which, however, Black has several adequate lines of defence, namely 10 .... P—B3, or 10 .... Q—Q3, or, chiefly, 10 .... R—Q1; 11 P—B4 (a second edition of the Queen's Gambit); 11 .... Kt—B3; 12 P×P, Q—Kt5 ch, etc., with simplification.

8	P—QB3

He could have eased the tension in the centre by an exchange of Knights, but prefers to commit himself in the centre. A game Bogoljubow-Spielmann (match, 1932) ran as follows: 8 .... Kt×Kt; 9 Q×Kt (more scientific than 9 P×Kt); 9 .... P—QB3; 10 B—Q3, P×P; 11 B×P, P—QKt3; 12 P—QKt4, P—QR4; 13 P—Kt5, P×P; 14 B×KtP, B—Kt2; 15 Castles KR, B×Kt; 16 P×B, Q—Kt4 ch, and White resigns (because of 17 .... Q×B).

9 B—Q3	

More lively play results from 9 Kt×Kt, P×Kt; 10 Kt—Q2 (or 10 Q×P, Q—Kt5 ch; 11 Kt—Q2, Q×KtP; 12 Q—Kt1, etc.); 10 .... P—KB4; 11 P—B5, etc.

9	P—KB4

A deferred *stonewall*.

10 Castles KR	Kt—Q2
11 QR—K1	P—QKt3

The demonstration 11 .... R—B3, followed by .... R—R3, is interesting.

12 Kt—Q2	B—Kt2
13 P—B3	Kt×KKt
14 Q×Kt	

White has now eliminated the troublesome KKt, but not without weakening his base.

14	P×P
15 B×QBP	QR—Q1
16 Q—QB2	K—R1
17 Q—R4	

He thinks he can decree that the Q side is the main theatre of war.

17	P—QR3
18 P—B4	

In order to prevent 18 .... P—K4, etc. If 18 P—K4, Q—Q3.

18	R—B3

The beginning of the attack. The "fork" 18 .... P—QKt4 would be ineffective, because of 19 Q—Kt3.

19 Q—Kt3	P—B4

With aggressive designs on both wings.

20 P—QR4	

Too dangerous would be 20 P×P, Kt×P; 21 Q×P, R—Q7, etc., but after the preventive text move also, Black resorts to direct action on the K side.

20	R—R3
21 R—B2	

In the belief that weakening pawn moves are not yet necessary. If 21 Q—B2, Q—R5; 22 P—KKt3, Q×KtP ch; 23 P×Q, R—R8 ch; 24 K—B2, R—R7 ch, followed by .... R×Q or 22 P—R3, Q—Kt6; 23 Q—B2, R×P, winning a pawn.

Relatively best is 21 R—K2.

21	Q—R5
22 P—Q5	

A sad awakening! If 22 P—Kt3, Q×KtP ch; 23 P×Q, R—R8 mate, and if 22 P—R3, B×P; 23 K×B, Q×P ch; 24 K—Kt1, Q—R8 mate. White is therefore compelled to allow his position to be invaded, with fatal results.

22	Q×P ch
23 K—B1	Q—Kt6

Threat: 24 .... R—R8 ch; 25 K—K2, R×R; 26 K×R, Q×P ch, etc. White has nothing better than to continue the King's flight.

24 K—K2	Q—Kt5 ch
25 K—Q2	P × P
26 B—K2	

For if 26 B × QP, Kt—B3, with a treble attack on Q4.

26	Q—Kt6
27 QR—KB1	P—Q5
28 Kt—Q1	P—B5
29 Q—R3	

A tactical necessity, for if 29 B × P, Kt—B4; 30 Q—R3, Kt—K5 ch, etc.

29	P × P ch
30 K—B1	

After 30 Q × P or 30 Kt × P, Kt—B4 dis ch is decisive.

30	Kt—B4
31 K—Kt1	

Still escaping; the threat was 31 .... Kt—Kt6 ch.

31	B—K5 ch
32 K—R2	Kt—Q6
33 B × Kt	P × B

More exacting than 33 .... B × B, which would be followed by 34 Q—K7, R—KKt1; 35 R—B3, P—K7; 36 R × Q, P × R (Q); 37 R × P, B—Kt8 ch; 38 K—R1, R × R; 39 Q—K8 ch, R—Kt1; 40 Q—K5 ch, and White would achieve a perpetual check.

34 Q—K7	R—KKt1
35 R—B3	B × R
36 R × B	P—K7
37 R × Q	P × Kt (Q)
38 R × KtP	

A last hope to obtain, after 38 .... R × R; 39 Q—K8 ch, etc., a surprise.

38	Q × P ch
Resigns	

A splendid performance.

380

White	Black
CAPABLANCA	ALEKHINE

(Match, Buenos Aires, 1927)

Refuting with great self-possession a hazardous innovation (9 .... P—B4), White accepts a general mêlée (19 B—Q3). The question of the two Kings' respective security is the deciding factor in this battle of giants.

1 P—Q4	P—Q4
2 P—QB4	P—K3
3 Kt—KB3	Kt—Q2
4 Kt—B3	KKt—B3
5 B—Kt5	P—B3

Instead of the academic continuation 5 .... B—K2, followed by .... Castles, Black contemplates a counter-offensive on the Q side.

6 P—K3	Q—R4

Defence (by unpinning) and attack (against White's QB3) at the same time. 7 .... Kt—K5 or .... B—Kt5 is intended.

7 Kt—Q2	

The best method of parrying the danger. Good also in its simplicity is 7 B × Kt, Kt × B; 8 B—Q3, etc., and not without guile, in spite of its peaceful appearance, is 7 P × P.

7	B—Kt5

The episode 7 .... P × P; 8 B × Kt (forced); 8 .... Kt × B; 9 Kt × P, Q—B2, etc., allows Black the advantage of the two Bishops, but leaves him with a cramped game.

8 Q—B2	Castles
9 B—R4	

Evading 9 .... P × P, in order, as far as possible, to preserve his two Bishops. A playable continuation is 9 B—K2. A curious mistake would be 9 B—Q3, because of 9 .... P × P, and both White's Bishops are attacked (10 B × P, Q × B, or 10 B × Kt, P × KB, etc.).

9	P—B4

Taking advantage of a short respite, in order to free his game, which, however, he could have done in a more propitious manner by 9 .... P—K4; e.g. 10 QP × P, Kt—K5, etc., or 10 Kt—Kt3, Q—B2, etc.

10 Kt—Kt3	Q—R5
11 B × Kt	Kt × B
12 QP × P	Kt—K5

Better is 12 .... Q—B3, or, at least, 12 .... B × Kt ch; 13 Q × B, Kt—K5.

13 P × P	

Definitely winning a pawn.

13	B × Kt ch
14 P × B	Kt × P (B4)

Better is 14 .... P × P

15 R—Q1	

Stressing the play in the centre (but not 15 P × P, B × P; 16 R—QKt1, QR—B1, etc.).

| 15 ...... | P×P |
| 16 R×P | Kt×Kt |

After this exchange, which rounds off White's position, Black remains a pawn to the bad without any compensation. 16 .... P—QKt3 offers better practical chances.

| 17 P×Kt | Q—B3 |
| 18 R—Q4 | R—K1 |

Preventing White from castling in the normal way (by 19 P—B3 or 19 P—K4, followed by B—Q3, etc.).

19 B—Q3

In great style! White incurs dangers, but feels that his future prospects warrant this course.

| 19 ...... | Q×P |

There is nothing better for Black than to seek to "fish in troubled waters." After, e.g., 19 .... P—KKt3; 20 Castles, etc., he would remain in a minority of a pawn without counter-chances of any kind.

20 B×P ch	K—B1
21 B—K4	Q—R6
22 Q—Q2	

Preventing 22 .... B—Q2, followed by .... B—B3.

22	B—K3
23 P—QB4	P—R4
24 R—Kt1	Q×P

Restoring the balance in material, but at what cost? For White's attack, on an open field, quickly becomes overwhelming.

| 25 R—R1 | Q—B2 |
| 26 Q—Kt2 | |

With the immediate threat of 27 Q—R3 ch (27 .... Q—K2; 28 R—R8 mate), but aiming at the same time at other important objectives (Pawn at KKt7).

| 26 ...... | Q—B4 |
| 27 B—Q5 | |

The struggle for strategic posts. After the early elimination of one of his Bishops, the position of Black's King becomes precarious.
Thoughtless would be 27 B×P, QR—Kt1; 28 B—Q5, Q—Kt5 ch, etc.

| 27 ...... | R—R3 |
| 28 R—K4 | |

Still not 28 B×P, R—Kt3, etc.

| 28 ...... | R—Q3 |

Clearly not 28 .... P—B3; 29 R—R8 ch, K—B2; 30 R×R, K×R; 31 B×B.

| 29 R—R7 | K—K2 |

The King takes to flight, because if 29 .... P—KKt3; 30 Q—B6.

| 30 Q×P | K—Q1 |
| 31 B×B | P×B |

If 31 .... Q—Kt5 ch; 32 K—B1.

| 32 Q×P | |

Whilst White's King is well guarded, his rival is held in a vice. The immediate threat is 33 Q—Kt8 ch, Q—B1; 34 Q×R ch.

| 32 ...... | Q—Kt5 ch |

Or, e.g., 32 .... Q—B1; 33 Q—R7 (threatening Q×P ch); 33 .... R—Q2; 34 R—Q4, R—K2; 35 Q×P ch, Q—B2; 36 R—R8 ch, R—K1; 37 R (Q4)×R ch, K×R; 38 Q×Q ch, K×Q; 39 R×R.

33 Q×Q	P×Q
34 P—B5	R—B3
35 R×KtP	R×P
36 R—R7	Resigns.

381

| *White* | *Black* |
| SPIELMANN | PIRC |

(Moscow, 1935)

The striking feature of this game is the prolonged King-hunt, from KKt1 to QKt1, culminating in a series of six shattering checks by White when he is himself in danger.

1 P—Q4	P—Q4
2 P—QB4	P—QB3
3 Kt—KB3	Kt—B3
4 Kt—B3	P—K3
5 B—Kt5	QKt—Q2
6 P—K3	Q—R4
7 P×P	

Localising the conflagration.

| 7 ...... | Kt×P |

The logical complement of the preceding move, of which his object was to render his KKt mobile. Much less consistent would be 7 .... KP×P; 8 B—Q3, Kt—K5; 9 Castles (this sacrifice of a pawn for the sake of rapid development is far more energetic than 9 Q—B2, Kt×Kt; 10 Kt×Kt, P—KR3; 11 Kt—B3, B—Q3, etc.; a blunder would be 9 B×Kt, P×B, and Black wins something); 9 .... Kt×Kt (or 9 ....

Kt×B; 10 Kt×Kt, Kt—B3; 11 R—K1, B—K2; 12 P—K4, P×P; 13 QKt×P, and White has by far the best of it); 10 P×Kt, Q×BP; 11 P—K4, and the first player has a dynamic advantage.

A hazardous try would be 7 .... Kt—K5 (8 P×KP, P×P; 9 Q—R4, etc.).

8 Q—Q2

A good reply, strengthening the attacked point QB3 and keeping the centre under observation. Much less propitious would be 8 Q—B2, B—Kt5; 9 R—B1, Q×P (winning a pawn with impunity), or 8 Q—Kt3, B—R6 (a beautiful counter).

8 ......   B—Kt5

There is a *finesse* here, namely 8 .... P—B3 (before White has played P—K4); 9 B—R4, and now only 9 .... B—Kt5; 10 R—B1, Castles, etc. Other ideas are 8 .... Kt×Kt; 9 P×Kt, Kt—Kt3, with a view to .... Kt—R5, or, as a preparation, 8 .... QKt—Kt3.

9 R—B1   Castles

He could first play 9 .... P—KR3; 10 B—R4, Castles. Over-hasty would be 9 .... P—QB4, on account of 10 P—K4, Kt×Kt; 11 P×Kt, B—R6; 12 R—QKt1, Castles; 13 B—Q3, and White has a preponderance in the centre.

10 P—K4   Kt×Kt
11 P×Kt   B—R6
12 R—QKt1   P—K4
13 B—Q3   B—Q3

Or at once 13 .... P—B3; 14 B—K3, Kt—Kt3; 15 Castles, etc., with a pitched battle. A simplified but no less stubborn battle results from 13 .... P×P; 14 P×P, Q×Q ch; 15 Kt×Q, Kt—Kt3, etc. The easiest line of play is 13 .... R—K1; 14 Castles, P—QKt3; 15 KR—K1, B—R3, etc.

14 Castles   P—B3
15 B—K3   R—Q1

To recapture with the Knight after 16 B—B4 ch, K—R1; 17 P×P.

16 KR—Q1

A curious assembly of seven pieces on the Q file.

16 ......   K—B1

If at once 16 .... Kt—Kt3; 17 P×P, P×P (not 17 .... B×P; 18 B—B4 ch, winning); 18 B×Kt, P×B; 19 B—B4 ch, followed by Kt—Kt5.

17 B—QB4   Kt—Kt3
18 B—Kt3   P×P

More resisting is at once 18 .... B—KKt5.

19 B×P   B—KKt5
20 Q—K3   Q—R4

Reverting to counter-threats.

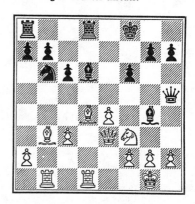

21 P—K5

Dividing the position in two.

21 ......   P×P

For if 21 .... B×Kt; 22 KP×B, B×R; 23 Q—K7 mate.

22 B—B5   B×B

If 22 .... Kt—B1; 23 R×B, Kt×R; 24 R—Q1, K—K2; 25 R×Kt, R×R; 26 Kt×P, etc.

23 Q×B ch   K—K1
24 R—K1   Kt—Q2

Against 24 .... K—Q2; 25 R×P is convincing.

25 R×P ch

Magnificent activity of concentrated pieces.

25 ......   Kt×R
26 Kt×Kt   B—K3

Ingeniously parrying 27 B—B7 ch (27 B×B, R—Q8 ch, followed by mate).

27 R—K1   R—Q7

Not 27 .... B×B; 28 Kt×P dis ch.

28 B×B   Q—K7

Pointing a pistol at White's head (for if 29 R×Q, R—Q8 ch, or if 29 R—KB1, R—Q8, and even if 29 Q—K3, Q×Q; 30 P×Q, QR—Q1, and Black still shows fight), but White now finds a way to bring matters to a conclusion in pandemonium.

29 B—B7 ch	K—Q1
30 Q—B8 ch	K—B2
31 Q—K7 ch	K—B1
32 B—K6 ch	K—Kt1
33 Kt—Q7 ch	K—B2
34 Kt—B5 dis ch	Resigns

(34 .... K—Kt3; 35 Q × P ch, K × Kt; 36 Q—Kt4 mate.)

382

| White | Black |
| ALEKHINE | CAPABLANCA |

(Match, Buenos Aires, 1927)

After an original opening Dr. Alekhine appears on four separate occasions to have a decisive advantage, but, in face of the most ferocious resistance, it is on the last occasion only that he is able to drive home his advantage. An epic battle!

1 P—Q4	Kt—KB3
2 P—QB4	P—K3
3 Kt—QB3	P—Q4
4 B—Kt5	QKt—Q2
5 P—K3	P—B3
6 P × P	

Instead of allowing the famous variation 6 Kt—B3, Q—R4, etc., White plays a continuation which might be termed "Anti-Cambridge-Springs."

| 6 ...... | KP × P |

Less good would be 6 .... BP × P.

| 7 B—Q3 | B—K2 |
| 8 KKt—K2 | |

A novelty, trying to avoid beaten tracks, such as 8 Kt—B3, Castles; 9 Castles, R—K1, etc. (a *Carlsbad Variation*, except for the fact that White's R—QB1 and Black's .... P—QR3 have not yet been played).

| 8 ...... | Castles |

The informative 8 .... P—KR3 before castling would have forced White to a decision concerning his QB. Another independent idea is 8 .... Kt—K5; 9 B × B, Kt × Kt; 10 P × Kt, Q × B, etc.

| 9 Kt—Kt3 | |

After 9 Q—B2, R—K1; 10 Castles QR, Black's best course is to launch an attack by pawns (10 .... P—QKt4).

| 9 ...... | Kt—K1 |

Trying to free his game. If 9 .... P—KR3; 10 P—KR4.

| 10 P—KR4 | |

White can no longer think of castling on the K side.

| 10 ...... | QKt—B3 |

If 10 .... B × B; 11 B × P ch.

| 11 Q—B2 | B—K3 |

Better is 11 .... P—KR3, followed by .... Kt—Q3.

12 Kt—B5	B × Kt
13 B × B	Kt—Q3
14 B—Q3	P—KR3
15 B—KB4	R—B1

With a view to action on the Q side, which White, however, forestalls.

| 16 P—KKt4 | |

A bayonet attack.

| 16 ...... | Kt (B3)—K5 |

Not 16 .... Kt × P; 17 B × Kt, followed by B—B5, nor 16 .... Kt (Q3)—K5; 17 P—Kt5. In order to minimise this latter threat, Black, by his last move, gives up a pawn.

17 P—Kt5	P—KR4
18 B × Kt (K5)	Kt × B
19 Kt × Kt	P × Kt
20 Q × KP	Q—R4 ch

More subtle than at once 20 .... Q—Q4; 21 Q × Q, P × Q; 22 R—Q1, etc.

21 K—B1	Q—Q4
22 Q × Q	P × Q
23 K—Kt2	R—B7

A promising invasion, for if White guards his pawn in a normal way (24 P—Kt3 or 24 QR—QKt1), there follows 24 .... KR—B1, and Black has sufficient compensation for his pawn.

| 24 KR—QB1 | |

This unexpected reply alters the course of events.

| 24 ...... | KR—B1 |

After 24 .... R × P; 25 R—B7, B—R6 (or 25 ..'.. R—K1; 26 R—Q7, R—Kt4; 27 P—R4); 26 R—Q7, R—Kt4; 27 R—Q1, R—B1; 28 R—Q3, B—B1; 29 R—Kt3, the white Rooks would take charge of affairs.

| 25 R × R | |

Black has won the struggle for this square (the junction of the open QB file and the seventh rank), but he has had to renounce the asset of the doubled Rooks.

25	......	R × R
26	R—QKt1	K—R2
27	K—Kt3	K—Kt3
28	P—B3	P—B3
29	P × P	B × P
30	P—R4	K—B4
31	P—R5	R—K7

He represses any idea of 32 R—K1, R × P; 33 P—K4 ch, and thinks himself master of the situation.

32 R—QB1

By this fresh sacrifice of a pawn, as unforeseen as it is profound, Alekhine gives a fresh impetus to the game.

32	......	R × KtP
33	R—B5	K—K3
34	P—K4	

The pith of the combination. If now 34 .... P × P, there follows 35 P—Q5 ch, K—B4 (or 35 .... K—Q2; 36 P × P, etc.); 36 P—Q6 dis ch, followed by P × P, and White's united passed pawns win the day.

34	......	B × P
35	R × P	

At this stage 35 P × P ch would be a mistake, because of 35 .... K—B4; 36 R—B4, B—B7 ch; 37 K—R3, R—Kt4, etc., and Black wins both territory and material.

35	......	B—B6

Better here would be 35 .... B—B7 ch; 36 K—R3, P—QKt4; 37 P × P e.p., P × P, etc., trying to turn his pawn to account, for his hope to "fix" White's weakness at QR5 will be disappointed.

36	R × P	P—R3
37	B—B7	B—K8 ch

If 37 .... R—Kt4; 38 K—Kt4.

38	K—Kt4	R—Kt7 ch
39	K—R3	R—KB7
40	K—Kt4	

Thoughtless would be 40 R—K5 ch, K—Q2, etc., as also 40 R—KB5, P—KKt3; 41 R—B8, K—K2, etc. The players are now indulging in a repetition of moves to gain time on the clock.

40	......	R—Kt7 ch
41	K—R3	R—KB7
42	P—B4	R—B6 ch
43	K—Kt2	R—B7 ch
44	K—R3	R—B6 ch
45	K—Kt2	R—B7 ch
46	K—Kt1	R—B7
47	B—Kt6	R—B5

In order to recover his pawn, save for the unexpected.

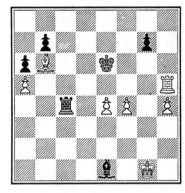

48 K—Kt2

The unexpected happens! By this almost miraculous King's move, not only is the KP indirectly defended (if 48 .... R × P ch; 49 K—B3, R any; 50 R—K5 ch, followed by R × B), but the King gets nearer the centre.

48	......	P—Kt3
49	R—K5 ch	K—Q2
50	P—R5	

Important. The lone pawn (which, in any event, could not be held, e.g. 50 K—R3, B—B6, or 50 B—B2, R—B7, etc.) is sacrificed in a good cause. The pawn mass in the centre acquires preponderance, whilst Black's isolated "forces" on the KR file will be able to advance only with difficulty.

50	......	P × P
51	K—B3	P—R5
52	R—R5	R—B6 ch
53	K—Kt4	R—B5
54	K—B5	B × P

An attempt at salvation, beautiful but unlucky.

55 R—R7 ch

The refutation. But not 55 B × B, R—B4 ch; 56 K—Kt4, R × R; 57 K × R, P—R6, and Black's passed pawn wins.

55	......	K—B3
56	B × B	

Calculated to a nicety, this liquidation is far more effective than the gain of the exchange by 56 R—B7 ch, K—Kt4; 57 R × R, B × B, etc.

56	......	R—B4 ch
57	K—K6	R × B
58	P—B5	R—R6
59	P—B6	

If 59 R × RP, R—KB6; 60 P—B6, P—Kt4, etc., and Black is not without resource.

59 ......   R—KB6
60 P—B7   P—Kt4
61 R—R5

A most telling final combination.

61 ......   P—R6
62 R—B5   R × R
63 P × R   Resigns

(63 .... P—R7; 64 P—B8 (Q), P—R8
(Q); 65 Q—R8 ch, followed by Q × Q.)

383

White	Black
CAPABLANCA	SPIELMANN

(New York, 1927)

*White's work on the Q side, especially the
forced-march of the QRP, is little short of
prodigious.*

1 P—Q4   P—Q4
2 Kt—KB3   P—K3
3 P—B4   Kt—Q2
4 Kt—B3   KKt—B3
5 B—Kt5   B—Kt5

Instead of trying for counter-play by
5 .... P—B3, followed by .... Q—R4, and
eventually .... B—Kt5 (*Cambridge Springs
Variation*), Black tones up the idea by first
playing 5 .... B—Kt5, intending ....
P—B4, and only then .... Q—R4 (the
Manhattan Variation).

6 P × P

Or 6 P—K3, P—B4, etc.

6 ......   P × P
7 Q—R4

A sound positional manœuvre. Much less
promising is 7 Q—B2 or 7 Q—Kt3, because
of 7 .... P—B4, followed by .... Q—R4.
An imaginative continuation is 7 P—K3,
P—B4; 8 B—Q3, Q—R4; 9 Castles, B × Kt;
10 P × B, Q × BP; 11 R—B1, Q—R4;
12 B × Kt, P × B; 13 P × P, Kt × P; 14 B—Kt1,
B—K3; 15 Q—Q4, and White is more than
compensated for the pawn given up.

7 ......   B × Kt ch

Unfortunate haste. By playing 7 ....
Q—K2, Black could have won an important
tempo.

8 P × B   Castles
9 P—K3   P—B4
10 B—Q3   P—B5

A move which carries responsibilities, for
soon White, by a natural reaction, will
threaten an advance in the centre by P—K4.

11 B—B2   Q—K2

Black's worries begin. If 11 .... P—QR3;
12 Kt—K5, P—Kt4; 13 Q—R3, etc., with
considerable advantage to White.

12 Castles KR   P—QR3

Black's first task is to consolidate his
Q side pawns. The question then will be
whether this pawn chain can be maintained
intact.

13 KR—K1

Preparing P—K4.

13 ......   Q—K3

He unpins the Knight in order to prevent
the thrust P—K4. If 13 .... P—Kt4;
14 Q—R5, threatening not only Q—B7,
but also P—QR4.

14 Kt—Q2

A very fine retrograde manœuvre, always
with a view to P—K4.

14 ......   P—Kt4

Not yet 14 .... Kt—K5, on account of
15 B × Kt, P × B; 16 Q × BP.

15 Q—R5   Kt—K5
16 Kt × Kt   P × Kt
17 P—QR4

The beginning of a phase, magnificent by
reason of its logic and precision.
Everything depends on a *tempo*, which
Black will lack for the maintenance of his
chain of pawns.

17 ......   Q—Q4

In the belief that he has time to attack
the hostile QB (for if now, e.g. 18 B—B4,
B—Kt2, and Black's position is once more
firm.

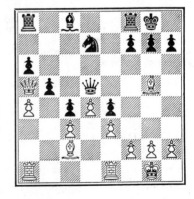

18 P×P

A profound sacrifice.

18 ......   Q×B

Asking for a demonstration of what looks like magic. Clearly not 18 .... Q×KtP; 19 Q×Q, and wins, nor 18 .... B—Kt2; 19 P×P, etc., nor, finally and chiefly, 18 .... R—Kt1; 19 P×P, R—Kt4; 20 Q—B7, Q×B; 21 P—R7, R—Kt2; 22 Q×Kt, B×Q; 23 P—R8 (Q), and the newly-born Queen being taboo, White remains a valuable pawn ahead.

19 B×P   R—Kt1

After 19 .... R—R2, there is another magnificent surprise by 20 P—Kt6, Q×Q; 21 P×R, and wins.

20 P×P

He is quite willing to exchange Queens, as after 20 .... Q×Q; 21 R×Q, R—Kt6; 22 P—R7, Kt—Kt3; 23 R—QB1, followed by P—R8 (Q), etc., White's advantage is decisive.

20 ......   R—Kt4
21 Q—B7   Kt—Kt3
22 P—R7

The triumphal advance. Threat: 23 Q×Kt.

22 ......   B—R6
23 KR—Kt1

Very elegant.

23 ......   R×R ch

For if 23 .... Kt—R1; 24 B×Kt, R×B; 25 Q—Kt8 ch.

24 R×R   P—B4
25 B—B3   P—B5
26 P×P   Resigns.

384

White   *Black*

PILLSBURY   LASKER

(St. Petersburg, 1896)

In this superb game, the contestants castle on opposite sides. But while White is still seeking a base for an attack, Black has already fully mobilised his Rooks on the open QB file. This purely technical factor causes Black to force a win by truly artistic means.

1 P—Q4   P—Q4
2 P—QB4   P—K3
3 Kt—QB3   Kt—KB3
4 Kt—B3

A sound developing move, instead of the popular pinning strategy 4 B—Kt5.

4 ......   P—B4
5 B—Kt5

A modest but very sound continuation is 5 P—K3. A very extensive chapter is opened up by 5 BP×P, Kt×P (better than 5 .... KP×P; 6 B—Kt5, etc.); 6 P—K4, Kt×Kt; 7 P×Kt, P×P; 8 P×P, B—Kt5 ch; 9 B—Q2, B×B ch; 10 Q×B, Castles, etc., a variation which requires most accurate manœuvres on the part of Black in order to counteract White's floating but flexible centre.

5 ......   BP×P
6 Q×P

More plastic play results from 6 KKt×P, and after 6 .... P—K4; 7 Kt—B3, P—Q5; 8 Kt—Q5, Kt—B3; 9 P—K4, etc.

6 ......   Kt—B3

Precipitate. The right move is *first* 6 .... B—K2, for to the text move White has a subtle reply.

7 Q—R4

After this impulsive move, Black can strengthen his defence. But by the fine intermediary measure 7 B×Kt, as shown in the next game, White can secure a tangible and lasting positional advantage.

7 ......   B—K2
8 Castles   Q—R4

Launching the attack.

9 P—K3   B—Q2
10 K—Kt1   P—KR3
11 P×P

White sees himself compelled to open the critical QB file, in order to establish at least one enduring weakness in his opponent's position, for if at once 11 Kt—Q4, Castles KR, would add to his own difficulties.

11 ......   P×P
12 Kt—Q4   Castles KR
13 B×Kt

If 13 B×P, White would not be without resources after 13 .... P×B; 14 Q×P, Kt—KKt5; 15 Q—B4, but Black's reply 13 .... Kt—K5 takes advantage of the fact that the imbroglio 14 KKt×Kt, Kt×Kt ch; 15 K—B2 (15 P×Kt, Q—Kt3 ch); 15 .... B×Q; 16 Kt×Q, Kt×R would lead to White's undoing. After the exchange in the text, Black's KB obtains a dominating post.

13	B × B
14 Q—R5	Kt × Kt
15 P × Kt	B—K3
16 P—B4	

He also tries to organise an attack. If relying on tactics, 16 Kt—K4, Black then simply plays 16 .... B—K2, maintaining and even increasing the tension. Or, modestly, 16 B—K2, QR—B1, and Black's attack grows.

| 16 ...... | QR—B1 |
| 17 P—B5 | |

Who has the attack?

| 17 ...... | R × Kt |

Partly calculated and partly intuitive, for the ultimate consequences of this first sacrifice are indeterminate.

18 P × B

For if, e.g. 18 P × R, Q × P; 19 P × B, R—B1; 20 Q—K2 (or 20 Q × P ch, K—R1, etc., or 20 B—K2, Q—Kt5 ch; 21 K—R1, R—B8 ch; 22 R × R, B × P ch, followed by mate); 20 .... B × P; 21 P × P ch (21 R × B, Q—B8 mate); 21 .... K—B1 (21 .... K × P; 22 Q—B3 ch); 22 Q—K8 ch, R × Q; 23 P × R (Q) ch, K × Q, and wins without difficulty.

| 18 ...... | R—QR6 |

Beautiful! Capture is compulsory, opening both the QKt file and the extremity of the long black diagonal.

19 P × P ch	R × P
20 P × R	Q—Kt3 ch
21 B—Kt5	

A propitiatory counter-sacrifice.

Or 21 K—R1, B × P ch; 22 R × B, Q × R ch; 23 K—Kt1, Q—K5 ch; 24 K—R1 (or 24 K—B1, R—B2 ch, etc., or 24 K—Kt2, R—B7 ch, etc.); 24 .... Q—K8 ch; 25 K—Kt2, R—B7 ch; 26 K—Kt3, Q—Kt8 ch, and wins; or 21 K—B2, R—B2 ch; 22 K—Q2, Q × P ch; 23 B—Q3, R—B7 ch; 24 K × R, Q—Kt7 mate.

| 21 ...... | Q × B ch |
| 22 K—R1 | R—B2 |

Preparing, at leisure, a fresh assault. Threat: 23 .... R—B8 ch; 24 R × R, B × P ch.

| 23 R—Q2 | R—B5 |
| 24 KR—Q1 | |

If 24 R—QKt1, Q—B3. If 24 Q—Kt4, Q—B3 (parrying counter-checks and threatening 25 .... R—B8 ch); 25 R—QKt1 (if 25 K—Kt2, Q—Kt3 ch; 26 K—R1, R × P;

27 Q—B8 ch, K—B2; 28 Q—Q7 ch, K—Kt3; 29 Q—K8 ch, K—R2, etc.); 25 .... P—KR4; 26 Q—B4, R × P; 27 R × R, Q—B6 ch; 28 R—Kt2, B × R, and wins.

| 24 ...... | R—B6 |
| 25 Q—B5 | Q—B5 |

The regrouping of Queen and Rook is achieved. Threat: 26 .... R—B8 ch.

26 K—Kt2

The King takes up his own defence, for if 26 R—QKt1, B × P is decisive (e.g. 27 Q—Kt4, R—Q6 dis ch, or 27 Q—K6 ch, K—R1; 28 Q—K8 ch, K—R2, etc.).

Similarly, if at once 26 Q—K6 ch, K—R1; 27 Q—K8 ch, K—R2, White's "perpetual check" has lasted only two moves.

| 26 ...... | R × P |

A fresh exploit! The surviving Rook tries to prove worthy of its companion.

| 27 Q—K6 ch | K—R2 |

The right method of avoiding a perpetual check, whereas after 27 .... K—R1; 28 Q—K8 ch, K—R2; 29 K × R, Q—B6 ch; 30 K—R4, Q—B5 ch; 31 K—R3 (31 K—R5, P—Kt3 mate); 31 .... Q—B6 ch, and Black must be satisfied with a draw.

28 K × R

Or 28 Q—B5 ch, K—R1, etc. If 28 K—R1, B × P ch, and even if 28 K—Kt1, B × P (less precise is 28 .... R × P; 29 R × R, Q—Kt6 ch; 30 K—B1, etc.); 29 Q—B5 ch, K—Kt1 (not 29 .... K—R1; 30 Q—KB8 ch); 30 Q—K6 ch, K—R1; 31 Q—K8 ch, K—R2; 32 R × B, Q × P ch; 33 K—B1, R—B6 mate.

| 28 ...... | Q—B6 ch |
| 29 K—R4 | P—Kt4 ch |

The finishing touch.

| 30 K × P | Q—B5 ch |
| 31 K—R5 | B—Q1 ch |

And Black mates next move.

385

| White | Black |
| PILLSBURY | LASKER |

(Cambridge Springs, 1904)

A worthy companion to the preceding game. In this case White finds an ingenious means (7 B × Kt, instead of 7 Q—R4) of obtaining a positional advantage, which he maintains with iron determination until victory is won.

1 P—Q4	P—Q4
2 P—QB4	P—K3
3 Kt—QB3	Kt—KB3
4 Kt—B3	P—B4
5 B—Kt5	BP×P
6 Q×P	Kt—B3

After a lapse of eight years, Dr. Lasker still prefers the text move to consolidation by 6 .... B—K2; 7 P×P, P×P; 8 P—K4, Kt—B3; 9 B—Kt5, Castles; 10 KB×Kt, P×B, etc., tending to equality.

7 B×Kt
A subtle intermediary manœuvre, which alters the outlook.

7 ...... P×B
He resigns himself to this square weakness, which is to influence the whole course of the game. He cannot play 7 .... Kt×Q; 8 B×Q, Kt—B7 ch (or 8 .... Kt×Kt ch; 9 KP×Kt, K×B; 10 P×P, etc.); 9 K—Q2, Kt×R; 10 B—R4, etc., nor 7 .... Q×B; 8 Q×Q, P×Q; 9 P×P, and Black has no compensation for his pawn.

8 Q—R4	P×P
9 R—Q1	

He refuses to release his hold on KB6 by playing 9 Q×QBP.

9 ...... B—Q2
Not 9 .... Q—Kt3; 10 Q×KBP, R—KKt1; 11 Kt—KKt5, etc., nor 9 .... Q—K2; 10 Kt—K4, etc.

10 P—K3	Kt—K4

After 10 .... P—QR3 or 10 .... B—K2, White plays 11 B×P, with fine concentric development of his forces.

11 Kt×Kt	P×Kt
12 Q×BP	Q—Kt3
13 B—K2	

On the strength of his superior development, White gives up a pawn.

13 ...... Q×KtP
An old story! The Queen should not waste time hunting distant pawns. But Black has now not much choice; if 13 .... R—B1; 14 Q—Q3, or if 13 .... Q—Kt5; 14 Q—B7, or finally, if 13 .... B—B3; 14 Castles, R—KKt1; 15 Kt—K4, B—K2; 16 B—R5, B—Q4; 17 R×B, P×R; 18 Q×P, R—KB1; 19 Q×KP, etc.

14 Castles	R—B1
15 Q—Q3	R—B2

If 15 .... B—B3; 16 B—B3.

16 Kt—K4
In the mobility of this Knight lies the reason of White's success.

16	B—K2
17 Kt—Q6 ch	K—B1

Or 17 .... B×Kt; 18 Q×B, K—Q1 (18 .... Q—Kt3; 19 Q×P (K5)); 19 R—Q2, Q—Kt3 (if 19 .... Q—B6; 20 B—Kt5, winning a piece); 20 Q×P (K5), and White has three files at his disposal for his attack.

18 Kt—B4	Q—Kt4
19 P—B4	P×P

If 19 .... P—K5, then not 20 Q×P, B—QB3; 21 Q—Q4, R—Kt1, etc., but 20 Q—Q4, R—Kt1; 21 Q×RP, B—B4; 22 Q—Kt8 ch, R—B1; 23 Q—K5, etc.

20 Q—Q4
Far more powerful than 20 R×P.

20 ...... P—B3
Compulsory weakness, for if 20 .... R—Kt1; 21 Q×BP, with a double threat.

21 Q×BP	Q—QB4
22 Kt—K5	B—K1
23 Kt—Kt4	P—B4

If 23 .... Q—B6; 24 R—Q3.

24 Q—R6 ch	K—B2
25 B—B4	

A fresh sensation (25 .... Q×B; 26 Kt—K5 ch).

25 ...... R—B3
Or 25 .... B—Q2; 26 R×B, R×R; 27 Q×KP ch, K—K1; 28 Kt—B6 ch, and mate to follow.

26 R×P ch
The principal threat (at K6) having been parried, the secondary threat now takes the stage.

26	Q×R
27 R—KB1	Q×R ch
28 K×Q	

And still White's Bishop cannot be taken (for if 28 .... R×B; 29 Kt—K5 ch).

28	B—Q2
29 Q—R5 ch	

More telling than 29 Kt—K5 ch, K—K1, etc.

29 ...... K—Kt1
Or, e.g. 29 .... K—Kt2; 30 Q—K5 ch, K—Kt1; 31 Kt—R6 ch, K—B1; 32 Q×R mate.

30 Kt—K5	Resigns

A splendid victory.

386

White	Black
LUNDIN	ALEXANDER

(Stockholm, 1937)

An exciting game, in which both sides stubbornly play for a win. But White's attack, directed against scattered and varied objectives, fails against Black's clever and active defence, the black isolated QP becoming in the end a winning asset.

	White	Black
1	Kt—KB3	Kt—KB3
2	P—B4	P—K3
3	Kt—B3	P—Q4
4	P—Q4	P—B4
5	B—Kt5	QP × P

Reverting to a species of *Queen's Gambit Accepted*, with the extended development of White's QB.

6	P—K3	Kt—B3
7	B × P	P × P
8	P × P	B—K2
9	Castles	Castles
10	R—K1	

Occupation of a potentially open file.

10	......	Kt—Q4

Black changes his plans, as he now considers that no pressure against the isolated QP could be successful (e.g. 10 .... Q—R4; 11 P—Q5, Kt × P; 12 Kt × Kt, B × B; 13 Kt × B, P × Kt; 14 B × P, etc.). Playable is 10 .... P—QKt3.

11	B × Kt	P × B

Sharper than 11 .... B × B.

12	B × B	Kt × B
13	Q—Kt3	

Beginning to lay siege to the weak points.

13	......	P—QKt3
14	Q—R3	B—K3

The well-knit black forces preclude access to the position.

15	Kt—KKt5	Kt—B3

Resorting to an active defence in preference to 15 .... Q—Q2.

16	Kt × B	

Ineffective would be 16 R × B, P × R; 17 Kt × KP, Q—B3; 18 Kt × R, R × Kt; 19 R—KB1, Q × P, etc.

16	......	P × Kt
17	Q—R4	

After 17 R × P, Kt × P; 18 R—Q6, Q—R5;

19 R—KB1, QR—B1, the rôles would suddenly be changed (e.g. 20 Kt × P, Q × BP ch, with mate in two, or 20 R × QP, R × Kt; 21 P × R, Kt—K7 ch; 22 K—R1, Kt—Kt6 ch; 23 K—Kt1, Kt × R, etc., or again, 20 Q × P, R × Kt, etc.)

17	......	R—B1

A file with a future.

18	R × P	Q—R5

Temporary spoils.

19	P—KKt3	Q × P
20	Q × Q	Kt × Q
21	R—Q6	Kt—B6 ch
22	K—Kt2	P—Q5
23	Kt—Q5	R—B7
24	Kt—B4	

Hatching a far from amiable plot against the Knight.

24	......	Kt—R5 ch

A very fine counter! 24 .... Kt—K4; 25 R × QP, P—KKt4; 26 Kt—R3, R × P; 27 R—K1, etc., would favour White's chances.

25	K—R3	

He disdains the more sheltered quarters at Kt1 (25 .... Kt—B6 ch; 26 K—Kt2, draw).

25	......	Kt—B4
26	R—Q7	R—K1

Here Black avoids a possible repetition of moves by 26 .... R—KB2; 27 R—Q8 ch, R—B1; 28 R—Q7, etc. Petty would be 26 .... R × KtP or 26 .... R × BP; 27 R—QB1.

27	R—Q1	

If 27 P—KKt4, R × BP.

27	......	P—KKt4

Alea jacta est.

28	Kt—R5	R—K3
29	R × QRP	

Serious complications would result from 29 P—KKt4.

29	......	R × BP
30	R—QB1	

Seizing immediately the accessible file (threat: 31 R—B8 ch), but his plans are met by Black with the utmost coolness.

30	......	Kt—K2
31	QR—B7	K—B2
32	R—Q7	R—K5

Defending the QP with a strong threat:

33 .... P—Kt5 ch; 34 K—R4, R×P ch;
35 K—Kt5, P—R3 ch; 36 K×P, R—K4,
and wins.

33 P—KKt4
This has become necessary, but, by
denuding his King's defences, he calls up
a new phase in this merciless struggle.

33 ...... R—K6 ch
34 Kt—Kt3 P—Q6
A direct threat of 35 .... P—Q7, with
.... R—K8 and .... P—Q8.

35 R—R3 R—Q7
36 P—Kt4
Intending 37 R—Kt3, with P—R4 and
P—R5, with new resources, but Black has
fresh reserves to throw into the *mêlée*.

36 ...... K—K3
The King, a strong piece!

37 R—Q4 Kt—Q4
The reserve cavalry.

38 R—K4 ch
Has White turned the corner?

38 ...... K—B3
A brilliant reply (39 R×R, Kt—B5 mate).

39 R—R8
He manages to get clear with the loss of
only the exchange, but Black's passed pawn
now decides the game.

39 ...... Kt—B5 ch
40 R×Kt ch P×R
41 R—B8 ch K—K4
42 R—B5 ch K—Q5
43 R×P ch K—B6
44 P—R4 R—R7
45 R—B8 P—Q7
46 R—B8 ch K×P
47 R—Q8 R—K8
Resigns.

387
White   Black
BURN   STEINITZ
(Cologne, 1898)

*An interesting feature of this fine game is
the ending of Rooks, Bishops and pawns. In
spite of Bishops of opposite colours, White
succeeds in exploiting minute advantages (disjointed black pawns, etc.) until the cumulative
effect of clever manœuvres leads to a decisive
win.*

1 P—Q4 P—Q4
2 P—QB4 P—K3
3 Kt—QB3 Kt—KB3
4 Kt—B3 P×P
Reverting to a *Queen's Gambit Accepted*;
this deferred decision is not without its
drawbacks.

5 P—K3
White could also adopt a more pretentious
policy by 5 P—K4, or revert to a purely
positional treatment of the opening by
5 Q—R4 ch, QKt—Q2; 6 P—KKt3 (more
precise than 6 Q×BP at once); 6 ....
P—QR3; 7 B—Kt2, P—B3 (if 7 ....
P—QKt4; 8 Kt×P); 8 Q×P (B4), etc.

5 ...... P—QR3
Black, having given up space in the centre,
tries to recoup himself on the Q side. Other
continuations could be, either 5 .... P—B4
at once, or, in a more restrained manner,
5 .... B—K2; 6 B×P, Castles; 7 Castles,
QKt—Q2; 8 P—K4, and White turns his
preponderance in the centre to account.

6 P—QR4 P—B4
7 B×P Kt—B3
8 Castles B—Q2
Black tries to solve the problem of the
QB without weakening the Q side by 8 ....
P—QKt3. Most pertinent, however, would
be mobilisation of the K side by 8 ....
B—K2; 9 Q—K2, Castles; 10 R—Q1, Q—B2,
with an even game.

9 Q—K2
A most important regrouping of Queen
and Rook.

9 ...... Q—Kt3
Black also goes in for an interesting
regroupment.

10 R—Q1 R—Q1
11 P—Q5 P×P
12 B×QP B—K2
If, instead, 12 .... B—B1 or 12 ....
B—Kt5, then 13 B×Kt ch, Q×B (or 13 ....
P×B, devaluing the pawns); 14 R×R ch,
K×R; 15 P—K4, with advantage to White.

13 P—K4
A bold idea.

13 ...... Kt—Q5
Black seeks simplification. After 13 ....
Castles; 14 P—K5, Kt×B; 15 Kt×Kt,
Q—R2; 16 Kt×B ch, Kt×Kt; 17 B—Kt5,
KR—K1; 18 R—Q2, etc. White's advant-
age becomes definite.

14 Q—B4 Kt×Kt ch
15 P×Kt Castles
16 B—B4
Again played with great freedom and a
keen appreciation of the hidden resources of
the position.

16 ...... Kt—R4
17 B—Kt3 Kt×B
18 RP×Kt B—KB3
Unpromising would be the expedition
18.... Q×P; 19 KR—Kt1 (or 19 QR—Kt1,
Q—B7; 20 QR—B1, Q—Kt7, with a repeti-
tion of moves); 19 .... Q—Q7 (if 19 ....
Q—B7; 20 R—R2, etc., and if 19 ....
P—QKt4; 20 R×Q, P×Q; 21 B×P,
B—KB3; 22 R—B2, etc., with advantage to
White); 20 R—R2, Q—Kt4; 21 R×P, and
White has the better game.

19 R—Q2 Q—Kt5
20 P—R5
In the coming end game, White relies on
his partial blockade of the Q side and his
control of the strategic point Q5.

20 ...... Q×Q
21 B×Q B—B3
22 B—Q5 R—Q2
Also after 22 .... B×Kt; 23 P×B, etc.,
White has sound winning assets.

23 Kt—R4 B×Kt
24 R×B
At first sight it seems that the ending
cannot be won (equality in material and
Bishops of opposite colours), but there is
much room for the unexpected.

24 ...... KR—Q1
25 R—B4 B—K2
Not 25 .... B—Q5; 26 P—QKt4.

26 R—Q3 K—B1
27 R—Kt3 R—Kt1
28 K—B1 P—B3
29 K—K2 R—B2
30 K—Q3 K—K1
31 R—B1 K—Q1
32 K—B4 R—Q2
33 R—KR1
A fresh perspective.

33 ...... P—R3
34 P—B4 K—B2
35 P—B5
Now the K side also is partially blockaded.

35 ...... R (Q2)—Q1
36 R—R4 B—B1
37 P—B4 B—Q3
38 K—B3 P—QKt4
Breaking at last the evil spell on the Q side,
but leaving there two depreciated pawns.

39 P×P e.p. ch KR×P
40 R×R R×R
41 R—R1 B—K2
42 P—Kt3 R—Q3
43 R—R1 R—Kt3
44 K—Q3 K—Kt1
The wrong direction.

45 K—K2 R—Q3
46 K—B3 K—B1
Returning at the double.

47 K—Kt4 K—Q1
48 K—R5 K—K1
49 K—Kt6
An uncompromising King.

49 ...... K—B1
50 R—R5 R—Kt3
51 B—B4 B—Q3
If 51 .... R—B3; 52 B×P, but now if
52 B×P, R×P.

52 R—R1 B—K2
53 K—R7 B—Q3
54 R—Q1 R—B3
55 R—Q5
After so much labour, here is a real, concrete threat: 56 P—K5.

55 ...... P—KR4
Setting a cruel trap: if now, unheedingly,
56 P—K5, there follows 56 .... P×P;
57 P×P, B×P, for if 58 R×B, R—R3 mate.
But White is wide-awake.

56 K—Kt6 P—R4
Or 56 .... P—R5; 57 P×P, B×P;
58 R—Q8 ch, K—K2; 59 R—QR8, B—R3;
60 R—R7 ch, etc.

57 K×P
Not 57 P—K5, P×P; 58 P×P, B×P
dis ch, etc.

57 ...... R—Kt3
58 P—K5 P×P
59 P×P B—K2
60 R—Q7 R—Kt1
61 R—R7
Methodical. Playable is also 61 P—B6,

P×P; 62 P×P, B—Q1 (62 .... B×P; 63 R—B7 ch); 63 K—Kt6, K—K1; 64 B—K6, etc.

61	R—Q1
62 R×P	R—Q7
63 R—R8 ch	R—Q1
64 R—R7	R—Q8
65 P—B6	

The final sanctions.

65	P×P
66 P×P	B—Q1
67 P—KKt4	R—KKt8
68 P—Kt5	R—Kt6
69 K—Kt6	K—K1
70 B—Kt5 ch	K—B1
71 R—B7 ch	K—Kt1
72 B—B4	Resigns.

388

White	Black
TARRASCH	WALBRODT

(Vienna, 1898)

In this game—reminiscent of a siege rather than a battle—we can follow, as in a slow-motion film, the workings of blockading strategy.

1 P—Q4	P—Q4
2 P—QB4	P—K3
3 Kt—QB3	Kt—KB3
4 Kt—B3	B—K2
5 B—B4	

Besides the pin by 5 B—Kt5, the text move is also a sound development of White's QB outside his lines. Another good plan is 5 P—K3, followed by B—Q3.

5	P—B3

Resorting, unnecessarily, to purely defensive play. A more enterprising policy is 5 .... Castles; 6 P—K3, P—B4, etc.

6 P—K3	QKt—Q2

If 6 .... Kt—R4; 7 B—K5, and if 6 .... B—Q3; 7 Kt—K5 (for if now 7 .... QKt—Q2; 8 Kt×KBP, K×Kt; 9 B×B, and White has won a pawn).

7 P—KR3

In order to preserve the KB in case of 7 .... Kt—R4.

7	Kt—B1

Or 7 .... Castles; 8 Q—B2, and White's game has the superior mechanism.

8 P—B5

To prevent, above all, 8 B—Q3 (and if 8 Kt—K5, Kt—Kt3).

8	Kt—Kt3
9 B—R2	Q—R4

The attempt to undermine White's pawn chain by 9 .... P—Kt3; 10 P—QKt4, P—QR4; 11 P—R3 would yield little. But at least, by continuing with 11 .... B—R3, Black would eliminate a dangerous combatant.

The *sortie* in the text is intended to make possible either 10 .... Kt—K5 or 10 .... P—Kt3, followed by .... B—R3.

10 P—R3

Very subtle. If now Black, unsuspecting, should play 10 .... P—Kt3, then 11 P—QKt4 wins the Queen on a full board!

10	Kt—K5

Hoping to weaken White's QB3, for if now 11 R—B1, P—Kt3, etc., and if 11 P—QKt4, Kt×Kt; 12 Q—B2, Q—R5; 13 Q×Kt, P—QR4; 14 R—QKt1, P×P; 15 P×P, Q—R6, and Black has succeeded in concentrating his forces on the extreme Queen's wing.

11 B—Q3	Kt×Kt

Or 11 .... P—B4; 12 B×Kt, BP×B; 13 Kt—Q2, Castles; 14 Castles, followed by P—B3, and White dominates the principal highways.

12 Q—Q2

An additional point. White not only avoids weakening his QB3, but also the exchange of Queens, which would ease Black's game.

12	Kt—KR5

Or, e.g. 12 .... P—Kt3; 13 P—QKt4, Q—R5; 14 Q×Kt, and now, already, neither 14 .... P—QR4 nor 14 .... B—R3 would be of any value.

13 Kt×Kt	B×Kt
14 P—QKt4	Q—Q1

Not to be recommended would be 14 .... Q—R5; 15 Q×Kt, P—QR4, because of 16 Castles (16 .... P×P; 17 P×P, winning the Queen).

15 Q×Kt

The local skirmishing has resulted in the completion of White's formidable pawn chain.

15	Castles
16 Castles KR	Q—Q2

With the opportunist plan of eliminating

another fighting unit after .... B—Q1 and .... B—B2.

17 Q—B2   P—B4

Allowing the adverse QB to occupy K5, but if 17 .... P—KR3; 18 Q—K2, B—Q1 19 B—Q6, B—K2; 20 B—K5, P—B3 (or 20 .... B—Q1; 21 Q—Kt4); 21 B—Kt3, B—Q1; 22 Q—R5, White will exploit the holes in the adverse King's position.

18 K—R1   B—Q1
19 B—K5   B—B2
20 P—B4   B × B
21 BP × B   Q—K2
22 P—Kt4

Bold, but scientific.

22 ......   P—KKt3

If 22 .... P × P; 23 R × R ch, Q × R; 24 R—KB1, Q—K2; 25 B × P ch, K—R1; 26 Q—Kt6, with the decisive threat 27 R—B7. And if 22 .... Q—R5; 23 R—B3, P × P; 24 B × P ch, and wins.

23 R—B4   B—Q2

If 23 .... P—KKt4; 24 R—B3, P × P; 25 B × P ch.

24 R—KKt1

White's concentration, on broad lines, is finished, but much remains to be done before the enemy position is ripe for the final assault.

24 .. ..   K—R1
25 Q—KKt2   P—QR4

Black thinks he has sufficient covering troops in the threatened sector, and tries to obtain breathing space on the opposite wing.

26 B—Kt1   P × QKtP
27 RP × P   R—R5

Taking the risk of temporarily leaving the first rank.

28 P × P

The right tactical moment when 28 .... KtP × P would be very risky.

28 ......   KP × P

Now White has an asset in his passed KP.

29 Q—Q2   R—KKt1
30 Q—K1   B—K3
31 P—R4   QR—R1
32 R (B4)—B1   R—Kt2
33 R—Kt2   QR—KKt1
34 R—KR2   Q—Q2
35 B—Q3   R—R1
36 Q—Kt3   Q—K2
37 R—KKt1   QR—KKt1
38 R (R2)—Kt2

Dissuading his opponent from playing

38 .... P—KKt4; 39 P × P, R × P; 40 Q × R, R × Q; 41 R × R, etc., which would be in White's favour.

38 ......   R—KB1
39 Q—B4   R (B)—KKt1
40 Q—R6   B—Q2
41 K—R2   B—K3
42 R—Kt5   B—Q2
43 K—Kt3   B—K1
44 K—B4   B—Q2
45 P—R5

The assault.

45 ......   B—K1
46 P × P   B × P

If 46 .... R × P; 47 B × P, R × Q; 48 R × R mate.

47 B—K2

Much more accurate than 47 B × P, Q—KB2.

47 ......   Q—Q1
48 B—R5

The beginning of the end.

48 ......   B × B
49 Q × B   R × R
50 R × R   R × R
51 Q × R   Q—KB1
52 P—K6   Resigns

A hard fight.

389

White	Black
ALEKHINE	LASKER

(New York, 1924)

A game in which an impetuous aggressor is gradually driven back. Technically, the value of the two Bishops is much in evidence.

1 P—Q4   P—Q4
2 P—QB4   P—K3
3 Kt—KB3   Kt—KB3
4 Kt—B3   QKt—Q2
5 P × P

Foreshadowing an attempt to obtain control of the central zone. If at once 5 B—B4, P × P; 6 P—K4, B—Kt5, etc., or 6 P—K3, Kt—Q4 (if 6 .... Kt—Kt3; 7 Kt—K5); 7 B × P, B—Kt5 (better than 7 .... Kt × B; 8 P × Kt); 8 R—QB1, Castles, and Black holds his own.

Restrained play would be 5 P—K3, whilst 5 B—Kt5 reverts to usual lines.

| 5 ...... | P×P |
| 6 B—B4 | |

Threatening 7 Kt—QKt5.

| 6 ...... | P—B3 |
| 7 P—K3 | |

With 7 P—KR3, White could preserve his QB.

| 7 ...... | Kt—R4 |

To eliminate a troublesome fighter, in preference to 7 .... B—K2; 8 P—KR3 or 7 .... B—Kt5; 8 B—Q3, which would gradually lead into normal lines of play, in which White quite naturally claims the initiative.

8 B—Q3

Alekhine decides on the most trenchant continuation. Ineffective would be 8 B—KKt5, B—K2; 9 B×B, Q×B, etc., and 8 B—Kt3, Kt×B; 9 RP×Kt lacks plastic character. The most tense would be 8 B—K5, P—B3; 9 B—Kt3, etc.

| 8 ...... | Kt×B |
| 9 P×Kt | |

White's QP is isolated, and his KBP doubled. As Black, moreover, will be the first to occupy the open K file, he will soon have a positional advantage.

| 9 ...... | B—Q3 |
| 10 P—KKt3 | |

He is forced to create a weakness, for if 10 Q—Q2, Q—K2 ch (e.g. 11 Kt—K5, P—B3, or 11 Kt—K2, B—Kt5, and wins).

10	Castles
11 Castles	R—K1
12 Q—B2	Kt—B1
13 Kt—Q1	

An artificial manœuvre. A more direct line of play would be 13 Kt—KKt5, P—KKt3; 14 P—KR4, etc.

13	P—B3
14 Kt—K3	B—K3
15 Kt—R4	

Too much manœuvring. Here again 15 P—KR4 has its points.

| 15 ...... | B—QB2 |

Heralding the concerted action of the *two Bishops*. The KB will aim at the isolated QP, and the QB will take White's weaknesses on the K side as its target.

16 P—QKt4

As the Q side, in view of Black's threats, is at present of secondary importance, 16 B—B5 is better, defending the QP by 17 QR—Q1, in case of 16 .... B—Kt3.

| 16 ...... | B—Kt3 |
| 17 Kt—B3 | B—KB2 |

A profound manœuvre.

18 P—Kt5

An unwise measure, as the opening of a file will benefit only his adversary. Sound again would be 18 B—B5, in order to oppose 18 .... B—KR4 with 19 B—Kt4 (if then 19 .... R×Kt; 20 B×B).

18	B—KR4
19 P—Kt4	B—KB2
20 P×P	R—B1
21 Q—Kt2	P×P
22 P—B5	Q—Q3

Threatening 23 .... Q—B5.

| 23 Kt—Kt2 | B—B2 |

Emphasising the weakness of White's King's field.

24 KR—K1

Too late to seek simplification. But if 24 P—KR4, R—K5, etc.

| 24 ...... | P—KR4 |

An important thrust.

25 P—KR3	Kt—R2
26 R×R ch	R×R
27 R—K1	R—Kt1
28 Q—B1	Kt—Kt4

Deadly, for if 29 Kt×Kt, Q—R7 ch; 30 K—B1, P×Kt, threatening 31 .... Q—R8 ch; 32 K—K2, Q×Kt.

29 Kt—K5

A most ingenious parry, which, however, does not meet all the threats.

| 29 ...... | P×Kt |

More exact than 29 .... Kt×P ch; 30 K—B1, B—K1.

| 30 Q×Kt | P—K5 |

Leaving White the choice between losing the Bishop or the Knight.

| 31 P—B6 | P—Kt3 |

More exacting than 31 .... Q×P.

32 P—B4

Trying to the last to find a way out. White now threatens 33 P×P, whilst if, at once, 32 P×P, Q—R7 ch; 33 K—B1, P×B, threatening 34 .... Q—R8 mate.

32 ......   P×P
A realist's policy.

33 B—K2   P×P
34 B—R5   R—Kt7
35 Kt—R4   Q×P (B5)
36 Q×Q   B×Q
Resigns.

390

White	Black
DUS-CHOTIMIRSKI	MARSHALL

(Moscow, 1925)

An interesting game, which demonstrates ad oculos *that a player with a genius for attack will nearly always succeed in engineering one, even as Black, and even in so staid an opening as the Queen's Gambit Declined. After six moves, Marshall assumes the lead (6 .... P—B4), and six moves later he already pierces White's outer defences.*

1 P—Q4   P—Q4
2 Kt—KB3   Kt—KB3
3 P—B4   P—K3
4 Kt—B3   B—Kt5
An enterprising continuation. Ulterior objects: .... P—QB4 and .... Q—R4.

5 P—K3
If 5 B—Kt5 seems here to be unpromising, White could upset his adversary's plans by 5 Q—R4 ch, Kt—B3; 6 Kt—K5.

5 ......   Castles
6 B—Q2
Resigning himself to the rôle of a defender. A sound positional measure would be 6 Q—Kt3, which would force Black to give up his original intentions: 6 .... P—B4 (on account of 7 QP×P, B×P; 8 B—K2, etc., with an advantage in development), and to have recourse to less bellicose stratagems, such as 6 .... Q—K2 or 6 .... Kt—B3.

6 ......   P—B4
Execution of his bold scheme.
Clearly not 6 .... Kt—K5, as 7 Kt×Kt wins.

7 R—B1
White hopes to have the last word on the QB file, whereas the affray will be located in the centre, around his King. More pertinent would be 7 B—K2.

7 ......   BP×P
8 KKt×P
After 8 KP×P, P×P; 9 B×P, Kt—B3, etc., Black would have an easy target in the isolated QP.

8 ......   P—K4
9 Kt—B2
If 9 Kt—B3, P—Q5, etc. (not 9 .... P—K5; 10 Kt—Q4, etc.).

9 ......   B×Kt
10 B×B   Kt—B3
If 10 .... P—Q5; 11 B—Kt4, R—K1; 12 B—K2, Kt—B3; 13 P—B3 (if 13 Castles, P—K5); 13 .... B—B4 (if 13 .... Q—Kt3; 14 P—B5, followed by Castles); 14 B—Q3, P—K5; 15 P×P, Kt×P; 16 Castles, and White is mastering his adversary's onslaught.

11 Kt—Kt4
He underestimates the latent energy of the black forces. A policy of retrenchment by 11 P×P, Kt×P; 12 B—Q2, etc., is preferable.

11 ......   B—Kt5
A most vigorous intermediary measure. It goes without saying that the peaceful line of play 11 .... Kt×Kt; 12 B×Kt, R—K1; 13 P×P, Kt×P; 14 B—Q2, etc., does not appeal to him.

12 Q—Q3
Of little use would be 12 B—K2, B×B; 13 Q×B, P—Q5; 14 Kt×Kt (not 14 B—Q2, P—Q6, etc., nor 14 P×P, P×P, threatening .... R—K1); 14 .... P×Kt; 15 B—Q2 (if 15 B—Kt4, P—B4; 16 B×P, P—Q6; 17 Q—Q1, P—Q7 ch; 18 Q×P, Q×Q ch; 19 K×Q, Kt—K5 ch, followed by .... Kt×B, winning a piece); 15 .... P—Q6, etc., and Black has the advantage. The lesser evil would be 12 P—B3, although it weakens the King's field.

12 ......   P—Q5
A pawn sacrifice for the sake of an open file.

13 Kt×Kt   P×Kt
14 P×P
After 14 B—Kt4, R—K1, White's position is no better.

14 ......   P×P
15 B×P
If 15 Q×QP, R—K1 ch; 16 K—Q2, Q—B2, and wins, whilst after the text move, if 15 .... R—K1 ch; 16 B—K3, and the K file is closed again.

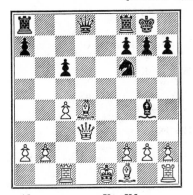

15 ......   Kt—K5

A beautiful manœuvre, avoiding the exchange 16 B × Kt, and threatening 16 .... Q—R4 ch.

16 P—QR3

In order to reply to 16 .... Q—R4 ch with 17 P—Kt4. If 16 Q × Kt, R—K1; 17 B—K5, Q—R4, and wins, and if 16 B—K3, Q—R4 ch, with vertical and diagonal effect.

| 16 ...... | R—K1 |
| 17 B—K3 | Q—B3 |

Threat: 18 .... Kt × P.

18 B—K2

If 18 P—B3, Q—R5 ch; 19 K—Q1 (or 19 P—KKt3, Kt × P; 20 P × Kt, Q × P ch, etc.); 19 .... QR—Q1, exploiting the central files.

18 ......   Kt × P

If 19 B × Kt, R × B ch, etc.

19 Q—B3	Kt × R
20 Q × Q	P × Q
21 B × B	R × B ch

And White soon resigned, being a Rook down. If 22 B—K2, QR—K1. If 22 K—Q2, Kt—B7; 23 K × R, Kt × B, with a piece ahead. Also after 22 K—B1, QR—K1, etc., White has nothing left.

391

| *White* | *Black* |
| BERGER | THOMAS |

(Hastings, 1926–7)

An important feature of this game is a new idea in the lay-out of the opening, which, carried out with the utmost logic and energy, leads to a speedy and conclusive win.

1 P—Q4	Kt—KB3
2 P—QB4	P—K3
3 Kt—KB3	P—Q4
4 B—Kt5	

White applies the *pinning strategy* before playing out his QKt.

4 ......   P—KR3

After 4 .... B—K2, White can either revert to the normal development by 5 Kt—B3 or play 5 P—K3, Castles; 6 QKt—Q2, etc., the *neo-orthodox* development. The same can occur after 4 .... QKt—Q2.

After 4 .... P—B3, White can, with even less misgivings, play 5 P—K3, followed by QKt—Q2 and B—Q3, etc. Therefore Black's most independent course is 4 .... P × P or, more accurately, 4 .... B—Kt5 ch; 5 Kt—B3, P × P (the *Vienna Variant*), trying, eventually, to hold the gambit pawn.

5 B × Kt

After 5 B—R4 he can still more comfortably capture and hold the gambit pawn by 5 .... B—Kt5 ch; 6 Kt—B3, P × P; for if then 7 P—K4, there follows 7 .... P—KKt4; 8 B—Kt3, P—Kt4 (the *Duras Trap*).

5 ......   Q × B

It is better first to give an intermediary check by 5 .... B—Kt5 ch.

6 Kt—B3   P—B3

If 6 .... B—Kt5; 7 Q—Kt3.

7 Q—Kt3

This positional sally (preventing 7 .... B—Kt5 and preparing P—K4) solves the problem of the position in a far more dynamic manner than would 7 P—K3. But 7 P—K4 would be premature, e.g. 7 .... P × KP; 8 Kt × P, B—Kt5 ch, liberating Black's position.

7 ......   Kt—Q2

After 7 .... B—Q3, White also plays 8 P—K4. Played in a game Winter—Perkins (cable match, 1926), this advance has, it may be said, livened up the rather stereotyped lines of the *Orthodox Variation*.

8 P—K4

An energetic advance, introduced for the first time in tournament practice in the present game. It changed the appreciation of the whole of this variation, and has been adopted since by several leading masters (amongst them Dr. Alekhine). It may be added that Mr. Berger's inventive spirit has enriched contemporary theory with a number of fertile and original ideas.

Languid would be 8 P—K3, B—Q3; 9 B—K2, Q—K2, etc., and Black's game is consolidated.

8	P×KP
9 Kt×P	

The beginning of the Queen hunt.

| 9 ...... | Q—B5 |

Insisting on remaining in enemy territory.
Against 9 .... Q—Q1; 10 Castles would be
justified.
Relatively best is 9 .... Q—B4.

10 B—Q3	B—K2
11 Castles	Castles
12 KR—K1	P—QKt3

Or, avoiding this weakness, 12 ....
R—Q1; 13 QR—Q1, Q—B2, etc., or, at
once, 12 .... Q—B2, but Black's game
remains difficult.

13 QR—Q1	R—Q1
14 B—Kt1	Kt—B1

Better would be the discreet retirement
14 .... Q—B2, although even then White
maintains a strong and lasting pressure after
15 Q—Q3, Kt—B1; 16 Kt—K5, B—Q3;
17 Q—KKt3, B×Kt; 18 P×B, R×R;
19 R×R, K—R1; 20 Kt—Q6, etc.

| 15 Kt—K5 |

Already decisive, as White now threatens
16 P—Kt3, Q—B4; 17 Kt—Q6, followed by
Kt(Q6)×P.

15	P—KR4
16 P—Kt3	Q—R3
17 Q—KB3	

In order to win, not only a pawn, but the
exchange as well, whereas 17 Kt×QBP,
R—K1 allowed Black some breathing space.

| 17 ...... | B—B3 |

If 17 .... P—KB4, then equally 18 Kt×P,
etc.

18 Kt×QBP	R—K1
19 Kt—Q6	B—Q2
20 Kt×R	R×Kt
21 Kt—K5	Resigns

An important game.

392

White	Black
FINE	GRÜNFELD

(Amsterdam, 1936)

A feature of this fine game is a positional
*Queen's sacrifice on the 13th move, an unusual
occurrence.*

1 P—Q4	P—Q4
2 Kt—KB3	Kt—KB3
3 P—B4	P—K3
4 Kt—B3	P×P

Deferred acceptance of the gambit.

| 5 P—K4 |

More violent than 5 P—K3.

5	B—Kt5
6 B—Kt5	

If 6 Q—R4 ch, Kt—B3, and if 6 P—K5,
Kt—Q4, in favour of Black.

| 6 ...... | P—B4 |

The position represents the main line of
the *Vienna Variant*.

| 7 P—K5 |

Accepting the challenge. After 7 P×P,
Black could either simplify by 7 ....
Q×Q ch; 8 R×Q, QKt—Q2, etc., remaining with an extra pawn, or complicate
matters by 7 .... Q—R4. Useless would
be 7 P—Q5 (7 .... P—KR3; 8 B×Kt,
P×B, etc.), or the exchange 7 B×Kt (7 ....
Q×B; 8 B×P, P×P; 9 Q×P, Kt—B3;
10 Q×Q, P×Q, etc. Therefore the simplest
is 7 B×P, P×P; 8 Kt×P, etc.

7	P×P
8 Q—R4 ch	

Well timed! 8 Kt×P, Q—R4; 9 P×Kt,
Q×B, etc., would be weak. After 8 P×Kt,
P×P; 9 B—R4 (if 9 Q×P, Q×Q; 10 Kt×Q,
P×B, etc., and if 9 Q—R4 ch, Kt—B3;
10 B—Q2, P×Kt, etc., with even chances);
9 .... Kt—B3 (and here clearly not 9 ....
P×Kt; 10 Q×Q ch, K×Q; 11 B×P ch,
K—B2; 12 P×P, etc.); 10 Kt×P, Kt×Kt;
11 KB×P, White has some compensation
for his pawn.

8	Kt—B3
9 Castles	

Wrong would be 9 P×Kt, P×Kt, and
Black gets in first.

| 9 ...... | B—Q2 |

An active defence. Unfavourable is 9 ....
B×Kt; 10 P×B, with increased pressure by
White.

| 10 Kt—K4 | B—K2 |

If 10 .... P—KR3; 11 Kt×Kt ch,
P×Kt; 12 B×KBP, and wins. That is why
Black intends to give up a piece for three
pawns, which plan White will soon thwart
by an orgy of sacrifices.

11 P×Kt	P×P
12 B—R4	Kt—Kt5
13 Q×Kt	

A striking, even though compulsory, sacrifice of the Queen. 13 Q—R3 looks a

possible expedient (13 .... Kt—Q6 ch; 14 R×Kt, B×Q; 15 Kt×P ch, etc., and White sacrifices his Queen in a far more sustained manner), but—Black would reply 13 .... Kt—Q4 with advantage.

13	B×Q
14 Kt×P ch	K—B1
15 R×P	

Another *finesse*. He refrains from recovering his Queen by 15 Kt×P ch, R×Kt; 16 B×Q, R×B; 17 R×P, P—Kt4, and if anything Black has the best of it!

| 15 ...... | Q—R4 |

This escape succeeds but partially. The best course is 15 .... B—K2; 16 Kt×B ch (not 16 R×B, B×Kt); 16 .... K—Kt2; 17 R—Kt4 ch, K—R3; 18 QKt—K5, the battle is in full swing.

16 Kt×B ch	K—K1
17 Kt—B6 ch	K—B1
18 B×P	

Disdaining the draw.

18	R—B1
19 K—Kt1	P—R4
20 KR—Q1	B—K2
21 Kt—Q7 ch	K—K1
22 B—KKt3	R—KKt1
23 P—KR3	R—Kt2
24 P—R3	P—Kt4

Priming a counter-attack.

25 B—Kt3	P—Kt5
26 P×P	B×P
27 B—K5	R×P
28 R×B	

A complementary sacrifice.

28	Q×R
29 Kt—B6 ch	K—K2
30 R—Q7 ch	K—B1
31 B—Q6 ch	Q×B
32 R×Q	R×P
33 R—Q3	

Guarding everything. In the subsequent struggle, the exchange of three minor pieces for Rook and two pawns is in favour of White.

| 33 ...... | K—K2 |

Or 33 .... P—R5; 34 Kt—Kt4, R—KB8 ch; 35 B—Q1, etc.

| 34 Kt×P | R—KB8 ch |
| 35 B—Q1 | |

Not 35 K—R2, R—QB4, with a double target.

35	R—KKt1
36 Kt—Q4	P—K4
37 Kt—B6 ch	K—K3
38 K—R2	R×B

Getting two pieces for the Rook, but as his pawns become doubled, the transaction is a poor one.

39 R×R	R—Kt4
40 Kt—B4 ch	P×Kt
41 Kt—Q4 ch	K—B3

If 41 .... K—K2; 42 R—KB1, R—R4; 43 P—R4.

| 42 R—KB1 | R—R4 ch |
| 43 K—Kt1 | |

If 43 K—Kt3, R—R4.

| 43 ...... | R—R5 |
| 44 Kt—B3 | |

Not 44 R×P ch, K—K4.

44	R—K5
45 R—K1	R—K3
46 R×R ch	P×R

On the surface, Black has improved his pawn formation and has better prospects, but the white King, arriving in time, decides the issue.

47 K—B2	P—K4
48 K—Q3	K—B4
49 Kt—Q2	K—Kt4
50 K—K4	K—R5
51 K×P	K×P
52 K×P	Resigns

A magnificent game.

393

| White | Black |
| JANOWSKI | MARSHALL |

(Cambridge Springs, 1904)

A desperate battle, in which White's attacking resources seem to be inexhaustible, but are thwarted by an ingenious and sound defence.

1 P—Q4	P—Q4
2 P—QB4	P—K3
3 Kt—QB3	P—QB4

Though simple in appearance, this, the *Tarrasch Defence*, leads to intricate and varied play. It is, however, less plastic than the orthodox defence (with 3 .... Kt—KB3).

4 P—K3
A very solid continuation.

4	Kt—QB3
5 Kt—B3	Kt—B3
6 P—QR3	

The question for White is how to utilise "the move" in order to put an end to symmetry. The text move intends the formation of an *Extended Fianchetto* by 7 QP×P, B×P; 8 P—QKt4 and 9 B—Kt2. After 6 B—Q3, Black can simplify matters by 6 .... QP×P; 7 B×P, B—K2; 8 Castles, Castles; 9 P×P, Q×Q; 10 R×Q, B×P, etc.

6 ......   Kt—K5
Trying to obtain the initiative.
A simplifying continuation is 6 .... QP×P; 7 B×P, P—QR3, etc. Desultory would be 6 .... B—Q3; 7 QP×P, B×BP; 8 P—QKt4, B—Q3; 9 B—Kt2, Castles; 10 Q—B2, Q—K2 (it would be fatal to keep up the symmetry, e.g. 10 .... P—QR3; 11 B—Q3, P×P; 12 B×P, P—QKt4; 13 B—Q3, Q—B2; 14 Kt—K4, Kt×Kt; 15 B×Kt, with a *double attack* on QB6 and KR7); 11 QR—Q1, R—Q1; 12 B—Q3, and White has preserved the advantage of the move.

7 B—Q3
After 7 Kt×Kt, P×Kt, Black gains territory, e.g. 8 Kt—Q2, P—B4.

7 ......   Kt×Kt
Here the supporting 7 .... P—B4 would have no substance.

| 8 P×Kt | B—Q3 |
| 9 Castles | Castles |

Maintaining the tension in the centre as long as possible. A premature cession of territory would be 9 .... QP×P; 10 B×BP, Castles; 11 P—K4, P—QKt3; 12 B—K3, and White has a distinct advantage.

10 Q—K2
He accumulates energy in the centre, in preference to releasing the tension by 10 P—K4 (e.g. P×KP; 11 B×P, and, although White has cleared the terrain, he has no longer his precious KP).
Not without inconvenience is also 10 BP×P, KP×P; 11 P—K4, easing his game, but also his adversary's. Best is 10 Q—B2.

10 ......   Kt—R4
Threatening, eventually, ... Kt—Kt6.
Not 10 .... QP×P; 11 B×P. Kt—R4; 12 B—R2, etc., nor 10 .... P—QKt3 (a particularly instructive mistake); 11 P—K4, P×KP; 12 Q×P, with a *double threat*.

11 P—K4
Opening up the game. Too dissolving would be 11 BP×P, KP×P; 12 P—K4, Kt—Kt6; 13 R—R2, Kt×B; 14 R×Kt, QP×P; 15 Q×P, P—KKt3, etc.

11 ......   P×BP
He undoubles his opponent's doubled pawn, but frees his own game. After 11 .... P×KP; 12 Q×P, he would have to weaken his position by 12 .... P—KKt3 or 12 .... P—B4.

12 B×P	Kt×B
13 Q×Kt	Q—B2
14 Q—Q3	B—Q2
15 P—K5	B—K2
16 Kt—Kt5	

If 16 B—Kt5, B—QB3.

| 16 ...... | B×Kt |
| 17 B×B | KR—B1 |

Not merely to meet the threat 18 B—K7, but also to intensify the pressure on the QB file.

18 Q—Kt3
Threatening to produce a mating attack by 19 B—B6, P—KKt3; 20 Q—Kt5, etc.
Here and in the sequel White pursues an aggressive policy, as, with positional manœuvres, his KP would be a dead weight, hindering his Bishop.
Doubtful would be the comprehensive liquidation 18 P×P, Q×KP; 19 Q×B, Q×B; 20 KR—B1, QR—Kt1, and Black stands distinctly better.

18	K—R1
19 KR—K1	P×P
20 P×P	Q—B6

An active defence.

21 Q—B4   K—Kt1
Too passive would be 21 .... B—K1. By playing, now or on the next move, 22 Q—Kt4, K—R1; 23 Q—B4, etc., White could propose a repetition of moves, but prefers to chance his luck.

| 22 QR—Kt1 | P—QKt3 |
| 23 P—KR4 | |

Neck or nothing! Of course not 23 R—K3, Q—B8 ch.

23 ......   Q×RP
An important capture.

| 24 P—R5 | P—KR3 |
| 25 B—R4 | |

After 25 B×P, P×B, neither 26 Q×P, Q—B1, etc., nor 26 R—K3, R—R6, etc., would be healthy for White.

| 25 ...... | R—B6 |
| 26 Q—Kt4 | QR—QB1 |

More precise would be first 26 ....
Q—B1, for after the text move 27 R—R1,
Q—B1; 28 R × P is possible.

| 27 K—R2 | Q—B1 |
| 28 R—K4 | B—B3 |

Less clear-cut would be 28 .... B—R5;
29 R—QR1, B—B7; 30 R—B4, etc.

29 R—B4	K—R2
30 P—B3	B—Q4
31 Q—Kt3	B—B5
32 R—QR1	P—R4
33 R—Kt4	B—Q6
34 B—B6	

Now or never—otherwise 34 .... B—B4
would drive the Rook from the KKt file.
The sacrifice holds also many practical
chances.

| 34 ...... | P × B |
| 35 P × P | R—Q1 |

In order to cope with 36 R—Kt7 ch,
K—R1; 37 Q—B4 by 37 .... Q—Q3.

| 36 R—K1 | K—R1 |
| 37 R—K5 | |

Exciting play! If 37 R—Kt7, R × P, and
if 37 Q—B4 (threat: 38 R—Kt7); 37 ....
R—Q4 (counter-threat: 38 .... R × P ch);
38 R—K5, R × R; 39 Q × R (or 39 P × R,
R—B5, etc.); 39 .... R—B3; 40 Q—Kt3
(if 40 .... Q—Q3; 41 R—Kt8 ch, with
perpetual check); 40 .... Q—Q1, and wins.

| 37 ...... | B—B4 |

Parrying the threat of 38 Q—B4, followed
by R—Kt7.

| 38 R—Kt7 | R × QP |

Stopping 39 Q—B4.

| 39 R—Kt5 | R (B6)—B5 |

Preventing the capture 40 R × KtP by the
counter-threat at KR5.

| 40 Q—K5 | |

Now he can reply to 40 .... R—R5 ch
by 41 K—Kt3.

40	Q—Q3
41 P—Kt4	Q × Q ch
42 R × Q	B × P

Giving back the piece at the right moment.
Otherwise 43 R × BP would be painful.

43 P × B	R—B7 ch
44 K—Kt3	R—Q6 ch
45 K—B4	R—B5 ch
46 R—K4	R × R ch
47 K × R	R—Q2

A new phase; the birth of a new black

Queen is obviously approaching. But what
of White's chances in that respect?

| 48 K—B4 | P—R5 |
| 49 P—Kt5 | P × P ch |

If 49 .... R—Q5 ch; 50 K—K3, P—R6;
51 P—Kt6, etc.

| 50 K × P | P—R6 |
| 51 K—R6 | R—R2 |

Disentangling the King and providing a
support for the passed pawn, for if 51 ....
P—R7; 52 R—R7 ch, K—Kt1; 53 R—Kt7
ch, K—B1; 54 R—R7, K—Kt1; draw.

52 R—R7 ch	K—Kt1
53 R—Kt7 ch	K—B1
54 K—R7	

Imaginative (55 R—Kt8 mate).

54	K—K1
55 K—Kt8	P—R7
56 P—R6	P—R8 (Q)
57 P—R7	

| 57 ...... | Q × P |

An elegant "dual" is 57 .... R—R1;
58 R × P, Q—Kt8 ch; 59 R—Kt7, Q × R ch;
60 K × Q (60 P × Q, K—K2 mate); 60 ....
R—R2 ch; 61 K—Kt6, R × P; 62 K × R,
K—B2, and wins.

58 P—R8 (Q)	K—K2
59 Q—R1	R—Q2
60 K—R7	Q—B4 ch
61 K—R6	P—K4
62 R—Kt1	R—Q1
63 Q—Kt7 ch	Q—Q2
64 Q—B3	Q—K3 ch

Or, ruthlessly, 64 .... Q—R6 ch;
65 Q × Q, R—R1 ch, etc.

65	K—R7	Q—Q4
66	Q—R3 ch	Q—Q3
67	Q—B1	P—K5

Very powerful, with the main threat of
68 .... Q—R7 ch.

68	R—Kt2	Q—B4
69	Q × Q ch	P × Q
70	R—Kt5	K—B3
71	R × P	R—K1
72	R—B1	P—K6
73	R—B1 ch	K—K4
74	K—R6	P—B4
75	K—R5	K—K5
76	R—QR1	P—B5

Resigns.

394

White   *Black*

ROTLEVI   RUBINSTEIN

(Lodz, 1907)

*If any criticism of the following magnificent
game can be made, it is that White's impetuous advance (19 P—K5) does not take
his own security sufficiently into account.
Black, on the other hand, has the great and
enviable gift of sensing the exact moment
of the crisis. Any stricture on White's play,
however, must needs be charitable, in view
of the transcending brilliance and depth of his
adversary's operations.*

1	P—Q4	P—Q4
2	Kt—KB3	

Accepted as more solid than at once
2 P—QB4, but it allows the trenchant reply
2 .... P—QB4, which frees Black's game.

2	......	P—K3
3	P—K3	P—QB4
4	P—B4	Kt—QB3
5	Kt—B3	Kt—B3

By an inversion of moves, we now have
the *normal position of the Tarrasch Defence.*

6 QP × P

Less consistent than 6 P—QR3 or
6 B—Q3, maintaining as long as possible
the tension in the centre.

6	......	B × P
7	P—QR3	P—QR3
8	P—QKt4	B—Q3

The Bishop has here a greater field of
action than at K2 or QR2.

9	B—Kt2	Castles
10	Q—Q2	

Loss of time—the Queen will soon have
to seek a better square (14 Q—K2). The
most useful move is 10 Q—B2.

10	......	Q—K2
11	B—Q3	P × P
12	B × P	P—QKt4
13	B—Q3	R—Q1
14	Q—K2	B—Kt2
15	Castles KR	

It can be seen that, owing to the time
wasted by White's Queen and KB, Black
now has the initiative.

15	......	Kt—K4
16	Kt × Kt	B × Kt

Threatening to win a pawn by 17 ....
B × P ch; 18 K × B, Q—Q3 ch, followed by
.... Q × B. White's next move provides
against this, but loosens the K side defences.

17	P—B4	B—B2
18	P—K4	QR—B1
19	P—K5	

This attempted offensive weakens the inner
lines. He should have played 18 QR—Q1.

19	......	B—Kt3 ch
20	K—R1	Kt—Kt5

A fine manœuvre, initiating a decisive
attack.

21 B—K4

After 21 Q × Kt, R × B. Black dominates
the field.

21	......	Q—R5

The invasion continues.

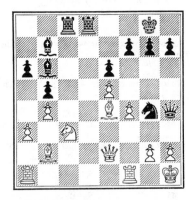

22 P—Kt3

The alternative 22 P—R3, parrying the
mate, would lead to the following brilliant

lines of play: 22 .... R×Kt (an *eliminating sacrifice*, getting rid of the Knight, which *overprotects* the KB); 23 B×R (or 23 Q×Kt, R×P ch; 24 Q×R, Q×Q ch; 25 P×Q, B×B ch; 26 K—R2, R—Q7 ch; 27 K—Kt3, R—Kt7 ch; 28 K—R4, B—Q1 ch; 29 K—R5, B—Kt3 mate); 23 .... B×B; 24 Q×Kt (or 24 Q×B, Q—Kt6; 25 P×Kt, Q—R5 mate); 24 .... Q×Q; 25 P×Q, R—Q6 (with the double threat of 26 .... R—R6 mate and 26 .... R×B); 26 K—R2, R×B, and Black wins. Beautiful as are these variations, the continuation in the text is still more splendid.

> 22 ...... R×Kt
> 23 P×Q

Or 23 B×R, B×B ch, leading to .... Q×P mate.

> 23 ...... R—Q7

A *deflecting sacrifice*. The whole series of events centres on White's K4, which is still guarded by the white Queen.

> 24 Q×R B×B ch
> 25 Q—Kt2 R—R6

The final point. White resigns, as mate at R2 cannot be prevented.

A memorable game.

395

White	Black
NIMZOWITSCH	TARRASCH

(St. Petersburg, 1914)

A famous game, in which the tension in the centre is suddenly relieved by a diversion on the K side, which comprises the extremely brilliant sacrifice of two Bishops. The fact that it is Black who is responsible for this deed of valour enhances the merit of the performance.

> 1 P—Q4 P—Q4
> 2 Kt—KB3 P—QB4
> 3 P—B4 P—K3
> 4 P—K3

One of the aspects of the *Tarrasch Defence* in which White reserves his decision to develop the QKt at QB3 or, eventually, at Q2.

> 4 ...... Kt—KB3
> 5 B—Q3 Kt—B3

He could gain a *tempo* by 5 .... QP×P;

6 B×BP, Kt—B3, etc., but he prefers to maintain the tension.

> 6 Castles B—Q3

More busy than 6 .... B—K2.

> 7 P—QKt3 Castles
> 8 B—Kt2 P—QKt3

Of little value at this stage would be 8 .... QP×P; 9 KtP×P, P×P; 10 P×P, and White's mobile centre would be a dangerous weapon.

> 9 QKt—Q2 B—Kt2
> 10 R—B1

Although the QB file is important in the scheme of things, work on the K file by 10 Q—K2 with Kt—K5 is more pressing.

> 10 ...... Q—K2
> 11 BP×P

If 11 QP×P, then 11 .... KtP×P, with a well-balanced game for Black, but not 11 .... B×P; 12 P×P, Kt×P; 13 Kt—K4, etc. The most patient course is 11 Q—K2.

> 11 ...... KP×P
> 12 Kt—R4

A provocative measure, comprising the loss of a pawn, in order to produce some weak points in the hostile K field.

If 12 Kt—Kt5, P×P; 13 P×P, P—KR3, etc., or, in quest of adventure, 13 R×Kt, B×R; 14 B×P, B—K4, etc., stopping his opponent's impetus.

> 12 ...... P—Kt3
> 13 Kt (R4)—B3 QR—Q1
> 14 P×P P×P
> 15 B—Kt5 Kt—K5
> 16 B×Kt B×B
> 17 Q—B2

After 17 Kt×Kt, P×Kt; 18 Kt—Q2, B×P ch; 19 K×B, Q—Q3 ch; 20 K—Kt1, Q×Kt; 21 Q×Q, R×Q; 22 R×P, R×B; 23 R×B, R×RP, Black has won a pawn.

> 17 ...... Kt×Kt
> 18 Kt×Kt

The guardian of the King's field leaves his post for a moment, assuming wrongly that 19 Q—B3 is a major threat.

If 18 Q×Kt, then also 18 .... P—Q5 (19 P×P, B×Kt; 20 P×B, Q—R5, etc.). (*Diagram. See p. 506.*)

> 18 ...... P—Q5

An *unmasking advance*.

> 19 P×P

Here 19 KR—K1 would soften, but not eliminate the shock.

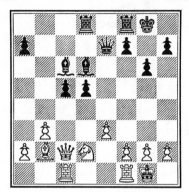

Position after 18 Kt × Kt

19 ......   B × P ch
The regulation sacrifice at KR7.

20 K × B   Q—R5 ch
21 K—Kt1   B × P
A *complementary sacrifice*: the King's field is entirely bare.

22 P—B3
For if 22 K × B, Q—Kt5 ch, followed by .... R—Q4 and .... R—R4 mate.

22 ......   KR—K1
A beautiful waiting move, cutting off the King's flight, for if 22 .... Q—R8 ch; 23 K—B2, Q—R7; 24 K—K1, etc., and if 22 .... Q—Kt6; 23 Kt—K4.

23 Kt—K4   Q—R8 ch
24 K—B2   B × R
25 P—Q5
A desperate resistance. If 25 R × B, Q—R7 ch, winning the Queen; and if 25 Kt—B6 ch, K—B1; 26 Kt × R, Q—Kt7 ch, etc.

25 ......   P—B4
26 Q—B3   Q—Kt7 ch
27 K—K3   R × Kt ch
Mass production in sacrifices!

28 P × R   P—B5 ch
Magnificent, and leading to a beautiful mate. However, there is a rigid mate in three by 28 .... Q—Kt6 ch; 29 K—Q2, Q—B7 ch; 30 K—Q1, Q—K7 mate.

29 K × P   R—B1 ch
30 K—K5   Q—R7 ch
31 K—K6   R—K1 ch
32 K—Q7   B—Kt4 mate
A *pure* mate.

396

White   *Black*
BURN   ZNOSKO-BOROVSKI

(Ostend, 1906)

In the following game, Black's QP—isolated but endowed with great striking powers—becomes the principal factor in the struggle.

1 P—Q4   P—Q4
2 P—QB4   P—K3
3 Kt—QB3   P—QB4
4 P × QP   KP × P
5 Kt—B3
If 5 P × P, P—Q5 (and not 5 .... Kt—KB3; 6 B—K3).

5 ......   Kt—QB3
Much more comfortable than 5 .... Kt—KB3, which allows the pin by 6 B—Kt5.

6 B—Kt5
This sally is more straightforward than 6 B—K3, and more assertive than 6 B—B4. 6 P × P would be less positional; 6 P—KR3, too slow; 6 P—K3, unambitious; while 6 P—KKt3 is very deep.

6 ......   B—K2
7 B × B   KKt × B
8 P—K3
If 8 P × P, P—Q5.

8 ......   P × P
After 8 .... Castles; 9 P × P, Q—R4; 10 B—Q3, Q × BP; 11 Castles, and White has the greater control of the position. Similarly, if 8 .... Q—Kt3; 9 P × P.

9 KKt × P   Q—Kt3
Already Black has the initiative. Less precise would be 9 .... Castles; 10 B—K2, Q—Kt3, because of 11 Q—Q2.

10 Kt—Kt3
If, instead, 10 Q—Q2, B—Kt5.

10 ......   B—K3
11 B—Q3   Castles KR
12 Castles   KR—Q1
13 Kt—R4   Q—B2
14 R—B1   Q—K4
15 Q—K2   QR—B1
16 P—B4
A doubtful advance, but if, e.g., 16 QKt—B5, P—QKt3; 17 Kt × B, P × Kt, and Black has succeeded in reinforcing his pawn structure.

16	Q—B3
17 P—B5	B—Q2

Clearly not 17 .... B×P; 18 B×B, Kt×B; 19 P—Kt4.

18 Kt(R4)—B5	P—QKt3
19 Kt×B	R×Kt
20 P—Kt4	

He overestimates the resources of his position. A waiting policy is called for, e.g. 20 Q—KB2.

20	QR—Q1
21 K—R1	R—Q3
22 R—KKt1	

With the transparent menace 23 P—Kt5.

22	Q—Kt4
23 QR—B1	

Caution calls for 23 QR—Q1.

23	P—Q5
24 P—K4	

After 24 P×P, Kt×P; 25 Kt×Kt, R×Kt; the black Rooks would soon play a chief rôle.

24	Kt—K4

The beginning of telling manœuvres by the black Knights.

25 R—Kt3

Now (and even more so on the next move) Kt—B1 is essential, in order to stop the terrible pawn.

25	Kt(K2)—B3
26 Kt—Q2	Kt×B
27 R×Kt	Kt—K4
28 R—KKt3	P—Q6
29 Q—Kt2	R—QB3
30 Kt—B3	Kt×Kt
31 Q×Kt	R—B8

Blasting White's position, for if 32 R×R, Q×R ch; 33 R—Kt1, P—Q7; 34 Q—Q1, R—QB1, etc.

32 R(Kt3)—Kt1	R×R
33 R×R	Q—Q7

Very powerful, for if now 34 Q—Kt2, Q—QB7, followed by .... P—Q7, and if 34 R—B2, Q×R; 35 Q×Q, P—Q7, etc.; similarly, 34 Q—B2, Q×Q, etc., or 34 R—Q1, Q×P; 35 R×P, Q—Kt8 ch, etc.

34 R—QKt1	Q—K7
35 Q—Kt2	Q—K6
36 R—Q1	P—Q7

Obtaining by this penultimate advance a curious *Zugzwang* position.

37 P—KR3	Q—K8 ch
38 Q—Kt1	Q—K7
39 P—K5	R—Q6

Resigns

The simple means by which Black enforces the victory deserve the greatest praise.

397

White	Black
RUBINSTEIN	CAPABLANCA

(San Sebastian, 1911)

In a game overflowing with the finer points of positional play, the outstanding feature is perhaps the problem-like turn 17 Q—B1, by which White very elegantly saves all his unguarded pieces and remains with an extra pawn.

1 P—Q4	P—Q4
2 Kt—KB3	P—QB4
3 P—B4	P—K3
4 BP×P	KP×P
5 Kt—B3	Kt—QB3
6 P—KKt3	

First introduced by Schlechter (Schlechter—Dus Chotimirsky, *Prague*, 1908), and systematised by Rubinstein, this positional manœuvre has all but refuted the *Tarrasch Defence.*

6 ......   B—K3

The instinctive desire to guard his QP incites Black, here and later, to stress operations on the Q side. Without being, as yet, faulty, this plan insensibly leads on to a thorny path. It is more rational to look after the development of the K side, which can be done in one of two ways, as follows:

(*a*) 6 .... Kt—B3 (with .... B—K2 and .... Castles to follow—*the main variation of the Tarrasch Defence*); 7 B—Kt2, B—K2 (against 7 .... B—Kt5 the counter-pin 8 B—Kt5 is effective; if 7 .... P×P; 8 KKt×P, B—QB4; 9 Kt—Kt3, B—Kt3; 10 Castles, with advantage to White); 8 Castles, Castles; 9 P×P (a more expectative plan is 9 B—Kt5, B—K3; 10 R—B1, etc.); 9 .... P—Q5 (the *Tarrasch Gambit*, instead of which 9 .... B×P, etc., can be played without palpable damage); 10 Kt—QR4 (or 10 Kt—QKt5, B×P, etc.); 10 .... B—KB4, with even chances.

(*b*) 6 .... P—B5 (with a view to .... B—QKt5; .... KKt—K2 and .... Castles

—the *Folkestone Variation*, which revived the interest in the *Tarrasch Defence*); 7 B—Kt2 (a bold idea is 7 P—K4, P×P; 8 Kt—KKt5, Q×P; 9 B—B4, etc.); 7 .... B—QKt5; 8 Castles, KKt—K2; 9 P—K4. Other possibilities: 9 B—Q2 (or 9 B—Kt5, P—B3; 10 B—Q2, or 10 Kt—K5); 9 .... P×P; 10 Kt×P, Castles, etc., with equal prospects.

7 B—Kt2	B—K2
8 Castles	R—B1

Too dogmatic; Black devotes too much attention to the Q side.

If he wishes to avoid being pinned by 8 .... Kt—B3; 9 B—Kt5, etc., 8 .... P—KR3 is playable.

9 P×P	B×P
10 Kt—KKt5	

Feeling for weak points in the enemy camp.

10	Kt—B3
11 Kt×B	P×Kt
12 B—R3	

Attack in the centre, as the black King is still in the danger zone.

12	Q—K2
13 B—Kt5	Castles

Too late, and yet—as the storm now breaks—not late enough. Better would be 13 .... R—Q1.

14 B×Kt	Q×B
15 Kt×P	

A very complicated conception.

15	Q—R3

Now two white pieces are "in the air." Black cannot play 15 .... P×Kt; 16 Q×P ch, K—R1; 17 B×R, etc., nor 15 .... B×P ch; 16 K—Kt2, Q—R3; 17 Kt—B4, etc., with an easy win for White.

16 K—Kt2

Guarding the Bishop as well as, indirectly, the Knight. But the last word is not yet said.

16	QR—Q1

The Knight is apparently doomed.

17 Q—B1

A beautiful and profound manœuvre, which leads to the gain of a pawn.

17	P×Kt

If 17 .... Q×Q; 18 B×P ch, followed by 19 QR×Q, and if 17 .... R×Kt; 18 Q×Q, P×Q; 19 B×P ch, with an immediate win.

18 Q×B	Q—Q7
19 Q—Kt5	

Having cleverly won a pawn, White shows that he also can hold what he has gained.

19	Kt—Q5
20 Q—Q3	Q×Q

Evidently not 20 .... Q×KtP; 21 KR—QKt1, winning a piece. After the exchange of Queens comes the technical phase.

21 P×Q	KR—K1
22 B—Kt4	

Far less good would be 22 KR—K1, Kt—B7; 23 R×R ch, R×R; 24 R—Q1 (compulsory inactivity, for if 24 R—QB1, Kt—Kt5, attacking two pawns); 24 .... K—B2, (a false hope would be 24 .... R—K7; 25 B—Kt4, Kt—K6 ch; 26 K—B3, Kt×R; 27 K×R, Kt×KtP; 28 B—K6 ch, K—B1; 29 B×P, etc.); 25 R—Q2, Kt—Q5, etc.

22	R—Q3
23 KR—K1	R×R
24 R×R	R—QKt3

Very cleverly Black obtains some counter-play which will bring in a pawn on the Q side.

25 R—K5

Seeking compensation in the centre. For if 25 P—Kt3, R—QR3, and, on the other hand, 25 R—QKt1 would be too passive.

25	R×P
26 R×P	Kt—B3

On a defensive mission. After 26 .... Kt—B7; 27 B—K6 ch, K—B1; 28 R—Q7, Black's house would be in flames.

27 B—K6 ch	K—B1
28 R—B5 ch	

If, instead, 28 R—Q7, Kt—K4.

28	K—K1

After 28 .... K—K2; 29 B—B4 threatens R—B7 ch.

29 B—B7 ch	K—Q2
30 B—B4	P—QR3

To avoid the exchange of Rooks, for if .... K—Q3; 31 R—QKt5.

31 R—B7 ch	K—Q3
32 R×KKtP	P—Kt4
33 B—Kt8	P—QR4
34 R×P	P—R5
35 P—R4	P—Kt5
36 R—R6 ch	K—B4
37 R—R5 ch	K—Kt3
38 B—Q5	

This energetic-looking move is in reality a mistake. The win—well deserved after the previous deeply conceived play—is as follows: 38 B—B4, e.g. 38 .... P—Kt6; 39 R—Kt5 ch, K—B2; 40 B×P, P×B; 41 P×P, with a winning pawn formation, or

38 .... R×P; 39 R—Kt5 ch (not 39 B×R,
P—Kt6, etc.); 39 .... K—B2; 40 B×R,
and wins.

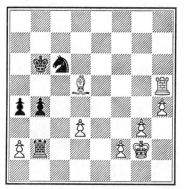

38 ......   P—Kt6

A rare instance of the Cuban missing an
opportunity. The solution, in great style,
is: 38 .... R×P; 39 B—B4 (making the
best of it, for after 39 B×R, P—Kt6 it
would be Black's game); 39 .... R—B7
(threat: 40 .... R×B); 40 R—Kt5 ch,
K—B2; 41 B—Kt8, and White's task is
exceedingly difficult.

39 P×P

The result of very precise calculations.
39 B×P is another way to win.

39 ......   P—R6
If 39 .... P×P; 40 R—R6.

40 B×Kt

This paradoxical capture is now feasible,
e.g. 40 .... P—R7; 41 R—Kt5 ch, K—R3;
42 R—Kt8, or if 40 .... K×B; 41 R—QR5,
etc.

40 ......   R×P
41 B—Q5   P—R7
42 R—R6 ch   Resigns

(If 42 .... K—R2 or 42 .... K—R4;
43 R—R8 ch, and if 42 .... K—Kt4;
43 B—B4 ch, followed by R—R6.)
A fine game.

398

White	Black
PIRC	ALEKHINE

(Bled, 1931)

*This whirlwind game proves conclusively
that the so-called "Morphy Style" is by no
means dead.*

1 P—Q4	P—Q4
2 P—QB4	P—K3
3 Kt—QB3	P—QB4
4 BP×P	BP×P

The *Duisburg Gambit,* which alters the
positional course of events. Black gives up
a pawn in order to get his pieces into
vigorous play.

5 Q—R4 ch

Or 5 Q×P, Kt—QB3; 6 Q—Q1, P×P;
7 Q×P, B—K3 (von Hennig's idea, which
allows the exchange of Queens, instead of
7 .... B—Q3; 8 B—Kt5, etc., or 7 ....
B—Q2; 8 P—QR3, etc.); 8 Q×Q ch,
R×Q, etc.

5 ......   B—Q2
More comfortable than 5 .... Q—Q2.

6 Q×QP   P×P
7 Q×QP

A realist's conception, but dynamically
7 Kt—B3 is better.

7 ......   Kt—QB3
If 7 .... Kt—KB3; 8 Q—Q1 is the wisest
course.

8 B—Kt5

A plausible but deceptive sally. More
rational is 8 P—K3, Kt—B3; 9 Q—Q1, etc.,
trying to castle as soon as possible, thus consolidating his game and remaining a pawn
ahead.

8 ......   Kt—B3
9 Q—Q2   P—KR3
10 B×Kt

He helps his opponent's development.
More self-reliant would be 10 B—R4,
P—KKt4; 11 B—Kt3, etc.

10 ......   Q×B
11 P—K3   Castles
12 Castles

Si duo faciunt idem, non est idem. Whereas
castling on the Q side on the part of Black
carries with it direct threats, it proves dis-
astrous for White, whose Queen is exposed.
But if 12 B—K2, B—KR6; 13 Kt—Q5,
B—QKt5; 14 Q×B, Kt×Q; 15 R—B1 ch,
K—Kt1; 16 Kt×Q, B×P, etc.
The best course is 12 Kt—Q5.

12 ......   B—KKt5
Decisive.

13 Kt—Q5
Compulsory.

13 ......   R×Kt
The beginning of the end!

14 Q×R   B—QR6
Another *coup.*

15 Q—Kt3
If 15 P×B, Q—R8 ch; 16 K—B2, B×R ch; 17 Q×B, Q×P ch; 18 K any, R—Q1, and wins.

15 ......   B×R
16 Q×KB   Q×P
A devastating irruption.

17 Q—Q3   B—Kt5
And not 17 .... R—Q1; 18 Kt—R3.

18 Kt—B3
He must at least develop his K side.

18 ......   B×Kt
19 Q—B5 ch
Holding on to his gains.

19 ......   K—Kt1
20 Q×B   Q—K8 ch
21 K—B2
After 21 Q—Q1, Q×P ch; 22 Q—Q2 is a simple theoretical win for Black.

21 ......   R—QB1
Very profound, as one might think that the text move allows a simplifying exchange of Queens.

22 Q—Kt3 ch   Kt—K4 dis ch
Black asserts himself.

23 K—Kt3   Q—Q8 ch
24 K—R3
The King at bay. If 24 K—Kt4, Q—Q3 ch, etc.

24 ......   R—B4
Resigns
For if 25 P—Kt4, R—B6 ch; 26 K—Kt2, Q—B8 mate; and if 25 P—Kt3, R—R4 ch; 26 K—Kt4, Q—Q7 mate.

399

White	Black
BURN	PERLIS

(Ostend, 1905)

Although it is at times possible to dispense with castling, in the majority of cases it is an essential of safety. Here Black neglects this precaution, with dire results.

1 P—Q4   P—Q4
2 P—QB4   P—K3
3 Kt—QB3
After 3 Kt—KB3, Black can also play 3 .... P—QR3.

3 ......   P—QR3
The *Janowski Defence*, which relies on tactical finessing.

4 P×P
Thwarting Black's primary intention to effect, for instance, after 4 P—K3 the development of his QB by 4 .... P×P; 5 B×P, P—QKt4, followed by .... B—Kt2.
The drawback of the text move is that it allows the hostile QB the freedom of the original diagonal QB1—KR6.
Too dogmatic is an attempted blockade by 4 P—B5, with the immediate reaction 4 .... P—QKt3; 5 P×P, P—QB4, etc. Against 4 Kt—B3 the reply 4 .... P×P; 5 P—QR4, P—QB4 is to be recommended.

4 ......   P×P
5 Kt—B3
Or, e.g., 5 B—B4, Kt—KB3; 6 P—K3, B—Q3; 7 B×B, Q×B, and Black has avoided all danger.

5 ......   P—QKt3
A time-wasting attempt to procure fresh prospects for the QB, already quite effective on the reopened diagonal QB1—KR6. However, the Bishop at QKt2 is better placed for the protection of the QP, whilst it prevents later on the thrust .... P—K4.
After 5 .... P—QB3 (the black square complex on Black's Q side proves to be

weak, which fact White will try to turn to account); 6 Q—B2, B—Q3; 7 P—KKt3 (preparing to oppose his Bishop, with the object of eliminating the guardian of the black squares in the opposite camp). The most steadfast is therefore 5 .... Kt—KB3; e.g. 6 B—Kt5, B—K2; 7 P—K3, Castles; 8 B—Q3, P—B3 (an afterthought); 9 B × Kt, B × B; 10 Q—B2, P—R3, leading to a pitched battle.

6 B—B4

Intensifying the development of his pieces, in preference to the more reserved 6 P—K3, or simplification by 6 B—Kt5, B—K2; 7 B × B, Kt × B, etc.

6 ......   B—Kt2

Not yet 6 .... B—Q3; 7 Kt × P, guarding the QB.

7 P—K3   B—Q3

Or 7 .... Kt—KB3, with greater expectations; 8 P—KR3 (making 8 .... Kt—R4 useless on account of 9 B—R2, maintaining his important Bishop); 8 .... B—K2, etc.

8 Kt—K5

Assuming control of the entire K side.

8 ......   Kt—Q2

Suddenly Black's situation has become difficult, for 8 .... P—KB3 is inadmissible on account of 9 Q—R5 ch, nor is 8 .... Kt—K2; 9 Q—R5, nor 8 .... Q—K2; 9 Q—Kt4 desirable.

Best is 8 .... Kt—KB3.

9 Q—Kt4

A telling manœuvre, which emphasises the desirability of having a defending Knight at KB3.

9 ......   B × Kt

More self-possessed is 9 .... P—Kt3.

10 P × B   K—B1
11 Castles   Kt—B4

With the triple function of guarding the QP and of keeping K5 and K3 under observation. If 11 .... Kt—K2; 12 Kt—K4, P × Kt; 13 R × Kt, Q—B1; 14 P—K6, etc.

12 P—K4   P—Q5
13 B—K3

The battle now rages around Q4.

13 ......   Kt—K3
14 B—QB4   B—B1
15 P—B4   Q—K2

He tries to take advantage of the situation by initiatng a counter-attack. 15 ....

P—QB4; 16 P—B5, Kt—B2; 17 B—KKt5, Q—K1; 18 Kt—Q5 is an artistic means of saving the forked pieces (18 .... Q × P; 19 B—B4, Q × KP; 20 B—Q6 ch, winning the Queen).

16 P—B5

Clearly not 16 QB × P, Kt × B, " 'ware the Queen," nor 16 Kt—Q5, " 'ware the two Bishops."

16 ......   P × Kt
17 P × Kt   Q—Kt5

Abandoning the King for an illusory prospect (18 B—Kt3, B × P, etc.). But 17 .... P × P ch; 18 K—Kt1, B × P; 19 B × B, Q × B; 20 Q × Q, P × Q; 21 R—Q7, etc.; and if 17 .... P—KR4; 18 Q—B3, which makes clear the desperate sally in the text.

18 R—Q8 ch

The finish is a perfect picture.

18 ......   K—K2
19 B—Kt5 ch   P—B3
20 B × P ch   Resigns
(20 .... P × B; 21 Q—Kt7 ch, K × R; 22 R—Q1 ch, Q—Q3; 23 Q—B8 mate.)

400

White	Black
STEINITZ	BIRD

(Hastings, 1895)

A fine game, full of vicissitudes. White's extended front strategy is badly upset by a riposte (18 .... P—B4), and his over-confidence in advanced passed pawns and the colourful play of the black Knight bring about an unavoidable mate.

1 P—Q4   P—Q4
2 P—QB4   P—K3
3 Kt—QB3   P—QB3

This *Semi-Slav Defence* contains a possible threat of taking and (by .... P—QKt4) maintaining the gambit pawn.

4 P—K3

A solid continuation. Against 4 Kt—B3 there are several possible replies:
(a) 4 .... P × P; 5 P—K4 (more solid is, however, 5 P—K3); 5 .... P—QKt4; 6 P—QR4, B—Kt5; 7 B—Q2, P—QR4, etc.

(b) 4 .... Kt—Q2; 5 P—K4, P×KP;
6 Kt×P, B—Kt5 ch; 7 Kt—B3, reverting to
the continuation in the text.

(c) 4 .... Kt—B3; 5 P—K3, QKt—Q2,
etc.

(d) 4 .... P—KB4: a *Stonewall Defence*,
which is not to be recommended in this
position because of 5 B—B4, B—Q3;
6 P—K3, etc.

| 4 ...... | Kt—Q2 |

Now that White has also shut in his QB,
the *Stonewall Defence* mentioned above,
4 .... P—KB4, would be justifiable.

| 5 Kt—B3 | B—Q3 |

Of little value would be 5 .... B—Kt5,
but here again 5 .... P—KB4 is playable.
The most usual is 5 .... KKt—B3, but
Black has a more *eccentric* development of
his KKt in view.

6 P—K4

He opens the centre without compunction,
and now his QB is freed. Nevertheless, the
text move weakens the centre (Q4). A more
patient continuation is 6 B—Q3, KKt—B3;
7 Castles, Castles (or 7 .... P×P; 8 B×BP,
P—K4); 8 P—K4, P×KP; 9 Kt×P, Kt×Kt;
10 B×Kt, and White has more space.

6	P×KP
7 Kt×P	B—Kt5 ch
8 Kt—B3	QKt—B3

An original development of the Knights.
Black wants to have them both on the K side,
but if at once 8 .... Kt—K2; 9 B—Kt5.

9 B—Q3

Preventing 9 .... Kt—K5.

9	Q—R4
10 B—Q2	Kt—K2
11 Castles	Castles
12 P—QR3	B×Kt
13 B×B	

He appropriates the hypothetical advantage of the *two Bishops*.

| 13 ...... | Q—B2 |
| 14 Kt—K5 | |

The strategy of *strong points*.

| 14 ...... | R—Q1 |
| 15 Q—K2 | P—QKt3 |

Heralding the counter-offensive.

16 P—QKt4

He decides to widen his front, anticipating
16 .... P—B4.

| 16 ...... | B—Kt2 |
| 17 P—B4 | |

Better is 17 QR—Q1.

| 17 ...... | Kt—B4 |

An active defence.

| 18 Q—KB2 | |

Or 18 B×Kt, P×B, obtaining a strong
point in the centre (K5).

| 18 ...... | P—B4 |

With this pawn sacrifice Black breaks up
the cohesion of the adverse pawns.

19 QP×P

He prefers simplification to 19 P—Q5,
with its ensuing complications, after which
the opening of lines by 19 .... Kt—K2;
20 QP×P, KBP×P, etc., would have
helped the black forces.

19	P×P
20 Q×P	Q×Q ch
21 P×Q	B—K5
22 KR—Q1	KR—QB1
23 P—B6	B×B
24 R×B	Kt—K5

Intending (e.g. after 25 B—R5) 25 ....
P—B3, with .... R×P, recovering his pawn
with advantage.

25 B—Kt4

He avoids the exchange and, incidentally,
deprives the adverse QKt of its flight squares.

| 25 ...... | P—QR4 |

A mistake would be 25 .... P—B3, on
account of 26 R—K1, P×Kt; 27 R×Kt,
P×P (or 27 .... R×P; 28 P×P); 28 R×P,
and White maintains the advantage.

26 QR—Q1

If 26 B—K1, P—B3, followed by ....
R×P. It looks as if White's trust in his
mass of pawns were justified.

| 26 ...... | P×B |
| 27 P—B7 | |

A threatening advance. But he has no
time to lose, for if at once 27 P×P, there
follows 27 .... P—B3, both driving off the
Knight and providing the King with a flight
square.

| 27 ...... | P—Kt4 |

The saving clause. The great English
player had an extraordinary gift for brilliant
and unexpected repartee.

| 28 R—Q8 ch | K—Kt2 |
| 29 RP×P | |

Another critical moment for Black, whose
Rooks seem to be inactive.

29 ......   Kt—K6

Powerful cavalry! As White's QR can move neither vertically (because of 30 .... R—R8 ch) nor horizontally (e.g. 30 R—K1, R×R; 31 P×R (Q), R×Q; 32 R×Kt, R—Q8 ch, followed by mate), White is compelled to exchange Rooks.

30 R×R   R×R
31 R—Q4

Or 31 R—Q7, R—QR1; 32 R×P ch, K—Kt1; 33 P—R4 (33 P—R3, R—R8 ch; 34 K—R2, Kt—B8 ch; 35 K—Kt1, Kt—Kt6 dis ch; 36 K—R2, R—R8 mate; and if 33 P—B8 (Q) ch, R×Q; 34 P×P, Kt×BP, etc.); 33 .... R—R8 ch; 34 K—R2, Kt—B8 ch; 35 K—R3, Kt—B7 mate. This illustrates the tremendous power of the "battery" set up by the two black Knights in the enemy camp.

31 ......   P—B4
32 R—Q7 ch   K—R3
33 P×P ch   K×P
34 P—R4 ch

Hoping to disengage his King. If 34 Kt—B7 ch, K—B3, etc.

34 ......   K—B3

And not 34 .... K×P; 35 Kt—B3 ch, K—Kt5; 36 R×P, etc.

35 Kt—B6

Trying to prevent the turning movement 35 .... R—QR1 by 36 Kt—R5, but in the meantime a frontal attack has become possible.

35 ......   R—KKt1

What a change in the situation!

Resigns—
for mate is inevitable.

SLAV DEFENCE

401

White	Black
ZUKERTORT	STEINITZ

(New York, 1886)

A clash of ideas: White's pawn strategy against Black's active handling of his pieces. A positional sacrifice by Black tips the scale in his favour and leads to lively happenings.

1 P—Q4   P—Q4
2 P—QB4   P—QB3

Whether this defence is called *Slav* (*vide* Tartakower), *Czech* (Tarrasch), or *Russian* (Bogoljubow), the fact remains that it was quoted by Polerio in 1590.

3 P—K3   B—B4

The idea underlying the *Slav Defence*, namely to preserve the mobility of the QB.

4 Kt—QB3

The restricted development by 4 Kt—Q2 will keep the long black diagonal clear.

After 4 B—Q3 the continuation is, not 4 .... B×B, nor 4 .... P—K3, but the far better 4 .... B—Kt3. Against 4 P×P Black must avoid 4 .... P×P; 5 Q—Kt3, etc., and play 4 .... B×Kt; 5 R×B, Q×P, etc. Against 4 Q—Kt3 the best reply is 4 .... Q—B1; 5 P×P, P×P; 6 Kt—QB3, P—K3, etc. A curious collapse could occur after 4 .... Q—Kt3, e.g. 5 P×P, Q×Q (5 .... B×Kt; 6 Q×Q, P×Q; 7 R×B, R×P; 8 B—B4, and White has the better game); 6 P×Q, B×Kt; 7 P×P, B—K5 (or 7 .... Kt×P; 8 R×B, winning a pawn); 8 R×P, R×R; 9 P—B7, and wins.

4 ......   P—K3

If 4 .... Kt—B3; 5 P×P, e.g. 5 .... P×P; 6 Q—Kt3, etc., or 5 .... Kt×P; 6 B—B4, with a slight advantage to White.

5 Kt—B3   Kt—Q2

This allows a more active policy than would 5 .... Kt—B3.

6 P—QR3

A passive move, which soon turns out to have been loss of time. The accurate application of a blockading plan is: 6 B—K2, B—Q3; 7 P—B5, B—B2; 8 P—QKt4, KKt—B3 (if 8 .... P—QR4; 9 P—Kt5, etc., but, as in the text, the continuation 8 .... P—K4 is playable); 9 B—Kt2, etc. The following continuations show little ambition: 6 B—Q3, or 6 P×P, KP×P, or 6 Q—Kt3, Q—Kt3, etc.

6 ......   B—Q3
7 P—B5

Initiating the blockade which, although a rather rigid undertaking, may be decisive unless opposed by timely and energetic measures.

7 ......   B—B2
8 P—QKt4   P—K4

Voilà! Prepared by the three preceding moves, this peremptory thrust overthrows the centre and is far more efficacious than

the quiet continuation 8 .... KKt—B3;
9 B—Kt2, Castles; 10 B—Q3, etc.

9 B—K2
Or 9 P × P, Kt × KP; 10 Kt—Q4, B—KKt3,
and Black has still kept his hold, e.g.
11 P—B4, Kt—Q2; 12 P—B5 (thinking to
win a piece); 12 .... Q—R5 ch; 13 P—Kt3
(or 13 K—Q2, QB × P; 14 Kt × B, Q—B7 ch,
followed by .... Q × Kt); 13 .... B × P
ch; 14 P × B, Q × R; 15 P × B, RP × P, etc.,
with the exchange and two pawns for a piece.

```
9  ......              KKt—B3
10 B—Kt2              P—K5
11 Kt—Q2
```
If 11 Kt—KR4, B—K3 threatens to win
a piece by 12 .... P—KKt4.

```
11 ......             P—KR4
```
Preventing 12 P—Kt4.

```
12 P—R3              Kt—B1
```
The reserve cavalry is being brought to
the critical sector.

13 P—QR4
Unaware of danger, White indulges in
quite inoffensive infantry manœuvres. Better
would be 13 Q—R4, Kt—Kt3 (if 13 ....
P—R4; 14 P—Kt5); 14 Castles QR, etc.,
with the issue uncertain.

```
13 ......             Kt—Kt3
14 P—Kt5             Kt—R5
15 P—Kt3
```
If 15 B—KB1, Q—Kt1, still preventing
16 P—Kt3, for then 16 .... KB × P;
17 P × B, Q × P ch; 18 K—K2, Kt—Kt5.

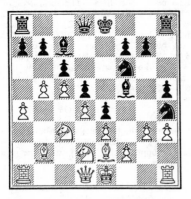

```
15 ......             Kt—Kt7 ch
16 K—B1              Kt × P ch
```
A very promising *positional sacrifice*.

```
17 P × Kt            B × P
18 K—Kt2             B—B2
19 Q—KKt1
```
Better is 19 Kt—B1 (R—R3; 20 K—B2,
etc.).

```
19 ......             R—R3
```
Substantially strengthening the attack on
three files.

```
20 K—B1              R—Kt3
21 Q—B2              Q—Q2
22 P × P             P × P
23 R—KKt1
```
He cannot prevent the loss of a third pawn.
If 23 P—R4, Kt—Kt5.

```
23 ......             B × P ch
24 K—K1              Kt—Kt5
25 B × Kt            B × B
26 Kt—K2             Q—K2
```
Preventing 27 Q—R4, and preparing,
eventually, against 27 .... P—R5.

```
27 Kt—KB4
```
Better is 27 K—Q1, with K—B2.

```
27 ......             R—R3
28 B—B3              P—Kt4
29 Kt—K2             R—B3
30 Q—Kt2             R—B6
31 Kt—KB1            R—Kt1
32 K—Q2              P—B4
33 P—R5
```
White can do nothing. If, e.g. 33 Kt—R2,
R—R6.

```
33 ......             P—B5
34 R—R1              Q—B2
35 R—K1              P × P ch
36 Kt × P            R—B7
37 Q × R
```
Despair. If 37 Q—Kt1, Q—B6; 38 Kt × B,
Q—Q6 ch, etc.

```
37 ......             Q × Q
38 Kt × B
```
Or 38 KR—B1, Q—R5, e.g. 39 R—KR1,
B—R6; 40 Kt—Kt1, P—Kt5, etc., or
39 Kt × B, Q × Kt, etc.

```
38 ......             B—B5 ch
39 K—B2              P × Kt
40 B—Q2              P—K6
41 B—B1              Q—Kt7
42 K—B3              K—Q2
43 R—R7 ch           K—K3
44 R—R6 ch           K—B4
45 B × P
```
A last trap.

45 ......   B × B
46 R—B1 ch
After which 46 .... Q × R; 47 Kt—Kt3
ch will not do. But if 46 .... K—K5;
47 R—K6 mate.

46 ......   B—B5
    Resigns.

402

White	Black
LANDAU	BERGER

(Match, 1932)

*The slow and progressive destruction of
White's King's field is a useful reminder of the
fact that "one evil begets another." If, however, the preparations for Black's counter-
attack are slow, its execution is swift and
overpowering.*

1 P—Q4	P—Q4
2 Kt—KB3	Kt—KB3
3 P—K3	B—B4
4 P—B4	P—B3
5 Kt—B3	

After 5 P × P, P × P the game would
become equalised after—

(*a*) 6 Kt—B3, P—K3; 7 Kt—K5 (or
7 Q—Kt3, Q—B1, etc.); 7 .... KKt—Q2
(not the plausible 7 .... QKt—Q2;
8 P—KKt4, B—Kt3; 9 P—KR4, with a
conclusive advantage to White); 8 Q—Kt3,
Q—B1; 9 B—Q2, Kt—QB3; 10 R—B1,
Kt × Kt; 11 P × Kt, B—K2, etc.; or

(*b*) 6 Q—Kt3, Q—B1; 7 Kt—R3 (the
better to exploit the open QB file); 7 ....
P—K3; 8 B—Q2, Kt—B3; 9 R—B1,
Kt—K5; 10 B—Kt5, Kt × B; 11 K × Kt,
B—Q3, etc.; or

(*c*) 6 B—Q3, B × B; 7 Q × B, Kt—B3, etc.

5 ......   P—K3
6 B—K2
After 6 Q—Kt3, Q—B2 Black has a good
game with a strong point in the centre (Q4),
and plenty of scope for his QB.
The simplest for White is 6 B—Q3.

6 ......   QKt—Q2
If at once 6 .... B—Q3; 7 P—B5, B—B2;
8 P—QKt4, P—QKt4 (8 .... P—QR4;
9 P—Kt5); 9 B—Kt2, etc. Whereas, after
the text move, if 7 P—B5, P—QR4 would
anticipate the formation of a chain of pawns
by White.

7 Kt—KR4
An ambitious but artificial plan.

7 ......   B—K5
8 Castles
If 8 P—B3, then, not 8 .... Kt—R4,
9 P—KKt3, etc., but 8 .... B—Kt3.

8 ......   B—Q3
9 P × P   BP × P
If 9 .... KP × P; 10 Kt × B, followed by
11 Kt—B5.

10 Kt × B	Kt × Kt
11 P—KKt3	Castles
12 P—B3	KKt—B3
13 Q—Kt3	

White's last five moves were meant to give
the game a positional tendency (pressure on
the Q side, early occupation of the open QB
file, the two Bishops, etc.).

13 ......   R—Kt1
Very calmly Black keeps watch on the
Q side, and reserves for himself freedom of
action on the K side (14 .... P—KKt4
15 Kt—Kt2, P—KR4, etc.) or in the centre
(14 .... P—K4).

14 P—B4
Anticipating the lines indicated, but sur-
rendering control of Black's K5.

14 ......   Kt—K5
15 B—Q3   Kt (Q2)—B3
Simple and energetic. Whilst maintaining
his hold on K5, Black again threatens 16 ....
P—KKt4.

16 Kt—B3   Q—K2
17 K—Kt2
Playing to win. But he should have
played 17 B—Q2, if only to put an end to the
drawback of having three pieces out of play
on the Q side.

17 ......   KR—B1
18 P—KR3   R—B2
19 P—Kt4   QR—QB1
20 Kt—Kt1
If 20 P—Kt5, Kt—R4, etc., and if
20 Kt—Q2, R × B; 21 Kt × Kt, P × Kt;
22 QR × R, R × R; 23 R × R, P × B;
24 R—B8 ch, Kt—K1; 25 Q × QP, P—B3,
etc., with advantage to Black.

20 ......   P—KR3
21 Q—Q1   P—R3
22 P—KR4
Running amuck. 22 B—Q2 is still better.

22 ......   Kt—R2
Reculer pour mieux sauter!

23 Kt—B3

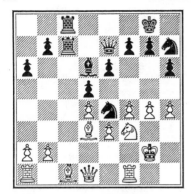

23 ......   P—KKt4
The storm breaks just before White has time to strike on the K side by 24 P—Kt5.

24 RP × P   P × P
25 Kt—Q2
Or, e.g. 25 P—B5, P × P; 26 P × P, P—Kt5; 27 Kt—R2, K—R1; 28 Kt × P, R—KKt1, and White's position collapses.

25 ......   P—B4
Thus the spirits White himself has evoked turn against him, as happened to the sorcerer's 'prentice.

26 P × BP   KP × P
27 Kt × Kt   BP × Kt
28 B—K2   P × P
In a trice the three K side files, previously thronged with pawns, have become a shambles.

29 P × P   Q—R5
Cutting off the white King's retreat.

Resigns
A fine example of a counter-attack.

403

White	Black
CAPABLANCA	LASKER

(New York, 1924)

Another battle of giants in which White's positional sacrifice of a piece is effective even in a simplified end-game.

1 P—Q4   Kt—KB3
2 P—QB4   P—B3
3 Kt—QB3   P—Q4
4 P × P
Reverting to the *Exchange Variation*, which is not so harmless as it looks.

4 ......   P × P
5 Kt—B3   Kt—B3
For in this *Four Knights Slav Variation* White is able to use his QB extensively, whilst Black cannot very well go in for symmetry.

6 B—B4
Less energetic is 6 P—K3 or 6 P—KKt3. If 6 Q—Kt3, Q—Kt3.

6 ......   P—K3
An important juncture. By shutting in his QB Black has to admit a measure of superiority in his adversary's position. He avoids symmetry by 6 .... B—B4, because of 7 Q—Kt3, e.g. 7 .... Q—Kt3; 8 Q × Q, P × Q; 9 B—B7, Kt—QKt5; 10 K—Q2, etc., or 7 .... Kt—QR4; 8 Q—R4 ch, B—Q2; 9 Q—B2, etc., with a small but enduring advantage to White.
Not without drawbacks would be other attempts: 6 .... Q—Kt3 or 6 .... Kt—K5 or 6 .... P—KKt3.

7 P—K3   B—K2
He adapts himself to the sinuous character of the position, and decides on a restricted development. Useless would be 7 .... B—Kt5 (8 B—Q3, Castles; 9 Castles, etc.). After 7 .... B—Q3; 8 B—Q3 would be hazardous (8 .... B × B; 9 P × B, etc.), and 8 B × B would lead to simplification (8 .... Q × B; 9 B—Q3, Castles; 10 Castles, P—K4, etc.).
The best move would be 8 B—Kt3 (e.g. 8 .... Castles; 9 B—Q3, R—K1; 10 R—B1, P—QR3; 11 Castles, Q—K2; 12 B—R4, with a steady pressure by White).

8 B—Q3   Castles
9 Castles
The straightforward path in preference to a waiting policy by 9 P—KR3 or 9 R—QB1.

9 ......   Kt—KR4
Trying to direct the course of events. The demonstration 9 .... Q—Kt3 would fail, as White gains space after 10 Kt—QR4, Q—R4; 11 P—QR3, B—Q2; 12 P—QKt4, Q—Q1; 13 Kt—B5, etc.

10 B—K5
Far more dynamic than 10 B—Kt3.

10 ......   P—B4
Black's plan is revealed. He plays for a *deferred stonewall*.
If 10 .... Kt × B; 11 Kt × Kt, Kt—B3; 12 P—B4, P—KKt3; 13 Q—B3, etc., White has a fine attack, and if 10 .... P—B3; 11 B—KB4 (not 11 Kt—KR4, P × B;

12 Q × Kt, P—K5; 13 Kt × KP, B × Kt, etc.,
nor 11 Kt—KKt5, P—KKt3, the only good
defence; 12 Kt × RP, P × B; 13 B × P,
Kt—Kt2; 14 Kt × R, B × Kt; 15 Q—Kt4,
Q—B3, etc., with the issue uncertain);
11 .... Kt × B; 12 P × Kt, and White has
the better prospects.

11 R—B1   Kt—B3
12 B × Kt
Preventing Black from completing his
stonewalling plans by .... Kt—K5, e.g.
12 B—KB4, Kt—K5; 13 Kt—K5, B—Q2,
etc., with an equalised position.

12 ......   P × B
More bellicose than 12 .... R × B or
12 .... B × B.

13 Kt—KR4   K—R1
14 P—B4   KR—Kt1
15 R—B3   B—Q2
16 R—R3
Hoping to be first with his attack. The
best is at once 16 R—Kt3.

16 ......   B—K1
He has to prevent 17 Q—R5, threatening
18 Kt—Kt6 ch. Against 16 .... Q—KB1
the sacrificial continuation 17 Kt × QP,
P × Kt; 18 Kt × P, B × Kt; 19 B × B, R—Kt2;
20 B—K6, etc., would be disturbing.

17 P—R3   R—Kt2
In order to reply to 18 Q—B2 by 18 ....
B—Q2, etc. If 17 .... R—QB1; 18 Kt × BP,
and if 17 .... B—B2; 18 Q—B2, R—Kt2;
19 Kt—R4, etc., gaining territory on the
Q side.

18 R—Kt3
Stamping his 16th move as too impetuous.

18 ......   R × R
In view of the threat of 19 R × R, K × R;
20 K—R1, followed by P—KKt4, but now
the KR file will serve White as a base of
action. Better would be 18 .... Q—Q2;
19 R × R, K × R; 20 P—KKt4, P × P;
21 Q × P ch, K—R1; 22 P—B5, B—B2, etc.,
and Black is not without resources.

19 P × R   R—B1
20 K—B2   Kt—R4
21 Q—B3
Unsound would be the sacrificial combination 21 P—KKt4, P × P; 22 Q × P,
P—B4; 23 Kt × BP, P × Kt; 24 B × P, R—B3,
etc. The correct manœuvre, combining
attack and defence, is 21 Q—K2.

21 ......   Kt—B5
22 Q—K2
To rectify the lack of precision in his preceding move.

22 ......   Kt—Q3
23 R—KR1   Kt—K5 ch
Too precipitate. The position is so complicated that both champions seem to grope
in the dark. Unprofitable would be × 23 ....
Q—Kt3 (24 Kt × QP, P × Kt; 25 Kt × P,
Kt × Kt; 26 B × Kt, etc.), as well as 23 ....
Q—Q2 (24 P—KKt4), but by playing
23 .... B—B2 Black could provide against
all dangers.

24 B × Kt   BP × B
Against 24 .... QP × P; the attack
25 P—KKt4, P × P; 26 P—B5, etc., would
succeed.

25 Q—Kt4   P—B4
The only way to parry the *double threat*
26 Q × P and 26 Kt—Kt6 ch. After 25 ....
R—B3; or 25 .... B—B2; there follows
26 P—B5.

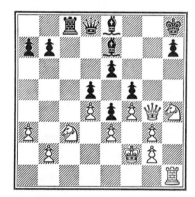

26 Kt × BP
This *positional sacrifice* has been impending for some time. After any other move
White's action would slacken, e.g. 26 Q—K2,
B × P, etc., or 26 Q—R3, K—Kt2; or finally,
26 Kt—Kt6 ch, B × Kt; 27 Q × B, Q—Kt1;
28 Q × Q ch, R × Q, and Black stands better.

26 ......   P × Kt
27 Q × P   P—KR4
28 P—KKt4
A draw would result from 28 Kt × QP,
R—B7 ch, etc.

28 ......   R—B3
29 P—Kt5
Not the best. At this point 29 Kt × QP

leads to success, e.g. 29 .... R—B7 ch;
30 K—Kt3, P—R5 ch; 31 K—R3, Q—Q3;
32 Q—K5 ch, Q × Q; 33 QP × Q, B—Q1;
34 R—Q1, etc., and White's advantage has
passed into the end-game phase.

29 ......   K—Kt1
If 29 .... R—Q3; 30 P—Kt4.

30 Kt × QP
Here again 30 Q × P ch would yield
nothing, but 30 P—KKt4 has points.

30 ......   B—B2
31 Kt × B ch   Q × Kt
32 P—KKt4   P × P
He scorns drawing variations: 32 ....
B—Kt3 (e.g. 33 Q—Q5 ch, B—B2, etc.) or,
even more safely, 32 .... R—B7 ch
(33 K—Kt3, R—K7; 34 P—Kt6, P—R5 ch;
35 R × P, R × P ch; 36 K—Kt2, R—K7 ch;
37 K—B1, R—K8 ch, with perpetual check).

33 Q—R7 ch   K—B1
34 R—R6   B—Kt1
35 Q—B5 ch   K—Kt2
If 35 .... K—K1; 36 R × R, P × R;
37 Q—Kt6 ch, winning the QBP.

36 R × R   P × R
37 K—Kt3
A skilful King. Not 37 Q × KtP, P—B4.

37 ......   Q—K3
A tactical error, presenting the adverse
King with an all-important *approach tempo*.
A mistake also would be 37 .... B—K3
38 Q—K5 ch, followed by P—B5. If 37 ....
B—Q4; 38 Q—B8, with multiple chances
(but not 38 Q × KtP, P—B4). All these
dangers would be avoided by 37 ....
B—B2; e.g. 38 Q × KtP, P—B4, or 38 Q—B8,
Q—K3; 39 Q—Kt7, Q—B5, and a draw is
in sight, as Black can penetrate into the
enemy camp.

38 K × P
The white King's activity is a token of
victory.

38 ......   Q × Q ch
If 38 .... Q—K2; 39 Q—K5 ch.
After the exchange of Queens the white
pawn phalanx, admirably seconded by their
King, ensures the win.

39 K × Q   B—Q4
40 P—Kt4
With a view to K—K5 and P—Kt5.

40 ......   P—R3
41 K—Kt4
Impeccable technique, which will allow the

pawns to advance in serried ranks. Less
methodical would be 41 K—K5, K—Kt3;
42 K—Q6, K—B4; 43 P—R4, B—Kt6;
44 K × P, etc.

41 ......   B—B5
42 P—B5   B—Kt6
43 K—B4   B—B7
44 K—K5   K—B2
45 P—R4
Proposing the transaction 45 .... B × P;
46 K × P, after which the three united passed
pawns would ensure a speedy decision.

45 ......   K—Kt2
46 P—Q5   B × P
47 P—Q6   P—B4
48 P × P   B—B3
49 K—K6   P—R4
50 P—B6 ch   Resigns
A very fine game.

404

White	Black
KLEIN	CAPABLANCA

(Margate, 1935)

*The interesting opening manœuvres in this
game result in a blockade of Black's position.
The game is also interesting in that it shows
how a moment's relaxation can throw away
the whole of a hard-earned advantage.*

1 P—Q4   Kt—KB3
2 P—QB4   P—B3
A preparatory move, leading back into
the *Slav Defence*.

3 Kt—QB3   P—Q4
4 Kt—B3
Offering the *Slav Gambit* in preference to
the more circumspect 4 P—K3.

4 ......   P × P
Accepting the challenge, instead of reverting to the *Semi-Slav Defence* by 4 ....
P—K3 or the *Fianchetto Variation* 4 ....
P—KKt3. Other, but freakish, continuations
are 4 .... Q—Kt3 or 4 .... B—B4 or
4 .... B—Kt5 or, finally, 4 .... Kt—K5.

5 P—QR4
Leading to the *primary variation* of the
Slav Gambit. Instead of preventing 5 ....
P—QKt4, White can also revert to the

secondary variation by 5 P—K3, P—QKt4; 6 P—QR4, etc., recovering the gambit pawn.

5 ......   B—B4

Effecting the main object of the *Slav Defence*, which is to bring the QB into play from the outset. A more reserved idea is 5 .... P—K3.

6 Kt—K5

With the twofold mission of regaining the gambit pawn and of challenging Black's QB by P—B3, followed by P—K4.

Apart from this *old Krause Attack*, White can also play the *new Krause Attack* by 6 Kt—R4, or else continue quietly with 6 P—K3, in which case Black must avoid the trap 6 .... Kt—R3; 7 B × P, QKt—Kt5; 8 Kt—K5, Kt—B7 ch; 9 Q × Kt, B × Q; 10 B × P mate.

6 ......   QKt—Q2

Unsubstantial would be the continuations 6 .... P—B4 (7 P—K4, Kt × P; 8 Q—B3) or 6 .... P—K3 (7 P—B3, B—QKt5; 8 Kt × P(B4), etc.).

7 Kt × P(B4)   Q—B2

Aiming at 8 .... P—K4. Less ambitious would be 7 .... P—K3; 8 P—B3, etc., or 7 .... Kt—Kt3.

8 P—KKt3

Suggested by Señor Capablanca himself, who is thus attacked with his own weapons. The sound move in the text assists both White's Bishops. After 8 P—B3, and even after 8 Q—Kt3, Black could still play 8 .... P—K4.

8 ......   P—K4
9 P × P   Kt × P
10 B—B4   KKt—Q2
11 B—Kt2   P—B3

A "mechanical" but sound protection of the square K4. Less consistent are other attempts, e.g. 11 .... B—K3 (12 Kt × Kt, Kt × Kt; 13 Castles, B—K2; 14 Q—B2, etc.) or 11 .... R—Q1 (12 Q—B1, P—B3; 13 Castles, B—K3; 14 Kt—K4, etc.).

12 Castles   B—K3

He wishes to clear up matters in the centre. If 12 .... R—Q1; 13 Q—B1.

13 Kt × Kt   P × Kt
14 B—K3   B—QB4
15 Q—B1

This fine manœuvre gets the Queen into play, whereas 15 B × B, Kt × B would further Black's emancipation. An unnecessary weakening of his own base would result from 15 Kt—K4, B × B; 16 P × B, Castles QR, with good prospects for Black.

15 ......   B × B

If 15 .... Q—Kt3; 16 P—R5, B × B; 17 P × Q, B × Q; 18 R × P, etc. The most self-possessed is 15 .... Castles KR.

16 Q × B   Q—Kt3

Trying to ease matters. Or 16 .... Castles KR; 17 P—R5.

17 P—R5

An important move.

17 ......   Q × Q
18 P × Q   P—QR3

He must prevent the outflanking manœuvre, but now White's blockade on the Q side ensures for him a positional advantage both sound and lasting. In spite of the absence of Queens, the struggle remains stubborn, and full of interesting and critical moments.

19 Kt—K4   K—K2
20 R—R4   KR—KB1
21 R—QB1   B—B4
22 Kt—Q2   QR—Kt1
23 R—QKt4   KR—Q1
24 B—K4   P—KKt3
25 B × B   P × B
26 Kt—B3

Not at once 26 R—KR4, on account of 26 .... Kt—B3, consolidating his position, whilst now White succeeds in nailing down not only his opponent's pawns, but his pieces as well.

26 ......   R—Kt1
27 R—KR4   R—Kt2
28 R—R5   R—KB1
29 R—B4   P—K5

Cutting the board in half, and so bisecting his centre, but at least preventing the serious threat of 30 R (B4)—KR4, winning a pawn.

30 Kt—Q4   R (Kt2)—B2

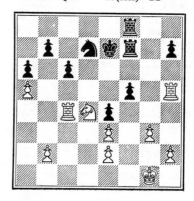

31 R—B1

Heedless play. By first playing 31 P—QKt4, White could have held his opponent's game in a vice. Not, however, 31 Kt—Kt3, R—B1, nor clearly 31 R—Kt4, P—B4.

31 ......   P—B4

At one stroke, Black frees himself.

32 Kt—Kt3   R—B1

Not 32 .... K—Q3; 33 R—R6 ch.

33 Kt—Q4

An artificial *equilibrium* is now established.

33 ......   R (B1)—B1
34 Kt—Kt3   R—B1

Draw.

An interesting game.

405

White	Black
ALEKHINE	EUWE

(Match, 1935)

A classic example of an attack based on the progressive occupation of strong points.

1 P—Q4   P—Q4
2 P—QB4   P—QB3

In both matches for the World Championship (1935 and 1937), the *Slav Defence* was selected by both players as the principal theme of the contests.

3 Kt—KB3   Kt—B3
4 Kt—B3   P×P

The *Slav Gambit*.

5 P—QR4   B—B4
6 Kt—K5

With a three-fold object: namely, to seize an outpost position, to recover the gambit pawn, and to vacate the KB file, eventually for P—KB3 and P—K4.

6 ......   QKt—Q2
7 Kt×P (B4)   Q—B2
8 P—KKt3

Helping the development of both the white Bishops (one at KKt2, the other at KB4).

8 ......   P—K4
9 P×P   Kt×P
10 B—B4

The pinning of the Knight now becomes the main topic for discussion.

10 ......   KKt—Q2
11 B—Kt2   B—K3

More tenacious is 11 .... P—B3.

12 Kt×Kt   Kt×Kt
13 Castles   B—K2

Here 13 .... P—B3 would still erect a sound barricade, but Black relies on the development of his pieces.

14 Q—B2   R—Q1

If, instead, 14 .... P—B3 or 14 .... Castles KR, then 15 Kt—Q5.

15 KR—Q1   Castles
16 Kt—Kt5

More active than 16 Kt—Q5, B×Kt; 17 B×B, etc. White already foresees the important rôle this Knight will be called upon to play.

16 ......   R×R ch

Instead of abandoning the open Q file of his own free will, he should at once have played 16 .... Q—R4.

17 R×R   Q—R4

This attempt at disengaging the pinned Knight will be refuted in a skilful and ingenious manner.

18 Kt—Q4   B—B1

He hopes to have surmounted the crisis, and to continue if possible with 18 .... Kt—Kt3 or 18 .... B—B3.

19 P—QKt4

A fine manœuvre with double action. The real Alekhine!

19 ......   Q—B2

Retreating in sackcloth and ashes, for if 19 .... B×P; 20 Kt—Kt3, Q—B2; 21 Q—K4, B—B6 (if 21 .... B—Q3, there comes the final point of the beautiful combination 22 Q—Q4, winning a piece); 22 R—QB1, and wins.

20 P—Kt5   P—QB4
21 Kt—B5   P—B3
At last, but at this stage 21 .... B—B3 would leave Black's position less cramped.

22 Kt—K3   B—K3
Watching the square at Q4, but the frank counter-thrust 22 .... P—Kt4 now affords the only chance of impeding the hostile impetus.

23 B—Q5
More useful than the plausible 23 Kt—Q5 (B × Kt; 24 B × B ch, K—R1, etc.).

23 ......   B × B
24 R × B   Q—R4
Prepared to leave some casualties on the way, if only he can obtain some counter-play. If 24 .... R—Q1; 25 Q—B5.

25 Kt—B5   Q—K8 ch
26 K—Kt2   B—Q1
27 B × Kt   P × B
28 R—Q7
Demonstrating that the preceding exchange was not intended to win a pawn of doubtful value (28 R × BP, B—Kt3, etc., or 28 R × KP, P—QKt3, etc.), but to enforce the occupation of the seventh rank.

28 ......   B—B3
Or 28 .... P—KKt3; 29 Kt—R6 ch, K—R1; 30 Q × BP. Now White is ready for a final *coup*.

29 Kt—R6 ch   K—R1
(For if 29 .... P × Kt; 30 Q × P mate.)

30 Q × P   Resigns
If 30 .... R—K1; 31 Q—Q5 (threatening a smothered mate); 31 .... P × Kt, 32 Q—B7, etc.

406
White   *Black*
GRÜNFELD   RUBINSTEIN
(Meran, 1924)

By means of profound manœuvres Black emancipates his Q side, and then concentrates on a triumphant K side attack; his play is beyond praise. Moves 6 to 10 by Black represent an appropriate defence for an enterprising player. Played for the first time in the present game, it has been named the Meran Variation.

1 P—Q4   P—Q4
2 P—QB4   P—QB3
3 P—K3   Kt—B3
4 Kt—QB3   P—K3
He avoids experiments (4 .... B—B4; 5 P × P, etc.) and reverts wisely to the *Semi-Slav Defence.*

5 Kt—B3   QKt—Q2
6 B—Q3   P × P
Deferred acceptance of the gambit.

7 B × BP   P—QKt4
8 B—Q3
More artificial is 8 B—Kt3 (8 .... P—Kt5; 9 Kt—K2, B—R3, etc.), and more passive, 8 B—K2.

8 ......   P—QR3
9 Castles
Or 9 P—QR4, P—Kt5; 10 Kt—K4, P—B4, etc., or 9 Q—K2, P—B4, etc., or 9 Kt—K4, P—B4, etc. The main variation is 9 P—K4.

9 ......   P—B4
The point of the whole of this line of play. We now have a very sound variation of the *Queen's Gambit Accepted.* The only difference is the number of moves played: Black has played his QBP, and White's KB has moved twice to reach its present square.
The *Meran Defence*—cleverly thought out by Rubinstein—keeps the flag of the defence to the *Queen's Gambit Declined* flying. Neither 9 .... B—K2; 10 P—K4 nor 9 .... B—Kt2; 10 P—K4 sufficiently safeguards Black's position. If 9 .... P—Kt5; 10 Kt—K4, etc.

10 P—QR4
Clearly not 10 P × P, Kt × P, etc. If 10 P—QKt3, B—Kt2 (preventing henceforth the advance of White's KP); 11 B—Kt2, B—K2, followed by .... Castles, etc. If 10 P—K4, P × P (now the exchange is justified); 11 KKt × P, B—Kt2 (threatening to win the KP by 12 .... P—Kt5); 12 P—QR3, Kt—B4, etc., with equality.
If quietly 10 Q—K2, B—Kt2; 11 R—Q1, Q—B2 (more astute than at once 11 .... Q—Kt3; 12 P—QR4, P—Kt5; 13 P—R5); 12 B—Q2 (slow but rational development); 12 .... B—K2; 13 QR—B1, Q—Kt3; 14 B—Kt1, Castles KR; 15 B—K1, KR—Q1, with an even game.
The move in the text is the most energetic continuation.

10 ......   P—Kt5
11 Kt—K4
Or 11 Kt—Kt1, B—Kt2; 12 QKt—Q2, B—K2, etc., as in the actual game.

11 ......   B—Kt2
12 QKt—Q2
Simplification by 12 Kt×Kt ch, Kt×Kt
would only further Black's plans. A favourable clearance in the centre would be
12 Kt×P, B×QKt; 13 P×B, Kt×P, gaining time as well as space. But 12 Q—B2
would strengthen the position.

12 ......   B—K2
13 Q—K2
Here on the next move a playable continuation is P—R5, isolating Black's QKtP,
but at some risk.

13 ......   Castles
14 R—Q1   P—QR4
More effective than 14 .... Q—B2;
15 P—R5, etc.

15 Kt—B4   Q—B2
16 B—Q2
The development by 16 P—QKt3 with
B—Kt2 is to be recommended.

16 ......   KR—Q1
The sequel will show that 16 .... KR—B1
is a better solution of the positional problem.

17 QR—B1
Again, 17 P—QKt3, which will have to be
played sooner or later, would be better.

17 ......   Q—B3
18 P—QKt3   Q—Q4
19 B—K1
The relief of the Q file is better effected by
19 Q—B1, followed by B—K2.

19 ......   P×P
20 P×P
Practically forced, as the KKt is immobilised by the threat of mate at KKt2, and if
20 B—Kt1, Kt—B4; 21 R×P, Q—R4, etc.,
with multiple threats.

20 ......   KR—QB1
Preparing for 21 .... Kt—K5, which at
present would be over-hasty by reason of
21 Kt—K3, Q×KtP; 22 R—B7, QR—Kt1;
23 R×B, R×R; 24 B×Kt, R—B2;
25 R—R1, with a winning position.

21 B—Q2
Retracting his 19th move, in order to concentrate his forces on the K file either by
22 R—K1 or by 22 B—K3, etc.

21 ......   Kt—K5
22 R—K1   Kt—Q3
23 Q—B1   Kt×Kt
24 P×Kt
He hopes that this additional *weak point*

will find compensation in the activities of
the passed QBP.
After 24 B×Kt, Q—R4; 25 Kt—K5,
Kt×Kt; 26 P×Kt, R—Q1, Black remains
master of the field.

24 ......   Q—R4
25 Kt—K5
Plausible, but fatal. White decides on
energetic measures, because after 25 B—K4,
B×B; 26 R×B, Kt—Kt3; 27 P—B5,
Kt—Q4 (but not 27 .... Kt×P; 28 Q—Q1);
28 Q—B4, P—R3, etc., his game remains
cramped, and his two centre pawns have no
vitality.

25 ......   Kt×Kt
26 R×Kt
After 26 P×Kt, White's weaknesses at
QB4 and QR4 would be still more marked.

26 ......   Q—R5
27 P—B4
If 27 B—K3, B—KB3, with the decisive
gain of a pawn, if not of the exchange.

27 ......   B—KB3
28 P—Kt3
This gives Black a chance for fireworks.
But otherwise a substantial loss of material
is unavoidable, e.g. 28 KR—K1, B×P ch,
winning the QP, or 28 B—K3, B×R;
29 BP×B, B—K5, etc., winning the exchange.

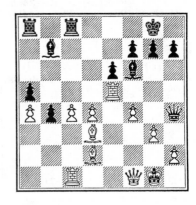

28 ......   B×R
Offering the Queen (29 P×Q, B×P ch,
with advantage).

29 QP×B   Q—K2
30 B—K3   Q—Q2
Threatening 31 .... Q—B3, winning the
QRP.

31 B—K2	Q×P
32 P—Kt4	P—Kt6
33 K—B2	B—K5
34 B—Q4	R—Q1
35 K—K3	B—B7
36 R—R1	Q—Kt5
Resigns.	

407

White	Black
CAPABLANCA	LÖWENFISCH

(Moscow, 1935)

A wrong conception of the spirit of the variation leads Black to lay too much stress on Q side manœuvres, and allows a fearful storm to break loose on the castled wing.

1 P—Q4	P—Q4
2 P—QB4	P—QB3
3 Kt—KB3	Kt—B3
4 P—K3	P—K3

Both sides play carefully (4 .... B—B4; 5 P×P, etc.).

5 Kt—B3
More straightforward than 5 QKt—Q2 (5 .... P—B4; 6 B—K2, Kt—B3; 7 Castles, B—Q3, etc.) or 5 B—Q3.

5 ......   QKt—Q2
The fight for the *tempo*. Other continuations:
(*a*) 5 .... P—QR3; doubtful, because of 6 P—B5.
(*b*) 5 .... P×P; presenting his opponent with an important *tempo*.
(*c*) 5 .... B—Kt5; too enterprising.
(*d*) 5 .... B—Q3; too optimistic.
(*e*) 5 .... B—K2; the fight for the *tempo* now takes the following course: 6 B—Q3, P×P; 7 B×BP, Castles; 8 Castles, P—QKt4; 9 B—Q3, P—Kt5; 10 Kt—K4, B—R3, etc. (the *pseudo Meran Defence*).
(*f*) 5 .... Kt—K5, followed by .... P—KB4; a *deferred stonewall*.

6 B—Q3
Or 6 Q—B2 (continuing the fight for the *tempo*) or 6 Kt—K5, the *Anti-Meran Attack*, or 6 P—QKt3, or even 6 P—QR4.

6	P×P
7 B×BP	P—QKt4
8 B—Q3	P—QR3

Less turbulent than it looks is the *Ultra-Meran Variation*, 8 .... P—Kt5.

9 P—K4
The *Main Variation*. But even here Black is able to effect the liberating advance of his QBP.

9 ......   P—B4
The thrust which characterises the whole of the *Meran Defence*—the wing reaction against the offensive in the centre. Unpromising would be 9 .... B—Kt2; 10 P—K5 or 9 .... B—K2; 10 Castles, B—Kt2; 11 P—K5, etc., but a playable idea is 9 .... P—Kt5, the *Neo-Meran Variant*.

10 P—K5   P×P
There follow exciting skirmishes. If 10 .... Kt—Q4; 11 Kt—Kt5.

11 QKt×P
The *Blumenfeld Attack*. Useless would be 11 P×Kt, P×Kt, etc.

11 ......   Kt×P
An ambitious reply, which causes White far more embarrassment than would 11 .... P×Kt; 12 P×Kt, etc. If 11 .... Kt—Kt5; 12 Kt—Q6 ch.

12 Kt×Kt   P×Kt
13 Q—B3
An ingenious continuation (Stahlberg's idea). Other attempts:
(*a*) Liquidation: 13 B×P ch, B—Q2; 14 Kt×B (or 14 B×B ch, Kt×B; 15 Kt—Q3, etc., with chances for both sides); 14 .... Q—R4 ch; 15 B—Q2, Q×B; 16 Kt×Kt ch, P×Kt; 17 Q—B3 (or 17 Q—K2, R—QKt1); 17 .... Q—K4 ch; 18 K—Q1, R—B1; 19 R—K1, Q—Q3; 20 Q×P, R—KKt1, etc., with even chances.
(*b*) Concentration: 13 Castles, Q—Q4; 14 Q—K2, R—QKt1 (better than 14 .... B—R3; 15 P—QR4); 15 B—Kt5 (more insistent than 15 B—Q2, B—Q3; 16 P—B4, Castles, etc.); 15 .... Kt—Q2 (a resilient retreat, for after 15 .... B—Q3, or even after 15 .... B—K2, White could launch a serious attack with 16 B—KB4); 16 B—KB4 (here 16 P—B4 would lead to disappointment after 16 .... Kt×Kt; 17 P×Kt, P—B4); 16 .... Kt×Kt; 17 Q×Kt (better than 17 B×Kt, Q—Q3); 17 .... R—Kt3 (fatal would be 17 .... Q×Q; 18 B×Q); 18 Q×Q, P×Q; 19 B—K5, and White recovers his pawn.

13 ......   R—R4
A painful choice. He can play neither 13 .... Q—Q4 (14 Q×Q, Kt×Q; 15 B×P ch, K—K2; 16 Kt—B6 ch, K—B3; 17 Kt×P, with a sound extra pawn) nor 13 .... B—Q2 (14 Kt×B, Kt×Kt; 15 B×P, with two Bishops).

If 13 .... R—QKt1; 14 B—KB4 (not impulsively 14 Kt—B6, B—Kt2; 15 B×P, Q—Kt3; 16 P—QR4, Kt—Q2, etc.), for if now 14 .... B—Q3; 15 Q—B6 ch.

Unpleasant would be 13 .... Q—R4 ch (14 K—K2, B—Q3; 15 Q—B6 ch, K—K2; 16 B—Q2, etc.)

Relatively the best would be the freeing check 13 .... B—Kt5 ch, with the continuation 14 K—K2 (the KR would remain cut off after 14 K—B1); 14 .... R—QKt1 (more artful than 14 .... B—Q2 or 14 .... Q—Q4); 15 Q—Kt3 (15 Kt—B6, B—Kt2); 15 .... Q—Q4; 16 Kt—B6 (or, more solidly, 16 Kt—B3); 16 .... Q×Kt; 17 Q×R, Castles, and Black, although the exchange down, is not without counter-chances.

14 Castles
Ineffective would be 14 Kt—B6, B—Kt2.

| 14 | ...... | P—Kt5 |
| 15 | B—KB4 | B—K2 |

If 15 .... B—Q3; 16 Q—B6 ch, K—K2; 17 Kt×P, K×Kt; 18 B×B.

| 16 | K R—B1 | Castles |
| 17 | Q—R3 | |

A powerful diversion, which threatens to win the exchange by 18 Kt—B6, and also 18 Kt—Kt4 and 18 B—KKt5.

| 17 | ...... | R—B4 |

After this error of judgment Black's resistance falls to pieces. He should have parried the main threat (18 Kt—B6) by 17 .... B—Kt2, e.g. 18 B—KKt5, P—R3, etc., or 18 Kt—Kt4, P—Kt3; 19 B—B7, Q—Q4; 20 B × R, Q × B, and Black can still hold out.

| 18 | R×R | B×R |
| 19 | B—KKt5 | |

With a decisive threat against KR7.

| 19 | ...... | P—R3 |

If 19 .... P—Kt3; 20 Kt—Kt4, B—K2; 21 Q—R4, and wins, and if 19 .... R—K1; 20 B×Kt, Q×B; 21 Q×P ch, K—B1; 22 B—Kt5, with a decisive gain in material.

| 20 | Kt—Kt4 | |

Elegant play.

| 20 | ...... | B—K2 |
| 21 | B×Kt | P×B |

Despair; but if 21 .... B×B; 22 Kt×P ch, P×Kt; 23 Q×RP, R—K1 (still trying to escape the mate); 24 B—R7 ch, etc.

| 22 | Kt×RP ch | K—Kt2 |
| 23 | Q—Kt4 ch | |

All runs smoothly (23 .... K×Kt; 24 Q—R4 ch, K—Kt2; 25 Q—R7 mate).

Position after 19 .... P—R3

23	......	K—R1
24	Q—R5	K—Kt2
25	Kt×P	

The final exploit (25 .... R×Kt; 26 Q—R7 ch, K—B1; 27 Q—R8 mate).

| 25 | ...... | R—R1 |
| 26 | Q—Kt6 ch | Resigns. |

408

| *White* | *Black* |
| FLOHR | MARÓCZY |

(Bled, 1931)

This game is exceptionally impressive, on account of the simplicity of the means employed. A battle of squares, lines and strong points.

1	P—Q4	P—Q4
2	P—QB4	P—QB3
3	Kt—QB3	Kt—B3
4	Kt—B3	P—K3

Semi-Slav contours.

| 5 | P—K3 | QKt—Q2 |
| 6 | B—Q3 | B—K2 |

He avoids 6 .... P×P (the *Meran Defence*), as well as 6 .... B—Q3 (7 P—K4, P×KP; 8 Kt×P, Kt×Kt; 9 B×Kt, Castles; 10 Castles, Q—B2; 11 B—B2, with the threat of Q—Q3, and White has the better game.

| 7 | Castles | Castles |
| 8 | P—QKt3 | |

Patience and strategic judgment. If White

were to open the centre in haste by 8 P—K4, P×KP; 9 Kt×P, Black, taking advantage of a breathing space, succeeds "under enemy fire" in developing his game by 9 .... P—QKt3—Fairhurst's discovery!

8	P—QKt3
9 B—Kt2	B—Kt2

Or 9 .... B—R3 (10 Q—K2, R—K1; 11 Kt—K5, Q—B2; 12 P—B4, with an increasing pressure).

10 Q—K2

A fine concentration of forces. White avoids undue haste either in the centre (10 Kt—K5) or on the wings (10 R—B1, R—B1, etc.). A kindred idea is 10 Q—B2.

10	R—B1

Instead of these preparations behind the front, Black could take more trenchant measures such as (a) 10 .... P×P; 11 P×P, P—B4; 12 KR—Q1, Q—B2; 13 Kt—K5, P—QR3 (of course not 13 .... Kt×Kt; 14 P×Kt, Q×P, because of 15 Kt—Q5); 14 P—B4, etc., or (b) 10 .... P—B4; 11 KR—Q1, BP×P; 12 KP×P, etc., controlling important sectors.

11 QR—Q1

Completing his preceding move, White now threatens 12 Kt—K5. This outpost manœuvre could have been effected at once (e.g. 11 Kt—K5, Kt×Kt; 12 P×Kt, Kt—K1; 13 P—B4, etc.), but it is White's intention to proceed methodically.

11	Q—B2
12 P—K4	

The crisis. Although the outpost manœuvre outlined above could now be carried out (e.g. 12 Kt—K5, Kt×Kt; 13 P×Kt, Q×P; 14 Kt×P, and wins), White decides on another lively line of play, opening the centre.

12	P×KP
13 Kt×P	P—B4

After 13 .... Kt×Kt; 14 Q×Kt, Kt—B3; 15 Q—R4 (threat: 16 P—Q5), 16 .... P—KR3; 17 Kt—K5, White energetically takes the lead.

14 P×P

Neither now nor later does White's lucid strategy shrink from large-scale liquidation.

14	P×P
15 KKt—Kt5	Kt×Kt

Still avoiding the devaluation of his pawns, which would result from 15 .... P—KR3; 16 Kt×Kt ch, Kt×Kt; 17 B×Kt, B×B;

18 Kt—R7, KR—Q1; 19 Kt×B ch, P×Kt; 20 Q—Kt4 ch, etc.

16 Kt×Kt	Q—B5

With the object of provoking some weakening of the opposing King's field.

17 P—Kt3	Q—B2

He rejects the bolder itinerary 17 .... Q—R3.

18 P—B4	Kt—B3
19 Kt×Kt ch	B×Kt
20 B×B	P×B
21 Q—Kt4 ch	K—R1
22 Q—R4	P—B4
23 Q—B6 ch	K—Kt1
24 B—K2	

With a double mission both defensive (24 .... Q—B3; 25 B—B3) and offensive (25 B—R5).

24	KR—K1

If 24 .... QR—Q1; 25 B—R5, threatening 26 B×P ch.

25 B—R5	Q—K2
26 Q×Q	R×Q
27 R—Q6	K—B1
28 KR—Q1	KR—B2
29 K—B2	

If 29 R—Q7, B—B3.

29	K—K2
30 B—B3	B—Q4
31 R—R6	B×B
32 K×B	R—Q1
33 R×R	K×R
34 K—K3	

A most instructive Rook ending now follows. During the whole of the transition period (moves 21 to 34), White has tried not so much to increase his palpable advantage, but to maintain the superiority in space already acquired, the result of which is the more active position of his Rook.

34	K—B1
35 R—R5	P—B3

If 35 .... K—Kt2; 36 R—Kt5 ch, maintaining his grip. But the text move will have equally unfortunate consequences.

36 R—R6	K—Q2

(*Diagram. See p. 526.*)

37 P—KKt4

Putting the finishing touch to his discreet manœuvres by a brilliant stratagem with a double break-through.

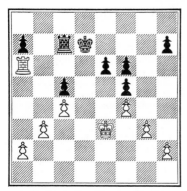

Position after 36 .... K—Q2

37	P × P
38 P—B5	R—B3
39 R × P ch	K—Q3
40 K—B4	P—R4

A stubborn resistance.

41 R—KB7	R—R3
42 R × P	R × P
43 R × P ch	K—Q2
44 K—Kt3	R—Kt7
45 R—K3	R—Kt8
46 K—R4	R—KB8
47 K × P	R—B6

The last cartridge!

48 R—K5	P—Kt6
49 P × P	R × KKtP
50 P—B6	R × P
51 P—B7	R—KB6
52 K—Kt6	Resigns.

409

| White | Black |
| PILLSBURY | GUNSBERG |

(Hastings, 1895)

In this game Black holds his own well in the opening, and brings about a comprehensive liquidation (moves 11 to 13). But with almost diabolical cunning, White effects a scintillating finish in a Knight ending.

1 P—Q4	P—Q4
2 P—QB4	P—QB3
3 P—K3	P—KKt3

A profound conception, a combination of the *Queen's Gambit* and the *King's Fianchetto*. The same idea was taken up in inverse order in the twentieth century (*Grünfeld's Variation*): 1 P—Q4, Kt—KB3; 2 P—QB4, P—KKt3 (first the *King's Fianchetto*); 3 Kt—QB3, P—Q4 (then the *Queen's Gambit*).

4 Kt—QB3	B—Kt2
5 Kt—B3	Kt—B3
6 B—Q3	

Nonchalant strategy which puts up, now or later, with the loss of a *tempo* by 6 .... P × P; 7 B × BP. A modern continuation, keeping up the battle for the *tempo*, is 6 Q—Kt3, Castles; 7 B—Q2, etc.

| 6 ...... | Castles |

If first 6 .... QKt—Q2; 7 P × P (not 7 Kt—K5, Kt × Kt; 8 P × Kt, Kt—Kt5; 9 P × P, Kt × P (K4); 10 B—K2, P × P; 11 Kt × P, Castles, with an even game); 7 .... P × P; 8 Kt—K5, etc., emphasising the pressure.

| 7 Kt—K5 | |

If 7 Castles, P × P, and if 7 P × P, P × P, soon to be followed by .... Kt—B3, closing the QB file.

| 7 ...... | P × P |

Hastening to neutralise White's impetus, for if 7 .... QKt—Q2; 8 P—B4, and White's pressure is far-reaching.

| 8 B × BP | Kt—Q4 |
| 9 P—B4 | B—K3 |

With the threat of 10 .... B × Kt, and if, unsuspectingly, 11 BP × B, then 11 .... Kt × Kt, and wins. After 9 .... P—K3, Black's game remains cramped.

| 10 Q—Kt3 | |

Without faltering, he allows a whole series of exchanges, which practically eliminate the middle game, for he hopes to create some interesting tensions in the ending.

10	P—QKt4
11 B × Kt	B × B
12 Kt × B	Q × Kt
13 Q × Q	P × Q
14 Kt—Q3	Kt—Q2
15 B—Q2	KR—B1
16 K—K2	P—K3
17 KR—QB1	B—B1
18 R × R	R × R
19 R—QB1	R × R
20 B × R	B—Q3

Better would be 20 .... P—Kt5.

21 B—Q2   K—B1
22 B—Kt4

In this battle of the minor pieces, White is looking for a strong point, which he will, in fact, create at QB5.

22 ......   K—K2
23 B—B5   P—QR3
24 P—QKt4   P—B3
25 P—Kt5   B×B

An optimistic exchange, allowing his opponent the potential asset of a passed pawn.

26 KtP×B   Kt—Kt1

Or, e.g. 26 .... P—QR4; 27 P—B6, Kt—Kt3; 28 Kt—B5, K—Q3; etc.

27 P—B5

A brilliant conception, giving this apparently humdrum Knight ending an epic character.

The threat is 28 P×KP, K×P; 29 Kt—B4 ch, etc.

27 ......   P—Kt4

After 27 .... KtP×P; 28 P×P, P×P; 29 Kt—B4, White would still have annexed the vital QP.

28 Kt—Kt4   P—QR4
29 P—B6

The unshackled pawn! Apart from the obvious 29 .... P×Kt; 30 P—B7, etc., there are other unexpected *finesses*.

29 ......   K—Q3
30 P×P   Kt×P

Again, if 30 .... P×Kt; 31 P—K7, K×KP; 32 P—B7.

31 Kt×Kt   K×Kt
32 P—K4

The last-but-one surprise.

32 ......   P×P
33 P—Q5 ch

The ultimate artifice.

33 ......   K—Q3
34 K—K3   P—Kt5
35 K×P   P—R5
36 K—Q4   P—R4

If 36 .... P—B4; 37 P×P, P—Kt6 (if at once 37 .... K—K2, there follows 38 K—B5, P—Kt6; 39 P—Q6 ch, K—Q1; 40 P—B6, P×P; 41 P—B7, etc.; and if 37 .... P—Kt5; 38 P—B6, P—R4; 39 P—B7, K—K2; 40 P—Q6 ch, K—B1; 41 P—Q7, and wins); 38 P×P, P×P (or 38 .... P—R6; 39 K—B3, K—K2; 40 P—Kt4, P—Kt5; 41 P—Kt5, etc.); 39 K—B3, K—K2; 40 K×P, P—Kt5; 41 K—B4, P—R4; 42 K—B5, P—R5; 43 P—Q6 ch, K—Q1; 44 P—B6, and wins; or 36 .... K—K2; 37 K—B4, P—Kt6; 38 P×P, P×P; 39 K×P, P—B4; 40 P×P, P—Kt5; 41 K—B4, P—R4; 42 K—B5, P—R5; 43 P—Q6 ch, K—Q1; 44 P—B6, and wins.

37 P×P   P—R6
38 K—B4   P—B4
39 P—R6   P—B5
40 P—R7   Resigns

An ending from practical play which, in beauty and depth, can be compared to any artistic end-game study.

410

White	Black
MENCHIK	*BECKER*

(Carlsbad, 1929)

Three notable features of this game are: White's strong opening strategy up to the exchange of Queens; impeccable technique thereafter; and, last but not least, the artistic touch which pervades the whole—a tribute to Miss Menchik's exceptional powers.

1 P—Q4   P—Q4
2 Kt—KB3   Kt—KB3
3 P—B4   P—B3
4 Kt—B3   P—K3
5 P—K3   Kt—K5

An independent idea.

6 B—Q3

A terrible *faux-pas* would be 6 Kt×Kt, P×Kt; 7 Kt—K5 (better in any event

7 Kt—Q2, P—KB4); 7 .... KB—Kt5 ch;
8 B—Q2, B×B ch; 9 Q×B, P—B3;
10 Kt—Kt4, P—KR4, appropriating the
Knight.

    6 ......   P—KB4

This deferred *stonewall formation* leads to
a difficult game for Black. It is playable in
this position because White's QB also
remains shut in.

    7 Kt—K5

Counter-stonewall. A splendid idea.

    7 ......   Q—R5

More enterprising than 7 .... Q—B3.

8 Castles	Kt—Q2
9 P—B4	B—K2
10 B—Q2	Kt×KKt

A less assertive continuation is 10 ....
Castles.

    11 QP×Kt

Better than 11 BP×Kt, which would
enlarge Black's field of action.

11	B—B4
12 B×Kt	BP×B

If 12 .... QP×B; 13 P—QKt4 (13 ....
B×P; 14 Kt×P).

    13 Q—Kt3

Threat: 14 P×P, KP×P; 15 Kt×QP,
winning a pawn.

    13 ......   Q—Q1

Not 13 .... Castles; 14 P×P, e.g. 14 ....
KP×P; 15 Kt×KP, etc., or 14 .... BP×P;
15 Kt×QP, etc., or finally, 14 .... R×P;
15 Kt—R4, and wins. Against 13 ....
Q—K2; 14 Kt—R4, as in the text, would
still prevent Black from castling, e.g. 14 ....
Castles; 15 Kt×B, Q×Kt; 16 B—Kt4, etc.

14 Kt—R4	B—K2
15 B—Kt4	P—QKt3
16 B×B	Q×B
17 P×P	KP×P

Hoping to obtain a well-balanced position
by .... B—Kt2 and .... P—B4, but White
prevents this important advance of the QBP.
Better would be 17 .... BP×P, followed by
.... Castles, with a cramped but playable
game.

    18 QR—B1   B—Kt2

After 18 .... B—R3, White would not
play 19 R×P, B×R; 20 Q×QP, R—Q1;
21 Q—Kt3, R—Q6, etc., but simply
19 KR—Q1, maintaining the pressure.

    19 Kt—B3   Q—KB2

Over-protecting the QP, with a view to
20 .... P—B4. He can play neither 19 ....
Castles nor 19 .... Q—K3, on account of
20 Kt×KP.

    20 Q—Kt4   R—Q1

Not 20 .... Q—K2, because of 21 Q×Q
ch, K×Q; 22 Kt×P ch, P×Kt; 23 R—B7
ch, followed by R×B.

Nor would 20 .... Q—B1 be desirable
(e.g. 21 Q×Q ch, R×Q; 22 P—QKt4, etc.),
whilst 20 .... Castles QR is too provocative.

Against 20 .... P—B4 the liquidation
by 21 Q—Kt5 ch, Q—Q2; 22 Q×Q ch,
K×Q; 23 KR—Q1, K—K3; 24 P—QKt4,
KR—QB1; 25 Kt—Kt5 would still keep the
black forces at bay.

    21 KR—Q1   B—R1

Not yet 21 .... Q—K2, by reason of
22 Q—R4, winning a pawn. Best, now or
on the next move, is 21 .... P—KR4,
followed by .... R—R3.

    22 P—KR3   Q—K2

An illusory relief.

    23 Q×Q ch   K×Q

    24 P—QKt4

Preventing 24 .... P—B4 (25 P×P, P×P;
26 Kt—Kt5).

    24 ......   R—Q2

If 24 .... R—QB1 (in order at last to play
the key move .... P—B4); 25 P—Kt5.

    25 R—Q2   KR—Q1

Not at once 25 .... R—QB1, because of
26 Kt×P ch.

26 Kt—K2	R—QB1
27 R (Q2)—B2	R (Q2)—B2
28 Kt—Q4	

The mobile Knight is manifestly superior
to the imprisoned Bishop.

28	P—Kt3
29 Kt—Kt5	R—Q2
30 K—B2	

Methodical procedure. The hasty
30 Kt—Q6 would allow the liberating sacrifice of the exchange by 30 .... R×Kt;
31 P×R ch, K×P, and Black's position
becomes tenable.

    30 ......   P—KR3

Black is reduced to makeshift moves. If
his KR moves, 31 Kt—Q4 wins the QBP.
If 30 .... QR—Q1, then equally 31 Kt—Q4,
and if 30 .... R—Kt2; 31 Kt—Q6, etc.

Finally, if 30 .... B—Kt2; 31 Kt×P, R—QR1; 32 Kt×P ch, B×Kt; 33 R×B, R×P ch; 34 R (B1)—B2, with a definite advantage.

31 P—Kt4
Preparing the break-through.

31 ......   P—R3
32 Kt—Q4   R (Q2)—B2
33 P—B5
The deluge!

33 ......   P—KKt4
34 K—Kt3   B—Kt2
If 34 .... P—B4; 35 Kt—K6.

35 P—KR4   P×P ch
Or else there follows 36 P×P, P×P; 37 R—KR1, a *turning manœuvre* which wins easily.

36 K×P   K—B2
37 K—R5   P—R4
Desperation.

38 P×P   P×P
39 Kt—Kt5   R—Q2
40 P—K6 ch   Resigns.

411

White	Black
ALEKHINE	EUWE

(Match, 1937)

This game is instructive in that it shows that even the greatest masters are at times not immune from errors under the stress of emotion.

Tactically, Dr. Alekhine presents us with one of his most effective attacks. Technically, it is worth noting that even such a steady opening as the Queen's Gambit *can, from the very beginning, turn into the fiercest of battles.*

1 P—Q4   P—Q4
2 P—QB4   P—QB3
3 Kt—QB3
Less used now than 3 Kt—KB3.

3 ......   P×P
The solid continuation on both parts is 3 .... Kt—B3; 4 P—K3. The *Winawer Counter Gambit* 3 .... P—K4 (4 QP×P, P—Q5 or 4 BP×P, BP×P, etc.) is not without its defects.

4 P—K4
An ambitious continuation. Less good is 4 P—K3, leading to the deceptive sequel 4 .... P—QKt4; 5 Kt×P (apparently favourable); 5 .... P×Kt; 6 Q—B3, Q—B2 (a decisive counter-sacrifice); 7 Q×R, B—Kt2; 8 Q×P, P—K4 (threat: 9 .... Kt—QB3); 9 B×P (if 9 P—Q5, B—B4, still harrying the Queen); 9 .... P×B; 10 P×P, Kt—QB3; 11 Q—R4, B—Kt5 ch, and Black has a dominating position.

4 ......   P—K4
Here (as against 4 P—K3) 4 .... P—QKt4 is indicated.

5 B×P   P×P
If 5 .... Q×P; 6 Q—Kt3.

6 Kt—B3
A sacrifice of a piece both unexpected and venturesome.

6 ......   P—QKt4
The reaction to the sudden shock, and an error of judgment which compromises his game. The most complicated line results from acceptance by 6 .... P×Kt; 7 B×P ch, K—K2; 8 Q—Kt3, etc. After 6 .... P—QB4; 7 Q—Kt3, Black's position would be critical, and even after the plausible 6 .... B—QB4, White keeps up the offensive with 7 Kt—K5. The most self-possessed reply is therefore 6 .... Kt—Q2.

7 QKt×P
A relentless episode (for if 7 .... P×Kt; 8 B—Q5).

7 ......   B—R3
8 Q—Kt3   Q—K2
Or 8 .... B×Kt; 9 B×P ch, K—Q2; 10 Kt×P, and White's attack—in the gambit style—prevails.

9 Castles   B×Kt
Or 9 .... P×Kt; 10 B—Q5, B—Kt2; 11 Q×P ch, and wins.

10 B×B   Kt—B3
If 10 .... P×B; 11 Q—Q5. By playing 10 .... Q—Kt2; 11 B—QB4 or 10 .... Q—Kt5; 11 B—QB4, Q×Q; 12 B×Q, P—QB4; 13 Kt—K5, Black could effect the exchange of Queens, without, however, avoiding serious damage.

11 B—QB4   QKt—Q2
12 Kt×P
He is content with the gain of a valuable pawn and refrains from 12 P—K5, with further complications.

12	R—QKt1
13 Q—B2	Q—B4
14 Kt—B5	

If 14 Kt×P, R—B1 (and not 14 ....
Q×Kt; 15 B×P ch).

| 14 ..... | Kt—K4 |
| 15 B—B4 | |

Reinforcing the pressure. A short-sighted
policy would be 15 Kt×P ch, to which Black
would reply, not 15 .... B×Kt; 16 B×P ch,
etc., but 15 .... K—Q2; 16 R—Q1 ch,
K—B2, etc., saving the situation.

| 15 ..... | Kt—R4 |

The counter-attempt meets with a telling
refutation. If 15 .... R—Q1; 16 Kt×P
ch, etc. The only possible defence is 15 ....
KKt—Q2

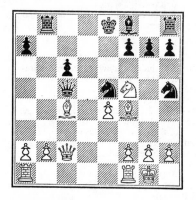

16 B×P ch
Obtaining, after liquidation, a second
pawn. Far less good would be 16 B×Kt,
Q×QB; 17 B—K2 (with a double threat:
18 B×Kt and 18 Q×P ch), but there follows
17 .... B—B4; 18 B×Kt, R×P, etc.

16	K×B
17 Q×Q	B×Q
18 B×Kt	R—Kt4

With the counter-threat of 19 .... B×P
ch, followed by .... R×B. If 18 ....
QR—K1; 19 B—Q6.

| 19 B—Q6 | B—Kt3 |
| 20 P—QKt4 | |

Persistent energy. The threat is now
21 P—QR4.

| 20 ..... | R—Q1 |

Intending to reply to 21 P—QR4 with
21 .... R×Kt; 22 P×R, R×B, etc. Nevertheless, 20 .... P—B4 at once is a little
better.

21 QR—Q1	P—B4
22 P×P	B×P
23 R—Q5	

The *coup-de-grâce*.
Black resigns.

UNUSUAL DEFENCES

412

| *White* | *Black* |
| ALEKHINE | MARSHALL |

(Baden-Baden, 1925)

*This game is characteristic of Dr. Alekhine's
forceful style. He first prevents the opposing
King from seeking safety on the Q side
(14 Q—K3), and then starts a hand-to-hand
fight on the K and KB files which soon
develops into a general mêlée. Notable is
the advance of the two pawns on the files
named, both of which penetrate into the heart
of the enemy position.*

| 1 P—Q4 | P—Q4 |
| 2 P—QB4 | Kt—KB3 |

The *American Defence*, which forgoes the
maintenance of a supported pawn at Q4.

3 P×P
The most assertive continuation.

| 3 ..... | Kt×P |

After 3 .... Q×P (akin to the *Centre
Counter*); 4 Kt—QB3, Q—QR4 (if not 4 ....
Q—Q1, reverting to the line in the text);
5 Kt—B3, Kt—B3; 6 B—Q2, etc., White
secures the advantage.

4 P—K4
Trying to register a concrete superiority
in the centre. A good positional continuation is 4 P—KKt3, with B—Kt2, but the
soundest is 4 Kt—KB3.

| 4 ..... | Kt—KB3 |

The retreat 4 .... Kt—Kt3 is playable.

5 B—Q3
The straightforward course—and the only
one by which an advantage in the opening
can be maintained—is 5 Kt—QB3, for after
5 .... P—K4; 6 P×P (or simply 6 Kt—B3);
6 .... Q×Q ch; 7 K×Q, Kt—Kt5, White
is the first to reap the harvest by 8 Kt—Q5.
Therefore, in reply to 5 Kt—QB3, Black's

best course is 5 .... P—K3; 6 Kt—B3, and White has an advantage in space.

5 ...... P—K4

Well countered!

6 P×P

Or 6 Kt—KB3, P×P; 7 Kt×P, B—QB4; 8 B—K3, with an even game.

6 ...... Kt—Kt5
7 Kt—KB3

After the mechanical defence of the pawn by 7 P—B4, the reply 7 .... B—QB4 would lead to a painful situation for White.

7 ...... Kt—QB3
8 B—KKt5

Unpromising would be 8 B—KB4, Kt—Kt5, etc.

8 ...... B—K2
9 B×B Q×B
10 Kt—B3 QKt×P
11 Kt×Kt Q×Kt

Black overestimates his resources, and attacks before he is fully developed. With 11 .... Kt×Kt he could obtain an approximately even game (e.g. 12 B—K2, P—QB3; 13 P—B4, Kt—Q2; 14 Q—Q4, Castles; 15 Castles QR, Q—B4, etc., or 12 Castles, Castles; 13 B—K2, B—K3, etc.).

12 P—KR3 Kt—B3
13 Q—Q2

After the plausible 13 Castles, Black could counter-attack by 13 .... P—KKt4, with advantage.

13 ...... B—Q2
14 Q—K3

Astute. If at once 14 Castles (QR,) Castles (QR) would tend to equality. White succeeds in castling on the Q side whilst preventing his opponent from doing likewise.

14 ...... B—B3
15 Castles QR

Not yet 15 P—B4, Q—QR4; 16 Castles QR, Castles QR, with equality.

15 ...... Castles KR

Useless is 15 .... Q—QR4; 16 B—B4.

16 P—B4 Q—K3

Or 16 .... Q—QR4; 17 P—K5, Kt—Q4; 18 Kt×Kt, B×Kt; 19 B×P ch, K×B; 20 Q—Q3 ch, followed by Q×B, with the gain of a pawn.

17 P—K5

Threatening 18 P—B5.

17 ...... KR—K1
18 KR—K1 QR—Q1

In order to play 19 .... Kt—Q4 at last without losing a pawn.

19 P—B5

Decisive.

19 ...... Q—K2
20 Q—Kt5 Kt—Q4
21 P—B6 Q—B1
22 B—B4

A vital diagonal.

22 ...... Kt×Kt
23 R×R R×R
24 P×P Kt×P ch

Or 24 .... Q—K1; 25 B×P ch, K×B; 26 P—Kt8 (Q) ch, Q×Q; 27 P—K6 ch, etc.

25 K—Kt1

After 25 B×Kt, there is the saving clause 25 .... Q—B4 ch.

25 ...... Q—K1
26 P—K6

A fresh exploit! Less convincing now would be 26 B×P ch, Q×B; 27 Q×R ch, K×P, etc.

26 ...... B—K5 ch
27 K—R1

Avoiding another pitfall: 27 R×B, R—Q8 ch; 28 K×Kt, Q—R5 mate.

27 ...... P—KB4

A desperate measure, but if 27 .... P×P; 28 B×P ch, Q×B; 29 Q×R ch, K×P; 30 Q—Q4 ch, followed by R×B, and wins.

28 P—K7 dis ch R—Q4
29 Q—B6 Q—B2
30 P—K8 (Q) ch Resigns.

White mates in two.

413

White	Black
VIENNA	ST. PETERSBURG

(By cable, 1897–99)

Black gives up a piece without any apparent compensation at the very beginning (6 .... P—QKt4), but his skilfu manœuvring of his massed pawns compels White to give back the booty and to be content with a draw.

| 1 P—Q4 | P—Q4 |
| 2 P—QB4 | Kt—QB3 |

The *Tchigorin Defence*, which is by no means obsolete.

3 Kt—QB3

The most stable continuation is 3 Kt—KB3, e.g. 3 .... B—Kt5ʹ (if 3 .... P—K4; 4 Kt×P); 4 Q—R4, still preventing .... P—K4; e.g. 4 .... B×Kt; 5 KP×B, P—K3 (if 5 .... P×P; 6 B×P, ˙Q×P; 7 Kt—B3, followed by B—K3, and White's forces are better placed); 6 Kt—B3, B—Kt5; 7 P—QR3 (a wise precaution); 7 .... B×Kt ch; 8 P×B, Kt—K2; 9 R—QKt1, R—QKt1; 10 B—Q3, P×P; 11 B×BP, Castles; 12 Castles, etc., with an advantage in territory.

3 ...... P×P

Already with a view to the *positional sacrifice* of a piece.

Lacking in consistency would be 3 .... P—K3, but a violent disturbance in the centre would result from 3 .... P—K4; 4 BP×P, Kt×P; 5 P—K3, Kt—B4; 6 P—K4, Kt—Q3 (not 6 .... Kt—Q5; 7 P—B4, etc.); 7 Kt—B3 (or 7 P—B4); 7 .... P—KB3, and Black consolidates his game.

4 P—Q5

Striking the iron whilst it is hot. Another continuation, 4 Kt—B3, Kt—B3; 5 P—K4, B—Kt5; 6 B—K3, concentrates its energies in the centre.

4	Kt—R4
5 Q—R4 ch	P—B3
6 P—QKt4	P—QKt4

Revealing his intentions. Short-sighted would be 6 .... P×Pep; 7 RP×P, P—QKt3; 8 P—QKt4, Kt—Kt2; 9 P×P, and White's advantage becomes manifest.

7 Q×Kt	Q×Q
8 P×Q	P—Kt5
9 Kt—Q1	P×P

Although Black has only two pawns for his piece, his well-organised chain of pawns, partially advanced and covering the whole board, redresses the balance.

10 P—K4

Seeking to create a weak point (at Q5) in the ominous phalanx.

10	P—K3
11 Kt—K3	Kt—B3
12 P×P	P×P
13 B—Kt2	B—K3

If 13 .... P—B6; 14 B—Kt5 ch.

| 14 B×Kt | P×B |
| 15 Kt—K2 | |

After 15 Castles, B—R3; 16 Kt—B3, R—QB1, followed by .... R—B4, Black obtains a dangerous attack.

15	R—B1
16 Kt—B4	R—B4
17 R—Q1	

The crisis.

17 ...... P—B6

If 17 .... R×P; 18 QKt×QP, to White's advantage.

| 18 P—R6 | B—Q3 |
| 19 KKt×P | |

Securing the draw.

After 19 P—Kt3, Castles; 20 B—Q3, P—Q5; 21 Kt×B, P×KKt; 22 Kt—B2, P—K4; 23 Kt×KtP, P—K5; 24 B×P, R—K4; 25 R×P, B×Kt; 26 R×B, KR—K1; 27 Castles, R×B; 28 R×R, R×R; 29 R—B1, R—QB5, and the Rook ending would also lead to a draw.

19	P—B7
20 R—B1	B×Kt
21 Kt×B	R×Kt
22 R×P	

After the elimination of the passed pawns, the Bishops of opposite colours herald a peaceful issue.

22	K—K2
23 P—Kt3	R—QR4
24 B—K2	B—K4
25 Castles	R—Q1

And after a few unimportant moves a draw was agreed.

25. ALBIN'S COUNTER-GAMBIT

414

White	Black
LASKER	ALBIN

(New York, 1893)

The parent game of this bold counter gambit. Although it was won by White, who imperceptibly kept on gaining territory, it does show that the first player can be forced to leave the beaten track.

1 P—Q4	P—Q4
2 P—QB4	P—K4
3 QP×P	P—Q5

In the manner of *Falkbeer's Counter Gambit.*

4 Kt—KB3
A well-known pitfall: 4 P—K3 (what could be more natural?), B—Kt5 ch; 5 B—Q2, P×P; 6 B×B (or 6 Q—R4 ch, Kt—B3; 7 B×B, P×P ch; 8 K×P, Q—R5 ch, and wins; the lesser evil is 6 P×P); 6 .... P×P ch; 7 K—K2, P×Kt (Kt) ch, and wins. Less critical continuations are 4 P—K4 or 4 P—QR3.

4 ...... Kt—QB3
More pertinent than 4 .... P—QB4 (5 P—K3, Kt—QB3; 6 B—K2, KKt—K2; 7 Castles, etc.).

5 P—QR3
The more energetic continuation 5 QKt—Q2 already threatens to win the QP by 6 Kt—Kt3.

5 ...... B—Kt5
Quite rightly hastening the development of his Q side, but this can be done with more insistence by 5 .. B—K3, attacking the QBP, with a view to .... Q—Q2 and .... Castles QR. An artificial line of play would be 5 .... P—QR4, intending .... B—QB4; .... KKt—K2; and .... Castles.

6 P—R3
He is not afraid of phantoms, and wishes to clear up the situation. A more scientific continuation is 6 QKt—Q2, e.g. 6 .... Q—K2; 7 P—R3, B×Kt; 8 Kt×B, Castles; 9 Q—Q3, P—KR3; 10 P—KKt3, followed by B—Kt2 and Castles, etc.

6	B×Kt
7 KtP×B	Kt×P
8 P—B4	

This pawn now drives away the QKt (8 .... Kt×P; 9 Q—R4 ch), and clears the long diagonal for White's eager KB, which has no outlet on the other wing.

8	Kt—QB3
9 B—Kt2	Q—Q2
10 P—Kt4	

Giving his adversary a foretaste of the attack which would break loose should he castle on the Q side.

10	P—QR3
11 B—Kt2	

Now both 11 P—Kt5 (11 .... P×P; 12 P×P, Kt—R4, etc.) and 11 Q—R4 would be premature.

11 ......
A change of plans. Black will not risk .... Castles QR, but .... Castles KR seems still very far off.

12 Kt—Q2 KKt—K2
A simpler line would be 12 .... Kt—B3; 13 Kt—Kt3, B—K2, in order to castle as soon as possible.

13 Kt—Kt3	Kt—B4
14 Q—Q3	B—K2
15 B—K4	Kt—Q3

One evil begets another! Black's position becomes increasingly cramped, but after 15 .... Kt—R5 or 15 .... Kt—R3 White increases the pressure by 16 Castles (QR.)

16 Kt—B5	Q—B1
17 B—KB3	Castles

His first strategic object is achieved, but under deplorable conditions.

18 R—KKt1
He rightly thinks that 18 Kt×RP, P×Kt; 19 B×Kt, etc., would, in the circumstances, be too paltry a plan.

18 ...... Kt—K1
This appears to parry some of his adversary's serious threats. 18 .... Q×P would clearly be suicidal (if only on account of 19 Kt×KtP, Kt×Kt; 20 R—R1, etc.), but

18 .... B—B3 provides a less melancholy defence.

19 Kt—Kt3
Maintaining a fine initiative. After 19 Kt × RP, Kt—R4; 20 P × Kt, P × Kt the Q side, where White wishes to castle, would be awkwardly disturbed.

19 ......   Q—Q2
Rejoicing in her newly-found freedom, the black Queen seeks adventure. But 19 .... Kt—B3 would be better.

20 Castles   Q—Q3
21 K—Kt1   Q × BP
A delusive satisfaction. Black wants to make up for the imminent loss of his QP.

22 R—Kt4   Q—R3
23 B × Kt   P × B
More resistance, at all events, would result from 23 .... Q × B (24 Kt × P, Q—R5; 25 QR—Kt1, B—B3, etc., or 24 R × P, R × R; 25 Kt × R, Q—KKt3; 26 Kt—B5, B—B3, etc.).

24 R × P   R—Q3
25 P—B5   R—K3
26 Q × P   Q × P
The balance in material is still maintained, but the co-ordination of the black pieces is deteriorating.

27 R (Q4)—Q3   Q—Kt7
28 Kt—Q4   R—B3
Or 28 .... R—Kt3; 29 R—KB3.

29 R—K3   B—Q1
30 Kt—B2
A curious gain of a piece, and of another soon afterwards.

30 ......   R × P
31 R × B   Resigns.

415

White   *Black*

DUS-CHOTIMIRSKI   MARSHALL

(Hamburg, 1910)

In the play of trap and counter-trap, White gets the last word in a manner both elegant and unexpected.

1 P—Q4   P—Q4
2 P—QB4   P—K4
3 QP × P   P—Q5
4 Kt—KB3   Kt—QB3
5 QKt—Q2   B—KKt5
Intending .... Q—Q2 and .... Castles QR (or at least .... R—Q1), he must keep his advanced post at Q5. After 5 .... P—QR4 or 5 .... KKt—K2; 6 Kt—Kt3 would win the QP.
A fairly well-grounded continuation after 5 .... B—QKt5 is 6 P—QR3, B × Kt ch; 7 B × B, B—Kt5; 8 Q—Kt3, KKt—K2; 9 P—Kt3, Castles; 10 B—Kt2, R—Kt1; 11 Castles (KR), Kt—Kt3, etc., and Black will recover his pawn with an approximately even game.
But after playing a "real gambit" by 5 .... P—B3; 6 P × P, Kt × P (more vigorous than 6 .... Q × P; 7 P—KKt3); 7 P—KKt3 (or 7 P—QR3, B—KKt5; 8 P—R3, B × Kt; 9 Kt × B, etc., with an equal game); 7 .... B—KB4; 8 P—QR3, P—QR4; 9 B—Kt2, Q—Q2; 10 Castles, Castles, and Black's dynamic resources are not to be despised.
An idea for the rapid mobilisation of the Q side is 5 .... Q—K2, e.g. 6 Kt—Kt3, B—Kt5, or 6 P—KKt3, B—QKt5 (better than 6 .... B—B4; 7 B—Kt2, Castles; 8 Castles, etc.); 7 B—Kt2, Castles; 8 Castles, P—Q6, etc., with a complex position.
Many and varied threats result from 5 .... B—K3, as is seen in a game O'Hanlon—Kostitsch (*Nice*, 1930): 6 P—QR3 (against 6 Kt—Kt3, Black has the choice between 6 .... B × P; 7 QKt × P, Q—Q4, etc., or, more simply, 6 .... B—Kt5 ch; 7 B—Q2, Q—K2, etc.); 6 .... Q—Q2; 7 P—KKt3, KKt—K2; 8 B—Kt2, Kt—Kt3; 9 Castles (more to the point is 9 P—QKt4); 9 .... B—K2; 10 P—QKt4 (too late! Now he should play 10 P—Kt3); 10 .... R—Q1; 11 B—Kt2, Castles; 12 R—B1, KKt × P; 13 Kt × Kt, Kt × Kt; 14 P—Kt5 (if 14 B × KtP, P—QB4, etc.; more rational would be 14 P—B5); 14 .... P—QB4; 15 Q—R4, P—QR3; 16 P—B4, Kt × P; 17 Kt × Kt, P × P; 18 Kt—K5, P × Q; 19 Kt × Q, R × Kt, and White resigns.

6 P—KR3
More phlegmatic would be 6 P—KKt3 (6 .... Q—K2; 7 B—Kt2, Castles; 8 Castles, etc.) or 6 P—QR3. Against 6 Kt—Kt3, Black has the choice between 6 .... B × Kt; 7 KP × B, etc., and 6 .... Q—K2

6 ......   B—R4
He could have continued 6 .... B × Kt; 7 Kt × B, and now, neither 7 .... B—B4; 8 P—R3, P—QR4; 9 P—KKt3, etc., nor

7 .... B—Kt5 ch; 8 B—Q2, B—B4;
9 P—R3, P—QR4; 10 P—KKt3, but—disdaining a pawn—7 .... P—B3; 8 P×P,
Kt×P, etc.

7 P—R3　　　　　P—R4
Or 7 .... Q—Q2; 8 P—QKt4, etc.

8 Q—R4
Preventing 8 .... B—B4, on account of
9 Kt—Kt3.

8 ......　　　　　Q—Q2
9 Q—Kt5　　　　 B—Kt3
He anticipates the threat 10 P—K6,
whereas the alternative threat 10 Q×KtP is
illusory because of 10 .... R—Kt1;
11 Q—R6, R—Kt3; 12 Q—R8 ch, R—Kt1,
with an early draw.

10 P—KKt3　　　 KKt—K2
11 Kt—Kt3　　　　P—R5
A deep trap.

12 Kt—B5
Wisely avoiding the shoals! If 12 QKt×P,
R—R4; 13 Q×KtP, Kt×Kt; 14 Q—Kt8 ch,
Kt—B1; 15 Kt×Kt, B—K5; 16 Kt—B3
(best); 16 .... R—R1; 17 Q—Kt5, B—B3;
18 P—K6, Q×P; 19 Q—KR5, P—Kt3;
20 Q—Kt4, P—B4, and the tables are turned
in Black's favour.

12 ......　　　　　Q—B1
13 B—Q2
A bad business would be 13 Q×KtP,
Q×Q; 14 Kt×Q, Kt—B1; 15 B—Kt2,
B—K5, and White's QKt is caught.

13 ......　　　　　P—Kt3
14 Kt×QP
A fine counter, which illustrates the main
idea underlying the opening (conquest of
the advanced QP), but also the line of play
characteristic of this variation (converging
action against QB6).

14 ......　　　　　P×Kt
15 Kt×Kt　　　　 B—K5
The counter-plot. If now 16 Kt—R7 dis
ch, Q—Q2.

16 Kt×Kt dis ch　 K×Kt
If, instead, 16 .... Q—Q2; 17 Q×Q ch,
K×Q; 18 P—B3, winning a piece.

17 P—B3　　　　　K—K3
The King gets under way in the hope of
catching the Queen. But there is a flaw in
the whole grandiose conception.

18 P×B　　　　　P—QB3
19 Q—Kt6　　　　R—R3
Jubilation.

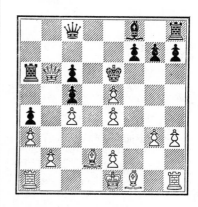

20 P—R4
The awakening! "An eye for an eye,
a Queen for a Queen."

20 ......　　　　　R×Q
The attempt 20 .... P—B4 would be
ineffective, e.g. 21 P×P e.p., K×P; 22 Q—Q8
ch, Q×Q; 23 B—Kt5 ch, recovering the
Queen and remaining with an extra piece.

21 B—R3 ch　　　 K×P
22 B×Q　　　　　 K×P
23 Castles KR　　　B—Q3
24 B—B5 ch　　　 K—Q5
25 QR—B1
Threat: 26 P—K3 ch, K—K4; 27 B—B3
mate.

25 ......　　　　　R—Kt6
Fighting desperately. If 25 .... B×P;
26 B—B3 ch, winning the Bishop as well.

26 P—K3 ch　　　 R×P
27 B×R ch　　　　K×B
28 QR—K1 ch　　 K—Q5
29 R—K4 ch　　　Resigns.

26. QUEEN'S PAWN GAME

COLLE SYSTEM

416

White	Black
COLLE	STOLTZ

(Bled, 1931)

This game presents an object lesson in the ill effects of a premature counter-attack.

1 P—Q4   P—Q4
2 Kt—KB3
A sound supporting move, which reserves the option of either P—QB4 or, quietly, P—K3, as in the present game. Peaceful only in appearance is 2 P—K3, with the possible continuation P—KB4, with Kt—KB3.

2 ......   Kt—KB3
3 P—K3
Shutting in the QB, in order to bring out the KB as quickly as possible.

3 ......   P—B4
The most usual reply is 3 .... P—K3.
A noteworthy scheme against the *Colle System*, preventing the exploitation of White's KB, is 3 .... P—K3, e.g. 4 P—B4, P—B3, etc., reverting to the *Slav Defence*, or 4 B—Q3, P—K3 (instead of either 4 .... B×B; 5 P×B, with a reinforced white centre, or 4 .... B—Kt3); 5 B×B, P×B; 6 Q—Q3, Q—B1; 7 Castles, B—K2; 8 P—QKt3, Castles; 9 P—B4, P—B3; 10 Kt—B3, Kt—R3, etc.

4 P—B3
The famous *Colle Triangle* (K3—Q4—QB3), characteristic of this opening.
Also sound is 4 P—QKt3.

4 ......   QKt—Q2
More wily than 4 .... Kt—B3, etc. Not without drawbacks would be 4 .... B—Kt5 (playing the orthodox *Queen's Gambit* with a *tempo* behind). The most academic continuation is 4 .... P—K3, e.g. 5 B—Q3, Kt—B3; 6 QKt—Q2, B—Q3 (a bold counter-scheme would be 6 .... Q—B2; 7 Castles, B—Q2; 8 Q—K2, Castles, etc.); 7 Castles, Castles (the *normal position of the Colle System*); 8 P×P, B×P; 9 P—K4,

P×P; 10 Kt×P, B—K2; 11 Q—K2, and White's game is slightly superior.

5 QKt—Q2   Q—B2
Instead of the usual move 5 .... P—K3 or 5 .... P—KKt3 (Fairhurst's idea).

6 B—Q3   P—K4
7 P—K4
White has now the superior chances in the centre and, being better developed, can seriously hamper the opposing King.

7 ......   P×KP
8 QKt×P   Kt×Kt
9 B×Kt   Kt—B3
10 B—B2
The Bishop retreats to a prepared position, and so, without loss of time, White has maintained a superiority in space.

10 ......   BP×P
If 10 .... B—Q3; 11 P×KP, B×P; 12 Q—K2, Castles; 13 Kt×B, R—K1; 14 P—KB4, and White keeps what he has gained.
More prudent is 10 .... KP×P; 11 Castles, B—K2, etc.

11 Castles
A sound reply. 11 P×P, B—Kt5 ch, etc., would only help Black.

11 ......   P×P
An ill-advised acceptance of a doubtful gift. He should try to avoid the worst by 11 .... B—Q3, followed by .... Castles.

12 Kt×P
A brilliant complement of the previous sacrifice.

12 ......   B—Q3
After 12 .... B—K2; 13 B—R4 ch, Black is in similar trouble.

13 B—R4 ch
Demonstrating that the black King's position is denuded both frontally and diagonally.

13 ......   K—B1
Or 13 .... B—Q2; 14 Kt×B, Kt×Kt; 15 R—K1 ch, K—B1; 16 B×Kt, Q×B; 17 P×P, and Black's game is tottering.

14 B—B4

Very skilful, for if 14 .... B×Kt; 15 B×B, Q×B; 16 Q—Q8 ch, Kt—K1; 17 QR—K1, and wins.

14 ......   B—KKt5

In trying to deal with the situation in combinative style (e.g. if 15 Kt×B, B×B, etc., or if 15 P—B3, B×Kt, etc.), Black himself becomes the victim of a cruel affray. He can only anticipate his opponent's threat by 14 .... K—Kt1.

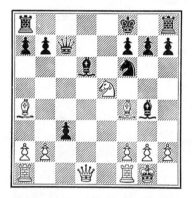

15 Kt—Kt6 ch   K—Kt1

A simple calculation: after 15 .... RP×Kt; 16 B×B ch, K—Kt1; 17 B×Q, B×Q; 18 QR×B, White remains a piece ahead.

16 B×B   B×Q
17 B×Q   B×B
18 Kt×R   Kt—Q4

If at once 18 .... K×Kt; 19 P—QKt3, B—Kt4; 20 KR—Q1.

19 B—R5   P—B7
20 B—Q2

Preventing 20 .... Kt—B5.

20 ......   K×Kt

In the end Black has only lost the exchange and has even a promising passed pawn, but White's impeccable technique solves the difficulty without much trouble.

21 KR—K1   K—Kt1
22 QR—B1   R—QB1

Necessary, on account of 23 P—QKt3.

23 R—K4   B—Q2
24 R—Q4   B—K3
25 P—QKt3   P—QKt4

Parrying the threat 26 R—QB4. If 25 .... Kt—B3; 26 R×P.

26 B—R5   P—Kt4
27 R—Q2   R—B3
28 QR×P   R—R3
29 P—QKt4   R—Q3
30 P—QR3   P—KR3
31 R—B5   P—R3
32 B—B7   R—Q2
33 B—K5   K—R2
34 P—R3   P—KR4
35 B—Kt2   K—Kt3
36 R—B6   Resigns.

417

White	Black
LANDAU	BERGER

(Match, 1932)

It is not that White, in this game, starts his attack with insufficient means, but rather that Black succeeds in imbuing each of his units with the maximum efficiency—an object lesson in the art of exploiting the full power of the pieces.

1 P—Q4   Kt—KB3
2 Kt—KB3   P—K3
3 P—K3   B—K2
4 QKt—Q2   P—Q4

Reverting to the *Colle Formation* proper, in preference to the *Colle Variation* of the *Indian Defence*, by 4 .... P—B4; 5 B—Q3, Kt—B3; 6 P—B3, P—QKt3; 7 Castles, B—Kt2, etc.

5 B—Q3   P—B4
6 P—B3   Castles
7 Q—K2

A conventional development could be 7 Castles, Kt—B3; 8 P×P (or 8 Q—K2); 8 .... B×P; 9 P—K4, P×P (or 9 .... P—K4, or 9 .... Q—B2); 10 Kt×P, B—K2 (best); 11 Q—K2, etc., but White thinks he can improve on this line of play.

7 ......   QKt—Q2

In order to reply to 8 P×P with 8 .... Kt×P, which could not be done after 7 .... Kt—B3.

8 Kt—K5

The immediate advance 8 P—K4 would have its drawbacks, e.g. 8 .... QP×P; 9 Kt×P, P×P; 10 Kt×P (10 P×P, B—Kt5 ch); 10 .... Kt—B4, and Black has a free game.

8 ......   Kt×Kt
If 8 .... Q—B2; 9 P—KB4.

9 P×Kt   Kt—Q2
10 P—KB4   P—B4
Energetic play. If 10 .... P—B3, trying
to undermine White's advanced post, then
11 P—K4 (in preference to the doubtful
attack 11 Q—R5, P—B4; 12 P—KKt4);
11 .... BP×P; 12 KP×P, etc.

11 P—QKt3   Kt—Kt1
A fine retrograde manœuvre. The Knight
has no future at QKt3, and seeks fresh
pastures.

12 B—Kt2
Better than no development, but it is
already clear that sooner or later the problem
of shifting the QBP will arise, and that the
pawn at K5 is nothing more than a dead
point in White's formation.

12 ......   Kt—B3
13 Castles KR   B—Q2
14 K—R1
As the attack in *front of the pawns* by
14 R—B3, followed by R—R3, would not
have sufficient substance, White decides on
the old stratagem of "major pieces behind
pawns."

14 ......   K—R1
15 P—KKt4   P—KKt3
16 R—KKt1   R—KKt1
17 R—Kt3   Q—KB1
18 QR—KKt1   Q—B2
19 Kt—B3
Supporting the advance of the KRP, but
after that White's action will be marking
time. The liquidation by 19 P×P, KtP×P;
20 R×R ch, R×R; 21 R×R ch, Q×R,
etc., would evidently be a mistake; and if
19 P—Kt5 (to be followed by P—KR4, and
then R—R3 and P—R5), then 19 ....
K—Kt2; 20 P—KR4, R—R1; 21 R—R3,
P—KR3; 22 P×P, R×P; 23 P—R5,
QR—R1; 24 R—Kt2 (24 R×P ch, Q×R,
etc.); 24 .... P—KKt4; 25 P×P, R×P;
26 R×R, Q×R ch, and Black would benefit
from the opening of the critical KKt and
KR files.

19 ......   QR—Q1
20 P—KR4   P—QR3
Preventing 21 B—Kt5, followed by the
exchange of an idle Bishop for an active
Knight, but aggressive as well, as it threatens
eventually 21 .... P—Kt4, followed by
.... P—B5.

21 P—B4
The threat 22 BP×P, KP×P; 23 P—K6

dis ch is alluring, but as it will be eliminated,
White has only added to his weaknesses.
Better is 21 R—R3.

21 ......   P×BP
22 P×QBP
At one stroke White has isolated both his
QBP and QRP, allowed the black Knight
access to QKt4, bared the long white
diagonal for Black's QB, and opened the
Q file for occupation by the black QR. His
opponent takes full and instant advantage
of his opportunities.

22 ......   Kt—Kt5
23 B—Kt1   B—QB3
A very timely occupation of the long
diagonal.

24 P—R3
An illusory measure of relief would be
24 P×P, KtP×P; 25 R×R ch, R×R;
26 R×R ch, Q×R, for now 27 P—R3,
Q—Kt6 wins, or 27 B×P, Q—Kt6 (not
27 .... P×B; 28 P—K6 dis ch), or
27 Q—Kt2, Q—Kt5; 28 Q×Q, P×Q;
29 P—K4, P×Kt; 30 P—R3, KB×P;
31 P×Kt, P×P, with a winning advantage,
or again, 27 K—R2, Q—Kt5; 28 Kt—Kt1,
Q×RP ch; 29 Kt—R3, B—K1, with a
definite advantage to Black.
Therefore the best course is 24 P—Kt5.

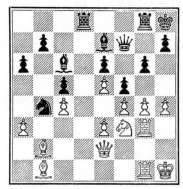

24 ......   Kt—Q6
A very fine surprise move! White expected
only 24 .... B×Kt ch; 25 R×B, Kt—B3,
etc.
If, after the text move, 25 B×Kt, P×P;
26 R×P, R×B; 27 Q×R, R×R ch;
28 K—R2, B×R; 29 R×B, R—Q1, and
Black has much the best of the bargain.

25 P×P   Q×P
26 K—R2   Q—R4
Again leaving the Knight errant to its fate
in view of promising operations.

27 B×Kt	B×Kt
28 R×B	R×B

If 28 .... B×P; 29 R—R3.

29 Q×R	Q×R

The balance in material is still undisturbed, but the white King's exposed position is irremediable.

30 R—Kt3	Q—B7 ch
31 K—R3	R—Q1
32 Q—Kt1	R—Q7

Irruption!

33 B—B3

The Bishop is saved, but not the King.

33	Q—R7 ch
34 K—Kt4	P—R4 ch
35 K—B3	Q—K7 ch

Better than capturing in passing the adverse Rook by 35 .... R—B7 ch; 36 K—K4, Q×R, etc.

36 K—K4	Q×BP ch
37 K—B3	Q—K7 ch
38 K—K4	R—Q8
39 Q×P	

Or 39 Q—Kt3, Q—Q6 ch; 40 K—B3, R—B8 ch; 41 K—Kt2, Q—K7 ch; 42 K—R3, R—R8 mate.

39	Q—B7 ch

Resigns

An impressive game.

418

White	*Black*
LANDAU	BÖÖK

(Kemeri, 1937)

In this magnificent example of the direct attack, *we witness a perfect "witches' sabbath" on the vulnerable squares in the defender's King's field, namely KR2, KR3, KKt3, KB3, KB2.*

1 P—Q4	P—Q4
2 Kt—KB3	Kt—KB3
3 P—K3	P—K3
4 B—Q3	P—B4
5 P—B3	QKt—Q2

Setting his adversary a more arduous problem than by 5 .... Kt—B3.

6 QKt—Q2	B—Q3
7 Castles	Castles
8 R—K1	

An important move. The immediate advance 8 P—K4 is of doubtful value, e.g.

8 .... BP×P; 9 BP×P, P×P; 10 Kt×P, Kt×Kt; 11 B×Kt, Q—Kt3, etc. As 8 P×P fails against 8 .... Kt×P, White, instead, consolidates his base. Another preparatory move could be 8 Q—K2 (e.g. 8 .... Q—B2; 9 P—K4, BP×P; 10 BP×P, P×P; 11 Kt×P, etc., with a fine attacking position. 8 P—KR3 is also playable. But after the text move the KR will show an astonishing versatility.

8	Q—B2

The advance 8 .... P—K4 is over-hasty, and 8 .... P—QKt3 is too dilatory.

After 8 .... R—K1 the following superb continuation occurred in a game Colle—O'Hanlon, *Nice*, 1930: 9 P—K4, QP×P; 10 Kt×P, Kt×Kt; 11 B×Kt, P×P (if 11 .... Kt—B3; 12 B—KKt5; the best move is 11 .... Kt—B1); 12 B×P ch (a familiar sacrifice, with, however, some additional points); 12 .... K×B; 13 Kt—Kt5 ch, K—Kt3 (or 13 .... K—Kt1; 14 Q—R5); 14 P—KR4, R—R1; 15 R×P ch (most artistic); 15 .... Kt—B3; 16 P—R5 ch, K—R3 (16 .... R×P; 17 Q—Q3 ch, K—R3; 18 Kt×P mate); 17 R×B, Q—R4; 18 Kt×P db ch, K—R2; 19 Kt—Kt5 ch, K—Kt1; 20 Q—Kt3 ch, resigns.

9 P—K4	P×QP
10 BP×P	P×P
11 Kt×P	Kt×Kt
12 R×Kt	

Much more effective than 12 B×Kt, Kt—B3; 13 B—B2.

12	R—K1
13 R—R4	Kt—B1
14 Kt—Kt5	P—KR3

Or 14 .... P—KKt3; 15 Q—B3.

15 Q—R5

A brilliant sally, initiating all kinds of problem-like turns.

15	P—K4
16 B—Q2	P×P
17 R—QB1	Q—K2
18 Kt—K4	Kt—Kt3

In view of the threat 19 B×P.

19 B—KKt5

The "orchestration" of the attack becomes more and more impressive.

19	Q—K4

If 19 .... P×B; 20 Q—R7 ch, K—B1; 21 Q—R8 ch, Kt×Q; 22 R×Kt mate (almost a smothered mate).

20 P—B4	Q—Q4

Better would be 20 .... Q—R4, after which, however, the attack continues ingeniously with 21 P—QKt4.

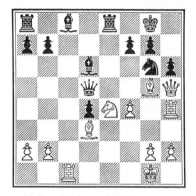

21 Kt—B6 ch   P×Kt
22 B×Kt   B—B1
Clearly not 22 .... P×KB; 23 Q×P ch,
K—B1; 24 Q×BP ch, etc., nor 22 ....
BP×QB; 23 Q×RP, etc. White has recovered
his piece, but Black hopes to exploit the
insecure position of the white Bishops.

23 R—B7   B—K3
Black must provide against the fresh
threat of 24 B×P ch.

24 B×BP   Q×Q
If 24 .... Q—Q3; 25 Q×P. But even
the exchange of Queens will not put a stop
to White's orgy of sacrifices.

25 B×Q   KR—B1
26 B×P ch
As 26 .... B×B; 27 R—Kt4 ch leads to
mate, Black must submit to the loss of
pawns, after which there is no hope.

26 ......   K—R2
27 R×R   B×R
28 B×P   B—KB4
29 R—R5   Resigns.

419

White   *Black*
TYLOR   ALEXANDER
(Hastings, 1938)

*During the period of transition leading into
the middle game (here from the 10th to the
14th move), Black wrests the strategic initiative from his opponent. Unexpectedly, instead
of trying to add to his worldly possessions
(turning a positional advantage into one in
material), he makes a positional sacrifice of*

*the exchange on his 23rd move.   The finish is
most attractive.*

1 Kt—KB3   Kt—KB3
2 P—Q4   P—K3
3 P—K3   P—Q4
4 B—Q3   P—B4
5 Castles   Kt—B3
6 P—QKt3
White prefers not to revert to the *Colle
System.*

6 ......   B—Q3
7 B—Kt2   Q—B2
Preventing 8 Kt—K5, and preparing for
8 .... P—K4. If, in a stereotyped manner,
7 .... Castles, there follows 8 Kt—K5,
Q—B2; 9 P—KB4, preserving the initiative.

8 Kt—B3
An unpositional manœuvre. As a rule,
in closed games one should avoid blocking
the QBP, which is nearly always needed to
support any action against Q5. Premature
would be 8 P—B4, QP×P, etc. The most
methodical line of play is 8 QKt—Q2,
Castles (not yet 8 .... P×P; 9 P×P,
Kt—QKt5; 10 B—Kt5 ch, B—Q2; 11 B×B
ch. Kt×B; 12 P—B4, etc.); 9 P—B4, etc.

8 ......   P—QR3
9 P×P   B×P
10 P—K4   P—Q5
11 Kt—K2   P—K4
12 K—R1
If 12 Kt—Kt3, P—KR4; and if 12 Kt—K1,
P—KKt4; and if 12 P—KR3, R—KKt1, an
uncomfortable situation.

12 ......   B—KKt5
13 KKt—Kt1   P—KKt4
Stopping 14 P—KB4.

14 Q—B1   R—KKt1
15 P—QB3   Castles
16 P×P   QKt×P
17 Kt×Kt   B×Kt
18 B×B   R×B
19 Q—K3
Although after 19 Q×Q ch, K×Q;
20 QR—B1 ch, K—Kt1; 21 B—Kt1,
KR—Q1, Black would still have the advantage, it would be more prudent for White to
adopt this simplifying course.

19 ......   K—Kt1
20 QR—B1   Q—Q3
21 B—B2   Kt—R4
Starting a K side attack and eliminating
the freeing manœuvre P—B3, for if
22 P—B3, Kt—Kt6 ch; 23 P×Kt, Q—R3
ch; 24 Kt—R3, B×Kt; 25 P×B, Q×P ch;
26 K—Kt1, Q×P ch; 27 K—R1, R—Kt3,
and mate follows.

22 P—KR3

If 22 Kt—K2, R—Q7; 23 KR—Q1, R—Q1 (23 .... R×Kt; 24 Q×R); 24 R×R, Q×R; 25 Q×Q, R×Q; 26 Kt—Kt3, R×P, etc., and Black has enough to win.

| 22 ...... | B—Q2 |
| 23 Kt—K2 | P—Kt5 |

A sacrifice which conforms to general principles—security in the centre, a break-through on the wing.

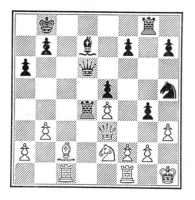

24 P—KR4

Hoping to be able to accept the sacrifice under more favourable conditions.

After 24 Kt×R, P×Kt; 25 KR—Q1 (relatively best, for if 25 QR—Q1, P×P; 26 P—Kt3, Q—KB3; etc., and if 25 Q—Q2, P×P; 26 P—Kt3, Q—KB3, etc.); 25 .... P×P; 26 P—Kt3, P×Q; 27 R×Q, P×P; 28 R×B, Kt×P ch; 29 K—R2, P—B8 (Q); 30 R×Q, Kt×R ch; 31 K×P, R—Kt6 ch; 32 K—R4, R—Kt7, and Black is a pawn ahead.

24	B—Kt4
25 Kt×R	P×Kt
26 KR—Q1	

After 26 Q—Q2, B×R; 27 R×B, P—Kt6, there is no hope for White.

26	P×Q
27 R×Q	P×P
28 B—Q3	B×B
29 R×B	P—Kt6

Pharaoh's tomb.

| 30 R—Q5 | Kt—B5 |

A quick mate is possible here by 30 .... R—Kt5; 31 R×Kt, R×P, etc.

31 R—KKt5	R×R
32 P×R	Kt—K3
	Resigns.

420

| *White* | *Black* |
| JANOWSKI | TARRASCH |

(Ostend, 1905)

As often happens in closed games, there is much manœuvring on the Q side, where Black actually obtains an advantage. But, suddenly, the black King finds himself menaced at long range, and White's sacrifice of a Knight in a good cause is the climax to a well co-ordinated attack.

1 P—Q4	P—Q4
2 Kt—KB3	P—QB4
3 P—B3	

Equal chances result from 3 P×P, P—K3; 4 P—K4, B×P; 5 P×P, P×P, etc. Assertive is 3 P—B4, Kt—KB3 (or 3 .... P—K3; 4 BP×P, KP×P; 5 P—KKt3, a variation of *Tarrasch's Defence*); 4 BP×P, P×P; 5 Q×P (if 5 Kt×P, Kt×P; 6 P—K4, Kt—Kt5); 5 .... Q×P; 6 Kt—B3, Q×Q; 7 Kt×Q, P—QR3, with an even game.

| 3 ...... | P—K3 |
| 4 B—B4 | |

A valid idea.

| 4 ...... | Q—Kt3 |

Other continuations are 4 .... B—Q3 or 4 .... Kt—QB3.

5 Q—Kt3

Too unassuming would be 5 P—QKt3 (5 .... P×P; 6 P×P, B—Kt5 ch; 7 QKt—Q2, Kt—KB3, etc.). The most ingenious is here 5 Q—B1, e.g. 5 .... Kt—QB3; 6 P—K3, Kt—B3; 7 QKt—Q2, B—Q2; 8 B—Q3, R—B1 (with the positional threat of 9 .... P×P; 10 KP×P, Kt—QKt5; 11 B—K2, B—Kt4, easing Black's game); 9 Q—Kt1, B—K2; 10 P—KR3, Castles; 11 Kt—K5, etc., stressing the centre.

| 5 ...... | Kt—KB3 |

If 5 .... P—B5, then not 6 Q×Q, P×Q, etc., but, as the QB file is now closed, 6 Q—B2.

| 6 P—K3 | Kt—B3 |
| 7 P—KR3 | |

Anticipating 7 .... Kt—KR4.

7	B—K2
8 QKt—Q2	B—Q2
9 B—K2	Castles KR
10 Castles KR	KR—B1

The most natural is 10 .... KR—Q1, leaving the QB file to the other Rook.

11 Kt—K5   B—K1
12 B—Kt3

Against 12 .... B—Q3 he can now play
13 Kt—Q7, Kt×Kt (or 13 .... Q×Q;
14 Kt×Kt ch, P×Kt; 15 P×Q, etc.);
14 Q×Q (14 B×B, Kt×P); 14 .... P×Q;
15 B×B, etc., remaining with the *two
Bishops*.

If 12 B—R2, B—Q3.

12 ......   Kt—Q2
13 Kt(Q2)—B3   Kt—B1
14 K R—Q1   Kt—R4
15 Q—B2   P—B5

An ambitious plan. He not only cramps
White's Q side, but he also threatens to gain
important territory on the K side by 16 ....
P—B3; 17 Kt—Kt4, P—R4; 18 Kt(Kt4)—R2,
P—Kt4; 19 Kt—B1, B—Kt3; 20 Q—B1,
P—R5; 21 B—R2, Kt—Q2, etc.

16 Kt—Q2   P—B3
17 Kt(K5)—B3   B—Kt3
18 Q—B1   P—KR3

He wishes to maintain the QB on the
diagonal, which he has gained, in case of
19 Kt—R4. Insensibly, Black has weakened
his King's field by moving his pawns. Yet
it hardly looks as if his King were in danger.

19 Kt—R2   Q—Q1

Preparing the advance of his Q side pawns,
without sufficiently heeding the latent power
of the adverse pieces. 19 .... B—Q3 provides an easier game.

20 B—B3

He prepares P—K4, the logical reaction
to the advance of Black's QBP.

20 ......   P—Kt4
21 P—K4   Kt—B3
22 P×P   P×P
23 R—K1   P—Kt5

Both sides play out their trumps.

24 Kt(Q2)—B1

The battlefield is clear, and the white
pieces in their modest formation gain in
value.

24 ......   P×P

Premature. Better would be 24 ....
P—QR4, giving the QR more freedom of
action.

25 P×P   Q—R4

Black still looks upon the Q side as the
main field of battle, and begins to direct his
forces to that quarter. More cautious would
be 25 .... Q—Q2, etc.

26 Kt—K3   B—B2
27 Q—Q2   B—R6

In view of the threat 28 Kt×BP, P×Kt;
29 B×Kt, R×B; 30 R×B. Even if 27 ....
R—K1; 28 Kt×BP, P×Kt; 29 B×Kt, etc.
A tactical expedient could be 27 .... B—Q1,
e.g. 28 QR—Kt1, B—QKt3 (with the improvised threat 29 .... B×P), or 28 Kt—B5,
B—B2, minimising the dangers.

28 QR—Kt1   Kt—Q2

He must find artificial means of defence
in the absence of natural ones. If, for
instance, 28 .... P—R3; 29 R—Kt7,
R—R2; 30 R×B, K×R; 31 B×P ch, etc.;
or 28 .... Kt—K2; 29 R—Kt7, Q—R3;
30 R×Kt, B×R; 31 Kt×QP, etc.

29 R—Kt7

This deeply calculated irruption bears the
stamp of genius. Note how smoothly and
effectively the two Bishops co-operate.

29 ......   Kt—Kt3

In seeking safety, the KKt over-protects
the critical point Q4, and appears to shut in
the invading Rook.

30 Kt—B5   Q—R3

He expects only the simplification
31 R—QB7, R×R; 32 B×R, Q—B1;
33 B×Kt, Q×Kt, etc.
The defensive measure 30 .... B—B1 is
essential.

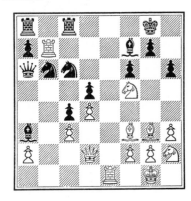

31 Kt×P ch
A *break-up sacrifice*.

31 ......   P×Kt
32 R×B

A complementary sacrifice. The black
King's sole defender disappears, and in
place of the defensive rampart of pawns,
there will soon be a void.

32 ...... K×R
33 Q×P

Threatening above all 34 B—R5 ch,
K—Kt1; 35 Q—Kt6 ch, K—R1; 36 Q×P
ch, etc., and also 34 Q—R7 ch, K—B1;
35 B—R5, etc.

33 ...... K—Kt1

The King defends himself desperately. If
33 .... R—B1; 34 Q—R7 mate. If 33 ....
B—B1; 34 Q—R7 ch, B—Kt2; 35 B—R5
ch, K—B1; 36 B—Q6 ch, Kt—K2; 37 B×Kt
mate; if 33 .... Kt—K2; 34 Q—R7 ch,
K—K1 (34 .... K—B1; 35 B—R5);
35 B—Kt4, Kt—Q2; 36 Q—R5 ch, K—Q1;
37 Q—R8 ch, Kt—Kt1; 38 Q×Kt ch,
Kt—B1 (38 .... B—B1; 39 Q—B7);
39 Q×P ch, enforcing capitulation. Black's
misfortune is that he cannot come to the
rescue of his second rank by 33 .... Q—Kt2,
on account of 34 Q—R7 ch.

34 Q—Kt6 ch K—R1
35 Q×P ch K—Kt1
36 Q—Kt6 ch K—R1

Or 36 .... K—B1; 37 B—B4. Black,
being a Rook ahead, and seeing White's
ingress via K5 and K7 guarded, hopes to
master 37 B—R4 by 37 .... R—B1, but
things turn out differently.

37 R—K5

The crowning glory!

37 ...... Resigns

A fine example of modern chess.

421

White	Black
BERNSTEIN	STAHLBERG

(Zürich, 1934)

*An outpost manœuvre in the Pillsbury
manner (7 Kt—K5) in the QP game (without
the support of the QBP) leads to a vigorous
K side attack. This game demonstrates that,
in spite of its reputed pacifism, the opening
can lead to brilliant and forceful play.*

1 Kt—KB3 P—Q4
2 P—Q4 Kt—KB3
3 B—B4 P—K3

Or, without shutting in the QB, 3 ....
P—B4; 4 P—K3, Kt—B3; 5 P—B3, Q—Kt3;
6 Q—B1 (6 Q—Kt3, P—B5, e.g. 7 Q×Q,

P×Q; 8 Kt—R3, P—K4; 9 Kt—QKt5
R—R4; 10 Kt—B7 ch, K—Q2; 11 P×P,
Kt—R4; 12 Kt×P, R×Kt; 13 B×P,
R—R4, etc., or 7 Q—B2, P—Kt3, followed
by .... B—KB4); 6 .... B—B4; 7 P×P
(7 Kt—R4, B—K5, etc., or 7 B—K2, P—K3,
etc.); 7 .... Q×BP; 8 QKt—Q2, R—B1,
and Black has overcome the difficulties of
the opening.

Too passive is 4 .... B—K2.

4 P—K3 B—K2
5 QKt—Q2 Castles
6 B—Q3 P—QKt3

More contentious would be 6 ....
QKt—Q2, or again, 6 .... P—B4.

7 Kt—K5 B—Kt2
8 Q—B3

Preventing 8 .... Kt—K5, and heralding
direct action in the best style of the classical
school.

8 ...... P—B4

Belated energy.

9 P—B3 QKt—Q2

Evidently not 9 .... P—B5; 10 B×P.

10 Q—R3

White's attack is already in full swing.

10 ...... R—K1

With the idea of protecting the critical
point at KR2 without disturbing the pawn
skeleton in the King's field, but the no less
critical point at KB2 will lack a defender.

11 QKt—B3 Kt×Kt

If 11 .... Kt—B1, as intended, 12 Kt—Kt5
wins.

12 Kt×Kt P—B5

Black deems his K side sufficiently secured
and seeks counter-chances on the opposite
wing.

13 B—B2 P—QKt4

If 13 .... B—Q3; 14 Kt—Kt4, and White
causes some weakening in the hostile pawn
formation.

14 P—KKt4 P—Kt3

Thus White has after all enforced a dislocation of the trio of hostile K side pawns.
If 14 .... P—KR3; 15 P—Kt5, forcing open
a file.

15 B—Q1

If 15 P—Kt5, Kt—R4, which the text move
prevents.

15 ......   B—KB1

Parrying the threat 16 P—Kt5, Kt—K5;
17 Kt×KBP, K×Kt; 18 Q×RP ch, K—B1;
19 B—K5, etc., but allowing another attacking stratagem—the *pin*.

16 B—Kt5   B—K2

After 16 .... B—Kt2; 17 Q—R4, the
diagonal pressure persists, and could be
intensified by KR—KKt1—KKt3—KB3.

17 Q—B3

But now the *vertical pressure* remains
(KB7). The ulterior threat is the advance
of the KRP.

17 ......   P—Kt5

Trying, at all costs, to obtain some counter-
play. If 17 .... R—KB1; 18 B—R6, R—K1;
19 P—Kt5, and wins.

18 P×P   B×P ch
19 K—B1   B—K2
20 K—Kt2

White threatens 21 Kt×QBP, which at this
point would still be premature (20 Kt×QBP,
B—R3). If 20 B—R6, threatening 21 P—Kt5,
B—KB1.

20 ......   R—Kt1
21 B—QR4

A fresh calamity.

21 ......   R—KB1
22 B—R6   Q—B2
23 P—R4   Kt—K5

Launching a counter-attack.

24 Kt—Q7

He threatens to win two exchanges
(25 B×R, and then Kt×R).

24 ......   B—QB3
25 B×B   Q×B
26 B×R   Q×Kt
27 B×R   R×P

The energy of despair, for after 27 ....
Q×B; 28 Q—K2, there is no hope.

28 B—B6

The holes in Black's King's field would
lead to instant loss after 28 .... R×P ch;
29 Q×R, Kt×Q; 30 K×Kt, P—K4;
31 QR—QKt1, Q—B1; 32 B×P, etc.

28 ......   Q—Kt2

He continues to fight, being a Rook down,
as his advanced passed pawn gives him an
illusive hope of a counter-chance. If 28 ....
P—K4 (intending 29 .... R×BP ch;
30 Q×R, Q×P ch, etc.); 29 QR—QKt1, e.g.
29 .... Kt×P; 30 R×R, or 29 ....

Kt—Q7; 30 R×R, or 29 .... R×P ch;
30 Q×R, Q×P ch; 31 K—B1, or, finally,
29 .... P—B6; 30 R×R, P×R; 31 R—QKt1,
Q—Kt4 (if 31 .... Kt—Q7; 32 R×P, and
if 31 .... Q—Kt2; 32 Q—K2, Kt—B6;
33 Q×P, etc.); 32 P—R4, Q—Kt6;
33 Q—K2, and wins without appeal.

29 QR—KB1   P—B6

If 29 .... Kt—Q7; 30 Q—B4, Kt×R;
31 Q—R6, etc.

30 P—Kt5

A buffer pawn. If at once 30 P—R5,
P—Kt4.

30 ......   Q—Kt4

Not 30 .... P—B7; 31 R—B1, etc., nor
30 .... Kt—Q7; 31 Q—B4, Kt×R;
32 R×Kt, P—B7; 33 R—B1, etc.

31 P—R5   Kt—Q7
32 P×P   BP×P
33 Q—Kt4   Q—Q2
34 R×P

A very beautiful touch.

34 ......   Q×R

After 34 .... K×R, there follows a mate
in four. If 34 .... Kt×R; 35 R×Q,
Kt×P ch; 36 K—B3, etc.

35 R—KR1

A convincing "point."

35 ......   Q×R ch
36 K×R   K—B2
37 Q—R3   R—Kt8 ch
38 K—Kt2   Resigns.

422

White	Black
JANOWSKI	ED. LASKER

(New York, 1924)

*The major part of this game (16th to 53rd
move) is a contest between Rook and Knight
against Queen, and it is surprising that the
weaker party has the better of the exchanges
and manages to win two pawns. But in the
moment of danger the power of the Queen
reasserts itself, and her mobility saves the day
against two Knights and masses of refractory
pawns. The ending is of the utmost piquancy.*

1 P—Q4	P—Q4
2 B—B4	

An archaic continuation.

Modern, if unusual, continuations are:

(a) 2 Kt—QB3: *Breyer's Opening*.

(b) 2 P—K4, P × P; 2 P—KB3: *Blackmar Gambit*, unsound because of 3 .... P—K4.

(c) 2 Kt—Q2.

(d) 2 P—KKt3: the *Catalan Opening*.

2	Kt—KB3

A wise reply.

Against the provocative 2 .... P—QB4 the curious continuation of a game Mason-Tchigorin, *New York*, 1889, was: 3 B × Kt, R × B; 4 P × P, Q—R4 ch; 5 Kt—B3, P—K3; 6 P—K4, B × P; 7 P × P (if 7 B—Kt5 ch, K—B1; 8 P × P, Q—Kt3, etc.); 7 .... Kt—B3; 8 B—Kt5 ch, K—K2; 9 Kt—B3, Kt × P (harmful greed; he should play 9 .... B—Kt5; 10 P—Q6 ch, B × P; 11 Castles, R—Q1; 12 Q—K2, with a fairly balanced game); 10 Q—Q2, Kt × Kt; 11 Q—Kt5 ch, P—B3; 12 Q × B ch, K—B2; 13 B—K8 ch, resigns.

3 P—K3	P—K3
4 B—Q3	P—B4
5 P—QB3	Q—Kt3

If not 5 .... Kt—B3, or at once 5 .... B—Q3, etc.

6 Q—B2

More precise is 6 Q—B1.

6	QKt—Q2

A valid plan is 6 .... Kt—B3; 7 Kt—B3, B—Q2; 8 QKt—Q2, R—B1, and White must play 9 Q—Kt1, on account of the positional threat 9 .... P × P; 10 KP × P, Kt—QKt5, etc.

7 Kt—Q2	B—Q3

After 7 .... B—K2; 8 P—KR3, etc., the white QB remains a source of danger.

8 B × B	Q × B
9 P—KB4	

The text move prevents 9 .... P—K4, and imparts to the game a fanciful character.

9	Kt—Kt5
10 Kt—B1	

Clearly not at once 10 K—K2, P—B5.

10	P × P
11 BP × P	Q—Kt5 ch
12 K—K2	Kt—Kt3
13 P—QR3	Q—K2
14 Kt—B3	

The development of this Knight could no longer be delayed. If at once 14 P—R3, Q—R5; 15 P—KKt3, Q—R4, Black remains within enemy territory.

14	B—Q2

Or 14 .... P—B4; 15 P—R3, Kt—B3, followed by .... Kt—K5.

15 P—R3	R—QB1
16 Q × R ch	

A fine *positional sacrifice of the Queen*, entailing various advantages: opportunities on the QB and KR files, cohesion of his pawns, etc.

16	Kt × Q
17 P × Kt	Kt—Q3
18 R—B1	Kt—B5

Ingeniously closing the open QB file. If 18 .... B—B3; 19 Kt—K5, Q—B2; 20 P—Kt4, P—QR3; 21 B × QRP.

19 B × Kt	P × B
20 QKt—Q2	P—QKt4
21 R—R5	P—B3

Not 21 .... Castles; 22 QR—KR1, P—KR3; 23 P—Kt5.

22 P—Kt5	K—Q1
23 QR—KR1	B—K1

If 23 .... P—Kt3; 24 P × P.

24 R × P

A hardly-earned pawn.

24	R × R
25 R × R	P × P
26 KKt × P	K—B1
27 R—R8	K—Kt2
28 QKt—K4	

Foreshadowing the threat 29 Kt × P.

28	K—Kt3
29 Kt—B5	B—B3

Neither 29 .... B—Q2 nor 29 .... B—B2, on account of 30 R—Kt8 ch, followed by R—Kt7.

30 KKt × P

A further and almost decisive gain, for the white pawn mass has become a power.

30	B—Q4

He must first of all drive the Knight from its dominant post, for if 30 .... B × P; 31 R—R7, followed by R × P.

31 Kt—Kt5	K—R4

If 31 .... B × P; 32 P—K4, cutting off the Bishop.

32 P—K4	B—B3
33 K—K3	B—K1
34 Kt—B3	P—Kt5

Regardless of further loss (the QBP), Black strives to relieve his game.

35 Kt—K5	B—Kt4

If 35 .... P—B6; 36 Kt—B4 ch, K—Kt4; 37 P—R4 ch (an attractive turn, particularly as he might have taken the wrong path by 37 R × B, Q × R; 38 Kt—Q6 ch, K—B3; 39 Kt × Q, BP × P, and the pawn queens); 37 .... K—B3 (37 .... K × Kt; 38 P—Kt3 mate); 38 P × P, P × P; 39 K—Q3, vastly increasing his gain.

36 P—R4	B × P
37 Kt × P ch	K—Kt4
38 Kt—K5	

Threatening 39 P—QKt3.

38	K—R4
39 R—QKt8	B—Kt4
40 P—KKt3	

If 40 R—Kt7, Q—R5.

40	P—Kt4
41 Kt—B3	

He must loosen his grip, in order to protect his inner lines.

41	P × P ch
42 P × P	Q—R2
43 P—B5	

The hope of spinning a mating web has vanished, and the prospect of guiding his pawns home becomes of first importance.

43	Q—R8
44 Kt—Kt3 ch	K—R5
45 Kt (Kt3)—Q2	Q—R3 ch
46 K—B2	B—Q6
47 R—Kt8	Q—B5
48 R—KR8	

An indirect defence of his KP.

48	P—Kt6
49 R—R4	Q—B2
50 P—B6	B—B5
51 R—R5	

Threat: 52 R—QB5. But a simple line of play would be 51 Kt × B, Q × Kt; 52 R—B4, e.g. 52 .... Q—B7 ch; 53 K—Kt3, Q × KtP; 54 P—B7, Q—R6; 55 P—B8 (Q), Q × Q; 56 R × Q, P—Kt7; 57 R—QKt8, K—R6; 58 Kt—Q2, and wins.

51	B—K3
52 R—K5	

Or 52 R—QB5, Q—B2; 53 P—K5.

52	Q—B2

Unexpectedly capturing a troublesome but important pawn. If 53 Kt—Kt5, Q × P ch.

53 R × B	Q × R
54 P—K5	

The ensuing end-game is most unusual (two Knights and a phalanx of three pawns against the Queen), and should automatically be won by the pigmies surrounding the giantess, unless Black manages to obtain a counter-chance.

54	K—Kt5
55 K—K3	P—R4
56 K—B4	P—R5
57 Kt—Kt5	Q—Q2
58 P—B7	Q—K2

And not 58 .... Q × QP ch; 59 Kt (Q2)—K4, Q—Q1; 60 Kt—K6, Q—R5 ch; 61 K—B5, etc.

59 P—Q5	P—R6
60 P × P ch	K—B6

Suddenly Black's QKtP affords a hope, and he fights brilliantly for his existence.

61 P—Q6	

The avalanche still continues.

61	Q—B1
62 Kt(Kt5)—K4 ch	K—Q6
63 P—K6	Q—R3 ch
64 K—B5	P—Kt7

With the threat (e.g. after 65 P—K7) of 65 .... Q—R2 ch; 66 K—K6, Q—R6 ch; 67 K—B6, Q—R3 ch, with perpetual check.

65 P—Q7	Q—B1
66 P—R4	Q—QR1
67 P—K7	

An extraordinary position.

67	Q—Q4 ch
68 K—B6	Q—Q5 ch

A most important check.

69 K—K6	P—Kt8 (Q)

Peremptory.

70 Kt × Q	

Compulsory. If 70 P—Q8 (Q), Q—R7 ch; 71 K—B5, Q × P ch, etc.

70	Q × Kt ch
71 K—B6	Q—R5 ch

Draw.

An ending full of the unexpected.

27. DUTCH DEFENCE

423

White	Black
HARRWITZ	MORPHY

(Match, Paris, 1858)

Both opponents play for the end-game, but White fails to maintain the balance in territory. Decisive is the superior mobility of the black King. The joint invasion of the white positions by the black King and Rook—thanks to the dissolving effect of the advance 50 .... P—R5—is very impressive.

1 P—Q4
A positional player, Harrwitz was one of the first to specialise in closed games.

1 ......   P—KB4
The *Dutch Defence* suits Morphy's aggressive temperament.

2 P—QB4   P—K3
3 Kt—QB3   Kt—KB3
4 B—Kt5
Treating the opening in the manner of the orthodox *Queen's Gambit Declined*, but here the *pinning strategy* yields little.

After 4 P—K3, a conventional line of play could be 4 .... P—QKt3 (contesting the strategic point K5; less flexible would be the *stonewall treatment* 4 .... P—Q4, with .... P—QB3 and .... B—Q3 to follow); 5 B—Q3, B—Kt2; 6 Kt—B3 (more artificial would be 6 P—B3 and KKt—K2, etc.); 6 .... B—Kt5; 7 B—Q2 (after 7 Castles, KB×Kt; 8 P×B, P—Q3, followed by .... P—B4, the weakened *white pawn complex*—doubled and blockaded—on the QB file would be vulnerable; or 7 Q—Kt3, P—B4); 7 .... Castles; 8 Castles, P—Q3; 9 P—QR3, KB×Kt; 10 B×B, Kt—K5, etc., as the situation is unclear. Black's *Queen Fianchetto* could be prevented by 4 P—KKt3, B—Kt5; 5 B—Q2, Castles; 6 B—Kt2, etc.

4 ......   B—K2
Or, more incisively, 4 .... B—Kt5; 5 Q—Kt3, P—B4; 6 P—K3 (or 6 P—Q5, P—K4, with a good game); 6 .... Castles; 7 B—Q3, Q—R4; 8 Kt—K2, Kt—B3, etc., with equal chances.

5 P—K3
Useless would be 5 B×Kt, B×B; 6 P—K4, P×P; 7 Kt×P, Castles, etc.

5 ......   Castles
6 B—Q3
After 6 Kt—B3, Kt—K5, unpinning, is playable.

6 ......   P—QKt3
Instead of the far less dynamic conception 6 .... P—Q4; 7 Kt—B3, P—B3; 8 Kt—K5, etc., Black applies the very modern idea of *distant control of the centre*. A violent episode would be 6 .... Kt—K5; 7 KKt—K2 (not 7 P—Q5, Kt×P, nor 7 P×P. Kt—R3, etc.); 7 .... P×P; 8 P×P, etc.

At this stage, unpinning would lead to a more difficult game after 6 .... Kt—K5; 7 B×B, Q×B (if 7 .... Kt×Kt; 8 B×Q, Kt×Q; 9 B—K7, Kt×KtP; 10 B×R, Kt×B ch; 11 K—K2, Kt×P; 12 K×Kt, K×B, etc., with a difficult game); 8 B×Kt (8 Kt×Kt, P×Kt; 9 B×P, Q—Kt5 ch, recovering both the pawn and territory); 8 .... P×B; 9 KKt—K2, and White stands better.

7 KKt—K2
More elastic than 7 Kt—B3, after which Black would continue the process of emancipation by 7 .... B—Kt2; 8 Castles, Q—K1; 9 Q—K2, Kt—K5.

7 ......   B—Kt2
8 Castles   Kt—R4
Again, less good would be 8 .... Kt—K5; 9 B×B, Q×B; 10 B×Kt, P×B; 11 Kt—Kt3, and Black's advanced KP would be a dead weight in his game.

9 B×B   Q×B
10 Kt—Kt3   Kt×Kt
11 RP×Kt   P—Q3
More methodical than at once 11 .... P—K4; 12 P×P, Q×P, etc. Black has solved the problem of the opening very satisfactorily.

12 P—B4
If 12 Q—Kt3, K—R1, and if 12 Q—B2 P—Kt3, preparing the advance of the KP. The text move prevents this thrust, but at the cost of a serious weakening of his base.

12 ......   Kt—B3
Preventing 13 P—K4, which advance might be effected after 12 .... Kt—Q2.

13 P—KKt4

White now tries to impart to the game the character of an open battle, while Black treats it positionally.

13	Kt—Kt5
14 P×P	

With the object, not only of eliminating his doubled pawn, but also of preventing once and for all the thrust .... P—K4, for if, e.g. 14 P—Kt5, P—Kt3; 15 B—Kt1, P—K4, etc.

14	P×P
15 Q—Q2	QR—K1
16 QR—K1	Q—R5

Sounding the attack. The factors will be the long-range effect of the Bishop and the irruption on the KR file.

17 B—Kt1	R—K3
18 Q—KB2	

Still warding off the assault.

18	Q—R4
19 P—Q5	R—R3
20 Q—B3	Q—R5
21 P—R3	Kt—R3
22 P—QKt4	

Preventing, of course, 22 .... Kt—B4, but Black need not worry about the Knight's future.

22	Kt—Kt1
23 Kt—K2	Kt—Q2
24 Kt—Kt3	

Digging himself in, instead of the doubtful enterprise 24 Kt—Q4, P—Kt3; 25 Kt—K6.

24	P—Kt3
25 K—B2	Kt—B3
26 R—R1	Kt—Kt5 ch
27. K—Kt1	Q—B3
28 R×R	Kt×R
29 Q—Q1	Kt—Kt5

Renewing the attack.

30 Q—Q2	Q—R5
31 Kt—B1	

He succeeds in warding off the fresh dangers.

31	R—K1
32 P—Kt3	Q—R6
33 P—Kt5	

Anticipating the chain-breakers (.... P—QB3 or .... P—QKt4), but offering a target for the subsequent opening of the QR file (35 .... P—QR3).

33	Kt—B3
34 Q—KKt2	

Forcing the exchange of Queens (34 ....

Q—Kt5; 35 Q—K2, etc.), but Black has no reason to avoid it.

34	Q×Q ch
35 K×Q	P—QR3

He opens the sluices.

36 P—R4	P×P
37 RP×P	R—R1
38 Kt—Q2	R—R6
39 P—K4	P×P
40 Kt×P	Kt×Kt
41 B×Kt	

If 41 R×Kt, K—B2. In this interesting end-game, it is still very difficult for Black to drive home his advantage.

41	R—QB6
42 B—B3	K—B2

For if 42 .... R×P; 43 R—K8 ch, K—B2; 44 R—QKt8, winning a piece.

43 R—K4	B—B1
44 B—K2	B—B4
45 R—Q4	P—R4

The text move prevents 46 P—Kt4; it has also—as the sequel will show—great attacking potentialities.

46 K—B2	K—B3
47 R—Q2	B—B7

This prevents 48 R—R2, and vacates a square for Black's King.

48 K—K1

An interesting position. If, passively, 48 R—Q4, then 48 .... K—B4; 49 R—Q2, P—R5 (or 49 .... K—K5; 50 B—B1, B—Q6, etc.); 50 P×P (a will-o'-the-wisp would be 50 R×B, R×R, for 51 B—Q3 ch cannot be played, as the Bishop is pinned); 50 .... K×P, etc., winning. The text move is thus both an active defence (48 .... R×KtP; 49 R×B) and a trap, for if 48 .... K—B4; 49 R×B wins.

48 ......   B—K5
This loses no time, as the KKtP is attacked. Playable is also 48 .... B—Kt6; 49 R—Q3, R—B8 ch; 50 K—Q2, R—B7 ch, etc., winning a pawn.

49 K—B2   K—B4
The King—a strong piece.

50 R—R2
Black had to take this counter-action carefully into account.

50 ......   P—R5
51 P×P   K×P
52 R—R7   R—KR6
An exemplary finish.

53 R×P   R—R7 ch
54 K—K1   K—K6
      Resigns.

424

White	Black
BLACKBURNE	DELMAR

(New York, 1889)

The storm breaks on the K file, let loose by White's 9th move (9 R—K1), breaking the dykes (10 P—K4), shattering embankments (11 P—B3), and, after sweeping aside all obstacles, ends up by carrying the enemy defences (16 B×Kt). Epic play in a swift-moving game.

1 P—Q4   P—KB4
2 P—KKt3
Blackburne's continuation, which has proved far more fertile than 2 P—QB4, an advance which here White delays until after he has castled, so that Black cannot give a relieving check, as after 2 P—QB4, P—K3; 3 P—KKt3, B—Kt5 ch, etc.

2 ......   Kt—KB3
3 B—Kt2   P—B3
An artificial idea. Apart from 3 .... P—Q3 or 3 .... P—KKt3, if Black prefers not to divulge his plans in the centre by 3 .... P—Q4, the move indicated is 3 .... P—K3, with a choice of three continuations:
(a) 4 Kt—KB3, B—K2 (if not a *stonewall* by 4 .... P—Q4; 5 Castles, B—Q3; 6 P—B4, P—B3; 7 Kt—B3, Castles; 8 Q—Q3, Kt—K5, etc.; hazardous would

be 4 .... P—B4; 5 Castles, etc.); 5 Castles, Castles; 6 P—B4, P—Q3 (with a restricted centre, or 6 .... P—Q4; 7 Kt—B3, P—B3, etc.); 7 Kt—B3, Q—K1, etc., with a complicated game.
(b) 4 Kt—KR3, complementing Blackburne's idea: the Knight's eventual route is to be *via* KB4 and Q3, guarding K5, e.g. 4 .... P—Q4 (risky would be 4 .... P—B4; 5 P×P, B×P; 6 Castles, P—Q4; 7 P—QB4, etc.); 5 Castles, B—Q3; 6 B—B4 (or 6 P—QB4, P—B3; 7 Kt—B3, Castles; 8 Q—Q3, etc.); 6 .... Castles; 7 Kt—Q2, P—B3; 8 Kt—B3, etc., fighting for squares.
(c) 4 P—QB4: less compact than the two preceding variations, for it eases Black's game after 4 .... B—Kt5 ch; 5 B—Q2, B×B ch, followed by .... Castles, etc.

4 Kt—KR3
Intent on leaving the long diagonal free for the KB.

4 ......   P—K4
An impulsive amplification of his preceding move, instead of the solid 4 .... P—Q4, strengthening the *stonewall*.

5 P×P   Q—R4 ch
6 Kt—B3   Q×KP
He has recovered his pawn, but at the expense of time, exposing his Queen to multiple molestations.

7 B—B4   Q—K2
If 7 .... Q—R4; 8 B—Q2. Better is 7 .... Q—B4.

8 Castles   P—Q4
This looks reassuring.

9 R—K1
Preparing a very vigorous assault.

9 ......   QKt—Q2
10 P—K4
Opening a central file in an unusual manner.

10 ......   BP×P
11 P—B3   Kt—B4
Still holding out. But after 11 .... Q—B4 ch; 12 K—R1, B—K2; 13 P×P, Castles; 14 P×P, the whole of Black's formation is fractured.

12 P×P   QKt×P
13 Kt—B2   B—B4
14 P—KKt4
A fresh resource.

14 ......   B—Kt3
15 P—Kt5   Kt—R4
16 B × Kt
The harvest.

16 ......   Kt × B
He hopes to calm the fury of the attack by giving up his Queen. If 16 .... P × B; 17 QKt × P, Kt × B; 18 Kt—Q6 ch, K—Q2; 19 Kt—B5 dis ch, followed by Kt × Q, and Black is hopelessly lost.

17 B × B ch   P × B
18 Q—Kt4
Precluding any attempt at a counter-attack.

18 ......   Kt—R4
19 Kt—Q3   K—B2
20 R × Q ch   B × R
21 Kt—K5 ch   Resigns.

425

White	Black
RUBINSTEIN	SPIELMANN

(San Sebastian, 1912)

The unusual manner in which Black handles his attack (17 .... P—B5), culminating in a splendid sacrifice (25 .... B × P), and succeeding, when a Rook down, in tying up the opposing King, is a treat for the connoisseur.

1 P—Q4   P—K3
A "chameleon" defence, which can be turned into one of several known openings.

2 P—QB4
After 2 P—K4, Black can revert to the *French Defence*, or by 2 .... P—QB4; 3 Kt—KB3, P × P; 4 Kt × P, etc., to the *Sicilian Defence*. After 2 Kt—KB3 we have a *QP game* by 2 .... P—Q4, or a *Dutch Defence* by 2 .... P—KB4, or an *Indian Defence* by 2 .... Kt—KB3, or again, a *Sicilian Defence* by 2 .... P—QB4; 3 P—K4, P × P; 4 Kt × P, etc.

2 ......   P—KB4
He now has his *Dutch Defence*, having first tempted White to play 2 P—QB4 before castling and avoided the dangerous *Staunton Gambit*, which occurs after 1 P—Q4, P—KB4; 2 P—K4. A possible continuation would be 2 .... B—Kt5 ch (3 B—Q2, Q—K2, etc., or 3 Kt—B3, P—QB4, etc.).

3 Kt—QB3   B—Kt5
4 B—Q2
More careful than at once 4 P—K3 or 4 P—KKt3.

4 ......   Kt—KB3
After 4 .... P—QKt3 the structure 5 P—K3, B—Kt2; 6 P—B3 is possible.

5 P—KKt3
A scientific line of play.

5 ......   Castles
6 B—Kt2   P—Q3
This *restricted centre* leads to a tense contest.

7 P—QR3
To preserve the two Bishops and, incidentally, to lay the foundation for a Q side attack. If 7 Kt—B3, B × Kt; 8 B × B, Kt—K5; 9 Q—B2, etc. If 7 Kt—R3, P—K4.

7 ......   B × Kt
8 B × B   QKt—Q2
9 Q—B2
To prevent 9 .... Kt—K5, which could be played both after 9 Kt—B3 and 9 Kt—R3.

9 ......   P—B4
Fighting indirectly for the junction at K5.

10 P × P
More pugnacious is 10 P—QKt4, P × QP; 11 B × QP, P—K4; 12 B—QB3, etc.

10 ......   Kt × P
Better than 10 .... P × P.

11 Kt—B3
If 11 P—B3, P—K4; 12 R—Q1, Q—K2, followed by Kt—K3.

11 ......   QKt—K5
12 Castles KR   B—Q2
13 KR—Q1   R—B1
14 B × Kt
Not 14 P—Kt3 nor 14 B—K1, on account of 14 .... P—QKt4. Nor would 14 B—Q4 or 14 B—Kt4 be desirable.

14 ......   Q × B
15 Q—Kt3   R—QB2
16 Kt—K1
If 16 Kt—Q4, then, as in the text, 16 .... Kt—B4; 17 Q—Kt4, P—B5, etc. If 16 P—K3, P—K4.

16 ......   Kt—B4
17 Q—Kt4
Not 17 Q—B2, as 17 .... B—R5 would win the exchange.

17 ......   P—B5
The direct attack now begins.

18 Kt—Q3
If 18 R×P, P×P; 19 BP×P, Q—B7 ch;
20 K—R1, Q×P; 21 P—R3 (21 R—Q2,
R—B8 ch, followed by mate); 21 ....
Kt—K5, and wins.

18 ......   P×P
19 BP×P   Kt×Kt
20 R×Kt
Or 20 P×Kt, Q—Q5 ch; 21 K—R1,
R—B7, etc.

20 ......   Q—B7 ch
21 K—R1   B—B3
The key to the converging attack.

22 P—K4
If 22 B×B, Q×KP; 23 KR—Q1
(23 R—Q2, R—B8 ch, followed by mate);
23 .... R—B7; 24 Q—K1, R×P ch;
25 K—Kt1, R×B; 26 Q×Q, R×Q, with
a certain win.

22 ......   QR—B2
23 R—K1
If 23 R×P, Q—K7; 24 Q—K1 (still
parrying the triple threat .... R—B8 ch or
.... B×P or .... R—B7); 24 ....
Q×QKtP; 25 R×P, R—B7, etc.

23 ......   P—QR4
24 Q—B3   Q—QB4
25 P—QKt4
After 25 R—B3, R×R; 26 B×R, P—R5,
etc., White's position remains distressing.

25 ......   B×P
Magnificent.

26 R×B
Not 26 P×Q, because of mate in two.
Very troublesome, too, for White, would
be 26 B×B, R—B8 ch; 27 R×R, R×R ch;
28 K—Kt2, R—Kt8 ch (if 28 .... R—B7
ch; 29 K—Kt1); 29 K—B3 (29 K—R3,
Q—R4 mate); 29 .... Q—R4 ch, etc.

26 ......   R—B8 ch
A complementary sacrifice of the exchange.
Now White is a Rook ahead, but his King
remains in danger.

27 B×R   R×B ch
28 K—Kt2   Q—B7 ch
29 K—R3   R—KR8
Threat: 30 .... R×P ch; 31 K—Kt4,
Q—B4 mate.

30 R—B3
If 30 R—B4, Q×RP ch; 31 K—Kt4,
Q—R4 mate, and if 30 R×KP, Q×RP ch;
31 K—Kt4, Q—R6 ch, followed by ....
Q×R.

30 ......   Q×RP ch
31 K—Kt4   Q—R4 ch
32 K—B4   Q—R3 ch
33 K—Kt4   P—KKt4
A splendid point, establishing a mating
net at one stroke; threat: 34 .... Q—R4.

34 R×P
Or 34 R—B8 ch, K×R; 35 K—B3, P×P;
36 P×P, K—B2, with 37 .... Q—B3 to
follow.

34 ......   Q×R ch
35 R—B5   P—R3
36 Q—Q3
If 36 Q—B3, Q×P ch; 37 R—B4, P×R;
38 Q×R, P—B6 dis ch, and wins easily.

36 ......   K—Kt2
A decisive reinforcement, threatening not
only 37 .... K—Kt3, but also (e.g. after
37 Q—Q5) 37 .... P—R4 ch; 38 K×P,
Q—R3 mate.

37 K—B3   R—B8 ch
Pretty and peremptory.

38 Q×R   Q×R ch
39 K—Kt2   Q×Q ch
40 K×Q   P×P
41 P×P   K—B3
42 K—B2   P—R4
    Resigns
A beautiful game.

426

White	*Black*
BOGOLJUBOW	ALEKHINE

(Hastings, 1922)

A feature of this magnificent game is the bi-lateral effect of Black's attack. The finish is of quite exceptional charm.

1 P—Q4	P—KB4
2 P—QB4	Kt—KB3
3 P—KKt3	P—K3
4 B—Kt2	B—Kt5 ch
5 B—Q2	

A sound reply; or 5 QKt—Q2 (5 .... Kt—K5; 6 P—QR3, Kt×Kt; 7 B×Kt, B×B ch; 8 Q×B, Castles; 9 Kt—R3, P—Q4, etc.), or 5 Kt—B3.

5	B×B ch
6 Kt×B	

But here a stronger plan would be 6 Q×B, Castles; 7 Kt—QB3, etc.

6	Kt—B3

Stressing the slight organic defect in White's last move, namely the encumbering of the Q file.

7 KKt—B3	Castles
8 Castles	

If 8 Q—B2, P—Q4; 9 Castles KR, P×P; 10 Q×QBP, Q—Q4, etc.

8	P—Q3

Effecting, in two stages, what White could not achieve: the advance of the KP.

9 Q—Kt3	K—R1
10 Q—B3	

He mistakenly thinks he can hinder Black's plan. Better would be 10 P—Q5, P×P; 11 P×P, Kt—K4; 12 Kt—Q4, etc., trying to complicate matters.

10	P—K4

Thanks to the forlorn position of White's QKt, this advance can be effected after all.

11 P—K3

After 11 P×P, P×P; 12 KR—Q1 (not 12 Kt×P, Kt×Kt; 13 Q×Kt, Q×Kt); 12 .... Q—K2, Black has a compact centre.

11	P—QR4

He must prevent the advance of the QKtP, for which White will now patiently prepare.

12 P—Kt3

And not at once 12 P—QR3, P—R5, and

this pawn now blockades by itself two hostile pawns, showing how this important end-game stratagem can be profitable in the middle game and even in the opening.

12	Q—K1
13 P—QR3	Q—R4

Black has energetically transferred the centre of gravity to the castled wing.

14 P—KR4

If 14 P—QKt4, P—K5; 15 Kt—K1, P×P, winning a pawn. Here again 14 P×P is not playable (14 .... P×P; 15 Kt×P, Kt×Kt; 16 Q×Kt, Kt—Kt5).

14	Kt—KKt5
15 Kt—Kt5	B—Q2
16 P—B3	Kt—B3

Threatening to break up White's pawn chain by 17 .... P—B5.

17 P—B4	P—K5

Closing the episode on the K side by blockading the respective pawn chain, but with the positive advantage of restricting the hostile Bishop and both Knights.

18 KR—Q1

Wiser would be to block the centre as well by 18 P—Q5.

18	P—R3
19 Kt—R3	P—Q4

He stirs up the centre to his advantage. White cannot play 20 P×P, KKt×P, followed by Kt×KP.

20 Kt—B1	Kt—K2

Threatening 21 .... P—R5; 22 P—QKt4, P×P; 23 Q×P, QKt—Q4, and a Knight is permanently posted on this important square.

21 P—R4

Better would be 21 P—B5, as Black, adapting himself to circumstance, will now exploit the accessible squares at QKt5 and Q6.

21	Kt—B3
22 R—Q2	Kt—QKt5
23 B—R1	

He tries to get up some sort of an attack on the K side by R—KKt2, Kt—B2, Kt—R2 and P—KKt4.

23	Q—K1
24 R—KKt2	

If 24 P—B5, P—QKt4 (stronger than 24 .... P—QKt3) would be damaging for White.

24 ......   P × P
25 P × P

He gives up a pawn of minor importance rather than allow 25 Q × P, KKt—Q4, threatening 26 .... P—QKt4.

25 ......   B × P
26 Kt—B2   B—Q2
27 Kt—Q2   P—QKt4
28 Kt—Q1

Not 28 P—B5, nor even 28 P × P, on account of 28 .... KKt—Q4. But now that White has guarded his KP and cleared the second rank, he could reply to 28 .... P × P by 29 Kt × BP, KKt—Q4; 30 Q—R3, followed by Kt—K5. For this reason Black gives back the pawn to turn his resources to better account.

28 ......   Kt—Q6
29 R × P

Or 29 P × P, B × P; 30 R × P, Kt—Q4; 31 Q—R3, R × R; 32 Q × R, Q—B3, threatening 33 .... R—R1.

29 ......   P—Kt5

The repercussions of this "exchange combination" are far-reaching.

30 R × R

Or 30 Q—R1, R × R; 31 Q × R, Q—R1, and Black penetrates into the hostile position *via* the QR file.

30 ......   P × Q
31 R × Q   P—B7

The point! Black, in the end, obtains a Queen for two disjointed Rooks.

32 R × R ch   K—R2
33 Kt—B2   P—B8 (Q) ch
34 Kt—B1   Kt—K8

Threat: 35 .... Kt—B6 mate.

35 R—R2   Q × BP

With fresh and powerful threats by 36 .... B—Kt4; 37 Kt—Q2, Q—B8, which forces White to lessen the pressure by giving up the exchange.

36 R—QKt8   B—Kt4
37 R × B   Q × R
38 P—Kt4   Kt—B6 ch
39 B × Kt   P × B
40 P × P   Q—K7

A *Zugzwang* position! White has only weary pawn moves, for if 41 R any, Kt—Kt5; if 41 Kt—Kt3, Q × P; and if 41 Kt—R3, there is a renewal of the Queen sacrifice by 41 .... Kt—Kt5; 42 R × Q, P × R, obtaining—once again—a new Queen!

41 P—Q5   K—Kt1
42 P—R5   K—R2
43 P—K4   Kt × KP
44 Kt × Kt   Q × Kt
45 P—Q6

Or 45 R—Q2, Q × P (B5).

45 ......   P × P
46 P—B6   P × P
47 R—Q2   Q—K7

An elegant finish.

48 R × Q   P × R
49 K—B2   P × Kt (Q) ch
50 K × Q   K—Kt2
51 K—B2   K—B2
52 K—K3   K—K3
53 K—K4   P—Q4 ch

Yet another Queen in sight! White resigns.

427

	White	Black
	HOROWITZ	FINE

(Match, 1934)

Black's attack, once launched, is kept up relentlessly. The decisive blow is struck by his cavalry.

1 P—Q4   P—KB4
2 Kt—KB3   Kt—KB3
3 P—KKt3   P—K3
4 B—Kt2   B—K2
5 Castles   Castles
6 P—B4

Note that, in accordance with modern technique, this advance is effected *after castling*, thus denying the opponent the relieving sally .... B—Kt5 ch.

6 ......   P—Q3

The strategy of the *restricted centre*. The *stonewall* formation is also admissible: 6.... P—Q4; 7 Kt—B3, P—B3, etc. Playable, too, is 6 .... Kt—K5.

7 Kt—B3   Q—K1

A regrouping, conforming to the spirit of the defence, which from the first foreshadows expansion on the K side.

8 Q—B2

At the cross-roads. White prepares the advance of his KP, which could also be effected by 8 R—K1, or even indirectly by 8 B—Kt5 (with a view to 9 B×Kt, B×B; 10 P—K4).

Useless would be the diversion 8 Kt—QKt5, B—Q1, but a sound, constructive idea is 8 P—Kt3, for after 8 .... Q—R4; 9 Q—B2, QKt—Q2; 10 B—QR3, the counter-thrust 10 .... P—K4 is still impeded.

    8 ......   Kt—B3
    9 P—QR3

Excessively cautious. As 9 P—K4 would be neutralised by 9 .... P—K4, he would do well to harass his opponent by 9 P—Q5 (e.g. 9 .... Kt—Q1; 10 Kt—Q4, etc., or 9 .... Kt—QKt5; 10 Q—Kt3, etc.).

    9 ......   P—K4

Thus Black has achieved this central advance ahead of his opponent.

    10 P—Q5   Kt—Q1
    11 P—QKt4

He underestimated the action preparing on the opposite wing. Better would be, now or on the next move, B—Kt5.

    11 ......   B—Q2
    12 Kt—Q2   Q—R4

The direct attack.

    13 P—B3   Kt—B2
    14 P—K4

A dead point which virtually immobilises six (!) of his pieces. He should have tried 14 R—B2, e.g. 14 .... P—B5; 15 Kt—B1, etc.

    14 ......   P—B5
    15 P—Kt4   Q—R5
    16 Kt—Kt3

Hoping, not so much for action on the Q side, as for relief, by blocking as far as possible the critical sector after 17 Q—B2, Q—R3; 18 P—KR4, P—KKt4; 19 P—R5. But Black's strong reply maintains his advantage. Best therefore would be at once 16 R—B2, with 17 Kt—B1.

    16 ......   P—KR4
    17 P×P

Compulsory. If 17 P—R3, Kt—Kt4.

    17 ......   Q×P
    18 R—B2   Kt—Kt4
    19 Kt—Q2   K—B2

Initiating a very instructive phase, in whch Black's artillery exploits the K R file and thence overruns the adjacent open file.

    20 Kt—B1   R—R1
    21 Kt—K2   Q—R5
    22 Q—Q2   Kt—R4
    23 Kt—B3   R—R3
    24 R—K2   R—Kt3˙
    25 K—R1   R—R1

Now things happen with a rush. Black's preceding move threatened 25 .... Kt×P ch; now he threatens 26 .... Kt—Kt6 ch.

    26 R—B2
White is condemned to passivity.

    26 ......   Kt—Kt6 ch
A telling finish.

    27 K—Kt1
A tottering King. He hopes to hold out after 27 .... Kt×Kt; 28 K×Kt, Q×P; 29 Kt—K2, etc.

    27 ......   Kt—R6 ch
The finishing stroke.

    28 B×Kt   Kt—K7 db ch
        Resigns.

428

White	*Black*
EUWE	ALEKHINE

(Match, 1935)

In this, the finest game in this match for the World Championship, White demonstrates that even in a closed game an impetuous idea can find expression. Especially remarkable is the immense amount of ground covered by White's KKt (moves 19 to 47), and most instructive the task accomplished by his centre pawns.

1 P—Q4	P—K3
2 P—QB4	P—KB4
3 P—KKt3	B—Kt5 ch
4 B—Q2	B—K2

An original idea. Black obviously did not want an exchange when checking on his preceding move, but merely to clog the Q file.

5 B—Kt2	Kt—KB3
6 Kt—QB3	Castles
7 Kt—B3	

A more concentric development of his forces than 7 Kt—R3, P—Q3; 8 Castles, etc. If 7 Q—B2, Kt—B3; 8 Kt—B3, P—Q4, with a satisfactory game.

7 ......   Kt—K5
He skilfully follows up the idea of his fourth move.

8 Castles
White calmly pursues his development, and is not tempted into experimenting by 8 P—Q5 or challenging the centre by 8 Q—B2, or manœuvring by 8 Kt—K5, P—Q3; 9 Kt—Q3, etc., or rushing matters by 8 Kt×Kt, P×Kt; 9 Kt—Kt1 (not 9 Kt—K5, P—Q3; 10 Kt—Kt4, P—K4, etc.); 9 .... P—Q4; 10 Kt—R3, etc.

8 ......   P—QKt3
Trying to preserve his outpost at K5. A less ambitious plan would be 8 .... B—B3; 9 Q—B2, Kt×B; 10 Q×Kt, etc.

9 Q—B2	B—Kt2
10 Kt—K5	Kt×Kt

A mistake would be 10 .... P—Q3; 11 Kt×Kt, etc.

11 B×Kt
A bad speculation for White would be 11 B×B, Kt×P ch; 12 K—Kt2, Kt×QP; 13 Q—Q3, QKt—B3, etc., with advantage to Black.

11	B×B
12 K×B	Q—B1

In order to drive off the intruding Knight by 13 .... P—Q3. Meanwhile, White gets a hold on the centre.

13 P—Q5	P—Q3
14 Kt—Q3	P—K4
15 K—R1	P—B3

Less bellicose would be 15 .... Kt—Q2, or, first, 15 .... P—B4.

16 Q—Kt3
With the threat of 17 P—B5, e.g. 17 ....

KtP×P; 18 Kt×KP, P×Kt; 19 P—Q6 dis ch, followed by P×B, and White has the better game.

16 ......   K—R1
After 16 .... P×P; 17 P×P, Black has opened the game to White's benefit.

17 P—B4	P—K5
18 Kt—Kt4	P—B4

Closing the Q side, otherwise 19 P×P, Kt×P; 20 Kt—Q5 would impede Black's game.

19 Kt—B2	Kt—Q2
20 Kt—K3	B—B3

By playing 20 .... Kt—B3 Black would have avoided the coming complication, but his position would still be inferior.

21 Kt×P
Giving up a piece for three pawns.

21	B×B
22 Kt×QP	Q—Kt1
23 Kt×P	B—B3
24 Kt—Q2	

To profit by his pawn phalanx.

24 ......   P—KKt4
Only a counter-attack can help Black.

25 P—K4	P×P
26 P×P	B—Q5
27 P—K5	Q—K1
28 P—K6	R—KKt1
29 Kt—B3	

Clearly not 29 P×Kt, Q—K7, etc. The text move, however, is not flawless. The most convincing is 29 Q—KR3, after which White's positional advantage is definite.

29	Q—Kt3
30 R—KKt1	

Forced (for if 30 Kt—R4, Q—Kt5, etc.), but forcible as well, as White maintains the initiative.

30	B×R
31 R×B	Q—B3

The best defence is 31 .... Q—B4; 32 P×Kt, R×R ch; 33 K×R, Q×P (Q2); 34 K—B2, and a draw is in sight.
(*Diagram. See p. 556.*)

32 Kt—Kt5
Brilliant play. Although a Rook down, White manœuvres with perfect ease in the enemy camp, and threatens an immediate decision by 33 Kt—B7 ch.

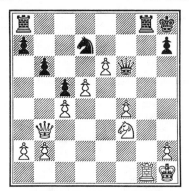

Position after 31 .... Q—B3

32 ......   R—Kt2
Against 32 .... P—KR3 there follows
33 Kt—B7 ch, K—R2; 34 Q—Q3 ch,
R—Kt3; 35 Kt—K5, Kt×Kt; 36 P×Kt,
Q—Kt2; 37 P—Q6, and White's passed
pawns cannot be mastered.
Note that, had Black played 31 ....
Q—B4 (instead of 31 .... Q—B3), the continuation in the text would be useless because
of 32 .... P—KR3; 33 Kt—B7 ch, K—R2,
and White's Queen has no diagonal check.

33 P×Kt   R×P
Or 33 .... Q×BP; 34 Q—QB3, Q—Q5;
35 Q×Q, P×Q; 36 Kt—K6, R×P;
37 Kt×P, etc., to White's advantage, for—
as actually played—his pawns are a powerful
lever.

34 Q—K3   R—K2
35 Kt—K6   R—KB1
If here 35 .... Q×KtP; 36 P—Q6.

36 Q—K5   Q×Q
37 P×Q   R—B4
In trying to maintain the "exchange,"
Black adds to his difficulties. The most
promising defence is 37 .... R×Kt;
38 P×R, R—B4, but even then, after
39 R—K1, K—Kt1; 40 R—K3, K—B1;
41 R—QR3, White has winning chances in
the Rook ending.

38 R—K1
The most precise is 38 R—Kt5, for, after
the text move, Black could have obtained the
variation cited above by 38 .... R×Kt;
39 P×R, K—Kt1, etc.

38 ......   P—KR3
Still underestimating the danger, Black
hesitates and—is lost.

39 Kt—Q8
This Knight's action is decisive.

39 ......   R—B7
40 P—K6   R—Q7
For if 40 .... R×KtP; 41 P—Q6, etc.

41 Kt—B6   R—K1
42 P—K7   P—Kt4
43 Kt—Q8   K—Kt2
Preventing 44 Kt—B7 ch.

44 Kt—Kt7   K—B3
45 R—K6 ch   K—Kt4
46 Kt—Q6   R×KP
Seeking some chances of salvation in case
of 47 R×R, R—Q8 ch; 48 K—Kt2, P×P;
49 Kt×P, R×P, etc., but White finds an
energetic way of breaking Black's resistance.

47 Kt—K4 ch   Resigns.

429

White   Black
MARÓCZY   TARTAKOWER
(Teplitz-Schönau, 1922)

*A rare occurrence: a positional sacrifice of
a Rook, based on general considerations only,
succeeds because the opposing forces are disorganised. The sacrifice fructifies nineteen
moves after its consummation.*

1 P—Q4   P—K3
2 P—QB4   P—KB4
The *Dutch Defence Deferred.*

3 Kt—QB3   Kt—KB3
4 P—QR3   B—K2
The first strategic object: the safety of the
King. 4 .... P—QKt3 is playable, but if
4 .... P—Q4; 5 B—B4.

5 P—K3   Castles
6 B—Q3   P—Q4
Reverting to the *stonewall formation* which,
besides its defensive rôle of preventing
7 P—K4, offers many attacking chances.

7 Kt—B3   P—B3
Premature would be 7 .... Kt—K5;
8 P×P, P×P; 9 Q—Kt3, with a double
attack on Q5 and K4.

8 Castles   Kt—K5
9 Q—B2
A waiting policy. A simple continuation
is the *counter-stonewall* 9 Kt—K5, B—Q3;
10 P—B4, with an almost symmetrical battle
array.

9 ......   B—Q3
The attack begins.

10 P—QKt3   Kt—Q2
11 B—Kt2   R—R3
The Rook, normally so ponderous, is to
co-operate with the "flying column." The
alternative, without its participation, is
11 .... Q—B3, to be followed by ....
P—KKt4 and .... P—Kt5.

12 KR—K1
After 12 Kt—K5, Black would have continued his action by 12 .... R—R3;
13 P—B3, Kt × Kt (K4); 14 QP × Kt, B × P,
etc., with a winning assault, or 13 P—B4,
B × Kt; 14 BP × B, Q—R5; 15 P—R3,
Kt—Kt4, etc., with a promising attack.

12 ......   R—R3
With the well-known threat 13 .... B × P
ch; 14 Kt × B, Q—R5, etc.

13 P—Kt3   Q—B3
14 B—KB1   P—KKt4
15 QR—Q1
After 15 B—Kt2, Black would regroup his
forces by 15 .... Q—Kt3, followed by ....
Q—R4, after which the arrival of the QKt
at KKt5 *via* KB3 would maintain the attack.

15 ......   P—Kt5
16 Kt × Kt
If 16 Kt—Q2, Kt × BP; 17 K × Kt, R × P
ch; 18 B—Kt2, B × P ch, and if 16 Kt—KR4,
R × Kt is decisive.

16 ......   BP × Kt
17 Kt—Q2
Hoping to consolidate his position in time,
e.g. 17 .... Kt—B1; 18 B—Kt2, Kt—Kt3;
19 Kt—B1, B—Q2; 20 R—K2, R—KB1;
21 P—Kt4, and White has nothing more
to fear.

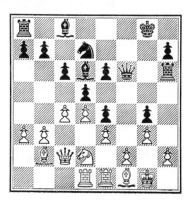

17 ......   R × P
This *break-up sacrifice* succeeds only
because Black is able for some time to tie up
White's relief troops.

18 K × R
Compulsory acceptance, for if 18 Kt × P,
Q—R3, threatening mate.

18 ......   Q × P ch
19 K—R1
Best. If 19 B—Kt2, Kt—B3, etc.

19 ......   Kt—B3
The "point" of the Rook's sacrifice.
White's second rank being paralysed, Black
is able to bring up his reserves at leisure,
whereas, if at once 19 .... Q × KtP;
20 Kt—Kt1, and White's Queen becomes
mobile.

20 R—K2   Q × KtP
21 Kt—Kt1   Kt—R4
Not 21 .... Q—R5 ch; 22 R—R2.

22 Q—Q2   B—Q2
Yet another quiet move. Insufficient
would be 22 .... Q—B6 ch (or ....
Q—R5 ch), because of 23 K—Kt1.

23 R—B2
To prevent 23 .... R—KB1. If 23 Q—K1,
Q—B6 ch; 24 R—Kt2, Q—R6 ch; 25 K—Kt1,
R—KB1; 26 Kt—Q2, B—Kt6; 27 R × B,
Q × R ch; 28 Q × Q, Kt × Q; 29 B—B3,
Kt—B4; 30 R—K1, P—KR4, and Black's
mobile pawns become effective.

23 ......   Q—R5 ch
24 K—Kt1   B—Kt6
25 B—B3
White is already forced to throw ballast overboard. If 25 R—R2, B × R ch;
26 Q × B, Q—Kt4, etc., or if 25 R—Kt2,
R—KB1; 26 Q—K2, R—B6, and in either
case Black wins.

25 ......   B × R ch
26 Q × B   P—Kt6
27 Q—KKt2   R—KB1
Black's game is developed at last, and he
threatens 28 .... R—B7; 29 Q—R1,
R—KR7, winning the Queen.

28 B—K1
Offering a compromise, for if Black now
recovers his piece by 28 .... Q—R7 ch;
29 Q × Q, P × Q ch; 30 K × P, R × B, the
game would be equalised after 31 Kt—Q2,
R—B1; 32 B—R4, etc.

28 ......   R × B ch
A fresh surprise, which wins the *tempo*

necessary to bring the idle Bishop into the fray.

29 K × R   P—K4
30 K—Kt1
Or 30 B × P, Kt × B ch; 31 K—B2, B—Kt5, etc.; or 30 K—K2, B—Kt5 ch; 31 K—Q2, Q—R7; 32 Q × Q, P × Q, and wins.

30 ......   B—Kt5
31 B × P
Sad but necessary, for if 31 R—Q2, KP × P; 32 KP × P, B—B6; 33 B × P, Kt × B; 34 Q—KR2, Q × Q ch; 35 R × Q, Kt—K7 ch, followed by .... Kt × P, with three pawns for the exchange.

31 ......   Kt × B
32 R—K1   Kt—B4
33 Q—KB2   Q—Kt4
34 QP × P
There is no saving the game. If 34 K—B1, Q—R4, threatening 35 .... Q—R8 ch; 36 Q—Kt1, Kt—Kt6 ch; 37 K—B2, Q—B6 mate.

34 ......   B—B6 dis ch
35 K—B1   Kt—Kt6 ch
          Resigns
(36 K—Kt1, Kt—R8 dis ch.)

BLACKMAR GAMBIT

430

| *White* | *Black* |
| VON FREYMANN | FORGACZ |

(St. Petersburg, 1909)

The salient point of this brilliant game is a triple pin, elegantly turned to account by a "mere nothing" (21 Kt—K4). A most instructive turn.

1 P—Q4   P—KB4
2 P—K4
The *Blackmar* or *Staunton Gambit*, which aims at opening up the game for the benefit of the assailant.

2 ......   P × P
3 Kt—QB3
There is little substance in the violent continuations 3 P—KB3 (3 .... P—Q4; 4 P—QB4, P—K3; 5 Kt—B3, B—QKt5, etc.), or the *Swedish Attack*, 3 P—KKt4.

3 ......   Kt—KB3
4 B—KKt5
Recovering his pawn. If 4 P—B3, P—Q4, and if, impetuously, 4 P—KKt4, P—KR3; 5 P—Kt5, P × P; 6 B × P, P—Q4, etc., with chances for both sides.

4 ......   P—B3
A catastrophe would result from 4 .... P—Q4, e.g. 5 B × Kt, KP × B; 6 Q—R5 ch, P—Kt3; 7 Q × QP, Q × Q; 8 Kt × Q, and White wins instead of losing a pawn. More or less ingenious ideas are 4 .... P—Q3 or 4 .... P—QKt3, or, stressing the development of the pieces, 4 .... Kt—B3.
After 4 .... P—KKt3, the powerful continuation in a game Réti-Euwe (Match, 1920) was as follows: 5 P—B3 (after 5 B × Kt, P × B; 6 Kt × P, P—Q4, etc., Black has nothing to fear); 5 .... P × P (5 .... P—Q4; 6 P × P, P × P; 7 B—QB4); 6 Kt × P, B—Kt2 (more to the point is 6 .... P—Q4; 7 B—Q3, Kt—B3, etc.); 7 B—Q3, P—B4; 8 P—Q5, Q—Kt3; 9 Q—Q2, Q × P; 10 R—QKt1, Kt × P; 11 Kt × Kt (a touch of genius; he sacrifices both Rooks); 11 .... Q × R ch; 12 K—B2, Q × R; 13 B × P, P—Q3; 14 B × P, Kt—B3; 15 B—Kt5, B—Q2; 16 B × Kt, P × B; 17 Q—K2 ch, resigns.

5 P—B3
Far better than 5 B × Kt, KP × B; 6 Kt × P, Q—Kt3; 7 Q—K2, Q × KtP; 8 Kt—Q6 db ch, K—Q1, or 7 R—Kt1, P—Q4, and Black has a good game.

5 ......   Q—R4
Best. After 5 .... Q—Kt3; 6 P × P, Q × KtP; 7 B—Q2, White's attack is maintained. This attack would be even more insistent after 5 .... P × P; 6 Kt × P, etc.

6 Q—Q2
Less good is 6 B × Kt, KP × B; 7 P × P, P—Q4; 8 P × P, B—QKt5, and Black has the initiative.

6 ......   P—K6
Already renouncing his prey, for his position would be unenviable after 6 .... P × P; 7 Kt × P, P—Q3; 8 B—Q3, etc., or 6 .... P—Q4; 7 P × P, P × P; 8 Kt × P, etc., or again, 6 .... P—K4; 7 B × Kt, P × B; 8 BP × P, etc.

7 B × P
More diplomatic than 7 Q × P.

7 ......   P—K4
More solid is 7 .... P—K3, although even then White maintains the initiative by 8 B—Q3, followed by KKt—K2, and Castles KR, etc.

8 P×P	Q×KP
9 Castles	P—Q4
10 B—KB4	Q—B4

If 10 .... Q—R4; 11 P—KKt4.

11 R—K1 ch	K—B2
12 B—Q3	Q—Q2
13 Kt—R3	Q—Q1

A more stoical resistance results from 13 .... P—KR3.

14 Kt—Kt5 ch	K—Kt1
15 Kt—K6	B×Kt
16 R×B	P—KKt3

He must attend to the development of his K side, but the pressure on his KB3 will soon overshadow all his other worries.

17 B—KKt5	QKt—Q2
18 Q—B4	K—B2
19 KR—K1	P—KR3
20 B—R4	B—Kt2

For if 20 .... P—KKt4; 21 Q—B5, R—KKt1; 22 B—B2, and Black's position remains precarious. Black can effect an artificial castling by 21 .... R—KB1, followed by .... P—KKt4 and .... K—Kt1, etc.

21 Kt—K4

Beautiful play. He forces open a hidden door on the diagonal QR2—KKt8.

21 ...... P×Kt

He must accept the sacrifice, otherwise things would flare up at his KB3. If, for instance, 21 .... R—KB1; 22 Kt×Kt,

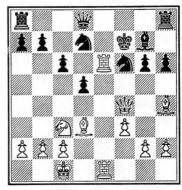

Position after 20 .... B—Kt2

Kt×Kt; 23 B×Kt, B×B; 24 R—Q6, P—KKt4; 25 Q—B5, Q×R; 26 Q—Kt6 mate.

22 B—B4

A vivid illustration of the power of the discovered check.

22	K—Kt1
23 R×Kt dis ch	K—R2
24 R×KtP	

Cutting the life line of both King and Queen, for after 24 .... K×R, there is a mate in two.

24	Kt—B3
25 Q—B5	Resigns.

28. BENONI COUNTER-GAMBIT

431

White   *Black*

HANSTEIN   VON DER LAZA

(Berlin, 1841–2)

The following game provides an interesting and very early example of an opening, which, after falling into disuse, has been taken up again lately with modern improvements.

1 P—Q4   **P—QB4**

"Un-positional" as this move may appear, it is playable. But, needless to say, the continuation requires the utmost care and precision.

2 P—Q5

Driving a wedge into the hostile position, and rendering cohesion between Black's two wings more difficult.

2 ......   **P—K4**

In some of the games in the match Staunton—St. Amant (1843), Black tried 2 .... P—B4, but without success.

Other moves usually played at this stage are 2 .... P—Q3 or 2 .... Kt—KB3 or 2 .... P—KKt3; 3 P—K4. After 3 P × P e. p., BP × P; 4 P—K4, Kt—QB3; 5 Kt—KB3, P—Q4; 6 P × P, P × P, etc., with an equal game.

3 P—K4   **P—Q3**
4 P—KB4

The most ambitious continuation. Concentric development by 4 B—Q3 is also good, while the slower 4 P—KKt3 would permit the counter-attempt 4 .... P—B4.

Other moves which have been tried here are 4 Kt—QB3, 4 Kt—K2, and 4 P—QB4.

4 ......   **P—B4**

Black's position is not secure enough to justify the violent advance of four pawns in the centre. Only White will profit by it in the end.

Best would have been 4 .... P × P.

5 B—Q3

Contesting the square at K4. Also good is 5 Kt—QB3, BP × P; 6 Kt × P, Kt—KB3; 7 B—Q3, as Black cannot reply with 7 .... Kt × P on account of 8 B—Kt5 ch.

5 ......   **BP × P**
6 B × P   **Kt—KB3**
7 Kt—QB3   **B—K2**
8 Kt—B3

By maintaining a piece centrally at K4, White has scored a point. He will soon score another by strengthening his advanced QP.

8 ......   **Castles**
9 P × P   **P × P**
10 Castles

It would have been premature to play 10 Kt × P, because of 10 .... Kt × B; 11 Kt × Kt, B—R5 ch; 12 P—Kt3, Q—K2; 13 P × B, Q × Kt; 14 Q—K2, R—K1; 15 Kt—Kt3, Q × Q ch; 16 Kt × Q, B—Kt5, with an imminent catastrophe due to the white King's exposed position.

10 ......   **Kt × B**
11 Kt × Kt   **B—B4**
12 R—K1

Leaving to the adverse KR the administration of the sterile KB file, White's KR seizes another and vital file.

12 ......   **Kt—Q2**
13 P—Q6   **B—R5**
14 B—Kt5

Well parried. Now all the white pieces get into play.

14 ......   **B × B**
15 QKt × B   **Q—B3**

This provides against a well-known stratagem (16 Q—Q5 ch, K—R1; 17 Kt—B7 ch, winning the exchange), without, however, avoiding some slight loss in material.

16 Q—Q5 ch   **K—R1**
17 Q × KtP   **QR—Kt1**
18 Q—Q5

Returning to the charge instead of being lured from the main battlefield by 18 Q × P, R × P, etc.

18 ......   **B × P**
19 Kt × KP

Bold-looking, but well calculated. Now neither 19 .... Q × QKt (20 Kt—B7 ch, winning the Queen) nor 19 .... Q—B7 ch (affording no real chance for Black) is playable.

19 ......   Kt×Kt
20 Q×Kt   Q—B7 ch

Here again this check represents no more than a purely transitory success. Also of no value would be 20 .... Q×Q; 21 R×Q, R×P (or 21 .... QR—Q1; 22 R×P); 22 R—K2, P—B5; 23 P—Q7, and wins.

21 K—R1   B—Kt3
22 Kt—K6   R—B3

Equally, if 22 .... R—B2; 23 P—Q7 wins a Rook for the advanced pawn.

23 P—Q7
And White wins.

432

White	Black
RUBINSTEIN	SPIELMANN

Pistyan, 1912

The building up of an attack by the second player—especially in an opening both peculiar and difficult to handle—is a special art. We shall be able to follow some of its guiding principles here.

1 P—Q4   P—QB4
2 P—Q5   P—Q3

Reserving the option of 3 .... P—K4, and of other plans of development.

3 P—QB4

The most incisive plan here is 3 P—K4, and, whether Black plays 3 .... P—K4 or 3 .... P—KKt3, the energetic continuation 4 P—KB4.

3 ......   P—KKt3

In this position, with the long diagonal remaining "wide open," this scheme of development is particularly suitable.

4 P—K4   B—Kt2
5 B—Q3

This Bishop would have more future after 5 P—KKt3, followed by B—Kt2.

5 ......   P—K3

It will be noticed that Black carefully refrains from blocking the long diagonal either by 5 .... P—K4 or, even temporarily, by 5 .... Kt—KB3.

6 Kt—QB3

After 6 P×P, P×P, Black's centre would be strengthened, and the KB file open to him for future action.

6 ......   Kt—K2
7 KKt—K2

Here 7 P—B4, followed by Kt—B3, leads to more straightforward development.

7 ......   P×P
8 KP×P   Kt—Q2
9 P—B4

If 9 Castles, Kt—K4, and White loses the "two Bishops." But it must be recognised that the move in the text renders the position of White's King more vulnerable.

9 ......   Kt—KB3
10 Kt—Kt3   P—KR4

Sounding the general attack.

11 Castles   P—R5
12 KKt—K4   Kt×Kt
13 B×Kt   B—Q5 ch
14 K—R1   Kt—B4

Black's attack has quickly assumed a concrete form. The text move announces the well-known attack by 15 .... Kt—Kt6 ch; 16 P×Kt, P×P dis ch, followed by mate.

15 B×Kt   B×B
16 R—K1 ch   K—B1

Leading to artificial castling (21 .... K—Kt2), by which all his troops are left undisturbed in their attacking positions.

17 Q—B3

White seeks to avoid fresh weaknesses, e.g. if 17 B—K3, B×Kt; 18 P×B, P—R6; 19 P—Kt3, B—K5 ch; 20 K—R1, P—B4 (or 20 .... B—Kt7), and White's position remains restricted.

17 ......   P—R6

This bold pawn assumes here, as in the sequel, the rôle of a piece.

18 P—KKt3

Evidently not 18 P—KKt4, because of 18 .... Q—R5, attacking White's KKtP as well as his Rook.

18 ......   Q—Q2
19 B—Q2   B—Kt5
20 Q—B1

Against 20 Q—Q3 Black would also play 20 .... Q—B4, because White could not reply with 21 Q×Q, on account of 21 .... B—B6 mate.

20 ......   Q—B4

With the threat of dissolution by 21 .... Q—B7.

21 QR—B1   K—Kt2
22 B—K3   B—B3
23 P—Kt3
He prefers carefully to consolidate his
position instead of trying 23 Kt—Kt5, after
which 23 .... Q—Q2 would without difficulty have subdued all White's attempts at
active play.

23 ......   R—K1
With all his forces in active participation,
Black's attack is at its height.

24 B—B2
Here again the false alarm by 24 Kt—Kt5
would, after 24 .... Q—Q2; 25 Kt×RP,
R—R1; 26 Kt—Kt5, R×P, etc., lead only
to increased pressure by Black. White's
grave situation stands out clearly in the
following curious variation: 24 B—Kt1,
R×R; 25 Q×R (or 25 R×R, B×Kt);
25 .... B—B6 mate.

24 ......   B—B6 ch
25 K—Kt1   B—Kt7
This mating of the white Queen is conclusive.

26 R×R   B×Q
27 R×R   Q—Q6
Stronger still than 27 .... K×R;
28 K×B.

28 R—K8   Q—B6
29 K×B   Q—R8 ch
30 B—Kt1   Q—Kt7 ch
31 K—K1   Q×B ch
32 K—Q2   Q×P ch
       Resigns
If 33 Kt—K2, Q—Kt7; 34 R—KKt1,
Q×R; 35 Kt×Q, P—R7.

433

White	Black
RUBINSTEIN	MIESES

(Kissingen, 1928)

*The opening of lines, either vertical or
diagonal—even at the cost of the positional
sacrifice of a pawn—nearly always benefits
the better-developed player. Neglect of this
old principle causes Black's downfall here.*

1 P—Q4   P—QB4
2 P—Q5   P—Q3
3 P—QB4   P—KKt3
4 P—KKt3
A positional continuation, which stores up
energy for the future.

4 ......   B—Kt2
5 B—Kt2   Kt—KB3
Black also adopts a closed style. Another
plan of opening is 5 .... P—K3, to be
followed by .... Kt—K2. An interesting
attempt to bring life into the game is 5 ....
P—QKt4.

6 P—K4   Castles
7 Kt—K2   QKt—Q2
Another type of development arises from
7 .... P—K4; 8 Castles, Kt—K1; 9 P—B4,
P—B4; 10 QKt—B3, and White's position
remains superior, thanks mainly to his
advanced pawn at Q5. That is why, for the
present, Black prefers avoiding a clinch on
the central squares K4 and K5 and pursues
a restrained development.

8 P—B4   Kt—Kt3
9 Q—B2   P—K3
10 Castles   P×P
11 BP×P
After 11 KP×P, B—B4, etc., Black's task
would be appreciably lighter.

11 ......   R—K1
Black now also has some definite plans on
the K file, which White, however, can easily
circumvent.

12 QKt—B3   B—Kt5
In the hope of being able to continue with
13 .... Q—Q2 and .... B—R6, but, needless to say, White does not allow these plans
to fructify.

13 P—KR3   B×Kt
14 Kt×B
Clearly not 14 Q×B, because of 14 ....
QKt×P.

14 ......   Q—K2
15 Kt—B3
Parrying without difficulty both threats:
15 .... Kt×KP and 15 .... QKt×P.

15 ......   Kt—R4
A critical moment. Black's plan to win
a pawn is unsound, and will cost him
valuable material.

16 K—R2   B×Kt
17 P×B
He readily falls in with his adversary's
intentions, because his two Bishops will go
from strength to strength. It would, however, be a mistake to play 17 Q×B, Kt—B3;
18 R—K1, on account of 18 .... KKt×QP.

17 ......   Kt—B3
18 P—B4
With the double mission of reinforcing the

QP (18 R—K1, KKt × QP) and of reopening the long black diagonal.

18 ......　　　Kt × KP

By capturing the pawn Black signs his death-warrant, for he loses time, commits his Knight, and gives new life to the K file for his opponent's benefit. However, there was not much to be said for a passive defence by 18 .... KKt—Q2; 19 B—Kt2, P—B3; 20 QR—K1, etc., as White's Bishops are far superior to Black's lame Knights.

19 B—Kt2

Already decisive.

19 ......　　　P—KR3

A belated effort to create a basis for defence, for after 19 .... Kt—B3; 20 Q—B3, QKt—Q2; 21 QR—K1, Q—B1; 22 P—Kt4 (threatening 23 P—Kt5), the end is near.

20 QR—K1　　　P—B4
21 P—Kt4

Preparing to open yet another vitally important file (KKt).

Still premature would be 21 B × Kt, P × B; 22 Q—B3, because of 22 .... K—R2.

21 ......　　　K—R2
22 P × P　　　　P × P
23 R—KKt1　　　R—KKt1
24 B × Kt　　　　Resigns

After 24 .... P × B; 25 R × P, the effect of the discovered check would be crushing.

434

White	*Black*
BOGOLJUBOW	ALEKHINE

(Match, 1934)

In this game, in which Black conducts the opening in a very original manner, it is particularly interesting to watch—from the 25th to the 37th move—the contest between the two Bishops and the two Knights.

1 P—Q4　　　　P—QB4
2 P—Q5　　　　P—K4

An old idea, successfully revived by Alekhine.

3 P—K4　　　　P—Q3
4 P—KB4

Trying as quickly as possible to capture the initiative. The sequel will show that the state of tension thus produced also affords Black some fighting resources.

Therefore the easier course here is 4 B—Q3, preventing the counter-thrust 4 .... P—B4, and developing his own K side at the same time.

4 ......　　　P × P
5 B × P　　　　Q—R5 ch

Instead of at once 5 .... Q—K2, Black's text move is intended to cause a slight weakness in the hostile position. 5 .... Q—B3 leads to nothing because of 6 Q—B1, guarding the two points attacked (the Bishop at KB4 and the pawn at QKt2).

If 5 .... Kt—Q2; 6 Kt—KB3 furthers White's development, and continues the pressure on K5.

6 P—Kt3

Clearly not 6 B—Kt3, because of 6 .... Q × P ch.

6 ......　　　Q—K2
7 Kt—QB3

Other ways of guarding the KP are 7 B—Q3 or 7 B—Kt2, but an ingenious idea is to sacrifice it as follows: 7 Kt—KB3, Q × P ch; 8 K—B2 (with the threat of 9 B—Kt5 ch, followed by R—K1 and R—K8); 8 .... Kt—KB3; 9 B—R3 (if 9 P—B4, B—B4, in order to exchange Queens by 10 .... Q—B7 ch); 9 .... K—Q1; 10 R—K1, Q—Kt3, with a most complicated position.

7 ......　　　P—KKt4
8 B—K3　　　　Kt—Q2
9 Kt—B3

Not a happy position for this undefended Knight, which can be attacked by .... P—Kt5, and which, moreover, obstructs the KB file.

A more promising plan of development would be 9 Q—Q2, P—KR3; 10 Castles, with interesting possibilities for White (e.g. P—KR4).

9 ......　　　P—KR3
10 Q—Q2　　　KKt—B3
11 Castles　　　Kt—Kt5

It would have been too risky to accept White's sacrifice of a pawn, e.g. 11 .... Kt × KP; 12 Kt × Kt, Q × Kt; 13 B—Kt2 (13 R—K1, Q × Kt; 14 B—Kt2, Q—R4; 15 B—Q4 dis ch, Kt—K4, remaining with a piece ahead); 13 .... Q—Kt3; 14 QR—K1, and White's frontal attack is very strong.

12 B—K2　　　　B—Kt2
13 KR—B1　　　Kt × B
14 Q × Kt　　　　P—R3
15 Kt—KKt1

Less passive would be 15 QR—K1.

15 ...... P—Kt4

An offensive on either wing. At the same time the move in the text frees the QB, so that Black will be able to castle on the Q side.

16 QR—K1   B—Kt2
17 Kt—Q1   Castles QR
18 B—Kt4   K—Kt1
19 B×Kt

Else 19 .... Kt—K4 or 19 .... Kt—Kt3 (and if 20 P—Kt3, Q—K4) might become awkward. But now the "two Bishops" will be in Black's favour.

19 ...... R×B
20 Q—Q2

A vacating manœuvre, allowing the QKt to occupy KB5, where, however, it will have no dynamic effect. If 20 Kt—K2 or 20 Kt—KB3, then 20 .... R—K1, reinforcing the pressure against the exposed KP.

20 ...... P—KKt5

Emphasising the poor rôle played by the opposing KKt. Black's superiority in space is evident.

21 Kt—K3   Q—K4
22 P—B3   P—KR4
23 Kt—B5   B—KB3
24 Q—B4

Strategically at a disadvantage, White seeks relief in the exchange of Queens.

24 ...... Q×Q
25 P×Q

Not 25 R×Q, B—Kt4.

25 ...... QR—Q1
26 P—B4

Hoping, in vain, to obtain freedom and to regain the pawn. The waiting move 26 K—B2 is better.

26 ...... P×P
27 Kt—K3   P—B6

The first hammer stroke, maintaining the pawn.

28 P—Kt3   B—Q5
29 Kt—B4   P—B4

The second hammer stroke, freeing the QB.

30 P—K5   P×P
31 P×P   B×QP
32 R×P   QR—KB1
33 R×R ch   R×R
34 P—K6   R—K1
35 P—K7   QB×Kt
36 P×B   B×Kt
37 R×B   R×P

After the liquidation, Black remains with

a decisive advantage for the ensuing Rook ending.

38 P—KR3   P×P
39 K—B2   P—R7
40 R—Kt1 ch R—Kt2
41 R—KR1   R—Kt7 ch
42 K×P   R×P
43 K—Q3   K—B2
44 K—K4   K—B3
45 K—B5   P—R4
46 K—Kt5   R—K7
    Resigns.

435

White   Black

ALATORZEV   PANOV

(Moscow, 1937)

After a period of "trench warfare," consisting in waiting manœuvres, Black succeeds in thrusting his shock battalions along the opened KR file and disrupting the enemy camp.

1 P—Q4   P—QB4
2 P—Q5   P—K4
3 P—K4   P—Q3
4 Kt—K2

Slower than the alternative development by 4 B—Q3 or 4 Kt—QB3, the text move enables Black to mobilise his forces without difficulty.

4 ...... Kt—KB3

Black's plan of campaign is first of all to complete the development of his K side by .... B—K2 and .... Castles, and after that to proceed methodically after .... Kt—K1 to the preparation of the thrust .... P—KB4.

If, however, 4 .... Kt—K2; 5 Kt—Kt3, P—KKt3, the impetuous advance of 6 P—KR4 is likely to undermine Black's K side.

5 P—KB3

Restrained play. If 5 Kt—Kt3, B—K2; 6 P—KB4, Black simply continues with 6 .... P×P; 7 B×P, Castles, followed by .... R—K1, and has full control of the vacated square at K4.

5 ......   B—K2
6 P—QB4   Castles
7 B—K3   Kt—K1

Patiently making his way, whereas 7 ....

Kt—R4, though more energetic in appearance, would be helping White after 8 P—KKt4.

8 Q—Q2   Kt—R3
Bilateral work, much favoured by modern strategists. Before embarking on .... P—B4; Black prefers to effect the active mobilisation of his Q side.

9 QKt—B3   QKt—B2
10 P—KKt4
This preventive measure against the above-mentioned thrust .... P—KB4; causes some disarrangement of White's position.

10 ......   B—R5 ch
The subsidiary idea underlying this check is to prevent a future advance by Black's KtP.

11 Kt—Kt3   B—Q2
12 B—Q3   P—KKt3
13 Castles KR
In view of Black's preparations, castling on the Q side would be too hazardous, e.g. 13 Castles QR, P—QR3, followed by .... P—QKt4, opening files for the attack.

13 ......   Kt—Kt2
14 K—R1   P—Kt3
15 R—KKt1   Q—K2
16 R—Kt2   K—R1
17 QR—KKt1
Simulating an intended K side attack, but really waiting on events.

17 ......   P—QR3
18 P—R4   QR—Kt1
Now the Q side is ready to strike.

19 P—Kt3   P—B3
And the K side is ready as well.

20 KKt—K2   P—QKt4
And so Black has decided to open hostilities on the Q side.

21 RP×P   P×P
22 P—B4
Refusing to await events passively.

22 ......   P—Kt5
23 Kt—Q1   P×P
24 Kt×P   K—Kt1
Here and in the sequel we see "manœuvres of attrition" carried out behind both fronts.

25 Q—K2   R—R1
26 B—Q2   B—KKt4
27 R—B1   B—B1
28 B—B2   Kt—R3
A "rejuvenating manœuvre." The Knight

proceeds *via* QKt1 and Q2 to K4, now that this square has become "alive" again.

29 Q—B2   Kt—Kt1
30 P—R4   B×Kt
31 Q×B   Kt—Q2
32 B—Kt1   Kt—K4
33 Kt—K3   Q—Q2
34 R(Kt2)—B2   R—B2
35 Q—Kt3   P—R3
36 Q—B4
Returning to the charge, without, however, making any impression on KR6.

36 ......   K—R2
37 B—B1
Because 37 Kt—B5, P×Kt; 38 Q×RP ch, K—Kt1 would lead to nothing, Black, unlike White, having nothing to fear.

37 ......   R—R8
38 R—QKt2   P—R4
Hitting out at last.

39 P×P   Kt×RP
40 Q—B2   K—Kt1
41 B—B2   R—KR2
With the immediate threat of 42 .... P—Kt4.

42 R—QKt1   R×R
43 B×R   P—Kt4
44 R—Kt1   Kt—Kt2
45 Kt—Kt2   Kt—Kt5
46 Q—Kt2   Kt—R4
Threatening an original mate by 47 .... Kt—Kt6.

47 R—K1   P×P
48 P—K5   P—R6
Resigns
A most piquant ending: after 49 B×R ch, Q×B; 50 Kt—B4 (or 50 Kt—K3, Q—K5 ch); 50 .... Kt—Kt6 ch; 51 K—Kt1, BP×P, White's position is hopeless.

436

White	Black
FINE	STAHLBERG

(Match, 1937)

This game is characteristic of the winner's methods—simple means, both discreet and logical, bring about the collapse of the hostile position with almost elemental force.

| 1 P—Q4 | Kt—KB3 |
| 2 P—QB4 | P—B4 |

A bold reply.

3 P—Q5

The only continuation likely to give White any advantage in the opening.

| 3 ...... | P—K4 |

If 3 .... P—K3, then simply 4 Kt—QB3.

| 4 Kt—QB3 | P—Q3 |
| 5 P—K4 | P—KKt3 |

Awkward, but after 5 .... B—K2, 6 P—KKt3, Castles; 7 B—Kt2, White has the better chances.

6 P—KKt3	B—Kt2
7 B—Kt2	Castles
8 KKt—K2	QKt—Q2
9 Castles	

White has treated the opening simply and powerfully, and can already boast of a superiority in territory.

| 9 ...... | Kt—K1 |
| 10 B—K3 | P—QR3 |

Black recognises that the thrust 10 .... P—B4 would be useless, as after 11 Q—Q2 this pawn's further progress would be stopped. On the other hand, 11 .... P × P, 12 Kt × P would be in favour of White. That is why Black seeks to get his QR into play.

11 Q—Q2	P—Kt3
12 QR—K1	R—R2
13 P—B4	

A well-prepared advance.

| 13 ...... | P × P |

This exchange is assuredly unfavourable. Normally exchanges can only benefit the better-developed side. 13 .... P—B3 would therefore have been better, followed by a regrouping of forces by .... Kt—Kt1 and QR—KB2.

| 14 P × P | P—B4 |

Continuing the faulty strategy of expansion, instead of prudently resigning himself to 14 .... P—B3.

15 P × P	P × P
16 Kt—Kt3	QKt—B3
17 B—R3	

This unpretentious looking move plays a decisive part in the attack. Black's reply is forced, after which White's troops penetrate victoriously into the enemy camp.

17	Kt—Kt5
18 B × Kt	P × B
19 P—B5	

With the twofold function of opening the way for White's Bishop and preventing 19 .... B—B4, which would have tended to consolidate Black's position.

| 19 ...... | QR—KB2 |
| 20 B—Kt5 | Q—B2 |

A little better would have been 20 .... B—B3, 21 B—R6, B—KKt2, and White would still have had to allow for the threat 22 .... B × P.

| 21 B—R6 | K—R1 |

White's KBP was indirectly defended, for after exchanges Black's Knight would be lost.

| 22 QKt—K4 | B × B |

Here again 22 .... QB × P; would be fatal on account of 23 Kt—Kt5, R—B3; 24 Kt × B, etc. Nor would 22 .... Kt—B3 save the situation because of 23 Kt—Kt5, R—K2; 24 Kt—K6, B × Kt; 25 BP × B, with complete control of the board.

| 23 Q × B | K—Kt1 |

The King *in extremis*.

24 P—B6	P—Kt4
25 Kt—R5	P—Kt6
26 R—K3	P × P ch
27 K × P	K—R1
28 Kt—Kt5	Resigns

White threatens not only 29 Kt × R ch, but also 29 Kt × P.

437

| *White* | *Black* |
| WEINITSCHKE | BOGOLJUBOW |

(Elster, 1938)

In the following extravaganza, Black gives up a piece for three pawns in the opening and succeeds in devastating the enemy camp.

| 1 P—Q4 | Kt—QB3 |

A fancy opening in the same class as:
(a) 1 .... P—QKt4: the *Polish Defence*.
(b) 1 .... P—K4: *Charlick's Gambit*.
(c) 1 .... P—Q3: the *Old Indian Defence*.
(d) 1 .... P—KKt3 and 1 .... P—QKt3: the *Fianchetto Defences*.

2 P—Q5

The simplest is 2 Kt—KB3 (reverting,

after 2 .... P—Q4; 3 P—B4, to the *Tchigorin Defence*). After 2 P—K4, P—Q4 we have the *Nimzowitsch-Fischer Defence*.

2	Kt—K4
3 P—KB4	

More solid is 3 P—K4.

3	Kt—Kt3

Thoughtless would be 3 .... Kt—Kt5; 4 P—K4, etc.

4 P—K4	P—K4
5 P—B5	

Obduracy. The wise course is 5 P×P e.p., BP×P, etc.

5	Q—R5 ch

Touching the spot. But after 5 .... QKt—K2; 6 B—KKt5, White would have the advantage.

6 K—Q2	Q×KP

Revealing his intentions.

7 P×Kt

Necessary, to make up for his loss in pawns, for if 7 B—Q3, Q×KtP ch; 8 Kt—K2, Q—Kt4 ch; 9 K—B3, Q—R5, and Black saves his piece.

7	Q×QP ch
8 K—K1	Q×Q ch
9 K×Q	RP×P

Result: three good pawns for the piece. A fresh battle begins.

10 Kt—QB3

Better, first, 10 P—B4.

10	P—QB3

Preparing a formidable pawn centre.

11 Kt—B3	P—B3
12 B—Q3	

More reserved would be 12 B—K2, but it is only natural for White to want to exploit his extra piece.

12	Kt—K2
13 R—K1	P—Q4
14 P—KR3	

White decides to give back the piece rather than lose yet another pawn.

14	P—K5
15 B×P	P×B
16 Kt×P	K—B2

Anticipating any frontal attack.

17 B—Q2

If 17 Kt—Q6 ch, K—Kt1.

17	Kt—B4
18 P—QKt3	P—KKt4

Black's play is remarkably aggressive, although his pieces are slow in getting into play, and he is only a doubled pawn ahead.

19 K—K2

Remaining on the K side, for if 19 P—B3, Kt—Q3; 20 Kt×Kt ch, B×Kt; 21 K—B2, P—Kt5, White's position would deteriorate rapidly.

19	Kt—Q3
20 Kt—B2	

After 20 Kt×Kt ch, B×Kt, Black's two Bishops would act promptly. After the text move, too, the thrust 20 .... P—Kt5 is prevented.

20	B—B4
21 Kt—Q4	B—Kt3
22 K—B1	Kt—B4
23 Kt—K2	B—B4
24 Kt—K4	B—Kt3

Now Black has two machine-guns in position (Bishop at KKt3 and Bishop at QKt3). Less patient would be 24 .... Kt—K6 ch; 25 B×Kt, B×B; 26 Kt—Q6 ch, K—B1; 27 Kt—Kt3, B—B5; 28 Kt(Kt3)—B5, P—Kt3; 29 P—B4, and there is no immediate decision in the contest between the Knights and the Bishops.

25 P—B4

If 25 P—KKt4, Kt—K6 ch; 26 B×Kt, B×Kt; 27 B×B, P×B, winning another pawn.

25	QR—Q1
26 KR—Q1	

If 26 P—B5, B×P; 27 Kt×B, R×B; 28 Kt×P, R—K1, and wins.

26	R×B

Elegant to the end.

27 Kt×R	Kt—K6 ch

The finishing touch; White loses everything after 28 K—K1, Kt×P ch; 29 K—B1, Kt—K6 ch; 30 K—K1, R×P, etc.

White resigns.

29. INDIAN DEFENCES

KING'S INDIAN DEFENCE

438

White	Black
COCHRANE	MOHESHUNDER BONNERJEE

(Calcutta, about 1847)

A temporary sacrifice by Black (9 .... Kt × KP) allows him to recover his material, but at the cost of territory (especially the square at his K3). A sacrifice of the exchange by Black on that square (16 .... R × Kt) is followed by the loss of another exchange, thanks to pretty play by White, which leads to a thrilling King hunt.

1 P—K4   P—Q3

In this *Old Indian Defence* we see the tendency, in vogue to-day, of avoiding an early clinch in the centre.

2 P—Q4   Kt—KB3

Gaining a slight moral success, for White must now assign to his KB the modest rôle of a guardian of pawns.

3 B—Q3   P—KKt3

The natural complement of Black's first move, opening up distant horizons for *both Bishops*.

4 P—QB4

Showing a wholly modern *positional judgment*, which requires that the QKt shall not be developed at QB3, before advancing the QBP in support of the centre.

4 ......   B—Kt2
5 Kt—QB3   Castles
6 P—B4

By this extension of his front (known to modern theory under the name of the *Indian Four Pawns' Attack*), instead of 6 Kt—B3 or 6 KKt—K2, Cochrane demonstrates his impetuous temperament. He refrains also from blocking his KBP by the nonchalant development 6 Kt—B3.

6 ......   P—K4

A vigorous counter-measure. According to the player's temperament, three other continuations can be tried here: the patient defence 6 .... QKt—Q2 (7 P—K5, Kt—K1; 8 Kt—B3, P—QB4, etc.); the constructive plan 6 .... B—Kt5; 7 Kt—B3, Kt—B3; 8 B—K3, P—K4, etc.; or, finally, the lateral demonstration 6 .... P—B4.

7 BP × P   P × P
8 P—Q5

Better than 8 P × P, Kt—Kt5, which would help Black's intentions.

8 ......   B—Kt5

Here again a policy of patience can be adopted, e.g. 8 .... QKt—Q2; 9 Kt—B3, Kt—B4; 10 B—B2, P—QR4; 11 Castles (not 11 Kt × P, R—K1; 12 B—B4, Kt—R4); 11 .... Q—Q3; 12 Q—K1, B—Q2; 13 Q—R4, QR—K1, with an even game.

9 Kt—B3   Kt × KP

Although this is but a *temporary sacrifice*, the recovery of the piece will cause a weakening of Black's formation. A more peaceful continuation is 9 .... Kt—R3; 10 P—KR3, B × Kt; 11 Q × B, Kt—B4; 12 B—B2, P—QR4; 13 Castles, Q—Q3, and although White can claim an advantage in space, Black can still hope to equalise.

10 Kt × Kt   P—KB4
11 QKt—Kt5   P—K5

A fine fork, but it can be mastered.

12 Castles

Safety first. If at once 12 Kt—K6, P × Kt; 13 P × P (not 13 Kt × Q, nor 13 Castles, on account of 13 .... P × P); 13 .... Q—R5 ch holds many dangers to White's King.

12 ......   R—K1

Better would be 12 .... Q—Q3, etc.

13 B—K2   P × Kt
14 B × P   B × B
15 Q × B   Kt—Q2

Although the balance of power is restored, Black's position is no longer sound. If, e.g. 15 .... Kt—R3; 16 P—KKt4.

16 Kt—K6   R × Kt

Paltry would be 16 .... Q—B1, etc. The idea of relieving the Knight's heavy pressure by the sacrifice of the exchange is sound, if the supporting pawn can be annexed at the same time.

17 P×R	Kt—B4
18 Q—Q5	Q—K2
19 R—K1	

Preparing a very fine turn, otherwise the immediate settlement by 19 B—Kt5 (e.g. 19 .... Q×B; 20 Q×Kt, etc., or 19 .... Q—Q3; 20 B—B4) has points.

| 19 ...... | R—Q1 |

Better is 19 .... P—B3.

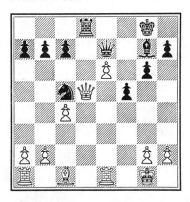

20 B—Kt5

Demonstrating the potential value of a discovered check.

20	Q×B
21 P—K7 dis ch	R×Q
22 P—K8 (Q) ch	B—B1
23 P×R	Q—B3

Black, although two exchanges down, is still full of fight. But 23 .... Kt—Q6 would be better, as now the Knight will remain in quarantine.

24 QR—Q1	P—B5
25 P—QKt4	Kt—R3
26 R—K4	K—Kt2

An amusing continuation would be 26 .... P—B6; 27 P×P, Q×P; 28 R—KB1, and Black succumbs without even a solitary "spite check."

| 27 P—QR3 | B—Q3 |
| 28 R—KB1 | Q—B6 |

Black leaves his King to fend for himself, in the hope of extricating his Knight. But 28 .... Q—Kt4 would be better.

29 R—K7 ch

A telling reply.

| 29 ...... | K—R3 |

If 29 .... B×R; 30 Q×B ch, K—Kt1; 31 R×P, and wins.

| 30 Q—B8 ch | K—Kt4 |
| 31 P—R4 ch | |

Intensifying the pursuit.

| 31 ...... | K×P |

Or 31 .... K—Kt5; 32 Q—B8 ch.

| 32 R×RP ch | K—Kt4 |

Or 32 .... K—Kt5; 33 Q—R6.

33 Q—R6 ch	K—B4
34 R—B7 ch	K—K5
35 Q×KtP ch	K×P
36 Q—B5 ch	B—K4
37 R—Q1 ch	K—B3

The fugitive still hopes.

38 P—Kt5 ch

The final blow.

| 38 ...... | K×P |
| 39 R—Q5 ch | |

And White wins.

439

| White | Black |
| ENGLISCH | TARRASCH |

(Hamburg, 1885)

Again an ultra-modern opening from long ago. The manner in which White exploits his advantage by forfeiting his Queen is worthy of all praise.

1 P—Q4	Kt—KB3
2 P—QB4	P—KKt3
3 Kt—QB3	B—Kt2
4 P—K4	

This *Indian Three Pawns' Attack* is more straightforward than 4 Kt—B3, 4 P—KKt3, or 4 P—K3.

| 4 ...... | P—Q3 |
| 5 P—B4 | |

But, plausible though it may appear, the *Indian Four Pawns' Attack* is less energetic than any of the other accepted continuations, which seem to be quieter, such as 5 Kt—B3, or 5 P—KKt3, or 5 P—B3, or, finally, 5 P—KR3.

| 5 ...... | Castles |
| 6 Kt—B3 | |

Ineffective would be 6 P—K5, KKt—Q2;

7 Kt—B3, P—QB4; and Black has counter-play in the centre.

6 ......   QKt—Q2
More provocative would be 6 ....
Kt—B3 (7 P—Q5, Kt—Kt1, followed by
.... QKt—Q2 and .... Kt—B4). An optimistic sally is 6 .... B—Kt5; 7 B—K2,
QKt—Q2, etc. An over-refinement would
be 6 .... Kt—K1, but an elastic retreat is
6 .... KKt—Q2, intending .... P—K4.
A trenchant advance is 6 .... P—K4;
7 BP×P, P×P; 8 P—Q5 (awkward would
be 8 Kt×P, P—B4); 8 .... QKt—Q2, etc.
Best is the demonstration on the wing,
6 .... P—B4 (e.g. 7 P×P, Q—R4, etc., or
7 P—Q5, P—K3, etc.), showing that White
has been building on sand.

7 B—K2
More reserved than 7 B—K3. Useless is
7 P—K5, Kt—K1.

7 ......   P—K4
Plausible, but ill-advised. If 7 .... P—B4;
8 P—Q5, and the restricted position of
Black's side affects the whole of his game.

8 QP×P   P×P
9 P×P   Kt—Kt5
10 B—Kt5
In conjunction with the next move, an
awkward episode for Black.

10 ......   Q—K1
11 Kt—Q5   KKt×KP
Intending, if 12 Kt×P, Kt×Kt ch;
13 B×Kt, Q—K4; 14 Kt×R, Q×B, etc., not
without practical chances for Black. But
White's next move shatters all illusions.
Tragi-comic would be 11 .... P—QB3;
12 Kt—B7, capturing the Queen.

12 B—K7   Kt×Kt ch
13 B×Kt   P—QB3
14 B×R   Q×B
After 14 .... P×Kt; 15 B×B, P×KP;
16 B—K2, K×B; 17 Q—Q4 ch, P—B3;
18 Castles KR, etc., White, in addition to
the exchange, has the initiative.

15 Kt—B3   Q—B4
16 Q—Kt3
After 16 Q—K2, B×Kt ch; 17 P×B,
Kt—K4; 18 Castles, B—K3, Black would
have the attack.

16 ......   Kt—K4
Not 16 .... Q—K6 ch; 17 Kt—K2,
Q×Q; 18 P×Q, B×P; 19 R—R2, etc.,

after which White remains the exchange
ahead (for a pawn).

17 Castles   Kt×P
Underestimating the force of White's
intention. The irruption of the heavy artillery could have been prevented by 17 ....
B—K3, e.g. 18 B—K2, P—QKt4, or
18 Q×P, R—K1, and Black could still
hold out.

18 R—Q8 ch   B—B1
19 KR—Q1   B—K3
This attempt, on which Black built all his
hopes, will be sternly refuted.

20 R×R   Q—Kt4 ch
21 K—Kt1   Kt—Q7 ch
22 R×Kt   B×Q
23 KR—Q8
Through this interpolation White obtains
more than an equivalent for his Queen.

23 ......   B—B5
24 R×B ch   K—Kt2
25 KR—Q8
This move eliminates Black's threat of
25 .... B—Q6 ch, followed by mate in two.

25 ......   P—Kt4
26 P—QKt3   B—B8
27 R—Q7   Q—QB4
28 Kt—Q1   P—Kt5
29 R—Q2   Q—K4
30 R×P   Q×RP
31 KR—Q7   K—R3
32 R×P   B—Q6 ch
33 K—B1   Q—K4
34 K—Q2   B×P
35 B×B   Q×B
36 Kt—K3
The field has been cleared, and White's
advantage is becoming manifest.

36 ......   Q—Kt8
37 K—K2   Q—Kt7 ch
38 K—B3   P—B4
39 QR—Q7   Q—B6
After 39 .... Q×RP, there is a mate in
three by 40 Kt—Kt4 ch, etc.

40 P—Kt4
Threat: 41 R—Q5. The black King is
trapped, and there is nothing to be done.

40 ......   Q—R8
41 R×P ch   K—Kt4
42 R—Q5 ch   K—B3
43 P—Kt5 ch   K—K3
44 R (Q5)—Q7   Resigns.

440

White	Black
SÄMISCH	EUWE

(Wiesbaden, 1925)

The fight for the initiative is the motif *of many a contest. But it is a curious fact that frequently the variations having the most war-like appearance (as in the present game, 5 P—B4) are apt to provide a weak point as a target for the counter-attack.*

1 P—Q4	Kt—KB3
2 P—QB4	P—KKt3
3 Kt—QB3	B—Kt2
4 P—K4	P—Q3
5 P—B4	

The present game has been instrumental in revealing that this attack on a widened front is not as powerful as it looks, because White's commitments in the centre are too heavy.

5	Castles
6 Kt—B3	P—B4

This *lateral demonstration* effects a thorough emancipation of Black's position.

7 P—Q5

If 7 P × P, then no simplification by 7 .... P × P; 8 Q × Q, R × Q; 9 P—K5, etc., but, assuming the offensive, 7 .... Q—R4, e.g. 8 P × P, Kt × P, etc., or 8 B—Q2, Q × BP, and Black keeps the lead.

7	P—K3
8 B—Q3	

Or 8 P × P, P × P; 9 B—K2, Kt—B3; 10 Castles, Q—K2, and Black has some advantage. More reserved than the text move is 8 B—K2, even though Black would maintain a slight pull after 8 .... P × P; 9 BP × P, P—QR3; 10 P—QR4, R—K1, etc.

8	P × P
9 BP × P	

Also after 9 KP × P, R—K1 ch, White would be in difficulties.

9 ...... Q—Kt3

Preventing White from castling (10 Castles, P—B5 dis ch).

10 Kt—Q2 Kt—Kt5

Maintaining his grip.

11 Kt—B4 Q—Q1

This move still prevents White's castling, although indirectly, e.g. 12 Castles, B—Q5 ch; 13 K—R1, Q—R5; 14 P—KR3, Q—Kt6; 15 P × Kt, Q—R5 mate.

12 B—K2	P—KR4
13 Kt—Kt5	

An unsuccessful counter-attempt, but White's position is already inferior, e.g. 13 B × Kt, B × B; 14 Q—B2, Q—R5 ch; 15 P—Kt3, Q—K2; 16 Castles, P—R5, and Black is busy.

13 ...... P—R3

He is not frightened of phantoms!

14 Kt (Kt5) × P

This costs a piece, but promises some counter-play, whilst White's game would become still more precarious after 14 Kt—B3, P—QKt4; 15 Kt—K3, Kt × Kt; 16 B × Kt, P—Kt5; 17 Kt—R4, Q—R4; 18 B—Q2, B—Q2.

14	P—QKt4
15 Kt × B	P × Kt
16 P—K5	Q × Kt
17 P—KR3	Kt—R3
18 P—KKt4	Kt—Q2
19 P × P	Q—Q1

Since the 9th move the black Queen has displayed remarkable activity. The threat is now 20 .... Q—R5 ch.

20 Castles Q—R5

21 R—B3

After 21 P × P, Q—Kt6 ch; 22 K—R1, Q × P ch; 23 K—Kt1, Q—Kt6 ch; 24 K—R1, Kt × P; 25 P × Kt, B × P, Black's attack would succeed.

21	P × P
22 R—B3	QR—K1
23 B—Q2	Kt × P
24 P × Kt	R × P
25 B—K1	Q—K2
26 P—Q6	Q—K3
27 B—B1	R—Kt4 ch

The final assault against the white King's depleted position.

28 R—Kt3	Q—K6 ch
29 K—Kt2	

Clearly not 29 B—B2, R × R ch.

29	B—Q5
30 R × R	Q × R ch

Resigns.

441

White	Black
ALEKHINE	YATES

(Carlsbad, 1923)

A very fine game by the British master. His final combination, beginning with the sacrifice of the exchange (33 .... R × Kt) and extending to twenty moves, is monumental.

1 P—Q4	Kt—KB3
2 P—QB4	P—KKt3
3 P—KKt3	

By this *counter-fianchetto* (*Przepiórka's Attack*), White adopts a purely positional treatment of the opening.

3	B—Kt2

An impassive reply which confers upon White the hegemony in the centre.

A solid idea is 3 .... P—B3, preparing for .... P—Q4, e.g. 4 B—Kt2, P—Q4; 5 P×P, P×P; 6 Kt—QB3, B—Kt2, etc., with an even game.

Ill-founded, however, is 3 .... P—Q4, as was shown, in harrowing fashion, in a game Grünfeld-Nagy, *Debreczen*, 1924: 4 P×P (not 4 B—Kt2, P×P; 5 Q—R4 ch, B—Q2; 6 Q×BP, Kt—B3, etc.); 4 .... Q×P; 5 Kt—KB3, B—Kt2; 6 B—Kt2 (very strong is also 6 Kt—B3, Q—KR4; 7 P—KR3, threatening B—Kt2, with Kt—K5 and B—B3, winning the Queen); 6 .... Castles; 7 Kt—B3, Q—KR4; 8 P—KR3, Kt—B3; 9 Kt—KKt5, R—Q1; 10 B—B3, R×P; 11 Q—Kt3, resigns.

4 B—Kt2	Castles

At this stage 4 .... P—B3 or 4 .... P—Q4 would be less propitious than on the preceding move.

5 Kt—QB3	

Still delaying P—K4.

5	P—Q3
6 Kt—B3	

By first playing 6 P—K4, White could preserve the option of developing this Knight at K2. On the other hand, the text move prevents Black's 6 .... P—K4.

6	Kt—B3

An interesting idea of Burn's, provoking 7 P—Q5, and freeing Black's QB4. A more usual continuation is 6 .... QKt—Q2; 7 P—K4, P—K4, etc.

7 P—Q5	Kt—Kt1
8 P—K4	

If 8 Castles, Black would avoid 8 .... P—K4 (9 P×P e.p., P×P; 10 B—Kt5, Kt—B3; 11 Q—Q2, etc.), but would start energetic counter-action by 8 .... P—QR4, followed by .... QKt—Q2 and .... Kt—B4.

8	QKt—Q2
9 Castles	P—QR4

Ensuring an influential post for his QKt at QB4, a well-known stratagem.

10 B—K3	

More prudent is, first, 10 P—KR3 (10 .... Kt—B4; 11 Q—B2, P—Kt3; 12 B—K3, etc.). Less plastic would be 10 .... P—K4, as his own pieces would lose this important square.

10	Kt—Kt5
11 B—Q4	KKt—K4
12 Kt×Kt	Kt×Kt
13 P—B5	P×P
14 B×P	P—Kt3
15 B—Q4	B—QR3
16 R—K1	Q—Q3
17 B—B1	B×B
18 R×B	P—QB4

Forcing the exchange of the adverse Bishop for the Knight, after which Black can claim to have won the *minor exchange,* for in this position the Bishop is stronger than the Knight.

19 B×Kt	Q×B
20 Q—Kt3	QR—Kt1
21 Q—Kt5	

He must prevent 21 .... P—QKt4 (22 Kt×P, Q×KtP; 23 QR—Kt1, Q×Q; 24 R×Q, P—B5; 25 QR—Kt1; P—B6. etc.).

21	P—B4

Cleverly taking advantage of the fact that the hostile pieces are not at hand, Black assumes the offensive.

22 QR—K1	

After 22 P×P, Q×BP, Black's Bishop gets into action.

22	P—KB5
23 Q—Q7	QR—Q1
24 P×P	Q×BP
25 Q—K6 ch	

If 25 Q×P, Q—Kt5 ch; 26 K—R1, Q—B6 ch; 27 K—Kt1, QR—K1, with a winning attack.

25	K—R1
26 P—B3	Q—Kt4 ch
27 K—R1	

Relatively better is 27 Q—Kt4.

27	R—Q3
28 Q—R3	B—K4
29 R—K2	QR—KB3
30 Kt—Q1	R—B5
31 Kt—K3	R—R5
32 Q—K6	

A better defence is 32 Q—Q7, for if then 32 .... Q—R4; 33 R (B1)—B2, R×BP; 34 Q—K8 ch, K—Kt2; 35 Q×KP ch, K—R3 (or 35 .... K—Kt1; 36 Q—K8 ch, K—Kt2; 37 Kt—B5 ch); 36 Kt—B5 ch, P×Kt; 37 Q—K6 ch, K—Kt4; 38 Q—Kt8 ch, K—R3 (not 38 .... K—B5; 39 Q—Kt3 mate); 39 Q—K6 ch, with perpetual check.

| 32 ...... | Q—R4 |
| 33 Kt—Kt4 | |

If 33 R (B1)—B2, R×BP, etc. By his ingenious reply White hopes to restore the balance.

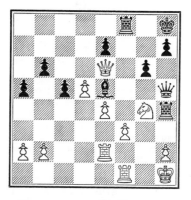

33 ......   R×Kt

As this is a *real sacrifice*, it could only be entertained after profound and minute calculations.

34 P×R	R×R ch
35 K—Kt2	Q×RP ch
36 K×R	Q—R8 ch
37 K—B2	B—Q5 ch
38 K—Kt3	Q—Kt8 ch
39 K—R3	

Or 39 R—Kt2, Q—K8 ch, etc.

39	Q—B8 ch
40 R—Kt2	Q—R8 ch
41 K—Kt3	

Or 41 R—R2, Q—B6 ch; 42 K—R4, B—B3 ch; 43 P—Kt5, P—R3; 44 P×B, P—Kt4 mate.

41	Q—K8 ch
42 K—R3	P—KKt4
43 R—QB2	

The only move to prevent mate or loss of a Rook.

43 ......   Q—B8 ch

Trying his luck (for perhaps 44 K—Kt3, Q--Q6 ch.).

44 K—R2	Q—Kt8 ch
45 K—R3	Q—R8 ch
46 K—Kt3	Q—Q8

Another quiet move, magically effective.

47 R—B3

Sad necessity of leaving the second rank, for if—

(*a*) 47 R—Kt2, Q—K8 ch is decisive.

(*b*) 47 R—R2, Q—Kt8 ch; 48 K—R3, Q—K6 ch; 49 K—Kt2, Q—B7 ch, followed by mate.

(*c*) 47 Q—B7, Q—Q6 ch; 48 Q—B3, B—K4 ch; 49 K—Kt2, Q×R ch, and wins.

47	Q—Kt8 ch
48 K—R3	Q—B8 ch
49 K—Kt3	B—B7 ch
50 K—B3	B—Kt8 dis ch

And Black mates in two.

442

| *White* | *Black* |
| GOGLIDSE | FLOHR |

(Moscow, 1935)

In a most elegant manner Black takes advantage of the weakness he has discovered in White's position at KB2, and never relaxes his grip. One of those interesting cases where the positional treatment of the game leads logically, so to speak, to a powerful and brilliant finish.

1 P—Q4	Kt—KB3
2 P—QB4	P—KKt3
3 Kt—KB3	B—Kt2
4 P—KKt3	Castles
5 B—Kt2	P—Q3
6 Castles	QKt—Q2
7 Q—B2	

More artificial than the simple developing move 7 Kt—B3 (7 .... P—K4; 8 P—K4, etc.).

| 7 ...... | P—K4 |
| 8 P×P | |

If 8 P—K4, P×P; 9 Kt×P, R—K1; 10·Kt—QB3, Kt×P, winning a pawn.

| 8 ...... | P×P |
| 9 R—Q1 | |

As the pressure on the Q file remains sterile, the initiative gradually passes into Black's hands. Better would be 9 Kt—B3 (9 .... P—B3; 10 P—Kt3, etc.).

9	Q—K2
10 Kt—B3	P—B3
11 Kt—QR4	

In this stage of transition from the opening

mobilisation to the complexities of the middle game, White pays too much attention to conventional manœuvres on the Q side. He should try to get his pieces into play (e.g. 11 Kt—Q2, with a view to KKt—K4 and Kt—Q6).

11 ......   R—K1

Placing the Rook on a "potentially open file."

12 P—KR3

Intending 13 B—K3, without fear of .... Kt—Kt5.

12 ......   Kt—R4

Pawn play on White's part, play by pieces on Black's.

13 P—B5

He underrates the dynamic potentialities which are hidden in the black formation. He should have put up a barrage against Black's coming onslaught in the centre by 13 P—K4.

13 ......   P—K5
14 Kt—Q4   P—K6

A fine combination, with the twofold object of clearing the K file and of weakening the white King's field.

15 B×KP   Kt×KtP
16 QR—B1   Kt—B3
17 Kt—QB3   Kt (B3)—K5

Consistently pursuing his plan of attack. After 17 .... Q×P Black would be threatened with many dangers, e.g. 18 Kt×P, R×B; 19 Kt—K4, Q×Q; 20 R—Q8 ch, B—B1; 21 Kt×Kt ch, K—Kt2; 22 Kt—K8 ch, K—R3; 23 R×Q, etc.

18 Kt×Kt

If 18 P×Kt, Kt×Kt, immediately and most advantageously recovering his piece.

18 ......   Kt×Kt
19 B—B4

A plausible mistake. His best course is 19 B×Kt, Q×B; 20 Q×Q, R×Q; 21 Kt—B3, B—B4; 22 R—Q2, and the fury of the battle dies down and Black's positional advantage loses its sting.

19 ......   Kt×KBP

A thunderbolt. The consequences of this move had to be calculated many moves ahead.

20 K×Kt   Q—R5 ch
21 K—B3   B×P
22 B×B   Q×KB ch
23 K—B2

If 23 B—Kt3, B—K4; 24 R—KKt1, B×Kt.

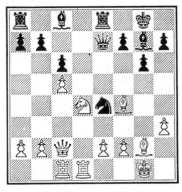

Position after 19 B—B4

23 ......   Q—R5 ch
24 K—B3   B—K4

A beautiful manœuvre, which eliminates the white King's only defender.

25 P—K3

Or, e.g. 25 B×B, R×B; 26 P—K4, Q—R6 ch; 27 K—B2 (or 27 K—K2, QR—K1, etc., or 27 K—B4, QR—K1, threatening 28 .... P—Kt4 mate); 27 .... R—Kt4; 28 Kt—K2, R—Kt7 ch; 29 K—K1, Q—K6, with a forced mate. Or 25 B—K3, Q—Kt6 ch; 26 K—K4, B×Kt dis ch; 27 K×B, Q×B ch; 28 K—B4, R—K5 ch. Or 25 Q—Q2, QR—Q1, etc. Or 25 Q—K4, P—B4; 26 Kt×KBP, Q—R4 ch. Or finally, 25 Kt—B5, Q—R4 ch.

25 ......   B×B
26 P×B   Q—R6 ch
27 K—B2   R—K6
28 R—KKt1   QR—K1
29 R—Kt2   Q—R5 ch
Resigns.

443

White	Black
KERES	FLOHR

(Semmering-Baden, 1937)

A grand game, which illustrates the winner's genius for sustained attack. Moves 11, 14 and 20 by White are admirable examples of well-timed aggression.

1 P—Q4	Kt—KB3
2 P—QB4	P—KKt3
3 Kt—KB3	B—Kt2
4 P—KKt3	P—B3
5 B—Kt2	

If, in order to prevent 5 .... P—Q4, White himself plays 5 P—Q5, there follows 5 .... P×P; 6 P×P, Q—R4 ch; 7 Kt—B3, Kt×P, with advantage to Black.

5	P—Q4
6 P×P	

White prefers not to spend time on guarding the QBP, and gives up the tension in the centre. After 6 Castles, P×P; 7 Kt—K5, B—K3; 8 Kt—R3, B—Q4; 9 QKt×P, B×B; 10 K×B, Castles, and, although White has his pawn back, the unrelaxed position is in Black's favour.

6	Kt×P

More solid is 6 .... P×P.

7 Castles

A doubtful enterprise would be 7 P—K4, Kt—Kt3; 8 Castles, Castles; 9 Kt—B3, B—Kt5 (an indirect attack on the now vulnerable QP); 10 B—K3, Kt—B5, and Black's counter-play must be taken seriously.

7	Castles
8 Kt—B3	Kt×Kt

A more cautious plan is 8 .... Kt—Kt3, to be followed by .... QKt—Q2 and .... P—QB4, undermining the centre.

9 P×Kt

But now White's centre is strengthened.

9	P—QB4

Hoping to continue with 10 .... Kt—B3, which White will prevent.

10 B—QR3	P×P
11 Kt×P	

Finely played. He cares not whether his pawns become isolated, relying on the action of his pieces, whilst hindering his adversary's. If 11 P×P, Kt—B3.

11	Q—B2
12 Q—Kt3	B—B3

His KP must be guarded if 13 .... Kt—Q2 is to follow. Examine—

(a) 12 .... R—K1; 13 B—Q5, P—K3; 14 Kt—Kt5, Q—Q2; 15 B—KKt2, threatening 16 QR—Q1, and the Queen is "mated."

(b) 12 .... Kt—R3; 13 QR—Kt1, Kt—B4; 14 Q—Kt4, Kt—R3; 15 Q×KP, Q×BP; 16 Kt—Kt5, Q—R4; 17 KR—Q1, commanding the field.

(c) 12 .... Kt—B3; 13 Kt×Kt, P×Kt;

14 KR—B1, and White's forces are the more effectively placed.

Nevertheless, 12 .... Kt—B3 is the best course in the circumstances.

13 KR—Q1	Kt—Q2

The proposed itinerary is *via* QKt3 to QB5.

14 P—QB4

Instead of needing protection, this pawn now becomes a powerful weapon of attack. If now 14 .... Kt—Kt3; 15 P—B5, Kt—Q2; 16 P—B6, P×P; 17 Kt×P, etc.

14	Kt—B4
15 Q—Kt4	Kt—K3

Black's position becomes more and more cramped. After 15 .... Kt—R3; 16 Q—Kt5, R—Kt1; 17 QR—Kt1, B—Q2; 18 Q—Kt3, Kt—B4; 19 Q—K3, White maintains his positional advantage.

16 Kt—Kt5	Q—K4

Threatening to win the Knight by 17 .... P—QR3.

17 QR—B1

Preventing the exchange of the Queen for two Rooks by 17 .... Q×R.

17	R—Q1

Here 17 .... P—QR3 no longer has any value because of 18 Kt—B3, with Kt—Q5. Disadvantageous would also be 17 .... Q×KP; 18 Kt—B3, B×Kt; 19 Q×B, R—K1; 20 B—B3, and wins, or 18 .... Q—K4; 19 Kt—Q5, R—K1; 20 Q—Kt5, K—B1; 21 P—B4, Q—B4; 22 P—Kt4, Q×KtP; 23 Kt×B, and wins; or 18 .... Q—R4; 19 Kt—Q5, and White is master of the situation.

18 R—Q5	R×R
19 P×R	P—QR3

A vain hope to slow down matters. Slightly better would be—

(a) 19 .... Kt—Q1; 20 P—Q6, P×P (or 20 .... Kt—B3; 21 B×Kt, P×B; 22 Kt—B7, and wins); 21 Kt—B7, R—Kt1; 22 Q×QP, Q×Q; 23 B×Q, etc.

(b) 19 .... Kt—Q5; 20 Kt×Kt, Q×Kt; 21 Q×Q, B×Q; 22 B×P, with a small—but comforting—advantage in material for White.

(c) 19 .... B—Q2; 20 P×Kt (20 Kt—B3 is less good, but 20 P—K4 is also very lively); 20 .... B×Kt; 21 R—B5, Q—R8 ch; 22 B—QB1, B—R3; 23 P×P ch, K×P; 24 B×P, B×B; 25 Q×B, with a distinct advantage to White.

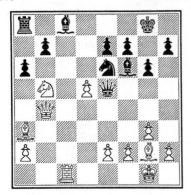

20 Kt—R7
A very original turn, which gains material.

20 ......   Kt—Q5
Or 20 .... R × Kt; 21 R × B ch, Kt—B1;
22 Q—Kt6, Q—R8 ch (if 22 .... Q—Q5;
23 B—B5); 23 B—KB1, B—Q5; 24 Q—Q8,
B—Kt2 (24 .... B × P ch; 25 K × B,
Q—Q5 ch; 26 K—K1, etc.); 25 B × P, and
Black has no defence.

21 R × B ch   R × R
22 Kt × R   Q × KP
A last attempt. If 22 .... Kt × P ch;
23 K—B1, Kt—Q5; 24 Kt × P ch, K—Kt2;
25 P—R4 (not 25 Kt—B5 ch, P × Kt;
26 Q—B8 ch, K—Kt3); 25 .... Kt—B7;
26 Kt—B5 ch, P × Kt (26 .... Q × Kt;
27 Q—B8 mate); 27 Q—B8 ch, K—Kt3;
28 Q—Kt8 ch, B—Kt2; 29 P—R5 ch,
winning.

23 P—R4   Kt—B4
24 Q—K4   Resigns.

444

White   Black
WINTER   KOLTANOWSKI
(Hastings, 1936–7)

*A game full of skilful manœuvres. At first
both players try to be the first to effect the
impetuous advance P—KB4. In the second
part, the salient point is the capture of the
KR file by White. In the sequel a turning
movement, cleverly contrived, decides the
issue.*

1 P—Q4   Kt—KB3
2 P—QB4   P—KKt3
3 Kt—QB3   B—Kt2
4 P—K4
This *Indian Three Pawns' Attack* henceforth prevents Black's .... P—Q4; which
he could have played on the preceding move.

4 ......   P—Q3
5 P—KKt3   Castles
6 B—Kt2   P—B3
Trying to build up a strong defensive
system. A little "airy" would be 6 ....
P—K4; 7 P × P, P × P; 8 Q × Q, R × Q;
9 Kt—Q5, Kt × Kt; 10 BP × Kt, etc., but
the most rational is 6 .... QKt—Q2; clearing the way for .... P—K4.

7 KKt—K2
More flexible than 7 Kt—B3, for, although
it does not oppose the advance of Black's
KP, it supports, on the other hand, the
forward thrust of his own KBP.

7 ......   P—K4
8 P—KR3
With multiple functions, such as:
(*a*) To prevent 8 .... B—Kt5.
(*b*) To avoid 9 .... Kt—Kt5; in case he
chooses to play 9 B—K3.
(*c*) To prevent the manœuvre possible
after 8 Castles, namely 8 .... B—Q2,
9 P—Kt3, Q—B1, followed by .... B—R6.
(*d*) To prepare the advance P—KKt4.

8 ......   B—K3
Provocative. As 8 .... B—Q2; 9 Castles,
Q—B1; 10 K—R2 also fails to open the way
into the enemy camp, 8 .... QKt—Q2 is
better.

9 P—Q5   P × P
Compulsory, on account of the weakness
of the QP. If at once 9 .... B—Q2;
10 P × P, B × BP; 11 B—K3, Kt—K1;
12 Q—Q2, P—B4; 13 Castles, and White
has the greater command of the board.

10 BP × P   B—Q2
This Bishop is restricted and, in addition,
it blocks the usual outlet for the QKt.
Nevertheless, he has succeeded in closing
the centre, with fair prospects of later
becoming aggressive on the K side.

11 Castles   Kt—K1
Clearing the way for his KBP.

12 B—K3
Not yet 12 P—B4, Q—Kt3 ch.

12 ......   P—Kt3
Discarding the aggressive 12 .... P—B4

which would turn to White's advantage after the counter-stroke 13 P—B4.

13 P—B4
The advance as planned by his 7th move. All White's pieces are well placed or available, and his attack increases in scope.

13 ...... P—B3
Black is definitely on the defensive. Neither 13 .... P×P; 14 P×P, etc., nor 13 .... P—B4; 14 Q—Q2, etc., would do.

14 P—B5
Far more trenchant than 14 P×P, BP×P, and the open KB file becomes neutral.

14 ...... P—KKt4
Trying to keep the K side hermetically sealed, in which, however, he will not be entirely successful. The manner in which White succeeds both in creating and exploiting a flaw in the opponent's formation is a fine example of modern technique of the attack.

15 P—KKt4 R—B2
The counter-attempt: 15 .... P—KR4; 16 P×P, B—R3; 17 P—KR4 would not shake White's grip.

16 Kt—Kt3 B—KB1
Black's forces find little useful employment, and those on the Q side none at all.

17 R—B2
The beginning of a clever regrouping.

17	Kt—Kt2
18 B—KB1	B—K1
19 R—R2	P—QR4
20 P—KR4	P—R3

If 20 .... P×P; 21 R×P, Kt—R3; 21 B×Kt, R×B; 22 Q—K2, QR—R2; 23 Q—R2, with R×P to follow. Or 20 .... B—Q2; 21 Q—Kt3, and Black's QKtP must fall.

21 P×P	RP×P
22 Q—B3	R—Kt2
23 Q—R1	

Completing most skilfully the regrouping begun on his 17th move. Note how important it is to have major pieces posted *behind* less important units.

23	Kt—Q2
24 R—R8 ch	K—B2
25 Q—R7	K—K2

Black must guard against the threat 26 Kt—R5, followed by R×B ch and Q×Kt mate.

26 Kt—R5 Resigns
If 26 .... B×Kt; 27 P×B, threatening 28 P—R6.

445

| White | Black |
| STAEHELIN | ELISKASES |

(Zürich, 1935)

Black wins this positional game only by the following manœuvres: the alternating play of his KKt, moves 10 to 13, intermediary evolutions before retaking the KBP, moves 14 to 17, irruption, moves 18 to 20, winning the exchange.

1 P—Q4	Kt—KB3
2 P—QB4	P—KKt3
3 Kt—QB3	B—Kt2
4 P—K4	P—Q3
5 Kt—B3	

Without any *finessing*, White proceeds with his normal development while preventing 5 .... P—K4.

5	QKt—Q2
6 B—K2	P—K4
7 P—Q5	

Breaking off the hand-to-hand fighting. But he could have waited by playing 7 Castles, e.g. 7 .... P×P; 8 Kt×P, Castles; 9 B—K3, R—K1; 10 P—B3, etc., with a fine formation in the centre, or 7 .... Castles; 8 P—QKt3, R—K1, and now only 9 P—Q5, after which the presence of Black's KR on the K file no longer has any object.

In any event, 7 P×P, P×P would be too simplifying.

| 7 ...... | Kt—B4 |
| 8 Q—B2 | P—QR4 |

A well-known supporting manœuvre.

9 Castles Castles
This might be called the *normal position* of the *King's Indian Defence*. As White has blocked the centre, he must now decide on which sector he will become active.

10 P—QKt3
A more lively action on the Q side results from 10 Kt—Q2, followed by Kt—Kt3. A sound plan of action in the centre is 10 B—K3.

10 ......   Kt—R4
He immediately organises counter-play on
the castled wing.

11 R—K1
Intending 12 B—B1, in reply to 11 ....
Kt—B5.

11 ......   P—B4
12 Kt—Q2   Kt—B3
Concentrating his energy on the present
objective: the point K5.

13 P—B3   Kt—R4
Having weakened the hostile K field,
Black "retracts" his last move, intending to
initiate a direct attack. It is of the art of
the strategist to be able to adapt himself to
circumstances, and to change his plans under
fire.

14 P×P
A little better is 14 B—R3, but White
seeks simplification, expecting nothing more
than 14 .... B×P; 15 KKt—K4, Q—R5;
16 B—K3, etc.

14 ......   Q—R5
This intermediary sally decisively
strengthens Black's initiative.

15 B—Kt2
Clearly not 15 P—Kt3, KKt×P; 16 P×Kt,
Q×P ch; 17 K—B1, B×P, threatening
.... B—R6 mate; and if 15 B—R3, P—K5;
16 Kt—B1, B—Q5 ch; 17 K—R1, Q—B7,
etc.; or 16 B×Kt, P×B; 17 KKt×P,
B—Q5 ch, etc.

15 ......   B—R3
Threatening mate in two.

16 Kt—B1   Q—Q5 ch
17 K—R1   B×P
18 Q—Q1
Or 18 Kt—K4, B×Kt; 19 P×B, Q×KP;
20 Q×Q, Kt×Q; 21 B×Kt, Kt—B7 ch;
22 K—Kt1, P×B, with a concrete advantage
to Black.

18 ......   Q—B7
19 B—B1
The text move holds, if artificially, all the
threatened points after 19 .... B×B;
20 Q×B, Kt—B5; 21 Kt—K3, QKt—Q6;
22 R—B1.

19 ......   B—B7
Winning the exchange in a most *piquant*
manner.

Position after 19 B—B1

20 Q×B   Q×R
The remainder of the play is only a
question of technique.

21 P—QR3
Liquidation by 21 B×B, Q×R; 22 B×R,
R×B would only clear the battlefield and
help the stronger side.

21 ......   B×B
22 R×B   Q—B7
23 Kt—Q1   Q—Q5
24 P—QKt4   P×P
25 P×P   Kt—R3
More methodical would be 25 ....
Kt—Q2, but Black looks for direct threats.

26 R—Kt1   Kt—B5
27 Kt—Kt3   P—B4
28 KtP×P
A little more tenacious would be 28 P×P
e.p., P×P; 29 Kt—B3, etc.

28 ......   QKt×P
Resigns.

446
White   Black
MENCHIK   THOMAS
(London, 1932)

*A game in which the players castle on
opposite wings. White's vehement measures
(10 P—KKt4, etc.) are based on purely
positional considerations, and score an impressive success. A sensational game, which
confirmed the opinion that Vera Menchik, the
first woman of full master strength in the
history of the game, could hold her own with
the strongest.*

1 P—Q4	Kt—KB3
2 P—QB4	P—KKt3
3 Kt—QB3	B—Kt2
4 P—K4	P—Q3
5 P—B3	

Forming a fine chain of pawns, behind which the pieces concentrate undisturbed, ready for the coming co-ordinated assault. The modernised form of the *Four Pawns' Attack*, thought out by Sämisch, allows the second player only slender chances of counter-attack.

| 5 ...... | Castles |

Immediate reaction in the centre by 5 .... QKt—Q2; 6 B—K3, P—K4 is preferable.

| 6 B—K3 | P—K4 |

Or 6 .... QKt—Q2; 7 Q—Q2, etc.

| 7 KKt—K2 | |

Vigorous play, and more promising than simplification by 7 P × P, P × P, etc., or the closing of the central zone by 7 P—Q5.

| 7 ...... | P—Kt3 |

After 7 .... QKt—Q2; 8 Q—Q2, Kt—K1, followed eventually by .... P—KB4, Black could hope for effective counter-play.

| 8 Q—Q2 | Kt—B3 |

Challenging a clearance in the centre at the cost of a *tempo*.

| 9 P—Q5 | Kt—K2 |

In spite of actual loss of time, 9 .... Kt—Kt1 with .... QKt—Q2 would be better.

| 10 P—KKt4 | |

This could superficially be taken as merely heralding the attack, but it is also a deep preparatory manœuvre which presently is to prevent .... P—KB4.

| 10 ...... | Kt—Q2 |
| 11 ...... | R—KKt1 |

Energetically following up the preceding move and preventing 11 .... P—KB4 (12 KtP × P, P × P; 13 B—R6, R—B2; 14 B × B, R × B; 15 R × R ch, K × R; 16 Q—Kt5 ch, followed by P × P, etc.), whereas, if conventionally 11 Castles, P—KB4, etc., is not without counter-chances for Black.

11	P—QR4
12 Castles	Kt—QB4
13 Kt—Kt3	B—Q2
14 P—KR4	P—R5

Black's counter-attack becomes concrete only after his opponent's invasion has succeeded. Preventive measures would therefore be more to the point (e.g. 14 .... P—KB3; and if 15 P—R5, P—KKt4) closing the door.

| 15 P—R5 | |

Forcing open a file.

15	Q—Kt1
16 B—R6	Q—R2
17 B × B	K × B

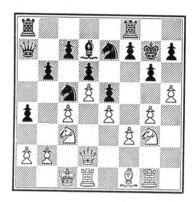

18 Kt—B5 ch

A very fine move, which threatens to clear the KKt file at one stroke of three hostile units. If 18 R—R1, R—R1.

| 18 ...... | Kt × Kt |

An immediate catastrophe results from 18 .... P × Kt; 19 P × P dis ch, K—R1; 20 Q—R6, etc.; and if 18 .... K—B3; 19 P—Kt5 mate.

| 19 KtP × Kt | P—R6 |

Intending, after 20 P—Kt3, to continue 20 .... Kt × P ch; 21 P × Kt, P—R7, advantageously regaining the piece. But this attempt gives White the opportunity for a magnificent finish; 19 .... R—KKt1 would prolong Black's resistance.

| 20 P—B6 ch | K—R1 |

Or 20 .... K × P; 21 Q—Kt5 ch, K—Kt2; 22 P—R6 ch, K—Kt1; 23 Q—B6, with unavoidable mate.

21 Q—R6	P × P ch
22 K—Kt1	R—KKt1
23 P × P	P × P
24 Q × RP ch	Resigns

(White mates in two moves.)

447

White	Black
FLOHR	TYLOR

(Hastings, 1929)

White here starts an attack (6 P—KKt4) with insufficient means. Its refutation by Black is both forceful and brilliant.

1 P—Q4	Kt—KB3
2 P—QB4	P—KKt3
3 P—B3	

An innovation at the time, due to Nimzowitsch. It results in a modernised form of the *Four Pawns' Attack*. But after 3 Kt—QB3, Black can revert to 3 .... P—Q4 (*Grünfeld's Defence*).

3	B—Kt2

Falling in with his adversary's intentions. He could experiment with counter-thrusts:

(*a*) 3 .... P—Q4; 4 P×P, Kt×P; 5 P—K4, Kt—Kt3; 6 Kt—B3, B—Kt2; 7 B—K3, Castles, etc.

(*b*) 3 .... P—B4; 4 P—Q5, P—Q3; 5 P—K4, B—Kt2; 6 Kt—B3, Castles, etc.

4 P—K4	P—Q3
5 Kt—B3	Castles
6 P—KKt4	

White takes the lead, in preference to the conventional line of play: 6 B—K3, QKt—Q2; 7 Q—Q2, P—K4; 8 P—Q5 (or 8 KKt—K2, Kt—K1, avoiding the pin by 9 B—Kt5, and preparing for 9 .... P—KB4, etc.); 8 .... Kt—K1; 9 Castles, etc.

6	P—K4
7 P—Q5	P—B3

There is no necessity for Black to attempt hazardous enterprises such as 7 .... Kt×KtP; 8 P×Kt, Q—R5 ch; 9 K—Q2, etc.

8 Kt—R3	P—QR3

In keeping with the idea underlying his preceding move, which is not only to undermine White's outpost at Q5, but also to prepare an offensive on the wing.

9 B—K3	P—QKt4
10 QP×P	

If 10 BP×P, P×KtP; and Black would benefit from the opening of the QB file, whereas, after the move in the text, White hopes to exert pressure on the Q file.

10	P—Kt5
11 Kt—Q5	QKt×P
12 Q—R4	

A double attack on the hostile QKt and QKtP. If 12 B—Kt5, P—R3, etc.; if 12 Q—Q2, Q—R4; if 12 B—Kt6, Q—Q2; and in all these cases Black's independent strategy ensures him equal prospects.

12	Kt—Q5
13 B×Kt	P×B
14 Kt×P	Kt—Q2

A clever retreat which has a multiple effect:

(*a*) Unmasking the Queen, as well as

(*b*) The long black diagonal.

(*c*) The threat of jumping back into play *via* K4 or QB4.

Incorrect would be 14 .... Kt×KP; 15 P×Kt, Q—R5 ch; 16 Kt—B2, etc.

15 Castles	

Relative security. After 15 Kt—Q3, P—B4 would roll up White's position.

15	Kt—B4
16 Q—R3	

Remaining in the danger zone. If 16 Q—B2, Q—R4; 17 P—R3, B—Q2, with reinforced pressure by Black.

16	P—KR4
17 P—Kt5	

If 17 P×P, Q—R5.

17	B×Kt
18 B×B	Q×P ch
19 K—Kt1	QR—Kt1

A converging assault against White's QKt2.

20 KR—K1	

If 20 Kt×P, R—R1; and if 20 P—Kt3, Q—B3; e.g. 21 KR—B1, P—Q6; or 21 Kt—Q3, Q×P.

20	P—Q6
21 Q—R5	

Or 21 P—Kt3, Q—K4; 22 Kt×QP, Q—R8 ch; 23 K—B2, Q—B6 ch, and White is helpless.

21	Q—K4
22 R—Q2	

Or 22 Q—R3, P—R4.

22	Kt×P
Resigns	

Black rarely scores with such energy in a closed game.

448

White	Black
ALEKHINE	BLÜMICH

(Dresden, 1926)

In this game, built up by White in a manner as confident as it is original, the tragedy of the KB file is vividly illustrated: penetration (11 P—KB4), sacrifice (14 R×P), vertical pin (20 Q—B3), all of which are executed with consummate ease, and depth of artistic conception.

1 P—Q4	Kt—KB3
2 Kt—KB3	

Quite as rational and, in a way, more solid than 2 P—QB4.

2	P—KKt3
3 B—Kt5	

Avoiding the usual development, White aims at a vigorous employment of his pieces. On the same lines, but less insistent, are: 3 B—B4, as there is no immediate employment for the Bishop; and 3 QKt—Q2, as the QB becomes obstructed; but a continuation worth considering is 3 Kt—B3, as played in a game Palau—te Kolsté, *London*, 1927: 3 .... P—Q4 (better than 3 .... B—Kt2; 4 P—K4, P—Q3; 5 P—KR3, Castles; 6 B—K3, etc.); 4 B—B4, Kt—R4; 5 B—K5, P—KB3; 6 B—Kt3, Kt×B; 7 RP×Kt, B—Kt2; 8 P—K3, P—B3; 9 B—Q3, P—K4; 10 R×P, K—B2; 11 B×P ch, K×B; 12 Kt×P ch, P×Kt; 13 Q—R5 ch, K—B3; 14 Q×P ch, K—B2; 15 Q×B ch, resigns.

3	B—Kt2
4 QKt—Q2	Castles

Better would be 4 .... P—B4, etc.

5 P—K3

White wishes to create a solid base by the pawn triangle K3—Q4—QB3, in preference to 5 P—K4, which would increase the range of the adverse KB.

5	P—Q3
6 B—QB4	Kt—B3

After 6 .... P—Q4; 7 B—Q3, P—B4; 8 P—B3, Kt—B3; 9 Kt—K5, followed by P—KB4, and White would have a strong attack in the Pillsbury manner.

7 P—B3	P—QR3
8 Q—K2	B—Kt5

As he has no intention of exchanging this Bishop for a Knight, this sally means the loss of a *tempo*. Better, therefore, would be

8 .... B—Q2 at once (9 P—KR3, P—K4, etc.).

9 P—KR3	B—Q2
10 Kt—R2	Q—B1

At once 10 .... P—K4 is better.

11 P—B4   P—K4

A belated attempt at emancipation, which will be brilliantly refuted. However, if Black resorts to a passive defence, White would gradually force forward the line of demarcation by P—K4 and P—K5.

12 BP×P	P×P
13 Castles KR	Kt—KR4

Relatively the best. If 13 .... Kt—K1; 14 P—Q5, followed by B—K7, winning the exchange.

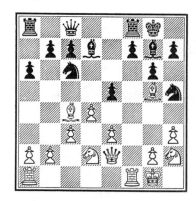

14 R×P

An elegant sacrifice with picturesque details.

14	R×R
15 B×R ch	K×B
16 Q—B4 ch	B—K3

Or 16 .... K—B1; 17 R—B1 ch, B—B4; 18 P—KKt4, etc., to White's advantage.

17 P—Q5   B×QP

After 17 .... K—K1; 18 P×B, Black's position would be no less grave.

18 R—B1 ch

This intermediary check prevents the reorganisation of the black forces, whilst after 18 Q×B ch, Q—K3; 19 R—B1 ch, B—B3; 20 Q—B3, K—Kt2, Black would have a chance of recovery.

18 ......   Kt—B3

After 18 .... K—K3; 19 Q—Kt4 ch,

K—Q3; 20 Kt—B4 ch, K—B4 (or 20 ....
B×Kt; 21 Q×B, etc.); 21 P—Kt4 ch,
Kt×P; 22 B—K7 ch, K—B3; 23 Kt—R5 ch,
the King hunt would be successful.
Or 18 .... B—B3; 19 Q—KR4, K—Kt1;
20 B×B, Kt×B; 21 Q×Kt, Q—B1;
22 Kt—Kt4, Q—Kt2; 23 P—B4, and
White's attack is in full cry.
Or, finally, 18 .... K—Kt1; 19 Q×B ch,
K—R1; 20 P—KKt4, P—R3 (not 20 ....
Kt—Kt6; 21 R—B2); 21 B—R4, P—KKt4;
22 P×Kt, P×B; 23 Kt—Kt4, Q—K1;
24 Q—B7, R—Q1; 25 Kt—K4, and White
maintains his superiority.

19 Q×B ch   Q—K3
20 Q—B3,
Threatening 21 Kt—Kt4, or if 20 ....
P—KR4; 21 Kt—K4, winning a piece.

20 ......   Q—B4
Or, e.g., 20 .... R—KB1; 21 Kt—K₁t4,
K—Kt1 (21 .... K—K2; 22 Kt—K4);
22 Q—Kt3, Q×P; 23 Q—R4.

21 B×Kt   Resigns
For after 21 .... B×B; 22 Kt—Kt4, etc.,
and White will remain a piece ahead.

Grünfeld Defence

449

White	Black
ATKINS	PRINS

(Anglo-Dutch Match, 1937)

*The feature of the following game is the
fight for the long diagonal. Black thinks he
is driving, but realises too late that he is being
driven. A faultless game by White.*

1 P—Q4	Kt—KB3
2 P—QB4	P—KKt3
3 Kt—QB3	

Preparing to play P—K4, as soon as
possible.

3 ......   P—Q4
Thwarting White's intentions. The *Grünfeld Defence*, which forms a connecting link
between the *Indian* idea and the *Queen's
Gambit*: it is a strong variation, so much so
that some move other than 3 Kt—QB3 is
frequently preferred.

4 P×P
The *principal variation*, and the most
plausible. Other sound lines are 4 Q—Kt3
(dogmatic) and 4 B—B4 (astute).
The sally 4 .... Kt—K5 is of little value on
account of 4 .... Kt—K5 (e.g. 5 P×P
Kt×B; 6 P—KR4, P—K3; 7 P×Kt, P×P,
etc.), but a more compact continuation is
4 Kt—B3, B—Kt2; 5 B—Kt5, etc. A placid
line of play is 4 P—K3, B—Kt2; 5 Kt—B3,
etc.; or 4 P—KKt3, P×P; 5 B—Kt2,
B—Kt2; 6 Q—R4 ch, followed by Q×BP,
reverting to a variation of the *Queen's
Gambit Accepted*.

4 ......   Kt×P
5 P—K4
After 5 Q—Kt3, Kt×Kt; 6 P×Kt,
P—QB4, etc., Black has a very good game.

5 ......   Kt×Kt
6 P×Kt
White has now gained territory in the
centre, but his pawn mass is liable to be
shaken.

6 ......   P—QB4
Energetic play. If, in preparation for this
advance, 6 .... B—Kt2; 7 B—R3, Castles;
8 Q—Kt3, Kt—Q2; 9 Kt—B3, P—QB4;
10 B—K2, etc., and White has the better
chances.

7 Kt—B3
Besides this purely developing move, there
are several tempting continuations, e.g.
7 B—Kt5 ch, Kt—Q2, etc.; or 7 B—QB4,
B—Kt2; 8 Kt—K2, etc.; or 7 B—K2; or
7 B—K3, B—Kt2; 8 Kt—B3, Kt—B3, etc.

7 ......   B—Kt2
8 B—K3
At the cross-roads. Alternative lines are:
(*a*) 8 B—Kt5 ch, B—Q2; 9 B×B ch,
Q×B; 10 Castles, P×P; 11 P×P, Kt—B3;
12 B—K3, Castles KR, and Black has nothing
to fear. He has even a slight potential
advantage for the end-game: two pawns to
one on the Q side.
(*b*) 8 B—K2 (as played in the game which
originated this variation, Becker—Grünfeld,
Vienna, 1922: 8 .... Castles; 9 Castles,
P×P; 10 P×P, Kt—B3; 11 B—K3, B—Kt5,
etc., and Black has a very good game.
(*c*) 8 B—QB4, Kt—B3 (if 8 .... B—Kt5;
9 B×P ch); 9 B—K3, Castles; 10 P—KR3,
P×P; 11 P×P, and White claims the initiative.
(*d*) 8 P—KR3, preventing the pin.

8 ......   Castles
9 Q—Q2
He strengthens his centre before proceeding with his development.

9 ...... B—Kt5
10 R—Kt1
He still attends to his Q side. If 10 B—K2,
Q—R4; or 10 P×P, Q—R4.

10 ...... P×P
11 P×P Kt—B3
12 P—Q5
Having become mobile, this pawn now
serves White as a lever.

12 ...... Kt—R4
After 12 .... B×Kt; 13 P×B, Kt—K4;
14 B—K2, Black's position remains tense.

13 B—K2 P—K3
A hazardous undertaking. If 13 ....
P—Kt3; 14 Castles, etc.

14 B—B5 R—K1
15 B—Kt5 P×P
16 B×R Q×B
Loss or sacrifice of the exchange. In any
event, Black's threats demand very careful
play on White's part.

17 Castles P×P
18 Q×Kt P×Kt
If, first, 18 .... Kt—Kt3; 19 Q—K1, e.g.
19 .... P×Kt; 20 Q×Q ch, R×Q;
21 B—K3, with the better game; or 19 ....
P×B; 20 Kt—Q2, P—K6; 21 Q×P, Q×Q;
22 P×Q, B—K3; 23 KR—K1, R—K1;
24 Kt—B1, etc., and White has a definite
advantage.

19 KR—K1
The balance in material is approximately
even, but the open lines favour White's game.

19 ...... B—K3
20 Q—Kt4 P—Kt3
Driving the Bishop to—better squares.
After 20 .... Q—Q2, there would be a much
harder fight.

21 B—Q4 KB—B1
Prudence demanded the exchange of
Bishops.

22 Q—B3 P×P
23 Q—B3 Q—Q1
If (in order to parry the threat 24 Q—B6)
23 .... B—K2; 24 R—B7 (threatening
25 R×B); 24 .... B—Q1; 25 R—Kt7, and
Black is in a vice.
Relatively better would be 23 ....
B—Kt2.

24 QR—Q1 B—Q4
25 Q—B4 R—B1
If 25 .... B—Q3; 26 R—K8 ch, Q×R;

27 Q—B6, K—B1; 28 Q×B ch, and wins
easily.

26 R—K8
A beautiful final stroke.

26 ...... Resigns
(26 .... Q×R; 27 Q—B6.)

450

White	Black
FINE	LILIENTHAL

(Moscow, 1937)

*A purely positional game in which, without
brilliant effects, each move is the result of
deep and exact calculation. The finish after
30 R—Q3, in which White, in spite of being
a pawn down, seeks liquidation—relying on
the paralysis of the opposing Q side—is a
revelation.*

1 P—Q4 Kt—KB3
2 P—QB4 P—KKt3
3 Kt—QB3 P—Q4
4 Q—Kt3
A Russian idea: its chief merit is that it is
fashionable, as its main idea, pressure
against the point Q5, can be met satisfactorily.

4 ...... P—B3
A passive reply. A far more independent
treatment is 4 .... P×P; 5 Q×BP, B—K3;
6 Q—Q3 (if 6 Q—Kt5 ch, Kt—B3;
7 Kt—B3, Kt—Q4, etc., not without danger
for White); 6 .... Kt—B3; 7 Kt—B3,
P—QR3; 8 P—K4, Kt—QKt5; 9 Q—Q1,
B—Kt5, and Black contests the initiative.

5 Kt—B3
Instead of playing impulsively 5 B—Kt5
or 5 P×P, P×P; 6 B—Kt5, White speeds
up his K side development.

5 ...... B—Kt2
6 P—K3 Castles
7 B—Q2
Fight for the tempo (7 B—Q3, P×P;
8 B×BP). Again, if 7 P×P, P×P; 8 B—Q3,
Kt—B3, etc., Black's development becomes
easier, and his QKt is better placed at QB3
than at Q2.

7 ...... P—K3
A waiting policy. He should try to free

his game by 7 .... P×P; 8 B×P, QKt—Q2;
9 Castles KR, Kt—Kt3; 10 B—K2, B—K3,
etc.

    8 B—Q3   QKt—Q2
    9 Castles KR   Kt—Kt3
An artificial idea. If—
(a) 9 .... R—K1; 10 KR—Q1, Q—K2;
11 QR—B1, and the White forces are better
placed.
(b) 9 .... P×P; 10 B×BP, P—QKt4;
11 B—K2, P—QR3, in order to effect the
freeing advance .... P—QB4.
(c) 9 .... P—Kt3, followed by ....
B—Kt2, deferring any trenchant decision.

    10 KR—Q1
A reply both deep and unexpected. White
allows his KB to be exchanged for a Knight,
because he foresees his increasing mastery of
the centre.

    10 ......   P×P
    11 B×BP   Kt×B
    12 Q×Kt   Kt—Q2
Better is 12 .... Kt—Q4.

    13 P—K4   Q—B2
    14 P—K5
With a lasting pressure and, incidentally,
providing a powerful support for a Knight
at Q6 or KB6.

    14 ......   Kt—Kt3
Or else (after 14 .... P—Kt3) 15 Kt—QKt5,
followed by Kt—Q6, etc.

    15 Q—K2   P—KB4
Eliminating an adverse *strong point*, but
at the cost of a serious weakness. More
steady would be 15 .... B—Q2, followed
by .... QR—Q1, etc.

    16 P×P e.p.   R×P
    17 Kt—K4   R—B4
More exact would be 17 .... R—B1;
18 B—Kt4, R—Q1, etc.

    18 B—Kt4   R—Q4
    19 Kt—K5
Very astute. Black begins to lack breathing space.

    19 ......   R—Q1
For if 19 .... B—Q2; 20 Kt—QB3,
winning the exchange. On the other hand,
after 19 .... B×Kt; 20 P×B, neither
20 .... R×P; 21 B—Q6, nor 20 .... Q×P;
21 B—B3 is playable.

    20 QR—B1   Kt—Q4
    21 B—R3   Kt—K2
If 21 .... B—Q2; 22 B—Q6, etc., and if
21 .... B×Kt; 22 P×B, Q×P; 23 B—K7,
with the double threat 24 B×R or
24 Kt—B6 ch.

    22 Q—B3   Kt—Q4
After 22 .... R—B1; 23 Q—R3, there
are many threats such as 24 B—Q6 or
24 Kt—Kt5. More enterprising would be
22 .... Kt—B4.

    23 Q—KKt3   B—R3
    24 R—B2   B—B1
The weakness of his Q3 still prevents Black
from getting his QB into play. Black's
game generally suffers from weakness on the
black squares.

    25 P—R4   B×B
    26 Q×B   R—B1
He must fortify his K side. If 26 ....
B—Q2; 27 P—R5.

    27 P—R5   R—B5
    28 R—K2   P×P
    29 Q—Kt3 ch   Q—Kt2
    30 R—Q3
A curious position, in which White can
afford to exchange Queens when minus
a pawn.

    30 ......   P—R5
    31 Q×Q ch   K×Q
    32 P—KKt3   P×P
    33 R×P ch   K—B1
    34 P—B3
The second Rook is called into play.

    34 ......   Kt—B3
Or 34 .... R—R5; 35 R (K2)—Kt2.

    35 R—R2   R×Kt
A despairing sacrifice. If 35 ....
Kt×Kt; 36 P×Kt, R×P; 37 R×P, R×P;
38 R (Kt3)—Kt7, forcing a speedy mate.

    36 P×R   Kt×P
    37 R—Kt4   Kt—B3
Losing a piece. But after 37 .... Kt—Q3;
38 R×P, there is no hope for Black.

    38 R—KB2   Resigns
Triumph of the *positional combination.*

451

White	*Black*
EUWE	ALEKHINE

(Match, 1935)

*White's work on the KR file, opened up
early in the game, is very effective (10 R×P).
A piquant feature is that White, on the 20th
move, overlooked a far from obvious chance
of a win, after which he had, so to speak, to
win the game a second time.*

1 P—Q4	Kt—KB3
2 P—QB4	P—KKt3
3 Kt—QB3	

After 3 P—Q5, anticipating the *Grünfeld Defence* (3 .... P—Q4), 3 .... B—Kt2; 4 Kt—QB3, P—Q3; 5 Kt—B3, Castles, White has prematurely committed himself in the centre.

| 3 ...... | P—Q4 |
| 4 B—B4 | Kt—R4 |

Too restless a reaction. Solid, if passive, is 4 .... P—B3. Unambitious is 4 .... B—Kt2, e.g. 5 B—K5, P—B3; 6 P—KR3, Castles; 7 Kt—B3, QKt—Q2, etc., or 5 P—K3, Castles, etc.

5 B—K5

Far more astute than at once 5 B—Kt3, for it causes a certain weakness on the opponent's K side.

5	P—KB3
6 B—Kt3	Kt × B
7 RP × Kt	

The *open KR file* becomes a powerful asset in White's hands.

7	P—B3
8 P—K3	B—Kt2
9 B—Q3	

Threat: 10 R × P, R × R; 11 B × P ch, followed by B × R, as in the game Palaute Kolsté.

9 ......   Castles

He tries to complicate matters, for a passive defence by 9 .... P—KB4 or 9 .... K—B2 would leave the black King in a precarious position.

10 R × P

Without being difficult to see, this offer of a sacrifice is elegant.

10 ......   P—KB4

Acceptance would be fatal, e.g. 10 .... K × R; 11 Q—R5 ch, K—Kt1; 12 B × P, and wins, whereas Black forces the invading Rook to retire, and can make use of the extra *tempo*.

11 R—R1   P—K4

Otherwise White has the blockading move 12 P—B4.

| 12 P × KP | B × P |
| 13 Kt—B3 | B × Kt ch |

The retreat 13 .... B—Kt2 preserves a useful piece for the defence, but Black would have to submit to a passive defence.

| 14 P × B | Q—B3 |
| 15 P × P | |

Both sides are imbued with the spirit of the attack. White also gives up a pawn rather than being satisfied with 15 Q—Kt3.

15	Q × P ch
16 K—B1	Q—B3
17 R—B1	P × P
18 R—B7	Kt—Q2

He naturally would like to block the second rank.

19 B—Kt5   Q—Q3

The only move, for if 19 .... Q—B2; 20 Kt—Kt5, and wins, and if 19 .... Kt—Kt3; 20 KR—R7.

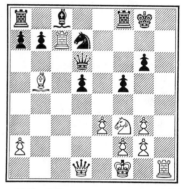

20 R—B4

Elegant as is this method of reconnecting his Rooks, he has a speedy win here by the following magnificent combination:
20 Q—Q4, Q × R (20 .... Kt—B3; 21 KR—R7); 21 R—R8 ch, K—B2; 22 Kt—Kt5 ch, K—K2 (if 22 .... K—K1; 23 R × R ch); 23 R—R7 ch, K—K1 (if 23 .... K—Q3; 24 Q—B4 ch); 24 Q × QP (powerful and simple, the threat being 25 Q—K6 ch; ineffective would be 24 Q—Kt7, Q—Q3); 24 .... Q—B8 ch; 25 K—K2, and Black has no defence.

20	Kt—B3
21 QR—KR4	Q—B4
22 B—R4	Q—B6
23 Kt—Kt5	

Renewing the attack while preventing 23 .... B—K3.

23 ......   K—Kt2
24 Kt—R7

Eliminating a stout defender of the hostile King, his Kt.

24 ......   R—Q1

Not 24 .... R—R1; 25 Kt × Kt, R × R; 26 Kt—K8 ch, etc.

25 Kt×Kt   K×Kt
26 R—R7   B—K3
27 R(R1)—R6

With the threat, eventually, of 28 R×P ch, K×R; 29 Q—R5 ch, etc. A deviation from the general plan of attack would be 27 R×P, which would allow a counter-thrust in the centre by 27 .... P—Q5.

27 ......   B—B2
28 K—Kt1   R—KKt1
29 P—Kt4

If 29 Q—R5, Q—Kt5, with a sufficient defence.

29 ......   R—Kt2
30 P×P   R×R
31 R×R   P×P
32 B—Kt3

Preventing 32 .... R—KKt1; 33 R×B ch, K×R; 34 Q×P ch.

32 ......   Q—K4
33 Q—B3   R—QB1

Looking for counter-play, but 33 .... R—Q1 is more solid.

34 P—Kt4   B—Kt3

Not 34 .... R—B8 ch; 35 K—Kt2, Q—K5; 36 R×B ch, K×R; 37 B×P ch, etc., nor 34 .... B—K3; 35 P—Kt5 ch, K×P; 36 Q—Kt2 ch, K—B3; 37 Q—Kt7 mate.

35 R×P   Q—R8 ch
36 K—Kt2   R—KR1

Threatening 37 .... Q—R8 ch, but White, taking advantage of the black King's insecure position, engineers a final assault of great precision.

37 P—Kt5 ch

A *sacrifice* which acts like a magnet.

37 ......   K×P
38 Q—B4 ch   K—B3

Or 38 .... K—R4; 39 Q—R2 ch, K—Kt4; 40 P—B4 ch, etc.

39 Q—Q6 ch   K—Kt4
40 P—B4 ch   K—R3
41 Q—K7   Resigns.

QUEEN'S INDIAN DEFENCE

452

White	Black
ALEKHINE	BOGOLJUBOW

(Triberg, 1921)

The main feature here is the consistency with which White sustains the frontal pressure which, after his 6th move, is inherent in his position.

1 P—Q4   Kt—KB3
2 Kt—KB3   P—K3

With a tendency to apply the various ideas underlying the orthodox defence of the *Queen's Gambit* (.... P—QKt3, or .... B—QKt5, or .... P—QB4, or .... Kt—K5) without committing himself in the centre by 2 .... P—Q4.

3 P—B4

Inviting Black to revert, by 3 .... P—Q4, to the classic lines of the orthodox *Queen's Gambit*.

3 ......   P—QKt3

The strategic objective of this line of play (the *Queen's Indian Defence*) is the control of the important square K5.

4 P—KKt3

A duel between the two Bishops, developed in the *fianchetto* manner, and in which the white KB has the better chances, Black's QB being undefended.

4 ......   B—Kt2
5 B—Kt2   P—B4
6 P×P

Intending to initiate frontal action on the open Q file. More dynamic, however, is 6 P—Q5, P×P; 7 Kt—R4 (or also, according to Berger's idea, 7 Kt—Kt5, stressing in either case the fact that Black's QB is unguarded); 7 .... P—Kt3 (after other replies such as 7 .... B—K2, or 7 .... Kt—B3, or 7 .... Q—B1, or 7 .... Q—B2, White recovers his pawn with some advantage); 8 Kt—B3, B—Kt2; 9 Castles, Castles; 10 P×P, with an enduring pressure by White in the centre.

6 ......   B×P

After 6 .... P×P; 7 Kt—B3, B—K2; 8 B—B4, Castles; 9 Castles, P—Q3 (9 .... P—Q4; 10 Kt—K5); 10 Q—Kt3, B—B3 (10.... Q—Kt3; 11 Kt—QKt5); 11 KR—Q1, etc., White's pressure would also be the main theme of the contest.

7 Castles

Not yet 7 Kt—B3, Kt—K5.

7 ......   Castles
8 Kt—B3   P—Q4

If, instead, 8 .... Kt—K5; 9 Kt×Kt, B×Kt; 10 Kt—Kt5, B×B; 11 Q—Q3, P—B4; 12 K×B, Kt—B3; 13 R—Q1, etc., with a fine initiative for White. Better than the text move is 8 .... Kt—R3; 9 B—Kt5, B—K2, etc., and, in spite of his backward QP, Black can hope for play on the Q side after .... R—QB1.

9 Kt—Q4

He takes advantage of the fact that Black's

QP is pinned. He could also play 9 Kt—K5 advantageously.

9 ......   B × Kt
If 9 .... Kt—B3; 10 B—K3.

10 Q × B   Kt—B3
11 Q—R4   P × P
Or 11 .... Kt—K4; 12 P—Kt3, followed by B—Kt2, bringing another piece into play.

12 R—Q1
Much more energetic than 12 Q × P, after which Black could ease his position by 12 .... Kt—QR4 and .... B × B.

12 ......   Q—B1
If 12 .... Q—K2; 13 B—Kt5, P—KR3; 14 QB × Kt, Q × B (not 14 .... P × B; 15 B—K4); 15 Q × Q, P × Q; 16 R—Q7, winning two minor pieces for a Rook.

13 B—Kt5   Kt—Q4
He anticipates only 14 Kt × Kt, P × Kt; 15 B × P, Kt—R4, with an easier game, but White ingeniously improves on this calculation.

14 Kt × Kt   P × Kt
15 R × P
With a most subtle *interceptive idea*.

15 ......   Kt—Kt5
16 B—K4
Without warning, trouble threatens at KR7.

16 ......   P—B4
Very attractive are also the two continuations:
(*a*) 16 .... P—Kt3; 17 B—B6, Q—K3; 18 Q × P ch, K × Q; 19 R—R5 ch, K—Kt1; 20 R—R8 mate.
(*b*) 16 .... P—KR3; 17 B × P, P—B4 (17 .... P × B; 18 R—Kt5 ch); 18 Q—Kt5, Q—B2; 19 B × KtP, Q × B; 20 Q × Q ch, K × Q; 21 R—Q7 ch, winning.

17 B × P   R × B
18 R—Q8 ch
The vertical pressure started on White's 6th move has done its work.

18 ......   Q × R
19 B × Q
Now White has to solve a fairly easy technical problem.

19 ......   R—QB1
20 R—Q1   R—KB2
21 Q—Kt4   Kt—Q6
Otherwise there follows 22 R—Q7.

22 P × Kt   R × B
23 P × P   QR—KB1
24 P—B4   R—K2
25 K—B2   P—KR3
26 R—K1   B—B1
27 Q—B3   R (K2)—KB2
28 Q—Q5   P—KKt4
29 R—K7   P × P
30 P × P   Resigns
An attractive game.

453

White	*Black*
ALEKHINE	SULTAN KHAN

(Prague, 1931)

The manner in which Black wards off his great opponent's furious onslaught is a model of coolness and sagacity.

1 Kt—KB3   Kt—KB3
2 P—B4   P—K3
3 P—Q4   P—QKt3
4 P—KKt3   B—Kt2
5 B—Kt2   P—Q4
Modern strategy prefers not to engage the centre at this early stage.

6 Kt—K5
Black's QP becomes the object of a lasting attack. 6 P × P, Kt × P would be tame.

6 ......   QKt—Q2
Or 6 .... B—Kt5 ch; 7 Kt—Q2, Castles; 8 Castles, QKt—Q2; 9 Kt—Q3, etc., or 6 .... B—K2; 7 Kt—QB3, Castles; 8 Castles, QKt—Q2; 9 Q—R4, etc., with a distinct advantage to White. Playable is 6 .... P—B3, with an artificial defence of his central formation.

7 Q—R4
A sound positional manœuvre.

7 ......   P—B4
Black tries for a settlement in the centre. If, passively, 7 .... B—K2; 8 Kt—B6, Q—B1 (8 .... B × Kt; 9 Q × B, winning the QP); 9 P × P, Kt × P; 10 Castles, etc., and White's advantage is clear-cut.

8 P × QP   Kt × P
After 8 .... B × P; 9 B × B, Kt × B; 10 Kt—QB3, White's advance in development would increase, whereas, after the text move, 9 Kt—QB3 is clearly impossible.

9 P×P   B×P
10 Castles   P—QR3

With the utmost self-possession, Black frees his game.

11 Q×Kt ch   Q×Q
12 Kt×Q   K×Kt
13 Kt—Q2   KR—Q1
14 Kt—Kt3   QR—B1

Renouncing for once his traditional preference for the two Bishops, he boldly manœuvres his Rook within the open space on the fourth rank.

15 Kt×B ch   R×Kt
16 P—K4   Kt—B3

Like a boomerang the Knight returns to attack the pawn.

17 B—K3

Continuing an untiring quest for some tangible advantage. The preliminary consolidating measure 17 R—K1 would be of no avail after 17 .... K—B1; 18 P—Kt3, B×P; 19 B×B, Kt×B; 20 B—R3 (not at once 20 R×Kt, R—Q8 ch, followed by .... R×B); 20 .... Kt—Q7 (not 20 .... R—K4; 21 B—Kt2, nor 20 .... R—QR4; 21 B—Kt4, and White wins); 21 B×R, Kt—B6 ch; 22 K—B1, Kt×R; 23 B×P, R—Q3, etc., and Black averts all danger.

17 ......   R—QKt4

He defends his QKtP, and now two hostile pawns are attacked.

18 KR—Q1 ch   K—K1
19 R×R ch   K×R
20 B—Q4   Kt×P

He accepts stoically his opponent's intentions, for if 20 .... K—K2; 21 R—QB1, and if 20 .... P—K4; 21 P—QR4.

21 B×P

Thus White now not only has the two Bishops, but his pawns are more compact, and Black's Rook has not yet found a fixed abode.

21 ......   Kt—Q3

The art of defence! If now 22 R—Q1, B×B; 23 R×Kt ch, K—K2, leading to absolute equality.

22 P—QR4   R—KB4

Fatal would be 22 .... R—Kt5; 23 R—Q1, B×B (or 23 .... B—Q4; 24 B×B, P×B; 25 R×P, K—K2; 26 R×Kt, etc.); 24 R×Kt ch, K—K2; 25 K×B, K×R; 26 B—B8 ch, followed by B×R.

23 B—Q4   P—Kt4
24 B—B1   K—Q2
25 P×P   P×P
26 B—K3

If 26 R—R7, R—Q4.

26 ......   P—R4

Preventing 27 P—KKt4, and thus maintaining the active Rook on the fourth rank.

27 P—B4

Hoping to play 28 B—R3, R—Q4; 29 K—B2, R—Q6; 30 K—K2, R—Kt6; 31 B—Q4, and the black Rook is at last dislodged.

27 ......   B—K5
28 R—R7 ch   K—K1
29 K—B2

If 29 P—QKt4, then again 29 .... R—Q4.

29 ......   R—Q4

Now that Black has effected a sound regrouping of his Rook and Bishop, the battle loses its intensity.

30 B—K2   B—Q6
31 B—B3   B—K5
32 B—Q2

Ineffective would be the attempt 32 R—R8 ch, K—K2; 33 R—KR8, B×B; 34 K×B, Kt—B5; 35 P—Kt3, Kt×B; 36 K×Kt, R—QB4, and the Rook ending would even be slightly in Black's favour.

32 ......   B—Q6
                Draw.

454

White   *Black*

GOLOMBEK   NORMAN-HANSEN

(Margate, 1937)

After positional manœuvring in the centre and on the Q side, the trenchant manner in which White breaks into the King's position deserves special mention.

1 P—Q4   Kt—KB3
2 Kt—KB3   P—K3
3 P—B4   P—QKt3
4 P—KKt3   B—Kt2
5 B—Kt2   B—K2

Restrained strategy.

A constructive idea is 5 .... Q—B1; 6 Castles, P—B4, or 6 Kt—B3, B—Kt5, etc.

6 Castles   Castles
7 Kt—B3

Intending Q—B2, and then P—K4. If, first, 7 Q—B2, then 7 .... Kt—B3; 8 Kt—B3, P—Q4; 9 P×P, Kt—QKt5; 10 Q—Kt3, QKt×QP, and Black's counterplay is satisfactory.

If 7 P—Kt3, Q—B1, guarding the QB, and thus clearing the way for the thrusts .... P—Q4 or .... P—B4.

7 ......   P—Q4

A more stubborn fight for the strategic point K5 results from 7 .... Kt—K5, e.g. 8 Q—B2, Kt×Kt; 9 Q×Kt, P—KB4, etc., or 8 Kt×Kt, B×Kt, with an even game.

8 Kt—K5

If 8 P×P, Kt×P; 9 Q—B2, Kt—R3, and Black's game is free.

8 ......   P—B3

Although artificial, this line of defence should be noted. If 8 .... P—B4; 9 B—K3. If 8 .... QKt—Q2; 9 P×P, P×P, etc. (not 9 .... Kt×Kt; 10 P—Q6, B×B; 11 P×B, Q×KP; 12 P×Kt, B×R; 13 P×Kt, Q×P; 14 Q×B and White obtains a conclusive advantage in material). After 8 .... Q—B1 the ruthless continuation of a game Tartakower—L. Steiner, *Warsaw*, 1935, was: 9 P×P, P×P; 10 Q—Kt3, P—B3; 11 B—Q2, Kt—R3; 12 QR—B1, Kt—B2; 13 P—K4, R—Q1; 14 KR—K1, P—B4; 15 QP×P, KtP×P; 16 P×P, QKt×P; 17 B—Kt5, R—Kt1; 18 QB×Kt, B×B; 19 Kt×P, P—B5; 20 Kt×R, resigns (20 .... P×Q; 21 R—K8 mate).

9 P—Kt3

Far-seeing policy.

Too simplifying is 9 P×P, BP×P; 10 B—B4, P—QR3; 11 R—B1, P—QKt4, and Black has recovered ground. Too optimistic is 9 B—B4, too quiet 9 P—K3, and again too expansive is 9 P—K4, P×BP; 10 Kt×P (B4), B—R3, and Black contests the initiative.

9 ......   QKt—Q2
10 B—Kt2   R—B1
11 R—B1   B—Q3

To be followed by .... Q—K2 and .... B—R6, in order to eliminate the adverse QB but this regrouping takes too much time A violent attempt at emancipation in the centre would be 11 .... P—B4.

12 P—B4

A position in the style of Pillsbury.

12 ......   Q—K2
13 P—K3

Intending to advance the KKtP as far as Kt5. Committing himself too definitely would be 13 P—K4, in view of the possibility .... P—B4.

13 ......   B—R6
14 B×B   Q×B
15 P—K4

Now that Black's KB has disappeared and his Queen is far away, this advance is energetic.

15   ....   Kt×Kt

Compulsory.

16 BP×Kt   Kt×P
17 B×Kt

A case in which this Bishop is less valuable than the Knight.

17 ......   P×B
18 Kt×P   Q—K2

Home again. Suicidal would be 18 .... Q×RP; 19 R—R1, Q—Kt7; 20 R—B2, winning the Queen.

19 Q—R5

With the summary threat 20 Kt—B6 ch.

19 ......   P—KB4

An attempt to slow down the enemy's impetus. If, instead, 19 .... K—R1; 20 Kt—Kt5, and if 19 .... P—KR3; 20 R—B6, P—B4; 21 R×RP, P×R; 22 Kt—B6 ch, K—Kt2; 23 Q—Kt4 ch, K—R1; 24 Q—R4, K—Kt2; 25 Kt—R5 ch, followed by Q×Q, and wins.

20 P×P e.p.   P×P
21 Kt×P ch

An elegant turn.

21 ......   K—R1

For if 21 .... R×Kt; 22 Q—Kt5 ch, K—B2; 23 R×R ch, Q×R; 24 R—B1, winning the Queen. The remainder is treated by White with the conciseness of a courtmartial.

22 Q—K5   Q—Kt2
23 R—B4   P—B4
24 QR—B1   P×P
25 Kt—R5

A beautiful final stroke.

25 ......   Resigns.

455

White	Black
EUWE	CAPABLANCA

(Match, 1931)

After a successful opening trap, White emerges the exchange to the good. The resulting duel between the Knight, beautifully handled by Capablanca, and the Rook is most exciting.

1 P—Q4	Kt—KB3
2 P—QB4	P—K3
3 Kt—KB3	P—QKt3
4 P—KKt3	B—Kt2

Or at once 4 .... B—Kt5 ch. An original development of the QB would be 4 .... B—R3 (5 QKt—Q2, B—Kt5, or 5 Q—B2, B—Kt5 ch, or 5 Q—R4, P—B3, etc.).

5 B—Kt2	B—Kt5 ch
6 B—Q2	B × B ch
7 Q × B	

To be followed by Kt—B3, with concerted pressure on Q5. Less good would be 7 QKt × B.

7 ...... Castles

Instead of disclosing at once the King's future abode, consolidating measures in the centre can be undertaken first. Even then there are shoals to be avoided, as is demonstrated by the game Becker—Fuss, *Vienna*, 1933: (1 P—Q4, P—K3; 2 Kt—KB3, Kt—KB3; 3 P—B4, B—Kt5 ch; 4 B—Q2, B × B ch; 5 Q × B, P—QKt3; 6 P—KKt3, B—Kt2; 7 B—Kt2, P—Q3) 8 Kt—B3, Kt—K5 (8 .... QKt—Q2 is better); 9 Q—B4, Kt × Kt; 10 Kt—Kt5, P—KB3; 11 B × B, P × Kt; 12 Q—K3, Kt—Q2; 13 Q × P ch, K—B1; 14 B × R, Q × B; 15 P—B3, resigns.

8 Kt—B3

More pertinent than 8 Castles, P—Q3; 9 Kt—B3, Kt—K5; 10 Q—B2, Kt × Kt; 11 Q × Kt (11 Kt—Kt5, Kt × P ch); 11 .... Kt—Q2; 12 QR—Q1, Q—K2, etc., with an even game.

8 ...... Kt—K5

Plausible, but not good. He should have been content with 8 .... P—Q3; 9 Q—B2, QKt—Q2; 10 Castles KR, Q—K2; 11 P—K4, P—K4, etc.

9 Q—B2

After 9 Kt × Kt, B × Kt; 10 Castles, P—Q3; 11 Kt—K1, B × B; 12 Kt × B, Kt—Q2, etc., a draw is in sight.

9 ...... Kt × Kt

After 9 .... P—KB4; 10 Kt—K5, White's advantage becomes apparent.

10 Kt—Kt5

The *Monticelli Trap*, aiming at KR7.

10 ...... Kt— K5

He finds the best means of avoiding the sudden danger. If 10 .... Q × Kt; 11 B × B, Kt—B3; 12 B × R, Kt × KP; 13 Q × Kt (not 13 B × Kt, Kt × QP; 14 Q—Q3, Kt × B, etc.); 13 .... Kt × P; 14 Q—Q3 (but not 14 Q—K4, Q—R4 ch; 15 K—B1, Kt—Kt6, etc.); 14 .... Q—K4 ch; 15 B—K4 (not 15 Q—K4, Q—R4 ch); 15 .... P—KB4; 16 Castles QR (White keeps the spoils); 16 .... P—B4 (16 .... P × B; 17 Q × Kt, winning); 17 B—B3, and Black's dream evaporates.

11 B × Kt	B × B
12 Q × B	Q × Kt
13 Q × R	Kt—B3

Although he is the exchange down, Black is able to put up a fierce fight. Another line of play is 13 .... Q—R4 ch; 14 K—B1, Kt—B3; 15 Q—Kt7, Q—Q7; 16 P—K3, Q—Q6 ch; 17 K—Kt2, Q—K5 ch (17 .... Q × BP; 18 KR—Q1); 18 K—B1, P—B4, and Black still has some shot in his locker.

14 Q—Kt7	Kt × P
15 R—Q1	Q—K4

Relatively best is 15 .... Q—QB4. After 15 .... P—QB4 there follows 16 P—K3, Kt—B7 ch; 17 K—Q2, and White still has winning chances.

16 P—K3

If 16 R—Q2, P—Q4.

16	Kt—B7 ch
17 K—K2	P—Q4
18 R—Q2	Q × QKtP
19 P × P	Q—Kt4 ch
20 K—B3	Kt—Kt5
21 R—QB1	Q—R4
22 P—Q6	

A skilful thrust, which brings about a desirable liquidation.

22	P × P
23 R—B8	P—Kt3
24 R × R ch	K × R
25 Q—B8 ch	K—K2
26 Q—B7 ch	K—B3
27 Q—B3 ch	K—K2
28 Q—B7 ch	K—B3
29 Q—Q8 ch	K—Kt2
30 Q × QP	Kt × P

As long as Black has two extra pawns, he has, theoretically if not practically, sufficient compensation for the exchange.

31 Q—Q4 ch	P—K4
32 Q—Q5	Q × Q
33 R × Q	

In the ensuing magnificent battle, the defence succeeds only by astute, problem-like turns.

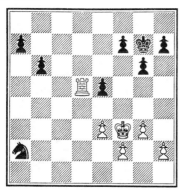

33	P—K5 ch

Now if 34 K × P, Kt—B6 ch; whereas neither 33 .... P—B3; 34 R—Q7 ch, followed by R × QRP, nor 33 .... K—B3; 34 R—Q7, P—QR4; 35 R—Q6 ch, followed by R × QKtP, would be encouraging.

34 K—B4	Kt—Kt5
35 R—QKt5	

In order to immobilise both hostile Q side pawns.

35	Kt—Q6 ch
36 K × P	Kt × P ch
37 K—Q4	P—B4
38 R—Kt2	Kt—Kt5
39 P—R3	Kt—B3
40 R—QB2	Kt—K5

The Knight's evolutions are intended, as far as possible, to reduce the number of pawns.

41 P—Kt4	K—B3
42 P × P	K × P

He allows his opponent to obtain a passed pawn rather than to let his own K side pawns be separated.

43 R—B7	Kt—Kt4
44 R × QRP	P—R4
45 R—R3	

A most astute defence of the KRP (if 45 .... Kt × P; 46 P—K4 ch, K—Kt5; 47 R × Kt, K × R; 48 P—K5, and wins).

45	Kt—B6 ch
46 K—Q3	

Artificial. After 46 K—Q5, Black would have arduous problems to solve.

46	Kt—Kt8
47 K—Q2	P—KKt4

He loses his Q side pawns, but re-forms a threatening mass on the other wing.

48 R—Kt3	P—R5
49 R × P	Kt × P
50 K—K2	P—Kt5
51 R—Kt5 ch	K—K5
52 R—Kt4 ch	K—B4
53 K—B1	K—Kt4
54 R—Kt5 ch	K—Kt3
55 R—Kt4	K—R4
56 R—Kt5 ch	Kt—Kt4

Draw.

Although normally, against a Rook, a Knight is less useful than a Bishop, the present game is a beautiful illustration of an exceptional case.

456

White	*Black*
CAPABLANCA	ALEKHINE

(Match, Buenos Aires, 1927)

The manner in which White harries the black forces after he has obtained a slight advantage is remarkably consistent and relentless.

1 P—Q4	Kt—KB3
2 Kt—KB3	P—QKt3
3 P—KKt3	B—Kt2
4 B—Kt2	P—B4

Trying to undermine the white centre, after which the formation of a second *fianchetto* will have a wider scope, thus: 5 P × P, P × P; 6 Castles, P—Kt3; 7 P—B4, B—Kt2. Awkward, however, would be the immediate *fianchetto* development by 4 .... P—Kt3; 5 Castles, B—Kt2; 6 P—B4, Castles; 7 Kt—B3, P—Q3; 8 Q—B2, QKt—Q2; 9 R—Q1, with superior mechanism for White.

Note that, where the formation of a *double fianchetto* demands the preliminary P—B4, it is better to avoid playing P—KR3, on account of the *hole* at KB3.

5 Castles

He allows simplification in preference to seeking doubtful tensions by 5 P × P, P × P; 6 Castles, P—Kt3, etc.

5	P × P

It is also possible calmly to play 5 ....

P—Kt3, and only after 6 P—B4 (threatening 7 P—Q5); 6 .... P × P, etc.

6 Kt × P
More awkward is 6 Q × P, Kt—B3.

| 6 ...... | B × B |
| 7 K × B | P—Q4 |

A doubtful advance. Much more sustained is the formation of a *second fianchetto* by 7 .... P—Kt3 (8 P—QB4, B—Kt2; 9 Kt—QB3, Q—B1; 10 P—Kt3, Kt—B3, etc., and Black has a strong game).

| 8 P—QB4 | P—K3 |

Or 8 .... P × P; 9 Q—R4 ch, QKt—Q2 (9 .... Q—Q2; 10 Kt—Kt5); 10 R—Q1, manifestly in favour of White.

| 9 Q—R4 ch | Q—Q2 |

If 9 .... QKt—Q2; 10 P × P.

| 10 Kt—Kt5 | Kt—B3 |
| 11 P × P | P × P |

Not 11 .... Kt × P; 12 R—Q1 (threat: 13 P—K4), nor 11 .... Q × P ch; 12 P—K4.

| 12 B—B4 | R—B1 |
| 13 R—B1 | |

The threat is 14 Kt—B7 ch, R × Kt; 15 B × R, Q × B; 16 Q × Kt ch, etc.

| 13 ...... | B—B4 |
| 14 P—QKt4 | |

A very fine conception, winning material.

| 14 ...... | B × KtP |

Or 14 .... Kt × P; 15 Kt—Q6 ch, K—Q1; 16 Q × Q ch, K × Q; 17 Kt × R, R × Kt; 18 Kt—Q2, Kt—Kt5; 19 P—QR3, etc.

| 15 R × Kt | R × R |
| 16 Q × B | |

A new phase begins which is far from plain sailing, for Black will offer the most stubborn resistance.

16	Kt—K5
17 Kt—Q2	Kt × Kt
18 Q × Kt	Castles
19 R—Q1	R—B4
20 Kt—Q4	R—K1
21 Kt—Kt3	QR—B1
22 P—K3	Q—R5

An enterprising idea; he tries to exchange his QP for White's QRP in order to eliminate a weakness and to create two united passed pawns for the end-game. But his support in the centre will disappear at the same time, and there his opponent will have full freedom of action. For this reason 22 ....

QR—Q1 in support of the QP—weak but effective—would be the soundest course.

| 23 Q × P | R—B7 |

Not at once 23 .... Q × P; 24 R—QR1, followed by R × P.

24 R—Q2	R × P
25 R × R	Q × R
26 Q—B6	R—KB1
27 Kt—Q4	

Preventing 27 .... Q—K3.

| 27 ...... | K—R1 |

In order to reply to 28 B—Q6 by 28 .... R—KKt1.

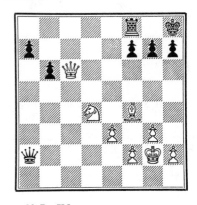

28 B—K5
Threatening 29 B × P ch, K × B; 30 Kt—B5 ch, K—Kt1; 31 Q—KB6.

| 28 ...... | P—B3 |

A more stubborn resistance would result from 28 .... R—KKt1.

29 Kt—K6	R—KKt1
30 B—Q4	P—KR3
31 P—R4	

He is in no hurry, but a more direct decision could be obtained by 31 Kt × P, e.g. 31 .... K × Kt; 32 Q × P ch, K—R2; 33 Q—B5 ch, R—Kt3; 34 Q—Q7 ch, K—Kt1; 35 Q—K8 ch, K—R2; 36 Q—R8 mate; or 31 .... R × Kt; 32 Q × BP, Q—Q4 ch; 33 P—B3, Q—KKt4; 34 Q × Q, P × Q; 35 K—B2, K—Kt1; 36 B × R, and White wins, his pawn phalanx being far the stronger.

| 31 ...... | Q—Kt8 |
| 32 Kt × P | Q—Kt3 |

If 32 .... R × Kt; 33 Q × BP, Q—K5 ch; 34 K—R2, Q—Kt5, and White's advantage in material is sufficient for a win.

33	P—R5	Q—B2
34	Kt—B5	K—R2
35	Q—K4	R—K1
36	Q—B4	Q—B1
37	Kt—Q6	R—K2
38	B × BP	Q—R1 ch
39	P—K4	R—KKt2
40	B × R	K × B
41	Kt—B5 ch	Resigns.

457

White	*Black*
SULTAN KHAN	CAPABLANCA

(Hastings, 1930)

The following titanic struggle is both tense and instructive. By subtle manœuvring the Indian master leads his forces to victory.

1	Kt—KB3	Kt—KB3
2	P—Q4	P—QKt3
3	P—B4	B—Kt2
4	Kt—B3	

He renounces the more scientific plan 4 P—KKt3, in order to accelerate his pressure in the centre.

4	......	P—K3
5	P—QR3	

If 5 Q—B2 or 5 B—Kt5, in order to play P—K4, Black would oppose White's intentions by 5 .... B—Kt5.

5	......	P—Q4

Reverting to the outlines of a regular *Queen's Gambit.*

6	P × P	P × P

Playable is also 6 .... Kt × P.

7	B—Kt5	B—K2
8	P—K3	Castles
9	B—Q3	Kt—K5
10	B—KB4	

Avoiding the more usual simplification 10 B × B.

10	......	Kt—Q2
11	Q—B2	P—KB4

Instead of this *quasi-stonewall*, he could also play 11 .... QKt—B3 (12 Kt—QKt5, P—B3).

12	Kt—QKt5	

A venture which succeeds.

12	......	B—Q3

Not 12 .... P—B3; 13 Kt—B7, R—B1; 14 Kt—K6, etc. A very deep scheme to neutralise White's efforts is 12 .... P—QR3, e.g. 13 B × P, Q—B1, or 13 Q × P, P × Kt; 14 Q × B, QKt—B4; 15 P × Kt, Kt × QBP; 16 Q—B7, Kt × B ch, etc., or, finally (and best), the retreat 13 Kt—B3, and White has lost some time.

13	Kt × B	

He deprives Black of the "two Bishops," and spoils his pawn formation into the bargain. Bad would be 13 Kt × BP, R—B1; 14 Kt—K6, Q—K2, etc.

13	......	P × Kt
14	P—KR4	

Against 14 Castles KR, Black has a violent counter-attack by 14 .... P—KKt4; 15 B—Kt3, P—KR4, etc.

14	......	R—B1
15	Q—Kt3	Q—K2

If at once 15 .... QKt—B3; 16 Kt—Kt5.

16	Kt—Q2	

If, instead, 16 Kt—Kt5, P—KR3.

16	......	QKt—B3

If 16 .... K—R1; 17 P—B3 (not 17 Kt × Kt, QP × Kt, etc., undoubling his pawns).

17	Kt × Kt	

Now that Black can no longer undouble his pawns, this exchange is effective.

17	......	P × Kt
18	B—K2	R—B3
19	P—Kt4	

A bold offensive.

19	......	KR—B1

Giving up a pawn is his best chance.

20	P—Kt5	Kt—K1
21	B—Kt4	

A grand conception, having already in view the exchange, if not the sacrifice of the Queen for two Rooks, which, in present circumstances, would favour White's chances. Short-sighted would be the gain of a pawn by 21 Q × P ch, K—R1; 22 Q—Kt3, R—B8 ch; 23 K—Q2, R × QR; 24 R × R, Q—QB2, and Black seizes the initiative.

21	......	R—B8 ch
22	K—Q2	KR—B7 ch

More prudent would be 22 .... R × QR; 23 R × R, R—B5, etc.

23 Q × R	R × Q ch
24 K × R	Q—B2 ch

A short-lived attack.

25 K—Q2	Q—B5

With the threat 26 .... Q—Q6 ch, etc.

26 B—K2	Q—Kt6
27 QR—QKt1	K—B2
28 KR—QB1	K—K2
29 R—B3	Q—R5

Not 29 .... Q—R7; 30 K—B1, followed
by B—Q1 and B—QKt3.

30 P—Kt4	

Containing a threat of immobilising the
black Queen by 31 P—Kt5, followed by
R—Kt4.

30	Q—Q2
31 QR—QB1	P—QR3
32 R—KKt1	Q—R5

Not 32 .... Q—R6; 33 B—Kt4,
Q × P; 34 R—Kt2, followed by R—B1,
R (B1)—KKt1, and then R—R2, and
Black's Queen is lost.

33 R (Kt1)—QB1	

Threatening 34 R—B7 ch, Kt × R;
35 R × Kt ch, followed by R × B.

33	Q—Q2
34 P—R5	K—Q1
35 R (B1)—B2	Q—R6
36 K—B1	Q—R5
37 K—Kt2	Q—R6

Not 37 .... Q × BP; 38 KB × P, and wins.

38 R—B1	Q—R5
39 R (B3)—B2	Q—R6
40 P—R4	Q—R5
41 K—R3	Q—R6
42 B—Kt3	

Having strengthened his base during the
last ten moves with truly Oriental patience,
White now passes on to more concrete action.

42	Q—B4
43 B—R4	P—Kt3

The only defence. If 43 .... Q—R6;
44 P—Kt6 dis ch, Q × B; 45 P × P, queening,
and if 43 .... K—Q2; 44 R—KKt1, threatening 45 B—Kt4.

44 P—R6	Q—Q2

Or 44 .... Q—R6; 45 B—Kt3, Q—B4;
46 B—KB4, a successful regrouping of
White's forces.

45 P—Kt5	P—R4

The closure; but if 45 .... P × P;
46 B × P, followed by B × Kt, and the irruption of the white Rooks on the seventh rank
would have a deadly effect.

46 B—Kt3	Q—B4
47 B—KB4	Q—R6
48 K—Kt2	Q—Kt7
49 K—Kt1	

A trap. If now 49 .... Q × BP; 50 B—R5,
Q—R5; 51 R—KR2, and the Queen is lost.

49	Q—R6
50 K—R1	Q—Kt7
51 K—Kt2	

The King's well-known triangular manœuvre, putting the onus to move on his
adversary.

51	Q—R6
52 R—KKt1	

With the astute threat 53 B—Kt4, Q—R5;
54 P—B3, P × P; 55 KB × P (not at once
55 R—R2, P—B7); 55 .... Q—R6;
56 B—Kt4, Q—R5; 57 R—R2, again
winning the Queen.

52	B—B1

After 52 .... Q—K3, or 52 .... Q—Q2,
White imposes his will by 53 B—Kt4, followed by R (Kt1)—QB1.

53 R—B6	

After winning the black QKtP, White's
passed pawn decides the game.

53	Q—R5

If 53 .... B—Kt2, then not impulsively
54 R × P, K—B2, etc., but 54 B—Kt4,
Q—R5; 55 R—B2, followed by P—B3, etc.,
winning the Queen.

54 R (Kt1)—QB1	B—Kt5

If instead, 54 .... B—Kt2; 55 R × P,
Q × BP; 56 R—B2, B—B1; 57 R—Kt8,
Kt—B2; 58 B—Kt4, forcing the win.

55 B—B1	

Most astute. If 55 B × B, Q × B; 56 R × P,
Q—K7 ch; 57 R—B2, Q—K8, etc.

55	Q—R4

After 55 .... Q × P ch, Black's Queen is
lost in one of several ways: 56 R (B6)—B2,
Q—R5; 57 R—R2, etc., or 56 .... Q—B6;
57 B—Kt2, etc., or 56 .... Q—Kt8;
57 R—Kt2, Q—R8; 58 R—R2, Q—Kt8 (or
58 .... Q—B6; 59 B—K2, etc.); 59 B—K2,
etc.

56 R—K1	

Not yet 56 R × P, B—K7; 57 B × B,
Q × B ch; 58 R—B2, Q—K8, and the black
Queen is active again.

56	Q—R8
57 R (K1)—B1	Q—R4
58 K—B3	

Crippling his opponent's efforts. Now the

white King, instead of a Rook, assumes the task of guarding the central zone.

58	......	Q—R5
59	B—Kt3	Q×KtP
60	K—Q2	Q—B4
61	R×P	

At last this decisive capture has become possible.

61	......	K—K2
62	R—Kt7 ch	K—K3
63	P—Kt6	Kt—B3
64	B—Kt5	

Immobilising the black Knight. Ineffective would be 64 R (B1)—B7, Q—B6.

| 64 | ...... | Q—B6 |
| 65 | R—Kt8 | Resigns |

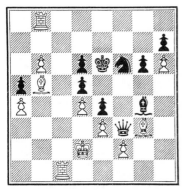

The continuation could be: 65 .... Kt—Q2 (65 .... Kt—R4; 66 R—K8 ch); 66 R—K8 ch, K—B2; 67 P—Kt7, B—R4; 68 R—K1 (not yet 68 B×Kt, Q—K7 ch); 68 .... B—Kt5; 69 B×Kt, and wins.

458

| *White* | *Black* |
| COLLE | GRÜNFELD |

(Berlin, 1926)

The most attractive feature of this beautiful game is the break-up of Black's well-guarded King's position by a sequence of brilliant and logical sacrifices.

1	P—Q4	Kt—KB3
2	Kt—KB3	P—K3
3	P—K3	

Inviting his adversary to revert to the *Colle Variation* of the *Queen's Pawn Game* (3 .... P—Q4; 4 B—Q3, P—B4; 5 P—B3, etc.).

| 3 | ...... | P—QKt3 |

In this *Colle Variation* of the *Indian Defence*, it is very difficult for White to obtain a strategic initiative.

| 4 | B—Q3 | B—Kt2 |
| 5 | QKt—Q2 | P—B4 |

Preventing, just in time, the thematic advance of the KP, for if now 6 P—K4, P—B5.

6 Castles

White reserves the option of effecting the *Colle Triangle* by 6 P—B3 (K3—Q4—QB3), or following an ordinary QP game by 6 P—B4.

| 6 | ...... | B—K2 |

More insistent is 6 .... Kt—B3, threatening 7 .... Kt—QKt5); 7 P—B3, Q—B2; 8 R—K1 (8 P×P, B×P); 8 .... B—K2, etc. Over-hasty would be 6 or 7 .... P×P, as is shown clearly in a game Tartakower-Najdorf, Match, *Thorn*, 1935: 1 P—Q4, Kt—KB3; 2 Kt—KB3, P—QKt3; 3 P—K3, B—Kt2; 4 B—Q3, P—B4; 5 QKt—Q2, P—K3; 6 Castles, B—K2; 7 R—K1, P×P; 8 P×P, Castles; 9 P—QKt3, Kt—B3; 10 P—B4, P—Q4; 11 B—Kt2, R—B1; 12 QR—B1, B—Kt5; 13 P—QR3, P×P; 14 P×P, B×Kt; 15 Q×B, Kt—QR4; 16 Q—K3, Kt—Q2; 17 Kt—K5, R—K1; 18 P—Q5, Kt—B1; 19 Q—Kt3, P—B3; 20 Kt—Kt4, K—R1; 21 QB×P, resigns.

7 P—QKt3

Or 7 R—K1, with a view to P—K4.

7	......	P×P
8	P×P	P—Q3
9	B—Kt2	QKt—Q2
10	P—B4	

Obtaining a "hanging" but flexible centre.

10	......	Castles
11	R—B1	R—K1
12	R—K1	Q—B2
13	Q—K2	QR—B1
14	Kt—B1	Q—Kt1

Black is confined to the first three ranks, and that his position is uncomfortable is shown by this bizarre plan of playing the Queen to QR1 in order to manœuvre the QB on to the long diagonal.

| 15 | Kt—Kt3 | Q—R1 |
| 16 | Kt—Kt5 | P—Kt3 |

White's outstanding strategy will demonstrate that this plausible move is a mistake.

A false solution would also be 16 .... B × P;
17 P—Q5, P × P; 18 Kt—B5, B—B1;
19 Q—R5, Kt × Q (or 19 .... P—Kt3;
20 Kt—R6 ch, and wins); 20 Kt—R6 ch,
followed by mate.

The *coup juste* is 16 .... B—B1.

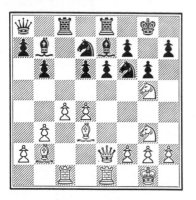

17 Kt × BP

The first of a series of sacrifices, for
Black's well-defended King's field is difficult
to disrupt.

17 ......   K × Kt
18 Q × P ch   K—Kt2

If 18 .... K—B1; 19 QR—Q1 (intending
20 B—QB1 and B—R6 mate); 19 ....
B—Q1; 20 Q × P ch, and White already has
three pawns for his piece.

19 P—Q5

An important link in White's conception,
this advance has been impending for some
time.

19 ......   Kt—B4
20 Kt—B5 ch

Completing White's work of destruction.

20 ......   K—B1

If 20 .... P × Kt; 21 Q × BP, with the
double threat 22 Q × P ch or (after 21 ....
Kt × B) 22 R × B ch and 23 Q × Kt (B6), etc.

21 Q—K3   P × Kt

And if 21 .... Kt—Kt1; 22 B—Kt7 ch,
K—B2; 23 Q—K6 ch, Kt × Q; 24 P × Kt
mate.

22 Q—R6 ch   K—B2
23 B × P

Threatening not only 24 R × B ch, followed by Q × Kt ch, but also 24 R—K6,
Kt × R; 25 B × Kt mate.

23 ......   B × P

In a desperate endeavour to parry one
danger, Black exposes himself to another.
After 23 .... B—Q1, however, White
calmly continues 24 B × P, etc.

24 R × B ch

Sweeping away the last obstacles.

24 ......   R × R
25 Q × Kt ch   K—K1
26 Q—R8 ch   K—B2
27 B × R   Resigns

The balance in material is even, but if
27 .... B × KtP; 28 Q—Kt7 ch, K—K1;
29 Q—Kt8 mate, and if 27 .... B—K3;
28 B × B ch, followed by Q × Q.

A very fine game.

459

White   Black

TÜRN   GOLOMBEK

(Stockholm, 1937)

*The contestants having castled on different
wings, Black's strategy aims at preventing the
opening of the KKt file, whilst forcing for
himself a passage on the Q side. Black's
conception and its accomplishment are worthy
of all praise.*

1 P—Q4   Kt—KB3
2 Kt—KB3   P—QKt3
3 B—Kt5

An impulsive sally, which is not to be
mistaken for *Janowski's Attack*, in which,
after 2 Kt—KB3, P—K3; 3 B—Kt5, the
Bishop's move has a definite object in view.

3 ......   Kt—K5
4 B—B4

If 4 B—R4, P—Kt3, whereas, after the
text move, if 4 .... P—Kt3; 5 Q—B1,
B—KKt2; 6 B—R6, with exchanges.

4 ......   B—Kt2
5 Kt—Kt5

If 5 QKt—Q2, P—KB4, but if now 5 ....
P—KB4; 6 P—KB3. However, White already
has to lose time.

5 ......   Kt × Kt
6 B × Kt   P—KB3

Firm play. Any other development such
as 6 .... P—KR3; 7 B—R4, etc., or 6 ....

P—Kt3; 7 Q—Q2, etc., would create fresh confusion in the black King's defences.

| 7 B—B4 | P—K3 |
| 8 P—K3 | P—KB4 |

Carrying out the idea of his 6th move (.... P—KB3), which was not to assign to this pawn an obstructive *rôle*.

| 9 Kt—Q2 | B—Q3 |

If 9 .... B—K2; 10 Q—R5 ch, P—Kt3; 11 Q—R6, B—KB1; 12 Q—R3, and White takes the lead.

| 10 B×B | P×B |

The doubling of the QP is compensated by the strengthening of his centre.

| 11 B—K2 | Castles |

If 11 .... B×P; 12 R—KKt1, and now he cannot play 12 .... Q—Kt4, because of 13 P—KR4, Q—Kt3; 14 B—R5, or 13 .... Q×RP; 14 R×B, Q—R8 ch; 15 B—B1, maintaining the extra piece.

12 B—B3

Conscious of the fact that his opening strategy has brought him nothing, White tries to simplify.

12	B×B
13 Q×B	Kt—B3
14 P—B3	

Intending 15 P—Q5 (Kt—K4; 16 Q—K2, P×P; 17 Q—Kt5, etc.), whilst if at once 14 P—Q5, Kt—Kt5.

| 14 ...... | P—Q4 |

Preventing 15 P—Q5 and other attempts at expansion such as 15 P—K4 or 15 Kt—B4.

15 Castles QR

Castles KR is safer.

| 15 ...... | P—QKt4 |

Heralding the battering-ram.

16 K—Kt1

If 16 P—QR3, P—QR4, preparing the further advance of the QKtP. But if, after the text move, 16 .... P—Kt5; 17 P—B4, avoiding all danger. That is why Black defers his assault by pawns and prepares for it by encircling manœuvres of his pieces.

| 16 ...... | Kt—R4 |
| 17 KR—Kt1 | |

A counter-attack.

| 17 ...... | Q—Kt3 |
| 18 P—KKt4 | P—B5 |

He does not allow the KKt file to be opened (either by 18 .... P×P; 19 Q×KtP, etc., or by 18 .... P—Kt3; 19 P×P, R×P;

20 Q—K2, etc.), but skilfully paralyses White's impetus.

19 P×P

He accepts the gift of a pawn, but 19 P—K4 is better.

| 19 ...... | P—Kt5 |

Black succeeds in forcing open the critical files.

20 K—R1	P×P
21 P×P	QR—B1
22 P—B5	Q—B3
23 R—Kt3	

He thinks he can still combine attack with defence. He would have done better to restrict himself to defensive measures such as 23 R—QB1.

| 23 ...... | Q—R5 |

Finely played. The immediate threat is 24 .... QR×P.

| 24 R—QB1 | R—QB3 |
| 25 Q—Q3 | |

He hopes at last to relieve the pin of the KBP and to prevent 25 .... R—R3 as well.

| 25 ...... | R—R3 |

For if 26 Q×R, Kt—Kt6 ch; 27 Kt×Kt, Q×Q, besides which he has a convincing threat of 26 .... Kt—Kt6 ch, followed by mate.

26 R—B2

Or 26 Q—B2, Q×Q; 27 R×Q, P×P, and Black has most advantageously recovered his pawn.

26	R—Kt1
27 R—Kt1	QR—Kt3
28 P×P	P×P
29 P—QB4	

This advance calls forth a catastrophe, but there is no valid defence against 29 .... Q—R6, followed by .... R—Kt7.

29	P×P
30 Kt×P	Kt—Kt6 ch
Resigns.	

460

| *White* | *Black* |
| NIMZOWITSCH | MARSHALL |

(Bad-Kissingen, 1928)

A whole series of surprising moves, intertwined with a positional *sacrifice (14 .... Kt×P), leads to a winning attack by Black. A game of outstanding merit.*

| 1 P—Q4 | Kt—KB3 |
| 2 P—QB4 | P—QKt3 |

As White's 2 P—QB4, unlike 2 Kt—KB3, exercises pressure on Q5, it is sounder to defer the text move until after 2 .... P—K3, and to hold a watching brief on the central square.

3 Kt—QB3

The most energetic continuation, preparing 4 P—K4, and getting a piece into play.

| 3 ...... | B—Kt2 |
| 4 B—Kt5 |

More expedient, in view of the pressure on K4, is at once 4 Q—B2, e.g. 4 .... P—Q4; 5 Kt—B3, or 4 .... P—K3; 5 BP×P, P—Q4; 6 BP×P, P×P; 7 P—K5, with an advantage in space to White.

Another good method of preparing the advance of the KP is 4 P—B3, P—Q4; 5 P×P, Kt×P; 6 P—K4, Kt×Kt; 7 P×Kt, P—K3, or 4 .... P—K3; 5 P—K4, P—Q4; 6 KP×P, P×P, with a complicated game.

| 4 ...... | P—K3 |
| 5 Q—B2 |

If 5 P—K4, P—KR3, forcing the exchange of the Bishop for the Knight.

| 5 ...... | P—KR3 |
| 6 B—R4 |

The desire to keep the Bishop costs two *tempi*. Simpler is therefore 6 B×Kt, Q×B; 7 P—K3, etc.

| 6 ...... | B—K2 |
| 7 P—K4 |

As this move carries too many responsibilities, the more solid alternative is 7 P—K3.

| 7 ...... | Castles |
| 8 P—K5 |

Having committed himself in the centre, he needs must continue a policy of violence. For instance, if—

(a) 8 B—Q3, Kt—B3, with the double threat of .... QKt×P and .... Kt—QKt5.

(b) 8 Kt—B3, Kt—B3 (threat: 9 .... P—KKt4; 10 B—Kt3, P—Kt5, etc.); 9 Castles, Kt—QKt5; 10 Q—Kt1, P—Q4, with counter-chances.

(c) 8 P—B3, P—Q4, opening the game.

(d) 8 Castles, P—Q4, freeing his game.

(e) 8 P—Q5, Kt×QP, etc.

| 8 ...... | Kt—Q4 |

The first minor surprise.

9 B—Kt3

More peaceful would be 9 B×B, Kt×B, etc.

| 9 ...... | Kt—Kt5 |
| 10 Q—Kt3 |

Better is 10 Q—Q2, followed by 11 P—QR3 and Kt—B3.

| 10 ...... | P—Q4 |

Another unexpected move. White can hardly play 11 P—QR3, P×P, neither 12 Q×P, Kt—B7 ch, nor 12 B×P, B×P, etc.

| 11 P×P e.p. | B×QP |
| 12 Castles |

Again, if 12 P—QR3, KKt—B3, and White's QP is under fire. Disappointing also would be the pawn hunt 12 B×B, Q×B; 13 Kt—Kt5, Q—K2; 14 Kt×BP, on account of 14 .... QKt—B3; 15 Kt×R, Kt×QP, with a winning position for Black.

| 12 ...... | QKt—B3 |

A very powerful move, threatening 13 .... Kt—R4, which paradoxically deprives the other Knight of its natural retreat. But Black sees that 13 .... Kt—R4; 14 Q—R4, B—B3; 15 Kt—Kt5, Kt—R7 ch; 16 K—Kt1, B×B; 17 RP×B, P—R3; 18 K×Kt, P×Kt; 19 P×P, B—Q4 ch; 20 K—Kt1, B—Kt6, and wins.

| 13 B×B | Q×B |
| 14 P—QR3 |

At last this move seems to be playable, but Black has in contemplation another problem-like manœuvre. If 14 Kt—B3, Kt—R4, and if 14 Kt—Kt5, Q—B5 ch; 15 Q—K3 (15 R—Q2, P—R3); 15 .... Q×Q ch; 16 P×Q, Kt×P ch; 17 K—Kt1, KKt—Kt5; 18 Kt×BP, Kt—R4, with the shattering threat 19 .... B—K5 ch.

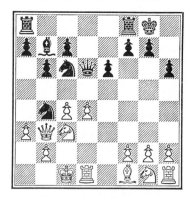

| 14 ...... | Kt×P |

The justification for this *positional sacrifice*

lies in the undeveloped state of the opposing K side.

15 R×Kt
Or 15 Q×Kt, P—QB4; 16 Q—R4, B—B3; 17 Q—R6 (the only refuge, for if 17 Kt—Kt5, Q—B5 ch, followed by 18 .... P—R3); 17 .... Q—B5 ch; 18 K—Kt1, Q×BP; 19 KKt—K2, KR—Q1, and Black's attack prevails.

| 15 ...... | Q×R |
| 16 P×Kt | |

After 16 Q×Kt, P—QB4, Black's advantage would be still more pronounced.

| 16 ...... | Q×KBP |

With the exchange and two pawns for the piece, Black is at no disadvantage in material, and the undeveloped state of White's forces ensures for Black a dynamic superiority.

17 Q—Q1	KR—Q1
18 Q—K2	Q—B5 ch
19 K—B2	P—QR4

Continuing the sequence of masterly moves.

20 P×P
This allows the second black Rook to get into active play, but if 20 P—Kt5, P—R5, followed by .... P—R6.

| 20 ...... | R×P |
| 21 Kt—B3 | R—R8 |

This invasion contains the threat 22 .... Q—B8 ch; 23 K—Kt3, KR—R1, followed by .... QR—R6 ch.

22 K—Kt3
In order to parry 22 .... Q—B8 by 23 Q—QB2.

| 22 ...... | P—QKt4 |

If (a) 23 P×P, B—Q4 ch; 24 Kt×B, Q—R5 ch; 25 K—B3, R×Kt, etc.
If (b) 23 Kt×P, B—K5, with numerous threats (24 .... B—Q6, or 24 .... P—QB3, followed by .... R—Kt1).

23 Q—K5	P×P ch
24 K—Kt4	Q—B8
25 Kt—QKt5	P—B4 ch

Elegant to the end.

Resigns
(26 K×P, R—Q4 ch, or 26 Q×P, Q×P ch; 27 K×P, R—B8 ch, followed by mate.)
Marshall at his best.

OLD INDIAN DEFENCE

461

White	Black
COHN	TCHIGORIN

(Carlsbad, 1907)

Loss or sacrifice? Whichever it may be, Black accepts the positional gift of a pawn (12 .... Kt×BP), and has to look on while White's attack gathers strength and speed. A boldly contested game.

| 1 P—Q4 | Kt—KB3 |
| 2 P—QB4 | P—Q3 |

The *Old Indian Defence,* also known as *Tchigorin's Variation* because it has been frequently adopted by him.

3 Kt—QB3
Preparing for P—K4.

| 3 ...... | QKt—Q2 |

In preparation for the counter-advance of the KP which, if effected at once, would result in Black forfeiting castling.

Black's position is now cramped but sound. 3 .... B—B4 would be doubtful (4 P—KKt3, P—B3; 5 B—Kt2, QKt—Q2; 6 P—K4, B—Kt3; 7 KKt—K2) and White's advantage is becoming definite. Black can revert to the *King's Indian Defence* by playing 3 .... P—KKt3.

4 P—K4   P—K4
He opens the game, which becomes a kind of *Philidor Defence (Hanham Variation).* This affinity between openings which seem to differ so greatly is curious and instructive.

| 5 KKt—K2 | B—K2 |
| 6 P—KKt3 | Castles |

A more artificial plan is 6 .... P—B3, followed by .... Q—B2.

7 B—Kt2	R—K1
8 Castles	B—B1
9 P—KR3	P×P
10 Q×P	

Bold play, but if 10 Kt×P, Kt—Kt3; 11 P—Kt3, P—B3, with .... P—Q4 to follow.

| 10 ...... | Kt—K4 |

With the double threat of 11 .... B×P and 11 .... P—B4. Less compromising is 10 .... P—KKt3.

| 11 P—B4 | P—B4 |
| 12 Q—B2 | Kt×BP |

Black has won a pawn, but at the cost of time and space, so that White is now able to develop his attack freely.

13 P—Kt3   Kt—QR4
14 B—Kt2   Kt—B3
15 QR—Q1   Q—R4
Evading the eventuality 16 P—K5.

16 P—KKt4
Conquest of Q5.
16 ......   Kt—Q5

17 Kt×Kt   P×Kt
18 P—Kt4
Maintaining the initiative.

18 ......   Q×KtP
19 R×P   Q—R4
20 P—Kt5   Kt—Q2
21 Kt—Q5   Q—Q1
22 P—KR4   Kt—Kt3
23 P—B5   Kt×Kt
24 R×Kt   B—Q2
25 P—K5   B—B3
If 25 .... P×P; 26 KR—Q1, etc.

26 P—K6   P×P
27 P×P   Q—K2
28 Q—B7 ch K—R1
29 R (Q5)—KB5 Q×Q
30 P×Q
And not 30 R×Q, B×B; 31 K×B,
K—Kt1, followed by .... R×P.

30 ......   R—K7
31 KR—B2   R×R
32 R×R   P—Q4
33 B—Q4   P—KR4
Or 33.... P—KR3; 34 P—Kt6 (threat:
R—B5, then R—R5 and R×P mate).

34 P—Kt6   B—Q2
Trying to prevent 35 R—B5, with mate.

35 R—K2   B—Q3
36 B—R3   B—Kt4
Or 36 .... B—R5; 37 R—K6, B—B1;
38 R—K5, B—Q8; 39 R—K8.

37 R—K6   Resigns
(37 .... B—B1; 38 R—K5.)

462

White	*Black*
APPEL	TARTAKOWER

(Lodz, 1938)

*Whilst White indulges in an excess of
manœuvring, Black engineers an increasingly
direct attack and succeeds in ransacking the
ill-guarded fortress.*

1 Kt—KB3   Kt—KB3
2 P—B4   P—Q3
3 P—Q4   B—Kt5
Less ambitious is 3 .... B—B4.

4 Q—Kt3
Trying to interfere with Black's mobilisa-
tion which, after 4 Kt—B3, would be
effected without any trouble by 4 ....
QKt—Q2; 5 P—K4, P—K4; 6 B—K2,
B—K2, etc.

4 ......   B×Kt
The waiting move 4 .... Q—B1 (exchanging the Bishop only in case of 5 P—KR3) is
also sound.

5 KtP×B
If 5 Q×B, Kt—B3; 6 P—Q5, Kt—K4;
7 Q—Kt3, Q—B1; 8 Kt—B3, P—KKt3,
and Black's game is in a good way.
5 KP×B also is not without drawbacks.

5 ......   Q—B1
6 P—B4
If 6 B—R3, QKt—Q2, or 6 P—K4,
P—K4.

6 ......   P—KKt3
As 6 .... P—K4 is prevented and 6 ....
P—K3 is too unassuming, the text move
provides a sound alternative development
for the KB.

7 B—Kt2   P—B3
8 Kt—Q2   B—Kt2
9 Castles   Castles
10 Kt—B3
White is too cautious. He should have
decided on shouldering the responsibilities
attached to 10 P—K4.

10 ......   QKt—Q2
11 B—K3   P—K3
Instead of .... P—K4, the thrust ....
P—Q4 is now intended.

12 QR—B1   R—Q1
13 KR—Q1   Q—Kt1
Preventing 14 P—Q5.

14 B—Q2   Q—B2
And now B—R5 is to be stopped.

15 Q—R3   P—QR4
16 Q—R4   Kt—K5
17 B—K3   P—KB4
18 Q—B2   QKt—B3
19 Kt—K1
Too much manœuvring. The best chance
of relieving an awkward situation is
19 Kt—Q2.

19 ......   P—Q4
20 P—B5   Kt—Kt5
All Black's forces will now co-operate in the common cause.

21 Kt—Q3   Q—K2
22 P—KR3
Weakening, but after 22 Kt—K1, Q—R5; 23 Kt—B3, Q—R4, etc., or 22 B—B3, Kt×B; 23 P×Kt, P—KKt4, etc., White's position remains poor.

22 ......   Kt×B
23 P×Kt   Q—R5
Threat: 24 .... Q—Kt6.

24 R—B1   K—R1
A daylight robbery is being planned.

25 Q—Q1   P—KKt4
26 Q—K1   Q—R3
27 K—R2   P—Kt5
28 R—KR1   R—KKt1
29 K—Kt1
As White has nothing to fear from the closure 29 .... P—Kt6, and as neither 29 .... P×P; 30 R×P, etc., nor 29 .... Q—Kt3; 30 P×P, Q×P; 31 Q—R4 is dangerous, he seems to have achieved the consolidation of his position.

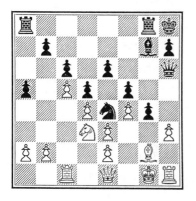

29 ......   B×P
This *irruptive sacrifice* gains an essential *tempo*, for Black thus succeeds in eliminating the three pieces which separated his Rook from the adverse King.

30 P×P
For if 30 P×B, P×P; 31 Q—B1, P×B, 32 R×Q, P×Q (Q) db ch; 33 K×Q, R—Kt5; 34 P—K3, QR—KKt1, winning with ease.

30 ......   B×P ch
31 K—B1   Q×R ch
This *Queen's sacrifice*, followed by a quiet move, is the most concise and elegant continuation.

32 B×Q   R×P
33 B—Kt2   Kt—Q7 ch
If 33 .... QR—KKt1; 34 Kt—K5, R×B; 35 Kt—B7 ch, K—Kt2; 36 K×R.

34 Q×Kt   B×Q
Resigns.

White   *Black*
TORRE   LASKER
(Moscow, 1925)

An unusual example of a swinging movement which, together with the combination preceding it, is of rare beauty.

1 P—Q4   Kt—KB3
2 Kt—KB3   P—K3
The policy of the *Neo-Indian Defence* is to realise the idea underlying the orthodox *Queen's Gambit*, but without .... P—Q4.

3 B—Kt5   P—B4
After the more passive 3 .... P—B3, the amusing sequel in a game Springe—Gebhard, *Munich*, 1927, was as follows:
4 P—K4, Q—Kt3; 5 QKt—Q2, Q×KtP (reprehensible greed); 6 B—Q3, P—Q4; 7 Castles, Q—Kt3; 8 Q—K2, P×P; 9 Kt×P, Kt×Kt; 10 Q×Kt, Kt—Q2; 11 P—B4, P—KR3; 12 Q×P ch, P×Q; 13 B—Kt6 mate.
Other unpretentious replies are 3 .... P—Q4 or 3 .... B—K2, etc. If 3 .... P—QKt3; 4 P—K4, but the following is playable: 3 .... P—KR3; 4 B—R4, P—QKt3; (for if now 5 P—K4, P—KKt4; 6 B—Kt3, Kt×P; winning a pawn).

4 P—K3
After the vigorous continuation 4 P—K4, a game H. Steiner—Opocensky, *Bad Striben*, 1930, went as follows: 4 .... Q—R4 ch; 5 QKt—Q2 (if 5 B—Q2, Q—Kt3, but best is 5 Q—Q2, Q—Kt3; 6 Kt—B3, etc.); 5 .... Kt×P; 6 P—QKt4, Q×KtP; 7 R—QKt1, Q—B6; 8 R—Kt3, Q—R4; 9 R—Kt5, Q—B6; drawn by repetition of moves, mutually compulsory.

4 ......   P × P

This decision might have been deferred, but could hardly be avoided. After 4 .... Kt—B3, the sensational continuation of a game Janowski—Sämisch, *Marienbad*, 1925, was: 5 QKt—Q2, P—QKt3; 6 P—B3, B—Kt2; 7 B—Q3, P × P; 8 KP × P, B—K2; 9 Kt—B4, Castles; 10 Q—K2, Q—B2; 11 P—KR4, P—KR3; 12 Q—Q2, Kt—KKt5; 13 B—B4, P—Q3; 14 Kt—K3, Kt × Kt; 15 Q × Kt, P—KR4; 16 R—R3, P—K4 (illusive emancipation; he should play 16 .... B—B3); 17 P × P, Kt × P; 18 Kt × Kt, P × Kt; 19 B × P, B—Q3; 20 Q—R6, resigns. An extraordinary finish.

5	P × P	B—K2
6	QKt—Q2	P—Q3
7	P—B3	QKt—Q2
8	B—Q3	P—QKt3
9	Kt—B4	B—Kt2
10	Q—K2	Q—B2
11	Castles KR	Castles KR
12	KR—K1	KR—K1
13	QR—Q1	Kt—B1
14	B—B1	Kt—Q4
15	Kt—Kt5	

Thinking only of his own attack, he allows his opponent to effect a serious counteraction on the opposite wing (P—QKt4—Kt5), which 15 Kt—R3, P—QR3; 16 Kt—B2, etc., could have prevented.

15	......	P—Kt4
16	Kt—R3	P—Kt5
17	P × P	Kt × P

Now White's QP is isolated.

18	Q—R5	B × Kt
19	B × B	Kt × B
20	R × Kt	Q—R4

He threatens to win a piece, and attacks the KR at the same time.

21 P—QKt4

An ingenious expedient.

21 ......   Q—KB4

The idea not to accept the doubtful gift, but to maintain the *horizontal pin*, is good, but its execution lacks precision. The *coup juste* is 21 .... Q—Q4, after which 22 R—KKt3, P—KR3; 23 B—B6, Kt—Kt3; 24 Q × Q, B × Q would cost White a Bishop, so that he would have to be content with 22 Q—Kt4, P—K4, and Black would obtain the initiative.

22	R—KKt3	P—KR3
23	Kt—B4	

Again the unexpected.

23 ......   Q—Q4

Simplification could be obtained by 23 .... P × B; 24 Kt × P, Q—Kt3; 25 Q × Q, Kt × Q; 26 Kt × B, KR—Kt1; 27 Kt—B5, R × P; 28 R × KtP, R × P, with approximately equal chances.

24 Kt—K3   Q—Kt4

A mistake! But after 24 .... Q × QP; 25 B × P, Kt—Kt3; 26 B—Kt5, threatening 27 R—R3, etc., White maintains an appreciable attack.

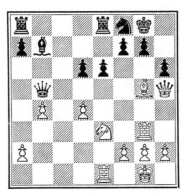

25 B—B6

Beautiful.

25	......	Q × Q
26	R × P ch	K—R1
27	R × P dis ch	

The swinging movement begins, and White recovers more than enough material.

27	......	K—Kt1
28	R—Kt7 ch	K—R1
29	R × B dis ch	K—Kt1
30	R—Kt7 ch	K—R1
31	R—Kt5 dis ch	K—R2
32	R × Q	K—Kt3

He recovers his piece, but remains three pawns to the bad. The rest requires no comment.

33	R—R3	K × B
34	R × P ch	K—Kt4
35	R—R3	KR—Kt1
36	R—Kt3 ch	K—B3
37	R—B3 ch	K—Kt3
38	P—QR3	P—R4
39	P × P	R × P
40	Kt—B4	R—Q4
41	R—B4	Kt—Q2
42	R × P ch	K—Kt4
43	P—Kt3	Resigns.

BLUMENFELD VARIATION

464

White	Black
TARRASCH	ALEKHINE

(Pistyan, 1922)

A fearless champion of new ideas in chess, Dr. Alekhine here introduces into master practice a counter-gambit (4 .... P—QKt4), and breaks down the defences of his dumbfounded opponent.

1 P—Q4	Kt—KB3
2 Kt—KB3	P—K3
3 P—B4	P—B4

The spirit of the initiative.

4 P—Q5
After 4 Kt—B3, P×P; 5 Kt×P, B—Kt5, Black has freed his game.

| 4 ...... | P—QKt4 |

The *Blumenfeld Counter Gambit*. Although White's defence has been strengthened since this game was played, the result of this gambit is always most interesting.

5 P×KP
Better than the text move, which reinforces Black's centre, or than 5 P—K3, is the pin by 5 B—Kt5, as illustrated by a game Grünfeld—Bogoljubow, *Vienna*, 1922: 5 .... P—KR3 (much preferable is 5 .... P×P; 6 P×QP, and only now 6 .... P—KR3); 6 B×Kt, Q×B; 7 Kt—B3, P—Kt5; 8 Kt—QKt5, Kt—R3; 9 P—K4, Q×P (he is too greedy); 10 B—Q3, Q—B3; 11 P—K5, Q—Q1; 12 P×P, QP×P; 13 B—K4, Q×Q ch; 14 R×Q, R—QKt1; 15 B—B6 ch, K—K2; 16 Kt×P, P—Kt4; 17 B—Kt5, B—KKt2; 18 Kt—B6 ch, K—B1; 19 R—Q8 mate.

| 5 ...... | BP×P |
| 6 P×P | P—Q4 |

Black's very strong centre more than compensates him for the lost pawn.

7 P—K3
Or 7 QKt—Q2, B—Q3; 8 P—QKt3, Q—R4, etc., or 7 P—KKt3, Q—R4 ch, and Black stands very well.

7	B—Q3
8 Kt—B3	Castles
9 B—K2	B—Kt2
10 P—QKt3	

He must develop his QB somehow.

10	QKt—Q2
11 B—Kt2	Q—K2
12 Castles	QR—Q1
13 Q—B2	P—K4

Beginning of a "war of movement."

14 KR—K1	P—K5
15 Kt—Q2	Kt—K4
16 Kt—Q1	Kt (B3)—Kt5

His target appears to be White's KR7.

17 B×Kt (Kt4)
After 17 P—KR3, a development similar to that in the text would follow by 17 .... Kt—R3, with .... Kt—B4, etc.

| 17 ...... | Kt×B |
| 18 Kt—B1 | Q—Kt4 |

Disclosing his real target: KKt7.

19 P—KR3	Kt—R3
20 K—R1	Kt—B4
21 Kt—R2	P—Q5

The beginning of the end. Premature would be 21 .... Kt—Kt6 ch.

22 B—B1
For if 22 P×P, P—K6; 23 R—KKt1, Kt—Kt6 ch; 24 P×Kt, Q×P; 25 Kt—KB3, B×Kt, and wins.

| 22 ...... | P—Q6 |

Crossing the line.

| 23 Q—B4 ch | K—R1 |
| 24 B—Kt2 | Kt—Kt6 ch |

The accumulated energy is now discharged.

25 K—Kt1
Clearly not 25 P×Kt, Q×KtP, etc.

25	B—Q4
26 Q—R4	Kt—K7 ch
27 K—R1	R—B2
28 Q—R6	P—R4
29 P—Kt6	Kt—Kt6 ch
30 K—Kt1	P×P
31 Q×KtP	P—Q7

The harvest.

32 R—KB1	Kt×R
33 Kt×Kt	B—K3
34 K—R1	

Allowing a startling finish. But there is no saving the game. If, e.g., 34 Q—B6, R—B6; 35 Q×KP, B—Q4; 36 Q—Q3, Q×P ch, with mate in four to follow.

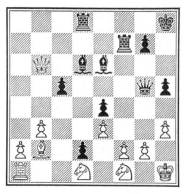

34 ......   B × RP

Carrying the fortress by storm.

35 P × B	R—B6
36 Kt—Kt3	P—R5
37 B—B6	Q × B
38 Kt × P	R × P ch
Resigns	

(39 K—Kt2, Q—B6 ch, or 39 K—Kt1, B—R7 ch.)

NIMZOWITSCH VARIATION

465

| *White* | *Black* |
| VIDMAR | NIMZOWITSCH |

(New York, 1927)

Owing to White's rather passive play (12 B—K1, and again, 23 B—K1), Black skilfully seizes the initiative on the semi-open K file, and shows the utmost vitality on the long white diagonal. Modern strategy at its best.

1 P—Q4	Kt—KB3
2 Kt—KB3	P—K3
3 P—B4	B—Kt5 ch

Whether this relieving check is credited to Bogoljubow—or at a far earlier date—to Buckle, it typifies the modern tendency to proceed with the development of the forces, without hastening to occupy the centre by .... P—Q4.

4 B—Q2

More artificial would be 4 QKt—Q2, and more superficial 4 Kt—B3.

4 ......   Q—K2

A very rational post for the Queen. A more conventional continuation for both sides, 4 .... B × B ch; 5 Q × B (better than 5 QKt × B); 5 .... P—QKt3; 6 P—KKt3, B—Kt2; 7 B—Kt2, leads to a well-known variation of *Queen's Indian Defence* proper, a remarkable affinity between two types of the "Indian complex."

5 Kt—B3

Unnecessarily interrupting the contact between the two contending Bishops, the text move helps Black's development. White evidently cannot play 5 B × B, Q × B ch, winning a pawn; a more scientific line of play is 5 P—KKt3. A continuation which, at the cost of a *tempo*, forces an immediate settlement is 5 P—QR3, B × B ch; 6 Q × B, followed by Kt—B3.

A nonchalant move is 5 P—K3, as played in a game Marshall—Petrov, *Hamburg*, 1930: 5 .... Castles; 6 B—Q3, P—Q4; 7 Castles, QKt—Q2; 8 Kt—B3, B × Kt; 9 B × B, P—QKt3; 10 R—B1, B—Kt2; 11 P × P, P × P; 12 Q—Kt3, P—B4 (better is 12 .... Kt—K5); 13 P × P, Kt × P; 14 B × Kt, P × B (14 .... Q × B; 15 R × Kt); 15 Q—Kt4, K—R1 (essential is 15 .... KR—K1); 16 R × Kt, resigns (16 .... P × R; 17 Q—KR4). A genuine Marshall game.

| 5 ...... | Castles |
| 6 P—K3 | P—Q3 |

Thanks to White's 5th move, Black can turn his attention to the centre and prepare .... P—K4. Less pertinent would be 6 .... P—QKt3; 7 B—Q3, B—Kt2; 8 Castles, KB × Kt; 9 B × B, Kt—K5; 10 B × Kt, B × B; 11 Kt—Q2, B—Kt2; 12 P—K4, and the white Bishop's diagonal is far more promising than its counterpart.

Poor strategy would be 6 .... B × Kt; 7 B × B, Kt—K5; 8 Q—B2, Kt × B; 9 Q × Kt, and White has the slightly better game.

7 B—K2

If 7 B—Q3, P—K4.

7 ......   P—QKt3

Strategy as well as psychology! Having restrained the white KB from controlling the strategic point K4, Black prepares to exercise that control himself.

8 Castles	B—Kt2
9 Q—B2	QKt—Q2
10 QR—Q1	

Intending, eventually, 11 Kt—Kt1, e.g. 11 .... B—K5; 12 B—Q3, or 11 .... B × B; 12 QKt × B, and White obtains full command of K4. Black's next move thwarts this plan.

| 10 ...... | B×QKt |
| 11 B×B | Kt—K5 |

The disputed square is conquered.

12 B—K1

A passive manœuvre, instigated by White's desire to preserve his two Bishops. Better at once 12 Kt—Q2, or, with some risk, 12 P—Q5.

| 12 ...... | P—KB4 |

A "posthumous" *Dutch Defence*, so to speak.

| 13 Q—Kt3 | P—B4 |

"Stopping" the centre.

| 14 Kt—Q2 | Kt×Kt |
| 15 R×Kt | P—K4 |

The typical advance. Black has the better game.

16 P×KP

Playing for the asset of the open Q file.

| 16 ...... | P×P |
| 17 P—B3 | |

An artificial plan must serve, when a more natural one, such as 17 P—B4, is fraught with danger.

| 17 ...... | P—KKt4 |

Preventing 18 B—R4, which could be played after 17 .... Kt—B3, or 17 .... QR—K1.

| 18 B—B2 | Kt—B3 |
| 19 KR—Q1 | QR—K1 |

A profound idea: Black rightly estimates that the adverse artillery on the open Q file is less dangerous than it looks, and, in consequence, he avoids exchanges and occupies a file which is *potentially open*.

| 20 Q—R4 | B—R1 |

Parrying the double threat 21 Q×P or 21 R—Q7, which would win a piece for the exchange.

21 R—Q6

Intending ultimately B—K1 and B—B3, and if possible even R (Q1)—Q2 and Q—Q1. But the manœuvre takes too much time.

| 21 ...... | Q—KKt2 |

Hoping to open the KKt file by 22 .... P—Kt5.

22 B—B1

In order to play 23 P—B4, in reply to 22 .... P—Kt5. But now Black opens a breach in another manner.

| 22 ...... | P—K5 |

Breaking the front.

23 B—K1

Not 23 P—B4, P×P; 24 P×P, P—K6, with a fork by .... P—K7.

| 23 ...... | P×P |
| 24 B—B3 | |

Threatening 25 B×Kt, R×B; 26 R×R, and wins.

| 24 ...... | Q—K2 |

Fatal would be 24 .... R×P; 25 R×Kt, R×R; 26 R—Q8 ch.

25 R (Q6)—Q3

Not 25 B×Kt, Q×P ch; 26 K—R1, P×P ch; 27 B×P, Q—K8 ch, with mate to follow, nor 25 R (Q1)—Q3, P×P; 26 B×P, B×B; 27 B×Kt, Q—K5; 28 Q—B2, B—R6, etc.

25	P×P
26 B×P	B×B
27 B×Kt	

After 27 K×B, Q—K5 ch, matters would run smoothly for Black.

| 27 ...... | Q—K5 |

Creating an expressive ending.

| 28 R (Q1)—Q2 | B—R6 |

Decisive. (But not 28 .... R×B; 29 R×B, Q×R; 30 Q×R ch, and White escapes.)

| 29 B—B3 | Q—Kt5 ch |

And Black mates in two.
(A game typical of the modern style.)

466

| *White* | *Black* |
| ENGLISCH | BLACKBURNE |

(London, 1883)

A moment of inattention in the opening, and Black loses a pawn. But the magnificent fight which he makes of it subsequently more than redeems his delinquency.

1 P—Q4	P—K3
2 P—QB4	Kt—KB3
3 Kt—QB3	B—Kt5

Thus, then, we have—with a slight inversion of moves—an ultra-modern line of play, the famous and frequently used *Nimzowitsch Variation*, applied before its sponsor was born.

Another example, also with an inversion of moves, is a game Steinitz—Englisch, *Vienna*, 1882: 1 P—Q4, P—K3; 2 P—QB4, B—Kt5 ch; 3 Kt—B3, Kt—KB3, etc.

4 B—Q2
Strengthening his QB3, and thus assuming, for the time being, a defensive rôle.

| 4 ...... | Castles |
| 5 Kt—B3 | P—QKt3 |

Fighting at long range—quite in the modern style—for the strategic square at his K5. A trenchant line of play, seeking a hand-to-hand fight in the centre, is 5 .... P—Q4; 6 P—K3, P—B4, and Black has sound prospects of speedily equalising the game.

| 6 P—K3 | B—Kt2 |

An important alternative is 6 .... B×Kt; 7 B×B, Kt—K5, and Black will be able, when necessary, to eliminate the adverse QB.

7 B—K2
More energetic is 7 B—Q3, for if in that case 7 .... KB×Kt; 8 B×B, Kt—K5, there follows 9 B×Kt, B×B; 10 Kt—Q2, B—Kt2 (10 .... B×P; 11 R—KKt1); 11 Q—Kt4, and White's QB has survived and becomes his principal weapon of attack.

| 7 ...... | P—Q4 |

More in keeping with the general scheme is the formation of a restricted centre 7 .... P—Q3, or, as mentioned before, 7 .... KB×Kt; 8 B×B, Kt—K5, etc.

| 8 Castles | QKt—Q2 |

A tactical inadvertence, which costs a pawn. Playable is 8 .... P×P or, if it is desired to keep up, or even to increase, the tension of the centre pawns, 8 .... P—B4.

9 Kt×P
Cruel! If now 9 .... P×Kt; 10 B×B, and if 9 .... B×B; 10 Kt×Kt ch, Kt×Kt; 11 Kt×B, etc., a good illustration of the danger of leaving pieces unguarded.

| 9 ...... | Kt×Kt |
| 10 P×Kt | B—Q3 |

If 10 .... B×B; 11 P×P, B×P; 12 P×B. Now Black has at least preserved his KB.

11 P×P	P×P
12 Kt—K1	Kt—B3
13 P—B3	

A simple plan is 13 B—KB3.

| 13 ...... | Kt—Kt5 |

Very pretty. (14 P×Kt, Q—R5, etc.)

14 P—B4	Kt—B3
15 Kt—Q3	Kt—K5
16 B—KB3	Q—K1

Black keeps up an active policy.

| 17 B—K1 | Q—Kt3 |
| 18 Kt—B2 | QR—Q1 |

This occupation of a potential open file contains the astute threat 19 .... P—B4.

19 Kt×Kt	B×Kt
20 B×B	Q×B
21 Q—B3	Q×Q
22 R×Q	P—B4

A sort of minority attack, for White sees himself beset in the centre where he has an extra pawn.

23 B—B3
Or 23 P×P, B×QBP; 24 B—B2, R—Q7, etc.; or 23 R—Q1, P×P; 24 R×P, B—B4; 25 R×R, R×R, etc.; or 23 P—KKt3, P—K4, etc. It is most remarkable that White's well-established points Q4, K3, KB4 should all three constitute weaknesses. Relatively best would be 23 B—Kt3.

| 23 ...... | P×P |
| 24 B×P | B×P |

Without succeeding in recovering the pawn, this pretty move brings about favourable exchanges.

25 R×B	R×R
26 B×QKtP	P×B
27 P×R	R—Q7

The seventh rank.

28 P—QKt3	K—B2
29 P—QR3	K—B3
30 P—QKt4	P—QKt4
31 R—K1	

Or 31 P—QR4, P×P; 32 R×P, R—Kt7.

31	R—Q6
32 R—K5	R×P
33 R×P	R—R7
34 P—R3	R—Kt7
35 K—R2	R—Kt6

"No exit."

36 P—R4	P—Kt3
37 P—Kt3	R—Kt7 ch
38 K—R3	P—R4

Preparing an artistic finish.

39 R—Kt7	K—B4
40 R—B7 ch	K—K5
41 R—B6	K—B6
42 R×KP	R—Kt8

Draw.

(43 K—R2, R—Kt7 ch; 44 K—Kt1, R—Kt8 ch.)

In spite of material advantages, the imprisoned King must pay the ransom of a draw.

467

White	Black
P. JOHNER	NIMZOWITSCH

(Dresden, 1926)

Black's scientific attack is mainly carried out on the KKt file. The feature of the game is the way in which this attack expands to the adjacent files with far-reaching results, thanks to the winner's deep conceptions.

1 P—Q4	Kt—KB3
2 P—QB4	P—K3
3 Kt—QB3	B—Kt5
4 P—K3	Castles

A neutral development. After 4 .... B×Kt ch, the disruption of White's pawn formation has its compensation in the strengthening of his centre, especially the key point Q4.

5 B—Q3

The natural development.

5	P—B4

Or 5 .... P—Q4; 6 Kt—K2.

6 Kt—B3

He continues to neglect the point QB3, whilst he could quite comfortably have played 6 Kt—K2.

6	Kt—B3
7 Castles	B×Kt

Black decides to make the weakening of the white pawn formation the theme of the contest.

8 P×B	P—Q3

Guarding the QBP, which in turn blockades the doubled pawn, and preparing for .... P—K4.

9 Kt—Q2	P—QKt3
10 Kt—Kt3	

He again protects the point Q4 to make 11 P—K4 possible. The KKt has now moved to QKt3 to prevent the stratagem .... B—R3, followed by .... P—QKt4 and .... R—QB1.

10	P—K4
11 P—B4	

After 11 P—Q5, P—K5; 12 P×Kt (12 B—K2, Kt—K4); 12 .... P×B; 13 Q×P, Q—B2, Black's position is preferable.

11	P—K5
12 B—K2	Q—Q2

Stopping 13 P—Kt4

13 P—KR3	Kt—K2
14 Q—K1	P—KR4

With a view to future operations, he decides definitely to prevent P—KKt4, which allows him to use his KB4 as a lever.

15 B—Q2

Disadvantageous would be 15 Q—R4, Kt—B4; 16 Q—Kt5, Kt—R2; 17 Q×P, Kt—Kt6, etc.

15	Q—B4

This manœuvre, by which the Queen is intended to move to KR2 and to direct operations from there, is both profound and original.

16 K—R2	Q—R2
17 P—QR4	Kt—B4

Threat: 18 .... Kt—Kt5 ch; 19 P×Kt, P×P dis ch; 20 K—Kt1, P—Kt6, etc.

18 P—Kt3	P—R4

Eliminating possible complications on the Q side.

19 R—KKt1	Kt—R3
20 B—KB1	

Not 20 Q—B2, Kt—Kt5 ch, etc.

20	B—Q2
21 B—B1	

The Bishop vacates Q2 to let the Knight into play, and the second rank to allow the Rook to strengthen it by R—R2.

21	QR—B1
22 P—Q5	K—R1
23 Kt—Q2	R—KKt1
24 B—KKt2	P—KKt4

Black now resorts to direct action.

25 Kt—B1

Better is 25 R—B1.

25	R—Kt2
26 R—R2	Kt—B4

White still cannot play 27 R—KB2, on account of 27 .... Kt—Kt5 ch.

27 B—R1	QR—KKt1
28 Q—Q1	P×P
29 KP×P	B—B1

Threatening 30 .... B—R3.

| 30 Q—Kt3 | B—R3 |
| 31 R—K2 | |

Having more or less guarded the vulnerable points (especially KKt3 and QB4), White in turn aims at Black's isolated KP.

| 31 ...... | Kt—R5 |

Triumphant tactics. The threat is 32 .... Kt—B6 ch; 33 B×Kt, P×B, forcing the entry of the Queen into the enemy camp.

32 R—K3

An amusing variation would be 32 Kt—Q2, B—B1; 33 Kt×P, Q—B4; 34 Kt—B2, Q×P ch; 35 Kt×Q, Kt—Kt5 mate.

| 32 ...... | B—B1 |
| 33 Q—B2 | B×P |

Not so much a sacrifice (if 34 K×B, Q—B4 ch, etc., with a speedy win) as a means of exchanging his KP against White's valuable KRP. Far less effective would be 33 .... B—B4, and if 33 .... Q—B4; 34 B—KKt2.

34 B×P	B—B4
35 B×B	Kt×B
36 R—K2	P—R5

Carefully prepared since Black's 16th move (.... Q—R2), this advance puts the finishing touch to Black's strategy.

37 R (Kt1)—Kt2	P×P db ch
38 K—Kt1	Q—R6
39 Kt—K3	Kt—R5

Threat: 40 .... Kt—B6 ch.

| 40 K—B1 | R—K1 |

The final stroke, threatening 41 .... Kt×R; 42 R×Kt, Q—R8 ch; 43 K—K2, Q×R ch.

Resigns.

468

| White | Black |
| FLOHR | LISSITZIN |

(Moscow, 1935)

White's scientifically prepared action culminates in a magnificent sacrifice of a Rook. A good illustration of the fact that the most profound strategic ideas lead quite naturally to concrete and conclusive measures.

1 P—Q4	Kt—KB3
2 P—QB4	P—K3
3 Kt—QB3	B—Kt5
4 P—K3	Castles
5 Kt—K2	

White renounces the most natural move, 5 B—Q3, in order to avoid the doubling of his QBP.

| 5 ...... | P—Q4 |

Straightforward strategy. An idea is 5 .... R—K1, intending to reply to 6 P—QR3 by 6 .... B—B1.

| 6 P—QR3 | B—K2 |

The simpler continuation 6 .... B×Kt ch; 7 Kt×B, P×P; 8 B×P, P—QR3; 9 P—QKt4, QKt—Q2, etc., tends to equalise the game.

| 7 P×P | P×P |
| 8 Kt—Kt3 | P—B4 |

It would be more solid to reserve this pawn for defensive purposes (.... P—QB3), and to play 8 .... R—K1.

| 9 B—Q3 | Kt—B3 |
| 10 Castles | |

If 10 .... P×P; 11 P×P, Kt×P; 12 B×P ch, K×B; 13 Q×Kt, B—K3; 14 QKt—K2, etc., in White's favour.

| 10 ...... | P—KKt3 |

There is no threat yet of 11 .... P×P; 12 P×P, Kt×P, because of 13 B×P ch. Black wishes, by his text move, to limit once and for all the scope of the adverse KKt, but the long black diagonal is weakened thereby.

11 P×P

Playing without delay for an *extended fianchetto.*

11	B×P
12 P—Kt4	B—Q3
13 P—Kt5	

Not yet 13 B—Kt2, P—Q5.

| 13 ...... | Kt—K4 |
| 14 B—K2 | QKt—Kt5 |

Instead of attacking with poorly co-ordinated forces, he would have done better

to regroup them by 14 .... R—K1, with
.... B—B1 and .... B—Kt2.

15 B—Kt2   P—KR4
16 P—R3   P—R5

Black tries to avoid loss of territory, but
his forces lose their cohesion. Bad would
be 16 .... Kt×KP; 17 P×Kt, B×Kt;
18 Q—Q4, Kt—Q2; 19 Q×QP, and White
dominates the situation.

17 P×Kt   P×Kt
18 Q—Q4

White's threats prevail. At the moment
19 Kt×P or 19 P—Kt5 are on the *tapis*.

18 ......   Kt—Q2
19 P—Kt5   P×P ch

Not 19 .... Q×P; 20 Kt—K4, Q—K4;
21 Kt×B, etc., nor 19 .... B—K4;
20 Q—KR4, R—K1; 21 P—B4, B—Kt2;
22 R—B3, followed by R×P

20 R×P   B—K4
21 Q—KR4

Here again 21 Q×QP, Q×P would help
Black's counter-attack.

21 ......   Kt—Kt3
22 P—Kt3

A shrewd plan (23 R—R2).

22 ......   P—B4

If 22 .... Q—B2; 23 R—R2, R—K1
(or 23 .... P—B4; 24 Kt×P, Kt×Kt;
25 B×B, and wins); 24 Kt×P, Kt×Kt;
25 Q—R8 ch, B×Q; 26 R×B mate.

23 P×P e.p.   B×BP
24 Q—R6   B—Kt2

If 24 .... B×Kt; 25 Q×P ch, and if
24 .... B—B4; 25 R×B, and, finally, if
24 .... Q—K1; 25 R×B, R×R; 26 Kt—K4,
Q×Kt; 27 B×R, and wins.

25 Q×P   R×R

26 Kt—K4

White even lets a Rook go in order to
gain a *tempo*—an example of the *passive
sacrifice* which consists in non-recapture.

26 ......   R—B2

This attempt to hold on to his gain only
hastens the *débâcle*, which could have been
deferred by 26 .... Q—K2; 27 Kt×R,
Q—KB2; 28 Q—Kt5, etc.

27 Kt—Kt5   R—B3

If 27 .... Q—K1; 28 Q—R7 ch, K—B1;
29 B×B ch, R×B (or 29 .... K—K2;
30 B—B6 ch); 30 R—B1 ch, K—K2;
31 Q×R ch, and wins.

28 B×R   Q×B
29 Q—R7 ch   K—B1
30 R—KB1   Q×R ch
31 B×Q   B—Q2
32 Q—Kt6   B—K1
33 Q—B5 ch   K—Kt1
34 B—R3   Resigns

(In view of the threat 35 Q—R7 ch,
K—B1; 36 Kt—K6 ch, winning a piece.)

469

White	Black
SÄMISCH	ENGELS

(Brünn, 1928)

In the following beautiful game, the
positional foundation *of the contest leads to
a scintillating finish, quite in the best Morphy
style.*

1 P—Q4   Kt—KB3
2 P—QB4   P—K3
3 Kt—QB3   B—Kt5
4 P—QR3

Trying out a vigorous continuation which
stood Sämisch in good stead on subsequent
occasions, but which must be credited to
Norman (*Hastings*, 1925).

4 ......   B×Kt ch
5 P×B   P—Q3

Intending to exploit the weakness of the
doubled pawn.

Complications result from 5 .... P—QKt3;
6 P—B3, P—Q4, as also from 5 .... P—Q4
at once (6 P—B3, P—QKt3). A constructive scheme is 5 .... Kt—K5; 6 Q—B2,
P—KB4. If 5 .... Castles; 6 Q—B2, intending P—K4.

6 Q—B2
Another method of preparing P—K4 is
6 P—B3.

6 ......   Q—K2
Or at once 6 .... P—K4; 7 P—K4,
Castles; 8 B—Q3, etc.

7 P—K4   P—K4
Neutralising each other's efforts in the
centre.

8 P—B3   Castles
9 B—Q3   Kt—B3
10 Kt—K2
Harmonious development, which preserves the flexibility of the central formation,
instead of 10 P—Q5, Kt—Q1, etc.

10 ......   Kt—K1
Too passive. Better is 10 .... Kt—Q2,
where the Knight continues to be useful.

11 Castles   P—QKt3
Intending .... Kt—R4, and eventually
.... B—R3, besieging the weak point in
White's formation, namely his pawn at QB4.

12 B—K3   Kt—R4
13 Kt—Kt3   B—K3
If 13 .... B—R3; 14 P—B5, B×B;
15 P×QP, B×Q; 16 P×Q, followed by
P×R, and White wins the exchange.

14 Q—K2   P—KB3
15 P—B4   P×BP
16 R×P   Q—B2
17 P—Q5
Black's partial success in having provoked
this advance is offset by his badly-placed
KKt. Nor is the centre hermetically sealed.
If 17 P—B5, QP×P; 18 P×P, B—B5, and
Black is able to effect exchanges.

17 ......   B—Q2
18 QR—KB1   Kt—Kt2
19 Kt—B5   Kt—B4
After 19 .... B×Kt; 20 R×B, Kt—B4;
21 B×Kt, KtP×B; 22 P—K5, QP×P;
23 R×KP, Black's position is still precarious.

20 B×Kt   KtP×B
After 20 .... QP×B the continuation in
the text would be still more decisive.

21 P—K5
A fine break-through of a type which is
found in several Morphy games.

21 ......   QP×P
Or 21 .... BP×P; 22 Kt—R6 ch, or
21 .... B×Kt; 22 B×B.

Position after 20 .... KtP×B

22 R—R4
Terrible threats such as 23 Kt—K7 ch or
23 R×P are in the air.

22 ......   P—KR3
23 R×P
Fall of the last defences.

23 ......   Kt—Q3
The Rook can be taken neither instead
of the text move nor after 23 .... B×Kt;
24 B×B, etc.

24 Kt—K7 ch!
The coping stone.

24 ......   Q×Kt
25 R—R8 ch   Resigns
(For there is a mate in three by 25 ....
K×R; 26 Q—R5 ch, K—Kt1; 27 Q—R7
ch, K—B2; 28 B—Kt6 mate; or 25 ....
K—B2; 26 B—Kt6 ch, K×B; 27 Q—R5
mate.)

470

White	Black
WINTER	SULTAN KHAN

(Hastings, 1933)

*After the exchange of Queens, Black seems
to be out of difficulty, whereas his troubles
only really begin. Ingenious counter-attacks
by the second player are countered by equally
ingenious measures, which lead to a winning
grand offensive by White.*

1 P—Q4	Kt—KB3
2 P—QB4	P—K3
3 Kt—QB3	B—Kt5
4 P—QR3	B×Kt ch
5 P×B	P—B4
6 P—B3	

In preparation for 7 P—K4. Once White's central structure is built up and secured, the KBP will, at an opportune moment, be able to continue its journey and to initiate a direct attack by P—KB4, etc. That is the strategic meaning of the *Sämisch Variation*.

If 6 Q—B2, Kt—B3; if 6 P—K3, Kt—K5; and if 6 Kt—B3, Q—R4.

6	Kt—B3

Inconsistent, for in order to prevent 7 P—K4, and at the same time to continue the attack on the hostile centre, 6 .... P—Q4 is indicated.

7 P—K4	P—Q3

If 7 .... Q—R4; 8 B—Q2.

8 B—K3
White seeks a harmonious grouping of his forces in preference to simplification by 8 P×P.

8	Q—R4
9 Q—Q2	P—K4
10 P—Q5	Kt—K2
11 B—Q3	Kt—Kt3
12 Kt—K2	Q—R5

The object of the text move is eventually to continue either with .... P—QKt3 and .... B—R3 or with .... P—QR3 and .... P—QKt4, whilst preventing 13 P—QR4 and immobilising the adverse KB.

13 Kt—Kt3
If 13 P—B4, Kt—Kt5, etc. Too slow would be the preparatory 13 P—R3.

13	P—KR4

As he cannot very well castle on either side (on the Q side after 13 .... B—Q2), he indulges in enfeebling demonstrations. Better would be 13 .... P—Kt3.

14 Q—Kt2
A skilful manœuvre. Perceiving that Black's weaknesses are of a permanent character, White resolutely plays for wholesale liquidation.

14	R—QKt1

In order to mobilise the QB. If 14 .... P—R5; 15 Kt—B5.

15 Q—Kt5 ch	Q×Q

He has to undouble his adversary's pawns,

for if 15 .... B—Q2; 16 Q×Q, B×Q; 17 Kt—B5.

16 P×Q	P—R5
17 Kt—K2	B—Q2
18 Kt—R4	K—K2
19 K—B2	Kt—R4
20 P—Kt3	

Played principally with a view to advancing the KBP, which will have very considerable dynamic effect.

20	R—R2
21 P—KB4	KP×P

If at once 21 .... B—Kt5; 22 P—B5, whereas now Black has freed the square K4.

22 P×BP	B—Kt5

An indirect attack on the KBP.

23 P—K5
Instead of the unimposing continuation 23 P—B5, Kt—K4, the thrust in the text livens up the game.

23	B×Kt
24 B×Kt	P×B
25 K×B	R—KB1

Seeking salvation in a counter-attack, according to a well-known formula.

26 QR—KB1	R—B4
27 KR—Kt1	P×P

If 27 .... R—R3; 28 R—Kt5.

28 B×P ch	K—Q2
29 P×P	R×P ch
30 K—Q3	R×P ch
31 K—B4	R—B4
32 R—Q1 ch	K—B2
33 KR—K1	

A telling move. White is not anxious to regain his pawn at once by 33 R×P, but, instead, he prepares a ruthless attack.

33	R—B2

Clearly not 33 .... P—Kt3; 34 R—K7 ch, K—B1; 35 R—K8 ch, K—B2; 36 B—Q6 ch, etc.

34 B×P	R—R1

If 34 .... P—Kt3; 35 R—K6.

35 R—K5	K—B1

Parrying the threat 36 R—B5 mate.

36 P—Kt6
Renewing the mating threat, whilst realising that the imprisonment of the Bishop is only temporary.

36	R—B3

Or 36 .... R—B5 ch; 37 K—Kt3,

R—B4; 38 R—K7, R—B4; 39 R (Q1)—Q7, which is decisive.

37 R—B5 ch	R—B3
38 R×R ch	P×R
39 P—R5	K—Kt2
40 R—Q7 ch	K—R3
41 B—Kt8	

The point! The Bishop is freed and the value of the QKtP increased.

41	K×P
42 K—B5	K—R5
43 B—K5	

The most precise move.

43	R—K1
44 R—R7 ch	K—Kt6
45 B—B7	Kt—B3
46 P—Kt7	K—B7
47 K×P	

Avoiding the last shoal. If 47 P—Kt8 (Q), Kt—Q2 ch; etc.

| 47 ...... | R—K3 ch |
| 48 B—Q6 | Resigns. |

471

| *White* | *Black* |
| BOGOLJUBOW | MONTICELLI |

(San Remo, 1930)

Although this game is interesting and well-fought throughout, its outstanding feature is a finish of quite exceptional liveliness, where three consecutive sacrifices by Black lead to a problem-like mate.

1 P—Q4	Kt—KB3
2 P—QB4	P—K3
3 Kt—QB3	B—Kt5
4 Kt—B3	

A nonchalant continuation, aiming at development pure and simple, without even reserving, as does 4 P—K3, the option of the KKt's alternative development at K2.

4	P—QKt3
5 B—Kt5	B×Kt ch
6 P×B	B—Kt2
7 P—K3	P—Q3

The *restricted centre*. With fine judgment Black refrains from castling in a hurried and conventional manner, which would favour White's attacking chances, as all his forces

are aimed at the King's wing. Unpinning by 7 .... Q—B1; is rather artificial, and its consequences are illustrated in a picturesque game Dyckhoff–Priwonitz (played by correspondence in 1929):

8 B×Kt, P×B; 9 Kt—R4, K—K2; 10 B—Q3, Q—Kt1 (threat: 11 .... Q—Kt4); 11 P—B4, P—KR4; 12 Q—K2, Q—Kt5; 13 Q—KB2, Kt—B3 (13 .... P—Q3, followed by .... Kt—Q2 tends to consolidation); 14 P—Q5 (not at once 14 Kt—Kt6 ch, P×Kt; 15 P—KR3, Kt—Kt5), resigns, for after 14 .... P×P; 15 P×P, Kt—R4; 16 Kt—Kt6 ch, P×Kt; 17 P—KR3, the black Queen is "on the spot."

| 8 B—Q3 | QKt—Q2 |
| 9 Castles | Q—K2 |

The thrust .... P—K4 is prepared, but in addition Black can castle on the Q side.

10 Kt—Q2

Preparing P—K4, which it would, however, have been better to have played at once e.g. 10 P—K4, P—KR3; 11 B×Kt, Q×B; 12 Q—Q2, etc., with an even game.

10 ......   P—KR3

Not at this stage, and still less on the next move, 10 .... Castles KR; because of 11 P—B4, and then P—K4, assuming the offensive.

| 11 B—R4 | P—KKt4 |
| 12 B—Kt3 | Castles QR |

A fighting scheme.

| 13 P—QR4 | P—QR4 |

Evidently necessary, in order to prevent 14 P—R5.

| 14 R—Kt1 | QR—Kt1 |
| 15 P—B3 | |

If 15 Kt—Kt3 (intending 16 P—B5), Black plays 15 .... B—B3, with the counter-threat .... B×RP.

15	P—R4
16 P—K4	P—R5
17 B—K1	

After 17 B—KB2, P—Kt5, followed by .... P—Kt6, would effect a break-through, whilst if, after the text move, 17 .... P—Kt5; 18 P—B4, P—Kt6; 19 P—R3.

| 17 ...... | P—K4 |
| 18 P—R3 | |

He hopes to prevent the counter-advance of the KKtP once and for all. But, instead of this plethora of preventive measures, he should hasten to seek chances in the advance 18 P—B5, QP×P; 19 P—Q5, etc.

| 18 ...... | Kt—R4 |
| 19 P—B5 | |

The chances afforded by this pawn sacrifice are considerable.

19	QP × P
20 P—Q5	Kt—B5
21 Kt—B4	

Threatening 22 P—Q6, P × P; 23 Kt × KtP ch.

| 21 ...... | R—R3 |

Preparing a *counter-sacrifice* of the exchange which will break down White's impetus.

22 R—B2

For if 22 P—Q6, R × P; 23 Kt × R ch, Q × Kt, and Black has the attack and two pawns for the exchange.

| 22 ...... | P—B4 |

Threatening to swamp the enemy sector by 23 .... P—Kt5, which forces White to join issue in the centre.

23 P—Q6	R × P
24 Kt × R ch	Q × Kt
25 B—B4	R—B1
26 P × P	R × P
27 R—Q2	

White overrates the results of this occupation of the open Q file. It would be wiser to exchange Queens.

| 27 ...... | Q—K2 |
| 28 Q—Kt3 | |

Leading to a direct threat after 29 QR—Q1 or 29 B—Kt5, but 28 B—Kt5 at once would be more effective.

| 28 ...... | R—B1 |

In order to reply to the scheme indicated above by 29 .... Kt—B3. White must now change his tactics and assume the defensive.

29 B—Q3   P—K5

He perseveres. If 29 .... Kt × B; 30 R × Kt, P—K5; 31 P × P, and neither 31 .... B × P; 32 R—K3, nor 31 .... Q × P; 32 Q—B2 would have the desired effect.

30 B × KP	B × B
31 P × B	Q × P
32 Q—B2	

The strongest resistance would result from 32 Q—Kt5.

| 32 ...... | Q—B3 |
| 33 P—B4 | |

In order to prevent *inter alia* 33 .... P—B5, followed by .... Kt—Q6.

| 33 ...... | P—Kt5 |

The break-through.

34 B × KRP

If 34 P × P, Kt—K4, stopping the breach.

| 34 ...... | P × P |
| 35 P—Kt3 | Kt—K4 |

A brilliant conception.

36 R—Kt3

If 36 P × Kt, Kt—B6 ch, winning. A little better would be 36 R—B2.

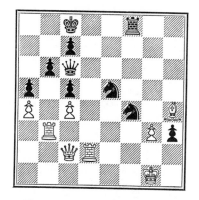

| 36 ...... | Kt—K7 ch |

A sacrifice with threefold effect: masking (37 K—R2, Q—Kt7 mate), unmasking his Rook, and depriving the King ultimately of a flight square.

| 37 R × Kt | R—B8 ch |
| 38 K × R | Q—R8 ch |

Forcing the King into a mating net reminiscent of a problem.

39 K—B2   Kt—Kt5 mate.

472

| White | Black |
| MICHELL | COLLE |

(Hastings, 1930-1)

The following game illustrates the folly of attempting too much. Its main feature is White's skilful defence against four black pieces which become mixed in their co-operation.

1 P—Q4	Kt—KB3
2 P—QB4	P—K3
3 Kt—QB3	B—Kt5
4 Q—Kt3	

A scientific continuation which strengthens the square at QB3 (4 .... B × Kt ch; 5 Q × B) and at the same time forces Black to guard the pinning Bishop.

| 4 ...... | P—B4 |

A less active defence is 4 .... Q—K2, but the *Zürich Variation* has many confirmed followers.

| 5 P × P | Kt—B3 |

A sound intermediary manœuvre, for if at once 5 .... B × P; 6 Kt—B3 (avoiding the pitfall 6 B—Kt5, B × P ch); 6 .... Castles; 7 B—Kt5, White has the better game.
More artificial is 5 .... Kt—R3.

| 6 Kt—B3 | |

Timid is 6 B—Q2, whilst 6 B—Kt5 presents no difficulties.

| 6 ...... | Kt—K5 |

Enterprising. . . . Increases the pressure on White's QB3 instead of relieving it by 6 .... B × P or neutralising it by 6 .... Castles; 7 B—Kt5, etc.
If 6 .... Q—R4 (a false alarm); 7 B—Q2, Q × BP; 8 P—QR3, B × Kt; 9 B × B, and White has slightly the better position.

| 7 B—Q2 | |

A curious miscalculation would be 7 Kt—Q2, Kt—Q5; 8 Q—R4 (or 8 Q—Q1), B × Kt; 9 P × B, Kt × QBP, and the Queen is lost.

| 7 ...... | Kt × P(B6) |

Continuing harrying tactics. As for 7 .... Kt × B, whilst it certainly deprives White of the *two Bishops*, it gives him chances on the Q file.

| 8 Q—B2 | P—B4 |

The turning point of the game. Black is under threat of 9 P—QR3, B × Kt; 10 B × B, Castles; 11 P—QKt4, and for that reason he wishes to create a point of support for his errant Knight at K5. Nevertheless, the advance in the text implies a certain weakness which White will exploit in a scientific manner.
Less impulsive is 8 .... Castles; 9 P—QR3 (best, for if 9 P—K4, Q—B3; and if 9 P—K3, P—Q4; or again, if 9 P—KKt3, P—Q4); 9 .... B × Kt; 10 B × B, and only now in face of the imminent threat 10 .... P—B4;

11 P—QKt4, Kt—K5; 12 B—Kt2, P—QKt3; 13 P—K3, B—Kt2; 14 B—K2, R—QB1; 15 Castles KR, Q—K2; 16 KR—Q1, P—Q3, and the struggle is at its height.

| 9 P—KKt3 | |

Very finely White no longer troubles about the massed black pieces on the Q side, and proceeds with his own purely positional plans.

| 9 ...... | Castles |

Perfunctory play. He should immediately apply the counter-measure 9 .... P—Q4.

| 10 B—Kt2 | P—Q4 |

A more reserved policy would be 10 .... P—QKt3; 11 Castles KR, B—Kt2; 12 KR—Q1, etc., but White would still have the easier game.

| 11 P × P | P × P |
| 12 P—QR3 | P—Q5 |

With this policy of constant surprises Colle has scored many a success, but on this occasion it fails against the rock-like defence of an opponent of no mean calibre.

| 13 P × B | Kt × P |
| 14 Q—Q1 | |

Clearly not 14 Q—B1, Kt—Q6 ch.

| 14 ...... | B—K3 |
| 15 Castles | B—Kt6 |

He fails to see that his attack has gone, or else he would have steered into calmer waters by playing 15 .... P × Kt; 16 B × P, Kt—Q4; 17 B—Q4, Q—K2, etc.

| 16 Q—B1 | P × Kt |
| 17 Q × P | |

A change of scene! Black's three minor pieces being unguarded, he can no longer avoid loss in material.

| 17 ...... | Kt—B7 |

For if 17 .... Kt (Kt5)—R3; 18 R × Kt, etc.

18 Q × Kt (B5)	Kt × R
19 R × Kt	Q—Q4
20 Q—Kt4	Q—B5
21 Kt—Q4	

Ruthlessly adding to his gains.

| 21 ...... | KR—Q1 |
| 22 Q × B | Resigns |

(22 .... R × Kt; 23 Q × Q ch, R × Q; 24 B—Q5 ch.)
A sad ending to a hazardous adventure.

473

White	Black
STAHLBERG	PETROV

(Lodz, 1938)

An impressive example of a blockade on a full board! The game, incidentally, demonstrates that the advantage of "the move" is at times overrated.

1 P—Q4	Kt—KB3
2 P—QB4	P—K3
3 Kt—QB3	B—Kt5
4 Q—Kt3	Kt—B3

The *Zürich Variation.* This active defence was already employed in a game Steinitz— Englisch, *Vienna*, 1882. But after 5 Kt—B3, P—Q4; 6 P—K3, etc., it ended in a listless draw in seventeen moves.

5 P—K3
Preserving the option of developing the KKt at K2. It is to be noted that 5 P—Q5, P×P; 6 P×P, Kt—Q5; 7 Q—Q1, B×Kt ch; 8 P×B, Kt—B4 gives White no more than equality.

| 5 ...... | P—Q4 |

Showing that besides the intended .... P—K4, Black, after ..... Castles and .... P—Q3, also intends to contest the centre.

6 P×P
He should play 6 Kt—B3. Premature would be 6 P—B5, on account of 6 .... P—K4.

| 6 ...... | P×P |
| 7 B—Kt5 | |

Continuing the sequence of conventional moves, which in no way hinders the adversary's plans. Better is 7 B—Q3.

7	Q—K2
8 P—QR3	B×Kt ch
9 P×B	Castles
10 B×Kt	

Consistent, but bad. By playing 10 Kt—B3, speeding up his mobilisation, White could still hope to redress the balance.

| 10 ...... | P×B |
| 11 Kt—K2 | B—R3 |

A powerful combatant.

12 Q—B2 Q—K5
Obtaining a favourable liquidation.

| 13 Q×Q | Kt×Q |

Threat: .... B×Kt, followed by .... Kt×QBP.

14 P—B3	Kt—Q3
15 P—QR4	QR—Kt1
16 K—B2	R—Kt6
17 B—R3	KR—Kt1

He increases the pressure and resists the bait 17 .... B×Kt; 18 K×B, R×P; 19 KR—QB1, and White will advantageously regain his pawn.

18 B—Kt4
Neither 18 KR—QB1, Kt—B5; 19 B—B5, R (Kt1)—Kt2, etc., nor 18 B×Kt, P×B; 19 QR—QB1, R—Kt7; 20 KR—K1, R—R7, etc., would enable White to redress the balance.

| 18 ...... | R—Kt7 |
| 19 KR—K1 | B—B5 |

Preventing 20 QR—Kt1, which now would lead to 20 .... R×R (not 20 .... R×Kt ch; 21 R×R, B×R; 22 K×B, P—QR4; 23 B×Kt, R×R; 24 B×P, followed by B×P); 21 R×R, P—QR4, winning a piece.

20 P—R5
Again threatening 21 QR—Kt1.

| 20 ...... | Kt—Kt4 |

Opposing the threat, which now would be answered by 21 QR—Kt1, R×Kt ch; 22 R×R, B×R; 23 K×B, Kt×BP ch.

21 QR—B1
If 21 P—K4, P×P; 22 P×P, R—K1; 23 P—K5, P—B3.

| 21 ...... | P—KB4 |

As the QKt file is blocked, Black concentrates his efforts on the K file.

22 P—B4
To eliminate the break-through .... P—B5, and also to relieve by K—B3 the permanent pin of the Knight. But the move has serious disadvantages.

| 22 ...... | Kt—Q3 |

A versatile Knight.

23 K—B3
Not 23 R—QKt1, Kt—K5 ch, nor 23 B×Kt, P×B; 24 K—B3, R—R7.

| 23 ...... | Kt—K5 |

A formidable blockade.

| 24 R—QR1 | P—KR3 |
| 25 P—R3 | P—Kt4 |

Already threatening 26 .... B×Kt ch; 27 R×B, P—Kt5 ch.

26 P×P   P×P
27 P—R4

Acquiescing in his fate. But White is beyond help, e.g. 27 P—Kt4, P×P ch; 28 P×P, P—B4; 29 B×P, Kt×B; 30 P×Kt, B×Kt ch (more conclusive than 30 .... R—B1 ch; 31 Kt—B4, P×Kt; 32 P×P, etc.); 31 R×B, R—B1 ch, forcing capitulation.

27 ......   B×Kt ch
Resigns

This game shines like a jewel against the frequently arid background of modern strategic conceptions.

474

White   *Black*

VIDMAR   ALEKHINE

(San Remo, 1930)

A game of the first rank, in which Dr. Alekhine's conceptions prove to be more profound than his tenacious adversary's. Opening finesse (7 .... Kt—QB3), skirmishing in the middle game (20 .... Kt—K5 ch), the final duel between Rook and Knight (51 .... R—Q4): how finely chiselled it all is!

1 P—Q4   P—K3
2 P—QB4   Kt—KB3
3 Kt—QB3   B—Kt5
4 Q—B2   P—Q4
5 P—QR3

Challenging a decision at the cost of a *tempo*. If 5 P—K3, or 5 Kt—B3, P—B4. A risky plan is 5 B—Kt5, P×P; 6 Castles, etc.; but midway between these various ideas lies the clear-cut continuation 5 P×P, Q×P (if 5 .... P×P; 6 B—Kt5, without any risk); 6 P—K3, P—B4; 7 P—QR3, B×Kt ch; 8 P×B, P—QKt3; 9 Kt—B3, QKt—Q2, etc., with equal chances.

5 ......   B×Kt ch
Playable also is 5 .... B—K2.

6 Q×B   Kt—K5
7 Q—B2   Kt—QB3

Intending 8 .... P—K4, and eventually .... B—B4. A more standardised line of play is 7 .... P—QB4; 8 P×BP, Kt—QB3; 9 P—K3 (or 9 Kt—B3, Q—R4 ch, etc., but not 9 P—QKt4, Q—B3); 9 .... Q—R4 ch; 10 B—Q2, Kt×B; 11 Q×Kt, Q×BP, with an even game.

8 P—K3

The continuation 8 Kt—B3 lends more support to the centre, but even then Black can play 8 .... P—K4 (e.g. 9 P—K3, B—B4, etc., or also 9 QP×P, B—B4, threatening 10 .... Kt—Kt6).

8 ......   P—K4
9 P—B3

Artificial. A continuation which creates widespread and perplexing complications is at once 9 BP×P, Q×P; 10 B—B4, Q—R4 ch; 11 P—Kt4, Kt×KtP; 12 Q×Kt, Kt—B7 db ch; 13 K—K2, and the white King's wanderings begin.

9 ......   Kt—B3
10 P×QP   Q×P
11 B—B4   Q—Q3
12 P×P   Kt×P
13 B—Q2   Castles
14 B—Kt4   P—B4

A subtle retort, for if now 15 B×P, Q×B; 16 B×P ch, R×B; 17 Q×Q, then 17 .... Kt—Q6 ch, followed by .... Kt×Q, shatters White's hopes.

15 R—Q1   Q—B3
16 B—Q2   B—B4

A fresh and well-managed surprise, by which Black obtains a favourable exchange.

17 Q×B   Kt×B
18 B—B1   KR—K1

Black now obtains an enduring initiative, as 19 P—K4 fails on account of 19 .... Kt×KP.

19 K—B2   R—K3

Making effective the threat 20 .... Kt—K5 ch; 21 P×Kt, R—B3.

20 Kt—R3   Kt—K5 ch
21 K—K1   KKt—Q3
22 Q—Q3

Or 22 Q—B4, QR—K1, etc.

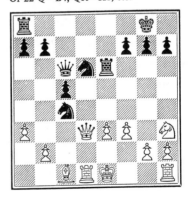

22 ...... Kt × KP

Black's harrying tactics are bearing fruit.

23 B × Kt P—B5

Recovering his piece, for if 24 Q—B3, Kt—B4.

24 Q—Q5	R × B ch
25 K—B2	Q × Q
26 R × Q	R—Q6
27 R × R	P × R
28 R—Q1	Kt—B5
29 R × P	Kt × KtP
30 R—Kt3	Kt—B5
31 R × P	Kt × P

After so much liveliness, here is a fairly prosaic ending, in which Black has not yet made sure of his extra pawn.

32 Kt—Kt5 P—QR4

If 32 .... P—B3; 33 Kt—K6.

33 Kt × BP	P—R5
34 Kt—Q6	Kt—B7
35 R—Kt2	P—R6
36 R × Kt	

White avoids the worst by giving up the exchange.

36	P—R7
37 R × P	R × R ch
38 K—Kt3	K—B1

The sequel is an outstanding object lesson of the Rook *v.* Knight ending.

39 P—R4	K—K2
40 Kt—K4	P—R3
41 Kt—B2	K—K3
42 Kt—Q3	K—B4
43 Kt—B2	R—R5
44 Kt—Q3	R—QB5
45 Kt—B2	R—B3
46 Kt—R3	K—K4
47 P—R5	R—B7
48 Kt—B4	R—Q7
49 Kt—R3	K—Q5
50 Kt—B4	K—K6
51 Kt—K6	

Hoping to simplify.

51 ...... R—Q4

After delicate preparatory manœuvres, here is something concrete.

52 P—B4 R—KB4

An efficient "frontier guard." White cannot now play 53 Kt × P, by reason of 53 .... R × BP; 54 Kt—K6, R—B3, and the Knight is cornered.

53 K—Kt4	R—B3
54 P—B5	R—B2
55 P—Kt3	

Or 55 P—B6, R × P; 56 Kt × P, K—K5, etc.

55	K—K5
56 Kt—B5 ch	K—Q5
57 Kt—Kt3 ch	K—K4
Resigns	

A masterly game.

475

White	*Black*
FINE	REYNOLDS

(Ostend, 1937)

In the following game Black rises to the heights of modern strategy.

1 P—Q4	Kt—KB3
2 P—QB4	P—K3
3 Kt—QB3	B—Kt5
4 Q—B2	Kt—B3

As also against 4 Q—Kt3, the *Zürich idea* aims at obtaining the control of the centre (.... P—K4, with or without .... Castles, and .... P—Q3).

5 Kt—B3

If 5 P—K3, P—K4.

5 ...... Castles

He could even play 5 .... P—Q3 at once, e.g. 6 B—Q2, P—K4.

A different and less flexible, although playable, line is 5 .... P—Q4.

6 B—Q2

A consolidating manœuvre. Either 6 B—Kt5, R—K1; 7 P—K3, P—Q3; 8 B—K2, P—K4, etc., or 6 P—K4, P—K4, or 6 P—KKt3, R—K1, or 6 P—QR3, B × Kt ch; 7 Q × B, Kt—K5; 8 Q—B2, P—B4; and Black contests the mastery of the centre.

6	P—Q3
7 P—QR3	B × Kt
8 B × B	R—K1

Another *open sesame* in the centre is 8 .... Q—K2; 9 P—K3, P—K4, etc.

9 R—Q1	Q—K2
10 P—K3	

If 10 P—K4, P—K4; 11 P—Q5, Kt—Q5.

10 ...... P—K4

At last!

11 P—Q5	Kt—Kt1
12 Kt—Q2	

Less sound is 12 B—K2.

| 12 ...... | QKt—Q2 |
| 13 P—K4 | Kt—R4 |

Initiating an action on a grand scale.

| 14 P—KKt3 | P—KB4 |

A temporary pawn sacrifice.

| 15 P×P | P—K5 |

Threatening 16 .... P—K6.

| 16 B—K2 | QKt—B3 |
| 17 Castles | |

If 17 QB×Kt, Kt×B; 18 P—KKt4, P—K6; 19 P×P, Kt×KtP; 20 B×Kt, Q—R5 ch.

17	B×P
18 KR—K1	Q—B2
19 Kt—B1	Kt—Kt5

Threatening 20 .... P—K6 or 20 .... Kt×BP.

20 Kt—K3	Kt×Kt
21 P×Kt	Q—Kt3
22 B—B1	

After 22 B×Kt, Q×B the Bishops of opposite colours would render White's defence more difficult, as Black's Bishop would become practically inexpugnable.

| 22 ...... | B—Kt5 |
| 23 R—Q4 | B—B4 |

But not 23 .... B—B6; 24 B—Kt2, simplifying. If, after the text move, 24 QR—Q1, Kt—B3. So White tries to tie the opposing forces to the defence of their advanced KP.

24 B—Kt2	Kt—B3
25 R—KB1	Kt—Kt5
26 B—Q2	Kt—K4

Artistic manœuvring. If now 27 B×P, Kt—B6 ch; 28 R×Kt, B×B, winning the exchange.

| 27 R—B4 | Kt—Q6 |
| 28 R—B1 | P—KR4 |

Black's evolutions are animated by a praiseworthy spirit of aggression.

29 B—QB3	R—K2
30 Q—K2	R—KB1
31 Q—Q2	

White, reduced to inactivity, awaits events.

| 31 ...... | R (K2)—B2 |

Threatening 32 .... P—R5; 33 P×P, B—R6; 34 R×R, R×R, followed by .... R—B7.

| 32 R—B4 | |

He throws ballast overboard.

32	Kt×R
33 KP×Kt	P—R5
34 Q—K3	P×P
35 P×P	R—K2
36 R—Q2	B—Kt5
37 R—KB2	R (B1)—K1
38 K—R2	Q—B4
39 B—Q4	P—KKt3

He skilfully provides his Rooks with an effective base of action.

40 B—QB3	R—R2 ch
41 K—Kt1	K—B2
42 P—B5	

Ineffective would be 42 Q—Q4.

| 42 ...... | B—B6 |
| 43 B×B | |

Or else 43 .... Q—Kt5.

| 43 ...... | P×B |
| 44 Q×P | Q—R6 |

Threatening 45 .... R—K6.

| 45 B—Q2 | R (K1)—KR1 |

Trebly impressive.

| 46 P—B5 | |

Fighting to the end.

46	Q—R8 ch
47 Q×Q	R×Q ch
48 K—Kt2	R (R1)—R7 ch
49 K—B3	R×R ch
50 K×R	KtP×P
51 P—B6	P×P
Resigns	

A jewel of aggressive chess!

CATALAN SYSTEM

476

| White | Black |
| RESHEVSKY | TREYSTMAN |

(New York, 1938)

Blockading strategy in the grand style, and highly characteristic of the winner's play.

1 P—Q4	Kt—KB3
2 P—QB4	P—K3
3 P—KKt3	

The *Catalan Gambit*, which avoids a pin after 3 Kt—QB3, B—Kt5, and at the same time prevents the *Queen's Fianchetto* (3 Kt—KB3, P—QKt3).

3 ......   B—Kt5 ch
Or 3 .... P—Q4; 4 B—Kt2, P×P;
5 Q—R4 ch, QKt—Q2, etc., a modern variation of the *Queen's Gambit Accepted*, in
which White's *fianchetto* formation would
be very effective.

4 B—Q2   Q—K2
5 B—Kt2   Castles
6 Kt—KB3
Bringing about a position which can result
from *Buckle's Defence* (1 P—Q4, Kt—KB3;
2 P—QB4, P—K3; 3 Kt—KB3, B—Kt5 ch;
4 B—Q2, Q—K2; 5 P—KKt3, Castles;
6 B—Kt2, etc.).

6 ......   P—Q4
Unpromising. A more stubborn defence
arises from 6 .... B×B ch; 7 Q×B,
Kt—K5; 8 Q—B2, P—KB4, etc.

7 Q—B2   Kt—K5
He unwisely relies on a policy of exchanges.
Stronger is 7 .... P—B3, and Black's game
is tenable in spite of the difficulty of exploiting his imprisoned QB.

8 Castles   Kt×B
If 8 .... B×B; 9 KKt×B.

9 QKt×Kt   P—QB3
10 P—K4   B×Kt
11 Kt×B   P×P
12 Kt×P   Kt—Q2
13 P—B5
White has a definite advantage: tactically,
the occupation of Q6 by a Knight is promised; and strategically, a blockade is foreshadowed.

13 ......   P—K4
A move dictated by the desire to open a
way for the Bishop, and by the general considerations of an active defence. But it is
too bold considering the K file is already
half open.

14 P×P   Kt×KP
After 14 .... Q×KP; 15 KR—K1. The
open K file would be exclusively White's own.

15 KR—K1   Kt—Kt3
Anticipating the latent threat by the Rook
against the Queen, e.g.:
(*a*) 15 .... B—Kt5; 16 P—B4, Kt—Kt3;
17 Kt—Q6, Q—Q2; 18 P—B5, Kt—K2;
19 Q—K4, and wins.
(*b*) 15 .... B—B4; 16 Q—B3, threatening
17 Kt—Q6, etc.
(*c*) 15 .... P—B3; 16 P—B4, Kt—B2;
17 Kt—Kt5, and wins.

16 Kt—Q6   Q—B2
17 P—B4   B—Q2
Or 17 .... R—Q1; 18 P—B5, Kt—B1;

19 Q—B3, and White threatens 20 Kt—K8.

18 P—B5   Kt—R1
19 R—K7   P—QKt3
20 P—QKt4   P×P
If 20 .... P—QR4; 21 P—Kt5.

21 Q×P   QR—Q1
22 P—Kt5   Q—Kt1
An ingenious attempt to free himself, for
if now 23 P×P, B×QBP; 24 B×B, R×Kt,
etc.

23 P—QR4   P×P
24 P×P   B—B1
Clearly not 24 .... B×KtP; 25 Kt×B,
nor 24 .... Q—Kt3; 25 Q×Q, P×Q;
26 Kt—Kt7, and wins.

25 R—B7   Q—Kt3
Or there follows 26 QR×P, threatening
R—R8.
The exchange of Queens eases Black's
task a little.

26 Q×Q   P×Q
27 R—B6   P—Kt3
28 P—Kt4   P—R4
29 P—R3   RP×P
30 RP×P   K—Kt2
Or 30 .... P×P; 31 P×P, B—Q2;
32 R×P, R—Kt1; 33 R×R, R×R;
34 B—B6, R—Q1 (if 34 .... R—Kt3;
35 Kt—B8, B×Kt; 36 R—R8, followed by
R×B); 35 B×B, R×B; 36 P—Kt6, R×Kt;
37 P—Kt7, R—QKt3; 38 R—R8 ch,
K—Kt2; 39 P—Kt8 (Q), R×Q; 40 R×R,
P—B3; 41 K—B2, Kt—B2; 42 K—K3, and
wins.

31 K—B2   B—Q2
32 R×P   R—QKt1
Better, first, 32 .... P×P, but then, after
33 P×P, R—QKt1; 34 R×R, R×R;
35 K—K3, etc., White's advantage is still
considerable.

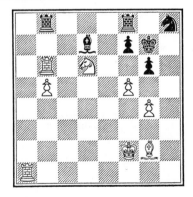

33 P—B6 ch

The pawn cannot be taken, e.g. 33 ....
K×P; 34 Kt—K8 dbl ch, followed by R×R.

33 ......   K—R3
34 K—Kt3

Splendid! The black King must make
way (34 .... R×R; 35 R—R1 ch, K—Kt4;
36 Kt—K4 mate).

34 ......   K—R2
35 R×R   R×R
36 P—Kt5

The Knight is permanently walled in.

36 ......   R—Kt3

For if 36 .... B×P; 37 R—QKt1.

37 R—R6   R—Kt1
38 B—B6   B—B4
39 R—R8   R×R
40 B×R   B—Q6
41 P—Kt6   B—R3
42 P—Kt7   Resigns.

BUDAPEST DEFENCE

477

White   Black

RUBINSTEIN   VIDMAR

(Berlin, 1918)

*The following encounter is the first example
of the* Budapest Defence *to be found in
a Masters' Tournament. The ultra-rapid
development of the black forces leads to a
decisive sacrifice of the exchange.*

1 P—Q4   Kt—KB3
2 P—QB4   P—K4

Thought out and elaborated in Budapest
chess circles in 1917, this defence, if not
altogether sound, is both brilliant and
interesting.

3 P×P   Kt—Kt5
4 B—B4   Kt—QB3

If 4 .... P—KKt4; 5 B—Q2, and White
tries to exploit the weakness of the adverse
formation.

5 Kt—KB3   B—Kt5 ch
6 Kt—B3

More solid is 6 QKt—Q2, e.g. 6 ....

Q—K2; 7 P—QR3, KKt×KP; 8 Kt×Kt
(of course, neither now nor on the next move
8 P×B, Kt—Q6 mate); 8 .... Kt×Kt;
9 P—K3, B×Kt ch; 10 Q×B, P—Q3, and
the fighting has died down.

6 ......   Q—K2

More precise is 6 .... B×Kt ch; 7 P×B,
Q—K2; for now White would have to play
8 Q—Kt3.

7 Q—Q5

Maintaining his gain.

7 ......   B×Kt ch
8 P×B   Q—R6

A critical moment. The following line of
play offers good practical chances: 8 ....
P—B3; 9 P×P, Kt×P (B3); 10 Q—Q3,
P—Q3, and the superior disposition of
Black's forces compensates for the pawn
invested.

9 R—B1

If 9 Q—Q2, Q—K2; 10 Q—Q5, etc.

9 ......   P—B3

Conceding the pawn, but claiming the
initiative.

10 P×P

Or 10 P—K6, P×P; 11 Q—R5 ch,
P—Kt3; 12 Q×Kt, P—K4, and Black
regains his piece with advantage.

10 ......   Kt×P (B3)
11 Q—Q2   P—Q3
12 Kt—Q4   Castles
13 P—K3

He underestimates Black's resources. His
best play would be 13 P—B3.

13 ......   Kt×Kt

He takes advantage of the moment when
14 Q×Kt is not available, to effect a break
either diagonally as in the text, or vertically
after 14 KP×Kt.

14 BP×Kt

Or 14 KP×Kt, Kt—K5; 15 Q—K3,
R—K1; 16 B—K2, Q×P, etc.

14 ......   Kt—K5
15 Q—B2   Q—R4 ch
16 K—K2

Or 16 K—Q1, B—B4; 17 B—Q3, Kt×P
ch, etc.

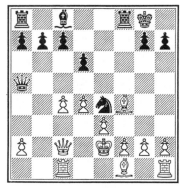

| 16 ...... | R × B |

A *clearance sacrifice.*

17	P × R	B—B4
18	Q—Kt2	R—K1
19	K—B3	Kt—Q7 ch
20	K—Kt3	Kt—K5 ch
21	K—R4	

His morale has weakened. Better is 21 K—B3, after which Black could reinforce his attack by 21 .... P—R4. But the "undecided decision" in the text brings about a débâcle.

21	......	R—K3
22	B—K2	R—R3 ch
23	B—R5	R × B ch
24	K × R	B—Kt3 db ch
	Resigns	

None too soon—25 K—Kt4, Q—R4 mate.

478

| *White* | *Black* |
| YATES | SPIELMANN |

(Carlsbad, 1923)

This game is noteworthy for the skill displayed by White in changing his advantage in mobility into one of territory, which in turn is translated into one of material. These most instructive changes are effected not only with an implacable logic, but with a light artistic touch.

1	P—Q4	Kt—KB3
2	P—QB4	P—K4
3	P × P	Kt—Kt5
4	P—K4	

He gives back the pawn in order to preserve an advantage in development.

| 4 | ...... | Kt × KP |

A natural reply, whereas the far more artificial conception 4 .... P—KR4; 5 Kt—QB3, Kt—QB3; 6 Kt—R3, KKt × KP; 7 B—K2 would favour White.

An astute idea propounded in Dr. Tartakower's *Die Hypermoderne Schach Partie* is, in true gambit style, 4 .... P—Q3, as played, with an inversion of moves, in a game Langner—Zander, *Berlin,* 1926: 5 P × P, B × P; 6 Kt—KB3 (plausible, but bad; weak would also be 6 P—KR3, Q—R5; 7 Q—B2, Kt × P; 8 Kt—KB3, Q × P ch, etc.; best is 6 B—K2, with interesting complications after 6 .... P—KB4; 7 P × P, Q—K2, etc.); 6 .... B—Kt5 ch; 7 B—Q2, B—QB4, and Black has won considerable material.

| 5 | P—B4 | KKt—B3 |

At the cross-roads. After 5 .... Kt—Kt3 a vigorous continuation is 6 Kt—KB3, B—B4; 7 P—B5, and Black's perplexities have only begun. The most satisfactory continuation, with an intermediary check, is 5 .... B—Kt5 ch; 6 B—Q2, B × B ch; 7 Q × B, KKt—B3; 8 Kt—QB3, Castles, etc., tending to equalisation.

| 6 | Kt—KB3 | |

With great calm and foresight he allows his opponent the temporary freedom of the weakened diagonal KKt1—QR7.

If 6 B—K3, B—Kt5 ch; 7 Kt—B3, B × Kt ch; 8 P × B, Q—R5 ch; 9 P—Kt3, Q—K2; 10 B—Q3, Kt—R3, followed by .... Kt—B4, and Black's game is not without resources; or 6 P—QR3, P—QR4; 7 B—K3, Kt—R3, followed by .... B—B4, etc.

6	......	B—B4
7	Kt—B3	P—Q3
8	B—Q3	Castles
9	P—QR3	P—QR4

A necessary counter-measure.

| 10 | Q—K2 | B—KKt5 |

The series of exchanges resulting from the move in the text will clear the battlefield without, however, making Black's task easier. A more violent course is 10 .... P—B4; 11 P × P, R—K1 (not 11 .... B × BP; 12 B × B, R × B; 13 Q—K6 ch, R—B2; 14 Kt—KKt5); 12 Kt—K4, B × BP, etc., or 11 P—K5, P × P; 12 P × P, R—K1, etc., but White replies advantageously 11 B—K3, P × P; 12 Kt × P, B × B; 13 Q × B, etc.

| 11 | B—K3 | Kt—Q5 |
| 12 | Q—KB2 | B × Kt |

Another manner of liquidating is 12 .... Kt × Kt ch; 13 P × Kt, B × B; 14 Q × B,

Q—R5 ch; 15 Q—B2 (or 15 K—K2); 15 .... Q×Q ch; 16 K×Q, B—K3; 17 P—KB5, B—Q2; 18 Kt—Q5, Kt—R3; 19 P—B6, and White's position remains very promising.

13 B×Kt	B×B
14 Q×B (Q4)	Kt—B3
15 Q—B2	B—R4

If 15 .... B—Kt5; 16 P—R3, B—Q2; 17 P—KKt4, etc., strengthening his hold on the centre. On the whole, Black has disentangled his game fairly well, but White, owing to the dynamic superiority of his minor pieces, has the advantage.

| 16 Castles | P—B4 |

A temporary sacrifice of a pawn in preference to the timid 16 .... P—B3.

| 17 P×P | B—Kt5 |
| 18 P—B6 | |

Returning the pawn under the most favourable conditions.

18	Q×P
19 Kt—Q5	Q—Q1
20 QR—K1	Kt—K4

Better is 20 .... B—B4. White refutes the text move very prettily.

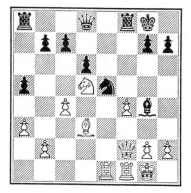

| 21 B×P ch |

A *temporary sacrifice.*

| 21 ...... | K×B |
| 22 Q—Kt3 | |

A subtle manœuvre, which is based on the fact that his opponent's two minor pieces are insecure.

22	P—B3
23 P×Kt	P×Kt
24 R×R	Q×R
25 Q—R4 ch	

More astute than at once 25 Q×B.

25	K—Kt1
26 Q×B	P×KP
27 Q—K6 ch	Q—B2
28 Q×QP	R—K1

Ever since his unfortunate 20th move, Black has offered a desperate resistance.

| 29 Q×Q ch | K×Q |
| 30 R—K3 | |

In this Rook ending, the victory of the extra pawn still appears problematical, but White solves all difficulties with virtuosity. If 30 R—Q1, K—K3, etc., whilst now the white Rook finds a way of getting into effective action on the Q side.

| 30 ...... | R—QB1 |

If 30 .... K—K3; 31 R—QKt3, R—K2; 32 R—Kt5, etc.

But a more stubborn defence results from 30 .... P—R5.

| 31 R×P | R×P |
| 32 R—QKt5 | |

Ineffective would be 32 R×P, R—B8 ch; 33 K—B2, R—B7 ch, followed by .... R×QKtP.

32	R—B2
33 K—B2	K—Kt3
34 K—B3	Resigns

The loss of a second pawn is inevitable.

479

| *White* | *Black* |
| THOMAS | RÉTI |

(Baden-Baden, 1925)

The simple means by which White obtains first a positional and then a material advantage are noteworthy, whilst his methodical persistance in turning his extra material to account equals the best performances of the great end-game virtuosi.

1 P—Q4	Kt—KB3
2 P—QB4	P—K4
3 P×P	Kt—Kt5
4 Kt—KB3	

He does not attempt to refute Black's defence (by 4 P—K4 or otherwise), and relies on simple and rational development.

| 4 ...... | Kt—QB3 |

Another possibility is 4 .... B—B4;

5 P—K3, Kt—QB3; 6 P—QR3, P—QR4, and Black regains his pawn, without inconvenience for the time being.

5 Kt—B3

A sober continuation, instead of holding on to his pawn by 5 B—B4.

5	KKt×P
6 P—K3	B—Kt5
7 B—Q2	Castles
8 P—QR3	B×Kt

Or 8 .... B—K2; 9 Kt—Q5, Kt×Kt ch (in order to preserve the *two Bishops*); 10 Q×Kt, B—Kt4; 11 P—KR4, B—R3 (for if 11 .... B×RP; 12 Q—R5); 12 P—KKt4, and Black's position fast becomes unsafe.

9 B×B	P—Q3
10 B—K2	Kt×Kt ch
11 B×Kt	Kt—K4
12 B—K2	B—K3
13 Castles	Q—Q2

Not 13 .... Kt×P; 14 B×Kt, B×B; 15 Q—Q4 (or 15 Q—Kt4), winning, nor yet 13 .... B×P; 14 B×B, Kt×B; 15 Q—Q5 (if 15 B×P, then, not 15 .... K×B; 16 Q—Kt4 ch, K—R1; 17 Q×Kt, to White's advantage, but 15 .... Kt×KP; 16 P×Kt, K×B, remaining with an extra pawn); 15 .... Kt—K4; 16 Q×KtP, and White has the better game owing to his more compact pawn formation.

14 P—B5

Finely played! White creates a lasting weakness in the opposing camp.

14	KR—Q1
15 P×P	Q×P
16 Q×Q	P×Q

After the exchange of Queens, Black's task becomes even more arduous.

| 17 KR—Q1 | QR—B1 |

If 17 .... B—B5; White would disdain the gain of a meagre pawn by 18 B×Kt, B×B; 19 R×P, etc., but would still play 18 K—B1.

18 R—Q4

An effective post for the Rook.

18	B—B5
19 K—B1	P—B3
20 QR—Q1	R—B3
21 B—QKt4	B—Kt6
22 R—Kt1	

Better than 22 R×P, KR×R; 23 R×R, for then, although neither *enterprise* (23 .... R—B8 ch; 24 B—K1, R—Kt8; 25 R—Q2, Kt—B5; 26 R—Q3, B—R7; 27 P—QKt4, etc.) nor *liquidation* (23 .... R×R; 24 B×R, Kt—B5; 25 B—B5, Kt×KtP; 26 B×P, etc.)

would ensure full equality for Black, White would at any rate have lost the initiative.

| 22 ...... | P—Q4 |

Fatal would be 22 .... R—B7; 23 B—Q1, B—B5 ch; 24 K—Kt1, and wins.

23 K—K1	KR—QB1
24 B—QB3	Kt—B5
25 B—B3	Kt—Kt3
26 B—Q1	B×B
27 QR×B	K—B2
28 P—QR4	R—B5
29 P—R5	Kt—R5
30 R×R	R×R

More resisting than 30 .... P×R; 31 R—Q7 ch, followed by R×QKtP.

| 31 R×P | Kt×B |
| 32 P×Kt | K—K3 |

After 32 .... R×P; 33 R—Q7 ch, K—Kt3; 34 R×P, White has won a second pawn.

33 R—QKt5

A new stage. White has not only made sure of his extra pawn, but the dominating position of his Rook promises to increase this advantage.

33	R—B2
34 K—Q2	R—Q2 ch
35 K—B2	K—Q3
36 P—B3	K—B3
37 P—QB4	P—QKt3
38 P—Kt4	R—K2
39 P×P	P×P
40 K—Q3	R—R2
41 P—Kt5	P×P
42 R×P	P—Kt3
43 P—R4	R—K2
44 P—R5	R—K3
45 P—B4	K—Q2
46 K—Q4	R—QB3

In order to bring his King to the critical corner, for if 46 .... K—K2; 47 R—K5, forces the exchange of Rooks.

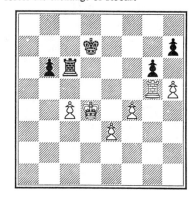

47 P—KB5
The battering-ram.

47	......	P×BP
48	R—Kt7 ch	K—K3
49	R×P	R—Q3 ch
50	K—B3	K—K4
51	P—R6	R—K3
52	R—R8	K—K5
53	P—R7	R—K2
54	K—Kt4	K×P

The balance in material is restored.

55 K—Kt5
Nothing could be achieved without the King's intervention, for after 55 R—KB8, R×P; 56 R×P, R—R6; 57 R—Q5, K—K5, etc., a draw would be in sight.

| 55 | ...... | P—B5 |
| 56 | K—B6 | |

Very shrewd play! After 56 K × P, P—B6, a draw would result, whereas, after the text move there is a threat of 57 K—Q6, R—KB2; 58 R—K8 ch, or 57 .... R—K5; 58 R—KB8.

| 56 | ...... | K—B7 |

If 56 .... P—B6; 57 K—Q6, P—B7; 58 K × R, P—B8 (Q); 59 R—K8, followed by P—R8 (Q), and wins.

57 K × P
Winning the decisive *tempo*.

| 57 | ...... | P—B6 |
| 58 | K—B6 | |

And again the King's progress (K—Q6) is all-important, and not the advance of the QBP.

| 58 | ...... | R—B2 |

After 58 .... R—KKt2; 59 P—B5, Black can play neither 59 .... K—B8; 60 R—KB8, nor 59 .... K—Kt7; 60 R—KKt8.

59	P—B5	K—B8
60	K—Kt6	P—B7
61	P—B6	K—K7
62	R—K8 ch	K—Q6
63	P—R8 (Q)	P—B8 (Q)

Black puts up a heroic resistance; he also has queened a pawn, and more *finessing* will be needed before White can finally secure the victory.

64	R—Q8 ch	K—B7
65	Q—R2 ch	R—B7
66	Q—K5	R—B5
67	Q—Q5	Q—K8
68	Q—Q3 ch	K—B8
69	Q—R3 ch	K—B7
70	Q—B5 ch	K—Kt7
71	R—QKt8	

In order to reply to 71 .... R—Kt5ch with 72 Q × R ch, etc.

71	......	R—QR5
72	K—B7 dis ch	K—R8
73	R—Kt3	

Preparing without more ado for a final liquidation.

| 73 | ...... | Resigns |

(73 .... K—R7; 74 Q—QB2 ch, or 73 .... Q—K7; 74 Q—B1 ch, etc.)

For once the great composer of end-game studies, Réti, found his master.

480

White	Black
ALEKHINE	TARTAKOWER

(London, 1932)

The effect of a fine retrograde manœuvre by White (8 Kt—QKt1) is most remarkable.
There is no doubt that no master has done as much as Dr. Alekhine to enrich chess strategy.

1	P—Q4	Kt—KB3
2	P—QB4	P—K4
3	P×P	

All kinds of methods of refusing the *Budapest Gambit* are ineffective, such as 3 Kt—KB3, P×P, or 3 B—Kt5, P×P, or 3 P—K4, Kt × P, or, timidly, 3 P—K3, P × P; 4 P×P, P—Q4, etc., and Black's game has reached emancipation without any trouble.

Against 3 P—Q5, the continuation of a game N.—Romano, *Rio de Janeiro*, 1936, was as follows: 3 .... B—B4; 4 P—QR3 (another dilatory measure; the storm breaks); 4 .... B × BP ch; 5 K × B, Kt—K5 ch; 6 K—K3, P—KB4; 7 Kt—KB3, P—Q3; 8 Kt—B3, P—B5 ch; 9 K × Kt, B—B4 ch; 10 K × B, Q—B3 ch; 11 K—K4 (or 11 K—Kt4, P—R4 ch, etc.); 11 .... Q—Kt3 mate. Beautiful!

| 3 | ...... | Kt—K5 |

The *Leipzig Variation*, recovering his pawn at once, but at some risk.

| 4 | Kt—Q2 | |

Or 4 Kt—KB3, Kt—QB3; 5 QKt—Q2, Kt—B4, etc. Less good is the precautionary measure 4 P—QR3, giving up a *tempo* to prevent .... B—Kt5 ch.

| 4 | ...... | Kt—B4 |

More useful than 4 .... B—Kt5.

5 KKt—B3   Kt—B3
6 P—KKt3
Scientific treatment. 6 P—QR3 yields
nothing, e.g. 6 .... Q—K2; 7 P—K3,
Kt×P; 8 Q—B2, P—QR4; 9 P—QKt3,
P—QKt3, etc., with an even game, but not
7 P—QKt4, Kt×P; 8 P—K3 (if 8 P×Kt,
Kt—Q6 mate; and if 8 Kt×Kt, Q×Kt,
etc.); 8 .... KKt—Q6 ch, to Black's
advantage.

6 ......   Q—K2
He prefers to recover his pawn rather than
to continue, in gambit style, 6 .... P—Q3;
7 P×P, B×P; 8 B—Kt2, B—B4, etc., not
without practical chances.

7 B—Kt2   P—KKt3
Not yet 7 .... Kt×P; 8 Kt×Kt, Q×Kt;
9 Kt—B3, which would favour White's
development.

8 Kt—QKt1
Profound as well as original. The Knight
is bound for Q5.

8 ......   Kt×P
9 Castles   Kt×Kt ch
He allows his adversary to obtain a powerful base of action on the K side. Far preferable is 9 .... P—Q3.

10 P×Kt   B—Kt2
11 R—K1   Kt—K3
12 Kt—B3   Castles
Not 12 .... P—QB3; 13 Kt—K4. The
lesser evil is 12 .... B×Kt.

13 Kt—Q5   Q—Q1
Not 13 .... Q—B4; 14 B—K3, Q×P;
15 B—KB1, Q—B3; 16 Kt—K7 ch, and
wins.

14 P—B4   P—QB3
Black's position is already difficult, but it
would be wiser to avoid this weakness by
playing at once 14 .... P—Q3.

15 Kt—B3   P—Q3
16 B—K3   Q—B2
17 R—QB1   B—Q2
18 Q—Q2   QR—Q1
19 KR—Q1   B—B1
Black has succeeded in consolidating his
position up to a point, but White finds a way
of reinforcing his pressure.

20 Kt—K4   Kt—B4
He decides on an *active defence*.

If 20 .... P—KB4; 21 Kt×P, B×P;

22 Q×B, R×Kt; 23 R×R, Q×R;
24 QB×P, and White has won a valuable
pawn. And if 20.... P—Kt3; 21 P—QKt4.

21 Kt×P   Kt—R5
22 P—QB5   Kt×KtP
23 R—K1
Black must now provide against the threat
24 B—Q4, Kt—R5; 25 B×B, K×B;
26 Q—Q4 ch, followed by Q×Kt.

23 ......   P—QKt4
This abrupt advance is magnificently
refuted. If 23 .... B—B4; 24 B—B1, and
if 23 .... B—K3; 24 B—Q4. He should
have made the best of 23 .... Kt—R5, with
the probable loss of two minor pieces for
a Rook.

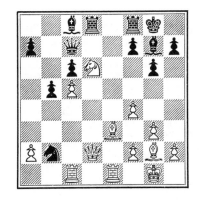

24 P×P e.p.
Giving up a piece in order to give his pawn
a chance to triumph.

24 ......   Q×Kt
If 24 .... P×P; 25 R×P.

25 Q×Q   R×Q
26 P×P   B—Kt2
Or 26 ... B—K3; 27 B—B5, QR—Q1;
28 B×R, followed by B×P and P—R8 (Q).

27 B—B5   QR—Q1
28 B×R   K×B
A pathetic moment. After 28 .... R×B
or 28 .... B×B; 29 B×P is decisive, and if
28 .... Kt—Q6; 29 R—Kt1.

29 B×P   B×B
30 R×B   R—R1
31 R—Kt6   R×P
32 R—Kt8 mate.

30. ENGLISH OPENING

481

White | Black
STAUNTON | HORWITZ
(London, 1851)

Here we see a methodical blockade—which would do credit to the technicians of modern times—allowing White gradually to increase his zone of influence and, at the right moment, to launch his final assault.

1 P—QB4

A remarkable feature of Staunton's play is the number of ultra-modern ideas with which he was familiar, e.g. the restricted centre, the *fianchetto* development, bilateral work, the theory of the local engagement, etc., and, last but not least, the *English Opening* (sometimes called the *Staunton Opening*).

1 ......   P—K3
2 Kt—QB3   P—KB4

Trying to revert to the *Dutch Defence*. But White, instead of playing 3 P—Q4, decides on a restricted centre (5 P—Q3), with action on the wings.

3 P—KKt3

A scientific treatment.

3 ......   Kt—KB3

Here and on the next move the thrust 3 .... P—K4 would react on the centre, but would, in effect, mean a loss of time.

4 B—Kt2   P—B3

Restricting the scope of the adverse KB, but his own development lags behind.

5 P—Q3   Kt—R3

He uses the respite accorded by White's last move for acrobatic evolutions, but 5 .... B—K2, or even 5 .... B—Kt5, would be more natural.

6 P—QR3   B—K2
7 P—K3

The restricted centre.

7 ......   Castles
8 KKt—K2   Kt—B2
9 Castles   P—Q4
10 P—Kt3   Q—K1

An aimless manœuvre. The spirit of enterprise demands, after due preparation, ... P—K4.

11 B—Kt2   Q—B2
12 R—B1

Another modern idea: the occupation of a potentially open file.

12 ......   B—Q2

Black's plan is to complete his mobilisation behind a curtain of pawns. White, however, does not wait, and himself starts an affray in the centre.

13 P—K4

He uses this pawn as a lever, as he foresees that the opening of the KB file and later on the QB will be of little use to his adversary.

13 ......   BP×P
14 QP×P   QR—Q1
15 P—K5

A far-sighted plan. Sooner or later White will succeed in reopening the long diagonal.

15 ......   KKt—K1
16 P—B4   P×P
17 P×P

White's pawn formation on the Q side is spoilt, but the striking force of his pieces becomes greater. Static warfare imperceptibly changes into a war of movement.

17 ......   B—B4 ch
18 K—R1   B—K6
19 R—QKt1   P—KKt3
20 Q—Kt3

A useful manœuvre.

20 ......   B—B1
21 Kt—K4   B—Kt3
22 QR—Q1   Kt—R3
23 Q—B3   R×R

If 23 .... Q—B2; 24 Kt—Q6. The potential value of the long black diagonal begins to make itself felt.

24 R×R   Kt—B4
25 Kt—Q6   Q—B2
26 Q—B2   Kt—Kt2
27 P—Kt4

The steam-roller.

27 ......   Q—K2
28 B—Q4   Q—QB2

It is clear that Black has been outmanœuvred.

29 P—QR4

Threat: 30 P—R5, B×P; 31 B×Kt.

29 ......   Kt—R3
30 P—QB5   B—R4
31 Q—Kt3   P—Kt3
32 Kt—K4   P×P
After 32 .... Kt—K1, Black's situation remains precarious.

33 Kt—B6 ch   K—R1
If 33 .... R×Kt; 34 P×R.

34 Q—KR3   Kt—K1
35 B—R1
Clearly, the pawn won by Black can have no influence in such a position.

35 ......   Kt×Kt
Necessary, in order to parry the threat 36 R—Q7, but now the long black diagonal definitely comes to life.

36 P×Kt   K—Kt1
37 B—K5   Q—QKt2
38 B—K4
Heralding the eventual threat of B×KtP.

38 ......   Q—KB2
39 Kt—Kt1   B—Q1
40 P—Kt5   B—Kt2
41 Kt—B3   R—K1
With a view to 42 .... B—B2; 43 B×B, Q×B.

42 B—Q6
With the cruel threat of mating the Queen by 43 Kt—K5.

42 ......   B×P
43 P×B   Q×P
44 Kt—Kt5
Harrying the disabled enemy.

44 ......   Q—Kt2
45 B—K5   Q—K2
46 B×KtP   Resigns.

482

White	Black
ZUKERTORT	BLACKBURNE

(London, 1883)

A memorable game. In reply to a carefully prepared action on the Q side by Black, White launches a violent counter-attack, which culminates in an exceptionally brilliant deflecting sacrifice of the Queen, with many scintillating ramifications.

1 P—QB4   P—K3
2 P—K3   Kt—KB3
3 Kt—KB3   P—QKt3
4 B—K2   B—Kt2
5 Castles   P—Q4
With 5 .... P—B4, followed by .... Kt—B3, Black could survey the central zone without committing himself there.

6 P—Q4
Reverting to the classical lines of the *Queen's Gambit Declined.*

6 ......   B—Q3
7 Kt—B3   Castles
8 P—QKt3   QKt—Q2
A more comfortable plan is 8 .... P—B4, with .... Kt—B3.

9 B—Kt2   Q—K2
He allows his enterprising Bishop to be exchanged for a Knight.

10 Kt—QKt5   Kt—K5
11 Kt×B   P×Kt
12 Kt—Q2   QKt—B3
Instead of the more active 12 .... Kt×Kt, followed by .... P—B4.

13 P—B3   Kt×Kt
14 Q×Kt   P×P
Instead of releasing the pressure in the centre, he could have intensified it by 14 .... P—K4.

15 B×P   P—Q4
Clearly so as to prevent P—K4.

16 B—Q3   KR—B1
The plan of exploiting the open QB file is good, but the hope of turning it into the main field of battle will prove too one-sided.

17 QR—K1
A deep conception, which rejects simplification by 17 QR—B1, and allows Black the mastery over the only open file on the board.
    Tactically, the thrust P—K4 is being prepared.

17 ......   R—B2
18 P—K4   QR—QB1
Without any precise target, but with hopes of the future.

19 P—K5   Kt—K1
20 P—B4   P—Kt3
21 R—K3
The Rook is making for KKt3 or KR3.

21 ......   P—B4
Too abrupt.

22 P×P e.p.　　　Kt×P
The frontal pin of the KP could be eliminated here by 22 .... Q×P.

23 P—B5　　　Kt—K5
He must close the critical K file even if only superficially. For if 23 .... KtP×P; 24 B×P.

24 B×Kt　　　P×B
25 P×KtP
Far-sighted calculation or foresight.

25 ......　　　R—B7
A hasty reply, which seems to win a piece, but unleashes the latent energy of the white forces. He should have played 25 .... P×P, although White still has a fine attack after 26 R—Kt3, Q—K1; 27 Q—R6, etc., or 26 .... Q—R2; 27 R—B6, R—Kt2; 28 R—R3, etc., or 26 .... Q—Kt2; 27 P—Q5, P—K4; 28 Q—Kt5, R—K1; 29 R—B6, etc.

26 P×P ch　　　K—R1
Hopeless would be 26 .... K×P; 27 R—R3 ch, K—Kt1; 28 R—Kt3 ch, K—R2; 29 Q—B4 (threat: 30 Q—Kt4); 29 .... P—K6; 30 R—R3 ch, K—Kt1; 31 Q—Kt4 ch, Q—Kt2; 32 Q×P ch, followed by mate.

27 P—Q5 dis ch　　　P—K4
The critical moment.

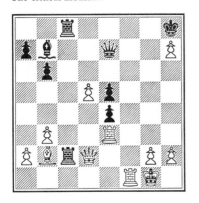

28 Q—Kt4
A Queen's sacrifice of exceptional splendour. If 28 P—Q6, Q—Kt2.

28 ......　　　QR—B4
If 28 .... Q×Q, there is a *mate in seven* by 29 B×P ch, K×P; 30 R—R3 ch, K—Kt3; 31 R—Kt3 ch, K—R3; 32 R—B6 ch, K—R2 (or 32 .... K—R4; 33 R—B5

ch, etc.); 33 R—B7 ch, K—R3; 34 B—B4 ch, K—R4; 35 R—R7 mate.
If 28 .... QR—B2; 29 R—B8 ch, and if 28 .... KR—B2; 29 P—Q6.

29 R—B8 ch
Again deflecting the hostile Queen from the vital point K4.

29 ......　　　K×P
If 29 .... Q×R; 30 B×P ch, K×P; 31 Q×P ch, followed by *mate in four*.

30 Q×P ch　　　K—Kt2
31 B×P ch　　　K×R
32 B—Kt7 ch
The climax! (32 .... Q×B; 33 Q—K8 mate.)

32 ......　　　K—Kt1
33 Q×Q　　　Resigns.

483

White　　　Black
TARTAKOWER　　LASKER
(St. Petersburg, 1909)

An interesting feature of this fine game is the highly modern method employed by Black in exploiting the weakness of the white square complex in his opponent's position, and the subtle means he uses in turning this advantage to account.

1 P—QB4　　　P—K4
An enterprising reply, after which White plays a *Sicilian Defence*, with a move in hand.

2 Kt—QB3　　　Kt—KB3
3 P—KKt3
The *Bremen System*, which eschews any immediate commitments.

3 ......　　　B—K2
Very reserved play. A heavy instrumentation results from 3 .... P—KKt3.
Black can obtain a free game by 3 .... P—Q4; 4 P×P, Kt×P; 5 B—Kt2, Kt—Kt3 (far more independent than 5 .... B—K3; 6 Kt—B3, Kt—QB3; 7 Castles, B—K2; 8 P—Q4, P×P; 9 Kt×P, or 5 .... P—QB3; 6 Kt—B3, Q—B2; 7 P—Q4, etc.); 6 Kt—B3, Kt—B3; 7 Castles, B—K2; 8 P—Q3, Castles; 9 B—K3, B—KKt5, and Black contests the initiative.

| 4 B—Kt2 | Castles |
| 5 Kt—B3 | P—Q3 |

To be followed by 6 .... QKt—Q2, keeping the Q file intact, whereas after 5 .... Kt—B3; 6 P—Q4, P×P; 7 Kt×P, the Q file is unmasked, to White's advantage. Not 5 .... P—K5; 6 Kt—KKt5, winning the KP.

| 6 Castles | QKt—Q2 |
| 7 P—Q3 | |

More straightforward would be 7 P—Q4, for now Black will himself try to push his QP forward.

7	P—B3
8 Kt—K1	Kt—Kt3
9 P—K4	P—Q4
10 BP×P	

He allows a weakness to emerge at his Q3 as he foresees its speedy elimination. Otherwise 10 Q—K2, or 10 KP×P, P×P; 11 Q—K2, etc., would be to the point.

10	P×P
11 P×P	KKt×P
12 Kt×Kt	Kt×Kt
13 P—Q4	P×P
14 Q×P	B—K3
15 Kt—B2	B—B3
16 Q—K4	Q—R4

Skilfully evading the threat 17 R—Q1.

| 17 Kt—Q4 | B×Kt |
| 18 Q×KB | KR—Q1 |

White controls a long diagonal while Black manœuvres on an open file. If White's Queen may be said to survey a wider territory, she is at the same time more exposed than her rival.

19 B—Kt5

The more modest 19 B—Q2 would give White a well-balanced game.

| 19 ...... | R—Q2 |
| 20 P—QR3 | |

If 20 B—Q2, Q—Q1.

20	Kt—Kt3
21 Q—KR4	Kt—B5
22 P—QKt4	

If 22 B—K4, P—B4.

| 22 ...... | Q—Kt3 |
| 23 KR—K1 | |

If 23 B—K4, then not 23 .... P—B4; 24 B×BP, but, without fear, 23....P—KR3; 24 B×RP, P×B; 25 Q×P, B—B4, and White's impetus is broken.

| 23 ...... | P—KR3 |

An important measure, which puts an end to an illusory attack.

24 B—K7

Incorrect would be 24 QB×P, P×B; 25 Q×P, B—Q4, etc.

24	Q—B2
25 B—B5	Kt—K4
26 B—K3	

If 26 KB×P, Kt—Kt3.

26	Kt—Q6
27 KR—Q1	B—Kt6
28 R—KB1	B—Q4

After much careful manœuvring, he succeeds in eliminating the guardian of the white squares in the enemy camp, which White can ill afford, in view of his weakness at KB3.

| 29 B×B | R×B |
| 30 Q—K4 | Q—Q2 |

All three open files are in Black's keeping.

31 R—R2

Not 31 QR—Q1, Kt×BP.

31	R—K1
32 Q—Kt2	P—QKt3
33 R—B2	R—Q1
34 Q—K4	P—QKt4
35 P—B4	

A risky advance, but White is fighting for air.

35	R—K1
36 Q—B3	Q—K3
37 B—B2	

Clearly not 37 B×P, Kt—K8, etc.

| 37 ...... | R—Q2 |
| 38 K—Kt2 | |

A little better is 38 R—B3. But not 38 R—Q2, Kt—K4.

| 38 ...... | Q—Kt6 |

Black stresses his opponent's weakness at QKt3. The harrying tactics employed by him from his 24th move onwards now give way to more concrete measures.

39 Q—B6

The only playable counter-measure. If 39 R—Q2, Q×RP; 40 KR—Q1, KR—Q1; 41 K—Kt1 (in order to play 42 B×P, without fear of .... Kt—K8 ch); 41 .... Q×P, and neither 42 R×Kt, R×R; 43 R×R, Q—Kt8 ch, etc., nor 42 B×P, Kt—K4; 43 R×R, Q—Kt8 ch, etc., will save White.

39	......	R (K1)—Q1
40	Q—QB3	Q—Q4 ch
41	K—Kt1	Q—K5
42	Q—Kt3	P—Kt4

As White cannot free his K4 by 43 P×P, Kt—K4, etc., he must incur some loss.

43	Q—R2	P×P
44	R—K2	Q—Kt3
45	Q—B2	K—R2
46	Q—B3	R—KKt1
47	K—R1	Q—R4
48	R—Q2	P×P
49	B×KtP	R×B
50	Q—QB6	

"Hope springs eternal . . ."

50	......	Kt—K4
51	Q—K4 ch	K—Kt1
52	R (Q2)—KB2	R—Kt4
	Resigns.	

484

| *White* | *Black* |
| FLOHR | SCHMIDT |

(Pärnu, 1937)

Black's 9th move may have been the loss or the sacrifice of a pawn, but his exploitation of the resulting positional advantage is masterly. For a long time White is prevented from castling, and when at last he does so on the Q side, the remedy proves worse than the disease.

1	P—QB4	P—K4
2	Kt—QB3	Kt—KB3
3	Kt—B3	Kt—B3

The *English Four Knights Game*, a vigorous conception of contemporary strategy.

4 P—K3
Preparing 5 P—Q4, which advance can quite well be effected at once, as in a game Müller—Duchamp, *The Hague*, 1928: 4 (P—Q4) P×P (if 4 .... P—K5; 5 Kt—Q2, Kt×P; 6 KKt×P, etc., with a clear advantage to White); 5 Kt×P, B—Kt5; 6 B—Kt5, P—KR3; 7 B—R4, Kt—K5 (a delusion; 7 .... Kt—K4; 8 P—K3, B×Kt ch; 9 P×B, Kt—Kt3; 10 B—Kt3, etc., leads to a stiff fight); 8 B×Q, Kt×Kt; 9 Kt×Kt (not 9 Q—Q3, Kt—K5 dis ch; 10 K—Q1, Kt×P ch, nor 9 Q—Kt3, Kt×Kt; 10 Q×B, Kt—B7 ch, and wins); 9 .... Kt×Q dis ch

(if 9 .... KtP×Kt; 10 Q—Kt3); 10 Kt×B, Resigns.

4 ...... P—Q3
Almost passive. If 4 .... B—Kt5; 5 Kt—Q5. The most enterprising line is 4 .... P—Q4; 5 P×P, Kt×P, etc.

| 5 | P—Q4 | B—K2 |
| 6 | P—Q5 | |

Closing the centre, for opening by 6 P×P, P×P, etc., yields nothing. On the other hand, after 6 B—K2, Castles; 7 Castles, B—Kt5, Black has freed his game.

6	......	Kt—QKt1
7	P—K4	QKt—Q2
8	B—K2	Castles
9	Q—B2	

Simplest is 9 Castles (9 .... Kt—B4; 10 Q—B2, P—QR4; 11 P—KR3, etc.), but White wants to reply to 9 .... Kt—B4 with 10 P—QKt4.

9 ...... Kt—R4
A feint. But it is the only way to avoid White's domination.

10 Kt×P
He thinks he sees farther than his adversary. If 10 P—KKt3, P—KKt3, guarding the KKt and preparing .... P—KB4.

10	......	Kt×Kt
11	B×Kt	Kt×P
12	Kt—Kt5	

He exults in the prospective gain of a pawn.

12 ...... P—QR3
Presence of mind.

13 Q×Kt
Obstinacy. White captures a unit, but his Queen gets out of play and he loses the initiative. The right move is 13 Kt—Q4.

| 13 | ...... | P×Kt |
| 14 | Q×KtP | P—KB4 |

Black takes the lead. This vigorous counter-thrust opens up wide fields of action.

15 B—B3
If 15 P×P, P—QKt3.

15 ...... P—QKt3
16 Q—Kt3
And not 16 Castles, B—R3. Now White himself threatens 17 P—K5.

| 16 | ...... | P×P |
| 17 | B×P | B—R5 |

Very strong. After 17 .... B—R3; 18 B—Q3, White gets out of trouble.

18 B—B3

After 18 Castles, B×P ch; 19 R×B, R×R; 20 K×R, Q—R5 ch; 21 K—K3, Q—K8 ch; 22 K—Q4, B—R3, White's King is in a bad way. If 23 B—Q3, Q—K4 mate; and if 23 Q—K3, Q—Kt5 mate. If 18 P—Kt3, Q—K2; and if 18 B—K3, Q—K1; 19 B—B3, B—Q2, maintaining the pressure.

| 18 ...... | Q—K1 ch |
| 19 B—K3 | |

Or 19 Q—K3, Q—Kt4.

| 19 ...... | B—Q2 |
| 20 P—QR3 | |

He still cannot castle. If 20 Castles KR, R×B; 21 P×R, B—R6; 22 K—R1, Q—R4, etc., and the attack increases in intensity; and if 20 Castles QR, B—R5.

| 20 ...... | R—R4 |

Threat: 21 .... R—Kt4; 22 Q—B3, R×KtP; 23 Q×R, Q×B ch; 24 K—B1, R×B; 25 P×R, Q×BP; 26 R—KKt1, B—Kt4 ch; 27 K—K1, Q—K6 ch; 28 K—Q1, B—R5 ch, and wins.

21 Q—Q3	B—QKt4
22 Q—Q2	Q—Kt3
23 Castles	

At last White can castle, but there is no safety even now.

| 23 ...... | R—R5 |
| 24 B—K2 | |

The only way to meet to some extent the terrible threat of 24 .... R—B5 ch, for if 24 B—K4, B—Kt4; if 24 P—QKt3, R×P; and if 24 QR—K1, R—B5 ch; 25 K—Q1, Q—Kt8 ch; 26 K—K2, R—B7 mate.

| 24 ...... | B×B |
| 25 Q×B | B×P |

A brilliant conception. If now 26 B×B, R×B; 27 Q×R, R—B5 ch; 28 K—Q2, Q—B7 ch; 29 K—K1 (or 29 K—K3, Q—K5 ch; 30 K—Q2, R—B7 mate); 29 .... R—K5 ch, with an early mate.

26 B—Q2	R—K5
27 Q—Kt5	R—Q5
28 Q—K2	

If 28 B—B3, B—K6 ch; and if 28 KR—B1, Q—K5.

| 28 ...... | R×P |
| 29 B—B3 | |

If 29 Q—B4, Q—Q6, as Black has an advantage in material.

29	QR—KB4
30 P—KKt3	P—Q4
31 KR—B1	B—K6 ch

Winning the exchange and avoiding a trap by 31 .... P—Q5; 32 B×P.

32 B—Q2	Q—B3 ch
33 K—Kt1	R×R
34 B×B	

Otherwise a piece is lost. The rest is *Kismet*.

34	R×R ch
35 Q×R	Q—B5
36 B—B4	P—Q5
37 Q—Kt4	Q—Q4
38 K—B2	P—B4
39 K—Q2	Q—K5
40 Q—Q7	R—K1
Resigns.	

485

| White | Black |
| NIMZOWITSCH | RUBINSTEIN |

(Dresden, 1926)

A beautiful example of ultra-modern chess. White's surprising conquest of the open K file, after a series of deep manœuvres contrived with great cunning, leads to a well-earned victory.

| 1 P—QB4 | P—QB4 |
| 2 Kt—KB3 | |

A very interesting scheme, tried out by Nimzowitsch in the same tournament, and sometimes called the *Dresden Variation*, is 2 Kt—QB3, Kt—KB3; 3 P—K4 (instead of 3 Kt—B3 or 3 P—KKt3); 3 .... Kt—B3; 4 P—B4, P—Q3; 5 Kt—B3, etc.

| 2 ...... | Kt—KB3 |
| 3 Kt—B3 | P—Q4 |

Preventing his opponent from gaining the initiative.

| 4 P×P | Kt×P |
| 5 P—K4 | |

Enterprising play.

If 5 P—KKt3, Kt×Kt; 6 KtP×Kt, P—KKt3; 7 B—Kt2, B—Kt2, etc., with equal chances.

| 5 ...... | Kt—Kt5 |

He could revert to *Grünfeld's Indian Variation* by 5 .... Kt×Kt; 6 KtP×Kt, P—KKt3; 7 P—Q4, etc.

6 B—B4

Much more energetic than 6 P—Q3. A warlike manœuvre is 6 Kt—K5, KKt—B3; 7 Q—R5, etc.

6 ......   P—K3

Useless is the episode 6 .... Kt—Q6 ch; 7 K—K2, Kt × B ch (or 7 .... Kt—B5 ch; 8 K—B1); 8 R × Kt, Kt—B3; 9 B—Kt5, and White has the better game. A preparatory measure is 6 .... P—QR3.

7 Castles

Clearly not 7 P—Q4, P × P; 8 Kt × P, Q × Kt.

7 ......   QKt—B3
8 P—Q3   Kt—Q5

He must vacate QB3 for the other Knight in view of the threat 9 P—QR3, which, while enabling Black to blockade Q4, would restrict the scope of his own pieces.

9 Kt × Kt	P × Kt
10 Kt—K2	P—QR3
11 Kt—Kt3	B—Q3
12 P—B4	Castles
13 Q—B3	K—R1
14 B—Q2	P—B4

A preventive manœuvre.

| 15 QR—K1 | Kt—B3 |
| 16 R—K2 | |

Henceforth, directly or indirectly, the K file will furnish the main theme of the contest. Premature, however, would be 16 P × P, P × P, followed by .... R—K1, and White's impetus is held.

16 ......   Q—B2

If 16 .... P × P; 17 Kt × P. But now Black actually threatens 17 .... P × P; 18 Kt × P, Kt—K4; 19 Q—Kt3, Kt × B; 20 P × Kt, Q × P, etc.

17 P × P   P × P
18 Kt—R1

Profound and original! The Knight returns to the fray via KB2, KR3 and KKt5. If at once 18 KR—K1, Kt—K2, followed by .... Kt—Kt3, whereas now 18 .... Kt—K2; 19 Kt—B2, Kt—Kt3; 20 Kt—R3 would not be to White's advantage.

18	B—Q2
19 Kt—B2	QR—K1
20 KR—K1	R × R
21 R × R	Kt—Q1

If 21 .... R—K1; 22 Q—Q5, Kt—K2 (22 .... Q—Kt1; 23 R × R ch, and wins); 23 Q—B7, etc.

Thus the open K file still remains under White's control.

22 Kt—R3	B—B3
23 Q—R5	P—KKt3
24 Q—R4	K—Kt2
25 Q—B2	

A very fine challenging manœuvre, intended to divert the KB from the control of the squares K5 and K7.

25 ......   B—B4

If 25 .... Q—Kt3, then not at once 26 B—B3, B—B4; 27 P—QKt4, P × B; 28 P × B, Q—Kt8 ch; 29 R—K1, P—B7, etc., but 26 P—QKt4.

26 P—QKt4	B—Kt3
27 Q—R4	R—K1
28 R—K5	

Maintaining his control of the K file.

28 ......   Kt—B2

For if 28 .... R × R; 29 P × R (threat: 30 Q—B6 mate); 29 .... Q × P; 30 Q—R6 ch, followed by mate.

29 B × Kt	Q × B
30 Kt—Kt5	Q—Kt1
31 R × R	B × R
32 Q—K1	B—B3
33 Q—K7 ch	K—R1

Or 33 .... K—R3; 34 Kt—K6.

34 P—Kt5

A beautiful final effort.

34 ......   Q—Kt2

Desperation; a victim falls by the wayside, for if 34 .... B × P; 35 Q—B6 ch, Q—Kt2; 36 Q × B, and if 34 .... P × P; 35 Kt—K6, P—R4; 36 Q—B6 ch, K—R2; 37 Kt—Kt5 ch, K—R3; 38 B—Kt4 (the move for which White was playing); 38 .... P—R5; 39 B—B8 ch, K—R4; 40 Kt—B3, or 34 .... P—R3; 35 Kt—K6, threatening 36 Q—B6 ch, K—R2; 37 Kt—B8 ch.

| 35 Q × Q ch | K × Q |
| 36 P × B | Resigns. |

486

| *White* | *Black* |
| ALEXANDER | FINE |

(Nottingham, 1936)

A game which impressively illustrates two features of the art of the contemporary technician: in rounding off the corners in the most complicated openings, and in exploitation in an inexorable end-game of the slightest weakness in the enemy camp.

1 P—QB4	Kt—KB3
2 Kt—QB3	

This and the following move preserve the character of the *English Opening*, while 2 Kt—KB3 reverts to the *Zukertort-Réti Opening*.

2	P—K3

Preparing to support the centre. Playable also, without any preparation, is 2 .... P—Q4 (3 P × P, Kt × P; 4 Kt—B3, P—KKt3, etc.); or as in the preceding game, 2 .... P—B4 (3 Kt—B3, P—Q4; 4 P × P, Kt × P, etc.). A close struggle results from 2 .... P—KKt3 (3 P—K4, P—Q3; 4 P—B4, etc.), or 2 .... P—Q3.

2 .... P—K4 leads to an *Inverted Sicilian*.

3 P—K4	

A modern line of attack.

3	P—Q4

Leading to a violent clash in the centre.

4 P—K5	

If, first, 4 BP × P, P × P; 5 P—K5, the reply 5 .... Kt—Kt5; 6 P—Q4, P—KR4, etc., is interesting.

4	P—Q5

If 4 .... KKt—Q2; 5 P—B4, etc., and if 4 .... Kt—K5; 5 Kt × Kt, P × Kt; 6 Q—Kt4, etc.

5 P × Kt	P × Kt
6 KtP × P	

After 6 BP × P, P × P ch; 7 B × P, B × P, Black has nothing to fear.

6	Q × P
7 P—Q4	

More precise is 7 Kt—B3, e.g. 7 .... P—B4; 8 P—Q4, P—KR3; 9 B—Q3, or 7 .... P—QKt3; 8 P—Kt3, B—Kt2; 9 B—Kt2, Kt—Q2; 10 P—Q4, etc., with a slight advantage to White.

7	P—QKt3

Here 7 .... P—B4 would be more likely to ease Black's game.

8 Kt—B3	B—Kt2
9 B—K2	

Evidently not yet 9 B—Kt5, but Black now hastens to prevent this move.

9	P—KR3

More to the point is 9 .... B—Q3.

10 Kt—K5

Instead of this abrupt manœuvre, the normal development 10 Castles, B—Q3; 11 Q—Kt3, P—B4; 12 B—K3, Q—K2; 13 P—Q5, Castles; 14 QR—Q1, P—B4, etc., leads to stabilisation.

10	B—Q3

Illusory would be 10 .... B × P; 11 Q—R4 ch, P—B3; 12 R—KKt1, B—K5; 13 P—B3, and Black's structure is tottering.

11 Q—R4 ch

The temptation to prevent Black's castling is great. If 11 Castles, B × Kt; 12 P × B, Black would do well to decline the offer of a pawn (12 .... Q × P; 13 B—B3, etc.) and to consolidate his base by 12 .... Q—K2.

A simplified position results from 11 B—B3, B × B; 12 Q × B, Q × Q; 13 Kt × Q, etc.

11	K—K2
12 B—B3	B × B
13 Kt × B	R—Q1
14 Castles	K—B1

Artificial castling! All is now safe.

15 R—K1	Kt—Q2
16 Q—B6	

Exposing the Queen without a real objective. Better is 16 Q—B2.

16	P—K4

A strategically sound move, which frees Black's game but contains also the threat of 17 .... P × P (18 P × P, B × P ch).

Tactically, the move in the text is made possible because after 17 Q—K4, White cannot gain material by 18 P × P, Kt × P; 19 Kt × Kt, B × Kt; 20 Q × B, Q × Q; 21 R × Q, because of 21 .... R—Q8 ch; etc.

17 Q—K4	K—Kt1
18 B—Kt2	

Artificial. Better is 17 B—K3.

18	R—K1
19 R—K2	Q—K3

Useless would be 19 .... P × P; 20 Q × R ch, R × Q; 21 R × R ch, followed by P × P, with two Rooks for the Queen. But now Black threatens both 20 .... Q × P and 20 .... P—KB4, gaining territory.

20 P × P

White himself brings about an end-game for which his position is too disjointed. By playing 20 Kt—Q2, White could still maintain the flexibility of his centre.

20	Kt × P
21 Kt × Kt	Q × Kt
22 Q × Q	R × Q
23 R × R	B × R

This ending, with so many weak points in

White's camp, can definitely be won by Black, but he will encounter a stubborn and ingenious resistance.

24 R—Q1	R—K1
25 K—B1	R—K3
26 R—K1	K—B1
27 P—Kt3	P—KKt4
28 R—K4	K—K2
29 K—K2	P—KB4
30 R—K3	K—B3
31 K—Q3	R—Q3 ch
32 K—B2	P—B5
33 R—K2	P—KR4
34 B—B1	R—B3
35 K—Q3	P—Kt4

A very fine move.

36 KtP × P   P × P

Cool, calm and collected! If 36 ....
P × P ch, then not 37 K—K4, B × KBP;
38 B × B, R—K3 ch; 39 K—B3, P—Kt5 ch, winning the exchange; but 37 K—B2, P × P; 38 P—B3 and the "dead points" in Black's position prevent the full deployment of his forces.

37 R—K4	K—B4
38 P—B3	R—Q3 ch
39 K—B2	

More resisting is 39 K—K2.

39	P × P
40 R × P	R—KKt3

A salient point. Although the forces are balanced, and all eight pawns equally weak, Black's prospective passed pawn proves more dynamic than its counterpart.

41 R—R4	R—Kt7 ch
42 B—Q2	R × P
43 R × P	P—R5
44 R—R8	P—R6
45 R—B8 ch	K—K3
46 R—QKt8	R—R8
47 R—K8 ch	K—Q3
Resigns.	

487

White	Black
GOLOMBEK	HOROWITZ

(Warsaw, 1935)

A fine game. White deserves credit for the ingenious way in which he wins a pawn, and still more for the clever and patient manner in which he turns this gain to account in a piquant Bishop's ending.

1 P—QB4	Kt—KB3
2 Kt—QB3	P—B3

Supporting the square Q4 in the same way as 2 .... P—K3, but more rigidly.

3 P—K4	P—Q4
4 P—K5	

The exchange by 4 BP × P, P × P; 5 P—K5, P—Q5, etc., would needlessly free the black forces.

4 ......   KKt—Q2

More independent is 4 .... P—Q5;
5 P × Kt, P × Kt.

5 P—Q4   P—K3

The game assumes the character of an *ultra-closed French Defence.*

6 Kt—B3

He wisely develops his pieces in preference to extending his front—and responsibilities —by 6 P—B4.

6	B—K2
7 B—Q3	P × P

Gaining a *tempo*, without, however, being able to free his centre.

8 B × BP	Kt—Kt3
9 B—Q3	Kt—Q4
10 Castles	Kt—Q2

The exchange 10 .... Kt × Kt; 11 P × Kt deserves consideration. While it reinforces White's centre, it reduces his chances of attack.

11 Kt—K4   P—KR3

He must provide against the threat of 12 B—KKt5, followed by B × B and Kt—Q6.

12 P—QR3	P—QB4
13 P × P	Kt × BP
14 Kt × Kt	B × Kt
15 P—QKt4	B—K2
16 B—Kt2	B—Q2

Black can develop his game only with difficulty, as neither 16 .... Castles nor 16 .... P—QKt3 is inviting. Even the attempt at simplification by 16 .... Kt—B5 would turn out to White's advantage after 17 B—Kt5 ch, B—Q2; 18 Kt—Q4, B × B; 19 Kt × B, etc.

17 Kt—Q4

A fine centralising manœuvre, resulting in the survey of four squares in hostile territory, the prevention of 17 .... B—B3, and the preparation for 18 Q—Kt4.

17 ......   Castles
18 Q—Kt4

The beginning of a direct attack which,

although difficult to sustain, will have a lasting effect.

18 ......   B—K1
19 QR—Q1

Leaving the other Rook for duty on its natural file. Ineffective would be 19 Q—K4, P—KKt3; 20 B—B1, K—Kt2, as Black, by his last move, has wisely strengthened his KKt3, which prevents the sacrifice 21 Kt × P.

19 ......   R—B1
20 B—K4

White has no intention of embarking on an altruistic combination by 21 Kt × P, P × Kt, etc., or 21 B × Kt, Q × B, etc. He wants rather to clear his third rank. Incorrect would be 20 Kt × P, P × Kt; 21 Q × KP ch, B—B2.

20 ......   R—B5
21 R—Q3

The "mountain artillery."

21 ......   Q—Q2
22 R—KKt3   P—KKt3

Having provoked this weakening of the adverse King's field, White takes up the attack with fresh vigour.

23 B—Q3   R—B1
24 P—B4   Kt—B6
25 P—B5   P × P
26 Kt × P

Masterly play. 26 B × P, which looks very forcible, would yield very little after 26 .... Q × Kt ch; 27 Q × Q, Kt—K7 ch; 28 K—B2 (or equally 28 K—R1, Kt × Q, etc.); 28 .... Kt × Q; 29 B × R, B—QKt4.

26 ......   B—Kt4
27 P—KR4   P × Kt
28 B × P   Q—Q7
29 P × B   Kt—K7 ch
30 K—R2   R—B5

Preventing the worst.

31 Q × R   Kt × R
32 K × Kt   Q × B
33 P × P

A quick win could have been obtained here by 33 Q—B4, B—B3; 34 R—B2, Q—B6 ch; 35 K—R2, R—K1; 36 P—K6. Both players were short of time.

33 ......   Q × KP ch
34 K—R3   K—R1
35 Q—B4   Q × Q
36 R × Q

In this interesting ending, White's extra pawn at KR6 is a host in itself.

36 ......   B—B3
37 R—Q4

Unavailing would be 37 B—Kt6, B × P ch; 38 K × B, R—KKt1; 39 R × P, R × B ch; 40 K—B3, R—QKt3, etc., and if 37 B—K6, R—KKt1 (not now 37 .... B × P ch; 38 K × B, R—Kt1 ch; 39 R—Kt4, P × B; 40 R × R ch, K × R; 41 K—B3, and wins).

37 ......   R—K1
38 P—Kt4   K—Kt1
39 K—R4   B—R5
40 K—Kt5   P—Kt3
41 K—B6   B—Kt6
42 P—QKt5   R—R1
43 P—Kt5   R—K1
44 R—Q7   R—R1
45 K—K7   B—B5
46 R—Q8 ch

Bringing about, with a sure hand, a *Bishop's ending* in which Black succumbs in spite of the temporary restoration of the balance in material.

46 ......   R × R
47 K × R   B × P
48 K—B7   B—B5
49 K—Kt7   B—K3
50 B—Q3   P—R4
51 K × P   P—R5
52 K—B6   B—Kt6
53 K—Q6   B—R7
54 K—K7   B—Kt6
55 K—B6   B—R7
56 B—Kt5   B—Kt6
57 B—K8   Resigns.

31. RÉTI-ZUKERTORT OPENING

488

White	Black
RÉTI	BOGOLJUBOW

(New York, 1924)

A magnificent example of ultra-modern strategy: delayed occupation of the centre, positional manœuvres with latent and powerful threats. The problem-like ending is worthy of the subtle operations that lead up to it.

1 Kt—KB3
An opening from the past, which became, towards 1923, the opening of the future.

1 ...... Kt—KB3
A non-committal reply. Against 1 .... P—Q4 the same incisive reply 2 P—B4 (the *Réti Gambit*) is available. But White can of course play 2 P—Q4, leading into a QP game as Zukertort used to do, and as happened in a game Owen—Burn, *Horton*, 1887: 1 Kt—KB3, P—Q4; 2 P—Q4, B—B4 (this reply is far from non-committal, and against it 3 P—B4, P—QB3; 4 Q—Kt3, stressing the absence of the QB, is to be recommended); 3 P—K3, P—K3; 4 Kt—B3, Kt—KB3; 5 P—QR3, P—B4; 6 B—Kt5 ch, QKt—Q2; 7 Kt—K5, B—Q3 (better is 7 .... P—QR3); 8 P—KKt4, B×Kt; 9 P×QB, B—Q3; 10 P×BP, B×BP; 11 P—Kt4, B—Q3; 12 B—Kt2, R—QB1; 13 Q—Q4, Castles (into the lion's mouth); 14 B×Kt, Q×B; 15 Kt×P, Kt—K1 (if 15 .... P×Kt; 16 Q×Kt; and if 15 .... P—K4; 16 Kt×Kt ch, P×Kt; 17 Q—Q3, with a valuable extra pawn); 16 Kt—B6 ch, P×Kt (or 16 .... Kt×Kt; 17 Q×Kt, P—K4; 18 R—KKt1, P—KKt3; 19 Castles, etc.); 17 R—Kt1 ch, K—R1; 18 Q×P ch, and mate next move.

2 P—B4 P—K3
In order to support the advance .... P—Q4.
Another method of effecting this thrust, but without shutting in the QB, is 2 .... P—B3, e.g. 3 P—KKt3 (or 3 P—Q4, P—Q4, the *Slav Defence* of the *Queen's Gambit*); 3 .... P—Q4; 4 P—Kt3 (with the double function of guarding the QBP and of effecting a *double fianchetto*); 4 .... B—B4, etc.
A sound counter-plan is 2 .... P—KKt3

(3 P—QKt4, B—Kt2; 4 B—Kt2, Castles, etc.).

3 P—KKt3 P—Q4
Instead of coming to grips in the centre, Black can quite well compromise in the *modern Indian style* by playing 3 .... P—QKt3; 4 B—Kt2, B—Kt2; 5 Castles, P—B4, etc.

4 B—Kt2 B—Q3
He concentrates his pieces in the centre, with a view to .... P—K4. Less attractive is 4 .... B—K2. Ineffective would be 4 .... P×P; 5 Q—R4 ch.

5 Castles Castles
6 P—Kt3
As a consequence of White's "centrophobe" policy, the *double fianchetto* is one of the basic ideas of the *Réti system*.

6 ...... R—K1
7 B—Kt2 QKt—Q2
8 P—Q4
He occupies the centre at the right moment. Less convincing would be 8 P—Q3.

8 ...... P—B3
Assigning to this pawn a *static rôle*. It could be employed *dynamically* by 8 .... P×P; 9 P×P, P—B4, etc.

9 QKt—Q2
Much more effective than 9 Kt—B3.

9 ...... Kt—K5
Seeing that the intended thrust 9 .... P—K4 would now not be without its drawbacks (10 BP×P, BP×P; 11 P×P, Kt×P 12 Kt×Kt, B×Kt; 13 B×B, R×B; 14 Kt—B4, R—K1; 15 Kt—K3, B—K3; 16 Q—Q4, and Black's isolated pawn is an easy mark), and that 9 .... Q—K2 would not release the tension, Black now engages in a hand-to-hand tussle, which, however, turns to White's advantage.
More steadfast is 9 .... P—QKt3.

10 Kt×Kt P×Kt
Thus the cohesion of his three centre pawns is destroyed, and, moreover, his outpost K5 requires support.

11 Kt—K5   P—KB4
The only possible defence of the KP, for neither 11 .... Kt—B3; 12 Q—B2, nor 11 .... B×Kt; 12 P×B, P—KB4; 13 P×P e.p. would save it.

12 P—B3
The well-known method of undermining an advanced post.

12 ......   P×P
13 B×P
A beautiful tactical *finesse*. Instead of 13 P×P, he reserves a more heroic part for his KP.

13 ......   Q—B2
He tries to eliminate the dominant factor at White's K5, for if 13 .... Kt—B3; 14 Q—B2, etc., White's resources are increased. The lesser evil would be 13 .... Kt×Kt; 14 P×Kt, B—B4 ch; 15 K—Kt2, B—Q2, trying to effect a regrouping of his forces—Q at B2, QR at Q1, and Bishop at QB1—but in that case the imprisonment of Black's QB would be a definite advantage for White.

14 Kt×Kt   B×Kt
15 P—K4
Disrupting the centre.

15 ......   P—K4
A hazardous counter-attempt. But neither 15 .... P×P; 16 B×P, nor 15 .... B—KB1; 16 Q—Q3, QR—Q1; 17 P—Q5, etc., nor 15 .... P—B4; 16 P—K5, B—KB1; 17 P—Q5, etc., would save Black's crumbling foundation.

16 P—B5   B—KB1
17 Q—B2
A double threat on Black's KP and KBP.

17 ......   P×QP
Or 17 .... P×KP; 18 B×P, P—KKt3; 19 P×P, etc.

18 P×P
The forces are still equal, but Black is the more exposed.

18 ......   QR—Q1
An indirect protection of the QP, for if now 19 QB×P, QB×P.

19 B—R5
The decisive assault.

19 ......   R—K4
Not 19 .... R—K2; 20 B×P, QB×P; 21 Q×B, R×B; 22 Q×B mate, nor 19 .... R—K6; 20 B×P.

20 B×P   R×KBP
This attempt at immediate reprisal will be magnificently refuted. A more stubborn resistance results from 20 .... R—Q4.

21 R×R   B×R
22 Q×B   R×B
And again the balance in material is even (and with Bishops of opposite colours as well), but in spite of the simplified position, a tactical *finesse* puts the finishing touch to White's wonderful strategy.

23 R—KB1
Not 23 Q—K6 ch, K—R1; 24 R—KB1, Q—K2, with an even game.

23 ......   R—Q1
Not 23 .... B—K2; 24 Q—B7 ch, with mate in two, nor, especially, 23 .... Q—K2; 24 B—B7 ch, K—R1; 25 B—Q5 (a problem-like manœuvre which prevents 25 .... R—Q1); 25 .... P—KKt3 (or 25 .... Q—B3; 26 Q—B8 ch); 26 Q×B ch, Q×Q; 27 R×Q ch, K—Kt2; 28 R—Kt8 ch, remaining a piece ahead.

24 B—B7 ch   K—R1
25 B—K8
A very beautiful final touch.

25 ......   Resigns
Mate in a few moves is unavoidable, e.g. 25 .... P—KR3; 26 Q×B ch, K—R2; 27 B—Kt6 ch, K×B; 28 Q—B5 mate.
A work of art.

489

White   *Black*
RÉTI   ROMANOVSKI

(Moscow, 1925)

If in the preceding game Réti succeeded in building up his opening with marvellous skill, in the present example he weaves on the same frame a most surprising ending in which space seems to be at his beck and call.

1 Kt—KB3	Kt—KB3
2 P—B4	P—B4

Assigning to this pawn an active rôle.

3 P—KKt3

True to his own system, White renounces the equally sound continuation 3 P—Q4, P × P; 4 Kt × P, etc.

3 ......   P—K3

The symmetrical variation 3 .... P—KKt3 (4 B—Kt2, B—Kt2; 5 Kt—B3, Kt—B3; 6 P—Q3, P—Q3; 7 B—Q2, etc.) would, in the long run, result in an advantage for the first player.

A sound idea is 3 .... P—QKt3, with a *double fianchetto* for Black after 4 B—Kt2, B—Kt2; 5 Castles, P—Kt3.

4 B—Kt2	B—K2
5 Castles	Castles

He refrains from revealing his plans in the centre. If 5 .... P—Q4; 6 P × P, Kt × P; 7 P—Q4, P × P; 8 Kt × P, and White has an easy objective in the centre.

6 P—Kt3	Kt—B3
7 B—Kt2	P—Q4
8 P × P	Kt × P

After 8 .... P × P; 9 P—Q4, White obtains a fairly favourable variation of the *Tarrasch Defence* to the *Queen's Gambit*.

9 Kt—B3	B—B3
10 R—B1	Kt × Kt
11 B × Kt	P—K4

Black treats the opening in an independent manner. After 11 .... B × B; 12 R × B, he would have difficulty in defending the QBP.

12 B—Kt2	Q—Q3

He even threatens to win a piece by 13 .... P—K5; 14 B × B, P × Kt, etc.

13 Kt—K1	B—B4
14 P—Q3	QR—Q1
15 Kt—B2	P—QKt3
16 Kt—K3	B—K3
17 P—B4	

A violent action, creating pressure on the K side, not, however, without weakening the K file.

17 ......   Kt—Q5

If 17 .... P × P; 18 B × B.

18 P—B5   B—Kt4

An active defence.

19 Kt—B4	B × Kt
20 R × B	B—K6 ch

An interesting episode would be 20 .... P—Kt4; 21 R—QB3, P—B5, etc.

21 K—R1	Q—R3
22 B × Kt	R × B
23 R × R	B × R
24 B—K4	

With *Bishops of opposite colours*, only a fine analytical brain could conceive that the problem can be solved.

24	R—Q1
25 K—Kt2	P—QKt4
26 Q—B1	Q × Q

Better would be 26 .... B—K6.

27 R × Q   P—Kt5

Intending to establish himself at QB6 after 28 K—B3 and P—K3.

28 R—B4	K—B1
29 K—B3	R—B1
30 P—K3	B—B6
31 P—QR4	

Bringing this pawn to life.

31	K—K2
32 B—Q5	R—B2
33 R—R4	P—KR3
34 K—K4	

The mechanism of all the white pieces functions admirably.

34	K—B3
35 R—R5	R—Q2
36 P—Kt4	

A formidable threat: 37 P—R4, followed by P—Kt5 ch, opening the way for the Rook on the KR file.

36 ......   P—Kt3

Inventing an ingenious parry.

37 R × P

An even more subtle refutation.

37	K—Kt4
38 R—R7	K × P

How can White now parry the threat 39 .... P × P mate? If 39 P × P, P—B4 mate, and if 39 P—B6, K—Kt4, draw.

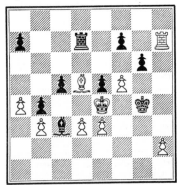

39 B—K6

A problem in an actual game!

| 39 | ...... | P × B |

He must accept the sacrifice, for if 39 ....
R—K2; 40 R × P, R × R; 41 P × P dis ch,
etc.

40 P × KtP

Again not 40 R × R, P × P mate.

| 40 | ...... | R—Q1 |
| 41 | R × P | |

On balance White has obtained three very
insistent passed pawns for his piece. If only
the black Bishop could come to the rescue in
time!

| 41 | ...... | K—Kt4 |

If 41 .... B—K8; 42 P—R5, B—R5;
43 P—R6, B—B3; 44 P—Kt7, R—KKt1;
45 R—Kt7, B × P; 46 P—R7 (threatening
47 R—Kt8; the black Bishop arrives one
tempo late on the battlefield); 46 ....
R—QR1; 47 R × B ch, and wins.

42	P—Kt7	K—R3
43	P—R5	K—R2
44	P—R6	R—Q3

Or else there follows 45 R—Kt7 and
P—R7.

45 P—R4

The third musketeer.

45	......	B—K8
46	P—R5	B—R5
47	P—R6	Resigns.

490

| *White* | *Black* |
| EUWE | ALEKHINE |

(Match, 1926)

*The way in which White obtains, in a pitched
battle, two advanced united passed pawns is
impressive, and gives this game a monumental
aspect. Once again the dead point at his Q5
serves Black badly.*

| 1 | Kt—KB3 | P—Q4 |
| 2 | P—B4 | P—Q5 |

Instead of giving the *Réti Gambit* the
go-by in this manner, Black can decline it
by 2 .... P—K3 or 2 .... P—QB3, or

accept it by 2 .... P × P. The text move
leads to many complications.

3 P —QKt4

The best course is the immediate challenge
by 3 P—K3.

| 3 | ...... | P—KKt3 |

White is faced with more difficult problems
should Black, taking advantage of the
momentary respite, play 3 .... P—KB3;
4 P—K3, P—K4.

4 P—K3 P—QR4

Or, without committing himself to this
episode, 4 .... P—QB4; 5 P × BP, Kt—QB3;
6 B—Kt2, B—Kt2, for he will sooner or
later recover his pawn.

5	P—Kt5	P—QB4
6	P × P	B—Kt2
7	P—Q3	P × P
8	P—Kt3	Kt—Q2
9	QKt—Q2	

He could, without encumbering the Q file,
play 9 B—KKt2 (Kt—B4; 10 B—QR3,
Q—Kt3; 11 Castles, etc.).

9	......	Kt—B4
10	Kt—Kt3	Q—Kt3
11	Kt × Kt	Q × Kt
12	B—KKt2	Kt—R3
13	Castles	Castles
14	P—QR4	

Positional judgment. White's superior pawn
mass on the Q side ensures his advantage, as
Black's pressure in the centre lacks useful
targets.

| 14 | ...... | R—K1 |

Black's position would be tenable if only
he could keep the QBP blockaded. But this
is not possible, e.g. 14 .... P—Kt3;
15 B—QR3, Q—B2; 16 Kt × P, R—Kt1;
17 Kt—B6, etc., and White has a definite
advantage.

15	R—K1	B—B4
16	B—QR3	Q—B2
17	P—B5	QR—Q1
18	Kt—Kt5	B—B3
19	Kt—K4	B—Kt2
20	Q—Q2	Kt—Kt5
21	P—Kt6	Q—B1

Black is in a precarious position, owing
to the lack of cohesion of his forces.
(*Diagram. See p. 640.*)

22 P—B6

The decisive advance, giving White
advanced and united passed pawns.

Position after 21 .... Q—B1

22 ......   P×P
If 22 .... Q×P; 23 Kt—Q6, winning the exchange.

23 Q×P   Kt—K4
24 Q—Q2   Q—R3
25 P—R5
Saving the QRP and QKtP, while the loss of the third pawn attacked (Q3) is of lesser importance.

25 ......   Kt×P
26 Kt—B5   Kt×Kt
27 B×Kt   Q—Kt4
As his game is strategically lost, Black has for a time been angling for some tactical *finesse*, but in vain.
If 27 .... Q—Kt2; 28 P—R6 is crushing, and if 27 .... P—Q6; 28 R—R3.

28 B×KP   QR—B1
29 B—B1   Q—Kt6
30 R—R3
Although in point of numbers the forces are still equal, and Black also has two passed pawns, White's lead is decisive.

30 ......   Q—Q4
31 P—Kt7   R—Kt1
32 P—R6
And White wins.

491

White	*Black*
NIMZOWITSCH	ROSSELLI DEL TURCO

(Baden-Baden, 1925)

An energetic game which, built up on strategic considerations, ends in crushing tactical hammer-blows.

1 Kt—KB3   P—Q4
2 P—QKt3
The object of this, the *Danish System*, is to exert a strong pressure on K5. White can also defer the text move by 2 P—K3, P—QB4; 3 P—QKt3, etc.

2 ......   P—QB4
Or, without disturbing the pawns, which may lead to weaknesses around QB3, 2 .... B—Kt5; 3 B—Kt2 (3 Kt—K5, B—R4); 3 .... Kt—Q2, 4 P—K3, KKt—B3; 5 P—KR3, B—R4; 6 B—K2, P—K3, with an even game.
The most independent reply is 2 .... B—B4, as the natural reaction 3 P—B4, followed by Q—Kt3, is not possible, and Black's Q side thus remains secure.

3 P—K3
Or at once 3 B—Kt2, for if then prematurely 3 .... P—Q5, White wins the local engagement around Q4 after 4 P—K3, Kt—QB3; 5 B—Kt5, etc. Generally speaking, the moves *P—QKt3 and P—K3* go together, as do *P—KKt3 and P—Q3* (not P—K3, as it would bring into being a most undesirable hole at KB3).

3 ......   Kt—QB3
4 B—Kt2   B—Kt5
If, instead, 4 .... P—K3; 5 B—Kt5 (attack on QB6, in order to conquer the square K5); 5 .... B—Q2; 6 Castles, Kt—B3; 7 P—Q3, B—K2; 8 QKt—Q2, Castles; 9 KB×Kt, B×B; 10 Kt—K5, R—B1; 11 P—KB4, etc., and White has a lasting initiative.
It may be noted that the advance of the KBP on the 11th move can also be made on the 1st move (1 P—KB4, P—Q4, etc.), leading gradually to the identical position.

5 P—KR3
More active than 5 B—K2, P—K3; 6 P—KR3, B×Kt; 7 B×B, Kt—B3, etc., for now the Queen gets into play.

5 ......   B×Kt
If 5 .... B—R4; 6 B—Kt5, R—B1; 7 P—KKt4, B—Kt3; 8 Kt—K5.

6 Q×B   P—K4
Preventive occupation of the point in dispute. Black hopes to restrict the opposing QB. If, more peaceably, 6 .... P—K3; 7 B—Kt5 favours White's chances.

7 B—Kt5   Q—Q3
8 P—K4   P—Q5
If 8 .... P×P; 9 Q×P, P—B3 (9 .... KKt—K2; 10 Q×KP); 10 P—KB4, and

White succeeds in spoiling Black's pawn formation. Or 8 .... R—Q1; 9 P×P, Q×P; 10 Q×Q, R×Q; 11 B×Kt ch, P×B; 12 Kt—B3, R—Q2; 13 Castles QR, etc., equally to White's advantage. Or again, 8 .... Kt—B3; 9 P×P, Kt×P; 10 Kt—B3, and White as before has the better game.

    9 Kt—R3   P—B3

A measure born of the desire of avoiding the doubling of the QBP, but White will now concentrate his efforts on breaking up the hostile chain of pawns.

    10 Kt—B4   Q—Q2

If 10 .... Q—K3; 11 Kt—R5, and if 10 .... Q—QB2; 11 Q—Kt4.

    11 Q—R5 ch

A provocative check intended to weaken the hostile KBP. If at once 11 Kt—R5, KKt—K2.

    11 ......   P—Kt3
    12 Q—B3   Q—QB2

Not only to prevent 13 Kt—R5, but also to make possible 13 .... P—QR3, which at this stage would be a mistake because of 12 .... P—QR3; 13 Kt—Kt6.

Another miscalculation would be 12 .... K—B2; 13 B×Kt, Q×B; 14 Kt×P ch, but after 12 .... Castles; 13 Kt—R5, White would succeed in doubling Black's QBP, as 13 .... KKt—K2 cannot be played (14 Q×P).

    13 Q—Kt4   K—B2

Artificial castling, for if 13 .... P—QR3; 14 Q—K6 ch.

    14 P—B4

Hammer-blows follow upon harrying tactics. White, so to speak, offers a deferred *King's Gambit.*

    14 ......   P—KR4
    15 Q—B3   P×P
    16 B×Kt   P×B
    17 Castles KR   P—Kt4

The barricade improvised by Black inspires little confidence.

    18 P—B3

A move of some importance. If, first, 18 QR—K1, B—Q3; 19 P—B3, B—K4.

    18 ......   R—Q1
    19 QR—K1   Kt—K2

If here 19 .... B—Q3; 20 P×P.

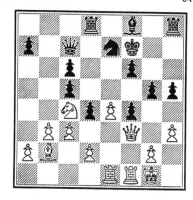

    20 P—K5

Gaining considerable territory.

    20 ......   Kt—B4

Or 20 .... P×P; 21 Kt×P ch, K—B3; 22 P—KR4.

    21 P×QP   Kt×P
    22 Q—K4   B—K2
    23 P—KR4

The decisive blow, eliminating the support of the gambit pawn.

    23 ......   Q—Q2
    24 P×BP   B×P
    25 P×P   Resigns

Not 25 .... B×P; 26 Kt—K5 ch, nor 25 .... B—Kt2; 26 R×P ch, K—Kt1; 27 Q—Kt6, and Black is defenceless.

A game which combines *finesse* with energy.

492

    White   *Black*
  BOTWINNIK   TCHECHOVER

(Moscow, 1935)

This fine game begins in the positional style with manœuvres around the centre. But, by a brilliant sacrifice, 22 Kt—Kt5, soon to be followed by another, 24 Kt×P, White starts an increasingly violent attack. A third sacrifice, 32 R×Kt, initiates a magnificent King hunt in which the black King is driven from his KR1 to QKt7 to meet his fate.

1 Kt—KB3	P—Q4
2 P—B4	P—K3
3 P—QKt3	

Combining the pressure against Q5 with that on K5.

3	Kt—KB3
4 B—Kt2	B—K2
5 P—K3	

The lines of the *Danish System*. With 5 P—Kt3, followed by B—Kt2, White reverts to the *Réti System*.

5	Castles
6 B—K2	P—B3
7 Castles	QKt—Q2
8 Kt—B3	P—QR3

In preparation for the contingency 9 R—B1, P—K4, without being exposed to molestation by 10 P×P, P×P; 11 Kt—QKt5.

9 Kt—Q4

An interesting manœuvre, which is intended to provoke 9 .... P—K4 (10 Kt—B5) or 9 .... P—B4 (10 Kt—B3), after which Black's pawn skeleton would be slightly disarranged.

| 9 ...... | P×P |
| 10 P×P | Kt—B4 |

He thinks he has time for 11 .... P—K4; 12 Kt—B3, P—K5; 13 Kt—Q4, Kt—Q6, etc., but in reality he loses precious moments. He should at once regroup his forces by 10 .... Q—B2, ... R—Q1, and eventually .... Kt—B1, with a cramped but defensible position.

11 P—B4	Q—B2
12 Kt—B3	R—Q1
13 Q—Q2	

Stopping not only 13 .... Kt—Q6, but also 13 .... QKt—K5.

| 13 ...... | QKt—Q2 |

Return of the prodigal Knight.

14 P—Q4

He is now ready for a grapple in the centre.

14	P—B4
15 Kt—K5	P—QKt3
16 B—Q3	P×P

If at once 16 .... B—Kt2; 17 P—Q5.

17 P×P	B—Kt2
18 Q—K2	Kt—B1
19 Kt—Q1	

Beginning of a lengthy but far-sighted peregrination directed towards the castled wing, which gradually becomes the main battlefield. Clearly not 19 Q—KB2, R×P.

| 19 ...... | R—R2 |

He almost instinctively strengthens the second rank (*especially KB2*), and allows for some rearrangement of his forces by .... Q—Kt1; followed by .... Q—R1; or by .... B—R1; followed by .... Q—Kt2. A less complicated plan of defence is 19 .... Kt—K1; with a view to .... B—KB3 or .... P—B3.

| 20 Kt—B2 | Q—Kt1 |
| 21 Kt—R3 | P—R3 |

He should have played 21 .... Kt—K1; 22 Kt—Kt5, B×Kt; 23 P×B, B—R1, etc.

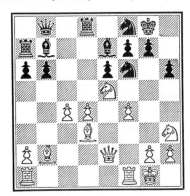

22 Kt—Kt5

A brilliant conception.

| 22 ...... | P×Kt |
| 23 P×P | Kt (B1)—Q2 |

Black is already anxious to give back the extra material, for if 23 .... Kt—K1; 24 Kt×P, with the telling menace 25 Q—R5.

24 Kt×P

Logic of circumstances: instead of recovering his piece by 24 P×Kt, Kt×P, which would allow the critical KB file to be masked, he even sacrifices his second Knight in order to force a way in.

A strong continuation, however, would also be 24 Kt×Kt, R×Kt (24 .... Kt×Kt; 25 Q—R5); 25 P×Kt, P×P (or 25 .... KB×P; 26 R×B, P×R; 27 Q—Kt4 ch, etc.); 26 Q—Kt4 ch, K—B1; 27 Q—R4, B—Q3; 28 R×P, etc., with a persistent attack.

| 24 ...... | K×Kt |
| 25 P—Kt6 ch | |

The wrong move would be 25 Q—R5 ch.

| 25 ...... | K—Kt1 |

He offers the strongest possible resistance.

26 Q×P ch	K—R1
27 Q—R3 ch	K—Kt1
28 B—B5	

An important reinforcement.

28	Kt—B1

Piquant would be 28 .... B—Q3; 29 B—K6 ch, K—B1; 30 Q—R8 ch, K—K2; 31 Q×P ch, K×B; 32 Q—B7 mate.

29 B—K6 ch	Kt×B
30 Q×Kt ch	K—R1
31 Q—R3 ch	K—Kt1
32 R×Kt	

Ruthless again!

32	B×R
33 Q—R7 ch	K—B1
34 R—K1	

Cutting off the King's flight.

34	B—K4

A desperate attempt at salvation.

35 Q—R8 ch	K—K2
36 Q×P ch	K—Q3
37 Q×B ch	K—Q2
38 Q—B5 ch	K—B3
39 P—Q5 ch	K—B4
40 B—R3 ch	K×P
41 Q—K4 ch	K—B6
42 B—Kt4 ch	K—Kt7
43 Q—Kt1 mate.	

493

White	*Black*
MIKENAS	ALEXANDER

(Hastings, 1938)

A short but impressive game. The means employed in refuting a premature attack can only be termed masterly.

1 Kt—KB3	Kt—KB3
2 P—B4	P—K3
3 P—QKt3	P—Q4
4 B—Kt2	QKt—Q2
5 P—K3	P—B3
6 B—K2	B—Q3

More enterprising than B—K2, as it has in view the advance 7 .... P—K4.

7 Kt—Q4	

Better, first, 7 Kt—B3, after which 7 .... P—K4 would be of doubtful expediency, on account of 8 P×P, P×P; 9 Kt—QKt5. As for Q4, White prefers to delay it in order to conserve greater elasticity in the centre.

7	P—K4

He accepts the challenge.

8 Kt—B5	B—B1
9 P—B4	

This attack is premature. Better is 9 Q—B2.

9	KP×P
10 KP×P	Kt—B4
11 Kt—Q4	

He is already on the retreat, and tries to mask the Q file. If 11 Q—B2, KKt—K5, and White is uneasy. If 11 Kt—K3, P—Q5, etc. But 11 Kt—Kt3 would be more plastic than the move in the text.

11	P×P
12 P×P	

If 12 B×P, B—Kt5.

12	B—Q3
13 Q—B2	

White has nothing better than to follow a hazardous course, for if 13 Castles, Q—B2; 14 P—Kt3, B—R6; 15 R—K1, Castles QR, and Black dominates the field.

13	B×P
14 Castles	

A little better is 14 P—Kt3.

14	Q—B2
15 Kt—B5	

Va banque! If 15 P—Kt3, B×KtP; 16 P×B, Q×P ch; 17 K—R1, KKt—K5, with decisive threats.

15	B×P ch
16 K—R1	B×Kt
17 R×B	

Or 17 Q×B, QKt—K5; 18 Q—R3, B—K4, forcing matters.

17	Kt (B4)—K5

A well-calculated *coup*, which is more effective than 17 .... Kt (B3)—K5.

18 B×Kt	Kt—Kt6 ch
19 K×B	Kt×R dis ch
20 K—Kt1	Kt—Kt6

A quiet move which decides the issue, for now both hostile Bishops are under fire.

21 B—Kt4	

Or 21 B×P, Kt×B ch; 22 K—B2, Q—Kt6 ch, etc.

21	P×B
22 Kt—B3	Q—K4
23 K—B2	

In view of the threat 23 .... Q—Q5 ch, followed by .... Q×B, White's King tries to take a hand, for after 23 B—B3, Castles, or 23 B—R3, Castles, White is hopelessly lost.

23	Q—B5 ch
24 B—B3	Castles QR
25 P—Q3	Kt—B4
26 R—K1	Q—Q5 ch
	Resigns

(27 K—B1, Kt—Kt6 mate; or 27 K—K2, Q—K6 ch; 28 K—Q1, R×P ch, etc.)
A *débâcle*.

494

| *White* | *Black* |
| SANTASIERE | REINFELD |

(New York, 1936)

A beautiful game, in which White skilfully effects and exploits a breach in the enemy lines: a success all the more praiseworthy, as it is gained against an outstanding theoretician.

| 1 Kt—KB3 | Kt—KB3 |
| 2 P—QKt4 | |

Besides the *Réti System* (2 P—B4) and the *Danish System* (2 P—QKt3), White can adopt quiet continuations such as 2 P—K3 or 2 P—KKt3. The *Extended Fianchetto* illustrated in the text is less fantastic than it looks, as it has a definite strategic tendency to anticipate any counter-play on the Q side.

In a similar manner, this opening was adopted in an extraordinary game Alekhine—Drewitt, *Portsmouth*, 1923: 1 Kt—KB3, P—Q4; 2 P—QKt4, P—K3; 3 B—Kt2, Kt—KB3; 4 P—QR3, P—B4; 5 P×P, B×P; 6 P—K3, Castles; 7 P—B4, Kt—B3; 8 P—Q4, B—Kt3; 9 QKt—Q2, Q—K2; 10 B—Q3, R—Q1; 11 Castles, B—Q2; 12 Kt—K5, B—K1; 13 P—B4, QR—Kt1; 14 R—B1, Kt—Q2; 15 Kt×Kt (B6), R×Kt (a *relieving sacrifice* of a piece for three pawns); 16 P—B5, Kt×P; 17 P×Kt, B×P; 18 R—KB3, B×P; 19 R×R, B×R; 20 B×P ch (the prelude to a double Bishop's sacrifice, a rare occurrence); 20 .... K×B; 21 R—R3 ch, K—Kt1; 22 B×P, resigns (22 .... K×B; 23 Q—Kt4 ch, with mate in two).

| 2 ...... | P—K3 |
| 3 P—QR3 | |

If 3 P—Kt5, P—QR3.

| 3 ...... | P—Q4 |
| 4 P—K3 | |

Combining a wing offensive with a quiet conception in the centre, which, by a curious psychological reaction, incites his opponent to become aggressive in turn.

| 4 ...... | P—QR4 |

If 4 .... P—B4; 5 P×P (exchanging an unimportant pawn for one which affects the centre); 5 .... B×P; 6 P—Q4, with advantage to White.

5 P—Kt5	P—B4
6 B—Kt2	B—Q3
7 P—B4	Castles
8 Kt—B3	QKt—Q2
9 Q—B2	Kt—Kt3

Better, at once, 9 .... R—K1, followed eventually by .... Kt—B1.

| 10 P×P | P×P |
| 11 B—Q3 | R—K1 |

If 11 .... B—Kt5; 12 Kt—K2, reserving the option of castling on either side.

| 12 Castles KR | P—R3 |
| 13 Kt—K2 | B—Q2 |

With a modest threat of 14 .... P—B5, followed by .... QB×P.

14 P—QR4	Kt—K5
15 Kt—Kt3	Q—K2
16 Kt—R5	P—B3

Quite distressing would be 16 ...., P—Kt3; 17 B×Kt, P×Kt; 18 B—R7 ch, K—B1; 19 Q—B3, etc.

17 Kt—Kt3	P—B5
18 B×Kt	P×B
19 Kt—Q4	P—Kt3

He must prevent 20 Kt—B5.

| 20 P—B3 | |

Having created a bulge in the hostile formation, White uses it to gain access to the enemy's lines.

| 20 ...... | P—B4 |

Compulsory, for if 20 .... P×P; 21 Q×P ch, and if 20 .... B×Kt; 21 P×B, B—B4; 22 Kt×B, P×Kt; 23 P×P, etc.

| 21 P×P | P×P |
| 22 Kt (Q4)—K2 | |

Black's position is ripe for storming.

| 22 ...... | K—R2 |

Or 22 .... B—K4; 23 Kt—B4.

23 R—B6   Kt—Q4
If 23 .... B—B2; 24 QR—KB1.

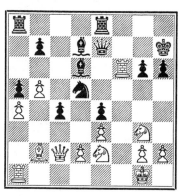

24 Kt × P

This *temporary sacrifice* gains time and space.

24 ......   B—K4
Evidently not 24 .... Kt × R; 25 Kt × Kt ch, nor 24 .... Q × Kt; 25 Q × Q, R × Q; 26 R—B7 ch, K—Kt1; 27 R × B, etc.

But the text move leads to a fresh *unmasking sacrifice*: from Charybdis into Scylla.

25 Kt—Kt5 ch
Decisive.   Black has to capture, otherwise there follows 25 .... K—R1; 26 Kt—B7 ch, followed by 27 Q × KtP ch.

25 ......   P × Kt
26 Q × P ch   K—R1
27 B × B   Q × B
28 Q—R6 ch   K—Kt1
29 R—Kt6 ch   K—B2
30 Q—R7 ch   K—B1
31 R—Kt8 mate.

32. BIRD'S OPENING

495

White   *Black*
BUCKLE   LÖWENTHAL

(London, 1851)

Buckle, one of the strongest players of his time, is seen in this game to have been as well versed in preparatory positional manœuvres as in the handling of a dashing direct attack.

1 P—KB4
A sound opening move, which, however, has the drawback of slightly weakening the King's field.

1 ......   **P—KB4**
With this symmetrical reply, Black declines to contest the initiative.

2 P—QKt3
Logically, White looks after the future of his QB, which is obstructed by the KBP. Or 2 P—K3. A violent continuation is the *Swiss Gambit*: 2 P—K4, P×P; 3 Kt—QB3, Kt—KB3; 4 P—KKt4, etc.

2 ......   **Kt—KB3**
Here, as in most closed openings, symmetry could be maintained a good deal further, e.g. 2 .... P—QKt3; 3 B—Kt2, B—Kt2; 4 P—K3, P—K3.

3 P—Kt3
Foreshadowing the modern trend of thought in which development on the wings precedes that of the centre.

3 ......   **P—K3**
4 B—QKt2   **B—K2**
5 B—Kt2   **P—B3**
Restricting the adverse KB without having recourse to the trenchant advance 5 .... P—Q4.

6 Kt—QB3
He accepts the neutralisation of the two centre files, instead of the more assertive 6 P—B4, followed by the text move.

6 ......   **Kt—R3**
7 Kt—R3
The players vie with one another in giving the game an original, if waiting, character.

7 ......   **P—Q3**
Preparing the thrust .... P—K4.

8 Castles   **Castles**
9 P—K3
If 9 P—K4, P×P; 10 Kt×P, Kt×Kt; 11 B×Kt, and if then 11 .... P—K4; 12 Q—R5, P—KKt3; 13 B×KtP, P×B; 14 Q×P ch, K—R1; 15 P×P, and wins. But Black would play, more cautiously, 11 .... Q—K1.

9 ......   **B—Q2**
10 Q—K2   **P—KR3**
11 KR—K1   **Q—B2**
12 Kt—B2   **P—K4**
13 P×P   **P×P**
14 Kt—Q3   **B—Q3**
15 P—K4   **P—B5**
He tries to mask the weaknesses in his game, and hopes to fish in troubled waters. 15 .... P×P; 16 Kt×P is hardly attractive for Black.

16 P×P   **B—KKt5**
Of course, neither here nor later 16 .... P×P, because of the fork by 17 P—K5.

17 Q—B2   **Q—Q2**
18 Q—R4   **Kt—R4**
19 P—B5
White keeps the material gained.

19 ......   **Kt—B3**
20 Kt—K2
A double threat (winning the KP or, after 20 .... QR—K1; 21 Kt—Kt3, with P—KR3).

20 ......   **B×Kt**
21 R×B   **QR—K1**
22 K—R1
Preparing a decisive action by the Rooks on the depleted KKt file.

22 ......   **P—QKt4**
Lacking a proper objective, Black is reduced to a waiting policy.

23 B—KB3   **Q—KB2**
24 R—KKt1   **K—R2**
Better would be 24 .... K—R1.

25 R—Kt6	R—KKt1
26 R (K2)—Kt2	Kt—Kt1
27 Kt—B2	QKt—Q2
28 P—Q3	

The QB is to take part in the general assault.

28	K—R1

If 28 .... Kt—B1; 29 B—B1, threatening 30 Q×P ch, P×Q; 31 R×P mate.

29 B—B1	B—K2

So as to be able to play 30 .... Kt—B1, which without this move would be catastrophic: 29 .... Kt—B1; 30 B×P, P×B; 31 R×Kt, or 30 .... Kt×R; 31 P×Kt, etc.

30 B—R5	

White's manœuvres are admirably timed. If now 30 .... Kt—B1; 31 R×P ch.

30	Q—B1
31 Q—R3	

Preventing consolidation by 31 .... Kt—R2.

31	Kt×B
32 Q×Kt	Kt—B3
33 Q—R3	B—R6

In order to reply to 34 B—Q2 by 34 .... R—K2.

34 B×P	

The long-expected sacrifice.

34	Kt—R2

It would be hopeless to accept the sacrifice: 34 .... P×B; 35 R×P ch, Q×R; 36 Q×Q ch, Kt—R2; 37 Kt—Kt4, etc.

35 B×P ch	R×B
36 R×R	Q×R
37 R×Q	K×R
38 Kt—Kt4	

Black could well resign here.

38	B—B8
39 Q—R5	R—K2
40 Q—Kt6 ch	K—B1
41 P—B6	Resigns

A brilliantly conducted attack.

496

White	Black
LASKER	BAUER

(Amsterdam, 1889)

In this celebrated game, Lasker enriches the repertoire of the combinative player with a double Bishop's sacrifice, a feat which has since been repeated (notably: Alekhine—Drewitt, Portsmouth, 1923; and—with the black pieces!—Nimzowitsch—Tarrasch, St. Petersburg, 1914).

1 P—KB4	P—Q4

A *Dutch Defence*, with a move in hand.

2 P—K3	Kt—KB3

If 2 .... P—KKt3 (as played by White in the *Blackburne Variation* of the *Dutch Defence*); 3 P—B4.

3 P—QKt3	

More precise is, first, 3 Kt—KB3, for after the text move Black could play 3 .... P—Q5.

3	P—K3

More active is 3 .... B—Kt5, e.g. 4 Kt—KB3, QKt—Q2, etc., or 4 B—K2, B×B, followed by 5 .... QKt—Q2.

4 B—Kt2	B—K2

Not without danger would be 4 .... P—B4; 5 B—Kt5 ch, Kt—B3; 6 Kt—KB3 (Bird, who was an expert in this opening, named after him, used to play 6 B×Kt ch, P×B; 7 Kt—KB3, Q—B2; 8 Kt—K5, etc.); 6 .... B—Q2; 7 Castles, B—Q3; 8 P—Q3, Castles; 9 QKt—Q2, R—B1; 10 KB×Kt, B×B; 11 Kt—K5, and the conquest of this strategic point secures White's advantage.

The same plan used to be followed by Nimzowitsch in devious ways: 1 Kt—KB3, P—Q4; 2 P—QKt3, playing P—KB4 at a much later stage.

5 B—Q3	

He avoids the standardised continuation 5 Kt—KB3, and obtains a rational co-operation of his two Bishops, reserving the possibility of 6 Q—B3, followed by Kt—KR3.

5 ......   P—QKt3
An original if cumbersome counter-plan.

6 Kt—QB3   B—Kt2
7 Kt—B3   QKt—Q2
8 Castles   Castles
9 Kt—K2   P—B4
After 9 .... Kt—B4, he would eliminate
the two Bishops, but White's centre would
be strengthened.

10 Kt—Kt3   Q—B2
With a view to 11 .... P—B5.

11 Kt—K5
If 11 Q—K2, QR—B1.

11 ......   Kt × Kt
12 B × Kt   Q—B3
If 12 .... B—Q3; 13 B × Kt, P × B;
14 Q—R5, P—B4; 15 Q—Kt5 ch, K—R1;
16 Q—B6 ch, K—Kt1; 17 Kt—R5, forcing
the mate. It can be seen that the clouds are
gathering around the black King's field.

13 Q—K2   P—QR3
Stopping 14 B—Kt5, and intending
14 .... P—QKt4. He can play neither
13 .... KR—B1; 14 B—Kt5, holding the
black Queen to ransom, nor 13 ....
KR—Q1, nor 13 .... P—KR3, nor even
13 .... K—R1; 14 Kt—R5, Kt × Kt;
15 B × RP, Kt—B3; 16 B × Kt, P × B;
17 Q—R5, R—KKt1; 18 R—B3, and wins.
Comparatively the best is 13 .... P—Kt3.

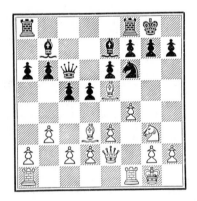

14 Kt—R5
Sounding the attack!

14 ......   Kt × Kt
There is no saving clause, e.g. if 14 ....
P—B5; 15 Kt × Kt ch, P × Kt; 16 B × P ch,

K × B; 17 Q—R5 ch, K—Kt1; 18 Q—Kt4
ch, K—R2; 19 R—B3, followed by R—R3
mate. Or if 14 .... P—R3; 15 Kt × Kt ch,
B × Kt (15 .... P × Kt; 16 Q—Kt4 ch,
K—R1; 17 Q—R4, K—Kt2; 18 R—B3,
etc.); 16 B × B, P × B; 17 Q—Kt4 ch, K—R1;
18 R—B3, R—KKt1; 19 Q—R4, K—Kt2;
20 R—Kt3 ch, K—B1; 21 Q × P, etc., with
enough to win.

After the text move, Black expects
15 Q × Kt, after which 15 .... P—B4 would
enable him to hold out. But a well prepared and miraculous combination frustrates
his hopes.

15 B × P ch   K × B
16 Q × Kt ch   K—Kt1
17 B × P
This *complementary sacrifice* of a second
Bishop completes the destruction of the
black King's position.

17 ......   K × B
18 Q—Kt4 ch   K—R2
If 18 .... K—B3; 19 Q—Kt5 mate.

19 R—B3
The reserve artillery.

19 ......   P—K4
The only means of saving the mate.

20 R—R3 ch   Q—R3
21 R × Q ch   K × R
22 Q—Q7
The final point!

22 ......   B—KB3
23 Q × B   K—Kt2
A better defence than 23 .... P × P;
24 R—KB1.

24 R—KB1   QR—Kt1
25 Q—Q7   KR—Q1
26 Q—Kt4 ch   K—B1
27 P × P   B—Kt2
If 27 .... B × P; 28 Q—K6.

28 P—K6   R—Kt2
29 Q—Kt6   P—B3
30 R × P ch
The final blow.

30 ......   B × R
31 Q × B ch   K—K1
32 Q—R8 ch   K—K2
33 Q—Kt7 ch   Resigns.

497

White	Black
TARTAKOWER	PRINS

(Zandvoort, 1936)

The feature of this game is White's sacrifice of the exchange at the very moment when he looks like gaining material, which in fact breaks down Black's resistance.

1 P—KB4	P—K4

A violent reply.

2 P×P

White can revert to the *King's Gambit* by 2 P—K4.

2	P—Q3
3 P×P	B×P

On the strength of the threat 4 .... Q—R5 ch (5 P—Kt3, Q×P ch; 6 P×Q, B×P mate), the *From Gambit* is not without practical chances.

4 Kt—KB3

More awkward is 4 P—KKt3, P—KR4, etc.

4	Kt—KB3

Aiming at both KKt5 and K5. A less varied route is available after 4 .... Kt—KR3; 5 P—Q4, Kt—Kt5; 6 Q—Q3, and Black's impetus will be gradually checked.

The most incisive continuation is 4 .... P—KKt4, as played in a consultation game Bird and Dobell—Gunsberg and Locock, *Hastings*, 1892: 5 P—B3 (the best is 5 P—Q4, P—Kt5, and now, not the chancy 6 Kt—Kt5, but 6 Kt—K5, B×Kt; 7 P×B, Q×Q ch; 8 K×Q, Kt—QB3; 9 B—Kt5, etc., and the straggling formation of Black's pawns tells against him); 5 .... P—Kt5; 6 Q—R4 ch, Kt—B3; 7 Kt—Q4, Q—R5 ch; 8 K—Q1, P—Kt6; 9 P—Kt3 (9 P—KR3 is necessary); 9 .... Q×P, and White resigns.

5 P—KKt3

If 5 P—Q4, Kt—K5 (instead of 5 .... Kt—Kt5; 6 Q—Q3, etc.); 6 Q—Q3, P—KB4, fishing in troubled waters.

5	P—KR4

A natural reaction.

6 P—Q4	P—R5
7 P×P	Kt—K5

Threat: 8 .... R×P.

8 Q—Q3	B—KB4

Not 8 .... R×P; 9 B—Kt5, Kt×B; 10 Kt×R.

9 B—R3

Only this duplication can stop Black's onslaught, which was already threatening

9 .... R×P or 9 .... Kt—Kt6. If 9 Kt—B3, B—QKt5.

9	B—Kt3

After 9 .... B×B; 10 Q×Kt ch, White would rapidly gain the upper hand.

10 R—Kt1

Openly announcing his intention of giving up the exchange.

Joyless would be 10 Q—Kt5 ch, P—B3; 11 Q×P, R×P, etc.

10	Q—K2
11 R×B	

An *eliminating sacrifice* with far-reaching effect.

11	P×R
12 Kt—B3	

If 12 QKt—Q2, R×P, whereas after the text move 12 .... R×P is inadmissible on account of 13 B—Kt5.

12	Kt×Kt
13 P×Kt	

White refrains from rushing his offensive. He could agree to an exchange of Queens by 13 Q×P ch, Q—B2; 14 Q×Q ch, K×Q; 15 P×Kt, remaining with three pawns for the exchange.

13	Castles

Rightly seeking salvation in a counter-attack.

14 Q×P	R—K1

If 14 .... R×Kt; 15 B—K6 ch, R—B2; 16 B—Kt5, Q—K1; 17 P—R5 (not 17 Castles, K—B1, nor 17 P—K4, Q—Q2, nor again, 17 R—Kt1, Kt—Q2, etc.); 17 .... K—B1; 18 Q—R7, R—B8 ch; 19 K—Q2, B—B5 ch; 20 K—Q3, Q—Kt4 ch; 21 P—B4, Q×B; 22 Q—Kt8 ch, K—K2; 23 Q—B7 ch, K—Q3; 24 R×R, and wins.

15 Q—Q3	Kt—Q2
16 Kt—Kt5	Kt—B3

If 16 .... Kt—B1; 17 B—K6 ch.

17 B—K6 ch	K—R1

After 17 .... K—B1, White maintains his grip by 18 Q—B5, e.g. 18 .... KR—Q1; 19 Kt—R7 ch, K—K1; 20 Q—Kt6 ch, or 18 .... Q—Q1; 19 Q—Kt6, Q—K2; 20 P—Q5, with the threat Q—R7. Giving up the Queen by 17 .... Q×B; 18 Kt×Q, R×Kt; 19 B—Kt5, etc., would be insufficient.

18 Kt—B7 ch	K—Kt1
19 B—Kt3	K—B1
20 Kt—R8	

This final stroke (threatening 21 Kt—Kt6 mate) is not without humour.

20	Resigns.

33. IRREGULAR OPENINGS

498

White	Black
BLACKBURNE	NIMZOWITSCH

(St. Petersburg, 1914)

The freshness and vitality with which the veteran conducts this game are reminiscent of his prime.

1 P—K3
Mentioned long ago by Lucena (1498), this, the *Van't Kruyz Opening*, is a highly modern opening showing a spirit of discretion in the centre. It frequently leads into variations of other openings.

1 ...... P—Q3
Reserved in his turn. After 1 .... P—K4 White can revert to the *Exchange Variation* of the *French Defence*, or seek untrodden paths by 2 Kt—QB3, P—Q4; 3 P—Q4, P×P; 4 Q×P, Kt—KB3; 5 P—K4, Kt—B3; 6 B—QKt5, etc.

2 P—KB4
A *Bird's Opening Deferred*.

2 ...... P—K4
The opening of the KB file is destined to be of great advantage to White. More reserved is 2 .... P—KKt3.

3 P×P P×P
4 Kt—QB3
In order to bring about an open game by 5 P—K4—a bold conception, which recks nothing of loss of time or of the depletion of the weakened diagonal KKt1—QR7. Of course, not at once 4 P—K4, Q—R5 ch, nor 4 Kt—KB3, P—K5.

4 ...... B—Q3
If 4 .... P—KB4; 5 P—K4.

5 P—K4
Evidently not 5 P—Q4, P×P; 6 P×P, Q—R5 ch; 7 P—Kt3, B×P ch, and wins, nor, prematurely, 5 Kt—B3, B—KKt5.

5 ...... B—K3
Preventing White from occupying the live diagonal QR2—KKt8 by 6 B—B4.

6 Kt—B3 P—KB3
Creating a fairly secure asylum for his King.

7 P—Q3 Kt—K2
If 7 .... B—QB4; 8 Kt—QR4.

8 B—K3 P—QB4
Foreshadowing his plan of blockading Q5, which, however, creates some dead points in his own position. Better is 8 .... Kt—Q2, with a view to 9 .... B—QB4.

9 Q—Q2 QKt—B3
10 B—K2 Kt—Q5
11 Castles KR Castles
12 Kt—Q1 KKt—B3
13 P—B3
Again White shows that he is not afraid of phantoms, for he risks weakening and exposing his base at Q3.

13 ...... Kt×B ch
14 Q×Kt R—K1
15 Kt—R4
The beginning of lengthy operations on the KB file.

15 ...... B—KB1
16 Kt—B5 K—R1
Simpler would be 16 .... B×Kt.

17 P—KKt4 Q—Q2
If 17 .... B×Kt; 18 KtP×B, and the KKt file becomes the base of action.

18 Kt—B2 P—QR4
Very naturally, he seeks counter-action on the opposite wing.

19 P—QR3
In order to render the QR mobile, which it would not be after 19 P—QR4.

19 ...... P—QKt4
20 QR—Q1 QR—Kt1
21 R—Q2 P—Kt5
22 RP×P RP×P
23 P—B4
He closes two files (QKt and QB) at one stroke. The open QR file will be of little use to Black.

23 ...... R—R1
24 Q—B3 R—R7
Beating the air.

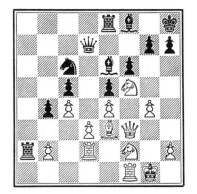

25 P—Kt5
A very fine break-through.

25 ......   P—Kt3
He hopes to escape with little harm.
Better is 25 .... B × Kt, in spite of hidden
or apparent dangers.

26 Kt—Kt4
A brilliant conception.

26 ......   P × Kt
Or 26 .... P × P; 27 Kt—B6, etc.

27 Kt × BP   Kt—Q5
Or 27 .... P × P; 28 Q × P, and the tension continues.

28 Q—B2   Q—B3
29 Kt × R   Q × Kt
30 B × Kt   KP × B
31 P × P   B—Q2
32 R—K1
On balance White has an advantage of the
exchange and two pawns for a piece. Nevertheless, the black Bishops could quickly
become an influential force unless White
succeeds in turning his Rooks to account on
the open K file, and in using his advanced
pawns as battering rams. The way White
effects both these operations is masterly.

32 ......   Q—B2
33 Q—R4   R—R1
Not 33 .... Q × KBP; 34 R—KB1, nor
33 .... B × P; 34 R—KB2, Q—Kt3;
35 R (K1)—KB1, and wins.

34 R—KB2   B—B3
35 Q—Kt4   R—K1
36 R × R   Q × R
37 R—K2
This Rook is to keep three hostile pieces
occupied.

37 ......   Q—Q2
38 R—K6   B—R1
With a view to 39 .... Q—QKt2 or
39 .... Q—R2 or 39 .... Q—R5.

39 P—Kt6
Refuting Black's intentions, for if 39 ....
Q—QKt2; 40 Q—K4, and if 39 ....
Q—R2; 40 R—K8, Q—R8 ch; 41 K—B2,
Q × P ch; 42 Q—K2, and wins; or 39 ....
Q—R5; 40 P × P, etc. On the other hand,
White already threatens 40 P × P.

39 ......   P × P
40 R × P
Triumph of the "twin-open files."

40 ......   Q—KR2
Or 40 .... Q—KB2; 41 Q—R4 ch,
Q—R2; 42 Q—B6 ch, B—Kt2; 43 Q—Q8
ch, Q—Kt1; 44 Q × Q ch, K × Q; 45 P—B6;
or 40 .... B—KKt2; 41 Q—R5 ch, K—Kt1;
42 P—B6.

41 Q—Kt3   Q—R4
42 R—Kt4
With the double effect of stopping 42 ....
Q—Q8 ch, and threatening 43 R—R4.

42 ......   Resigns
If 42 .... B—K2; 43 Q—K5 ch, etc.

499

White	Black
White	*Black*
BARATZ	MENCHIK

(Hastings, 1927)

*A pretty game, in which Black wins, one
after another, no less than four pawns with
astuteness worthy of the former woman
Champion of the World.*

1 P—QKt3
The *Queen's Fianchetto Opening*, men-
tioned by Lucena (1498), leads to a slow
development.
More risky is the *Extended Queen's
Fianchetto*, as shown in a game Fleissig—
Schlechter, *Vienna*, 1895: 1 P—QKt4, P—K3;
2 B—Kt2, Kt—KB3; 3 P—QR3, P—B4;
4 P—Kt5, P—Q4; 5 P—Q4, Q—R4 ch;
6 Kt—B3, Kt—K5; 7 Q—Q3, P × P; 8 Q × P,
B—B4; 9 Q × KtP, B × P ch; 10 K—Q1,
P—Q5; 11 Q × R ch, K—K2; 12 Q × B,
P × Kt; 13 B—B1, Kt—Q2; 14 Q × R,

Q×KtP; 15 B—B4, Q—Q4 ch; 16 K—B1,
B—K6 ch; 17 B×B, Kt—B7, and White
resigns.

    1 ......   P—Q4
Or 1 .... P—K4; 2 B—Kt2, P—KB3.

    2 B—Kt2   Kt—KB3
    3 P—K3   P—KKt3
A good idea. In the duel between the
two Bishops on the black squares, the second
player's Bishop will have the advantage,
after castling, of being protected.

    4 Kt—KB3
Useless would be 4 B×Kt, P×B, whilst
fresh responsibilities would be incurred by
4 P—KB4, B—Kt2; 5 Kt—KB3.

    4 ......   B—Kt2
    5 P—KR3   Castles
    6 P—KKt4
Intimidation.

    6 ......   P—B4
    7 B—Kt2   Kt—B3
    8 P—Q3
Against this restricted centre Black will
intensify her activity in the centre by preparing the advance .... P—K4.

    8 ......   B—Q2
    9 QKt—Q2
Nothing would come of 9 P—Kt5,
Kt—KR4.

    9 ......   Q—B2
    10 Kt—B1
Heading for a mistake, but White's
position is already invidious. If 10 Q—K2,
thinking of castling on the Q side, then
10 .... Kt—QKt5; 11 Kt—B1, Q—R4;
12 B—B3, KKt×P; 13 B×B, Kt×QP
db ch; 14 K—Q1, KKt×BP ch, and wins.
The simplest is therefore 10 Castles.

    10 ......   KR—Q1
Intending the full deployment of her forces
by .... B—K1 and .... QR—B1 before
deciding on .... P—K4.

    11 Kt—Kt3
What could be more plausible?

    11 ......   Kt×P
Astonishing.

    12 P×Kt
For if 12 B×B, Kt×KP, with the two
unfortunate sequels by 13 P×Kt, Q×Kt ch,
or 13 Q—Q2, Kt×B ch, etc.

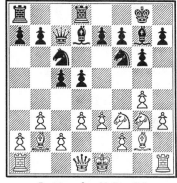

Position after 11 Kt—Kt3

    12 ......   B × B
    13 QR—Kt1   B—B6 ch
Although White has only lost a pawn, his
game suffers from other organic weaknesses.

    14 Kt—Q2
Compulsory, for otherwise there follows
14 .... B×P.

    14 ......   Kt—K4
    15 B—B3
If 15 P—B3, Kt×P

    15 ......   Q—R4
Tightening her grip.

    16 Kt—B1   Q×P
Severe reprisals.

    17 B—K2   Q—R4
    18 P—B4   Kt—B3
    19 K—B2
White's King is paying dearly for having
scorned humdrum castling.

    19 ......   Q—B2
    20 B—B3
Or 20 K—B3, P—K4.

    20 ......   P—Q5
    21 Kt—K4   P×P ch
    22 K—Kt3   B—Kt2
If 22 .... B—Q5; 23 P—B3.

    23 Kt×KP   B—K1
Turning the Rook to account whilst fore-
stalling the threat 24 Kt×P, for now 24 ....
B—Q5.

    24 Q—KB1   P—KR3
An astute double threat.

    25 P—B3
Or 25 Kt—Kt2, P—KKt4.

25 ...... Q × P ch
A superb move, winning a third pawn.

26 K—B2
He hopes for the miscalculation 26 ....
B—K4; 27 Kt—Kt2, B—Q5 ch; 28 P × B,
Q—B2; 29 P × P, etc., winning.

26 ...... Kt—K4
Black wins a fourth pawn.

Resigns.

500

White	Black
RÉTI	ALEKHINE

(Baden-Baden, 1925)

In this encounter between two great players, both outstanding strategists who knew the last word about tactics, there is a profusion of the most intricate and fascinating combinations.

1 P—KKt3
The *King's Fianchetto Opening* gives Black a free hand in the centre, which is not the case in the *Réti-Zukertort* or *Catalan* systems. White assumes an arduous task.

1 ...... P—K4
Black boldly takes the initiative. More reserved is 1 .... P—Q4; 2 B—Kt2, P—QB3, restricting the action of White's KB on the long diagonal.

2 Kt—KB3
Alekhine's Defence with a move in hand, which move is, however, of doubtful value.

2 ...... P—K5
Or 2 .... Kt—QB3; 3 P—Q4, P × P (3 .... P—K5; 4 KKt—Q2); 4 Kt × P, B—B4; 5 Kt × Kt, KtP × Kt; 6 B—Kt2, and White has the superior formation.

3 Kt—Q4 P—Q4
4 P—Q3 P × P
More insistent is 4 .... P—QB4, as after the text move White's development puts on a spurt and takes advantage of the long white diagonal.

5 Q × P
If now 5 .... P—QB4; 6 Kt—KB3.

5 ...... Kt—KB3
6 B—Kt2 B—Kt5 ch
7 B—Q2 B × B ch
8 Kt × B Castles
9 P—QB4 Kt—R3
A good reply. Black wants to establish a piece at Q4.

10 P × P Kt—QKt5
11 Q—B4 QKt × QP
12 QKt—Kt3 P—B3
13 Castles KR R—K1
14 KR—Q1 B—Kt5
15 R—Q2 Q—B1
Scientific manœuvres by both players. His mobilisation hardly completed, Black already aims at the slight weakness in the white King's field. For his part, White has taken timely measures to preserve his valuable KB.

16 Kt—QB5
A "red herring."

16 ...... B—R6
17 B—B3
A line, full of the unexpected, would be 17 B × B, Q × B; 18 Kt × KtP, Kt—KKt5; 19 Kt—B3, Kt (Q4)—K6; 20 P × Kt, Kt × KP; 21 Q × P ch, K—R1 (not 21 .... K × Q; 22 Kt—Kt5 ch); 22 Kt—R4, R—KB1; 23 Q—Kt3, Q—B8 ch; 24 R × Q, R × R mate.

17 ...... B—Kt5
18 B—Kt2 B—R6
19 B—B3 B—Kt5
20 B—R1
The crucial moment. Underestimating his opponent's resources, White avoids the draw by repetition of moves—the legitimate outcome of the potentialities of the position.

20 ...... P—KR4
The well-proven procedure against the *fianchetto*.

21 P—Kt4 P—R3
22 R—QB1 P—R5
23 P—R4 P × P
24 RP × P Q—B2
25 P—Kt5
It would be better to suspend the action on the Q side and to attend to the centre by 25 P—K4.

25 ...... RP × P
26 P × P
White's strategic plan has consistently been to undermine first the outpost at Black's K5 (4 P—Q3), then the semi-advanced post at his Q4 (9 P—QB4), and

even the hostile base at QB3. But now a tactical *coup* prevails over strategic considerations.

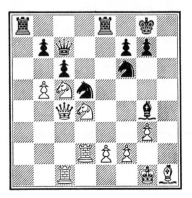

26 ......   R—K6
A magnificent irruption. If now 27 P × R, Q × P ch; 28 B—Kt2, Kt—K6, with a forced mate. In addition, Black's text move threatens 27 .... R × P ch.

27 Kt—B3
Relatively the best defence is 27 B—B3.

27 ......   P × P
28 Q × P   Kt—B6
29 Q × P
If 29 Q—B4, P—QKt4.

29 ......   Q × Q
Curiously enough, in spite of the exchange of Queens, Black's attack loses none of its intensity.

30 Kt × Q   Kt × P ch
A most complicated affair.

If, instead of the text move, 30 .... R × P, then neither 31 R × Kt, B × Kt, etc., nor 31 R—Q3, QKt—K5, but 31 R (Q2)—B2, R × R; 32 R × R, R—R8 ch; 33 K—Kt2 (if 33 K—R2, R × B ch; 34 K × R, B × Kt ch, and Black has two minor pieces for a Rook); 33 .... Kt—Kt4 (threatening 34 .... B × Kt ch); 34 Kt—K5, and White is out of the danger zone.

31 K—R2
If 31 K—B1, Kt × P ch; 32 P × Kt, B × Kt; 33 B × B, R × B ch; 34 K—Kt2, QR—R6, and wins.

31 ......   Kt—K5
A powerful reinforcement.

32 R—B4
If 32 P × Kt, KKt × R, and White loses at least the exchange.

32 ......   Kt × BP
33 B—Kt2   B—K3
The final combination.

34 R (B4)—B2   Kt—Kt5 ch
35 K—R3
He can do no other: if 35 K—R1, R—R8 ch.

35 ......   Kt—K4 dis ch
36 K—R2
If 36 K—R4, R—K5 ch.

36 ......   R × Kt
37 R × Kt   Kt—Kt5 ch
38 K—R3   Kt—K6 dis ch
39 K—R2   Kt × R
40 B × R   Kt—Q5
The key to the whole combination; a white piece is lost in lamentable circumstances. White resigns.
A great feat.

GAMES AT ODDS, BLINDFOLD, ETC.

GAMES AT ODDS

I. PAWN AND MOVE (REMOVE BLACK'S KBP)

White	Black
ATWOOD	PHILIDOR

(London, 1795)

Undisputed champion of his time and the founder of modern chess, Philidor was a firm believer in pawn strategy. His motto was: The pawns are the soul of chess. In the following game, won from a player of the first rank, he effects his favourite stratagem— assault by pawns—by means of a pretty sacrifice of a Bishop.

	White	Black
1	P—K4	
2	P—Q4	P—K3
3	P—KB4	P—Q4
4	P—K5	P—B4
5	P—B3	QKt—B3
6	Kt—B3	Q—Kt3
7	B—Q3	Kt—R3
8	Q—Kt3	P—B5
9	Q×Q	P×Q
10	B—B2	P—QKt4
11	P—QKt4	B×P
12	P×B	Kt×KtP
13	K—Q2	Kt×B
14	K×Kt	P—Kt5
15	B—Q2	R—R5
16	P—KR3	R—B1
17	P—Kt4	Kt—B2
18	Kt—Kt5	Kt×Kt
19	P×Kt	R—B7
20	P—R4	P—Kt4
21	P—R5	P—Kt6 ch
22	K—Kt2	P—Kt5
23	P—Kt6	RP×P
24	KRP×P	B—R3
25	R—R8 ch	K—Q2

And Black won.

E.g. 26 R—KKt8, P×P; 27 R×P ch, K—B3; 28 R×P, R×B ch; 29 Kt×R, P—B6 ch; 30 K—Kt3, R×R; 31 R—B7 ch, K×R; 32 P—Kt7, R—Kt7 ch; 33 K—R4, P×Kt, etc.

II. PAWN AND TWO (REMOVE BLACK'S KBP)

White	Black
McDONNELL	LEWIS

(London, about 1825)

After a premature attack (9 Q—R5 ch, instead of 9 KP×P), White not only loses his pawn, but is himself exposed to attack. Black pursues his advantage with notable energy, and finishes the game with a beautiful and decisive stroke.

	White	Black
1	P—K4	
2	P—Q4	Kt—QB3
3	B—Q3	P—K4
4	P—KB4	P—Q3
5	P—Q5	QKt—K2
6	P—B5	P—KKt3
7	Kt—KR3	P—B3
8	P—B4	KtP×P
9	Q—R5 ch	K—Q2
10	Q—B7	Q—K1
11	Kt—Kt5	P—KR3
12	Q×Q ch	K×Q
13	Kt—K6	B×Kt
14	P×B	P×P
15	B×KP	Kt—B3
16	Kt—B3	P—Q4
17	P×P	P×P
18	B—B2	R—B1
19	Castles	B—Kt2
20	B—R4 ch	K—Q1
21	Kt—Kt5	R—B3
22	B—Q2	R×P
23	B—R5 ch	P—Kt3
24	B—Kt4	Kt—B3
25	B—R3	B—B1
26	QR—B1	B×B
27	Kt×B	Kt—Q5
28	KR—K1	R—Kt1
29	K—B1	Kt—K5
30	B—Q1	Kt—Q7 ch
31	K—B2	R—B3 ch
32	K—K3	R×P
33	B—K2	Kt—K5
34	B—R5	Kt—B4 ch
35	K—B3	Kt—R5 db ch
36	K—K3	R—B6 ch
37	B×R	Kt—B4 ch
38	K—Q3	R—Q7 mate

Without trying to push his name forward

or courting public favour, Lewis was one of the foremost players of his day.

III. Pawn and Two (Remove Black's KBP)

White	Black
COCHRANE	DESCHAPELLES

(Paris, between 1815 and 1832)

A pitched battle in which the contestants fight desperately for the initiative, until a stroke of genius (22 .... Q—R5) decides the day in favour of Black.

	White	Black
1	P—K4	
2	P—Q4	P—K3
3	P—KB4	P—Q4
4	P—K5	P—B4
5	P—B3	Kt—QB3
6	Kt—B3	P × P
7	P × P	Q—Kt3
8	Kt—B3	B—Q2
9	P—QR3	Kt—R3
10	P—R3	Kt—B4
11	Kt—K2	B—K2
12	P—KKt4	B—R5 ch
13	Kt × B	Kt × Kt
14	K—B2	Castles KR
15	K—Kt3	Kt—Kt3
16	P—Kt4	P—QR4
17	B—Q2	P × P
18	B × P	Kt × B
19	P × Kt	Q × KtP
20	R—QKt1	R—R6 ch
21	K—R2	Q—K2
22	R × P	Q—R5
23	R × B	Q—B7 ch
24	B—Kt2	R × P ch
25	K × R	Q—R5 mate.

IV. Pawn and Two (Remove Black's KBP)

White	Black
MONGREDIEN	ST. AMANT

(London, between 1834 and 1844)

A feature of this game is the ingenious manner in which Black regains his pawn, and the no less ingenious way in which, on a full board, he wins a piece.

	White	Black
1	P—K4	
2	P—Q4	P—K3
3	B—Q3	P—B4
4	P—QB3	P × P
5	P × P	Kt—QB3
6	P—K5	Q—Kt3
7	Q—R5 ch	K—Q1
8	Kt—K2	KKt—K2
9	Q—Kt4	Q—Kt5 ch
10	B—Q2	Kt × KP
11	B × Q	Kt × Q
12	Kt—Q2	Kt—Q4
13	B—B3	P—QKt3
14	P—KR3	Kt (Kt5)—B3
15	Castles KR	P—KKt4
16	P—QR4	B—QKt2
17	P—R5	P—R4
18	P × P	P × P
19	R × R ch	B × R
20	R—R1	B—QKt2
21	R—R7	K—B1
22	B—R6	B × B
23	R × B	K—Kt2
24	R—R1	P—Kt5
25	P—R4	B—Q3
26	P—KKt3	R—QB1
27	R—R4	P—Kt4
28	R—R1	P—Kt5

And Black wins.

V. Odds of the Knight (Remove White's KKt)

White	Black
GRECO	N.

(1622–34)

A "storm in a teacup." In this short skirmish one can almost feel the hope, the triumph, and then the sad disillusionment of the odds taker in quick and exciting sequence.

	White	Black
1	P—K4	P—K4
2	B—B4	Kt—KB3
3	P—Q4	Kt × P
4	P × P	Kt × P
5	Castles	Kt × Q
6	B × P ch	K—Q2
7	B—Kt5 mate.	

VI. Odds of the Knight (Remove White's QKt)

White	Black
PHILIDOR	ATWOOD

(London, 1794)

Philidor's method of besieging the critical point KB7 positionally is very remarkable. Remarkable, because in those days rapid and brilliant decisions were the order of the day, because the King's Gambit *does not lend itself to a slow and scientific treatment, and, finally, because a player, giving the odds of a piece, usually seeks the solution of the problem in surprise moves, and not in methodical play.*

1 P—K4	P—K4
2 P—KB4	P × P
3 Kt—B3	P—KKt4
4 B—B4	B—Kt2
5 P—B3	Q—K2
6 P—Q4	P—Q3
7 Castles	P—KR4
8 P—KR4	P—Kt5
9 Kt—Kt5	Kt—KR3
10 B × P	Castles
11 Q—Kt3	Kt—B3
12 B—Q2	Kt—Q1
13 Q—B2	K—R1
14 QR—K1	Kt—K3
15 P—K5	Kt × Kt
16 P × Kt	Kt—Kt1
17 P × P	Q × QP
18 B × P	Q—QB3
19 P—Q5	Q—Q2
20 Q—Kt6	Resigns.

VII. Odds of the Knight (Remove White's QKt)

White	Black
McDONNELL	SLOUS

(London, between 1832 and 1835)

Before embarking on his final assault (17 B—Kt8), White succeeds in obtaining a plethora of open files and diagonals. One is reminded of an anecdote which tells how the great Morphy, at the odds of the Queen, had to sacrifice the whole of his material, and yet his depressed adversary resigned, because of an open file which he thought was still in Morphy's power.

1 P—K4	P—K4
2 Kt—B3	Kt—QB3
3 B—B4	B—B4
4 P—QKt4	B × P
5 P—B3	B—B4
6 Castles	P—Q3
7 P—Q4	B—Kt3
8 P × P	Kt × P
9 Kt × Kt	P × Kt
10 B × P ch	K—K2
11 B—R3 ch	P—B4
12 Q—Kt3	Kt—B3
13 QR—Q1	Q—B2
14 P—KB4	Kt—Kt5
15 P × P	Q × P
16 P—Kt3	Kt—K6
17 B—Kt8	B—K3
18 R—B7 ch	K—K1
19 Q—Kt5 ch	B—Q2
20 Q × B mate.	

VIII. Odds of the Knight (Remove White's QKt)

White	Black
MORPHY	MAURIAN

(New Orleans, 1857)

An amazing number of sacrifices takes place in the following short game: besides the QKt given at the outset, the KKt is offered (5 P—Q4, Ghulam Kassim's Attack, a variant of the Muzio Gambit), *then the KB, two innocent pawns, and, finally, the Rook. A real "Morphy."*

1 P—K4	P—K4
2 P—KB4	P × P
3 Kt—B3	P—KKt4
4 B—B4	P—Kt5
5 P—Q4	P × Kt
6 Q × P	P—Q4
7 KB × P	P—QB3
8 B × KBP ch	K × B
9 Q—R5 ch	K—Kt2
10 B × P	B—K2
11 Castles KR	Q × P ch
12 K—R1	Q × KP
13 QR—K1	Q—Kt3
14 R × B ch	K—B1 (a)

(a) If 14 .... Kt × R; 15 B—R6 ch and mate next move.

15 B—Q6 dis ch   Resigns (b)

(b) For 15 .... Kt—B3; 16 R × Kt ch, Q × R; 17 Q—K8 mate.

IX. ODDS OF THE KNIGHT (REMOVE WHITE'S· QKt)

White	Black
MORPHY	THOMPSON

(New York, 1859)

Although Black puts up a strong defence, he is not proof against Morphy's encircling stratagems. The finish, with a Queen's sacrifice leading to a "two Bishops' mate," is very brilliant.

1 P—K4	P—K4
2 Kt—B3	Kt—QB3
3 B—B4	B—B4
4 P—QKt4	B × P
5 P—B3	B—R4
6 Castles	B—Kt3
7 P—Q4	P—Q3
8 P × P	Kt × P
9 Kt × Kt	P × Kt
10 B × P ch	K—K2
11 Q—Kt3	Kt—B3
12 B—R3 ch	P—B4
13 QR—Q1	Q—B2
14 P—KB4	R—B1
15 B—B4	R—Q1
16 QR—K1	B—Q2
17 B—B1	R—KB1
18 P × P	Q × P
19 B—B4	Q—R4
20 R—Q1	K—Q1
21 P—K5	Kt—K1
22 Q—R4	Q—Kt5
23 P—K6	Kt—B3

White announced mate in three (24 R × B ch, etc.).

X. ODDS OF THE KNIGHT (REMOVE WHITE'S QKt)

White	Black
ANDERSSEN	HILLEL

(Breslau, 1859)

With his peremptory advance on his 9th move, Black "sows the wind and reaps the whirlwind." The resources of unmasking and deviation sacrifices break down his defences with elemental force.

1 P—K4	P—K4
2 Kt—B3	Kt—QB3
3 P—B3	P—Q4

4 B—Kt5	P × P
5 Kt × P	B—Q2
6 Kt × B	Q × Kt
7 Castles	Castles
8 P—B3	B—B4 ch
9 K—R1	P—K6
10 P—Q4	Q—K3
11 R—K1	Kt × P
12 P × Kt	R × P
13 Q—B2	B—Kt3
14 B × P	R—Q1
15 QR—Q1	Q—K4
16 B—Kt5	Q × QB
17 Q—B5 ch	Q × Q
18 R × R ch	K × R
19 R—K8 mate.	

XI. ODDS OF THE KNIGHT (REMOVE WHITE'S QKt)

White	Black
CAPABLANCA	N.

(1919)

In the best classical tradition, the Cuban genius forces a free passage through the KB file, after which he willingly allows all exchanges offered by his adversary. The mate, effected, so to speak, by the Queen alone, is impressive.

1 P—K4	P—K4
2 P—KB4	P × P
3 Kt—B3	P—KKt4
4 B—B4	B—Kt2
5 Castles	P—KR3
6 P—KKt3	P—Kt5
7 Kt—R4	P—B6
8 Kt × P	P × Kt
9 B × P ch	K × B
10 Q × P ch	Kt—B3
11 P—K5	R—B1
12 P × Kt	B × P
13 P—Q4	K—Kt2
14 Q—R5	B—Kt4
15 R × R	K × R
16 B × B	Q × B
17 R—B1 ch	K—K2
18 Q—B7 ch	K—Q3
19 R—B6 ch	Q × R
20 Q × Q ch	K—Q4
21 Q—K5 ch	K—B3
22 Q—B5 mate.	

XII. Odds of Knight and Move
(Remove Black's QKt)

White	Black
ALDERTON	du MONT

(London, 1931)

In this game at unusual and difficult odds, Black submits to and encourages a violent attack by White. White overruns the KKt file, doubles and trebles the pressure on the KKt pawn, the presumed centre of Black's resistance, displaces the obstacle, wins the Queen, only to find that the pawn in question has become Black's winning asset, and cannot be prevented from queening.

	White	Black
1	P—Q4	P—KB4
2	P—QB4	P—K3
3	Kt—QB3	Kt—B3
4	Kt—B3	P—QKt3
5	P—KKt3	B—Kt2
6	B—Kt2	B—K2
7	Castles	Castles
8	Q—B2	R—B1
9	B—K3	Q—K1
10	P—KR3	Q—R4
11	Kt—R2	B × B
12	K × B	P—KKt4
13	P—B3	K—R1
14	P—KKt4	Q—Kt3
15	B—B2	P—KR4
16	R—R1	K—Kt2
17	QR—KKt1	B—Q3
18	K—B1	RP × P
19	RP × P	R—KR1
20	P × P	P × P
21	B—K3	R—R4
22	Q—Q2	P—Kt5
23	P × P	P × P
24	R—Kt2	R—B1
25	K—K1	P—Kt6
26	R(R1)—Kt1	R × Kt
27	R × R	P × R
28	R × Q ch	K × R
29	Q—Q3 ch	K—B2
	Resigns.	

XIII. Odds of the Queen (Remove White's Queen)

White	Black
COCHRANE	N.

(London, between 1815 and 1832)

Giving the odds of the Queen implies remuneration of an immediate attack, and waiting until the presumably inexperienced opponent commits himself to some sterile

expedition. The co-operation of White's three minor pieces in the weaving of a mating net is very effective.

	White	Black
1	P—K4	P—K4
2	P—KB4	P × P
3	B—B4	Q—R5 ch
4	K—Q1	B—B4
5	Kt—KB3	Q—Q1
6	P—Q4	B—Kt3
7	B × P	P—KB3
8	P—K5	Kt—K2
9	P × P	P × P
10	Kt—B3	QKt—B3
11	R—K1	B—R4
12	Kt—K4	B × R
13	Kt × P ch	K—B1
14	B—R6 mate.	

BLINDFOLD GAMES

XIV

White	Black
BRUHL	PHILIDOR

(London, 1787)

Philidor introduced the art of blindfold play, then new to Europe, playing usually three games at the same time. This number has, in modern times, been increased to an incredible extent. Philidor, however, having no competitor, lacked the incentive to try for more.

In the present game, against one of the strongest players of the period, Philidor shows the depth of his conceptions in the middle game and his flawless technique in a Rook ending.

	White	Black
1	P—K4	P—K4
2	B—B4	P—QB3
3	Q—K2	P—Q3
4	P—QB3	P—KB4
5	P—Q3	Kt—B3
6	P × P	B × P
7	P—Q4	P—K5
8	B—KKt5	P—Q4
9	B—Kt3	B—Q3
10	Kt—Q2	QKt—Q2
11	P—KR3	P—KR3
12	B—K3	Q—K2
13	P—KB4	P—KR4
14	P—B4	P—R3
15	P × P	P × P
16	Q—B2	Castles KR
17	Kt—K2	P—QKt4
18	Castles KR	Kt—Kt3

19	Kt—Kt3	P—Kt3	
20	QR—B1	Kt—B5	
21	Kt×B	P×Kt	
22	Q—Kt3 ch	Q—Kt2	
23	Q×Q ch	K×Q	
24	B×Kt	KtP×B	
25	P—KKt3	QR—Kt1	
26	P—Kt3	B—R6	
27	R—QB2	P×P	
28	P×P	KR—B1	
29	R×R	R×R	
30	R—R1	B—Kt5	
31	R×P	R—B6	
32	K—B2	R—Q6	
33	R—R2	B×Kt	
34	R×B	R×KtP	
35	R—B2	P—R5	
36	R—B7 ch	K—Kt3	
37	P×P	Kt—R4	
38	R—Q7	Kt×P	
39	B×Kt	R—B6 ch	
40	K—Kt2	R×B	
41	R×P	R—B6	
42	R—Q8	R—Q6	
43	P—Q5	P—B5	
44	P—Q6	R—Q7 ch	
45	K—B1	K—B2	
46	P—R5	P—K6	
47	P—R6	P—B6	

And Black wins.

XV

White   *Black*

MORPHY   AMATEUR

One of six simultaneous blindfold games

(New Orleans, 1858)

Playing over one of Morphy's masterpieces, such as the following game, is to the enthusiast like drinking from the fountain of youth.

1	P—K4	P—K4
2	Kt—KB3	Kt—QB3
3	B—B4	B—B4
4	P—QKt4	B×P
5	P—B3	B—R4
6	P—Q4	P×P
7	Castles	P×P
8	B—R3	P—Q3
9	Q—Kt3	Kt—R3
10	Kt×P	B×Kt
11	Q×B	Castles
12	QR—Q1	Kt—KKt5
13	P—R3	KKt—K4

14	Kt×Kt	Kt×Kt
15	B—K2	P—KB4
16	P—B4	Kt—B3
17	B—B4 ch	K—R1
18	B—Kt2	Q—K2
19	QR—K1	R—B3
20	P×P	Q—B1
21	R—K8	Q×R
22	Q×R	Q—K2
23	Q×P ch	Q×Q
24	P—B6	Q×P ch
25	K×Q	B×P ch
26	K×B	P—KR4
27	R—KKt1	Resigns.

XVI

White   *Black*

MORPHY   FREEMAN

One of eight blindfold games

(Birmingham, 1858)

In this game, Black makes an early attempt to obtain the initiative (8 .... Kt×P), which, however, is refuted by admirably forceful play.

1	P—K4	P—K4
2	B—B4	B—B4
3	P—QKt4	B—Kt3
4	Kt—KB3	P—Q3
5	P—Q4	P×P
6	Kt×P	Kt—KB3
7	Kt—QB3	Castles
8	Castles	Kt×P
9	Kt×Kt	P—Q4
10	B—KKt5	Q—K1
11	B×P	P—B3
12	R—K1	Q—Q2
13	Kt—B6 ch	P×Kt
14	QB×P	Q—Q3
15	Kt—K6	B×Kt
16	Q—R5	B×P ch
17	K—R1	Q—B5
18	R×B	Kt—Q2
19	B—Kt2	B—Q5
20	P—Kt3	Kt—B3
21	P×Q	Kt×Q
22	B×B	Kt×P
23	R—Kt1 ch	Kt—Kt3
24	QR×Kt ch	RP×R
25	R×P ch	K—R2
26	R—Kt7 ch	K—R3
27	B—K4	P—KB4
28	B—Q3	P—Kt3
29	R—Kt3	R—B2
30	B—K5	R—K1
31	B—B4 ch	K—R2
32	R—Kt5	R—K8 ch

33	K—Kt2	R—KKt2
34	B × P ch	K—R1
35	P—KR4	R × R ch
36	B × R	R—K1
37	K—B3	Resigns.

XVII

White	*Black*
BLACKBURNE	O'HANLON

One of eight simultaneous blindfold games
(Belfast, 1896)

Himself an expert in combinative and imaginative play, J. J. O'Hanlon, who later several times became Champion of Ireland, is here drawn into the complications of the Hamppe-Allgaier Gambit, *and succumbs to surprise manœuvres imagined by his great opponent.*

1	P—K4	P—K4
2	Kt—QB3	Kt—QB3
3	P—B4	P × P
4	Kt—B3	P—KKt4
5	P—KR4	P—Kt5
6	Kt—KKt5	P—KR3
7	Kt × P	K × Kt
8	B—B4 ch	P—Q4
9	Kt × P	B—K3
10	P—Q4	Kt—B3
11	Q—Q3	K—Kt2
12	Kt × KBP	B × B
13	Q × B	Q—K2
14	P—K5	Kt—Q1
15	Castles	Kt—R2
16	Kt—R5 ch	K—Kt3
17	Q—Q3 ch	K × Kt
18	Q—B5 ch	Kt—Kt4
19	P × Kt	P × P
20	K—B2	K—R3
21	B × P ch	Q × B
22	R—R1 ch	Resigns.

XVIII

White	*Black*
PILLSBURY	HOWELL

One of twelve simultaneous blindfold games
(London, 1902)

Joining imagination to elegance, Pillsbury was one of the greatest masters of blindfold play. He was said to see everything and a little more, as in this game the prodigious coup *16 R—Kt7.*

1	P—K4	P—K4
2	Kt—QB3	Kt—QB3
3	P—B4	P × P
4	Kt—B3	P—KKt4
5	P—KR4	P—Kt5
6	Kt—KKt5	P—KR3
7	Kt × P	K × Kt
8	P—Q4	P—Q4
9	B × P	B—Kt2
10	B—K3	B—B3
11	P—KKt3	P × P
12	B—B4 ch	K—Kt2
13	Castles	B × QP
14	R—B7 ch	K—Kt3
15	P—R5 ch	K × P
16	R—Kt7	Kt—K4
17	B × B	Kt—Kt3
18	K—Kt2	R—R2
19	Q—R1 ch	Kt—R5 ch
20	Q × Kt ch	Q × Q
21	B—B7 mate.	

XIX

White	*Black*
PILLSBURY	MÖLLER

One of 21 simultaneous blindfold games

(Hanover, 1902)

A memorable séance *against first-class opponents, many of them of master strength. His opponent in this game is a Danish master and an outstanding theoretician. He treats the opening in excellent fashion, only to find, in a Rook ending, that the "blindfold" player has "seen" one move further.*

1	P—K4	P—K4
2	Kt—KB3	Kt—QB3
3	P—Q4	P × P
4	B—B4	Kt—B3
5	Castles	B—B4
6	P—K5	P—Q4
7	P × Kt	P × B
8	R—K1 ch	B—K3
9	Kt—Kt5	P—KKt3
10	Q—Kt4	Q—Q4
11	B—B4	K—Q2
12	Kt × B	P × Kt
13	Kt—Q2	Q—B4
14	Q × Q	KP × Q
15	Kt × P	KR—K1
16	K—B1	P—QKt4
17	Kt—K5 ch	Kt × Kt
18	B × Kt	K—B3
19	QR—Q1	QR—Q1
20	P—KB4	R—Q2

21 R—Q3	KR—Q1
22 P—KR3	P—QR4
23 K—B2	B—Kt3
24 K—B3	K—Kt2
25 P—KKt4	P×P ch
26 P×P	P—B4
27 P—Kt5	K—B3
28 P—B5	R—K1
29 K—B4	B—B2
30 QR—Q1	R—Q4
31 B×B	R×P ch
32 K—Kt4	R×R
33 R×R	K×B
34 R—K7 ch	K—Q3
35 R×P	P—B5
36 R—R3	K—K4
37 R—KB3	K—K5
38 R×R	P×R ch
39 K—Kt3	Resigns.

XX

White *Black*

ALEKHINE H. STEINER

One of 26 simultaneous blindfold games

(New York, 1924)

Here, again, the blindfold player meets an opponent of master strength, against whom a surprise attack has little chance of succeeding. And so we witness trench warfare and positional play. The resulting ending is worth careful study, and the finish would do credit to any player in a normal single-handed contest.

1 P—K4	P—QB4
2 Kt—KB3	P—KKt3
3 P—Q4	P×P
4 Kt×P	B—Kt2
5 P—QB4	Kt—QB3
6 B—K3	Kt—B3
7 Kt—QB3	P—Q3
8 B—K2	B—Q2
9 P—B3	Castles
10 R—QB1	R—B1
11 Castles	P—QR3
12 Kt—Q5	KKt×Kt
13 KP×Kt	Kt—Kt1
14 Q—Q2	P—QR4
15 KR—K1	Kt—R3
16 P—QKt3	Kt—B4
17 QR—Q1	Q—B2
18 B—R6	B×B
19 Q×B	P—K4
20 P×P e p	P×P
21 Kt—Kt5	B×Kt
22 P×B	P—Q4
23 B—B1	R—B4
24 Q—K3	Q—Q3
25 P—QR3	R—K1
26 P—QKt4	P×P
27 P×P	Kt—Q2
28 Q—B3	R—R4
29 P—Kt3	Q—Kt3 ch
30 K—Kt2	R—KB1
31 Q—Q4	Q×Q
32 R×Q	Kt—K4
33 P—B4	R×P ch
34 K×R	Kt—B6 ch
35 K—Kt2	Kt×QR
36 R—B1	R—B2
37 P—Kt6	Kt—B3
38 B—R6	Kt×P
39 B×P	R—K2
40 B—B8	K—B2
41 P—Kt7	Kt—R3
42 R—QR1	Kt—Kt1
43 R—R8	Kt—B3
44 P—Kt8 (Q)	Kt×Q
45 R×Kt	K—B3
46 K—B3	P—R3
47 R—Kt6	P—Kt4
48 P×P ch	P×P
49 K—Kt4	R—K1
50 B—Q7	R—K2
51 B—B6	P—Q5
52 B—K4	K—K4
53 B—Q3	R—QB2
54 R—Kt5 ch	K—B3
55 K—B3	R—B8
56 R—Kt1	R—B6
57 R—Q1	K—K4
58 K—Kt4	K—Q4
59 K×P	P—K4
60 K—B5	R×B
61 R×R	P—K5
62 R—Q1	P—Q6
63 K—B4	K—Q5
64 R—QR1	P—Q7
65 R—R8	Resigns.

XXI

White *Black*

ALEKHINE FREEMAN

One of 26 simultaneous blindfold games

(New York, 1924)

Unlike the preceding game, this one displays a lively attack, leading to a neat and sparkling ending. Dr. Alekhine, at a later date, raised his record for blindfold play to 32 simultaneous games, a feature of the exhibition being the strength of the opposition.

1	P—K4	P—K4
2	P—Q4	P×P
3	P—QB3	P—Q4
4	KP×P	Q×P
5	P×P	B—Kt5 ch
6	Kt—B3	Kt—QB3
7	Kt—B3	Kt—B3
8	B—K2	Castles
9	Castles	B×Kt
10	P×B	P—QKt3
11	P—B4	Q—Q1
12	P—Q5	Kt—K2
13	Kt—Q4	B—Kt2
14	B—Kt2	P—B3
15	B—KB3	P×P
16	R—K1	R—K1
17	Q—B1	R—Kt1
18	Q—Kt5	Kt—Kt3
19	Kt—B5	R×R ch
20	R×R	P×P
21	B×B	R×B
22	B×Kt	Q×B
23	R—K8 ch	Kt—B1
24	Kt—R6 ch	Q×Kt
25	R×Kt ch	K×R
26	Q—Q8 mate.	

18	Q—B5 ch	K—B2
19	Q—R5 ch	K—Kt1
20	Q—R6	B—B1
21	Q×P	Kt—K2
22	B—R6	B×B
23	Q×B	Resigns.

SIMULTANEOUS CHESS

XXIII

White	Black
ALEKHINE	KUSSMAN

From a simultaneous performance
(New York, 1924)

After an exemplary treatment of the opening, the champion obtains here a solid positional advantage. From this he evolves a combination of surpassing charm, leading to a powerful finish.

1	P—Q4	P—Q4
2	Kt—KB3	Kt—KB3
3	P—B4	P—K3
4	Kt—B3	P—B4
5	P×QP	KP×P
6	B—Kt5	B—K3
7	B×Kt	Q×B
8	P—K4	P×KP
9	B—Kt5 ch	B—Q2
10	Kt×P	Q—QKt3
11	B×B ch	Kt×B
12	Castles	P×P
13	Kt×P	R—Q1
14	Kt—KB5	Kt—K4
15	Q—K2	P—Kt3
16	Q—Kt5 ch	Kt—Q2
17	KR—K1	B—Kt5
18	Kt—B6 db ch	K—B1
19	Kt×Kt ch	R×Kt
20	Q—K5	Resigns

There are three distinct and separate threats of mate.

XXII

White	Black
KOLTANOWSKI	BURNETT

One of 34 simultaneous blindfold games
(Edinburgh, 1937)

An admirable performance, which probably reaches the limit of mental and physical endurance. In this game the "theory" goes as far as the 17th move, but the Belgian master had the satisfaction, in these difficult circumstances, to foretell accurately the compulsory course of the next six moves.

1	P—K4	P—K4
2	Kt—KB3	Kt—QB3
3	B—B4	B—B4
4	Castles	Kt—B3
5	P—Q4	P×P
6	P—K5	P—Q4
7	P×Kt	P×B
8	R—K1 ch	B—K3
9	Kt—Kt5	Q—Q4
10	Kt—QB3	Q—B4
11	QKt—K4	B—KB1
12	Kt×BP	K×Kt
13	Kt—Kt5 ch	K—Kt3
14	Kt×B	P×P
15	P—KKt4	Q—QR4
16	B—Q2	Q—Kt3
17	Q—B3	B—K2

XXIV

White	Black
TARTAKOWER	N.

From a simultaneous performance
(Paris, 1933)

In order to cope with a large number of opponents at the same time, the simultaneous player must be well equipped with a theoretical knowledge of all phases of the game. Only thus can he hope to take instant advantage of every opportunity. For instance, in the following game, if 14 .... Q×P ch; 15 Q×Q, B×Q; 16 P—B7 mate.

A humorous feature is the repetition of the same stratagem on moves 17 and 19 by White: R—K7.

1	P—K4	P—K4
2	Kt—KB3	Kt—QB3
3	B—B4	B—B4
4	P—Q4	P×P
5	Castles	Kt—B3
6	P—K5	P—Q4
7	P×Kt	P×B
8	R—K1 ch	B—K3
9	Kt—Kt5	Q—Q4
10	Kt—QB3	Q—B4
11	QKt—K4	B—KB1
12	Kt×BP	K×Kt
13	Kt—Kt5 ch	K—Kt1
14	P—KKt4	Q×P (B3)
15	R×B	Q—Q1
16	Q—B3	Q—Q2
17	R—K7	Kt—K4
18	R×Kt	P—KR3
19	R—K7	Resigns.

9	Q—Kt1	P—B3
10	P—QR3	Kt—R3
11	B—K2	P—R3
12	Q—B2	B—KB4
13	Castles KR	QR—Q1
14	QR—B1	KR—K1
15	P—K4	P×KP
16	P×P	B—R2
17	P—QKt4	B—Kt1
18	KR—Q1	Kt—Q2
19	R—K1	Kt—B1
20	P—B5	Kt—Kt3
21	P—Kt3	Kt—B2
22	Kt—B4	Kt—Kt4
23	QR—Q1	P—B3
24	P—QR4	Kt—Q5
25	Kt×Kt	P×Kt
26	Q—Kt3	K—R1
27	P—B3	B—K4
28	P—B4	B—QKt1
29	B—KB3	B×P
30	P×B	Kt×P
31	R×P	R×R
32	B×R	Q—Q2
33	Kt—Q6	R—K2
34	R—KB1	Q—R6
35	Kt—B7 ch	R×Kt
36	Q×R	B—Kt1
37	Q—B7	B—B5
38	R—B2	Kt—Q6
39	R—KKt2	Resigns.

LIGHTNING CHESS

XXV

White	Black
DU MONT	RÉTI

Lightning Tournament

(London Congress, 1922)

The following game is an example of modern positional play at ten seconds a move.

Both players are on the watch; up to the last moment, Black effects dangerous threats, in the hope of catching his opponent off guard, but in the end the co-operation of the well-directed white pieces (Queen, Rook and Bishop) prevails.

1	P—QKt3	P—K4
2	B—Kt2	Kt—QB3
3	P—K3	P—Q4
4	Kt—KB3	B—Q3
5	P—B4	Kt—B3
6	P—Q3	Castles
7	QKt—Q2	Q—K2
8	Q—B2	Kt—QKt5

LIVING CHESS

XXVI

White	Black
MICHELL	GRIFFITH

Living Chess

(Hurlingham, 1936)

A game played with living pieces at great speed, for whoever was the first to use up five minutes lost the game. The winner used two and a half minutes, or less than seven seconds a move—a tribute to his quick sight, and to the nimbleness of the living pieces.

The sacrificial combination which Black manages to evolve, despite the speed, is masterly.

1	P—K4	P—QB3
2	P—Q4	P—Q4
3	P×P	P×P
4	P—QB4	P—K3
5	Kt—QB3	Kt—KB3

6 Kt—B3	B—K2	15 B × B	Q × B
7 B—Q3	Castles	16 Q—B2	QR—B1
8 Castles	Kt—B3	17 Q—K2	P—B4
9 R—K1	Kt—QKt5	18 P—KR3	B × Kt
10 B—B1	P × P	19 P × B	Q—Kt4 ch
11 B × P	QKt—Q4	20 K—R1	Q—R5
12 Kt × Kt	P × Kt	21 P × Kt	BP × P
13 B—Q3	B—KKt5	22 Q—B1	R × P
14 B—KKt5	Kt—K5		Resigns.

INDEX

Page numbers in italics refer to players of additional games quoted for reference
Pages 1–304 comprise Book I and pages 305–665 Books II and III

A CATALOG OF SELECTED DOVER
BOOKS IN ALL FIELDS OF INTEREST

CONCERNING THE SPIRITUAL IN ART, Wassily Kandinsky. Pioneering work by father of abstract art. Thoughts on color theory, nature of art. Analysis of earlier masters. 12 illustrations. 80pp. of text. 5⅜ × 8½. 23411-8 Pa. $3.95

ANIMALS: 1,419 Copyright-Free Illustrations of Mammals, Birds, Fish, Insects, etc., Jim Harter (ed.). Clear wood engravings present, in extremely lifelike poses, over 1,000 species of animals. One of the most extensive pictorial sourcebooks of its kind. Captions. Index. 284pp. 9 × 12. 23766-4 Pa. $11.95

CELTIC ART: The Methods of Construction, George Bain. Simple geometric techniques for making Celtic interlacements, spirals, Kells-type initials, animals, humans, etc. Over 500 illustrations. 160pp. 9 × 12. (USO) 22923-8 Pa. $9.95

AN ATLAS OF ANATOMY FOR ARTISTS, Fritz Schider. Most thorough reference work on art anatomy in the world. Hundreds of illustrations, including selections from works by Vesalius, Leonardo, Goya, Ingres, Michelangelo, others. 593 illustrations. 192pp. 7⅛ × 10¼. 20241-0 Pa. $8.95

CELTIC HAND STROKE-BY-STROKE (Irish Half-Uncial from "The Book of Kells"): An Arthur Baker Calligraphy Manual, Arthur Baker. Complete guide to creating each letter of the alphabet in distinctive Celtic manner. Covers hand position, strokes, pens, inks, paper, more. Illustrated. 48pp. 8¼ × 11.
24336-2 Pa. $3.95

EASY ORIGAMI, John Montroll. Charming collection of 32 projects (hat, cup, pelican, piano, swan, many more) specially designed for the novice origami hobbyist. Clearly illustrated easy-to-follow instructions insure that even beginning papercrafters will achieve successful results. 48pp. 8¼ × 11. 27298-2 Pa. $2.95

THE COMPLETE BOOK OF BIRDHOUSE CONSTRUCTION FOR WOOD-WORKERS, Scott D. Campbell. Detailed instructions, illustrations, tables. Also data on bird habitat and instinct patterns. Bibliography. 3 tables. 63 illustrations in 15 figures. 48pp. 5¼ × 8½. 24407-5 Pa. $1.95

BLOOMINGDALE'S ILLUSTRATED 1886 CATALOG: Fashions, Dry Goods and Housewares, Bloomingdale Brothers. Famed merchants' extremely rare catalog depicting about 1,700 products: clothing, housewares, firearms, dry goods, jewelry, more. Invaluable for dating, identifying vintage items. Also, copyright-free graphics for artists, designers. Co-published with Henry Ford Museum & Greenfield Village. 160pp. 8¼ × 11. 25780-0 Pa. $9.95

HISTORIC COSTUME IN PICTURES, Braun & Schneider. Over 1,450 costumed figures in clearly detailed engravings—from dawn of civilization to end of 19th century. Captions. Many folk costumes. 256pp. 8⅜ × 11¾. 23150-X Pa. $11.95

STICKLEY CRAFTSMAN FURNITURE CATALOGS, Gustav Stickley and L. & J. G. Stickley. Beautiful, functional furniture in two authentic catalogs from 1910. 594 illustrations, including 277 photos, show settles, rockers, armchairs, reclining chairs, bookcases, desks, tables. 183pp. 6½ × 9¼. 23838-5 Pa. $8.95

AMERICAN LOCOMOTIVES IN HISTORIC PHOTOGRAPHS: 1858 to 1949, Ron Ziel (ed.). A rare collection of 126 meticulously detailed official photographs, called "builder portraits," of American locomotives that majestically chronicle the rise of steam locomotive power in America. Introduction. Detailed captions. xi + 129pp. 9 × 12. 27393-8 Pa. $12.95

AMERICA'S LIGHTHOUSES: An Illustrated History, Francis Ross Holland, Jr. Delightfully written, profusely illustrated fact-filled survey of over 200 American lighthouses since 1716. History, anecdotes, technological advances, more. 240pp. 8 × 10¾. 25576-X Pa. $11.95

TOWARDS A NEW ARCHITECTURE, Le Corbusier. Pioneering manifesto by founder of "International School." Technical and aesthetic theories, views of industry, economics, relation of form to function, "mass-production split" and much more. Profusely illustrated. 320pp. 6⅛ × 9¼. (USO) 25023-7 Pa. $8.95

HOW THE OTHER HALF LIVES, Jacob Riis. Famous journalistic record, exposing poverty and degradation of New York slums around 1900, by major social reformer. 100 striking and influential photographs. 233pp. 10 × 7⅞. 22012-5 Pa $10.95

FRUIT KEY AND TWIG KEY TO TREES AND SHRUBS, William M. Harlow. One of the handiest and most widely used identification aids. Fruit key covers 120 deciduous and evergreen species; twig key 160 deciduous species. Easily used. Over 300 photographs. 126pp. 5⅜ × 8½. 20511-8 Pa. $3.95

COMMON BIRD SONGS, Dr. Donald J. Borror. Songs of 60 most common U.S. birds: robins, sparrows, cardinals, bluejays, finches, more—arranged in order of increasing complexity. Up to 9 variations of songs of each species. Cassette and manual 99911-4 $8.95

ORCHIDS AS HOUSE PLANTS, Rebecca Tyson Northen. Grow cattleyas and many other kinds of orchids—in a window, in a case, or under artificial light. 63 illustrations. 148pp. 5⅜ × 8½. 23261-1 Pa. $3.95

MONSTER MAZES, Dave Phillips. Masterful mazes at four levels of difficulty. Avoid deadly perils and evil creatures to find magical treasures. Solutions for all 32 exciting illustrated puzzles. 48pp. 8¼ × 11. 26005-4 Pa. $2.95

MOZART'S DON GIOVANNI (DOVER OPERA LIBRETTO SERIES), Wolfgang Amadeus Mozart. Introduced and translated by Ellen H. Bleiler. Standard Italian libretto, with complete English translation. Convenient and thoroughly portable—an ideal companion for reading along with a recording or the performance itself. Introduction. List of characters. Plot summary. 121pp. 5¼ × 8½. 24944-1 Pa. $2.95

TECHNICAL MANUAL AND DICTIONARY OF CLASSICAL BALLET, Gail Grant. Defines, explains, comments on steps, movements, poses and concepts. 15-page pictorial section. Basic book for student, viewer. 127pp. 5⅜ × 8½. 21843-0 Pa. $3.95

BRASS INSTRUMENTS: Their History and Development, Anthony Baines. Authoritative, updated survey of the evolution of trumpets, trombones, bugles, cornets, French horns, tubas and other brass wind instruments. Over 140 illustrations and 48 music examples. Corrected and updated by author. New preface. Bibliography. 320pp. 5⅜ × 8½. 27574-4 Pa. $9.95

HOLLYWOOD GLAMOR PORTRAITS, John Kobal (ed.). 145 photos from 1926–49. Harlow, Gable, Bogart, Bacall; 94 stars in all. Full background on photographers, technical aspects. 160pp. 8⅜ × 11¼. 23352-9 Pa. $11.95

MAX AND MORITZ, Wilhelm Busch. Great humor classic in both German and English. Also 10 other works: "Cat and Mouse," "Plisch and Plumm," etc. 216pp. 5⅜ × 8½. 20181-3 Pa. $5.95

THE RAVEN AND OTHER FAVORITE POEMS, Edgar Allan Poe. Over 40 of the author's most memorable poems: "The Bells," "Ulalume," "Israfel," "To Helen," "The Conqueror Worm," "Eldorado," "Annabel Lee," many more. Alphabetic lists of titles and first lines. 64pp. 5³⁄₁₆ × 8¼. 26685-0 Pa. $1.00

SEVEN SCIENCE FICTION NOVELS, H. G. Wells. The standard collection of the great novels. Complete, unabridged. First Men in the Moon, Island of Dr. Moreau, War of the Worlds, Food of the Gods, Invisible Man, Time Machine, In the Days of the Comet. Total of 1,015pp. 5⅜ × 8½. (USO) 20264-X Clothbd. $29.95

AMULETS AND SUPERSTITIONS, E. A. Wallis Budge. Comprehensive discourse on origin, powers of amulets in many ancient cultures: Arab, Persian, Babylonian, Assyrian, Egyptian, Gnostic, Hebrew, Phoenician, Syriac, etc. Covers cross, swastika, crucifix, seals, rings, stones, etc. 584pp. 5⅜ × 8½. 23573-4 Pa. $12.95

RUSSIAN STORIES/PYCCKNE PACCKA3bl: A Dual-Language Book, edited by Gleb Struve. Twelve tales by such masters as Chekhov, Tolstoy, Dostoevsky, Pushkin, others. Excellent word-for-word English translations on facing pages, plus teaching and study aids, Russian/English vocabulary, biographical/critical introductions, more. 416pp. 5⅜ × 8½. 26244-8 Pa. $8.95

PHILADELPHIA THEN AND NOW: 60 Sites Photographed in the Past and Present, Kenneth Finkel and Susan Oyama. Rare photographs of City Hall, Logan Square, Independence Hall, Betsy Ross House, other landmarks juxtaposed with contemporary views. Captures changing face of historic city. Introduction. Captions. 128pp. 8¼ × 11. 25790-8 Pa. $9.95

AIA ARCHITECTURAL GUIDE TO NASSAU AND SUFFOLK COUNTIES, LONG ISLAND, The American Institute of Architects, Long Island Chapter, and the Society for the Preservation of Long Island Antiquities. Comprehensive, well-researched and generously illustrated volume brings to life over three centuries of Long Island's great architectural heritage. More than 240 photographs with authoritative, extensively detailed captions. 176pp. 8¼ × 11. 26946-9 Pa. $14.95

NORTH AMERICAN INDIAN LIFE: Customs and Traditions of 23 Tribes, Elsie Clews Parsons (ed.). 27 fictionalized essays by noted anthropologists examine religion, customs, government, additional facets of life among the Winnebago, Crow, Zuni, Eskimo, other tribes. 480pp. 6⅛ × 9¼. 27377-6 Pa. $10.95

FRANK LLOYD WRIGHT'S HOLLYHOCK HOUSE, Donald Hoffmann. Lavishly illustrated, carefully documented study of one of Wright's most controversial residential designs. Over 120 photographs, floor plans, elevations, etc. Detailed perceptive text by noted Wright scholar. Index. 128pp. 9¼ × 10¾.
27133-1 Pa. $11.95

THE MALE AND FEMALE FIGURE IN MOTION: 60 Classic Photographic Sequences, Eadweard Muybridge. 60 true-action photographs of men and women walking, running, climbing, bending, turning, etc., reproduced from rare 19th-century masterpiece. vi + 121pp. 9 × 12. 24745-7 Pa. $10.95

1001 QUESTIONS ANSWERED ABOUT THE SEASHORE, N. J. Berrill and Jacquelyn Berrill. Queries answered about dolphins, sea snails, sponges, starfish, fishes, shore birds, many others. Covers appearance, breeding, growth, feeding, much more. 305pp. 5¼ × 8¼. 23366-9 Pa. $7.95

GUIDE TO OWL WATCHING IN NORTH AMERICA, Donald S. Heintzelman. Superb guide offers complete data and descriptions of 19 species: barn owl, screech owl, snowy owl, many more. Expert coverage of owl-watching equipment, conservation, migrations and invasions, etc. Guide to observing sites. 84 illustrations. xiii + 193pp. 5⅜ × 8½. 27344-X Pa. $7.95

MEDICINAL AND OTHER USES OF NORTH AMERICAN PLANTS: A Historical Survey with Special Reference to the Eastern Indian Tribes, Charlotte Erichsen-Brown. Chronological historical citations document 500 years of usage of plants, trees, shrubs native to eastern Canada, northeastern U.S. Also complete identifying information. 343 illustrations. 544pp. 6½ × 9¼. 25951-X Pa. $12.95

STORYBOOK MAZES, Dave Phillips. 23 stories and mazes on two-page spreads: Wizard of Oz, Treasure Island, Robin Hood, etc. Solutions. 64pp. 8¼ × 11.
23628-5 Pa. $2.95

NEGRO FOLK MUSIC, U.S.A., Harold Courlander. Noted folklorist's scholarly yet readable analysis of rich and varied musical tradition. Includes authentic versions of over 40 folk songs. Valuable bibliography and discography. xi + 324pp. 5⅜ × 8½. 27350-4 Pa. $7.95

MOVIE-STAR PORTRAITS OF THE FORTIES, John Kobal (ed.). 163 glamor, studio photos of 106 stars of the 1940s: Rita Hayworth, Ava Gardner, Marlon Brando, Clark Gable, many more. 176pp. 8⅜ × 11¼. 23546-7 Pa. $10.95

BENCHLEY LOST AND FOUND, Robert Benchley. Finest humor from early 30s, about pet peeves, child psychologists, post office and others. Mostly unavailable elsewhere. 73 illustrations by Peter Arno and others. 183pp. 5⅜ × 8½.
22410-4 Pa. $5.95

YEKL and THE IMPORTED BRIDEGROOM AND OTHER STORIES OF YIDDISH NEW YORK, Abraham Cahan. Film Hester Street based on Yekl (1896). Novel, other stories among first about Jewish immigrants on N.Y.'s East Side. 240pp. 5⅜ × 8½. 22427-9 Pa. $6.95

SELECTED POEMS, Walt Whitman. Generous sampling from *Leaves of Grass*. Twenty-four poems include "I Hear America Singing," "Song of the Open Road," "I Sing the Body Electric," "When Lilacs Last in the Dooryard Bloom'd," "O Captain! My Captain!"—all reprinted from an authoritative edition. Lists of titles and first lines. 128pp. 5$\frac{3}{16}$ × 8¼. 26878-0 Pa. $1.00

THE BEST TALES OF HOFFMANN, E. T. A. Hoffmann. 10 of Hoffmann's most important stories: "Nutcracker and the King of Mice," "The Golden Flowerpot," etc. 458pp. 5⅜ × 8½. 21793-0 Pa. $8.95

FROM FETISH TO GOD IN ANCIENT EGYPT, E. A. Wallis Budge. Rich detailed survey of Egyptian conception of "God" and gods, magic, cult of animals, Osiris, more. Also, superb English translations of hymns and legends. 240 illustrations. 545pp. 5⅜ × 8½. 25803-3 Pa. $11.95

FRENCH STORIES/CONTES FRANÇAIS: A Dual-Language Book, Wallace Fowlie. Ten stories by French masters, Voltaire to Camus: "Micromegas" by Voltaire; "The Atheist's Mass" by Balzac; "Minuet" by de Maupassant; "The Guest" by Camus, six more. Excellent English translations on facing pages. Also French-English vocabulary list, exercises, more. 352pp. 5⅜ × 8½. 26443-2 Pa. $8.95

CHICAGO AT THE TURN OF THE CENTURY IN PHOTOGRAPHS: 122 Historic Views from the Collections of the Chicago Historical Society, Larry A. Viskochil. Rare large-format prints offer detailed views of City Hall, State Street, the Loop, Hull House, Union Station, many other landmarks, circa 1904–1913. Introduction. Captions. Maps. 144pp. 9⅜ × 12¼. 24656-6 Pa. $12.95

OLD BROOKLYN IN EARLY PHOTOGRAPHS, 1865–1929, William Lee Younger. Luna Park, Gravesend race track, construction of Grand Army Plaza, moving of Hotel Brighton, etc. 157 previously unpublished photographs. 165pp. 8⅞ × 11¾. 23587-4 Pa. $13.95

THE MYTHS OF THE NORTH AMERICAN INDIANS, Lewis Spence. Rich anthology of the myths and legends of the Algonquins, Iroquois, Pawnees and Sioux, prefaced by an extensive historical and ethnological commentary. 36 illustrations. 480pp. 5⅜ × 8½. 25967-6 Pa. $8.95

AN ENCYCLOPEDIA OF BATTLES: Accounts of Over 1,560 Battles from 1479 B.C. to the Present, David Eggenberger. Essential details of every major battle in recorded history from the first battle of Megiddo in 1479 B.C. to Grenada in 1984. List of Battle Maps. New Appendix covering the years 1967–1984. Index. 99 illustrations. 544pp. 6½ × 9¼. 24913-1 Pa. $14.95

SAILING ALONE AROUND THE WORLD, Captain Joshua Slocum. First man to sail around the world, alone, in small boat. One of great feats of seamanship told in delightful manner. 67 illustrations. 294pp. 5⅜ × 8½. 20326-3 Pa. $5.95

ANARCHISM AND OTHER ESSAYS, Emma Goldman. Powerful, penetrating, prophetic essays on direct action, role of minorities, prison reform, puritan hypocrisy, violence, etc. 271pp. 5⅜ × 8½. 22484-8 Pa. $5.95

MYTHS OF THE HINDUS AND BUDDHISTS, Ananda K. Coomaraswamy and Sister Nivedita. Great stories of the epics; deeds of Krishna, Shiva, taken from puranas, Vedas, folk tales; etc. 32 illustrations. 400pp. 5⅜ × 8½. 21759-0 Pa. $9.95

BEYOND PSYCHOLOGY, Otto Rank. Fear of death, desire of immortality, nature of sexuality, social organization, creativity, according to Rankian system. 291pp. 5⅜ × 8½. 20485-5 Pa. $7.95

A THEOLOGICO-POLITICAL TREATISE, Benedict Spinoza. Also contains unfinished Political Treatise. Great classic on religious liberty, theory of government on common consent. R. Elwes translation. Total of 421pp. 5⅜ × 8½. 20249-6 Pa. $8.95

MY BONDAGE AND MY FREEDOM, Frederick Douglass. Born a slave, Douglass became outspoken force in antislavery movement. The best of Douglass' autobiographies. Graphic description of slave life. 464pp. 5⅜ × 8½.   22457-0 Pa. $8.95

FOLLOWING THE EQUATOR: A Journey Around the World, Mark Twain. Fascinating humorous account of 1897 voyage to Hawaii, Australia, India, New Zealand, etc. Ironic, bemused reports on peoples, customs, climate, flora and fauna, politics, much more. 197 illustrations. 720pp. 5⅜ × 8½.   26113-1 Pa. $15.95

THE PEOPLE CALLED SHAKERS, Edward D. Andrews. Definitive study of Shakers: origins, beliefs, practices, dances, social organization, furniture and crafts, etc. 33 illustrations. 351pp. 5⅜ × 8½.   21081-2 Pa. $8.95

THE MYTHS OF GREECE AND ROME, H. A. Guerber. A classic of mythology, generously illustrated, long prized for its simple, graphic, accurate retelling of the principal myths of Greece and Rome, and for its commentary on their origins and significance. With 64 illustrations by Michelangelo, Raphael, Titian, Rubens, Canova, Bernini and others. 480pp. 5⅜ × 8½.   27584-1 Pa. $9.95

PSYCHOLOGY OF MUSIC, Carl E. Seashore. Classic work discusses music as a medium from psychological viewpoint. Clear treatment of physical acoustics, auditory apparatus, sound perception, development of musical skills, nature of musical feeling, host of other topics. 88 figures. 408pp. 5⅜ × 8½. 21851-1 Pa. $9.95

THE PHILOSOPHY OF HISTORY, Georg W. Hegel. Great classic of Western thought develops concept that history is not chance but rational process, the evolution of freedom. 457pp. 5⅜ × 8½.   20112-0 Pa. $9.95

THE BOOK OF TEA, Kakuzo Okakura. Minor classic of the Orient: entertaining, charming explanation, interpretation of traditional Japanese culture in terms of tea ceremony. 94pp. 5⅜ × 8½.   20070-1 Pa. $2.95

LIFE IN ANCIENT EGYPT, Adolf Erman. Fullest, most thorough, detailed older account with much not in more recent books, domestic life, religion, magic, medicine, commerce, much more. Many illustrations reproduce tomb paintings, carvings, hieroglyphs, etc. 597pp. 5⅜ × 8½.   22632-8 Pa. $10.95

SUNDIALS, Their Theory and Construction, Albert Waugh. Far and away the best, most thorough coverage of ideas, mathematics concerned, types, construction, adjusting anywhere. Simple, nontechnical treatment allows even children to build several of these dials. Over 100 illustrations. 230pp. 5⅜ × 8½.   22947-5 Pa. $7.95

DYNAMICS OF FLUIDS IN POROUS MEDIA, Jacob Bear. For advanced students of ground water hydrology, soil mechanics and physics, drainage and irrigation engineering, and more. 335 illustrations. Exercises, with answers. 784pp. 6⅛ × 9¼.   65675-6 Pa. $19.95

SONGS OF EXPERIENCE: Facsimile Reproduction with 26 Plates in Full Color, William Blake. 26 full-color plates from a rare 1826 edition. Includes "The Tyger," "London," "Holy Thursday," and other poems. Printed text of poems. 48pp. 5¼ × 7.
  24636-1 Pa. $4.95

OLD-TIME VIGNETTES IN FULL COLOR, Carol Belanger Grafton (ed.). Over 390 charming, often sentimental illustrations, selected from archives of Victorian graphics—pretty women posing, children playing, food, flowers, kittens and puppies, smiling cherubs, birds and butterflies, much more. All copyright-free. 48pp. 9¼ × 12¼.   27269-9 Pa. $5.95

PERSPECTIVE FOR ARTISTS, Rex Vicat Cole. Depth, perspective of sky and sea, shadows, much more, not usually covered. 391 diagrams, 81 reproductions of drawings and paintings. 279pp. 5⅜ × 8½. 22487-2 Pa. $6.95

DRAWING THE LIVING FIGURE, Joseph Sheppard. Innovative approach to artistic anatomy focuses on specifics of surface anatomy, rather than muscles and bones. Over 170 drawings of live models in front, back and side views, and in widely varying poses. Accompanying diagrams. 177 illustrations. Introduction. Index. 144pp. 8⅜ × 11¼. 26723-7 Pa. $7.95

GOTHIC AND OLD ENGLISH ALPHABETS: 100 Complete Fonts, Dan X. Solo. Add power, elegance to posters, signs, other graphics with 100 stunning copyright-free alphabets: Blackstone, Dolbey, Germania, 97 more—including many lower-case, numerals, punctuation marks. 104pp. 8⅛ × 11. 24695-7 Pa. $7.95

HOW TO DO BEADWORK, Mary White. Fundamental book on craft from simple projects to five-bead chains and woven works. 106 illustrations. 142pp. 5⅜ × 8. 20697-1 Pa. $4.95

THE BOOK OF WOOD CARVING, Charles Marshall Sayers. Finest book for beginners discusses fundamentals and offers 34 designs. "Absolutely first rate . . . well thought out and well executed."—E. J. Tangerman. 118pp. 7¾ × 10⅝. 23654-4 Pa. $5.95

ILLUSTRATED CATALOG OF CIVIL WAR MILITARY GOODS: Union Army Weapons, Insignia, Uniform Accessories, and Other Equipment, Schuyler, Hartley, and Graham. Rare, profusely illustrated 1846 catalog includes Union Army uniform and dress regulations, arms and ammunition, coats, insignia, flags, swords, rifles, etc. 226 illustrations. 160pp. 9 × 12. 24939-5 Pa. $10.95

WOMEN'S FASHIONS OF THE EARLY 1900s: An Unabridged Republication of "New York Fashions, 1909," National Cloak & Suit Co. Rare catalog of mail-order fashions documents women's and children's clothing styles shortly after the turn of the century. Captions offer full descriptions, prices. Invaluable resource for fashion, costume historians. Approximately 725 illustrations. 128pp. 8⅜ × 11¼. 27276-1 Pa. $11.95

THE 1912 AND 1915 GUSTAV STICKLEY FURNITURE CATALOGS, Gustav Stickley. With over 200 detailed illustrations and descriptions, these two catalogs are essential reading and reference materials and identification guides for Stickley furniture. Captions cite materials, dimensions and prices. 112pp. 6½ × 9¼. 26676-1 Pa. $9.95

EARLY AMERICAN LOCOMOTIVES, John H. White, Jr. Finest locomotive engravings from early 19th century: historical (1804–74), main-line (after 1870), special, foreign, etc. 147 plates. 142pp. 11⅜ × 8¼. 22772-3 Pa. $8.95

THE TALL SHIPS OF TODAY IN PHOTOGRAPHS, Frank O. Braynard. Lavishly illustrated tribute to nearly 100 majestic contemporary sailing vessels: Amerigo Vespucci, Clearwater, Constitution, Eagle, Mayflower, Sea Cloud, Victory, many more. Authoritative captions provide statistics, background on each ship. 190 black-and-white photographs and illustrations. Introduction. 128pp. 8⅞ × 11¾. 27163-3 Pa. $13.95

EARLY NINETEENTH-CENTURY CRAFTS AND TRADES, Peter Stockham (ed.). Extremely rare 1807 volume describes to youngsters the crafts and trades of the day: brickmaker, weaver, dressmaker, bookbinder, ropemaker, saddler, many more. Quaint prose, charming illustrations for each craft. 20 black-and-white line illustrations. 192pp. 4⅜ × 6. 27293-1 Pa. $4.95

VICTORIAN FASHIONS AND COSTUMES FROM HARPER'S BAZAR, 1867–1898, Stella Blum (ed.). Day costumes, evening wear, sports clothes, shoes, hats, other accessories in over 1,000 detailed engravings. 320pp. 9⅜ × 12¼. 22990-4 Pa. $13.95

GUSTAV STICKLEY, THE CRAFTSMAN, Mary Ann Smith. Superb study surveys broad scope of Stickley's achievement, especially in architecture. Design philosophy, rise and fall of the Craftsman empire, descriptions and floor plans for many Craftsman houses, more. 86 black-and-white halftones. 31 line illustrations. Introduction. 208pp. 6½ × 9¼. 27210-9 Pa. $9.95

THE LONG ISLAND RAIL ROAD IN EARLY PHOTOGRAPHS, Ron Ziel. Over 220 rare photos, informative text document origin (1844) and development of rail service on Long Island. Vintage views of early trains, locomotives, stations, passengers, crews, much more. Captions. 8⅞ × 11¾. 26301-0 Pa. $13.95

THE BOOK OF OLD SHIPS: From Egyptian Galleys to Clipper Ships, Henry B. Culver. Superb, authoritative history of sailing vessels, with 80 magnificent line illustrations. Galley, bark, caravel, longship, whaler, many more. Detailed, informative text on each vessel by noted naval historian. Introduction. 256pp. 5⅜ × 8½. 27332-6 Pa. $6.95

TEN BOOKS ON ARCHITECTURE, Vitruvius. The most important book ever written on architecture. Early Roman aesthetics, technology, classical orders, site selection, all other aspects. Morgan translation. 331pp. 5⅜ × 8½. 20645-9 Pa. $8.95

THE HUMAN FIGURE IN MOTION, Eadweard Muybridge. More than 4,500 stopped-action photos, in action series, showing undraped men, women, children jumping, lying down, throwing, sitting, wrestling, carrying, etc. 390pp. 7⅞ × 10⅝. 20204-6 Clothbd. $24.95

TREES OF THE EASTERN AND CENTRAL UNITED STATES AND CANADA, William M. Harlow. Best one-volume guide to 140 trees. Full descriptions, woodlore, range, etc. Over 600 illustrations. Handy size. 288pp. 4½ × 6⅜. 20395-6 Pa. $5.95

SONGS OF WESTERN BIRDS, Dr. Donald J. Borror. Complete song and call repertoire of 60 western species, including flycatchers, juncoes, cactus wrens, many more—includes fully illustrated booklet. Cassette and manual 99913-0 $8.95

GROWING AND USING HERBS AND SPICES, Milo Miloradovich. Versatile handbook provides all the information needed for cultivation and use of all the herbs and spices available in North America. 4 illustrations. Index. Glossary. 236pp. 5⅜ × 8½. 25058-X Pa. $5.95

BIG BOOK OF MAZES AND LABYRINTHS, Walter Shepherd. 50 mazes and labyrinths in all—classical, solid, ripple, and more—in one great volume. Perfect inexpensive puzzler for clever youngsters. Full solutions. 112pp. 8⅛ × 11. 22951-3 Pa. $3.95

PIANO TUNING, J. Cree Fischer. Clearest, best book for beginner, amateur. Simple repairs, raising dropped notes, tuning by easy method of flattened fifths. No previous skills needed. 4 illustrations. 201pp. 5⅜ × 8½. 23267-0 Pa. $5.95

A SOURCE BOOK IN THEATRICAL HISTORY, A. M. Nagler. Contemporary observers on acting, directing, make-up, costuming, stage props, machinery, scene design, from Ancient Greece to Chekhov. 611pp. 5⅜ × 8½. 20515-0 Pa. $11.95

THE COMPLETE NONSENSE OF EDWARD LEAR, Edward Lear. All nonsense limericks, zany alphabets, Owl and Pussycat, songs, nonsense botany, etc., illustrated by Lear. Total of 320pp. 5⅜ × 8½. (USO) 20167-8 Pa. $6.95

VICTORIAN PARLOUR POETRY: An Annotated Anthology, Michael R. Turner. 117 gems by Longfellow, Tennyson, Browning, many lesser-known poets. "The Village Blacksmith," "Curfew Must Not Ring Tonight," "Only a Baby Small," dozens more, often difficult to find elsewhere. Index of poets, titles, first lines. xxiii + 325pp. 5⅜ × 8¼. 27044-0 Pa. $8.95

DUBLINERS, James Joyce. Fifteen stories offer vivid, tightly focused observations of the lives of Dublin's poorer classes. At least one, "The Dead," is considered a masterpiece. Reprinted complete and unabridged from standard edition. 160pp. 5³⁄₁₆ × 8¼. 26870-5 Pa. $1.00

THE HAUNTED MONASTERY and THE CHINESE MAZE MURDERS, Robert van Gulik. Two full novels by van Gulik, set in 7th-century China, continue adventures of Judge Dee and his companions. An evil Taoist monastery, seemingly supernatural events; overgrown topiary maze hides strange crimes. 27 illustrations. 328pp. 5⅜ × 8½. 23502-5 Pa. $7.95

THE BOOK OF THE SACRED MAGIC OF ABRAMELIN THE MAGE, translated by S. MacGregor Mathers. Medieval manuscript of ceremonial magic. Basic document in Aleister Crowley, Golden Dawn groups. 268pp. 5⅜ × 8½.
23211-5 Pa. $8.95

NEW RUSSIAN-ENGLISH AND ENGLISH-RUSSIAN DICTIONARY, M. A. O'Brien. This is a remarkably handy Russian dictionary, containing a surprising amount of information, including over 70,000 entries. 366pp. 4½ × 6⅛.
20208-9 Pa. $9.95

HISTORIC HOMES OF THE AMERICAN PRESIDENTS, Second, Revised Edition, Irvin Haas. A traveler's guide to American Presidential homes, most open to the public, depicting and describing homes occupied by every American President from George Washington to George Bush. With visiting hours, admission charges, travel routes. 175 photographs. Index. 160pp. 8¼ × 11. 26751-2 Pa. $10.95

NEW YORK IN THE FORTIES, Andreas Feininger. 162 brilliant photographs by the well-known photographer, formerly with *Life* magazine. Commuters, shoppers, Times Square at night, much else from city at its peak. Captions by John von Hartz. 181pp. 9¼ × 10¾. 23585-8 Pa. $12.95

INDIAN SIGN LANGUAGE, William Tomkins. Over 525 signs developed by Sioux and other tribes. Written instructions and diagrams. Also 290 pictographs. 111pp. 6⅛ × 9¼. 22029-X Pa. $3.50

CATALOG OF DOVER BOOKS

ANATOMY: A Complete Guide for Artists, Joseph Sheppard. A master of figure drawing shows artists how to render human anatomy convincingly. Over 460 illustrations. 224pp. 8⅜ × 11¼. 27279-6 Pa. $9.95

MEDIEVAL CALLIGRAPHY: Its History and Technique, Marc Drogin. Spirited history, comprehensive instruction manual covers 13 styles (ca. 4th century thru 15th). Excellent photographs; directions for duplicating medieval techniques with modern tools. 224pp. 8⅜ × 11¼. 26142-5 Pa. $11.95

DRIED FLOWERS: How to Prepare Them, Sarah Whitlock and Martha Rankin. Complete instructions on how to use silica gel, meal and borax, perlite aggregate, sand and borax, glycerine and water to create attractive permanent flower arrangements. 12 illustrations. 32pp. 5⅜ × 8½. 21802-3 Pa. $1.00

EASY-TO-MAKE BIRD FEEDERS FOR WOODWORKERS, Scott D. Campbell. Detailed, simple-to-use guide for designing, constructing, caring for and using feeders. Text, illustrations for 12 classic and contemporary designs. 96pp. 5⅜ × 8½. 25847-5 Pa. $2.95

OLD-TIME CRAFTS AND TRADES, Peter Stockham. An 1807 book created to teach children about crafts and trades open to them as future careers. It describes in detailed, nontechnical terms 24 different occupations, among them coachmaker, gardener, hairdresser, lacemaker, shoemaker, wheelwright, copper-plate printer, milliner, trunkmaker, merchant and brewer. Finely detailed engravings illustrate each occupation. 192pp. 4⅝ × 6. 27398-9 Pa. $4.95

THE HISTORY OF UNDERCLOTHES, C. Willett Cunnington and Phyllis Cunnington. Fascinating, well-documented survey covering six centuries of English undergarments, enhanced with over 100 illustrations: 12th-century laced-up bodice, footed long drawers (1795), 19th-century bustles, 19th-century corsets for men, Victorian "bust improvers," much more. 272pp. 5⅜ × 8¼. 27124-2 Pa. $9.95

ARTS AND CRAFTS FURNITURE: The Complete Brooks Catalog of 1912, Brooks Manufacturing Co. Photos and detailed descriptions of more than 150 now very collectible furniture designs from the Arts and Crafts movement depict davenports, settees, buffets, desks, tables, chairs, bedsteads, dressers and more, all built of solid, quarter-sawed oak. Invaluable for students and enthusiasts of antiques, Americana and the decorative arts. 80pp. 6½ × 9¼. 27471-3 Pa. $7.95

HOW WE INVENTED THE AIRPLANE: An Illustrated History, Orville Wright. Fascinating firsthand account covers early experiments, construction of planes and motors, first flights, much more. Introduction and commentary by Fred C. Kelly. 76 photographs. 96pp. 8¼ × 11. 25662-6 Pa. $8.95

THE ARTS OF THE SAILOR: Knotting, Splicing and Ropework, Hervey Garrett Smith. Indispensable shipboard reference covers tools, basic knots and useful hitches; handsewing and canvas work, more. Over 100 illustrations. Delightful reading for sea lovers. 256pp. 5⅜ × 8½. 26440-8 Pa. $7.95

FRANK LLOYD WRIGHT'S FALLINGWATER: The House and Its History, Second, Revised Edition, Donald Hoffmann. A total revision—both in text and illustrations—of the standard document on Fallingwater, the boldest, most personal architectural statement of Wright's mature years, updated with valuable new material from the recently opened Frank Lloyd Wright Archives. "Fascinating"—*The New York Times*. 116 illustrations. 128pp. 9¼ × 10¾. 27430-6 Pa. $10.95

PHOTOGRAPHIC SKETCHBOOK OF THE CIVIL WAR, Alexander Gardner. 100 photos taken on field during the Civil War. Famous shots of Manassas, Harper's Ferry, Lincoln, Richmond, slave pens, etc. 244pp. 10⅝ × 8¼.
22731-6 Pa. $9.95

FIVE ACRES AND INDEPENDENCE, Maurice G. Kains. Great back-to-the-land classic explains basics of self-sufficient farming. The one book to get. 95 illustrations. 397pp. 5⅜ × 8½. 20974-1 Pa. $7.95

SONGS OF EASTERN BIRDS, Dr. Donald J. Borror. Songs and calls of 60 species most common to eastern U.S.: warblers, woodpeckers, flycatchers, thrushes, larks, many more in high-quality recording. Cassette and manual 99912-2 $8.95

A MODERN HERBAL, Margaret Grieve. Much the fullest, most exact, most useful compilation of herbal material. Gigantic alphabetical encyclopedia, from aconite to zedoary, gives botanical information, medical properties, folklore, economic uses, much else. Indispensable to serious reader. 161 illustrations. 888pp. 6½ × 9¼. 2-vol. set. (USO) Vol. I: 22798-7 Pa. $9.95
Vol. II: 22799-5 Pa. $9.95

HIDDEN TREASURE MAZE BOOK, Dave Phillips. Solve 34 challenging mazes accompanied by heroic tales of adventure. Evil dragons, people-eating plants, bloodthirsty giants, many more dangerous adversaries lurk at every twist and turn. 34 mazes, stories, solutions. 48pp. 8¼ × 11. 24566-7 Pa. $2.95

LETTERS OF W. A. MOZART, Wolfgang A. Mozart. Remarkable letters show bawdy wit, humor, imagination, musical insights, contemporary musical world; includes some letters from Leopold Mozart. 276pp. 5⅜ × 8½. 22859-2 Pa. $6.95

BASIC PRINCIPLES OF CLASSICAL BALLET, Agrippina Vaganova. Great Russian theoretician, teacher explains methods for teaching classical ballet. 118 illustrations. 175pp. 5⅜ × 8½. 22036-2 Pa. $4.95

THE JUMPING FROG, Mark Twain. Revenge edition. The original story of The Celebrated Jumping Frog of Calaveras County, a hapless French translation, and Twain's hilarious "retranslation" from the French. 12 illustrations. 66pp. 5⅜ × 8½. 22686-7 Pa. $3.95

BEST REMEMBERED POEMS, Martin Gardner (ed.). The 126 poems in this superb collection of 19th- and 20th-century British and American verse range from Shelley's "To a Skylark" to the impassioned "Renascence" of Edna St. Vincent Millay and to Edward Lear's whimsical "The Owl and the Pussycat." 224pp. 5⅜ × 8½. 27165-X Pa. $4.95

COMPLETE SONNETS, William Shakespeare. Over 150 exquisite poems deal with love, friendship, the tyranny of time, beauty's evanescence, death and other themes in language of remarkable power, precision and beauty. Glossary of archaic terms. 80pp. 5³⁄₁₆ × 8¼. 26686-9 Pa. $1.00

BODIES IN A BOOKSHOP, R. T. Campbell. Challenging mystery of blackmail and murder with ingenious plot and superbly drawn characters. In the best tradition of British suspense fiction. 192pp. 5⅜ × 8½. 24720-1 Pa. $5.95

THE WIT AND HUMOR OF OSCAR WILDE, Alvin Redman (ed.). More than 1,000 ripostes, paradoxes, wisecracks: Work is the curse of the drinking classes; I can resist everything except temptation; etc. 258pp. 5⅜ × 8½. 20602-5 Pa. $5.95

SHAKESPEARE LEXICON AND QUOTATION DICTIONARY, Alexander Schmidt. Full definitions, locations, shades of meaning in every word in plays and poems. More than 50,000 exact quotations. 1,485pp. 6½ × 9¼. 2-vol. set.
Vol. 1: 22726-X Pa. $15.95
Vol. 2: 22727-8 Pa. $15.95

SELECTED POEMS, Emily Dickinson. Over 100 best-known, best-loved poems by one of America's foremost poets, reprinted from authoritative early editions. No comparable edition at this price. Index of first lines. 64pp. 5³⁄₁₆ × 8¼.
26466-1 Pa. $1.00

CELEBRATED CASES OF JUDGE DEE (DEE GOONG AN), translated by Robert van Gulik. Authentic 18th-century Chinese detective novel; Dee and associates solve three interlocked cases. Led to van Gulik's own stories with same characters. Extensive introduction. 9 illustrations. 237pp. 5⅜ × 8½.
23337-5 Pa. $6.95

THE MALLEUS MALEFICARUM OF KRAMER AND SPRENGER, translated by Montague Summers. Full text of most important witchhunter's "bible," used by both Catholics and Protestants. 278pp. 6⅝ × 10. 22802-9 Pa. $10.95

SPANISH STORIES/CUENTOS ESPAÑOLES: A Dual-Language Book, Angel Flores (ed.). Unique format offers 13 great stories in Spanish by Cervantes, Borges, others. Faithful English translations on facing pages. 352pp. 5⅜ × 8½.
25399-6 Pa. $8.95

THE CHICAGO WORLD'S FAIR OF 1893: A Photographic Record, Stanley Appelbaum (ed.). 128 rare photos show 200 buildings, Beaux-Arts architecture, Midway, original Ferris Wheel, Edison's kinetoscope, more. Architectural emphasis; full text. 116pp. 8¼ × 11. 23990-X Pa. $9.95

OLD QUEENS, N.Y., IN EARLY PHOTOGRAPHS, Vincent F. Seyfried and William Asadorian. Over 160 rare photographs of Maspeth, Jamaica, Jackson Heights, and other areas. Vintage views of DeWitt Clinton mansion, 1939 World's Fair and more. Captions. 192pp. 8⅞ × 11. 26358-4 Pa. $12.95

CAPTURED BY THE INDIANS: 15 Firsthand Accounts, 1750–1870, Frederick Drimmer. Astounding true historical accounts of grisly torture, bloody conflicts, relentless pursuits, miraculous escapes and more, by people who lived to tell the tale. 384pp. 5⅜ × 8½. 24901-8 Pa. $8.95

THE WORLD'S GREAT SPEECHES, Lewis Copeland and Lawrence W. Lamm (eds.). Vast collection of 278 speeches of Greeks to 1970. Powerful and effective models; unique look at history. 842pp. 5⅜ × 8½. 20468-5 Pa. $13.95

THE BOOK OF THE SWORD, Sir Richard F. Burton. Great Victorian scholar/adventurer's eloquent, erudite history of the "queen of weapons"—from prehistory to early Roman Empire. Evolution and development of early swords, variations (sabre, broadsword, cutlass, scimitar, etc.), much more. 336pp. 6⅛ × 9¼. 25434-8 Pa. $8.95

CATALOG OF DOVER BOOKS

AUTOBIOGRAPHY: The Story of My Experiments with Truth, Mohandas K. Gandhi. Boyhood, legal studies, purification, the growth of the Satyagraha (nonviolent protest) movement. Critical, inspiring work of the man responsible for the freedom of India. 480pp. 5⅜ × 8½. (USO) 24593-4 Pa. $7.95

CELTIC MYTHS AND LEGENDS, T. W. Rolleston. Masterful retelling of Irish and Welsh stories and tales. Cuchulain, King Arthur, Deirdre, the Grail, many more. First paperback edition. 58 full-page illustrations. 512pp. 5⅜ × 8½. 26507-2 Pa. $9.95

THE PRINCIPLES OF PSYCHOLOGY, William James. Famous long course complete, unabridged. Stream of thought, time perception, memory, experimental methods; great work decades ahead of its time. 94 figures. 1,391pp. 5⅜ × 8½. 2-vol. set.
Vol. I: 20381-6 Pa. $12.95
Vol. II: 20382-4 Pa. $12.95

THE WORLD AS WILL AND REPRESENTATION, Arthur Schopenhauer. Definitive English translation of Schopenhauer's life work, correcting more than 1,000 errors, omissions in earlier translations. Translated by E. F. J. Payne. Total of 1,269pp. 5⅜ × 8½. 2-vol. set.
Vol. 1: 21761-2 Pa. $11.95
Vol. 2: 21762-0 Pa. $11.95

MAGIC AND MYSTERY IN TIBET, Madame Alexandra David-Neel. Experiences among lamas, magicians, sages, sorcerers, Bonpa wizards. A true psychic discovery. 32 illustrations. 321pp. 5⅜ × 8½. (USO) 22682-4 Pa. $8.95

THE EGYPTIAN BOOK OF THE DEAD, E. A. Wallis Budge. Complete reproduction of Ani's papyrus, finest ever found. Full hieroglyphic text, interlinear transliteration, word-for-word translation, smooth translation. 533pp. 6½ × 9¼. 21866-X Pa. $9.95

MATHEMATICS FOR THE NONMATHEMATICIAN, Morris Kline. Detailed, college-level treatment of mathematics in cultural and historical context, with numerous exercises. Recommended Reading Lists. Tables. Numerous figures. 641pp. 5⅜ × 8½. 24823-2 Pa. $11.95

THEORY OF WING SECTIONS: Including a Summary of Airfoil Data, Ira H. Abbott and A. E. von Doenhoff. Concise compilation of subsonic aerodynamic characteristics of NACA wing sections, plus description of theory. 350pp. of tables. 693pp. 5⅜ × 8½. 60586-8 Pa. $13.95

THE RIME OF THE ANCIENT MARINER, Gustave Doré, S. T. Coleridge. Doré's finest work; 34 plates capture moods, subtleties of poem. Flawless full-size reproductions printed on facing pages with authoritative text of poem. "Beautiful. Simply beautiful."—*Publisher's Weekly*. 77pp. 9¼ × 12. 22305-1 Pa. $5.95

NORTH AMERICAN INDIAN DESIGNS FOR ARTISTS AND CRAFTSPEOPLE, Eva Wilson. Over 360 authentic copyright-free designs adapted from Navajo blankets, Hopi pottery, Sioux buffalo hides, more. Geometrics, symbolic figures, plant and animal motifs, etc. 128pp. 8⅜ × 11. (EUK) 25341-4 Pa. $7.95

SCULPTURE: Principles and Practice, Louis Slobodkin. Step-by-step approach to clay, plaster, metals, stone; classical and modern. 253 drawings, photos. 255pp. 8⅛ × 11. 22960-2 Pa. $10.95

CATALOG OF DOVER BOOKS

THE INFLUENCE OF SEA POWER UPON HISTORY, 1660–1783, A. T. Mahan. Influential classic of naval history and tactics still used as text in war colleges. First paperback edition. 4 maps. 24 battle plans. 640pp. 5⅜ × 8½.
25509-3 Pa. $12.95

THE STORY OF THE TITANIC AS TOLD BY ITS SURVIVORS, Jack Winocour (ed.). What it was really like. Panic, despair, shocking inefficiency, and a little heroism. More thrilling than any fictional account. 26 illustrations. 320pp. 5⅜ × 8½.
20610-6 Pa. $7.95

FAIRY AND FOLK TALES OF THE IRISH PEASANTRY, William Butler Yeats (ed.). Treasury of 64 tales from the twilight world of Celtic myth and legend: "The Soul Cages," "The Kildare Pooka," "King O'Toole and his Goose," many more. Introduction and Notes by W. B. Yeats. 352pp. 5⅜ × 8½.
26941-8 Pa. $8.95

BUDDHIST MAHAYANA TEXTS, E. B. Cowell and Others (eds.). Superb, accurate translations of basic documents in Mahayana Buddhism, highly important in history of religions. The Buddha-karita of Asvaghosha, Larger Sukhavativyuha, more. 448pp. 5⅜ × 8½. ,
25552-2 Pa. $9.95

ONE TWO THREE . . . INFINITY: Facts and Speculations of Science, George Gamow. Great physicist's fascinating, readable overview of contemporary science: number theory, relativity, fourth dimension, entropy, genes, atomic structure, much more. 128 illustrations. Index. 352pp. 5⅜ × 8½.
25664-2 Pa. $8.95

ENGINEERING IN HISTORY, Richard Shelton Kirby, et al. Broad, nontechnical survey of history's major technological advances: birth of Greek science, industrial revolution, electricity and applied science, 20th-century automation, much more. 181 illustrations. ". . . excellent . . ."—Isis. Bibliography. vii + 530pp. 5⅜ × 8¼.
26412-2 Pa. $14.95